M000276485

How to use your Connected Casebook

Step 1: Go to **www.CasebookConnect.com** and redeem your access code to get started.

Access Code:  SANDEPRP60845197

Step 2: Go to your **BOOKSHELF** and select your Connected Casebook to start reading, highlighting, and taking notes in the margins of your e-book.

Step 3: Select the **STUDY** tab in your toolbar to access a variety of practice materials designed to help you master the course material. These materials may include explanations, videos, multiple-choice questions, flashcards, short answer, essays, and issue spotting.

Step 4: Select the **OUTLINE** tab in your toolbar to access chapter outlines that automatically incorporate your highlights and annotations from the e-book. Use the My Notes area for copying, pasting, and editing your book notes or creating new notes.

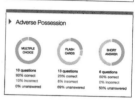

Step 5: If your professor has enrolled your class, you can select the **CLASS INSIGHTS** tab and compare your own study center results against the average of your classmates.

Is this a used casebook? Access code already scratched off?

You can purchase the Digital Version and still access all of the powerful tools listed above.
Please visit CasebookConnect.com and select Catalog to learn more.

PLEASE NOTE: Each access code can only be used once. This access code will expire one year after the discontinuation of the corresponding print title and must be redeemed before then. CCH reserves the right to discontinue this program at any time for any business reason. For further details, please see the Casebook Connect End User Agreement.

PIN: 10052995-0002 ANPRO2

2862

PROPERTY LAW

ASPEN CASEBOOK SERIES

PROPERTY LAW

Practice, Problems, and Perspectives

SECOND EDITION

Jerry L. Anderson

Dean and Calkins Distinguished Professor of Law
Drake University Law School

Daniel B. Bogart

Bolinger Chair in Real Estate, Land Use and Environmental Law
Dale E. Fowler School of Law at Chapman University

Published by Wolters Kluwer in New York.

Wolters Kluwer Legal & Regulatory U.S. serves customers worldwide with CCH, Aspen Publishers, and Kluwer Law International products. (www.WKLegaledu.com)

To contact Customer Service, e-mail customer.service@wolterskluwer.com, call 1-800-234-1660, fax 1-800-901-9075, or mail correspondence to:

Wolters Kluwer
Attn: Order Department
PO Box 990
Frederick, MD 21705

Printed in the United States of America.

2 3 4 5 6 7 8 9 0

ISBN 978-1-4548-9789-7

Library of Congress Cataloging-in-Publication Data

Names: Anderson, Jerry L. (Jerry Linn), 1959- author. | Bogart, Daniel B.,
    1960- author.
Title: Property law : practice, problems, and perspectives / Jerry L.
    Anderson, Dean and Calkins Distinguished Professor of Law, Drake
    University Law School; Daniel B. Bogart, Bolinger Chair in Real Estate,
    Land Use and Environmental Law; Dale E. Fowler School of Law at Chapman University.
Description: Second edition. | New York : Wolters Kluwer, [2019] | Series:
    Aspen Casebook series | Includes bibliographical references and index.
Identifiers: LCCN 2018055948 | ISBN 9781454897897
Subjects: LCSH: Property—United States. | LCGFT: Casebooks (Law)
Classification: LCC KF561.A53 2019 | DDC 346.7304—dc23
LC record available at https://lccn.loc.gov/2018055948

About Wolters Kluwer Legal & Regulatory U.S.

Wolters Kluwer Legal & Regulatory U.S. delivers expert content and solutions in the areas of law, corporate compliance, health compliance, reimbursement, and legal education. Its practical solutions help customers successfully navigate the demands of a changing environment to drive their daily activities, enhance decision quality and inspire confident outcomes.

Serving customers worldwide, its legal and regulatory portfolio includes products under the Aspen Publishers, CCH Incorporated, Kluwer Law International, ftwilliam.com and MediRegs names. They are regarded as exceptional and trusted resources for general legal and practice-specific knowledge, compliance and risk management, dynamic workflow solutions, and expert commentary.

To Susan, Peter, and Evan—*omnia propter vos*
JLA

To Larry I. Bogart, my father, and an exceptional real property attorney
DBB

PART II SPLITTING UP THE BUNDLE OF STICKS

4. CONCURRENT INTERESTS 175

PART III TRANSFER OF OWNERSHIP

Writing a Property text is daunting; Property covers a huge array of topics, but in one sense or another, each addresses the *creation, transfer,* and *destruction of wealth*. This wealth may arise in the form of personal property, intellectual property, or real property. This book therefore requires students to become familiar with the considerable body of legal rules and doctrine that make up Property law. Still, we hope to do more than provide a solid platform for teaching and learning doctrine, as crucial as that objective is to a first-year course. We have several additional and important goals for this book.

- This book represents a truly contemporary Property law text. Our goal is to make this intellectually challenging material as *accessible* and *understandable* as possible. We endeavor to explain the law clearly, but without oversimplification. We speak to student lawyers directly, in first person. We often use boxes, charts, photographs, and online interactive exercises to supplement case opinions and text. When you see this icon: ⌨, that will signal you to access the Simulation for additional content.
- We include videos that will acquaint student lawyers with the role of attorneys in various fields of Property law. These videos also serve as an opportunity to begin a conversation about what it means to be a *professional* and *ethical* practitioner. We believe this is a conversation that must begin in the very first year of law school. When you see this icon: 🎥, that will signal you to access the video content in the Simulation.
- We embrace the task of training law students as attorneys. We continually place the discussion of Property law squarely within the context of the *practice of law*. From time-to-time we refer to documents and other materials that lawyers use in practice. We regularly ask student lawyers to resolve problems and hypotheticals from the perspective of an attorney; our goal is to help student lawyers begin the difficult process of developing *professional judgment*.
- We wish to impart a lesson that is sometimes underemphasized in law schools. Legal rules underlie *transactions* and not just *litigation*. A transaction that "works" will allow the parties to avoid later disputes. This book does not focus solely on judicial resolution of disputes. We also examine Property law rules through the lens of a transactional attorney. This is particularly important in the chapters devoted to the land and loan transactions.
- We are fascinated by the *evolution of Property law*, and we regularly confront student lawyers with the policy arguments for and against different legal rules. We want student lawyers who use this book to understand that, in practice, they must consider policy to be able to resolve property issues they will encounter in their professional lives.

- We forge the connection between *traditional, historic cases* and *the modern world*, and we consider the profound effects on the law wrought by both science and a rapidly changing society. Rules governing property are often old, and sometimes ancient. Courts, legislators, and lawyers must adapt these rules to modern, cutting-edge problems. For example, the drafters of the U.S. Constitution anticipated the need to protect intellectual property, and provided for patents. But the founders could not have possibly imagined gene research, the enormous wealth this science makes possible, and the legal disputes that have arisen in their wake.
- Finally, we wish to transmit our love for Property law: the colorful characters who inhabit its case opinions, the rules and doctrine of which it is made, and the attorneys who practice it.

We hope that you find this book an engaging, effective tool for teaching or learning Property law.

Jerry L. Anderson
Daniel B. Bogart

December 2018

ACKNOWLEDGEMENTS FOR THE SECOND EDITION:

The authors want to thank again the editorial staff at Wolters Kluwer, especially Darren Kelly and Patrick Cline, for their excellent work on this edition.

Dean Anderson wishes to thank his research assistants for this edition, Cody Reimer and Rob Howard, as well as his administrative assistant, Leslie Herman.

Professor Bogart wishes to thank Sherry Leysen, Associate Director for Library Services and Heather Joy, Research/Instruction Librarian at the Dale E. Fowler School of Law, for their extraordinary assistance during the process of creating a second edition of this text.

ACKNOWLEDGEMENTS FOR THE FIRST EDITION:

The authors want to thank the editorial staff at Wolters Kluwer, particularly Darren Kelly and Thomas Daughhetee, for making the production process a pleasure. In addition, we appreciate the constructive comments of the anonymous professors who reviewed drafts of the book.

Special thanks to Susan Anderson for her meticulous proofreading and editing. Although the authors take full responsibility for any errors that remain, the book would not have been in the shape it is without her expert guidance.

Professor Anderson: Sincere thanks to Drake Law School students Erin Toomey, Jonathon Schroeder, Emily Ertel, Jeffrey Kappelman, and Matthew Hohenstein for their helpful research assistance. I want to especially commend Mr. Kappelman for doing a citation edit of the entire manuscript under significant time pressure. My wonderful colleagues, Drake Law Professors Martin Begleiter, Shontavia Johnson, Maura Strassberg, and Jonathan Rosenbloom, provided very valuable suggestions and feedback on earlier drafts. I greatly appreciate being able to call upon their expertise. Professor Cathy Mansfield took to the field to get me a picture of the property at issue in the *Martin* case. *Gratius ago* to Jack Blais for his Latin assistance.

Kristi Longtin went above the call of duty in preparing copy, formatting the book, and providing some of the special illustrations. The Drake Law Librarians were a tremendous help in acquiring obscure sources quickly.

I spoke with several lawyers who very kindly provided me with helpful background information on cases in this book: Patrick Dewane, Jr., of Manitowoc, Wisconsin, who represented the plaintiffs in *Jacque v. Steenberg Homes*, and James D. Mosteller III, of Barnwell, South Carolina, who represented the owners of the historic property in the *Boyd* case about implied easements. I also had helpful conversations with the plaintiffs, John and Caroline Boyd.

I am indebted to my own Property professor, Robert C. Ellickson, for inspiring my love of this area of the law and for instilling in me the theoretical framework that permeates my parts of the book. As Ellickson's research assistant, I began my acquaintance with the Coase theorem plotting car/cow accidents for his groundbreaking article, "Of Coase and Cattle," an opportunity for which I remain grateful. Similarly, I thank Judge Alex Kozinski for expanding my methods of legal analysis and teaching me how to write a pithy sentence.

I thank my friend and colleague Danny Bogart — first of all, for calling on me to join him in this endeavor, and secondly, for putting up with me throughout. He is a true "dirt lawyer," one of the few law professors who is equally at home in the worlds of practice and scholarship and so can bridge the gap for the rest of us.

Finally, I warmly thank my family—Susan, Peter, and Evan—for their love, support, and understanding during this project.

Professor Bogart: I am grateful for the excellent assistance of law students Evan Cote and Marissa McDonald. Ms. McDonald was especially helpful as we moved toward completion of this project. Many thanks are due to colleagues for their time and comments; I am particularly thankful to Donald Kochan, Jayne Kacer, Mario Mainero, and Tom Campbell.

I want to thank a number of attorneys who permitted us to use materials they developed in practice. I asked (and received) many suggestions for teachable materials from the lawyers participating on the DIRT Listserve maintained by the Law School at the University of Missouri, Kansas City. I was not able to use all that I received, but I gratefully used documents provided by Michael G. Kerman of Sutherland Asbill & Brennan, Joshua Stein of Joshua Stein, PLLC, and Charles D. Calvin of Faegre Baker Daniels. Similarly, Professor Tanya Marsh of the Wake Forest University School of Law kindly allowed us to use several forms in this book.

I am exceedingly fortunate to have Jerry Anderson as a co-author. Jerry is a rare person: a true Property scholar, a clear and careful writer, and an enthusiastic and creative teacher.

As always, I thank Lisa and my two sons, Alex and Ethan (for pretty much everything, and not just this book).

Finally, I would like to thank the many generations of Property students who I have had the honor and pleasure to teach.

A note about the format of this book: We include many problems based on reported decisions. The problems often use the names of the parties in one of the cases, but note that we have changed and simplified the facts for our purposes and do not intend to make any representation about the actual facts of the cases cited.

In many of the case opinions excerpted, we have eliminated some of the court's citations to increase readability.

All of the footnotes in the book, including those embedded in the cases, are numbered sequentially. Therefore, be aware that the footnote numbers in a particular case do not match the actual footnote numbers in the case opinion.

The authors gratefully acknowledge permission to excerpt or reprint the following materials:

All publications of the American Land Title Association®, including ALTA® Policy Forms, Endorsements, and Related Documents, are copyrighted and are reprinted herein by specific permission from: American Land Title Association® (ALTA®), copyright © 2006-2018 American Land Title Association. All rights reserved. The use of these forms is restricted to ALTA licensees and ALTA members in good standing as of the date of use. All other uses are prohibited. Reprinted under license from the American Land Title Association.

Anderson, Jerry, photograph of bike trail.

Anderson, Jerry, photograph of Black Acre Realty sign.

Becker, David, foreclosed development photograph, copyright David Becker/ZUMA Press.

Bedford County deed room, photograph courtesy of the Register of Deeds, Bedford County, Tennessee.

Blach, Mariusz, Lake Tahoe photograph, copyright Mariusz Blach - Fotolia.com.

Bogart, Daniel, photograph of Grand Central terminal.

Bogart, Daniel, photograph of Nordstrom storefront.

Boxes in Royal Albert Hall, copyright © Associated Newspapers /REX/Shutterstock.

Calvin, Charles D., Sample Purchase and Sale Agreement.

Downing, Larry, eviction photograph, courtesy of Reuters/Larry Downing.

Ellickson, Robert C., Cities and Homeowners Associations, 130 U. Pa. L. Rev. 1519, 1526-30 (1982). Reprinted by permission of the author and the University of Pennsylvania Law Review.

Fischel, William A., photograph and map of David Lucas's two lots, courtesy of William A. Fischel.

Foreclosure sign, photograph, Moodboard/123RF.

Marsh, Tanya, Promissory Note.

Freed, Leonard, photograph of a rental sign showing discrimination, copyright Leonard Freed/ Magnum Photos.

Hair, Rodney W., photographs of Boyd antique store. Used by permission from Rodney W. Hair and Caroline E. Boyd.

Hartley's North Park Addition poster, copyright © San Diego History Center.

Hughes, Langston, portion of the poem Ballad of the Landlord (1940), from The Collected Poems of Langston Hughes, edited by Arnold Rampersad, with David Roessel, Associate Editor, copyright © 1994 by the Estate of Langston Hughes. Used by permission of Alfred A. Knopf, an imprint of the Knopf Doubleday Publishing Group, a division of Random House LLC. All rights reserved.

Jackson County Recorder of Deeds Official Public Records online search page, used by permission of the Senior Deputy County Counselor, Jackson County, Missouri.

Kades, Eric, The Dark Side of Efficiency: Johnson v. M'Intosh and the Expropriation of American Indian Lands, 148 U. Pa. L. Rev. 1065, 1071 (2000). Reprinted by permission of the author and the University of Pennsylvania Law Review.

Kelly, Darren, photograph of Pepto Bismol bottles.

Kingsbury Place neighborhood, photograph courtesy of the Missouri History Museum, St. Louis.

Leicester Square, c. 1808, courtesy of Private Collection, copyright © Look and Learn/ Bridgeman Images.

Leicester Square, today, courtesy of Romazur via Creative Commons.

Mansfield, Cathy Lesser, photograph of Prince Street, Alexandria, Virginia.

McNeece, Joel /Calhoun County Journal, photograph of Webster County, Mississippi, courthouse fire.

Neponsit development, postcard, courtesy of rockawaymemories.com.

No trespassing sign, photograph copyright ejmphotos - Fotolia.com.

Nolon, Sean, Ona Ferguson, and Pat Field, Land in Conflict: Managing and Resolving Land Use Disputes 14 (2013). Copyright © 2013 Lincoln Institute of Land Policy. Reprinted with permission.

North Carolina Association of Realtors, sample forms and agreements. These forms are property of the North Carolina Association of Realtors (NCAR) and are reprinted with the permission of NCAR.

Oil wells, California, 1923, photograph courtesy of Everett Collection.

Peale, Rembrandt, painting of Chief Justice John Marshall, from the Collection of the Supreme Court of the United States.

Riedel, Charlie, sinkhole photograph, AP Photo/Charlie Riedel.

Smith, Henry E., Property as the Law of Things, 125 Harv. L. Rev. 1691, 1697, 1718-19 (2012). Reprinted by permission of the author and Harvard Law Review Association.

Stein, Joshua, Model Simple Office Lease, Model Residential House Apartment Lease, Commercial Mortgage Agreement.

Symphony Space, photograph courtesy of Symphony Space, Inc.

Texas Bar Association, forms from the Texas Real Estate Forms Manual, 3rd Edition, copyright © 2017 TexasBarBooks.

Trant, Lucy, image of Dower petition of Delilah Black, 1848.

Vetstein, Richard, Vetstein Law Group, P.C., beachfront access sign photo.

Woolworth Building, c.1913, courtesy of the Library of Congress.

> This land, this red land, is us; and the flood years and the dust years and the drought years are us.
>
> —*John Steinbeck, The Grapes of Wrath*

We know that it's possible you are entering into your study of Property law with some trepidation. You may not own much property other than a laptop or a car at this point, so you have little experience to draw on. And you might be afraid that this class will be a boring exercise in dusty old doctrines that have more to do with shifting property lines and money around than with the vital issues of our time.

Consider, however, that how a society defines, distributes, and protects property is one of the most fundamental factors influencing what life in that society will be like. The law of property will determine who has wealth and power—the extent to which those who own the property will call the shots in any community. Property law was—and is—crucially responsible for our country's development and prosperity.

In addition to these societal, macro issues, there is drama at the micro level as well. We urge you to recognize that the cases in this book are not only about land or other property—they are also about the lives of the people involved, the likes of whom may someday be your clients.

A real-life story to illustrate this point: one of the authors was recently consulted by a couple who had lived for years on farm land that had been in their family for generations. Their neighbor across the road decided to transform his cornfield into a confinement operation for about 5,000 hogs. Hogs produce a lot of manure—roughly three times the amount produced by an average human—which will sit in a lagoon until the farmer applies it to his fields.

The odors from the lagoon are tremendous—hydrogen sulfide and ammonia, enough to make your nose burn and your eyes water. If you hang your laundry out to dry, it becomes permeated with the odor. You can't open your windows for fresh air anymore, you can't have company over for a picnic. You start to worry about the health impacts on your kids after reading studies showing higher rates of asthma for those living near hog lots.

The farm couple says that their lives have been ruined. Expressed purely in terms of property value, you could say that their house is now worth about half of what it was before. But this case isn't about money—it's about this family being driven from their home and having their lives turned upside down by what a neighbor has decided to do with his land.

There are countless situations like this—people care deeply about their land in ways that go far beyond monetary value. We hope that when you read these cases, you will see behind the legal claims to get a sense of the impact of property law on peoples' lives. When you read about a foreclosure or a leasehold eviction, think about the children who might be homeless depending on the outcome. A case about eminent domain is not just about compensation; it's about the government's power to force people off their land. Go to any zoning meeting and you may be surprised to see the passion people have about these issues.

The beginning quote from *The Grapes of Wrath* is one of numerous illustrations from popular culture about our intense relationship with the land. The tragic center of Steinbeck's classic novel is the eviction of the Joad family (like countless others) from their farm during the Great Depression, which takes away their livelihood and leaves them rootless. A neighbor, Muley, refuses to leave, because he feels so strongly tied to the land, such as the place where his father died: "An' his blood is right in that groun', right now.... An' I put my han' on that groun' where my own pa's blood is part of it." Their blood is in the land, and the land in turn is in their veins; it has become a part of them. Land—and property in general—was here before us and will be here long after we're gone, providing us with a strong connection to the past, and also to the future. Again, remember when you read these cases that more is at stake than property value.

In this book, we will emphasize the place of the lawyer in property law. In many ways, your role in this field may be different from the courtroom litigator students often have in the back of their minds. For example, you may act as an estate planner, counseling people about the best way to ensure that their property will descend to loved ones when they die. In a zoning case, you may spend time talking to neighborhood groups and city council members, trying to determine possible objections and allay concerns. In real estate transactions, your role may be to "get the deal done" by negotiating contract terms and examining title documents to determine possible pitfalls and how to guard against them.

As you can see, a firm grasp of Property law will help prepare you for a variety of possible career options. In this course, you will acquire the foundation you need for numerous upper-level subjects, such as:

- Family law, which involves the division of marital property;
- Wills and Trusts (Estate Planning), which uses the building blocks you will learn here to transfer property at death;
- Real Estate Transactions, from making deals to leasing;
- Land Use Control, from zoning to homeowners associations;
- Natural Resources law, which uses property concepts to protect sensitive areas and allocate scarce resources;
- Debtor-Creditor or Bankruptcy, which uses Property law to determine the rights of creditors;
- Intellectual Property, which deals with establishing and protecting rights to creative property interests.

So, let's start the journey. We hope, by the end, you will be as excited and engaged by this branch of the law as we are.

PROPERTY LAW

PART I

Definition and Acquisition of Property

Have you ever seen one of those stereograms, such as the *Magic Eye*™ posters? After you stare at it awhile and learn how to relax your eyes, an incredible 3-D image pops out at you. You learn, in other words, that there was a lot more going on beneath the surface than you thought at first glance.

In a way, law school is like that. Property law, in particular, involves setting aside your preconceived notions of how the world works and looking at things differently. You might come into this course thinking about property as a relatively static, absolute, concrete thing: "This land is mine; I can do what I want with it." It is our job in the first part of this book to get you to see below the surface, to understand the complex set of rights and obligations that make up property ownership, as well as the balance of interests that determine what they are. After this course, we hope you will never drive by a "For Sale" sign again without thinking about the layers of interests involved.

This takes some doing—we spend the whole first chapter thinking about this thing we call *property* and what we really mean by that term. We will discover that property rights are grounded in important policy goals that help explain most of the cases in this book. Moreover, those rights evolve over time, as societal circumstances and policies change.

Chapter 2 explores those policies further in discovering how property rights are acquired in the first place. Of course, most property rights now are acquired by purchase or inheritance, which we discuss fully later in the book. In Chapter 2, however, we will focus on the acquisition of property by capture, by find, or by gift—all of which require an understanding of the fundamental concept of *possession*. Be careful of a tendency to dismiss this as marginally relevant in today's society—you will find out that these same concepts are behind important modern problems such as how we allocate water and internet domain names.

In Chapter 3, we focus on another important way property rights are acquired—by creation. We have developed *intellectual property rights* to reward inventors, songwriters, authors, and other creators for the fruits of their labor.

We will learn the basic forms of intellectual property protection, as well as the balance of public and private interests behind them.

By the end of Part I, you should have a solid grasp of how property rights are acquired and how society has defined those rights to further important policies.

The Foundations of Property Law

> Government is instituted no less for protection of the property, than of the persons, of individuals.
>
> —*James Madison, The Federalist No. 54*

> The great and chief end, therefore, of men's uniting into commonwealths, and putting themselves under government, is the preservation of their property.
>
> —*John Locke, Second Treatise of Civil Government*[1]

> The theory of the Communists may be summed up in the single sentence: Abolition of private property.
>
> —*Karl Marx, The Communist Manifesto*[2]

A INTRODUCTION

A few students come into this class having some extensive experience with property ownership—perhaps you have already bought a house or may even own

---

[1] John Locke, The Second Treatise of Civil Government 67 (Barnes & Noble 2004) (1690).
[2] Karl Marx, Manifesto of the Communist Party 25 (Start Publishing 2012) (1888).

your own business. Most students, however, have very limited experience with property—you might own a laptop, or a few other electronic devices, and maybe a car, but that's about it. Regardless of which category you fall into, you likely have never considered what it really means to *own* property, in a legal sense. Moreover, you probably have never thought about *why* we protect property rights in the first place—you just accept property ownership and its rights as a given state of affairs.

In this chapter, we ask you to think more carefully about the foundational policies of property law—why is it that we protect private property rights? As you will see, property rights are not unlimited and are often disputed. Therefore, we first need to understand the basic policies our system is trying to promote in order to decide the proper scope of property rights.

Second, we need to understand what we mean when we say something is your "property." It turns out that the term *property* is a concept that includes a bundle of various rights. In many instances, these rights may be split up among different people. Even if you have a particular right in the bundle, it may be trumped by the superior interests of society or other property owners. In the second part of this chapter, we will detail the various rights in the ownership bundle and explore how and why they might be limited.

B   WHAT IS PROPERTY?

Before we start to explore the theoretical foundations of property law, we should at least briefly discuss what we mean when we say something is your "property." Until now, you may think of property primarily in terms of its physical attributes or spatial location. As a lawyer, however, you need to start thinking of property in terms of rights and interests in the thing.

Think about your laptop, your car, or some other piece of property you have. What are the attributes of your ownership? In other words, what can you do with it?

This aggregation of rights in a particular piece of property is often referred to as the "bundle of sticks," by property professors who prefer to have concrete metaphors for abstract concepts. In many cases, you might hold some of the sticks in the bundle, while someone else holds the remainder. For example, if you rent an apartment, you have the right of occupancy and the right to exclude, although your landlord may have modified your right to exclude by retaining the ability to enter under certain circumstances. You don't have the right to sell the apartment or will it to your sister, although you may have a limited right to transfer by sublease. Your right

The Bundle of Sticks

1. The right to possess or occupy.
2. The right to use or exploit.
3. The right to exclude others.
4. The right to transfer (by sale, gift, or will, for example).
5. The right to modify or destroy.

to modify the structure is probably very limited, and you certainly don't have the right to destroy! Can you think of other circumstances in which the bundle of sticks may be divided?

Moreover, your rights may change depending on who is on the other side. For example, your right to exclude may depend on whether we are talking about your annoying neighbor, or the police with a valid warrant, or the landlord under a clause in the lease. Property rights are therefore *relational*.

At the end of this chapter, we will explore some of the sticks in this bundle in greater detail. For now, begin to think about property as *legal rights among persons with respect to things*.

The Definition of Property

Professor Morris Cohen noted the relational nature of property rights:

> Whatever technical definition of property we may prefer, we must recognize that a property right is a relation not between an owner and a thing, but between the owner and other individuals with reference to a thing.
>
> —*Morris Cohen, Property and Sovereignty (1927)*

By contrast, the English jurist William Blackstone referred to property as

> the sole and despotic dominion which one man claims and exercises over the external things of the world, in total exclusion of the right of any other individual in the universe.
>
> —*Sir William Blackstone, 2 William Blackstone, Commentaries *2*

Does Blackstone's definition fail to acount for the relational aspects of property we just discussed?

■ PROBLEM: WHAT IS PROPERTY?

Determining whether a particular interest can be called "property" has important consequences. For example, as we will see in the final chapter, the government owes you compensation when it confiscates your property, but this protection applies only if you can define your interest as "property."

Assume Jenna and Marta are getting a divorce after five years of marriage. In their state, marital property is equitably divided between the spouses upon dissolution of the marriage. Jenna has spent the last three years working as a firefighter to put Marta through law school. Since all their money went to that goal, the couple accumulated no other substantial assets. Just after the dissolution proceedings were filed, Marta landed a good job with a law firm.

In this context, should a graduate school degree be considered "property"? Marta paid good money to help acquire the degree; its existence, while not physical, is evidenced by a diploma, a piece of paper akin to a stock certificate. Which of the attributes that we think of as normally attached to "property" might apply to a graduate degree? Despite the lack of some of these attributes, might a court consider a degree "property" in the context of a divorce?

An Example of the Bundle of Sticks: The World Trade Center [3]

To begin thinking about property in terms of "rights among persons with respect to things," consider the example of a piece of property we all know about and now think of as hallowed ground: The World Trade Center site in New York City. We tend to think about this property in terms of its physical structures: most notably, the massive Twin Towers, which at the time they were constructed, in 1973, were the tallest buildings in the world.

Consider the layers of property interests involved at this site at the time of the terrorist attack of September 11, 2001. The towers were constructed on land owned by the Port Authority of New York and New Jersey, a bi-state agency established by interstate compact. While the Port Authority continued to own the land and buildings, it entered into a 99-year lease of the Twin Towers with a company owned by World Trade Center Properties, L.L.C. (WTC). It also entered into a 99-year lease with Westfield WTC, L.L.C. (Westfield) for retail areas within and beneath the towers. The leases required WTC and Westfield to pay hundreds of millions of dollars up front, plus annual rent in excess of $100 million. In order to finance these obligations, WTC obtained financing from GMAC Commercial Mortgage Corporation, which subsequently assigned the loan to Wells Fargo Bank Minnesota, N.A. Likewise, Westfield obtained a loan to finance the retail lease, from UBS Warburg Real Estate Investments. These loans were secured by mortgages on the leasehold interest.

The lessees subleased space—for offices, restaurants, and stores—to a wide variety of sub-tenants. Some of these sub-tenants then subleased space to other tenants (sub-sub-tenants). The entire World Trade Center complex included 435 tenants representing 26 countries. At the time it opened, the World Trade Center was the largest commercial real estate development project in the United States.

---

[3] Most of the facts regarding property interests in the World Trade Center site were taken from Lucien J. Dhooge, *A Previously Unimaginable Risk Potential: September 11 and the Insurance Industry*, 40 Am. Bus. L.J. 687 (2003).

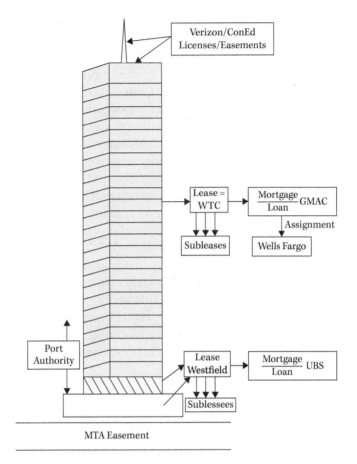

Property interests in the World Trade Center

New York's Metropolitan Transit Authority owned the two subway lines running underneath the Twin Towers. Numerous other entities, such as Verizon, Con Edison, and TV stations, also had rights to use the property, including the right to install and use satellite dishes and antennae on the tops of the towers.

In addition, the lessees had insurance on their property interests of approximately $3.5 billion per occurrence, from two dozen insurers.[4]

Given this complex web of interests, does it make any sense to talk about the "ownership" of the WTC site? All of these entities had some sort of legal rights with respect to the property. With this example, you can start thinking of property rights in terms of these layers of interests, considering property to be allocated functionally as well as spatially. Although the World Trade Center represents an extreme example, most land involves multiple holders of various types of property rights. Even in rural settings, an owner's land might be subject to a farm lease, a pipeline easement, an oil and gas lease, a mortgage, or other sorts of interests.

---

[4] *See* World Trade Ctr. Props., L.L.C. v. Hartford Fire Ins. Co., 345 F.3d 154, 158 (2d Cir. 2003).

THE POLICIES BEHIND PROPERTY LAW

Think about the quotations at the beginning of this chapter. On one hand, we know that the Framers of the United States Constitution thought that the protection of property was crucially important—so much so that they placed it alongside life and liberty in the triad of things that cannot be taken from you without due process under the Fifth Amendment. John Locke, a philosopher whose writings heavily influenced the Founders, went even further, calling the protection of property the "chief end" of government.[5] By contrast, Karl Marx made the *abolition* of private property the central tenet of communist philosophy.[6] As Professor Robert Ellickson put it, property systems are "a major battleground" on which the conflict "between individual liberty and privacy on the one hand and community and equality on the other" is resolved.[7]

What is it about property that makes it the focal point of this dispute? How property is distributed in a society involves deciding who will control fundamental resources and wealth. In this section, we suggest a few of the most common policy goals behind property rights protection. In the chapters that follow, you will see that these policies can be used to explain many of the cases in which property rights are in conflict. Note, however, that these policies do not always line up in the same direction!

The Policies of Property Law

The most important public policies behind property law may be summarized as follows:

1. **Economic efficiency:** The protection of property gives people an incentive to produce and therefore leads to wealth maximization for society. By making property *alienable* (that is, able to be transferred), the free market system should help ensure that the property will end up in the use most valued by society (the "highest and best use," the term used by real estate experts to describe the maximally productive and feasible use of property).[8]
2. **Fairness:** Property rights are a reward for the labor spent in creating or improving property. Fairness invokes the moral case for property ownership.
3. **Certainty:** Property law should create a system in which purchasers can easily determine that the seller is the rightful owner of a particular

---

[5] Locke, *supra* note 1, at 2.
[6] Marx, *supra* note 2, at 25.
[7] Robert C. Ellickson, *Property in Land*, 102 Yale L.J. 1315, 1345 (1993).
[8] Stephen Sussna, *The Concept of Highest and Best Use Under Taking Theory*, 21 Urb. L. 113, 113-14 (1989).

piece of property, thereby lowering the costs of transactions. Property rules should be clear and easy to administer. Secure property rights promote peace and order.

4. **Personhood:** Owning property allows people to express themselves through creative uses of property and serves important ends like privacy and security. Property often has sentimental value that is not accounted for by the market.

5. **Democracy:** Unless one's property is protected, all other freedoms may become meaningless. A nation of property owners provides stability, as more people have a stake in maintaining the rule of law.

Although these are the most commonly advanced policy reasons for property rights rules, we will explore even more policies in the chapters ahead.

1. Economic Efficiency: Wealth Maximization

The success of capitalistic societies can be traced directly to their protection of property rights. Simply put, protecting property gives people the incentive to produce. What farmer will work for months plowing, planting, fertilizing, and weeding, if someone else can come along and reap the crop? What company will invest millions of dollars building a new plant, or creating a new medicine, if it cannot be assured that its investment will be secure?

Thus, private property rights promote the economically efficient use of resources. We will use the term *economic efficiency* to refer to the use of resources (such as land or water) in the manner that will maximize economic benefits (i.e., the production of goods and services). In many cases throughout this book, you will see courts striving to allocate property rights in a manner that will achieve the greatest wealth for society.

Marx pointed out, however, that protecting property in the hands of those who own it works only because we are depriving everyone else of its enjoyment.[9] Even though our society is not based on Marxism, his point still has relevance. As we will see, when private property rights are protected, the interests of other owners or the public at large are often diminished. Thus, a balance must be struck when determining how far to protect the property interests of the private owner.

The institution of private property itself generally furthers efficient resource use. In a *communal property* system, a group of people hold property rights in common. We still have many instances of these common-pool resources: for example, the world's ocean fisheries or the lake owned by a gated housing community. In some cases, communal property schemes work well—typically where there is low demand for the resource, or where it is governed by a community

---

[9] *See* Marx, *supra* note 2.

group (such as a homeowners association) that can limit use and easily enforce those limits.

But in many instances, holding resources in common leads to economic inefficiency. Garrett Hardin described this problem in his classic article, *The Tragedy of the Commons*.[10] He used the example of a field owned in common by a group of herders. We have adapted his example to illustrate the tragedy of the commons problem.

The Tragedy of the Commons

Assume that 10 dairy cattle herders own a 100-acre field in common. If the demand for milk is low, so that each herder basically uses the field for her family's dairy needs, each herder grazes one cow and the field's capacity is never reached. When the demand for milk increases, however, each herder can make an extra $100 for each cow she places in the field. Assume that each additional cow that exceeds the field's capacity causes $120 in damage to the field through overgrazing. That cost, however, is borne by the entire group, and not the individual herder. Moreover, each herder knows that even if she "does the right thing" and refrains from adding cattle, she cannot prevent others from doing so. Therefore, it is in each herder's self-interest to continue to add cattle until the common field is destroyed, constituting the tragedy of the commons.

There are four possible ways to avoid this result:

1) Some herders might be *altruistic* and voluntarily reduce their herds in recognition of the collective impacts.
2) The government could *regulate* the field, set an allowable herd limit, and then enforce it.
3) The herders could join together and reach a collective agreement about the appropriate size of each person's herd. This *collaborative* approach would involve certain *transaction costs*—difficulties such as meeting, deciding limits, and then monitoring and enforcing those limits.
4) The field could be *privatized*: instead of 100 acres owned in common, the field would be divided into ten lots and each herder given 10 acres. Now, if Herder A wants to add another cow to her field, she will not only receive the benefit of the cow, but will also bear its full cost. Presumably, then, she will make the right economic decision and stop adding cows when the field's capacity is reached.

Thus, the introduction of private property helps avoid the tragedy of the commons and furthers the most economically efficient use of resources. In fact, this is exactly what happened during the enclosure period[11] in England, when millions of acres of common lands were converted to privately owned property. While this had some

---

[10] Garrett Hardin, *The Tragedy of the Commons*, 162 Science 1243 (1968).
[11] The most intense period of enclosure took place from 1700-1840.

positive economic consequences, it also profoundly changed the structure of English society.

Another feature of private property that promotes economic efficiency is *transferability*. By making property freely alienable, it is more likely to end up in the hands of the highest and best user, i.e., the person who can use it to create the greatest benefit for society. Throughout the book, you will see that courts strive to remove unreasonable impediments to the free movement of property in the market.

Common Pool Issues: Fishing Rights

The fish in the sea are a common pool, and ownership rights are acquired only by possession. In fact, H. Scott Gordon used a fishery to describe the tragedy of the commons 14 years before Garrett Hardin's classic article gave the problem a name.[12] As a result, according to the Food and Agriculture Organization of the United Nations, about 30 percent of the world's fish stocks, including such important species as bluefin tuna and Atlantic cod, are being fished at biologically-unsustainable levels, while another 57 percent are "fully exploited."[13]

Various measures to control overfishing have been attempted, with little success. Limiting the length of the fishing season just encouraged the overinvestment in bigger boats and bigger nets. Limiting the catch per boat just encouraged the overinvestment in more boats.

A relatively recent idea is the introduction of private property rights to fish in the form of individual transferable quotas (ITQs). An ITQ gives each fisher the right to a share of the total allowable catch. The fisher no longer has an incentive to overinvest in fishing equipment, because there is no longer a race to catch more fish. There are, however, administrative costs involved in setting up the system, and in determining and enforcing the allowable quotas. In developing countries without a regulatory infrastructure, communal rights may be the optimal choice to control overfishing.[14]

Externalities

The overgrazing costs in the communal property system are called *externalities*, which is defined as either a cost or benefit that the person taking the action does not have to consider. Externalities can be either positive or negative. Overgrazing is a negative externality because the negative consequences are spread throughout the community. A positive externality example: if one of the herders decided to spend $100 on fertilizer for the field, the community, rather than the individual herder, would get most of the benefit.

Privatizing property is one way to *internalize externalities*. Once Herder A has her own ten-acre plot, she will have to consider the full costs of adding an additional cow, but will also receive the full benefits of adding fertilizer.

---

[12] H. Scott Gordon, *The Economic Theory of a Common-Property Resource: The Fishery*, 62 J. Pol. Econ. 124 (1954).
[13] FAO, *The State of World Aquaculture and Fisheries*, 2016.
[14] *See* Katrina M. Wyman, *The Property Rights Challenge in Marine Fisheries*, 50 Ariz. L. Rev. 511, 542 (2008).

■ POINTS TO CONSIDER

1. **Do private property rights internalize all externalities?** Assume Herder A, after acquiring her ten acres, decides to straighten a stream that meanders through her land in order to maximize the available grazing land. As a result, water travels faster through A's land, resulting in erosion and flooding damage on B's land, which is downstream. The cost to A to straighten the stream is $1,000, but she will receive $300 annually in additional grazing profit. However, B must bear an additional $400 a year in erosion and flooding costs. What role could property rights play to internalize externalities and maximize wealth here? How might A's decision change if she had to bear the full costs of her actions?

   We will see that many of our land use laws serve to internalize or minimize the negative externalities of landowner behavior, which encourages owners to make economically efficient decisions.

2. **Are there alternatives to private property regimes?** Elinor Ostrom won the Nobel Prize for Economics in 2009 for her work on the management of common pool resources. Ostrom's research teaches us that the tragedy of the commons is not an inevitable result of common pool situations. Based on numerous field studies, she identified certain principles that characterize successful common pool management systems, such as collective agreements on resource use and effective monitoring.[15] Can you think of examples of resources that are still successfully managed communally rather than privatized?

3. **Transaction costs.** Ostrom's research indicates that communal property systems can work to achieve efficient results, in the right set of circumstances. Note that the parties would have to get together, reach agreement on sustainable resource use limits, and then monitor and enforce those limits. These are examples of *transaction costs*—which include any impediments that must be overcome to achieve a certain result. For example, if you are deciding whether to drive or take the bus to work, you compare not only the actual cost of the bus ticket and the cost of gas and parking, but also the amount of time you have to wait for the bus, the distance you have to walk, whether you have to make a transfer, and so on, compared to the difficulty of finding a parking space, the effort of convincing your friend to loan you the car, etc.

   Economist Ronald Coase illustrated that in many resource conflicts, transaction costs are of paramount importance.[16] If transaction costs are low or non-existent, interested parties are likely to reach the most efficient allocation of property rights on their own. On the other hand, when transaction costs are high, the parties are less likely to reach the most efficient result, so a legal rule may be necessary to achieve it.

---

[15] Elinor Ostrom, Governing the Commons: The Evolution of Institutions for Collective Action (Cambridge Univ. Press 1990).
[16] Ronald Coase, *The Problem of Social Cost*, 3 J.L. & Econ. 1 (1960).

2. Fairness: Rewarding Labor

In his Second Treatise on Government, philosopher John Locke argued that private property rights can be justified using natural law theory.[17] Natural law theory posits that every person has a property right in her own body and the labor of her body. Mixing that labor with an unowned object to increase its value makes that object the property of the laborer. For example, if Alice cuts down a tree in a communal forest and turns it into a coffee table, she has increased its value due to her labor and therefore has a natural right to it.

In modern terms, we usually believe it is *fair* to reward labor by granting the laborer a property right in the fruits of her labor. Note that this result usually also furthers our economic efficiency policy, because it creates an incentive to work, which increases our productivity. However, the fairness policy would grant the laborer a property right solely because she deserves it, not because it would make society better off. Thus, fairness involves a moral case for property rights, in which we believe the owner should receive her "just deserts." [18]

Homestead and Mining Acts

From 1862 through the early twentieth century, about 10 percent of the property in the United States was settled under the various Homestead Acts, which awarded property to anyone who lived on the land for a certain period of years. In order to acquire title, the occupant had to improve the land, which typically required construction of a house and cultivation of crops. Similarly, the General Mining Act of 1872 awarded property rights to those who discovered valuable minerals on public lands. The Homestead and Mining Acts are good examples of American property laws that both reward labor and incentivize economic activity.

The following case illustrates how a court might use labor theory to determine the rights of claimants to particular property. In this case, the plaintiff clearly did not create the "product" at issue, but made it more valuable through his labor. Do you think this was the sort of thing Locke had in mind?

HASLEM v. LOCKWOOD

37 Conn. 500 (1871)
Supreme Court of Errors of Connecticut

[In the borough of Stamford, large quantities of horse manure accumulated in the public streets. Plaintiff hired two men to scrape the manure into heaps,

---

[17] *See* Locke, *supra* note 1.
[18] Although many people want to spell this term "dessert," thinking that a tasty concoction is a better reward than a bit of sand, the word "desert" comes from "deserve" and is spelled accordingly.

intending to cart it off to his land the next evening, where presumably it would be used for fertilizer. Before he could do so, however, defendant saw the manure and carted it away himself. Plaintiff sued defendant for trover, a cause of action for damages for the wrongful confiscation of another's personal property. The case depended on whether the manure was plaintiff's *property*, merely because he had caused it to be gathered up. The trial court ruled against plaintiff, on the ground that he had not established a sufficient property interest in the manure.]

PARK, J.

[Defendant first argued that plaintiff could not acquire a property right in the manure, because it should be considered part of the street, which is the real property of the borough.] We think the manure scattered upon the ground, under the circumstances of this case, was personal property. The cases referred to by the defendant to show that it was real estate are not in point. The principle of those cases is, that manure made in the usual course of husbandry upon a farm is so attached to and connected with the realty that, in the absence of any express stipulation to the contrary, it becomes appurtenant to it. The principle was established for the benefit of agriculture. It found its origin in the fact that it is essential to the successful cultivation of a farm that the manure, produced from the droppings of cattle and swine fed upon the products of the farm, and composted with earth and vegetable matter taken from the land, should be used to supply the drain made upon the soil in the production of crops, which otherwise would become impoverished and barren; and in the fact that manure so produced is generally regarded by farmers in this country as a part of the realty and has been so treated by landlords and tenants from time immemorial. . . .

But this principle does not apply to the droppings of animals driven by travelers upon the highway. The highway is not used, and cannot be used, for the purpose of agriculture. The manure is of no benefit whatsoever to it, but on the contrary is a detriment; and in cities and large villages it becomes a nuisance, and is removed by public officers at public expense. The finding in this case is, "that the removal of the manure and scrapings was calculated to improve the appearance and health of the borough." It is therefore evident that the cases relied upon by the defendant have no application to the case.

The manure originally belonged to the travelers whose animals dropped it, but it being worthless to them was immediately abandoned; and whether it then became the property of the borough of Stamford which owned the fee of the land on which the manure lay, it is unnecessary to determine; for, if it did, the case finds that the removal of the filth would be an improvement to the borough, and no objection was made by any one to the use that the plaintiff attempted to make of it. Considering the character of such accumulations upon highways in cities and villages, and the light in which they are everywhere regarded in closely settled communities, we cannot believe that the borough in this instance would have had any objection to the act of the plaintiff in removing a nuisance that affected the public health and the appearance of the streets. At all events, we think the facts of the case show a sufficient right in the plaintiff to the immediate possession of the property as against a mere wrong doer.

The defendant appears before the court in no enviable light. He does not pretend that he had a right to the manure, even when scattered upon the highway, superior to that of the plaintiff; but after the plaintiff had changed its original condition and greatly enhanced its value by his labor, he seized and appropriated to his own use the fruits of the plaintiff's outlay, and now seeks immunity from responsibility on the ground that the plaintiff was a wrong doer as well as himself. The conduct of the defendant is in keeping with his claim, and neither commends itself to the favorable consideration of the court. The plaintiff had the peaceable and quiet possession of the property; and we deem this sufficient until the borough of Stamford shall make complaint.

. . . But the question is, if a party finds property comparatively worthless, as the plaintiff found the property in question, owing to its scattered condition upon the highway, and greatly increases its value by his labor and expense, does he lose his right if he leaves it a reasonable time to procure the means to take it away, when such means are necessary for its removal?

Suppose a teamster with a load of grain, while traveling the highway, discovers a rent in one of his bags, and finds that his grain is scattered upon the road for the distance of a mile. He considers the labor of collecting his corn of more value than the property itself, and he therefore abandons it, and pursues his way. A afterwards finds the grain in this condition and gathers it kernel by kernel into heaps by the side of the road, and leaves it a reasonable time to procure the means necessary for its removal. While he is gone for his bag, B discovers the grain thus conveniently collected in heaps and appropriates it to his own use. Has A any remedy? If he has not, the law in this instance is open to just reproach. We think under such circumstances A would have a reasonable time to remove the property, and during such reasonable time his right to it would be protected. If this is so, then the principle applies to the case under consideration.

A reasonable time for the removal of this manure had not elapsed when the defendant seized and converted it to his own use. The statute regulating the rights of parties in the gathering of sea-weed, gives the party who heaps it upon a public beach twenty-four hours in which to remove it, and that length of time for the removal of the property we think would not be unreasonable in most cases like the present one.

We therefore advise the Court of Common Pleas to grant a new trial.

Inheritance and Labor Theory

If we base our recognition of property at least in part on rewarding labor, does that suggest that those who inherit property have a weaker claim? Interestingly, James Madison, one of our strongest proponents of property rights, also favored limits on the ability to pass property down indefinitely to future generations. *See* John F. Hart, *"A Less Proportion of Idle Proprietors": Madison, Property Rights and the Abolition of Fee Tail*, 58 Wash. & Lee L. Rev. 167, 170 (2001). We will study limitations on the right to will property in Chapter 5.

■ POINTS TO CONSIDER

1. **Property policy.** How does *Haslem* illustrate the labor theory of property? Did the court's decision also further economic efficiency? Do you see any possible drawbacks to the court's decision?

2. **Labor and intellectual property.** The labor theory plays a large role in intellectual property rights—if you work to create a new invention or new song, the law recognizes your right to reap the benefits of your effort. Can you see how the principles of *Haslem* might be used to give property rights to someone who has taken another person's creation (e.g., a song or book) and transformed it into something new?

3. **Property classification.** There are many ways to classify property interests. One division is between *real property* and *personal property*. Real property generally consists of land and anything attached to or appurtenant to the land. Personal property generally refers to all property other than real estate. Your furniture, your bank account, and your car are all classified as personal property. *Immovable* property is generally the same as real property while *movable* property generally encompasses personal property.

    The court in *Haslem* indicates that manure is sometimes considered real property and sometimes personal property. What is the distinction?

    Property can also be classified as *tangible* or *intangible*. Tangible property has a physical existence that gives it value, while intangible property does not. Your jewelry is tangible; its value arises from its physical qualities. Your shares of stock are intangible; even though you might have a stock certificate that represents the shares, the certificate itself does not give the stock its value. How would you classify the various types of *intellectual property*, such as patents, trademarks, and copyrights?

■ PROBLEMS

1. **Tangible or intangible?** Assume Testa's will left all her tangible property to her son Alphonse and all her intangible property to her daughter, Beatrice. Upon her death, we discover that Testa, who didn't trust banks, had stuffed $100,000 in cash in her mattress. Who should get the money? For Judge

① rewarding putting value into something.

① Tang. -A

② would require repayment?

bankruptcy context, see In re Oakley, 344 F.3d 709 (7th
ontext (will versus bankruptcy) matter?

the law of accession. Suppose Seurat is sharing an
sse. He sees some paint and a canvas in a closet and mis-
were left there by a previous occupant. So, he uses the
create a little thing he calls *A Sunday Afternoon on the*
atte. Matisse returns and informs Seurat that the paint
ged to him and that the painting is now his as well.
urt rule, using the labor theory of property? Would it make
ad known all along that the canvas and paint belonged to
ds, would Seurat's "deserts" no longer be "just"?

3. Certainty

Certainty refers to creating a system in which purchasers may easily determine whether the seller has the rights to the property he purports to be selling. Certainty may seem like a rather mundane policy goal for a property rights regime. Yet, you will see that a substantial portion of the cases we will read are based on assuring that our system of rights is certain.

Certainty can also refer to a preference for property rules that can be *easily administered and applied.* A rule that is more certain allows people to plan accordingly and reduces time and money spent on dispute resolution. Certainty also contributes to *peace and order*: one of the primary goals of property rights is to prevent constant fights over who should have what.

Uncertainty and the Developing World

The Peruvian economist Hernando de Soto Polar has argued that a poorly functioning property system is one of the main reasons that developing countries have been unable to achieve greater economic progress:

> It would be hard to think of anything which discourages investment as much as uncertainty. . . . Greater certainty would increase the value of both the labor and the capital of the nation. In any country, uncertainty or legal instability reduces the volume of long-term investment and investment in plant and equipment. People save less and invest the little they do save in such socially unproductive goods as jewelry, gold, or luxury property. The flight of capital from countries like Peru is only one more result of the desire to avoid uncertainty.

Hernando de Soto Polar, The Other Path : The Invisible Revolution in the Third World 180-81 (1990). De Soto has also detailed the enormous transaction costs caused by uncertainty in property systems:

> Any asset whose economic and social aspects are not fixed in a formal property system is extremely hard to move in the market. . . . Without such a system, any trade

of an asset, say a piece of real estate, requires an enormous effort just to determine the basics of the transaction: Does the seller own the real estate and have the right to transfer it? Can he pledge it? Will the new owner be accepted as such by those who enforce property rights? What are the effective means to exclude other claimants? In developing and former communist nations, such questions are difficult to answer. For most goods, there is no place where the answers are reliably fixed. That is why the sale or lease of a house may involve lengthy and cumbersome procedures of approval involving all the neighbors. This is often the only way to verify that the owner actually owns the house and there are no other claims on it. It is also why the exchange of most assets outside the West is restricted to local circles of trading partners.

Hernando de Soto Polar, The Mystery of Capital: Why Capitalism Triumphs in the West and Fails Everywhere Else 47 (2000).

Discussion Question

After the unsuccessful Bay of Pigs invasion in 1961, Fidel Castro nationalized the property of U.S. companies doing business in Cuba. Those companies have property claims valued at almost $2 billion, still awaiting settlement.[19] How might that experience impact the current Cuban government's attempt to entice foreign investment?

The problem of informal property records is not confined to the developing world. In the United States, title to land in low-income families may be passed from generation to generation without formal documentation, resulting in much uncertainty about true ownership. For example, an estimated 15 percent of homeowners affected by Hurricane Katrina had clouded title, which impeded their ability to obtain assistance. Heather K. Way, *Informal Homeownership in the United States and the Law*, 29 St. Louis U. Pub. L. Rev. 113, 118 (2009).

■ PROBLEMS

1. **The rule of increase.** A mule is born on a ranch in Montana. The mule is claimed by (1) the owner of the mare (the mother); (2) the owner of the ranch, whose grass the mule and his mother have been eating; and (3) the owner of the sire (the father). Who owns the mule? Is your proposed decision based on certainty, fairness (labor theory), economic efficiency, or something else?[20]

---

[19] Nick Miroff, *The 20 Largest U.S. Property Claims in Cuba*, Wash. Post, Dec. 8, 2015
[20] This problem is drawn from Felix Cohen, *Dialogue on Private Property*, 9 Rutgers L. Rev. 357, 365-69 (1954).

2. The law of the sea? The *RMS Titanic* has struck an iceberg and the captain is deciding how to allocate lifeboat space.[21] One lieutenant suggests that the captain adopt "the law of the sea," a custom that allows women and children to board before any men. Another suggests that the law of the sea is outdated and sexist; instead, the captain should allow first class passengers to board before second class, and second before third, because those passengers paid more for their passage. After all, this lieutenant argues, don't

> **Blackstone on Property Rights**
>
> Blackstone, in discussing the origins of property law, noted that property rights arose, in large part, to prevent endless disputes over resources:
>
> > Otherwise innumerable tumults must have arisen, and the good order of the world have been continually broken and disturbed, while a variety of persons were striving who should get the first occupation of the same thing, or disputing which of them had actually gained it.
>
> *—Sir William Blackstone, 2 William Blackstone, Commentaries *4*

we think that passengers such as John Jacob Astor—the wealthy investor, developer, inventor, and writer—would be more valuable to society than the average steerage passenger? Another lieutenant objects violently to this approach and suggests that the crew should just board whoever gets there first.

Which rule is most certain? Which rule would be most efficient economically? Which would be the fairest, based on labor theory?

Certainty and the Root of Title

In the following case, the Supreme Court was faced with the issue of what to do about the title to land first granted by Native American tribes to certain individuals and then later granted by the U.S. government to someone else. The case concerns property in what is now Illinois. This territory was claimed for France in 1673 by Marquette and Joliet. In 1763, at the end of the French and Indian War, the Treaty of Paris ceded the territory to the British. After the Revolutionary War, of course, the newly formed United States ended up with this land. The territory would not become the state of Illinois until 1818.

Just before the Revolutionary War, land speculators formed corporations to purchase land from the Native American tribes who occupied the territory. In

---

[21] By the way, a seat on the lifeboat would be classified as a *license*, a property right that gives you the revocable right to use someone else's property for a particular purpose. In these circumstances, this license is the most valuable property a passenger could own.

this case, the Illinois and Wabash Corporations, whose shareholders included the future governors of Virginia and Maryland, paid the tribes in possession of the land a total of $55,000 in goods for two huge tracts. The deals were struck with the Kaskaskia, Peoria, and Cahokia (referred to collectively as the Illinois) tribes in 1773 and the Piankeshaw tribe in 1775. Plaintiffs in the case below claimed under title acquired by Thomas Johnson in this manner.

In the early 1800s, the tribes entered into several treaties ceding their rights to this territory to the United States. By 1814, the United States had opened a land office in Kaskaskia, Illinois, to begin selling land to settlers. William McIntosh purchased 53 tracts of land, amounting to almost 12,000 acres, all over southern Illinois. McIntosh received what is called a *patent*, a document issued by a state or federal government conveying a portion of the public domain. (Do you see any similarity between a land patent and a patent for a new invention?)

The case resolving the dispute between these rival titleholders had enormous importance for the certainty of property ownership in the United States; it established a grant from the sovereign as the *root* or beginning of most titles in this country.

Chief Justice John Marshall

The author of the *Johnson v. M'Intosh* opinion, Chief Justice John Marshall, is one of the country's most celebrated jurists. Appointed to the United States Supreme Court as Chief Justice in 1801, he served for 34 years, the longest tenure of any chief justice in history. Among his most notable opinions are *Marbury v. Madison*, which established the right of the courts to review legislation for constitutionality, and *McCulloch v. Maryland*, which set out the basic principles of federalism.

Collection of the Supreme Court of the United States
Painting by Rembrandt Peale

JOHNSON v. M'INTOSH

21 U.S. 543 (1823)
Supreme Court of the United States

Mr. Chief Justice MARSHALL delivered the opinion of the Court.

The plaintiffs in this cause claim the land, in their declaration mentioned, under two grants, purporting to be made, the first in 1773, and the last in 1775, by the chiefs of certain Indian tribes, constituting the Illinois and the Piankeshaw nations; and the question is, whether this title can be recognised in the Courts of the United States?

The facts, as stated in the case agreed, show the authority of the chiefs who executed this conveyance, so far as it could be given by their own people; and likewise show, that the particular tribes for whom these chiefs acted were in rightful possession of the land they sold. The inquiry, therefore, is, in a great measure, confined to the power of Indians to give, and of private individuals to receive, a title which can be sustained in the Courts of this country.

As the right of society, to prescribe those rules by which property may be acquired and preserved is not, and cannot be drawn into question; as the title to lands, especially, is and must be admitted to depend entirely on the law of the nation in which they lie; it will be necessary, in pursuing this inquiry, to examine, not singly those principles of abstract justice, which the Creator of all things has impressed on the mind of his creature man, and which are admitted to regulate, in a great degree, the rights of civilized nations, whose perfect independence is acknowledged; but those principles also which our own government has adopted in the particular case, and given us as the rule for our decision.

On the discovery of this immense continent, the great nations of Europe were eager to appropriate to themselves so much of it as they could respectively acquire. Its vast extent offered an ample field to the ambition and enterprise of all; and the character and religion of its inhabitants afforded an apology for considering them as a people over whom the superior genius of Europe might claim an ascendency. The potentates of the old world found no difficulty in convincing themselves that they made ample compensation to the inhabitants of the new, by bestowing on them civilization and Christianity, in exchange for unlimited independence. But, as they were all in pursuit of nearly the same object, it was necessary, in order to avoid conflicting settlements, and consequent war with each other, to establish a principle, which all should acknowledge as the law by which the right of acquisition, which they all asserted, should be regulated as between themselves. This principle was, that discovery gave title to the government by whose subjects, or by whose authority, it was made, against all other European governments, which title might be consummated by possession.

The exclusion of all other Europeans, necessarily gave to the nation making the discovery the sole right of acquiring the soil from the natives, and establishing settlements upon it. It was a right with which no Europeans could interfere.

It was a right which all asserted for themselves, and to the assertion of which, by others, all assented.

Those relations which were to exist between the discoverer and the natives, were to be regulated by themselves. The rights thus acquired being exclusive, no other power could interpose between them.

In the establishment of these relations, the rights of the original inhabitants were, in no instance, entirely disregarded; but were necessarily, to a considerable extent, impaired. They were admitted to be the rightful occupants of the soil, with a legal as well as just claim to retain possession of it, and to use it according to their own discretion; but their rights to complete sovereignty, as independent nations, were necessarily diminished, and their power to dispose of the soil at their own will, to whomsoever they pleased, was denied by the original fundamental principle, that discovery gave exclusive title to those who made it.

While the different nations of Europe respected the right of the natives, as occupants, they asserted the ultimate dominion to be in themselves; and claimed and exercised, as a consequence of this ultimate dominion, a power to grant the soil, while yet in possession of the natives. These grants have been understood by all, to convey a title to the grantees, subject only to the Indian right of occupancy.

The history of America, from its discovery to the present day, proves, we think, the universal recognition of these principles. [The Court discusses various charters given by the English Crown to the American colonies claiming to vest title.]

Thus has our whole country been granted by the crown while in the occupation of the Indians. These grants purport to convey the soil as well as the right of dominion to the grantees. . . . It has never been objected to this, or to any other similar grant, that the title as well as possession was in the Indians when it was made, and that it passed nothing on that account.

These various patents cannot be considered as nullities; nor can they be limited to a mere grant of the powers of government. . . .

Thus, all the nations of Europe, who have acquired territory on this continent, have asserted in themselves, and have recognised in others, the exclusive right of the discoverer to appropriate the lands occupied by the Indians. Have the American States rejected or adopted this principle?

By the treaty which concluded the war of our revolution, Great Britain relinquished all claim, not only to the government, but to the "propriety and territorial rights of the United States," whose boundaries were fixed in the second article. By this treaty, the powers of government, and the right to soil, which had previously been in Great Britain, passed definitively to these States. We had before taken possession of them, by declaring independence; but neither the declaration of independence, nor the treaty confirming it, could give us more than that which we before possessed, or to which Great Britain was before entitled. It has never been doubted, that either the United States, or the several States, had a clear title to all the lands within the boundary lines described in the treaty, subject only to the Indian right of occupancy, and that the exclusive power to extinguish that right, was vested in that government which might constitutionally exercise it. . . .

The ceded territory was occupied by numerous and warlike tribes of Indians; but the exclusive right of the United States to extinguish their title, and to grant the soil, has never, we believe, been doubted. . . .

The United States, then, have unequivocally acceded to that great and broad rule by which its civilized inhabitants now hold this country. They hold, and assert in themselves, the title by which it was acquired. They maintain, as all others have maintained, that discovery gave an exclusive right to extinguish the Indian title of occupancy, either by purchase or by conquest; and gave also a right to such a degree of sovereignty, as the circumstances of the people would allow them to exercise.

. . . An absolute title to lands cannot exist, at the same time, in different persons, or in different governments. An absolute [title], must be an exclusive title, or at least a title which excludes all others not compatible with it. All our institutions recognise the absolute title of the crown, subject only to the Indian right of occupancy, and recognise the absolute title of the crown to extinguish that right. This is incompatible with an absolute and complete title in the Indians.

. . . Conquest gives a title which the Courts of the conqueror cannot deny, whatever the private and speculative opinions of individuals may be, respecting the original justice of the claim which has been successfully asserted. The British government, which was then our government, and whose rights have passed to the United States, asserted title to all the lands occupied by Indians, within the chartered limits of the British colonies. It asserted also a limited sovereignty over them, and the exclusive right of extinguishing the title which occupancy gave to them. These claims have been maintained and established as far west as the river Mississippi, by the sword. The title to a vast portion of the lands we now hold, originates in them. It is not for the Courts of this country to question the validity of this title, or to sustain one which is incompatible with it. . . .

The title by conquest is acquired and maintained by force. The conqueror prescribes its limits. Humanity, however, acting on public opinion, has established, as a general rule, that the conquered shall not be wantonly oppressed, and that their condition shall remain as eligible as is compatible with the objects of the conquest. Most usually, they are incorporated with the victorious nation, and become subjects or citizens of the government with which they are connected. The new and old members of the society mingle with each other; the distinction between them is gradually lost, and they make one people. Where this incorporation is practicable, humanity demands, and a wise policy requires, that the rights of the conquered to property should remain unimpaired; that the new subjects should be governed as equitably as the old, and that confidence in their security should gradually banish the painful sense of being separated from their ancient connexions, and united by force to strangers.

When the conquest is complete, and the conquered inhabitants can be blended with the conquerors, or safely governed as a distinct people, public opinion, which not even the conqueror can disregard, imposes these restraints upon him; and he cannot neglect them without injury to his fame, and hazard to his power.

But the tribes of Indians inhabiting this country were fierce savages, whose occupation was war, and whose subsistence was drawn chiefly from the forest. To leave them in possession of their country, was to leave the country a wilderness; to govern them as a distinct people, was impossible, because they were as brave and as high spirited as they were fierce, and were ready to repel by arms every attempt on their independence.

What was the inevitable consequence of this state of things? The Europeans were under the necessity either of abandoning the country, and relinquishing their pompous claims to it, or of enforcing those claims by the sword, and by the adoption of principles adapted to the condition of a people with whom it was impossible to mix, and who could not be governed as a distinct society, or of remaining in their neighbourhood, and exposing themselves and their families to the perpetual hazard of being massacred.

Frequent and bloody wars, in which the whites were not always the aggressors, unavoidably ensued. European policy, numbers, and skill, prevailed. As the white population advanced, that of the Indians necessarily receded. The country in the immediate neighbourhood of agriculturists became unfit for them. The game fled into thicker and more unbroken forests, and the Indians followed. The soil, to which the crown originally claimed title, being no longer occupied by its ancient inhabitants, was parcelled out according to the will of the sovereign power, and taken possession of by persons who claimed immediately from the crown, or mediately, through its grantees or deputies.

That law which regulates, and ought to regulate in general, the relations between the conqueror and conquered, was incapable of application to a people under such circumstances. The resort to some new and different rule, better adapted to the actual state of things, was unavoidable. Every rule which can be suggested will be found to be attended with great difficulty.

However extravagant the pretension of converting the discovery of an inhabited country into conquest may appear; if the principle has been asserted in the first instance, and afterwards sustained; if a country has been acquired and held under it; if the property of the great mass of the community originates in it, it becomes the law of the land, and cannot be questioned. So, too, with respect to the concomitant principle, that the Indian inhabitants are to be considered merely as occupants, to be protected, indeed, while in peace, in the possession of their lands, but to be deemed incapable of transferring the absolute title to others. However this restriction may be opposed to natural right, and to the usages of civilized nations, yet, if it be indispensable to that system under which the country has been settled, and be adapted to the actual condition of the two people, it may, perhaps, be supported by reason, and certainly cannot be rejected by Courts of justice. . . .

It has never been contended, that the Indian title amounted to nothing. Their right of possession has never been questioned. The claim of government extends to the complete ultimate title, charged with this right of possession, and to the exclusive power of acquiring that right. . . .

After bestowing on this subject a degree of attention which was more required by the magnitude of the interest in litigation, and the able and elaborate arguments of the bar, than by its intrinsic difficulty, the Court is decidedly of opinion, that the plaintiffs do not exhibit a title which can be sustained in the Courts of the United States; and that there is no error in the judgment which was rendered against them in the District Court of Illinois.

Judgment affirmed, with costs.

■ POINTS TO CONSIDER

1. **What happened?** Note that the Native American tribes that Chief Justice Marshall spends most of his opinion discussing were not actually represented in this case, which pits wealthy land speculators against another real estate investor, William McIntosh. The subsequent history of the tribes involved in *M'Intosh* is typical, but tragic. By 1818, the Piankeshaw tribe had diminished significantly, and its chief signed a treaty selling most of its land to the United States. The remaining members of the tribe moved to Missouri, then Kansas, and eventually ended up on a reservation in Oklahoma. The Illinois tribes had been decimated by a war with the Lake tribes in the late 1700s, and by 1800 there were only about 150 members of the combined tribes. The survivors had sold all their land in Illinois by 1833 and moved to the same Oklahoma reservation with the Piankeshaw. In 1759, the Piankeshaw alone were estimated at 1,500; in 1885, the combined Piankeshaw and Illinois tribes numbered fewer than 200.

2. **The bundle of sticks.** Chief Justice Marshall's decision leaves the Native Americans with *some* property rights, but not others—which of the rights in our bundle of sticks does Marshall indicate they have and which do they not have? Some American Indian law scholars have called Marshall's decision "a brilliant compromise" between giving the tribes full title or no rights at all, which would have allowed unhindered expropriation[22] of their lands. *See, e.g.,* Nell Jessup Newton, *At the Whim of the Sovereign: Aboriginal Title Reconsidered,* 31 Hastings L.J. 1215, 1223 (1980).

3. **Discovery and conquest.** *M'Intosh* also illustrates the *relational* nature of property rights—your rights to property may depend on who is on the other side. As between European nations, the Court indicates that "discovery" is the relevant rule: title goes to the first nation to discover the land and claim it. As we will see in the next chapter, this is a rule of "first possession," which is the most common way of allocating rights in unowned property.

   But of course, the Europeans didn't "discover" America; the Native Americans were there first. Why doesn't the discovery rule apply to them?

   For Europeans versus Native Americans, the Court uses a different rule: *conquest.* Again, the Court adjusts the rule of conquest to fit the

---

[22] Expropriation means the deprivation of someone's property by the government.

circumstances. In most cases of conquest, the Court says, the "rights of the conquered to property should remain unimpaired," but in this case, the conquered were not eligible for that rule. Why not?

4. **Certainty.** Can you see how this decision laid the foundation for protecting the certainty of land titles in the United States? When Abraham and Mary Lincoln bought their house in 1844 in Springfield, Illinois, they were buying, for $1,200, a small piece of the tract that had been purchased by the Illinois Company in 1773 from the Indian tribes. In order to be sure he was getting good title, Lincoln presumably would have traced the ownership of the parcel back to the "root of title," which in this case would be a grant or patent from the United States. But had *M'Intosh* not been decided as it was, could the Lincolns be sure that they were getting good title to the property?

5. **The "dark side" of economic efficiency?** Professor Eric Kades has written extensively on the history and implications of the *M'Intosh* case:

> Those with a dark view of the process of expropriation argue that European settlers used (or perhaps more accurately, abused) laws either with specific intent to take land and exterminate the aboriginal population, or with deliberate indifference to these inevitable results of their policies. Observers who view European actions as relatively benevolent insist that legal rules softened the process of expropriation....
>
> ... [N]either view is consistent with even the most basic facts in the legal and historical record. Massacres, and even battles, were quite rare in the process of expropriating Indian lands—a fact difficult to harmonize with a theory of intentional genocide. On the other hand, it is hard to reconcile a benevolent view of the expropriation process with the end result—the knowing and intentional expropriation of a continent accompanied by the destruction of tribe after tribe.

Eric Kades, *The Dark Side of Efficiency:* Johnson v. M'Intosh *and the Expropriation of American Indian Lands*, 148 U. Pa. L. Rev. 1065, 1071 (2000). Professor Kades argues that the *M'Intosh* decision was economically efficient, because it eliminated competition for the purchase of these lands, thereby allowing the government to obtain them at a lower cost, which Kades labels "the dark side of efficiency." *Id.* at 1190. Do the policies of economic efficiency and fairness cut in different directions in this case?

6. **Legal positivism and utilitarianism.** Compare the reasoning of Chief Justice Marshall with the utilitarian philosophy of Jeremy Bentham, who published these thoughts on property in 1802, about 20 years before the *M'Intosh* decision:

Bentham's Utilitarian Theory of Property

We shall see that there is no natural property—that property is entirely the creature of law....

> . . . [T]here have always been circumstances in which a man could secure by his own means the enjoyment of certain things—but the catalogue of these cases is very limited. The savage, who has hidden his prey, may hope to keep it for himself so long as his cave is not discovered; so long as he is awake to defend it; whilst he is stronger than his rivals: but this is all. How miserable and precarious is this method of possession!— Suppose, then, the slightest agreement among these savages reciprocally to respect each other's booty: this is the introduction, of a principle, to which you can only give the name of law. . . .
>
> Property and law are born and must die together. Before the laws, there was no property: take away the laws, all property ceases.
>
> *—Jeremy Bentham, The Works of Jeremy Bentham 308-09 (John Bowring ed., William Tait)*

Bentham's utilitarian philosophy rests on the assumption that property rights arose to serve human needs, such as security, peace, and order, and should be recognized only to the extent that they serve those ends.[23] You can also label this approach *positivism*, because Bentham believes that property rights come from the law itself, and no other source, so that we are free to define the limits of property rights when necessary to achieve societal goals.[24] Compare Locke's philosophy, based on fairness and *natural law*, which emphasizes the moral case for property rights. Which philosophy is behind Chief Justice Marshall's reasoning in *M'Intosh*? If property rights can be manipulated to serve societal needs, do we really have any property protection? Can the government simply redefine property, so we have no assurance that what we have will not be taken away from us? In other words, if the Native Americans (and those who purchased from them) can have their property rights redefined to suit the needs of the country, why can't the government redefine property to prevent you from building on land that society prefers to keep in its natural condition? These are tough questions, which we will consider further in the final chapter of this book, when we discuss constitutional limitations on government regulation of property. For now, we should at least note that the utilitarian, positivist philosophy of Bentham and *M'Intosh* must have limits—property rights cannot mean only what society says they mean.

4. Democracy

Thomas Jefferson and other Founders believed that the widespread, secure ownership of property was essential to liberty. John Adams declared: "Property must be

---

[23] Jeremy Bentham, The Works of Jeremy Bentham 308-09 (John Bowring ed., William Tait).

[24] *Id.*

secured or liberty cannot exist."[25] In a 1776 letter, Adams wondered whether "men in general, in every society, who are wholly destitute of property, are . . . too dependent on other men to have a will of their own?"[26] A person who owned his own land would be largely self-sufficient and therefore would not be dependent on the state for survival. Such a person would be at liberty to oppose the current government, or speak freely against its policies, without fear of reprisal. That freedom, of course, depended on the person's property being secure from governmental appropriation.

Property and Political Stability

Private Property is arguably the single most important institution of social and political integration. Ownership of property creates a commitment to the political and legal order since the latter guarantees property rights: it makes the citizen into a co-sovereign, as it were. . . . Historical evidence indicates that societies with a wide distribution of property, notably in land and residential housing, are more conservative and stabler, and for that reason more resilient to upheavals of all sorts.

—*Richard Pipes, The Russian Revolution (1991)*

Property and Democracy—The Red Scare

During the decade following World War II, thousands of Americans were accused of being Communists or communist sympathizers, which placed them in danger of being "blacklisted" and having their careers destroyed. Often accusations were made on the basis of rumors or questionable evidence.

In one famous episode during the Army-McCarthy hearings, Senator Joseph McCarthy chastised Joseph Welch, head counsel for the United States Army, for continuing to employ an attorney, Fred Fisher, who was accused of associating with the National Lawyers Guild (which the FBI had labeled a "communist front") while in law school. It was this attempt to coerce Welch into firing Fisher that prompted Welch to ask, "Senator, may we not drop this? . . . Let us not assassinate this lad further, Senator. You've done enough. Have you no sense of decency, sir? At long last, have you left no sense of decency?"

Does the Red Scare illustrate why Adams insisted that the protection of property is essential to liberty? In modern society, in which few Americans are the type of self-sufficient landed yeomen Jefferson envisaged, should protection of "property" include protection of employment rights? *See Board of Regents v. Roth*, 408 U.S. 564, 577 (1972) ("It is a purpose

---

[25] Discourses on Davila, *in* 6 The Works of John Adams 280 (Charles Francis Adams ed., 1851).

[26] John Adams to James Sullivan (April 26, 1776), *in* 9 The Works of John Adams 376 (Charles Francis Adams ed., 1854).

of the ancient institution of property to protect those claims upon which people rely in their daily lives, reliance that must not be arbitrarily undermined").

We can see the link between property and democracy arising in several modern contexts. Internationally, the issue of property distribution is of crucial importance in countries with emerging democracies. Modern social scientists confirm that democracy is much more likely to take root in societies with broad distribution of land and relative social equality.[27] In the United States, this policy is behind laws that discourage concentrations of land ownership and subsidize the purchase of homes. This policy helps explain limitations on the ability to pass property from generation to generation indefinitely—if accumulated property cannot be distributed more broadly, the democratic ideal may be compromised. It may also partially account for laws that prohibit the foreign ownership of agricultural land.[28]

Most importantly, the principle of democracy is behind the dual protection of property found in the U.S. Constitution. Property cannot be taken from you without the due process of law and without just compensation, thus ensuring that you are free to criticize the government without fear that your political enemies will deprive you of your possessions.

5. Personhood

One of the chilling aspects of the imaginary communal society in Thomas More's *Utopia* was that everyone wore clothes of exactly the same color and style and lived in houses of identical design.[29] The society he envisioned in 1516, in which private property was abolished, became a reality in the communist countries of the twentieth century, such as the former Soviet Union and China. After the Chinese Revolution in 1949, almost everyone—men and women alike—wore the same style of clothes, often the formless outfit known as the "Mao suit"; cosmetics and jewelry virtually disappeared. Communist housing, at least in urban

> ### Bentham on Property
>
> [O]ur property becomes a part of our being, and cannot be torn from us without rending us to the quick.
>
> —*Jeremy Bentham, The Theory of Legislation 115 (1789)*

---

[27] *See* Jeffrey Riedinger, *Property Rights and Democracy: Philosophical and Economic Considerations*, 22 Cap. U. L. Rev. 893, 895-97 (1993) (summarizing research on property distribution and democracy).

[28] *See, e.g.*, Mo. Ann. Stat. §442.571 (West 2013) (prohibiting ownership of agricultural land by non-citizens).

[29] *See* Thomas More, Utopia (Arc Manor 2008) (1516).

areas, consisted largely of standardized concrete block apartment buildings. Before the Berlin Wall came down in 1989, going from West to East Berlin was often described as similar to switching your television set from color to black and white.

Think about how owning property allows you to express yourself. Everyone who has bought a house understands the joy that comes from stepping onto property that you now control. This *autonomy* allows you to decide whether to paint the shutters green or red. You can decide whether to plant roses or bushes along the front walk. Even a person who has only rented an apartment or lived in a dorm room knows that the ability to "make it your own" by hanging your pictures has important psychological benefits. Whether you choose to drive a grey sedan or a red sports car says something about you. All these decisions are expressions of your personality and therefore bring a sense of fulfillment to property ownership.

We also recognize that individuals may place a value on property that far exceeds the amount of money the item could bring in the marketplace. For example, a picture of a deceased relative or the letter your father wrote to you on your eighteenth birthday may have no real economic value, but may be a priceless treasure to you. Therefore, we must temper our economic efficiency calculus in many cases by recognizing that property carries with it a personal value that cannot be measured accurately. *See generally* Jeremy Blumenthal, *"To Be Human": A Psychological Perspective on Property Law*, 83 Tul. L. Rev. 609 (2009) (reviewing the literature on the psychological aspects of property ownership).

We can also put in this category the values of *privacy* and *security* that property carries with it. Owning property gives you an enclave where you can be free from the tumult of society. As Judge Jerome Frank put it:

> A man can still control a small part of his environment, his house; he can retreat thence from outsiders, secure in the knowledge that they cannot get at him without disobeying the Constitution. That is still a sizable hunk of liberty—worth protecting from encroachment. A sane, decent, civilized society must provide some such oasis, some shelter from public scrutiny, some insulated enclosure, some enclave, some inviolate place—which is a man's castle.

United States v. On Lee, 193 F.2d 306, 315-16 (2d Cir. 1951) (Frank, J., dissenting), *aff'd*, 343 U.S. 747 (1952). The Fourth Amendment protection against unreasonable searches gives constitutional protection to the privacy aspect of property.

The personhood policy can be seen in a variety of other property laws. Almost every state protects the *homestead* of a debtor from the reach of creditors, for example.[30] These homestead laws are intended to protect what one court called "the inviolable sanctuary of the family." Wilson v. Cochran, 31 Tex. 677 (1869). Similarly, the bankruptcy code exempts "household furnishings, household goods, wearing apparel, appliances, books, animals, crops, musical instruments,

---

[30] *See* Alison D. Morantz, *There's No Place Like Home: Homestead Exemption and Judicial Constructions of Family in Nineteenth-Century America*, 24 Law & Hist. Rev. 245, 255 (2006) (homestead exemption found in all but two states).

or jewelry that are held primarily for the personal, family, or household use of the debtor or a dependent of the debtor." [31] Many of our zoning laws balance personhood interests against other societal interests such as economic efficiency.

In the chapters that follow, look for cases that implicate the personhood element of property. In this chapter, we will see that an owner's right to exclude rests largely on this ideal of privacy and security.

D   THE BUNDLE OF STICKS

As we noted at the start of this chapter, property law consists of legal rights among persons with respect to things. An owner's property interest can be described as an aggregation of various rights, such as the right to occupy; the right to exploit the resources; the right to transfer by sale, gift, or will; the right to exclude others, and so on. In many cases, some of the sticks in this bundle of interests may be held by others—when an owner sells off the mineral interests in her property, for example, or rents her pasture to a farmer to graze his cattle.

These rights are not absolute. As we have just learned, property rights developed to serve certain policy goals and sometimes may be limited when those policies are outweighed by other societal interests. A few examples:

> ➤ As we will see in subsequent chapters, the right to will property has been limited in many ways: one spouse cannot completely disinherit the other spouse, for example, and society has limited your ability to control property indefinitely after you die.
> ➤ A landowner has the right to transfer, but may not refuse to sell based on discriminatory reasons; similarly, a landlord has the right to exclude potential tenants, but may not discriminate.
> ➤ Chapters 12 and 13 describe various limitations on your right to use your property (e.g., zoning control or nuisance law).

In this chapter, we explore a couple of the sticks in the bundle, to illustrate the *relational* and *mutable* nature of property interests. You should see that, far from being static and absolute, property rights evolve over time to serve more closely the interests of society.

1.   The Right to Exclude

The Supreme Court has noted that the right to exclude others from your property is "universally held to be a fundamental element of the property right,"[32] and is

---

[31] 11 U.S.C. §522(f)(1)(B)(i) (2013).
[32] Kaiser Aetna v. United States, 444 U.S. 164, 179-80 (1979).

"one of the most essential sticks in the bundle of rights."[33] A landowner's fence is a visible dividing line distinguishing her property from her neighbor's. When we say you "own" your laptop, we understand that means not only that you have the right to use it, but that you also have the right to keep others from using it, even if that means it sits in the storage room and gathers dust.

While this seems to be a given part of what property ownership entails, we need to think more carefully about *why* we protect the right to exclude and *under what circumstances* we might consider limiting that right.

The following case involves an action for *trespass*, the legal action claiming the breach of the boundaries of someone's property. Trespass can be a criminal action, if the intruder knows he is not authorized or privileged to be on the property, and has been told to leave, or the land is posted or enclosed in such a way that he should know his presence is unauthorized. Trespass can also be a civil action, in which the landowner seeks damages for the intrusion.

At common law, every unauthorized boundary breach was deemed to be an actionable trespass. Under the modern rule, the intruder is liable for a harmless entry only if it is intentional. Restatement (Second) of Torts §158 (1965). A reckless or negligent entry, or one that results from an abnormally dangerous activity, is also actionable, but only if it causes harm. Restatement (Second) of Torts §165 (1965). Someone may be liable for a trespass by causing the entry of a thing or another person onto the land; for example, if A released water onto B's land, or launched a rocket, which landed on B's property, the action would constitute a trespass. *See, e.g.*, Wilen v. Falkenstien, 191 S.W.3d 791 (Tex. App. 2006) (neighbor who hired tree service to trim plaintiff's trees while he was on vacation in order to improve view liable for trespass).

In the following case, the court recognized that determining the remedy for a trespass has important implications for the right to exclude.

JACQUE v. STEENBERG HOMES

563 N.W.2d 154, 209 Wis. 2d 605 (1997)
Supreme Court of Wisconsin

WILLIAM A. BABLITCH, Justice.

Steenberg Homes had a mobile home to deliver. Unfortunately for Harvey and Lois Jacque (the Jacques), the easiest route of delivery was across their land. Despite adamant protests by the Jacques, Steenberg plowed a path through the Jacques' snow-covered field and via that path, delivered the mobile home. Consequently, the Jacques sued Steenberg Homes for intentional trespass. At trial, Steenberg Homes conceded the intentional trespass, but argued that no compensatory damages had been proved, and that punitive damages could not

---

[33]Loretto v. Teleprompter Manhattan CATV Corp., 458 U.S. 419, 433 (1982).

be awarded without compensatory damages. Although the jury awarded the Jacques $1 in nominal damages and $100,000 in punitive damages, the circuit court set aside the jury's award of $100,000. The court of appeals affirmed, reluctantly concluding that it could not reinstate the punitive damages because it was bound by precedent establishing that an award of nominal damages will not sustain a punitive damage award. We conclude that when nominal damages are awarded for an intentional trespass to land, punitive damages may, in the discretion of the jury, be awarded. We further conclude that the $100,000 awarded by the jury is not excessive. Accordingly, we reverse and remand for reinstatement of the punitive damage award.

decision

> **Damages**
>
> Compensatory damages are sometimes called actual damages and are intended to compensate for the harm or injury caused by the tort.
>
> Nominal damages are very small awards intended to show that a violation of the law occurred, but that no damage resulted.
>
> Punitive damages are intended to punish the wrongdoer and deter future wrongful conduct. They are typically allowed only when the conduct is especially egregious or malicious.

I.

The relevant facts follow. Plaintiffs, Lois and Harvey Jacque, are an elderly couple, now retired from farming, who own roughly 170 acres near Wilke's Lake in the town of Schleswig. The defendant, Steenberg Homes, Inc. (Steenberg), is in the business of selling mobile homes. In the fall of 1993, a neighbor of the Jacques purchased a mobile home from Steenberg. Delivery of the mobile home was included in the sales price.

Steenberg determined that the easiest route to deliver the mobile home was across the Jacques' land. Steenberg preferred transporting the home across the Jacques' land because the only alternative was a private road which was covered in up to seven feet of snow and contained a sharp curve which would require sets of "rollers" to be used when maneuvering the home around the curve. Steenberg asked the Jacques on several separate occasions whether it could move the home across the Jacques' farm field. The Jacques refused. The Jacques were sensitive about allowing others on their land because they had lost property valued at over $10,000 to other neighbors in an adverse possession action[34] in the mid-1980's. Despite repeated refusals from the Jacques, Steenberg decided to sell the mobile home, which was to be used as a summer cottage, and delivered it on February 15, 1994.

---

[34] Adverse possession refers to a method of acquiring title to land through continuous, long-term possession. We will discuss the elements of and theory behind adverse possession in Chapter 2.—Eds.

On the morning of delivery, Mr. Jacque observed the mobile home parked on the corner of the town road adjacent to his property. He decided to find out where the movers planned to take the home. The movers, who were Steenberg employees, showed Mr. Jacque the path they planned to take with the mobile home to reach the neighbor's lot. The path cut across the Jacques' land. Mr. Jacque informed the movers that it was the Jacques' land they were planning to cross and that Steenberg did not have permission to cross their land. He told them that Steenberg had been refused permission to cross the Jacques' land.

One of Steenberg's employees called the assistant manager, who then came out to the Jacques' home. In the meantime, the Jacques called and asked some of their neighbors and the town chairman to come over immediately. Once everyone was present, the Jacques showed the assistant manager an aerial map and plat book of the township to prove their ownership of the land, and reiterated their demand that the home not be moved across their land.

At that point, the assistant manager asked Mr. Jacque how much money it would take to get permission. Mr. Jacque responded that it was not a question of money; the Jacques just did not want Steenberg to cross their land. Mr. Jacque testified that he told Steenberg to "[F]ollow the road, that is what the road is for." Steenberg employees left the meeting without permission to cross the land.

At trial, one of Steenberg's employees testified that, upon coming out of the Jacques' home, the assistant manager stated: "I don't give a—what [Mr. Jacque] said, just get the home in there any way you can." The other Steenberg employee confirmed this testimony and further testified that the assistant manager told him to park the company truck in such a way that no one could get down the town road to see the route the employees were taking with the home. The assistant manager denied giving these instructions, and Steenberg argued that the road was blocked for safety reasons.

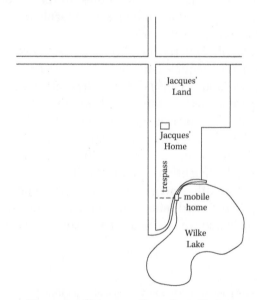

Diagram of Jacque v. Steenberg Homes
Thanks to Pat Dewane, plaintiff's counsel

The employees, after beginning down the private road, ultimately used a "bobcat" to cut a path through the Jacques' snow-covered field and hauled the home across the Jacques' land to the neighbor's lot. One employee testified that upon returning to the office and informing the assistant manager that they had gone across the field, the assistant manager reacted by giggling and laughing. The other employee confirmed this testimony. The assistant manager disputed this testimony.

When a neighbor informed the Jacques that Steenberg had, in fact, moved the mobile home across the Jacques' land, Mr. Jacque called the Manitowoc County Sheriff's Department. After interviewing the parties and observing the scene, an officer from the sheriff's department issued a $30 citation to Steenberg's assistant manager.

The Jacques commenced an intentional tort action in Manitowoc County Circuit Court . . . seeking compensatory and punitive damages from Steenberg. The case was tried before a jury on December 1, 1994. . . . The jury awarded the Jacques $1 nominal damages and $100,000 punitive damages. Steenberg filed post-verdict motions claiming that the punitive damage award must be set aside because Wisconsin law did not allow a punitive damage award unless the jury also awarded compensatory damages. . . . The circuit court granted Steenberg's motion to set aside the award.

Steenberg argues that, as a matter of law, punitive damages could not be awarded by the jury because punitive damages must be supported by an award of compensatory damages and here the jury awarded only nominal and punitive damages. The Jacques contend that the rationale supporting the compensatory damage award requirement is inapposite when the wrongful act is an intentional trespass to land. We agree with the Jacques.

. . . The rationale for the compensatory damage requirement is that if the individual cannot show actual harm, he or she has but a nominal interest, hence, society has little interest in having the unlawful, but otherwise harmless, conduct deterred, therefore, punitive damages are inappropriate. . . .

However, whether nominal damages can support a punitive damage award in the case of an intentional trespass to land has never been squarely addressed by this court. Nonetheless, Wisconsin law is not without reference to this situation. In 1854 the court established punitive damages, allowing the assessment of "damages as a punishment to the defendant for the purpose of making an example." McWilliams v. Bragg, 3 Wis. 424, 425 (1854). The *McWilliams* court related the facts and an illustrative tale from the English case of Merest v. Harvey, 128 Eng. Rep. 761 (C.P. 1814), to explain the rationale underlying punitive damages.

In *Merest*, a landowner was shooting birds in his field when he was approached by the local magistrate who wanted to hunt with him. Although the landowner refused, the magistrate proceeded to hunt. When the landowner continued to object, the magistrate threatened to have him jailed and dared him to file suit. Although little actual harm had been caused, the English court upheld damages of 500 pounds, explaining "in a case where a man disregards every principle which actuates the conduct of gentlemen, what is to restrain him except large damages?" *McWilliams*, 3 Wis. 424 at 428.

To explain the need for punitive damages, even where actual harm is slight, *McWilliams* related the hypothetical tale from *Merest* of an intentional trespasser:

> Suppose a gentleman has a paved walk in his paddock, before his window, and that a man intrudes and walks up and down before the window of his house, and looks in while the owner is at dinner, is the trespasser permitted to say "here is a halfpenny for you which is the full extent of the mischief I have done." Would that be a compensation? I cannot say that it would be. . . .

McWilliams, 3 Wis. at 428. Thus, in the case establishing punitive damages in this state, this court recognized that in certain situations of trespass, the actual harm is not in the damage done to the land, which may be minimal, but in the loss of the individual's right to exclude others from his or her property and, the court implied that this right may be punished by a large damage award despite the lack of measurable harm.

. . . The Jacques argue that the rationale for not allowing nominal damages to support a punitive damage award is inapposite when the wrongful act involved is an intentional trespass to land. The Jacques argue that both the individual and society have significant interests in deterring intentional trespass to land, regardless of the lack of measurable harm that results. We agree with the Jacques. An examination of the individual interests invaded by an intentional trespass to land, and society's interests in preventing intentional trespass to land, leads us to the conclusion that the [compensatory damages requirement] should not apply when the tort supporting the award is intentional trespass to land.

We turn first to the individual landowner's interest in protecting his or her land from trespass. The United States Supreme Court has recognized that the private landowner's right to exclude others from his or her land is "one of the most essential sticks in the bundle of rights that are commonly characterized as property." . . . This court has long recognized "[e]very person['s] constitutional right to the exclusive enjoyment of his own property for any purpose which does not invade the rights of another person." Diana Shooting Club v. Lamoreux, 114 Wis. 44, 59, 89 N.W. 880 (1902) (holding that the victim of an intentional trespass should have been allowed to take judgment for nominal damages and costs). Thus, both this court and the Supreme Court recognize the individual's legal right to exclude others from private property.

Yet a right is hollow if the legal system provides insufficient means to protect it. Felix Cohen offers the following analysis summarizing the relationship between the individual and the state regarding property rights:

> [T]hat is property to which the following label can be attached:
>
> To the world:
>
> Keep off X unless you have my permission, which I may grant or withhold.

Signed: Private Citizen

Endorsed: The state

Felix S. Cohen, *Dialogue on Private Property*, IX Rutgers Law Review 357, 374 (1954). Harvey and Lois Jacque have the right to tell Steenberg Homes and any other trespasser, "No, you cannot cross our land." But that right has no practical meaning unless protected by the State. And, as this court recognized as early as 1854, a "halfpenny" award does not constitute state protection.

The nature of the nominal damage award in an intentional trespass to land case further supports an exception to [the general rule for punitive damages]. Because a legal right is involved, the law recognizes that actual harm occurs in every trespass. The action for intentional trespass to land is directed at vindication of the legal right. W. Page Keeton, *Prosser and Keeton on Torts*, §13 (5th ed. 1984). The law infers some damage from every direct entry upon the land of another. *Id.* The law recognizes actual harm in every trespass to land whether or not compensatory damages are awarded. *Id.* Thus, in the case of intentional trespass to land, the nominal damage award represents the recognition that, although immeasurable in mere dollars, actual harm has occurred.

The potential for harm resulting from intentional trespass also supports an exception to [the general rule]. A series of intentional trespasses, as the Jacques had the misfortune to discover in an unrelated action, can threaten the individual's very ownership of the land. The conduct of an intentional trespasser, if repeated, might ripen into prescription or adverse possession and, as a consequence, the individual landowner can lose his or her property rights to the trespasser. *See* Wis. Stat. §893.28.

In sum, the individual has a strong interest in excluding trespassers from his or her land. Although only nominal damages were awarded to the Jacques, Steenberg's intentional trespass caused actual harm. We turn next to society's interest in protecting private property from the intentional trespasser.

Society has an interest in punishing and deterring intentional trespassers beyond that of protecting the interests of the individual landowner. Society has an interest in preserving the integrity of the legal system. Private landowners should feel confident that wrongdoers who trespass upon their land will be appropriately punished. When landowners have confidence in the legal system, they are less likely to resort to "self-help" remedies. In *McWilliams*, the court recognized the importance of "'prevent[ing] the practice of dueling, [by permitting] juries [] to *punish* insult by exemplary damages.'" *McWilliams*, 3 Wis. at 428. Although dueling is rarely a modern form of self-help, one can easily imagine a frustrated landowner taking the law into his or her own hands when faced with a brazen trespasser, like Steenberg, who refuses to heed no trespass warnings.

People expect wrongdoers to be appropriately punished. Punitive damages have the effect of bringing to punishment types of conduct that, though oppressive and hurtful to the individual, almost invariably go unpunished by the public prosecutor. Kink v. Combs, 28 Wis. 2d 65, 135 N.W.2d 789 (1965). The

$30 forfeiture was certainly not an appropriate punishment for Steenberg's egregious trespass in the eyes of the Jacques. It was more akin to Merest's "halfpenny." If punitive damages are not allowed in a situation like this, what punishment will prohibit the intentional trespass to land? Moreover, what is to stop Steenberg Homes from concluding, in the future, that delivering its mobile homes via an intentional trespass and paying the resulting Class B forfeiture, is not more profitable than obeying the law? Steenberg Homes plowed a path across the Jacques' land and dragged the mobile home across that path, in the face of the Jacques' adamant refusal. A $30 forfeiture and a $1 nominal damage award are unlikely to restrain Steenberg Homes from similar conduct in the future. An appropriate punitive damage award probably will.

[The court then affirmed the amount of the punitive damages award, finding that the conduct of Steenberg Homes was "deceitful" and "egregious."]

Accordingly, we reverse and remand to the circuit court for reinstatement of the punitive damage award.

■ POINTS TO CONSIDER

1. **The case for a strong right to exclude.** We tend to think of the right to exclude as inherently part of property ownership, but it helps to think about why this is so. The *Jacque* opinion highlights some of the policy reasons for recognizing a strong right to exclude. What are they? Can you think of others?

2. **Remedies.** If the damages to the Jacques' property really amounted to only $1 and the benefit to Steenberg Homes far exceeded that, can the court's decision be considered economically efficient? How do you measure damages to the Jacques' privacy, security, or personhood interests?

   In this case, are the Jacques' rights protected by a *property rule* or a *liability rule*? Consider this explanation provided by the classic work on this distinction:

   > An entitlement is protected by a property rule to the extent that someone who wishes to remove the entitlement from its holder must buy it from him in a voluntary transaction in which the value of the entitlement is agreed upon by the seller. It is the form of entitlement which gives rise to the least amount of state intervention: once the original entitlement is decided upon, the state does not try to decide its value. It lets each of the parties say how much the entitlement is worth to him, and gives the seller a veto if the buyer does not offer enough. . . .

> Whenever someone may destroy the initial entitlement if he is willing to pay an objectively determined value for it, an entitlement is protected by a liability rule. This value may be what it is thought the original holder of the entitlement would have sold it for. But the holder's complaint that he would have demanded more will not avail him once the objectively determined value is set.

Guido Calabresi & A. Douglas Melamed, *Property Rules, Liability Rules, and Inalienability: One View of the Cathedral*, 85 Harv. L. Rev. 1089, 1092 (1972). In what circumstances do you think a liability rule might be appropriate?

3. **Privileged entry.** The *Jacque* case presents good arguments for protecting the landowner's right to exclude. Nevertheless, you can surely think of *some* circumstances that might trump this right. For example, assume a small airplane has run out of fuel and needs to use the Jacques' field to make an emergency landing. Or assume the fire department needs to take the same path Steenberg Homes used in order to rescue someone from a burning house. These are examples of *privileged entry*, justified by the necessity of entry in order to protect life or property.

    What is the difference between Steenberg Homes' asserted need to use the Jacques' property and those needs the law recognizes as a valid defense to trespass? Is it just a matter of degree? If the road around the Jacques' property became impassable, so that using it became impossible rather than merely difficult, would we have a different case? If a utility company needed to put a cable through the Jacques' property, in most cases the law would allow the utility to force its way through, upon payment of just compensation. Why do we not respect the Jacques' right to exclude in that instance?

> **Animal Cruelty**
>
> Should the necessity principle allow a neighbor priviliged entry to give food and water to a neglected animal? *See* Cal. Penal Code §597(e) (West 2012) (allowing entry after 12 consecutive hours without food or water and allowing recovery of costs against owner).

a. Exclusion and the Public Interest

Are there any other circumstances in which public interests might outweigh the landowner's right to exclude? Consider these cases:

CASE SUMMARY: State v. Shack, 277 A.2d 369 (N.J. 1971)

The landowner, Tedesco, hired migrant workers for seasonal agricultural work, housing the workers in a camp on his land. Defendant Tejeras was employed by a nonprofit corporation whose mission included providing health services to migrant workers. He sought to enter the camp to provide aid to a worker who had been injured and needed help removing his sutures. Tejeras was accompanied by defendant Shack, an attorney with a legal services office that provided legal advice to migrant workers. Shack wanted to discuss a legal problem with another worker.

Tedesco confronted Tejeras and Shack as they neared the camp. When he learned their mission, he offered to find the injured worker and bring him out. As for legal advice, he would allow Shack to meet with the worker only in his office under his supervision. The defendants declined the offers, contending they had the right to meet with the workers in their living quarters, without supervision. Tedesco then summoned a state trooper and filed written complaints charging the defendants with criminal trespass.

The court held that the right to exclude must yield when public policy demands it:

> Property rights serve human values. They are recognized to that end, and are limited by it. Title to real property cannot include dominion over the destiny of persons the owner permits to come upon the premises. Their well-being must remain the paramount concern of a system of law. Indeed the needs of the occupants may be so imperative and their strength so weak, that the law will deny the occupants the power to contract away what is deemed essential to their health, welfare, or dignity.

State v. Shack, 277 A.2d 369, 372 (N.J. 1971). The court then noted that migrant workers were "a highly disadvantaged segment of our society," for whom the government had created programs to assist. The programs would be ineffective, however, if "the intended beneficiaries could be insulated from efforts to reach them." Using the principle of "necessity" as an example, the court noted that property rights are not absolute:

> The subject is not static. As pointed out in 5 Powell, Real Property (Rohan 1970) §745, pp. 493-494, while society will protect the owner in his permissible interests in land, yet
>
> > . . . (s)uch an owner must expect to find the absoluteness of his property rights curtailed by the organs of society, for the promotion of the best interests of others for whom these organs also operate as protective agencies. The necessity for such curtailments is greater in a modern industrialized and urbanized society than it was in the relatively simple American society of fifty, 100, or 200 years ago. The current balance between individualism and dominance of the social interest depends not only upon political and social ideologies, but also upon the physical and social facts of the time and place under discussion.

Id. at 373. The court held that "the defendants invaded no possessory right of the farmer" and therefore could not be convicted of trespass. The court denied that it was opening up the property to the general public, but stated:

> [W]e find it unthinkable that the farmer-employer can assert a right to isolate the migrant worker in any respect significant for the worker's well-being. The farmer, of course, is entitled to pursue his farming activities without interference, and this defendants readily concede. But we see no legitimate need for a right in the farmer

to deny the worker the opportunity for aid available from federal, State, or local services, or from recognized charitable groups seeking to assist him. Hence representatives of these agencies and organizations may enter upon the premises to seek out the worker at his living quarters. So, too, the migrant worker must be allowed to receive visitors there of his own choice, so long as there is no behavior hurtful to others, and members of the press may not be denied reasonable access to workers who do not object to seeing them.

Id. at 374.

CASE SUMMARY: Robins v. Pruneyard Shopping Center, 592 P.2d 341 (Cal. 1979)

In *Robins v. Pruneyard Shopping Center*, the California Supreme Court held that the state constitution protects the right to petition, if reasonably exercised, at privately owned shopping centers. The center had a uniformly enforced policy prohibiting any non-commercial expressive activities. A group of high school students attempted to solicit signatures for a petition opposing a United Nations resolution against Zionism. The court noted that the shopping mall had become the modern town square: "Shopping centers to which the public is invited can provide an essential and invaluable forum for exercising [constitutional speech and petition] rights."

Subsequently, the U.S. Supreme Court held that limiting the shopping center's right to exclude in this manner did not amount to a governmental "taking" of a property interest under the federal Constitution. Pruneyard Shopping Ctr. v. Robins, 447 U.S. 74 (1980). The Court noted that the normal interests of privacy and security promoted by the right to exclude were diminished in the case of a public center and that allowing this expressive activity would not unreasonably impair the value or use of the property.

Note that the majority of jurisdictions have not adopted the California approach to free speech rights on quasi-public property. Instead, most states prohibit only state action that infringes free speech. *See, e.g.,* Citizens for Ethical Gov't, Inc. v. Gwinnett Place Assocs., L.P., 392 S.E.2d 8 (Ga. 1990) (owners of shopping center entitled to prohibit distribution of petitions).

■ POINTS TO CONSIDER

1. **Private versus quasi-public property.** The property involved in both *Shack* and *Pruneyard* was privately owned, but was not as highly private as the land in *Jacque.* Does that help explain the different holdings in these cases? The New Jersey Supreme Court commented on this distinction in a case similar to *Pruneyard*, which required the owner of a regional shopping mall to allow anti-war protesters to distribute leaflets:

    [P]rivate property does not "lose its private character merely because the public is generally invited to use it for designated purposes." Nevertheless, as private property becomes, on a sliding scale, committed either more or less to public use and enjoyment, there is actuated, in effect, a counterbalancing between expressional and property rights.

New Jersey Coalition Against War in the Middle East v. J.M.B. Realty Corp., 650 A.2d 757 (N.J. 1994). The New Jersey court found that the mall had become so public that its private property interests had been diminished and were outweighed by the speech interests of the protesters.

2. **Certainty.** If you agree that owners of "quasi-public" property have a weaker right to exclude, where should we draw the line? For example, does Wal-Mart have to allow protesters to stand at the entrance and hand out leaflets accusing the company of discriminatory hiring practices? Do the Dallas Cowboys have to allow war protestors to set up a table in the concourse for a petition drive? *See* Albertson's, Inc. v. Young, 131 Cal. Rptr. 2d 721 (Cal. Ct. App. 2003) (distinguishing supermarket from large shopping center).

   Which of these "right to exclude" decisions provides greater certainty to our property law system? Do *Shack* and *Pruneyard* open courts to ad hoc balancing in these situations, which was precisely what the *Jacque* court tried to avoid?

3. Google Maps has a feature called "Street View," which offers internet access to panoramic, navigable street-level photographs in and around major cities. In order to create this feature, Google attaches digital cameras to cars, which drive around photographing areas along the street. Aaron and Christine Boring live on a private road in Pittsburgh, clearly marked with a "No Trespassing" sign. They discovered that Google had taken photographs of their residence, without any authorization, from a vehicle parked in their private drive. Google claims that the Borings were not harmed by this temporary entry and that their mapping project serves a significant public purpose. Do the Borings have a trespass claim? If Google had taken the same picture from a public street, would the Borings' alleged harms be any different? *See* Boring v. Google Inc., 362 Fed. Appx. 273 (3d Cir. 2010). Assuming this is a trespass, would these facts support a $100,000 punitive damages award, as in *Jacque*, or is this case different?

Occupy London Movement

The Occupy London movement originally targeted Paternoster Square, the home of the London Stock Exchange. Because the square was privately owned, however, the owners were able to get an injunction banning the protesters. The owners now limit entry to preserve the private nature of the square and their right to control access.

The square contains several restaurants and the stock exchange, as well as the offices of investment banks. If the British courts followed *Pruneyard*, would they enjoin the Occupy protests? From the point of view of the protesters, does it have the same impact and significance to "occupy" only public parks?

The Right to Exclude: A Comparative Perspective

Recognizing a landowner's right to exclude inherently limits the public's right of access, as Steenberg Homes discovered in *Jacque*. For example, when a gated community shuts off public access to its streets and sidewalks, it furthers the privacy and security interests of the owners, but at a significant cost of inconvenience to the public. What might have been a short walk to the grocery store, if you could cut through the community, might now be a long walk around it to the next public street.

In Britain, the balance tips more toward public interests. For example, there are numerous public footpaths criss-crossing private land, which are jealously guarded against private infringement. Composer Andrew Lloyd Webber's attempt to relocate a footpath that ran within 50 meters of his home was denied, because moving the path would have had a detrimental effect on the public's view of historic buildings. Madonna and her then-husband Guy Ritchie likewise had to tolerate a public footpath running through their 1,200-acre estate in Wiltshire.

In 2000, the British Parliament went even further, enacting a "right to roam" in the Countryside and Rights of Way Act, which opened up millions of acres of private land for public wandering. The public now has the right to hike and picnic on any private land classified as "open country," consisting of mountains, moors, heath, and downland (grassy pasture over chalk or limestone).

In Scandinavia, the custom of *allemansrätten* similarly allows public access to private land to gather wildflowers, hunt mushrooms, or even to camp along rivers.

Are these limitations on the right to exclude consistent with the foundational property policies we have discussed so far? Can you imagine any American jurisdictions opening up private rangeland, for example, to public hiking? Why not? *See* Jerry L. Anderson, *Britain's Right to Roam: Redefining the Landowner's Bundle of Sticks*, 19 Geo. Int'l Envtl. L. Rev. 375 (2007).

Professor Thomas Merrill has written that the right to exclude is "the *sine qua non*" of property: "Deny someone the exclusion right and they do not have property." Thomas W. Merrill, *Property and the Right to Exclude*, 77 Neb. L. Rev. 730, 730 (1998). Do the owners of "open country" in Britain still have anything we can recognize as property, now that their right to exclude has been compromised? What sticks are left in the bundle?

b. *Exclusion and Personal Property*

The right to exclude typically applies to personal property as well. If a private investigator places a tracking device on your car without a warrant, it may be a trespass. If your neighbor borrows your lawn tractor without your permission and bends an axle, you can sue for trespass to chattels. *Chattel* is another word for personal property, in some contexts restricted to tangible, movable property. Note the difference between *trespass to chattels*, which involves injury to or temporary deprivation of personal property, and *conversion*, which is the wrongful appropriation (in other words, permanent deprivation) of personal property.

What about your email in-box: Is it your personal property and can you sue for trespass when someone repeatedly ignores your requests to stop emailing you? Or can your employer, who owns the email servers, sue to exclude certain emails from "invading" its cyberspace? *Compare* CompuServe, Inc. v. Cyber Promotions, Inc., 962 F. Supp. 1015 (S.D. Ohio 1997) (plaintiff has possessory interest in computer system and spam messages substantially interfere with possession), *with* Intel Corp. v. Hamidi, 71 P.3d 296 (Cal. 2003) (no trespass where messages critical of company sent by former employee did not interfere with system). If you think it is the mailbox owner's responsibility to set up an adequate spam filter, does that mean anyone can trespass on your land if you don't have a tall enough fence?

c. *The* Ad Coelum *Doctrine*

Another interesting aspect of the right to exclude is its physical dimensions. American landowners are commonly said to hold title according to the ancient doctrine of *cujus est solum, ejus est usque ad coelum et ad inferos*, or *ad coelum* for short, which is roughly translated as "whoever owns the soil, it is theirs all the way up to Heaven and down to Hell." Generally, ownership of land includes possession of not only the surface, but also the airspace above the surface and the subsurface below. A very common transaction—a landowner's sale of the "mineral rights" to Blackacre, technically known as the *mineral estate*—is a perfect illustration of the *ad coelum* nature of property ownership.

Certainly, the *ad coelum* doctrine would prevent your neighbor from building a garage with a roof that overhangs your land, even though it never touches the surface. The doctrine also gives you the right to trim your neighbor's trees that are scraping against the side of your house or the roof of your car. Moreover, the doctrine allows you to enjoin (i.e., legally put a stop to) an oil well that has been drilled diagonally into the area below your land.

Nevertheless, it is generally conceded today that the literal reach of the doctrine—to the heavens and to the center of the earth—was poetic hyperbole, created in a time when airplanes and modern oil and gas drilling techniques were beyond comprehension.

Consider the proper scope of the right to exclude above and below the surface of land.

CASE SUMMARY: United States v. Causby, 328 U.S. 256 (1946)

The Causbys owned a few acres of land near an airport in Greensboro, North Carolina, on which they had a house and some chickens. The federal government used the airport for various military aircraft, which frequently passed over the Causbys' land. The flights passed just above the trees on the land, causing a great deal of noise, which disturbed the owners' sleep and made chicken production impossible. The trial court held that the United States had effectively taken an easement over the Causbys' land and awarded them $2,000 for the value of this right.

The U.S. Supreme Court refused to base its decision on the *ad coelum* doctrine:

It is ancient doctrine that at common law ownership of the land extended to the periphery of the universe—*Cujus est solum ejus est usque ad coelum.* But that doctrine has no place in the modern world. The air is a public highway, as Congress has declared. Were that not true, every transcontinental flight would subject the operator to countless trespass suits. Common sense revolts at the idea. To recognize such private claims to the airspace would clog these highways, seriously interfere with their control and development in the public interest, and transfer into private ownership that to which only the public has a just claim.

United States v. Causby, 328 U.S. 256, 260-61(1946). Note how the Court used legal positivism and economic efficiency to determine the scope of the owner's right to exclude. Using similar economic considerations, the Court found that these particular flights did invade the Causbys' property interests:

We have said that the airspace is a public highway. Yet it is obvious that if the landowner is to have full enjoyment of the land, he must have exclusive control of the immediate reaches of the enveloping atmosphere. Otherwise buildings could not be erected, trees could not be planted, and even fences could not be run. The principle is recognized when the law gives a remedy in case overhanging structures are erected on adjoining land. The landowner owns at least as much of the space above the ground as he can occupy or use in connection with the land. . . . The fact that he does not occupy it in a physical sense—by the erection of buildings and the like—is not material. As we have said, the flight of airplanes, which skim the surface but do not touch it, is as much an appropriation of the use of the land as a more conventional entry upon it.

Id. at 264.

■ PROBLEMS: THE *AD COELUM* DOCTRINE

1. Modern natural gas drilling techniques include hydraulic fracturing, commonly called "fracking." In this process, fluid is pumped down a well at high pressure to create cracks in the subsurface rock, which are then propped open with a slurry containing sand or other granules, or "proppants." This allows gas that would otherwise be trapped to flow through the cracks to the well. Geologists cannot control precisely in which direction the fractures will occur. Alpha Oil buys the mineral rights to Blackacre, drills a well on it, and begins a fracturing operation, two miles below the surface. The fracture travels beneath the adjoining property, Whiteacre, owned by Beta. The proppants injected into the fracture also travel and lodge beneath Whiteacre. Beta sues Alpha Oil, asserting a trespass. What result? *See* Coastal Oil & Gas Corp. v. Garza Energy Trust, 268 S.W.3d 1 (Tex. 2008) (no trespass if there is no injury).

2. The entrance to a cave lies on Edwards' property and he has begun offering tours. Lee, who owns the adjoining property, believes that a portion of the cave lies below his property and that the cave visitors are trespassing. Should

Lee be able to prevent Edwards from accessing that portion of the cave or require him to pay a fee, even though Lee cannot access the cave from his own land? *See* Edwards v. Sims, 24 S.W.2d 619 (Ky. 1929) (requiring Edwards to allow Lee to survey cave).

CASE SUMMARY: Orr v. Mortvedt, 735 N.W.2d 610 (Iowa 2007)

The owner of a rock quarry discontinued mining, and the excavated area filled with water, turning into a small lake. The owner divided the property into several pieces and sold them to several different purchasers. Each lot contained a portion of the lake bed and the land adjacent to it. Some of the owners wanted to drain the lake and reopen the quarry. The Mortvedts, however, objected. The other owners wanted to erect a fence or other structure in the lake, to restrict the Mortvedts' use of the lake to only the part above their own land. The other owners also wanted to begin draining the water from their portion of the lake. As the court explained, jurisdictions are divided on the use of private lakes owned in common"

The majority rule, often referred to as the "common law rule," dictates that one is entitled to exclusive use and enjoyment of that portion of the nonnavigable lake covering the lake bed one owns. . . . In jurisdictions following the common law rule, owners of the lake bed may fence off their lake bed to promote their exclusive use and enjoyment. The common law rule thus conforms to the familiar legal maxim *cujus est solum, ejus est usque ad coelum et ad inferos*—"[w]hoever owns the soil owns everything up to the sky and down to the depths." Nichols v. City of Evansdale, 687 N.W.2d 562, 566 (Iowa 2004) (citing Black's Law Dictionary 1712 (8th ed. 2004)).

A lesser number of jurisdictions have adopted what has been described as the "civil law rule." This rule holds that owners of any part of a nonnavigable lake are entitled to reasonable use and enjoyment of the entire surface of the lake, not merely that part covering the bed they own.

Navigable

In water law, a "navigable" lake refers to one that has been or may be used for purposes of commerce. The bed of navigable waters is owned by the state and the public enjoys the right to use these waters. *Mortvedt* involved a private lake, which is not "navigable" in the sense that it is used for commerce.

Orr v. Mortvedt, 735 N.W.2d 610, 616-17 (Iowa 2007). Should the right to exclude be absolute in these circumstances? Do you think the parties purchased the property with the expectation of being able to use the whole lake?

The majority in *Mortvedt* adopted the "common law" rule:

The principal advantage of the rule we adopt today is its consistency with prevailing norms of real estate ownership in this state. The common law rule recognizes the legal significance of property boundaries and protects the interests of owners when neighbors are unwilling or unable to coexist cooperatively. Finally, we adopt the common law rule as the default rule, realizing that the several owners of nonnavigable lakes may bargain among themselves to adopt other mutually acceptable arrangements for the use and mutual enjoyment of water resources.

Id. at 618. In contrast, Justice Cady in dissent preferred a "free access" rule, which would allow reasonable use of the surface waters by all the owners. The majority's decision, according to Justice Cady, was "based on the anachronistic rule that our property rights 'extend from heaven to hell.' . . . The march of time, the evolution of society, and the inherent differences between land, water, and air clearly demonstrate they do not. The majority's adoption of what is called the 'common law rule' only furthers this antiquated abstraction."[35]

Justice Cady believed that the majority's rule would cause uncertainty about underwater property lines, leading to trespass claims whenever an owner mistakenly casts a fishing line on the wrong side. Citing *Johnson v. M'Intosh*, Justice Cady believed that property rights must be molded to fit the circumstances and modern expectations:

> The policy behind the free access rule best reflects life in Iowa in the twenty-first century. Rigid property rights of the past centuries should give way to the simple and fair solution of boundary disputes offered by the better reasoned free access rule. Our laws pertaining to land, air, and water must begin to reflect that we coexist on Earth as one.

Id. Which of our foundational property policies are furthered by the rule adopted by the majority in *Mortvedt*? Are the policies the dissent favors different, or does the dissent just disagree about which rule best accomplishes those policies?

2. The Right to Use

The right to use your property in whatever manner you see fit is one of the most important sticks in the bundle. "Property is composed of constituent elements and of these elements the right to *use* the physical thing to the exclusion of others is the most essential and beneficial. Without this right all other elements would be of little value. . . ." Passailaigue v. United States, 224 F. Supp. 682, 686 (M.D. Ga. 1963) (emphasis in original) (quoted in Dickman v. C.I.R., 465 U.S. 330, 336 (1984); *see also* Barker v. Publishers' Paper Co., 103 A. 757, 758 (N.H. 1918) ("In its final analysis, the property in anything consists in the use").

Yet, we also know that the use of property must have limitations, in order to preserve the rights of other landowners and the public in general. Many of these restrictions, such as zoning, we now take for granted. As we will see in the final chapter of this book, restrictions on the use of property may become so severe that we consider the property to have been appropriated, even though bare legal title may remain in the landowner.

At common law, *nuisance* was the primary legal mechanism for balancing conflicting rights to use property. The general principle was often expressed in

---

[35] *Id.* at 621 (Cady, J., dissenting) (quoting Professor Andrea B. Carroll, *Examining a Comparative Law Myth: Two Hundred Years of Riparian Misconception*, 80 Tul. L. Rev. 901 (2006)).

the Latin maxim: *sic utere tuo ut alienum non laedas*. As applied by the courts, *sic utere tuo* meant that one may not use property in a manner that causes unreasonable harm to the use and enjoyment of another's land. Note the rule is not that a landowner can't cause *any* harm; only *unreasonable* harm is prohibited. What harms are *unreasonable*, of course, is difficult to determine and will require some analysis in Chapter 12 of this book.

For now, we will look at one example of how courts deal with these land use conflicts—the law of *spite fences*. You may be surprised to find that, even in property cases, the *intentions* of the landowner can be relevant. Here again, we find that the courts use our foundational property policies to determine the limits of acceptable use of property.

BURKE v. SMITH

69 Mich. 380 (1888)
Supreme Court of Michigan

MORSE, J.

The parties to this suit own adjoining lots in the city of Kalamazoo. The complainant built two dwelling-houses on his lot for the purposes of rental. . . . These houses came up within about two feet of the line between him and the defendant. . . . These parties got into a quarrel, and, as a result of petty annoyances on both sides, the defendant finally put up a screen or fence in front of the lower side windows of the complainant, as it is claimed, covering, obscuring, and darkening the same, and shutting out the light and air therefrom. The evidence shows these screens to be two in number, and about eleven feet high, coming up to the top of the lower windows of complainant's houses. They were built by setting posts in the ground, and nailing boards against them. They were open at the bottom below the windows.

I think it is established by the evidence that these screens were not put up for a fence, or any other necessary or useful or ornamental purpose, but simply to shut out the view of defendant's premises from complainant's windows. Smith claims that he did not wish the occupants of complainant's houses to gaze into his windows, or to witness the getting out of and into carriages of his family at the horse block beside the drive-way, and for that reason put up these barriers. There is plenty of evidence that when he was erecting these screens he said he was doing it to shut the light out of Burke's windows. I think there was nothing but malice in his motives. The complainant . . . alleges that these screens were unnecessarily erected from malicious motives, and for the express and avowed purpose of darkening the windows of his two houses, and cutting off the light from entering the windows of said houses, obstructing the view from them, and thereby injuring the value of the houses. Avers that they are an intolerable nuisance; that, by their existence, light and air are prevented from freely entering his houses, the view from the windows is wholly obstructed and cut off, the looks and appearance of the houses greatly injured, their desirability as homes greatly lessened, their rental value depreciated, and their actual market value reduced more than $500. Prays that said screens may be abated as a nuisance, and a perpetual injunction allowed against a continuation or renewal of the same. The court below granted the prayer of the complainant's bill.

These screens are erected entirely upon the lot of the defendant, and he appeals to this court, claiming that he has a perfect right to erect and maintain them, and that the question of his motives has nothing to do with the legal aspects of the case, though he disclaims any malice against complainant. It must be taken for granted, in discussing this case, that these screens were not erected for the purposes of a fence, or for any other necessary, useful, or ornamental purpose. The pretense that they were built to keep prying eyes from observing what was going on in the houses or yard of the defendant is not supported by the proofs. The evidence is clear to my mind that malice alone entered into the reason and motive of their erection. . . . It is admitted by the counsel for the complainant that he would have no redress had the defendant erected houses or useful buildings or structures as near to complainant's line as these screens are, even though the consequent damage of such erection would have been as great or greater than it has been and now is from the effect of these screens upon the dwellings of complainant in every respect here complained of. But his contention is that these screens being a damage to the houses of complainant, and being erected for no good or useful purpose, but with the malicious motive of doing injury, they become and are such a nuisance to the property of complainant that equity will cause their removal, and enjoin their future erection or continuance. He invokes the legal maxim that "every man in the use of his own property must avoid injury to his neighbor's property as much as possible;" and argues that, while it is true that when one pursues a strictly legal right his motives are immaterial, yet no man has a right to build and maintain an entirely useless structure for the sole purpose of injuring his neighbor.

The argument has force, and appears irresistible, in the light of the moral law that ought to govern all human action. And the civil law, coming close to the moral law, declares that "he who, in making a new work upon his own estate, uses his right without trespassing either against any law, custom, title, or possession, which may subject him to any service towards his neighbors, is not answerable for the damages which they may chance to sustain thereby, unless it be that he made that chance merely with a view to hurt others without advantage to himself." Thus the civil law recognizes the moral law, and does not permit the owner of land to do an act upon his own premises for the express purpose of injuring his neighbor, when the act brings no profit or advantage to himself. The law furnishes redress, because the injury is malicious and unjustifiable. The moral law imposes upon every man the duty of doing unto others as he would that they should do unto him; and the common law ought to, and in my opinion does, require him to so use his own privileges and property as not to injure the rights of others maliciously, and without necessity.

It is true that he can use his own property, if for his own benefit or advantage, in many cases to the injury of his neighbor; and such neighbor has no redress, because the owner of the property is exercising a legal right which infringes on no legal right of the other. Therefore, and under this principle, the defendant might have erected a building for useful or ornamental purposes, and shut out the light and air from complainant's windows; but when he erected these "screens" or "obscurers" for no useful or ornamental purpose, but out of pure malice against his neighbor, it seems to me a different principle must prevail. I do not think the common law permits a man to be deprived of water, air, or light for the mere gratification of malice. No one has an exclusive property in any of these elements except as the same may exist or be confined entirely on his own premises. . . . The complainant in this case had a right to the use of the air and light about his houses, and over defendant's lands, until such right came in conflict with the defendant's enjoyment of his property. This air and light was free and unconfined, and the common property of all. . . .

In a well-reasoned case in 74 Me. 164, (Chesley v. King,) the authorities are reviewed, and the court reach[es] the conclusion "that it cannot be regarded as a maxim of universal application that malicious motives cannot make that a wrong which in its own essence is lawful." In that case the defendant dug a well upon his own land, which cut off the sources of supply from a spring upon plaintiff's premises. There was a special finding that defendant dug the well for the "mere, sole, and malicious purpose of diverting the veins of water which supplied the spring, and not for the purpose of procuring a better supply of water for himself and improving his estate." The supreme court . . . [held], in substance, that, if the special finding had been true, the plaintiff's action would have been sustained. . . . If a man has no right to dig a hole upon his premises, not for any benefit to himself or his premises, but for the express purpose of destroying his neighbor's spring, why can he be permitted to shut out air and light from his neighbor's windows, maliciously, and without profit or benefit to himself. By analogy, it seems to me that the same principle applies in both cases, and that the law will interpose and prevent the wanton injury in each instance.

In Phelps v. Nowlen, supra, it is stated that the doctrine is settled in New York "that, if a man has a legal right, courts will not inquire into the motive by which he is actuated in enforcing the same. A different rule would lead to the encouragement of litigation, and prevent, in many instances, a complete and full enjoyment of the right of the property which inheres to the owner of the soil. An idle threat to do what is perfectly lawful, or declarations which assert the intention of the owner, might often be construed as evincing an improper motive and a malignant spirit, when in point of fact they merely stated the actual rights of the party. Malice might be easily inferred, sometimes, from idle and loose declarations, and a wide door be opened by such evidence to deprive an owner of what the law regards as well-defined rights."

But it must be remembered that no man has a legal right to make a malicious use of his property, not for any benefit or advantage to himself, but for the avowed purpose of damaging his neighbor. To hold otherwise would make the law a convenient engine, in cases like the present, to injure and destroy the peace and comfort, and to damage the property, of one's neighbor for no other than a wicked purpose, which in itself is, or ought to be, unlawful. The right to do this cannot, in an enlightened country, exist, either in the use of property, or in any way or manner. There is no doubt in my mind that these uncouth screens or "obscurers" as they are named in the record, are a nuisance, and were erected without right, and for a malicious purpose. What right has the defendant, in the light of the just and beneficent principles of equity, to shut out God's free air and sunlight from the windows of his neighbor, not for any benefit or advantage to himself, or profit to his land, but simply to gratify his own wicked malice against his neighbor? None whatever. The wanton infliction of damage can never be a right. It is a wrong, and a violation of right, and is not without remedy. The right to breath[e] the air, and to enjoy the sunshine, is a natural one; and no man can pollute the atmosphere, or shut out the light of heaven, for no better reason than that the situation of his property is such that he is given the opportunity of so doing, and wishes to gratify his spite and malice towards his neighbor.

It is said that the adoption of statutes in several of the states making this kind of injury actionable shows that the courts have no right to furnish the redress without statutory authority. It has always been the pride of the common law that it permitted no wrong with damage, without a remedy. In all the cases where this class of injuries have occurred, proceeding alone from the malice of the defendant, it is held to be a wrong accompanied by damage. That courts have failed to apply the remedy has ever been felt a reproach to the administration of the law; and the fact that the people have regarded this neglect of duty on the part of the courts so gross as to make that duty imperative by statutory law furnishes no evidence of the creation of a new right or the giving of a new remedy, but is a severe criticism upon the courts for an omission of duty already existing, and now imposed by statute upon them, which is only confirmatory of the common law. The decree of the court below is affirmed, with costs of both courts.

SHERWOOD, J., concurred.

CAMPBELL, C.J., (dissenting).

This case, assuming all that is claimed for complainant, is one where he opened windows on the side of his house near defendant's line, and defendant built a screen entirely on his own land high enough to keep his own house, so far as its lower story and side porch and entrances are concerned, from being open to the views from complainant's windows. No authority has been found, and I am satisfied there is no authority, at least in any region from which we have borrowed our law, which controverts defendant's right to secure his privacy in that way. If we should grant the complainant relief, we should not only be going beyond the judicial provinces in making the law, but we should also make a rule in conflict with universal weight of authority.

It was urged on the argument that there was at least foundation for such relief in the civil law, and that we might follow that if we chose. I have searched diligently, and found no such authority. On the other hand, the civil law reckoned the right of one proprietor to secure a prospect over his neighbor's land as an easement which could only be gained by grant, or possibly by such prescription as would be equivalent to a grant. [The dissent reviews various European authorities, which hold that there is no right of view or air over another's property unless it has been expressly granted or acquired by usage over time.] The right to overlook a neighbor's premises seems, by the civil law, to be one depending entirely on whether such a servitude has been created; and, if it has not been, there can be no doubt of the right of the neighbor to stop it. . . .

Our law rests on our own American common-law usages; and a somewhat careful search has failed to bring to light any authority for holding that any one is bound to permit his privacy to be invaded by his neighbors, without the right to screen his premises against them. . . . There can be no question about the character of such a right as complainant claims. It is the right to have his prospect into defendant's property left unobstructed. It is an easement in the strictest sense of the term, and is among those expressly designated as such by all systems of laws. No man can create an easement for himself. If he has no such right, then he cannot complain that it is interfered with, either at law or in equity. . . .

It was held in Roberts v. Macord, 1 Moody & R. 230, that there was no easement in a prospect, and that rights in windows did not go so far. And in Wheeldon v. Burrows, above cited, it was held that the sale of a house by one owning also the adjacent lot involved no implied covenant not to darken the windows. And in Wynstanley v. Lee, 2 Swanst. 333, it was recognized that in London there never was any presumption of a right to light. This has been always recognized as the custom of London, and was the law there until the passage of an act of parliament which changed the disputable presumption which sometimes arose, after long time, into an absolute right, after 20 years, to have windows left clear, and made the rule applicable in spite of local customs. In Yates v. Jack, L. R. 1 Ch. 295, it was held that the statute now in force abolished the custom of London and of other cities; and the court, while commenting on the absurd consequences in a city, felt bound to apply the statute, and require the owner of buildings only 20 or 30 feet high on one side of a London street to abstain from raising them higher, and thus lessening the light that would fall on the other side. The result of such a rule is to destroy the value of property, and prevent its owners from using it for natural and proper purposes.

In the nature of things, there can be no wrong in preventing another from doing what he has no right to insist upon. It was held by this court in Allen v. Kinyon, 41 Mich. 281, that the motive is of no consequence when the party does not violate the rights of another; and in support of this doctrine reliance was had on Mahan v. Brown, 13 Wend. 261, where the case was like the present one in its circumstances, but much more serious. There a fence was put up, as the screen was here, for the express purpose of preventing the view from 15 windows over defendant's ground. The court held that, where there was no right to the prospect, there was no wrong in fencing it out, and that the defendant's motive was of no consequence, as he was in the exercise of his own right. . . . It was held by this court in Hawkins v. Sanders, 45 Mich. 491, 8 N.W. Rep. 98, that there was no right of prospect which would prevent the erection of an awning on a neighboring lot. In Durant v. Riddell, 12 La. Ann. 746, the same rule was applied to a veranda covering the sidewalk. The doctrine of Mahan v. Brown has been repeatedly enforced in Illinois in very strong language; the court holding that a fence or screen of any height was lawful to shut off the view from a neighboring window. Honsel v. Conant, 12 Bradw. 259; Guest v. Reynolds, 68 Ill. 478. . . .

It certainly cannot be any man's duty to rebuild or to build when he has no occasion for so doing, and when an open yard or grounds may be desirable for his comfort. No one disputes his right to shut off windows in that way; and there is no authority for holding that, if he does not wish to build, he may not in any other effective way secure the privacy which is his right on his own premises. That, according to the sense of all civilized nations, is a valuable domestic right, and, if we deny it, we shall find no standing point in jurisprudence to justify it.

I think complainant has no right whatever to complain of defendant's screen, and that his bill should be dismissed, with costs of both courts.

CHAMPLIN, J.

I concur with my Brother Campbell that the decree should be reversed. The decisions have been quite uniform to the effect that the motives of a party in doing a legal act cannot form the basis upon which to found a remedy against such party. Under these circumstances, it should be left to the legislature to define and prohibit the act and declare the remedy, as has been recently done in Massachusetts, Vermont, and some of the other states. Pub. Acts Mass. 1887, c. 348; Pub. Acts Vt. 1886, p. 59. I think, also, that legislation of the character contained in the statutes above cited is required, and would meet my hearty approval. We should then have a rule certain in its provisions and operative upon all alike with due and proper safeguards to the owners of private property.

■ POINTS TO CONSIDER

1. **Policy.** The majority's limitation on the right to use seems to be based on moral principle. Can you explain the majority's decision on economic efficiency grounds? On the other hand, what property policies support the dissent's approach?

2. **Easement of view?** Was Burke seeking to impose an *easement of view* over Smith's property? An *easement* is "an interest in land in the possession of another," which "entitles the owner of such interest to a limited use or enjoyment of the land in which the interest exists." Restatement (First) of Property §450 (1944). An easement can be either *affirmative* (a right to do something on someone else's property) or *negative* (the right to prevent a landowner

from doing something on her land that she would otherwise be able to do). For example, conservation easements prevent the landowner from developing the land, by requiring it to be maintained in its natural state.

The dissent viewed this situation as an attempt by Burke to impose a negative easement of view on Smith, without Smith's agreement and without compensation. The majority, on the other hand, viewed the case as one in which Smith imposed unreasonable harm on his neighbor. The case highlights the reciprocal nature of land use conflicts—recognition of rights in one landowner may limit the rights of another.

3. **Common law versus statutes.** About half of the states have enacted statutes prohibiting the erection of fences or other structures with the intent to annoy or injure adjoining property owners. In other jurisdictions, the problem is partially addressed by city ordinances or neighborhood agreements regarding the height of fences and minimum set-backs for buildings. In the rest of the jurisdictions, the courts have established common law rules for resolving the conflict. As you probably know by now, *common law* refers to a rule derived from no other source than previous judicial decisions based on customary norms of behavior, as opposed to legislative or constitutional provisions.

> **Practice Tip**
>
> Always check first for a statute or local ordinance. Property law is largely a matter of state and even local law (such as zoning ordinances), and many of the property issues we will cover are at least partially governed by legislative enactments.

In *Burke*, Justice Champlin preferred a legislative solution to this problem. What advantages would legislation have over the common law approach? Do those advantages necessarily require the court to wait for legislative action?

4. **Spite trees?** Many statutes and cases extend the spite fence doctrine to other types of structures, such as walls or buildings. In *Dowdell v. Bloomquist*, the defendant planted a row of 40-foot-high arborvitae trees to block his neighbor's view of the water. Defendant's purpose was to exact revenge for the neighbor's opposition to defendant's application for a zoning variance. The Rhode Island statute prohibited "a fence or other structure in the nature of a fence" that unnecessarily exceeds six feet and was maliciously erected. The Rhode Island Supreme Court held the trees were the equivalent of a spite fence and upheld the trial court's order to remove the trees or cut them down to no more than six feet in height.[36]

3. The Right to Destroy

Generally, ownership of property includes the right to destroy it. If you are drafting a novel, the manuscript is protected as your personal property; you alone

---

[36] Dowdell v. Bloomquist, 847 A.2d 827 (R.I. 2004).

can decide whether and when to throw it in the fireplace and start over. Similarly, if your old barn is falling down and needs extensive repairs, you alone can decide to tear it down and put up a new three-car garage in its place.[37]

But does ownership always include the right to destroy? What if the old barn has historic or architectural significance? What if the manuscript you are about to destroy was something you inherited from your great-great-grandfather, Charles Dickens?

CASE SUMMARY: Eyerman v. Mercantile Trust Co., N.A., 524 S.W.2d 210 (Mo. Ct. App. 1975)

Destruction Might Be Cathartic

One of the most famous acts of destruction occurred in 2004, when restaurateur Grant DePorter paid about $114,000 for the baseball that featured in the Chicago Cubs defeat in the 2003 National League Championship Series. In the eighth inning, when the Cubs were ahead in the game and the series, a fan interfered with a foul ball that would have assuredly been caught by the Cubs' left fielder. The Cubs' opponents (the Florida Marlins) went on to score eight runs that inning and won not only the game but the series. The ball was destroyed in a symbolic public ceremony held at Harry Caray's Restaurant.

Louise Woodruff Johnston died, leaving a will that directed her executor to tear down her St. Louis home and sell the land and add the proceeds of the sale to her estate. Other residents of the Kingsbury Place subdivision, a neighborhood of historic homes of "high architectural significance," sued to enjoin the destruction of the house. The court determined that razing the house would depreciate the values of neighboring properties, while costing the estate almost $40,000. The court concluded that "no individual, group of individuals nor the community generally benefits from the senseless destruction of the house; instead, all are harmed and only the caprice of the dead testatrix is served." The court therefore invalidated that provision of Johnston's will as against public policy.

■ POINTS TO CONSIDER

1. **Economic efficiency.** The *Eyerman* court emphasized that the right to destroy property may be more limited in the context of a will, when the property's owner is deceased. Can economic efficiency principles help explain this difference?

2. **Public interest.** Historic preservation acts often limit the ability to destroy or even modify historic buildings. Similarly, the Presidential Records Act of 1978 prevents the destruction of any presidential papers that have "administrative,

---

[37] We will see that there are often disputes *between co-owners* about destruction—either between co-tenants or between current owners and those with future ownership interests. Here we are talking about the rights of an owner vis-à-vis the public rather than against other co-owners.

Kingsbury Place neighborhood at issue in Eyerman
Missouri Historical Society

historical, informational, or evidentiary value."[38] Should owners of other property with significant cultural value be similarly limited? Could you buy and destroy the Mona Lisa, for example? *See* Joseph L. Sax, Playing Darts with a Rembrandt: Public and Private Rights in Cultural Treasures (1999); Lior Jacob Strahilevitz, *The Right to Destroy*, 113 Yale L.J. 781 (2005).

3. **Moral rights—personhood.** The Visual Artists Rights Act of 1990 gives the creator of an artwork of "recognized stature" the right to prevent its modification or destruction. 17 U.S.C. §106A (1990). Similar protections in the Massachusetts Art Preservation Act last 50 years beyond the death of the artist. In 2010, David Ascalon sued the Jewish Federation of Harrisburg, Pennsylvania, claiming that their restoration work on his steel and barbed wire Holocaust memorial sculpture changed its meaning and was "completely contrary to the core vision of the memorial."[39] Can you explain this limitation on the right to destroy using our fundamental property policies?

4. Limitations of the Bundle of Sticks Metaphor

Even though most Property professors and most courts, including the Supreme Court, use "bundle of sticks" to convey the idea that property consists of an

---

[38] 44 U.S.C. §2203(c) (1996).

[39] Ascalon v. Dep't of Parks & Recreation, et al., 2012 WL 4232377 (M.D. Pa.) (complaint).

aggregation of rights, the metaphor has some limitations. On one hand, some commentators believe that the metaphor furthers a formalistic conception of property and does not adequately convey the way property rights evolve over time and have to be tailored to balance private and public interests.

On the other hand, other scholars wonder whether the metaphor leads to a dangerous focus on individual sticks in the bundle, which fails to take into account how they all work together. They find that the bundle theory encourages a policy-oriented approach that fails to take into account the essential core of rights that constitute property ownership. One scholar compares the contingent quality of the bundle of sticks to a shopping bag of fruit—"people are free to pack in and rearrange it in whatever way they see fit. A person may take out the apples, for instance, and they still possess a 'shopping bag of fruit.' "[40]

Thus, while we will use the bundle of sticks metaphor as a useful tool for explaining how property law works and how it develops, keep in mind its limitations and pitfalls. Although you should recognize that property rights serve the policies we have identified, and therefore evolve when necessary, they are not infinitely malleable. Moreover, stability in our property rights system serves to protect the legitimate expectations of owners, promoting the values of fairness and certainty.

Coda: Reconsidering the Bundle of Sticks

We have now thoroughly indoctrinated you into thinking of property rights as a bundle of sticks, which may be limited or modified in certain cases when the public interest requires it. To close the chapter, we add a balancing note of caution from Professor Henry Smith, who urges us to consider the dangers of this approach:

> The problem with the bundle of rights is that it is treated as a theory of how our world works rather than as an analytical device or as a theoretical baseline. In the realist era, the benefits of tinkering with property were expressed in bundle terms without a corresponding theory of the costs of that tinkering. . . . "Property" is simply a conclusory label we might attach to the collection. In its classic formulation, the bundle picture puts no particular constraints on the contents of bundles: they are totally malleable and should respond to policy concerns in a fairly direct fashion. These policy-motivated adjustments usually involve adding or subtracting sticks and reallocating them among concerned parties or to society. This version of the bundle explains everything and so explains nothing. . . .
>
> . . . Just as water molecules do not have to be wet for water to be wet, so each stick in the bundle and each doctrine of property need not have the desirable features we want the system to have. Wetness is an emergent property of water. So with property law. Allowing owners to exclude others seems nasty and selfish, but whether it is efficient, fair, just, or virtue-promoting is sometimes only assessable in the context of the system as a whole. For example, the law of trespass in its individual applications can look very arbitrary, unfair, and even irrational, but it permits owners the space (literally, in the case of land) to pursue projects without having to answer to others,

---

[40] Adam Mossoff, *What Is Property? Putting the Pieces Back Together*, 45 Ariz. L. Rev. 371, 374 (2003).

thus generally promoting efficiency and liberty. One need not endorse the reasons invoked by the Jacques in Jacque v. Steenberg Homes, Inc. for excluding Steenberg Homes to see the Jacques as deserving robust protection for their refusal. . . .

Properties like efficiency, fairness, justice, and virtue promotion are emergent properties of the property system. It is certainly relatively easy to ask whether isolated individual rules—like the doctrine of necessity, antidiscrimination law, and the exemption of high-altitude airplane overflights from trespass—serve a given purpose. And sometimes isolating the purposes of individual rules makes some sense, but it makes more sense if we realize that our decision in any such situation is not a freestanding one but one that impacts the rest of the owner's rights and the working of the system. By making the pieces of the bundle fully congruent with their purposes and obscuring the means-ends relation between property law and the purposes it serves, the bundle theory leads to a fallacy of division—like expecting a water molecule to be wet. Requiring that each piece of the system and each stick in the bundle transparently reflect or promote our purposes is not necessary.

Henry E. Smith, *Property as the Law of Things*, 125 Harv. L. Rev. 1691, 1697, 1718-19 (2012).

■ PROBLEM: PROPERTY AND THE BUNDLE OF STICKS

Vera Beech loved to use Facebook (FB). She posted lots of deep thoughts on her page, along with lots of pictures she took of unusual things that caught her attention. She also was an author, and her books gradually became fairly successful. Tragically, she died while trying to climb Mount Everest. During this last journey, Vera posted a series of messages on her FB page, which were filled with inspirational messages coupled with dramatic photographs.

Vera left a will giving all of her property to her mother, Sunny. After Vera's death, Sunny decided the best way to honor her legacy would be to publish the FB photographs and messages in a book, which would be called "Vera's Last Journey." There seems to be no other record of these images and messages. In addition, Sunny would like to keep Vera's FB page going and make it a tribute to Vera and her work; it would also direct visitors to a webpage where they could purchase the "Last Journey" book.

Vera's FB page was password-protected and FB refused to give Sunny access.[41] In fact, within hours of being informed of her death, FB took down Vera's page at the request of Vera's brother, Rocky, who thinks that Vera would not have wanted her private thoughts exploited for commercial gain. In addition, FB refuses to give Sunny or anyone else access to Vera's page or to the images or messages that were stored there.

Sunny has now brought suit against FB claiming (1) Vera's FB page and all the information stored thereon constituted Vera's digital property, and (2) this digital property was part of Vera's estate, which Vera was therefore entitled to devise by

---

[41] This hypothetical is not intended to describe Facebook's actual approach to these issues.

will to whomever she wanted. FB, in response, claims that anything stored on company servers is its property. Moreover, even if the page and its contents could be considered Vera's property, it was personal to her and could not be willed. However, nothing in the user agreement covers this issue.

a) In a jurisdiction that has not adopted legislation concerning digital assets, do you consider Vera's FB page and its content to be her digital property? Does this property interest extend to the right to devise?

b) Most states have now enacted the Fiduciary Access to Digital Assets Act, Revised (2015). The legislation allows you to specify in a will or trust what should happen to your digital assets, and it allows you to designate someone to control those assets upon your death, regardless of the contractual terms of service. What should be the default rule if a decedent did not leave testamentary instructions regarding these assets?

SUMMARY

■ Property consists of legal relations among persons with respect to things.

■ Ownership of property entails an aggregation of rights, referred to as the "bundle of sticks."

■ One person may have some of the sticks in the bundle but not others—the right to occupy, for example, but not the right to transfer.

■ The sticks may vary depending on who is on the other side: the landowner should be able to keep out a travelling salesman, but may not be able to prevent social service workers from accessing migrant laborers.

■ The extent of a property owner's rights may be dependent on and defined by fundamental policies for property protection: fairness, economic efficiency, certainty, democracy, and personhood (including freedom of expression, privacy, and security).

Property Acquisition

> [T]he presumption of law is that the person who has possession has the property.
>
> —*Jeffries v. Great W. Ry. Co. (1856) 119 Eng. Rep. 680 (K.B.)*

In this chapter, we will look at various ways to acquire ownership of property. We will set aside, for the time being, the two most common means of property acquisition—purchase and inheritance—because these involve more complex issues that deserve separate treatment. We will also deal with gifts of real property, as opposed to personal property, in the chapter on real estate transactions.

So, what is left? In this chapter, we will focus initially on acquiring rights to property that is unowned—*res nullius*—or where the true owner is unknown—i.e., the law of finders. We will then consider the law concerning gifts of personal property. A common theme runs through all of these topics: the importance of *possession* in establishing a legal right to property. It turns out the concept of possession is more indeterminate than you might think at first.

In keeping with this theme, we will then examine the law of *adverse possession*, a doctrine that allows the true owner to be divested of ownership by another party's occupancy over a long period of time. The idea of adverse possession may surprise you, but you will find that it remains a very important way to further the policies of property we learned in Chapter 1.

A THE RULE OF CAPTURE

We begin our discussion of property acquisition with the *rule of capture*, which governs the allocation of *res nullius*, or unowned property. The rule awards ownership to the first possessor; it developed in Roman law as a simple way to assign property rights in disputes between hunters over the ownership of wild animals and similar situations. You might think that, at this point, there isn't much *res nullius* left to which the rule could apply and that it is therefore of limited importance.

We will find, however, that the rule of capture is the basis of the allocation of property rights in water, oil and gas, and ocean fishing. The rule of capture also governs the initial allocation of domain names on the internet, which might be the most valuable piece of property a business owns. More generally, studying the rule of capture helps us understand the concept of *possession*, which remains fundamentally important to property law.

Our first case is a classic, which deals with the rule in its original context of hunting *ferae naturae*—wild animals. The court answers the important question of who may claim the carcass of a fox. We don't expect you will have many fox hunting cases in your career, but think about the implications of this case for more modern problems. Which policies of property is each judge trying to promote?

PIERSON v. POST

3 Cai. R. 175 (1805)
Supreme Court of New York

This was an action of trespass on the case commenced in a justice's court, by the present defendant against the now plaintiff.

The declaration stated that Post, being in possession of certain dogs and hounds under his command, did, "upon a certain wild and uninhabited, unpossessed and waste land, called the beach, find and start one of those noxious beasts called a fox," and whilst there hunting, chasing and pursuing the same with his dogs and hounds, and when in view thereof, Pierson, well knowing the fox was so hunted and pursued, did, in the sight of Post, to prevent his catching the same, kill and carry it off. A verdict having been rendered for the plaintiff below, the defendant there sued out a certiorari, and now assigned for error, that the declaration and the matters therein contained were not sufficient in law to maintain an action.

TOMPKINS, J. delivered the opinion of the court.

. . . The question submitted by the counsel in this cause for our determination is, whether Lodowick Post, by the pursuit with his hounds in the manner alleged in his declaration, acquired such a right to, or property in, the fox, as will sustain an action against Pierson for killing and taking him away?

The cause was argued with much ability by the counsel on both sides, and presents for our decision a novel and nice question. It is admitted that a fox is an animal *ferae naturae*, and that property in such animals is acquired by occupancy only. These admissions narrow the discussion to the simple question of what acts amount to occupancy, applied to acquiring right to wild animals?

If we have recourse to the ancient writers upon general principles of law, the judgment below is obviously erroneous. Justinian's Institutes . . . and Fleta . . . adopt the principle, that pursuit alone vests no property or right in the huntsman; and that even pursuit, accompanied with wounding, is equally ineffectual for that purpose, unless the animal be actually taken. The same principle is recognised by Bracton. . . .

Puffendorf . . . defines occupancy of beasts *feræ naturæ*, to be the actual corporal possession of them, and Bynkershoek is cited as coinciding in this definition. It is indeed with hesitation that Puffendorf affirms that a wild beast mortally wounded, or greatly maimed, cannot be fairly intercepted by another, whilst the pursuit of the person inflicting the wound continues. The foregoing authorities are decisive to show that mere pursuit gave Post no legal right to the fox, but that he became the property of Pierson, who intercepted and killed him.

It therefore only remains to inquire whether there are any contrary principles, or authorities, to be found in other books, which ought to induce a different decision. Most of the cases which have occurred in England, relating to property in wild animals, have either been discussed and decided upon the principles of their positive statute regulations, or have arisen between the huntsman and the owner of the land upon which beasts *feræ naturæ* have been apprehended; the former claiming them by title of occupancy, and the latter *ratione soli*.[1] Little satisfactory aid can, therefore, be derived from the English reporters.

Barbeyrac, in his notes on Puffendorf, does not accede to the definition of occupancy by the latter, but, on the contrary, affirms, that actual bodily seizure is not, in all cases, necessary to constitute possession of wild animals. He does not, however, *describe* the acts which, according to his ideas, will amount to an appropriation of such animals to private use, so as to exclude the claims of all other persons, by title of occupancy, to the same animals; and he is far from averring that pursuit alone is sufficient for that purpose. To a certain extent, and as far as Barbeyrac appears to me to go, his objections to Puffendorf's definition of occupancy are reasonable and correct. That is to say, that actual bodily seizure is not indispensable to acquire right to, or possession of, wild beasts; but that, on the contrary, the mortal wounding of such beasts, by one not abandoning his pursuit, may, with the utmost propriety, be deemed possession of him; since, thereby, the pursuer manifests an unequivocal intention of appropriating the animal to his individual use, has deprived him of his natural liberty, and brought him within his certain control. So also, encompassing and securing such animals with nets and toils, or otherwise intercepting them in such a manner as to deprive them of their natural liberty, and render escape impossible, may justly be deemed to give possession of them to those persons who, by their industry and labour, have used such means of apprehending them. . . . The case now under consideration is one of mere pursuit, and presents no circumstances or acts which can bring it within

---

[1] *Ratione soli* is Latin for "according to the soil"; in other words, ownership of animals based on owning the land upon which they are found.—EDS.

the definition of occupancy by Puffendorf, or Grotius, or the ideas of Barbeyrac upon that subject.

The case cited from 11 Mod. 74-130 [*Keeble*] I think clearly distinguishable from the present; inasmuch as there the action was for maliciously hindering and disturbing the plaintiff in the exercise and enjoyment of a private franchise; and in the report of the same case, 3 Salk. 9. Holt, Ch. J. states, that the ducks were in the plaintiff's decoy pond, and so in his possession, from which it is obvious the court laid much stress in their opinion upon the plaintiff's possession of the ducks, *ratione soli.*

We are the more readily inclined to confine possession or occupancy of beasts *feræ naturæ*, within the limits prescribed by the learned authors above cited, for the sake of certainty, and preserving peace and order in society. If the first seeing, starting, or pursuing such animals, without having so wounded, circumvented or ensnared them, so as to deprive them of their natural liberty, and subject them to the control of their pursuer, should afford the basis of actions against others for intercepting and killing them, it would prove a fertile source of quarrels and litigation.

However uncourteous or unkind the conduct of Pierson towards Post, in this instance, may have been, yet his act was productive of no injury or damage for which a legal remedy can be applied. We are of opinion the judgment below was erroneous, and ought to be reversed.

LIVINGSTON, J.

My opinion differs from that of the court.

Of six exceptions, taken to the proceedings below, all are abandoned except the third, which reduces the controversy to a single question.

Whether a person who, with his own hounds, starts and hunts a fox on waste and uninhabited ground, and is on the point of seizing his prey, acquires such an interest in the animal, as to have a right of action against another, who in view of the huntsman and his dogs in full pursuit, and with knowledge of the chase, shall kill and carry him away?

This is a knotty point, and should have been submitted to the arbitration of sportsmen, without poring over Justinian, Fleta, Bracton, Puffendorf, Locke, Barbeyrac, or Blackstone, all of whom have been cited; they would have had no difficulty in coming to a prompt and correct conclusion. In a court thus constituted, the skin and carcass of poor *reynard*[2] would have been properly disposed of, and a precedent set, interfering with no usage or custom which the experience of ages has sanctioned, and which must be so well known to every votary of *Diana*.[3] But the parties have referred the question to our judgment, and we must dispose of it as well as we can, from the partial lights we possess, leaving to a higher tribunal, the correction of any mistake which we may be so unfortunate as to make. By the pleadings it is admitted that a fox is a "wild and noxious beast." Both parties have regarded him, as the law of nations does a pirate, "*hostem*

---

[2] The word for fox in Middle English and French (renard). Renard was often used as the name for a fox in medieval tales.—EDS.

[3] Diana was the Roman goddess of the hunt. A votary is a devout adherent.—EDS.

humani generis,"[4] and although "*de mortuis nil nisi bonum*,"[5] be a maxim of our profession, the memory of the deceased has not been spared. His depredations on farmers and on barn yards, have not been forgotten; and to put him to death wherever found, is allowed to be meritorious, and of public benefit. Hence it follows, that our decision should have in view the greatest possible encouragement to the destruction of an animal, so cunning and ruthless in his career. But who would keep a pack of hounds; or what gentleman, at the sound of the horn, and at peep of day, would mount his steed, and for hours together, "*sub jove frigido*,"[6] or a vertical sun, pursue the windings of this wily quadruped, if, just as night came on, and his stratagems and strength were nearly exhausted, a saucy intruder, who had not shared in the honours or labours of the chase, were permitted to come in at the death, and bear away in triumph the object of pursuit? Whatever Justinian may have thought of the matter, it must be recollected that his code was compiled many hundred years ago, and it would be very hard indeed, at the distance of so many centuries, not to have a right to establish a rule for ourselves. In his day, we read of no order of men who made it a business, in the language of the declaration in this cause, "with hounds and dogs to find, start, pursue, hunt, and chase," these animals, and that, too, without any other motive than the preservation of Roman poultry; if this diversion had been then in fashion, the lawyers who composed his institutes, would have taken care not to pass it by, without suitable encouragement. If any thing, therefore, in the digests or pandects shall appear to militate against the defendant in error, who, on this occasion, was the foxhunter, we have only to say *tempora mutantur*;[7] and if men themselves change with the times, why should not laws also undergo an alteration?

It may be expected, however, by the learned counsel, that more particular notice be taken of their authorities. I have examined them all, and feel great difficulty in determining, whether to acquire dominion over a thing, before in common, it be sufficient that we barely see it, or know where it is, or wish for it, or make a declaration of our will respecting it; or whether, in the case of wild beasts, setting a trap, or lying in wait, or starting, or pursuing, be enough; or if an actual wounding, or killing, or bodily tact and occupation be necessary. Writers on general law, who have favoured us with their speculations on these points, differ on them all; but, great as is the diversity of sentiment among them, some conclusion must be adopted on the question immediately before us. After mature deliberation, I embrace that of Barbeyrac, as the most rational, and least liable to objection. If at liberty, we might imitate the courtesy of a certain emperor, who, to avoid giving offence to the advocates of any of these different doctrines, adopted a middle course, and by ingenious distinctions, rendered it difficult to say (as often

---

[4] Latin for "enemy of mankind." The term originated in admiralty law and referred to pirates and slavers, who, as enemies of mankind, could be dealt with by any country as it saw fit without offending international law.—EDS.
[5] Latin for "speak no ill of the dead."—EDS.
[6] Latin for "under the cold heavens." This is a reference from the Roman lyric poet Horace, who writes about a hunter who, "unmindful of his tender spouse," "tarries beneath the chill sky (or cold heavens)." Horace, *Odes*, bk. 1, ode 1. Nineteenth-century schools often used this Ode from Horace to teach Latin.—EDS.
[7] Latin for "times change."—EDS.

happens after a fierce and angry contest) to whom the palm of victory belonged. He ordained, that if a beast be followed with *large dogs and hounds*, he shall belong to the hunter, not to the chance occupant; and in like manner, if he be killed or wounded with a lance or sword; but if chased with *beagles only*, then he passed to the captor, not to the first pursuer. If slain with a dart, a sling, or a bow, he fell to the hunter, if still in chase, and not to him who might afterwards find and seize him.

Now, as we are without any municipal regulations of our own, and the pursuit here, for aught that appears on the case, being with dogs and hounds of *imperial stature*, we are at liberty to adopt one of the provisions just cited, which comports also with the learned conclusion of Barbeyrac, that property in animals *feræ naturæ* may be acquired without bodily touch or manucaption,[8] provided the pursuer be within reach, or have a *reasonable* prospect (which certainly existed here) of taking, what he has *thus* discovered an intention of converting to his own use.

When we reflect also that the interest of our husbandmen, the most useful of men in any community, will be advanced by the destruction of a beast so pernicious and incorrigible, we cannot greatly err, in saying, that a pursuit like the present, through waste and unoccupied lands, and which must inevitably and speedily have terminated in corporal possession, or bodily *seisin*, confers such a right to the object of it, as to make any one a wrongdoer, who shall interfere and shoulder the spoil. The justice's judgment ought, therefore, in my opinion, to be affirmed.

Judgment of reversal.

■ POINTS TO CONSIDER

1. **Who are those guys?** The majority opinion relies on an array of legal theorists, who have had significant influence on the development of the law. A quick introduction to these jurists illustrates how ancient the roots of the rule of capture are.

   > *Justinian*, Byzantine emperor from 527-565 C.E., ordered the comprehensive codification of law known as the Corpus Juris Civilis ("Body of Civil Law") or Code of Justinian, which was a major influence on legal thought in the Western world. Justinian's *Institutes* was a textbook for jurists in training.

   > *Henry de Bracton* was an English jurist of the thirteenth century, who compiled and organized judical decisions while incorporating elements of Roman law in his monumental work, *De Legibus et Consuetudinibus Angliae* ("The Laws and Customs of England").

   > *Fleta* refers to a treatise on the common law of England written about 1290 C.E., whose anonymous author is supposed to have been a judge imprisoned by Edward I in London's Fleet prison (hence the moniker Fleta).

---

[8] Manucaption means "seizure by hand," i.e., actual physical control.—EDS.

> *Hugo Grotius*, an early-seventeenth-century Dutch jurist and scholar, was known for establishing the foundations of international law and for his contributions to natural law theory.

> *Baron Samuel von Pufendorf*, a German jurist and philosopher of the late seventeenth century, wrote commentaries on the natural law theories of Grotius and Thomas Hobbes.

> *Cornelius van Bynkershoek* was a Dutch legal scholar of the early eighteenth century, whose most significant contributions concerned the Law of the Sea. He agreed with Grotius that nations should have control over their territorial seas, which is the area adjacent to the coastline. He argued that the width of this territory should match the practical means of controlling it—i.e., the range of the nation's weaponry. This idea was translated into an international standard of three nautical miles for territorial waters, a width that corresponds to the range of the best cannons of that time. Since the mid-twentieth century, a 12-mile limit has become the norm. Note how the concepts of possession, based on control, applied to this property question as well.

2. **The rule of capture.** The acquisition of rights in unowned property follows a simple rule: the first possessor wins. Both Justice Tompkins and Justice Livingston seem to agree that the rule of capture applies to this case, but they disagree about what degree of possession is sufficient to fulfill the rule.

We all understand the concept of *physical (corporeal) possession*: actually holding something in your hand or carrying it in a bag or in your pocket. But most of us have far more possessions than we carry around with us. Therefore, we say we are in possession of those items not in our physical possession that we have *control* over. Are you in possession, right now, of the books in your locker or the stuff in the back seat of your car?

Constructive Possession

Constructive possession is defined as "being in a position to exercise dominion or control over a thing." United States v. DiNovo, 523 F.2d 197, 201 (7th Cir. 1975). Therefore, a hunter might be said to have constructive possession of a fox caught in his trap. The term *constructive* is used in a variety of legal contexts to mean "deemed to be, by operation of law." So, in this sense, the hunter is deemed to be in possession even if he has not actually taken physical custody of the animal.

The U.S. Supreme Court has cautioned:

[B]oth in common speech and in legal terminology, there is no word more ambiguous in its meaning than possession. It is interchangeably used to describe actual possession and constructive possession which often so shade into one another that it is difficult to say where one ends and the other begins.

National Safe Deposit Co. v. Stead,
232 U.S. 58 (1914).

What exactly does the majority believe is sufficient possession to acquire a property interest in a wild animal? Is actual physical possession—i.e., holding the dead fox up by the tail—required? How does Livingston's test differ?

3. **The policies behind possession.** Think about how deeply engrained the rule of first possession is in our culture: How do you decide who gets to order first in a fast-food restaurant? The person with the shortest lunch hour? The person with the easiest order? The person of greatest social stature? The person who is hungriest? In all these common situations of priority, we easily and naturally defer to the person who got there first. "First come, first served" is a universally accepted principle.

So, too, in property law. We believe that the first person to acquire occupancy of unowned property is entitled to ownership of it. But why? Which of our foundational policies of property law are furthered by the rule of capture? Would Livingston's definition of possession serve those policies better or worse? If we assume economic efficiency, in this case, means the greatest number of foxes killed, which definition of possession furthers that policy best?

4. *Ferae naturae.* Two facts are critically important to understanding *Pierson v. Post.* First, what kind of animal is under consideration? And where does the hunt take place? Why do those two facts matter? To flesh out the reasons, consider the following problems:

   a) Assume that you are riding your bike on a public nature trail and come across a cow standing in your path. Can you call home and announce that you've just found dinner? Why would a cow not be subject to the same rule of capture as *ferae naturae*?

   b) Assume that, instead of uninhabited wasteland, the fox Post is chasing runs onto land owned by Pierson. Is the fox still subject to capture by Post?

   c) The rule of capture states that you acquire a property right once you have possession. Assume Post catches the fox in a trap he has set. If Pierson happens upon the fox while it is struggling to free itself, can he kill the fox and establish first possession?

   d) What happens if the fox caught in Post's trap frees itself and runs past Pierson? If it comes past Pierson now, can he kill it and fulfill the rule of capture? How is this possible if the fox belonged to Post while it was caught in the trap?

   e) If a lion—surely the epitome of *ferae naturae*—escapes from the local zoo and you manage to capture it on your nearby land, who gets it? What accounts for the difference between this and the fox case?

5. **The role of custom.** Livingston suggested that the issue in this case could be easily answered by a jury of sportsmen, who would not need to rely on legal scholars to know what to do. What should be the role of custom in applying the law in a case like this? What advantages are there in conforming law to custom? In answering that question, consider the following case involving custom and capture.

CASE SUMMARY: Ghen v. Rich, 8 F. 159 (D. Mass. 1881)

Whalers in Massachusetts Bay used an identifiable bomb-lance to shoot finback whales. When killed in this manner, the whale sinks, but then later floats to the surface. Some of these whales would then wash up on the beach. Customarily, the person who found the whale notified the whaler, who removed the blubber and paid the finder a small fee.

In this case, the finder of a whale on the beach did not notify the whaler, but instead sold the whale at auction. The whaler sued for damages based on the market value of the oil obtained from the whale. The court held that the customary method of acquiring a property right in the whale should be followed:

> It has been recognized and acquiesced in for many years. It requires in the first taker the only act of appropriation that is possible in the nature of the case. Unless it is sustained, this branch of industry must necessarily cease, for no person would engage in it if the fruits of his labor could be appropriated by any chance finder. It gives reasonable salvage for securing or reporting the property. That the rule works well in practice is shown by the extent of the industry which has grown up under it, and the general acquiescence of a whole community interested to dispute it. It is by no means clear that without regard to usage the common law would not reach the same result. . . . If the fisherman does all that it is possible to do to make the animal his own, that would seem to be sufficient.

Ghen v. Rich, 8 F. 159, 162 (D. Mass. 1881). If the rule of capture requires that the hunter exercise *control* over the animal, why did the whaler win?

The Rule of Capture and Baseball

In 2001, Barry Bonds broke the record for most home runs in a season. His record-setting 73rd home run was hit at PacBell Park in San Francisco. The home run ball sailed into a standing-room area near right field. Alex Popov reached for the ball with his softball glove, and it hit the webbing. Just as Popov attempted to secure the ball, he was jostled by the crowd and eventually ended up on the ground under several people. Meanwhile, the ball rolled away, and it eventually came into the hands of Patrick Hayashi, who put it in his pocket.

Popov sued Hayashi for conversion. The parties agreed that before Bonds swung the bat, the ball was the property of Major League Baseball. Once it cleared the fence it was intentionally abandoned property (like the manure in *Haslem*) and became, literally, up for grabs. The court applied the rule of capture, citing *Pierson v. Post, Ghen v. Rich*, and the testimony of no less than four distinguished law professors, who disagreed on what constituted possession in this case.

The court noted that the rule of capture must be tailored to the circumstances:

> A stable economic environment requires rules of conduct which are understandable and consistent with the fundamental customs and practices of the industry they regulate. Without that, rules will be difficult to enforce and economic instability will

result. Because each industry has different customs and practices, a single definition of possession cannot be applied to different industries without creating havoc.

Popov v. Hayashi, No. 400545, 2002 WL 31833731, at *9 (Cal. Super. Ct. Dec. 18, 2002). What constitutes a "catch" according to the customary rules of baseball? Would a runner be out at first if the ball popped out of the webbing of the first baseman's glove? On the other hand, what if the ball popped out because the runner intentionally jostled the fielder?

The court held that Popov could not establish that he would have retained control of the ball even had he not been jostled, and therefore he did not have possession of the ball. However, the court felt that it was unfair that Popov was prevented by the crowd from trying to complete the catch. Moreover, the court did not want to encourage the type of violence that occurred in this case.

Therefore, the court deemed that both Popov and Hayashi had an interest in the ball. The court labeled Popov's interest "pre-possessory": "where an actor undertakes significant but incomplete steps to achieve possession of a piece of abandoned personal property and the effort is interrupted by the unlawful acts of others, the actor has a legally cognizable pre-possessory interest in the property." Applying the concept of *equitable division,* the court determined that each had a half interest. *Id.* at *8. Does that rule fulfill our fairness policy, or is it simply a judicial cop-out?

Would recognition of a "pre-possessory" interest have changed the result in *Pierson v. Post*?

Should the court in *Pierson v. Post* have awarded each hunter a share of the fox in accordance with the amount of their labor? Why do you think it didn't adopt that approach? Is the application of a rule designed for wild animals appropriate for "wild baseballs"?

The Rule of Capture Applied

As we noted earlier, the law of first possession governs many instances of property allocation. The Homestead Acts and the Mining Acts we mentioned in Chapter 1, for example, gave (or, in the case of the Mining Act, still give) property rights to the first person to stake a claim to unowned land or minerals, providing that the person makes use of them (thereby fulfilling the policy of economic efficiency).

The opening of the Unassigned Lands in the Oklahoma Territory was one of the most striking examples of the rule of capture at work. This description of the first Land Run in 1889 paints the picture:

> In its picturesque aspects the rush across the border at noon on the opening day must go down in history as one of the most noteworthy events of Western civilization. At the time fixed, thousands of hungry home-seekers, who had gathered from all parts of the country, and particularly from Kansas and Missouri, were arranged in line along the border, ready to lash their horses into furious speed in the race for fertile spots in the beautiful land before them. . . .

As the expectant home-seekers waited with restless patience, the clear, sweet notes of a cavalry bugle rose and hung a moment upon the startled air. It was noon. The last barrier of savagery in the United States was broken down. Moved by the same impulse, each driver lashed his horses furiously; each rider dug his spurs into his willing steed, and each man on foot caught his breath hard and darted forward. A cloud of dust rose where the home-seekers had stood in line, and when it had drifted away before the gentle breeze, the horses and wagons and men were tearing across the open country like fiends. The horsemen had the best of it from the start. It was a fine race for a few minutes, but soon the riders began to spread out like a fan, and by the time they had reached the horizon they were scattered about as far as eye could see.

William Willard Howard, *The Rush to Oklahoma*, Harper's Weekly, May 18, 1889, at 391.

The rule of capture is of critical importance to more modern property issues as well. The world wide web, for example, is not that different from the territory of Oklahoma, with millions of domain names available for the first person to stake a claim and pay a fee.

In *Pierson v. Post*, the court applied the rule of capture to wild animals due to their nature as "fugitive resources;" that is, things that do not stay in one place and therefore cannot be considered part of any particular land. Should courts and legislatures apply the rule of capture to other types of fugitive resources, such as water, oil, and gas? The materials below explore the rule of capture in these contexts.

1.   Surface Water Allocation

There are two basic systems of allocating surface water in the United States. In nine states, all located in the western part of the country, the *prior appropriation* system is used.[9] The *riparian* doctrine governs the water rights system that prevails in 31 states, all but one of which (Hawaii is the exception) are located in the eastern half of the United States.[10] The remaining ten states use a hybrid that incorporates elements of both systems. All of the hybrid states except one (Mississippi) are located west of the Mississippi River.[11]

---

[9] Prior appropriation states include: Alaska, Arizona, Colorado, Idaho, Montana, Nevada, New Mexico, Utah, and Wyoming.

[10] Riparian states include: Alabama, Arkansas, Connecticut, Delaware, Florida, Georgia, Hawaii, Illinois, Indiana, Iowa, Kentucky, Louisiana, Maine, Maryland, Massachusetts, Michigan, Minnesota, Missouri, New Hampshire, New Jersey, New York, North Carolina, Ohio, Pennsylvania, Rhode Island, South Carolina, Tennessee, Vermont, Virginia, West Virginia, and Wisconsin.

[11] Hybrid states include California, Kansas, Mississippi, Nebraska, North Dakota, Oklahoma, Oregon, South Dakota, Texas, and Washington. *See generally* A. Dan Tarlock, Law of Water Rights and Resources (West 2011).

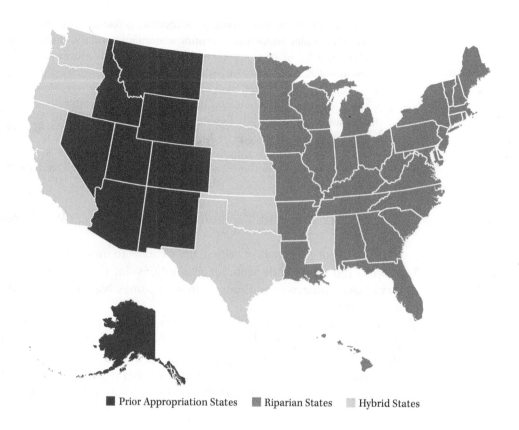

■ Prior Appropriation States   ■ Riparian States   ■ Hybrid States

Under the *prior appropriation* system, water rights are acquired by diverting water from a watercourse and putting it to beneficial use. *See* Colorado v. New Mexico, 459 U.S. 176, 179 (1982). This doctrine is based on the rule of capture: the first in time to "possess" the water is first in right, so long as the use lasts. If there is insufficient flow to satisfy all users, the *senior appropriator* (i.e., the user with the oldest priority date) is entitled to its full appropriation before junior users get any water. Water rights are generally transferable and may be used in a different location and for a different purpose, as long as the transfer doesn't injure junior appropriators. As you can imagine, water rights in the arid West are very valuable interests and are essential for any new development.

In contrast, the *riparian* system assigns the right to use water to *riparian* and *littoral* landowners. Riparian land borders a river or stream, while littoral land borders an ocean, sea, or lake. The term *riparian* is often used to encompass both of these types of land. Riparian landowners are entitled to make *reasonable use* of the water. The test for reasonableness involves balancing the benefits of the use against the rights and uses of the other riparians. A Michigan court described the factors to be considered:

First, attention should be given to the size, character and natural state of the water course. Second, consideration should be given the type and purpose of the uses proposed and their effect on the water course. Third, the court should balance the benefit that would inure to the proposed user with the injury to the other riparian owners.

Three Lakes Ass'n v. Kessler, 285 N.W.2d 300, 303 (Mich. Ct. App. 1979). When a new appropriation of water is proposed, note the difference in the two systems:

- In a riparian jurisdiction, other users may object and the court will need to determine whether the new use is reasonable. This will involve a judgment about the value of the new use as compared to the value of the existing uses.
- In a prior appropriation jurisdiction, there is no inquiry into relative value. The new appropriator takes its place at the bottom of the priority ladder and gets water if there is any left when the senior appropriations have been satisfied. Because the rights generally are transferable,[12] the market will (at least theoretically) ensure that the water gets to its highest and best use.

The 100th meridian, which runs through the Dakotas, Nebraska, Kansas, Oklahoma, and Texas, has traditionally been considered the nation's "dry line." To the east of this line, rainfall averages over 20 inches a year, and irrigation is typically not necessary for agriculture. To the west, however, annual rainfall averages less than 20 inches, and irrigation is common. Does the scarcity of water in the West help explain why we have two systems of water rights? Do you see any drawbacks to using the rule of capture in this situation?

■ PROBLEM: COMPARING RIPARIAN AND PRIOR APPROPRIATION SYSTEMS

A stream runs through land owned by Aupperle (upstream) and Koch (downstream). In 1989, Koch built a dam on the stream and impounded enough water to fill a small pond, which he uses for recreational fishing and watering livestock. In 2005, Aupperle began construction of a dam on his property and he plans to use the water to irrigate a Christmas tree farm he is starting. Koch believes that this diversion of water will severely impact his use of the water downstream. Koch admits, however, that he could water his livestock by using well water, so he is mostly concerned about the fishing.

Koch has sued Aupperle to enjoin his diversion of water from the stream. How would you evaluate this claim under the riparian and prior appropriation systems? *See* Koch v. Aupperle, 737 N.W.2d 869 (Neb. 2007). What property policies are furthered by each system?

---

[12] There are limits on the ability to transfer water rights, but we will save that complexity for upper-level courses in water law.

2. Groundwater

As we learned in Chapter 1, the *ad coelum* doctrine suggests that ownership of land carries with it the ownership of all that lies beneath. Certainly, this doctrine applies in the case of hard minerals, such as coal or precious metals. But what about water or oil, resources that lie in reservoirs in and between layers of sedimentary rock, far beneath the surface? If Alice drills a well near Barney's land and starts pumping out water that was originally under Barney's land, can Barney sue to stop her, arguing that she is taking his property?

These pools of water, or oil and gas, have two qualities that make them different from hard rock minerals. First, these materials are *fugacious*, meaning that they can travel through porous sedimentary rock. Second, they are fungible, meaning that once you start drilling, there is no way to tell whether the particular oil coming through the wellhead at the surface came from under your land or mine. In this sense, water and petroleum resources have some of the qualities of wild animals, and the courts have used wild animal cases as precedent.

But does the analogy always make sense? In the case of groundwater, many states historically followed the rule of "absolute ownership" of groundwater announced in the English case of Acton v. Blundell, 152 Eng. Rep. 1223 (1843), which was based on the rule of capture and the *ad coelum* doctrine:

> [W]e think the present case, for the reasons above given, is not to be governed by the law which applies to rivers and flowing streams, but that it rather falls within that principle, which gives to the owner of the soil all that lies beneath his surface; that the land immediately below is his property, whether it is solid rock, or porous ground, or venous earth, or part soil, part water; that the person who owns the surface may dig therein, and apply all that is there found to his own purposes at his free will and pleasure; and that if, in the exercise of such right, he intercepts or drains off the water collected from underground springs in his neighbour's well, this inconvenience to his neighbour falls within the description of *damnum absque injuria*,[13] which cannot become the ground of an action.

Id. at 1235. The absolute ownership rule for groundwater has now been modified, in all but a few states, either by requiring reasonable use, similar to the riparian system; or by prior appropriation; or by a system of *correlative rights*, which limits the user in times of shortage to an equitable share of the available water. *See* Restatement (Second) of Torts §858 (1939) (withdrawal of groundwater that "unreasonably causes harm" to neighbor's use or exceeds "reasonable share" is actionable).

A few states, however, such as Maine, Massachusetts, and Texas, continue to adhere to the absolute ownership rule. *See, e.g.,* Maddocks v. Giles, 728 A.2d 150, 153 (Me. 1999). Texas's continued adherence to the absolute ownership rule despite the depletion of aquifers has been the source of considerable political

---

[13] Latin for "loss without (legal) injury."

and legal debate. *See* Ronald Kaiser & Frank F. Skillern, *Deep Trouble: Options for Managing the Hidden Threat of Aquifer Depletion in Texas*, 32 Tex. Tech. L. Rev. 249 (2001). Texas law allows for the regulation of water withdrawal to prevent depletion of aquifers, but because groundwater is deemed to be the "property" of the landowner, limiting groundwater use may require the government to compensate the owner. See Edwards Aquifer Auth. v. Bragg, 421 S.W.3d 118 (Tx. Ct. App. 2013) (landowner denied groundwater withdrawal permit to irrigate pecan orchard entitled to compensation for taking of property).

How would you use the property policies we have learned so far to argue in favor of retaining or changing the absolute ownership rule for groundwater? In what ways is groundwater not like a wild animal?

■ PROBLEM: GROUNDWATER EXTRACTION

The Muddy Waters Company purchases land in Michigan and builds a bottled-water plant. It begins to withdraw 500,000 gallons of water per day from its groundwater wells. The Love-R-Lake community, located nearby, begins to notice that its lake, which is fed by the groundwater aquifer, has lost significant volume; recreational uses, such as fishing and waterskiing, have been impacted. Michigan has adopted the reasonable use approach. Does Love-R-Lake have any recourse against Muddy Waters? Does your answer change under an absolute ownership or prior appropriation system?

3. Oil and Gas

Assume Allison owns Blackacre and Beau owns Whiteacre, two adjacent properties that lie over the Big Oil Reservoir. Allison drills a well on her property and begins extracting oil from the reservoir. This causes the petroleum under Beau's land to migrate over to Allison's land, where it is drawn into her well. Can Beau enjoin Allison's production or at least require her to compensate him for the damage to his mineral resources? Is oil any different from groundwater in this regard?

Early on, the courts dealing with these issues realized that allowing an injunction or damages in a case like this would make oil production difficult if not impossible. By using an analogy to wild animals, the courts instead held that the owner of land did not own the oil and gas until it was "captured"—that is, until it came up out of the ground into the owner's possession. The classic approach to classifying oil and gas as fugitive resources is set out in Westmoreland & Cambria Natural Gas Co. v. De Witt, 18 A. 724, 725 (Pa. 1889):

> Water and oil, and still more strongly gas, may be classed by themselves, if the analogy be not too fanciful, as minerals *ferae naturae*. In common with animals, and unlike other minerals, they have the power and the tendency to escape

without the volition of the owner. Their "fugitive and wandering existence within the limits of a particular tract was uncertain," as said by Chief Justice Agnew in Brown v. Vandegrift, 80 Pa. St. 147, 148. They belong to the owner of the land, and are part of it, so long as they are on or in it, and are subject to his control; but when they escape, and go into other land, or come under another's control, the title of the former owner is gone. Possession of the land, therefore, is not necessarily possession of the gas. If an adjoining, or even a distant, owner, drills his own land, and taps your gas, so that it comes into his well and under his control, it is no longer yours, but his. . . . [O]ne who controls the gas—has it in his grasp, so to speak—is the one who has possession in the legal as well as in the ordinary sense of the word.

How does this application of the rule of capture further our property policies of certainty, economic efficiency, and fairness?

■ PROBLEM: RULE OF "RECAPTURE"?

After Allison captures a large quantity of natural gas from her well on Blackacre, she needs a place to store it until demand increases, along with the price. She therefore decides to store the gas in an underground sandstone formation on her land, which is impervious and therefore perfect for holding the gas. A small part of the formation, however, lies under Beau's property. Beau drills a well on Whiteacre and begins to extract the gas stored by Allison. Can Allison enjoin Beau?

An early decision, Hammonds v. Cent. Ky. Natural Gas Co., 75 S.W.2d 204, 206 (Ky. 1934), likened this situation to a release of the fox back into the wild, where it was once again up for grabs. Later decisions, however, rejected that analogy:

> The analogy of wild animals upon which *Hammonds* is founded fails to undergird the ultimate decision of that case. Gas has no similarity to wild animals. Gas is an inanimate, diminishing non-reproductive substance lacking any will of its own, and instead of running wild and roaming at large as animals do, is subject to be moved solely by pressure or mechanical means. It cannot be logically regarded as personal property of the human race as are wild animals[;] instead of being turned loose in the woods as the fanciful fox or placed in the streams as the fictitious fish, gas, a privately owned commodity, has been stored for use, as required by the consuming public being, as alleged by appellant, subject to its control and withdrawal at any time. Logic and reason dictates . . . that in Texas, the owner of gas does not lose title thereof by storing the same in a well-defined underground reservoir.

Lone Star Gas Co. v. Murchison, 353 S.W.2d 870, 879 (Tex. Civ. App. 1962); *see also* Texas Am. Energy Corp. v. Citizens Fid. Bank & Trust Co., 736 S.W.2d 25 (Ky. 1987) (overruling *Hammonds*).

In some states, such as Kansas, this issue has been addressed by statute:

Kansas Statutes §55-1210:

(a) All natural gas which has previously been reduced to possession, and which is subsequently injected into underground storage fields, sands, reservoirs and facilities, whether such storage rights were acquired by eminent domain or otherwise, shall at all times be the property of the injector, such injector's heirs, successors or assigns, whether owned by the injector or stored under contract.

(b) In no event shall such gas be subject to the right of the owner of the surface of such lands or of any mineral interest therein, under which such gas storage fields, sands, reservoirs and facilities lie, or of any person, other than the injector, such injector's heirs, successors and assigns, to produce, take, reduce to possession, either by means of the law of capture or otherwise, waste, or otherwise interfere with or exercise any control over such gas.

The downside of the rule of capture. Knowing that Allison has drilled her well and that his oil is migrating to Blackacre, Beau does the only thing a self-interested landowner could do: he drills his own well. Allison responds by drilling another well, to increase her rate of production, and Beau responds in kind. Soon we have overproduction, and inefficient production. In fact, this sort of drilling technique usually results in causing otherwise recoverable petroleum to be trapped in pockets that are not recoverable. This should remind you of our discussion of the problem of common pool resources in Chapter 1. In this case, we have privatized the surface of the land, but left the fugitive mineral resource in communal ownership, leading to a tragedy of the commons.

Oil and gas states responded to the problems of a pure rule of capture by enacting conservation laws, such as well-spacing requirements, production limits, and compulsory pooling. *See* Bruce M. Kramer & Owen L. Anderson, *The Rule of Capture—An Oil and Gas Perspective*, 35 Envtl. L. 899, 953-54 (2005). Pooling arrangements provide a share of the profits from an oil well to all the landowners in a particular drilling area. As we noted in Chapter 1, regulation is one way to deal with a tragedy of the commons.

Oil wells, California, 1923
Everett Collection

4. The Internet

An internet address can be an extremely valuable property interest. A domain name may lead customers to your site and provide consumers with valuable information and assistance. On a personal level, a web site may fulfill the values of self-expression we discussed in Chapter 1.

Acquiring the rights to a domain name is based on the rule of capture. The Internet Corporation for Assigned Names and Numbers (ICANN) oversees the rights to use particular domain names. The first person to register a particular domain name with ICANN (through delegated domain name registrars) acquires the exclusive right to use that name.

■ PROBLEM: WWW.THEBEETLES.COM

Professor Scarab conducts research on *coleoptera*, an order of insects commonly called "beetles." He was fortunate enough to obtain the rights to *www.thebeetles.com*, and has used the site to display his pictures of various types of beetles and links to his research, particularly with regard to his dung beetle findings.

A company called Apple Corps represents the interests of a rock band from Liverpool with the name "The Beatles." Although the company owns the rights to www.thebeatles.com, it finds that many fans of the group, who want information on their songs and the doings of Paul McCartney and Ringo Starr, are confused by the spelling and often end up looking at pictures of dung beetles.

Apple Corps contacts Professor Scarab and offers him $50,000 for the web site. He refuses, however, and maintains that the site is not for sale at any price.

Does the rule of capture fulfill the fundamental policies of property law in this instance? Are the considerations in this case any different from the real estate context, where someone owns land near a business that wants to expand? What if Scarab was *not* a scientist, but rather an entrepreneur who is sitting on the site knowing that the rock group would eventually want it?

> ### Most Expensive Domain Names
>
> Some of the most expensive domain name sales include:
>
> - Insurance.com: $35.6 million in 2010.
> - Vacationrentals.com: $35 million in 2007.
> - Internet.com: $18 million in 2009.
> - Sex.com: $13 million in 2010
>
> Times change: The American Farm Bureau Federation acquired FB.com before Facebook was a "thing". In 2009, Facebook bought the name for $8.5 million.

■ ■ ■

A name that is protected as a trademark, as we will see in our introduction to intellectual property below, modifies the pure rule of capture on the internet. If someone other than the trademark owner acquires a web address with that name, the trademark owner may have recourse if the use of the site *dilutes* the distinctive quality of the mark. Lanham Act, 15 U.S.C. §1114 (2005). A plaintiff must prove (1) that it possesses a mark; (2) that the defendant used the mark; (3) that the defendant's use of the mark occurred "in commerce"; (4) that the defendant used the mark "in connection with the sale, offering for sale, distribution, or advertising" of goods or services; and (5) that the defendant used the mark in a manner likely to confuse consumers. Would this apply to Professor Scarab?

Courts have often found that the consumer confusion caused by web sites using the name of famous companies or services is sufficient to prove dilution. However, courts sometimes protect sites if they are being used to criticize the trademark owner, because they are not used "in commerce" or in connection with goods and services. Compare these decisions:

> ➤ Planned Parenthood Fed'n of Am., Inc. v. Bucci, No. 97CIV0629, 1997 WL 133313 (S.D.N.Y. Mar. 24, 1997). Anti-abortion advocate registered domain name "plannedparenthood.com" and used it to promote a book about abortion. The court enjoined the use of the site.
> ➤ Lamparello v. Falwell, 420 F.3d 309 (4th Cir. 2005). Site owner used www. fallwell.com to criticize the opinions of the Rev. Jerry Falwell on homosexuality. The court refused to enjoin the site, finding no likelihood of consumer confusion.
> ➤ People for the Ethical Treatment of Animals v. Doughney, 263 F.3d 359 (4th Cir. 2001). Defendant registered peta.org and used it for a web site called "People Eating Tasty Animals." The court found the use of site was likely to prevent prospective users from reaching PETA's web site and therefore enjoined use.

Note that the Lanham Act only allows the trademark owner to *enjoin* the use of the confusing web site; it does not allow the trademark owner to demand the transfer of the domain name. However, the Anticybersquatting Consumer Protection Act (ACPA), 15 U.S.C. §1125 (2012), does allow the court to transfer the domain name to the mark owner if the use of the mark was in *bad faith*. The following case should remind you of the *spite fence* policies outlined in Chapter 1.

VIRTUAL WORKS, INC. v. VOLKSWAGEN OF AMERICA, INC.

238 F.3d 264 (2001)
U.S. Court of Appeals, Fourth Circuit

WILKINSON, Chief Judge:
Volkswagen challenges Virtual Works, Inc.'s use of the domain name vw.net under the 1999 Anticybersquatting Consumer Protection Act (ACPA). Volkswagen claims that Virtual Works registered vw.net with the purpose of one

day selling it to Volkswagen. The district court agreed, holding that Virtual Works had a bad faith intent to profit from the vw.net domain name and that its use of vw.net diluted and infringed upon the VW mark.... The district court therefore ordered Virtual Works to relinquish to Volkswagen the rights to vw.net. Because the district court did not err in holding that Virtual Works violated the ACPA, we affirm the judgment.

I.

On October 23, 1996, Virtual Works registered the domain name vw.net with Network Solutions, Inc. (NSI).... At the time Virtual Works registered vw.net, two of its principals, Christopher Grimes and James Anderson, were aware that some Internet users might think that vw.net was affiliated with Volkswagen. According to Grimes, he and Anderson "talked about Volkswagen and decided that [they] would use the domain name for [the] company, but if Volkswagen offered to work out a deal for services or products, that [they] would sell it to [Volkswagen] for a lot of money." When Virtual Works registered vw.net, many other domain names were available for its use. For instance, vwi.net, vwi.org, virtualworks.net, and virtualworks.org, were still available.

Virtual Works used the vw.net domain name for approximately two years as a part of its ISP [Internet Service Provider] business. In December 1998, various Volkswagen dealerships contacted Virtual Works and expressed an interest in purchasing the rights to the vw.net domain name. Virtual Works, in turn, called Volkswagen, offering to sell vw.net. The terms of Virtual Works' offer, however, were somewhat unusual. Anderson left a voice mail message for Linda Scipione in Volkswagen's trademark department. In the message, Anderson stated that he owned the rights to vw.net. He also said that unless Volkswagen bought the rights to vw.net, Virtual Works would sell the domain name to the highest bidder. Anderson gave Volkswagen twenty-four hours to respond....

II.

A.

The ACPA was enacted in 1999 in response to concerns over the proliferation of cybersquatting—the Internet version of a land grab. According to the Senate Report accompanying the Act: "Trademark owners are facing a new form of piracy on the Internet caused by acts of 'cybersquatting,' which refers to the deliberate, bad-faith, and abusive registration of Internet domain names in violation of the rights of trademark owners." S. Rep. No. 106-140, at 4 (1999). Cybersquatting is the practice of registering "well-known brand names as Internet domain names" in order to force the rightful owners of the marks "to pay for the right to engage in electronic commerce under their own brand name." Id. at 5. See also H.R. Rep. No. 106-412, at 5-7 (1999). Cybersquatting is profitable because while it is inexpensive for a cybersquatter to register the mark of an established company as a domain name, such companies are often vulnerable to being forced into paying substantial sums to get their names back. Sporty's Farm, L.L.C. v. Sportsman's Market, Inc., 202 F.3d 489, 493 (2d Cir. 2000).

Congress viewed the practice of cybersquatting as harmful because it threatened "the continued growth and vitality of the Internet as a platform" for "communication, electronic commerce, education, entertainment, and countless other yet-to-be-determined uses." S. Rep. No. 106-140, at 8. New legislation was required to address this situation because then-current law did not expressly prohibit the act of cybersquatting and cybersquatters had started to take the necessary precautions to insulate themselves from liability under the Federal Trademark Dilution Act. Id. at 7. Accordingly, Congress passed, and the President signed, the ACPA in 1999. Pub. L. No. 106-113, 113 Stat. 1536 (codified at 15 U.S.C. §1125(d)).

B.

Under the ACPA, a person alleged to be a cybersquatter is liable to the owner of a protected mark if that person:

    (i) has a bad faith intent to profit from that mark . . . ; and

    (ii) registers, traffics in, or uses a domain name that—

        (I) in the case of a mark that is distinctive . . . , is identical or confusingly similar to that mark;

        (II) in the case of a famous mark . . . , is identical or confusingly similar to or dilutive of that mark;

15 U.S.C. §1125(d)(1)(A). With respect to the bad faith determination, the statute provides that:

    (B) (i) In determining whether a person has a bad faith intent . . . a court may consider factors such as, but not limited to

        (I) the trademark or other intellectual property rights of the person, if any, in the domain name;

        (II) the extent to which the domain name consists of the legal name of the person or a name that is otherwise commonly used to identify that person;

        (III) the person's prior use, if any, of the domain name in connection with the bona fide offering of any goods or services;

        (IV) the person's bona fide noncommercial or fair use of the mark in a site accessible under the domain name;

        (V) the person's intent to divert consumers from the mark owner's online location to a site . . . that could harm the goodwill represented by the mark, either for commercial gain or with the intent to tarnish or disparage the mark . . . ;

        (VI) the person's offer to transfer, sell, or otherwise assign the domain name to the mark owner or any third party for financial gain without having used . . . the domain name in the bona fide offering of any goods or services . . . ;

(VII)   the person's provision of material and misleading false contact information when applying for the registration of the domain name . . . ;

(VIII)   the person's registration or acquisition of multiple domain names which the person knows are identical or confusingly similar to marks of others . . . ; and

(IX)   the extent to which the mark incorporated in the person's domain name registration is or is not distinctive and famous. . . .

15 U.S.C. §1125(d)(1)(B)(i). In addition to listing these nine factors, the Act contains a safe harbor. The safe harbor provision states that bad faith intent "shall not be found in any case in which the court determines that the person believed and had reasonable grounds to believe that the use of the domain name was fair use or otherwise lawful." 15 U.S.C. §1225(d)(1)(B)(ii). . . .

A.

The first inquiry under the ACPA is whether Virtual Works acted with a bad faith intent to profit from a protected mark. . . .

We are mindful that the instant case comes to us on summary judgment and involves a contested determination of Virtual Works' intent. Unfortunately for Virtual Works, however, there is both circumstantial and direct evidence establishing bad faith. The following uncontested facts all provide circumstantial evidence of Virtual Works' bad faith with respect to the VW mark: 1) the famousness of the VW mark; 2) the similarity of vw.net to the VW mark; 3) the admission that Virtual Works never once did business as VW nor identified itself as such; and 4) the availability of vwi.org and vwi.net at the time Virtual Works registered vw.net. Notably, either of these domain names would have satisfied Virtual Works' own stated criterion of registering a domain name that used only two or three letters and would have eliminated any risk of confusion with respect to the VW mark.

We consider such circumstantial factors cautiously, however. We do not suggest that these four facts would alone resolve the question of Virtual Works' intent on summary judgment. The fact that a domain resembles a famous trademark, for example, hardly in and of itself establishes bad faith. Moreover, domain names that are abbreviations of a company's formal name are quite common. To view the use of such names as tantamount to bad faith would chill Internet entrepreneurship with the prospect of endless litigation.

Volkswagen, however, points to direct evidence regarding Virtual Works' intent—the statements made at registration. Grimes' deposition reveals that when registering vw.net, he and Anderson specifically acknowledged that vw.net might be confused with Volkswagen by some Internet users. They nevertheless decided to register the address for their own use, but left open the possibility of one day selling the site to Volkswagen "for a lot of money." Volkswagen claims that this is sufficient to establish bad faith registration in violation of the ACPA.

Viewing the facts in the light most favorable to Virtual Works, as we must on summary judgment, the statement at registration establishes that Virtual Works had a dual purpose in selecting vw.net. Contrary to Virtual Works' claim, the fact that it used vw.net for two years as a part of an ISP business is not dispositive of the question of intent. Virtual Works chose vw.net over other domain names not just because "vw" reflected the company's own initials, but also because it foresaw the ability to profit from the natural association of vw.net with the VW mark. Indeed, it is obvious even to a casual observer that the similarity between vw.net and the VW mark is overwhelming.

Moreover, the facts in the summary judgment record affirmatively support the claim that Virtual Works had a bad faith intent to profit when it attempted to sell vw.net to Volkswagen. It is true that a mere offer to sell a domain name is not itself evidence of unlawful trafficking. H.R. Conf. Rep. No. 106-464, at 111 (1999). The ACPA was not enacted to put an end to the sale of all domain names. This case, however, involves much more than a plain vanilla offer to sell a domain name.

Indeed, the second piece of direct evidence regarding Virtual Works' intent is the terms of its offer to Volkswagen. Virtual Works told Volkswagen that vw.net would be sold to the highest bidder if Volkswagen did not make an offer within twenty-four hours. Virtual Works also stated that others would jump at the chance to own a valuable domain name like vw.net because Internet users would instinctively associate the site with Volkswagen. Virtual Works knew, both when it registered vw.net and when it offered to sell the site, that consumers would associate vw.net with Volkswagen. It sought to maximize the advantage of this association by threatening to auction off the site. And it hoped that in an effort to protect its mark, Volkswagen would respond with a hefty offer of its own.

Likewise, Virtual Works cannot take refuge in the ACPA's safe harbor provision. The safe harbor is only available when the defendant both "believed and had reasonable grounds to believe that the use of the domain name was fair use or otherwise lawful." 15 U.S.C. §1125(d)(1)(B)(ii). The openly admitted hope of profiting from consumer confusion of vw.net with the VW mark disqualifies Virtual Works from the ACPA's safe harbor. . . .

Viewed in its totality, the evidence establishes that at the time Virtual Works proposed to sell vw.net to Volkswagen, it was motivated by a bad faith intent to profit from the famousness of the VW mark. This is the sort of misconduct that Congress sought to discourage. . . .

IV.

The remedy that Volkswagen sought in district court was the right to use vw.net for itself. The ACPA allows a court to order "the transfer of the domain name to the owner of the mark" if the Act is violated. 15 U.S.C. §1125(d)(2)(D)(i). Because Virtual Works' violation of the ACPA supports the remedy Volkswagen seeks, we need not address Volkswagen's claims of trademark infringement or dilution.

The ACPA was not enacted to give companies the right to fence off every possible combination of letters that bears any similarity to a protected mark. Rather, it was enacted to prevent the expropriation of protected marks in cyberspace and to abate the consumer confusion resulting therefrom. The resolution of this case turns on the unique facts and circumstances which it presents. Ultimately, we believe the evidence is sufficient to establish that, as a matter of law, Virtual Works attempted to profit in bad faith from Volkswagen's famous mark. 15 U.S.C. §1125(d)(1)(A). The district court thus did not err in ordering Virtual Works to turn over vw.net to Volkswagen. For the foregoing reasons, we affirm the judgment.

AFFIRMED.

■ POINTS TO CONSIDER

1. **The internet versus land or foxes.** Chief Judge Wilkinson likened cybersquatting to "the Internet version of a land grab." But we allow savvy investors to buy land they think might be valuable in the future and hold it for a profit. If Virtual Works bought land next to a Volkswagen assembly plant, we wouldn't force them to transfer it to the car company (although whether such government power exists will be discussed in the chapter on eminent domain). So why is the internet different? Are the policies behind the rule of capture better served by this exception to the rule of first possession?

2. **Bad faith.** Do you agree that Virtual Works' conduct here meets the definition of "bad faith" under the ACPA? Which of the factors weigh most heavily in favor of Virtual Works?

3. **Preparing to practice.** If the owners of Virtual Works, Anderson and Grimes, had come to you shortly after purchasing vw.net, how would you have advised them to conduct themselves in order to avoid a violation of the Act? Or is avoiding a violation even possible in this case?

4. **Selling domain names.** Can you offer to sell a domain name without triggering a claim of bad faith? In other words, what makes this more than a "plain vanilla" offer to sell, as the court puts it?

5. **Beatles again.** Consider Professor Scarab in the "www.thebeetles.com" problem above. Would Apple Corps have a case against him under the ACPA? Should it?

B THE LAW OF FINDERS

Everyone knows the basic rule with respect to finding lost property: finders keepers, meaning the one who finds lost property gets to keep it, at least until the true owner reclaims it, and even then the finder might, by law or by custom, expect to receive some sort of reward for recovering the lost item.

Valuable property is lost every day, and you may be surprised to discover how often these cases arise. But even if you never have a finders case, exploring the law of finders will give us a chance to apply the concept of possession in a different context.

The classic finders case below pits a goldsmith, at the top of the social ladder, against a chimney sweeper's assistant, occupying a rung near the bottom. The goldsmith in question is Paul de Lamerie, who was appointed royal goldsmith to King George I in 1716, just five years before the case reported here. His work in silver gained special renown, and he is generally regarded as the most accomplished English silversmith of the eighteenth century. As it happens, he was also known for flouting guild regulations, so his behavior in this case may not surprise you.[14] We have no historical record of how a chimney sweeper's boy managed to retain counsel to represent him in a case against the King's goldsmith.

ARMORY v. DELAMIRIE

1 Strange 505, 93 Eng. Rep. 664 (1721)
King's Bench

PRATT, C.J.

The plaintiff being a chimney sweeper's boy found a jewel and carried it to the defendant's shop (who was a goldsmith) to know what it was, and delivered it into the hands of the apprentice, who under pretence of weighing it, took out the stones, and calling to the master to let him know it came to three halfpence, the master offered the boy the money, who refused to take it, and insisted to have the thing again; whereupon the apprentice delivered him back the socket without the stones. And now in trover against the master these points were ruled:

1. That the finder of a jewel, though he does not by such finding acquire an absolute property or ownership, yet he has such a property as will enable him to keep it against all but the rightful owner, and consequently may maintain trover.
2. That the action well lay against the master, who gives a credit to his apprentice, and is answerable for his neglect.
3. As to the value of the jewel several of the trade were examined to prove what a jewel of the finest water that would fit the socket would be worth; and the Chief Justice directed the jury, that unless the defendant did produce the jewel, and shew it not to be of the finest water, they should presume the strongest against him, and make the value of the best jewels the measure of their damages: which they accordingly did.

---

[14] Philippa Glanville, *Paul Jacques de Lamerie*, Oxford Dictionary of National Biography (Oxford Univ. Press 2004).

The Chimney Sweep

The life of a chimney sweeper's boy was appallingly difficult. Often taken at a very young age from orphanages or sold into work by impoverished parents, the boys would work from dawn to dusk crawling up flues with their brushes. The boys had a high incidence of cancer and were often seriously injured or deformed.[15]

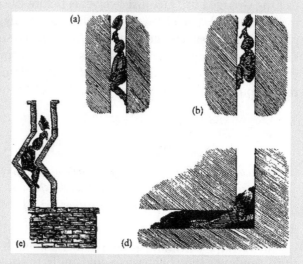

Four diagrams of boys in flues.
Kathleen H. Strange, Climbing Boys: A Study
of Sweeps' Apprentices 1773-1875, 13 (1982)

Reform came slowly. In 1788, the Chimney Sweepers Act set a minimum age of 8 years, but the law was rarely enforced. In 1875, a 12-year-old boy smothered while stuck in a flue, and Parliament responded with an act finally ending the practice of climbing boys.

Armory is especially remarkable, given that a chimney sweeper's boy was at the bottom of the social ladder, while goldsmith Paul de Lamerie was near the top. Does it also make you wonder where the boy found the jewel?

---

[15] Kathleen H. Strange, Climbing Boys: A Study of Sweeps' Apprentices 1773-1875, 15 (1982). Strange quotes a master-sweep's statement to a parliamentary commission:

> No one knows the cruelty which a boy has to undergo in learning. The flesh must be hardened. This is done by rubbing it, chiefly on the elbow and knees with the strongest brine, as that got from a pork-shop, close by a hot fire. You must stand over them with a cane, or coax them by a promise of a halfpenny, etc. if they will stand a few more rubs.

■ POINTS TO CONSIDER

1. **Black letter law.** In short order, the report of Chief Justice Pratt's opinion gives us three important rules of law. In paragraph 1, he gives us the finder's rule in one sentence. In paragraph 2, he sets out the tort rule of *respondeat superior*, which provides that the master is liable for the acts of a servant done in the course of his employment. In paragraph 3, the court announces what we now call the "spoliation" doctrine, which punishes a party for the destruction of evidence. "If spoliation has occurred, then a court may impose a variety of sanctions, ranging from dismissal or judgment by default, preclusion of evidence, imposition of an adverse inference, or assessment of attorney's fees and costs." Goodman v. Praxair Services, Inc., 632 F. Supp. 2d 494, 506 (D. Md. 2009); *see also id.* at 518 n.12 (tracing spoliation doctrine back to *Armory*, "a Dickensian tale of avarice and trickery"). Of course, for this class, we are primarily concerned with point number one!

2. **Trover.** As noted in Chapter 1, *trover* is the form of action for the wrongful appropriation of personal property, which today is usually called *conversion*. Conversion seeks damages for the misappropriation, while *replevin* seeks the return of the property. A few jurisdictions continue to use the common law action of trover. Each of these claims depends, of course, on the plaintiff's ability to establish a superior property right in the item taken.

3. **Relative title.** What does Justice Pratt mean when he says that Armory did not acquire "absolute property or ownership"? Recall that in *Haslem*, the manure case from Chapter 1, the court held that the person who gathered the manure had a relatively better property interest than the person who carted off the piles. He might well have lost, however, if the Borough had claimed the manure as owner of the public street.

   Similarly, in this case the finder does not have *absolute* ownership, but has title good against "all but the rightful owner." Is that statement true in all finders cases? Suppose that the sweep dropped the jewel on the way to the goldsmith's shop and it was found in the street by a street urchin. Retracing his steps, the sweep finds the urchin admiring his acquisition. Who gets the jewel (assuming, of course, there were plenty of witnesses to the sweep's earlier find)?

Recall *Haslem v. Lockwood*

The court in *Haslem* determined that the manure was *abandoned* property to which the original owner had relinquished any claim. The first possessor's title to abandoned property is no longer subject to the rights of the true owner.

4. **Finders.** The law of finders is another application of the rule of first possession. Although this property is not *res nullius*, it is "up for grabs" until the true owner reclaims it. What property policies are fulfilled by this rule?

- ■ **Fairness.** The finder labored to discover the property. Think of those folks on the beach with metal detectors hoping to uncover lost change.
- ■ **Efficiency.** By giving a property interest to the finder, we allow the property to be used. If we can't find the true owner, we don't want the property to just go to waste. The property interest gives the finder an incentive to retrieve lost items, rather than simply allowing them to continue lying there.
- ■ **Certainty.** By protecting possession, we avoid all kinds of questions about ownership (do you have the receipt to your laptop with you?) and preserve peace and order by preventing endless dispossession from those who can't prove ownership. If we don't protect the sweep, why can't someone else take the jewel from the goldsmith?

■ ■ ■

Note how the court in the case below used the policies behind the finders rule to decide this property dispute over historical documents. The case is a perfect illustration of the ancient maxim that "possession is nine-tenths of the law."

WILLCOX v. STROUP

467 F.3d 409 (2006)
U.S. Court of Appeals, Fourth Circuit

[After his stepmother died, Thomas Law Willcox found a shopping bag in one of her closets, which contained over 400 documents from the administrations of two Civil War–era governors of South Carolina. The collection was valued at over $2 million. Willcox's great-great-uncle was a Confederate General who presumably took possession of the papers during General Sherman's 1865 attack on the South Carolina capital. The State of South Carolina claimed that the papers constituted public property which should be returned to the state. The district court held that the State had failed to establish that the papers were public property.]

WILKINSON, Circuit Judge.

The exceptional nature of the papers in dispute—their early vintage, their unknown history—presents issues distinct from those of the typical personal property case. Without the benefit of clear chain of title, evidence of original ownership, eyewitness testimony, and any number of documentary aids usually helpful in the determination of ownership, the court must utilize the legal tools that remain at its disposal. In this situation, tenets of the common law that usually remain in the background of ownership determinations come to the forefront, their logic and utility revealed anew.

That possession is nine-tenths of the law is a truism hardly bearing repetition. Statements to this effect have existed almost as long as the common law itself. . . .

The importance of possession gave rise to the principle that "[p]ossession of property is indicia of ownership, and a rebuttable presumption exists that those in possession of property are rightly in possession." 73 C.J.S. Property §70 (2004). The common law has long recognized that "actual possession is, prima facie, evidence of a legal title in the possessor." William Blackstone, 2 Commentaries *196. See, e.g., Edward Coke, 1 Commentary upon Littleton 6.b. (19th ed. 1832) (strong presumption of ownership created by "continual and quiet possession"); Jeffries v. Great W. Ry. Co. (1856) 119 Eng. Rep. 680 (K.B.) ("[T]he presumption of law is that the person who has possession has the property.").

This presumption has been a feature of American law almost since its inception. "Undoubtedly," noted the Supreme Court, "if a person be found in possession . . . it is prima facie evidence of his ownership." Ricard v. Williams, 20 U.S. (7 Wheat.) 59, 105 (1822). Almost eighty years later, the Court reaffirmed, "If there be no evidence to the contrary, proof of possession, at least under a color of right, is sufficient proof of title." Bradshaw v. Ashley, 180 U.S. 59, 63 (1901). See also, Oliver Wendell Holmes, The Common Law 241 (1881) ("The consequences attached to possession are substantially those attached to ownership, subject to the question of the continuance of possessory rights. . . . ").

In South Carolina law, too, it is well established that, absent evidence of superior title, "[t]he law ever presumes in favor of possession, for possession alone is prima facie evidence of a good title." . . . In this case, the possession of the Law and Willcox families triggers the presumption of their ownership of the papers. . . . The unusual circumstances of this case . . . provide a notable illustration of why such a presumption exists in the first place.

First and foremost, the presumption operates to resolve otherwise impenetrable difficulties. Where neither party can establish title by a preponderance of the evidence, the presumption cuts the Gordian knot, determining ownership in favor of the possessor. This case shows the need for such a default rule. It presents questions the answers to which remain a mystery. Little is known of the papers' whereabouts, status, or movements from their creation to their acquisition by General Law. There is no evidence of how General Law acquired the papers. Not even the chain of possession within the Law and Willcox families has yet been determined with any certainty. . . .

. . . Where the party not in possession is able to establish superior title by satisfactory evidence, the presumption gives way in favor of this evidence. But where no such evidence is produced—where, as here, the events at issue are impossible to reconstruct—the presumption recognizes and averts the possibility of a court's presiding over a historical goose chase. See Richard A. Posner, Economic Analysis of Law 78 (6th ed. 2003).

Second, the presumption of ownership in the possessor promotes stability. "It is the policy and even the duty of the law, to have personal property vested as early as practicable." Collins v. Bankhead, 32 S.C.L. (1 Strob.) 25, 29 (S.C. Ct.

App. 1846). The presumption of ownership from possession is one of an array of legal principles designed to this end. The presumption means that, absent proof to the contrary, settled distributions and expectations will continue undisturbed. Even where evidence overcomes the presumption, other principles work to protect settled expectations, including the statute of limitations, the doctrine of adverse possession, and equitable defenses such as laches, staleness, abandonment, and waiver.

Such principles, working in concert, favor status-quo distributions over great upsets in property rights. At the most basic level, this fosters "the policy of protecting the public peace against violence and disorder." See Sabariego v. Maverick, 124 U.S. 261, 297 (1888). In contemporary commercial society, it protects the expectations of those in possession, thus encouraging them to make improvements that increase social wealth. See, e.g., Richard A. Posner, Economic Analysis of Law 80-84 (6th ed. 2003); Thomas W. Merrill & Henry E. Smith, *What Happened to Property in Law and Economics?,* 111 Yale L.J. 357, 398 (2001) ("[T]he refined problems of concern in advanced economies exist at the apex of a pyramid, the base of which consists of the security of property rights."). Without rules such as the presumption of ownership, whether public or private, such valuable goals would give way to uncertainty.

In this case, the resulting confusion is not difficult to imagine. If the State were not required to defeat the presumption in order to gain title, a whole system of archival practice could be thrown into question. The State could claim ownership of other papers of Governors Pickens and Bonham held by the Library of Congress and Duke University, as well as papers of other South Carolina governors currently at institutions other than the State Archives. The result would be immense litigation over papers held by private owners, universities, historical societies, and federal depositories. It would upset settled archival arrangements and the expectations of institutions and historical scholars alike. Disregard of possession as presumptive evidence of ownership would throw the whole of this important area into turmoil. . . .

In short, the common law, through the presumption of ownership in the possessor, resolves otherwise insoluble historical puzzles in favor of longstanding distributions and long-held expectations. Such a rule both protects the private interests of longtime possessors and increases social utility. Of course, this presumption will not always cut in one direction. In many instances, the State will possess the papers, and it will then be entitled to the strong presumption that the private party claims here. In this case, however, where the Law and Willcox families have been in possession for well over a century, the presumption favors plaintiff Willcox.Having recognized the presumption in favor of Willcox's ownership, the court must consider whether the State has rebutted this presumption. Under South Carolina law, the burden is on the party not in possession to prove title superior to that of the possessor. See *Hammond*, 336 S.E.2d at 497. In most cases, the party not in possession would attempt to meet its burden through factual evidence, such as evidence of title or of recent prior possession.

Even if the State had been able to show evidence of superior title, however, that would not be the end of the matter. After the party out of possession establishes superior title, the possessor may still raise a number of defenses, including the statute of limitations and equitable defenses such as staleness, laches, waiver, and abandonment. See, e.g., O'Keeffe v. Snyder, 83 N.J. 478, 416 A.2d 862 (1980) (artist barred from reclaiming stolen paintings where she did not diligently pursue recovery of stolen works).

In this case, the State has been unable to provide such evidence. There is no documentary evidence of the State's title, nor is there evidence of its recent possession. While there is no suggestion that the Law and Willcox families are bona fide purchasers, since no purchase was involved, there is also no indication that they acquired the papers in bad faith. In any case, the State's burden may not be met by challenging the sufficiency of the possessor's title but only by proving the superior strength of its claim. See id.

Given the insufficient factual evidence, the State's remaining argument for ownership is that, under the law at the time of the documents' creation (1860-64) or their acquisition by General Law (1865), they were public property. South Carolina law of the relevant time period provides no basis for the State's claim of ownership.

[The court reviews the historical evidence and finds it is inconclusive as to what documents were considered public property during the relevant period.]

We conclude that the State has failed to establish that South Carolina law at the relevant time treated gubernatorial papers as public property. This conclusion leaves the State with no basis upon which to rebut the strong presumption of possession in the Law and Willcox families and no basis upon which to claim title superior to that of plaintiff Willcox....

The judgment of the district court is hereby affirmed.

AFFIRMED.

■ POINTS TO CONSIDER

1. **Policy.** Are there any policies that would favor giving these documents to the State of South Carolina—for example, the cultural property policies we discussed in Chapter 1? In terms of fairness, do these documents more properly belong to the people of South Carolina rather than to the person who happened to uncover them? Or is it enough that the government can buy the papers if it wants them?

2. **Presumption from possession.** The court states that a party in possession is presumed to be the owner and gives us the policies in favor of that presumption. Should the circumstances matter? In this case, there is a plausible explanation for how the papers ended up in Willcox's possession. But what if the finder was the son of a clerk at the state historical building and we strongly suspect, but can't prove, that the documents were stolen from the state's archives? The clerk's son has no explanation for his possession of the

documents, but claims the benefit of the presumption given possessors. Do you still think the presumption makes sense in those circumstances? For that matter, what if you suspect that the chimney sweeper's boy didn't so much "find" the jewel in *Armory* as lift it from a customer's house?

Finders and the Locus in Quo

The finders rule of first possession is fairly easy to apply when the property is found on public property, like the middle of the street. But what if the item is found on private property? It turns out the *locus in quo*, or the place where the item is found, makes a big difference.

If you invite someone over for dinner, you don't expect them to lay claim to items they "find" around your house, do you? In general, we consider you to be in *constructive possession* of items in your house, so these possessions are not lost property subject to the finder's rule.

As the next case illustrates, it is sometimes difficult to tell when a landowner has constructive possession. The case is also a useful example of how courts and attorneys deal with conflicting precedents.

HANNAH v. PEEL

[1945] K.B. 509
King's Bench

On December 13, 1938, the freehold of Gwernhaylod House, Overton-on-Dee, Shropshire, was conveyed to the defendant, Major Hugh Edward Ethelston Peel, who from that time to the end of 1940 never himself occupied the house and it remained unoccupied until October 5, 1939, when it was requisitioned,[16] but after some months was released from requisition. Thereafter it remained unoccupied until July 18, 1940, when it was again requisitioned, the defendant being compensated by a payment at the rate of 250£ a year. In August, 1940, the plaintiff, Duncan Hannah, a lance-corporal, serving in a battery of the Royal Artillery, was stationed at the house and on the 21st of that month, when in a bedroom, used as a sick-bay, he was adjusting the black-out curtains when his hand touched something on the top of a window-frame, loose in a crevice, which he thought was a piece of dirt or plaster. The plaintiff grasped it and dropped it on the outside window ledge. On the following morning he saw that it was a brooch covered with cobwebs and dirt. Later, he took it with him when he went home on leave and his wife having told him it might be of value, at the end of October, 1940, he informed his commanding officer of his find and, on his advice, handed it over to the police, receiving a receipt for it. In August, 1942, the owner not having been found the police handed the brooch to the defendant, who sold

---

[16] "Requisition" here refers to acquisition by the government for military purposes.—EDS.

it in October, 1942, for £66,[17] to Messrs. Spink & Son, Ltd., of London, who resold it in the following month for £88. There was no evidence that the defendant had any knowledge of the existence of the brooch before it was found by the plaintiff. The defendant had offered the plaintiff a reward for the brooch, but the plaintiff refused to accept this and maintained throughout his right to the possession of the brooch as against all persons other than the owner, who was unknown. By a letter, dated October 5, 1942, the plaintiff's solicitors demanded the return of the brooch from the defendant, but it was not returned and on October 21, 1943, the plaintiff issued his writ claiming the return of the brooch, or its value, and damages for its detention. By his defence, the defendant claimed the brooch on the ground that he was the owner of Gwernhaylod House and in possession thereof.

BIRKETT, J.

There is no issue of fact in this case between the parties. As to the issue in law, the rival claims of the parties can be stated in this way: The plaintiff says: "I claim the brooch as its finder and I have a good title against all the world, save only the true owner." The defendant says: "My claim is superior to yours inasmuch as I am the freeholder.[18] The brooch was found on my property, although I was never in occupation, and my title, therefore, ousts yours and in the absence of the true owner I am entitled to the brooch or its value." Unhappily the law on this issue is in a very uncertain state and there is need of an authoritative decision of a higher court. Obviously if it could be said with certainty that this is the law, that the finder of a lost article, wherever found, has a good title against all the world save the true owner, then, of course, all my difficulties would be resolved; or again, if it could be said with equal certainty that this is the law, that the possessor of land is entitled as against the finder to all chattels found on the land, again my difficulties would be resolved. But, unfortunately, the authorities give some support to each of these conflicting propositions.

In the famous case of *Armory v. Delamirie*, . . . it was ruled "that the finder of a jewel, though he does not by such finding acquire an absolute property or ownership, yet he has such a property as will enable him to keep it against all but the rightful owner, and consequently may maintain trover." The case of *Bridges v. Hawkesworth* is in process of becoming almost equally as famous because of the disputation which has raged around it. The headnote in the Jurist is as follows: "The place in which a lost article is found does not constitute any exception to the general rule of law, that the finder is entitled to it as against all persons except the owner." . . . The facts appear to have been that in the year 1847 the plaintiff, who was a commercial traveller, called on a firm named Byfield & Hawkesworth on business, as he was in the habit of doing, and as he was leaving the shop he picked up a small parcel which was lying on the floor. He immediately showed it to the shopman, and opened it in his presence, when it was

---

[17] The value of £66 in 1942 would be approximately $4,000 today. —EDS.

[18] As we will see in Chapter 5 covering estates in land, a freehold refers to the ownership of real property.—EDS.

found to consist of a quantity of Bank of England notes, to the amount of £65. The defendant, who was a partner in the firm of Byfield & Hawkesworth, was then called, and the plaintiff told him he had found the notes, and asked the defendant to keep them until the owner appeared to claim them. Then various advertisements were put in the papers asking for the owner, but the true owner was never found. No person having appeared to claim them, and three years having elapsed since they were found, the plaintiff applied to the defendant to have the notes returned to him, and offered to pay the expenses of the advertisements, and to give an indemnity. The defendant refused to deliver them up to the plaintiff, and an action was brought in the county court of Westminster in consequence of that refusal. The county court judge decided that the defendant, the shopkeeper, was entitled to the custody of the notes as against the plaintiff, and gave judgment for the defendant. Thereupon the appeal was brought. . . . Patteson J. said: ". . . The case, therefore, resolves itself into the single point on which it appears that the learned judge decided it, namely, whether the circumstance of the notes being found inside the defendant's shop gives him, the defendant, the right to have them as against the plaintiff, who found them." After discussing the cases, and the argument, the learned judge said: "If the discovery had never been communicated to the defendant, could the real owner have had any cause of action against him because they were found in his house? Certainly not. The notes never were in the custody of the defendant, nor within the protection of his house, before they were found, as they would have been had they been intentionally deposited there. . . . We find, therefore, no circumstances in this case to take it out of the general rule of law, that the finder of a lost article is entitled to it as against all persons except the real owner, and we think that that rule must prevail, and that the learned judge was mistaken in holding that the place in which they were found makes any legal difference. Our judgment, therefore, is that the plaintiff is entitled to these notes as against the defendant."

It is to be observed that in *Bridges v. Hawkesworth* . . . neither counsel put forward any argument on the fact that the notes were found in a shop. . . . The case for the appellant was that the shopkeeper never knew of the notes. Again, what is curious is that there was no suggestion that the place where the notes were found was in any way material; indeed, the judge in giving the judgment of the court expressly repudiates this and said in terms "The learned judge was mistaken in holding that the place in which they were found makes any legal difference." It is, therefore, a little remarkable that in *South Staffordshire Water Co. v. Sharman*, Lord Russell of Killowen C.J. said: "The case of *Bridges v. Hawkesworth* stands by itself, and on special grounds; . . . the ground of the decision being, as was pointed out by Patteson J., that the notes, being dropped in the public part of the shop, were never in the custody of the shopkeeper, or 'within the protection of his house.'" Patteson J. never made any reference to the public part of the shop and, indeed, went out of his way to say that the learned county court judge was wrong in holding that the place where they were found made any legal difference.

Bridges v. Hawkesworth has been the subject of considerable comment by text-book writers and, amongst others, by Mr. Justice Oliver Wendell Holmes, Sir

Frederick Pollock and Sir John Salmond. All three agree that the case was rightly decided, but they differ as to the grounds on which it was decided and put forward grounds, none of which, so far as I can discover, were ever advanced by the judges who decided the case. Mr. Justice Oliver Wendell Holmes wrote: "Common law judges and civilians would agree that the finder got possession first and so could keep it as against the shopkeeper. For the shopkeeper, not knowing of the thing, could not have the intent to appropriate it, and, having invited the public to his shop, he could not have the intent to exclude them from it." So he introduces the matter of two intents which are not referred to by the judges who heard the case. Sir Frederick Pollock, whilst he agreed with Mr. Justice Holmes that *Bridges v. Hawkesworth* was properly decided wrote: "In such a case as *Bridges v. Hawkesworth*, where a parcel of banknotes was dropped on the floor in the part of a shop frequented by customers, it is impossible to say that the shopkeeper has any possession in fact. He does not expect objects of that kind to be on the floor of his shop, and some customer is more likely than the shopkeeper or his servant to see and take them up if they do come there." He emphasizes the lack of de facto control on the part of the shopkeeper. . . . It is clear from the decision in *Bridges v. Hawkesworth* that an occupier of land does not in all cases possess an unattached thing on his land even though the true owner has lost possession.

With regard to *South Staffordshire Water Co. v. Sharman*, the first two lines of the headnote are: "The possessor of land is generally entitled, as against the finder, to chattels found on the land." I am not sure that this is accurate. The facts were that the defendant Sharman, while cleaning out, under the orders of the plaintiffs, the South Staffordshire Water Company, a pool of water on their land, found two rings embedded in the mud at the bottom of the pool. He declined to deliver them to the plaintiffs, but failed to discover the real owner. In an action brought by the company against Sharman in detinue[19] it was held that the company were entitled to the rings. Lord Russell of Killowen C.J. said: "The plaintiffs are the freeholders of the locus in quo, and as such they have the right to forbid anybody coming on their land or in any way interfering with it. They had the right to say that their pool should be cleaned out in any way that they thought fit, and to direct what should be done with anything found in the pool in the course of such cleaning out. It is no doubt right, as the counsel for the defendant contended, to say that the plaintiffs must show that they had actual control over the locus in quo and the things in it; but under the circumstances, can it be said that the Minster Pool and whatever might be in that pool were not under the control of the plaintiffs? In my opinion they were. . . . The principle on which this case must be decided, and the distinction which must be drawn between this case and that of *Bridges v. Hawkesworth*, is to be found in a passage in Pollock and Wright's 'Essay on Possession in the Common Law,' p. 41: 'The possession of land carries with it in general, by our law, possession of everything which is attached to or under that land, and, in the absence of a better title elsewhere, the right to possess it also.'" If that is right, it would clearly cover the case of the rings embedded

---

[19] "Detinue" is an old form of action for recovery of personal property.—EDS.

in the mud of the pool, the words used being "attached to or under that land." . . . Then Lord Russell cited the passage which I read earlier in this judgment and continued: "It is somewhat strange"—I venture to echo those words—"that there is no more direct authority on the question; but the general principle seems to me to be that where a person has possession of house or land, with a manifest intention to exercise control over it and the things which may be upon or in it, then, if something is found on that land, whether by an employee of the owner or by a stranger, the presumption is that the possession of that thing is in the owner of the locus in quo." . . . *South Staffordshire Water Co. v. Sharman* . . . has also been the subject of some discussion. It has been said that it establishes that if a man finds a thing as the servant or agent of another, he finds it not for himself, but for that other, and indeed that seems to afford a sufficient explanation of the case. The rings found at the bottom of the pool were not in the possession of the company, but it seems that though Sharman was the first to obtain possession of them, he obtained them for his employers and could claim no title for himself.

The only other case to which I need refer is *Elwes v. Brigg Gas Co.*, in which land had been demised to a gas company for ninety-nine years with a reservation to the lessor of all mines and minerals. A pre-historic boat embedded in the soil was discovered by the lessees when they were digging to make a gasholder. It was held that the boat, whether regarded as a mineral or as part of the soil in which it was embedded when discovered, or as a chattel, did not pass to the lessees by the demise, but was the property of the lessor though he was ignorant of its existence at the time of granting the lease. . . .

A review of these judgments shows that the authorities are in an unsatisfactory state. . . . It is fairly clear from the authorities that a man possesses everything which is attached to or under his land. Secondly, it would appear to be the law from the authorities I have cited, and particularly from *Bridges v. Hawkesworth*, that a man does not necessarily possess a thing which is lying unattached on the surface of his land even though the thing is not possessed by someone else. A difficulty however, arises, because the rule which governs things an occupier possesses as against those which he does not, has never been very clearly formulated in our law. He may possess everything on the land from which he intends to exclude others, if Mr. Justice Holmes is right; or he may possess those things of which he has a de facto control, if Sir Frederick Pollock is right.

There is no doubt that in this case the brooch was lost in the ordinary meaning of that term, and I should imagine it had been lost for a very considerable time. . . . But the moment the plaintiff discovered that the brooch might be of some value, he took the advice of his commanding officer and handed it to the police. His conduct was commendable and meritorious. The defendant was never physically in possession of these premises at any time. It is clear that the brooch was never his, in the ordinary acceptation of the term, in that he had the prior possession. He had no knowledge of it, until it was brought to his notice by the finder. . . . In those circumstances I propose to follow the decision in *Bridges v. Hawkesworth*, and to give judgment in this case for the plaintiff for £66. Judgment for plaintiff.

■ POINTS TO CONSIDER

1. **Constructive possession and control.** Does *Hannah v. Peel* mean that strangers are now free to acquire property by find when they visit other people's houses? If not, why not? In *Pierson* and the rule of capture, we noted that possession depends on *control*. Do you see how control plays a central role in determining whether a landowner has constructive possession of lost items on the land?

   - Would it have made a difference if Major Peel had "taken possession" of the house, by moving in, at least a little while, before it was requisitioned?
   - Would it have made a difference if Major Peel had seen the brooch in a quick inspection of his new house? Perhaps he intended to pick it up later and examine it, but simply forgot in his haste.
   - Would it have made a difference if Corporal Hannah had been hired by Major Peel to fix the window and had found the brooch while doing his job?
   - What if the brooch had been dropped *outside* the window and had become partially buried in the dirt?

2. **Policy.** In addition to the policies already mentioned, finders cases usually involve an additional aim: to facilitate the return of the property, if possible, to its true owner. Does awarding the brooch to Corporal Hannah further that policy? What additional policies are furthered by the decision for Corporal Hannah?

■ PROBLEMS

Assume Aamir finds a lottery ticket, which turns out to be a $1 million winner. Discuss the merits of the landowner's claim against him in these circumstances:

1) Aamir found the ticket on the front sidewalk of Shanice's house.
2) Aamir found the ticket on the front porch of Shanice's house.
3) Aamir found the ticket just inside the front door of Shanice's house.
4) Aamir found the ticket in the backyard of Shanice's house, while he was helping her clean up after a big party.
5) Aamir found the ticket in the hallway of the law school.
6) Aamir found the ticket on the floor of the dean's office.

If your answer was not the same for each of these cases, can you explain why your answer changes?

Classification of Found Property

Courts tend to classify found property into one of four categories and the classification may affect the rights of the finder:

- **Abandoned property.** The owner has voluntarily relinquished rights to the property; the finder obtains ownership of the property against all others, including the former owner.
- **Lost property.** The owner has involuntarily and unintentionally lost possession; the finder obtains title subject to the rights of the original owner.
- **Mislaid property.** The owner voluntarily and intentionally places the property somewhere and then neglects to return for it or forgets where it is; the owner of the locus in quo, rather than the finder, obtains the right of possession against all but the true owner.
- **Treasure trove.** Coins, currency, jewels, gold, or silver found hidden in the earth or another private place; belongs to the finder, not the owner of the land where found, subject to the rights of the true owner.

These categories are sometimes more misleading than helpful. Certainly, it makes sense to say that if a true owner has relinquished her rights to the property, as with abandoned property, her interests should no longer be considered when determining ownership.

But what about treasure trove? From *Hannah v. Peel*, we determined that one solid rule we could rely on is that anything buried or embedded in the land belongs to the landowner. Now we have a treasure trove rule that says buried *treasure* doesn't follow that rule; it belongs to the finder. Apparently, the purpose of the rule, which originated in Roman law, was to encourage discovery, but what about discouraging trespassing? Although the doctrine of treasure trove has been mentioned and applied from time to time, many courts have rejected the notion as archaic.

> [We] find the rule with respect to treasure-trove to be out of harmony with modern notions of fair play. The common-law rule of treasure-trove invites trespassers to roam at large over the property of others with their metal detecting devices and to dig wherever such devices tell them property might be found. If the discovery happens to fit the definition of treasure-trove, the trespasser may claim it as his own. To paraphrase another court: The mind refuses consent to the proposition that one may go upon the lands of another and dig up and take away anything he discovers there which does not belong to the owner of the land [citation omitted].
>
> The invitation to trespassers inherent in the rule with respect to treasure-trove is repugnant to the common law rules dealing with trespassers in general.

Morgan v. Wiser, 711 S.W.2d 220, 222-23 (Tenn. Ct. App. 1985); *see also* Corliss v. Wenner, 34 P.3d 1100, 1105 (Idaho 2001) ("[W]e conclude that the rule of treasure trove is of dubious heritage and misunderstood application, inconsistent with our values and traditions."); Schley v. Couch, 284 S.W.2d 333 (Tex. 1955) (rejecting treasure trove).

Treasure Trove

With the Treasure Act of 1996, the United Kingdom changed its common law of treasure trove to better balance the interests involved. Treasure is carefully defined: for example, a hoard of coins over 300 years old, or two or more prehistoric base metal objects. The finder must report the find to a local official, and museums are then allowed to purchase the items at fair market value from the finder, with the price being set by an independent board of antiquities experts. The finder and the landowner share a reward, with the amount and shares determined by this Treasure Valuation Committee. What values are served by this system?

Mislaid property.   One more factor may play a role in finder's cases: whether the property is considered *lost* or *mislaid. Mislaid* property has been intentionally placed somewhere, but then the owner neglects to retrieve it. You might put your purse on the counter of a shop while you're writing a check, for example, and then go off without it. Property is *lost*, on the other hand, when the owner has unintentionally and unknowingly parted with its possession.

Unlike lost property, courts have ruled that mislaid property belongs to the owner of the premises on which the property is found, as against all persons other than the true owner. Ritz v. Selma United Methodist Church, 467 N.W.2d 266, 269 (Iowa 1991). One of the earliest cases to make this distinction was McAvoy v. Medina, 11 Allen 548 (Mass. 1866), in which the court ruled that a pocketbook lying on a table in a shop belonged to the shopkeeper, rather than the customer who discovered it. The court noted that *Bridges v. Hawkesworth* (cited and followed in *Hannah v. Peel*) was distinguishable, because there the banknotes were found on the floor of the shop, so they had not been placed there voluntarily by the owner. The court's only reason for the distinction was that awarding mislaid property to the owner of the locus "was better adapted to secure the rights of the true owner." *Id.* at 549.

Apparently, the court thought that the true owner might come back for the mislaid property when the true owner remembered where he left it, so allowing a finder to carry it away would make it harder to recover. Is there any difference between lost and mislaid property in that regard? Would it be possible to protect the interests of the true owner by requiring the finder to advertise or leave the property in the hands of the shopkeeper for a certain period of time, while still allowing the finder to retain rights to it?

Scholars have found the lost/mislaid distinction problematic, both because it requires an uncertain excursion into the intentions of the original owner and because it does not necessarily promote the policies of finders law. It is often difficult to tell whether something has been placed somewhere deliberately or not. For example, was the brooch in *Hannah v. Peel* lost or mislaid? Can you imagine circumstances that would support either conclusion? Should it matter? Do you think the owner of that brooch is ever coming back to reclaim it?

The best argument in support of the distinction is that often the item has been placed in an area, such as the checkout counter, that is more under the control of the shopkeeper than the rest of the store. As a 1939 Harvard Law Review article noted, "there is something akin to a bailment relation created when an article is mislaid."[20] Courts continue to rely on the distinction. Some recent examples:

> ➤ Terry v. Lock, 37 S.W.3d 202 (Ark. 2001). Terry was preparing a Best Western motel for renovation when he discovered a cardboard box containing old currency that, due to its historic nature, may have been worth far more than its face value of $38,310.00. The trial court's finding that the box was mislaid property was not clearly erroneous, and therefore the property belonged to the owner of the premises.
> ➤ Benjamin v. Lindner Aviation, Inc., 534 N.W.2d 400 (Iowa 1995). Employee of aviation service company found $18,000 hidden behind panel in wing of airplane. Court determined property was mislaid and therefore belonged to the owner of the plane.
> ➤ Grande v. Jennings, 278 P.3d 1287 (Ariz. Ct. App. 2012). New homeowners hired remodeling contractor, who found $500,000 hidden in walls of the home. Court held the money was mislaid and therefore belonged to home-owner.

Is it not more likely in all of these cases that the true owner of the property has abandoned it? If the original intent of the mislaid distinction is to facilitate the return of the property to the true owner, do these cases achieve that goal? In other words, do you think that the true owner is likely to show up? Would it make more sense to consider the *agency* and *control* aspects of these cases, rather than the artificial distinction between lost and mislaid property?

Bailments

A *bailment* is created when one person has possession of the personal property of another for some particular purpose. The bailment may be for the benefit of the bailor (the one who delivers the property) or the bailee (the one holding the property) or both.

■ Charlie borrows Darcy's lawnmower to mow his lawn. Darcy is the bailor, Charlie is the bailee, and the bailment benefits the bailee.
■ Ingrid asks Joan to hold on to her purse while she goes to the restroom. Ingrid is the bailor, Joan is the bailee, and the bailment benefits the bailor.
■ Vikram gives his car to the valet when he goes to a restaurant and pays the valet $10. Vikram is the bailor, the valet is the bailee, and the bailment is for their mutual benefit.

---

[20] David Riesman, *Possession and the Law of Finders*, 52 Harv. L. Rev. 1105, 1120 (1939).

These are all examples of *voluntary bailments*, when the bailee agrees to accept the property. A bailment can also be involuntary. For example, when someone comes to your house for dinner and leaves without her purse, you have become an *involuntary bailee.*

Historically, courts have distinguished between the types of bailments in determining the duty of care owed by the bailee. If the bailment solely benefits the bailee, the bailee must exercise great care. If the bailment solely benefits the bailor, the bailee is liable only for gross negligence. For mutually beneficial bailments, the standard is ordinary care. *See, e.g.,* Ryan v. Schwab, 261 S.W.2d 605, 608 (Tex. Civ. App. 1953). Normally, a bailee is liable for any loss or injury to the bailed goods caused by her failure to exercise the degree of care of a reasonably careful owner. In many cases, contractual provisions may affect the liability question.

Statutory solutions. Many states have statutes pertaining to lost, mislaid, and abandoned property, which attempt to balance the interests of the finder and the true owner. The statutes often require the finder to report the find to public officials so that a public record may be made. The finder may have to advertise for the true owner. If the owner doesn't appear and prove ownership within a certain period of time, the finder is declared the new owner. Note that the finder's title is now unconditional. *See, e.g.,* Mich. Comp. Laws Ann. §434 (West 2017). If the true owner does claim the property, the finder may receive a fee. *See, e.g.,* Iowa Code Ann. §556F.13 (West 2017) (10 percent finder's fee).

Who Owns the Shipwreck?

The law regarding ownership of shipwrecks is a complex mixture of statutory and common law. The first question is whether the owner of the wreck has abandoned the property—if the ship was owned by a government, for example, it may claim the property. If the wreck is not deemed abandoned, the wreck may be salvaged for the owner and the salvor entitled to a salvage award. For example, the company that discovered the RMS *Titanic,* in 12,000 feet of water in the North Atlantic, was deemed a salvor. R.M.S. Titanic, Inc. v. The Wrecked and Abandoned Vessel, 435 F.3d 521 (4th Cir. 2006). In addition, if the wrecked vessel is embedded in the soil within the territorial waters of a state, the government may have

In rem Actions

In shipwreck cases, the party who discovers the wreck often files an *in rem* action against the ship and its cargo. An *in rem* action differs from an *in personam* action in that it is against the property itself, rather than against the owner. Under admiralty rules of procedure, in order to get jurisdiction, the plaintiff must post notice *on the wreck* (i.e., under water!) and publish the notice in a newspaper. Then the court will issue a *warrant for the arrest* of the vessel or other property at issue. Any party who may have an interest in the property may then intervene.

a claim. *Compare* Klein v. Unidentified Wrecked and Abandoned Sailing Vessel, 758 F.2d 1511 (11th Cir. 1985) (United States had constructive possession of ship buried in soil of Biscayne National Park) *with* Aqua Log, Inc. v. Abandoned Pre-Cut Logs, 94 F. Supp. 3d 1345 M.D. Ga. 2015)(submerged logs from 1800s logging operation were not embedded in Flint River bed and therefore could be claimed by finder).

If the wreck is abandoned and either not embedded or not in territorial waters, the law of finders applies and ownership is given to the first possessor. *How do you get possession of a shipwreck?*

Applying *Pierson v. Post*, the court in Eads v. Brazelton, 22 Ark. 499 (1861), determined that the finder of a wrecked steamboat in the Mississippi River had not sufficiently reduced it to his possession to prevent its appropriation by third parties. He had marked trees on the shore and attached a buoy to the wreck to indicate its location, but did not place his boat over the wreck and make persistent efforts to salvage its contents.

 ACQUISITION BY GIFT

In this section, we discuss another common way to acquire personal property—acquisition by gift. We will not discuss acquisition by will or inheritance in this chapter, because that concerns the more general topic of succession on death, which is covered later in the book. We will also save the topic of gifts of real property for the chapter on real estate transactions, because the rules of transfer are similar, whether it is a gift or sale of real estate. The topic of *gifts of personal property* fits well in this chapter, because it is another example of how possession plays a large role in property rights.

Elements of a Gift

A gift of personal property requires three elements:

1) donative *intent*;
2) *delivery* of the gift to the donee; and
3) *acceptance* of the gift by the donee.

Donative intent. The donor must exhibit the clear and unmistakable intention to make a gift. In addition, there must be an intention to make a *present* transfer of an interest in the property; the intent to make the gift sometime in the future won't do. In addition, the donor must intend to *irrevocably and completely* part with the property; a tentative or conditional intent is not sufficient.[21]

---

[21] There are a few instances in which we recognize conditional gifts, such as gifts in contemplation of marriage. In some states, if the marriage does not occur, the donor can recover possession of the engagement ring or other personal property transferred in expectation of the marriage. *See, e.g.,* N.Y. Civ. Rights Law §80-b (McKinney 2013).

Delivery. In addition, the donor must *deliver* the gift to the donee. Requiring an actual transfer of possession serves *three fundamental purposes*, nicely summarized in a 1926 article by Professor Phillip Mechem:

> In the first place, the delivery makes vivid and concrete to the donor the significance of the act he is doing. . . . The *wrench* of delivery . . . the little mental twinge at seeing his property pass from his hands into those of another, is an important element to the protection of the donor. . . .
>
> Second, the act of manual tradition is as unequivocal to actual witnesses of the transaction as the donor himself. . . . Perhaps he hesitated and contradicted himself so that the outcome of his thought was not readily to be ascertained by witnesses in the flurry of the moment. If he hands over the property, he has done an act that will settle many doubts. . . .
>
> Thirdly, and lastly, the fact of the delivery gives the donee . . . at least prima facie evidence in favor of the alleged gift.

Philip Mechem, *The Requirement of Delivery in Gifts of Chattels and Choses in Action Evidenced by Commercial Instruments*, 21 U. Ill. L. Rev. 341, 348-49 (1926).

Professor Mechem's last point should remind you of the presumption of ownership that arises from possession in the finders context.

You can imagine instances of delivery without the requisite donative intent. For example, you may ask a friend to take care of your pet iguana while you are abroad; you have transferred possession, but have no intent to make a gift. Conversely, you may have a clear donative intent, but without delivery there is no gift. You may announce in front of a hundred witnesses: "For his 21st birthday, I hereby give to my son Andrew this heirloom gold watch I am wearing." Unless you take the watch off and give it to Andrew, the most that can be said is that you have announced your *intention* to make a gift, but you haven't yet completed the gift.

Acceptance. The last item, acceptance, is generally *presumed* when the gift is valuable. In other words, you do not need to present direct evidence of acceptance if there is no reason to suspect the gift would not be welcomed by the recipient. Moreover, once the donee exercises dominion over the gift or makes any assertion of ownership, acceptance is implied. But the presumption is rebuttable by any evidence that the donee rejected the gift. Can you imagine situations in which a donee might not accept a gift?

Diamonds Aren't Forever

In 2005, Jerry Townsend, a high school football player who had been paralyzed while making a tackle, was invited to attend an NFL awards ceremony. At the ceremony, he asked Minnesota Vikings quarterback Daunte

Culpepper, "Can I get some of that ice?"—referring to two diamond necklaces Culpepper was wearing. Without saying anything, Culpepper jumped up and put the necklaces—worth about $75,000—around Townsend's neck. After the ceremony, Culpepper asked for the jewelry back and promised to give Townsend something else. Was there a completed gift?

■ PROBLEM: ACCEPTANCE

Grandfather was near death and decided to give $10,000 to each of his six grandchildren. His accountant advised him that this would reduce the size of his estate, with favorable tax consequences. While five of the donees cashed their checks immediately, grandson Mickey did not because he was advised by his mother to seek the advice of a lawyer before acting. His lawyer advised him to cash the check. Before he could do so, however, his grandfather died and his executor stopped payment on the check. Mickey wants the money. Was there acceptance of the gift before it was revoked by the executor? *See* Sinclair v. Fleischman, 773 P.2d 101 (Wash. Ct. App. 1989).

The Delivery Requirement

The delivery requirement for donative transfers requires a bit more analysis. The delivery of the gift serves to confirm and provide evidence of the donor's intent, so the intent and delivery elements are closely related, as we will see in the cases below. Courts generally require the best form of delivery available under the circumstances.

In general, there are *three types of delivery*:

- **Manual delivery.** The actual physical transfer of possession, i.e., the item is actually handed over to the donee. Generally, courts *require* manual delivery if it is possible.
  - □ *Example*: Dad announces at Son's birthday party that he wants him to have his grandfather's gold watch. He takes it out and hands it to Son.
- **Constructive delivery.** Giving *control* over the property, rather than the item itself. Constructive delivery is acceptable if manual delivery is impossible or impracticable.
  - □ *Example*: In Thompson v. Thompson, 16 Pa. D. & C.3d 778 (1981), husband "with great ceremony," in front of several witnesses, handed keys to car to wife, saying he was giving it to her as birthday gift. *See also* In re Lines' Estate, 201 N.Y.S.2d 290 (1959) (handing over keys to car sufficient delivery where "observance of the niceties of title transfers cannot be expected" of donor in last illness).

■ **Symbolic delivery.** Handing over something that represents the gift.
   □ ***Example*:** In Mirvish v. Mott, 965 N.E.2d 906 (N.Y. 2012), Yulla Lipchitz inherited "The Cry," a 1,100-pound bronze sculpture, from her husband, the sculptor Jacques Lipchitz. In 1973, she took a picture of the sculpture and wrote on the back that she was giving it to her friend Biond Fury "in appreciation for all he did for me during my long illness." She then handed the picture to Fury, but the sculpture itself remained in storage at a New York art gallery. The court held that a valid gift had been made.

Note that some courts confuse the terms *symbolic* and *constructive*, treating them as equivalent.

As the following case illustrates, not all courts accept symbolic delivery as sufficient, especially where there might be a question about the intent of the donor. *Newman v. Bost* involves a special kind of gift, called *causa mortis*, or in anticipation of death. The main difference between a gift *inter vivos*, or between living persons, and a gift *causa mortis* is that a gift in contemplation of death is *revocable* if the donor recovers. In contrast, a gift *inter vivos* is irrevocable once it is complete (i.e., once there is delivery and acceptance).

Gifts *causa mortis* are used as a substitute for *testamentary* gifts (i.e., legacies made by will). Because *causa mortis* gifts avoid the safeguards of the Statute of Wills, courts are very strict about requiring evidence of donative intent and delivery. After all, in the case of a gift *causa mortis*, we know that at least one witness to the transaction typically will not be available to testify should a dispute occur later!

N E W M A N v. B O S T

29 S.E. 848, 122 N.C. 524 (1898)
Supreme Court of North Carolina

[In 1896, J.F. Van Pelt died *intestate*, which means without a will. By statute his nearest relatives inherited his estate, which consisted of the property he owned at death. His wife had died about ten years before and they had no children. The issue in this case is whether Van Pelt gave away most of his personal property before he died; if so, it would not pass through his estate to his heirs.

Shortly after his wife's death, Van Pelt employed the plaintiff, Julia Newman, an orphan of about 18 years of age, to be his housekeeper. Newman resided alone in the house with Van Pelt and in 1895, he announced his intention to marry her within the next year.

On March 31, 1896, however, Van Pelt was stricken with paralysis, confining him to bed until he died about two weeks later. He sent for Enos Houston to nurse him in his last illness. When he was near death, Van Pelt asked Houston to call Newman into his room. The court described the deathbed scene, according to the trial testimony:

[Van Pelt] then asked plaintiff [Newman] to hand him his private keys . . . she having gotten them from a place over the mantel in intestate's bedroom and by his direction; he then handed plaintiff the bunch of keys and told her to take them and keep them, that he desired her to have them and everything in the house; he then pointed out the bureau, the clock, and other articles of furniture in the house and asked his chamber door to be opened and pointed in the direction of the hall and other rooms and repeated that everything in the house was hers . . . ; his voice failed him soon after the delivery of the keys and these declarations, so that he could never talk again to be understood . . . ; the bunch of keys . . . included one which unlocked the bureau pointed out to plaintiff as hers . . . and the bureau drawer, which this key unlocked, contained in it a life insurance policy payable to intestate's estate . . . , this bureau drawer was the place where intestate kept all his valuable papers.

Newman claimed the property she says that Van Pelt gave to her before he died. Bost, the administrator of Van Pelt's estate, defended the suit on behalf of the heirs.]

FURCHES, J.

The plaintiff in her complaint demands $3,000 collected by defendant, as the administrator of J. F. Van Pelt, on a life insurance policy, and now in his hands; $300, the value of a piano upon which said Van Pelt collected that amount of insurance money; $200.94, the value of household property sold by defendant . . . ; and $45, the value of property in the plaintiff's bed room. . . .

The $3,000 money collected on the life insurance policy, and the $200.94, the price for which the household property sold, plaintiff claims belonged to her by reason of a *donatio causa mortis* from said Van Pelt. The $45, the price for which her bedroom property sold, and the $300, insurance money on the piano, belonged to her also by reason of gifts *inter vivos*. The rules of law governing all of these claims of the plaintiff are in many respects the same, and the discussion of one will be to a considerable extent a discussion of all.

To constitute a *donatio causa mortis*, two things are indispensably necessary: an intention to make the gift, and a delivery of the thing given. . . .

[W]hat constitutes or may constitute delivery, has been the subject of discussion and adjudication in most or all the courts of the Union and of England, and they have by no means been uniform; some of them holding that a symbolical delivery—that is, some other article delivered in the name and stead of the thing intended to be given—is sufficient; others holding that a symbolical delivery is not sufficient, but that a constructive delivery is,—that is, the delivery of a key to a locked house, trunk, or other receptacle is sufficient. They distinguish this from a symbolical delivery, and say that this is in *substance* a delivery of the *thing*, as it is the means of using and enjoying the thing given; while others hold that there must be an actual manual delivery to perfect a gift *causa mortis*.

This doctrine of *donatio causa mortis* was borrowed from the Roman civil law by our English ancestors. There was much greater need for such a law at the time it was incorporated into the civil law and into the English law than there is now. Learning was not so general, nor the facilities for making wills so great, then as now. . . . [T]his doctrine of causa mortis is in direct conflict with the spirit and purpose of [the Statute of Frauds and the Statute of Wills]—the prevention of fraud. It is a doctrine, in our opinion, not to be extended, but to be strictly construed, and confined within the bounds of our adjudged cases. . . .

The case of Thomas v. Lewis (a Virginia case) 37 Am. St. Rep. 878, 15 S.E. 389, . . . is distinguishable from the case under consideration. There, the articles present were taken out of the bureau drawer, handed to the donor, and then delivered by him to the donee. According to all the authorities, this was a good gift *causa mortis*. The box and safe, the key to which the donor delivered to the donee, were not present, but were deposited in the vault of the bank; and, so far as shown by the case, it will be presumed, from the place where they were and the purpose for which things are usually deposited in a bank vault, that they were only valuable as a depository for such purposes, as holding and preserving money and valuable papers, bonds, stocks, and the like. This box and safe would have been of little value to the donee for any other purpose. But, more than this, the donor expressly stated that "all you find in this box and this safe is yours." There is no mistake that it was the intention of the donor to give what was contained in the box and in the safe.

As my Lord Coke would say, "Note the diversity" between that case and the case at bar. There, the evidences of debt contained in the bureau which was present, were taken out, given to the donor, and by him delivered to the donee. This was an actual manual delivery, good under all the authorities. But no such thing was done in this case as to the life insurance policy. It was neither taken out of the drawer, nor mentioned by the donor, unless it is included in the testimony of Enos Houston, who . . . says that Van Pelt gave [Newman] the keys, saying "what is in this house is yours". . . . The bureau in which was found the life insurance policy, after the death of Van Pelt, was present in the room where the keys were handed to Julia, and the life insurance policy could easily have been taken out and handed to Van Pelt, and by him delivered to Julia, as was done in the case of *Thomas v. Lewis*, supra. But this was not done. The safe and box, in *Thomas v. Lewis*, were not present, so that the contents could not have been taken out and delivered to the donee by the donor. The ordinary use of a stand of bureaus is not for the purpose of holding and securing such things as a life insurance policy, though they may often be used for that purpose, while a safe and a box deposited in the vault of a bank are. A bureau is an article of household furniture, used for domestic purposes, and generally belongs to the ladies' department of the household government, while the safe and box, in *Thomas v. Lewis*, are not. The bureau itself, mentioned in this case, was such property as would be valuable to the plaintiff. . . .

It is held that the law of delivery in this State is the same in gifts *inter vivos* and *causa mortis*. Adams v. Hayes, 24 N.C. 361. And there are expressions used . . . that would justify us in holding that in all cases of gifts, whether *inter vivos* or *causa mortis*, there must be an absolute manual delivery, to constitute, or probably more correctly speaking, to complete, a gift. . . .

Following [*Adams*], we feel bound to give effect to *constructive delivery*, where it plainly appears that it was the intention of the donor to make the gift, and where the things intended to be given are *not* present, or, where present, are incapable of *manual* delivery from their size or weight. But where the articles are present, and are capable of manual delivery, *this must be had.* This is as far as we can go. It may be thought by some that this is a hard rule—that a dying man cannot dispose of his own. But we are satisfied, when properly considered, it will be found to be a just rule. . . . The law provides that every man may dispose of all of his property by will, when made in writing. And it is most singular how guarded the law is to protect the testator against fraud and imposition by requiring that every word of the will must be written and signed by the testator, or, if written by some one else, it must be attested by at least two subscribing witnesses, who shall sign the same in his presence and at his request, or the will is void. . . .

In gifts *causa mortis* it requires but one witness, probably one servant, as a witness to a gift of all the estate a man has; no publicity is to be given that the gift has been made, and no probate or registration is required.

The Statute of Wills is a statute against fraud, considered in England and in this state to be demanded by public policy. And yet, if symbolical deliveries of gifts *causa mortis* are to be allowed, or if constructive deliveries be allowed to the extent claimed by the plaintiff, the statute of wills may prove to be of little value. For such considerations, we see every reason for restricting, and none for extending, the rules heretofore established, as applicable to gifts *causa mortis.*

It being claimed and admitted that the life insurance policy was present in the bureau drawers in the room where it is claimed the gift was made, and being capable of actual manual delivery, we are of the opinion that the title to the insurance policy did not pass to the plaintiff, but remained the property of the intestate of the defendant.

But we are of the opinion that the bureau and any other article of furniture, locked and unlocked by any of the keys given to the plaintiff, did pass, and she became the owner thereof. This is upon the ground that while these articles were present, from their size and weight, they were incapable of actual manual delivery; and that the delivery of the keys was a constructive delivery of these articles, equivalent to an actual delivery if the articles had been capable of manual delivery.

[W]e are of the opinion that the other articles of household furniture (except those in the plaintiff's private bedchamber) did not pass to the plaintiff, but remained the property of the defendant's intestate.

We do not think the articles in the plaintiff's bedchamber passed by the *donatio causa mortis,* for the same reason that the other articles of household furniture did not pass—want of delivery—either constructive or manual. But, as to the furniture in the plaintiff's bedroom ($45), it seems to us that there was sufficient evidence of both gift and delivery to support the finding of the jury, as a gift *inter vivos.* The intention to give this property is shown by a number of witnesses and contradicted by none.

The only debatable ground is as to the sufficiency of the delivery. But, when we recall the express terms in which he repeatedly declared that it was hers; that he had bought it for her, and had given it to her; that it was placed in her private chamber, her bedroom, where we must suppose that she had the entire use and control of the same, it would seem that this was sufficient to constitute a delivery. . . .

As to the piano there was much evidence tending to show the intention of Van Pelt to give it to the plaintiff, and that he had given it to her, and we remember no evidence to the contrary. And as to this, like the bedroom furniture, the debatable ground, if there is any debatable ground, is the question of delivery. It was placed in the intestate's parlor, where it remained until it was burned. The intestate insured it as his property, collected and used the insurance money as his own, often saying that he intended to buy the plaintiff another piano, which he never did. It must be presumed that the parlor was under the dominion of the intestate, and not of his cook, housekeeper, and hired servant. And unless there is something more shown than the fact that the piano was bought by the intestate, placed in his parlor, and called by him "Miss Julia's piano," we cannot think this constituted a delivery. But as the case goes back for a new trial, if the plaintiff thinks she can show a delivery, she will have an opportunity of doing so. But she will understand that she must do so according to the rules laid down in this opinion—that she must show actual or constructive delivery, equivalent to actual manual delivery. We see no ground upon which the plaintiff can recover the insurance money if the piano was not hers.

We do not understand that there was any controversy as to the plaintiff's right to recover for her services, which the jury have estimated to be $125. . . . There is no such thing in this State as *symbolical delivery* in gifts either *inter vivos* or *causa mortis*. . . .

New trial.

■ POINTS TO CONSIDER

1. **The relationship between delivery and intent.** This case illustrates how the delivery requirement bolsters intent. Why does the court mention, for example, that the ordinary use of a bureau is not for keeping life insurance policies? If, in handing Julia the keys, Van Pelt had said "Julia, I want you to have this bureau and the life insurance policy it contains," would we have a different case? Would we have a different case if Julia were his daughter, instead of, as the court describes Julia, "his cook, housekeeper, and hired servant"?

   For example, in Carlson v. Bankers Trust Co., 50 N.W.2d 1 (Iowa 1951), a dying mother gave her daughter the keys to the house and to a safety box, telling her (allegedly) that she was giving her thereby "all the personal property I own." The mother's will, on the other hand, left her personal property to her cousin. The court held this was a valid constructive delivery of the contents of the bank box and the household effects, neither of which could be manually delivered. The court commented that "[i]t was natural for testatrix to hand down the contents of the home to her only child." However, the court affirmed the trial court's finding that bank accounts were not constructively delivered, when the bank books were readily available (in the china cabinet) and could have been handed over.

2. **Delivery and control.** A common theme in this chapter is the importance of control in determining possession. For example, why does the court determine that Julia's bedroom furniture was delivered, but other furniture in the house, which also was not opened by the keys, was not? This emphasis on control should remind you of the discussion of control and possession in *Pierson v. Post*.

3. **Symbolic delivery.** Most courts accept symbolic delivery in cases where manual or constructive delivery would be impossible or impracticable. In fact, the Restatement takes the position that symbolic delivery should suffice, even when manual delivery would be possible. Restatement (Third) of Property: Wills and Other Donative Transfers §6.2 (2003). Why does the North Carolina Supreme Court refuse to allow symbolic delivery? Why do you think the Restatement doesn't agree? Given the stance of the court in *Newman*, how could Van Pelt have completed a gift of the piano to Julia? Can you think of any reason why Van Pelt might not have wanted to simply write a will giving Julia Newman the property at issue? Why do people continue to rely on these deathbed gifts so frequently?

CASE SUMMARY: Gruen v. Gruen, 496 N.E.2d 869 (N.Y. 1986)

Victor Gruen escaped from Vienna in 1938 just as the Nazis took over. Settling in New York, he became an internationally renowned architect, known as the "father" of the modern shopping mall. In 1959, he purchased a painting by Gustav Klimt for $8,000. The painting sold for over $23.5 million in 1997. In 1963, Victor wrote a letter to his son Michael, who was at school at Harvard, stating that he was giving Michael the painting for his 21st birthday. Victor, however, wrote that he wanted to keep the painting for the remainder of his life, so Michael never took possession of it. Upon his father's death in 1980, Michael requested the painting from his stepmother (the defendant Gruen in the case), who refused to relinquish it. Was there a valid gift *inter vivos*? It was not a gift *causa mortis*—do you see why?

The court noted that an *inter vivos* gift requires "that the donor intend to make an irrevocable present transfer of ownership," and thus a transfer effective only at death requires a will. In this case, the court found that Victor *did* transfer ownership

Present vs. Future Transfer

Do you see the difference between a *present* transfer of a *future* possessory interest, which is a valid gift, and the *future* transfer (at death) of a *present* possessory interest, which must be done by will? Consider the difference in the wording of the letter from Victor to Michael:

➤ "Michael, I intend to give you the Klimt painting upon my death."

   Versus

➤ "Michael, I am giving you the Klimt painting, but you will not receive possession of it until my death."

of the painting in 1963. Although Victor retained possession for life, he transferred to Michael ownership and the right to possess the painting in the future.

The court also held that the delivery requirement was met by the letter, despite the lack of manual delivery of the painting itself. The court noted that the delivery requirement "must be tailored to suit the circumstances of the case." *Id.* at 874 (quoting Matter of Szabo, 176 N.E.2d 395 (N.Y. 1961)). It would have been "illogical" to require Michael to have taken possession when his father intended to retain possession for life.

■ POINTS TO CONSIDER

1. Consider the purposes of the delivery requirement. Does the letter in *Gruen* (which Victor Gruen drafted after consulting with lawyers) meet those purposes? If the Statute of Wills requires transfers on death to have an instrument signed in the presence of two witnesses, why does the court allow Gruen's letter to accomplish the same thing?

2. In Chapter 5, we will discuss ways to divide ownership of property by time: between present and future interests. We will see that Victor Gruen retained a *life estate* in the painting, while giving Michael a future interest called a *remainder*.

■ PROBLEMS: GIFT OR NOT?

1. Note that the requirements of intent, delivery, and acceptance do not necessarily have to occur simultaneously or in that order. Assume Kate borrows her grandmother Elizabeth's diamond necklace to wear to a fancy dinner party. After the party, Kate calls up Elizabeth to gush about how beautiful the necklace was. Elizabeth tells Kate, "Honey, why don't you just keep the necklace. I want you to have it." Has Elizabeth made a valid gift?

2. Assume that Van Pelt kept his insurance policy and bundles of cash in his safe. He hands Newman a piece of paper with the combination to the safe written on it, saying, "I want you to have everything in that safe when I die." Valid gift? Would the case be different if he gave her the only keys to his safety deposit box at the bank? Why?

D ADVERSE POSSESSION

Until now, we have been focusing on the acquisition of property rights in personal property, and in all these situations—capture, finders, and gift—*possession* has been of paramount importance. We will now consider how possession plays a role in acquiring rights to real property. As you recall from Chapter 1, possession was the foundation of the rule of conquest, discussed in *Johnson v. M'Intosh*, and in the acquisition of unowned property through homestead laws. After initial acquisition, rights to real property are most commonly acquired by sale, gift, or inheritance. However, we now consider how real property may be acquired another way—by the hostile possession of one who is not the true owner.

Adverse possession is basically a statute of limitations. If someone occupies your land without legal right, he is a trespasser, and you have a cause of action for ejectment in order to recover possession. If you do not bring an action to eject the trespasser within the statutory limitations period, you have lost your right to do so. Once you have lost the right to exclude, the law concludes that you are no longer the owner and awards title to the trespasser.[22]

The statute in your jurisdiction will tell you how long you have to bring an action: the majority of jurisdictions have statutes of limitation of between 5 and 15 years.[23] The shortest adverse possession period in the United States is 3 years in Arizona, Florida, and Texas (providing certain conditions are met), and the longest is 60 years in New Jersey for woodlands and uncultivated land.[24]

The doctrine of adverse possession may strike you, at first, as nothing more than legalized theft. In fact, we are talking about how someone can wrest ownership from the true owner of real property merely by wrongfully possessing it for a long period of time. The doctrine violates the "right to exclude," which is consistently declared to be a fundamental stick in the property owner's bundle. Nevertheless, by the end of this section you should discover that the doctrine serves many of our foundational property policies.

Adverse possession has a long pedigree. The first Statute of Westminster (1275) prohibited claims to recover possession of land that arose before the beginning of the reign of Richard I (1189). Thus, anyone whose chain of possession dated back to Richard's reign could not be ejected. In 1623, England limited the action of ejectment to 20 years from the time the entry occurred.[25]

Early cases in this country include McIver v. Ragan, 15 U.S. 25 (1817), in which Chief Justice Marshall upheld a possessor's claim to 5,000 acres in North

---

[22] To make this title marketable, the adverse possessor will need some sort of judicial declaration that the elements of adverse possession have been successfully established, so that the record accurately reflects the true state of title.

[23] *See* Robert C. Ellickson, *Adverse Possession and Perpetuities Law: Two Dents in the Libertarian Model of Property Rights*, 64 Wash. Univ. L.Q. 723, 733 (1986).

[24] Lynn Foster & J. Cliff McKinney, II, *Adverse Possession and Boundary Acquiescence in Arkansas: Some Suggestions for Reform*, 33 U. Ark. Little Rock L. Rev. 199, 201 (2011). *See* N.J. Stat. Ann. §2A:14-30 (West 2013) (60-year period for woodlands and uncultivated land). New Jersey takes the unusual approach of distinguishing between a limitations period on actions for ejectment (20 years) and acquisition of title by adverse possession (30 or 60 years depending on nature of property). *See* J&M Land Co. v. First Union Nat'l Bank, 766 A.2d 1110 (N.J. 2001).

[25] 21 James I, c. 16 (1623).

Carolina, despite the objections of the superior title holder. In early American history, deeds to land were often not recorded in a central location, so it was quite difficult to confirm with any certainty that someone really owned Blackacre. Marshall confirmed, as he did in *M'Intosh* a few years later, that certainty of title was of paramount importance, and he recognized that erasing conflicting claims after a period of time would remove "clouds" on the title from impeding efficient land use.

As you will see when we get to the material on land titles, our system of recording documents relating to land ownership has greatly improved. Nevertheless, the opportunities for error abound. Property may be described improperly in a deed; a deed may be improperly recorded; a legal interest may have been overlooked; parties may be mistaken about boundary lines. Somehow these uncertainties must be resolved—the doctrine of adverse possession remains centrally important in clearing these clouds on the title.

> **Conflicts of Title**
>
> Conflicts of title were unfortunately so numerous that no one knew from whom to buy or take lands with safety; nor could improvements be made without great hazard, by those in possession, who had conflicting claims hanging over them. . . .
>
> —*Clark v. Smith, 38 U.S. 195 (1839)*

The Policies Behind Adverse Possession

■ INTRODUCTORY PROBLEM

Assume that Rod owns 80 acres of cropland called Blackacre, adjacent to 80 acres owned by Cindy, called Whiteacre. A small creek meanders down the border between the properties, so neither owner has farmed the area close to the boundary. In 1990, a big storm resulted in flooding that changed the location of the creek. After that, five acres of Whiteacre ended up on the other side of the creek, which we can call Parcel A. From that time on, Rod planted Parcel A and treated it as part of Blackacre. If Cindy realized the change, she said nothing about it and probably thought it would be impracticable for her to farm those acres anyway.

Cindy died in 1995, leaving her property by will to her son Peter, who lived in a big city far away. Peter rented the land to another farmer and rarely visited the property. He had no idea that the land on the other side of the creek was part of Whiteacre and neither did the farmer who rented the land. All the while, Rod continued to plow, plant, fertilize, and harvest Parcel A.

This situation continued until 2014, when a new highway brought development potential to the area. Big Deals, Inc. approached Peter and offered him

$10,000 per acre for his land, which it believes is a perfect place for a shopping center. Rod, however, claims that Parcel A is his and it is not for sale. Big Deals needs the whole 80 acres for its planned development and threatens to cancel the deal if this title problem can't be resolved. What should be the result?

In many jurisdictions, Peter would be deemed to have lost title to Parcel A to Rod through adverse possession. In some jurisdictions, as we will see below, Rod's claim would depend on some additional facts.

Various justifications for adverse possession have been proposed. As we will see in the cases that follow, the policies have important implications for how the doctrine is applied.

1) *Certainty.* As noted above, the primary objective of adverse possession is to remove clouds on the title of the possessor. There may be conflicting instruments that might encumber ownership, but these disappear with the passage of time so that we can rely on the secure title of the one in possession.

2) *Economic productivity.* Adverse possession rewards the person who makes productive use of the property, rather than leaving it in the hands of an owner who is neglecting it. The 5 acres in our hypothetical would have been idle for 24 years if not for Rod's productive efforts.

   Assume that in 1845, Stephen Austin sold a 100-acre parcel of land in Texas to Rafael Vasquez, an immigrant from Mexico. Vasquez paid $25 and received a valid deed to the land, but soon after returned to Mexico and was never heard from again. Austin took possession of the land and eventually sold it to someone else. These 100 acres are now in the center of Dallas. Do we want them to remain vacant and idle, waiting for the return of Rafael Vasquez? After all, he has valid legal title to the land. Or do we think that, at some point, any claim Vasquez had must be extinguished by the passage of time so that the land can be put to productive use?

   Note that adverse possession also imposes costs on the owner— increased vigilance is necessary, which increases the *costs of monitoring.* In theory, the statutory period and the elements of a claim that require notice to the true owner attempt to minimize these monitoring costs.

3) *Fairness.* Labor theory suggests that one who works to improve property should acquire property interests. In our hypothetical, Rod has done a lot of work on this land and it would be fair to reward his labor. Of course, one could also argue Rod got the benefit of land that wasn't his for a long time, which may not seem fair, either.

4) *Personhood.* The longer you occupy property, the more it becomes a part of you and the more reluctant we are to force you to part with it. Imagine that you find a stray puppy and begin to care for it. After a few days, the owner comes to reclaim it. No one would argue that the dog should stay with the finder. But what if the owner doesn't come for a year? For five

years? At some point, do we think the finder has more of a psychological attachment to the dog than the original owner?

The same thing is true for real property. In the introductory problem, Rod has worked with those 5 acres of land for 24 years and, in so doing, has probably formed a deeper association with it than Peter, who has hardly even seen the land.

Thus, the doctrine of adverse possession can be seen either as punishing the true owner for sleeping on his rights, or as rewarding the possessor for putting the land to productive use. Which theory a court adopts will affect how it applies the elements of adverse possession.

Holmes on the Acquisition of Rights by Lapse of Time

I should suggest that the foundation of the acquisition of rights by lapse of time is to be looked for in the position of the person who gains them, not in that of the loser. . . . It is in the nature of man's mind. A thing which you have enjoyed and used as your own for a long time . . . takes root in your being and cannot be torn away without your resenting the act and trying to defend yourself, however you came by it. The law can ask for no better justification than the deepest instincts of man.

—Justice Oliver Wendell Holmes, The Path of the Law,
10 Harv. L. Rev. 457, 476-77 (1897)

Elements of Adverse Possession

In every case, the claim of adverse possession starts with the state statute establishing a limitation on actions for ejectment or recovery of possession. In addition to setting forth the length of possession necessary, the statute may specify other requirements, such as the payment of taxes. Courts have then created additional elements that must be met for adverse possession to be established:

1) *Actual.* Use of the land in the same manner a reasonable owner would use it. Cases often turn on whether the occupier has done enough to establish actual possession. What is sufficient will vary according to the type of land involved. The possession has to be enough to warn the true owner that he should act, and enough to merit a "reward" under the theories outlined above.

2) *Exclusive.* The possessor should not share possession with others, including the true owner. By exercising the right to exclude, the possessor gives notice that she is making a claim of ownership to the property. Practically

speaking, in our hypothetical, if Rod farmed Parcel A but then Janie grazed her sheep there and Diego stored his machinery there, how would Peter, the true owner, know who, if anyone, was claiming the land?

3) *Open and notorious.* Open means that the possession can't be furtive or hidden, while notorious connotes conspicuous or prominent possession. In other words, this element means that the possession must be reasonably discoverable by the true owner. If you sneak onto a remote section of Peter's land every night and pitch a tent, but then sneak off again at the crack of dawn, you are not going to trigger the statute of limitations. Again, the question boils down to whether the true owner was put on *notice* that he should take action.

4) *Continuous.* The possession must be uninterrupted for the length of the statutory period. Again, this depends on the type of property involved and what is sufficient to put the true owner on notice. The adverse possessor need not occupy the property all the time, but must be at least in *constructive possession* during this entire period. If the true owner inspects the property while you aren't there, will she be on notice that you are in possession? Was Rod in continuous possession of Parcel A, even though he didn't set foot on the property for several months each winter?

Notice

Note carefully that *knowledge* by the true owner is not the same as *notice* and is usually not required—do you see the difference? Courts may require actual knowledge only in those cases in which the true owner would have had to undertake the expense of a survey to discern a minor border encroachment by the adverse possessor. *See, e.g.,* Manillo v. Gorski, 255 A.2d 258 (N.J. 1969). In that case, the possession might be open, but it is not notorious!

---

5) *Adverse, under claim of right.* The possession must be contrary to the interests of the true owner. If you are occupying the land with the owner's permission—for example, pursuant to a lease—you cannot be adverse. Again, does the occupation make a reasonable owner think she needs to bring an action to eject the occupier?

■ Some jurisdictions interpret this last element to require a *good faith* claim of right—in other words, that the occupation is the result of a mistake. Those jurisdictions emphasize the reward theory of adverse possession and reason that only innocent possessors should be awarded title. In these jurisdictions, the good faith requirement is often stated as a sixth element, in addition to the "adverse" requirement of no permission.

■ A few jurisdictions require the possession to be not only adverse, but *hostile.* These courts require the possessor to know the land is not hers, but to intend to take it anyway.

Would Rod meet the requirements of a good faith jurisdiction? Of a jurisdiction that requires hostility?

■ PROBLEM: APPLYING THE ELEMENTS

The border between Kate and Ashley's properties ran through a ravine covered with brush and trees. In 1995, Kate's children began building a treehouse in a tree about 20 feet on Ashley's side of the line. In addition, they cleared some of the brush around the site and stored various bikes and toys there. Kate had many children, so this occupation continued for the ten-year statute of limitations. In 2017, Ashley planned to build a stone wall around her property, but Kate objected on the ground that she established adverse possession to the treehouse area. What result? *See* Aud-War Realty Co. v. Ellis, 557 A.2d 69 (R.I. 1989).

■   ■   ■

The following case illustrates one type of adverse possession situation, in which a neighbor has taken advantage of the absence and neglect of the owner of adjacent land. The parties in this case were colorful characters, who had a relationship similar to the Hatfields and the McCoys. You will find that the elements of adverse possession we have just learned are sometimes difficult to apply to real world evidence and that the test is pliable enough to lead to inconsistent results.

VAN VALKENBURGH v. LUTZ

106 N.E.2d 28 (1952)
New York Court of Appeals

[In 1912, William and Mary Lutz bought lots 14 and 15 in the newly laid out Murray Estate subdivision in Yonkers, New York, which lies just north of New York City.[26] At the time, the land was hilly, rocky, and wild, and the roads were unpaved. William and his brother Charlie built a house on their lots, and the family (which included five children) moved in around 1920. Most of the other lots in the area, however, remained unimproved for a long time.

From the beginning, the Lutz family used a "traveled way" across a triangular lot to the west of their property, called Lot 19, to reach a street called Gibson Place, because that way was flatter than the steep descent to what would become Leroy Avenue, which ran in front of their house. William Lutz left his job in 1928 and at that point, their use of the triangular lot increased. Lutz cleared part of the lot and began using it to grow vegetables to sell. He also stored junk and built a chicken coop on Lot 19. At some point, he built a small shed on the property, which Charlie lived in. In addition, he built a garage, part of which encroached onto Lot 19.

In 1946, bad blood developed between the Lutzes and the Van Valkenburghs, who owned another property nearby. Apparently, the Van Valkenburgh children

---

[26] Many of the background facts for this case were taken from R.H. Helmholz, *The Saga of* Van Valkenburgh v. Lutz: *Animosity and Adverse Possession in Yonkers, in* Property Stories (Gerald Korngold & Andrew Morriss eds. 2004).

played on Lot 19, and at one point Lutz chased the children off the lot with an iron pipe, yelling, "I'll kill you," according to testimony. As a result he was arrested and convicted of assault. Later Lutz may have tried to have Van Valkenburgh arrested for criminal trespass.

The original owner of Lot 19 did not pay taxes on the property, and the Van Valkenburghs purchased the lot at a tax sale in 1947, probably motivated by the opportunity of kicking out the Lutzes. They soon asserted their rights to the parcel, demanding that Lutz vacate the property and blocking access to the traveled way. They had a survey done, which indicated that Lutz had built his garage over the property line, which they demanded be rectified.

Lutz first sued the Van Valkenburghs to establish his right to use the travelled way across the lot. He claimed an easement by *prescription*, which we will learn is a method to establish a right-of-way based on continuous use, very similar to adverse possession. The problem, however, is that you can acquire an easement only on *someone else's* land. Lutz won that case, but in so doing made an admission that the Van Valkenburghs owned Lot 19.

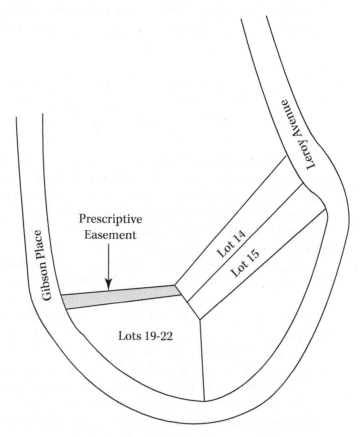

Diagram of **Van Valkenburgh v. Lutz**

In 1948, the Van Valkenburghs sued the Lutzes for ejectment, claiming that they had not fully removed the structures on Lot 19. With new counsel, the Lutzes now raised adverse possession as a defense, claiming that their use of the property in excess of the 15-year statutory period made them the owners of Lot 19.]

DYE, Judge.

These consolidated actions were brought to compel the removal of certain encroachments upon plaintiffs' lands, for delivery of possession and incidental relief.... The subject premises were purchased by the plaintiffs from the city of Yonkers by deed dated April 14, 1947. At that time the defendants were, and had been since 1912, owners of premises designated as lots 14 and 15 in block 54, as shown on the same map. The defendants' lots front on Leroy Avenue and adjoin lot 19 owned by the plaintiffs at the rear boundary line.... At that time that part of the Murray subdivision was covered with a natural wild growth of brush and small trees.

The defendants interposed an answer denying generally the allegations of the complaint and alleging as an affirmative defense, and as a counterclaim, that William Lutz had acquired title to the subject premises by virtue of having held and possessed the same adversely to plaintiffs and predecessors for upwards of thirty years.

The issue thus joined was tried before Hon. Frederick P. Close, Official Referee, who found that title to said lots "was perfected in William Lutz by virtue of adverse possession by the year 1935" and not thereafter disseized....

To acquire title to real property by adverse possession not founded upon a written instrument, it must be shown by clear and convincing proof that for at least fifteen years (formerly twenty years) there was an "actual" occupation under a claim of title, for it is only the premises so actually occupied "and no others" that are deemed to have been held adversely. Civil Practice Act, §§34, 38, 39. The essential elements of proof being either that the premises (1) are protected by a substantial inclosure, or are (2) usually cultivated or improved. Civil Practice Act, §40.

Concededly, there is no proof here that the subject premises were "protected by a substantial inclosure" which leaves for consideration only whether there is evidence showing that the premises were cultivated or improved sufficiently to satisfy the statute.

We think not. The proof concededly fails to show that the cultivation incident to the garden utilized the whole of the premises claimed. Such lack may not be supplied by inference on the showing that the cultivation of a smaller area, whose boundaries are neither defined nor its location fixed with certainty, "must have been ... substantial" as several neighbors were "supplied ... with vegetables." This introduces an element of speculation and surmise which may not be considered since the statute clearly limits the premises adversely held to those "actually" occupied "and no others," Civil Practice Act, §39, which we have recently interpreted as requiring definition by clear and positive proof....

Furthermore, on this record, the proof fails to show that the premises were improved. Civil Practice Act, §40. According to the proof the small shed or shack (about 5 by 10 ½ feet) which, as shown by survey map, was located on the subject premises about 14 feet from the Lutz boundary line. This was built in about the year 1923 and, as Lutz himself testified, he knew at the time it was not on his land and, his wife, a defendant here, also testified to the same effect.

The statute requires as an essential element of proof, recognized as fundamental on the concept of adversity since ancient times, that the occupation of premises be 'under a claim of title' Civil Practice Act, §39, in other words, hostile, and when lacking will not operate to bar the legal title, no matter how long the occupation may have continued....

Similarly, the garage encroachment, extending a few inches over the boundary line, fails to supply proof of occupation by improvement. Lutz himself testified that when he built the garage he had no survey and thought he was getting it on his own property, which certainly falls short of establishing that he did it under a claim of title hostile to the true owner. The other acts committed by Lutz over the years, such as placing a portable chicken coop on the premises which he moved about, the cutting of brush and some of the trees, and the littering of the property with odds and ends of salvaged building materials, cast-off items of house furnishings and parts of automobiles which the defendants and their witnesses described as "personal belongings," "junk," "rubbish" and "debris," were acts which under no stretch of the imagination could be deemed an occupation by improvement within the meaning of the statute, and which, of course, are of no avail in establishing adverse possession.

We are also persuaded that the defendant's subsequent words and conduct confirms the view that his occupation was not "under a claim of title." When the defendant had the opportunity to declare his hostility and assert his rights against the true owner, he voluntarily chose to concede that the plaintiffs' legal title conferred actual ownership entitling them to the possession of these and other premises in order to provide a basis for establishing defendant's right to an easement by adverse possession the use of a well-defined "traveled way" that crossed the said premises. . . . Declarations against interest made by a prescriptive tenant are always available on the issue of his intent. 6 Wigmore on Evidence, §1778.

On this record we do not reach the question of disseisin by oral disclaimer, since the proof fails to establish actual occupation for such time or in such manner as to establish title. What we are saying is that the proof fails to establish actual occupation for such a time or in such a manner as to establish title by adverse possession....

The judgments should be reversed, the counter-claim dismissed and judgment directed to be entered in favor of plaintiff Joseph D. Van Valkenburgh for the relief prayed for in the complaint subject to the existing easement . . . with costs in all courts.

FULD, Judge (dissenting).

In my Judgment, the weight of evidence lies with the determination made by the court at Special Term and affirmed by the Appellate Division. . . .

Wild and overgrown when the Lutzes first moved into the neighborhood, the property was cleared by defendant's husband and had been, by 1916, the referee found, developed into a truck farm "of substantial size." Lutz, together with his children, worked the farm continuously until his death in 1948; indeed, after 1928, he had no other employment. Each year, a new crop was planted and the harvest of vegetables was sold to neighbors. Lutz also raised chickens on the premises, and constructed coops or sheds for them. Fruit trees were planted, and timber was cut from that portion of the property not used for the farm. On one of the lots, Lutz in 1920 built a one-room dwelling, in which his brother Charles has lived ever since.

Although disputing the referee's finding that the dimensions of Lutz's farm were substantial, the court's opinion fails to remark the plentiful evidence in support thereof. For instance, there is credible testimony in the record that "nearly all" of the property comprised by the four lots was cultivated during the period to which the referee's finding relates. A survey introduced in evidence indicates the very considerable extent to which the property was cultivated in 1950, and many witnesses testified that the farm was no larger at that time than it had ever been. There is evidence, moreover, that the cultivated area extended from the "traveled way" on one side of the property to a row of logs and brush placed by Lutz for the express purpose of marking the farm's boundary at the opposite end of the premises.

According to defendant's testimony, she and her husband, knowing that they did not have record title to the premises, intended from the first nevertheless to occupy the property as their own. Bearing this out is the fact that Lutz put down the row of logs and brush, which was over 100 feet in length, to mark the southwestern boundary of his farm; this marker, only roughly approximating the lot lines, extended beyond them into the bed of Gibson Place. The property was, moreover, known in the neighborhood as "Mr. Lutz's gardens," and the one-room dwelling on it as "Charlie's house"; the evidence clearly indicates that people living in the vicinity believed the property to be owned by Lutz. And it is undisputed that for upwards of thirty-five years until 1947, when plaintiffs became the record owners no other person ever asserted title to the parcel.

With evidence such as that in the record, I am at a loss to understand how this court can say that support is lacking for the finding that the premises had been occupied by Lutz under a claim of title. The referee was fully justified in concluding that the character of Lutz's possession was akin to that of a true owner and indicated, more dramatically and effectively than could words, an intent to claim the property as his own. . . . That Lutz knew that he did not have the record title to the property—a circumstance relied upon by the court—is of no consequence, so long as he intended, notwithstanding that fact, to acquire and use the property as his own. . . .

Quite obviously, the fact that Lutz alleged in the 1947 easement action twelve years after title had, according to the referee, vested in him through adverse possession that one of the plaintiffs was the owner of [Lot 19], simply constituted evidence pointing the other way, to be weighed with the other proof by the courts below. While it is true that a disclaimer of title by the occupant of property, made before the statutory period has run, indelibly stamps his possession as nonadverse and prevents title from vesting in him, . . . a disclaimer made after the statute has run carries with it totally different legal consequences. Once title has vested by virtue of adverse possession, it is elementary that it may be divested, not by an oral disclaimer, but only by a transfer complying with the formalities prescribed by law. . . .

"Usually Cultivated or Improved"

The New York statute limits adverse possession to cases in which the occupier either encloses the land or cultivates or improves it. An *improvement* is generally defined as a permanent addition to the land, which increases its productivity or value. For example, we normally consider buildings or parking lots to be improvements.

In view of the extensive cultivation of the parcel in suit, there is no substance to the argument that the requirements of sections 39 and 40 of the Civil Practice Act were not met. Under those provisions, only the premises "actually occupied" in the manner prescribed that is, "protected by a substantial inclosure" or "usually cultivated or improved" are deemed to have been held adversely. The object of the statute, we have recognized, "is that the real owner may, by unequivocal acts of the usurper, have notice of the hostile claim, and be thereby called upon to assert his legal title." . . . Since the character of the acts sufficient to afford such notice "depends upon the nature and situation of the property and the uses to which it can be applied," it is settled that the provisions of sections 39 and 40 are to be construed, not in a narrow or technical sense, but with reference to the nature, character, condition, and location of the property under consideration. . . .

Judge Dye considers it significant that the proof "fails to show that the cultivation incident to the garden utilized the whole of the premises claimed." . . . There surely is no requirement in either statute or decision that proof of adverse possession depends upon cultivation of "the whole" plot or of every foot of the property in question. And, indeed, the statute which, as noted, reads "usually cultivated or improved" has been construed to mean only that the claimant's occupation must "consist of acts such as are usual in the ordinary cultivation and improvement of similar lands by thrifty owners." Ramapo Mfg. Co. v. Mapes, supra, 216 N.Y. 362, 373, 110 N.E. 772, 776[.] The evidence demonstrates that by far the greater part of [Lot 19] was regularly and continuously used for farming, and, that being so, the fact that a portion of the property was not cleared should not affect the claimant's ability to acquire title by adverse possession: any frugal person, owning and occupying lands similar to those here involved, would have permitted, as Lutz did, some of the trees to stand while clearing the bulk of the property in order to provide a source of lumber and other tree products for his usual needs. . . . The nature of the cultivation engaged in by Lutz was more than adequate, as his neighbors' testimony establishes, to give the owner notice of an adverse claim and to delimit the property to which the claim related. . . .

In short, there is ample evidence to sustain the finding that William Lutz actually occupied the property in suit for over fifteen years under a claim of title. Since, then, title vested in Lutz by 1935, the judgment must be affirmed....

I would affirm the judgment reached by both of the courts below.

LEWIS, CONWAY and FROESSEL, JJ., concur with DYE, J.

FULD, J., dissents in opinion in which LOUGHRAN, C.J., and DESMOND, J., concur.

■ POINTS TO CONSIDER

1. **Statutory variations.** To what extent did the particular language of New York's statute of limitations play a role in Lutz's defeat? Had the statute specified only the required length of possession, as many statutes do, would the case have come out differently? Even statutes such as this one do not set out the elements of adverse possession as traditionally applied by courts: do any of the requirements of the New York statute correspond to and help define the traditional elements?

2. **Reputation?** Is it relevant that the neighbors thought the property belonged to the Lutz family? As a lawyer, would you put a witness on the stand to testify to that fact?

3. **Color of title.** Note that the statute the court applied in *Van Valkenburgh* refers to claims "not founded on a written instrument." In many cases, the occupier has a deed or will with a mistaken property description, so that her possession is based on *color of title*.

   In many states, an adverse possessor who claims under color of title gains certain advantages by statute. In some states, the limitations period is shorter for color of title claims. *Compare* Tex. Civ. Prac. & Rem. Code Ann. §16.024 (three-year period if under color of title) *and* §16.026 (West 2013) (ten-year period without color of title). In addition, under color of title, occupation of part of the property is typically deemed

   > **Color of ...**
   >
   > You will encounter the term "color of" in different contexts in law. The term means "under the supposed authority of" or "under the pretense of." For example, the Civil Rights Act punishes law enforcement officials who violate the constitutional rights of others, if they act "under color of law"—in other words, while asserting their legal authority. 18 U.S.C. §242 (2013).

   constructive possession of the entire property described in the written instrument. Without color of title, the adverse possessor is entitled only to the portion of the property actually occupied.

Problem. Assume that Lutz's grandfather George signed a contract to buy Lot 19, then rewrote his will to make sure the property would go to Lutz when he died. George never fulfilled the contract, however, and so never got title to the property. He died soon thereafter, and never changed his will, so Lutz thought that he owned Lot 19 when he started his truck farm and built the chicken coops, etc. How do you think that would change the court's analysis in the case? The theory behind color of title is that the occupancy of part of the tract should give the true owner notice of a claim to the whole property described in the written instrument. You can imagine that Van Valkenburgh would say to Lutz, "Get off of my property," and Lutz would reply, "No, I got Lot 19 in my grandfather's will." Without a written instrument, the only indication of the extent of Lutz's claim is the occupation itself.

4. **State of mind.** American jurisdictions are split between three approaches to the requisite state of mind to establish "adversity" in adverse possession:

    ☐ **Objective.** A large number of states use this approach, which does not inquire into the possessor's state of mind, letting the possessive acts speak for themselves. In these jurisdictions, adversity is destroyed only if the occupation is permissive, or if the possessor overtly acknowledges the true owner's superior title during the statutory period.

    ☐ **Good faith.** A minority of jurisdictions require the possessor to have a good faith belief that he owns the property in question. *See, e.g.,* N.M. Stat. Ann. §37-1-22 (West 2013); Or. Rev. Stat. Ann. §105.620 (West 2013); Carpenter v. Ruperto, 315 N.W.2d 782 (Iowa 1982). This theory awards title only to those who make a legitimate mistake. One commentator has argued that even states that do not overtly require good faith implicitly favor mistaken possessors. R.H. Helmholz, *Adverse Possession and Subjective Intent,* 61 Wash. U. L.Q. 331, 331-32 (1983).

    ☐ **Hostile or aggressive trespasser.** A few states take the term *hostile* literally, and require the trespasser to know she is trespassing, but nevertheless intend to claim the property as her own, or at least intend to claim it regardless of whether she owns it. This is known as the "Maine rule," because it was spelled out in the early case of Preble v. Maine Cent. R. Co., 27 A. 149 (Me. 1893). Because this approach seems to reward bad actors over those who make an honest mistake, a "shrinking minority of jurisdictions" continues to use some version of this rule, and even Maine itself has reversed the rule by statute. Lee Anne Fennell, *Efficient Trespass: The Case for "Bad Faith" Adverse Possession,* 100 Nw. U. L. Rev. 1037, 1039 n.10 (2006).

Can you tell which approach the majority and dissent take in *Van Valkenburgh*? For example, why does the majority in *Van Valkenburgh* consider that the "small shed or shack" does not qualify as an "improvement" sufficient to meet the requirements of adverse possession? Why does the garage encroachment not qualify either? What state of mind does the majority want an adverse possessor to have? What does the dissent say about the requisite state of mind? Which property policies from Chapter 1 do you think are emphasized by the state of mind approach taken by the majority and the dissent? Many commentators have criticized the majority opinion in *Van Valkenburgh* for its contradictory position on the element of "adversity." A more recent New York decision, Walling v. Przybylo, 804 N.Y.S.2d 435, 438-39 (N.Y. App. Div. 2005), characterized the majority's statement in *Van Valkenburgh* about the required state of mind to be "*dictum*." Instead, the court held that "the possessor's knowledge or belief as to who owns the disputed parcel is immaterial to a claim of adverse possession." This is known as the *objective* standard because it pays no attention to the *subjective* intent of the occupier. The *Walling* court did say, however, that the adverse possessor's "overt acknowledgement" of the true owner's superior title, *before* the statutory period runs, negates the claim of right required. *Id.* at 437. Do you see the difference?

Professionalism and State of Mind

Recall our introductory problem involving Rod farming Peter's land for the statutory period. Assume Rod came to you, described the situation, and wanted to know if he could claim the land by adverse possession. You carefully explain that the law in your jurisdiction requires that the adverse possessor have a good faith belief that he owned the property. Do you think Rod would now be more likely to claim that he was confused about exactly where the property line was? As a lawyer, what do you think your ethical obligation would be in that case? Can you think of any way to avoid this situation? Does it make sense to make adverse possession turn on the state of mind of the occupier, when the occupier is typically the only source of that evidence?

Hostility or Good Faith? Adverse Possession in Lower Manhattan

We have already seen that property law sometimes takes into account the intentions of the parties. In the spite fence cases, for example, a structure that might be allowed if built with a valid purpose is not allowed if done out of malice. In accession cases, the mistaken appropriation of another's property is treated differently than purposeful misappropriation. In adverse possession, should courts consider the fact that the possessor *knew* the land wasn't hers? What possible theory supports the "bad faith" approach?

CASE SUMMARY: Humbert v. Rector, Churchwardens & Vestrymen of Trinity Church, 24 Wend. 587 (1840)

One of the earliest American cases rejecting a good faith requirement involved Trinity Church's claims to what is now a large section of Tribeca in Manhattan.

The plaintiffs in *Humbert* claimed title to almost 200 acres of New York City, tracing their title back to Anneke Jans Bogardus, whose husband had been granted the land (in what was then New Amsterdam) in 1636. Anneke devised her property to her children and grandchildren and by the time of this case, there were a large number of descendants claiming an interest in the land. Trinity Church, on the other hand, had been granted the land directly south of this property in 1705, but its deed left the northern boundary ambiguous.

From that time on, the court found, the church "entertained a settled design . . . to claim the Bogardus lands in severalty as a part of their grant. They had prosecuted that design through the instrumentality of threats, of persecution, of riotous invasion and on some occasions in a spirit of vandal ferocity." *Id.* at 601. Evidence showed, for example, that the defendants pulled down the plaintiffs' fences and other improvements and burned them, and turned their cattle onto plaintiffs' cropland to destroy it. *Id.* at 598-99.

The Church claimed the land through adverse possession for over 50 years. Plaintiffs argued that the Church's bad faith and knowledge that it didn't own the land should preclude its claim. The court disagreed:

> [I]t cannot be denied that the bill makes out a case of strong moral transgression; and the question thus raised is, whether a plaintiff, lying by and forbearing to bring his action till after the time in the statute of limitations shall have run against him, can excuse his negligence by the fact *that the defendant knew all along he was in the wrong.*

Id. at 603. The court noted that other limitations provisions, such as those for debt or trespass, do not inquire into the bad faith of the defendant, but rather are based on time only.

> Possession by the defendant with a claim of title for twenty years, can no more be answered by averring that he knew he was wrong, than could the bar for two years, in slander, by the known falsehood of the libel for which it is prosecuted. . . . It is of the nature of the statute of limitations when applied to civil actions, in effect, to mature a wrong into a right, by cutting off the remedy.

Id. at 604.

A variety of policy reasons supported the court's decision. The court noted, for example, that adverse possession rewards *productive use* of property:

> Statutes limiting real actions generally operate in favor of the men who cultivate the soil, or inhabit the dwelling houses of the country; and cannot discriminate between the rich and the poor, the powerful and the weak, the wise and the ignorant. Looking at their tendency to encourage men not only in the pursuits of agriculture, but every great interest of the nation, an argument of policy arises for their equal and steady application, even more strong than of statutes which passed to limit personal actions.

Id. at 609. Moreover, the court stressed that adverse possession promotes *certainty*. The plaintiffs' claims originated in 1663 and raised numerous issues regarding inconsistent descriptions of property boundaries, uncertain laws of descent and inheritance, and difficulties in tracing heirs.

> If parties have legal claims to property, they should settle their controversies before time has drawn its veil over all the transactions connected with it; before the witnesses who could testify . . . are all departed to their long account; and before the documents and written evidences which would explain and make clear many things now in doubt and obscurity, are destroyed or lost.

Id. at 633.

The Trinity Church thus gained control over much of the Tribeca neighborhood of lower Manhattan. Over the last two centuries, the property was sold to raise money or granted to other churches or organization. Trinity Real Estate now owns about 15 acres in the city, which still makes it one of the largest landholders in Manhattan.[27]

Oddly, Trinity was not the only church to obtain large parts of Manhattan by adverse possession in the 1800s. In 1842, the U.S. Supreme Court ruled in favor of the Reformed Dutch Church in its claim to 16 acres north and east of Maiden Lane and Broadway. Smith Harpending v. Minister, Elders and Deacons of the Reformed Protestant Dutch Church, 41 U.S. 455 (1842). The property was originally granted to John Haberdinck, a shoemaker, in 1696, and he willed it to the Church when he died in 1722. The church took possession, but heirs of Haberdinck claimed that the law then prohibited churches from taking property by will.[28] The court affirmed the dismissal of the suit, holding that even if the church could not take by will, it was entitled to the property by adverse possession. The Reformed Dutch Church is now known as the Collegiate Church and continues to own much property in the area. In 2004, the church estimated that the value of the property at issue in the Haberdinck will was $365 million. Thus, the title to a large section of lower Manhattan rests on adverse possession!

Do we really want to reward the sort of intimidation and "riotous invasion" the Trinity Church was alleged to have used against the Bogardus heirs in lower Manhattan? Contrast with *Trinity* the opinion in the following case, which expresses the view of the "good faith" jurisdictions:

CASE SUMMARY: Jasperson v. Scharnikow, 150 F. 571 (9th Cir. 1907)

Uriah Bryant arrived in the town of Ballard, Washington, in 1888, found 160 acres of land that was vacant, and went into possession. He built a log cabin and barn, cleared part of the land, and began cutting wood to take to market. He did this until his death 12 years later, which exceeded the 10-year statute of limitations in the state.

The real owner of the property, Higgens, had been granted a patent to the property in 1872 and paid taxes on it annually, but resided in Montana. The testimony

---

[27] https://www.trinitywallstreet.org/campus-directory.
[28] This prohibition, dating from King Edward I in 1279, is called a *mortmain* statute.

showed that Bryant knew full well that Higgens owned the property, but determined to "squat" on the property to attempt to acquire it by adverse possession.

The court found that Bryant could not claim title by adverse possession under these circumstances:

> These facts fully justified, we think, the trial court in saying at the close of the evidence that the entry of Bryant and his wife was without any pretense "of having a right as owner of the property at the inception of their entry, which is necessary to make out a title by adverse possession. This idea of acquiring title by larceny does not go in this country. A man must have a bona fide claim, or believe in his own mind that he has got a right as owner, when he goes upon land that does not belong to him, in order to acquire title by occupation and possession. The defendant's evidence fails to show any claim of right in Bryant when he went on the land. There is not a particle of testimony that squints in the direction that he supposed that he had any right, or that he went there for any other purpose than to acquire right, if he could do so by holding long enough without molestation."

Jasperson v. Scharnikow, 150 F. 571, 572 (9th Cir. 1907). Which policies of property law do you think are furthered by the states that require the adverse possession to be in "good faith"?

Which approach to the state of mind of the possessor do you prefer? Do you think that the appropriate state of mind requirement might depend on whether the situation involves a squatter or a mistaken boundary? Might the desire to mold the requirement to the context explain the court's apparent waffling on the state of mind requirement in *Van Valkenburgh*? *See* Luke Meier, A Contextual Approach to Claim of Right in Adverse Possession Cases, 19 Lewis & Clark L. Rev. 47 (2015).

■ PROBLEMS: ADVERSE POSSESSION

Assume the jurisdiction has a 20-year statute of limitations for ejectment.

1. **Abandonment.** A school district built a school building on its land, but mistakenly constructed a storage shed on Benson's land. This situation continued for 25 years, when the school district proposed to build a new shed. A survey determined the current shed was on the wrong property, and the school board voted to tear down the shed and vacate the land, which was promptly done. A few months later, however, the board's attorney suggested that the district might have acquired title by adverse possession. Did the board's action in abandoning the property negate any right the district may have had to it? *See* School Dist. No. 4 v. Benson, 31 Me. 381 (1850) (once adverse possessor meets elements, title is vested and may only be divested by written conveyance or adverse possession of another).

2. **Adversity.** Franklin's lot is bordered on the west by Murphy's lot. There is a row of bushes bordering Murphy's driveway, about 20 feet west of the

property line. In 1995, Murphy became ill and Franklin began to mow up to the bushes, "to help old man Murphy." In 1998, Murphy died and the property descended to Murphy, Jr. Franklin continued to mow the grass and in 2000, began to store some scrap lumber on the 20-foot strip. In 2002, he began to park a recreational vehicle there. In 2019, Murphy, Jr. wants to sell the property and sues Franklin to eject him from the parcel. Has Franklin established adverse possession?

3. **Interruption.** In the previous problem, the adverse possession period does not start over just because Murphy died and Murphy, Jr. inherited the property. In order to interrupt the running of the statute, the owner must *oust* the adverse possessor, which means retaking possession of the disputed land. What if Murphy, Jr. sent Franklin a letter, five days before the limitations period would have run, requesting that he vacate the disputed parcel? What if he sent Franklin a letter, on the same date, saying that he didn't mind him using the parcel but wanted to make it clear that it was by *permission*, which could be revoked at any time?

4. **Tacking.** Assume Franklin sells his house in 2007 to Norton, who continues using the strip of land in a similar manner. Can Norton use Franklin's period of possession, or does he need to start over? Generally, courts allow subsequent possessors to *tack* on the occupancy of previous possessors, if there is *privity* between them and continuity of possession. In other words, if Franklin took his lumber and RV with him when he moved out and Norton didn't start using the strip again for several years, the adverse possession might be deemed to have been interrupted, especially if Murphy, Jr. started mowing the grass again.

Privity simply requires some reasonable connection between the successive adverse possessors. By purchasing Franklin's property, Norton could be said to have purchased whatever possessory interests were appurtenant to the property. Could the same be said if Norton had been given the property in Franklin's will? How about if Franklin gave Norton the property as a gift? Can you think of any instances in which privity between successive occupiers would *not* exist?

It is important to know whether Franklin had already fulfilled the adverse possession requirements by the time he transferred his property to Norton. If so, it wouldn't matter whether Norton continued to use the strip of land in a hostile manner. Franklin was the true owner, at that point, of the strip of land, whether he knew it or not—the question should be whether Franklin *intended* to convey that strip to Norton along with the deeded parcel. *See* Doty v. Chalk, 632 P.2d 664 (Colo. App. 1981) (adverse possessor did not intend to convey disputed parcel in deed to other land, but retained ownership herself, even though she didn't know she owned it).

Legal disabilities. Limitations statutes typically provide that the period does not run against those who are minors or under another legal disability to

Video Problem: *Mitchell v. Daniels*

🎞 Applying the "good faith" test can be difficult. In this video, which is available on the Simulation, Lee Mitchell has been using a ten-foot strip of his neighbor's land for a very long time. He seems to think that he had the right to use it. You should assess whether the occupation is sufficient to meet the adverse possession standards in a good faith jurisdiction with a 15-year statute.

bring suit at the time the cause of action accrues. *See, e.g.*, Utah Code Ann. §78B-2-223 (West 2018). Legal disabilities usually include mental incapacity, but may also include imprisonment, at least if the prisoner was unable to discover the adverse possession by the exercise of reasonable diligence. *See, e.g.*, Ariz. Rev. Stat. Ann. §12-528(B) (2018).

In order to toll the statute, the disability must exist either at the time of the adverse entry giving rise to a cause of action, or in some states, at the time the owner acquired a possessory interest. In some jurisdictions, the disability statute simply starts the limitations period when the disability is removed, while in others, the statute provides for a different period in cases of disability. In some states, there is also an absolute maximum limitation period, even if a disability exists. *See* Cal. Civ. Proc. Code §328 (West 2018) (normal 5-year adverse possession period is extended to 5 years from disability removal, not exceeding 20 years from time cause accrues).

Here is an example of a disability statute from Arkansas:

Ark. Code Ann. §18-61-101 (West 2018). Lands, tenements or hereditaments

(a) (1) No person or his or her heirs shall have, sue, or maintain any action or suit, either in law or equity, for any lands, tenements, or hereditaments after seven (7) years once his or her right to commence, have, or maintain the suit shall have come, fallen, or accrued.

(2) All suits, either in law or equity, for the recovery of any lands, tenements, or hereditaments shall be had and sued within seven (7) years next after the title or cause of action accrued and no time after the seven (7) years shall have passed.

(b) If any person who is, or shall be, entitled to commence and prosecute a suit or action in law or equity is, or shall be, at the time the right or title first accrued come or fallen within the age of twenty-one (21) or non compos mentis, the person or his or her heirs, shall and may, notwithstanding the seven (7) years may have expired, bring his or her suit or action if the infant or non compos mentis, or his or her heirs, shall bring it within three (3) years next after full age or coming of sound mind.

(c) No cumulative disability shall prevent the bar formed and constituted by the saving of this section.

■ PROBLEMS: DISABILITIES AND ADVERSE POSSESSION

Apply the Arkansas statute to these facts: Assume that Omar is the title holder of Blackacre as of January 1, 2005. Alf enters Blackacre on that date and begins building a house. Omar or his successor brings suit to eject Alf on January 1, 2013.

1. As of January 1, 2005, Omar was confined in the Alzheimer's unit of a care facility. His daughter, Danielle, has power of attorney to take care of his legal matters. Omar dies on January 1, 2011, and Danielle inherits Blackacre.
2. As of January 1, 2005, Omar is 17 years old. From 2007 to 2010, he served in an Army unit in Afghanistan, and returned home on January 1, 2010, after being diagnosed with post-traumatic stress disorder. On January 1, 2012, a doctor issued an opinion certifying that Omar remained in treatment for this disorder.

Consider your role as an attorney if you were consulted by Alf, the adverse possessor. If all you know is the evidence concerning Alf's possession—the amount of enclosure and improvement; the length of time; the continuous, open, and notorious nature of the occupation; and Alf's state of mind—can you give Alf an accurate opinion on the case? Do you see why you need to know some facts about Omar as well?

Adverse Possession Against the Government

The general rule is that an individual cannot gain title to the government's real property through adverse possession. If you have any thoughts about heading into the vast federal lands of Alaska to begin establishing a claim, you can forget it. But the rule also applies when you mistakenly build your garage on a paper street (i.e., planned but never built) that the municipality has never gotten around to using.

With respect to the federal government, 28 U.S.C. §2409a(n) (2018) explicitly states that sovereign immunity is not waived for claims of adverse possession by private parties. The majority of states also prohibit adverse possession of government property by statute[29] or state constitution.[30] Even in states without a statutory or constitutional ban on adverse possession, courts have been reluctant to allow adverse possession claims against the government's real property. They reason that the burden on government to police all of its property would be too great and that the government should not be bound by the negligent acts of its agents. Moreover, as one court stated, the public should not lose its land to "one of its own members whose duty it was, as much as any other citizen, to protect

---

[29] *See, e.g.,* Alaska Stat. §09.45.052 (2018); Ark. Code Ann. §14-301-113 (2018); Cal. Civ. Code §1007 (West 2018); Colo. Rev. Stat. §38-41-101(b) (2018); Wash. Rev. Code §4.16.160 (2018).
[30] *See* La. Const. art. XII, §13; Miss. Const. art. IV, §104.

Nullum Tempus Occurit Regi

The rule banning adverse possession claims against the government is an application of this general principle, which is Latin for "no time runs against the state." According to Black's Law Dictionary, "the purpose of the rule is to fully protect public rights and property from injury."[31]

---

the state." Stone v. Rhodes, 752 P.2d 1112, 1114-15 (N.M. Ct. App. 1988). Theoretically, a citizen cannot adversely possess property she already shares ownership of as a member of the public.

Some states have tempered this ban on adverse possession claims against the government by allowing adverse possession claims in limited circumstances.[32] For example, some states require double the statutory length of time for possession,[33] while some courts have allowed adverse possession only for property not actually being used for a public purpose.[34] A minority of states allow adverse possession against the government without any barriers, treating adverse possession claims against the government the same as those against a private party.[35]

The limitations do not go both ways, however. Generally, the government at all levels can obtain title to property through adverse possession by fulfilling the same elements a private party would need to satisfy.[36] Exceptions arise when different levels of government are both the plaintiff and defendant in the same case. The U.S. Supreme Court in *Texas v. Louisiana* stated that a state cannot obtain title to property through adverse possession against the federal government.[37] Similarly, at least one court has held that local municipalities (considered a subdivision of the state) cannot claim adverse possession of state property.[38]

■ PROBLEM: ADVERSE POSSESSION AGAINST THE GOVERNMENT

In 1975, the original plat of the Greenwood Subdivision granted the Town of Sedgwick ownership of a three-acre plot of land to be used as a park for the

---

[31] Black's Law Dictionary 1096 (7th ed. 1999).

[32] A very thorough law review article on this topic is Paula R. Latovick, *Adverse Possession Against the States: The Hornbooks Have It Wrong*, 29 U. Mich. J.L. Reform 939 (1996).

[33] *Compare* Cal. Civ. Proc. Code §315 (West 2012) (requiring 10-year period for state land), *with* Cal. Civ. Proc. Code §318 (West 2012) (providing for a 5-year period generally); *compare* N.D. Cent. Code §28-01-01 (2012) (requiring 40-year period for state land), *with* N.D. Cent. Code §47-06-03 (2012) (requiring 20-year period generally).

[34] *See* Ortiz v. Pac. States Props., 215 P.2d 514 (Cal. Ct. App. 1950).

[35] *See, e.g.*, Meade v. Sturgill, 467 S.W.2d 363 (Ky. 1971); Mass. Gen. Laws ch. 260, §31 (2012).

[36] *See* Alaska Stat. §09.45.052 (2012) (disallowing adverse possession against the state or United States, yet allowing the public, state, or political subdivision of the state to adversely possess land for public transportation or public access purposes).

[37] Texas v. Louisiana, 410 U.S. 702, 714 (1973) (citing United States v. California, 332 U.S. 19, 39-40 (1947)) ("Texas claims any such islands existing prior to 1848 by prescription and acquiescence, but, plainly, a State may not acquire property from the United States in this manner.").

[38] Trustees of Univ. of S.C. v. City of Columbia, 93 S.E. 934, 937 (S.C. 1917) (indicating a city can adversely possess an individual's property but that "[t]he city governing is the state governing through the city in a circumscribed locality; and for a city to claim the property of the state adversely to the state is the same thing as to claim against itself, a manifest incongruity").

residents of the subdivision. The Town never actually built the park, however, and the vacant area began to be used by the adjacent landowners as if it were their own. Several of the adjacent owners planted bushes on the parcel to mark the area of their use. In 2019, the city plans a new bike trail, and the route goes through the middle of the three-acre plot. The adjacent residents claim that the city must compensate them for the right-of-way, because the property has become theirs by adverse possession. What result?

Adverse Possession of Chattels

In July 2017, Ethan asks Manuel if he can borrow his new $3,000, commercial-grade wood chipper to help with a little land clearing project he is working on. After a week, Manuel asks for the chipper back, but Ethan says he needs to repair a belt that broke on it. Another few weeks go by, and Ethan still has not returned the chipper, despite Manuel's repeated requests. At that point, Manuel is distracted by life events—his mother dies and shortly thereafter he is called to active duty overseas. When he finally returns, in September 2019, he finds that Ethan has been using the wood chipper the whole time. Ethan refuses to give it back and claims that he has made some expensive repairs he should be compensated for. Can Ethan claim adverse possession of this chattel?

Manuel has an action for conversion (or trover or replevin) of his personal property, and the question would be when the statute of limitations for such actions began to run. The general elements for adverse possession of real property also apply to adverse possession of personal property. Therefore, Ethan's possession must be hostile, actual, visible, exclusive, and continuous. Statutes of limitation for conversion of personal property are generally shorter than those required for adverse possession of real property and typically span from two to six years, although some states have the same time requirements for adverse possession of both real and personal property. Typically, courts hold that the statutory time period begins to run from the time the adverse possessor gains hostile possession of the personal property.

However, personal property creates several unique problems under the elements of adverse possession because—unlike real property—personal property can be readily moved and even concealed. Thus, personal property may be adversely possessed visibly and continuously in Florida, yet the true owner may not be put on notice of the adverse possession if he lives in Maine and never visits Florida. These problems often arise in the case of stolen artwork that is resold to an innocent buyer who is unaware he is purchasing stolen property and keeps the stolen artwork for an extended period of time. Under the traditional rules, as long as the possession was "open," the statute is running.

In Dunbar v. Seger-Thomschitz, 638 F. Supp. 2d 659 (E.D. La. 2009), for example, the plaintiff inherited an Oskar Kokoschka painting from her mother in 1973. Defendant alleged that the painting had been stolen by the Nazis and that plaintiff's mother should have known that when she bought it in 1946. The court held, however, that Louisiana's ten-year statute had been fulfilled by plaintiff's open and continuous possession. She displayed it openly in her home and loaned it to galleries for exhibitions. Therefore, she acquired ownership "irrespective of her good or bad faith." *Id.* at 663.

Discovery rule. Some jurisdictions that frequently have cases involving valuable, stolen chattels like artwork have adopted modified rules for the date the statutory time period begins running. One such approach is the *discovery rule.* The discovery rule begins the statutory period for adverse possession when the true owner discovers or should have discovered through reasonable diligence the adverse possessor's possession of the property. Due diligence is measured on a case-by-case basis, and the burden is on the true owner to prove that he has exercised due diligence in recovering his personal property.

The rationale behind the discovery rule is fairness to the true owner, who may not be able to ascertain who has possession of the personal property if it is concealed. As one court noted, how can a plaintiff who is unable to determine the possessor be expected to bring an action for replevin when a required element of such a claim is the identity of the one in possession?[39] The original case adopting the discovery rule, O'Keeffe v. Snyder, 416 A.2d 862, 869 (N.J. 1980), concerned adverse possession of three Georgia O'Keeffe paintings. The New Jersey Supreme Court noted that the art world had experienced an explosion of thefts and the only way to combat theft was to adopt a rule that was fair to true owners. Several other jurisdictions have now adopted this approach.[40]

Holocaust

In 2016, Congress enacted the Holocaust Expropriated Art Recovery Act of 2016, P.L. 114-308. The Act is intended to make it easier for the heirs of victims of Nazi persecution to recover stolen works of art. It adopts a uniform six-year statute of limitations and uses a strong version the discovery rule—the limitations period begins only upon the claimant's actual discovery of: (1) the identity and location of the artwork or other property, and (2) a possessory interest in the artwork or property. The legislation passed unanimously and has already been used to recover valuable art. *See, e.g.,* Cassirer v. Thyssen-Bornemisza Collection Found., 862 F.3d 951 (9th Cir. 2017), *cert. denied*, 138 S. Ct. 1992 (2018). Would this change the result in *Dunbar*, noted above?

Demand and refuse rule. A second approach to the statutory time period issue is the demand and refuse rule. *See* Solomon R. Guggenheim Found. v. Lubell, 569

---

[39] Autocephalous Greek Orthodox Church of Cyprus v. Goldberg & Feldman Fine Arts, 717 F. Supp. 1374, 1389 (S.D. Ind. 1989).
[40] Museum of Fine Arts, Bos. v. Seger-Thomschitz, 623 F.3d 1 (1st Cir. 2010); Erisoty v. Rizik, No. CIV. A. 93-6215, 1995 WL 91406 (E.D. Pa. Feb. 23, 1995); Cal. Civ. Proc. Code §338(c)(2) (West 2012).

N.E.2d 426, 429 (N.Y. 1991). The demand and refuse rule requires that (1) the true owner must demand the personal property be returned, and (2) the possessor must refuse to return it. At that point, the possessor's possession becomes clearly adverse and the statutory time period begins to run.

The demand and refuse rule provides the strongest protection to the true owner. As long as the true owner doesn't know who has her property, the time period cannot run, because no demand has been made. Additionally, the demand and refuse rule avoids the discovery rule's difficult determination of what constitutes reasonable diligence on the part of the true owner in regaining his personal property. Instead, the burden is placed on the individual adversely possessing the personal property, since the true owner is the more innocent party. This approach has been predominately followed by New York and Illinois.

How would a jurisdiction's adoption of the discovery rule or the demand and refuse rule apply to the wood chipper problem above? In that case, Manuel knew all along who had his chipper, but at what point should he have realized that Ethan's possession was adverse? At what point did Manuel have a cause of action for conversion?

■ PROBLEM: ADVERSE POSSESSION OF CHATTELS

In the early 1970s, a jazzman from New Orleans named Henry Roeland Byrd (a/k/a "Professor Longhair") sent some master tapes to Albert Grossman, who ran a New York record company. Nothing came of it, so, in 1975, Byrd sent two letters to Grossman demanding his tapes back. Grossman did not respond. In 1986, Grossman's estate licensed some of these recordings to Rounder Records, which released an album for which Byrd received a posthumous Grammy Award. In 1995, Byrd's successors brought suit against Grossman's estate for wrongful conversion of the tapes. The jurisdiction has a three-year statute of limitations for conversion. If you apply the elements of adverse possession, should the claims of Byrd's successors be barred? Would the discovery or demand and refuse rules affect this case? *See* SongByrd, Inc. v. Estate of Grossman, 206 F.3d 172 (2d Cir. 2000).

Continuing Relevance of Adverse Possession

Does the doctrine of adverse possession still make sense? In early American history, title to land was notoriously uncertain (remember the Trinity Church case, with title based on a will from the 1600s), so possession was the clearest evidence of ownership. Moreover, we wanted to encourage those who made the land productive, rather than absent owners who may have gotten a patent to the land for a small amount, but then never used it. See Larissa Katz, *The Moral Paradox of Adverse Possession: Sovereignty and Revolution in Property Law*, 55 McGill L. Rev. 47 (2010)(when the West was being settled, "it was seen as socially beneficial to encourage land-hungry locals to take over from absentee paper title holders").

Those policies no longer seem as strong. We now have a system of recording title documents and probate that makes it relatively easy to tell who owns property. Furthermore, we no longer need the adverse possession doctrine to give people an incentive to make productive use of land. As one commentator put it:

> Years ago when the Cowboy roamed the West, land barons purchased large tracts of land consisting of hundreds of thousands of acres. In part, to prevent stagnation of the land and under-use of natural resources, American courts imported two English doctrines—prescription and adverse possession. The courts believed these two legal devices would provide an incentive to landowners to work all portions of their holdings.
>
> Although these tools remain in effect today, the public policy supporting their usage has long since gone the way of the cattle drive and the chuckwagon. . . . [C]urrent public policy prefers land and resource preservation versus exploitation.

William G. Ackerman & Shane T. Johnson, *Outlaws of the Past: A Western Perspective on Prescription and Adverse Possession*, 31 Land & Water L. Rev. 79, 94 (1996); *see also* Gorman v. City of Woodinville, 283 P.3d 1082 (Wash. 2012) (Madsen, C.J., concurring) ("Insofar as the [adverse possession] doctrine serves the goal of utilization of land, we are now at a point where preserving unused land is not considered to be a poor use of land. The doctrine of adverse possession can wreak havoc in recorded title transfers and is fundamentally at odds with our usual recognition and enforcement of documented land ownership and transfers.").

Rather than simply dispossessing the true owner, would it make sense to at least require the adverse possessor to pay the original owner some compensation for the loss of her land, such as reimbursement for any property taxes or other costs incurred by the original owner during the period of occupation? In other words, after the limitations period, should we protect the property owner with a liability rule rather than a property rule? *See* Thomas W. Merrill, *Property Rules, Liability Rules, and Adverse Possession*, 79 Nw. U. L. Rev. 1122, 1145-54 (1984).

In Meyer v. Law, 287 So. 2d 37 (Fla. 1973), the Florida Supreme Court questioned whether the adverse possession doctrine was still consistent with modern policy goals for land development:

> The concept of adverse possession is an ancient and, perhaps, somewhat outdated one. It stems from a time when an ever-increasing use of land was to be, and was, encouraged. Today, however, faced, as we are, with problems of unchecked overdevelopment, depletion of precious natural resources, and pollution of our environment, the policy reasons that once supported the idea of adverse possession may well be succumbing to new priorities. A man who owns some virgin land, who refrains from despoiling that land, even to the extent of erecting a fence to mark its boundaries, and who makes no greater use of that land than an occasional rejuvenating walk in the woods, can hardly be faulted in today's increasingly "modern" world. Public policy and stability of our society, therefore, require strict

compliance with the appropriate statutes by those seeking ownership through adverse possession.

Id. at 41.

In dissent, Justice Adkins believed the policies behind adverse possession continued to be relevant:

> For seven long years, this man was allowed to believe that he was openly and notoriously tilling, improving, and fencing his own land. Under the rationale of the majority opinion, he was actually toiling for the benefit of his neighbor. Under the rationale of the statute, he acquired title by adverse possession.
>
> Neither neighbor is actually in the wrong; and, the best result would be that neither had to suffer. However, this is not possible within the limitations of land, and the Legislature has determined that, under the facts of the case *sub judice*, the man who had, through a good faith mistake, protected, enclosed and improved the land in question for seven years without complaint of his neighbor should have the benefit of his toils. The majority opinion gives the land to the man who did not bother to check his boundaries for seven years to determine whether or not his land has been invaded.

Id. at 42-43 (Adkins, J., dissenting).

Do you believe the doctrine of adverse possession promotes the appropriate policies for modern society? Should the doctrine be modified to better promote those goals? For example, does the doctrine place too much emphasis on "using" the land, when in many cases society would rather see it preserved? *See generally* John G. Sprankling, *An Environmental Critique of Adverse Possession*, 79 Cornell L. Rev. 816 (1994) (arguing that adverse possession doctrine encourages development instead of preservation of sensitive lands).

You may want to reserve judgment on this question until we have covered the material on real estate transactions. Adverse possession often helps cure defects that otherwise might be *clouds on the title*. For example, there might be a small discrepancy in the legal description of the property you're buying, in a deed from 30 years ago. Or there is some question about whether a spouse of an owner of the property back then properly released his marital rights. These could be difficult problems to "fix," but adverse possession cures most of them. That spouse, *if* he had any rights and *if* he wanted to claim them, slept on whatever rights he had and lost them. The title is now clean and can be transferred without fear. Of course, there might be other ways to achieve this purpose, but adverse possession continues to play an important role in clearing title. To be sure, the doctrine doesn't always increase the certainty of land transactions; by now, you can tell that adverse possession may *create* a few clouds on title as well!

You might be surprised to learn that Westlaw reported over 1,200 cases involving the term *adverse possession* just in the years 2014-17. This suggests that the doctrine remains useful and relevant in the modern world.

SUMMARY

■ The *rule of capture* awards ownership to the first person to acquire possession of unowned property, called *res nullius.*

■ What constitutes sufficient possession in a particular context may depend on custom and policy goals such as certainty, fairness, and economic efficiency. *Constructive possession* may be sufficient in some circumstances.

■ The rule of capture governs water allocation in the western states, where a *prior appropriation* system is used. The rest of the states use a *riparian* system, which allows landowners whose property borders a body of water to make *reasonable use* of it.

■ Although the *ad coelum* doctrine suggests that a landowner owns everything beneath the ground, *fugitive resources* such as oil and gas are not considered owned until they are captured by being brought to the surface. This capture rule led to overproduction, prompting legislative reforms. The example illustrates one negative consequence of the rule of capture, which can also be seen in other common pool situations.

■ The rule of capture also governs the initial allocation of *internet domain names*, which are given to the first person to apply. However, Congress has modified the pure capture rule in order to protect trademark owners from *cybersquatters* who hold domain names for ransom.

■ A *finder* of lost property acquires a property right good against all but the true owner or a previous finder. The presumption of ownership given to a possessor of property furthers important policies such as certainty, fairness, economic efficiency, and peace and order.

■ The place where property is found may affect the result. Property found on someone's land may be constructively possessed by the owner of the locus in quo, especially if it is buried or attached, the owner knows it is there, or if it is in a highly private location.

■ *Mislaid property*, which has been intentionally placed somewhere, may be more likely to be awarded to the owner of the locus in quo rather than the finder.

■ A *gift* of personal property requires *donative intent, delivery to the donee,* and *acceptance.*

■ *Delivery* may be manual, constructive, or symbolic, but courts typically require the best form of delivery possible in the circumstances and may be stricter about delivery requirements where intent is questionable.

■ A gift *causa mortis* is one made in contemplation of death, and may be revoked if the donor recovers. Otherwise, a completed *inter vivos* gift is irrevocable.

■ *Adverse possession* awards property to one who is in actual, adverse, open and notorious, exclusive, and continuous possession of another's property for the period specified by statute.

■ Jurisdictions vary on the *state of mind* required for adverse possession. Some states require *good faith* (i.e., the possessor thought the property was his), while a few seem to require that the possessor know the property belongs to someone else and intend to take it anyway as an "aggressive trespasser." Many jurisdictions, however, use an *objective* standard, which makes the state of mind irrelevant and focuses solely on whether the possessor acted as a true owner.

■ A subsequent possessor may *tack* on a previous possession if there is *privity* between the possessors.

■ *Disability* statutes extend the required period of adverse possession if the true owner has some sort of disability (such as mental incapacity or being under the age of majority) at the time adverse possession begins.

■ In general, *public property* is not subject to claims of adverse possession, although some states have modified that rule in certain limited circumstances.

■ Adverse possession also applies to the *possession of chattels*. However, because personal property is moveable, some states do not begin the statutory period until the true owner knows or should have known about the adverse possession under the discovery rule. A couple of jurisdictions use the "demand and refuse" rule, which does not start the period until the true owner demands the return of the chattel and the possessor refuses.

CHAPTER 3

Creation: An Introduction to Intellectual Property

A. The Policies of Intellectual Property Protection

B. The Principal Sources of Intellectual Property Protection
   1. Patent
   2. Copyright
   3. Trademark
   4. Trade Secret

C. The Balance of Interests in Intellectual Property Law
   1. The Balance of Interests in Trademark Law
   2. The Balance of Interests in Copyright Law
   3. The Balance of Interests in Patent Law

> There is certainly no kind of property, in the nature of things, so much his own, as the works which a person originates from his own creative imagination....
>
> —*Joel Barlow, Letter to the Continental Congress (1783)*[1]

Traditionally, we think of property in terms of physical, tangible objects—such as land, jewelry, or boats—of which we can acquire ownership by sale, gift, or possession (in the case of finders or adverse possession). In some cases, however, property does not exist until it is created by someone. For example, *MacBeth* was merely an idea in Shakespeare's head until he put quill to parchment and brought the Scottish play to life. This category, which the law protects by patents, copyrights, trademarks, and trade secrets, is called intellectual property or IP.

Intellectual property has become increasingly important. The Department of Commerce estimates that IP-intensive industries directly accounted for, or indirectly supported, 45.5 million jobs in 2014, almost 30 percent of all jobs in America. These activities added about $6.6 trillion in value to the U.S. economy, about 38 percent of the gross national product.[2]

---

[1] Letter from Joel Barlow to the Continental Congress (1783) (on file with the National Archives).
[2] Econ. and Statistics Admin., *Intellectual Property and the U.S. Economy: 2016 Update*, U.S. Dep't of Commerce ii (2016) https://www.uspto.gov/sites/default/files/documents/IPandtheUSEconomySept2016.pdf.

Some recent examples help illustrate the value of IP interests:

➤ In 2016, Idenix was awarded $2.54 billion in royalties for the infringement of its patent on hepatitis C drugs.
➤ In 2016, a jury awarded Epic Systems $940 million for the theft of its trade secrets related to healthcare software.
➤ In 2009, a jury in Minnesota penalized a woman $1.9 million for illegally downloading 24 songs on the Internet.

Of course, it is probably not necessary to convince students who have grown up with Microsoft, YouTube, and peer-to-peer file sharing of the importance of intellectual property issues.

In a first-year Property course, our goal is not to make you an expert in IP law. Instead, we have two aims in this chapter. First, we want to introduce the basic categories of IP protection, so that you are at least conversant with the building blocks of this area of law. Second, we want you to understand how IP law furthers the fundamental property policies discussed in Chapter 1 and how courts and legislatures attempt to strike the proper balance between public and private interests in ideas.

THE POLICIES OF INTELLECTUAL PROPERTY PROTECTION

> The Congress shall have Power . . . To promote the Progress of Science and useful Arts, by securing for limited Times to Authors and Inventors the exclusive Right to their respective Writings and Discoveries.
>
> —*U.S. Const. art. I, §8, cl. 8*

Intellectual property protection generally grants the holder the right to exclude others from using her work or invention, in essence giving the owner a monopoly. For copyrights and patents, this protection has a constitutional basis, in the clause authorizing Congress to provide this form of monopoly "for limited Times," in order to promote the progress of science and the arts.

Two of the fundamental property law policies outlined in Chapter 1 provided the impetus for including IP protection in the Constitution. In part, the motive stemmed from fairness, based on natural law theory: a person who works to invent a new product or write a new novel should reap the benefits.

Labor Theory and IP

The labor theory goal of IP protection is captured nicely in a letter from author Joel Barlow to the Continental Congress in 1783:

> There is certainly no kind of property, in the nature of things, so much his own, as the works which a person originates from his own creative imagination. And when he has spent great part of his life in study, wasted his time, his fortune & perhaps his health in improving his knowledge & correcting his taste, it is a principle of natural justice that he should be entitled to the profits arising from the sale of his works as a compensation for his labor in producing them, & his risque of reputation in offering them to the Public.
>
> *—Joel Barlow, Letter to the Continental Congress (1783)*[3]

But as the constitutional language suggests, there is also a strong utilitarian, or economic efficiency, principle at work. We want to reward creative labor, because we want to encourage invention in science and the arts. Just as no farmer will spend the time necessary to plow a field and sow the seed if he cannot be assured of a property right to the harvest, no inventor or writer will invest the time, energy, and money necessary to produce new works unless he can be assured of profiting in the end.

By some estimates, it costs around $4 billion to bring a new drug to market, given the costs of research and development and the high failure rate of potential drug candidates.[4] The cost is similar for the development of new pesticides. No manufacturer will make that investment unless it can be assured of a period of monopoly pricing, free from copycat competition. Similarly, in the trade secret and trademark context, business owners have an incentive to create the best formula for a soft drink or to invest in advertising to build a particular brand, knowing that they alone will enjoy the fruits of that labor.

In the *Federalist Papers*, James Madison noted how happily the policy goals of fairness and economic productivity work together in this context: "The public good fully coincides in both cases [patents and copyrights] with the claims of individuals."[5] Similarly, the Report of the Continental Congress committee assigned to consider the question of copyright protection clearly recognized these two principles, when it declared that "nothing is more properly a man's own than the fruit of his study, and . . . the protection and security of literary property would greatly tend to encourage genius, [and] to promote useful discoveries . . . ."[6]

One of the earliest discussions of the twin policies behind IP law is found in Davoll v. Brown, 7 F. Cas. 197 (C.C. D. Mass. 1845) (No. 3,622), in which the court was called upon to determine whether an inventor had sufficiently described his new bow-flyer invention for purposes of obtaining a patent:

---

[3] Barlow, *supra* note 1.

[4] Matthew Herper, *The Truly Staggering Costs of Inventing New Drugs*, Forbes (Feb. 10, 2012), http://www.forbes.com/sites/matthewherper/2012/02/10/the-truly-staggering-cost-of-inventing-new-drugs/.

[5] The Federalist No. 43, at 239 (James Madison) (Barnes & Noble Classics 2006).

[6] 24 Journals of the Continental Congress 1774-1789, at 326 (Worthington Chauncey Ford ed. 1922).

[A] liberal construction is to be given to a patent, and inventors sustained, if practicable, without a departure from sound principles. Only thus can ingenuity and perseverance be encouraged to exert themselves in this way usefully to the community; and only in this way can we protect intellectual property, the labors of the mind, productions and interests as much a man's own, and as much the fruit of his honest industry, as the wheat he cultivates, or the flocks he rears.

Similarly, Chief Justice John Marshall declared that the patent laws must be construed broadly to achieve their dual purpose: "the reward stipulated for the advantages derived by the public for the exertions of the individual, and . . . a stimulus to those exertions." Grant v. Raymond, 31 U.S. 218, 242 (1832).

Despite the importance of these principles, strong IP protection comes at a substantial social cost. Just as we recognize that the right to exclude, in the context of land, must be balanced against the public interest, we understand that giving a monopoly to the creator means that the public will have limited access to the product or idea, probably at a higher price.

Because monopolies violate our free market principles, the right to exclude others from a creator's ideas is typically limited by time. Eventually, we want ideas to be available to all, so they can be built upon, expanded, and used in new creations. Too much protection may stifle that constructive productivity. For example, over 150 films have been based on Shakespeare's classic tale of Romeo and Juliet. Disney pirated the ideas of classic fairy tales to create many of its cinematic masterpieces. In contrast, no one can create a Broadway production called "Hulk: The Musical," unless Marvel gives its consent.

So, we try to grant the inventor or creator a right to exclude others from her invention or creation only as long as necessary to give a sufficient incentive to produce and to allow her a fair return on her efforts. In some cases, like trademarks or trade secrets, the period lasts as long as the owner continues to use and protect its rights. In addition, we create exceptions, such as *fair use*, that serve other values and do not detract too much from the overall incentive to create. These background principles inform the balance to be struck between public and private rights in intellectual property, which we explore below.

The Cost of IP Protection

Have you noticed that the price of a particular drug goes down when the patent expires and generic versions begin to be offered? The difference between the generic price and the price commanded by the patent holder roughly approximates the patent's cost to the public.

Similarly, think about why the latest Danielle Steele novel costs $28, but you can buy *Great Expectations* for $3.50, not much more than it cost to print. Is that because Steele is a better novelist than Dickens?

B   THE PRINCIPAL SOURCES OF INTELLECTUAL PROPERTY PROTECTION

Intellectual property is a blend of federal and state statutory law, supplemented in a few instances by common law. As noted above, the U.S. Constitution grants the federal government the power to create protections for "Authors and Inventors."[7] Therefore, federal statutes provide the primary protection for patents and copyrights. In general, a federal system of IP protection furthers many of our property goals. It would be tremendously inefficient, for example, to require an inventor to file 50 separate patent applications in 50 different states. Moreover, having one central decision maker provides greater certainty to inventors and authors about how the rules will be interpreted and whether they

> ### Preemption and Displacement
>
> Under the Supremacy Clause of the U.S. Constitution, federal statutes are the "supreme Law of the Land ... any Thing in the Constitution or Laws of any State to the Contrary notwithstanding."[8] Some federal laws *expressly preempt* state law on the same subject. In other cases, preemption is *implied* either because federal regulation is so pervasive that it occupies the field or because state law conflicts with the federal provisions.
>
> In addition, federal statutes *displace* federal common law concerning the same subject under the concept of legislative supremacy.

can expect protection. We will explore below whether the policies are the same in the case of trademarks and trade secrets.

The question of common law copyright. Does the federal copyright statutory scheme supplant state or federal common law claims for the protection of ideas? International News Service v. Associated Press, 248 U.S. 215 (1918), recognized a "quasi-property" right in news gathering. Plaintiff AP, a wire service, invested a great deal of money in investigating and gathering news, which it then sold to its client newspapers. The defendant INS took early editions of newspapers that used AP's news and then rewrote the stories for its own publications, thereby avoiding the need to gather the news itself.

The Court was careful to point out that, while the news story as written was copyrightable, no one could establish a copyright in the news itself. If I hear on the radio that there was an earthquake in China, nothing prevents me from spreading the news to my students in class. As Justice Pitney explained:

> [T]he news element—the information respecting current events contained in the literary production—is not the creation of the writer, but is a report of matters that ordinarily are *publici juris*; it is the history of the day.

Id. at 234. However, the Court found INS's conduct actionable as a species of *unfair competition*:

> In doing this defendant, by its very act, admits that it is taking material that has been acquired by complainant as the result of organization and the expenditure of labor,

---

[7] U.S. Const. art. I, §8, cl. 8.
[8] U.S. Const. art. VI, cl. 2.

skill, and money, and which is salable by complainant for money, and that defendant in appropriating it and selling it as its own is endeavoring to reap where it has not sown, and by disposing of it to newspapers that are competitors of complainant's members is appropriating to itself the harvest of those who have sown.

Id. at 239-40. Does this rationale remind you of the *Haslem* case from Chapter 1, involving manure gathering? How do the policies of economic efficiency and fairness play a role here?

In Erie Railroad v. Tompkins, 304 U.S. 64 (1938), the Supreme Court greatly curtailed the use of federal common law. Nevertheless, some courts have adopted the analysis used in *INS* in allowing a state common law misappropriation claim in similar circumstances. Thus, there is a limited "supplement" to federal copyright law for this "hot news" situation, where plaintiff generates or collects information at considerable expense and defendant uses the information in direct competition. The issue has arisen recently with respect to news "aggregators," web sites that collect headlines and excerpts of news stories. *See, e.g.*, Barclays Capital Inc. v. Theflyonthewall.com, Inc., 650 F.3d 876 (2d Cir. 2011) (Copyright Act preempts state common law misappropriation claim for release of securities recommendations by web site).

Outside of the "hot news" context, courts have determined that the limited copyright protection created by Congress preempts more expansive state common law rights. In Cheney Brothers v. Doris Silk Corp., 35 F.2d 279 (1929), Judge Learned Hand wrote an influential opinion denying a silk fabric designer common law protection against knock-off designs. The copycat designers would simply wait to see which of plaintiff's designs were most popular and then imitate them. At the time, the designer could not get statutory copyright or patent protection for the designs. Certainly, the designers had strong arguments for the common law recognition of their property interests, based on fundamental principles of fairness (labor) and economic efficiency. Just as certainly, the knock-off artists were "reaping where they had not sown."

Nevertheless, Judge Hand noted that the Constitution gave the power to protect copyrights to Congress, not to the courts. In deciding that no common law copyright existed, Judge Hand minimized the importance of the Supreme Court's decision in *INS*. He refused to believe that the Court intended to allow a general common law copyright claim:

> While it is of course true that law ordinarily speaks in general terms, there are cases where the occasion is at once the justification for, and the limit of, what is decided. This appears to us such an instance; we think that no more was covered than situations substantially similar to those then at bar. The difficulties of understanding it otherwise are insuperable. We are to suppose that the court meant to create a sort of common-law patent or copyright for reasons of justice. Either would flagrantly conflict with the scheme which Congress has for more than a century devised to cover the subject-matter.

Cheney Bros. v. Doris Silk Corp., 35 F.2d 279, 280 (2d Cir. 1929). In any case, Judge Hand believed that courts were not equipped to draw the sort of lines the subject requires. For example, how long would the designs be protected? What sort of copying would be prohibited?

> It appears to us incredible that the Supreme Court [in *INS*] should have had in mind any such consequences. To exclude others from the enjoyment of a chattel is one thing; . . . to set up a monopoly . . . gives the author a power over his fellows vastly greater, a power which the Constitution allows only Congress to create.

Id. Thus, the "hot news" situation is a narrow exception to the general rule that federal copyright law preempts state common law protections of ideas and designs.

The material below provides you with a brief introduction to the different species of intellectual property. You will see that IP law is a blend of state and federal statutory protections, with some state common law.

The Sources of IP Law

- For **patent law,** federal statutes provide the exclusive source of protection.
- **Copyright** is also primarily protected by federal statutes, with the "hot news" area supplemented by state common law.
- In **trademark law,** both federal statutes and state law (statutory or common law) may be relevant.
- **Trade secret** protection, on the other hand, is primarily a creature of state law, although federal statutes also provide some criminal remedies for trade secret theft.

---

1. Patent

Under the U.S. Patent Act, 35 U.S.C. §§1-329 (2018), the U.S. Patent and Trademark Office (USPTO) issues patents for the invention or discovery of "any new and useful process, machine, manufacture, or composition of matter, or any new and useful improvement thereof." 35 U.S.C. §101 (2018). A patent gives the inventor or discoverer the exclusive right to make or sell the invention for *a term of 20 years* from the date of application. 35 U.S.C. §154 (2013).

In order to qualify for patent protection, the process or product must meet the requirements of *usefulness*, *novelty*, and *nonobviousness*:

- **Usefulness.** The invention must be capable of performing some beneficial function. Ironman will not get a patent for his awesome flying suit of armor unless the patent office can be convinced it really works.

- **Novelty.** The invention must be new and not known or used by others. If you want to patent a mousetrap, you must truly build a better mousetrap. Mere change in form will not suffice; as Jefferson noted, we don't want to grant a patent for "a square bucket instead of a round one."
- **Nonobviousness.** Even if the invention is novel, it must not be "obvious at the time the invention was made to a person having ordinary skill" in the field. As the Supreme Court said in Hotchkiss v. Greenwood, 11 How. 248, 267 (1851):

  [U]nless more ingenuity and skill . . . were required . . . than were possessed by an ordinary mechanic acquainted with the business, there was an absence of that degree of skill and ingenuity which constitute essential elements of every invention. In other words, the improvement is the work of the skilful [*sic*] mechanic, not that of the inventor.

In 1790, the first year of the Patent Act, Thomas Jefferson, the nation's first patent examiner, approved three patents—for inventions relating to milling flour and making soap and candles. By 1900, over 25,000 patents were awarded annually. In 2015, the USPTO received over 600,000 patent applications and issued over 325,000 patents.

Starting in 1931, the USPTO began patenting plants. The plant must have been altered or invented and must differ from other known plants. So, genetically modified varieties of seed may be patented. As a result, a farmer who uses patented seed can't save some seed from the harvest and plant it next year, because that would violate the patent. In 2015, over 1,000 plant patents were issued.

Designs can also be patented. For example, Apple obtained design patent No. D675,612 for its "ornamental design of an electronic device"—specifically, the rounded corners found on the iPhone. It also has a patent on the iPhone's "slide to unlock" design feature.

2. Copyright

What may be copyrighted? Copyright protects "original works of authorship fixed in any tangible medium of expression." 17 U.S.C. §102 (2018). A broad range of works may be copyrighted, including writings, music, art, photographs, and movies. Since 1989, it is also possible to copyright architectural works, giving the architect protection for the design of a building as embodied in plans or drawings, or in the building itself. 17 U.S.C. §§102(a)(5), (a)(8) (2018).

Copyright requires the work to be *fixed in a tangible form.* Assume you make up a song in your head and decide to sing it for a group of friends. No copyright. But if you write down the music and lyrics to the song, it is protected. If you record the performance of the song, it is also fixed in a tangible medium of expression.

You may register your creation with the Copyright Office, but that is strictly *voluntary*; your work is automatically protected from the moment it is fixed in a tangible form. Registration does have important advantages: it helps inform the public of your copyright claim and provides evidence of it. Owners of registered works also can get statutory damages and litigation costs if they bring a successful infringement claim. It is also not necessary to use the © symbol or otherwise indicate that the material is copyrighted. Nevertheless, such notice informs the public of your claim and helps prevent unintended infringement.

How long does a copyright last? For works created on or after January 1, 1978, copyrights now lapse after the *lifetime of the author plus 70 years*. In the case of anonymous or pseudonymous work, or a work made for hire, the term is 95 years from the date of first publication or 120 years from creation, whichever is shorter.

So, for most books it is not enough to look inside the front cover to see when it was first published; you need to know when the author died. For example, James Michener published *Chesapeake* in 1978, but he died in 1997, so that book will be protected by copyright until 2067. John Irving, who published *The World According to Garp* that same year, is still alive (as of this book's publication), so we don't yet know the date when this copyright term will lapse. An article written by a staff reporter for *The New York Times* published in 2018 will be protected by copyright until 2113, because it falls in the "work for hire" category.

Is that too long? The monopoly period has grown longer over the last century. Under the 1909 Copyright Act, a copyright lasted for 28 years from first publication, although the author could extend it for another 28 years, so it was unlikely to expire before the author did. In 1976, Congress changed the term to the author's life plus 50 years. As a congressional committee noted: "The debate over how long a copyright should last is as old as the oldest copyright statute and will doubtless continue as long as there is a copyright law."[9] In 1998, this statement proved true, as significant controversy surrounded the Copyright Term Extension Act (known derisively as the "Mickey Mouse Protection Act"), which lengthened all the copyright terms by 20 years,[10] making the term the lifetime of the author plus 70 years.

How long should the term be? If you believe IP law should primarily serve to incentivize production of creative works, the question would be whether an author needs 70 years of post-death monopoly to have an adequate incentive to produce. If, however, you believe IP law should serve to reward labor, or is based on a Lockean concept of natural rights, the question might be how long the period should be to ensure a fair return on the author's labor. Remember that the desire to protect the creator's interests must be balanced against the social costs of this protection.

---

[9] H.R. Rep. No. 94-1476, at 1 (1978), *reprinted in* 17 U.S.C. §302 (2006).
[10] Mickey Mouse began life in the 1928 silent film, *Mickey Mouse in Plane Crazy*. Thus, without the extension, the copyright on the character might have expired in 2003. With the extension, Disney can enjoy the copyright until at least 2023.

CASE SUMMARY: Eldred v. Ashcroft, 537 U.S. 186 (2003)

Is there any constitutional limit to Congress's ability to lengthen copyright terms? After all, Article I, §8, cl. 8, suggests that the term must be limited to the time necessary to give authors an adequate incentive to produce: "[t]o promote the Progress of Science . . . by securing [to Authors] for limited Times . . . the exclusive Right to their . . . Writings."

In *Eldred*, plaintiffs challenged the extension of existing copyrights by 20 years under the 1998 Copyright Term Extension Act, arguing that it violated the constitutional language allowing Congress to grant protection only for "limited Times." The Supreme Court refused to be drawn into the debate about the appropriate length of the copyright term: "[W]e are not at liberty to second-guess congressional determinations and policy judgments of this order, however debatable or arguably unwise they may be." 537 U.S., at 208.

Justice Stevens dissented, arguing that there should be a categorical rule against extending existing copyrights, because obviously such extensions cannot serve to incentivize creative production that has already occurred. Moreover, he believed the Court has a responsibility to recognize and protect the public interest involved in such extensions:

> By failing to protect the public interest in free access to the products of inventive and artistic genius—indeed, by virtually ignoring the central purpose of the Copyright/Patent Clause—the Court has quitclaimed to Congress its principal responsibility in this area of the law. Fairly read, the Court has stated that Congress' actions under the Copyright/Patent Clause are, for all intents and purposes, judicially unreviewable.

Id. at 242 (Stevens, J., dissenting). Justice Breyer also dissented, believing that Congress had violated its *limited* constitutional authority to grant monopolies to authors.

> The economic effect of this 20-year extension—the longest blanket extension since the Nation's founding—is to make the copyright term not limited, but virtually perpetual. Its primary legal effect is to grant the extended term not to authors, but to their heirs, estates, or corporate successors. And most importantly, its practical effect is not to promote, but to inhibit, the progress of "Science"—by which word the Framers meant learning or knowledge. . . .

Id. at 243 (Breyer, J., dissenting) (citing E. Walterscheid, The Nature of the Intellectual Property Clause: A Study in Historical Perspective 125-26 (2002)). Justice Breyer emphasized the *public costs of copyright protection*, which he termed "especially serious here." The public will have to pay 20 more years of royalties "that may be higher than necessary to evoke creation." *Id.*, at 248. In addition, having to seek the permission of the author may significantly inhibit the use of the work in research, writing, or teaching.

Do you agree that a *perpetual* copyright would be constitutionally unsound? If so, is there a length short of perpetuity that would also be problematic? Should the Court attempt to determine where that line should be drawn?

3. Trademark

The idea behind a trademark is to allow businesses to identify their products and services and distinguish them from others. In addition to helping the business by protecting its reputation and investment in a particular mark, this protection also helps consumers, who know that when they buy a product with a certain brand, they are getting the real thing.

Although trademarks also may be protected by state common law and statutes, the main source of trademark law is the federal Lanham Act, 15 U.S.C. §§1051-1129 (2018). The Lanham Act protects any *word*, *name*, *symbol*, or *device* used by a manufacturer or merchant to identify and distinguish its goods from others. 15 U.S.C. §1127 (2018). The right to a particular mark can be acquired only by actually using it in commerce. Restatement (Third) of Unfair Competition §18 (1995).

Registration of the mark with the U.S. Patent and Trademark Office provides prima facie evidence of the ownership and validity of a mark. After registration, the mark owner may give notice to others by displaying the ® symbol; if no notice is given, the owner can still enjoin the infringement, but will have to prove that an infringer knew the trademark was protected in order to get damages.

Even without registration, simply using a mark in commerce gives you certain rights. An unregistered trademark may be protected under state common law, for example. In addition, the Lanham Act prohibits the use of words or symbols that may mislead consumers regarding the origin of goods and services. 15 U.S.C. §1125 (2018). So Chevrolet could prevent another company from selling "Camaro" cars, even if it had never registered its trademark.

The range of trademark protection is quite broad, encompassing almost anything that identifies a particular product or company. For example, Coca-Cola trademarked the distinctive shape of its bottle, Microsoft trademarked the four-second sound a computer makes when Windows starts up, and even a particular scent may be trademarked.

Distinctive

A bottle is obviously functional, and if you invented a new bottle that was truly different (novel, nonobvious, and useful), such as the vortex bottle with special grooves in the neck, which Miller Lite debuted in 2010, you could get a patent.[11] A *trademark* is available if the bottle has a *distinctive* design.[12]

A good example is Coca-Cola's "contour" bottle, with its pinched-in waist, which is recognized all over the world. The bottle was designed in 1915

---

[11] In fact, the inventor, Owens-Illinois, Inc., has a patent pending on the vortex bottle.

[12] There is some overlap here now that you can also get a design patent. Coca-Cola had a design patent on its original bottle as well.

when the company asked its suppliers to create a new bottle that would be instantly recognizable even in the dark. Although its design is trademarked, Coke lost a European trademark infringement suit in 2010 against Pepsi's use of a "Carolina" bottle, with a similar pinched-in waist. The court noted that the "scallops" on the bottle were horizontal while Coke's were vertical.

To be protectable, a word or logo must be "distinctive," which means it must distinguish the goods or services of your company from those of others. In other words, we would not want to grant an automobile manufacturer a trademark on the word "car." A word or symbol may be *inherently distinctive* in one of three ways:

- **Fanciful.** A mark consisting of a word that was created especially for this product, such as "Clorox" for bleach.
- **Arbitrary.** The word exists, but it has no relationship to the particular product it is used to identify. For example, Apple can be trademarked for selling computers and iPods, but not for selling apples.
- **Suggestive.** A word that suggests the features of the product, but is not descriptive of the product. For example, Coppertone is suggestive of suntan oil.

If a word is *descriptive* of the product or service, it is protectable only if it has acquired *secondary meaning* in the minds of consumers. For example, "Weight Watchers" is certainly descriptive, but the public associates it with a particular organization and it is therefore eligible for trademark protection.

If a word is (or becomes) *generic*, it is not entitled to trademark protection. For example, "aspirin" was originally a trademark of the German pharmaceutical company Bayer AG (and still is trademarked in many countries), but lost its U.S. trademark protection by becoming a common name for pain relievers. The fastener everyone calls a "zipper" was originally the trademark of B.F. Goodrich.

Trademark protection lasts as long as the company continues to use the mark for its product or services. If the trademark holder *abandons* the mark by non-use with no intent to resume use, it is no longer protected. The holder must also be *reasonably vigilant* in taking action against infringement, or it may be deemed to have waived or abandoned its rights.

In addition to protecting and incentivizing companies that produce unique products or services, trademark law also protects consumers who may be confused or misled by products with similar names or logos.

4. Trade Secret

Unlike the forms of IP protection described above, which are principally based on federal law, trade secret is primarily a creature of state law. About 40 states have adopted the Uniform Trade Secrets Act (UTSA), which defines a trade secret as:

[I]nformation . . . that: (i) derives independent economic value, actual or potential, from not being generally known to, and not being readily ascertainable by proper means by, other persons who can obtain economic value from its disclosure or use, and (ii) is the subject of [reasonable] efforts . . . to maintain its secrecy.

Uniform Law Commission, UTSA §1(4) (1985). The UTSA provides civil remedies for trade secret violations, including injunctions and damages. Federal and state laws also criminalize the theft of trade secrets. *See* 18 U.S.C. §1832 (2018).

Examples of trade secrets include:

- **Formulas** — such as the recipe for Coca-Cola or Kentucky Fried Chicken.
- **Pattern, plans, or designs** — such as a company's marketing strategy or design for its new manufacturing facility.
- **Processes or physical devices** — such as a unique way of separating cream from milk or spraying paint on cars.

Some of these items might be patentable as well, but trade secret can protect them before a patent application is filed, or provide protection in addition to or instead of a patent. Trade secret has some *advantages* over patent protection:

- The *duration* of trade secret protection is unlimited, as long as the owner continues to take reasonable measures to maintain secrecy.
- A patent requires *disclosure* of the invention on the patent application, whereas trade secret is kept confidential.

The *disadvantage*, however, is that a trade secret is lost if someone else figures out the same thing independently or by reverse engineering. The protection is only against illegal *acquisition* of the secret. In contrast, a patent (or copyright) guarantees the exclusive rights to the invention or creation for a specific period of time.

■ PROBLEMS: RECOGNIZING IP ISSUES

Pepto Bismol
Photo by Darren Kelly

1. How might the four types of IP protection apply to Pepto-Bismol', a well-known upset stomach reliever, which has the active ingredient bismuth subsalicylate? The product was invented back in 1901 by a New York doctor and is now sold by Procter & Gamble (P&G). Which types of IP protection might be involved in producing and marketing this product?

   - ■ **Patent.** Can P&G get a patent for the Pepto-Bismol formula?
   - ■ **Copyright.** Can P&G get copyright protection for its ad copy, its television advertisements, and its jingle for Pepto-Bismol?
   - ■ **Trademark.** Can P&G get trademark protection for the product name, Pepto-Bismol? How about the logo on the box and the usual shape of its bottle?
   - ■ **Trade secret.** Can you think of anything associated with the Pepto-Bismol product that might be protected by trade secret? *See, e.g.,* Procter & Gamble Co. v. Alberto Culver Co., 1999 WL 319224 (N.D. Ill. 1999) (P&G alleged former employee pirated marketing plan).

Color Trademarks

Can P&G also get protection for Pepto-Bismol's distinctive pink color, at least for use in stomach remedies? In 1995, the U.S. Supreme Court ruled in *Qualitex v. Jacobson Products Co.* that color can be trademarked if it has acquired a secondary meaning and is not functional.[13] Owens-Corning was able to get protection for pink house insulation, for example, because the color had nothing to do with its function.[14] In Pepto-Bismol's case, a court in 1959 refused to protect Pepto-Bismol's color as a trademark, noting that the pink color might have a soothing quality that was functional.[15]

More recently, Christian Louboutin was able to get trademark protection for the distinctive red color it uses on the soles of its shoes. Christian Louboutin S.A. v. Yves Saint Laurent America, 696 F.3d 206 (2d Cir. 2012).

---

2. **Identifying IP protections.** In each of the following situations, advise your client as to the IP protections involved:

   a) A company called Testinator has developed new computer software for taking exams on computers.

   b) Your roommate has written a movie screenplay she says is "sure to be a hit." She wants to send it to a friend of hers in Hollywood but is afraid her ideas will be stolen.

   c) Dr. Faust genetically modifies a mouse, such that it is unusually susceptible to cancer. He believes his "Faust-mouse" will be incredibly valuable for researchers testing cancer treatments. He would like to be the exclusive provider of these mice.

   d) A local restaurant decides to collect the email addresses of its customers so it can send them periodic messages with coupons or specials. One of the cooks copies the database. She then opens her

---

[13] Qualitex Co. v. Jacobson Prods. Co., 514 U.S. 159 (1995).
[14] In re Owens-Corning Fiberglas Corp., 774 F.2d 1116 (Fed. Cir. 1985).
[15] Norwich Pharm. Co. v. Sterling Drug, Inc., 271 F.2d 569, 572 (2d Cir. 1959).

own restaurant and sends out an email, using the email database, to announce the grand opening.

Practice Tip

How would you advise a company to ensure that its trade secrets are adequately protected? Remember that the owner of a trade secret must make reasonable efforts to protect its secrecy.

- The company will want to have employment agreements that prevent the dissemination of confidential business information.
- Non-compete agreements: In a case where a key employee leaves to work for a competitor, the company will want to ensure that none of its secrets are being used by the former employee.

   An example of an employment agreement with a trade secret provision can be found on the Simulation.

---

3. Assume that one of your classmates secretly videotapes part of your professor's lecture today and wants to post it online. Can your professor prevent it, because the lecture was a copyrighted performance? Is it different from videotaping an NFL game and posting it online?

THE BALANCE OF INTERESTS IN INTELLECTUAL PROPERTY LAW

As we discussed earlier, the primary policies behind intellectual property laws include rewarding creators for their labor as well as incentivizing that creation. In addition, protections such as trademarks prevent consumer confusion over the nature and origin of products and services. Just as we discovered with other types of property, a strong right to exclude has social costs that must be weighed in the balance.

1. The Balance of Interests in Trademark Law

The next case illustrates how trademark law attempts to balance these interests and explores how giving one party monopoly power over a particular word might affect other people. Is there any constitutional limit to Congress's ability to grant a private entity the *exclusive right to use* certain words?

SAN FRANCISCO ARTS & ATHLETICS, INC. v. U.S. OLYMPIC COMMITTEE

483 U.S. 522 (1987)
Supreme Court of the United States

[In the Amateur Sports Act of 1978, Congress granted the United States Olympic Committee (USOC) the exclusive right to certain commercial and promotional uses of the word "Olympic." San Francisco Arts and Athletics (SFAA), a nonprofit corporation, promoted an event to be held in 1982 called the "Gay Olympic Games." In the past, the USOC had authorized various other uses of its trademark, such as the Special Olympics and the Junior Olympics, both of which Congress encouraged. However, in this case USOC requested that SFAA discontinue its use of the word "Olympic" in connection with this event. It had similarly denied senior citizens the right to use the "Golden Age Olympics." When SFAA refused to comply, the USOC brought suit to enjoin the use.]

Justice POWELL delivered the opinion of the Court:

. . . This Court has recognized that "[n]ational protection of trademarks is desirable . . . because trade-marks foster competition and the maintenance of quality by securing to the producer the benefits of good reputation." Park 'N Fly, Inc. v. Dollar Park and Fly, Inc., 469 U.S. 189, 198 (1985). In the Lanham Act, 15 U.S.C. §1051 et seq., Congress established a system for protecting such trademarks. Section 45 of the Lanham Act defines a trademark as "any word, name, symbol, or device or any combination thereof adopted and used by a manufacturer or merchant to identify and distinguish his goods, including a unique product, from those manufactured or sold by others." 15 U.S.C. §1127 (1982 ed., Supp. III). Under §32 of the Lanham Act, the owner of a trademark is protected from un-authorized uses that are "likely to cause confusion, or to cause mistake, or to deceive." §1114(1)(a). Section 33 of the Lanham Act grants several statutory defenses to an alleged trademark infringer. §1115.

The protection granted to the USOC's use of the Olympic words and symbols [in §110 of the Amateur Sports Act] differs from the normal trademark protection in two respects: the USOC need not prove that a contested use is likely to cause confusion, and an unauthorized user of the word does not have available the normal statutory defenses. The SFAA argues, in effect, that the differences between the Lanham Act and §110 are of constitutional dimension. First, the SFAA contends that the word "Olympic" is a generic[16] word that could not gain trademark protection under the Lanham Act. The SFAA argues that this prohibition is constitutionally required and thus that the First Amendment prohibits Congress from granting a trademark in the word "Olympic." Second, the SFAA argues that the First Amendment prohibits Congress from granting exclusive use

---

[16] A common descriptive name of a product or service is generic. Because a generic name by definition does not distinguish the identity of a particular product, it cannot be registered as a trademark under the Lanham Act. . . .

of a word absent a requirement that the authorized user prove that an unauthorized use is likely to cause confusion. We address these contentions in turn.

A.

This Court has recognized that words are not always fungible, and that the suppression of particular words "run[s] a substantial risk of suppressing ideas in the process." Cohen v. California, 403 U.S. 15, 26 (1971). The SFAA argues that this principle prohibits Congress from granting the USOC exclusive control of uses of the word "Olympic," a word that the SFAA views as generic.[17] Yet this recognition always has been balanced against the principle that when a word acquires value "as the result of organization and the expenditure of labor, skill, and money" by an entity, that entity constitutionally may obtain a limited property right in the word. . . .

There is no need in this case to decide whether Congress ever could grant a private entity exclusive use of a generic word. Congress reasonably could conclude that the commercial and promotional value of the word "Olympic" was the product of the USOC's "own talents and energy, the end result of much time, effort, and expense." Zacchini v. Scripps-Howard Broadcasting Co., 433 U.S. 562, 575 (1977). The USOC, together with respondent International Olympic Committee (IOC), have used the word "Olympic" at least since 1896, when the modern Olympic Games began. . . . Under the IOC Charter, the USOC is the national olympic committee for the United States with the sole authority to represent the United States at the Olympic Games. Pursuant to this authority, the USOC has used the Olympic words and symbols extensively in this country to fulfill its object under the Olympic Charter of "ensur[ing] the development and safeguarding of the Olympic Movement and sport." Olympic Charter, Rule 24.

The history of the origins and associations of the word "Olympic" demonstrates the meritlessness of the SFAA's contention that Congress simply plucked a generic word out of the English vocabulary and granted its exclusive use to the USOC. Congress reasonably could find that since 1896, the word "Olympic" has acquired what in trademark law is known as a secondary meaning—it "has become distinctive of [the USOC's] goods in commerce." Lanham Act, §2(f), 15 U.S.C. §1052(f). *See* Park 'N Fly, Inc. v. Dollar Park and Fly, Inc., 469 U.S., at 194. The right to adopt and use such a word "to distinguish the goods or property [of] the person whose mark it is, to the exclusion of use by all other persons, has been long recognized." *Trade-Mark Cases*, supra, 100 U.S. (10 Otto), at 92. Because

---

[17] This grant by statute of exclusive use of distinctive words and symbols by Congress is not unique. Violation of some of these statutes may result in criminal penalties. See, e.g., 18 U.S.C. §705 (veterans' organizations); §706 (American National Red Cross); §707 (4-H Club); §711 ("Smokey Bear"); §711a ("Woodsy Owl"). *See also* FTC v. A.P.W. Paper Co., 328 U.S. 193 (1946) (reviewing application of Red Cross statute). Others, like the USOC statute, provide for civil enforcement. *See, e.g.,* 36 U.S.C. §18c (Daughters of the American Revolution); §27 (Boy Scouts); §36 (Girl Scouts); §1086 (Little League Baseball); §3305 (1982 ed., Supp. III) (American National Theater and Academy).

Congress reasonably could conclude that the USOC has distinguished the word "Olympic" through its own efforts, Congress' decision to grant the USOC a limited property right in the word "Olympic" falls within the scope of trademark law protections, and thus certainly within constitutional bounds.

B.

... In this case, the SFAA claims that its use of the word "Olympic" was intended to convey a political statement about the status of homosexuals in society.[18]

Thus, the SFAA claims that in this case §110 suppresses political speech.

By prohibiting the use of one word for particular purposes, neither Congress nor the USOC has prohibited the SFAA from conveying its message. The SFAA held its athletic event in its planned format under the names "Gay Games I" and "Gay Games II" in 1982 and 1986, respectively. See n.2, supra. Nor is it clear that §110 restricts purely expressive uses of the word "Olympic." Section 110 restricts only the manner in which the SFAA may convey its message....

One reason for Congress to grant the USOC exclusive control of the word "Olympic," as with other trademarks, is to ensure that the USOC receives the benefit of its own efforts so that the USOC will have an incentive to continue to produce a "quality product," that, in turn, benefits the public. See 1 J. McCarthy, Trademarks and Unfair Competition §2:1, pp. 44-47 (1984). But in the special circumstance of the USOC, Congress has a broader public interest in promoting, through the activities of the USOC, the participation of amateur athletes from the United States in "the great four-yearly sport festival, the Olympic Games." Olympic Charter, Rule 1 (1985). ... Section 110 directly advances these governmental interests by supplying the USOC with the means to raise money to support the Olympics and encourages the USOC's activities by ensuring that it will receive the benefits of its efforts.

The restrictions of §110 are not broader than Congress reasonably could have determined to be necessary to further these interests. Section 110 primarily applies to all uses of the word "Olympic" to induce the sale of goods or services. Although the Lanham Act protects only against confusing uses, Congress' judgment respecting a certain word is not so limited. Congress reasonably could conclude that most commercial uses of the Olympic words and symbols are likely to be confusing. It also could determine that unauthorized uses, even if not confusing, nevertheless may harm the USOC by lessening the distinctiveness and thus the commercial value of the marks. See Schechter, The Rational Basis of

---

[18] According to the SFAA's president, the Gay Olympic Games would have offered three "very important opportunities":

    "1) To provide a healthy recreational alternative to a suppressed minority.

    "2) To educate the public at large towards a more reasonable characterization of gay men and women.

    "3) To attempt, through athletics, to bring about a positive and gradual assimilation of gay men and women, as well as gays and non-gays, and to diminish the ageist, sexist and racist divisiveness existing in all communities regardless of sexual orientation." App. 93.

... He thought "[t]he term 'Olympic' best describe[d] [the SFAA's] undertaking" because it embodied the concepts of "peace, friendship and positive social interaction." Id., at 99.

Trademark Protection, 40 Harv. L. Rev. 813, 825 (1927) (one injury to a trademark owner may be "the gradual whittling away or dispersion of the identity and hold upon the public mind of the mark or name" by non-confusing uses).

. . . Here, the SFAA's proposed use of the word "Olympic" was a clear attempt to exploit the imagery and goodwill created by the USOC.

[The Court then determined that the USOC was not a state actor for purposes of the equal protection provision of the Fifth Amendment.]

[Justices O'Connor and Blackmun dissented in part on the ground that USOC was a state actor.]

Justice BRENNAN, with whom Justice MARSHALL joins, dissenting.

[The dissent first argues that the action of USOC was government action and therefore subject to the Equal Protection Clause.]

A.

. . . The Amateur Sports Act is substantially overbroad in two respects. First, it grants the USOC the remedies of a commercial trademark to regulate the use of the word "Olympic," but refuses to interpret the Act to incorporate the defenses to trademark infringement provided in the Lanham Act. These defenses are essential safeguards which prevent trademark power from infringing upon constitutionally protected speech. Second, the Court construes §110(a)(4) to grant the USOC unconstitutional authority to prohibit use of "Olympic" in the "promotion of theatrical and athletic events," even if the promotional activities are noncommercial or expressive.

Trademark protection has been carefully confined to the realm of commercial speech by two important limitations in the Lanham Act. First, the danger of substantial regulation of noncommercial speech is diminished by denying enforcement of a trademark against uses of words that are not likely "to cause confusion, to cause mistake, or to deceive." See 15 U.S.C. §1066. Confusion occurs when consumers make an incorrect mental association between the involved commercial products or their producers. See E. Vandenburgh, Trademark Law and Procedure §5.20, p. 139 (2d ed. 1968). In contrast, §110(a)(4) regulates even nonconfusing uses of "Olympic." For example, it may be that while SFAA's use of the word "Olympic" would draw attention to certain similarities between the "Gay Olympic Games" and the "Olympic Games," its use might nevertheless not confuse consumers. Because §110 does not incorporate the requirement that a defendant's use of the word be confusing to consumers, it regulates an extraordinary range of noncommercial speech.

. . .

A key Lanham Act requirement that limits the impact of trademarks on noncommercial speech is the rule that a trademark violation occurs only when an offending trademark is applied to commercial goods and services. See 15 U.S.C. §§1066 and 1127. The Amateur Sports Act is not similarly qualified. Section 110(a)

(4) "allows the USOC to prohibit the use of 'Olympic' for promotion of theatrical and athletic events," even if such uses "go beyond the 'strictly business' context." . . .

While the USOC has unquestioned authority to enforce its "Olympic" trademark against the SFAA, §110(a)(4) gives it additional authority to regulate a substantial amount of noncommercial speech that serves to promote social and political ideas. The SFAA sponsors a number of nonprofit-making theatrical and athletic events, including concerts, film screenings, and plays. These public events are aimed at educating the public about society's alleged discrimination based on sexual orientation, age, sex, and nationality. App. 93-99. In conjunction with these events, the SFAA distributes literature describing the meaning of the Gay Olympic Games. References to "Olympic" in this literature were deleted in response to the injunction, because of §110's application to the promotion of athletic and theatrical events. Id., at 88-89, 94, 97.

B.

The Court concedes that "some" uses of "Olympic" prohibited under §110 may involve expressive speech. But it contends that "[b]y prohibiting the use of one word for particular purposes, neither Congress nor the USOC has prohibited the SFAA from conveying its message. . . . Section 110 restricts only the manner in which the SFAA may convey its message." Section 110(a)(4) cannot be regarded as a mere time, place, and manner statute, however. By preventing the use of the word "Olympic," the statute violates the First Amendment by prohibiting dissemination of a message for which there is no adequate translation.

In Cohen v. California, 403 U.S. 15 (1971), we rejected the very notion advanced today by the Court when considering the censorship of a single four-letter expletive:

> [W]e cannot indulge the facile assumption that one can forbid particular words without also running a substantial risk of suppressing ideas in the process. Indeed, governments might soon seize upon the censorship of particular words as a convenient guise for banning the expression of unpopular views. We have been able . . . to discern little social benefit that might result from running the risk of opening the door to such grave results.

Id., at 26.

The Amateur Sports Act gives a single entity exclusive control over a wide range of uses of a word with a deep history in the English language and Western culture. Here, the SFAA intended, by use of the word "Olympic," to promote a realistic image of homosexual men and women that would help them move into the mainstream of their communities. As Judge Kozinski observed in dissent in the Court of Appeals, just as a jacket reading "I Strongly Resent the Draft" would not have conveyed Cohen's message, so a title such as "The Best and Most Accomplished Amateur Gay Athletes Competition" would not serve as an adequate translation of petitioners' message. 789 F.2d 1319, 1321 (CA9 1986). Indeed, because individual words carry "a life and force of their own," translations never fully capture the sense of the original. The First Amendment protects more than the right to a mere translation. By prohibiting use of the word "Olympic," the USOC substantially infringes upon the SFAA's right to communicate ideas.

C.

The Amateur Sports Act also violates the First Amendment because it restricts speech in a way that is not content neutral. A wide variety of groups apparently wish to express particular sociopolitical messages through the use of the word "Olympic," but the Amateur Sports Act singles out certain of the groups for favorable treatment. As the Court observes, Congress encouraged the USOC to allow the use of "Olympic" in athletic competitions held for youth ("Junior Olympics" and "Explorer Olympics") and handicapped persons ("Special Olympics"), 36 U.S.C. §374(13), while leaving to the USOC's unfettered discretion the question whether other groups may use it.

The statute thus encourages the USOC to endorse particular noncommercial messages, while prohibiting others. Such a scheme is unacceptable under the First Amendment. "[A]bove all else, the First Amendment means that government has no power to restrict expression because of its message, its ideas, its subject matter, or its content." Police Department of Chicago v. Mosley, 408 U.S. 92, 95, (1972). . . .

I dissent.

■ POINTS TO CONSIDER

1. **The power of language.** In the case cited by both the majority and dissent, *Cohen v. California*, Cohen was convicted of disturbing the peace because he wore a jacket that said "F**k the Draft" inside the Los Angeles courthouse.[19] The Supreme Court overturned Cohen's conviction, holding that his First Amendment rights were violated. How does the Supreme Court's recognition of the power of certain words inform the opinions in the *USOC* case?

2. **The purpose of trademark protection.** What policies does the majority identify that are promoted by granting the exclusive control over the word "Olympic" to the USOC? What policies provide the limits to granting that degree of control? Are they in any way different from the fundamental property policies considered in Chapter 1? Is trademark protection essentially a "rule of capture" applied to words and symbols? How are words different from foxes or oil?

---

[19] Cohen v. California, 403 U.S. 15 (1971).

3. **Generics.** Has the word "Olympic" become generic since the IOC first started using the term in 1896 (or since the Greeks started using it in 776 B.C.)? In his dissent from the Ninth Circuit's refusal to hear the case en banc, Judge Alex Kozinski noted that over 200 businesses and other entities in Los Angeles and Manhattan had telephone book listings starting with the word "Olympic."[20] Why do generic terms not receive trademark protection under the Lanham Act?

CASE SUMMARY: Louis Vuitton Malletier S.A. v. Haute Diggity Dog, 507 F.3d 252 (4th Cir. 2007)

Louis Vuitton Malletier (LVM) manufactures luxury luggage and handbags. LVM has a trademark not only for its name, but also for its stylized monogram "LV" and for its canvas design, which features repetitions of the monogram along with four-pointed stars and four-pointed flowers inset in circles. At the time of the suit, Vuitton handbags retailed for between $995 and $4,500 and LVM had spent over $48 million over a three-year period marketing products using its marks and designs.

Haute Diggity Dog (Dog) manufactures and markets nationally a line of pet chew toys that parody famous products. There is a "Furcedes," a stuffed car that imitates Mercedes; a "Dog Perignon," a stuffed champagne bottle that imitates Dom Perignon; and even a "Sniffany & Co.," a stuffed toy imitating the jewelry box of Tiffany & Co. At issue in this suit was a plush toy called "Chewy Vuiton," a stuffed toy handbag that loosely resembled the Vuitton version, using a "CV" design instead of "LV."

LVM sued Dog for trademark infringement. There was no doubt that LVM had a valid and protectable trademark and that the chew toy was an imitation of it. However, LVM also had to show that Dog's use of the mark was likely to cause consumer confusion. If the item is instead a *successful parody*, consumers will probably not be confused. In order to be a successful parody, the item must convey some element of satire or amusement.

The court held that the chew toys were indeed successful parodies: "The dog toy irreverently presents haute couture as an object for casual canine destruction." 507 F.3d, at 261. In the parody context, the strength of LVM's mark did not aid its case, because the fact that its design is readily recognized contributed to the success of the parody. The differences between the dog toy and real LVM products were sufficient to ensure that consumers would not believe the toy was a real Vuitton.

---

[20] International Olympic Comm. v. S.F. Arts & Athletics, 789 F.2d 1319, 1326 n.4 (9th Cir. 1986) (Kozinski, J., dissenting).

■ POINTS TO CONSIDER

1. **The balance of interests.** LVM has spent billions of dollars building consumer recognition of its trademarks, which have been in use since 1896. Is it fair to allow another company to take advantage of that work? Is it like allowing Pierson to scoop up the fox chased by Post? How does Dog's use of the mark harm LVM, if at all? Why does the element of satire make imitating a product acceptable?

2. **Right of publicity.** In White v. Samsung Electronics America, Inc., 971 F.2d 1395 (9th Cir. 1992), the court held that Vanna White could sue Samsung for running a humorous ad depicting a robot that resembled White turning letters on a game board much like the "Wheel of Fortune." The court found there was a common law right of publicity in California, which prevented exploitation of a celebrity's persona for profit without permission. The court emphasized the labor theory, noting that the creation of celebrity identity value was the result of "[c]onsiderable energy and ingenuity."[21]

   Is *White* distinguishable from *Louis Vuitton*? Does the "personhood" element of property law explain the distinction?

   Judge Kozinski, dissenting from the court's refusal to rehear the *White* case en banc, thought the decision was "a classic case of overprotection,"[22] which upset the balance between private and public rights and threatened to squelch creative endeavors:

   > Intellectual property law assures authors the right to their original expression, but encourages others to build freely on the ideas that underlie it. This result is neither unfair nor unfortunate: It is the means by which intellectual property law advances the progress of science and art.

   Id. at 1517. In what ways would protecting the interests of LVM and Vanna White hurt the public interest?

2. The Balance of Interests in Copyright Law

The Olympics and Louis Vuitton cases help us understand that granting monopoly power over intellectual property does have social costs and that the rights should be carefully tailored to promote the public interest. Is the balance of interests the same in copyright law?

The federal Copyright Act contains an exception for "fair use" of copyrighted material, which codifies judicial decisions that had long recognized

---

[21] White v. Samsung Electronics Am., 971 F.2d 1395, 1399 (9th Cir. 1992).
[22] White v. Samsung Electronics Am., 989 F.2d 1512, 1514 (9th Cir. 1993) (Kozonski, J., dissenting).

this exception. This exception attempts to strike a balance between the legitimate public interest in using copyrighted material and the creator's right to exclude:

> [T]he fair use of a copyrighted work, including such use by reproduction in copies or phonorecords or by any other means specified by that section, for purposes such as criticism, comment, news reporting, teaching (including multiple copies for classroom use), scholarship, or research, is not an infringement of copyright. In determining whether the use made of a work in any particular case is a fair use the factors to be considered shall include—
>
> (1) the purpose and character of the use, including whether such use is of a commercial nature or is for nonprofit educational purposes;
> (2) the nature of the copyrighted work;
> (3) the amount and substantiality of the portion used in relation to the copyrighted work as a whole; and
> (4) the effect of the use upon the potential market for or value of the copyrighted work.

17 U.S.C. §107 (2018). For this reason, a book review in *The New Yorker* that describes the plot and reproduces several paragraphs of the latest novel by J.K. Rowling is not a violation of the author's copyright.

The next case illustrates how the *parody exception* to copyright helps courts strike the balance in the copyright fair use context.

CASE SUMMARY: Campbell v. Acuff-Rose Music, Inc., 510 U.S. 569 (1994)

In a notable Supreme Court case applying this exception, 2 Live Crew recorded a parody of Roy Orbison's song, "Pretty Woman," using a recognizable, hip-hop version of the tune, but substituting lyrics like "big hairy woman" for the original. Campbell v. Acuff-Rose Music, Inc., 510 U.S. 569 (1994). The copyright holder sued, but 2 Live Crew claimed its version was a parody, which constituted "fair use" of the original. The Supreme Court held, for the first time, that a parody may constitute fair use:

> The central purpose of this investigation is to see, in Justice Story's words, whether the new work merely "supersede[s] the objects" of the original creation . . . or instead adds something new, with a further purpose or different character, altering the first with new expression, meaning, or message; it asks, in other words, whether and to what extent the new work is "transformative." Although such transformative use is not absolutely necessary for a finding of fair use, the goal of copyright, to promote science and the arts, is generally furthered by the creation of transformative works. Such works thus lie at the heart of the fair use doctrine's guarantee of breathing space within the confines of copyright, and the more transformative the new work, the less will be the significance of other factors, like commercialism, that may weigh against a finding of fair use.

Id. at 579 (citations omitted). A parody must make some comment on the original, and the Court agreed with the district court that 2 Live Crew's song "derisively demonstrates how bland and banal the Roy Orbison song seems to them." *Id.* at 582. The Court refused to base its judgment on its perception of the parody's quality, quoting Justice Holmes: "It would be a dangerous undertaking for persons trained only to the law to constitute themselves final judges of the worth of [a work]." *Id.*

■ POINT TO CONSIDER

The policy of parody. Why does the fact that 2 Live Crew is "commenting" on Roy Orbison's song give them the right to use it without permission? Many hip-hop songs use "samples" of other songs. When Eminem uses the chorus from Aerosmith's "Dream On" in his song "Sing for the Moment," does it fall within the fair use exception?

■ PROBLEMS

Apply the fair use factors outlined above to the following problems:

1. Assume you are preparing PowerPoint slides for a class presentation on copyright law and you want to use a picture of the Chewy Vuiton toy from Haute Diggity Dog's online catalog in order to illustrate your explanation of the case. Is that fair use?

2. Steve Vander Ark created a book entitled "The Lexicon," which is an encyclopedia of the Harry Potter book series. The entries (over 2,400) include descriptions of the people, places, spells, and creatures contained in the books. Does that constitute fair use of J.K. Rowling's work? *See* Warner Bros. Entm't, Inc. v. RDR Books, 575 F. Supp. 2d 513 (S.D.N.Y. 2008).

3. Your garage band wants to perform a country version of the hard rock anthem "Highway to Hell," by AC/DC. Does the fact that you have "transformed" the original work into something different protect you from a copyright

> ### When Law School Hypo Becomes Reality
>
> Law students at the University of Pennsylvania had their own run-in with Louis Vuitton in 2012. For a school-sponsored event called "IP Issues in Fashion Law," a student group came up with a poster and invitation that imitated the Louis Vuitton design—in place of the interlocking LV they used TM (for trademark) and replaced some of the four-leaf flowers in circles with the copyright symbol ©. Louis Vuitton sent the school a "cease and desist" letter, calling the action "egregious" and a "serious willful infringement." Do you agree?
>
> To see the poster, along with the cease and desist letter and Penn's response, go to the Simulation.

infringement claim? Does it matter that you are performing it at a high school dance, where you and the band will net $50 each?

4. Lombardo writes a play called Who's Holiday based on the characters made famous in "How the Grinch Stole Christmas!" by Dr. Seuss. The play features a down-and-out 45-year-old named Cindy-Lou, who lives in a trailer in the hills by Mount Crumpit. Cindy-Lou speaks in rhyming couplets, drinks a lot of hard liquor, abuses prescription pills, and smokes "Who Hash." She recounts her story, including her sexual relationship with the Grinch. Can the copyright holder for Seuss stop the play? *See* Lombardo v. Dr. Seuss Enter., L.P., 279 F.Supp.3d 497 (S.D.N.Y. 2017).

3. The Balance of Interests in Patent Law

We have considered the basic balance of interests presented by copyright and trademark protection issues. We now turn to patent law, to see whether the balance is any different.

The introductory material gave you the basic elements of patentability: the inventor or discoveror of "any new and useful process, machine, manufacture, or composition of matter, or any new and useful improvement thereof" is given the exclusive right to make or sell the invention for a period of 20 years. 35 U.S.C. §§101, 154 (2018). To be patentable, the process or product must be *useful, novel,* and *nonobvious.*

Can the discoverer of a naturally occurring substance acquire a patent to it, especially when that discovery involves a great expenditure of effort? The following case elucidates the goals of patent law in the important context of genetics.

ASSOCIATION FOR MOLECULAR PATHOLOGY v. MYRIAD GENETICS, INC.

569 U.S. 576 (2013)
Supreme Court of the United States

Justice THOMAS delivered the opinion of the Court.

Respondent Myriad Genetics, Inc. (Myriad), discovered the precise location and sequence of two human genes, mutations of which can substantially increase the risks of breast and ovarian cancer. Myriad obtained a number of patents based upon its discovery. This case involves claims from three of them and requires us to resolve whether a naturally occurring segment of deoxyribonucleic acid (DNA) is patent eligible under 35 U.S.C. §101 by virtue of its isolation from the rest of the human genome. We also address the patent eligibility of synthetically created DNA known as complementary DNA (cDNA), which contains the same protein-coding information found in a segment of natural DNA but omits portions within the DNA segment that do not code for proteins. For the reasons that follow, we hold that a naturally occurring DNA segment is a product of nature and not patent eligible merely because it has been isolated, but that cDNA is patent eligible because it is not naturally occurring. We, therefore, affirm in part and reverse in part the decision of the United States Court of Appeals for the Federal Circuit.

I.

A.

Genes form the basis for hereditary traits in living organisms. . . . The human genome consists of approximately 22,000 genes packed into 23 pairs of chromosomes. Each gene is encoded as DNA, which takes the shape of the familiar "double helix" that Doctors James Watson and Francis Crick first described in 1953. Each "cross-bar" in the DNA helix consists of two chemically joined nucleotides. The possible nucleotides are adenine (A), thymine (T), cytosine (C), and guanine (G), each of which binds naturally with another nucleotide: A pairs with T; C pairs with G. The nucleotide cross-bars are chemically connected to a sugar-phosphate backbone that forms the outside framework of the DNA helix. Sequences of DNA nucleotides contain the information necessary to create strings of amino acids, which in turn are used in the body to build proteins. . . .

DNA's informational sequences and the processes that create mRNA, amino acids, and proteins occur naturally within cells. Scientists can, however, extract DNA from cells using well known laboratory methods. These methods allow scientists to isolate specific segments of DNA—for instance, a particular gene or part of a gene—which can then be further studied, manipulated, or used. It is also possible to create DNA synthetically through processes similarly well known in the field of genetics. One such method begins with an mRNA molecule and uses the natural bonding properties of nucleotides to create a new, synthetic DNA molecule. . . . This synthetic DNA created in the laboratory from mRNA is known as complementary DNA (cDNA).

Changes in the genetic sequence are called mutations. Mutations can be as small as the alteration of a single nucleotide—a change affecting only one letter in the genetic code. Such small-scale changes can produce an entirely different amino acid or can end protein production altogether. Large changes, involving the deletion, rearrangement, or duplication of hundreds or even millions of nucleotides, can result in the elimination, misplacement, or duplication of entire genes. Some mutations are harmless, but others can cause disease or increase the risk of disease. As a result, the study of genetics can lead to valuable medical breakthroughs.

B.

This case involves patents filed by Myriad after it made one such medical breakthrough. Myriad discovered the precise location and sequence of what are now known as the BRCA1 and BRCA2 genes. Mutations in these genes can dramatically increase an individual's risk of developing breast and ovarian cancer. The average American woman has a 12- to 13-percent risk of developing breast cancer, but for women with certain genetic mutations, the risk can range between 50 and 80 percent for breast cancer and between 20 and 50 percent for ovarian cancer. Before Myriad's discovery of the BRCA1 and BRCA2 genes, scientists knew that heredity played a role in establishing a woman's risk of developing breast and ovarian cancer, but they did not know which genes were associated with those cancers.

Myriad identified the exact location of the BRCA1 and BRCA2 genes on chromosomes 17 and 13. Chromosome 17 has approximately 80 million nucleotides, and chromosome 13 has approximately 114 million. . . . Knowledge of the location of the BRCA1 and BRCA2 genes allowed Myriad to determine their typical nucleotide sequence. That information, in turn, enabled Myriad to develop medical tests that are useful for detecting mutations in a patient's BRCA1 and BRCA2 genes and thereby assessing whether the patient has an increased risk of cancer.

Once it found the location and sequence of the BRCA1 and BRCA2 genes, Myriad sought and obtained a number of patents. . . .

C.

Myriad's patents would, if valid, give it the exclusive right to isolate an individual's BRCA1 and BRCA2 genes (or any strand of 15 or more nucleotides within the genes) by breaking the covalent bonds that connect the DNA to the rest of the individual's genome. The patents would also give Myriad the exclusive right to synthetically create BRCA cDNA. In Myriad's view, manipulating BRCA DNA in either of these fashions triggers its "right to exclude others from making" its patented composition of matter under the Patent Act. 35 U.S.C. §154(a)(1); see also §271(a) ("[W]hoever without authority makes . . . any patented invention . . . infringes the patent").

But isolation is necessary to conduct genetic testing, and Myriad was not the only entity to offer BRCA testing after it discovered the genes. The University of Pennsylvania's Genetic Diagnostic Laboratory (GDL) and others provided genetic testing services to women. Petitioner Dr. Harry Ostrer, then a researcher at New York University School of Medicine, routinely sent his patients' DNA samples to GDL for testing. After learning of GDL's testing and Ostrer's activities, Myriad sent letters to them asserting that the genetic testing infringed Myriad's patents. App. 94-95 (Ostrer letter). In response, GDL agreed to stop testing and informed Ostrer that it would no longer accept patient samples. Myriad also filed patent infringement suits against other entities that performed BRCA testing, resulting in settlements in which the defendants agreed to cease all allegedly infringing activity. 689 F.3d, at 1315. Myriad, thus, solidified its position as the only entity providing BRCA testing.

Some years later, petitioner Ostrer, along with medical patients, advocacy groups, and other doctors, filed this lawsuit seeking a declaration that Myriad's patents are invalid under 35 U.S.C. §101. . . .

II.

A.

Section 101 of the Patent Act provides:

> "Whoever invents or discovers any new and useful ... composition of matter, or any new and useful improvement thereof, may obtain a patent therefor, subject to the conditions and requirements of this title." 35 U.S.C. §101.

We have "long held that this provision contains an important implicit exception[:] Laws of nature, natural phenomena, and abstract ideas are not patentable." *Mayo*, 566 U.S., at _____ (slip op., at 1) (internal quotation marks and brackets omitted). Rather, "'they are the basic tools of scientific and technological work'" that lie beyond the domain of patent protection. Id., at _____ (slip op., at 2). As the Court has explained, without this exception, there would be considerable danger that the grant of patents would "tie up" the use of such tools and thereby "inhibit future innovation premised upon them." Id., at _____ (slip op., at 17). This would be at odds with the very point of patents, which exist to promote creation. Diamond v. Chakrabarty, 447 U.S. 303, 309 (1980) (Products of nature are not created, and "'manifestations ... of nature [are] free to all men and reserved exclusively to none'").

The rule against patents on naturally occurring things is not without limits, however, for "all inventions at some level embody, use, reflect, rest upon, or apply laws of nature, natural phenomena, or abstract ideas," and "too broad an interpretation of this exclusionary principle could eviscerate patent law." 566 U.S., at _____ (slip op., at 2). As we have recognized before, patent protection strikes a delicate balance between creating "incentives that lead to creation, invention, and discovery" and "imped[ing] the flow of information that might permit, indeed spur, invention." Id., at _____ (slip op., at 23). We must apply this well-established standard to determine whether Myriad's patents claim any "new and useful ... composition of matter," §101, or instead claim naturally occurring phenomena.

B.

It is undisputed that Myriad did not create or alter any of the genetic information encoded in the BRCA1 and BRCA2 genes. The location and order of the nucleotides existed in nature before Myriad found them. Nor did Myriad create or alter the genetic structure of DNA. Instead, Myriad's principal contribution was uncovering the precise location and genetic sequence of the BRCA1 and BRCA2 genes within chromosomes 17 and 13. The question is whether this renders the genes patentable.

Myriad recognizes that our decision in *Chakrabarty* is central to this inquiry. Brief for Respondents 14, 23-27. In *Chakrabarty*, scientists added four plasmids to a bacterium, which enabled it to break down various components of crude oil.

447 U.S., at 305, and n.1. The Court held that the modified bacterium was patentable. It explained that the patent claim was "not to a hitherto unknown natural phenomenon, but to a nonnaturally occurring manufacture or composition of matter—a product of human ingenuity 'having a distinctive name, character [and] use.'" Id., at 309-310. The *Chakrabarty* bacterium was new "with markedly different characteristics from any found in nature," 447 U.S., at 310, due to the additional plasmids and resultant "capacity for degrading oil." Id., at 305, n.1. In this case, by contrast, Myriad did not create anything. To be sure, it found an important and useful gene, but separating that gene from its surrounding genetic material is not an act of invention.

Groundbreaking, innovative, or even brilliant discovery does not by itself satisfy the §101 inquiry. In Funk Brothers Seed Co. v. Kalo Inoculant Co., 333 U.S. 127 (1948), this Court considered a composition patent that claimed a mixture of naturally occurring strains of bacteria that helped leguminous plants take nitrogen from the air and fix it in the soil. Id., at 128-129. The ability of the bacteria to fix nitrogen was well known, and farmers commonly "inoculated" their crops with them to improve soil nitrogen levels. But farmers could not use the same inoculant for all crops, both because plants use different bacteria and because certain bacteria inhibit each other. Id., at 129-130. Upon learning that several nitrogen-fixing bacteria did not inhibit each other, however, the patent applicant combined them into a single inoculant and obtained a patent. Id., at 130. The Court held that the composition was not patent eligible because the patent holder did not alter the bacteria in any way. Id., at 132 ("There is no way in which we could call [the bacteria mixture a product of invention] unless we borrowed invention from the discovery of the natural principle itself"). His patent claim thus fell squarely within the law of nature exception. So do Myriad's. Myriad found the location of the BRCA1 and BRCA2 genes, but that discovery, by itself, does not render the BRCA genes "new . . . composition[s] of matter," §101, that are patent eligible.

. . . Myriad explains that the location of the gene was unknown until Myriad found it among the approximately eight million nucleotide pairs contained in a subpart of chromosome 17. See Ibid. The '473 and '492 patents contain similar language as well. See id., at 854, 947. Many of Myriad's patent descriptions simply detail the "iterative process" of discovery by which Myriad narrowed the possible locations for the gene sequences that it sought. See, e.g., id., at 750. Myriad seeks to import these extensive research efforts into the §101 patent-eligibility inquiry. Brief for Respondents 8-10, 34. But extensive effort alone is insufficient to satisfy the demands of §101. . . .

C.

cDNA does not present the same obstacles to patentability as naturally occurring, isolated DNA segments. As already explained, creation of a cDNA sequence from mRNA results in an exons-only molecule that is not naturally occurring. Petitioners concede that cDNA differs from natural DNA in that "the non-coding regions have been removed." Brief for Petitioners 49. They nevertheless argue that cDNA is not patent eligible because "[t]he nucleotide sequence of cDNA is dictated by nature, not by the lab technician." Id., at 51. That may be so, but the lab technician unquestionably creates something new when cDNA is made. cDNA retains the naturally occurring exons of DNA, but it is distinct from the DNA from which it was derived. As a result, cDNA is not a "product of nature" and is patent eligible under §101, except insofar as very short series of DNA may have no intervening introns to remove when creating cDNA. In that situation, a short strand of cDNA may be indistinguishable from natural DNA.[23]

III.

It is important to note what is not implicated by this decision. First, there are no method claims before this Court. Had Myriad created an innovative method of manipulating genes while searching for the BRCA1 and BRCA2 genes, it could possibly have sought a method patent. . . .

Nor do we consider the patentability of DNA in which the order of the naturally occurring nucleotides has been altered. Scientific alteration of the genetic code presents a different inquiry, and we express no opinion about the application of §101 to such endeavors. We merely hold that genes and the information they encode are not patent eligible under §101 simply because they have been isolated from the surrounding genetic material.

■ POINT TO CONSIDER

Labor theory. There is no question that Myriad expended a great deal of effort to discover and isolate the BRCA1 and BRCA2 genes. In other contexts, we have found that labor may create property rights, both on the ground of fairness (or natural law) and to spur economic productivity. Why does the Supreme Court find in this case that the expenditure of labor is insufficient to create a property right? After all, the manure in *Haslem* was "naturally occurring" as well, but the one who gathered it was granted a right to exclude others. Is this situation different or does patent law simply not comport with our fundamental property principles?

---

[23] We express no opinion whether cDNA satisfies the other statutory requirements of patentability. See, e.g., 35 U.S.C. §§102, 103, and 112. . . .

SUMMARY

- The principal policies behind intellectual property protection are providing an incentive to creators and rewarding their labor. In addition, in the case of trademarks, we want to prevent consumer confusion.
- These reasons to protect intellectual property must be balanced against the social cost of allowing a limited monopoly.
- The Constitution provides that Congress may provide protection for authors and inventors "for limited Times."
- *Patents* are granted under federal law for useful, novel, and nonobvious inventions for a period of 20 years.
- Federal *copyright* law protects original works of authorship fixed in a tangible medium of expression, for a period of the lifetime of the author plus 70 years.
- The federal Lanham Act protects *trademarks*, which consist of any word, name, symbol, or device used by a manufacturer or merchant to distinguish its goods. The trademark must be "distinctive," and the right lasts as long as the company continues to use the mark.
- State *trade secret* laws protect confidential business information of economic value, such as formulas or strategies, for an unlimited time, as long as the business makes reasonable efforts to keep it secret.
- Although granting one entity control over the use of a particular word may limit the expressions of others, the Supreme Court has so far not found that any trademark protections violate the First Amendment.
- A parody may imitate a trademarked product for the purpose of satire or amusement, as long as consumers would not mistake the imitation for the original. Similarly, a parody of a copyrighted work constitutes "fair use" if it is transformative.

PART II

Splitting Up the Bundle of Sticks

At this point, you should have a good handle on the various rights that make up a property owner's bundle of sticks and the balance of interests behind them. In addition, you have learned the basic ways that property rights are acquired, other than by sale or inheritance.

Until now, we have been discussing ownership as if one person held the entire bundle of sticks. We are now going to introduce various ways in which these bundles of rights can be split up among multiple parties.

First, the bundle of sticks may be shared by co-owners of the property who have rights to it at the same time. The most common form of this co-ownership is marital property, but other forms of *concurrent ownership* are also frequently encountered. In Chapter 4, we introduce the various types of co-ownership and discuss the rights and responsibilities of co-owners.

Second, property rights can be split according to *time*—one person could hold the ownership rights to Blackacre for the present, while another person may hold the rights to it in the future. For example, Alice may have a life estate in Blackacre, and then her son Bart will come into ownership at her death. We call Alice's present interest an *estate in land* and Bart's property right a *future interest*. The categories and characteristics of these interests are the subject of Chapter 5.

Finally, the bundle of sticks may be split between *landlord* and *tenant*. The tenant (*lessee*) has the right of possession, for a particular period of time, while the landlord (*lessor*) continues to hold the remaining sticks in the bundle. The landlord-tenant relationship is governed by three sources: contract (the lease), statute (e.g., the state's Residential Landlord-Tenant Act), and the common law. In Chapter 6, you will be introduced to how landlord-tenant issues are resolved by reference to those three sources.

Concurrent Interests

> I told my mother-in-law that my house was her house, and she said, "Get the hell off my property."
>
> —*Joan Rivers*

A INTRODUCTION

In this chapter, we introduce the idea that the bundle of sticks constituting property ownership may be divided "length-wise," if you will, between two or more co-owners. The law refers to the concurrent ownership of property as a "co-tenancy": in this context, the word "tenancy" refers to the ownership or right to possess the property, rather than the landlord-tenant context you might be thinking of.

Suppose, for example, you want to buy a condo in a Colorado ski resort, but you don't quite have sufficient financial resources, so you ask your friend Selma to go in on the purchase with you. How do you hold title? What happens to Selma's interest when she dies? What if Selma wants to put a hot tub on the back deck and wants you to pay half of the cost? What if you decide that Selma is too hard to get along with and you want to end this relationship?

You can imagine all kinds of situations in which property is owned by co-tenants. For example, heirs often inherit property in an estate as co-tenants. Business partners sometimes hold title as co-tenants. Aging parents may decide to add their children as joint tenants of their real property as a form of estate planning. Of course, the most common form of co-ownership is between married couples.

In this chapter, we will cover the different types of co-tenancies and their characteristics. We will also discuss the rights and responsibilities of co-owners. Finally, we will introduce the most important form of co-ownership—marital property—along with the various mechanisms the law has provided to protect the property interests of married couples.

B   TYPES OF CO-OWNERSHIP

The first concept to grasp about co-tenancies is that we are talking about dividing ownership of the *rights* in the property, not dividing the *physical* property itself. If A and B own the 40-acre parcel of Blackacre as co-tenants, each owns a half *share* of the property as a *whole*. A and B do not own 20 acres each; they both own the entire 40 acres. In this way, co-ownership of property is somewhat like owning shares of stock in a corporation. You might own ten shares of McDonald's stock, but you could not walk into a McDonald's and point to any particular chair as your exclusive property—you own an *interest* in that property (along with about 1.3 million other shareholders). In legal parlance, we say that each co-tenant's interest is *undivided*, meaning that the property has not been separated into pieces, but rather is owned together as a whole.

This also means that each co-tenant has an equal right, along with other co-tenants, to *possess* the whole. Since it is physically impossible for two people to possess the same thing at the same time, this raises some interesting questions concerning co-tenant relations, which we will discuss below.

There are three types of concurrent ownership in current use: *tenancy in common*, *joint tenancy*, and *tenancy by the entirety*. We will start by discussing the creation and characteristics of each type of co-tenancy.

1. Tenancy in Common

a. Creation

The tenancy in common is the *default* form of co-tenancy. In most states, statutes provide that a tenancy in common is created by a conveyance or devise to two or more people that does not create either a joint tenancy or a tenancy by the entirety, described below. *See, e.g.*, Ind. Code §32-17-2-1 (2018). Therefore, a deed that simply conveys Blackacre "to A and B" would be held to create a tenancy in common. Similarly, a will in which T leaves Whiteacre "to my three children—A, B, and C" would create a tenancy in common.

b. *Characteristics*

- ■ Any number of owners can be co-tenants and they may have unequal shares.
  - □ For example, assume T willed Blackacre "half to the then-living children of my daughter A and half to the then-living children of my son B." When T died, A had two children, A1 and A2, and B had one child, B1. Therefore, A1 and A2 would each own an undivided quarter interest in Blackacre, while B1 would own an undivided half interest, and all would be tenants in common.
  - □ Unless the deed or will specifies otherwise, there is a presumption that tenants in common have equal shares, so any other arrangement must be clearly indicated by the facts. For example, assume that when Frank decided to buy a Colorado condo with his friend Ernest, Ernest could only come up with 25 percent of the necessary cash. The friends agreed that Ernest would have only a one-fourth ownership interest. The deed, however, says simply: "to Frank and Ernest, as tenants in common." If there is any dispute over the proceeds when the friends decide to sell the condo, a court will probably accept extrinsic evidence to prove the respective shares, but it had better be clear and convincing evidence to overcome the equal shares presumption.
- ■ Each co-owner in a tenancy in common has the right to sell, lease, or encumber[1] her share without the permission of the other co-tenants (absent some agreement to the contrary).
- ■ Upon death, each co-tenant's share passes with his or her estate. The other co-tenants have no right to succeed to the deceased co-tenant's share.

2. Joint Tenancy

The main difference between the joint tenancy and the tenancy in common is the *right of survivorship*. Unlike the tenancy in common, when one joint tenant dies, her interest is automatically absorbed by the surviving co-tenants. If Blackacre is owned by A and B in joint tenancy and A dies, B "survives to the whole." Thus, the

---

[1] For example, one co-tenant could pledge her share of Blackacre as collateral for a loan without the permission of the others.

deceased joint tenant's share of Blackacre will not pass through her will or even become part of her estate.

The joint tenancy is like a pie crust—hard to create, yet easy to break. Special requirements must be carefully met to create a joint tenancy. However, once it is created, it is easy to break: we will see that the joint tenancy may easily be converted at any time into a tenancy in common, even unintentionally.

a. Creation

First, every jurisdiction requires that the intent to create a joint tenancy be clearly specified in the deed or will, to overcome the modern presumption in favor of tenancy in common.[2] At early English common law, a conveyance or devise in a will "to A and B" was presumed to create a joint tenancy, but American jurisdictions switched gears early on, seeking to eliminate the unintended disinheritance of the deceased tenant's heirs. Banks v. Banks, 135 A.3d 311 (Del. Ch. 2016). Now, deed or will provisions must clearly indicate the intention to create a joint tenancy.

In most jurisdictions, the preferred language is "to A and B, as joint tenants with the right of survivorship." Some jurisdictions go even further, declaring that the language "as joint tenants with rights of survivorship, and not as tenants in common" is necessary to conclusively create a joint tenancy. S.C. Code Ann. §27-7-40 (2017); compare Banks v. Banks, 135 A.3d 311 (Del. Ch. 2016) (language specifically negating tenancy in common unnecessary, as long as intent to create joint tenancy is clear). Language conveying merely "to A and B as joint tenants," although not preferred, should be sufficient in most jurisdictions. *See, e.g.*, N.M. Stat. Ann. §47-1-16 (2017) ("joint tenants" prima facie evidence of joint tenancy).

Certainly, anything short of "as joint tenants" will cause difficulties. For example, in Montgomery v. Clarkson, 585 S.W.2d 483 (Mo. 1979), the court held that property deeded to two grantees "jointly" failed to create a joint tenancy. Similarly, a deed to A and B "jointly and severally," was held to be an ambiguous conveyance that could not overcome the statutory presumption in favor of tenancy in common. James v. Taylor, 969 S.W.2d 672 (Ark. Ct. App. 1998).

The Four Unities

In addition to using language to clearly express the intention to create a joint tenancy, at common law the "four unities" also had to exist:

---

[2] Two jurisdictions, Alaska and Oregon, do not allow a joint tenancy to be created at all, with limited exceptions. Or. Rev. Stat. §93.180 (2013). As we will see in the next chapter, a similar result might be achieved using life estates and remainders. If the co-tenants are married, the jurisdiction may have a presumption that any property acquired jointly is held in tenancy by the entirety (described below).

1. **Time.** The joint tenants had to acquire their interests in the property at the same time. For example, if O deeded a half interest in Blackacre to A in 2012 and then deeded the other half interest in Blackacre to B in 2013, a joint tenancy could not exist between A and B.
2. **Title.** The joint tenants must have acquired their interests by the same instrument. The previous example would also fail to meet this test, because O used two deeds to convey the interests to A and B.
3. **Interest.** The joint tenants must have the same type of interest, for the same duration. For example, suppose O wants Blackacre to go to his sons A and B, but wants B to keep the property only for life. He could not devise Blackacre in joint tenancy, giving A complete ownership and B a life interest. Some jurisdictions interpret "interest" to require equal shares in the tenancy, as discussed below.
4. **Possession.** Joint tenants have equal rights to possess the whole. Just as with a tenancy in common, the tenants own one estate together, rather than separate parts of the estate. Of course, this does not preclude the joint tenants from agreeing among themselves about how to share their possessory rights.

As we will see below, there has been significant movement, both statutory and judicial, away from strict adherence to the four unities concept. Nevertheless, the unities remain the underlying foundation for many of the modern property rules regarding joint tenancy.

The *unity of interest* originally referred to the type and duration of each joint tenant's interest in the property.[3] 2 William Blackstone, Commentaries *181. However, modern courts have often interpreted the unity of interest to mean that joint tenants must have *equal ownership shares. See, e.g.,* Ruffel v. Ruffel, 900 A.2d 1178, 1188 (R.I. 2006) ("joint tenants are required to have equal interests"). If A and B buy property as joint tenants and A pays 90 percent of the purchase price, the court may presume that A intended to make a gift to B of a half interest in the property, because it could not be a joint tenancy if B had only a 10 percent share. *See, e.g.,* Ramer v. Smith, 896 N.E.2d 563 (Ind. Ct. App. 2008) (court refused to equitably apportion the shares of joint tenants based on their contribution to the estate, based on the principle that all must have equal interests).

In contrast, in In re Estate of Lasater, 54 P.3d 511 (Kan. Ct. App. 2002), the court determined that a deed from a mother to herself and her son, which stipulated that the son had only a 1 percent share, created a joint tenancy, such that the property passed to the son on the mother's death. The court held that the "unity of interest" meant only that the tenants must have interests of the same *type*, not

---

[3] We will study the types of estates in the next chapter. For now, the easiest example would be that you couldn't create a joint tenancy that said: "to A for the remainder of her life, and to B for 20 years, as joint tenants."

that they have equal shares. Why do you think the mother deeded the property in that manner? Similarly, in Ballard v. Dornic, 140 A.3d 1147 (D.C. 2016), the court held that the unequal contributions of the joint tenants could create unequal shares so that the proceeds on partition and sale should be divided accordingly.

Some state statutes specifically allow unequal shares for joint tenants. Colo. Rev. Stat. §38-31-101 (2017) (interests of joint tenants may be unequal). Nevertheless, the presumption is that the shares of joint tenants are equal unless a contrary agreement is clearly established (e.g., stated in the deed or in a written agreement). As always, start by checking the statutes of the controlling jurisdiction.

b. Characteristics

As noted above, the signal characteristic of the joint tenancy is the right of survivorship among the co-tenants. When one of the joint tenants dies, her interest simply ends and the other joint tenants remain as owners, with proportionally larger shares. Of course, if there were only two joint tenants to begin with, the surviving joint tenant is now the sole owner. We do not say that the survivor "inherits" the deceased tenant's interest, because the deceased tenant's interest simply terminates on death and does not pass through her estate. The surviving joint tenant takes pursuant to the terms of the original grant.

This characteristic of joint tenancy makes this form of ownership a popular estate planning tool. For example, assume Paul and Megan have decided to move in together and start a family, but do not want to get married. If they buy a house and take title as joint tenants, they know that the house will go to the survivor even if neither has a will. Elderly or ill parents often decide to add a child (or other heir) to their real property title as a joint tenant, with the idea that the property will automatically go to that person when the parents die, without the necessity of probate.

Unlike the complex probate process, if A and B own Blackacre in joint tenancy and A dies, B automatically and immediately becomes the sole owner of Blackacre. B should file A's death certificate with the recorder's office to ensure that the record reflects this (see Chapter 8 regarding recording).

The fact that property held in joint tenancy is not part of A's estate and does not go through probate does *not* mean that there are no estate or gift tax consequences, however. Although estate and gift tax is beyond the scope of the

Probate

The term *probate* refers to the legal process of proving the validity of a will or determining heirs and distributing the decedent's estate after paying claims against it. The process takes time, because creditors must be notified and given time to make claims; an executor or administrator must be appointed by the court, and must then file inventories of the estate assets; and the court must determine the will's validity and interpret its provisions. Finally, the court must enter orders formally approving the estate distribution and transferring the title to assets such as automobiles and real property. Even though there are streamlined probate procedures for smaller estates, this process takes time and money.

first-year course, note that the main advantage of the joint tenancy is avoidance of *probate*, not avoidance of estate or gift tax.

■ PROBLEM: USING JOINT TENANCY TO AVOID PROBATE

Assume that Wendy, a widow aged about 70, asks you to draft a deed to "put her daughter Dottie on the title to her house, Blackacre" so Dottie will be sure to get the house when Wendy dies. Wendy doesn't have many assets and figures it's not worthwhile to do a will and have it probated when the time comes. She has one other child, Sonny, who is irresponsible and untrustworthy. She hasn't seen Sonny for years and does not want him to have any part of the house. Wendy knows that, under state law, if she dies without a will Sonny would be entitled to an equal share of her estate with Dottie. She is afraid that, even if she makes a will, Sonny could challenge it.

Will the joint tenancy fulfill her intent? What advice should you give Wendy about the possible drawbacks to this estate planning approach?

c. *Severance and Partition*

The term *severance* refers to an action of a joint tenant that converts the joint tenancy into a tenancy in common.[4] The right of survivorship as to that share is severed from the estate. In theory, any action that destroys one of the four unities (time, title, interest, and possession) will effect a severance, because a joint tenancy cannot exist if the unities are broken.

Most commonly, severance occurs when one joint tenant *transfers her interest* to someone else. In general, a joint tenant is absolutely free to alienate her undivided interest at any time, without the permission of the other co-owners. However, the transfer cannot create a joint tenancy, because the unities of time and title are thereby destroyed. If A and B own Blackacre as joint tenants and A conveys her interest to C, B and C now own Blackacre as tenants in common. Even if A clearly specified in the deed, "A hereby grants and conveys Blackacre to C in joint tenancy with right of survivorship with B," it would not work, at least if the court respects the unities. *If A really wants to convey her interest to C without severing the joint tenancy, how could it be accomplished?*

As explored below, severance issues arise when other unilateral actions, such as entering into a mortgage or lease, arguably destroy the unities. Joint tenants may also mutually agree to convert the joint tenancy into a tenancy in common (for example, by deed: "A and B, grantors, convey to A and B, as tenants in common").

---

[4] At least one court refers to the conversion to a tenancy in common as a "termination" of the joint tenancy. *See, e.g.,* Edwin Smith LLC v. Synergy Operating, LLC, 285 P.3d 656 (N.M. 2012). While we recognize the different terminology, we will use "severance" for consistency.

You should carefully distinguish the term *partition* from the term *severance*. A *partition* ends the co-ownership of property and divides the property between the co-owners. It applies to any of the forms of co-ownership. A joint tenant or tenant in common generally has the right to partition the property at any time; as discussed below, the only issue is whether to divide the property *in kind* or to sell the property and divide the proceeds. In any case, once the property is partitioned, the property will no longer be in concurrent ownership. In contrast, when a joint tenancy is *severed*, the co-tenants remain in concurrent ownership; only the right of survivorship has been terminated.

■ PROBLEMS: SEVERANCE

1. O wanted Blackacre to stay in the family, so he conveyed Blackacre to his daughter A and A's son B as joint tenants, figuring that when A died, B would get the property. In 2013, A was diagnosed with a terminal illness. A wanted to make sure that her third husband C could live on Blackacre the rest of his life after she died. On January 1, 2014, A conveyed her undivided half interest in Blackacre to C, specifying that C "shall be a joint tenant with my son B."

   a) A died on January 15, 2014, and C died on June 1, 2014, leaving a will giving all his property to X, a daughter by a previous marriage. Who owns Blackacre?

   b) How would you have advised O to achieve his purpose? How about advice to A?

2. After Pa died, Ma conveyed Blackacre "to Ma and Son, as joint tenants with right of survivorship." Even though Son was in prison, she wanted to make sure that Son would get the property when she died. In her 80s, she became ill and her granddaughter Gigi came to stay with her and nurse her. To show her gratitude, Ma decided that she wanted Gigi to have Blackacre, so she gave Gigi a deed conveying to her "any and all of my interest in Blackacre." Ma died shortly thereafter. What is the state of the title to Blackacre? *See* Bryant v. Bryant, 522 S.W.3d 392 (Tenn. 2017).

3. A conveyance by a joint tenant can affect only *her* relationship with the other joint tenants. So, if A, B, and C hold title to Blackacre as joint tenants and C conveys her share to D, what happens when B dies?

The Bundle of Sticks Revisited

In Chapter 1, we noted that sometimes owners have some, but not all, of the sticks in the bundle. Which of the sticks does the owner of an interest in joint tenancy have? Which does she not have, or at least not completely?

---

d. Personal Property

Joint tenancies may also be created in tangible personal property, such as boats or cars, and in intangible personal property, such as bank accounts. In general, the same principles apply.

In many cases, stock accounts or mutual funds are set up to be "payable on death" (POD) to a named beneficiary, which avoids probate, but, unlike a joint tenancy, gives the beneficiary no current interest in the property.

With regard to bank accounts, confusion often arises regarding the parties' intentions. In many cases, an elderly person adds another person's name to a bank account merely for convenience, not intending to make a gift of a current interest or a survivorship interest. Consider the Pennsylvania Multi-Party Account Act, 20 Pa. Cons. Stat. §6304(a) (2014):

> Joint account—any sum remaining on deposit at the death of a party to a joint account belongs to the surviving party or parties as against the estate of the decedent unless there is clear and convincing evidence of a different intent at the time the account is created.

Some banks offer a true "convenience" account, which is more formally known as a multi-party account without right of survivorship, which helps to clarify the intention of the owner. The Uniform Multiple-Person Accounts Act encourages financial institutions to provide accounts that clearly establish rights of survivorship among joint owners.

Otherwise, when adding a person's name to a bank account, the owner of the account should specify her intentions in writing to help avoid later confusion. For example, the account owner could specify in her will that the account is part of her estate and was set up for convenience only and not with donative intent.

e. *Intellectual Property*

Can intellectual property be held in a co-tenancy? How might owning a trademark, for example, as co-tenants differ from the co-ownership of real estate? *See, e.g.*, Hart v. Weinstein, 737 So. 2d 72 (La. Ct. App. 1999) (two groups of heirs owned trademark on family name in common and could not claim infringement against each other). Suppose Anderson and Bogart have a falling out and one of them seeks partition for the copyright of this book. How might a court partition such an asset? *See* McMunigal v. Bloch, 2010 WL 5399219 (N.D. Cal. 2010) (holding that court has no authority to partition copyright on Aspen casebook held jointly by two law professors because it would force transfer in violation of copyright law).

3. The Tenancy by the Entirety

The *tenancy by the entirety* (TBE) may exist only between *married* co-owners, who are treated as a unit, under the common law fiction that viewed a married couple as one person. Only about half of the states recognize this form of concurrent ownership. Moreover, some of those states recognize TBE only for real property, not personal property. As we'll see below, the TBE is one way in which states provide spousal protection for marital property and it is therefore a very important and common form of ownership in those states that allow it.

a. Creation

The tenancy by the entirety should be created by a conveyance "to H and W, a married couple, as tenants by the entirety." In many states that recognize TBE, however, a conveyance to a married couple is presumed to create a tenancy by the entirety unless a contrary intention is clearly stated. *See, e.g,* Ronollo v. Jacobs, 775 S.W.2d 121 (Mo. 1989) (conveyance of real property to "Carl Ronollo and Virginia Ronollo, his wife" with no other language created TBE due to presumption). In Michigan, a court held that even a conveyance to "Jasper Winstanley and Elizabeth J. Winstanley, his wife, as joint tenants," was not sufficient to overcome the presumption, because a TBE is a form of joint tenancy and the terms are often used interchangeably! Hoyt v. Winstanley, 191 N.W. 213 (Mich. 1922); *compare* Underwood v. Bunger, 70 N.E. 3d 338 (Ind. 2017) (language conveying "to A and B, husband and wife, as tenants in common" sufficient to overcome TBE presumption despite recitation of spousal relationship). How would you draft a deed in Michigan to a married couple if you wanted to avoid this presumption and create a joint tenancy?

The same four unities required for a joint tenancy must exist for a TBE, plus the *fifth unity of marriage*. The couple must be married at the time of the conveyance. If they marry after the conveyance, they have to reconvey the property (i.e., "A and B, grantors, hereby convey Blackacre to A and B, a married couple, grantees, as tenants by the entirety") in order to fulfill the fifth unity of marriage.

b. Characteristics

Just like a joint tenancy, spouses holding property in TBE have a *right of survivorship*, along with the other attributes of a joint tenancy. The biggest difference is that there is *no possibility of unilateral severance*; one spouse acting alone cannot affect the other spouse's right of survivorship.

The idea of treating the married couple as one unit also means that both spouses must agree to any transfer of an interest in TBE property. While we know that a typical joint tenant is certainly free to sell or give away her interest in Blackacre at any time, a person holding property in TBE needs his or her spouse's agreement to convey or encumber it (e.g., enter into a mortgage).

As the Mississippi Supreme Court explained:

An estate by entirety may exist only in a husband and wife and may not be terminated by the unilateral action of one of them because they take by the entireties and not by moieties [i.e., shares]. While the marriage exists, neither husband nor wife can sever this title so as to defeat or prejudice the right of survivorship in the other, and a conveyance executed by only one of them does not pass title.

Ayers v. Petro, 417 So. 2d 912, 914 (Miss. 1982); *see also* Jones v. Jones, 497 S.W.3d 334 (Mo. Ct. App. 2016). Similarly, while a joint tenant is generally free to demand partition, TBE property may be partitioned only with the agreement of both spouses, or upon dissolution of the marriage.

We will explore below the effect that the TBE form of ownership has on the interests of creditors.

C JOINT TENANCY CREATION ISSUES

As noted above, common law required strict adherence to the four unities of time, title, interest, and possession in order to create a joint tenancy. The failure to meet any of the unities would result in a tenancy in common, despite the intention of the parties.

For example, in Deslauriers v. Senesac, 163 N.E. 327 (Ill. 1928), Ida Boudreau owned a lot, which she conveyed to herself and her husband Homer after they married. The deed indicated: "Said grantors intend and declare that their title shall and does hereby pass to grantees not in tenancy in common but in joint tenancy." After Ida died intestate, Homer tried to sell the property, but the purchasers' lawyer questioned the validity of Homer's title. The court held that a tenancy in common was created, despite the express language of the deed, because two of the essential unities were lacking: Ida could not convey property to herself and therefore acquired her interest in the property before Homer (time), and through a different instrument (title). In consequence, her half interest in the property descended to her heirs at law.

In jurisdictions adhering to the common law, the only way for a sole owner of property to create a joint tenancy in himself and another was to use a *straw person*. The sole owner (A) conveyed Blackacre to X (perhaps her lawyer) and then X immediately conveyed it back to A and B as joint tenants. In that way, A and B acquired the property with the same instrument at the same time, fulfilling the required unities. In Riddle v. Harmon, 162 Cal. Rptr. 530 (Cal. Ct. App. 1980), the court discussed the origins of this requirement:

That "two-to-transfer" notion stems from the English common law feoffment ceremony with livery of seisin. If the ceremony took place upon the land being conveyed, the grantor (feoffor) would hand a symbol of the land, such as a lump of earth or a twig, to the grantee (feoffee). In order to complete the investiture of seisin it was necessary that the feoffor completely relinquish possession of the land to the feoffee. It is

> apparent from the requirement of livery of seisin that one could not enfeoff oneself—that is, one could not be both grantor and grantee in a single transaction. Handing oneself a dirt clod is ungainly.

Id. at 528-29 (citations omitted).

The court in *Riddle* dispensed with the need to go through this charade: "Just as livery of seisin has become obsolete, so should ancient vestiges of that ceremony give way to modern conveyancing realities." *Id.* at 529. Most jurisdictions have now eliminated the "two to transfer" requirement, either by statute or judicial decision. *See, e.g.,* Cal. Civ. Code §683 (West 2018) (joint tenancy may be created by conveyance from a "sole owner to himself and others"); Littleton v. Plybon, 395 S.W.3d 505 (Ky. Ct. App. 2012); Taylor v. Canterbury, 92 P.3d 961 (Colo. 2004). Thus, in most states, A as sole owner of Blackacre may create a joint tenancy by a simple deed conveying Blackacre from A as grantor "to A and B as joint tenants."

As noted above, most jurisdictions require clear language to create a joint tenancy, to overcome the presumption in favor of tenancy in common. In North Carolina, for example, if a joint tenancy conveyance does not specifically refer to the "right of survivorship," a survivorship interest will not be created. N.C. Gen. Stat. Ann. §41-2(a) (West 2013). Other courts focus more on the intent of the parties and are willing to interpret ambiguous language to fulfill that intent. In Downing v. Downing, 606 A.2d 208 (Md. 1992), the court noted that a conveyance to a mother and son "as joint tenants" was not completely clear without a reference to the right of survivorship, but the court held that it was sufficient to indicate an intent to create a joint tenancy.

■ PROBLEMS: JOINT TENANCY CREATION

How do you think a court would construe title in the following situations?

1. Deed conveys to father and son "as joint tenants and as in common with the right of survivorship." *See* Zomisky v. Zamiska, 296 A.2d 722 (Pa. 1972).

2. Two brothers are conveyed property as "tenants by the entirety." *See* Powell v. Estate of Powell, 14 N.E.3d 46 (Ind. Ct. App. 2014).

3. T devises Blackacre in his will "to my daughters A and B jointly and to the survivor of them."

4. O conveys Greenacre "to my daughter W and her husband H as tenants by the entirety and to my son S, as joint tenants with right of survivorship." In this case, what interests do W and S have if H dies?

5. A deed to conveys a condominium "to A and B as sole owners." A and B lease the condo to C, and the lease identifies A and B as "owners in joint tenancy with right of survivorship." A dies, leaving his property to H. Does B have a right of survivorship? *See* Herskovitz v. Steinmetz, 965 N.Y.S.2d 333 (2013).

D JOINT TENANCY SEVERANCE ISSUES

As we noted above, at common law any action that destroyed one of the four unities of time, title, interest, and possession would sever the joint tenancy, converting it into a tenancy in common. As a result, if a joint tenant conveyed her undivided interest to a third party, it would clearly work a severance as to that interest. In addition, at common law a joint tenant could not effect a severance by a conveyance to herself, without the use of a straw person, because the unities would not thereby be broken.

Just as courts have abandoned the "two to transfer" requirement for the creation of joint tenancies, they have also moved away from requiring the use of a straw person to sever joint tenancies. Instead, courts have begun to focus more on the *intention* of the joint tenant, rather than strictly requiring one of the unities to be destroyed. Thus, if A and B hold Blackacre as joint tenants, A should be able to convert the estate to a tenancy in common by a unilateral conveyance of her undivided interest "to A as tenant in common." As the next case illustrates, the new focus on intent raises some issues of fairness and certainty, as courts define which actions are sufficient to accomplish a severance.

IN THE MATTER OF THE ESTATE OF JOHNSON

739 N.W.2d 493 (2007)
Supreme Court of Iowa

CADY, Justice.

The right of survivorship makes joint tenancies a popular form of property ownership. Yet, the concomitant right of each joint tenant to destroy the joint tenancy, and thus the right of survivorship, is not always popular, particularly for the surviving joint tenant. As Hamlet observed in a different context, "ay, there's the rub"[5] and, in this case, the seeds of the issue presented. A district court decision found a joint tenant successfully exercised his right to destroy the right of survivorship prior to his death, and the surviving joint tenant appeals. We agree with the surviving joint tenant, now the executor of the surviving joint tenant's estate, and find the property remained in joint tenancy until the death of the joint tenant, at which time full title vested in the survivor. We reverse the district court's decision and remand.

I. BACKGROUND FACTS AND PROCEEDINGS

Roy and Emogene Johnson purchased a home in Van Meter, Iowa, in 1963. They were married and took title to the home as joint tenants with the right of

---

[5] William Shakespeare, *Hamlet* act 3, sc. 1, line 64.

survivorship. They continued to live in their Van Meter home for over thirty-five years, where they raised a family and established the property as their homestead. *See* Iowa Code §561.1 (2007) (defining homestead).

In the fall of 1998 Emogene suffered a severe stroke. The prognosis for her recovery was bleak, and she required intensive medical attention. Roy and the children felt Emogene would not live long, and they assumed Roy would survive her. Because of these circumstances, the family decided Emogene should transfer title in her automobile to Roy, as well as her interest in the homestead.[6] . . .

On [December 21, 1998], a quitclaim deed was drafted to convey Emogene and Roy's interest in their homestead solely to Roy. The deed stated "ROY N. JOHNSON and EMOGENE F. JOHNSON, husband and wife[,] do hereby Quit Claim to ROY N. JOHNSON all our right, title, interest, estate, claim and demand in the [homestead]." Roy signed the deed on December 21, and his signature was notarized. Emogene (or an agent for her), however, did not sign the deed that day, perhaps because the power of attorney did not authorize Emogene's agents to sell or encumber the homestead.

On January 4, 1999, Emogene purportedly executed another power of attorney. This power of attorney specified the legal description of the homestead and authorized [her daughter] Janice to convey or encumber Emogene's interest in the homestead. Then on January 6, 1999, Janice signed the quitclaim deed on behalf of Emogene, as indicated by the notary's seal. The deed was recorded the same day.

The earlier assumptions made by the family that gave rise to the transfers of property were proven wrong when Roy suddenly passed away on December 17, 1999, survived by his ailing wife Emogene and the three children, Janice, Beverly, and William. Roy left a will that gave all of his property to his three children in equal shares, although he did not specifically disinherit Emogene. Janice was named executor of Roy's estate in his will, but Beverly took her place after Janice's death in June of 2004. . . .

The district court found Emogene was clearly incompetent at the time she signed the powers of attorney, which invalidated the transfer of her interest in the property to Roy under the deed. Nevertheless, the court held Roy unilaterally terminated the joint tenancy in the homestead by his act of conveying his interest to himself in fee simple because the deed constituted an expression of his intent to destroy the joint tenancy. The court further held that Emogene's statutory homestead rights to the property did not prevent Roy from destroying the joint tenancy because the effect of Roy's self-conveyance of his interest only created a tenancy in common, which meant Emogene still maintained her homestead rights to possess the property.

As a result, the district court concluded title to the homestead was split between Emogene and Roy's estate as tenants in common in "undivided one-half"

---

[6] The record suggests the family made these decisions to help Emogene qualify for Medicaid, although the decisions were likely based on erroneous assumptions.

shares.[7] . . . Emogene appealed the district court ruling concerning the title to the homestead.

Emogene died in March of 2007, during the pendency of this appeal. As a result, Emogene's son and executor of her estate, William Johnson, is the named appellant.

II. ISSUE AND STANDARD OF REVIEW

The question presented is whether the joint tenancy in the parties' homestead was severed under the circumstances of this case. . . .

III. DETERMINING THE EXISTENCE OF JOINT TENANCIES IN IOWA

Traditionally, questions concerning the existence of joint tenancies were answered by resorting to the "four unities" of interest, title, time, and possession. *See, e.g.,* 48A C.J.S. Joint Tenancy §8, at 240 (2004) ("[I]n order that a joint tenancy may exist, there must coexist four unities: unity of interest, unity of title, unity of time, and unity of possession."). To create a joint tenancy the four unities had to be present—"[t]hat is, one and the same interest arising by the same conveyance, commencing at the same time and held by the one and the same undivided possession." Switzer v. Pratt, 237 Iowa 788, 791, 23 N.W.2d 837, 839 (1946). To sever or terminate a joint tenancy, a joint tenant simply had to destroy one of the unities. *See* Stuehm v. Mikulski, 139 Neb. 374, 297 N.W. 595, 597 (1941) ("The four unities heretofore listed must not only come into being with the creation of such an estate, but must also continue to exist while the estate exists, and the destruction of any one of them as to all holders will destroy the estate. . . .").

This common-law approach to the existence of joint tenancies began losing steam over fifty years ago. *See* R.H. Helmholz, *Realism & Formalism in the Severance of Joint Tenancies*, 77 Neb. L. Rev. 1, 1-2 (1998) [hereinafter Helmholz, *Severance of Joint Tenancies*]. Critics derided the approach as too formalistic, and declared it to be outdated. *See* Paul Basye, *Joint Tenancy: A Reappraisal*, 30 Cal. St. B.J. 504, 507 (1955) (describing the four unities as "an outstanding example of persisting medieval formalism"); Robert W. Swenson & Ronan E. Degnan, *Severance of Joint Tenancies*, 38 Minn. L. Rev. 466, 503 (1954) (describing the four unities as "useless concepts today"). Moreover, critics recognized the four unities often worked. . .to "frustrate the legitimate expectations of too many joint tenants [or

---

[7] It is admittedly a paradox, and perhaps an oxymoron, to state property could be divided in undivided one-half shares or interests. But it is consistently referred to in this manner, and the reason for doing so is that the individual tenants are entitled to possess the whole of the property while they remain co-tenants (therefore their possession is undivided), but should they choose to alienate the property, they only have a proportional interest (which could be a one-half interest depending on the circumstances) to alienate. (Citations omitted.)

would-be joint tenants], and for no discernable purpose," Helmholz, *Severance of Joint Tenancies*, 77 Neb. L. Rev. at 2.

As a result, courts began adopting an alternative intent-based approach to determine the existence of joint tenancies. *Id.* at 9, 162 Cal. Rptr. 530. We recognized this approach many years ago and have gravitated towards it since that time. *See, e.g.*, In re Baker's Estate, 247 Iowa 1380, 1384, 78 N.W.2d 863, 865 (1956) (noting cases in which we primarily relied on the intention of the parties rather than the four unities to determine the existence of a joint tenancy). Today, the approach generally enjoys favorable acceptance among other courts and scholars as the more appropriate and realistic means for determining the existence of joint tenancies. *See* Taylor v. Canterbury, 92 P.3d 961, 966 (Colo. 2004) ("Thus, in determining whether a joint tenancy has been created or severed, we look not to the four unities, but rather to the intent of the parties."); Nicholas v. Nicholas, 277 Kan. 171, 83 P.3d 214, 225 (2004) (recognizing "the modern trend of looking to the parties' intent as the operative test of whether a joint tenancy has been severed rather than depending upon the traditional doctrine of the four unities"); In re Estate of Knickerbocker, 912 P.2d 969, 975 (Utah 1996) ("There is substantial support for the concept that it is the intent of the parties, not the destruction of one of the four unities, that should govern."); Helmholz, *Severance of Joint Tenancies*, 77 Neb. L. Rev. at 9 ("A survey of the decisions on the subject during the past forty years . . . leaves one with the distinct sense of the traditional approach's substantive irrelevance.").

While we have not formally and expressly adopted the intent-based approach, we do so today. Our review of the case law and commentary confirms our position that strict reliance on the four unities is not the proper test for determining the existence of joint tenancies in Iowa. Instead, the intent of the parties should prevail when possible. . . . In addition, we see no reason to distinguish our approach based on whether the joint tenancy is sought to be created, severed, or terminated. *But see* Hyland v. Standiford, 253 Iowa 294, 299, 111 N.W.2d 260, 264 (1961) ("The common law unities of interest, title, time and possession necessary for the *creation or determination* of joint tenancies have lost their importance. There has been no comparable diminution of importance in questions of *termination or severance*." (Emphasis added.)). The modern case law clearly suggests uniformity under an intent-based approach. *See, e.g.*, Chrystyan v. Feinberg, 156 Ill. App. 3d 781, 510 N.E.2d 33, 36 (1987) ("Severance should not be governed more strictly than the creation of joint tenancies.").

Although an intent-based test is the best and more realistic approach, we recognize it is not without its own difficulties, as this case illustrates. When and under what circumstances a joint tenancy can be created, severed, or terminated remains a subject of great debate, and we must enter this discourse to consider the extent to which the intent-based analysis may alter the resolution of these questions provided under the common law. *See* Helmholz, *Severance of Joint Tenancies*, 77 Neb. L. Rev. at 24. Indeed, abandonment of the theoretical litmus test provided by the four unities may sacrifice some of the clarity it presumably provided. Clarity in the law is necessary, but we see no reason why it cannot be achieved under an intent-based approach when proper attention is paid to the individual facts and circumstances of each case. Yet, this goal also requires us to properly frame the intent-based concept, something we have not fully accomplished in the past.

In drawing the contours of the intent-based test, it is important to recognize this approach does not simply permit a court to determine the intent of a party under the facts and then fulfill it.[8] *See Nicholas*, 83 P.3d at 225 ("[I]ntent alone will not sever the joint tenancy. Sheryl's intent is irrelevant if he took no effective action."). In fact, we know of no court that has ever held intent alone is enough to determine the existence of a joint tenancy.[9] Instead, it seems fundamental that intent must be derived from an instrument effectuating the intent to sever the joint tenancy. Thus, we begin with the premise that intent unaccompanied by some action or instrument sufficient to corroborate and give effect to that intent will not create, sever, or terminate a joint tenancy. This approach, of course, leads us back to the district court holding that derived intent to sever from a deed characterized as a self-conveyance of one joint tenant.

IV. WAS THE JOINT TENANCY SEVERED IN THIS CASE?

The surrounding circumstances in this case inevitably point to a void deed. Under the common law, a void deed could not work a severance, but only because a failed conveyance could not disturb the original unities of time, title, interest and possession. *See* Helmholz, *Severance of Joint Tenancies*, 77 Neb. L. Rev. at 9 (recognizing that in cases of void deeds the conclusion that there is no severance "follows as a matter of course" under the common law). Of course, we must decide if this same result occurs under an intent-based approach.

Emogene's incompetence rendered the conveyance of her interest invalid. *See* 23 Am. Jur. 2d Deeds §23, at 89-90 (2d ed. 2002) ("A competent grantor is essential for a proper deed."). Additionally, the homestead nature of the property rendered the conveyance of Roy's interest invalid because Emogene did not provide her competent approval.[10] Normally, Emogene's incompetence would not

---

[8] The "intent of the parties" typically refers to the intent of the joint tenants—i.e., whether the alleged joint tenants intended to create a joint tenancy or if the actual joint tenants intended to sever or terminate the joint tenancy. *See, e.g., Baker's Estate*, 247 Iowa at 1385-88, 78 N.W.2d at 866-68 (discussing the creation and severance of joint tenancies, and examining the intent of the joint tenants). However, in cases of unilateral action, the "intent of the parties" really refers to just one joint tenant. *See, e.g.,* Keokuk Sav. Bank & Trust Co. v. Desvaux, 259 Iowa 387, 392, 143 N.W.2d 296, 299 (1966) (recognizing a joint tenant may unilaterally sever a joint tenancy). Thus, in cases of unilateral severance, the question would be what the singular joint tenant's, or party's, intent was, rather than the parties' intent.

[9] It appears from our review of the case law the closest a court came to relying solely on the party's intent was in Hendrickson v. Minneapolis Fed. Sav. & Loan Ass'n, 281 Minn. 462, 161 N.W.2d 688 (1968); but even in *Hendrickson*, the tenant's intent was accompanied by a "duly . . . executed Declaration of Election to Sever Survivorship of Joint Tenancy." 161 N.W.2d at 689.

[10] Of course, under the common law the conveyance of Roy's interest to himself would be invalid because it would violate the "two-to-transfer" rule. *See Riddle*, 162 Cal. Rptr. at 533. Iowa has, like most states, largely abandoned the common-law rule that prohibited conveyances between one person as grantor and grantee. . . .

prohibit Roy from conveying his own property interest held in joint tenancy with her. However, the interest of a spouse in homestead property is protected by statute. Iowa Code section 561.13 provides "[a] conveyance . . . of . . . the homestead, if the owner is married, is not valid, unless and until the spouse of the owner executes the same or a like instrument, or a power of attorney for the execution of the same or a like instrument." Iowa Code §561.13 (2005). Roy was clearly attempting to convey the homestead, albeit his own interest to himself. Thus, the plain language of the statute prohibited Roy from doing so unless Emogene joined in the pursuit pursuant to the statute. The deed was totally void.

Notwithstanding, Roy's estate argues, as the district court held, a deed that is void or ineffective as a conveyance may nevertheless remain a viable source of intent to sever a joint tenancy with a spouse in homestead property because mere severance of the joint tenancy in homestead property only creates a tenancy in common and does not jeopardize or destroy the statutory homestead rights of the spouse. Instead, severance would only change the form of ownership without compromising the spouse's right of possession provided under the homestead statute. . . . We reject this application of the intent-based test for two core reasons.

First, it is obvious that Roy's intent under the deed in this case was to take sole title to the homestead, and the joint tenancy would have been destroyed, not severed, as a consequence of that intent. Under an intent-based test, it is fundamental that the underlying instrument must effectuate the intent to sever. We conclude it would be inappropriate to utilize an intent-based approach to achieve a result the parties never intended.[11] As a result, Roy's lack of intent to sever the joint tenancy to create a tenancy in common with Emogene makes it unnecessary for us in this case to decide whether a spouse can unilaterally sever a joint tenancy in homestead property by means of a proper self-conveyance. *See Taylor*, 92 P.3d at 967 (permitting a unilateral severance by self-conveyance); *Knickerbocker*, 912 P.2d at 976 (same). The deed relied upon to supply intent did not express an intent to sever the joint tenancy.

Secondly, we are convinced an intent to sever a joint tenancy under the intent-based test must normally, if not in every instance, be derived from an instrument that is legally effective to carry out the intent. While we have always recognized a conveyance will sever or terminate a joint tenancy, *see Baker's Estate*, 247 Iowa at 1385, 78 N.W.2d at 866, we have never recognized an invalid conveyance, i.e., a void deed, will do so. A relatively recent law review article stated that, even under an intent-based approach when the joint tenant's intent is clear, if the deed is

---

Switzer, 237 Iowa at 790-92, 23 N.W.2d at 839-40 (permitting a husband to deed his own land to himself and his wife as joint tenants). There is no doubt courts have recently permitted such a conveyance even when the grantor was the sole grantee. *See Taylor*, 92 P.3d at 967; *Knickerbocker*, 912 P.2d at 975.

[11] We recognize a joint tenancy may be severed even when the joint tenant did not intend to create a tenancy in common. Such a result, however, is usually the inescapable conclusion of involuntary conveyances, seizures, or severances under the law. . . . It seems to us that in a voluntary situation such as this, when a joint tenant's intent is not to create a tenancy in common, but to obtain sole legal title, such intent is not a basis for severing the joint tenancy under a void deed.

void, "[t]he law has long been, and still is, that there is no severance." Helmholz, *Severance of Joint Tenancies*, 77 Neb. L. Rev. at 27-28. We find ample support for this statement from other jurisdictions. *See Chrystyan*, 510 N.E.2d at 36 (holding an invalid deed could not be used to establish intent to sever because the intent was not exercised in a way consistent with the law). . . .

The requirement for the intent under an intent-based analysis to be derived from a valid deed or similar instrument adds symmetry to the law and is consistent with our general principles governing property rights. In particular, we have never allowed a tenancy of any kind to be created without a valid deed or similar instrument. The same should hold true for the severance of a joint tenancy. *See, e.g., Bates*, 492 N.W.2d at 707 (permitting a severance under a valid but unexecuted mutual agreement); *Hendrickson*, 161 N.W.2d at 691 (permitting a " duly executed Declaration of Election to Sever Survivorship of Joint Tenancy" to sever the joint tenancy).[12]

V. CONCLUSION

In the final analysis, we think the circumstances of this case do not support a conclusion that the joint tenancy was severed. Not only was Roy's intent not aligned with the objective his estate seeks to accomplish in this proceeding, but it was accompanied by a void deed concerning homestead property. The district court erroneously determined the joint tenancy was severed. As a result, the property remained in joint tenancy, and Emogene's right of survivorship took effect upon Roy's death. The property should now be distributed in accordance with Emogene's will. We remand this case to the district court for proceedings consistent with this opinion.

Reversed and Remanded.

■ POINTS TO CONSIDER

1. **Homestead.** In *Johnson*, why did it matter that the property at issue was classified as "homestead" property? The homestead exemption places a certain amount of core property beyond the reach of creditors. As the Florida Supreme Court explained, homestead attempts to strike a balance between protecting creditors' rights and providing a safety net for debtors:

   As a matter of public policy, the purpose of the homestead exemption is to promote the stability and welfare of the state by securing to the householder a home, so that the homeowner and his or her heirs may live beyond the reach of financial misfortune and the demands of creditors who have given credit under such law.

---

[12] In addition, such an agreement or instrument should be recorded or otherwise public so as to allay the possibility of fraud. *See Knickerbocker*, 912 P.2d at 976 (noting "an unrecorded and unwitnessed unilateral transaction may allow one joint tenant to defraud the other").

Public Health Trust of Dade Cnty. v. Lopez, 531 So. 2d 946, 948 (Fla. 1988). Homestead protects only the premises actually occupied by the debtor as a *permanent residence* and a certain amount of appurtenant (attached) land. So, for example, a Minnesota resident could not claim a Florida condominium as his homestead just because it is worth more, if he could not prove that it was his permanent place of residence. *See* In re Cochrane, 178 B.R. 1011 (D. Minn. 1995) (debtor stayed in Naples condo only a few weeks a year). Similarly, a South Dakota farmer could only claim the "home place," not the more valuable crop land several miles away. Homestead protections vary widely by state. In some states, the exemption is of minimal importance due to very restrictive caps on value. *See, e.g.*, 42 Pa. Cons. Stat. §8123 (2014) ($300 limit); Mich. Comp. Laws §600.6023 (2018) (limit $3,500). In contrast, some states place no direct value cap on the homestead exemption, but limit the exemption by acreage. *See, e.g.*, Tex. Const. art. XVI, §51 (1876) (10 acres of property within city or 200 acres outside); Kan. Stat. Ann. §60-2301 (2017) (one acre within an incorporated town or 160 acres outside). *See also* Alison D. Morantz, *There's No Place Like Home: Homestead Exemption and Judicial Constructions of Family in Nineteenth-Century America*, 24 Law & Hist. Rev. 245, 255 (2006) (homestead exemption found in all but two states). In many states, homestead laws also require both spouses to join in any conveyance or mortgage of the homestead property, even if title to the property is in one spouse only. *See, e.g.*, Ala. Code 1975 §6-10-3 (2017). This provides, for this limited property at least, protection in some ways similar to the tenancy by the entirety. For a history and summary of homestead laws, see Ryan P. Rivera, *State Homestead Exemptions and Their Effect on Federal Bankruptcy Laws*, 39 Real Prop. Prob. & Tr. J. 71 (2004). Do homestead protections further the *personhood policies* of property law? *See* Benjamin Barros, *Home as a Legal Concept*, 46 Santa Clara L. Rev. 255 (2006).

2. **Fairness concerns.** The *Johnson* court indicates in a footnote that an instrument of severance should be recorded or "otherwise public" to avoid fraud. As we will discuss in Chapter 7, a deed is the instrument of conveyance for real property interests. Deeds normally do not need to be recorded (or made "otherwise public") in order to be valid; in fact, a deed is considered valid and effective the moment it is executed and delivered to the grantee. So why does the Iowa court state that this sort of instrument should be recorded or made public, "to allay the possibility of fraud"? Consider the case of Riddle v. Harmon, 162 Cal. Rptr. 530 (Cal. Ct. App. 1980), which the Iowa court refers to as one of the leading cases abandoning strict adherence to the four unities. The court describes Mrs. Riddle's attempt to unilaterally sever the joint tenancy:

Mr. and Mrs. Riddle purchased a parcel of real estate, taking title as joint tenants. Several months before her death, Mrs. Riddle retained an attorney to plan her estate. After reviewing pertinent documents, he advised her that the property was held in joint tenancy and that, upon her death, the property would pass to her husband. Distressed upon learning this, she requested that the joint tenancy be terminated so that she could dispose of her interest by will. As a result, the attorney prepared a grant deed whereby Mrs. Riddle granted to herself an undivided one-half interest in the subject property. The document also provided that "The purpose of this Grant Deed is to terminate those joint tenancies formerly existing between the Grantor, FRANCES P. RIDDLE, and JACK C. RIDDLE, her husband. . . ." He also prepared a will disposing of Mrs. Riddle's interest in the property. Both the grant deed and will were executed on December 8, 1975. Mrs. Riddle died 20 days later.

Id. at 525. The trial court "refused to sanction her plan to sever the joint tenancy and quieted title to the property in her husband." *Id.* The California Court of Appeal reversed, holding that Frances successfully severed the joint tenancy. The court noted: "An indisputable right of each joint tenant is the power to convey his or her separate estate by way of gift or otherwise without the knowledge or consent of the other joint tenant and to thereby terminate the joint tenancy." *Id.* at 527.

One joint tenant certainly could accomplish a unilateral severance by using a straw person—conveying to someone (e.g., her lawyer) who would then convey it immediately back. As noted above, California had already dispensed with the "two to transfer" rule in the *creation* of joint tenancies, allowing a sole owner of property to convey to himself and others in joint tenancy, without going through a straw. Therefore, the *Riddle* court found no reason to require the use of a straw to sever the joint tenancy either.

Note that Frances accomplished this severance of the joint tenancy without the knowledge or consent of her husband Jack. What issues do you see with this type of *"secret severance"*? Assume that Jack and Frances poured most of their retirement savings into buying Blackacre as an investment, taking title as joint tenants. They also made mirror image wills granting each other all of their estates. But soon thereafter, Frances began an affair with her dancing instructor, Felipe, and in the thrall of passion, executed a deed conveying her share of Blackacre to herself, as tenant in common, which she placed in an envelope in the custody of her executor, along with her new will, which devised her interest in Blackacre to Felipe. Jack knows nothing about these developments. If Jack dies first, she can simply tear up the deed, with what result? However, if she dies first, she has directed her executor to open the envelope and reveal to the world her severance of the joint tenancy. *See also* Wood v. Pavlin, 467 S.W.3d 323 (Mo. Ct. App. 2015) (severance when one brother conveyed his share of joint tenancy secretly into a revocable trust).

How would the Iowa Supreme Court's requirement of recording ameliorate the unfairness of this result? Note that some states now have statutes to prevent a "secret severance." *See, e.g.,* Cal. Civ. Code §683.2(c) (2018) (deed not effective as severance unless recorded before the severing tenant's death—unless it is made less than three days before death and recorded shortly after). *See generally* John V. Orth, *The Perils of Joint Tenancies,* 44 Real Prop. Tr. & Est. L.J. 427 (2009). How would Jack's protection be stronger if Blackacre had been held in a tenancy by the entirety? Would Jack's interests be protected if the property was the couple's homestead, instead of an investment? We will consider this problem again when we discuss marital property protections in further detail below.

■ PROBLEMS: SEVERANCE OF JOINT TENANCY

Assume a court applies the intent-based analysis of the *Johnson* case. Assume A and B hold Blackacre in joint tenancy. What would be result of the following situations:

1. A states in her will, "I hereby declare my intent to sever the joint tenancy in Blackacre and to pass my undivided interest through this will." The will devises her interest in Blackacre to X.
2. A signs a notarized "declaration," stating her intention to sever the joint tenancy in Blackacre and attaches it to her will, which provides for her interest in Blackacre to go to X.
3. A signs a deed conveying her interest in Blackacre to herself as tenant in common. She does not record the deed, but instead places it in an envelope along with her will, which devises her interest in Blackacre to X.
4. A not only signs the deed conveying her interest to herself as tenant in common, but she records the deed. She then devises her interest in Blackacre to X in her will.

If you think that some of these attempts at severance would be ineffective, explain why, given that A's intent seems clear in each case.

Other Actions That Sever the Joint Tenancy

We know that a conveyance by one joint tenant of his or her interest effects a severance. What other actions could destroy the unities, perhaps inadvertently? Courts have considered severance issues in the following situations:

(1) Mortgage. What if one joint tenant mortgages her individual interest? In some jurisdictions, the mortgage may be held to have destroyed the unities and severed the joint tenancy. As we will discuss in relation to real estate financing, some states view a mortgage as a conveyance of title to the lender or a trustee, who holds the property interest in trust until the debt is paid, much like a pawnbroker holds personal property as security for a loan. In those "title theory" states, the borrower actually signs a "deed of trust" conveying the property as security for the loan. Arguably, this conveyance destroys the unities.

Most states, however, view the mortgage simply as a *lien* on the property. The borrower retains title, but it is now encumbered by the mortgage. Those "lien theory" states have held that a mortgage by one joint tenant does not effect a severance.

> ➤ A recent example is Smith v. Bank of America, 957 N.Y.S.2d 705 (N.Y. App. Div. 2012), Teresa Smith deeded Blackacre to herself and her boyfriend David Hassid as joint tenants with the right of survivorship in 1999. Unbeknownst to Smith, in 2006 Hassid obtained a $300,000 loan from Bank

of America (BoA) secured by a mortgage on Blackacre. When Hassad died in 2009, BoA declared the loan to be in default and attempted to foreclose on Blackacre. BoA argued that the mortgage severed the joint tenancy, such that Hassid and Smith were tenants in common when he died. Smith argued that, while Hassid could encumber his interest, his share of the joint tenancy was extinguished upon his death, so the mortgage was no longer valid. The court held the mortgage did not sever the joint tenancy:

> Hence, since a mortgage is only a lien, Hassid's act of giving a mortgage on the subject property did not act to sever the joint tenancy relationship between him and the plaintiff.

Id. at 709. Because Hassid could mortgage only his own interest, the court held that the lien was extinguished by his death. Thus, Smith owned the property free and clear, while BoA was left holding the bag. *See also* CitiMortgage, Inc. v. Brown, 45 N.E.3d 258 (Ohio Ct. App. 2015)(mortgage entered into by one joint tenant extinguished by death).

Of course, if the loan is in default while the debtor tenant is alive, the lender can foreclose on the debtor's interest. Once that interest is transferred to a new owner during the foreclosure process, the unities are clearly destroyed and a severance has occurred. Otherwise, the lien's value depends on whether the debtor tenant survives the non-debtor tenant. In states that follow the lien theory, lenders can protect themselves by never lending to joint tenants unless all joint tenants sign the mortgage. *See also* Harms v. Sprague, 473 N.E.2d 930 (Ill. 1984).

In contrast, some states taking the *title theory* approach to mortgages continue to find a severance if less than all joint tenants join in the mortgage.

> ➤ In Countrywide Home Loans, Inc. v. Reed, 725 S.E.2d 667 (N.C. Ct. App. 2012), for example, Mrs. Smith took title to Blackacre in joint tenancy with Judy and Troy Reed, who lived with and cared for her (the Reeds held an undivided half interest together). Mrs. Smith then entered into a mortgage on Blackacre with Countryside, but neither Judy nor Troy signed the mortgage instruments. After Mrs. Smith died, Countryside sought clarification of its interest in the property. The court held that, because North Carolina is a title theory state, the mortgage entered into by Mrs. Smith severed the joint tenancy, converting it to a tenancy in common. Upon her death, her half interest in Blackacre did not pass to the Reeds by right of survivorship, but passed through her estate and remained encumbered by the mortgage. *See also* Franklin Credit Mgmt. Corp. v. Hanney, 262 P.3d 406 (Utah Ct. App. 2011) (mortgage by one joint tenant severs joint tenancy).

Not all title theory states agree, however. In Arizona, for example, a court concluded that even though a deed of trust conveys a form of legal title to the trustees, and "clearly destroys the common law unity of title," it does not carry any of the incidents of ownership of property (such as possession). Thus, there was no reason to treat the conveyance of a trust deed as any different from a mortgage. As the Arizona court put it: "We do not believe that dogged adherence to the requirements of the four unities in the context of severance is required by our case law." Brant v. Hargrove, 632 P.2d 978, 984 (Ariz. Ct. App. 1981). Because there was no evidence of an *intent to sever*, the court held that a deed of trust by one joint tenant did not sever the joint tenancy. *Id.*; *see also* Hamel v. Gootkin, 20 Cal. Rptr. 372 (Cal. Ct. App. 1962) (deed of trust by one joint tenant does not sever joint tenancy).

In some states, the issue has been resolved by the legislature. South Carolina, for example, simply prohibits encumbrances, such as mortgages, unless all joint tenants join in the instrument. S.C. Code Ann. §27-7-40(a)(iii) (2011). Wisconsin takes a compromise approach: a statute provides that a mortgage by one joint tenant does not sever the joint tenancy, but the mortgage survives the death of the joint tenant as an encumbrance on that interest. Wis. Stat. §700.24 (2018). Which solution do you think makes most sense?

(2) Lease. If one joint tenant enters into a long-term lease, is the joint tenancy severed? English courts said yes, reasoning that the conveyance of a leasehold destroys the unity of interest, because the joint tenant who entered into the lease has given up the right to present possession. One American jurisdiction seems to agree. *See* Alexander v. Boyer, 253 A.2d 359, 366 (Md. 1969).

Most jurisdictions, however, find no severance in the lease situation, as exemplified by the following influential case.

CASE SUMMARY: Tenhet v. Boswell, 554 P.2d 330 (Cal. 1976)

Johnson and Tenhet owned property as joint tenants. Apparently without Tenhet's knowledge or consent, Johnson leased the property to Boswell for a period of ten years, including a right of first refusal to purchase the property. Johnson died three months later and Boswell sought sole ownership of the property, free and clear of the leasehold. The court's reasoning is another illustration of modern courts' retreat from a formalist application of the four unities test, in favor of considering the intent of the parties:

> It could be argued that a lease destroys the unities of interest and possession because the leasing joint tenant transfers to the lessee his present possessory interest and retains a mere reversion. . . . Moreover, the possibility that the term of the lease may continue beyond the lifetime of the lessor is inconsistent with a complete right of survivorship. . . .
>
> We are mindful that the issue here presented is "an ancient controversy, going back to Coke and Littleton." (2 Am. Law of Prop. (1952) §6.2, p. 10.) Yet the problem is like a comet in our law: though its existence in theory has been frequently recognized its observed passages are few. Some authorities support the view that a lease

by a joint tenant to a third person effects a complete and final severance of the joint tenancy. . . . Such a view is generally based upon what is thought to be the English common law rule. . . .

As we shall explain, it is our opinion that a lease is not so inherently inconsistent with joint tenancy as to create a severance, either temporary or permanent.

If plaintiff and Johnson did not choose to continue the joint tenancy, they might have converted it into a tenancy in common by written mutual agreement. . . . They might also have jointly conveyed the property to a third person and divided the proceeds. Even if they could not agree to act in concert, either plaintiff or Johnson might have severed the joint tenancy, with or without the consent of the other, by an act which was clearly indicative of an intent to terminate, such as a conveyance of her or his entire interest. Either might also have brought an action to partition the property, which, upon judgment, would have effected a severance. Because a joint tenancy may be created only by express intent, and because there are alternative and unambiguous means of altering the nature of that estate, we hold that the lease here in issue did not operate to sever the joint tenancy.

Having concluded that the joint tenancy was not severed by the lease and that sole ownership of the property therefore vested in plaintiff upon her joint tenant's death by operation of her right of survivorship, we turn next to the issue whether she takes the property unencumbered by the lease. . . . By the very nature of joint tenancy. . .the interest of the nonsurviving joint tenant extinguishes upon his death. And as the lease is valid only "in so far as the interest of the lessor in the joint property is concerned," it follows that the lease of the joint tenancy property also expires when the lessor dies. . . .

As these decisions demonstrate, a joint tenant may, during his lifetime, grant certain rights in the joint property without severing the tenancy. But when such a joint tenant dies his interest dies with him, and any encumbrances placed by him on the property become unenforceable against the surviving joint tenant. For the reasons stated a lease falls within this rule.

Any other result would defeat the justifiable expectations of the surviving joint tenant.

Id. at 334-37. Would it matter to you whether the lease was a periodic, year-to-year lease, or a 10-year lease? How about a 99-year lease? At some point, would you agree with the English rule that a conveyance of a long-term leasehold has destroyed the unity of interest? What if the joint tenant grants a third party a life estate or remainder interest in her share of the property? Klouda v. Pechousek, 110 N.E.2d 258 (Ill. 1953) (conveyance of remainder interest, reserving a life estate, destroys the unity of interest and severs joint tenancy). Is a leasehold any different?

■ PROBLEMS: MORE SEVERANCE ISSUES

1. Bean and Quick owned Blackacre in Kissimmee, Florida as joint tenants. An oil and gas company wanted to drill on Blackacre. Bean, who lived in Kissimmee, signed a lease with the company on June 14, 1979. Quick, who

lived in Long Island, New York, signed an identical lease with the company on September 15, 1979. Both leases were recorded on September 20, 1979. Quick then died and his estate claimed that Bean no longer had a right of survivorship to Quick's half interest. The royalties from the lease turned out to be substantial. Was there a severance? *See* Estate of Quick, 905 A.2d 471 (Pa. 2006).

2. Nina and Larry Garland owned Blackacre, a house in Helena, Montana, as joint tenants. Nina died and Larry was convicted of murdering her. Her will leaves her estate to her two daughters. Who now owns Blackacre? *See* Estate of Garland, 928 P.2d 928 (Mont. 1996); In re Estate of Thomann, 649 N.W. 2d 1 (Iowa 2002). What if Larry had been convicted of involuntary manslaughter instead?

3. Two cousins, Richard and Douglas, owned an 80-acre farm as joint tenants. On December 18, 2009, without Doug's knowledge or consent, Richard executed a deed conveying his half interest to himself as tenant in common. He gave the deed to his lawyer, who mailed it to the county recorder's office on December 22. Richard died on December 28 and the recorder's office recorded the deed on December 29.

As you will learn in a subsequent chapter, a deed is valid when it has been "delivered" to the grantee; recording is not necessary for the validity of the deed. When a grantor is conveying a property interest to himself, when has the deed been delivered? Douglas argued in this case that there was no effective severance before Richard died; is he correct? *See* Reicherter v. McCauley, 283 P.3d 219 (Kan. Ct. App. 2012).

E PARTITION ISSUES

Partition ends the co-ownership of the property and divides it up between the owners. In general, any co-tenant holding an interest in joint tenancy or tenancy in common can request a court to partition the property at any time. A tenancy by the entirety, by contrast, cannot be partitioned (except through divorce) unless both spouses consent.

Notice that the joint tenant or tenant in common of real estate generally has the absolute right to obtain partition, absent some agreement or limitation in the deed or will granting the interest. As one court noted, partition has advantages favored by the law "because it secures peace, promotes industry and enterprise, and avoids compelling unwilling persons to use their property in common." Miller v. Miller, 564 P.2d 524 (Kan. 1977) (citing 59 Am. Jur. 2d Partition §3 (2003)). There are some limited exceptions to this rule:

- Some courts state that partition may be denied if it would violate public policy. So, for example, partition may be delayed if it would result in the minor children of one of the co-tenants being thrown out of their home.

Lawrence v. Harvey, 607 P.2d 55 (Mont. 1980). The court, suggested that partition can be barred in their state due to a public policy to keep usable land intact and able to be marketable.

■ The deed or will creating the co-tenancy may prohibit partition. Or, the co-tenants may contract between themselves to limit partition. Courts generally uphold such provisions, as long as they are of reasonable duration. Otherwise, they can be struck down as unreasonable restraints on alienation. *See* Succession of Crute v. Crute, 226 So.3d 1161 (La. Ct. App. 2017) (restraint on partition for indefinite time held void).

In the absence of one of these limited exceptions, if one co-tenant seeks partition, there is no question of *whether* partition will occur, the only issue is *how*. There are two possibilities:

■ *Partition in kind* (also called *actual* or *physical* partition), in which the property is physically divided into pieces and given to each co-tenant as separate property; or

■ *Partition by sale*, in which the property is sold by the court and the proceeds divided according to the ownership shares of each co-tenant.

Obviously, if the parties can agree as to an equitable division, they can simply end the co-tenancy by deed. For example, if A and B own an office building as tenants in common and are not getting along, A may offer to buy B's share and end the concurrent ownership. Or, the parties may agree to sell the property and divide the proceeds. If the parties can't agree, however, a judicial partition may be obtained.

Most jurisdictions have a statute setting forth the procedure for partition. Often the statutes call for commissioners or referees (who may be real estate experts) to be appointed to examine the property and recommend a fair division—or to determine that the property is not susceptible to a fair physical partition.

The general rule is that *partition in kind is favored*. Why do you think that is the rule? In general, a *partition by sale* will be ordered only if a partition in kind cannot be made without prejudice to the interests of the parties. In most states, this means that the property will be sold only if splitting it into shares is impracticable or will significantly reduce the value of the property. Note how the South Dakota Supreme Court interpreted this test in the following case.

E L I v. E L I

557 N.W.2d 405 (1997) Supreme Court of South Dakota

GILBERTSON, Justice.

Jody Eli appeals the trial court's judgment ordering the sale at public auction of property in which she owned an undivided one-third interest. We reverse and remand for further proceedings consistent with this opinion.

FACTS AND PROCEDURE

The property at issue in this case consists of 112.5 acres in Turner County, South Dakota. This property was formerly owned by Myrtle J. Eli and has been owned by members of Myrtle's family for almost one hundred years. In May 1992, Myrtle deeded 117 acres, which included the subject property, to her three sons: Chester, James and Dale. The deed gave each of the sons a one-third undivided interest. In July 1993, Dale transferred his one-third undivided interest to his daughter, Jody Eli, by quit claim deed.

This property consists of agricultural land and sits in a backward "L" shape. It is divided into two parcels for tax purposes. In 1995, the eastern strip, containing 74.92 acres, was assessed at $40,565 or $541.44 per acre. The western parcel, containing 37.35 acres, was assessed that same year at $20,790 or $556.63 per acre. A small portion of the original 117 acres is excepted out of the southeastern quarter of the property, leaving the 112.5 acres at issue. This small portion belongs to Dale Eli, by virtue of his receiving the land separately from Myrtle prior to her death, and is not in dispute here. Dale currently resides on this small outlot.

There are no material improvements on the property. It has no wells and rural water is not available to it at the present time. All parts of the property contain comparable soil type and crop production with an estimated 27 acres of tillable ground on each of three approximately 40-acre parcels. Each tract has approximately 5-10 acres of pasture with a creek running through them. The land has been tested and classified by the Soil Conservation Service as prime farmland, with a lesser quality, rough terrain surrounding the creek bed that runs through all three parcels. The two approximately 40-acre parcels which lie in the bottom portion of the "L" to the south enjoy separate highway access, while the only access to the northern 40 acres, the upper portion of the "L," is through one of the southern two parcels. Currently, access to the northern parcel is through the 40 acres lying directly to the south.

Following presentation of all the evidence, the trial court determined the ownership interests of the parties and ordered the property sold at public auction. The court further ordered a referee be appointed to oversee the sale. Jody, who had requested the trial court partition the property and order the sale of all but her one-third undivided interest, appeals the judgment raising the following issue:

Whether the Elis established by a preponderance of the evidence that great prejudice would result if the subject property were partitioned rather than sold as a whole unit?

ANALYSIS AND DECISION

Partition of real property actions are governed by SDCL Ch. 21-45. SDCL 21-45-1 provides cotenants the right to bring a partition action and to have the property, or any part thereof, sold:

When several cotenants hold and are in possession of real property as partners, joint tenants, or tenants in common, in which one or more of them have an estate of inheritance or for life or lives or for years, an action may be brought by one or more of such persons for a partition thereof according to the respective rights of the persons interested therein *and for a sale of such property or a part thereof, if it appear [sic] that a partition cannot be made without great prejudice to the owners.* (emphasis added).

SDCL 21-45-28 provides the statutory test the court must apply in determining whether partition or a sale is appropriate:

If it appear [sic] to the satisfaction of the court that the property, or any part of it, is so situated that partition cannot be made without great prejudice to the owners, the court may order a sale thereof, for which purpose it may appoint one or more, but not exceeding three referees, in its discretion. (emphasis added).

. . . In Johnson v. Hendrickson, 71 S.D. 392, 396, 24 N.W.2d 914, 916 (1946), we interpreted the predecessor statute to SDCL 21-45-28 to mean that a trial court may order a sale of the property if the court is satisfied that, were the property partitioned, the value of each cotenant's share "would be materially less than his share of the money equivalent that could probably be obtained for the whole." (citing Kluthe v. Hammerquist, 45 S.D. 476, 188 N.W. 749 (1922)). "A sale is justified if it appears to the satisfaction of the court that the value of the land when divided into parcels is substantially less than its value when owned by one person." *Id.*

When applying the above definition, it is also necessary to heed the following policy considerations. Where it can be had without great prejudice to the owners, the law favors a partition in kind rather than a sale and a division of the proceeds among the owners. *Berg*, 181 N.W.2d at 735 (applying a statute similar to SDCL 21-45-28 and quoting *Swogger*, 243 Minn. 458, 68 N.W.2d 376). "Unless great prejudice is shown, a presumption prevails that partition in kind should be made. Forced sales are strongly disfavored." Schnell v. Schnell, 346 N.W.2d 713, 716 (N.D. 1984) (citing *Berg*, 181 N.W.2d at 735 and Richmond v. Dofflemyer, 105 Cal. App. 3d 745, 164 Cal. Rptr. 727, 733 (1980)).

The burden of proof to establish great prejudice such that partition is not feasible rests with the party seeking the sale. *Nelson*, 74 S.D. at 442, 54 N.W.2d at 324: *Kluthe*, 45 S.D. at 479, 188 N.W. at 750. The court must decide in a partition action whether the premises can be physically partitioned, or whether the parties seeking partition have met their burden of proof that the premises should be sold at a partition sale and the proceeds divided among the tenants in common. Murphy v. Connolly, 81 S.D. 644, 653, 140 N.W.2d 394, 399 (1966).

The trial court found the subject property would sell for $50-$100 more per acre if sold as a whole 112.5-acre unit rather than as separate parcels. This finding is not clearly erroneous. It was based, in part, on testimony regarding the cost of digging wells that would be required to get water to the property so the individual parcels could be used as pastureland. It was also based on the distance the property lies from any town and the relatively small size of the entire unit. Testimony indicated a potential purchaser of this property might be a neighboring farmer who would wish to add to his own acreage, rather than someone attempting to sustain a farm operation on the 112.5 acres alone or a person looking to reside in the country. Testimony was offered that, considering the greater capabilities of modern farming machinery, smaller tracts of land are not as popular as they once were and the number of potential buyers would be decreased if the property were divided. It was estimated this property, sold as an entire unit, would sell for $400-$500 per acre. Based on these estimates, testimony was offered that the property would be worth 10-20% more if sold as a whole than if divided into smaller units. The land appraiser who testified to these figures characterized this as a "significant" difference.

Following trial, the court ordered the entire property to be sold at public auction and appointed a referee to oversee the sale. In making this determination, the trial court considered the lesser value of the land if it were partitioned rather than sold as a whole. The trial court further considered the character and location of the land and, noting inaccessibility to the northeast parcel, indicated the property would be impractical to partition. The court also reflected on the size of the land and the respective usefulness of the parcels if the property were sold as a single unit. The court stated this was farmland which, based on the testimony and the farming practices in the area, would be less useful if the property were partitioned in kind than if sold as one 112.5-acre unit. As there were no improvements of any consequence to the subject property, this was not a factor in the court's decision.

In *Johnson*, 71 S.D. at 396, 24 N.W.2d at 916, we reviewed a trial court's decision in a partition action in which the court ordered the sale of 160 acres of farmland in Clark County. In affirming the trial court's order to sell the property as an entire unit rather than divide it into "four or more separate tracts," we held that in this case, such division would result in material depreciation in the value of the property, both in terms of salability and as to the property's use for agricultural purposes. *Id.* (citations omitted)....

However, monetary considerations, while admittedly significant, do not rise to the level of excluding all other appropriate considerations.[13] SDCL 21-45-1 and 21-45-28 speak of "great prejudice," not "great financial prejudice." The sale of property "without [the owner's] consent is an extreme exercise of power warranted only in clear cases." Delfino v. Vealencis, 181 Conn. 533, 436 A.2d 27, 30 (1980) (quoting Ford v. Kirk, 41 Conn. 9, 12 (Conn. 1874)). We believe this to be especially so when the land in question has descended from generation to generation. While it is true that the Eli brothers' expert testified that if partitioned, the separate parcels would sell for $50 to $100 less per acre, this fact alone is not dispositive. One's land possesses more than mere economic utility; it "means the full range of the benefit the parties may be expected to derive from their ownership of their respective shares." Eaton v. Hackett, 352 A.2d 748, 750 (Me. 1976).

---

[13] One such appropriate consideration is ownership of agricultural lands by family members. The Legislature has recognized the value of the family-owned farm in South Dakota and has enacted statutes to protect its family ownership status. See SDCL Ch. 47-9A, Corporate Farming Restrictions, and SDCL Ch. 43-2A, Alien Ownership Act. Further, this Court has sought to protect ownership of agricultural land by families in property divisions arising out of divorce cases....

Such value must be weighed for its effect upon all parties involved, not just those advocating a sale. Butte Creek Island Ranch v. Crim, 136 Cal. App. 3d 360, 186 Cal. Rptr. 252, 255 (1982); Brown v. Boger, 263 N.C. 248, 139 S.E.2d 577, 583 (1965) (noting sale instead of partition "should not be done except in cases of imperious necessity . . . it is no objection to a partition in kind that some of the cotenants prefer a sale to a partition"). To this extent, the previous monetary definition of "great prejudice" as found in *Johnson, supra*, is modified to include consideration of the totality of the circumstances.

The case of *Schnell*, 346 N.W.2d 713, is particularly instructive. The North Dakota Supreme Court remanded a forced sale of a family ranch and required a partition in kind, which could have been accomplished without great prejudice to the owners. *Id.* at 721. It held:

> Given the duration of [one party's] involvement with the ranch and her sentimental attachment to the land, her resistance to a partition and sale is logical. In this respect we note that the sale of real property against the wishes of a joint owner can be likened to a forced sale. Forced sales seldom produce the highest return on property. In Vesper v. Farnsworth, 40 Wis. 357, 362 (1876), the court said that the power to convert real estate into money against the will of an owner "is an extraordinary and dangerous power, and ought never to be exercised unless the necessity therefor is clearly established." Similarly, in Haggerty v. Nobles, 244 Or. 428, 419 P.2d 9, 12 (1966), the court observed that although a court must occasionally order a sale in an appropriate case, "it is obnoxious to compel a person to sell his property."

Id. Therefore, the court held, "[i]f only two persons are owners of property and each treasures its heritage, partition in kind will generally preserve those personal interests better than a partition and sale." *Id.* In so holding, the court took several factors into account in determining value, including the financial abilities of the parties to repurchase the land through the sale, the location and size of the property, the use of the property before and after the sale, and the sentimental value attached to the parcel, although the court noted that sentimental reasons are subordinate to the parties' pecuniary interests. *Id.* at 716. Applying a definition of "great prejudice" identical to this Court's interpretation of that term in *Johnson*, the North Dakota Supreme Court noted that the primary question, contrary to the trial court's formulation, is not solely "which alternative would provide optimal economic value or maximum functional use." *Id.*

We agree with the North Dakota Supreme Court's treatment of the issue, and its application of stringent standards to those advocating sale and attempting to prove "great prejudice" from partition in kind. The Elis' piece of land is easily separable into three physically equal parcels, with similar soil content and physical layout. It can still be used for farmland as it was before the partition. There may be some interested in buying the three parcels as a whole; however, there was no mention that there would be a dearth of buyers interested in buying them separately. In fact, Jody Eli's father testified that he had had a neighbor express interest in one of the parcels. The Eli brothers' expert even admitted that the parcels could be bought and farmed separately. *Cf. Nelson*, 74 S.D. 441, 54 N.W.2d 324 (wherein this Court affirmed the trial court's order of sale of a ranch as a whole unit with one set of buildings which could not be divided and in which testimony indicated division, if possible, would not be practical).

It is apparent from our review of the record that Jody's primary concern in resisting a sale of the entire property is keeping a portion of land that has been in her family for almost a century and that she plans to continue to use as rented farmland. She has not been intractable over what parcel she desires or whether she wants exclusive use of it. She even consented to an easement over the parcel she eventually retains in favor of the other subservient parcels. Jody has a right, equal to that of her uncles, to pursue her personal interests regarding her own property. The law favors partition in kind because it does not compel a person to sell property against a person's will and it does not disturb the existing form of inheritance. Phillips v. Phillips, 170 Neb. 733, 104 N.W.2d 52, 56 (1960). Moreover, under the concept known as owelty, and in order to retain ownership of her property, Jody has offered to pay compensatory adjustments to the Eli brothers to make up the $50 to $100 difference in price per acre, if in fact the difference exists after the sale and should the court find that equity requires her to do so. *See* SDCL 21-45-19 (under principles of equity, trial court may order compensatory payments between parties to make equal their respective rights).

We find the trial court in this case placed too little emphasis on all of the other factors save the monetary difference. While it is true that the land may bring a lower price when sold in separate parcels, it is not so low that it could not be rectified by reasonable compensatory adjustments, nor so low that it alone carries the day when balanced against the competing interests of land ownership and inheritance and Jody's amenable attitude to equitable adjustments. The parties seeking the sale have the burden of proof to establish great prejudice and overturn the presumption favoring partition in kind. Weighing all of these factors, we believe a $50 to $100 per acre diminution in selling price is not enough to "greatly prejudice" the Eli brothers and they have failed to sustain their burden under SDCL 21-45-1.

We reverse and remand for further proceedings consistent with this opinion.

■ POINTS TO CONSIDER

1. **What's the test?** We noted above that most courts will order a sale if physical partition is impracticable or will be prejudicial to the interests of the parties. What test does the *Eli* court use for deciding which form of partition to use? How does it interpret the term *great prejudice*? If the court believes that a sale is not required merely because the property would lose value if divided, what does a co-tenant have to show to require a sale? Can you list some of the factors a court should consider using a "totality of the circumstances" test?

   The South Dakota court is not alone in determining that reduced economic value does not always justify a partition by sale. *See, e.g.,* Ark Land Co. v. Harper, 599 S.E.2d 754, 761 (W. Va. 2004) ("economic value of the property is not the exclusive test for deciding whether to partition in kind or by sale. Evidence of longstanding ownership, coupled with sentimental or emotional interests in the property, may also be considered in deciding whether the interests of the party opposing the sale will be prejudiced by the property's sale.").

Nevertheless, there are plenty of cases in which courts have ordered partition by sale over the objection of one or more co-tenants, especially where there are many co-tenants and the property is impracticable to divide. In fact, studies show that most partition actions result in a sale, despite the stated preference for partition in kind. *See* Yun-Chien Chang & Lee Anne Fennell, *Partition and Revelation,* 81 U. Chi. L. Rev. 27, 30 (2014) ("Most American jurisdictions have a common law rule that purports to favor partition in kind, but scholars suggest that courts usually order partition by sale.").

Contrary to the majority rule, Iowa has a statute that establishes a preference for partition by sale unless one of the co-tenants proves that physical partition is "equitable and practicable." This shifts the burden of proof to the party seeking partition in kind. Iowa Code 651.2; *see* Newhall v. Roll, 888 N.W.2d 636 (Iowa 2016).

2. **Policy.** What property policies explored in Chapter 1 are behind the preference for partition in kind? What policy motivated the *Eli* court to focus on the party's attachment to the land? On the other hand, what property policies would be furthered by deciding in favor of sale rather than physical partition? What do you think inspired the Iowa legislature to adopt this preference?

3. **Owelty.** The equitable remedy of "owelty" can be used by courts to make partition in kind possible in many cases. If there is a clear way to physically divide the property, but the parcels have unequal value, the court can order a monetary payment from one co-tenant to another to even up the shares. *See, e.g.,* Ala. Code §35-6-24 (2017); Dewrell v. Lawrence, 58 P.3d 223, 227 (Okla. Civ. App. 2002). For example, assume A and B own a 160-acre farm as tenants in common, of which 80 acres is pasture and 80 acres is more valuable crop land. It would hurt the overall value of the property to give each co-tenant 40 acres of each type of land. Instead, the court could award A the crop land, on the condition that she pay to B an amount representing the difference in value. Does the *Eli* court's use of owelty differ from this typical use?

4. **Prohibiting partition.** Assume that Elizabeth wants to leave the family's ancestral home, Balmoral, to her grandchildren, Harry and William. Elizabeth knows that Harry is a bit irresponsible and she is afraid he will immediately want to partition the estate and sell it, whereas she wants them to live there and make it home. Can she devise Balmoral "to Harry and William in joint tenancy with the right of survivorship, but without the right to partition the property during their lives"? Could Harry and William agree between themselves not to partition? Or more importantly, would (or should) a court enforce such an agreement?

5. **Unequal shares.** Although there is a presumption that co-tenants have equal shares, a court need not divide the property evenly if there is evidence

presented that the co-tenants contributed unequal amounts toward the purchase of the property. Even then, the court might be persuaded that the co-tenant who paid more of the purchase price had the intent to make a gift of a pro rata share.

> ➤ In Jones v. Graphia, 95 So. 3d 751 (Miss. Ct. App. 2012), a couple had dated for two years and purchased a house in Mississippi as joint tenants. Graphia testified that he paid the entire $274,000 purchase price of the house, as well as all the utilities, insurance, taxes, and homeowners association dues. After the couple broke up, Graphia sought partition, but asked the court to award him the entire property, based on the couple's unequal contributions. The trial court agreed to that result and the appellate court affirmed. In dissent, Justice Carlton pointed out that when Graphia agreed to put Jones' name on the title, the law presumes that he intended to make her a gift of a half interest in the property. Although adjustments may be made to account for taxes and maintenance, e.g., equity cannot completely disregard how title is held to deny Jones her share of the estate.

Do you agree with the majority or the dissent? *See also* Hoit v. Rankin, 320 S.W.3d 761 (Mo. Ct. App. 2010) (the Hoits held property in joint tenancy with adult child and his wife; upon partition, court awarded Hoits 98 percent of proceeds because house was bought with their money); Maskill v. Cummins, 397 S.W.3d 27 (Mo. Ct. App. 2013)(husband awarded 87 percent of proceeds of joint tenancy property due to relative contributions).

How would the case have come out differently if Jones and Graphia had been married? As we will soon discover, a court dividing the assets of a married couple can "equitably" distribute that property, including real estate held in common. Thus, the court may decide that the house, held by H and W as joint tenants, should go to W, while allocating the car to H. If H and W are not married, however, that sort of equitable allocation is not available.

6. **A third way.** Should an alternative to partition in kind or by sale be allowed?

> ➤ Consider Fernandes v. Rodriguez, 761 A.2d 1283 (Conn. 2000). Eyvind and Maria bought a small apartment house as an investment and took title as joint tenants. Maria lived in one of the apartments and took care of the premises. The evidence showed that Maria did the maintenance and made repairs and that Eyvind did nothing but contribute $1,000 toward the closing costs of the purchase. Eyvind sought partition of the property, now worth about $60,000. Rather than ordering partition by sale or in kind (which would have been difficult), the trial court ordered Eyvind to relinquish his interest in the property upon payment by Maria of $4,605, which the court determined his interest to be worth. On appeal, the Connecticut Supreme Court held that this sort of equitable remedy was beyond the power of the court. If partition in kind was

impracticable, it had to order a sale, but then could exercise its equitable powers in determining how to split the proceeds. The court held: "On the basis of the history of the right to partition, and in light of the legislative treatment of that right, we have held repeatedly that in resolving partition actions, the only two modes of relief within the power of the court are partition by division of real estate and partition by sale." *Id.* at 1288-89.

Is that fair to Maria? Why do you think she opposed a sale? In response to *Fernandes*, the Connecticut legislature amended its partition statute to allow a court to adopt the *Fernandes* remedy if it determines that one or more of the persons owning the property have only a minimal interest in the property and a sale would not promote the interest of the owners. Conn. Gen Stat. § 52-500 (2017). Do you support that change?

The Uniform Partition of Heirs Property Act

The National Conference of Commissioners on Uniform State Laws (NCCUSL), also known as the Uniform Law Commission, drafts model legislation in a wide variety of legal areas, which then may be adopted by state legislatures. The most well known is the Uniform Commercial Code (a joint project with the American Law Institute), which you study in Contracts. The organization (which was established in 1892) has produced many other uniform laws that have been widely adopted and have brought greater uniformity as well as needed clarity to state law.

   One of NCCUSL's recent efforts is the Uniform Partition of Heirs Property Act (UPHPA), which addresses the issue of the forced sale of inherited property, at issue in the *Eli* case. NCCUSL describes the problem:

> Most higher-income families engage in sophisticated estate planning, ensuring a smooth transfer of wealth to the next generation. In contrast, lower-income landowners are more likely to use a simple will to divide property among children, or to die intestate. Unless a property owner specifies a different form of ownership, the heirs of the owner will inherit real estate as tenants-in-common under state property statutes. A tenant-in-common may sell his or her interest without the consent of the co-tenants, making it easy for non-family members—including real estate speculators—to acquire an interest in the property.[14]

---

[14] These quotes are taken from NCCUSL, Partition by Heirs Property Act Summary, *available at* www.uniform-laws.org.

The Commission describes a typical situation in which a widow dies intestate, so that her three children inherit her small farm as tenants in common. While two of the children want to keep the farm and live in the house, the third sells her share to an investor.

> [T]he investor can petition the court for a partition of the farm. If the property contains only one farmhouse, dividing it into shares of equal value would likely be difficult. Therefore, a court would likely order a partition-by-sale, forcing the two siblings to sell the property against their will. Even worse, forced sales often bring meager returns. The property could sell for a price well below market value, and the siblings would have little to show for their inheritance.

Typically, the property is sold at auction and a co-tenant will not have the access to ready capital necessary to buy the entire property. Studies have shown that the problem is especially acute among rural African Americans in the South, who owned between 16-19 million acres of agricultural land in the 1920s but now retain only about 7 million acres. *See, e.g.*, Faith Rivers, *Inequity in Equity: The Tragedy of Tenancy in Common for Heirs' Property Owners Facing Partition in Equity*, 17 Temp. Pol. & Civ. Rts. L. Rev. 1 (2007).

The UPHPA would change the rules for partition actions in cases where a co-tenant received his or her property interest from a relative. In those cases, if any co-tenant files a partition action, the Act essentially gives the other co-tenants a right of first refusal. The property is first appraised. Then, any co-tenant is permitted to buy the share of the co-tenant seeking partition at the appraised fair market value. The Act gives the co-tenants 45 days to elect that option and then another 60 days to arrange financing. If no co-tenant elects this option, the court is directed to favor partition in kind, unless "great prejudice" to the co-tenants would result. The Act specifically requires the court to consider, in making this determination, a co-tenant's "sentimental attachment" to the property and "the collective duration" of ownership of a co-tenant and his predecessors. Those factors are to be considered along with the question of whether physical partition would decrease the economic value of the property.

Even if a sale is ordered, the court is directed to first attempt to sell the property on the open market, rather than by auction. Why do you think the property might bring in a higher price using that method?

As of 2018, the Act has been enacted in ten states. Would you support the enactment of UPHPA in your state? Do you see any drawbacks to the Act? Are there any differences between the UPHPA and the court's test in *Eli v. Eli*?

■ PROBLEMS: PARTITION BY SALE OR IN KIND

Using the test applied in *Eli*, make an argument in each of these cases that partition by sale is most appropriate. Then argue the other side, in favor of partition in kind.

1. Seven co-tenants own a 100-acre parcel of land, containing 20 acres of timber, 70 acres of pasture, a farm pond, and a farm house. The farm has been in the family for generations. There appears to be a deposit of valuable gravel beneath at least 30 acres of the land, but the exact extent of the deposit is unclear.

2. Two business associates own an office building and an adjacent parking garage in the downtown business district as tenants in common. One of the co-tenants uses a floor of the building for her chiropractic office and has been doing so for several years. *See* Ferguson v. Ferris, 882 P.2d 1119 (Or. Ct. App. 1994).

F   TENANCY BY THE ENTIRETY

The *tenancy by the entirety* (TBE) is a form of ownership available to married couples in about half of U.S. jurisdictions. As we discussed above, the TBE is like a joint tenancy, in that each owner has a right of survivorship, but is unlike a joint tenancy in that one co-tenant cannot unilaterally transfer an interest in the property or partition it. Thus, the TBE is an important form of spousal security.

Because one spouse cannot unilaterally convey an interest in TBE property, this form of tenancy has significant implications for creditors, as the next case illustrates.

RBS CITIZENS, N.A. v. OUHRABKA

190 Vt. 251, 30 A.3d 1266 (2011)
Supreme Court of Vermont

REIBER, C.J.

This is an interlocutory appeal from the trial court's denial of appellant RBS's motion for a writ of attachment of appellee Jan Ouhrabka's property, which Ouhrabka owns jointly with his wife as tenants by entirety. The trial court held that a creditor, like RBS, cannot attach property owned jointly by a debtor and a nondebtor when they hold that property as tenants by entirety. RBS contends that the estate of tenancy by entirety is an anachronism whose continuing utility should be reconsidered. In the alternative, RBS argues that Vermont law does not explicitly preclude granting a creditor prejudgment attachment where the property is held jointly by the debtor and a nondebtor in a tenancy by entirety. We disagree and affirm.

The facts in the matter before us are uncontested. Ouhrabka is the sole owner of Providence Chain Co., a Rhode Island jewelry corporation with a principal place of business located in Providence, Rhode Island. On June 7, 2010, the Rhode Island superior court placed Providence Chain into receivership. As of that date, Providence Chain's outstanding indebtedness to RBS exceeded $15,000,000.

By execution of a personal guaranty, signed on August 31, 2006, Ouhrabka became personally liable up to $500,000 for loans to Providence Chain. Ouhrabka signed an amendment to this guaranty on March 18, 2009 which made his personal liability for debts of Providence Chain unlimited. As part of the loan process, Ouhrabka submitted a personal financial statement which listed the Vermont property in East Ryegate as a joint asset with a stated value of $250,000.

At the time Providence Chain was placed into receivership financial records demonstrated that liquidating the company could satisfy approximately $3,000,000 of the debt owed to RBS. RBS filed the underlying complaint, seeking to recover amounts owed by Ouhrabka to RBS pursuant to his individual unlimited guaranty with an estimated balance of $10,000,000. In conjunction with its complaint, RBS filed a motion pursuant to Vermont Rule of Civil Procedure 4.1(g) requesting the trial court place a prejudgment writ of attachment against Ouhrabka's real estate holdings, including the Vermont property. The court denied the writ, holding that under Vermont common law a creditor of a single debtor can not attach property owned jointly by a debtor and a nondebtor when held as tenants by entirety.

RBS contends that because the original purpose of the estate of tenancy by entirety was to protect the survivorship rights of married women at a time when those were the only property rights which could be held by married women, such an estate is an anachronism with no place in our modern jurisprudence. In making this argument RBS points to women's historical coverture disabilities and the changes wrought by subsequent statutes. "At common law, the legal existence of a wife was suspended during the marriage . . . [u]pon marriage, a husband acquired vested interests in his wife's property." R. & E. Builders, Inc. v. Chandler, 144 Vt. 302, 303-04, 476 A.2d 540, 541 (1984). Thus the "husband ha[d] the right of possession and control of property so owned by himself and wife, for their joint lives, and he [could] convey, lease, or [e]ncumber it by mortgage for the same period." Laird v. Perry, 74 Vt. 454, 460, 52 A. 1040, 1041 (1902), *abrogated on other grounds by* Estate of Girard v. Laird, 159 Vt. 508, 513, 621 A.2d 1265, 1268 (1993). These "rights and powers of alienation in the husband, and of attachment and levy of execution in his creditors, [we]re limited only by the wife's contingent right to the property or income by survivorship." *Id.* at 461, 52 A. at 1041.

"Starting in the late nineteenth century, Vermont, like other states, began to enact statutes, such as the Rights of Married Women Act, see 15 V.S.A. §§61-69, to grant married women property and contractual rights independent of their husbands." Baker v. State, 170 Vt. 194, 257, 744 A.2d 864, 908-09 (1999) (Johnson, J., concurring in part and dissenting in part) (citing Med. Ctr. Hosp. v. Lorrain, 165 Vt. 12, 14, 675 A.2d 1326, 1328 (1996)). "The Legislature's intent in enacting the Rights of Married Women Act was to reject the archaic principle that husband and wife are one person, and to set a married woman free from the thralldom of the common law." *Id.* at 257, 744 A.2d at 909 (quotations omitted). After enactment of these statutes, the legal existence of married women was no longer merged into that of their husbands. . . .

RBS seems to contend that the estate of tenancy by entirety was based in married women's inability to control and manage marital property at common law and that once the disabilities of coverture were removed, the entire "theoretical basis" for the estate was abrogated. But the estate never flowed from the married woman's common law disabilities, rather, it "result[ed] from the common-law principle of marital unity." Lang v. Comm'r of Internal Revenue, 289 U.S. 109, 111 (1933). . . . Historically, marital unity has always been distinct from the antiquated concepts of a wife's coverture disabilities and a husband's common law right to possession and management of marital property. The unity of estate is the defining characteristic of a tenancy by entirety and results from the manner in which the parties take title. In an early case delineating the difference between joint tenants and tenants by entirety, this Court explained: "in [the] case of joint tenants each [party] has a seizin of the whole but a title only to his aliquot part." Park v. Pratt, 38 Vt. 545, 550 (1866). A tenancy by entirety "differs from a joint tenancy in the entirety of title as well as seizin of each grantee in the whole estate; they have but one title and each owns the whole." *Id.* Thus the "theoretical basis" of tenancy by entirety was and is premised on the manner in which the spouses take title—in its entirety—and the manner in which the parties are seized—of the whole. It is not, as RBS contends, based in the concept of a married woman's inability to freely own property at common law. While the Rights of Married Women Act vested married women with equal rights to manage marital property, it did nothing, explicitly or implicitly, to alter the quality of the marital unity, seizing, or title.

The Hawaii Supreme Court came to a similar conclusion in addressing the question of the effect of an analogous statute on the estate of tenancy by entirety:

> **Coverture**
>
> At common law, upon marriage a woman became a *feme covert* (literally "covered woman"), which meant that she was not able to own property or make contracts on her own. The principle of coverture arose from the idea that husband and wife were one person, an entity speaking and acting only through the husband. In the mid- to late nineteenth century, most U.S. states enacted Married Women's Property Acts, which expanded the rights of married women.

The effect of the Married Women's Property Acts was to abrogate the husband's common law dominance over the marital estate and to place the wife on a level of equality with him as regards the exercise of ownership over the whole estate. The tenancy was and still is predicated upon the legal unity of husband and wife, but the Acts converted it into a unity of equals and not of unequals as at common law. No longer could the husband convey, lease, mortgage or otherwise encumber the property without her consent. The Acts confirmed her right to the use and enjoyment of the whole estate, and all the privileges that ownership of property confers, including the right to convey the property in its entirety, jointly with her husband, during the marriage relation.

Sawada v. Endo, 57 Haw. 608, 561 P.2d 1291, 1295 (1977) (citations omitted). We conclude the theoretical basis of tenancy by entireties remains intact and that the estate enjoys continued validity in Vermont.[15]

This Court has long held that "[t]he estate of the wife and the husband's interest in her tenancy by the entirety, if validly created, is protected from the husband's sole creditors." Rose v. Morrell, 128 Vt. 110, 112, 259 A.2d 8, 10 (1969); see also Bellows Falls Trust Co. v. Gibbs, 148 Vt. 633, 633, 534 A.2d 210, 211 (1987) (mem.) (holding that "[n]either spouse has a share [of tenancy by entirety property] which can be disposed of or encumbered without the joinder of the other spouse.) . . . RBS admits that when property is held in tenancy by entirety neither spouse may convey their interest voluntarily, without the consent of the other. However, RBS draws a distinction between voluntary conveyances and involuntary attachments. . . .

Our past decisions do not distinguish voluntary conveyances of tenancy by entirety property from involuntary attachments. *See, e.g.*, Corey v. McLean, 100 Vt. 90, 91, 135 A. 10, 11 (1926) (holding that marital property "was not attachable for the [sole] debts of the husband" because it was held in tenancy by entirety). Furthermore, despite RBS's contention that numerous decisions from other jurisdictions support its proposition that tenancy by entirety property may be attached, most jurisdictions recognizing the estate do not allow a creditor of a single debtor to attach property held jointly by the debtor and the nondebtor in a tenancy by entirety. See Brown, *supra*, §6:84 ("Most jurisdictions that recognize tenancies by the entirety hold that a creditor of one spouse cannot reach the debtor spouse's share in the property."). . .

RBS advances the policy argument that distinguishing between voluntary conveyance and involuntary attachment is of great importance because to prohibit involuntary attachment of tenancy by entirety properties would allow assets to be unfairly shielded from one spouse's creditors. This argument is unpersuasive. If a spouse transfers property into a tenancy by entirety to evade his creditors, the creditor is not without remedy: it can pursue an action for fraud. See 12 V.S.A. §2808 (providing for action in superior court when property "is held in fraud of the levying creditor's rights"). Of course, if the asset was held in a tenancy by entirety before the issuance of the debt, an action for fraud would not lie—but neither could the creditor argue the asset was *unfairly* shielded from attachment. At the time of contracting, a creditor may always require both tenants by entirety to assume liability for a debt; it may also decline to issue credit absent sufficient security. RBS here is a sophisticated lender and was aware that Ouhrabka's property was held in tenancy by entirety. RBS could have required Ouhrabka's spouse to cosign the loan and unlimited guaranty. It failed to do so. This Court will not now correct RBS's error through wholesale revision of Vermont entireties law.

Affirmed.

---

[15] Our holding today is by no means unique. While some jurisdictions treat tenancy by entirety as having been abolished by enactment of statutes similar to Vermont's Rights of Married Women Act, the majority of those that recognized the estate at common law continue to do so. See O. Phipps, *Tenancy by Entireties*, 25 Temp. L.Q. 24, 29 (1951); 1 W. Brown, The Law of Debtors and Creditors §684, n.3 (June 2011).

■ POINTS TO CONSIDER

1. **Are all creditors the same?** The TBE allows married couples to protect their assets from the creditors of one spouse alone. The *RBS Citizens* court notes that creditors may take action to protect themselves by requiring both spouses to join in any pledge of assets to secure indebtedness. But what about tort judgment creditors who cannot take such precautions?

    In Sawada v. Endo, 561 P.2d 1291 (Haw. 1977), the Hawaii Supreme Court held that a judgment creditor could not reach assets held in TBE. The case has been influential and was noted in the *RBS Citizens* opinion. Mrs. Sawada was injured in an accident with a car driven by Mr. Endo. The Sawadas obtained a judgment against Mr. Endo, who did not have automobile insurance. Mr. and Mrs. Endo's primary asset was their house, which they attempted to protect by conveying title to their sons. The Sawadas then sued to set aside this conveyance as fraudulent.

    The court held that the conveyance was not fraudulent, because the house was not subject to the judgment debt anyway. Creditors of one spouse alone cannot reach property held in TBE. The court held that the policy of protecting the security of the family outweighed the interests of creditors. Do you agree? Is the case of Mrs. Sawada different from the case of RBS Citizens? In what circumstances, if any, would a tort judgment creditor be able to reach TBE property; for example, what would the Sawadas have to prove against the Endos to reach the house?

2. **The minority view.** Although *RBS* and *Sawada* represent the majority view, some states have adopted different approaches. A few states, such as New Jersey and Arkansas, adopt a compromise between the interests of the creditor and the non-debtor spouse: the creditor may reach only the debtor spouse's interest in TBE property, but cannot disturb the non-debtor spouse's interest in possession or survivorship. What would a creditor of one spouse in those states obtain, then, by executing on TBE property? *See* Morris v. Solesbee, 892 S.W.2d 281 (Ark. Ct. App. 1995). The Alaska legislature has gone further in protecting the interests of creditors by enacting this statute:

    > If an individual and another own property in this state as tenants in common or tenants by the entirety, a creditor of the individual . . . may obtain a levy on and sale of the interest of the individual in the property. A creditor who has obtained a levy, or a purchaser who has purchased the individual's interest at the sale, may have the property partitioned or the individual's interest severed.

    Alaska Stat. §09.38.100(a) (2017). Would you support such a statute?

3. **Limits on TBE property?** Does it matter how much or what kind of property is held in this form of ownership? For example, assume Harry has allowed his automobile insurance to lapse and in fact is barred from driving because of

multiple convictions for operating while intoxicated. Nevertheless, one night Harry gets drunk, decides to drive, and causes an accident that causes Crista to be permanently disabled. Crista sues Harry for negligence and obtains a $5 million judgment against him.

In seeking to enforce her judgment, Crista discovers that Harry owns the following assets: a condo in town worth $1 million, a beach house worth $2 million, an office building he rents to several businesses worth $10 million, a yacht worth $2 million, a stock account worth $3 million, and a collection of vintage cars worth $2 million. That's $20 million total.

- If Harry is single, Crista can easily enforce her judgment against him by attaching some of the assets listed above.
- But what if, instead, Harry is married to Wendy and holds all of the above-named assets in tenancy by the entirety with her? Should Crista be barred from satisfying her judgment?
- Would it be possible to take a compromise approach and allow Crista to reach Harry's interest, without disturbing Wendy's rights?
- Does it make more sense to protect core family interests with home-stead laws?
- In some states, only real property can be held in TBE. Would that approach make more sense? Or would it be better to limit the total value of property that can be held in TBE?

4. **Joint tenancy and creditors' rights.** Note the difference between TBE and joint tenancy in these situations. Because each joint tenant could, acting alone and without the permission of the other joint tenants, alienate his or her interest, it follows that creditors of one joint tenant may attach that tenant's share. It also follows, however, that if the debtor co-tenant dies before the joint tenancy is severed, the creditor's interest in the property is extinguished. In contrast, other property in the debtor's estate, passed on by will or inheritance, is subject to the claims of creditors.

■ PROBLEM: TENANCY BY THE ENTIRETY AND CREDITORS

H and W live in a state that allows only *real property* to be held in TBE. H and W own Blackacre in TBE. H defaults on a substantial debt to C, and C obtains a judgment against H. Thereafter, the house on Blackacre burns to the ground and C seeks to attach the $500,000 insurance proceeds, on the ground that it is personal property. What result? *See* Hawthorne v. Hawthorne, 192 N.E.2d 20 (N.Y. 1963).

G   RIGHTS AND RELATIONS BETWEEN CO-TENANTS

Everyone who has had a college roommate knows that when two or more people share possession of the same space, disagreements are almost inevitable. Much of the litigation arising from concurrent ownership involves this sort of dispute over competing plans for the use of the property. Other litigation arises from the refusal of co-tenants to share the revenues or costs associated with the property.

Assume that a relative dies, leaving a house to you and your sister as co-tenants. Your sister, who lives in that town, immediately moves in. You are in another state, going to law school, so are unable to take advantage of this property. Does your sister owe you money? Would it be different if she decided to rent out the basement to a local college student? Why? What if she calls and tells you the furnace isn't working properly and needs to be replaced? Do you have to pay half of the costs? What if she wants to put in a new swimming pool?

Even in a relatively simple situation, the rights and responsibilities of property co-ownership can quickly become complicated. The situation works if the co-owners have a good relationship and there is an agreement between them concerning their relative rights to possession and obligations with respect to maintenance, taxes, insurance, and so on. If the co-owners do not get along, and can't agree on these issues, co-tenancy becomes an unworkable form of ownership.

1. Ouster and Duty to Pay Rent

In theory, each co-tenant has an equal right to possess the whole of the property. Sole possession of the property by one co-tenant, therefore, is entirely consistent with the co-tenancy and, in most jurisdictions, does not give rise to an obligation to compensate the other co-tenants, absent *ouster*. Ouster is defined as the denial of a co-tenant's right to possession. As the court explains in *Spiller*, it is often difficult to tell if ouster has occurred.

SPILLER v. MACKERETH

334 So. 2d 859 (1976)
Supreme Court of Alabama

JONES, Justice.

This is an appeal from a suit based upon a complaint by John Robert Spiller seeking sale for division [i.e., partition by sale] among tenants in common and a counterclaim by Hettie Mackereth and others seeking an accounting for Spiller's alleged "ouster" of his cotenants. . . .

The pertinent facts are undisputed. In February, 1973, Spiller purchased an undivided one-half interest in a lot in downtown Tuscaloosa. Spiller's cotenants were Mackereth and the other appellees. At the time Spiller bought his interest, the lot was being rented by an automobile supply business called Auto-Rite. In May, 1973, Spiller offered to purchase Mackereth's interest in the property. Mackereth refused and made a counteroffer to purchase Spiller's interest which Spiller refused. Spiller then filed the complaint seeking sale for division on July 11, 1973.

In October, 1973, Auto-Rite vacated the building which it had been renting for $350 per month and Spiller begun [*sic*] to use the entire building as a warehouse. On November 15, 1973, Mackereth's attorney sent a letter to Spiller demanding that he either vacate one-half of the building or pay rent. Spiller did not respond to the letter, vacate the premises, or pay rent; therefore, Mackereth brought this counterclaim to collect the rental she claimed Spiller owed her.

On the question of Spiller's liability for rent, we start with the general rule that in absence of an agreement to pay rent or an ouster of a cotenant, a cotenant in possession is not liable to his cotenants for the value of his use and occupation of the property. . . . Since there was no agreement to pay rent, there must be evidence which establishes an ouster before Spiller is required to pay rent to Mackereth. The difficulty in this determination lies in the definition of the word "ouster." Ouster is a conclusory word which is used loosely in cotenancy cases to describe two distinct fact situations. The two fact situations are (1) the beginning of the running of the statute of limitations for adverse possession and (2) the liability of an occupying cotenant for rent to other cotenants. Although the cases do not acknowledge a distinction between the two uses of "ouster," it is clear that the two fact situations require different elements of proof to support a conclusion of ouster.

The Alabama cases involving adverse possession require a finding that the possessing co-tenant asserted complete ownership to the land to support a conclusion of ouster. The finding of assertion of ownership may be established in several ways. Some cases find an assertion of complete ownership from a composite of activities such as renting part of the land without accounting, hunting the land, cutting timber, assessing and paying taxes and generally treating the land as if it were owned in fee for the statutory period. See Howard v. Harrell, 275 Ala. 454, 156 So. 2d 140 (1963). Other cases find the assertion of complete ownership from more overt activities such as a sale of the property under a deed purporting to convey the entire fee. Elsheimer v. Parker Bank & Trust Co., 237 Ala. 24, 185 So. 385 (1938). But whatever factual elements are present, the essence of the finding of an ouster in the adverse possession cases is a claim of absolute ownership and a denial of the cotenancy relationship by the occupying cotenant.

In the Alabama cases which adjudicate the occupying cotenant's liability for rent, a claim of absolute ownership has not been an essential element. The normal fact situation which will render an occupying cotenant liable to out of possession cotenants is one in which the occupying cotenant refuses a demand of the other cotenants to be allowed into use and enjoyment of the land, regardless of a claim of absolute ownership. . . .

The instant case involves a cotenant's liability for rent. Indeed, the adverse possession rule is precluded in this case by Spiller's acknowledgment of the cotenancy relationship as evidenced by filing the bill for partition. We can affirm the trial Court if the record reveals some evidence that Mackereth actually sought to occupy the building but was prevented from moving in by Spiller. To prove ouster, Mackereth's attorney relies upon the letter of November 15, 1973, as a sufficient demand and refusal to establish Spiller's liability for rent. This letter, however, did not demand equal use and enjoyment of the premises; rather, it demanded only that Spiller either vacate half of the building or pay rent. The question of whether a demand to vacate or pay rent is sufficient to establish an occupying cotenant's liability for rent has not been addressed in Alabama; however, it has been addressed by courts in other jurisdictions. In jurisdictions which adhere to the majority and Alabama rule of nonliability for mere occupancy, several cases have held that the occupying cotenant is not liable for rent notwithstanding a demand to vacate or pay rent. Grieder v. Marsh, 247 S.W.2d 590 (Tex. Civ. App. 1952); Brown v. Havens, 17 N.J. Super. 235, 85 A.2d 812 (1952).

There is a minority view which establishes liability for rents on a continued occupancy after a demand to vacate or pay rent. Re Holt's Estate, 14 Misc. 2d 971, 177 N.Y.S.2d 192 (1958). We believe that the majority view on this question is consistent with Alabama's approach to the law of occupancy by cotenants. As one of the early Alabama cases on the subject explains:

> "Tenants in common are seized *per my et per tout.*[16] Each has an equal right to occupy; and unless the one in actual possession denies to the other the right to enter, or agrees to pay rent, nothing can be claimed for such occupation." Newbold v. Smart, supra.

Thus, before an occupying cotenant can be liable for rent in Alabama, he must have denied his cotenants the right to enter. It is axiomatic that there can be no denial of the right to enter unless there is a demand or an attempt to enter. Simply requesting the occupying cotenant to vacate is not sufficient because the occupying cotenant holds title to the whole and may rightfully occupy the whole unless the other cotenants assert their possessory rights.

Besides the November 15 letter, Mackereth's only attempt to prove ouster is a showing that Spiller put locks on the building. However, there is no evidence that Spiller was attempting to do anything other than protect the merchandise he had stored in the building. . . . There is no evidence that either Mackereth or any of the other cotenants ever requested keys to the locks or were ever prevented from entering the building because of the locks. There is no evidence that Spiller intended to exclude his cotenants by use of the locks. Again, we emphasize that as

---

[16] "Per my et per tout" is roughly translated as "by the half (or moeity or share) and by the whole," which the court uses here to indicate that the co-tenant has the right to possess the whole. The phrase has often been used to refer to joint tenancies, because of the concept of "unity of title," such that each joint tenant is seised of the whole. *See* Chambers v. Cardinal, 177 Md. App. 418, 935 A.2d 502, 507 n.4 (2007) (discussing origin of phrase in fifteenth century).—EDS.

long as Spiller did not deny access to his cotenants, any activity of possession and occupancy of the building was consistent with his rights of ownership. Thus, the fact that Spiller placed locks on the building, without evidence that he intended to exclude the other cotenants, is insufficient to establish his liability to pay rent.

After reviewing all of the testimony and evidence presented at trial, we are unable to find any evidence which supports a legal conclusion of ouster. We are, therefore, compelled to reverse the trial Court's judgment awarding Mackereth $2,100. . . .

■ POINTS TO CONSIDER

1. **Ouster.** What exactly would you have advised Mackereth to do in order to establish ouster in this case? What policies do you think are behind this requirement?

2. **Actions speak louder than words?** In most cases, a co-tenant will not simply state, in writing, "I hereby deny your right to possess Blackacre." Instead, ouster will be shown by the actions of the tenant in possession. Why was the fact that Spiller changed the locks (and didn't give Mackereth a key) insufficient to prove ouster?

   Compare Morga v. Friedlander, 680 P.2d 1267 (Ariz. Ct. App. 1984), in which two parties agreed to be co-tenants in the leasehold of an office building. After Friedlander moved out of his office and stopped paying his share of the rent, Morga changed the locks and took Friedlander's name off of the door. He sent Friedlander a letter, stating:

   > Since you have now removed all of your belongings, there is no further need for you to have access to this complex, unless you decide to move back in, and the locks on the doors have been changed accordingly.

   The court held that the actions of Morga amounted to an ouster of Friedlander. The court also found it significant that Friedlander attempted to rent out his office to a third party, but Morga refused to accept a new co-tenant. As a result of the ouster, Morga could not get contribution from Friedlander for the back rent. Do you agree that Morga's actions were sufficient to constitute an ouster? Were they different from Spiller's?

3. **Minority rule.** As noted in *Spiller*, in a few jurisdictions, a co-tenant who takes sole possession of the property may be liable to the other co-tenants for their proportionate share of the premises' fair rental value. These decisions are commonly based on a statute. For example, Iowa Code §557.16 (2013) provides:

   > In all cases in which any real estate is now or shall be hereafter held by two or more persons as tenants in common, and one or more of said tenants shall have been or shall hereafter be in possession of said real estate, it shall be lawful for any one or

more of said tenants in common, not in possession, to sue for and recover from such tenants in possession, their proportionate part of the rental value of said real estate for the time, not exceeding a period of five years, such real estate shall have been in possession as aforesaid.

Does this solution seem more or less fair than the *Spiller v. Mackereth* disposition?

4. **Constructive Ouster.** *Spiller* suggests that ouster occurs only when one co-tenant refuses to permit possession by another co-tenant. Are there situations in which the circumstances render it unnecessary to demand the right to occupy? Some courts have used the concept of *constructive ouster* in such situations. For example, one New Mexico case applied this concept in the context of marital dissolution:

> Applying the notion of constructive ouster in the marital context is simply another way of saying that when the emotions of a divorce make it impossible for spouses to continue to share the marital residence pending a property division, the spouse who—often through mutual agreement—therefore departs the residence may be entitled to rent from the remaining spouse.
>
> Common law precedents support the proposition that the remaining spouse should pay rent to the cotenant when both cannot be expected to live together on the property. For example, when it is impractical for all cotenants to occupy the premises jointly, it is unnecessary that those claiming rent from the cotenant in possession first demand the right to move in and occupy the premises.

Olivas v. Olivas, 780 P.2d 640, 643 (N.M. Ct. App. 1989).

Should constructive ouster apply in other circumstances? If the property owned by A and B in co-tenancy is a single-family house and A has already moved in with her family, does that establish an ouster *per se*? Does B really have to attempt to be let into joint possession? What if A doesn't deny B's right to possession, but says the only room left is in the basement. Has an ouster occurred? *See* Martin v. DeWitt, 334 P.3d 123 (Wy. 2014)(finding ouster where single-family house occupied by co-tenant who did not get along with other co-tenants and refused to leave).

■ PROBLEMS: OUSTER

1. Cathy and Charles had been dating a long time, so they decided to buy a house together and took title as joint tenants. Each of them contributed 50 percent of the purchase price. A couple of years later, amid allegations of infidelity, they had a huge fight. Cathy claims that Charles got so angry that he punched a hole in the wall. She moved out and began living in an apartment. Over the next year, they made several attempts to patch things up, but to no avail. Cathy now seeks partition and would like, in addition to half of the

sale price of the property, one half of the fair rental value during the period of Charles's sole occupancy. Should she get it? *See* Cox v. Cox, 71 P.3d 1028, 1033-34 (Idaho 2003).

2. The Atkinsons and the Andersons bought a Florida condominium together as an investment. After the Andersons fell on hard times, they sold their house and moved into the condo unit. The Atkinsons objected to the Andersons' exclusive possession. The Andersons replied: "If you want to use the unit, give us reasonable notice, and we will have one of the bedrooms available for you." The Atkinsons have five children and would need the use of the entire condominium. They also cannot rent it to others given the Andersons' occupation. Has an ouster occurred? *See* Anderson v. Atkinson, 77 So. 3d 768 (Fla. Dist. Ct. App. 2011).

2. Ouster and Adverse Possession

A surprising number of adverse possession cases involve co-tenants, where one of the co-tenants has long been in sole possession of the property. Because each co-tenant has the right to possess all of the property, however, such possession becomes adverse only if there is an ouster of the other co-tenants. *See, e.g.,* Van Nhu Huynh v. Leung Hing Li, 193 Wash.App. 1035 (2016) (exclusive occupancy by one co-tenant for long time period insufficient to establish adverse possession). Consider whether the test for ouster in the following case is different than in *Spiller.*

O'CONNOR v. LAROCQUE

302 Conn. 562, 31 A.3d 1 (2011)
Supreme Court of Connecticut

[In 1971, a widow inherited a one-third interest in a vacant lot from her deceased husband; the other two-thirds was split between four siblings. The mother, mistakenly believing she owned the entire lot, deeded her interest to Theresa, one of the siblings. In 1987, Theresa discovered that she did not own the entire lot. She was able to acquire the interests of two of the other siblings, but her sister Dorothy wouldn't sell and instead sought partition. Theresa claimed that she owned Dorothy's share by adverse possession. The Connecticut Supreme Court disagreed.]

In cases involving claims by one cotenant against another, we have added to this heavy burden by applying a presumption against adverse possession. The rationale for this presumption is that, "in view of the undivided interest held by cotenants . . . possession taken by one is ordinarily considered to be the possession by all and not adverse to any cotenant." . . . In other words, the presumption is based on a recognition that one cotenant's possession is not necessarily inconsistent with the title of the others. . . .

Although the presumption may be overcome in certain circumstances, it is not easily done. "[A] cotenant claiming adversely to other cotenants must show actions of such an unequivocal nature and so distinctly hostile to the rights of the other cotenants that the intention to disseize is clear and unmistakable."... Not only must an actual intent to exclude others be demonstrated;...but there also must be proof of "an ouster and exclusive possession so openly and notoriously hostile that the cotenant will have notice of the adverse claim."

In discussing the type of conduct required to overcome the presumption, we explained in Newell v. Woodruff, supra, 30 Conn. 492, that acts "consistent with an honest intent to account to his co-tenant for his share of the rents and profits, as the collection of all the rents, payment of all the taxes, occupation and enjoyment of the entire premises and the like, are termed 'equivocal,' because one may possess for all and be willing or compelled to account to all, [whereas] other acts necessarily evince an intent to exclude and hold adversely to his co-tenants, such as refusing to account on the ground that the co-tenant has no right in the property, making explicit claim to the whole and occupying under an avowed or notorious claim of right to the whole...denying the right of the co-tenant to possession, and refusing to acknowledge his right or to let him into possession upon demand made.... [T]he difference is only in the kind of evidence by which it may be proved in the two cases. As against a co-tenant it cannot be proved merely by acts which are consistent with an honest intent to acknowledge and conform to the rights of the co-tenant, although such acts might be sufficient evidence of an ouster between the parties if there was no tenancy in common and each claimed the whole. Hence it has been deemed eminently proper and safe, before bringing an action of ejectment against a tenant in common, to test the intent with which the property is holden by a formal demand to be let into the enjoyment of the right claimed; and a refusal furnishes that clear evidence of ouster which a demand and refusal furnish of a conversion in trover." Id., at 497-98.

Connecticut is not alone in establishing a very high bar to overcoming the presumption. It is generally agreed across jurisdictions that, because a relationship of trust between cotenants is presumed whereby one tenant in common holds the property for the benefit of the others, "there must be some hostile act, conduct, or declaration on the part of the possessor amounting to a repudiation of [the] cotenants' rights and an assertion of exclusive title in the possessor, of which the cotenants have knowledge or notice." The mere unannounced intention or exclusive possession of one cotenant is not sufficient to support a claim of adverse possession in cases involving tenants in common....

Furthermore, there is no evidence in the record that the plaintiff's possession and use of the lot was so openly and notoriously hostile that the defendant had notice of her adverse possession claim because of that conduct alone. The trial court found that the plaintiff's adverse use of the lot consisted of her payment of property taxes, maintenance activities such as mowing and cleanup, the planting of trees around the perimeter of the lot and her granting the town permission to use the lot for parking during the annual town fair. All of these activities, however, were entirely consistent with the actions of a tenant in common who shares an interest in the property without an intent to dispossess. . . .

■ POINT TO CONSIDER

Ouster in context. How does the test for ouster differ in this context? Would Theresa's actions have been sufficient to establish adverse possession in a case not involving co-tenants?

3.   General Rules of Co-Tenant Relations

Co-tenants may (and should) agree among themselves as to each party's rights and responsibilities. If you decide to buy a vacation condo with a couple of your friends, you can already see some of the issues you would want to spell out ahead of time in a written agreement. For example, how will the right to occupy the condo be split among you? How will you handle repairs and maintenance? How will you split expenses such as association fees, taxes, and insurance?

In the absence of agreement, courts may be called upon to resolve disputes. This typically happens in one of several ways:

> ➢ **Accounting.** Every partition action will include a final *accounting* of the expenses and benefits of the tenancy, in assessing how to divide the shares. A co-tenant also may bring a separate action for an accounting, without seeking partition, if another co-tenant receives rents or profits or otherwise benefits from the property in excess of his or her interest. *See, e.g.*, Conn. Gen. Stat. §52-404 (2017) (accounting action).
> ➢ **Contribution.** A co-tenant may seek *contribution* from the other co-tenants for their share of expenses he has paid, such as taxes, mortgage payments, or repairs. *See, e.g.*, N.C. Gen. Stat. Ann. §105-363 (2017) (authorizing suit for contribution for taxes).
> ➢ **Waste.** A co-tenant might seek an injunction against or compensation for the actions of another co-tenant that might harm or have harmed the property. This would be an action for *waste*.

Here are some general rules regarding these types of actions:

(1) Rents received. We already know that in most jurisdictions a co-tenant who occupies the premises herself is not liable to the other co-tenants, absent ouster. After all, each co-tenant is entitled to occupy the whole, subject only to the concurrent possessory rights of the other co-tenants. However, if a co-tenant leases out the premises to a third party, she will need to account to the other co-tenants for rents received. Why? Because the lease of the entire premises to a third party gives that party the right to exclusive possession during the lease term, which

necessarily involves an ouster of the other co-tenants. If a co-tenant leases out only her undivided interest in the property, giving the lessee only the same rights to possession that she had, some courts have held that the other co-tenants are not entitled to a share.

(2) Carrying costs. Co-tenants have a mutual obligation to pay the necessary costs of maintaining the property, including mortgage payments, insurance, taxes, and other costs necessary for the preservation of the property. *See, e.g.,* Biondo v. Powers, 743 So. 2d 161 (Fla. Dist. Ct. App. 1999). The co-tenant paying such costs may bring an action for contribution against the other co-tenants. In this case, however, a tenant in sole possession of the property may have to offset the value of his possession against the claim for reimbursement. *See, e.g.,* Christen v. Christen, 38 S.W.3d 488 (Mo. Ct. App. 2001). Does that affect your view of the ouster rule?

(3) Repairs and improvements. In most states, a co-tenant who makes repairs to the property, even if they are necessary, does not have the right to demand contribution from the other co-tenants. However, in an accounting action or upon partition, the paying co-tenant should get a credit for necessary repairs.

> ➢ For example, assume Maybelle and Junebug inherit a farm. Maybelle lives in another state and can't be bothered, so Junebug takes control. She first decides to fix the leaky roof on the barn. She wants Maybelle to pay for half of this repair, but she refuses. Junebug cannot bring a contribution action to force Maybelle to pay her share. But then Junebug decides to rent the pasture to Farmer. Maybelle finds out about the arrangement with Farmer and sues for an accounting. Maybelle is entitled to half the rent received from Farmer, but Junebug should receive a credit for the cost of fixing the roof.

This result makes sense if you think about it. Repairs, even necessary ones, involve a lot of discretionary decisions: Was fixing the roof really necessary or could it have waited another couple of years? Could they have used cheaper shingles or hired a cheaper contractor? The court does not want to get involved with these disputes every time co-tenants disagree about repairs.

But when there is an accounting to distribute profits, the repairs have been made and have undoubtedly contributed to the ability of the property to be rented. The court is already involved and unless the other co-tenants can prove the repairs were truly unnecessary, it seems fair to give the paying co-tenant credit. *See* Anderson v. Joseph, 26 A.3d 1050 (Md. Ct. Spec. App. 2011) (court refused credit for repairs not shown to be necessary).

The rule regarding *improvements* is slightly different. In that case, the co-tenant making the expenditure receives a credit upon partition for the increase in property value attributable to the improvement. For example, assume that A spent $50,000 on a new swimming pool for a house owned in common with B. Ten years later, the house is sold for $400,000 and an appraiser attributes $30,000 of this value to the swimming pool. A is entitled to a $30,000 credit, not the $50,000 spent. Why do you think this rule is different from the rule for repairs?

(4) Waste. The doctrine of waste is often used when one owner of an interest in property takes action (or fails to take action) that adversely impacts others with ownership interests in the property. A co-tenant may be able to enjoin actions that damage the property or, if the action has already occurred, may obtain damages for the decline in property value. Many of the cases involve timber cutting or mining without the consent of all owners. Note, however, that a court will not allow an action for waste to resolve every disagreement between concurrent owners over the best way to use the property. If co-tenant A wants to farm Blackacre and co-tenant B wants to turn it into a shopping mall, they should seek partition rather than requesting the courts to arbitrate.

Thinking Like a Lawyer

One of your clients, Mikayla, is thinking of buying a condominium in Florida with her sister, Nikita. The purchase price is $300,000. They plan to make a $100,000 down payment (Mikayla will provide $80,000 and Nikita $20,000), and then finance the rest. Mikayla is single at the moment, but Nikita is married, with one child. Nikita's spouse is not very keen on the condo idea, but Nikita says that is irrelevant because she plans to use her own money. The condo is in pretty good shape right now, but Mikayla thinks the kitchen needs some updating and probably new carpet soon.

What advice would you give Mikayla about entering into this deal? What questions would you need to ask her? How would you draft appropriate instruments to best protect her interests?

H   MARITAL PROPERTY

Marital property is the most common form of concurrent ownership. As we will see, the law has developed numerous ways to protect the property interests of spouses. Although newlyweds may not realize it, their property rights changed significantly the moment they said "I do." The modern trend toward recognition of same-sex marriage has increased the amount of property subject to these rules, as well as raising new issues. Although we will save most of the complicated issues for an upper-level course in family law, a first-year study of property would not be complete without understanding the basic concepts of marital property. In particular, we will focus on how rights to marital property are affected by death and divorce.

In general, the state has an interest in encouraging marriage, which is thought to stabilize family relationships and therefore society in general. It also has an interest in ensuring that the partners in the marriage arrangement are treated fairly and are not thrown upon the welfare of the state unnecessarily.

We have already covered two important forms of marital property protection. The *tenancy by the entirety*, unlike a joint tenancy, prohibits one of the co-tenants from unilaterally impacting the spouse's current interest in the property and right of survivorship. Similarly, *homestead* laws protect the family by providing a core of property that cannot be taken by creditors. Of course, homestead also protects single property owners, but one of its advantages is to protect a spouse and children from suffering calamity from the reckless actions of the other spouse.

In this section, we will introduce the two major systems of marital property in the United States: *community property* and *separate property*. We will then discuss how separate property jurisdictions protect a spouse at the death of the other spouse (through dower and elective share concepts) and at divorce (through equitable distribution), and compare the results under a community property system.

While the eastern part of the United States borrowed the law of England, including its treatment of marital property, the West was more heavily influenced by Spanish law. As a result, we have two very different systems of marital property in the United States.

The majority of jurisdictions (41) use what is known as the *separate property* system (also referred to as the "common law" approach). Upon marriage, each spouse may continue to hold and manage separate property, titled in his or her sole name. For example, assume H saves $80,000 from his job and keeps it in a separate savings account. He decides to use it to buy a new speedboat he's had his eye on. His wife, W, objects on the ground that they really should use the money to pay off the mortgage. H ignores her and buys the boat, titling it in his own name. A couple of years later, his friend offers to buy it from him for $50,000. W again objects, thinking that the price is too low. Under a separate property system, H can do whatever he wants. The rights of W to these assets will be determined only upon H's death or upon divorce (which may be likely in this case!). Those rules will be discussed in detail below.

In contrast, nine states (located primarily in jurisdictions influenced by Spanish law) use a form of *community property*: Arizona, California, Idaho, Louisiana, Nevada, New Mexico, Texas, Washington, and Wisconsin. In addition, Alaska allows a couple to elect community property treatment. This system treats the earnings of either spouse, or property purchased with those earnings, as jointly owned, regardless of how it is titled.

Here is a little more detail about these two systems:

1. Community Property

In community property jurisdictions, during the marriage the earnings of either spouse, and any property acquired with those earnings, becomes *community property*, owned equally and jointly by the couple, regardless of how it is titled.

- Typically, property owned by either spouse before the marriage, or received as a gift or inheritance after the marriage, is deemed *separate property*.

- All other property acquired during the marriage by either spouse is community property.
- However, separate property may lose its character and be *transmuted* into community property by being commingled with community property or by being used in the marriage.

Some common questions arise with respect to *characterization* of property as *separate* or *community*:

- **Increase in value.** Generally, if separate property *appreciates* in value during the marriage through inflation or market forces, the increased value retains its separate character; however, if the growth is due to the efforts of one of the spouses, the increase is marital property.
  - ☐ For example, if W owned a $10,000 stock account before marriage and it appreciated in value to $20,000 over the course of the marriage due to a rise in stock values, the entire amount would be deemed W's separate property.
  - ☐ If the increase in value was *active* rather than *passive*, attributable to the efforts of one of the spouses, then the increase is marital property. If W's stock account increased to $20,000 due to active day trading, for example, the $10,000 increase would be marital.
- **Commingling.** Separate property that is *commingled* with marital property retains its separate character *if* it can be traced and identified. For example, if W had a $10,000 money market account before marriage and she added to it another $20,000 of her earnings during marriage, the original $10,000 and whatever appreciation it earned could still be considered her separate property, even though it was commingled, because it was *traceable. See, e.g.,* Baruch v. Clark, 154 Idaho 732, 302 P.3d 357 (2013) (husband's retirement account community property because frequent withdrawals for development projects and other purposes constituted co-mingling).

  The characterization of property as separate or marital also affects the *management* of the property—that is, the right to sell, give away, modify, or encumber it. Any separate property may continue to be managed by the spouse who owns it. With regard to community property, however, the management rules become complex:
- In some states, each spouse may manage community property independently. In those states, H would still be able to buy and sell his speed boat without W's consent in the example above. Even though a spouse may have management control over community property, he or she acts in a fiduciary capacity, which includes a duty to not impair the interests of the nonmanaging spouse. The managing spouse may have to account for waste or bad faith in the management of these assets. *See, e.g.,* Wheeling v. Wheeling, 546 S.W.3d 216 (Tex. Ct. App. 2017) ("fraud on the community"

claim); La. Civ. Code Ann. art. 2354 (2014) (spouse liable for losses caused by bad faith in management of community property).

- In other jurisdictions, however, both spouses must join in transactions regarding community property. In still other jurisdictions, management authority may depend on the type of community property or the type of transaction at issue. For example, in Texas, each spouse has sole management authority over his or her earnings, but if those earnings are used to purchase a house, then both spouses become joint managers of it. Tex. Fam. Code §3.102. In California, either spouse may manage community personal property, but both must consent to gifts of personal property (or transfers for less than fair market value). Cal. Fam. Code §1100 (West 2014). Both spouses must join in mortgages or conveyances of community real property. Cal. Fam. Code §1102 (West 2014). How would the speedboat issue above be resolved in California?

Community property automatically protects each spouse's interests at death or dissolution of the marriage:

- **Death.** When one spouse dies, half of the community property and all of the decedent's separate property passes through the decedent's estate, while the other half of the community property is retained by the surviving spouse and does not pass through the estate.
- **Divorce.** On dissolution, jurisdictions vary on how to divide community property assets. Three states (California, Louisiana, and New Mexico) simply split community property 50/50, following the theory of equal ownership. The other jurisdictions, however, divide the assets "equitably," a test that may be interpreted to allow a court discretion to adjust the division to achieve fairness.

Is Dodger Stadium Community Property?

A prominent example of the importance of community property characterization was the divorce battle between Jamie and Frank McCourt over the status of the Los Angeles Dodgers baseball franchise. The couple lived for many years in Massachusetts, a separate property jurisdiction, where Frank amassed a fortune as a real estate developer. In 2004, the couple moved to California, a community property state, and Frank bought the Dodgers for $330 million, using assets from his company, which he held in his own name. Frank argued that the team was separate property, while Jamie argued that, after 30 years of marriage, all of the couple's assets were community property. The court never ruled on the issue, however, as the parties reached a settlement (after spending a reported $20 million in legal fees), providing Jamie with $191 million plus several pieces of very valuable real estate. After the settlement, Frank sold the team to a group led by Magic Johnson for $2 billion.

See James R. Ratner, *Distribution of Marital Assets in Community Property Jurisdictions: Equitable Doesn't Equal Equal*, 72 La. L. Rev. 21 (2011). For example, in Texas, the court is to order a division of the community property that is "just and right, having due regard for the rights of each party and any children of the marriage." Tex. Fam. Code Ann. §7.001 (2018). The division of property in these jurisdictions may therefore resemble the approach of separate property jurisdictions, described below.

■ PROBLEMS: COMMUNITY PROPERTY

Assume the following situations arose in a community property jurisdiction:

1. Michael and Trudy were married in 1999. In 2005, Michael's uncle gave him a horse named Pepper for his birthday. In 2008, the horse was injured in an explosion at his stable and Michael received $10,000 in insurance proceeds and settlement of a lawsuit regarding the horse's injuries. Michael used the money to buy another horse, named Lady. In 2014, the couple is getting divorced. Are Pepper and Lady separate or community property? *See* Bush v. Bush, 336 S.W.3d 722 (Tex. Ct. App. 2010).

2. Assume the explosion also injured Michael and he spent six months recovering. He filed a lawsuit for personal injury. After a trial, the jury awarded Michael $100,000 for lost wages and medical expenses, along with $50,000 for pain and suffering, and awarded Trudy $30,000 for loss of consortium. Both Trudy and Michael kept these amounts in separate accounts. In the subsequent divorce, should these amounts be deemed separate or community property?

3. Estaban and Christina married in 1998. Estaban, a professional baseball player, began carrying on an affair with Ashley. In 2000, without Christina's knowledge, he bought Ashley a new Lexus worth $70,000 and new cars for his mother, brother, and sister worth a total of $120,000. He also spent about $150,000 on hotel and airfare for trips with Ashley, and on gifts to Ashley's mother. The couple divorced shortly thereafter. Can Christina reclaim the loss caused by these community property expenditures? *See* Loaiza v. Loaiza, 130 S.W.3d 894 (Tex. Ct. App. 2004).

4. Prior to marriage, Mr. Bourgeois owned his "baby," a 1960 Chevy Brookwood. After marriage, Mr. Bourgeois used about $2,000 of community property assets to repair and renovate the Chevy. The car now runs like a top and is worth $20,000. When the Bourgeoises divorce, is this asset considered separate or community property? Bourgeois v. Bourgeois, 981 So. 2d 788 (La. Ct. App. 2008).

5. Kerry owned 160 head of cattle when he married Julie. When they divorced four years later, he had 181 cattle. Should the cattle, or at least some of them, now be considered community property? In Matter of Marriage of Stegall, 519 S.W.3d 668 (Tex. Ct. App. 2017).

2. Rights upon Death

Separate property jurisdictions focus on protecting the spouse only when the marriage ends, either by death or dissolution. During the marriage, property may be titled in and managed by either spouse alone. When the marriage ends, however, society steps in to ensure fairness and to further other public policies.

At death, this protection begins with the *intestacy* statutes, discussed in more depth in the next chapter, which apply when someone dies *without a will*. The state statutes vary as to the treatment of the spouse and the share often depends on whether there are children (or whether there are children from the decedent's previous marriage). In a few states, the spouse's share depends on whether the decedent has a surviving parent. In all separate property states, however, the spouse is given a substantial share of the decedent's estate.

Although the intestacy scheme adopts the distribution the legislature believes most people would want, it cannot take into account individual circumstances and desires. Thus, married couples should be advised that a will is desirable if they want to avoid the cookie-cutter result of intestacy.

Even for those couples who make wills, society has an interest in ensuring that a spouse is not disinherited completely. From a policy standpoint, would it make sense to allow someone like Oprah Winfrey to leave her entire fortune to the Alien Space Society, leaving her spouse destitute and forced on the charity of the state? Thus, marriage imposes an obligation of support that continues even at death. The common law method of spousal security—dower and curtesy— gave the surviving spouse a life interest in a portion of the decedent's real property, which historically was the primary source of wealth and the natural source of spousal support. While those concepts retain significance in a small group of states, they have now been replaced in most jurisdictions by statutory limitations on a spouse's ability to disinherit the surviving spouse, called "elective share" statutes. We discuss these spousal protection methods below.

In contrast, community property jurisdictions do not use spousal protection devices such as elective share or dower and curtesy, because the spouse already automatically owns half of the community property.

a. Dower and Curtesy

Assume you are interested in a piece of property called Blackacre, located in North Carolina. You search the title and discover that the title is in the name of Daniel Boone. He bought the property in 2005 and the conveyance was "to Daniel Boone, a married person." You contact Boone and quickly arrange to purchase Blackacre. Boone signs the deed conveying the property to you and you assume all is well.

Or is it? In some states, real estate agents quickly learn the phrase, "it takes one to buy, two to sell." They are referring to the spouse's *dower* interest, which must be released by a spouse, even if the property is titled solely in the name of the

Dower

Dower is referenced in the marriage ceremony in the Book of Common Prayer, which contains the phrase "with all my worldly goods I thee endow." The term *dowager*, used to refer to widows of noblemen (e.g., the Dowager Countess of Grantham, played by Maggie Smith, in *Downton Abbey*), refers to the dower right.

other spouse. Unless Daniel Boone's wife Becky signed the deed and released her dower interest, it remains an encumbrance on Blackacre.

The common law concept of dower originated in Germanic and Anglo-Saxon customs designed to protect a wife in the event of her husband's death. The practice continued in the Middle Ages, when it was customary for a husband, on his wedding day, to name specific lands that his wife would be allowed to enjoy for life, if she survived him. Common law eventually enshrined this custom in law and this dower right was expressly protected in a clause of the Magna Carta in 1217.

> In the middle ages, as in modern times, dower provided a widow with a measure of economic and social security. It also afforded support for younger children who, because of the rule of primogeniture, ordinarily took no rights in their father's land. Land was the chief source of subsistence at that time; unless she had lands of her own, a widow would frequently have been destitute without some rights in the lands of her husband. The husband's chattels were generally few, and not often of great value; and even if his personal property were considerable, his widow's assurance of any share therein was uncertain.

George L. Haskins, *The Development of Common Law Dower*, 62 Harv. L. Rev. 42, 46-47 (1948). Thus, dower rights arose to allow the wife to continue receiving support from the estate upon the husband's death, regardless of the provisions of his will.

At common law, the dower right consisted of a one-third life estate in all inheritable property of which the husband was seized during marriage. The restriction to "inheritable" means that it would not apply, for example, to a life interest held by the husband, because that interest is not inheritable, nor to property held in joint tenancy. A couple of important points to recognize about *dower*:

- During the life of the husband, the wife's dower interest is *inchoate*, which in this context means it is like a seed that has not yet sprouted and borne fruit. Instead, the dower right ripens only when and if the wife survives her husband. At that point, she is entitled to claim her interest in the property.
- Dower applies to *any* inheritable property the husband owned *during the marriage*, not just to the property he still owned at death. One of the main purposes of dower was to protect the spouse from being disinherited by her husband, which he could also do by simply giving all of his property away as he neared death.
- A similar protection, called *curtesy*, gave the husband a share of his wife's property at her death. Modern statutes generally use the term *dower* for both spouses.

As you will see, U.S. states have now adopted other forms of protection for spouses at death, including intestacy statutes that provide for inheritance by the spouse and elective share provisions that prevent complete disinheritance. In most states, these protections have replaced the older devices of dower and curtesy.

However, a small group of states retains the concept of dower, although most have modified it by statute. In those states in which it exists, dower applies to husbands as well as wives, and typically gives the spouse a *one-third fee simple interest in any real property of which the deceased spouse was seised during the marriage*. States that retain a dower concept include Arkansas, Iowa, Kentucky, Michigan, North Carolina, and Ohio. Dower does not exist in community property jurisdictions.

Widow Delilah Black's Petition to Court, 1848 English translation: "Your petitioner respectfully prays that her dower as the widow of the said William Black deceased may be allotted in the Lands above specified. . . ."
Provided by Lucy Trant (Delilah's great-great-great-great granddaughter)

While most jurisdictions retaining the dower concept have equalized its application to both sexes, Michigan's dower statute applies only to widows and it remains a one-third life interest rather than a fee simple. Mich. Comp. Laws Ann. §558.1 (West 2018). The statute survived an equal protection challenge, because the court found that the gender classification was substantially related to an important governmental interest, in that women are disproportionately disadvantaged by the death of their husbands. In re Miltenberger Estate, 482 Mich. 901, 753 N.W.2d 219 (2008). It remains to be seen how the statute will be interpreted with regard to same-sex marriages.

In those states retaining the dower right, it is important in any deed to identify whether the grantor and grantee are married or single. If a deed indicates Blackacre was conveyed "to John Smith, a married man" and you want to buy the property from John Smith, you know that dower must be released by his spouse, even though her name is not on the title.[17] Similarly, even if the original conveyance was "to John Smith, a single man," you would want the conveyance to indicate that the grantor is "John Smith, a single man" to ensure that he didn't get married in the interim and to ensure that the lack of a dower interest is apparent on the face of the title documents.

Another way dower issues can arise is under the Statute of Frauds, when a party wants to get out of a real estate purchase agreement on the ground that a spouse with a dower interest did not sign the purchase agreement. *See* Slater Mgmt. Corp. v. Nash, 536 N.W.2d 843 (Mich. Ct. App. 1995) (both spouse who owns the property and spouse with dower interest must sign to create valid real estate contract).

b. *Elective Share*

Elective share statutes have replaced the older dower and curtesy rights in most separate property states, although in the states noted above the rights co-exist. Every separate property state except Georgia now has a version of the elective share.[18] The basic idea is that, on the death of a spouse, the surviving spouse is entitled to take a certain share of the deceased spouse's estate, *regardless* of the provisions of the will. Thus, the elective share goes beyond the intestacy statute, because it trumps the testator's estate plan and prevents a spouse from being disinherited. The amount of the elective share ranges from one-third to one-half of the spouse's estate.

The elective share is truly *elective*, meaning that it is up to the surviving spouse to claim it. In the alternative, he or she can simply accept the provisions of the decedent's will. The right differs from dower in that it applies only to the property the decedent owned at death. Thus, jurisdictions that replaced the dower right with elective share simplified real estate transactions. State statutes differ, however, on the assets subject to the elective share calculation. For example, a spouse might try to defeat the elective share provision by making gifts *causa mortis* or converting real property to joint tenancy just before death. Some jurisdictions use a broadened concept of property owned at death (called the "augmented estate") that attempts to prevent this type of circumvention. You can study those complexities in upper-level classes on wills and trusts.

In community property states, elective share provisions do not exist, because the spouse already is deemed owner of half of the marital property. Thus, only half of the marital property, however it is titled, is subject to the decedent spouse's testamentary disposition.

You may have noted that the elective share represents a significant limitation on the right to will one's property. Regardless of the circumstances, or how clearly

---

[17] Remember, too, if the property is homestead, in many states both spouses must sign regardless of how the property is titled.

[18] In Georgia, the surviving spouse or minor children may seek an award of one year's support, much like alimony, to be paid out of the estate. *See* Ga. Code Ann. §§53-3-1 to 53-3-20 (West 2013).

the contrary is expressed in the decedent's will, the surviving spouse is entitled to claim the elective share of the estate.[19] As we discussed in Chapter 1, the right to determine how your property will be distrubuted at your death is one of the fundamental sticks in the property bundle. *Can this curtailment of the right to will your property be constitutional?* In the next case, the daughters of a wealthy decedent argue that the elective share statute deprives them of the right to receive their father's property.

HAMILTON v. HAMILTON

317 Ark. 572, 879 S.W.2d 416 (1994)
Supreme Court of Arkansas

This case challenges the right of the surviving spouse, appellee Virginia D. Hamilton, to take against her deceased husband's will. On January 22, 1992, Barrett Hamilton died. He and Virginia Hamilton had been married since 1981. They had separated in May 1990, and Barrett Hamilton had filed for absolute divorce on August 17, 1990. Barrett Hamilton had two adult daughters at the time of his death by a previous marriage. They are the appellants in this case, Melinda R. Hamilton and Maron M. Hamilton.

Under his will, Barrett Hamilton provided for his wife as follows:

(c) I give and bequeath to my Wife, VIRGINIA DALTON HAMILTON, if she survives me, and as along as she shall remain my lawful wife but not longer, all distributions, benefits, and allowances from my real and personal property, to which she is entitled from my estate as her dower interest under Arkansas law.

The residuary clause in the will left the remainder of all property to his two daughters.

On February 21, 1992, Virginia Hamilton renounced her rights under the will and filed her election to take her share against the will of her husband under Ark. Code Ann. §28-39-401 (1987). On January 8, 1993, Melinda and Maron Hamilton filed a motion to declare §28-39-401 unconstitutional on its face and as applied because the statute violates the Equal Protection and Due Process Clauses of both the federal and state constitutions. The motion further urged that with respect to the decedent and Virginia Hamilton, the probate court "treat the parties as divorced." On August 5, 1993, the probate court found that the elective share statute was constitutional and that Virginia Hamilton was entitled to take against the will. [The court first decided that the spouse's share under the Arkansas elective share statute would be greater than her dower interest.] Thus, the surviving spouse would realize more by taking her elective share in this instance than

---

[19] Unless the right is waived in a valid prenuptial (or possibly postnuptial) agreement. This possibility is discussed further below.

under the will where her distribution is limited to her dower interest, and the daughters' shares in the residuary estate would, accordingly, be reduced by the election. Because this is the case, the daughters do have a financial interest which is diminished by the election, and standing to file their motion exists.

B. CONSTITUTIONAL ARGUMENTS

We turn next to the constitutional arguments raised by the two Hamilton daughters. . . .

The Equal Protection Clause does not preclude all statutory classifications. Urrey Ceramic Tile Co. v. Mosley, 304 Ark. 711, 805 S.W.2d 54 (1991). Indeed, statutory classifications which have a rational basis and are reasonably related to the purpose of the statute are permissible. Id. . . .

> On an equal protection challenge to a statute, it is not our role to discover the actual basis for the legislation. Instead we are merely to consider whether any rational basis exists which demonstrates the possibility of a deliberate nexus with state objectives, so that the legislation is not the product of utterly arbitrary and capricious government purpose and void of any hint of deliberate and lawful purpose. Streight v. Ragland, 280 Ark. 206, 655 S.W.2d 459 (1983). Further, the party challenging the legislation has the burden of proving that the act is not rationally related to achieving any legitimate objective of state government under any reasonably conceivable state of facts. *Streight*, 280 Ark. at 214, 655 S.W.2d 459.

Arkansas Hosp. Ass'n v. Arkansas State Bd. Pharmacy, 297 Ark. 454, 456, 763 S.W.2d 73, 74 (1989).

The daughters advance the policy argument that the concept of an election statute for the economic protection of surviving spouses is outmoded. Moreover, they continue, the elective share concept runs counter to the testator's intent and is unfair to the beneficiaries under the will. They further highlight the disparate treatment in our statutes between divorced spouses with division of property under Ark. Code Ann. §9-12-315 (Repl. 1993) and surviving spouses with their elective share rights under §28-39-401. They assert that both classifications of spouses are similarly situated because regardless of the cause—divorce or death—the result is a termination of the marriage. Accordingly, they should be treated the same. In the case at hand, the daughters point out that Virginia Hamilton stands to gain much more by taking her elective share than she would under our divorce laws because, as the subsequent wife, her contribution to the property in Barrett Hamilton's estate was minimal.

This reasoning, though, is flawed. The policy consideration behind the statutory division of property as part and parcel of a divorce is not the same as the policy consideration giving rise to the elective share statute. The former policy deals with the dissolution of the marriage contract and the division of property. The latter is designed to prevent injustices when a marriage endures until the death of the husband or the wife. We easily discern a rational basis behind the

General Assembly's distinct handling of the two classes of spouses. Furthermore, any effort to amend the treatment afforded to the two groups is more appropriately addressed to the General Assembly. In sum, we decline to strike down §9-12-315 as violative of the Equal Protection Clause, either facially or as applied. *See* In the Matter of Patrick, 303 S.C. 559, 402 S.E.2d 664 (1991) (providing for surviving spouses is a legitimate legislative purpose and salvages the elective share statute from an equal protection attack).

Nor do we view the fact that Barrett Hamilton and Virginia Hamilton were estranged at the time of his death and that a divorce action was pending as altering our conclusion in this matter. Hamilton's death had the effect of terminating the divorce action. Childress v. McManus, 282 Ark. 255, 668 S.W.2d 9 (1984); Pendergist v. Pendergist, 267 Ark. 1114, 593 S.W.2d 502 (Ark. App. 1980). Hence, the parties were still married under our laws when Hamilton died. His widow's election to take against his will was appropriate, the pending divorce action notwithstanding. *See* In the Matter of the Estate of Kueber, 390 N.W.2d 22 (Minn. App. 1986) (estranged wife who was never divorced from testator entitled to her elective share).

The daughters also assert that Virginia Hamilton's elective share amounts to a taking of their property without compensation under the Due Process Clause of the state and federal constitutions. This court has recognized that the surviving spouse's right to an elective share is inviolate. *See* Gregory v. Estate of H.T. Gregory, 315 Ark. 187, 866 S.W.2d 379 (1993). This is true despite our acknowledgment that a spouse's decision to elect to take against the will at times rebuffs the testator's testamentary wishes. Id. The elective share provisions are designed to strike a balance between a testator's right to control the distribution of his or her property for life, while preserving the State's interest in protecting the surviving spouse. *See* Holland v. Willis, 293 Ark. 518, 739 S.W.2d 529 (1987); Estate of Dahlmann v. Estate of Dahlmann, 282 Ark. 296, 668 S.W.2d 520 (1984). As in the case of the classification discussed above, a legitimate government interest supports the diminishment in the daughters' shares caused by the widow's election.

Affirmed.

■ POINTS TO CONSIDER

1. **Background.** Barrett Hamilton, Jr., the decedent in this case, inherited a substantial fortune from his father, who founded one of Arkansas' most successful liquor distributorships shortly after Prohibition ended. Hamilton was found dead in his luxury suite at a New York City hotel, at the age of 47, of an apparent cocaine overdose. His estate was valued at over $16 million.

2. **Elective share constitutional.** The Arkansas court noted a 1991 South Carolina decision also upholding that state's elective share provision against an equal protection challenge. The Florida Court of Appeals has also rejected constitutional arguments to its elective share statute. In re Estate of Magee, 988 So. 2d 1 (Fla. Dist. Ct. App. 2007). No court has held to the contrary.

The elective share provision can thwart the estate planning goals of the couple. For example, in *Estate of Shipman*, Husband spent half of the couple's assets to pay for Wife's nursing home care, intending to leave the other half to the couple's children. The Medicaid provider insisted that the surviving spouse take her elective share. In re Estate of Shipman, 832 N.W.2d 335 (S.D. 2013).

3. **Are all spouses equal?** Should the amount of the elective share be the same regardless of the circumstances? For example, assume that H and W enter into marriage at the age of 60, the third marriage for each of them. Each has substantial assets and children from the previous marriages. One day after entering into marriage, W dies of a heart attack. W's will leaves all of her estate to her children. Should H be entitled to claim a one-third share of W's estate?

   The Uniform Probate Code attempts to provide for a greater variety of situations by adjusting the percentage allowed to the surviving spouse based on both the length of the marriage and the surviving spouse's own assets. Uniform Probate Code §2-202 (amended 2010). If the purpose of the elective share is to ensure that a spouse is treated fairly and is not thrown on the welfare of the state, does this model statute better accomplish those goals?

Thinking Like a Lawyer: Comparing Spousal Protections

Martha and George got married in 2006, at the age of 55. Both had first marriages that ended upon the death of their spouses. Each had significant assets resulting from their own successful careers and the life insurance proceeds and other assets inherited from their deceased spouses. In entering this second marriage, they discussed a prenuptial agreement, but decided that it would "spoil the romance." After marriage, they bought a house together for which each paid half and titled it in both their names as joint tenants. Other than that, they kept most of their assets separate. In 2011, they decided to make "mirror image" wills, in which they left certain investment accounts to their children, but all other property to each other. In 2013, Martha decided to retire. She purchased a beachfront vacation condo, which she bought with her separate assets and titled it in her name only. Martha lived in the condo several months of each year and George often stayed with her. In 2016, however, Martha had a big fight with George. In a moment of anger, she decided to convey the condo as a gift to Abigail, one of her children from her first marriage, over George's objection. George objected because they had been living mostly on his income since Martha retired and her conveyance violated their verbal agreement on how to distribute their assets.

Assume Martha died in 2018. Consider how the spousal protection concepts we have discussed in this chapter might be applied. These issues are complicated because questions regarding real property are governed by the law of the *situs* of the property—i.e., where the property is located. Legal issues regarding the distribution of estates, however, are governed by the law of the decedent's *domicile* at death. Domicile refers to the decedent's permanent principal home.

To avoid that complexity, assume at first that the couple lives in the same state as the condo property. How would George's rights to the condo differ in each situation:

1. The jurisdiction retains the concept of dower or curtesy.
2. The jurisdiction has an elective share provision.
3. The jurisdiction is a community property state.
4. The condo had been conveyed "to Martha and George, as joint tenants with the right of survivorship," rather than in Martha's name alone.
5. The condo had been conveyed "to Martha and George as tenants by the entirety."

Now, assume that Martha's domicile is a community property state, but she bought the condo in a separate property state. How would your answers change, if at all?

3. Rights upon Dissolution

In separate property jurisdictions, statutes determine how property will be distributed upon the dissolution of marriage. Under most of these statutes, courts are to make an "equitable distribution" of the marital property. Equitable does not mean "equal" division, although some statutes start with a presumption of equal distribution, which may be rebutted. *See* Ind. Code Ann. §31-15-7-5 (2018). Instead, the court attempts to distribute the assets fairly and reasonably according to the circumstances, and the trial court has broad discretion in that regard.

Only marital property is subject to distribution. Any property acquired prior to the marriage and gifts or inheritance received during the marriage constitute separate property. Separate property may be transmuted into marital property if it becomes commingled with marital property such that it is not traceable, or if it is used in the marriage in a manner that evidences an intent to make it marital property. Most statutes then direct the court to divide these marital assets to achieve an equitable result and specify the factors to be taken into account. Factors may include the contribution of each spouse to the accumulation of the assets; the dissipation of the assets by either spouse; the duration of the marriage; the economic circumstances of each party after divorce and their employability or other sources of income; and who will get custody of and have the costs of caring for any children. *See, e.g.,* 750 Ill. Comp. Stat. Ann. 5/503 (2016).

Misconduct or fault on the part of either spouse (such as cruelty or infidelity) may be considered in some jurisdictions in making the division. *See, e.g.,* Levi v. Levi, 848 N.Y.S.2d 225 (N.Y. App. Div. 2007) (misconduct included trying to bribe the trial judge); Vermaelen v. Vermaelen, 240 So.3d 1004 (La. Ct. App. 2018) (wife did not commit marital misconduct by leaving her husband's home and refusing sexual advances).

In other jurisdictions, consideration of misconduct is precluded either by court decision or by statute. *See, e.g.,* Tenn. Code Ann. §36-4-121 (West 2017) (court should equitably divide marital property "without regard to marital fault").

■ PROBLEMS: DISSOLUTION

1. Fletcher owned a house before he married Belle. After marrying, the couple lived in the house for 17 years, but never changed the title. Over the years, Belle performed a lot of routine maintenance on the house and chipped in when it needed a paint job. Belle now seeks a divorce. Is the house a marital asset, subject to division? What additional evidence would you consider? *See* Murray v. Murray, 439 S.E.2d 312 (S.C. Ct. App. 1993).

2. Simon and Greg were married in 2015. Over the next four years, Simon tooled around with his guitar writing songs, while Greg worked as a waiter to pay the rent and buy food for the couple. In 2019, the couple is getting a divorce. Greg wants the court to treat the copyright on Simon's music as a marital asset, even though until now none of the songs has made any money. Simon claims that, if and when the songs make money, it will be through his post-dissolution efforts to market them. How should the court deal with this issue? *See, e.g.,* In re Marriage of Feliciano, 2009 WL 1364420 (Cal. Dist. Ct. App. 2009) (spouse of José Feliciano engaged in 30-year battle over performance royalties for songs José recorded during marriage, including "Feliz Navidad").

Prenuptial or Postnuptial Agreements

In many cases in which a couple enters into marriage with significant assets, lawyers recommend the use of a prenuptial (also called *antenuptial*) agreement, in order to settle ahead of time the expectations of the parties in the event of divorce or death. These agreements historically were deemed unenforceable as against public policy, because they seemed to encourage, or at least enable, divorce. Today, they are recognized in all states, as long as they meet certain requirements. *See* Gentry v. Gentry, 798 S.W.2d 928 (Ky. 1990) (one of the last jurisdictions to hold that antenuptial agreements are enforceable).

In general, states will enforce a prenuptial agreement if it is in writing, signed, and notarized. States take a variety of approaches to claims of unfairness:

- In some states, the agreement will be enforced as long as there was *full disclosure* of the assets involved, and therefore a knowing and willing waiver of rights. In these jurisdictions, a spouse cannot later claim the agreement was unfair, as long as there was full disclosure at the time. *See, e.g.,* In re Marriage of Stokes, 608 P.2d 824 (Colo. App. 1979) (only appropriate inquiry is whether parties entered into agreement with full knowledge of consequences).

- In other states, courts will require that the disposition of property meet a certain minimal standard of fairness. These jurisdictions are split as to whether fairness is to be judged as of the time the agreement was entered into or at the time of the divorce. Some courts invalidate agreements based on "changed circumstances," such that an agreement that seemed fair at the time it was signed "no longer comports with the reasonable expectations of the parties." *See, e.g.,* Krejci v. Krejci, 667 N.W.2d 780 (Wis. Ct. App. 2003).

- Some states use a more relaxed standard of "unconscionability," rather than requiring agreements to meet a "fairness" test. *See* Chen v. Hoeflinger, 127 Hawai'i 346, 279 P.3d 11, 22 (2012) (unconscionability means "unjustly disproportionate" rather than merely inequitable).

Consider this situation, which illustrates the difference in jurisdictional approaches:

➤ In 1985, a restaurant hostess, W, became pregnant and was considering an abortion. H, a business owner and the father, asked her to marry him instead. She agreed. Several days later, H asked W to sign a prenuptial agreement prepared by his attorney. The agreement called for a basic alimony amount, which would be increased by the years of marriage, and the assets would belong to whomever owned them originally or received them during marriage. According to W, H assured W that the agreement was "just a formality," and that he would "take care of her." At the time, W had a net worth of $10,000 and H was worth at least $8.5 million. The agreement included a short statement of each party's assets and liabilities, but did not include a statement of their incomes. W says she was aware that H made a lot of money, but not how much.

Over the course of an 18-year marriage, and the birth of four children, H's net worth grew to almost $23 million. At that point, the parties divorced. In the dissolution proceeding, the trial court enforced the antenuptial agreement and awarded W $2,900 per month in alimony for four years (totaling about $140,000). H was awarded all the assets he had when he entered the marriage and all assets accumulated during the marriage.

See Mallen v. Mallen, 622 S.E.2d 812 (Ga. 2005). Should this antenuptial agreement be enforced? Why do you think some courts refuse to consider the fairness of prenuptial agreements? Even if the test is one of full disclosure, do these facts meet that test?

Although some states do not require *consideration* for this type of contract, those that do consider the marriage itself adequate consideration. This also means that *postnuptial* agreements may be harder to enforce. At that point, the consideration of entering into the marriage no longer exists, and some courts find it more likely that undue influence or duress occurs in this context.

Because public policy favors settlement, most courts will enforce a post-nuptial agreement and some state statutes specifically validate them. *See, e.g.,* In re Estate of Wilbur, 165 N.H. 246, 75 A.3d 1096 (N.J. 2013) (postnuptial agreements consistent with public policy of encouraging settlement of own financial affairs). Courts may accord a "mid-marriage" agreement (as opposed to one entered into at the end of marriage) closer scrutiny, however, as a New Jersey court explained:

> We are persuaded that placing a mid-marriage agreement in the same category as a pre-nuptial agreement is inappropriate. As previously indicated, the dynamics and pressures involved in a mid-marriage context are qualitatively different. Similarly, there are significant differences between a mid-marriage agreement and a property settlement agreement made in the context of termination of the marriage. In the latter circumstances, knowing that the marriage is over, though one party may wish to continue it, each party can pursue his or her economic self interest. Mid-marriage agreements closely resemble so-called reconciliation agreements. We must be aware, however, that such circumstances are pregnant with the opportunity for one party to use the threat of dissolution "to bargain themselves into positions of advantage."

Pacelli v. Pacelli, 725 A.2d 56 (N.J. Super. Ct. App. Div. 1999). *See also* Devney v. Devney, 886 N.W.2d 61 (Neb. 2016) (post-nuptial agreements not valid in Nebraska unless concurrent with separation or divorce).

4. Cohabiting Couples

We have already discussed several important property laws applicable to married couples of which unmarried cohabitants cannot take advantage. For example, marriage allows the couple to hold property as tenants by the entirety. In a community property state, the income of one spouse would be automatically owned in common. In a separate property state, each spouse would be protected by dower and elective share statutes.

These rights, in addition to many others, helped to convince the United States Supreme Court that same-sex couples were not being treated equally under the law. In Obergefell v. Hodges, 135 S.Ct. 2584 (U.S. 2015), the Supreme Court upheld the constitutional right of same-sex couples to marry, thereby giving these couples the option of triggering the protections that state and federal law gives to married couples.

Of course, cohabiting couples, whether same-sex or opposite-sex, may choose not to marry. The Census Bureau reports that the number of opposite-sex couples living together without being married has more than doubled since the 1990s, rising to over 8 million couples in 2016. These unmarried couples often have property issues as result of long periods of living together. Only a few states recognize "common law marriage," which applies if the couple intends to be married and holds themselves out as being married. Otherwise, these cohabiting couples may wish to enter into some kind of property agreement—akin to an antenuptial agreement—to solidify their expectations.

> ➤ Some jurisdictions refuse to enforce such agreements, on the ground that they involve "immoral consideration" (i.e., inducing someone to live with you in exchange for property). *See, e.g.,* Long v. Marino, 441 S.E.2d 475 (Ga. Ct. App. 1994) (unmarried cohabitation agreement unlawful and unenforceable).

> ➤ Most modern courts, however, enforce cohabitation agreements. *See, e.g.,* Salzman v. Bachrach, 996 P.2d 1263 (Colo. 2000) (joining majority of jurisdictions upholding cohabitation agreements "so long as sexual relations are merely incidental to the agreement").

Thinking Like a Lawyer: Cohabiting Couples

Martin and Erica have been living together for several years and are getting ready to buy a house together. They come to your office and seek your advice about how to arrange their property affairs in order to voluntarily provide as much of the same protections for each other as the law provides married couples. They want to adopt a child, and one of them may decide to stay home and care for the child while the other continues to work. At the moment, they are fully committed to each other, but they recognize that, like any other couple, they may split up at some point down the road.

What advice would you give to Martin and Erica? If you recommend that they enter into a cohabitation or partnership agreement, what would it contain? Would such an agreement be enforceable? Are there any protections the law provides for married couples that you could not mimic with voluntary agreements that provide equivalent protection?

We have not considered tax implications of marital status, as they are beyond the scope of this course, but we should at least note that significant issues exist. For example, if Erica pays all the living expenses, that would not be considered a gift, subject to gift tax, if the couple were married. It might be, though, if they are not. If Erica dies early, her spouse could roll over Erica's retirement funds into her own account tax-free, while a non-spouse could not. On death, the estate tax has a marital deduction, for which Martin would not qualify.

SUMMARY

- The three major types of *concurrent ownership* are tenancy in common, joint tenancy, and tenancy by the entirety (allowed in about half of U.S. jurisdictions).

- *Joint tenancy* must be created by clear language to overcome presumption of tenancy in common. The signal characteristic of joint tenancy is right of survivorship.

- In states allowing *tenancy by the entirety*, property conveyed to a married couple may be presumed to be TBE.

- At common law, the *four unities* of time, title, interest, and possession must exist to create and maintain joint tenancy. Modern courts may consider *intent* rather than strictly adhering to the four unities.

- *Severance* converts joint tenancy to tenancy in common, destroying the right of survivorship. Severance occurs when one of the unities is broken, most often by a conveyance of an undivided interest by one of the joint tenants.

- Most jurisdictions have eliminated the need to use a straw person to create or sever joint tenancy, as long as intent is clear. This results in a problem of "secret severance," however.

- Joint tenancy may be severed by a mortgage entered into by one joint tenant in some "title theory" states. Lease by one joint tenant is less likely to result in severance.

- In general, a joint tenancy or tenancy in common may be *partitioned* upon the request of any co-tenant at any time. Partition in kind is favored, but partition by sale may be ordered if physical partition is impracticable or would prejudice parties. Courts are split on whether prejudice includes sentimental considerations in addition to economic loss.

- *Tenancy by the entirety* must include the four unities, plus fifth unity of marriage. TBE includes the right of survivorship. TBE property may not be conveyed, encumbered, severed, or partitioned except with the consent of both spouses.

- In most states that allow TBE, a creditor of one spouse alone may not reach TBE property. This may raise fairness issues with regard to judgment creditors.

- *Homestead* laws protect core property used as a permanent residence from the reach of creditors.

- Most courts hold that a co-tenant who takes sole possession of the property does not owe the other co-tenants rent absent *ouster*.

- A co-tenant may claim adverse possession against other co-tenants by ouster, but acts must establish not only possession, but unequivocal denial of other co-tenants' rights to possession.

- In *community property* jurisdictions, property acquired during the marriage by either spouse, other than by gift or inheritance, is considered owned equally by both spouses. At death, a spouse may devise his or her separate property and half of the community property.

■ In *separate property* jurisdictions, the spouse is protected by *dower* or *elective share* provisions. The elective share gives the surviving spouse a certain percentage of the decedent spouse's estate regardless of the provisions of the will.

■ Upon dissolution, separate property jurisdictions apply the concept of equitable distribution of marital property.

■ *Unmarried cohabitants* may want to enter into an agreement that attempts to replicate some of the property protections the law provides to married couples.

Estates and Future Interests

> I do think it is the hardest thing in the world, that your estate should be
> entailed away from your own children; and I am sure, if I had been you,
> I should have tried long ago to do something or other about it.
> —*Mrs. Bennet, in Jane Austen, Pride and Prejudice*

A INTRODUCTION

■ INTRODUCTORY PROBLEM

Alice was married to Bill for many years and they had one child, Chrissy. The family lived for many years on a ranch called Blackacre, which was their main asset. Bill died in 2014. Now, Alice is contemplating marriage to Hank, who, like her, is in his mid-60s. Hank has agreed to give his house to his daughter and come to live with Alice. If Alice dies before Hank, she would like him to be able to stay on Blackacre for the rest of his life, but eventually she wants the property to go to Chrissy, rather than to Hank's relatives. How can she arrange her affairs to ensure this?

This is a typical problem in *estate planning*, the branch of law that deals with property distribution at death. A property owner often wants to give property to one person now, but then have the property go to another person (or persons) in the future. Thus, the property rights need to be divided *temporally*—that is, by time—between present and future owners.

The law has long accommodated this desire by developing an elaborate system of *present estates* and *future interests*. In our example, Alice could convey title to Blackacre to Chrissy, while reserving possession of Blackacre for Hank and herself for the rest of their lives. Alice and Hank would have a present estate, measured by their lives, called a life estate. Chrissy would then have a future interest, called a remainder. Alice has now split the bundle of sticks and given Chrissy a part of the bundle that will give her the right to possess Blackacre sometime in the future.

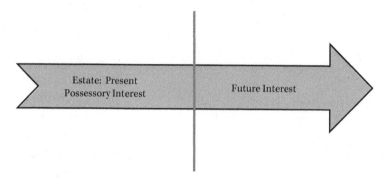

Meaning of "Estate"

The term *estate* has two meanings in property law. In probate, estate refers to the property the decedent owns at death. Estate also refers to a possessory interest in land. When we ask "what type of estate does A have?" we are referring to this latter definition.

In this chapter, we will learn the different ways property can be divided in terms of time. In part, this will be an exercise in vocabulary—learning which labels are attached to the different types of interests lawyers can use to serve different purposes. More important, however, is learning to grasp the concept of a *future interest*—the idea that Chrissy has something, a property interest, *right now*, even though she will not take possession until some time in the future.

To make sure you understand this concept from the very beginning, consider this question:

> ➢ What happens if, after Alice has deeded the property as described above, Chrissy dies first?

Chrissy has left a will giving all of her property to the Alien Space Society, a group that believes aliens are living among us. Her mother has been very opposed to Chrissy's involvement with this group.

If Alice had not conveyed a remainder interest to Chrissy and instead merely left Blackacre to Chrissy in her will, she could change it now and give the property to someone else.

Instead, Alice has conveyed to Chrissy a *property interest*, called a *future interest*. It is just as much Chrissy's property as her bank account or a piece of furniture in her house. Therefore, when Chrissy dies, that future interest goes by her will, and there is nothing Alice can do about it. Even if Chrissy hadn't died, nothing would prevent her from immediately selling her future interest in Blackacre to the Acme Chemical Company and going off to live in France.

> ➤ In other words, a future interest is not an expectancy, i.e., the anticipation of owning Blackacre in the future. It is instead the *present* ownership of a right to future possession.

The division of property rights into present and future interests is accomplished either in a *conveyance* (an *inter vivos* transfer by gift or sale, either directly to the beneficiary or to a trust) or in a will (a *testamentary* transfer). In this chapter, we provide some basic information about wills and trusts, to make sure you know the essentials of those methods of property transfer.

If you didn't understand the previous paragraphs fully, come back to them after you have read more of the chapter. As we said, the concept of a future interest is fundamental to understanding this chapter.

B │ AN INTRODUCTION TO WILLS

We are going to discuss the basics of wills, just enough for you to understand the material on estates and future interests. To learn more, you need to take an upper-level course on wills. Some students then take further courses in estate tax and estate planning, if they plan to specialize.

A *will* is the legal instrument by which a person directs how his or her property is to be distributed at death. Each jurisdiction has statutory requirements for the valid execution of a will, in order to prevent fraud and to regularize the process. Typically, these statutes require that two witnesses sign the will (a couple of states require three) and certify that the person making it was of sound mind and acted of her own volition.

Last Will and Testament

At common law, only real property passed through a will, while personal property was distributed by a *testament*. Today, a will disposes of both real and personal property, but you often still see this instrument entitled *Last Will and Testament*.

Wills Terminology

The following terms are used in most jurisdictions, with some minor variations:

Testator. The person who makes a will. Formerly, a female testator was called a *testatrix*, but today the term refers to either gender. If a person dies with a will, she is said to die *testate*. If a person dies without a will, he is *intestate*.

Holographic will. As noted above, most jurisdictions require two witnesses to sign the will. However, in some jurisdictions, a *holographic* will, which is handwritten and signed by the testator, is valid without witnesses. While it might be easy to forge someone's signature, it would be very difficult to forge an entire document in someone's handwriting. Holographic wills often raise interpretation issues, because they are usually drafted by persons without legal training.

Estate. The assets the decedent owns at death. Property held by the decedent in joint tenancy would not be considered part of the estate, because the decedent's interest was extinguished at death.

Devise. The gift of real property in a will. A testator *devises* Blackacre to someone, who is called a *devisee*. Technically, a gift of personal property by will is called a *bequest* or *legacy* and the person who receives it a *legatee*. However, the term *devise* is sometimes used for both. *See* Uniform Probate Code §1-201(10) (defining "devise" as testamentary disposition of real or personal property). In general, anyone designated to receive part of the estate is a *beneficiary*.

Residuary clause. After making specific devises and bequests, a will should include a paragraph designating who should receive "the rest, residue, and remainder" of the estate. Even if a testator believes she has disposed of her entire estate, the residuary clause may come into play if one of those devises is declared invalid or lapses due to the previous death of a named beneficiary. In addition, a beneficiary may decline to accept a devise or bequest (called a *disclaimer*).

Executor. The person named in the will and appointed by the court to carry out its provisions. In intestacy, or when the named executor cannot serve, the court will appoint an *administrator*.

Probate. The legal process for proving the validity of a will and distributing the estate according to its terms. Technically, the process of distributing an intestate estate is called *administration*, but since probate courts have jurisdiction over both processes, the term *probate* is commonly used to refer to both.

Intestate succession. Distribution of the estate of a person who dies without a will. Each state has statutes that designate who will *inherit* the decedent's property. Technically, the term *inherit* refers only to the receipt of property by intestate succession, but it is commonly used for devises and bequests as well. Intestacy statutes vary, but typically provide for distribution to:

- *Surviving spouse.* Usually takes the entire estate if there are no children (or descendants of children).
  - ☐ There are variations, however: In North Carolina, if there are no children, but the decedent has a surviving parent, the spouse takes only half of the real property and the parent takes the other half.
- *Issue.* Any descendants of the decedent. The issue typically take *per stirpes* (Latin for "by branch or roots"), which means that a pre-deceased child's share would be split among her children.
  - ☐ Assume Alice is a widow with two children, Bart and Carly. Carly died, leaving two children, David and Emily. If Alice then dies intestate, typically Bart will take half of the estate and David and Emily will split the other half.
- *Ancestor.* Any predecessor in the family lineage, such as a parent, grandparent, etc.
- *Collateral.* Descendant from the same ancestor. Collaterals take according to the degree of relationship—siblings would take before aunts and uncles, who would take before cousins.
- *Escheat.* If there are no heirs at law, the intestate's estate goes to the state treasury. Intestacy statutes typically limit descent to fairly close relatives. If the intestate dies without surviving relatives as defined by the statutes, the estate will escheat to the state.

Heirs. A person who inherits property by intestate succession. Note carefully that the legal definition of heir does NOT refer to a devisee or legatee. Note also that you do not have heirs until you die—before then, you have *heirs apparent,* who would be your heirs if you died today, but they will not become heirs until your death.

Revocation. The testator may revoke a will in many states either by drafting a new will, which explicitly or impliedly revokes the old one, or by a physical act, such as tearing up the old one or marking it void.

- ➤ This makes a will different from a deed, which is the instrument used to convey property *inter vivos.* Once a deed is signed and delivered, it may not be revoked by the grantor, while a will can always be changed or revoked (at least until death or incompetency).

We know that the preceding terminology is a lot to absorb right away. As you read the rest of the material, go back to this glossary and re-read it to solidify your understanding.

■ PROBLEMS: WILLS

1. In 2005, Alice granted Blackacre by deed "to my friend Betty for life, then to my heirs at law." Alice had one child, Chrissy. In 2015, Alice and Chrissy had a huge fight, and Alice wrote a will leaving her entire estate to the Alien Space Society. In 2012, Alice died, survived by Chrissy. In 2019, Betty died. Who owns Blackacre? Now assume Chrissy died in 2010, leaving one child, George, and a surviving spouse, Hank. Her will left her entire estate to Hank. Now who owns Blackacre upon Betty's death in 2019?

2. Lawyer is drafting a will for Alice. Alice has a son, Bart, and a daughter, Chrissy. She loves her daughter, Chrissy, but hates Chrissy's husband, Dirk, and wants to make sure he doesn't take Chrissy's share. Alice proposes the following: "I devise Blackacre to those of my children who survive me." That way, if Chrissy predeceases Alice, her share will go to Bart. Lawyer suggests changing that provision to "I devise Blackacre to those of my issue who survive me, per stirpes." What would be the effect of this change? Is there any other possible language you might suggest?

3. Alice was a single parent who had two children, Bart and Chrissy. Chrissy died, survived by her husband, Dirk, and her children, Emily, Fabian, and Gandalf. Fabian died, survived by his children, Harry and Inez. Alice then died intestate, survived by Bart, Dirk, Emily, Gandalf, Inez, and Harry. How should Alice's estate be distributed if the issue take *per stirpes*? How would a *per capita* (by the head, or per person) distribution differ? Which seems the most likely to correspond to Alice's wishes?

C   TYPES OF ESTATES AND FUTURE INTERESTS

In this section, you will learn the labels we attach to the various present estates and future interests in property. In some ways, this is like learning a foreign language—you need to know what things are called in order to converse with other property lawyers.

Present interests in property, called *estates,* are classified according to the *length of time* they may last. The longest, the *fee simple absolute,* lasts forever and is therefore the most complete estate. The other types are at least potentially shorter and therefore are accompanied by a *future interest* in someone else. The grantor (the person conveying the property by deed) or the testator may retain the future interest or create it in a third party. Here are the basic estates we will learn in this chapter:

Estate	Future Interest Retained by Grantor/Testator	Future Interest in Third Party
Fee simple absolute	None	None
Fee simple determinable	Possibility of reverter	Executory interest
Fee simple subject to condition subsequent	Right of entry or power of termination	Executory interest
Life estate	Reversion	Remainder
Term of years	Reversion	Remainder

These are the building blocks of estate planning. Thus, if Alice wanted Bart to be able to live on Blackacre for the rest of his life and then have the property go to Chrissy, she could grant a *life estate* in Bart and give Chrissy a *remainder*. Alternatively, Alice could decide to have Blackacre come back to her when Bart died, which would give Alice a *reversion*. She could then devise that reversion to whomever she wanted in her will.

We will now explore each estate and future interest in more detail. Note, however, that we are going to cover only the *basics* of estates and future interests. We are not going to discuss certain complexities, such as the Rule in Shelley's Case or the Doctrine of Worthier Title, preferring to save such topics for upper-level classes. Instead, we will focus on making sure you understand the fundamentals.

1. Fee Simple Absolute

The *fee simple absolute* (often abbreviated to "fee simple") is the most complete temporal ownership recognized. The fee simple owner has the entire timeline; there are no future interests. Most owners of property hold fee simple absolute ownership.

Fee Simple Absolute

- ■ "Fee" was derived from the Old English word "fief," which meant a landholding. It refers to an estate that is inheritable and might continue forever.
- ■ "Simple" refers to the fact that the grant does not have any limitations on alienability or inheritability attached to it.
- ■ "Absolute" indicates the estate lasts forever, as distinguished from other "fee simple" estates that might terminate earlier (as described below).

At common law, it was necessary to use special words of inheritance to create a fee simple. If Alice wanted to convey a fee simple absolute to Bart, she would need to say "Alice grants Blackacre to Bart and his heirs." If she just said "to Bart," it would be construed to be a life estate.

> ➤ Alice conveys Blackacre "to Bart and his heirs, successors, and assigns." Bart has a fee simple absolute.

This language has a historical basis, as most things in this area of law do, so we digress for a moment to consider where our current system of estates originated.

In 1066, William the Conquerer declared that all land in England belonged to the crown. The king would then grant property rights to noblemen in exchange for services, such as providing knights for battle. The noblemen (*lords* or *tenants-in-chief*) would in turn parcel out rights (or *tenancies*) to lower-level vassals who would actually work the land, in exchange for the provision of goods and services to the lord. The grant to the vassal would not be absolute, but rather subject to various conditions. If the vassal died, for example, you might want the property back so you could choose another tenant. If the vassal did not perform the required services or provide the required rent, you would want the property back. So, merely granting Blackacre to someone normally would not allow the grantee to sell the property to someone else or to have it descend to the grantee's heirs on death.

> ### Knights in Shining Armor: You Think *Your* Rent Is High!
>
> Next time you watch a movie about a battle in the Middle Ages (for example, *Henry V*), think about where all those knights in shining armor came from, without a draft and without army recruiters. Many of those knights probably held their tenancies by knight service, owing their lords service in the field in exchange for their use of the land. *Tenure by knight-service* was finally abolished by the Tenures Abolition Act of 1660.

As the Tennessee Supreme Court explained nicely:

> Because the feudal lord granted land solely as compensation for personal services, the grant was for no longer than the life of the grantee. Later the grant was extended to the sons and other issue of the grantee under the designation of "heirs." Heirs were thus entitled to stand in the place of their ancestor after his death if mentioned in the grant but only if specifically mentioned. Thereafter, the word "heirs," when used in a conveyance to a man "and his heirs," came to include collateral as well as lineal heirs, ultimately indicating that such grantee took an estate which would pass to his heirs or the heirs of anyone to whom he aliened it.

White v. Brown, 559 S.W.2d 938, 939 n.1 (Tenn. 1977). In other words, the use of the word "heirs" indicated that the recipient could transfer or devise the property, and it could be inherited by his heirs.

Today, some deed forms (which you will study in Chapter 7) conveying property in fee simple abolute continue to use language stating that the Grantor conveys to the Grantee "and the Grantee's heirs and assigns forever" or something similar. This language is used to clarify that a fee simple absolute, rather than a life estate or some other limited grant, is intended. The language referencing heirs and assigns simply means that the estate granted is *inheritable, devisable,* and *alienable*; it does not actually give the heirs any interest in the property. Many modern deed forms omit this language and simply state that Grantor conveys Blackacre to Grantee.

> ➢ Unlike common law, the law now assumes, unless a limitation is specifically noted, that the grantor/testator intends to convey/devise a fee simple absolute. *See, e.g.*, Ala. Code §35-4-2 (2017) (estate taken as fee simple unless expressly limited).
>   - ▪ In a deed: "Alice, grantor, hereby grants and conveys Blackacre to Bart, grantee." If Alice had a fee simple absolute, this language is sufficient to create a fee simple absolute in Bart.
>   - ▪ In a will: Alice's estate includes fee simple absolute ownership of Blackacre. In her will, after giving away a few minor legacies, testator Alice "leaves the rest, residue, and remainder of my estate to Bart." This devise creates a fee simple absolute in Blackacre in Bart.

Fee Simple Obsolete?

Professor Lee Ann Fennell has suggested that we may need to re-think whether the fee simple absolute represents the best form of packaging property rights in land in the modern era.

"[The fee simple absolute] purports to grant a 'chunk of the world'— a unique piece of the earth's surface and atmosphere—indefinitely to the party designated as owner. This formulation provided a useful shorthand for pairing inputs and outcomes in the mostly agrarian society in which the fee simple developed. Over time, however, it has become an anachronistic fiction that misses most of how urban property creates value." Lee Anne Fennell, *Fee Simple Obsolete*, 91 N.Y.U. L. Rev. 1457, 1459-60 (2016).

Professor Fennell notes that modern society, especially in the urban setting, involves the need for nimble, shifting land uses and minimization of externalities, which the FSA can impede. She concludes:

"We must loosen the grip of the rooted, everlasting estate on our imaginations if we want to build cities that are flexible enough to flourish."

Id., at 1515. Think about this critique as you study land use conflicts later in the semester.

In contrast, Katrina Wyman argues that the alleged economic impediments presented by the fee simple have not been established. She also emphasizes that "[l]and ownership is not only about the efficient use of land, but also about individual freedom." Katrina M. Wyman, *In Defense of the Fee Simple*, 93 Notre Dame L. Rev. 1, 6 (2017).

2. Life Estate

After the fee simple absolute, the most common variety of present possessory interest is the life estate. As we saw in the example beginning this chapter, in some situations the property owner wants to give the property to A for the remainder of A's life and then have the property go to B.

For example, assume Alice wants Blackacre to go to her son Bart. Bart is now married to Wilma, but he has a child, Carly, from his first marriage. Alice loves Bart and Carly, but she hates Wilma and does not want Blackacre to ever end up with Wilma and her family. She doesn't trust Wilma, in fact, to give Blackacre to Carly if Bart dies first. So, a will devising Blackacre to Bart in fee simple absolute will not fulfill her wishes. In that case, Blackacre would be marital property, so that Wilma could get a portion of it in the event of a divorce. Moreover, if Bart predeceased Wilma, he might devise Blackacre to Wilma and even if he didn't, she would have the right to a portion of Bart's property at death regardless of his will.

To fulfill her desires, Alice can devise Blackacre

➤ "to my son Bart for his use and benefit for the remainder of his life, and upon his death, to my granddaughter Carly."

This will ensure that Blackacre will get to Carly (assuming she outlives Bart). When Bart dies, his interest is extinguished, so Wilma will not be able to use his will, intestacy statutes, or elective share provisions to reach it.

We call Bart's present possessory interest a *life estate.* The future interest in Carly created by this devise is called a *remainder*—the part of the bundle of sticks remaining after the life estate is carved out. In this case, it is a remainder in fee simple absolute (that is, Carly will have a fee simple absolute when she takes possession). Alice could also have granted Carly only a remainder in life estate, and then created another remainder following that, say in Carly's children.

➤ "to my son Bart for life, then to my granddaughter Carly for life, then to Carly's children." Bart has a life estate, Carly has a remainder in life estate, and Carly's children have remainder in fee simple absolute.

The grantor or testator may also retain the future interest themselves—in other words, after the life estate terminates, the possessory interest in Blackacre will revert back to the grantor (or the testator's estate). This is called a *reversion.* It can be created explicitly ("and upon the death of Bart, Blackacre shall revert to the Grantor"), but it can also be created by simply failing to provide for a remainder interest after a life estate, or for a remainder that is certain to take (more about *contingent* remainders below).

➤ Alice grants Blackacre "to Bart for life, then to Carly if then living." Alice has a reversion, because the remainder to Carly is not certain to take. If Carly dies before Bart, the estate will revert to Alice upon the death of Bart.

The *creation of a life estate* is not difficult. The deed or will simply must use language indicating that the conveyance or devise is limited to the life of the holder. All of these phrases are sufficient to create a life estate:

- ➢ "to B for life"
- ➢ "to B in life estate"
- ➢ "to B during the term of his life"
- ➢ "the full use and possession of the described property to B for and during the term of her natural life."

Sometimes, the life estate will be created by a *reservation* in a deed granting a fee simple to someone else.

- ➢ Grantor Alice conveys Blackacre "to Bart, his heirs and assigns forever. Grantor reserves to herself the exclusive possession, use, and enjoyment of the above-granted property for and during her natural life."

The reservation of a life estate in a fee simple deed results in a remainder interest in the grantee (in the example, Bart).

Unless otherwise provided in the grant, a life estate is *alienable*: the life tenant may sell or give the estate to someone else. Assume Alice grants a life estate in Blackacre to Bart, with a remainder in Carly. Bart decides to move to Tasmania and so sells his life interest to David. David now has a life estate *pur autre vie* (for the life of another)—in other words, David's interest will still be measured by Bart's life. *What happens if David dies before Bart?*

In order to buy the entire fee simple, a purchaser will have to obtain both the present and future interests (the life estate and remainder). This makes property subject to a life estate difficult to buy and sell, or obtain a mortgage on, and is a key consideration for those thinking of using this device. The material on trusts at the end of this chapter will show you how to avoid some of these drawbacks.

As discussed above, the creation of a life estate is relatively simple. However, as the following case illustrates, it is sometimes not clear whether a fee simple or life estate was intended, especially when the language is drafted without the aid of an attorney. The case also gives us our first opportunity to examine the judicial construction (that is, interpretation) of wills, and how courts apply the cardinal rule of following the testator's intent.

WHITE v. BROWN

559 S.W.2d 937 (1977)
Supreme Court of Tennessee

BROCK, Justice.

This is a suit for the construction of a will. The Chancellor held that the will passed a life estate, but not the remainder, in certain realty, leaving the remainder to pass by inheritance to the testatrix's heirs at law. The Court of Appeals affirmed.

Mrs. Jessie Lide died on February 15, 1973, leaving a holographic will which, in its entirety, reads as follows:

> *April 19, 1972*
>
> *I, Jessie Lide, being in sound mind declare this to be my last will and testament. I appoint my niece Sandra White Perry to be the executrix of my estate. I wish Evelyn White to have my home to live in and not to be sold.*
>
> *I also leave my personal property to Sandra White Perry. My house is not to be sold. Jessie Lide*

(Underscoring by testatrix.)

Mrs. Lide was a widow and had no children. Although she had nine brothers and sisters, only two sisters residing in Ohio survived her. These two sisters quit-claimed any interest they might have in the residence to Mrs. White. The nieces and nephews of the testatrix, her heirs at law, are defendants in this action.

> **Glossary of Will Terminology**
>
> Remember to go back to the glossary of will terminology if you've forgotten what words like "heirs at law" mean!

Mrs. [Evelyn] White, her husband, who was the testatrix's brother, and her daughter, Sandra White Perry, lived with Mrs. Lide as a family for some twenty-five years. After Sandra married in 1969 and Mrs. White's husband died in 1971, Evelyn White continued to live with Mrs. Lide until Mrs. Lide's death in 1973 at age 88.

Mrs. White, joined by her daughter as executrix, filed this action to obtain construction of the will, alleging that she is vested with a fee simple title to the home. The defendants contend that the will conveyed only a life estate to Mrs. White, leaving the remainder to go to them under our laws of intestate succession. The Chancellor held that the will unambiguously conveyed only a life interest in the home to Mrs. White and refused to consider extrinsic evidence concerning Mrs. Lide's relationship with her surviving relatives. Due to the debilitated condition of the property and in accordance with the desire of all parties, the Chancellor ordered the property sold with the proceeds distributed in designated shares among the beneficiaries.

I.

Our cases have repeatedly acknowledged that the intention of the testator is to be ascertained from the language of the entire instrument when read in the light of surrounding circumstances. . . . But, the practical difficulty in this case, as in so many other cases involving wills drafted by lay persons, is that the words chosen by the testatrix are not specific enough to clearly state her intent. Thus, in our opinion, it is not clear whether Mrs. Lide intended to convey a life estate in the home to Mrs. White, leaving the remainder interest to descend by operation of law, or a fee interest with a restraint on alienation. Moreover, the will might even be read as conveying a fee interest subject to a condition subsequent (Mrs. White's failure to live in the home).

In such ambiguous cases it is obvious that rules of construction, always yielding to the cardinal rule of the testator's intent, must be employed as auxiliary aids in the courts' endeavor to ascertain the testator's intent.

In 1851 our General Assembly enacted two such statutes of construction, thereby creating a statutory presumption against partial intestacy.

Chapter 33 of the Public Acts of 1851 (now codified as T.C.A. §§64-101 and 64-501) reversed the common law presumption that a life estate was intended unless the intent to pass a fee simple was clearly expressed in the instrument. T.C.A. §64-501 provides:

> Every grant or devise of real estate, or any interest therein, shall pass all the estate or interest of the grantor or devisor, unless the intent to pass a less estate or interest shall appear by express terms, or be necessarily implied in the terms of the instrument.

Chapter 180, Section 2 of the Public Acts of 1851 (now codified as T.C.A. §32-301) was specifically directed to the operation of a devise. In relevant part, T.C.A. §32-301 provides:

> A will . . . shall convey all the real estate belonging to (the testator) or in which he had any interest at his decease, unless a contrary intention appear by its words and context.

Thus, under our law, unless the "words and context" of Mrs. Lide's will clearly evidence her intention to convey only a life estate to Mrs. White, the will should be construed as passing the home to Mrs. White in fee. "'If the expression in the will is doubtful, the doubt is resolved against the limitation and in favor of the absolute estate.'" Meacham v. Graham, 98 Tenn. 190, 206, 39 S.W. 12, 15 (1897) (quoting Washbon v. Cope, 144 N.Y. 287, 39 N.E. 388). . . .

Several of our cases demonstrate the effect of these statutory presumptions against intestacy by construing language which might seem to convey an estate for life, without provision for a gift over after the termination of such life estate, as passing a fee simple instead. In Green v. Young, 163 Tenn. 16, 40 S.W.2d 793 (1931), the testatrix's disposition of all of her property to her husband "to be used by him for his support and comfort during his life" was held to pass a fee estate. Similarly, in Williams v. Williams, 167 Tenn. 26, 65 S.W.2d 561 (1933), the testator's devise of real property to his children "for and during their natural lives" without provision for a gift over was held to convey a fee. And, in Webb v. Webb, 53 Tenn. App. 609, 385 S.W.2d 295 (1964), a devise of personal property to the testator's wife "for her maintenance, support and comfort, for the full period of her natural life" with complete powers of alienation but without provision for the remainder passed absolute title to the widow.

II.

Thus, if the sole question for our determination were whether the will's conveyance of the home to Mrs. White "to live in" gave her a life interest or a fee in the home, a conclusion favoring the absolute estate would be clearly required. The question, however, is complicated somewhat by the caveat contained in the will that the home is "not to be sold," a restriction conflicting with the free alienation of property, one of the most significant incidents of fee ownership. We must determine, therefore, whether Mrs. Lide's will, when taken as a whole, clearly evidences her intent to convey only a life estate in her home to Mrs. White.

Under ordinary circumstances a person makes a will to dispose of his or her entire estate. If, therefore, a will is susceptible of two constructions, by one of which the testator disposes of the whole of his estate and by the other of which he disposes of only a part of his estate, dying intestate as to the remainder, this Court has always preferred that construction which disposes of the whole of the testator's estate if that construction is reasonable and consistent with the general scope and provisions of the will. . . . A construction which results in partial intestacy will not be adopted unless such intention clearly appears. . . . It has been said that the courts will prefer any reasonable construction or any construction which does not do violence to a testator's language, to a construction which results in partial intestacy. . . .

The intent to create a fee simple or other absolute interest and, at the same time to impose a restraint upon its alienation can be clearly expressed. If the testator specifically declares that he devises land to A "in fee simple" or to A "and his heirs" but that A shall not have the power to alienate the land, there is but one tenable construction, *viz.*, the testator's intent is to impose a restraint upon a fee simple. To construe such language to create a life estate would conflict with the express specification of a fee simple as well as with the presumption of intent to make a complete testamentary disposition of all of a testator's property. By extension, as noted by Professor Casner in his treatise on the law of real property:

"Since it is now generally presumed that a conveyor intends to transfer his whole interest in the property, it may be reasonable to adopt the same construction, (conveyance of a fee simple) even in the absence of words of inheritance, if there is no language that can be construed to create a remainder." 6 American Law of Property §26.58 (A. J. Casner ed. 1952).

In our opinion, testatrix's apparent testamentary restraint on the alienation of the home devised to Mrs. White does not evidence such a clear intent to pass only a life estate as is sufficient to overcome the law's strong presumption that a fee simple interest was conveyed.

Accordingly, we conclude that Mrs. Lide's will passed a fee simple absolute in the home to Mrs. White. Her attempted restraint on alienation must be declared void as inconsistent with the incidents and nature of the estate devised and contrary to public policy. Nashville C & S.L. Ry. v. Bell, 162 Tenn. 661, 39 S.W.2d 1026 (1931). . . .

COOPER and FONES, JJ., concur.

HARBISON, J., dissents. HENRY, C.J., joins in dissent.

HARBISON, Justice, dissenting.

With deference to the views of the majority, and recognizing the principles of law contained in the majority opinion, I am unable to agree that the language of the will of Mrs. Lide did or was intended to convey a fee simple interest in her residence to her sister-in-law, Mrs. Evelyn White.

The testatrix expressed the wish that Mrs. White was "to have my home to live in and *not* to be *sold.*" The emphasis is that of the testatrix, and her desire that Mrs. White was not to have an unlimited estate in the property was reiterated in the last sentence of the will, to wit: "My house is not to be sold."

The testatrix appointed her niece, Mrs. Perry, executrix and made an outright bequest to her of all personal property.

The will does not seem to me to be particularly ambiguous, and like the Chancellor and the Court of Appeals, I am of the opinion that the testatrix gave Mrs. White a life estate only, and that upon the death of Mrs. White the remainder will pass to the heirs at law of the testatrix.

The cases cited by petitioners in support of their contention that a fee simple was conveyed are not persuasive, in my opinion. Possibly the strongest case cited by the appellants is Green v. Young, 163 Tenn. 16, 40 S.W.2d 793 (1931), in which the testatrix bequeathed all of her real and personal property to her husband "to be used by him for his support and comfort during his life." The will expressly stated that it included all of the property, real and personal, which the testatrix owned at the time of her death. There was no limitation whatever upon the power of the husband to use, consume, or dispose of the property, and the Court concluded that a fee simple was intended.

In the case of Williams v. Williams, 167 Tenn. 26, 65 S.W.2d 561 (1933), a father devised property to his children "for and during their natural lives" but the will contained other provisions not mentioned in the majority opinion which seem to me to distinguish the case. Unlike the provisions of the present will, other clauses in the Williams will contained provisions that these same children were to have "all the residue of my estate personal or mixed of which I shall die possessed or seized, or to which I shall be entitled at the time of my decease, to have and to hold the same to them and their executors and administrators and assigns forever."

Further, following some specific gifts to grandchildren, there was another bequest of the remainder of the testator's money to these same three children. The language used by the testator in that case was held to convey the fee simple interest in real estate to the children, but its provisions hardly seem analogous to the language employed by the testatrix in the instant case. . . .

In the present case the testatrix knew how to make an outright gift, if desired. She left all of her personal property to her niece without restraint or limitation.

As to her sister-in-law, however, she merely wished the latter have her house "to live in," and expressly withheld from her any power of sale.

The majority opinion holds that the testatrix violated a rule of law by attempting to restrict the power of the donee to dispose of the real estate. Only by thus striking a portion of the will, and holding it inoperative, is the conclusion reached that an unlimited estate resulted.

In my opinion, this interpretation conflicts more greatly with the apparent intention of the testatrix than did the conclusion of the courts below, limiting the gift to Mrs. White to a life estate. I have serious doubt that the testatrix intended to create any illegal restraint on alienation or to violate any other rules of law. It seems to me that she rather emphatically intended to provide that her sister-in-law was not to be able to sell the house during the lifetime of the latter, a result which is both legal and consistent with the creation of a life estate. . . .

■ POINTS TO CONSIDER

1. **Competing canons.** The primary job of the court in probate matters, as the Tennessee Supreme Court noted, is to fulfill the testator's intent. If the language of the will is clear, they do not go further. If there is ambiguity, however, courts have adopted "canons of construction" (i.e., rules) to assist their interpretation and provide some uniformity. In some cases, legislatures have provided statutes that either confirm, overrule, or modify the common law canons. What tools of construction does the court use in *White v. Brown*?

2. **Intent of the testator.** A later case out of Tennessee concerned another ambiguous devise. G.A. Williams died in 1944, survived by nine children. His will contained the following provision:

   I, G.A. WILLIAMS, being of sound mind make this my last will and Testament: At my death I want Ida Williams, Mallie Williams, and Ethel Williams, three of my daughters to have my home farm where I now live, consisting of one hundred and eighty-eight acres, to have and to hold during their lives, and not to be sold during their lifetime. If any of them marry their interest ceases and the ones that remain single have full control of same. I am making this will because they have stayed at home and taken care of the home and cared for their mother during her sickness, and I do not want them sold out of a home. If any one tries to contest this will I want them debarred from any interest in my estate.

   Ethel Williams, the sole survivor of the three sisters, still unmarried, claimed the farm in fee simple absolute. Several other heirs of G.A. Williams claimed that Ethel was devised only a life estate and that they inherited a share of the reversionary interest. *Can you distinguish the language used by Williams from the language used in Jessie Lide's will?* Williams v. Estate of

Williams, 865 S.W.2d 3 (Tenn. 1993) (holding that Ethel had a life estate determinable only, plus a share of the reversion). *Also compare* Chin v. Estate of Chin, 15 So. 2d 894 (Fla. Dist. Ct. App. 2009), where the court held that a provision that directed certain property "shall not be sold as long as my . . . sister desires to occupy same" created a life estate.

3. **Restraints on alienation.** The general rule is that an *unreasonable* restraint on alienation on a fee simple absolute is void. If Alice conveys Blackacre to Bart in fee simple with a deed indicating that it is "subject to the condition that Bart, his heirs and successors, never sell or otherwise transfer any interest in Blackacre," the court will strike down this restriction as invalid. The policy behind this rule is that the free transferability of property is necessary to ensure that property remains economically productive and is able to be transferred to the person who will put it to the most valuable use. However, note that only *unreasonable* restraints on alienation are impermissible. Courts have approved of some types of limited restraints. For example, if the Hatfields sell Blackacre, but specify that the property cannot be sold for the next 20 years to anyone from the McCoy family, a court may uphold it, because it does not unduly interfere with alienability.Some jurisdictions allow a restraint on alienation of a life estate. The restraint is of limited duration, and it seems reasonable to control who owns the life interest, to ensure that the property is used or maintained in a way that does not impair the remainder interest. Moreover, in some cases, the whole reason for creating the life interest is to allow a certain person to live on the property, not for just anyone to live there. How did the rule on restraints on alienation factor into the decision in *White*?

Practice Tip—Estate Planning

As you go through law school, part of your task is to contemplate the kind of lawyer you would like to be. Although movies and television focus on courtroom drama, you know that many more lawyers do other kinds of work, including estate planning. In this role, you are really a "counselor-at-law," because you are advising clients on how to achieve their goals. When someone dies, you are assisting bereaved survivors to work through probate and estate distribution. This can be very difficult, but also very rewarding.

■ PROBLEMS: LIFE ESTATES

1. In the section on fee simple absolute, we noted that the traditional way to convey a fee simple is "to A and her heirs." Assume that O conveys Blackacre "to William and Judy, for and during their life and upon their death, then to their heirs in fee simple." Do William and Judy have a life estate or a

fee simple? *See* Priest v. Ernest W. Ball & Associates, Inc., 62 So.3d 1013 (Ala. 2010).

2. Vada leaves her 316-acre ranch along with other property as follows:

> NOW BOBBY, I leave the rest to you, everything, certificates of deposit, land, cattle, and machinery. Understand the land is not to be sold but passed on down to your children, ANNETTE KNOPF, ALLISON KILWAY, AND STANLEY GRAY. TAKE CARE OF IT AND TRY TO BE HAPPY.

What type of estate does Bobby have? *See* Knopf v. Gray, 545 S.W.3d 542 (Tex. 2018).

a. Relations Between Present and Future Owners

In Chapter 4 on concurrent interests, we learned that when property interests are split between multiple owners, thorny disputes can often occur concerning the management of the property. The same thing is true in the context of future interests. The owner of a remainder (or other future interest), waiting for her possessory rights to ripen, may be seriously troubled by some action, or failure to act, on the part of the owner of the present possessory interest.

We learned that concurrent owners have a couple of ways to resolve these disputes. A co-tenant can bring an action for waste or for an accounting to protect her interests. As we discuss below, these actions are usually also available for holders of future interests. In addition, the co-tenant may simply end the relationship by partitioning the interests and usually has the absolute right to do so for any reason. Should the remedy of *partition* be available in the context of future interests? Is the situation different in any material way? Consider the following case, which discusses the common law rule and the impact of partition statutes.

i. Partition

BEACH v. BEACH

74 P.3d 1 (2003)
Supreme Court of Colorado

MULLARKEY, C.J., delivered the opinion of the court:

I. INTRODUCTION

This case involves a property dispute between a mother and daughter. The mother is the holder of a life estate interest in a 3-room addition to the daughter's house. The daughter holds the remainder interest in the addition, and the mother seeks to partition her life estate interest from the remainder. The court of appeals held that, as a life tenant, the mother has a right to seek partition from the daughter's non-concurrent remainder interest pursuant to section 38-28-101, 10 C.R.S. (2002). We reverse. Section 38-28-101 does not abrogate the common law rule that a life estate interest cannot be partitioned from a successive, non-concurrent remainder interest in the same property. Because we hold that partition under these circumstances is prohibited as a matter of law, we do not address the issue of whether the parties in this case impliedly waived their partition rights.

II. FACTS AND PROCEDURAL HISTORY

In 1993, Karen K. Beach ("the daughter") entered into an oral agreement with her parents Mary L. Beach ("the mother") and Ralph W. Beach ("the father"). The agreement arose when the father's health began to fail and the daughter offered the parents the option of building an addition to her own home where they could live for the rest of their lives. The daughter's home is a modest log house located on a 19-acre lot where the daughter runs a small working ranch. In return for the daughter's offer to let the parents build an addition to her home, the parents agreed to pay for the addition and agreed that the daughter would acquire the addition, at no cost, upon their deaths. The addition is equivalent to a small apartment, and consists of two bedrooms, a bathroom, and a living room with a kitchen. The addition is connected to the side of the daughter's house and the two areas share a common hallway.

After the father's death, the relationship between the mother and daughter deteriorated and the mother eventually sued the daughter to partition her interest in the addition from the daughter's property interests. At trial, the court found that the parties' oral agreement regarding the addition implicitly created a limited life estate in the parents measured by their joint lives, and that the daughter held the remainder interest. The court also found that because the parties impliedly intended for only the parents to occupy the addition during their lifetimes, the agreement prohibited either party from selling her interest in the addition. As a result of the above findings, the court held that the mother impliedly waived any partition rights when she entered into the contract because partition would be "a violation of the intent of the original agreement."

The court of appeals reversed. First, the court held that the mother had a statutory right to compel partition, interpreting section 38-28-101, 10 C.R.S. (2002), to allow partition between the mother's life estate in the addition and the daughter's successive, non-concurrent remainder interest in the addition. Beach v. Beach, 56 P.3d 1125, 1127 (Colo. App. 2002). Second, the court held that the mother had not impliedly waived her partition rights. *Id.* at 1129. The court reasoned that partition would not violate the intent of the original agreement because the daughter would retain her contractual right to the monetary value of her remainder interest in the addition when their property interests were liquidated. *See id.*[1]

We reverse the decision of the court of appeals. Section 38-28-101 does not abrogate the common law rule that a life estate interest cannot be partitioned from a successive, non-concurrent remainder interest in the same property. Therefore, as a matter of law, the mother cannot partition her life estate in the addition from the daughter's remainder interest in the addition.

III. ANALYSIS

A. *The Common Law Rule*

Under the common law, partition applies only to concurrent interests, meaning interests that are held simultaneously in time. Thus, a present life estate cannot be partitioned from a future remainder interest because the holders of the two interests possess the property successively, rather than concurrently. *See, e.g.,* 3 Richard R. Powell, Powell on Real Property §21.05 [3][b], at 21-78 (Michael Allan Wolf ed., 2003) ("Historically, partition serves to sever concurrent interests and is not to be used for an attempted severance of successive interests."); Restatement (First) of Prop. §172, cmt. b (1936) (The rule that holders of successive interests cannot compel partition is an "aspect of the general rule that concurrent ownership is a prerequisite for partition").[2]

The overwhelming majority rule among the states conforms with the common law rule, namely that the parties to a partition action must have concurrent interests in the property. Most state statutes effectuate this rule by explicitly limiting partition to present estates held by joint tenants, tenants in common, or other concurrent owners. *See, e.g.,* Nev. Rev. Stat. §39.010 (2002) ("When several persons hold and are in possession of real property as joint tenants or as tenants in common ... an action may be brought by one or more of such persons for a partial partition thereof"); Va. Code Ann. §8.01-81 (2002) ("Tenants in common, joint tenants, executors with the power to sell, and coparceners ... may compel partition"). . . .

A concurrent interest is a prerequisite for partition because the purpose of partition is to sever unity of possession. *See* Keith v. El-Kareh, 729 P.2d 377, 379 (Colo. App. 1986). There is no unity of possession to sever when the property interests at stake are not concurrent in time.

By definition, the holder of a *present* life estate and the holder of a *future* remainder interest do not own concurrent interests because each holder uses the property exclusively during her respective time of possession. Although the holders of the life

---

[1] The court of appeals held that if the daughter chose not to purchase the mother's life estate interest in the addition, the trial court should order a sale of the addition and distribute the proceeds according to the parties' respective interests in the addition. Id. at 1131-32.

[2] Although subsequent Restatements of Property have since been published, the language of section 172 has not changed.

estate and successive remainder interest do share a *common* interest in the property, "[t]his variety of simultaneously existent interests does not constitute the *concurrent* ownership, the splitting of which is the function of partition." Restatement (First) of Prop. §172 (1936) (emphasis added). Therefore, as holders of a life estate and successive remainder interest, the mother and daughter in this case do not share the necessary concurrent interest in the addition as required by common law.

B. The Colorado Partition Statute

The court of appeals acknowledged the above common law rule that life estates are not subject to partition from remainder interests, but then went on to hold that Colorado statute abrogates the common law rule. *Beach*, 56 P.3d at 1127. To test the validity of the court of appeals' conclusion, we turn first to Colorado's partition statute. Section 38-28-101, 10 C.R.S. (2002), provides:

> Actions for the division and partition of real or personal property or interest therein may be maintained by any person having an interest in such property.

The plain language of the statute makes no reference to the common law. However, the court of appeals reasoned that, because the statute allows "any person" having any interest in real or personal property to maintain an action for partition, and because a life estate is an interest in real property, the mother must be able partition her life estate from the daughter's non-concurrent remainder interest. *Beach*, 56 P.3d at 1127. The court also noted that even though partition would cause the daughter to lose her actual remainder interest in the addition, she would still retain the liquidated value of her remainder interest when the addition was sold. *See id.* at 1129.

In interpreting a statute, we must give effect to the intent of the legislature. Lagae v. Lackner, 996 P.2d 1281, 1284 (Colo. 2000). Although the General Assembly possesses the authority to abrogate common law remedies, statutes may not be interpreted to abrogate the common law absent a clear expression of intent. *See* Preston v. Dupont, 35 P.3d 433, 440 (Colo. 2001). A statute is not presumed to alter the common law except to the extent that such statute expressly provides. *See id.*

In this case, we conclude that section 38-28-101 does not abrogate the common law rule requiring concurrent ownership in partition actions. We base this conclusion on two grounds. First, section 38-28-101 is silent as to whether successive, non-concurrent property interests are partitionable. Second, the partition of non-concurrent interests would run counter to the ordinary meaning of partition and destroy the parties' property interests.

First, section 38-28-101 contains no clear expression of intent by the General Assembly to abrogate the common law rule. The very general language of section 38-28-101 stands in sharp contrast to the clear and specific language of other state statutes explicitly overriding the common law rule requiring concurrent ownership. For example, California's partition statute expressly provides: "[p]artition *as to successive estates* in the property shall be allowed if it is in the best interest of all the parties." Cal. Civ. Pro. §872.710(c) (2002) (emphasis added). Similarly, Rhode Island's statute explicitly contemplates partition between present and future interests. . . .

In contrast to the California and Rhode Island statutes, Colorado's statute is silent as to the availability of partition between successive property interests where the parties share no concurrent ownership or possession of the property. Although the statute has been in effect for over fifty years, it has never before been interpreted as overturning the settled expectations created by the common law of future interests. The language of the statute provides only a general declaration of who has standing to bring a partition action, and does not substantively extend a right of partition to holders of non-concurrent property interests. Absent a clearer and more specific statutory indication that the General Assembly actually intended to abrogate the fundamental common law rule that non-concurrent interests are not partitionable, we must presume that the General Assembly did not intend to change the common law rule. *See Preston*, 35 P.3d at 440.

Second, we conclude that the General Assembly did not intend to abrogate the common law rule that a life estate cannot be partitioned from a non-concurrent remainder interest because such partition would be incongruous with the meaning and purpose of partition. As discussed earlier, a court's function in a partition action is to sever unity of possession by physically dividing a parcel of property. *See Keith*, 729 P.2d at 379. Here, where the addition is not concurrently owned at any point in time, there is simply no unity of possession to physically sever—partition is logically impossible.

The practical result of allowing partition where physical division is inherently impossible due to a lack of concurrent interests is that partition becomes nothing more than an automatic forced sale—one party's "partition" right becomes the right to force another party to liquidate her property interests entirely. As a result, a party's right to actually enjoy her respective interest in the property is destroyed and the only available "remedy" for the lost interest is some inadequate dollar amount.

Here, for example, the daughter's remainder interest is destroyed upon sale of the addition because once the addition is liquidated, there is nothing left in which to have a remainder. As a practical matter, "partition" via liquidation then leaves the daughter with no choice but to either buy the present value of the mother's life estate interest for approximately $48,000, or have the court sell the addition to strangers and divide the proceeds according to the mother and daughter's present and future interests in the addition.[3] Because the addition in this case is attached to the daughter's own home and located on her own private property, it may be impossible to sell only the addition. If so, the end result of the "partition" would be the sale of the daughter's entire property in order to provide the mother with the proper monetary value of her present life estate interest. . . .

---

[3] The full property value of the addition is approximately $90,000. The court of appeals calculated the mother's life estate interest at the time of trial to be $47,834.10, and the court also went into great detail regarding the proper methodology of valuating a life estate interest. *Beach*, 56 P.3d at 1130-31. This valuation issue was not raised before this court, therefore we do not address the issue here.

IV. CONCLUSION

In sum, we hold that section 38-28-101 does not abrogate the common law rule that, as a matter of law, a life estate and non-concurrent remainder interest cannot be partitioned. We therefore reverse the holding of the court of appeals and do not reach the issue of whether the parties in this case impliedly waived their partition rights by virtue of their oral contract. We remand this case to the court of appeals with directions to return this case to the trial court.

■ POINTS TO CONSIDER

1. **Policy.** Can you identify a good policy reason to treat holders of future interests differently from co-tenants for purposes of partition? The court notes that the remedy in this context would always have to be a sale of the property, because physical partition of these interests is impossible. Is that always the case? Doesn't property often get sold in concurrent interest cases, too?

2. **Counter-policy.** The court notes that at least some states—including California and Rhode Island—have statutorily abrogated the common law rule against partition. Why do think the legislatures in these states decided to allow partition by owners of successive interests? Should it be allowed in all circumstances or only in certain cases?

Valuation

In cases involving future interests, valuation can be tricky. The need to value the interest comes up in various contexts: when the property is sold voluntarily or when it is condemned (for a highway project, for example), or when the holder of a life estate wants to qualify for Medicaid or other aid. Typically, in the case of a life interest, valuation is based on the life expectancy tables.

For example, assume Alice owns a life estate in Blackacre and Bart has the remainder. Alice is 87 years old. According to the actuarial tables, Alice has a life expectancy of about six years.[4] If the property is worth $100,000 and interest rates are 5 percent, the IRS calculates the present value of Bart's remainder to be about $78,000 and Alice's life estate to be worth about $22,000. If the property involved is Alice's home, do you see why she might resist partition? If Alice were only 20, on the other hand, the life estate would be worth about $93,000, using a 5 percent interest rate.

---

[4] This may surprise you, given that the average life expectancy of a female born in the United States is nearly 87. But those who reach 87 live, on average, six more years.

ii. Waste Even though a remainderman may not have an action for partition, the court in *Beach* noted that the doctrine of waste provides some protection for the future interest. As we discussed in Chapter 4, the owner of a property interest may sue the party in possession to prevent (by injunction), or to seek damages for, any action that injures or diminishes the value of her interest. Just as one co-tenant may sue another for waste, the holder of a remainder or a reversion may sue the life tenant to prevent damage to her future interest.

Certainly, the owner of a life estate is entitled to make full use of the property, which may include making changes in building structure or use. In order to win a waste case, the owner of the reversion or remainder must show that the action will diminish the value of her interest. The remedy may include an injunction, damages, or—in extreme cases—termination of the life estate.

> ### Without Impeachment for Waste
>
> A testator leaving a loved one a life interest may include a statement that the life tenant is "without impeachment for waste." This generally leaves the life tenant free to deal with the property without interference or second-guessing of management decisions by the remaindermen. Do you see any drawbacks to including this phrase in the devise?

For example, in Matteson v. Walsh, 947 N.E.2d 44 (Mass. App. Ct. 2011), a mother left her house on Cape Cod to her son Robert for life, with a remainder to his heirs and to his sisters Elizabeth and Carrie and their heirs. Robert failed to pay taxes on the property, causing the local authorities to threaten foreclosure. In addition, he failed to maintain the property, resulting in exposure to the weather and threats of rot. His sister Elizabeth (one of the remaindermen) stepped in and paid for necessary repairs and taxes. In an action for waste, the court terminated Robert's life interest, vesting the right to possession immediately in the remaindermen.

A couple of important points about *remedies for waste*:

> ➤ First, many states include a penalty of *treble damages* (the proven damages to the future interest are tripled) in order to provide a strong disincentive to commit waste. *See, e.g.,* Mo. Ann. Stat. §537.420 (West 2016); Or. Rev. Stat. Ann. §105.805 (West 2017). This is an ancient remedy, going back to the Statute of Marlbridge in 1267. Even in the absence of such a statute, punitive damages may be awarded.
>
> ➤ Second, the drastic remedy of *forfeiture* of the life estate is available only if authorized by statute and is invoked only when the damage caused by the waste equals or exceeds the remaining value of the life interest or when the conduct is especially egregious or intentional. Remember the maxim "equity abhors a forfeiture."

b. *Contingent and Vested Remainders*

After classifying an interest as a remainder, in many situations it is important to further classify the remainder as *contingent* or *vested*.

a)   A *contingent remainder* is either
  1)   subject to a *condition precedent* that is not certain to happen, or
  2)   granted to a person that is *not in existence or ascertained*.
    ➢ "To A for life, then to B if she survives A." B's remainder is contingent because it is subject to a condition precedent.
    ➢ "To A for life, then to A's heirs." The remainder in A's heirs would be contingent because we will not know who A's heirs are until A's death.[5]

b)   A *vested remainder* is
  1)   given to an *ascertained person in existence*, and
  2)   *not subject to a condition precedent*(other than one that is certain to happen, such as the end of a life estate).
    ➢ "To A for life, then to B." B has a vested remainder. The fact that it is subject to the condition of A dying is not relevant, because the natural termination of the preceding estate is a condition of all remainders and it is, unfortunately for A, certain to happen.
    ➢ "To A for life, then to B's heirs." If B is alive, this is a contingent remainder. But when B dies, leaving C as his only heir, C then has a vested remainder.
    ➢ "To A for life, then to B's heirs then living." B dies, leaving C as his only heir. C still has only a contingent remainder, because even though the grantee is now ascertained, it is still subject to the condition precedent of C surviving A.

c)   *Vested remainder subject to open.* Assume a remainder is granted to a *class* of persons, such as "A's children." If A has no children, the remainder is contingent, because there are no ascertained takers. When one child is born, however, it *vests* in her, but is *subject to open*, which means that more takers could join the class:
    ➢ "To A for life, then to A's children." A has two children, B and C. B and C have a *vested remainder subject to open*, because if A has more children, they would join the class.

d)   A remainder is *vested subject to divestment* if the condition is subsequent, rather than precedent. In other words, we know who the taker is and he doesn't have to meet any conditions to take; however, the interest could be taken away from him:

---

[5] Assume A has one child, B, and no other heirs. A is 90 years old and B is 60. The law still classifies this as contingent even though B is the probable heir. Certainly, B could die before A and would therefore not take the remainder.

> ➢ "To A for life, then to B. If B dies before A and leaves issue, then to B's issue." B has a vested remainder, because there is no condition precedent to meet. However, the remainder could be taken away from B (*divested*) if a certain condition occurs (B dies first, leaving issue).

Why does it matter whether a remainder is vested or contingent?

> ➢ Vested interests generally are devisable, while contingent interests may not be.
>   ■ "To A for life, then to A's children, B and C." B dies before A. B's vested remainder interest will pass by his will or by intestacy statutes.
>   ■ "To A for life, then to A's children who survive A." A has two children, B and C. B dies before A. B's contingent remainder interest is extinguished.
> ➢ Contingent remainders do not accelerate into possession upon the termination of the preceding estate:
>   ■ O conveys "to A for life, then to B if she reaches the age of 21." Until B reaches the age of 21, B has a contingent remainder and O has a reversion. Assume A dies when B is 17. The estate returns to O until B reaches 21. If B does not reach 21, her interest is extinguished and O has a fee simple absolute.
> ➢ O conveys "to A for life, then to B, but if B dies before the age of 21, then to C." Assume B is 17. B has a vested remainder subject to divestment. If A dies, the estate will go to B immediately, but it is subject to divestment until B reaches 21.[6] Contingent remainders are subject to the Rule Against Perpetuities, discussed below, while vested remainders are not.
> ➢ Contingent remaindermen may have fewer rights and remedies than vested remaindermen. For example, contingent remaindermen may not be entitled to damages or forfeiture for waste committed by a life tenant, although they may still obtain injunctive relief.

CASE SUMMARY: Hammons v. Hammons, 327 S.W.2d 444 (Ky. 2010)

Dr. James Hammons, died in 2006, with a will providing for his wife, Rosa, and his children by a former marriage, Janet and Jillisa. James devised Rosa a life estate in all of his estate and devised the remainder interest to Janet and Jillisa. The will provided that Rosa could not only use the income, as in a normal life estate, but could also use the principal (or *corpus*) of the estate if necessary to provide for her maintenance and medical care. With respect to the remainder, the will stated:

> On the death of my said wife, I give, devise, and bequeath, absolutely and in fee simple, all of the assets devised and bequeathed under this Item then remaining, to my daughters, JANET P. HAMMONS and JILLISA S. HAMMONS, to be divided equally

---

[6] As we will discuss below, C's interest is called an *executory interest*.

between. In the event either of my daughters should fail to survive me and my said wife leaving no issue surviving her, then such deceased daughter's part shall pass to her surviving sibling.

The daughters challenged Rosa's right to sell property without meeting the necessary conditions specified in the will and sought an accounting, so they (and the court) could review her transactions. Rosa responded that the daughters had only a contingent remainder and therefore had no right to an accounting. The court of appeals agreed that the remainder was contingent, because it depended on (a) Rosa not depleting the estate, and (b) the daughters surviving Rosa.

The Supreme Court of Kentucky held that, in fact, the daughters had a *vested remainder subject to divestment*. The remainder was given to an ascertained person and there was no condition precedent specified.

These contingencies in the colloquial sense—that there be something left in the estate and that Janet and Jillisa either survive Rosa or leave a child—do not prevent Janet and Jillisa's interest from vesting immediately upon the death of the testator. They simply create the possibility that Janet and Jillisa may be divested of their interests.

Id. at 451.

Nevertheless, the court held that Rosa was not required to provide an accounting to the remaindermen:

Whether . . . the life tenant must provide notice or an accounting of his use of the property is a matter of first impression for this Court. However, courts in other states have considered this issue and have held, seemingly uniformly, that, absent evidence the life tenant is abusing her authority, no notice or accounting is required. . . .

We find the logic and conclusions of these courts consistent with our duty to give effect to the testator's intent and thus hold that when a life tenant is explicitly given the right to consume or invade the corpus of the estate, absent a showing of waste, she may do so at her discretion without need to petition the court for permission or provide notice of the invasion or an accounting of her use of the property. To require such a life tenant to provide notice or an accounting would be overly burdensome and would run counter to the trust the testator expressly reposed in the life tenant.

Id. at 452-53. The court noted that the remaindermen were protected by the availability of an action for waste if the life tenant improperly used the estate assets, and a Kentucky statute provided for treble damages in that event. *Id.* at 454.

■ POINTS TO CONSIDER

Should the rights of a remaindermen depend on whether his interest is vested or contingent? Should all future interest holders be treated equally, or is there another basis for distinguishing between them?

◼ PROBLEM: CONTINGENT REMAINDERS AND WASTE

Tasha devised Blackacre "to Alice for life, then to Bart if he survives Alice, but if he does not survive Alice, then to Bart's issue then living per stirpes." Bart has one child, Carly. Bart discovers that Alice has leased the forested area of Blackacre to a timber company for $100,000, allowing it to cut down most of the trees on Blackacre. By the time Bart discovers this, about half of the trees have already been cut down.

Bart and Carly believe that this constitutes waste and bring a suit asking for an injunction against further cutting, as well as damages for the trees already cut down. Should they win? Are there any other facts you believe are relevant to this case? *See* Sermon v. Sullivan, 640 S.W.2d 486 (Mo. Ct. App. 1982).

◼ PROBLEMS: IDENTIFY THE INTERESTS

1. Alfredo wants to leave his condo, Steelacre, to his granddaughter Sha-tehl, but he wants her to have an incentive to continue her education. He writes a will leaving Steelacre "to my son Braden for life, then to my granddaughter Sha-Tehl if she graduates from college." What interests are created?

2. After her first husband died, Wanda married Harry and they live together on her ranch, Blackacre. If Harry outlives her, she wants him to be able to live on Blackacre the rest of his life, but she does NOT want the property to go to his children. In fact, eventually she wants Blackacre to go to her favorite charity, the Alien Space Society, if it can't go to her descendants. She executes a will devising Blackacre "to Harry for life, then to my daughter Zoey and my son Xavier for life, then to the Alien Space Society if neither Zoey or Xavier have children." What interests are created? How would you have drafted this provision to better fulfill Wanda's wishes?

3. Defeasible Fees

Assume your client Lisa Bogart owns a large tract of land adjacent to her house, called Greenacre, which she would like to donate to the city to use as a nature trail. She has never made use of Greenacre, so the donation will save her maintenance, property tax, and insurance costs; plus, she can take a charitable contribution deduction on her income taxes. Moreover, she really wants to provide a quiet place for people to go for a walk through nature. She envisions the "Bogart Nature Trail" as her legacy, which will be enjoyed by generations to come.

However, she fears that, a few years from now, the city may decide that the investment in development and maintenance of the park isn't worth it and that the city may want to sell Greenacre to a developer or an industry. She could enter into some kind of contract with the city in which it promises to use Greenacre as a park, but if the city breaches the agreement, she might be entitled only to damages, which would be hard to prove. Moreover, after she dies, who would (or could) enforce the contract?

How can she better protect her interests? Property law developed a special kind of estate for this situation: the *defeasible* fee simple. Bogart can convey Greenacre to the city "only so long as it is used for park or nature trail purposes." The deed can provide that, if and when the city fails to use Greenacre for these purposes, title to the property will revert to Bogart (or her heirs or assigns).

> ➤ This estate is called a *fee simple* because it could potentially last forever; however, it is *defeasible*, which means that it could be completely taken away upon the happening of a particular condition.

Defeasible fees are commonly found in conveyances involving:

> ➤ railroads (grants limited to railroad purposes);
> ➤ school districts (grants limited to school purposes); and
> ➤ charitable donations, such as our park example.

Defeasible fees are categorized as one of two types: *fee simple determinable* and *fee simple subject to a condition subsequent*. In many cases, it does not matter which type it is and the courts do not bother classifying it precisely. But in some cases, which we will discuss, it does matter, so you should learn to distinguish between the two types.

Fee simple determinable (FSD):[7]

> ▪ A limitation of a *durational character* is built into the *granting language*, such as "so long as" or "until."
>> ☐ Alice grants Blackacre "to the Rock Island Railroad so long as it is used for railroad purposes."
> ▪ If a violation occurs, the property *automatically reverts* to the grantor.
>> ☐ "If Blackacre is not used for railroad purposes, it shall revert to Alice, her successors or assigns."
> ▪ The future interest retained by the grantor is called a *possibility of reverter.*

Fee simple subject to a condition subsequent (FSS):

> ▪ A limitation with *conditional language* ("on the condition that" or "provided, however") follows language granting a fee simple absolute.
>> ☐ Alice grants Blackacre "to the Rock Island Railroad, its successors and assigns forever." In another clause of the deed, she attaches this condition: "Provided, however, that the grantee must use the property only for railroad purposes."

---

[7] In this context, "determinable" means that the interest may "determine"—that is, come to an end.

■ If a violation occurs, the grantor has the *option* of retaking the property.
  ☐ "Should the grantee cease using the property for railroad purposes, grantor may re-enter and retake possession."
■ The future interest retained by the grantor is called a *right of entry* or *power of termination*.

The FSD is a limited grant—Alice is not giving away the entire timeline of Blackacre, but only that part of it that lasts as long as the railroad uses it as a railroad. In contrast, with the FSS, Alice gives the entire timeline to the railroad, but can decide to take it back again if the condition is violated.

Unfortunately, it is not always clear whether the grantor intended to create a FSD or FSS. For example, in some cases these defining characteristics may cut in opposite directions—the grantor might use conditional language, but then include an automatic reversion. In cases of ambiguity, courts typically favor the FSS, because they prefer to avoid automatic forfeiture. Swaby v. N. Hills Reg'l R.R. Auth., 769 N.W.2d 798, 811 (S.D. 2009) (construing deeds to be FSS despite automatic reversion language); Singer v. State, 391 S.W.3d 627, 633 (Tex. App. 2012) (same).

■ PROBLEM: FSS VERSUS FSD

Determinable Life Estate

You can also create a life estate that will end upon the happening of some event. For example, if Alice wants to allow her second husband, Sam, to live on Blackacre until he dies, she could stipulate that this interest will terminate before then if Sam remarries. This is called a *life estate determinable*.

In 1885, Olive conveyed part of Blackacre "to Railroad, its successors and assigns, for use as a railroad; provided however, that if it is not used for railroad purposes, title shall revert to Olive and she may retake possession." In 1995, Railroad discontinued service on the line on Blackacre. In 2000, it decided to remove the rails. In 2013, however, Railroad decided to re-activate the line and spent considerable money preparing it for service. Alice, who is Olive's great-grandchild and sole heir, brings suit to quiet title in 2014, claiming that the property reverted to her, either in 1995 or 2000. Should she win? Does it make any difference whether the Railroad's interest is a FSS or FSD?

In addition to questions of what type of defeasible fee was created and whether there was a breach, defeasible fee cases often raise these issues:

1) *Did the grantor intend to create a fee interest or merely an easement?*
   ■ As you will see in Chapter 10, an easement allows the use of another's property for a particular purpose. If the language indicates the grantor intended only to allow use for a limited purpose (such as a right-of-way), rather than conveying the possessory fee interest, an easement may result.
2) *Did the grantor intend to create a defeasible fee or merely a covenant?*

■ As you will see in Chapter 11, a covenant is a promise respecting the use of the land. If the grantee merely promises to use the land in a particular way, without reversionary language, it may be construed to be a covenant.

☐ Bogart conveys Blackacre "to the City, for the purpose of creating a nature preserve. City hereby promises to use the land solely for this purpose." This language would probably be construed as a covenant, rather than a defeasible fee.

■ Covenants are enforced by damages or injunctions, but a breach does not typically result in a forfeiture of the estate.

3) *If a defeasible fee was created and there was a breach, did delay in enforcement constitute a* waiver *of the breach or allow the grantee to establish fee simple absolute title by* adverse possession?

■ With a FSD, a breach results in the automatic reversion of title to the grantor. If the grantee continues to use the property for the improper purpose, the time period for adverse possession has begun.

■ In contrast, with a FSS, the breach starts the grantor's right to retake the property. A court may deem that right *waived,* or invoke the equitable defense of *laches* if the grantor fails to take action within a reasonable time and the grantee acts in reliance on that failure to its detriment.

■ DEFEASIBLE FEE PROBLEMS: WAS THERE A BREACH?

1. In 1954, Thelma Ator conveyed seven acres of land to the School District "for so long as said real property shall be used as a part of a regularly organized and fully scheduled program of football practice and playing." The School District constructed a stadium ("Ator Field") on the land and for many years thereafter held high school football games there. In 2005, the District built a new high school stadium and ceased playing high school games at Ator Field. It did, however, allow a youth sports organization to use the field for football practices and games for younger children. Thelma's sole heir, Reuel, sues to quiet title to the property. What should be the result? *See* Ator v. Unknown Heirs, 146 P.3d 821 (Okla. Civ. App. 2006). *See also* Atlanta Development Authority v. Clark Atlanta Univ., Inc., 784 S.E.2d 353 (Ga. 2016)(breach of FSD to university for educational purposes only).

2. In 1908, George and Sarah Haley donated a parcel of land to the County to be used only "for school purposes." The county built an elementary school on the property, which operated until 2001, when it closed due to low enrollment. Since then, the county has used the building to store school food service supplies and has announced that it might use the building for instruction should enrollment increase. Has the property reverted to the heirs of the Haleys? Griffis v. Davidson Cnty. Metro. Gov't, 164 S.W.3d 267 (Tenn. 2005).

The Executory Interest

The future interest following a defeasible fee may also be created in a *transferee* (i.e., someone other than the grantor/testator). Suppose Alice wants her second husband Sam to have Blackacre when she dies, but only as long as he remains unmarried. If Sam remarries, Alice wants the property to go to her son, Bart.

> ➢ Alice devises Blackacre "to Sam, but if he remarries, then to Bart."

Sam has a fee simple subject to a condition subsequent. In our previous examples of this estate, the grantor retained a right of entry; in this case, there is a gift over to Bart. We call Bart's interest an *executory interest.* An executory interest follows a FSD or FSS, when the future interest is created in a transferee.

More generally, an executory interest is created whenever an estate may be divested before its *natural termination* in favor of a person other than the grantor/testator. So, if Alice created a life estate determinable in Sam, with a gift over to Bart, Bart would have an executory interest.

Some courts label a FSS or FSD that is followed by an executory interest a *fee simple subject to an executory limitation* (FSE). When the future interest is in a transferee, violation of the condition results in an *automatic* termination and transfer to the transferee. There is no optional right of entry in a transferee.

> ➢ O conveys Blackacre "to the Church, but if it is not used for church purposes, then to the Salvation Army."

> ■ The Salvation Army has an executory interest. The Church has a fee simple subject to an executory limitation (FSE). The Church's interest will automatically be divested in favor of the Salvation Army if Blackacre is not used for church purposes.

This example illustrates a *shifting* executory interest, in which the possessory interest shifts from one transferee (the Church) to another (the Salvation Army) upon the occurrence of some event (no longer used for church purposes). The previous example, giving the interest to Sam with the future interest in Bart, was also a shifting executory interest.

An executory interest may also be of the *springing* type, which springs out of the grantor's own estate.

Executory

The term *executory* in law refers to something that is dependent upon the fulfillment of a contingency. You will see the word again in the chapter on real estate transactions.

> ➢ O places $100,000 in trust, to be distributed "to my son Sam, if he graduates from college." The grantor retains the present interest in the trust and Sam will take only upon the occurrence of the stated condition (graduating from college).

> ■ O has a FSS (or FSE); Sam has an executory interest.

■ PROBLEM: EXECUTORY INTEREST

Muldrow's son Adam was convicted of a drug offense in 1983. He absconded and has not been heard from since. Muldrow's will divided his estate into equal shares for his three children. However, Adam's share was subject to the condition that he appear and claim it within ten years. If at the end of ten years he had not appeared, his share was to be distributed to Muldrow's issue then living. Muldrow died in 1995. Adam's share turned out to be worth about $60,000. In 2000, although Adam had not yet appeared, his ex-wife sought to attach his share to satisfy a judgment against him for unpaid child support. Does Muldrow's will give Adam a fee simple subject to a condition subsequent or a springing executory interest? Why might it make a difference? *See* Scott v. Brunson, 569 S.E.2d 385 (S.C. Ct. App. 2002).

4. Estate for Years

An *estate for years* has a fixed duration of certain or ascertainable units of years or subdivisions of years (i.e., days, weeks, months).

> ➤ If O conveys "to A for 99 years," A has an *estate for years* and O has a *reversion.*

For example, assume that Harry wants his second wife, Wendy, to be able to live on Blackacre until her daughter, Dora, graduates from high school. After that, however, he wants Blackacre to go to his children from his first marriage, Carl and Cindy. His will could devise Blackacre to Wendy "until Dora graduates from high school," but do you see a problem with that language? Instead, Harry could devise Blackacre "to Wendy, until her daughter Dora reaches the age of 19, then to Carl and Cindy."

> ➤ Assume Harry dies when Dora has just turned 15. Wendy has an estate for years, because it is certain to terminate in four years.[8]
> ➤ Carl and Cindy have a vested remainder in fee simple. If Harry had not created a remainder, his estate would have a reversion.
> ➤ *See* Buchanan v. Buchanan, 698 S.E.2d 485, 489 (N.C. Ct. App. 2010) (similar will provision deemed estate for years).

Traditionally, the estate for years was classified as a *nonfreehold* interest. In contrast, the other estates (fee simple, life estate) are termed *freehold* estates.

---

[8] Do you see why this is not a fee simple determinable or fee simple subject to an executory limitation? A FSD or FSE *may* be divested upon the happening of some event, which is not certain to occur at any particular time. Thus, the duration of the estate is uncertain. Here, we know exactly when the term will end.

The idea, at common law, was that the owner of a freehold had *seisin,* which for our purposes connotes actual title to the land, whereas the nonfreehold owner merely had possession, but not title. In other words, the term of years is deemed a leasehold, rather than a freehold.

However, you should note that estates for years are sometimes created outside the lease context, as in our first example. In that case, the holder of an estate for years has all of the rights of any other present estate owner, which means that he or she can assign or sell the interest and use the property just like the owner of a life estate could, subject to a claim of waste by the owner of the reversion or the remaindermen.

Although estates for years are not as commonly used in estate planning and conveyancing as life estates are, there are some interesting and prominent examples of this type of interest:

> ➢ About 90 percent of Cumberland Island off the coast of Georgia was owned by Lucy Carnegie and her husband Thomas, brother of steel baron Andrew Carnegie. In the 1970s, the Carnegie heirs sold the island to the National Park Service to create the Cumberland Island National Seashore. However, the conveyance was subject to a 40-year estate for years granted to Andrew Carnegie III and his heirs, limited to building one single-family residence. Controversy arose in 2008, when the estate (through a series of subleases) came into the hands of Ben Jenkins, who started expanding the house and digging a septic tank, which the NPS claimed was injuring the natural resources on the island. *See* United States v. Jenkins, 714 F. Supp. 2d 1213 (S.D. Ga. 2008).

> ➢ In 1885, the territorial legislature of Hawaii enacted a type of homestead law that gave homesteaders a 999-year interest instead of a fee simple. Unlike a normal estate for years, however, the 999-year homestead interest could not be encumbered, alienated, or devised, although it could descend to designated statutory heirs. In 1950, the law changed to allow a homestead to be converted to fee simple upon payment of a fair price, which turned out to be the full value of the property. *See, e.g.,* Keliipuleole v. Wilson, 941 P.2d 300 (Haw. 1997) (market value of homestead interest was negligible given inability to convey).

> ➢ In the late 1800s, railroads often granted rights to rail lines to other railroads for a 999-year term, because their charters prohibited the conveyance of these rights in fee simple. This method also was used to avoid laws against railroad mergers. *See* State ex rel. Leese v. Atchison & N.R. Co., 38 N.W. 43 (Neb. 1888).

> ➢ Boxes in London's Royal Albert Hall were sold for 999-year terms to help finance the original construction costs in 1871. The estate for years in these boxes can be bought and sold like any other private property, although the owner then becomes liable for an annual maintenance and administrative fee. In 2008, one of the nicest boxes with ten seats sold for about $2 million. In 2018, a 12-seat box near the Queen's box was offered for sale at $3.9 million.

Boxes in Royal Albert Hall
© Daily Mail/Rex/Alamy

In some cases, courts have distinguished between a grant of an *estate* for years, which grants the full possessory fee for that period, and the mere *usufruct* interest granted by a leasehold. A *usufruct* connotes that the holder has the right to use and enjoy the property, but has no ownership interest in it. In contrast, the holder of an *estate* for years may be considered the actual owner of the estate for that period of time and does not hold "under" the true owner. *See* Diversified Golf, LLC v. Hart Cnty. Bd. of Tax Assessors, 598 S.E.2d 791 (Ga. Ct. App. 2004) (provisions of conveyance must be scrutinized to determine whether legal effect is to grant estate or merely a right of use). *See also* Stuttering Found., Inc. v. Glynn County, 801 S.E.2d 793 (Ga. 2017).

In many cases, a term of years tenancy is created by a contract called a lease, which therefore carries with it the obligations and rights provided by the contract, as well as an overlay of statutory provisions designed to promote fairness. In that situation, the fee ownership remains with the landlord and the tenant has only a limited right of possession. A continuing relationship between the lessor and lessee is contemplated, as well as periodic payment of rent. We will study this type of "term of years" as well as other types of leaseholds and the complexities of the landlord-tenant relationship in Chapter 6.

D LIMITATIONS ON DEAD HAND CONTROL

A property owner's bundle of sticks includes the right to devise or convey Blackacre as she pleases. If a person could not control who gets her property after she dies, then one of the biggest incentives for accumulating wealth, especially in one's later years, would be taken away. So, in general, our property laws favor the freedom of property owners to devise and convey property.

Yet, there are limits on that freedom. For example, the elective share provision is a significant governmental intrusion on the freedom of testation, because the property owner's interest is outweighed by our public policy in favor of spousal support. Similarly, courts also do not allow testators or grantors to attach unreasonable restraints on alienation to property. One of the primary policies of property law is economic efficiency. Furtherance of that goal typically requires property to be freely transferable, so it can be owned by those who will put it to the most valuable use.

You may have already realized, in reading this chapter, that allowing testators or grantors to tie up property in future interests also has an impact on the free alienability of property. Even if O devises Blackacre to A for life, with a remainder to B, anyone wanting to buy Blackacre will have to get both A and B to agree to sell. The problem is compounded by multiple persons holding interests, some of whom may not even be born yet.

> ➤ Imagine that T wanted to keep Blackacre in the family, so she devised Blackacre to her children for life, then to her grandchildren for life, then to her great-grandchildren. Now assume that Blackacre is in the perfect spot for the community's new hospital and the hospital wants to buy Blackacre. The owners of the current possessory interest, T's children, want to sell. How do the parties accomplish the sale?
>
> ➤ Or suppose the ancient mansion on Blackacre falls into disrepair and T's children want to take out a loan. The Bank is willing to loan the money, but only if it can obtain a mortgage on Blackacre, which must be signed by all those with an interest in the property. Is that possible?

Land is for the living, after all, and at some point it must be available for the needs of the current generation, rather than tied up according to the desires of past generations. We would not want a valuable tract of land in downtown Manhattan to be a vacant lot, merely because it was tied up by indefinite remote[9] interests created by a testator in the 1700s.

Long ago, courts and legislatures became involved in providing some limitations on the absolute right of a property owner to determine the future ownership of Blackacre. In this section, we will learn about the outright prohibition on

---

[9] In this section, we use the word "remote" to refer to far away in *time*, not in distance.

one type of problematic estate, the fee tail. Then, we will introduce you to the infamous Rule Against Perpetuities, the primary limitation on the ability to control property from the grave.

1. Abolition of Fee Tail

The *fee tail* estate is like your appendix—even though it does not serve much, if any, purpose today, you still need to recognize it when you see it, know where it came from, and know what to do about it if it presents a problem. It also provides a good example of the need to limit the ability of property owners to control property after their deaths.

The fee tail was invented by medieval English lawyers to ensure that the family's land, the primary source of wealth, remained in the family indefinitely.[10] By tying up the property in fee tail, the family's estate would be assured of passing intact to future generations and could not be dissipated by any weak link in the gene pool. It was also a way for a lord to grant land to a certain tenant and his descendants, while retaining control of who would succeed to the property if the tenant's line died out.

To create a fee tail, the grantor or testator would convey or devise Blackacre "to my son Arthur and the *heirs of his body*." The phrase "heirs of his body" indicated that, when Arthur died, Blackacre would pass to Arthur's issue, and when they died, to their issue, and so on until the line died out. At that point, the estate would revert to the grantor or to his heirs. The fee tail could also be followed by a remainder interest in a transferee.

The fee tail thus created a potentially endless series of life interests. The present holder, say Arthur, could sell only what he had—the possessory interest until his death. Anyone wishing to purchase Blackacre in fee simple would find it impossible because of the future interests held by unborn heirs.

The fee tail proved popular with the landed gentry in England. Not only did it keep large estates intact, it preserved feudal relationships as well. However, it

Pride and Prejudice

The plot of Jane Austen's most celebrated novel is driven largely by the fact that Mr. and Mrs. Bennet have five daughters. Their estate, Longbourn, is held in *fee tail male*, restricted to only male lineal descendants, which meant that none of the young ladies qualified as a potential heir. Thus, the family knows that when Mr. Bennet dies, the estate will go to the next male heir in line—their cousin Mr. Collins—putting the women at his mercy. You can see then why marrying the daughters into good families was of paramount importance, in a society in which women had few options for salaried employment!

---

[10] This description of the long and complex history of the fee tail has been greatly simplified for our limited purposes here. Fascinating details about the early history of the device and mechanisms for avoiding it can be found in Joseph Biancalana, The Fee Tail and the Common Recovery in Medieval England 1176-1502 (2001).

also meant that a large proportion of the land in England could not be bought or sold or even mortgaged. Therefore, various legal remedies emerged, such as the *common recovery*, which allowed the present possessory owner to "bar the entail" and convert the estate into a fee simple through an elaborate judicial action. The fee tail was finally abolished in England in 1925.

In the United States, the vast majority of states either never allowed fee tail, or abolished it many years ago. In most states, an attempt to create a fee tail results in the creation of a fee simple absolute. In others, the result is a life estate in the grantee and a remainder to the grantee's issue.

In the few states that still allow a fee tail to be created, the grantee in current possession has the power to convey a fee simple absolute, making it very easy to bar the entail. *See, e.g.*, Mass. Gen. Laws Ann. ch. 183, §45 (West 2017). In Arkansas, a fee tail may be conveyed by the current holder and the remaindermen then living. Ark. Code Ann. §18-12-302 (West 2017). Rhode Island limits the duration of a fee tail to one generation. *See* R.I. Gen. Laws Ann. §33-6-10 (West 2017).

As a result, the fee tail is only rarely seen, even in those states where it has not been abolished.

The Fee Tail

Thomas Jefferson led the effort to abolish the fee tail in Virginia, which he counted among his proudest accomplishments. The preamble to the state's 1776 statute abolishing the fee tail described the complaints against this form of estate:

> [T]he perpetuation of property in certain families, by means of gifts made to them in fee taille, is contrary to good policy, tends to deceive fair traders, who give a credit on the visible possession of estates, discourages the holder thereof from taking care and improving the same, and sometimes does injury to the morals of youth, by rendering them independent of and disobedient to their parents. . . .

For Jefferson, the fee tail was a remnant of aristocratic English society that was antithetical to the goals of a democratic republic. Do you understand how the fee tail could (at least arguably) lead to the social ills described? *See* John F. Hart, *"A Less Proportion of Idle Proprietors": Madison, Property Rights, and the Abolition of Fee Tail*, 58 Wash. & Lee L. Rev. 167 (2001).

2. Rule Against Perpetuities

The Rule Against Perpetuities ["the Rule"] is notorious for being one of the most difficult concepts for first-year law students to grasp. Our objective here is to give you a basic understanding of the Rule, saving more in-depth study for upper-level courses in wills and trusts. We will also briefly discuss some of the modern reforms that have reduced the importance of the classic common law formulation.

The Rule's object is to *prevent the remote vesting* of interests. As we saw in our example beginning this section, the problem with creating a string of contingent future interests is that it interferes with alienability. Someone wanting to buy Blackacre will be unable to do so if he can't even identify who owns the future interests.

Therefore, the law developed a limitation on the ability of property owners to create contingent future interests. Not all contingencies were prohibited, however. It seemed reasonable to allow contingencies to exist for some period of time.

> ➤ For example, assume Tony wants to devise Blackacre "to my daughter, Danielle, for life, then to Danielle's children."

He doesn't know yet who all the children might be (some or all of whom may not yet be born), so the future interest is necessarily contingent. That seems reasonable and will not tie up the property too long. At the end of Danielle's life, we will know who the owners of Blackacre will be. But we want those contingencies cleared up, at the latest, within the present generation.

Then, too, Tony might not want Danielle's children to take the estate until they reach the age of majority. So, Tony would like to make the remainder "to Danielle's children who reach the age of 21." That seems reasonable as well.

Therefore, the classic Rule Against Perpetuities is a compromise: it allows the creation of contingent future interests, but only if the interests will *vest or fail* (i.e., if Danielle has no children who meet the condition) *within the present generation plus 21 years.*

> **Rule Against Perpetuities**
>
> No interest is good unless it must vest or fail within lives in being at the creation of the interest plus 21 years.

Apply the Rule to Tony's devise:

> ➤ Tony devises Blackacre "to my daughter, Danielle, for life, then to Danielle's children who reach 21."

The Rule applies to a devise at the time the will takes effect (i.e., at Tony's death) because that is when the interests are "created." At that point, Danielle's interest will be a life estate, vested in possession, so it is fine. The remainder to Danielle's children, however, is contingent—all the potential takers will not be known until Danielle's death. Then, within 21 years, we will know if the children met the condition precedent (living to age 21). Because the remainder will vest in the children (or fail, if there are no children or none reach 21) within Danielle's life (a "life in being at the creation of the interest") plus 21 years, the devise is *valid under the Rule.*

Suppose, however, that Tony wanted to devise the remainder to Danielle's *grandchildren* instead. Assume Danielle has two children, Alpha and Beta, who Tony just doesn't like very much. Danielle may have more children, of course, but Tony just wants to skip that generation altogether. So he devises Blackacre:

> ➢ "To Danielle for life, then to Danielle's grandchildren."

Now we have a remainder whose potential takers will not be known until all of Danielle's children die. Therefore, the remainder may remain contingent until then. Can we say that the interests will necessarily vest or fail within the lifetimes of those living at the creation of the interest: Danielle, Alpha, and Beta? Consider this possibility:

> ➢ 2020: Tony dies, survived by Danielle, Alpha, and Beta. [This is now the "creation of the interest" because it is when Tony's devise takes effect].
> ➢ 2021: Danielle has another child, Gamma.
> ➢ 2022: Danielle, Alpha, and Beta die in a car accident; Gamma survives.
> ➢ 2050: Gamma has a child, Zeta. As a grandchild named in the devise, the remainder would vest in Zeta at that time.

The interest here vested too remotely. It did not vest within the lives of those living at the creation of the interest—Danielle, Alpha, and Beta. It did not vest within 21 years after their deaths.

It does not matter whether this scenario *actually happens* or not. The Rule asks, at the time the interest is created (at Tony's death, in this case), whether there is *any possibility* that the interest might vest too remotely. Thus, because the contingent remainder interest created by Tony will not *necessarily* vest or fail within the lives in being at the creation of the interest, plus 21 years, it *violates the Rule.*

When an interest violates the Rule, it is simply struck out and the rest of the conveyance or devise remains as written. So, in our example, Danielle would still receive her life estate, but the remainder would be struck out, leaving Tony's estate with a reversion.

Applying the Rule: A Four-Step Approach

Applying the Rule can be a bit intimidating unless you break it down into a step-by-step process. If you learn this approach, it will eliminate a lot of headaches.

1. Identify the future interests created by the conveyance or devise.

> ➢ The Rule does *not* apply to present estates vested in possession.

> *Tony devises Blackacre "to Danielle for life, then to Danielle's children."*
>
> Danielle's life estate is not subject to the Rule, but the remainder to Danielle's children is.

Concentrating only on the future interests will immediately avoid a lot of mistakes. Consider a conveyance "to Bogart University for 999 years." Your first instinct might be that such a long term must violate the Rule, because it will last much longer than any life in being, even with the 21 years tacked on. Nevertheless, the interest is perfectly valid, because it is a *present estate* (an estate for years), not a *future interest*. The estate for years might be followed by a remainder, however, which we *will* have to test under the Rule.

2. Look for contingent remainders and executory interests.

  ➤ The Rule applies only to *contingent remainders* and *executory interests*.
  ➤ It does *not* apply to interests *retained by the grantor* (reversion, possibility of reverter, or right of entry).
  ➤ It does *not* apply to *vested remainders*.

> *Tony devises Blackacre "to Danielle for life, then to Danielle's children."*
>
> The remainder in Danielle's children is *contingent*, so it must be tested against the Rule. Remember that a remainder is contingent if the taker is not ascertained or in existence, or if it is subject to a condition precedent.

Class gifts. For class gifts such as this, the interest is not considered vested for purposes of the Rule until *all members of the class* are known and have met any conditions precedent.

Charitable gifts. The Restatement indicates that the Rule should *not* apply where *both the present and future interests are to charities*, in keeping with the general policy of encouraging charitable gifts. Restatement (Second) of Property: Donative Transfers §1.6 (1983). Statutes in some states contain broad exceptions to the Rule for charitable gifts. Mich. Comp. Laws §554.351 (West 2017).

The fact that the Rule does not apply to interests retained by the grantor, or to vested remainders, will also save you a lot of headaches. Again, consider a conveyance by Tony "to Bogart University for 999 years."

  ➤ If Tony retains the future interest himself—a reversion in this case—it is perfectly valid under the Rule. It is vested in Tony from inception, even though Tony (or his heirs or assignees) will not actually take possession of Blackacre for almost a millennium.

- If Tony creates a "gift over"—a remainder—it will also be valid, if it is vested. So, consider a devise "to Bogart University for 999 years, then to Danielle." The remainder interest is valid, because it is vested.
- This may seem strange to you, but consider that vested interests have a minimal impact on alienability. If the interest is vested, you know who to deal with if you want to buy Blackacre. In the first example, you need the agreement of Bogart University and Tony; in the second example, you need the agreement of Bogart University and Danielle.

3. Determine the latest point at which the future interest may vest or fail.

- If it is a contingent remainder, what makes it contingent? What will have to happen to clear up the contingency?
- If it is an executory interest, what event will cause it to come into possession?

> *Tony devises Blackacre "to Danielle for life, then to Danielle's children."*
>
> This remainder is contingent because the takers are not ascertained. We will know who all of the takers are only at the end of Danielle's life. Until then, we have to assume that more children could be born.

In our Bogart University example, assume that Tony conveyed "to Bogart University for 999 years, then to my issue then living." The remainder is now contingent, and the contingency will not be resolved until the end of the 999-year period, so the interest is invalid under the Rule.

Assume Tony conveys Blackacre "to Bogart University so long as it is used for a football stadium, then to Danielle." In this case, Danielle has an executory interest, so we have to ask when it will vest in possession. Danielle (or her heirs or assigns) will get Blackacre whenever Bogart U stops using the property for a football stadium. We cannot say that Danielle will get the property within her life, or anyone else's life, plus 21 years. Therefore, the interest is void under the Rule.

4. Determine whether the contingency will necessarily be resolved within the lifetime of a person alive at the creation of the interest, plus 21 years.

- "Creation of the interest" means at the time of conveyance or at the testator's death, for a devise.
- Forget about the 21 years unless the language of the interest contains some year limitation (otherwise, it is irrelevant).
- Look at the lives that affect vesting; anyone else's life won't help you.

Tony devises Blackacre "to Danielle for life, then to Danielle's children."

We said that the contingency will be resolved at the end of Danielle's life. Because Danielle is a person in being at the creation of the interest, her life is the *validating life* for this interest. The interest is good.

Try one more example using this four-step approach:

> Oliver conveys "to my wife Laura for life, then to my grandchildren." Note that because this is a conveyance, Oliver is alive "at the creation of the interest."

1. **Identify the future interests created.** Life estate in Laura, contingent remainder in the grandchildren. The life estate to Laura is a present estate, which is not subject to the Rule, so we will focus only on the remainder.
2. **Look for contingent remainders and executory interests.** The remainder to the grandchildren (a class gift) is contingent, because we don't yet know who all the takers might be.
3. **Determine the latest point at which the future interest may vest or fail.** We will know who all of Oliver's children are only when Oliver dies. Until then, we assume he could have more children. We will know for sure who all of the *grandchildren* of Oliver are only when all of his *children* die. Thus, this interest will vest, at the latest, when the last surviving child of Oliver dies.
4. **Will the contingency necessarily be resolved within the lifetime of a person alive at the creation of the interest plus 21 years?** The potential *validating lives* here are Oliver's children. However, his children might not all be lives in being at the creation of the interest (when the conveyance is made), because he might have more children later. Therefore, we cannot use the children to validate this interest. We cannot say that we will know the identities of all the members of this class within lives in being plus 21 years when the interest was created. The remainder is struck as invalid and Oliver ends up with a reversion.

Note: What would be the result in the previous example if, instead of an *inter vivos* conveyance, Oliver had created this same gift to his grandchildren as *a devise in his will*? The analysis is the same for the first three steps, but when you get to step 4, the "creation of the interest" is upon the death of the testator. Because Oliver is dead, he will not be having any more children. Therefore, we can use his children as the validating lives: when the last of his children dies, we will know who all of the grandchildren are and the class will necessarily be complete. The remainder would therefore be *valid*.

Practice Tips

Many violations of the Rule, such as those described above, could be avoided by simply rewording the language of the devise or conveyance.

- ➢ **Names help if you know them.** The law assumes that Oliver can have more children, even though he might be 80 years old and have no intention to do so (this is known as the *fertile octogenarian* rule). Assume Oliver has two children, Dick and Jane, and does not plan to have more. Instead of conveying a remainder "to his grandchildren," he can just make the remainder "to the children of my son Dick and my daughter Jane." Now the gift is good because we can use Dick and Jane as the validating lives.

- ➢ **"Then living" may help, too.** Consider the conveyance "to my daughter Danielle for life, then to my great-great-grandchildren then living." You might consider, since we just had an invalid remainder to grandchildren, that a remainder in great-great-grandchildren must certainly be void. But when will we know who all the takers are (if any)? Upon Danielle's death, the remainder will vest in the great-great-grandchildren then living or fail if there are none. We don't have to wait to find out who they all are, because the remainder is limited to those then in existence. The remainder is valid.

- ➢ **If you put a year in, make it 21.** Assume O wants to convey a life estate to Danielle, with a remainder to her children. A remainder "to those of Danielle's children who reach 21" is valid; a remainder "to those of Danielle's children who reach 25" is not.

Of course, the client's planning goals are of paramount importance, so the client must be made aware of how a change in language might result in a different distribution.

■ PROBLEMS: RULE AGAINST PERPETUTITIES

1. O conveys Blackacre "to the School District so long as it is used as a school, then to my daughter Danielle." O then dies, leaving all of his estate to his daughter Danielle.

2. O conveys Blackacre "to the School District, its successors and assigns; provided, however, that if Blackacre is not used as a school, it shall revert to my daughter Danielle."

3. T devises Blackacre "to A for life, then to B if and when B becomes a priest."

4. T devises Blackacre "to my daughter Alice for life, then to my grandson Bart for life, then to my great-grandson Carl for life, then to my best friend Debra for life, then to my issue then living."

5. O conveys Blackacre "to Alice for 100 years, then to Bart, but if Bart remarries, then to Cindy."

a. *Modern Reforms of the Rule Against Perpetuities*

As you can imagine, the application of the Rule can be harsh in some instances, significantly impacting the plans of the testator or grantor for no apparent social policy reason. In response, courts and legislatures have adopted reforms that soften the Rule's impact. Note, however, that the analysis always *starts* with the common law rule—it is only when the Rule is violated that courts apply these reforms:

1. "Wait and see." Rather than dwell on "what might happen," the court waits to see what actually *does* happen to determine the validity of the future interest. *See, e.g.*, Iowa Code Ann. §558.68 (West 2018). For example, assume O places property in an *inter vivos* trust, paying the interest to A for life, with the remainder "to my grandchildren who reach the age of 21." The future interest is invalid, because O could have more children after the conveyance to the trust, so we can't use the children as validating lives. But if O does not have any more children, the gift is valid, because the remainder will vest or fail at the end of the lives of the children now living plus 21 years. The court may be willing to wait and see whether O has any more children after the conveyance. This is especially useful to remedy the "fertile octogenarian" problem, which requires the court to assume that a person might have a child, no matter how old they are.

> ➤ Absent a statutory provision authorizing this reform, some courts have been reluctant to modify the Rule as a matter of common law. *See, e.g.*, The Arundel Corp. v. Marie, 860 A.2d 886, 895-96 (Md. 2004). Other courts have rejected the wait and see approach due to the uncertainty involved in determining how long to wait (whose lives should be used).

2. Cy pres or reformation. Some courts are empowered by statute to revise the terms of a conveyance or devise to fulfill its intent while coming within the Rule. For example, if a conveyance "to my grandchildren who reach 25" would be void, the court can reform it to provide for vesting at age 21.

> ➤ For example, assume testator's will sets up a trust fund to provide scholarships to those of the testator's issue who go to college. Because the issue who could qualify for this interest might not be born yet, the devise is void under the Rule. However, the court could revise the devise to limit the

beneficiaries to those who qualify by 21 years after the death of the last heir of the testator living at his death. *See* Estate of Keenan, 519 N.W.2d 373, 375 (Iowa 1994).

3. Uniform Statutory Rule Against Perpetuities (USRAP). In 1986, the Uniform Law Commission proposed a new solution to this issue, the Uniform Statutory Rule Against Perpetuities. The USRAP basically adopts the wait and see approach, but avoids the problem of deciding how long to wait by providing for a standard 90-year permissible vesting period. If an interest violates the common law rule, it may still be valid if it actually vests or fails within 90 years of its creation. The USRAP also empowers a court to reform an interest to require vesting within the 90-year period. Some version of this approach has been adopted in at least half of the states.

In addition to these reforms, some states have repealed the Rule completely or significantly lengthened the permissible vesting period, in particular with respect to assets held in trust. *See, e.g.*, Fla. Stat. Ann. §689.225(2)(f) (West 2018) (360-year period); Utah Code Ann. §75-2-1203 (West 2018) (1,000-year period). We will explore this development briefly in the last section of this chapter. We believe, however, that it remains important to understand the basic common law rule, if nothing else, so that you realize the benefits of creating a trust. In addition, you should know that some modern reforms are not retroactive, so that the common law rule still applies to older devises and conveyances.

Preparing to Practice: Savings Clause

Many lawyers add the following clause, or something similar, to their wills and trusts. This one was originally drafted by Harvard Law Professor W. Barton Leach, one of the greatest authorities on the Rule:

> Any interest in real or personal property which would violate the rule against perpetuities shall be reformed, within the limits of that rule, to approximate most closely the intention of the creator of the interest. In determining whether an interest would violate said rule and in reforming an interest the period of perpetuities shall be measured by actual rather than possible events.

W. Barton Leach, *Perpetuities: The Nutshell Revisited*, 78 Harv. L. Rev. 973, 989 (1965). Do you understand why you might want to include this? Does it allow you to no longer worry about violating the Rule?

b. The Rule and Options to Purchase

In the case of a conveyance to a corporation, the "lives in being" measurement is not applicable and the perpetuities period is a flat 21 years. This issue arises most frequently with respect to contracts that contain contingencies, which may or may not be fulfilled within 21 years. In particular, the real estate "option" agreement, which gives a party the right to purchase the property for a specified price, may raise perpetuities issues, as the following case illustrates. Do you think the result is fair? Are there more important public policies that outweigh any fairness concerns?

CASE SUMMARY: Symphony Space, Inc. v. Pergola Properties, Inc., 669 N.E.2d 799 (N.Y. 1996)

In this case, the New York Court of Appeals held that the Rule Against Perpetuities applied to options to purchase commercial property. The case involved a two-story building on the Upper West Side. Broadwest owned the building, which housed a theater and some commercial space. Broadwest had been unable to find a permanent tenant for the theater and had been operating the property at a loss.

Symphony Space is a multi-disciplinary performing arts center located
on the Upper West Side of Manhattan
Symphony Space, Inc.

In 1978, Broadwest entered into a complex arrangement with a nonprofit entity, Symphony Space, Inc. Under the agreement, Broadwest would sell the entire building to Symphony Space for $10,010, but then would lease back the commercial space for $1 per year. The arrangement would allow Symphony

Space, as a nonprofit, to seek property tax abatement for the building, which would save about $30,000 per year.

Crucially, the contract also gave Broadwest the option to repurchase the property "at any time after July 1, 1979, so long as the Notice of Election specifies the Closing is to occur during any of the calendar years 1987, 1993, 1998, and 2003." The option would also accrue at other times, such as if Symphony Space defaulted on its mortgage.

In the mid-1980s, the successors to Broadwest wanted to redevelop the entire block. If they could include the Symphony Space property in the plan, the deal's value increased by over $20 million. The option, in contrast, gave Broadwest's successors the right to purchase the building for just $15,000. They gave notice of their intention to close the purchase in 1987. Symphony Space claimed, however, that the option was void under the Rule Against Perpetuities.

The court recognized that, under the common law, options to purchase are subject to the Rule, because they give the holder a contingent future interest in the property. Think of the transaction this way:

> ➢ Broadwest conveys "to Symphony Space, provided however, that Broadwest may re-enter and retake possession by paying $X at the time of its choosing."

The court held that this was "precisely the sort of control over future disposition of the property that . . . the common law rule against remote vesting—and thus [the New York statute]—seeks to prevent."

> [T]he option grants its holder absolute power to purchase the property at the holder's whim and at a token price set far below market value. This Sword of Damocles necessarily discourages the property owner from investing in improvements to the property. Furthermore, the option's existence significantly impedes the owner's ability to sell the property to a third party, as a practical matter rendering it inalienable.

Id. at 805.

But did the option violate the Rule? The court held that because the parties to the transaction were corporations and there were no measuring lives stated in the agreement, the permissible vesting period was 21 years. Because the option could be exercised as late as 2003, 24 years after its creation in 1978, it was void. *Id.* at 806-07.

Under the "wait and see" modern reform, a court can validate an interest if it actually vests within the perpetuities period. Here, the option holders argued that the wait and see principle should save the option, since they actually exercised it by 1987, only nine years after it was created. New York, however, has never used a wait and see approach, and the court refused to adopt the reform here. The court will look only at "what might have happened," the court stated, "rather than to what has actually happened." *Id.* at 808.

■ POINTS TO CONSIDER

1. **Statutory reform.** Some states have specifically exempted commercial option agreements from the Rule. Would you support such a statute?

2. **Drafting.** If you were drafting this option, how could you have drafted it differently in order to avoid the Rule violation? *See, e.g.,* OneWest Bank Group, LLC v. Prime Venturers, 223 Md. App. 777 (2015) (ten-year option valid under RAP). The result here was the loss of an option agreement worth millions of dollars. Did the attorney who drafted this contract commit malpractice?

3. **First refusal compared.** A "right of first refusal" gives the holder the primary right to purchase the property if and when the owner decides to offer it for sale. The *Symphony Space* court distinguished such first refusal rights from options: the court noted that, unlike an option, a right of first refusal "does not affect transferability." Whereas an option agreement forces the owner to sell at the behest of the option holder, the right of first refusal "merely requires the owner, when and if he decides to sell, to offer the property first to the party holding the preemptive right. . . . " *Id.* at 805 (quoting Metropolitan Transp. Auth. v. Burken Realty Corp., 492 N.E.2d 379 (N.Y. 1986)). Does this distinction convince you? In most cases, New York now follows the majority rule, which applies the RAP to rights of first refusal. Kozak v. Porada, 154 A.D.3d 1242 (N.Y. App. Div. 2017). *See* Note, Heather M. Marshall, *Why the Rule Against Perpetuities Should Not Apply to Rights of First Refusal*, 44 New Eng. L. Rev. 763, 773 (2010) (collecting cases). A sizable minority of jurisdictions, however, hold that the RAP does not apply to such rights. *See, e.g.,* Bortolotti v. Hayden, 449 Mass. 193, 866 N.E.2d 882 (2007).

4. **Stock options.** Should the Rule be applied to option agreements involving personal, rather than real, property? For example, assume that Company gave Executive a stock option, consisting of the right to purchase 1,000 shares of Company stock at $5 per share. The stock option did not contain a particular time limitation. Twenty-five years later, the children of Executive seek to exercise the option, because Company stock has now hit $100 per share. Should the option be deemed invalid under the Rule? Are the same policy reasons applicable? *See* Smith v. Stuckey, 503 S.E.2d 284 (Ga. Ct. App. 1998) (rule applies to stock options).[11]

E   AN INTRODUCTION TO TRUSTS

It probably has occurred to you that dividing property rights between present and future owners can create numerous practical difficulties. Suppose Larry

---

[11] Thanks to Prof. Keith Sealing and Prof. Maureen Markey for the reference to this case.

(age 80) holds a life estate in Blackacre, with a remainder in "his issue then living." Larry thinks the old mansion needs a new roof, which will cost $10,000. He doesn't have that kind of money himself and besides, given his age, the roof may primarily benefit the remaindermen. His issue now include his daughter Debbie and the two daughters (Darla and Dana) of his deceased son. Of course, their remainder is still contingent—they must survive Larry to take—and they disagree on how much, if anything, they should contribute to this project. The bank won't give Larry a home improvement loan, even if Debbie, Darla, and Dana sign the note and mortgage (which they won't), because there may be other issue born who end up taking a share of the remainder. As a result, the roof won't get fixed.

This is just one example of the many practical issues that can arise using estates and future interests. For that reason, knowledgeable estate planners often use a trust to create these arrangments. A trust can be created either while the owner of the property is living—an *inter vivos* trust—or upon the owner's death—a *testamentary* trust. The vast majority of future interests issues arise in the context of trusts.

How a Trust Works

Oliver conveys his property, including Blackacre, to a Trustee. Oliver is called the Grantor, or the Trustor, or the Settlor (one who "settles" property on another). The property contained in the trust is called the *corpus* or principal. Oliver directs the Trustee to manage the corpus (including Blackacre) for the benefit of Larry during Larry's life. At Larry's death, the Trustee is directed to distribute the property to the issue of Larry then living. The Trustee is given specific management authority over the corpus—for example, she may have the right to sell, lease, or mortgage the property.

> ➢ Whereas in our previous example, Larry had a *legal life estate*, he now has an *equitable life estate*. In other words, legal title to Blackacre is in the Trustee, but the equitable interest is in Larry.

Now, if Blackacre needs a new roof, the Trustee can get a loan and mortgage Blackacre, without the need to get the agreement of everyone involved. If Larry can no longer live on Blackacre and needs to go to a nursing home, the Trustee can lease the property, or sell the property and invest the proceeds. In either case, Larry will get the income. In other words, the trust provides the *necessary flexibility* for dealing with property, while still fulfilling the grantor's desire for successive ownership.

Trusts may also provide other advantages:

> ➢ **Avoidance of probate.** Placing a family business or farm operation, for example, in an *inter vivos* trust means that there will be a smooth transition when one of the owners dies.

> ➤ **Custodial trusts.** The trustee can manage property on behalf of a minor or incompetent beneficiary.
> ➤ **Tax savings.** For example, property may be given to charity, while the trustor retains a life interest. The trustor can take an income tax deduction now and the principal will not be included in the estate for estate tax purposes.

The *income* to which a life tenant is ordinarily entitled would include the net rental income from rental property, the interest on bonds or certificates of deposit, and the dividends from stock. The trust document will be the most important source to consider for most issues that arise. For example, the trust may allow the life tenant to consume the principal, instead of being confined to the income from the principal. Even if the life tenant is to be paid only the income, the trust may allow the trustee considerable leeway in determining what to allocate to income and principal. Almost every state has adopted the Uniform Principal and Income Act, which provides a set of guidelines for trustees to follow.

The *prudent investor rule* requires the trustee to manage the trust and invest its funds as a prudent investor would under the circumstances, which include the terms and purposes of the trust. Restatement (Third) of Trusts §90 (2018). The trustee is a *fiduciary* and has a duty to exercise reasonable care in management of the trust assets. Thus, the trustee should not only act to preserve the trust property, but should also make it productive. Unless the trust instrument specifies otherwise, the trustee has *duty of impartiality* toward all of the trust's beneficiaries.

Inter vivos trusts may be *revocable* or *irrevocable*. In some states, a trust is considered revocable unless the trust instrument expressly provides otherwise. *See, e.g.,* Cal. Prob. Code §15400 (West 2018). The tax consequences are different for revocable trusts, since the gift is not considered complete until the trustor dies, so in many cases the trustor may want to make the trust irrevocable.

Creating a trust is not difficult. The trustor need only transfer the property to the trustee with some indication of an intention to create a trust relationship.

> ➤ For example, O conveys Blackacre by deed "to T, as trustee for my son S for life, then to S's issue then living per stirpes." O has created a trust in favor of S and his issue.

The trustor may also be the trustee, which is perfectly permissible. In that case, however, a conveyance won't work (O could not convey Blackacre to himself). In that case, a *declaration* of trust by the trustor is required.

Although it does not take much to create a trust, it is preferable to spell out the trustor's intentions fully in a trust document (or in the will, if it is a testamentary trust). The trust can contain, for example, specific instructions about the management of the property and allocation of principal and income. In the absence of trust provisions, however, there are state statutes that spell out the general principles to be followed. The Simulation for this book contains a sample form of a trust instrument.

■ PROBLEM: PRINCIPAL AND INCOME

Gertie's will placed $200,000 in trust for the benefit of her sister, Sophie, for life, remainder to the Temple. The trust names her banker, Tamara, as the trustee. The trust allows the trustee to invade the principal to provide for Sophie's health and welfare. Tamara has invested most of the principal in growth stocks, which tend to increase in value but do not produce much dividend income (about $1,000 per year). Sophie is a retired schoolteacher whose income consists of Social Security and a small pension. In the last three years, the value of the stock account has grown to $250,000. May Tamara distribute more than $1,000 per year to Sophie?

The perpetual trust.   Some states have decided that the Rule Against Perpetuities should not apply to certain types of trusts. Recall that the main policy reason behind the Rule is the fact that remote contingent interests make the property inalienable. If property is placed in trust, and the trustee has the power to sell, lease, or mortgage the property, this concern is no longer valid. A growing number of states have abolished the Rule's applicability to trusts that allow the trustee to alienate the corpus property, in effect allowing *perpetual trusts. See, e.g.*, Mo. Ann. Stat. §456.025. Do these trust arrangements resolve all of the policy concerns behind the Rule?

Video Problem
Thinking Like a Lawyer: Estate Planning

🎥 In this video, which is available on the Simulation, your client, Wilma, comes to you for advice. Her first husband died several years ago, and she is contemplating marriage to Hank. She is the owner of Blackacre, and she wants to ensure that Hank can use the property while he is alive, but on his death she wants it to go to her daughter, Dana. She does not under any circumstances want the property to go outright to Hank, because it might end up with his son Stewart. Consider these alternatives:

1. Putting the property in a joint tenancy between Wilma, and Dana and Hank.
2. Conveying the property to Dana, but reserving a life estate in Wilma and Hank.
3. Using a trust and a prenuptial agreement.

Can you now point out some advantages of the third option?

SUMMARY

- The bundle of sticks may be divided between *present estates* and *future interests*. The owner of a future interest has *present ownership* of the right to possess Blackacre in the future.

- A *fee simple absolute* is the most complete form of ownership, consisting of the right to possess Blackacre forever. At common law, words of inheritance (to A *and his heirs*) were required, but today a conveyance of a fee simple is presumed unless otherwise indicated.

- A *life estate* grants the possessory interest for the duration of the grantee's life. It is followed by either a *remainder* in a transferee, or a *reversion* in the grantor. A life estate may be transferred, resulting in a life estate *pur autre vie*.

- Absolute *restraints on alienation* are void, but reasonable restraints may be upheld. Thus, many courts will allow a restraint on the alienation of a life interest.

- At common law, property divided between present and future owners could not be *partitioned*. A few states have abrogated this rule by statute. Owners of future interests can sue for *waste*, however.

- Remainders are *vested* when the takers are ascertained and in existence. They are *contingent* when either of those conditions is not met.

- *Defeasible fees* could potentially last forever, but may terminate earlier upon the happening of some event. They include the *fee simple determinable* and the *fee simple subject to a condition subsequent*.

- The FSD uses *durational* language and has an *automatic* termination; the grantor retains a *possibility of reverter*.

- The FSS uses *conditional* language and has an *optional* termination; the grantor retains a *right of entry*.

- A *fee simple subject to an executory limitation* has an automatic termination upon the happening of some event, and the future interest, called an *executory interest*, is in a transferee.

- An *estate for years* has a term of fixed duration measured in ascertainable units of years or subdivisions of years.

- The *fee tail*, created by a conveyance or devise "to A and the heirs of his body," historically created a potentially endless series of life interests in the grantee and his issue. The estate has now been *abolished* in most American jurisdictions and, even where it still exists, may be *disentailed* easily.

- The *Rule Against Perpetuities*, in its classic form, requires contingent future interests to vest or fail within some life in being at the creation of the interest plus 21 years.

- The Rule applies only to *contingent remainders* and *executory interests* that vest too remotely.

- Many jurisdictions have enacted *reforms of the Rule*, either legislatively or judicially, including wait and see, cy pres, and the Uniform Statutory Rule Against Perpetuities.
- In some jurisdictions, the Rule applies to option agreements.
- Using a trust, which gives the trustee management authority over the corpus, avoids many of the difficulties presented by future interests. In some jurisdictions, the Rule does not apply to certain trusts.

Landlord-Tenant

Landlord, landlord,
My roof has sprung a leak.
Don't you 'member I told you about it
Way last week?
Landlord, landlord,
These steps is broken down.
When you come up yourself
It's a wonder you don't fall down.
Ten Bucks you say I owe you?
Ten Bucks you say is due?
Well, that's Ten Bucks more'n I'll pay you
Till you fix this house up new.
What? You gonna get eviction orders?
You gonna cut off my heat?

> You gonna take my furniture and
> Throw it in the street?
> —*Langston Hughes, Ballad of the Landlord (1940)*

 # INTRODUCTION

Although the leasehold is ancient in origin, it remains one of the most common mechanisms for the possession of residential and commercial property. You have probably signed a lease, in college or in law school. And you may be involved in many more during the course of your life, in many different scenarios. The law that governs the lease is based in Property, but in recent decades courts have come to recognize that a purely property law view of the leasehold leads to unexpected and socially harmful results. Today, courts increasingly evaluate leases under the rubric of contract law. In this chapter, we will look at the formation, operation, and termination of leasehold relationships, and the duties that a tenant and landlord owe to one another.

We will see that there is a very real and sometimes dramatic conflict between the expectations of the modern world and the traditional property law structure on which lease law is based. This conflict will continue for some time, and probably throughout your professional careers.

The leasehold is a *relationship*. The tenant goes into possession of the landlord's real property, accepting obligations regarding the use of the property and the payment of rent. The landlord, in turn, may have obligations to the tenant regarding the condition of the premises. Depending on the term (duration) of the lease, and the relative satisfaction of the parties, the lease relationship might continue for years. In a sense, the landlord and tenant have to "live with one another" until the end of the term. A well-crafted lease therefore spells out the expectations and rights of the parties.

A lease may be commercial or residential in nature. Langston Hughes, in his poem *Ballad of the Landlord*, describes the relationship between a *residential* landlord and his tenant. The relationship he describes is not a fair or happy one. The 1940 poem accurately depicts a common tenant predicament during that era. The landlord in Hughes's poem is the owner of a tenement or slum, and the law provided the tenant in that relationship with few protections. The tenant, having little in the way of money or leverage, was placed in a particularly precarious position. Disparity between the wealth and resources of residential landlords and their tenants remains a part of the landscape. But, as you read through this chapter, you should ask whether, since the time Hughes penned *Ballad of the Landlord*, the law has changed to provide residential tenants with greater protection from the callous disregard of landlords and whether those legal changes have altered the dynamic between the parties.

Hughes's poem describes the residential tenant, and the poor tenant at that. The poem says nothing about the *commercial* tenant. The leasehold is the primary means by which businesses possess and use real property. For example, few law firms—even the largest, national firms—own the property in which they have offices. Instead, they may lease a part of a building for an initial term of five years, with the right to extend for multiple, successive periods. Leasing gives them desirable flexibility. Centers of business activity often move as cities develop. If business moves from one part of a city to another, law firms are apt to follow as their leases expire. It is easier for a law firm to move if it leases, rather than owns, a building. As business expands or contracts, the firm can increase or decrease the amount of space it leases. Commercial tenants usually, though not always, have a greater degree of leverage when dealing with the landlord and therefore more equal bargaining power. Unlike residential tenants, commercial tenants are often represented by attorneys. As we move through this chapter, we will from time to time distinguish the commercial from the residential leasing context, when it may affect the legal rule.

Leasing as Life Blood of Commercial Property Development

Shopping centers, office towers, and industrial parks come into being only because a real property developer anticipates receiving rents from tenants. Developers almost never have the money necessary to acquire and develop real property, and they must therefore borrow the money. Lenders loan money to commercial property owners to cover the costs of property acquisition and construction only because lenders believe that the rental streams of the completed projects will allow the owners to pay their monthly mortgage payments. The owners of commercial property routinely employ lawyers to negotiate and draft complex, sophisticated leases. Lease law is therefore an extremely important component of the real property lawyer's practice. *See* Daniel B. Bogart, *The Right Way to Teach Transactional Lawyers: Commercial Leasing and the Forgotten "Dirt Lawyer,"* 62 U. Pitt. L. Rev. 335 (2001).

A modern analysis of lease law requires you to work with three *sources of law*. You must be able to examine and understand the provisions in the *lease contract* into which the landlord and tenant enter. State statutes often regulate the landlord-tenant relationship. These statutes may override the language of the contract. You must therefore also work with *statutory law*. This is particularly true of the residential lease relationship. Both courts and legislators view the residential tenant as a party with little leverage to challenge the language of lease contracts, and as vulnerable to occasionally exploitative behavior by landlords.

Finally, we must keep an eye on the *common law*. You might have an impression that the common law changes and develops at a glacial pace (and in some instances this may be true.) But judge-made law governing landlords and tenants has in fact changed over time. For example, we see this when we examine the duties that landlords are said to owe residential tenants to provide minimally habitable property. Older common law suggested that the landlord owed no duties to tenant whatsoever to provide leased property of a certain quality. The tenant purchased an interest in property and was subject to the concept of *caveat emptor*—buyer beware, or more precisely in this context, *caveat lessee*. If the tenant leased a farmhouse that subsequently leaked, the older common law placed the burden squarely on the tenant to repair. We will see in this chapter that this older common law doctrine has come under significant attack.

Restatement versus Uniform Law

We will refer to both the Restatement (Second) of Property: Landlord and Tenant, and the Uniform Residential Landlord and Tenant Act. The Restatement (Second) of Property: Landlord and Tenant is a product of the American Law Institute and was adopted in 1977. The Restatement represents an attempt not only to summarize, but also to clarify and improve the application of the common law by lawyers and judges. The Restatement only "becomes law" to the extent that courts choose to apply it. The Restatement is therefore a resource that informs judges and lawyers. (The American Law Institute recently began a 10-year process of crafting a new, comprehensive Restatement of Property.) By contrast, the Uniform Residential Landlord and Tenant Act (URLTA), created by the National Conference of Commissioners on Uniform State Laws, more recently known as the Uniform Law Commission, has been adopted by state legislatures in 21 jurisdictions. Where adopted, URLTA supersedes contrary common law governing landlords and tenants, in the residential sphere. The goals of both the Restatement and URLTA are the same: to modernize the law, to provide a greater degree of certainty and efficiency to the operation of landlord-tenant law, and to more fairly protect tenants, while not undermining the legitimate objectives of landlords. The Uniform Law Commission adopted a Revised Uniform Landlord Tenant Act in 2015, but as of this writing, no state legislature has adopted this model act.

B   WHAT IS A LEASE: THE BASICS

1. Essential Nature of the Landlord-Tenant Relationship

The essence of a lease is this: the landlord grants a *right of exclusive possession* of specific real property to the tenant for a term (period of time), with a *reversion* in the landlord at the end of the term. In other words, the lease creates a present possessory estate in the tenant, and a future interest in the landlord. We will see that the duration of the term varies. There are three categories of leases; the distinguishing characteristic of each is the nature of the lease term. However, regardless of the type of lease at issue, the landlord always has a reversion entitling the landlord to possession at the end of the term. Exclusive possession means just that: the tenant acquires the right to exclude anyone it wishes from the leased property during the term. Many lease agreements refer to the landlord as "lessor" and the tenant as "lessee."

One court explains the basics of a lease in this way: a lease, at the least, must contain "a description of the specific premises to be occupied by [the tenant],"... "the amount of rent to be paid, and [provide] for the [tenant's] exclusive use and occupancy for a fixed period of time." Coinmach Corp. v. Harton Assocs., 758 N.Y.S.2d 388, 389 (N.Y. App. Div. 2003).

If you own a building with an apartment in the basement and rent it to your friend for one month, then you have not really parted with that much. But if you rent the apartment to your friend for a significant period of time, then you are relying on his promise not to damage the property and not to allow it to fall into disrepair. It is not surprising therefore that most jurisdictions subject leases of greater than one year (or in some jurisdictions, three years) to the Statute of Frauds. The Statute of Frauds will require the three "P"s—Property (the specific leased premises), Price (the amount of rent), and the Parties (identity of the landlord and tenant) to be in a signed writing.

The tenant's common law right of exclusive possession even permits the tenant to exclude the landlord. After all, if you execute a lease for an apartment with the landlord, do you expect the landlord to visit your apartment, unannounced, with a master key? What rights would you have if the landlord chose to raid your refrigerator while you were at work? For this reason, in many leases, both residential and commercial, the landlord will reserve the right to enter the premises of a tenant if necessary, perhaps to undertake repairs or in an emergency to prevent damage to the property.

In many instances, a person may have a more limited right to use real property of another, for a limited purpose. This right is typically called a *license*. A license is a personal right based in contract

> **North Carolina provides:**
>
> All contracts to sell or convey any lands, tenements or hereditaments, or any interest in or concerning them, and all leases and contracts for leasing land for the purpose of digging for gold or other minerals, or for mining generally, of whatever duration; and all other leases and contracts for leasing lands exceeding in duration three years from the making thereof, shall be void unless said contract, or some memorandum or note thereof, be put in writing and signed by the party to be charged therewith, or by some other person by him thereto lawfully authorized.
>
> N.C. Gen. Stat. §22-2 (2015).

and is revocable by the licensor. A licensor gives the licensee a narrow right to use real property for a specific reason. Is a lease always so easy to identify? Distinguishing a license from a lease can be difficult.

Once a court identifies a relationship as a lease, tenant and landlord will be subject to the burdens and benefits conferred by landlord-tenant law. For example, in most jurisdictions, if the relationship is a lease rather than a license, a landlord will be able to remove the tenant from the leased premises only if the landlord follows the statutory requirements for eviction.

Keep in mind the basic point of the lease—the transfer of exclusive possession—and consider the following two fact patterns:

CASE SUMMARY: Township of Sandyston v. Angerman, 341 A.2d 682 (N.J. Super. Ct. App. Div. 1975)

Mr. and Mrs. Angerman signed an agreement with the Department of the Interior permitting the couple to occupy property that was part of the Delaware Water Gap National Recreation Area. The local township wished to assess taxes against the Angermans, arguing that the Angermans' occupancy amounted to a lease. The Angermans asserted instead that their relationship with the Department of Interior was a license, and not taxable as a lease. According to the terms of the written agreement, the Angermans were "authorized . . . to use" a cabin and approximately two acres of land as their personal residence, from September 15, 1971, to September 1, 1976. The agreement provided that the Angermans' rights could be terminated at the discretion of the Director of the National Park Service. After signing the agreement, the Angermans moved into the cabin. The Angermans were not required to pay cash in exchange for the right to occupy the property. Instead, they were required to rehabilitate, restore, and maintain the cabin, and to "assist park personnel in the detection and immediate reporting of building, forest or grass fires which may occur on the land in the vicinity," and to "make frequent checks of the other National Park Service property in the vicinity and immediately report any incidents, violations or apparent damage to a representative of the National Park Service." The cabin was in very poor condition at the time the Angermans signed the agreement. According to Mrs. Angerman, the couple "fixed it up" and then lived in it. The agreement specified that any improvements that the Angermans made became the property of the government. The agreement also provided the government with "the right to enter the premises at any time for inspection." According to the court, "there is nothing in the record to indicate that either Mr. Angerman or Mrs. Angerman was employed by the National Park Service in any capacity. . . ." *Id.* at 684.

■ POINTS TO CONSIDER

1. **Lease versus license.** Do you think that the agreement permitting the Angermans to occupy the cabin was a lease or a license? How can you tell?

2. **Focus on the language.** What language in the agreement grants to the Angermans a right to occupy the cabin, and should this language be controlling? How should the other provisions of the agreement mentioned in the case summary suggest or affect the outcome? Does it matter that the Director of the National Park Service could terminate the agreement at his discretion?

CASE SUMMARY: Muniz v. Kravis, 757 A.2d 1207 (Conn. App. Ct. 2000)

The defendants, Henry Kravis and Caroline Roehm, were partners in a business at a building they owned called "Weatherstone." The plaintiff, Mercedes Muniz, was employed as a cook at Weatherstone, and her husband was employed as a butler. According to the court, the Munizes' "employment compensation included a salary and the use of a private apartment on the premises of Weatherstone." In July of 1993, while Mr. Muniz was in the apartment in Weatherstone recovering from surgery, and Mercedes Muniz and her daughter were on a plane en route to Spain, Mr. Muniz received a visit from an armed guard employed by the defendants. The armed guard informed Mr. Muniz that his employment (and the employment of his wife Mercedes) was terminated immediately and that the family had 24 hours to vacate the apartment. As a result, Mrs. Muniz sued Kravis and Roehm for violation of Connecticut's Unfair Trade Practices Act. Among other things, that Act "provides for the protection of an individual's rights to due process when an employment relationship gives rise to a tenancy." Therefore, Mrs. Muniz asserted that she was a tenant of Kravis and Roehm.

■ POINTS TO CONSIDER

1. **Normal indicia of a leasehold?** Do you think that Mrs. Muniz was a tenant? Did the arrangement create a leasehold relationship? Consider the normal indicia of leasehold. Does this relationship qualify? If it is not a lease, what is it?

2. **Downton Abbey: were those servants tenants?** The Angermans were not employees of the Department of the Interior. By contrast, the Munizes were employees of Mr. Kravis and Ms. Roehm. Does this matter? Keep in mind that the law is not always kind; the fact that we sympathize with a plaintiff does not automatically translate into an emotionally satisfying result.

3. **Lease versus license: a recurring problem.** Whether one party has a lease or something less is a recurring issue, and it is one for which you should be on the lookout. Imagine that a university grants the owner of a food truck the right to park on campus every day and directs the food truck vendor to a particular spot. This becomes a very successful venture for the vendor because the spot is "prime"; the food truck owner positions the truck in a convenient place for students to order lunch when rushing from class to class. The university begins to construct a new building and "directs the truck" to a newer, less

profitable location. The food truck owner is livid. Can the University take this action? What facts would help you decide whether this is a lease or a license?

4. **Is a lease a contract or a conveyance?** The court in *Angerman* determined that the Angermans possessed their cabin pursuant to a lease. The Angermans received the exclusive right to possession until the end of their term. In other words, they received a present possessory estate, and the government had a reversion in the property. This is the nature of a lease conveyance; in that respect, it is no different from the conveyance of a life estate or other estate in land. But it is also true that the Angermans were required under the lease to repair and maintain the property. The landlord, the Department of Interior, bargained for and received the right to terminate the lease at its discretion prior to the stated endpoint. The lease therefore has contractual elements: promises and rights that extend beyond the mere transfer of the right of exclusive possession. For many years, leases were evaluated almost *purely* as creatures of property law and not as creatures of contract law, but that time is now over.

Sir Henry Maine, a noted legal theorist of the 1800s, famously stated that law in "progressive societies" could be seen as moving *"from Status to Contract."* Sir Henry Maine, Ancient Law: Its Connection with the Early History of Society, and Its Relation to Modern Ideas 170 (London: John Murray, Albermarle Street, 1861) (italics in the original). Sir Henry's statement seems prescient as applied to property law in general, and to landlord-tenant law in particular.

The conflict between the contract view and the property-based conveyance view of landlord-tenant law is perhaps most evident in the context of landlord obligations. We will examine obligations of the landlord to the tenant later in this chapter. For now, consider how differently the parties to a lease may be treated if the lease is evaluated as a contract rather than a conveyance.

At common law a landlord was not obligated to repair or restore leased property if it was damaged or destroyed. The tenant would have to continue to make rent payments, even if the subject property—perhaps his farm—burned to the ground. After all, the landlord conveyed the exclusive right to possess to the tenant, and that was the extent of the landlord's obligation. If the landlord had no right to enter into or possess the property, why would he have an obligation to repair it? To the extent that the tenant wished to see his house, barn, or building repaired, he would have to do it himself, all the while paying rent. Placing the burden of repair on the tenant may have made historical and practical sense in years past. The agrarian tenant understood his property and how to effect repairs, and even may have viewed a landlord's attempt to repair as interference. Does this expectation define your relationship with your landlord if you are subject to a lease today? A more contractual approach would view the subject of the contract—the premises—to be very important. If we viewed the lease purely as a contract, destruction of the property might relieve the tenant of an obligation to pay rent.

Similarly, under a property law approach, the landlord had no obligation to mitigate damages if the tenant abandoned the leased premises and thereby breached the lease. Again, the landlord conveys to the tenant the exclusive right to possession; whether the tenant chooses to actually possess the property is his decision. Nothing about a tenant's abandonment changes the fundamental nature of the conveyance. But contract law today commonly requires one party to minimize the damages caused by the breach of the other party. In terms of a lease, this might mean that the landlord would be required to find a replacement tenant.

Perhaps the most significant aspect of viewing a lease as a conveyance is the uniquely property law idea that covenants in the lease are independent. In other words, even if the landlord breaches an express promise in the lease, the tenant must still pay rent. Under this approach to lease law, the tenant is left only with a suit in damages for the landlord's breach of promise. A normal contractual analysis might relieve one party of the obligation to perform if the other materially breaches. On the whole, contract law has been on the ascendancy, but as we will see in coming sections, the property law approach to the lease continues to have vitality and the tension between contract and conveyance is ongoing. *See* Gerald Korngold, *Whatever Happened to Landlord-Tenant Law?*, 77 Neb. L. Rev. 703 (1998); Robert H. Kelley, *Any Reports of the Death of the Property Law Paradigm Have Been Greatly Exaggerated*, 41 Wayne L. Rev. 1563 (1995).

◼ PROBLEM: THE OBSTINATE "EX"

Alexandra and Anthony reconnect at a law school reunion. The two former classmates become a couple and begin living together not long afterwards. For the first year of their relationship, Alexandra lives part of the week in Anthony's home and the remainder of the week in her apartment. After Alexandra's law firm names her a partner, Alexandra purchases a home, which she titles solely in her name. Anthony moves into Alexandra's home. Anthony then makes his existing home available to strangers using a short-term Internet rental app. Alexandra and Anthony live together in Alexandra's home. Anthony and Alexandra do not execute a lease, and Anthony does not pay monthly rent to Alexandra. However, Anthony pays the phone and Internet bills, as well as the bill for groceries. Three years after purchasing her home, Alexandra spends a week with her elderly parents in a nearby town. At the beginning of her stay, Alexandra informs Anthony in a phone call that she is calling it quits on their relationship and asks Anthony to move out of her home. She makes this request repeatedly in phone calls during the course of the week. Anthony refuses. Anthony then sends Alexandra an email asserting a property interest in Alexandra's home and suggesting that he might be willing to vacate Alexandra's home in exchange for a cash settlement. Anthony's email cites the following state statute:

> A person in the possession of real estate, with the assent of the owner, is presumed to be a tenant at will until the contrary is shown, and thirty days' notice in writing must be served upon either party or a successor of the party before termination of the tenancy.

Alexandra asks for your advice. What is Anthony's position vis-à-vis Alexandra? *See* Bernet v. Rogers, 519 N.W. 2d 808 (Iowa 1994).

2. Categories of Leases

You may categorize a leasehold relationship by the manner in which it terminates the lease term. There are three "true" leasehold relationships—tenancy for a term of years, periodic tenancy, and tenancy at will. These three relationships are "true" because in each the landlord and tenant voluntarily and mutually agree to the arrangement. There is a fourth type of leasehold, but it is not the result of a consensual arrangement between landlord and tenant. If a tenant under a lease decides not to leave at the end of his term, this will create a tenancy at sufferance. This is not the result the landlord bargained for, and as a result, the law will grant the landlord an election to treat the tenant as a trespasser or a tenant under a new lease. In the meantime, however, the tenant holds a tenancy at the landlord's sufferance, by operation of law.

> **Three Types of True Leases**
>
> - **Term of years tenancy.** The leasehold terminates on a date certain.
> - **Periodic tenancy.** The leasehold continues for successive periods of equal length (e.g., month-to-month), unless one party notifies the other of its intention to terminate.
> - **Tenancy at will.** The leasehold does not have a term of a fixed period and lasts until one party informs the other that the lease is terminated.

a. Tenancy for a Term of Years

The lease for a term of years is probably the easiest of the three lease forms to identify. If, on January 1, 2020, Ursula states to Isaac: "I hereby lease my home to you for five years, and the lease shall terminate on December 31, 2025," then the lease is a term of years. December 31, 2025 is a date certain. Isaac knows exactly when the lease will end. He does not have to give Ursula notice that he wishes the lease to end, and neither does Ursula have to give Isaac notice of her decision to end the lease. The phrase "term of years" does not require the actual term to last years. It merely means that there is a fixed date of termination. Thus, if Ursula leased property to Isaac from January 1, 2020, to November 15, 2020, that is still referred to as a term of years.

A landlord could lease property via a term of years to a tenant (imagine a corporation) for *1,000 years*. Although leases of such lengths do exist, as we saw in Chapter 5, a lease of such significant length raises concerns. It is possible that the parties will trap one another into a relationship far into the future and far beyond their ability to see if the lease is the best use of the property, or even in the parties' interest. The landlord gives up essential control over the real property for a term of generations. Indeed, a lease of such considerable length begins to look much like a transfer of fee. Some states limit the maximum duration of leases by statute. *See, e.g.,* Cal. Civ. Code §717 (West 2007) (limiting agricultural leases to 51 years); Cal. Civ. Code §718 (West 2007) (limiting city lot leases to 99 years).

b. *Periodic Tenancy*

If you signed an apartment lease, there is a good chance that it is a periodic tenancy. The word "periodic" tells the story. The lease continues from period to period, and only terminates if either the landlord or the tenant notifies the other of an intention to terminate. The lease does not end in the middle of a period. The period may be one week, one month, a half-year, or a year. There are two key questions when encountering a periodic tenancy: How is the tenancy created? How is it terminated?

In most instances, a periodic tenancy is created by express language in a lease. If a landlord leases premises to the tenant "from year to year," then the landlord has expressed his intent to create a periodic tenancy with a year as the period. Residential leases are usually, but not always, periodic, although a layperson reading the lease may not realize that the lease will continue indefinitely.[1] A periodic tenancy may also be implied. A landlord may simply point to a particular apartment unit and then tell the tenant "you will pay me $200 rent every two months." This is likely a periodic tenancy, and unless there is more to the agreement (and in these kinds of oral agreements, there often is nothing else to the agreement), the period of tenancy is two months.

The landlord or tenant terminates the periodic tenancy by giving *notice*. A written lease agreement usually spells out how and to whom notice should be given—by mail, by hand delivery, or perhaps electronically.

The real question, however, is how much notice the tenant or landlord must give to the other party. Under the basic common law rule, the amount of notice equals the period of the periodic tenancy. For example, assume that landlord leases a house to tenant for successive two-month periods. If the tenant wishes to terminate the lease, he must give two months' notice to the landlord. This is one more example of a harsh common law rule, if you think about it a moment. A tenant with a six-month periodic tenancy lease would actually have to decide *six months in advance* to terminate. The common law did not take this rule to its complete logical extent, however. Even under the common law, periodic tenancies with periods of a year or more require only six months' notice. Many jurisdictions have adopted statutes deliberately reducing the days of notice required by one party to terminate a periodic tenancy. For example, Iowa, which has adopted the Uniform Residential Landlord and Tenant Act (the "URLTA"), requires at least 10 days' notice for periodic lease with a week-to-week period, and at least 30 days' notice for a periodic leases with periods of one month or greater. Iowa Code §562A.34 (2017). These rules typically are not waivable by the parties, and will override language in the lease to the contrary.

---

[1] Often, residential leases have an initial fixed term (e.g., one year) and then convert automatically to a periodic tenancy after the initial term.

■ PROBLEM: NOTICE IN THE ALTERNATIVE

- ➤ George leases an apartment to Winston on a year-to-year basis, beginning on January 1, 2010 at a rent of $500 per month.
- ➤ George believes that he can obtain a higher rent if he were to look for a new tenant; market rental rates have increased since Winston leased the apartment.
- ➤ George sends Winston a letter on December 31, 2020, notifying Winston that the lease is terminated on December 31, 2021. The letter states, however, that Winston "may in the alternative choose to stay in the apartment and continue the lease if Winston agrees to pay increased rent of $700 per month beginning on January 1, 2022."
- ➤ Winston does not respond to the letter, and he does not move out.

George asks for your advice in January 2022. Is Winston still a tenant? How much rent does Winston owe George per month after January 1, 2022? *See* Garrity v. United States, 67 F. Supp. 821 (Ct. Cl. 1946); Maguire v. Haddad, 91 N.E.2d 769 (Mass. 1950).

c. *Tenancy at Will*

The idea of a tenancy at will is simple: landlord and tenant each want the right to walk away from the leasehold relationship. The term in an at-will lease does not move from period to period. Instead, the landlord tells tenant, "I hereby lease the apartment to you for as long as I want to do so, and for as long as you wish to be a tenant." At any time, either party can tell the other party that the lease is terminated. When this happens, tenant must vacate.

As you can imagine, tenants tend to find the demand that they immediately vacate to be a bit harsh. In many American jurisdictions today, statutes require parties to a residential lease to give a minimum amount of notice to end a tenancy at will. The notice periods vary. Some jurisdictions require that parties give 30 days' notice if rent is paid on a monthly basis. In essence, this turns a tenancy at will into a month-to-month tenancy. URLTA converts a tenancy at will into a periodic tenancy: "Unless the rental agreement fixes a definite term, the tenancy is week-to-week in case of a roomer who pays weekly rent, and in all other cases month-to-month." In addition, under URLTA, the parties must give 10 days' notice if rent is paid weekly.

There is one peculiar common law attribute to a tenancy at will. At common law, a tenancy at will was always mutual. In other words, if a landlord had a right to terminate a lease at will, then the tenant would be granted that right by the court, even if the express written language of the lease did not do so. For example, assume a lease provided that "this lease shall last for a term of one year, but landlord may, at his election, terminate this lease at will at an earlier date." The clear intention of the language of the lease is to grant landlord a unilateral termination right. However, the common law would have none of this. Under the common law rule, the tenant in the example also would have the right to terminate the lease, even though the express language of the lease did not grant this right.

A tenancy at will was a defined creature of property law, and it admitted no contractual variance. This is just one example of the tension between property law and contract law in the development of lease law. Some courts have rejected this older property law approach and instead allow the parties to provide a right to terminate to one party by contract. Consider the following problem.

■ PROBLEM: THE OPEN-ENDED LEASE

> ➢ Daniel leases an apartment to Jerry using a form lease; the parties do not use lawyers and instead fill in the blanks.
> ➢ In the blank for "Rent" the parties handwrite "$100 per month."
> ➢ The paragraph titled "Term" reads "tenant shall have the exclusive possession and quiet enjoyment of the premises for a period of _____." The parties fill in the blank with the following language: "Jerry has the privilege of terminating this lease at a date of his own choosing."
> ➢ Jerry and Daniel execute the lease and Jerry moves into the apartment.
> ➢ Two years later Daniel dies and the executor of Daniel's estate sends a letter to Jerry informing him that "the lease is hereby terminated."

Jerry comes to you for advice. Has Daniel's executor terminated the lease? Must Jerry move out of the apartment? What type of estate do you think the parties were trying to create? *See* Garner v. Gerrish, 473 N.E.2d 223 (N.Y. 1984). *See also* Restatement (Second) of Property: Landlord and Tenant §1.6 cmt. g illus. 7 (1977).

Landlord and tenant may simply fail to set a term. In the absence of language defining term, courts will deem the lease to be at will. What happens if the lease fails to define the term, but the tenant pays his rent on a monthly basis?

Practice Tip

💻 An example of a Sample Residential Lease can be found on the Simulation. Look at the first page (it sets out the basic business terms) and Provision 1 ("Term.") This is a well-drafted form. But note that the lease anticipates that the parties will choose either a fixed term (a term of years), or a month-to-month term (a periodic tenancy). The nature of the term is dependent on the parties filling in the form.

d. *Tenancy at Sufferance and Holdover Tenancy*

We described three categories of leases at the start of this section: tenancy at will, tenancy for a term of years, and periodic tenancy. What happens if a tenant remains in his premises after his term has expired? Tenants engage in this behavior frequently, both in residential and commercial leases. This is known as a *tenancy at sufferance.* The tenant's decision to "hold over" has consequences, and may even result in a new lease. We will see that the tenant's holding over places leverage entirely in the hands of the landlord.

In the commercial world, a landlord will generally know the exact day that a tenant is supposed to vacate because most commercial tenants are subject to a term of years lease. Imagine the following:

> ➤ Bradbury Illustrations is a commercial art firm that leases offices in Downtown Tower from the owner Downtown, Inc. Bradbury Illustrations has a lease that expires on December 31, 2020. Downtown, Inc. is aware that the Bradbury Illustrations lease will expire at the end of the year and plans to quickly fix up the space when the tenant is out, to make it possible to lease the space to a new tenant. Rental rates have been rising in Downtown Tower because new businesses are opening in the area and Downtown, Inc., wishes to capitalize on this improving local economy. On January 2, 2021, representatives of Downtown, Inc. visit the premises expecting to find it empty. Instead, they discover Bradbury Illustrations still occupies the space. They encounter the president of Bradbury Illustrations, who explains: "We are planning to move into a new location, but it is not ready yet, so we will stay in this location until our new space is ready." Assume that you represent the landlord, Downtown, Inc. What is the status of Bradbury Illustrations as tenant? Is there even a leasehold relationship in place? Why do you think a tenant would choose to stay put?

A Nice Metaphor

"Tenancy at sufferance is as illusory as the rings of Saturn viewed edge-on. It arises in one narrow situation only: when one who is tenant in one of the three other tenancies holds over (wrongfully) after the termination of that tenancy." William B. Stoebuck & Dale A. Whitman, The Law of Property §6.20, at 267 (3d ed. 2000).

The common law grants the landlord an *election.* An election is an irrevocable choice that binds a party's legal rights. Downtown, Inc. may elect to treat Bradbury Illustrations as either (1) a trespasser or (2) a tenant under a new lease. Basically, the law interprets the decision of the tenant to remain in the space as an invitation to the landlord to keep the tenant in a leasehold relationship.

Prior to Downtown's election, Bradbury Illustrations is known as a *tenant at sufferance*—in other words, the landlord is suffering the presence of its tenant until the landlord makes a decision. Bradbury Illustrations does not get to occupy the premises for free during this period and must pay (or if necessary, be sued for) fair market rental. In most states, the landlord does not have to give the tenant notice of intention to treat the tenant as a trespasser; it simply begins dispossessory proceedings. The landlord can recover actual damages from the tenant (which may include the loss of a new tenant due to the delay). In some jurisdictions, the law gives the landlord double or even treble rent as a penalty for a willful holdover. *See, e.g.*, 735 Ill. Comp. Stat. 5/9-202 (2017).

What happens if the landlord elects to treat the tenant as a tenant under a new lease? Remember, the parties did not sign a new agreement. Most courts will say that the provisions of the old lease govern the new relationship. The old lease sets out the rental rate, tenant duties, and landlord obligations. Some commercial leases (as opposed to residential leases) have terms of greater than a year, often five years. If the terms of the old lease

Adverse Possession and Holdover Tenancies

One clear implication of the tenancy at sufferance is that tenant is considered legally in possession of the premises until landlord elects not to hold tenant to a new lease. The tenant's period for adverse possession of the premises begins to run only when the tenant is informed that tenant is in fact trespassing.

govern, then presumably the tenant is now stuck with a new five-year term. What does this mean for Bradbury Illustrations?

American jurisdictions, either by statute or case law, typically say that the new holdover term will be periodic and not a term of years. Some courts fix the period at the term under the older lease (but never longer than a year). In other jurisdictions, courts set the period at the rental payment period. Rent is almost always paid monthly, in both commercial and residential leases, and a holdover tenant thus receives a month-to-month lease in those jurisdictions.

Notice the effect of transforming all holdover leases to periodic tenancies: now the tenant and landlord must notify the other of their desire to terminate.

■ PROBLEM: ACCEPT THE CHECK?

> ➤ Bill leases property from Sam pursuant to a one-year term, for an annual rental of $12,000, payable in equal monthly installments of $1,000.
> ➤ Bill does not vacate at the end of the term, and instead delivers a check to Sam in the amount of $1,000, and a cover letter stating that "we did not leave because we like the office, and we have enclosed a check as usual."
> ➤ Sam cashes the check.

What just happened?

MANAGING THE RELATIONSHIP: RIGHTS AND OBLIGATIONS OF LANDLORD AND TENANT

The landlord and tenant will find themselves in a very real and meaningful relationship once they execute the lease and the tenant goes into possession. The lease agreement may place a number of obligations at the feet of either party. The lease agreement does not operate in a vacuum. We will see that the common law and statutes governing the landlord-tenant relationship also grant rights and impose obligations. 🖥 Visit the Simulation to see a Sample Commercial Lease. We will refer to it from time to time as we move through this material.

Let's look at the obligations of the landlord first, and then at those of the tenant. As you read these materials, you will discover additional examples of the ongoing battle between contract law and property law. As you encounter duties and obligations of landlord and tenant, you should also ask whether they are simply default rules that may be altered in the leases, or whether they are beyond the negotiation of the parties.

1. Landlord's Duties and the Consequences of Failure

> ### Primary Obligations of the Landlord
>
> The landlord's baseline obligations to the tenant vary, but you should consider:
>
> 1. whether the landlord is required to place the tenant into physical possession on the first day of the lease;
> 2. whether the landlord has interfered with the tenant's right of "quiet enjoyment";
> 3. in the residential context, whether the landlord must provide property meeting a minimal level of "habitability."

a. The Right to Possession

Let's begin with a basic yet profound insight: at common law, the landlord owed very, very little to the tenant. The landlord's duties (or rather, the lack thereof) emerged from the nature of the leasehold as a conveyance: the transfer of the exclusive right to possession of the premises. The landlord was required to deliver only a *right* to exclusive possession on the first day of the lease term, rather than actually *placing* the tenant into possession. This was not a relationship that bespoke equality, but it made sense at the time it arose. This relationship arose in the feudal era, in which agricultural leases were predominate and tenants were largely self-sufficient. Does this conception make sense today? Consider the following example:

> Assume Anderson owns an office building and that he leases a prime suite to Bogart. Bogart's term comes to an end, but Bogart rather creepily stays put. Bogart is a tenant at sufferance. As you know, Anderson may treat Bogart as a trespasser; this is exactly what Anderson does. He informs Bogart that his lease really is over and that he is trespassing. Anderson now has done all that is required under the law to eliminate Bogart's legal right to the space. *Keep in mind that Anderson is aware that Bogart is trespassing.* Anderson has not bothered to evict Bogart. Instead, he leases the office suite to Smith. On the day Smith is supposed to take possession of the office premises, Smith discovers that Bogart has barricaded himself into the office. Bogart can be heard, through locked doors, promising a "nasty surprise to anyone foolish enough to try to pry me from my office." Smith is concerned and calls Anderson. A pure property law analysis does not provide Smith much solace. Viewed solely from the perspective of property law, Anderson conveyed Smith the exclusive possessory rights to the offices, and retains only a reversion. At common law, it is Smith's job to remove Bogart (no easy task), all the while paying Anderson rent. This older common law rule is called the "American Rule." Other courts, now in the majority, require the landlord to place the tenant in actual physical possession. This is known as the "English Rule." Which rule makes the most sense?

Consider the following problem.

■ PROBLEM: BETTY RELOCATES HER BUSINESS

The fact pattern in this problem is based on Dieffenbach v. McIntyre, 254 P.2d 346 (Okla. 1953). We will follow this fact pattern with excerpts from two well-known and well-reasoned case opinions. Assume that the tenant and landlord in that fact pattern litigate; tenant claims that landlord did not meet her obligations regarding possession, and of course, landlord disagrees. How would you analyze the case? In other words, pretend that you are the judge and apply the law as best you can.

Betty operates a beauty salon in a downtown building and serves professionals who commute to and from work. Betty's lease is set to expire at the end of February. Betty decides that moving to a new location would improve her business. Therefore, she begins her search for a new business location in January. She locates Miriam, who owns a small building in a more exclusive part of the city. The building has a first level that will be perfect for a beauty salon, and a second floor with offices. Tenants presently occupy the second story offices on a month-to-month basis. Miriam offers to lease the building to Betty. Miriam promises Betty that Miriam will give notice and terminate these tenants so that Betty can take possession of the entire building. Betty plans to sublease the second story offices to new tenants at a higher rental rate. Betty ultimately executes a lease covering Miriam's entire building on February 1. This lease will begin March 1 and will have a term of three years. Miriam informs Betty on February 25 that the existing tenants will not depart until March 30, but promises that the remaining tenants will be gone by that date. Based on this assurance, Betty begins to operate her beauty salon on March 1. However, the second-story tenants remain in their offices after March 30, even after Betty makes a request to Miriam that she remove the tenants. Frustrated that tenants remain in the upstairs units, Betty eventually vacates Miriam's building and takes up space in a nearby location.

HANNAN v. DUSCH

153 S.E. 824 (1930)
Supreme Court of Virginia

[The most well-known opinion applying and supporting the American Rule is *Hannan v. Dusch,* which is cited by the court in *Dieffenbach*. Plaintiff Hannan leased real property from defendant Dusch for a term of 15 years. Unfortunately for Hannan, the prior tenant remained in the premises on the day that Hannan was to take possession. Hannan demanded that Dusch evict the tenant. Dusch refused to do so and argued that Hannan was required to evict the holdover. The court applied the American Rule and sided with the landlord.]

. . . The single question of law therefore presented in this case is whether a landlord, who without any express covenant as to delivery of possession leases property to a tenant, is required under the law to oust trespassers and wrongdoers so as to have it open for entry by the tenant at the beginning of the term—that is, whether without an express covenant there is nevertheless an implied covenant to deliver possession. . . .

Of course, the landlord assures to the tenant quiet possession as against all who rightfully claim through or under the landlord.

The discussion then is limited to the precise legal duty of the landlord in the absence of an express covenant, in case a former tenant, who wrongfully holds over, illegally refuses to surrender possession to the new tenant. This is a question about which there is a hopeless conflict of the authorities. It is generally claimed that the weight of the authority favors the particular view contended for. There are, however, no scales upon which we can weigh the authorities. In numbers and respectability they may be quite equally balanced.

It is then a question about which no one should be dogmatic, but all should seek for that rule which is supported by the better reason.

That great annotator, Hon. A.C. Freeman, has collected the authorities as they were at the time he wrote, in 1909, in a note to Sloan v. Hart (150 N.C. 269, 63 S.E. 1037). We shall quote from and paraphrase that note freely because it is the most succinct and the most comprehensive discussion of the question with which we are familiar.

It is conceded by all that the two rules, one called the English rule, which implies a covenant requiring the lessor to put the lessee in possession, and that called the American rule, which recognizes the lessee's legal right to possession, but implies no such duty upon the lessor as against wrongdoers, are irreconcilable....

In commenting on [the English rule] line of cases, Mr. Freeman says this: "The above rule practically prohibits the landlord from leasing the premises while in the possession of a tenant whose term is about to expire, because notwithstanding the assurance on the part of the tenant that he will vacate on the expiration of his term, he may change his mind and wrongfully hold over. It is true that the landlord may provide for such a contingency by suitable provisions in the lease to the prospective tenant, but it is equally true that the prospective tenant has the privilege of insisting that his prospective landlord expressly agree to put him in possession of the premises if he imagines there may be a chance for a lawsuit by the tenant in possession holding over. It seems to us that to raise by implication a covenant on the part of the landlord to put the tenant into possession is to make a contract for the parties in regard to a matter which is equally within the knowledge of both the landlord and tenant."

So let us not lose sight of the fact that under the English rule a covenant which might have been but was not made is nevertheless implied by the court, though it is manifest that each of the parties might have provided for that and for every other possible contingency relating to possession by having express covenants which would unquestionably have protected both.

Referring then to the American rule: Under that rule, in such cases, "the landlord is not bound to put the tenant into actual possession, but is bound only to put him in legal possession, so that no obstacle in the form of superior right of possession will be interposed to prevent the tenant from obtaining actual possession of the demised premises. If the landlord gives the tenant a right of possession he has done all that he is required to do by the terms of an ordinary lease, and the tenant assumes the burden of enforcing such right of possession as against all persons wrongfully in possession, whether they be trespassers or former tenants wrongfully holding over."...

So that, under the American rule, where the new tenant fails to obtain possession of the premises only because a former tenant wrongfully holds over, his remedy is against such wrongdoer and not against the landlord—this because the landlord has not covenanted against the wrongful acts of another and should not be held responsible for such a tort unless he has expressly so contracted. This accords with the general rule as to other wrongdoers, whereas the English rule appears to create a specific exception against lessors. It does not occur to us now that there is any other instance in which one clearly without fault is held responsible for the independent tort of another in which he has neither participated nor concurred and whose misdoings he cannot control. . . .

Mr. Freeman supports the American rule with a calm cogency which should be convincing. He summarizes this conclusion thus: "The gist of the reason advanced in favor of the English rule is that under the American rule, in case the demised premises are in the possession of a person wrongfully holding over or of some trespasser at the beginning of the tenant's term, and the tenant is forced to resort to litigation to oust the one in such possession, all he obtains by his lease is a chance for a lawsuit. It is conceded that under the English rule it becomes the duty of the tenant to maintain his possession at his own expense after once being placed in possession. It is also conceded that if the premises are withheld by the landlord, or someone holding a paramount title, that the tenant has a right of recovery against the landlord for a breach of his covenant of quiet possession. It must be conceded also that if the premises are withheld from the possession of the tenant by reason of the wrongful act of a trespasser or of some former tenant who wrongfully holds over, the tenant has a right to recover his damages from such person. In other words, the tenant is protected, no matter in what manner the possession is withheld from him. It is, of course, true that the tenant will suffer delay in obtaining possession if he is forced to sue for it, but so would the landlord under the same circumstances. It is not, we believe, customary for a person who contracts in respect to any subject to insure the other party against lawsuits. Indeed, both the landlord and tenant have a right to presume that a former tenant will vacate at the end of his term, and that no one will unlawfully prevent the new tenant from going into possession. To sue or be sued is a privilege or misfortune which may occur to anyone. We believe that the American, or New York rule as it is sometimes called, under which it is held that there is no implied covenant that the premises shall be open to entry by the tenant at the time fixed for the beginning of the term, but merely that the tenant shall have a right to the possession at that time is more in accord with substantial justice to both the landlord and tenant, and in accordance with the general course of business dealings in respect to insurance against the chances of a lawsuit in a court of justice."

KEYDATA CORP. v. UNITED STATES

504 F.2d 1115 (1974)
United States Court of Claims

[In *Keydata*, NASA and the Keydata Corporation both leased computer space in a building owned by the landlord, Wyman. NASA desired to expand the size of its computer facilities and Keydata Corporation desired to move to a new location. These desires therefore meshed: NASA would take over the Keydata computer space. Each of the two tenants entered into agreements with Wyman. Wyman agreed to "accept the surrender" of Keydata's computer room (thus terminating Keydata's lease), and Wyman agreed to lease that same computer room to NASA.

Keydata had installed $39,000 worth of air conditioning fixtures in the computer room (computers require considerable cooling). Wyman and Keydata agreed that Keydata would leave the air conditioning equipment in the space, and Wyman would pay Keydata $39,000 to cover its value. Similarly, NASA agreed to pay Wyman $39,000 to buy the improvements. NASA and Wyman agreed that NASA would be able to move into the computer room on January 1, 1969. When January 1, 1969, rolled around, Keydata had not moved out of the computer room. As a result, NASA sent Wyman a letter informing it that its lease of the computer room was terminated because the landlord had not placed it into physical possession on the date set for occupancy. Ultimately, Keydata did vacate and sued NASA for the $39,000 owing for the air conditioning equipment. NASA responded by saying that it was justified in terminating the lease, because the landlord had not put NASA into actual possession. The court applied the English Rule and sided with the tenant, NASA.]

On the merits, there is one important legal issue which can now be resolved. Keydata's motion for summary judgment asserts that the Government had no legal right to rescind its lease agreement with Wyman, despite plaintiff's holding-over. The argument is that the lease amendment obligated Wyman to do no more than convey to the Government the right to take possession of the computer room, that Wyman did not explicitly promise to deliver actual possession, and that no such promise can be implied.

Keydata's description of the lack of obligation of a landlord to secure his tenant in possession (in the absence of an express undertaking) is an accurate reflection of the present Massachusetts law. But there is a clear split among the states between the "American" and "English" rules on the liability of a landlord when the demised premises are occupied by a third party at the commencement of the lease term. See 49 Am. Jur. 2d, Landlord and Tenant §217 (1970). Under the so-called "American" rule, the landlord merely covenants that possession will not be withheld by himself or by one having paramount title. Ibid. This is the current rule in Massachusetts. Snider v. Deban, 249 Mass. 59, 144 N.E. 69 (1924). It is sometimes justified on the ground that, since the lessor has conveyed the sole and exclusive right of possession to the new lessee, he cannot maintain an action for possession in his own name. Snider v. Deban, *supra*, 249 Mass. at 66, 144 N.E. at 72.

The other doctrine, called the "English" rule, requires that, when the lease is silent on the point, the landlord deliver actual possession of the premises at the beginning of the term. 49 Am. Jur. 2d, Landlord and Tenant §217, at 235 (1970). The lessee's rights are based on breach of the lessor's implied covenant that he has a right to lease the premises, or of the implied undertaking that the lessor will deliver possession to the lessee. 2 R. Powell, Real Property (Rohan ed. 1966) §225(1). If the lessee cannot take possession because of a holdover tenant, or some other obstructing third person, the landlord is in breach of his obligation.

This division in view compels us to face the problems of whether we are bound to follow the Massachusetts rule because the real property is located there—and, if not, what standard to apply. It will prove simpler to reverse these questions and first take up the issue of what rule to adopt if we are free to choose on the merits of the competing principles. In such an area of free choice, we "should take account of the best in modern decision and discussion." Padbloc Co. v. United States, 161 Ct. Cl. 369, 377 (1963); Groves v. United States, 202 Ct. Cl. 660, 674 (1973).

The American Law Institute's most recent formulation, accepting the "English" rule, seems to us to represent "the best in modern decision and discussion." The Institute's phrasing (Restatement of the Law, Second, Property, Landlord and Tenant, §6.2, p. 137 (Tent. Draft No. 2, 1974) is this:

> Except to the extent the parties to the lease validly agree otherwise, there is a breach of the landlord's obligations if a third person is improperly in possession of the leased property on the date the tenant is entitled to possession and the landlord does not act promptly to remove such person and does not in fact remove him within a reasonable period of time. For such breach, the tenant may
>
> > (1) terminate the lease. . . .

The Restatement gives persuasive reasons in support of this choice (Restatement of the Law, Second, Property, Landlord and Tenant, §6.2, Comment a, p. 139 (Tent. Draft No. 2, 1974):

> (1) The landlord knows, or should know, the status of the possession of the leased property better than the tenant in the period prior to the date the tenant is entitled to possession.
>
> (2) The landlord knows, or should know, better than the tenant whether a person in possession of the leased property prior to the date the tenant is entitled to possession is properly or improperly on the leased property.
>
> (3) Prior to the date the tenant is entitled to possession of the leased property, the landlord is the only one of the two who can evict a person improperly in possession of the leased property.
>
> (4) In the situation where the person in possession of the leased property is entitled to be there until the date the tenant is entitled to possession, the case of the possible holdover prior tenant, the landlord is the only one of the two who had an opportunity to get some assurance that the prior tenant would not hold over.
>
> (5) The tenant will have received less than he bargained for if he must go forward with the lease and bear the cost of legal proceedings to clear the way for his entry on the leased property.

[handwritten margin note: • English rule supported by the ALI + the Restatement]

This "English" rule conforms to the commonsense notion of what a lease is. The tenant is buying space—in a building or in the open—and not merely the right to bring a lawsuit to try to get the space. The "American" (or Massachusetts) rule, on the other hand, rests on an abstruse technicality—the separation of legal title (which remains in the landlord) from the right to possession (which is conveyed to the new tenant)—and represents an unfortunate example of mechanical jurisprudence, grinding out a result without any regard for the true interests or policies involved.

Plaintiff objects that adoption for federal leases of the rule requiring the landlord to deliver actual possession places a Massachusetts lessor in a dilemma—he must deliver possession but cannot evict a third party or holdover tenant after the lease term has begun. *See* Snider v. Deban, *supra*, 249 Mass. at 66, 144 N.E. at 72. As the ALI comment suggests this difficulty is not insuperable. First, a landlord is able to protect himself in the lease document by expressly limiting or disclaiming his obligation to deliver possession, or else by requiring security of a prior tenant in possession that he will not hold over. Second, the landlord may have a remedy in damages against a holdover tenant; such at least is the majority American rule. 49 Am. Jur. 2d, Landlord and Tenant, §1123, at 1074 (1970). Third, the landlord is still in a better position to appraise, anticipate and bear the risk of this loss than a prospective tenant not yet in possession. The risk ought to be upon the owner, unless the prospective tenant expressly agrees to shoulder it.

■ POINTS TO CONSIDER

1. **Policies behind the two rules.** Identify the policies that support or undermine the English and American Rules. Do the *Hannan* and *Keydata* opinions address the weaknesses in the rules they propose, or do they focus only upon the weaknesses of the contrary rules?

2. **Apply the rules.** Now apply the rationales and arguments advanced by the courts in *Hannan* and *Keydata* to the fact set "Betty Relocates her Business." Make your best case for Betty and then for Miriam. If you were not representing one party or the other, but simply had to pick the best rule to resolve the dispute, which would you choose, and why?

3. **The present state of the law.** Although the jurisdictions are divided, it appears that a weak majority of states have adopted the English Rule and require the landlord to place the tenant into actual possession of the premises. *Keydata* noted that the Restatement (Second) of Property: Landlord and Tenant §6.2 (1977) takes the English Rule position. At the time of *Keydata*, the Restatement (Second) of Property was in draft form, but was since adopted in 1977. The Uniform Residential Landlord and Tenant Act (URLTA) §2.103 similarly adopts the English Rule. You can find an excellent discussion of the nature and development of the English and American Rules regarding the landlord's obligation to place tenant in possession of the premises in Glen Weissenberger, *The Landlord's Duty to Deliver Possession: The Overlooked Reform*, 46 U. Cin. L. Rev. 937 (1977). *See also* Kristine Karnezis, Annotation, *Implied Covenant or Obligation to Provide Lessee with Actual Possession*, 96 A.L.R.3d 1155 (1979). At least one writer has suggested that the American Rule is the preferable and more efficient approach to possession disputes in commercial leaseholds, and that the English Rule may be more appropriate in the context of residential lease disputes. *See* Matthew J. Heiser, *What's Good for the Goose Isn't Always Good for the Gander: The Inefficiencies of a Single Default Rule for Delivery of Possession of Leasehold Estates*, 38 Colum. J.L. & Soc. Probs. 171 (2004).

4. **What's a tenant to do?** The landlord has a remedy when a tenant holds over or when someone unrelated to the landlord simply trespasses on property while in the landlord's possession. The landlord may bring an eviction action and have the interloper removed. The landlord may also sue for any damage to the property. In addition, in the case of a holdover, the landlord may sue the tenant for rent for the time between the termination of the tenant's lease until the moment the tenant is removed. *See* Restatement (Second) of Property: Landlord and Tenant §6.2 (1977).

5. **Review the lease.** 🖥 Does the Sample Commercial Lease from the Simulation require the landlord to place the tenant in physical possession of the premises? Does it address the issue at all?

6. **Preparing to practice.** Assume you are representing a large commercial tenant negotiating a lease for office space. What would you put into the lease regarding this issue, to protect your client? If you represented the landlord, what might you agree to?

◼ PROBLEM: THREE DAYS LATE AND A DOLLAR SHORT?

Wells owns an apartment building in a desirable area in Silicon Valley. Traveler is a young software engineer who has just graduated from an engineering college on the East Coast. Traveler has been hired by one of the major social networking firms. Traveler will start work on January 9. Traveler sees an advertisement for an apartment unit in Wells's apartment building on-line and contacts Wells to discuss the unit. After some back-and-forth via email, Traveler and Wells execute a lease agreement for Unit 101 in the apartment building. The term (and Traveler's possession) is to commence on January 1. Wells sends Traveler a key to the apartment unit.

Traveler arranges the cross-continent move. Both Traveler and the moving truck arrive at the apartment building promptly at 7 A.M. on January 1. However, when approaching the front door of the unit, the door opens and a woman appears. She is distraught and tells Traveler, "I am so terribly sorry; I came down with the flu last month and I am still getting ready to move back to my parents' house in Southern California. I just need a week to get my act together, then I will be out of here. Can you just give me a week before you move in?" Traveler is a bit put out, but he is sympathetic. He responds, "I suppose that will be okay. I will tell the moving company to store my stuff for a week and then return on January 8 to move me into the apartment. You know, though, they will charge me a storage fee." The woman responds gratefully, "Thank you so much, you have done me a great kindness." Traveler informs the truck driver of his plan and then they leave.

On January 8, Traveler and the moving truck return to the apartment building. Traveler knocks on the door and again the woman answers. However, this time she appears healthy and happy. She says: "Sorry, I am still here. I'm over the flu, but I just had a fight with my parents. I cannot move back in with them now. I am sure I can find time to look around for a new apartment in about a month or so. Look, I know that this is inconvenient for you. I will pay the storage fees for your stuff if you'd like." Traveler responds: "That is not acceptable. I need this place because I start work tomorrow. Please give me access to the apartment." The woman replies by shutting the door in Traveler's face.

Traveler calls Wells to inform him that there is a holdover in the apartment, but Wells refuses to act.

Traveler comes to you for advice. What is his position relative to the holdover tenant and Wells? Will your answer change depending on whether the apartment is located in an American Rule or English Rule jurisdiction?

b. *The Right of Quiet Enjoyment*

As we have seen, the tenant's real goal in a lease is to obtain the exclusive right to possession of defined premises. In other words, the tenant leases space—an apartment or a business location—only because the tenant thinks that he will have the right to use the space and exclude others from its use. If you live in an apartment, you expect to be able to live in it undisturbed during the term. You live there; you sleep there; you entertain there. You rely on the fact that you have a place to go at the end of the day. Our homes are central to our day-to-day lives and the ability to feel secure.

The same is true for businesses. Although a business may be a legal entity, such as a corporation, in the end it is comprised of people, and when businesses lease property, these people expect to carry on their affairs in the leased premises. In fact, the leased property can become so central to the lives of the individuals who work in the businesses that they may become second homes. You may discover this fact of working life when you graduate from law school and begin your career as a practicing attorney. You may well spend as much time in your office as in your personal residence.

Life in an Office and What It May Mean

Alan M. Di Sciullo is a New York real estate attorney and co-author of an acclaimed treatise, John B. Wood & Alan M. Di Sciullo, Negotiating and Drafting Office Leases (Law Journal Press 2008). He added "A Comment on September 11" following the tragic events of 9/11. Mr. Di Sciullo's offices were located on the 65th floor of Tower 2 at the World Trade Center in Manhattan. Mr. Di Sciullo was on his way to work on the subway when the planes hit. In his Comment, Mr. Di Sciullo explains that the World Trade Center "was as much a home for many of us as our family residences. We spent more time in these offices than we did in our homes. Those of us who had offices in the towers took some delight in seeing tourists pay to wait oftentimes for hours to see a view very similar to the one we saw daily from our offices only forty-five floors below the observatory deck. . . . The Trade Center was a source of my children's . . . childhood memories as they attended the Company's holiday parties. . . ." Mr. Di Sciullo lost friends, as did so many people on that terrible day. But he also lost a *home*. You do not have to have had offices in the World Trade Center to empathize with Mr. Di Sciullo; you only have to live the life of a professional in rented offices. Our leased premises are incorporated into the fabric of our daily lives.

The tenant's right to exclude means that even the landlord does not have the right to enter into the tenant's property. Although this is a dramatic rule, it is also a default rule; the tenant may always grant the landlord a right in the lease to enter the premises for particular reasons.

At common law, the landlord did not have the right to enter *even to prevent waste*. The landlord could bring an action for damages as a result of waste, or for an injunction to prevent the tenant from wasting the property. But the landlord could not simply unlock the door and stop the wasteful activity. *See* 1 Andrew R. Berman, Friedman on Leases §4:3.2 (6th ed. 2017).

Similarly, the landlord could not generally enter property if he believed that the tenant was engaging in illegal activity. If the tenant began manufacturing drugs, the landlord's property might be subject to incursion by law enforcement. But the right of exclusive possession meant that landlord could not use a master key and enter on the landlord's own initiative. Some courts seem to be backing away from this strict common law rule, and may permit the landlord to enter the premises if necessary to safeguard other tenants or prevent severe damage, even if the lease does not so provide. *See, e.g.*, People v. Plane, 78 Cal. Rptr. 528 (Cal. Ct. App. 1969).

The tenant's very powerful common law right of exclusive possession explains portions of both commercial and residential lease agreements. Landlord typically drafts the lease, not tenant. Residential and commercial landlords often include provisions granting landlord the right to enter in the case of an "emergency," to effect repairs to structural or other systems integral to the building, and to prevent waste. Commercial landlords might include additional provisions, such as the right to enter the premises near the end of the term to show the space to prospective future tenants. Tenants need to read their leases carefully to make sure that the landlord does not have too broad or intrusive a right to enter. 🖳 You will find examples of the landlord's contractual right to enter the premises in the Sample Residential and Commercial Leases available on the Simulation.

The deal a tenant makes with her landlord can be complicated and involve many contractual promises and conditions. But at its core it remains as follows: "I pay you rent, and you leave me be in my space." This means, at the least, that the landlord (or anyone claiming under the landlord) may not physically interfere with the tenant's use and enjoyment of the premises. If the landlord fails to follow this basic rule, then the landlord is said to be violating the *implied covenant of quiet enjoyment*. Lease law flows from an early common law understanding that the covenants (read promises) that the landlord and tenant made to one another were *independent*. As a result, the landlord's breach of a covenant to the tenant did not relieve the tenant of the tenant's primary obligation—to pay the landlord rent. At most, the tenant could sue the landlord for damages arising from the landlord's breach of a promise, but the tenant could not withhold rent. The common law did provide a way around this rather harsh rule: if the landlord, or a party claiming under landlord, *physically removed* the tenant from the premises, then the tenant was relieved of the obligation to pay rent.

The courts extended this exception to *constructive evictions*. If the landlord, or some party claiming under landlord, interfered with the tenant's use of the leased premises to such a significant extent that the tenant was essentially forced out of the premises, this would also relieve the tenant from the duty to pay rent. For example, if the landlord cut off water to an office building, then fairly soon the tenant would be forced to leave, terminating the tenant's obligation to pay rent. If the landlord interfered with the tenant's quiet enjoyment, but not to a degree that forced the tenant to leave, the tenant could still sue landlord for damages based on a breach of the implied covenant of quiet enjoyment.

At its most basic level, this means that the landlord cannot remove the tenant physically from the premises or bar tenant from all or a portion of the leased space. The landlord cannot say to the tenant, for instance, that tenant is barred from one half of the leased space but not the other half; this action would terminate the lease and relieve the tenant from paying rent. Courts often stated simply that a landlord could not unilaterally apportion its wrong. In other words, the landlord could not violate the covenant partially and remain partially in compliance with the lease. The covenant of quiet enjoyment called for *total* compliance.

Consider the following problems. Do any of these fact patterns constitute a violation of the landlord's covenant of quiet enjoyment?

■ PROBLEM: THE WEEKEND LOCKOUT

> ➤ Jerry leases space in an office tower to Daniel to be used as law offices for a term of one year. The lease does not specifically address the hours in which the building will be open. It requires only that heating, ventilation, and air conditioning will be turned on during the hours of 8 A.M. until 7 P.M. Monday through Friday.
> ➤ Daniel expects to be able to work on the weekends, and understands that the offices may be hot or cold depending on the weather.
> ➤ One month into the lease, Jerry begins the practice of locking the front doors to the building on weekends and the security guard refuses Daniel entry. Daniel calls Jerry to complain, but Jerry responds: "It raises my insurance to have just a few tenants in the building on the weekend. It is much easier and cheaper for me to lock it down."

■ PROBLEM: THE UNEXPECTED TENANT

➢ Again, Jerry leases space in an office tower to Daniel to be used as law offices for a term of one year.

➢ One month into the lease, Jerry's son Barry graduates from law school and asks his father for help setting up a law practice. Jerry sends a note to his son Barry stating, "Look, you can have Suite 2101 in the Office Tower. It is presently occupied by Daniel. I will give you a master key and you can just put his stuff on the curb on the weekend."

➢ Barry follows his father's instructions and moves Daniel's office belongings to the curb.

➢ Daniel arrives at work the following Monday morning and discovers his desk, chair, file cabinet, and other detritus of work on the curb. He calls Jerry and is told, "I'll give you substitute space and I'll knock some money off your monthly rent. You will be even happier."

➢ Daniel is not "even happier."

Constructive Eviction

It is pretty rare nowadays that a landlord will physically remove a tenant from leased space before the end of the term. It may happen, but this is not the usual manner in which the covenant of quiet enjoyment comes to the attention of parties and courts. Courts today recognize that a landlord may make a tenant so utterly miserable in her occupancy of the space that the tenant must "quit" or vacate. That is, the landlord, through its action or inaction, will render the premises "untenantable"; the tenant's situation is just as bad as if the landlord picked up the tenant by the pants and kicked her out. Thus, she has been "constructively evicted."

Compare constructive eviction with actual eviction. The remedy for tenant is the same—tenant is relieved from paying rent and the lease is terminated. Physical eviction suggests that the tenant does not occupy all or a portion of the leased premises. We do not usually see physical eviction happen in slow motion; the tenant finds (as in the problem above) that he simply no longer occupies property promised him in the lease.

> **Practice Tip: Words Only Lawyers Use**
>
> Do not try to find the word "untenantable" in the dictionary. If you use it when writing a letter or document, your word processing program will flag it as incorrect. Like so many other unusual words we find in cases and documents, and in the conversations of lawyers, this is a term of art that exists only in the lawyering world. Untenantable property is property that a hypothetical tenant would find so unbearable as to leave within a short period of time.

We would expect the same to be roughly true of constructive eviction. The basic elements of constructive eviction are described differently by courts and commentators, but this is a general statement that works for most cases:

- the interference must be substantial and of a kind that would cause a reasonable person in tenant's position to be forced to leave the premises right away, or as soon as possible under the circumstances;
- the tenant must notify the landlord of the interference, and give the landlord an opportunity to fix the problem if possible within a reasonable time frame;
- the tenant must actually vacate; and
- the interference must result from a breach of an express or implied promise made by the landlord to the tenant in the lease.

Consider the last element. If the landlord never promised to provide a parking garage to the tenant, the decision of the landlord to remove a garage and insist that tenant park on the streets is not a constructive eviction. *The landlord cannot be in breach of a promise that he never made. See* 3 Andrew R. Berman, Friedman on Leases §29:3.1 (6th ed. 2017) ("It must be emphasized, however, that the conditions complained of by tenant must be due to an affirmative breach of duty by the landlord. Hence, if the landlord has no duty to tenant to prevent certain conditions from occurring, these conditions, no matter how horrible, do not give rise to a claim of constructive eviction.").

For example, in Charlotte Eastland Mall, LLC v. Sole Survivor, Inc., 608 S.E.2d 70 (N.C. Ct. App. 2004), tenant Sole Survivor was a shoe repair shop that vacated its space prior to the end of its ten-year term, because, according to the tenant:

> (1) in July 1994 Sole Survivor was the victim of an armed robbery; (2) during the eight years defendants leased space at Eastland, the police received many reports of criminal activity at Eastland; (3) during the same time period, several businesses vacated Eastland; and (4) Eastland had been made aware of the problem of criminal activity occurring at the mall.

Id. at 72. The court noted that although the landlord/owner of the mall reserved the sole right to provide security to the common areas, the lease did not place an affirmative duty on the landlord to do so. As a result, the failure of the landlord to provide security was not deemed by the court to be a constructive eviction. Do you think that this is a fair and correct result?

Constructive eviction is most often asserted by the tenant as a defense against the landlord's demand for rent. However, it is a risky defense. Imagine that you are the tenant's lawyer. You receive a call from tenant who says, "The air conditioning is out in our building, and this is Dallas in the summertime. It is so hot that I cannot meet my clients at the office and I am borrowing a friend's space. The landlord will not tell me when the AC will be fixed. When can I move out and lease other space?" How would you respond? Consider the following case:

RESTE REALTY CORP. v. COOPER

251 A.2d 268 (1969)
Supreme Court of New Jersey

FRANCIS, J.

Plaintiff-lessor sued defendant-lessee to recover rent allegedly due under a written lease. The suit was based upon a charge that defendant had unlawfully abandoned the premises two and a quarter years before the termination date of the lease. The trial court, sitting without a jury, sustained tenant's defense of constructive eviction and entered judgment for defendant. The Appellate Division reversed, holding (1) the proof did not support a finding of any wrongful act or omission on the part of the lessor sufficient to constitute a constructive eviction, and (2) if such act or omission could be found, defendant waived it by failing to remove from the premises within a reasonable time thereafter. We granted defendant's petition for certification. 51 N.J. 574, 242 A.2d 378 (1968).

On May 13, 1958 defendant Joy M. Cooper, leased from plaintiff's predecessor in title a portion of the ground or basement floor of a commercial (office) building at 207 Union Street, Hackensack, N.J. The term was five years, but after about a year of occupancy the parties made a new five-year lease dated April 1959 covering the entire floor except the furnace room. The leased premises were to be used as "commercial offices" and "not for any other purpose without the prior written consent of the Landlord." More particularly, the lessee utilized the offices for meetings and training of sales personnel in connection with the business of a jewelry firm of which Mrs. Cooper was branch manager at the time. No merchandise was sold there.

A driveway ran along the north side of the building from front to rear. Its inside edge was at the exterior foundation wall of the ground floor. The driveway was not part of Mrs. Cooper's leasehold. Apparently it was provided for use of all tenants. Whenever it rained during the first year of defendant's occupancy, water ran off the driveway and into the offices and meeting rooms either through or under the exterior or foundation wall. At this time Arthur A. Donigian, a member of the bar of this State, had his office in the building. In addition, he was an officer and resident manager of the then corporate-owner. Whenever water came into the leased floor, defendant would notify him and he would take steps immediately to remove it. Obviously Donigian was fully aware of the recurrent flooding. He had some personal files in the furnace room which he undertook to protect by putting them on 2×4's in order to raise them above the floor surface. When negotiating with defendant for the substitute five-year lease for the larger space, Donigian promised to remedy the water problem by resurfacing the driveway. (It is important to note here that Donigian told Walter T. Wittman, an attorney, who had offices in the building and who later became executor of Donigian's estate, that the driveway needed "regrading and some kind of sealing of the area between the driveway which lay to the north of the premises and the wall." He also told Wittman that the grading was improper and was "letting the water into

Procedural history

the basement rather than away from it.") The work was done as promised and although the record is not entirely clear, apparently the seepage was somewhat improved for a time. Subsequently it worsened, but Donigian responded immediately to each complaint and removed the water from the floor.

Donigian died on March 30, 1961, approximately two years after commencement of the second lease. Whenever it rained thereafter and water flooded into the leased floor, no one paid any attention to defendant's complaints, so she and her employees did their best to remove it. During this time sales personnel and trainees came to defendant's premises at frequent intervals for meetings and classes. Sometimes as many as 50 persons were in attendance in the morning and an equal number in the afternoon. The flooding greatly inconvenienced the conduct of these meetings. At times after heavy rainstorms there was as much as two inches of water in various places and "every cabinet, desk and chair had to be raised above the floor." On one occasion jewelry kits that had been sitting on the floor, as well as the contents of file cabinets, became "soaked." Mrs. Cooper testified that once when she was conducting a sales training class and it began to rain, water came into the room making it necessary to move all the chairs and "gear" into another room on the south side of the building. On some occasions the meetings had to be taken to other quarters for which rent had to be paid; on others the meetings were adjourned to a later date. Complaints to the lessor were ignored. What was described as the "crowning blow" occurred on December 20, 1961. A meeting of sales representatives from four states had been arranged. A rainstorm intervened and the resulting flooding placed five inches of water in the rooms. According to Mrs. Cooper it was impossible to hold the meeting in any place on the ground floor; they took it to a nearby inn. That evening she saw an attorney who advised her to send a notice of vacation. On December 21 she asked that the place be cleaned up. This was not done, and after notifying the lessor of her intention she left the premises on December 30, 1961.

Plaintiff acquired the building and an assignment of defendant's lease January 19, 1962. On November 9, 1964 it instituted this action to recover rent for the unexpired term of defendant's lease, i.e., until March 31, 1964.

At trial of the case defendant's proofs showed the facts outlined above. Plaintiff offered very little in the way of contradiction. It seemed to acknowledge that a water problem existed but as defense counsel told the court in his opening statement, he was "prepared to show that the water receded any number of times, and therefore the damage, if it was caused by an act that can be traced to the landlord, (the condition) was not a permanent interference" with the use and enjoyment of the premises. Plaintiff contended further that the water condition would not justify defendant's abandonment of the premises because in the lease she had stipulated that prior to execution thereof she had "examined the demised premises, and accept(ed) them in their (then) condition . . . , and without any representations on the part of the landlord or its agents as to the present or future condition of the said premises"; moreover she had agreed "to keep the demised premises in good condition" and to "redecorate, paint and

P's argument [handwritten marginalia]

renovate the said premises as may be necessary to keep them in good repair and good appearance."

The trial judge found that the "testimony is just undisputed and overwhelming that after every rainstorm water flowed into the leased premises of the defendant" and nothing was done to remedy the condition despite repeated complaints to the lessor. He declared also that the condition was intolerable and so substantially deprived the lessee of the use of the premises as to constitute a constructive eviction and therefore legal justification for vacating them.

On this appeal the plaintiff-landlord claims that under the long-settled law, delivery of the leased premises to defendant-tenant was not accompanied by any implied warranty or covenant of fitness for use for commercial offices or for any other purpose. He asserts also that by express provision of both the first and second leases (which are identical printed forms, except that the second instrument covers the additional portion of basement floor), the tenant acknowledged having examined the "demised premises," having agreed to accept them in their "present condition," and having agreed to keep them in good repair, which acknowledgment, as a matter of law, has the effect of excluding any such implied warranty or covenant.

It is true that as the law of leasing an estate for years developed historically, no implied warranty or covenant of habitability or fitness for the agreed use was imposed on the landlord. Because the interest of the lessee was considered personal property the doctrine of Caveat emptor was applied, and in the absence of an express agreement otherwise, or misrepresentation by the lessor, the tenant took the premises "as is." 1 American Law of Property (Casner ed. 1952) §3.45, p. 267. . . . Modern social and economic conditions have produced many variant uses and types of leases, e.g., sale and leaseback transactions, mortgaging of leasehold interests, shopping center leases, long-term leases. Moreover, an awareness by legislatures of the inequality of bargaining power between landlord and tenant in many cases, and the need for tenant protection, has produced remedial tenement house and multiple dwelling statutes. . . . It has come to be recognized that ordinarily the lessee does not have as much knowledge of the condition of the premises as the lessor. Building code requirements and violations are known or made known to the lessor, not the lessee. He is in a better position to know of latent defects, structural and otherwise, in a building which might go unnoticed by a lessee who rarely has sufficient knowledge or expertise to see or to discover them. A prospective lessee, such as a small businessman, cannot be expected to know if the plumbing or wiring systems are adequate or conform to local codes. Nor should he be expected to hire experts to advise him. Ordinarily all this information should be considered readily available to the lessor who in turn can inform the prospective lessee. These factors have produced persuasive arguments for reevaluation of the Caveat emptor doctrine and, for imposition of an implied warranty that the premises are suitable for the leased purposes and conform to local codes and zoning laws. Proponents of more liberal treatment of tenants say, among other things, that if a lease is a demise of land and a sale of an interest in land in the commercial sense, more realistic consideration should be given to the contractual nature of the relationship. . . .

Since the language of the two leases is the same, except that the second one describes the larger portion of the basement taken by the tenant, evaluation of the landlord's contentions will be facilitated by first considering the original lease and the factual setting attending its execution. Although the second or substitutionary lease is the controlling instrument, we take this approach in order to focus more clearly upon the effect of the change in the factual setting when the second lease was executed. This course brings us immediately to the landlord's reliance upon the provisions of the first lease (which also appear in the second) that the tenant inspected the "demised premises," accepted them in their "present condition" and agreed to keep them in good condition. The word "premises," construed most favorably to the tenant, means so much of the ground floor as was leased to Mrs. Cooper for commercial offices. The driveway or its surfacing or the exterior wall or foundation under it cannot be considered included as part of the "premises." In any event there is nothing to show that the inspection by Mrs. Cooper of the driveway or the ground floor exterior wall and foundation under it prior to the execution of the first lease would have given or did give her notice that they were so defective as to permit rainwater to flood into the leased portion of the interior. The condition should have been and probably was known to the lessor. If known, there was a duty to disclose it to the prospective tenant. Certainly as to Mrs. Cooper, it was a latent defect, and it would be a wholly inequitable application of Caveat emptor to charge her with knowledge of it. The attempted reliance upon the agreement of the tenant in both leases to keep the "demised premises" in repair furnishes no support for the landlord's position. The driveway, exterior ground floor wall and foundation are not part of the demised premises. Latent defects in this context, I.e., those the existence and significance of which are not reasonably apparent to the ordinary prospective tenant, certainly were not assumed by Mrs. Cooper.

. . .

But the landlord says that whatever the factual and legal situation may have been when the original lease was made, the relationship underwent a change to its advantage when the second was executed. This contention is based upon the undisputed fact that in April 1959, after a year of occupancy, defendant, with knowledge that the premises were subject to recurrent flooding, accepted a new lease containing the same provisions as the first one. This acceptance, the argument runs, eliminates any possible reliance upon a covenant or warranty of fitness because the premises were truly taken then "as is." While it is true that a tenant's knowing acceptance of a defective leasehold would normally preclude reliance upon any implied warranties, the landlord's position here is not sustainable because it is asserted in disregard of certain vital facts—the agent's promise to remedy the condition and the existence of an express covenant of quiet enjoyment in the lease.

The evidence is clear that prior to execution of the substitutionary lease, the tenant complained to the owner's agent about the incursion of water whenever it rained. The agent conceded the problem existed and promised to remedy the condition. Relying upon the promise Mrs. Cooper accepted the new lease, and the landlord resurfaced the driveway. Unfortunately, either the work was not sufficiently extensive or it was not done properly because at some unstated time thereafter the water continued to come into the tenant's offices. The complaints about it resumed, and as noted above, until the building manager died he made prompt efforts to remove the water. In our opinion the tenant was entitled to rely upon the promise of its agent to provide a remedy. Thus it cannot be said as a matter of law that by taking the second lease she accepted the premises in their defective condition. . . .

This brings us to the crucial question whether the landlord was guilty of a breach of a covenant which justified the tenant's removal from the premises on December 30, 1961. We are satisfied there was such a breach.

The great weight of authority throughout the country is to the effect that ordinarily a covenant of quiet enjoyment is implied in a lease. . . . We need not deal here with problems of current serviceability of that rule because as has been indicated above, the lease in question contains an express covenant of quiet enjoyment for the term fixed. Where there is such a covenant, whether express or implied, and it is breached substantially by the landlord, the courts have applied the doctrine of constructive eviction as a remedy for the tenant. Under this rule any act or omission of the landlord or of anyone who acts under authority or legal right from the landlord, or of someone having superior title to that of the landlord, which renders the premises substantially unsuitable for the purpose for which they are leased, or which seriously interferes with the beneficial enjoyment of the premises, is a breach of the covenant of quiet enjoyment and constitutes a constructive eviction of the tenant. . . .

Examples of constructive eviction having close analogy to the present case are easily found. Failure to supply heat as covenanted in the lease so that the apartment was "unlivable" on cold days amounted to constructive eviction. *Higgins v. Whiting*, supra; Anderson v. Walker Realty Co., 1 N.J. Misc. 287 (Sup. Ct. 1923). So too, when the main waste pipe of an apartment building was permitted to become and remain clogged with sewage for a long period of time causing offensive odors and danger to health, the covenant of quiet enjoyment was breached and justified the tenant's abandonment of his premises. *McCurdy v. Wyckoff*, supra. If a landlord lets an apartment in his building to a tenant as a dwelling and knowingly permits another part to be used for lewd purposes which use renders the tenant's premises "unfit for occupancy by a respectable family," his failure to terminate the use when he has the legal power to do so constitutes a constructive eviction. *Weiler v. Pancoast*, supra. The same rule was applied in White v. Hannon, 11 N.J.L.J. 338 (Dist. Ct. 1888) where it appeared that the plumbing in the rooms to the rear of the demised premises became so old and worn out as to emit strong and unhealthy odors which came through into the tenant's quarters. The tenant's removal was held justified. . . .

As noted above, the trial court found sufficient interference with the use and enjoyment of the leased premises to justify the tenant's departure and to relieve her from the obligation to pay further rent. In our view the evidence was sufficient to warrant that conclusion, and the Appellate Division erred in reversing it. Plaintiff argued and the Appellate Division agreed that a constructive eviction cannot arise unless the condition interferes with the use in a permanent sense. It is true that the word "permanent" appears in many of the early cases. See e.g., Stewart v. Childs Co., 86 N.J.L. 648, 650, 92 A. 392, L.R.A. 1915C, 649 (E.&A. 1914). But it is equally obvious that permanent does not signify that water in a basement in a case like this one must be an everlasting and unending condition. If its recurrence follows regularly upon rainstorms and is sufficiently serious in extent to amount to a substantial interference with use and enjoyment of the premises for the purpose of the lease, the test for constructive eviction has been met. Additionally in our case, the defective condition of the driveway, exterior and foundation walls which permitted the recurrent flooding was obviously permanent in the sense that it would continue and probably worsen if not remedied. There was no obligation on the tenant to remedy it.

Plaintiff claims further that *Stewart v. Childs Co.*, supra, strongly supports its right to recovery. Under the lease in that case the landlord covenanted that at all times he would keep the cellar waterproof. The cellar was known to be necessary to the conduct of the tenant's business. After the business opened, water flooded into the cellar, at times to a depth of two and three feet. There was no doubt the flooding resulted from failure of the landlord to make the place waterproof. But when the tenant moved out, a suit for rent for the unexpired term was instituted and the landlord was allowed to recover. It was held that the agreement to pay rent and the agreement to waterproof the cellar were independent covenants and breach of the covenant to waterproof was not a defense to the action for rent. We regard this holding as basically contrary to that in *Higgins v. Whiting*, supra, where the agreement by the landlord to heat the leased premises and the tenant's agreement to pay rent during the term were declared to be mutually dependent covenants. Thus failure to heat constituted a failure of consideration and justified vacation by the tenant without liability for further rent. We reject the rule of *Stewart v. Childs Co.* and espouse *Higgins v. Whiting* as propounding the sounder doctrine. . . .

Similarly whether the landlord's default in the present case is treated as a substantial breach of the express covenant of quiet enjoyment resulting in a constructive eviction of the tenant or as a material failure of consideration, (i.e., such failure as amounts to a substantial interference with the beneficial enjoyment of the premises) the tenant's vacation was legal. Thus it is apparent from our discussion that a tenant's right to vacate leased premises is the same from a doctrinal standpoint whether treated as stemming from breach of a covenant of quiet enjoyment or from breach of any other dependent covenant. Both breaches constitute failure of consideration. The inference to be drawn from the cases is that the remedy of constructive eviction probably evolved from a desire by the courts to relieve the tenant from the harsh burden imposed by common law rules which applied principles of Caveat emptor to the letting, rejected an implied warranty of habitability, and ordinarily treated undertakings of the landlord in a lease as independent covenants. To alleviate the tenant's burden, the courts broadened the scope of the long-recognized implied covenant of quiet enjoyment (apparently designed originally to protect the tenant against ouster by a title superior to that of his lessor) to include the right of the tenant to have the beneficial enjoyment and use of the premises for the agreed term. It was but a short step then to the rule that when the landlord or someone acting for him or by virtue of a right acquired through him causes a substantial interference with that enjoyment and use, the tenant may claim a constructive eviction. In our view, therefore, at the present time whenever a tenant's right to vacate leased premises comes into existence because he is deprived of their beneficial enjoyment and use on account of acts chargeable to the landlord, it is immaterial whether the right is expressed in terms of breach of a covenant of quiet enjoyment, or material failure of consideration, or material breach of an implied warranty against latent defects.

Plaintiff's final claim is that assuming the tenant was exposed to a constructive eviction, she waived it by remaining on the premises for an unreasonable period of time thereafter. The general rule is, of course, that a tenant's right to claim a constructive eviction will be lost if he does not vacate the premises within a reasonable time after the right comes into existence. Weiss v. I. Zapinsky, Inc., 65 N.J. Super. 351, 167 A.2d 802 (App. Div. 1961); Duncan Development Co. v. Duncan Hardware, Inc., 34 N.J. Super. 293, 112 A.2d 274 (App. Div. 1955); 1 American Law of Property, supra, §3.51, p. 282. What constitutes a reasonable time depends upon the circumstances of each case. In considering the problem courts must be sympathetic toward the tenant's plight. Vacation of the premises is a drastic course and must be taken at his peril. If he vacates, and it is held at a later time in a suit for rent for the unexpired term that the landlord's course of action did not reach the dimensions of constructive eviction, a substantial liability may be imposed upon him. That risk and the practical inconvenience and difficulties attendant upon finding and moving to suitable quarters counsel caution.

Here, plaintiff's cooperative building manager died about nine months before the removal. During that period the tenant complained, patiently waited, hoped for relief from the landlord, and tried to take care of the water problem that accompanied the recurring rainstorms. But when relief did not come and the "crowning blow" put five inches of water in the leased offices and meeting rooms on December 20, 1961, the tolerance ended and the vacation came ten days later after notice to the landlord. The trial court found as a fact that under the circumstances such vacation was within a reasonable time, and the delay was not sufficient to establish a waiver of the constructive eviction. We find adequate evidence to support the conclusion and are of the view that the Appellate Division should not have reversed it....

For the reasons expressed above, we hold the view that the trial court was correct in deciding that defendant had been constructively evicted from the premises in question, and therefore was not liable for the rent claimed. Accordingly, the judgment of the Appellate Division is reversed and that of the trial court is reinstated.

■ POINTS TO CONSIDER

1. **The death of caveat lessee?** The court explicitly discusses the change in the nature of the landlord-tenant relationship, and places a burden on the landlord rather than the tenant to bear the risk of defective property. What is the court's rationale? Would this rationale apply equally well (or better) in the residential context? Some courts have chosen to ditch the property law doctrine of independence of covenants entirely. This has implications for constructive eviction doctrine. *See* Wesson v. Leone Enters., Inc., 774 N.E.2d 611 (Mass. 2002). The leased building in *Wesson* contained a leaky roof and provided only minimal heat. The tenant did not prove that these problems rendered the premises untenantable. The court nevertheless held for the tenant. The court stated, succinctly, "because we adopt the rule of mutually dependent covenants for commercial leases and conclude that the plaintiff landlord breached his covenant to maintain the roof, the tenant was entitled to terminate the lease and recover relocation costs." *Id.* at 615-16.

2. **Establish the elements.** Apply the elements of constructive eviction to the facts of *Reste Realty*. Where do you find weak spots?

3. **Constructive eviction requires a permanent interference that is substantial in nature.** If that is the case, how can the court call the interference in *Reste Realty* permanent? Was the water constantly in the premises?

4. **Time to go; how fast is fast enough?** The tenant in *Reste Realty* signed a lease in 1958, and then a second revised lease in 1959. The space accumulated water during the first year as soon as the first rainstorm occurred. The tenant signed the replacement lease with the landlord in 1959 despite the fact that the problem continued. Then Mr. Donigian—the agent for the landlord and the individual with whom the tenant had been dealing—died in 1961. The court ultimately holds for the tenant and suggests that the tenant had been constructively evicted. How is this possible? Shouldn't the tenant have vacated months before? *See, e.g.,* Bakersfield Laundry Ass'n v. Rubin, 280 P.2d 921 (Cal. Ct. App. 1955).

5. **Some courts are harsh; other courts are generous.** Consider the post–World War II case of Thirteenth & Washington Sts. Corp. v. Neslen, 254 P.2d 847 (Utah 1953). In *Neslen,* a law firm entered into a lease with the landlord for space in an office building. The lease required the building to be open from 8 A.M. until 9 P.M. The landlord also promised the tenant that the building would be "first class." This is an important promise to a law firm or other similar tenant. The tenant wishes to project prestige and success to existing and

future clients. "First class" status suggested that the building would help create this image for tenant. Unfortunately for the tenant, the landlord placed a shoeshine and barbershop at the entrance of the building. The court deemed the tenant constructively evicted, referring to these vendors as creating an "obstacle course" for the tenant and tenant's clients. The obstacle course so confused the lawyers' clients that they sometimes missed the entrance to the office building altogether. In addition, the attorneys and their clients could not get into the building early or after 8 P.M., notwithstanding the language in the lease, because the landlord did not unlock the building during the agreed-upon hours. Does this sound like a *substantial* interference to you? Is the "obstacle course" of a shoeshine and barbershop equivalent to water filling the leased premises as occurred in *Reste Realty*? Do you think that landlord constructively evicted tenant?

6. **What happens if the tenant does not vacate?** Think again about *Thirteenth & Washington Sts. Corp. v. Neslen*, discussed in the note above. The tenant stayed in its offices for quite some time after encountering the behavior of the landlord that ultimately drove the tenant from the building. This delay might have deprived the lawyers of their constructive eviction defense. Another court might have concluded that the tenant was not constructively evicted because the tenant continued to have use of the premises largely, if not completely, as promised. What happens if they decide to stay put? *See* Echo Consulting Servs., Inc. v. N. Conway Bank, 669 A.2d 227 (N.H. 1995).

7. **Is intent a factor?** Do we care whether the landlord intended to make the tenant so uncomfortable as to be forced to leave? Is the landlord's intent relevant to constructive eviction?

■ PROBLEM: PROTESTORS

➤ Dr. Smith signs a lease for a fixed term of five years for space owned by landlord Medical Offices. Dr. Smith is an OB/GYN.

➤ Dr. Smith becomes a source of local controversy because he performs abortions in his Medical Offices location. Crowds regularly gather in front of the building, as well as in the atrium lobby of the building, to protest his practice. These protests grow in size and intensity. Most protests take place on weekends, rather than during the work week. Protestors carry picket signs, distribute reading material, and attempt to discourage patients from entering the building. On several occasions, protestors proceed beyond the atrium and enter Dr. Smith's offices proper.

➤ Dr. Smith calls the landlord on many occasions to ask landlord to remove the protestors and to ensure that Dr. Smith's patients could access his office. The landlord responds by printing written statements that are distributed by its onsite agent. The statement instructs protestors that they

[handwritten margin note: — landlord can prov. only control who/what is actually on the property]

risk arrest and criminal prosecution for their behavior. Landlord does not provide security personnel on weekends, although the lease requires such personnel to be present.

➤ Dr. Smith ultimately vacates the premises after four weeks of protests and leases other space.

  ➤ Dr. Smith's lease contains the following provision: "Tenant, on paying Rent, shall and may peaceably and quietly have, hold and enjoy the Leased Premises for said term." The lease also contains a provision stating that the tenant shall use the office for the practice of medicine.

  ➤ Landlord files suit against Dr. Smith for rent and claims that the lease is in full force and effect.

Assume that you represent Dr. Smith. Advise your client of his position vis-à-vis Landlord. *See* Fidelity Mut. Life Ins. Co. v. Kaminsky, 768 S.W.2d 818 (Tex. Ct. App. 1989).

c. Minimum Levels of Habitability

Reste Realty involved a commercial lease. Commercial leases are subject to significant negotiation, and commercial tenants are often (but not always) represented by counsel. There is typically more money "on the table" than in a residential lease. In the residential scenario, the tenant is usually presented with a form document that he cannot negotiate: if he does not like it, he is free to find another apartment complex. Moreover, the typical residential tenant has even less ability than his commercial counterpart to fully examine the leased space in advance in a way that would reveal problems.

Finally, as important as commercial space is to the tenant (recall the sentiments of Mr. Di Sciullo and the loss of offices in the World Trade Center), a home is just that: a home. Even the most primitive apartment leased to a residential tenant is a home to the person living there. We value our homes in a much more personal manner than just about any other kind of property.

In the context of an individual person's leased home, the problem with the doctrine of quiet enjoyment, and the related defense of constructive eviction, is as follows: the tenant must move out and then discover, after being sued for rent,

> **Caveat Lessee**
>
> We will see in Chapter 7 that purchasers of property are subject to the rule of *caveat emptor*, or "buyer beware." Under the common law, the purchaser took property subject to any physical defects then existing in the property. The tenant also purchases an interest in property, even if it is less than the fee simple. And under the common law, the tenant was subjected to the same rule, now called *caveat lessee*. This landlord-tenant rule has been under sharp attack in residential leaseholds.

whether the court deems the tenant's departure justified. Imagine what this means to a financially strapped (i.e., *poor*) tenant. She may move into an apartment and make it her home, only to discover that her landlord does not repair or maintain her unit. In essence, she comes to realize that she is the tenant in the Langston Hughes poem reprinted at the start of this chapter. Of course, she could sue, but at most she will receive damages for the breach of the contract. She can leave, but the landlord is holding her security deposit, and she may not be able to scrape together enough cash to make a second deposit. And it is unlikely that this sort of landlord will return a deposit once he has it. If the tenant does leave, and is sued by the landlord, she will have to prove that she was constructively evicted. This is risky; if she loses, she will owe rent payments to both her old landlord and her new landlord. Moreover, if she holds down a job and/or is taking care of children, she will have little time for any of this. More likely, she will be willing to live with the problem while trying to fix it, but that will cost her the constructive eviction defense.

Is this fair and right? Should the law protect this tenant, and if so, how?

HILDER v. ST. PETER

478 A.2d 202 (1984)
Supreme Court of Vermont

BILLINGS, Chief Justice.

Defendants appeal from a judgment rendered by the Rutland Superior Court. The court ordered defendants to pay plaintiff damages in the amount of $4,945.00, which represented "reimbursement of all rent paid and additional compensatory damages" for the rental of a residential apartment over a fourteen month period in defendants' Rutland apartment building. . . .

The facts are uncontested. In October, 1974, plaintiff began occupying an apartment at defendants' 10-12 Church Street apartment building in Rutland with her three children and new-born grandson. Plaintiff orally agreed to pay defendant Stuart St. Peter $140 a month and a damage deposit of $50; plaintiff paid defendant the first month's rent and the damage deposit prior to moving in. Plaintiff has paid all rent due under her tenancy. Because the previous tenants had left behind garbage and items of personal belongings, defendant offered to refund plaintiff's damage deposit if she would clean the apartment herself prior to taking possession. Plaintiff did clean the apartment, but never received her deposit back because the defendant denied ever receiving it. Upon moving into the apartment, plaintiff discovered a broken kitchen window. Defendant promised to repair it, but after waiting a week and fearing that her two-year-old child might cut herself on the shards of glass, plaintiff repaired the window at her own expense. Although defendant promised to provide a front door key, he never did. For a period of time, whenever plaintiff left the apartment, a member of her family would remain behind for security reasons. Eventually, plaintiff purchased and installed a padlock, again at her own expense. After moving in, plaintiff discovered that the bathroom toilet was clogged with paper and feces and would flush only by dumping pails of water into it. Although plaintiff repeatedly complained about the toilet, and defendant promised to have it repaired, the toilet remained clogged and mechanically inoperable throughout the period of plaintiff's tenancy. In addition, the bathroom light and wall outlet were inoperable. Again, the defendant agreed to repair the fixtures, but never did. In order to have light in the bathroom, plaintiff attached a fixture to the wall and connected it to an extension cord that was plugged into an adjoining room. Plaintiff also discovered that water leaked from the water pipes of the upstairs apartment down the ceilings and walls of both her kitchen and back bedroom. Again, defendant promised to fix the leakage, but never did. As a result of this leakage, a large section of plaster fell from the back bedroom ceiling onto her bed and her grandson's crib. Other sections of plaster remained dangling from the ceiling. This condition was brought to the attention of the defendant, but he never corrected it. Fearing that the remaining plaster might fall when the room was occupied, plaintiff moved her and her grandson's bedroom furniture into the living room and ceased using the back bedroom. During the summer months an odor of raw sewage permeated plaintiff's apartment. The odor was so strong that the plaintiff was ashamed to have company in her apartment. Responding to plaintiff's complaints, Rutland City workers unearthed a broken sewage pipe in the basement of defendants' building. Raw sewage littered the floor of the basement, but defendant failed to clean it up. Plaintiff also discovered that the electric service for her furnace was attached to her breaker box, although defendant had agreed, at the commencement of plaintiff's tenancy, to furnish heat.

In its conclusions of law, the court held that the state of disrepair of plaintiff's apartment, which was known to the defendants, substantially reduced the value of the leasehold from the agreed rental value, thus constituting a breach of the implied warranty of habitability. The court based its award of damages on the breach of this warranty and on breach of an express contract. Defendant argues that the court misapplied the law of Vermont relating to habitability because the plaintiff never abandoned the demised premises and, therefore, it was error to award her the full amount of rent paid. Plaintiff counters that, while never expressly recognized by this Court, the trial court was correct in applying an implied warranty of habitability and that under this warranty, abandonment of the premises is not required. Plaintiff urges this Court to affirmatively adopt the implied warranty of habitability.

Historically, relations between landlords and tenants have been defined by the law of property. Under these traditional common law property concepts, a lease was viewed as a conveyance of real property. See Note, *Judicial Expansion of Tenants' Private Law Rights: Implied Warranties of Habitability and Safety in Residential Urban Leases*, 56 Cornell L.Q. 489, 489-90 (1971) (hereinafter cited as *Expansion of Tenants' Rights*). The relationship between landlord and tenant was controlled by the doctrine of caveat lessee; that is, the tenant took possession of the demised premises irrespective of their state of disrepair. Love, *Landlord's Liability for Defective Premises: Caveat Lessee, Negligence, or Strict Liability?*, 1975 Wis. L. Rev. 19, 27-28. The landlord's only covenant was to deliver possession to the tenant. The tenant's obligation to pay rent existed independently of the landlord's duty to deliver possession, so that as long as possession remained in the tenant, the tenant remained liable for payment of rent. The landlord was under no duty to render the premises habitable unless there was an express covenant to repair in the written lease. *Expansion of Tenants' Rights, supra,* at 490. The land, not the dwelling, was regarded as the essence of the conveyance.

An exception to the rule of caveat lessee was the doctrine of constructive eviction. Here, if the landlord wrongfully interfered with the tenant's enjoyment of the demised premises, or failed to render a duty to the tenant as expressly required under the terms of the lease, the tenant could abandon the premises and cease paying rent.

Beginning in the 1960's, American courts began recognizing that this approach to landlord and tenant relations, which had originated during the Middle Ages, had become an anachronism in twentieth century, urban society. Today's tenant enters into lease agreements, not to obtain arable land, but to obtain safe, sanitary and comfortable housing.

> [T]hey seek a well known package of goods and services—a package which includes not merely walls and ceilings, but also adequate heat, light and ventilation, serviceable plumbing facilities, secure windows and doors, proper sanitation, and proper maintenance.

Javins v. First National Realty Corp., 428 F.2d 1071, 1074 (D.C. Cir.), *cert. denied,* 400 U.S. 925 (1970).

Not only has the subject matter of today's lease changed, but the characteristics of today's tenant have similarly evolved. The tenant of the Middle Ages was a farmer, capable of making whatever repairs were necessary to his primitive dwelling. Additionally, "the common law courts assumed that an equal bargaining position existed between landlord and tenant. . . ." Note, *The Implied Warranty of Habitability: A Dream Deferred,* 48 UMKC L. Rev. 237, 238 (1980) (hereinafter cited as *A Dream Deferred*).

In sharp contrast, today's residential tenant, most commonly a city dweller, is not experienced in performing maintenance work on urban, complex living units. The landlord is more familiar with the dwelling unit and mechanical equipment attached to that unit, and is more financially able to "discover and cure" any faults and break-downs. . . . Tenants vying for this limited housing are "virtually powerless to compel the performance of essential services."

In light of these changes in the relationship between tenants and landlords, it would be wrong for the law to continue to impose the doctrine of caveat lessee on residential leases.

> The modern view favors a new approach which recognizes that a lease is essentially a contract between the landlord and the tenant wherein the landlord promises to deliver and maintain the demised premises in habitable condition and the tenant promises to pay rent for such habitable premises. These promises constitute interdependent and mutual considerations. Thus, the tenant's obligation to pay rent is

predicated on the landlord's obligation to deliver and maintain the premises in habitable condition.

Boston Housing Authority v. Hemingway, 363 Mass. 184, 198, 293 N.E.2d 831, 842 (1973).

Recognition of residential leases as contracts embodying the mutual covenants of habitability and payment of rent does not represent an abrupt change in Vermont law.... More significantly, our legislature, in establishing local housing authorities, 24 V.S.A. §4003, has officially recognized the need for assuring the existence of adequate housing.

> [S]ubstandard and decadent areas exist in certain portions of the state of Vermont and ... there is not ... an adequate supply of decent, safe and sanitary housing for persons of low income and/or elderly persons of low income, available for rents which such persons can afford to pay.... This situation tends to cause an increase and spread of communicable and chronic disease ... [and] constitutes a menace to the health, safety, welfare and comfort of the inhabitants of the state and is detrimental to property values in the localities in which it exists....

24 V.S.A. §4001(4). In addition, this Court has assumed the existence of an implied warranty of habitability in residential leases. Birkenhead v. Coombs, 143 Vt. 167, 172, 465 A.2d 244, 246 (1983).

Therefore, we now hold expressly that in the rental of any residential dwelling unit an implied warranty exists in the lease, whether oral or written, that the landlord will deliver over and maintain, throughout the period of the tenancy, premises that are safe, clean and fit for human habitation. This warranty of habitability is implied in tenancies for a specific period or at will. Additionally, the implied warranty of habitability covers all latent and patent defects in the essential facilities of the residential unit.[2] *Id.* Essential facilities are "facilities vital to the use of the premises for residential purposes...." Kline v. Burns, 111 N.H. 87, 92, 276 A.2d 248, 252 (1971). This means that a tenant who enters into a lease agreement with knowledge of any defect in the essential facilities cannot be said to have assumed the risk, thereby losing the protection of the warranty. Nor can this implied warranty of habitability be waived by any written provision in the lease or by oral agreement.

In determining whether there has been a breach of the implied warranty of habitability, the courts may first look to any relevant local or municipal housing code; they may also make reference to the minimum housing code standards enunciated in 24 V.S.A. §5003(c)(1)-5003(c)(5). A substantial violation of an applicable housing code shall constitute prima facie evidence that there has been a breach of the warranty of habitability. "[O]ne or two minor violations standing alone which do not affect" the health or safety of the tenant, shall be considered

---

[2] The warranty also covers those facilities located in the common areas of an apartment building or duplex that may affect the health or safety of a tenant, such as common stairways, or porches. Javins v. First National Realty Corp., supra, 428 F.2d at 1082 n.62; King v. Moorehead, 495 S.W.2d 65, 76 (Mo. Ct. App. 1973).

de minimus and not a breach of the warranty. In addition, the landlord will not be liable for defects caused by the tenant. Javins v. First National Realty Corp., *supra*, 428 F.2d at 1082 n.62.

However, these codes and standards merely provide a starting point in determining whether there has been a breach. Not all towns and municipalities have housing codes; where there are codes, the particular problem complained of may not be addressed. In determining whether there has been a breach of the implied warranty of habitability, courts should inquire whether the claimed defect has an impact on the safety or health of the tenant. *Id.*

In order to bring a cause of action for breach of the implied warranty of habitability, the tenant must first show that he or she notified the landlord "of the deficiency or defect not known to the landlord and [allowed] a reasonable time for its correction." King v. Moorehead, *supra*, 495 S.W.2d at 76.

Because we hold that the lease of a residential dwelling creates a contractual relationship between the landlord and tenant, the standard contract remedies of rescission, reformation and damages are available to the tenant when suing for breach of the implied warranty of habitability. The measure of damages shall be the difference between the value of the dwelling as warranted and the value of the dwelling as it exists in its defective condition. Birkenhead v. Coombs, *supra*, 143 Vt. at 172, 465 A.2d at 246. In determining the fair rental value of the dwelling as warranted, the court may look to the agreed upon rent as evidence on this issue. *Id.* "[I]n residential lease disputes involving a breach of the implied warranty of habitability, public policy militates against requiring expert testimony" concerning the value of the defect. *Id.* at 173, 465 A.2d at 247. The tenant will be liable only for "the reasonable rental value [if any] of the property in its imperfect condition during his period of occupancy." Berzito v. Gambino, 63 N.J. 460, 469, 308 A.2d 17, 22 (1973).

We also find persuasive the reasoning of some commentators that damages should be allowed for a tenant's discomfort and annoyance arising from the landlord's breach of the implied warranty of habitability. See Moskovitz, *The Implied Warranty of Habitability: A New Doctrine Raising New Issues*, 62 Calif. L. Rev. 1444, 1470-73 (1974) (hereinafter cited as *A New Doctrine*); *A Dream Deferred*, *supra*, at 250-51. Damages for annoyance and discomfort are reasonable in light of the fact that

> the residential tenant who has suffered a breach of the warranty . . . cannot bathe as frequently as he would like or at all if there is inadequate hot water; he must worry about rodents harassing his children or spreading disease if the premises are infested; or he must avoid certain rooms or worry about catching a cold if there is inadequate weather protection or heat. Thus, discomfort and annoyance are the common injuries caused by each breach and hence the true nature of the general damages the tenant is claiming.

Moskovitz, *A New Doctrine*, *supra*, at 1470-71. Damages for discomfort and annoyance may be difficult to compute; however, "[t]he trier [of fact] is not to be deterred from this duty by the fact that the damages are not susceptible of reduction to an exact money standard." Vermont Electric Supply Co. v. Andrus, 132 Vt. 195, 200, 315 A.2d 456, 459 (1974).

Another remedy available to the tenant when there has been a breach of the implied warranty of habitability is to withhold the payment of future rent.[3] The burden and expense of bringing suit will then be on the landlord who can better afford to bring the action. In an action for ejectment for nonpayment of rent, 12 V.S.A. §4773, "[t]he trier of fact, upon evaluating the seriousness of the breach and the ramification of the defect upon the health and safety of the tenant, will abate the rent at the landlord's expense in accordance with its findings." *A Dream Deferred, supra*, at 248. The tenant must show that: (1) the landlord had notice of the previously unknown defect and failed, within a reasonable time, to repair it; and (2) the defect, affecting habitability, existed during the time for which rent was withheld. See *A Dream Deferred, supra*, at 248-50. Whether a portion, all or none of the rent will be awarded to the landlord will depend on the findings relative to the extent and duration of the breach. Javins v. First National Realty Corp., *supra*, 428 F.2d at 1082-83. Of course, once the landlord corrects the defect, the tenant's obligation to pay rent becomes due again. *Id.* at 1083 n.64.

Additionally, we hold that when the landlord is notified of the defect but fails to repair it within a reasonable amount of time, and the tenant subsequently repairs the defect, the tenant may deduct the expense of the repair from future rent. 11 Williston on Contracts §1404 (3d ed. W. Jaeger 1968); Marini v. Ireland, 56 N.J. 130, 146, 265 A.2d 526, 535 (1970).

In addition to general damages, we hold that punitive damages may be available to a tenant in the appropriate case. Although punitive damages are generally not recoverable in actions for breach of contract, there are cases in which the breach is of such a willful and wanton or fraudulent nature as to make appropriate the award of exemplary damages. Clarendon Mobile Home Sales, Inc. v. Fitzgerald, *supra*, 135 Vt. at 596, 381 A.2d at 1065. A willful and wanton or fraudulent breach may be shown "by conduct manifesting personal ill will, or carried out under circumstances of insult or oppression, or even by conduct manifesting . . . a reckless or wanton disregard of [one's] rights. . . ." Sparrow v. Vermont Savings Bank, 95 Vt. 29, 33, 112 A. 205, 207 (1921). When a landlord, after receiving notice of a defect, fails to repair the facility that is essential to the health and safety of his or her tenant, an award of punitive damages is proper. 111 East 88th Partners v. Simon, 106 Misc. 2d 693, 434 N.Y.S.2d 886, 889 (N.Y. Civ. Ct. 1980).

> The purpose of punitive damages . . . is to punish conduct which is morally culpable. . . . Such an award serves to deter a wrongdoer . . . from repetitions of the same

---

[3] Because we hold that the tenant's obligation to pay rent is contingent on the landlord's duty to provide and maintain a habitable dwelling, it is no longer necessary for the tenant to first abandon the premises; thus, the doctrine of constructive eviction is no longer a viable or needed defense in an action by the landlord for unpaid rent. . . .

or similar actions. And it tends to encourage prosecution of a claim by a victim who might not otherwise incur the expense or inconvenience of private action. . . . The public benefit and a display of ethical indignation are among the ends of the policy to grant punitive damages.

Davis v. Williams, 92 Misc. 2d 1051, 402 N.Y.S.2d 92, 94 (N.Y. Civ. Ct. 1977).

In the instant case, the trial court's award of damages, based in part on a breach of the implied warranty of habitability, was not a misapplication of the law relative to habitability. Because of our holding in this case, the doctrine of constructive eviction, wherein the tenant must abandon in order to escape liability for rent, is no longer viable. When, as in the instant case, the tenant seeks, not to escape rent liability, but to receive compensatory damages in the amount of rent already paid, abandonment is similarly unnecessary. Northern Terminals, Inc. v. Smith Grocery & Variety, Inc., *supra*, 138 Vt. at 396-97, 418 A.2d at 26-27. Under our holding, when a landlord breaches the implied warranty of habitability, the tenant may withhold future rent, and may also seek damages in the amount of rent previously paid.

In its conclusions of law the trial court stated that the defendants' failure to make repairs was compensable by damages to the extent of reimbursement of all rent paid and additional compensatory damages. The court awarded plaintiff a total of $4,945.00; $3,445.00 represents the entire amount of rent plaintiff paid, plus the $50.00 deposit. This appears to leave $1500.00 as the "additional compensatory damages." However, although the court made findings which clearly demonstrate the appropriateness of an award of compensatory damages, there is no indication as to how the court reached a figure of $1500.00. It is "crucial that this Court and the parties be able to determine what was decided and how the decision was reached." Fox v. McLain, 142 Vt. 11, 16, 451 A.2d 1122, 1124 (1982).

Additionally, the court denied an award to plaintiff of punitive damages on the ground that the evidence failed to support a finding of willful and wanton or fraudulent conduct. The facts in this case, which defendants do not contest, evince a pattern of intentional conduct on the part of defendants for which the term "slumlord" surely was coined. Defendants' conduct was culpable and demeaning to plaintiff and clearly expressive of a wanton disregard of plaintiff's rights. The trial court found that defendants were aware of defects in the essential facilities of plaintiff's apartment, promised plaintiff that repairs would be made, but never fulfilled those promises. The court also found that plaintiff continued, throughout her tenancy, to pay her rent, often in the face of verbal threats made by defendant Stuart St. Peter. These findings point to the "bad spirit and wrong intention" of the defendants, Glidden v. Skinner, 142 Vt. 644, 648, 458 A.2d 1142, 1144 (1983), and would support a finding of willful and wanton or fraudulent conduct, contrary to the conclusions of law and judgment of the trial judge. However, the plaintiff did not appeal the court's denial of punitive damages, and issues not appealed and briefed are waived.

R. Brown & Sons, Inc. v. International Harvester Corp., 142 Vt. 140, 142, 453 A.2d 83, 84 (1982)....

Affirmed in part; reversed in part and remanded for hearing on additional compensable damages, consistent with the views herein.

■ POINTS TO CONSIDER

1. **Floor wax, dessert topping, or both?** *What is the essential nature of the implied warranty of habitability?* A warranty is contractual in nature. The implied warranty of habitability is said to exist because it reflects a modern understanding of the expectation of parties to a lease. The court in *Hilder* notes this change explicitly when it mentions what tenants expected in an agrarian society, and what tenants expect today. When contract law operates correctly, it enforces the expectations of parties to an agreement. The implied warranty of habitability suggests that, even if a lease fails to specify that the tenant expects a habitable property, both tenant and landlord know that this was intended. But note that the tenant in *Hilder* sued for punitive damages in addition to compensatory damages. Punitive damages typically result from *tort* actions. Indeed, tort lies quietly alongside contract law at the heart of the warranty. A landlord can reasonably foresee the damage that will result to a tenant if the premises are not habitable. This creates a duty enforceable in tort law. Under this approach, we say that the law should punish and deter a landlord who ignores significant risks to the health and safety of her tenant. Years ago, a *Saturday Night Live* sketch depicted a couple in their kitchen arguing over a new product called "Shimmer." One spouse used Shimmer to mop the floor, the other as a dessert topping. A spokesman for the product, played by Chevy Chase, emerged on set and settled the argument by happily explaining: "[It's] a floor wax and a dessert topping!" And so it is with the implied warranty of habitability: It's a contract remedy; it's a tort remedy; it's both.

2. **Distinguish the implied warranty of habitability from constructive eviction.** This is a mistake the landlord in *Hilder* makes right at the start. The landlord argued incorrectly that the tenant lost any rights she might have had because she did not vacate the unit. This goes to the heart of the implied warranty of habitability. Must the tenant leave the unit to argue a breach of the warranty? The answer is "No." Unlike constructive eviction, the tenant does not need to abandon the premises in order to make a claim under the implied warranty of habitability.

   Look back at the list of defects in the premises that the tenant in *Hilder* encountered. It was an undeniably terrible apartment. Imagine that you move to a new city to attend law school and that you rent an apartment, sight unseen, before arriving. You discover the exact same problems in your new apartment as the tenant did in *Hilder*. How long would you stay in the unit?

Would you last even one night? *Why then didn't the tenant in* Hilder *just leave?* A strong majority of states have adopted the implied warranty of habitability by court decision or statute. URLTA contains a statutory version of the warranty. Nevertheless, a few states hold tight to the older rule of *caveat lessee.* Tenants in these states are left with the difficult decision of whether to leave uninhabitable space and then defend the landlord's suit for rent with a claim that they were constructively evicted. *See, e.g.,* Ortega v. Flaim, 902 P.2d 199 (Wyo. 1995) (tenant's guest fell down stairs and brought suit against landlord; among other holdings, court rejected implied warranty of habitability); Martin v. Springdale Stores, Inc., 354 So. 2d 1144 (Ala. Civ. App. 1978) (faulty wiring in residential apartment led to a fire that damaged unit and landlord offered a replacement unit; court rejected implied warranty of habitability). The Alabama court stated, simply, that "as between the landlord and tenant, where there is no fraud, false representations or knowing concealment of defects, there is no implied covenant or warranty that the premises are suitable for occupation or for the particular use which the tenant intends to make or that they are in a safe condition to use." *Martin,* 354 So. 2d, at 1145- 46.

However, in states in which courts have maintained a rule of *caveat lessee,* the legislature may override this result and incorporate the implied warranty of habitability into statute. For example, the South Carolina Supreme Court rejected the implied warranty of habitability. *See* Young v. Morrisey, 329 S.E.2d 426 (S.C. 1985). A year later, the South Carolina legislature statutorily overruled *Young,* enacting the URLTA, codified at S.C. Code Ann. §27-40-440(a)(1) and (2) (2007). The South Carolina legislature made one change to the implied warranty of habitability as enacted in that state's version of the URLTA: It inserted the word "reasonably" into the requirement that landlord effect repairs necessary to make the premises fit and habitable. Section 2.104 of the URLTA provided that the landlord "shall . . . (2) make all repairs and do whatever is necessary to put and keep the premises in a fit and habitable condition . . . ." As enacted in South Carolina, that section requires that landlord shall "make all repairs and do whatever is *reasonably* necessary to put and keep the premises in a fit and habitable condition." How does this change to the URLTA alter the landlord's obligation to the tenant? States that enact model laws may choose to do so verbatim, or, as in this instance, the legislature may make changes.

3. **Find the test in *Hilder.*** Section 5.1 of the Restatement (Second) of Property: Landlord and Tenant (1977) adopts the implied warranty of habitability. That section says that the residential landlord must provide the tenant with property that is "suitable for residential use." This phrase is broad. Look back at *Hilder,* and consider again the parade of horribles that confronted the tenant. At some point, it just seems obvious that the premises were "unsuitable." No legal rule is workable without something approximating a test. Reading the opinion, you would rightfully assume that the landlord in *Hilder* would fail just about any test, but not all cases and fact patterns are so clear-cut. Comment e to Restatement §5.1 provides one test for unsuitability.

According to the Restatement, property is unsuitable if "it would be unsafe or unhealthy for the tenant to enter on the leased property and use it as a residence." The Restatement continues:

> It need not be shown that the leased premises were ever in a better condition than at the time the lease was made. A significant violation of any controlling building or sanitary code, or similar public regulation, which has a substantial impact upon safety or health, is conclusive proof that the premises are unsafe or unhealthy, but other modes of proof are acceptable.

What test did the court in *Hilder* use to determine whether the landlord's behavior violated the warranty? How does that test comport with the Restatement? In the absence of a specific local code provision governing the problem, is it possible for a tenant to show that the leased premises violate the implied warranty of habitability? Assume that Jerry leases a house to Daniel for a one-year term. Daniel notices that the roof makes buckling sounds whenever a winter storm leaves more than five inches of snow, which is a common occurrence in the region where the house is located. An engineer informs Daniel that the roof is not adequately supported and needs to be braced. Although unlikely, the roof may buckle catastrophically during a major winter storm. Daniel does not move out, but he does temporarily leave the home during winter storms. After several months of this activity, Daniel becomes fed up with moving to hotels whenever he sees snow. He asks you whether Jerry has violated the implied warranty of habitability. What is your answer? *See* Restatement (Second) of Property: Landlord and Tenant §5.1, illus. 6. Here is the test applied in one often-cited opinion:

> Among those factors to be considered in determining whether a breach is material are 1) whether the condition violates a housing law, regulation or ordinance; 2) the nature and seriousness of the defect; 3) the effect of the defect on safety and sanitation; 4) the length of time for which the condition has persisted; and 5) the age of the structure. This proposed list of factors is not designed to be exclusive; the lower court, in its discretion, may consider any other factors it deems appropriate.

Pugh v. Holmes, 384 A.2d 1234, 1240 (Pa. Super. Ct. 1978).

4. **Notice.** Often, the landlord will know of the problem that renders the premises "unsuitable" for habitation before the tenant encounters it. As the facts of *Hilder* make clear, the ugly nature of the defect will probably cause the tenant to complain (and complain loudly) to the landlord. Both the Restatement and court opinions suggest that the tenant must notify the landlord and give the landlord a reasonable period of time under the circumstances to effect a remedy. *See* Restatement (Second) of Property: Landlord and Tenant §5.1, cmt. d (1977) ("Landlord's knowledge of the condition"). What is "reasonable" is a matter of debate. The tenant will argue that the condition is both nasty and the type of which a landlord could fix quickly. The landlord may argue the opposite. Did the tenant give adequate notice to the landlord in *Hilder*?

5. **The tenant got back all of her money; how is that possible?** Let's just stipulate that the living conditions faced by the tenant in *Hilder* were bad—really, really bad. But at the same time, the tenant had a roof over her head (most of the time, anyway). She was not living on the street, or in a car, or in a shelter. She was miserable, but she had an apartment. The court determined that she was entitled to all of her rent back. According to the court, what value did the apartment provide to the tenant? From the perspective of an economist, is this correct? How does the court arrive at the conclusion that the tenant was entitled to all of her rent back? What test does the court use to determine *damages* under the implied warranty? Courts apply different tests. Some permit the tenant to recover the difference between the rental rate specifically set in the contract and the reasonable rental value of the property. *See generally* James Charles Smith, *Tenant Remedies for Breach of Habitability: Tort Dimensions of a Contract Concept*, 35 U. Kan. L. Rev. 505 (1987).

6. **A matter of tactics.** Assume that Ben lives in a jurisdiction that adopts the implied warranty of habitability. What should he do if presented with unsanitary or unhealthy premises? First, he may be forced to move out. If *Hilder* is correct, Ben can sue after the fact for compensatory damages (based on the formula in that case) and possibly punitive damages. He will argue that the lease was terminated due to the landlord's violation of the implied warranty. Unlike constructive eviction, not only will Ben defeat the landlord's demand for rent, he also will recover damages associated with that period of time in which he occupied uninhabitable premises. However, Ben may not be in a position to vacate his apartment. If he stays, he can continue to pay rent and then sue the landlord for damages associated with a breach of the warranty. Can you see why Ben will not be comfortable with this second alternative? What is Ben's more likely response? *See* Javins v. First Nat'l Realty Corp., 428 F.2d 1071 (D.C. Cir. 1970). Another powerful tenant remedy is *repair and deduct*, which the *Hilder* court authorizes. Rather than wait for the landlord to repair the dangerous electrical outlet or the broken window, the tenant can notify the landlord, wait a reasonable time, and then simply pay for the repair and deduct it from the rent. Note, however, that this remedy might be *too* powerful in some cases—the tenant may start making expensive repairs right and left. For that reason, the URLTA limits this remedy to "minor" defects, for which the repair costs less than half a month's rent. Other states are more generous, but still limit the remedy to certain types of repairs.

7. **Retaliatory eviction.** A landlord who violates the implied warranty of habitability is probably the kind of person who holds a grudge. Let's embellish the facts of *Hilder* (as if that were really possible). Assume that the tenant in *Hilder* is a tenant under a *month-to-month* lease. Recall that this means that the landlord may give the tenant a month's notice and terminate the lease. As you might guess, the landlord is unhappy with the tenant, and just two weeks after tenant wins her case against the landlord, the landlord notifies tenant

that he has decided to terminate the lease. Should the landlord be able to evict tenant? *See* Edwards v. Habib, 397 F.2d 687 (D.C. Cir. 1968), *cert. denied*, 393 U.S. 1016 (1969) (holding the eviction to be invalid and in retaliation for tenant's housing code complaints). Where adopted, the Uniform Residential Landlord and Tenant Act accomplishes by statute what *Habib* provides judicially and extends the protection to retaliatory increases in rent or decreases in services. URLTA §5.101.

Residential versus commercial. As we have seen, commercial tenants are sometimes treated differently from residential tenants. One theory underlying the implied warranty of habitability is that a residential tenant is simply not in an adequate position to evaluate the physical condition of the leased premises, and even if he could do so, is not capable (nor permitted) to alter the property to fix defects. To put it simply, residential tenants are thought to be at the mercy of their landlords. The Restatement (Second) of Property deliberately punted on the issue of whether the implied warranty would apply in commercial lease transactions. In a "caveat" directly following the text of §5.1, the Restatement provides: "The Institute takes no position at this time as to whether the rule of this section is or should be available to the tenant of property leased for commercial or industrial purposes." Restatement (Second) of Property: Landlord and Tenant §5.1 (1977). The Reporter for the Restatement (Second) of Property, Professor A. James Casner, explained that "the failure to so extend [the rule to commercial leases] is not to be taken as any indication that it should or should not be so extended," and noted that parties to commercial leases are "free to modify the rule by arm's length agreement." Restatement (Second) of Property: Landlord and Tenant §5.1, reporter's note 2 (1977). In the years following adoption of the Restatement (Second) of Property, the implied warranty of habitability has been confined largely to residential leases. *See, e.g.*, J.B. Stein & Co. v. Sandberg, 419 N.E.2d 652 (Ill. App. Ct. 1981) (declining to extend the IWH to commercial leases). Texas seems to have moved in the direction of applying the warranty, in a somewhat modified form, in commercial leaseholds. *See* Davidow v. Inwood N. Prof'l Grp., 747 S.W.2d 373 (Tex. 1988) (poor air conditioning, leaky roof, mildewed carpet; court finds an implied warranty of "suitability" in commercial leases).

Do you think the same policies that justify implying a warranty as to condition of the property in a residential lease apply to a commercial lease? If you and friends start a law firm immediately upon graduation from law school, and lease a small office, would you be in a better or worse position than a residential tenant? What if the tenant is "big box retailer" and leases a large building for a 15-year term? Would that tenant be in a better or worse position than the typical residential tenant? *See* Fred William Bopp III, *The Unwarranted Implication of a Warranty of Fitness in Commercial Leases—An Alternative Approach*, 41 Vand. L. Rev. 1057 (1988).

Let's test some of the limits of the implied warranty of habitability.

■ PROBLEM: MOM AND POP'S LIQUOR STORE

[handwritten margin notes: • implied warranty at least applies to 2nd floor—used be residential—need to give reasonable time • if not, caveat constructive eviction.]

David and Kay own a liquor and convenience store near a major urban university in New Mexico. They sell many things that students need and look for on a daily basis (and many of the things their parents rather hope their children do not buy). David and Kay lease the first floor of a two-story building to house their store. By a separate lease document, David and Kay lease the second story as their residential apartment. The building is served by a single central air conditioning system.

During a brutally hot September, the air conditioning fails. David and Kay quickly telephone the landlord to notify him of the problem. The landlord responds: "Look, just open the front and back door and let the breeze come in; those students do not really care about air conditioning. I will get to the air conditioning unit in your building later in the month."

➤ David and Kay leave the front and back doors open but the temperature in the store rises to 90 degrees during the day. In fact, the students do care, and begin to patronize a convenience store that is further away from the university but air conditioned. Worse, the temperature in their second-story apartment reaches 100 degrees in the day and falls only a bit at night.

David and Kay ask you for advice. How should they respond to the landlord's behavior? What steps are open to them? *See* Charles E. Burt, Inc. v. Seven Grand Corp., 163 N.E.2d 4 (Mass. 1959).

■ PROBLEM: THE VERY DESPERATE DAD

➤ Daniel, a single dad with two children, loses his job at an automobile manufacturing plant and cannot make his mortgage payment. As a result, Daniel loses his home to foreclosure. With little money in the bank, and no salary, Daniel begins to search for an apartment and a job.

➤ Daniel finds a job as a handyman, but it pays only a fraction of his prior employment.

➤ Greg, Daniel's friend, owns a dilapidated house that needs serious repair. The ceiling leaks, the plumbing is unreliable, and there is obvious mold in corners of closets. Daniel asks Greg if he can lease the house.

➤ Here is their conversation:

■ Greg: "Daniel, you are a good friend. I simply cannot lease you that house. It is a dump and it is unsafe. I would be worried every day about the safety of your kids. I simply cannot do it."

■ Daniel: "Greg, I cannot afford anything else. I need a place to live, and I am a handyman. I can keep the house functioning, although some of the problems are beyond my ability to remedy. But here is the cruel truth; if you do not lease me the house, my kids and I will be on the street. I am not making this up. I really have no resources to lease any other place. Please, I am *begging you, for the love of God*, rent me the house."

➤ Greg relents and leases the house to Daniel at a low rent, thinking it will at least be enough to pay the taxes and the utility bills.

➤ One year later, Daniel gets a real job and moves to a new and better home. Daniel then sues Greg for return of his rental payments, alleging a violation of the implied warranty of habitability.

Greg contacts you for advice. What is his position vis-à-vis Daniel? Does Greg have a leg to stand on? *See* Restatement (Second) of Property: Landlord and Tenant §5.6 (1977). Does this problem suggest a policy drawback to the implied warranty of habitability? *But see* URLTA §2.104(c) (tenant may take on limited duty to repair). Would your answer change if Daniel begged Greg to lease Daniel a similarly dilapidated *commercial* premises for Daniel's business? Why or why not? *See* Gym-N-I Playgrounds, Inc. v. Snider, 220 S.W.3d 905 (Tex. 2007).

■ PROBLEM: ASSAULTS AND CRIME

➤ Debra is a student at a community college and is a tenant in Garden Apartments.

➤ The apartment project is old and is not gated.

➤ One evening, Debra returns from school and parks her car in a parking area designated for residents. While still in her car, a man forcibly enters the vehicle and assaults her.

➤ The assailant is arrested and criminally prosecuted, but he has no money and a civil trial against him for damages is useless.

➤ Debra therefore brings a suit against landlord based on a breach of the implied warranty of habitability

Advise the landlord. *See* Walls v. Oxford Mgmt. Co., Inc., 633 A.2d 103 (N.H. 1993).

2. Tenant's Duties and the Consequences of Failure

Now that we have looked at the obligations of the landlord to the tenant, it seems only fair to discuss the primary obligations of the tenant to landlord. Keep in mind that the driving point of lease law is that the landlord conveys to tenant an exclusive right to possession in particular real property. The landlord anticipates that the tenant will make good on his promise to pay rent. In addition, from the moment the tenant takes possession of the property, the tenant controls something of tremendous value to the landlord—the real property that makes up the leased premises. Not surprisingly, the landlord expects that the tenant will take physical care of the premises. The lease may expressly place other duties on the tenant, but the duty to pay rent and the duty to avoid waste arise uniformly in lease arrangements.

Much of the time, the question of whether a tenant has breached a lease is not in doubt. The tenant either ceases to pay rent while occupying the premises or ceases to pay rent and vacates the premises. When the tenant stops paying rent and stays put in the property, the tenant is inviting an eviction proceeding. Generally speaking, a tenant should not presume to be able to stay in his leased premises when he stops paying rent without a valid reason.

The tenant who simply vacates (or announces his intention to vacate) the premises prior to expiration of the term presents the harder question.

a. "I Surrender"; Giving Back the Keys and Walking Away

We have already described one important landlord election in this chapter: if a tenant holds over, the landlord can treat the tenant as a trespasser or as a tenant under a new lease. Something similar occurs when a tenant abandons the premises. *Abandonment* means that a tenant walks away from the premises and relinquishes any intention to return. A tenant who abandons leased premises typically stops paying rent. The landlord granted the tenant the exclusive right to possession; this fact does not change just because the tenant chooses temporarily to vacate the property. However, if the tenant *abandons*, the landlord has another election under the common law. The landlord may treat the lease as continuing and in full force and effect. If the landlord chooses to do so, rent continues to accrue and the landlord may sue tenant for rent until the end of the term.

On the other hand, the landlord may choose to "accept surrender" of the premises. This means that the landlord treats the lease as terminated from the moment of acceptance. This usually plays out as follows: tenant sends landlord a letter informing landlord that tenant is leaving the space and enclosing the keys. The tenant will then ask the landlord to treat the lease as terminated. If the landlord accepts surrender, the landlord can sue the tenant for any damage to the premises and unpaid back rent, but landlord cannot sue for future rents because the lease no longer exists. Taking the keys is akin to accepting a check; a landlord that accepts keys appears to have acquiesced to termination of the leasehold. But this is not always the case. The landlord may wish to retake the space, if only to make sure that it is safe and maintained.

Landlord's Response to the Tenant's Abandonment of the Premises

1. The landlord may "accept surrender" and terminate the lease; the landlord will not be entitled to future rents, but can recover past due rents.

2. The landlord may reject surrender. The jurisdictions are split on the effect of the landlord's decision to reject surrender:

- In most jurisdictions, under a modern contract law approach, the landlord would be *required* to use reasonable efforts to find a replacement tenant in order to mitigate damages from the breach of the lease.
- In jurisdictions holding fast to the common law, the landlord may choose to leave the premises vacant and continue to hold the tenant liable for rent for the remainder of the term.

Put yourself in the shoes of the landlord after being told that a tenant is vacating leased space: you would want to enter the premises to make sure that it is "locked down and safe." However, you might not want the lease to automatically terminate just because you are acting as a responsible landlord. Your chief concern, after assuring the safe maintenance of the premises, is money. You want to take steps that are likely to bring you the most money, in rent or damages, as possible. Therefore, the landlord may hold the keys (and possession) for the tenant in order to secure the property without accepting surrender. But if this is the course the landlord wishes to take, it must make clear to the tenant that the landlord is just acting out of caution and does not view taking the keys as termination.

The Market

If the landlord relets "for the benefit of tenant," all of the money that the landlord receives from the replacement tenant really belongs to the original tenant. If the market has plummeted, it is unlikely that a landlord will find a replacement tenant at the rental rate that the breaching tenant is obligated to pay. The landlord should not accept surrender and should instead relet for the tenant's benefit. This way, the landlord can pursue the tenant for the difference between the rent the landlord actually receives and the contract amount owed by the tenant. But if the market rate has *increased*, then it would be a mistake for the landlord to relet for the tenant's benefit, because the "profit" will belong to the tenant. It makes more sense for the landlord to simply accept surrender, and then rent to the new tenant at a higher rate, and keep all of the rents.

Early in this chapter, we explained that contract law and property law can lead to very different results. We see this conflict very clearly when looking at the obligations of the landlord when the tenant departs before the end of the term. If the tenant ditches the premises and the landlord finds itself in control of the property, can the landlord just allow the property to remain vacant and continue to demand rent? Or must the landlord try to find a tenant for the space in an effort to offset the rent?

The opinion below addresses that question in two separate cases: *Sommer* and *Riverview Realty Co.* These two cases do not present similarly sympathetic tenants, even if the two cases implicate the same basic legal proposition. The court combined the cases so that it could resolve the key legal issue.

SOMMER v. KRIDEL

378 A.2d 767 (1977)
Supreme Court of New Jersey

PASHMAN, J.

We granted certification in these cases to consider whether a landlord seeking damages from a defaulting tenant is under a duty to mitigate damages by making reasonable efforts to re-let an apartment wrongfully vacated by the tenant. . . .

I.

A.

Sommer v. Kridel

This case was tried on stipulated facts. On March 10, 1972 the defendant, James Kridel, entered into a lease with the plaintiff, Abraham Sommer, owner of the "Pierre Apartments" in Hackensack, to rent apartment 6-L in that building.[4] The term of the lease was from May 1, 1972 until April 30, 1974, with a rent concession for the first six weeks, so that the first month's rent was not due until June 15, 1972.

One week after signing the agreement, Kridel paid Sommer $690. Half of that sum was used to satisfy the first month's rent. The remainder was paid under the lease provision requiring a security deposit of $345. Although defendant had expected to begin occupancy around May 1, his plans were changed. He wrote to Sommer on May 19, 1972, explaining

> I was to be married on June 3, 1972. Unhappily the engagement was broken and the wedding plans cancelled. Both parents were to assume responsibility for the rent after our marriage. I was discharged from the U.S. Army in October 1971 and am now a student. I have no funds of my own, and am supported by my stepfather.

---

[4] Among other provisions, the lease prohibited the tenant from assigning or transferring the lease without the consent of the landlord. If the tenant defaulted, the lease gave the landlord the option of re-entering or re-letting, but stipulated that failure to re-let or to recover the full rental would not discharge the tenant's liability for rent.

In view of the above, I cannot take possession of the apartment and am surrendering all rights to it. Never having received a key, I cannot return same to you.

I beg your understanding and compassion in releasing me from the lease, and will of course, in consideration thereof, forfeit the 2 month's rent already paid.

Please notify me at your earliest convenience.

Plaintiff did not answer the letter.

Subsequently, a third party went to the apartment house and inquired about renting apartment 6-L. Although the parties agreed that she was ready, willing and able to rent the apartment, the person in charge told her that the apartment was not being shown since it was already rented to Kridel. In fact, the landlord did not re-enter the apartment or exhibit it to anyone until August 1, 1973. At that time it was rented to a new tenant for a term beginning on September 1, 1973. The new rental was for $345 per month with a six week concession similar to that granted Kridel.

Prior to re-letting the new premises, plaintiff sued Kridel in August 1972, demanding $7,590, the total amount due for the full two-year term of the lease. Following a mistrial, plaintiff filed an amended complaint asking for $5,865, the amount due between May 1, 1972 and September 1, 1973. The amended complaint included no reduction in the claim to reflect the six week concession provided for in the lease or the $690 payment made to plaintiff after signing the agreement. Defendant filed an amended answer to the complaint, alleging that plaintiff breached the contract, failed to mitigate damages and accepted defendant's surrender of the premises. He also counterclaimed to demand repayment of the $345 paid as a security deposit.

The trial judge ruled in favor of defendant. Despite his conclusion that the lease had been drawn to reflect "the 'settled law' of this state," he found that "justice and fair dealing" imposed upon the landlord the duty to attempt to re-let the premises and thereby mitigate damages. He also held that plaintiff's failure to make any response to defendant's unequivocal offer of surrender was tantamount to an acceptance, thereby terminating the tenancy and any obligation to pay rent. As a result, he dismissed both the complaint and the counterclaim. The Appellate Division reversed in a per curiam opinion, 153 N.J.Super. 1 (1976), and we granted certification. 69 N.J. 395, 354 A.2d 323 (1976).

B.

Riverview Realty Co. v. Perosio

This controversy arose in a similar manner. On December 27, 1972, Carlos Perosio entered into a written lease with plaintiff Riverview Realty Co. The agreement covered the rental of apartment 5-G in a building owned by the realty company at 2175 Hudson Terrace in Fort Lee. As in the companion case, the lease prohibited the tenant from subletting or assigning the apartment without the consent of the landlord. It was to run for a two-year term, from February 1, 1973 until January 31, 1975, and provided for a monthly rental of $450. The defendant took possession of the apartment and occupied it until February 1974. At that time he vacated the premises, after having paid the rent through January 31, 1974.

The landlord filed a complaint on October 31, 1974, demanding $4,500 in payment for the monthly rental from February 1, 1974 through October 31, 1974. Defendant answered the complaint by alleging that there had been a valid surrender of the premises and that plaintiff failed to mitigate damages. The trial court granted the landlord's motion for summary judgment against the defendant, fixing the damages at $4,050 plus $182.25 interest.

The Appellate Division affirmed the trial court, holding that it was bound by prior precedents, including Joyce v. Bauman, *supra.* 138 N.J. Super. 270, 350 A.2d 517 (App. Div. 1976). Nevertheless, it freely criticized the rule which it found itself obliged to follow:

> There appears to be no reason in equity or justice to perpetuate such an unrealistic and uneconomic rule of law which encourages an owner to let valuable rented space lie fallow because he is assured of full recovery from a defaulting tenant. Since courts in New Jersey and elsewhere have abandoned ancient real property concepts and applied ordinary contract principles in other conflicts between landlord and tenant there is no sound reason for a continuation of a special real property rule to the issue of mitigation.... (138 N.J. Super. at 273-74, 350 A.2d at 519; citations omitted).

...

II.

As the lower courts in both appeals found, the weight of authority in this State supports the rule that a landlord is under no duty to mitigate damages caused by a defaulting tenant. *See* Joyce v. Bauman, *supra.* ... This rule has been followed in a majority of states, Annot. 21 A.L.R.3d 534, §2(a) at 541 (1968), and has been tentatively adopted in the American Law Institute's Restatement of Property. Restatement (Second) of Property, §11.1(3) (Tent. Draft No. 3, 1975).

Nevertheless, while there is still a split of authority over this question, the trend among recent cases appears to be in favor of a mitigation requirement....

The majority rule is based on principles of property law which equate a lease with a transfer of a property interest in the owner's estate. Under this rationale the lease conveys to a tenant an interest in the property which forecloses any control by the landlord; thus, it would be anomalous to require the landlord to concern himself with the tenant's abandonment of his own property. Wright v. Baumann, 239 Or. 410, 398 P.2d 119, 120-21 (1965).

For instance, in Muller v. Beck, *supra*, where essentially the same issue was posed, the court clearly treated the lease as governed by property, as opposed to contract, precepts.[5] The court there observed that the "tenant had an estate

---

[5] It is well settled that a party claiming damages for a breach of contract has a duty to mitigate his loss....

for years, but it was an estate qualified by this right of the landlord to prevent its transfer," 94 N.J.L. at 313, 110 A. at 832, and that "the tenant has an estate with which the landlord may not interfere." Id. at 314, 110 A. at 832. Similarly, in Heckel v. Griese, *supra*, the court noted the absolute nature of the tenant's interest in the property while the lease was in effect, stating that "when the tenant vacated, . . . no one, in the circumstances, had any right to interfere with the defendant's possession of the premises." 12 N.J. Misc. at 213, 171 A. 148, 149. Other cases simply cite the rule announced in Muller v. Beck, *supra*, without discussing the underlying rationale. . . .

Yet the distinction between a lease for ordinary residential purposes and an ordinary contract can no longer be considered viable. As Professor Powell observed, evolving "social factors have exerted increasing influence on the law of estates for years." 2 Powell on Real Property (1977 ed.), §221(1) at 180-81. The result has been that

> (t)he complexities of city life, and the proliferated problems of modern society in general, have created new problems for lessors and lessees and these have been commonly handled by specific clauses in leases. This growth in the number and detail of specific lease covenants has reintroduced into the law of estates for years a predominantly contractual ingredient. (Id. at 181.)

Application of the contract rule requiring mitigation of damages to a residential lease may be justified as a matter of basic fairness.[6] Professor McCormick first commented upon the inequity under the majority rule when he predicted in 1925 that eventually

> the logic, inescapable according to the standards of a "jurisprudence of conceptions" which permits the landlord to stand idly by the vacant, abandoned premises and treat them as the property of the tenant and recover full rent, [will] yield to the more realistic notions of social advantage which in other fields of the law have forbidden a recovery for damages which the plaintiff by reasonable efforts could have avoided. (McCormick, "The Rights of the Landlord Upon Abandonment of the Premises by the Tenant," 23 Mich. L. Rev. 211, 221-22 (1925).)

Various courts have adopted this position. *See* Annot., *supra*, §7(a) at 565, and *ante* at 770-771.

The pre-existing rule cannot be predicated upon the possibility that a landlord may lose the opportunity to rent another empty apartment because he must first rent the apartment vacated by the defaulting tenant. Even where the breach occurs in a multi-dwelling building, each apartment may have unique qualities which make it attractive to certain individuals. Significantly, in *Sommer v. Kridel*, there was a specific request to rent the apartment vacated by the defendant;

---

[6] We see no distinction between the leases involved in the instant appeals and those which might arise in other types of residential housing. However, we reserve for another day the question of whether a landlord must mitigate damages in a commercial setting. . . .

there is no reason to believe that absent this vacancy the landlord could have succeeded in renting a different apartment to this individual.

We therefore hold that antiquated real property concepts which served as the basis for the pre-existing rule, shall no longer be controlling where there is a claim for damages under a residential lease. Such claims must be governed by more modern notions of fairness and equity. A landlord has a duty to mitigate damages where he seeks to recover rents due from a defaulting tenant.

If the landlord has other vacant apartments besides the one which the tenant has abandoned, the landlord's duty to mitigate consists of making reasonable efforts to re-let the apartment. In such cases he must treat the apartment in question as if it was one of his vacant stock.

As part of his cause of action, the landlord shall be required to carry the burden of proving that he used reasonable diligence in attempting to re-let the premises. We note that there has been a divergence of opinion concerning the allocation of the burden of proof on this issue. See Annot., *supra*, §12 at 577. While generally in contract actions the breaching party has the burden of proving that damages are capable of mitigation, *see* Sandler v. Lawn-A-Mat Chem. & Equip. Corp., 141 N.J. Super. 437, 455, 358 A.2d 805 (App. Div. 1976); McCormick, Damages, §33 at 130 (1935), here the landlord will be in a better position to demonstrate whether he exercised reasonable diligence in attempting to re-let the premises. *Cf.* Kulm v. Coast to Coast Stores Central Org., 248 Or. 436, 432 P.2d 1006 (1967) (burden on lessor in contract to renew a lease).

III.

The *Sommer v. Kridel* case presents a classic example of the unfairness which occurs when a landlord has no responsibility to minimize damages. Sommer waited 15 months and allowed $4658.50 in damages to accrue before attempting to re-let the apartment. Despite the availability of a tenant who was ready, willing and able to rent the apartment, the landlord needlessly increased the damages by turning her away. While a tenant will not necessarily be excused from his obligations under a lease simply by finding another person who is willing to rent the vacated premises, *see, e.g.*, Reget v. Dempsey-Tegler & Co., 70 Ill. App. 2d 32, 216 N.E.2d 500 (Ill. App. 1966) (new tenant insisted on leasing the premises under different terms); Edmands v. Rust & Richardson Drug Co., 191 Mass. 123, 77 N.E. 713 (1906) (landlord need not accept insolvent tenant), here there has been no showing that the new tenant would not have been suitable. We therefore find that plaintiff could have avoided the damages which eventually accrued, and that the defendant was relieved of his duty to continue paying rent. Ordinarily we would require the tenant to bear the cost of any reasonable expenses incurred by a landlord in attempting to re-let the premises, see Ross v. Smigelski, *supra*, 166 N.W.2d at 248-49; 22 Am. Jur. 2d, Damages, §169 at 238, but no such expenses were incurred in this case.

In *Riverview Realty Co. v. Perosio*, no factual determination was made regarding the landlord's efforts to mitigate damages, and defendant contends that

Holding for
K.K.

plaintiff never answered his interrogatories. Consequently, the judgment is reversed and the case remanded for a new trial. Upon remand and after discovery has been completed, . . . the trial court shall determine whether plaintiff attempted to mitigate damages with reasonable diligence,. . .and if so, the extent of damages remaining and assessable to the tenant. As we have held above, the burden of proving that reasonable diligence was used to re-let the premises shall be upon the plaintiff. See Annot., *supra*, §11 at 575.

In assessing whether the landlord has satisfactorily carried his burden, the trial court shall consider, among other factors, whether the landlord, either personally or through an agency, offered or showed the apartment to any prospective tenants, or advertised it in local newspapers. Additionally, the tenant may attempt to rebut such evidence by showing that he proffered suitable tenants who were rejected. However, there is no standard formula for measuring whether the landlord has utilized satisfactory efforts in attempting to mitigate damages, and each case must be judged upon its own facts. Compare Hershorin v. La Vista, Inc., 110 Ga. App. 435, 138 S.E.2d 703 (App. 1964) ("reasonable effort" of landlord by showing the apartment to all prospective tenants); Carpenter v. Wisniewski, 139 Ind. App. 325, 215 N.E.2d 882 (App. 1966) (duty satisfied where landlord advertised the premises through a newspaper, placed a sign in the window, and employed a realtor); Re Garment Center Capitol, Inc., 93 F.2d 667, 115 A.L.R. 202 (2 Cir. 1938) (landlord's duty not breached where higher rental was asked since it was known that this was merely a basis for negotiations); Foggia v. Dix, 265 Or. 315, 509 P.2d 412, 414 (1973) (in mitigating damages, landlord need not accept less than fair market value or "substantially alter his obligations as established in the pre-existing lease"); with Anderson v. Andy Darling Pontiac, Inc., 257 Wis. 371, 43 N.W.2d 362 (1950) (reasonable diligence not established where newspaper advertisement placed in one issue of local paper by a broker); Scheinfeld v. Muntz T.V., Inc., 67 Ill. App. 2d 8, 214 N.E.2d 506 (Ill. App. 1966) (duty breached where landlord refused to accept suitable subtenant); Consolidated Sun Ray, Inc. v. Oppenstein, 335 F.2d 801, 811 (8 Cir. 1964) (dictum) (demand for rent which is "far greater than the provisions of the lease called for" negates landlord's assertion that he acted in good faith in seeking a new tenant).

IV.

The judgment in *Sommer v. Kridel* is reversed. In *Riverview Realty Co. v. Perosio*, the judgment is reversed and the case is remanded to the trial court for proceedings in accordance with this opinion.

■ POINTS TO CONSIDER

1. **On the facts.** Take a moment and distinguish the factual scenarios presented by the two cases decided by the court. Why is *Sommer* simply reversed, while the court reverses and remands *Riverview Realty Co.* for further consideration

by the trial court? Why would Mr. Sommer (the landlord) simply refuse to accept surrender as he did? What reasons can you surmise for this sort of behavior? Does the nature of the economy and the market come into play?

2. **Competing rules.** The two sister cases in *Sommer* present the scenario of the tenant who does not occupy the space—either because the tenant never moves into the space in the first place (*Sommer*), or moves in but later vacates (*Riverview Realty Co.*). The landlord refused surrender and did not terminate the lease. This is why the case presents, in stark relief, the question of whether the landlord must try to mitigate damages. What rule does the court adopt, and what impact will the choice of rule have on landlord behavior? *See* Restatement (Second) of Property: Landlord and Tenant §12.1 (1977). Note again the divide between contract law and property law. Can you see property law reasons for the older no-mitigation rule? What reasons underlie the newer contract-based mitigation rule? At the time *Sommer* arose, the older common law no-mitigation rule was the majority rule. This is no longer the case. A prominent case addressing this issue is Austin Hill Country Realty, Inc. v. Palisades Plaza, Inc., 948 S.W.2d 293 (Tex. 1997), in which the Texas Supreme Court adopted a duty to mitigate. The court exhaustively reviewed the status of the mitigation rule and concluded: "Forty-two states and the District of Columbia have recognized that a landlord has a duty to mitigate damages in at least some situations: when there is a breach of a residential lease, a commercial lease, or both." *Id.* at 296. The Texas Supreme Court apparently persuaded its legislature. The Texas legislature codified the requirement that a landlord take steps to mitigate damages from tenant's breach of the contract. *See* Tex. Prop. Code Ann. §91.006(a) (West 2007). *See also*, White v. Harrison, 390 S.W.3d 666, 675 (Tex. Ct. App. 2012) ("The rule in *Palisades Plaza* has since been codified.")

3. **What constitutes acceptance of surrender?** The only reason that the landlord in either *Sommer* or *Riverview Realty Co.* might be subject to a duty to find a replacement tenant is that in each case the landlord was not willing to accept surrender by the tenant. What actions or inaction on the part of landlord constitute acceptance of surrender? The answer has to do with *landlord's intent*: do landlord's actions or inaction suggest his *intent* to accept surrender of the premises and the lease? According to the trial court, what landlord behavior constituted acceptance of surrender in the *Sommer* fact pattern?

Which of the following landlord actions should be deemed by a court as an acceptance of surrender?

■ The tenant slips the keys under the landlord's door along with a check marked "final payment," which the landlord cashes. The landlord keeps the keys.

- The tenant slips the keys under the landlord's door along with a check marked "final payment," which the landlord does not cash but does not return. The landlord keeps the keys.
- The tenant slips the keys under the landlord's door along with a check marked "final payment," which the landlord cashes. But the landlord then sends tenant a letter saying that acceptance of the keys and cashing of the check is not acceptance of surrender.
- The tenant slips the keys under the door. The landlord keeps the keys. The landlord leases the unit to a third party.

4. **Landlord and tenant view "reasonable steps" to mitigate very differently.** What is "reasonable" is in the eyes of the beholder. If a court adopts the modern contract approach, then the landlord will interpret "reasonable steps" very narrowly; the tenant will take a diametrically opposed position. A court determining whether a landlord has taken reasonable steps will typically examine acts customarily undertaken by landlords to rent space.

   ➢ Assume the following: Jerry lives in a mitigation-rule jurisdiction and leases an apartment from Daniel for a two-year term. However, one month into the term, Jerry receives a job offer "too good to be true" from a company on the other side of the country. Jerry orders a moving truck and high-tails it to his new city. He sends Daniel an email from the road explaining that he has moved out and asking that Daniel "take steps to fill my apartment, so that I do not owe you any more rent than necessary." Daniel does not respond to Jerry directly, but he does list the unit as "available for rent" on his company web page, along with all of the other units in his building that are vacant. Daniel's web page listings include photographs of some, but not all, of his vacant units. There is no photograph for the listing of Jerry's unit. Because Jerry moved out so suddenly, the unit has that "lived-in look." Daniel does not have it repainted, but he does have his maintenance service do a routine cleaning. Ultimately, ten individuals visit Daniel's building looking for an apartment unit. Daniel takes these individuals on a tour of the available apartment units—and he visits Jerry's unit on two out of ten occasions. Jerry's entire term passes and Daniel is not successful in renting out Jerry's unit. Has Daniel acted "reasonably" in an attempt to mitigate damages?
   ➢ Let's change the question a bit. What if one of the ten individuals offers to lease the space from Daniel, *but at 70 percent of the rent that Jerry is required to pay under his lease.* Daniel responds to the offer by saying, "That is just ridiculously low. I would be a fool to accept. I reject the offer." Has Daniel failed the mitigation requirement?

5. **Burden of proof.** Is it the landlord's burden to show that he reasonably mitigated, or the tenant's burden to show that the landlord failed to do so? *See*

Practice Tip: Papering the Trail

Landlord and tenant each have a reason to behave in a self-serving manner when the tenant vacates the premises prior to the end of the term. The landlord should answer tenant's letters to show that she has not accepted surrender, if that is her decision. But the landlord should also send the tenant who abandons a letter (or letters) identifying each of the steps landlord has taken, presumably without luck, to locate a third party to take the space in the tenant's absence. This is called "papering the trail"; the landlord will want to be able to demonstrate in litigation that she acted reasonably to fulfill her duty to mitigate.

Neel v. Tenet Healthsystem Hosps. Dall., Inc., 378 S.W.3d 597 (Tex. Ct. App. 2012) (commercial tenant failed to show that landlord did not mitigate where landlord located a tenant a year after tenant abandoned the premises). There is a difference of opinion among jurisdictions. *See* Stephanie G. Flynn, *Duty to Mitigate Damages upon a Tenant's Abandonment*, 34 Real Prop. Prob. & Tr. J. 721 (2000).

Commercial versus residential. Commercial tenants are often, but not always, represented by counsel. They do negotiate their leases, and the documents are not usually "take it or leave it." The mitigation rule protects the tenant, and a commercial tenant has a greater ability to negotiate a mitigation requirement into his lease. Friedman on Leases suggests that the no-mitigation rule is still the majority rule in commercial lease disputes. *See* 2 Andrew R. Berman, Friedman on Leases §16:3.1 (6th ed. 2017). Other scholarship suggests otherwise. *See* Stephanie G. Flynn, *supra* ("However, despite these differences in bargaining power between the residential and commercial tenants the vast majority of courts continue to make rulings without distinguishing between residential and commercial landlords"). May a commercial landlord avoid the mitigation obligation by putting a no-mitigation clause in the lease?

b. *The Opposite of Surrender: The Tenant Defaults but Stays in Possession*

Practice Tip: An Incentive to Leave

The landlord can provide the tenant with an incentive to leave at the end of the term and not hold over. Although not always effective, the landlord may include a provision in the lease establishing specific remedies if the tenant holds over. 🖥 Read Provision 21 of the Sample Commercial Lease available on the Simulation. Would this grab your attention if you were a tenant pursuant to this lease and you planned to stay in the premises after the end of the term?

A tenant might breach a lease during the term, most often by failing to pay rent, or might simply remain in the space at the end of the term. Either way, the landlord is faced with the same problem: how can he remove a recalcitrant tenant?

A tenant can do a lot of damage to the premises, if he wants to. Moreover, if a tenant remains in his space when he has lost his legal right to possession, the landlord cannot lease the space to a new, paying tenant. This is the cruelest cut for a landlord. And if the space is occupied, the landlord may have to continue to maintain it at a certain level and pay increased insurance and utilities. The landlord would like to bring this sad state of affairs to a quick end. *See* 2 Andrew R. Berman, Friedman on Leases §18:6 (6th ed. 2017). As we will see, the landlord has the option of resorting to a specialized judicial remedy known as *summary proceedings* (often called "unlawful detainer actions"). The end result is that a sheriff removes the tenant under the auspices of the court. In a few jurisdictions, the landlord may exercise a remedy known as *self-help* and personally remove the tenant. We now will spend some time with these two possible approaches to handling a tenant who does not want to pay or to leave.

The landlord does not want to sit on his hands when the tenant fails to pay rent. State statutes provide that the landlord does not have to do so. The landlord is permitted to (relatively) quickly evict a tenant and take possession if the tenant fails to pay rent. Statutes permit the landlord to retake possession after giving tenant a statutorily prescribed notice period and opportunity to cure. The notice periods are short (typically about ten days). These statutes apply to both residential and commercial leases. If the tenant does not pay within the time period but remains in the premises, the tenant is subject to a "summary" judicial proceeding. The statutes vary considerably. At the least, the landlord may obtain possession of the space. Some of the statutes also grant damages to the landlord. Some permit the landlord to use summary proceedings only if tenant fails to pay rent, while others give landlord a right to a summary proceeding for a non-monetary default under the lease. In many states, the tenant really has little in the way of defense other than "I paid the landlord; please do not evict me." Only those defenses that negate the landlord's right to possession are typically allowed. In other words, the fact that landlord breached a promise in the lease is not considered a defense at the summary proceeding.

Eviction
Larry Downing/Reuters/Landov

Summary Proceedings and the Implied Warranty of Habitability

The idea behind summary proceedings is that landlord should be able to retake possession quickly if the tenant is a deadbeat. But what if the reason the tenant has failed to pay rent is that the tenant is suffering a breach of the implied warranty of habitability? What if the tenant is the grandmother from *Hilder*? This question has vexed courts: does it seem fair to you to grant the landlord expedited recovery of his premises if the reason that the tenant fails to pay rent is that she is offsetting rent against the cost of maintaining a nasty and otherwise uninhabitable premises? Some jurisdictions permit tenant to show a breach of the implied warranty of habitability as a defense to a summary proceeding. *See* Tulley v. Sheldon, 982 A.2d 954 (N.H. 2009); N.H. Rev. Stat. Ann. §540:13-d (2013).

Of course, the tenant is likely to see things quite differently. In many instances, the tenant will argue that she is not in breach or is otherwise entitled to possession, only to see the landlord engage in self-help and evict the tenant. Should a landlord be able to evict a tenant without having to go to court?

BENDER v. NORTH MERIDIAN MOBILE HOME PARK

636 So. 2d 385 (1994)
Supreme Court of Mississippi

PITTMAN, JUSTICE, for the Court:

. . .

FACTS

Richard Bender (Bender) entered into a six month lease on July 13, 1987, to rent trailer No. 4 from North Meridian Mobile Home Park, Inc., (landlord). The lease specified that the rent was $195.00 per month, but did not state when such rent was due. [Clyde Rose was president of North Meridian Mobile Home Park, Inc., and Lannie Ritter was the mobile home park manager. Bender named the corporation, Mr. Ritter, and Mr. Rose as defendants in his suit; the court refers collectively to these parties as "landlord" in its opinion.]

Bender paid rent at various intervals and in varying amounts. Bender was behind on his rent from the beginning of the lease. Bender testified that no one complained about the way that he paid his rent. However, Lannie Ritter testified that he had talked with Bender many times about getting his rent paid. Through the end of November 1987, Bender was in arrears in the amount of $165.00.

The facts are disputed as to when Bender was locked out of the trailer. Bender testified that he had gone by to see Mr. Ritter on December 5, 1987, so that he would know that he was planning on bringing partial payment of the rent. He stated that he went to see Mr. Ritter because Mrs. Ritter had come by his trailer earlier to see if he had anything toward the rent. Bender stated that later that day when he returned to make a payment towards rent that he was locked out of his trailer. Bender testified that he received the eviction notice after he had been locked out of the trailer. Bender stated that all these events occurred on the same day.

After finding that the locks had been changed on the trailer, Bender stated that he went to see Mr. Ritter and attempted to give him some money towards rent, but Mr. Ritter would not accept it. Bender testified that Ritter told him not to come back to the trailer park, and if he did he would be shot as a trespasser.

Bender testified that he made several pleas with Mr. Ritter to allow him in the trailer to get some medication for his back injury but Ritter refused. Bender stated that he returned to the trailer three or four days after he had been locked out (Dec. 8 or 9, 1987) to get some papers for the Social Security Administration. He testified that he was not allowed to take any other items from the trailer.

Lannie Ritter did not testify at trial, but his deposition was admitted into evidence. Ritter testified that he and Clyde Rose decided that Bender must be evicted. Ritter testified that he served Bender with the eviction notice on December 5, 1987. He stated that he did not take further action until December 8 or 9, 1987. On either December 8 or 9 Ritter stated that he changed the locks on the trailer Bender was renting while Bender was away. Ritter stated that when Bender came back to the trailer park, he wanted to be let back in his trailer. Ritter stated that his wife went to the trailer with Bender and allowed him to get his medication out of the trailer. Ritter stated that the day after he locked Bender out of the trailer he (Bender) returned to the trailer park and threatened him with a gun. Ritter stated that when he threatened to call the sheriff, Bender left the trailer park. Ritter said that was the last time that he saw Bender.

Landlord kept Bender's property locked in the rental trailer No. 4 for about two months, until some date in February. At that time, landlord moved Bender's property to a storage trailer and prepared an inventory. Bender's property remained in the storage trailer until May or June 1988. The landlord sold the inventoried items at a general rummage sale in June 1988. An advertisement announcing the rummage sale was published in the local newspaper, but no reference was made to Bender's possessions being put up for sale. Bender was not notified of the sale. According to the landlord, the rummage sale of all items, including the inventoried property of the tenant, brought in thirty-five ($35.00) dollars.

DISCUSSION

I.

1.

Bender asserted that he was wrongfully evicted. The landlord stated that it had a landlord's lien pursuant to Miss. Code Ann. §89-7-51(2) for non-payment of rent. Section 89-7-51(2) states:

> All articles of personal property, except a stock of merchandise sold in the normal course of business, owned by the lessee of real property and situated on the leased premises shall be subject to a lien in favor of the lessor to secure the payment of rent for such premises as has been contracted to be paid, whether or not then due. Such lien shall be subject to all prior liens or other security interests perfected according to law. No such articles of personal property may be removed from the leased premises until such rent is paid except with the written consent of the lessor. **All of the provisions of law as to attachment for rent and proceedings thereunder *shall* be applicable with reference to the lessor's lien under this section.**

Landlord claimed that the Landlord Lien Statute permitted him to lock tenant out of the trailer and thereby eject Bender from the premises. The trial court agreed with the Landlord and found that the Landlord Lien Statute, §89-7-51(2) (1972), permitted a landlord to seize possession of the leased premises without legal process and that the statute was an additional method of evicting a tenant. . . .

Bender argued that the Landlord Lien Statute §89-7-51 does not provide for the ejectment of a tenant from the leased premises for failure to pay rent. This Court agrees. Section 89-7-51(2) is not an alternative remedy for removal of a tenant from the leased premises as the lower court stated. Section 89-7-51(2) gives a landlord a subordinate lien on all articles of personal property.[7] The landlord's reliance on the Landlord Lien Statute, §89-7-51, as some form of legal process or sanction to eject the tenant from his home was misplaced. There is nothing in the statute that indicates that a landlord is allowed to resort to lockout. The statute specifically states the means by which the lien should be enforced. The last sentence of §89-7-51(2) states "*All of the provisions of law as to attachment for rent and proceedings thereunder shall be applicable with reference to the lessor's lien under this subsection.*" This means that in order for the landlord to enforce his statutorily created lien on the tenant's personal property they must follow the attachment for rent statutes. Sections 89-7-55 through 89-7-125 set forth how a landlord attaches for rent. The landlord clearly did not follow this

---

[7] The statute provides that "[s]uch lien shall be subject to all prior liens or other security interests perfected according to law."

procedure. Since §89-7-51(2) did not provide for the actions taken by the land-lord, the Court finds that the trial court erred in finding that Bender was not (sic) properly evicted.[8]

<p style="text-align:center">

2.

Not only were landlord's actions of lockout not allowed by statute, but case law also prohibited the action. This Court has held that a landlord could not regain possession of leased premises by breaking in or by threats of personal violence or the exercise of such violence, but where the lease provided for reentry by the landlord for tenant's failure to pay rent, the landlord may exercise such reentry if done so without breaking in, violence or threats of violence. Clark v. Service Auto Co., 143 Miss. 602, 108 So. 704 (1926). In *Clark*, the lease between the land-lord and the tenant included a provision which gave the landlord the right to remove the tenant and take possession of the premises without notice for ten-ant's failure to pay rent. The Court stated that without such provision in the lease the landlord would have been required to follow the statutory process.

The lease between the landlord and tenant in the case *sub judice* had no provision which would have allowed the landlord to regain possession without notice and hearing. Since there was no such provision, the landlord should have used the statutory process and not resorted to a self-help procedure.

. . .

<p style="text-align:center">

IV.

Bender argued that the trial court erred in assessing the amount of damages for conversion. At the trial of the case *sub judice*, landlord introduced an inventory done by the landlord's manager about two months after Bender's property was locked up in his trailer. Bender's testimony as to what specific items were in the trailer and their value differed vastly from the inventory made by landlord.

Bender argued that a review of the record would clearly show that the trial court erred in its findings. Bender introduced an exhibit that listed the items he claimed were in the trailer at the time of landlord's seizure of property. This exhibit stated a total value of the listed items at $4,793.00. Bender testified that the seized property was worth at least $3,500.00. Bender introduced ten photo-graphs which portrayed items of personal property that Bender alleged were in the trailer at the time of the seizure by landlord.

The trial court found that "there was no credible evidence produced at trial convincing the court as to the value of said possessions, whatever they were, at the time of conversion." However, the trial court assessed Bender's conversion damages at $296.45. This was the same amount that the court found Bender owed to landlord for past due rent and deposit.

---

[8] The court must mean to say that "the trial court erred in finding that Bender *was* property evicted."—EDS.

The measure of damages for conversion is the fair market value of the property at the time and place of its conversion. Universal Underwriters v. Bob Burnham, Inc., 408 So. 2d 1010, 1015 (Miss. 1982). This Court has stated that when a trial judge sits without a jury, the judge has the sole authority to determine credibility of witnesses. Rice Researchers, Inc. v. Hiter, 512 So. 2d 1259, 1265 (Miss. 1987). Where a circuit judge sits without a jury, the Supreme Court must affirm his judgment unless the trial court was manifestly wrong.

After reviewing the record, there is nothing to indicate that the trial judge was manifestly wrong in his damage assessment for conversion. As the trier of fact, the trial judge determined the value of items that he believed to be in the trailer. The Court finds this assignment of error to be without merit.

CONCLUSION

This Court reverses the lower court's finding that Bender was not wrongfully evicted. We leave to the lower court to determine whether or not Bender suffered any damages from this wrongful eviction. We affirm the lower court's conversion damage assessment. Accordingly, the Court affirms in part and reverses in part.

■ POINTS TO CONSIDER

1. **A patchwork of laws.** At early common law, if the tenant ceased paying rent, the landlord would simply send in his men and remove the tenant. If it took genuine force to do so, the law permitted it. *See* Jean Pierre Nogues, *Defects in the Current Forcible Entry and Detainer Laws of the United States and England*, 25 UCLA L. Rev. 1067 (1978). The idea that a landlord may enter the premises and *roughly* remove the tenant is a thing of the past. Still, some jurisdictions permit a landlord to use the remedy of self-help to *peaceably* enter the premises of a tenant who no longer has the right of possession, so long as the landlord uses only that minimal physical intrusion necessary to obtain possession. This means that the landlord can enter the property when the tenant is out and change the locks. In many cases, the landlord removes the tenant's personal belongings, often to the street, or stores the tenant's personal belongings and charges the tenant a fee for doing so.

   The common law rule permitting self-help was long considered the majority rule. However, the tide has turned in favor of tenants, particularly residential tenants. A number of states have adopted statutes that forbid self-help, thus overruling the common law rule. *See, e.g.*, Ariz. Rev. Stat. Ann. §33-1374 (2014). North Carolina courts held to the common law rule as late as 1981 (Spinks v. Taylor, 278 S.E.2d 501 (N.C. 1981)), but this rule was supplanted by a statute that forbids self-help removal of residential tenants. N.C. Gen. Stat. §42-25.6 (2015). *See also* Ohio Rev. Code Ann. §5321.15(A) (West 2016) (limiting the right of residential landlords to exercise self-help eviction). The Uniform Residential Landlord and Tenant Act §4.207 bars landlords from self-help, limiting landlords to judicial process and summary proceedings. The Restatement (Second) of Property: Landlord and Tenant §14.2 (1977) takes a similar position. What rule does the court in *Bender* adopt? What policies justify the court's approach?

Jurisdictions vary on the question of whether courts should afford the same protection to commercial tenants as they do to residential tenants. In some jurisdictions, commercial tenants remain subject to a landlord's self-help remedy, but only if the lease reserves this right to the landlord. *See, e.g.,* Sol De Ibiza, LLC v. Panjo Realty, Inc., 911 N.Y.S.2d 567 (N.Y. App. 2010) (stating that "it is well established that a landlord may, under certain circumstances, utilize self-help to regain possession of demised commercial premises," where the lease agreement reserved to landlord the right to regain possession upon the tenant's failure to pay rent).

Other courts take the position that self-help is impermissible in the commercial context, even in those instances in which the landlord reserves this right in the lease. For example, in Berg v. Wiley, 264 N.W.2d 145 (Minn. 1978), the landlord, in the company of the sheriff, retook possession of a restaurant and locked out the tenant. The tenant had closed the restaurant, but had not actually vacated the premises. The court rejected the argument that the tenant abandoned the premises (which would have entitled landlord to enter). The court held that under the common law rule, the entry and eviction would have been unlawful, because the landlord's actions amounted to a breach of the peace. But the court went further and stated that in future cases it would reject the common law rule altogether. The *Berg* court reasoned that the landlord is afforded quick possession via summary proceedings, and that the availability of summary proceedings represents the legislature's desire to make this a landlord's *sole method* of retaking possession of a leasehold. *See also,* Palm Beach Fla. Hotel v. Nantucket Enter., Inc. 211 So. 3d 42 (Fla. Dist. Ct. App. 2016) (court invalidates landlord's self-help lock-out of commercial tenant; landlord must utilize statutory process notwithstanding self-help provision reserved in commercial lease). Does the rationale developed by the court in *Berg* help you understand the decision in *Bender*? If you were a landlord, why might you consider the judicial process, even summary proceedings, insufficient to protect your interests?

2. **Breach of the peace.** Some jurisdictions continue to allow self-help evictions if they are accomplished peaceably. What constitutes a breach of the peace? Do you think that the landlord in *Bender* breached the peace? Assume that you represent the landlord in *Bender*. Make your best case that landlord did *not* breach the peace.

3. **A slim reed.** The landlord in *Bender* claimed a right to enter and evict based on a landlord's lien statute. Should this statute provide the basis for the landlord's eviction of a tenant?

4. **Waiver.** According to the court in *Bender*, the landlord would have been permitted to engage in self-help had the lease provided the landlord this right. Does this make sense? The rationale often given for forbidding

self-help is that a breach of the peace, and even violence, might result when the landlord attempts to retake possession. Does this risk diminish if the tenant agrees in the lease, at the outset, that the landlord has the right to self-help? In jurisdictions that maintain statutes explicitly forbidding self-help, courts often divine a public policy forbidding a tenant from *waiving* this protection. These cases usually limit the rule against waiver to residential and not commercial leases. In other words, these courts permit commercial tenants to waive the right against self-help. *See, e.g.,* Design Ctr. Venture v. Overseas Multi-Prospects Corp., 748 S.W.2d 469 (Tex. App. 1988). Again, we see a distinction between the treatment of commercial and residential tenants. Other courts simply forbid self-help and, in addition, do not permit the parties to waive this rule. *See, e.g.,* Gorman v. Ratliff, 712 S.W.2d 888 (Ark. 1986). 💻 Take a look at a Basic Texas Commercial Lease available on the Simulation. Does it permit self-help? Does the Sample Commercial Lease we presented earlier in the chapter address the issue of self-help?

5. **The unexpected application of a statute.** Statutes have a way of affecting a wider set of cases than the legislature may have anticipated. This is true of statutes forbidding self-help. For instance, in one case, a landlord asked her resident manager to enter the tenant's apartment and look through the tenant's personal papers. The manager, being a person of good conscience, refused and was promptly fired. The manager then brought suit for unlawful discharge, and won, largely on the basis that the landlord had no right to engage in self-help of this sort and could therefore not fire the employee for refusing to comply. *See* Kessler v. Equity Mgmt., Inc., 572 A.2d 1144 (Md. Ct. Spec. App. 1990).

   The party who actually evicted the tenant in *Bender* was the landlord. The landlord changed the locks and allegedly threatened to shoot the tenant. Locating an eviction in *Bender* is rather easy. Is this always the case? Consider the following problem.

■ PROBLEM: SELF-HELP IN OTHER FORMS

Tenant fails to pay rent for an apartment and refuses the landlord's demand that the tenant vacate the space. Tenant then barricades himself in a bathroom. Landlord responds by doing what seems to make sense to the landlord—he calls the police. A police officer comes to the scene and, after failing to persuade the tenant to leave, enters the premises. The officer ultimately arrests the tenant and takes him to the station. The landlord presses criminal trespass charges; the tenant is found guilty and receives several months in the county jail. The state maintains a summary proceeding statute. The tenant asks for your advice. *See* People v. Evans, 516 N.E.2d 817 (Ill. App. Ct. 1987).

c. The Duty to Not Commit Waste

We have talked about waste in the context of both concurrent estates and future interests. We will discuss waste again in Chapter 9, which covers the real estate loan transaction. Waste is a tort. It is not really an action based in property law, and it is certainly not an action based in contract. Waste provides a remedy to a party who has an interest in real property, but who does not possess it, when the party in possession causes or allows physical damage to the real property.

In the case of landlord-tenant law, the tenant is in possession, and the landlord has a reversion giving the landlord the right to possession in the future. A tenant who deliberately changes the property in a way that diminishes its value is engaging in *affirmative* (or voluntary or commissive) waste. A tenant who simply allows the property to deteriorate by failing to take appropriate steps to protect or repair is engaging in *permissive* waste. The tenant is not allowed to waste the property that he leases. In the case of permissive waste, this really means that the tenant must make reasonable repairs or notify the landlord of a problem if the repair obligation falls to landlord under the lease.

On some occasions, a tenant might actually alter the premises in such a way as to increase its value. This is still a form of waste, but the landlord has less reason to be upset about it. This is called *ameliorative waste*, and in some limited instances, the tenant will not be liable in damages to the landlord for such ameliorative waste. Professors Stoebuck and Whitman suggest that "decisions allowing tenants to clear farmland of timber may be analyzed as meliorating waste cases and would be the commonest application of the doctrine." William B. Stoebuck & Dale A. Whitman, The Law of Property §6.23, at 273 (3d ed. 2000). *See also* Melms v. Pabst Brewing Co., 79 N.W. 738 (Wis. 1899). Do you think that it would make sense to apply the doctrine of ameliorative waste to a typical leasehold estate? One of the finest and most clearly written recent treatments of the doctrine of waste is found in John A. Lovett, *Doctrines of Waste in a Landscape of Waste*, 72 Mo. L. Rev. 1209 (2007).

As always, it will be important to consult the lease to determine whether it has anything to say about what actions of tenant might be considered waste. ⌨ Does the Sample Commercial Lease on the Simulation address the issue of waste? If so, what does it say?

Waste: Three Categories

- **Affirmative.** Tenant acts deliberately to alter the premises and lower its value.
- **Permissive.** Tenant fails to take reasonable steps to repair or protect the premises.
- **Ameliorative.** Tenant alters premises but increases its value.

Controlling Moral Hazard

What is the point of the doctrine of waste? The tenant knows that, at the end of the term, the landlord will retake possession of the property. What incentive does the tenant have to take care of the property? Why not just leave the windows open in the rain and invite a biker gang to hold meetings in the basement? After all, the damage to the property that results will be the landlord's problem. This is a good example of a *moral hazard*. At the start of the lease term, it makes sense for the tenant to watch over the property, in much the same way that a new car owner dotes on a new car. But as the end of the term comes close, the tenant will not care nearly as much. We want the tenant to treat the property as if it were his own. This is precisely what waste doctrine tries to accomplish. Tenant will be liable for any damage he causes or allows, and perhaps punitive damages, if the tenant intentionally acts to damage the property.

■ PROBLEM: GOPHERS!

> ➤ Ben and Jerry are law students. They are also co-tenants and have signed a lease with their landlord for a two-bedroom apartment in the Piedmont Park apartments. Ben occupies one bedroom and Jerry the other. Ben graduates a semester early and moves out of the apartment. Ben shuts the door to his room and never returns.
> ➤ Ben continues to pay his share of the rent. Jerry similarly continues to pay his share of the rent and all payments to the landlord are made on time.
> ➤ The day after Ben leaves, a heavy thunderstorm moves through the area; a single thunderclap breaks the bedroom window in Ben's room. In the following months, a number of animals, including a family of gophers, move into Ben's bedroom. Jerry hears the animal noises but assumes that the noises come from outside the apartment; he does not enter Ben's room.
> ➤ The lease term ends and Jerry moves out. The landlord enters the apartment unit after expiration of the term and discovers a veritable wild animal park in Ben's room. The room is considerably damaged.

The landlord asks for your advice. What are Ben's liability and Jerry's liability for the damage, if any? What steps would have protected Ben and Jerry from liability?

D   TRANSFER OF THE PREMISES

Imagine that, following graduation from law school, you "hang out a shingle" and open your own law practice. The first thing that you will probably do is lease an office. Let's assume that your lease is for a two-year term. You are now on the hook for rental payments for two years; you know (from prior sections) that if you vacate the office, the landlord may not have an obligation to mitigate the loss. And even in those jurisdictions that require mitigation, the landlord may not succeed. In either case, if you decide to vacate, you will owe your landlord money.

Your decision to lease the office therefore rests on two assumptions: that you will want to stay in the office and that you will have the financial ability to pay the rent for the term of the lease. What if your assumptions prove wrong? Perhaps business only trickles in and you find it difficult to make your monthly rent payment. Or perhaps a friend from law school invites you to join her in a more profitable law practice in a different city. Either way, you can do so only if you can find an "out" from your lease.

One way to do this would be to offer the landlord money to release you from your lease agreement. No doubt, if you name your landlord's price, your landlord will gladly give you a release. When is a landlord likely to negotiate a release?

However, there is another possible "out" from the lease: you may locate someone to take your place in the office and to start paying rent to the landlord. If this happens, you will have either "assigned" your interest in the lease or "subleased" the premises. In both situations, *you will have granted your exclusive right to possession to a third party*, who for the moment we will simply call the "transferee." This section will look at this possibility.

The tenant's decision to transfer the leasehold raises a number of issues: First, what is the nature of the transfer? Is it an "assignment" or a "sublease" and why does it matter? Second, if the tenant transfers the leasehold, who is liable to the landlord for rent—the original tenant, the transferee, or both? Third, is the tenant even allowed to transfer the leasehold to a third party? Most leases restrict the ability of the tenant to do so.

1. Distinguishing an Assignment from a Sublease

The landlord really does not care who makes the rent payments, so long as *someone* does. Here is the typical scenario: Isaac leases an apartment to Julio. Julio marries and moves to a new state prior to the end of the term to live with his spouse, and leases another apartment there. Julio realizes that someone must pay the piper—that is, Isaac. However, Julio cannot afford two rental payments, so he convinces a third person, Anne, to take over the apartment leased to him by Isaac. Anne moves in and dutifully pays rent for three months thereafter. However, Anne loses her job in the fourth month and ceases paying rent altogether. Anne continues to live in the apartment. Isaac may attempt to evict Anne, and he will win if he does so. But what Isaac really wants is the rental payment. Julio lives far away. Isaac can sue Julio, but then Isaac will be presented with the hard job of collecting on the judgment against a judgment debtor who lives in another state, assuming he can find Julio and Julio is not judgment-proof. Isaac would rather pin liability for rent on the transferee, Anne. To do so, he will be forced to locate a basis for Anne's liability in either contract law or property law. Can Isaac do so?

ERNST v. CONDITT

390 S.W.2d 703 (1965)
Tennessee Court of Appeals

CHATTIN, Judge.

Complainants, B. Walter Ernst and wife, Emily Ernst, leased a certain tract of land in Davidson County, Tennessee, to Frank D. Rogers on June 18, 1960, for a term of one year and seven days, commencing on June 23, 1960.

Rogers went into possession of the property and constructed an asphalt race track and enclosed the premises with a fence. He also constructed other improvements thereon such as floodlights for use in the operation of a Go-Cart track.

We quote those paragraphs of the lease pertinent to the question for consideration in this controversy:

"3. Lessee covenants to pay as rent for said leased premises the sum of $4,200 per annum, payable at the rate of $350 per month or 15% of all gross receipts, whether from sales or services occurring on the leased premises, whichever is the larger amount. The gross receipts shall be computed on a quarterly basis and if any amount in addition to the $350 per month is due, such payment shall be made immediately after the quarterly computation. All payments shall be payable to the office of Lessors' agent, Guaranty Mortgage Company, at 316 Union Street, Nashville, Tennessee, on the first day of each month in advance. Lessee shall have the first right of refusal in the event Lessors desire to lease said premises for a period of time commencing immediately after the termination date hereof....

"5. Lessee shall have no right to assign or sublet the leased premises without prior written approval of Lessors. In the event of any assignment or sublease, Lessee is still liable to perform the covenants of this lease, including the covenant to pay rent, and nothing herein shall be construed as releasing Lessee from his liabilities and obligations hereunder.

...

"9. Lessee agrees that upon termination of this contract, or any extensions or renewals thereof, that all improvements above the ground will be moved at Lessee's expense and the property cleared. This shall not be construed as removing or digging up any surface paving; but if any pits or holes are dug, they shall be leveled at Lessors' request."

Rogers operated the business for a short time. In July, 1960, he entered into negotiations with the defendant, A.K. Conditt, for the sale of the business to him. During these negotiations, the question of the term of the lease arose. Defendant desired a two-year lease of the property. He and Rogers went to the home of complainants and negotiated an extension of the term of the lease which resulted in the following amendment to the lease, and the sublease or assignment of the lease as amended to Conditt by Rogers:

"By mutual consent of the parties, the lease executed the 18th day of June 1960, between B. Walter Ernst and wife, Emily H. Ernst, as Lessors, and Frank G. Rogers as Lessee, is amended as follows:

"1. Paragraph 2 of said lease is amended so as to provide that the term will end July 31, 1962 and not June 30, 1961.

"2. The minimum rent of $350 per month called for in paragraph 3 of said lease shall be payable by the month and the percentage rental called for by said lease shall be payable on the first day of the month following the month for which the percentage is computed. In computing gross receipts, no deduction or credit shall be given the Lessee for the payment of sales taxes or any other assessments by governmental agencies.

"5. Lessor hereby consents to the subletting of the premises to A.K. Conditt, but upon the express condition and understanding that the original Lessee, Frank K. Rogers, will remain personally liable for the faithful performance of all the terms and conditions of the original lease and of this amendment to the original lease.

"Except as modified by this amendment, all terms and conditions of the original lease dated the 18th day of June, 1960, by and between the parties shall remain in full force and effect.

"In witness whereof the parties have executed this amendment to lease on this the 4 day of August, 1960.

B. Walter Ernst
Emily H. Ernst
Lessors

Frank D. Rogers
Lessee

"For value received and in consideration of the promise to faithfully perform all conditions of the within lease as amended,

"This 4 day of Aug, 1960.

Frank D. Rogers

Frank D. Rogers

"The foregoing subletting of the premises is accepted, this the 4 day of Aug, 1960.

A.K. Conditt

A.K. Conditt."

Conditt operated the Go-Cart track from August until November, 1960. He paid the rent for the months of August, September and October, 1960, directly to complainants. In December, 1960, complainants contacted defendant with reference to the November rent and at that time defendant stated he had been advised he was not liable to them for rent. However, defendant paid the basic monthly rental of $350.00 to complainants in June, 1961. This was the final payment received by complainants during the term of the lease as amended. The record is not clear whether defendant continued to operate the business after the last payment of rent or abandoned it. Defendant, however, remained in possession of the property until the expiration of the leasehold.

On July 10, 1962, complainants, through their Attorneys, notified Conditt by letter the lease would expire as of midnight July 31, 1962; and they were demanding a settlement of the past due rent and unless the improvements on the property were removed by him as provided in paragraph 9 of the original lease; then, in that event, they would have same removed at his expense. Defendant did not reply to this demand.

On August 1, 1962, complainants filed their bill in this cause seeking a recovery of $2,404.58 which they alleged was the balance due on the basic rent of $350.00 per month for the first year of the lease and the sum of $4,200.00, the basic rent for the second year, and the further sum necessary for the removal of the improvements constructed on the property.

The theory of the bill is that the agreement between Rogers, the original lessee, and the defendant, Conditt, is an assignment of the lease; and, therefore, defendant is directly and primarily liable to complainants.

The defendant by his answer insists the agreement between Rogers and himself is a sublease and therefore Rogers is directly and primarily liable to complainants.

The Chancellor heard the matter on the depositions of both complainants and three other witnesses offered in behalf of complainants and documentary evidence filed in the record. The defendant did not testify nor did he offer any evidence in his behalf.

The Chancellor found the instrument to be an assignment. A decree was entered sustaining the bill and entering judgment for complainants in the sum of $6,904.58 against defendant.

Defendant has appealed to this Court and has assigned errors insisting the Chancellor erred in failing to hold the instrument to be a sublease rather than an assignment.

To support his theory the instrument is a sublease, the defendant insists the amendment to the lease entered into between Rogers and complainants was for the express purpose of extending the term of the lease and obtaining the consent of the lessors to a "subletting" of the premises to defendant. That by the use of the words "sublet" and "subletting" no other construction can be placed on the amendment and the agreement of Rogers and the acceptance of defendant attached thereto.

Further, since complainants agreed to the subletting of the premises to defendant "upon the express condition and understanding that the original lessee, Frank D. Rogers, will remain personally liable for the faithful performance of all the terms and conditions of the original lease and this amendment to the original lease," no construction can be placed upon this language other than it was the intention of complainants to hold Rogers primarily liable for the performance of the original lease and the amendment thereto. And, therefore, Rogers, for his own protection, would have the implied right to re-enter and perform the lease in the event of a default on the part of the defendant. This being true, Rogers retained a reversionary interest in the property sufficient to satisfy the legal distinction between a sublease and an assignment of a lease.

It is then urged the following rules of construction of written instruments support the above argument:

"Where words or terms having a definite legal meaning and effect are knowingly used in a written instrument the parties thereto will be presumed to have intended such words or terms to have their proper legal meaning and effect, in the absence of any contrary intention appearing in the instrument." 12 Am. Jur., Contracts, Section 238.

"Technical terms or words of art will be given their technical meaning unless the context, or local usage shows a contrary intention." 3 Williston on Contracts, Section 68, Sub. S. 2.

As stated in complainants' brief, the liability of defendant to complainants depends upon whether the transfer of the leasehold interest in the premises from Rogers is an assignment of the lease or a sublease. If the transfer is a sublease, no privity of contract exists between complainants and defendant; and, therefore, defendant could not be liable to complainants on the covenant to pay rent and the expense of the removal of the improvements. But, if the transfer is an assignment of the lease, privity of contract does exist between complainants and defendant; and defendant would be liable directly and primarily for the amount of the judgment. Brummitt Tire Company v. Sinclair Refining Company, 18 Tenn. App. 270, 75 S.W.2d 1022; Commercial Club v. Epperson, 15 Tenn. App. 649.

The general rule as to the distinction between an assignment of a lease and a sublease is an assignment conveys the whole term, leaving no interest nor reversionary interest in the grantor or assignor. Whereas, a sublease may be generally defined as a transaction whereby a tenant grants an interest in the leased premises less than his own, or reserves to himself a reversionary interest in the term.

The common law distinction between an assignment of a lease and a sublease is succinctly stated in the case of Jaber v. Miller, 219 Ark. 59, 239 S.W.2d 760:

"If the instrument purports to transfer the lessee's estate for the entire remainder of his term it is an assignment, regardless of its form or of the parties' intention. Conversely, if the instrument purports to transfer the lessee's estate for less than the entire term—even for a day less—it is a sublease, regardless of its form or of the parties' intention."

The modern rule which has been adopted in this State for construing written instruments is stated in the case of City of Nashville v. Lawrence, 153 Tenn. 606, 284 S.W. 882:

"The cardinal rule to be followed in this state, in construing deeds and other written instruments, is to ascertain the intention of the parties."

In Williams v. Williams, 84 Tenn. 164, 171, it was said:

"We have most wisely abandoned technical rules in the construction of conveyances in this State, and look to the intention of the instrument alone for our guide, that intention to be arrived at from the language of the instrument read in the light of the surrounding circumstances."

It is our opinion under either the common law or modern rule of construction the agreement between Rogers and defendant is an assignment of the lease.

The fact that Rogers expressly agreed to remain liable to complainants for the performance of the lease did not create a reversion nor a right to re-enter in Rogers either express or implied. The obligations and liabilities of a lessee to a lessor, under the express covenants of a lease, are not in anywise affected by an assignment or a subletting to a third party, in the absence of an express or implied agreement or some action on his part which amounts to a waiver or estops him from insisting upon compliance with the covenants. This is true even though the assignment or sublease is made with the consent of the lessor. By an assignment of a lease the privity of estate between the lessor and lessee is terminated, but the privity of contract between them still remains and is unaffected. Neither the privity of estate or contract between the lessor and lessee are affected by a sublease. 32 Am. Jur., Landlord and Tenant, Sections 356, 413, pages 310, 339.

Thus, the express agreement of Rogers to remain personally liable for the performance of the covenants of the lease created no greater obligation on his part or interest in the leasehold, other than as set forth in the original lease.

The argument that since the agreement between Rogers and defendant contains the words, "sublet" and "subletting" is conclusive the instrument is to be construed as a sublease is, we think, unsound.

"A consent to sublet has been held to include the consent to assign or mortgage the lease; and a consent to assign has been held to authorize a subletting." 51 C.J.S. Landlord and Tenant §36, page 552.

Prior to the consummation of the sale of the Go-Cart business to defendant, he insisted upon the execution of the amendment to the lease extending the term of the original lease. For value received and on the promise of the defendant to perform all of the conditions of the lease as amended, Rogers parted with his entire interest in the property. Defendant went into possession of the property and paid the rent to complainants. He remained in possession of the property for the entire term. By virtue of the sale of the business, defendant became the owner of the improvements with the right to their removal at the expiration of the lease.

Rogers reserved no part or interest in the lease; nor did he reserve a right of re-entry in event of a breach of any of the conditions or covenants of the lease on the part of defendant.

It is our opinion the defendant, under the terms of the agreement with Rogers, had a right to the possession of the property for the entire term of the lease as amended, including the right to remove the improvements after the expiration of the lease. Rogers merely agreed to become personally liable for the rent and the expense of the removal of the improvements upon the default of defendant. He neither expressly, nor by implication, reserved the right to re-enter for a condition broken by defendant.

Thus, we are of the opinion the use of the words, "sublet" and "subletting" is not conclusive of the construction to be placed on the instrument in this case; it plainly appearing from the context of the instrument and the facts and circumstances surrounding the execution of it the parties thereto intended an assignment rather than a sublease.

It results the assignments are overruled and the decree of the Chancellor is affirmed with costs.

SHRIVER and HUMPHREYS, JJ., concur.

■ POINTS TO CONSIDER

1. **What is an assignment? Find the test.** An assignment suggests that the tenant transferred his status as tenant to a third party. For courts using the traditional test, determining whether a transfer is an assignment is straightforward. Courts ask: did the tenant transfer his right to exclusive possession *for the entire remainder of the term*? If the tenant retained the right to return into exclusive possession, for even an hour, the transfer would not be considered an assignment. *See* Joseph Bros. Co. v. F.W. Woolworth Co., 844 F.2d 369 (6th Cir. 1988) (court holds that landlord's reservation of even a day renders a transfer a sublease rather than an assignment); Northside Station Assocs. P'ship v. Maddry, 413 S.E.2d 319 (N.C. Ct. App. 1992) (expressly rejecting the intent test).

   The legal dividing line between assignment and sublease is an old one, but remains vigorously part of the law. *See* William G. Coskran, *Assignment and Sublease Restrictions: The Tribulations of Leasehold Transfers*, 22 Loy. L.A. L. Rev. 405 (1989), and for a lovely older discussion, *see* W.W. Ferrier, Jr., *Can There Be a Sublease for the Entire Unexpired Portion of the Term?*, 18 Cal. L. Rev. 1 (1929) (noting, after a discussion of more ancient sources, the majority American Rule that a transfer of the entire term creates an assignment). Mark Senn, a highly respected commercial leasing lawyer, traces the rule back to Blackstone: the owner of an interest in the lease creates an assignment if "he parts with the whole property, and the assignee stands to all intents and purposes in the place of the assignor." *See* Mark A. Senn, Commercial Real Estate Leases: Preparation, Negotiation and Forms §13.02 (5th ed. 2012), *quoting* 2 Blackstone, Commentaries 326-27 (1765-1769). By the process of elimination, if the transfer of exclusive possession is not an assignment, it must be a sublease—there are only two possibilities where the tenant transfers the exclusive right of possession.

   In *Ernst*, the document executed on August 4 referred to the arrangement between Rogers and Conditt as a sublease. Look back at the document signed by the parties; locate instances in which the agreement uses the terms "sublease" or "sublet." How then does the court reach the conclusion that the transfer was an assignment? What is the approach of the court: does form matter, or substance? *See* Siragusa v. Park, 913 S.W.2d 915 (Mo. Ct. App. 1996) (transfer deemed an assignment, even though it was labeled a sublease). *See also* Ann Peldo Cargile & Michael B. Noble, *Assignments and Subleases: The Basics*, Prob. & Prop., Sept./Oct. 2003, at 40. Would it have mattered if the August 4 document had been formally titled as "Amendment and Sublease"? The court also suggested that there is a more modern approach to determining whether a transfer is an assignment or sublease. Instead of strictly looking at whether the tenant transferred his estate for the remainder of the term, some courts might ask whether the tenant "intended" to assign its interest. Exactly what does this mean? On what basis can we tell whether the tenant intended to assign? If an assignment is a property law creature transferring status to the assignee, then presumably we should ask whether the tenant intended to assign this status. Do you think that tenants consider this so thoughtfully when transferring rights?

2. **Finding liability and parsing "privity."** The *Ernst* court spends considerable effort describing the meaning and effect of the terms *privity of estate* and *privity of contract*. These terms may seem arcane, but they are part of the property lawyer's lexicon. "Privity" has different meanings in different contexts. Broadly, though, one party needs to be in privity with another to hold that other person liable for an action. To put it another way, you cannot sue someone unless you can show that you have an adequate, legally recognized connection with the person you are suing.

    Contract law creates privity. If you contract to provide a service to a company and then fail to do so, the company can sue you for breach of contract because you are in *privity of contract*.

    Property law creates relationships that are based in status and carry rights and responsibilities. The words *status* and *estate* flow from a common root. When one party in a property-based relationship fails to meet a duty that attaches to the relationship, the other party may sue based on *privity of estate*. A person who borrows money and secures the loan by giving the lender a mortgage on real property is in a property law relationship. Similarly, a tenant is in privity of estate with the landlord, because the landlord has transferred a possessory estate to tenant, and tenant therefore may be sued by landlord for rent. Any party "stepping into the shoes of the tenant" via an assignment is in privity of estate with the landlord. But this property-based privity, and thus the liability that the assignee has for rent to the landlord, *ceases as soon as the assignee assigns to another party. See* OTR v. Flakey Jake's, Inc., 770 P.2d 629, 633 (Wash. 1989) ("[A]n assignee incurs liability for rent only while in possession of the premises, and such liability is based solely upon privity of estate. . . . In such a situation, an *assignment* would release the assignor from any obligation to pay rent because it would terminate all privity of estate.").

    The *Ernst* court does a largely solid job in its explanation, but it nevertheless confuses these terms at one point. Look back at the court's use of the terms *privity of contract* and *privity of estate*. Can you find the court's error?

3. **Three agreements or two?** We do not see all of the signatures of the three parties (Ernst, Rogers, and Conditt) following a single set of provisions. Instead, we see three separate signature blocks. Does this matter?

4. **Is the original tenant still liable for the rent?** In the August 4 agreement, Rogers states, "I hereby sublet the premises to A.K. Conditt *upon the understanding that I will individually remain liable for the performance of the lease.*" (Emphasis added.) Did Rogers really need to add that language? Think about your Contracts course for a minute. Imagine that two parties enter into a contract. (If it will help, it is a contract for "widgets." Contracts professors like "widgets.") One party is supposed to supply to the other 1,000 widgets by a certain date and for a particular price. Now assume that the widget supplier decides he cannot supply the widgets on the date promised. Can the supplier just announce that he is no longer liable on the contract? If you answered "no," and we hope that you did, then you are correct. When is one party ordinarily off the hook for performance of a contract? Is there anything in *Ernst* to suggest (1) that Rogers fully performed the lease (i.e., paid all rents through the end of the term); (2) that Ernst materially breached the lease contract; or (3) that Ernst released Rogers from performance?

> ### What Is a Release?
>
> A release is a voluntary and knowing decision of one party to a contract to relieve the other party from its obligation to perform.

5. **What if the transfer in *Ernst* was deemed a sublease?** Assume for a minute that the *Ernst* court found (however wrongly) that the August 4 agreement in fact created a sublease between Rogers and Conditt. Based on the August 4 agreement, can you still argue that Conditt would be liable to Ernst for the rent? *See also* Restatement (Second) of Property: Landlord and Tenant §16.1, cmt. c (1977).

6. **What is the nature of the relationship between a sub-tenant and sub-landlord?** In a sublease, the tenant becomes a sub-landlord to the sub-tenant. The relationship between a sub-landord and sub-tenant is that of a landlord and tenant. For example, the sub-landlord has the same duty to place the sub-tenant in possession of the premises and the same duty of quiet enjoyment as the landlord owes the tenant.

7. **Who keeps the profit?** Let's assume the following: The lease between Ernst and Rogers is for a two-year term. The rental for the second year is $2,000 per month. It turns out that market rentals for that location have been going up dramatically. In the fourth month of the second year, Rogers subleases the space to Conditt for $3,000 per month for the remainder of the term. Who gets to keep this profit—the landlord or the original tenant? Commercial leases will often include "profit sharing provisions"; these

provisions specify at the outset whether and what percentage of the profit the landlord will receive upon a transfer. Why would the landlord allow the tenant to recapture even a portion of the profits? *See* Mark A. Senn, Commercial Real Estate Leases: Preparation, Negotiation and Forms §13.10[B] (5th ed. 2012).

Practice Tip: Assignment and Assumption Agreements

Landlords often require the tenant and assignee to execute an "assignment and assumption" agreement as a condition to obtaining the landlord's consent to transfer. The assignment makes clear that the assignee is liable to the landlord for rent and other lease obligations as a matter of property law. The assumption makes clear under contract law that the assignee *will continue* to be personally liable for rent, even if the assignee later transfers the lease.

---

2. May Tenant Transfer His Lease Rights (Either by Assignment or Sublease)?

In *Ernst*, paragraph 5 of the original lease between Ernst and Rogers contained the following language: "Lessee shall have no right to assign or sublet the leased premises without prior written approval of Lessors." This is typical of lease agreements, both in the residential and the commercial contexts. The restrictions on transfer in a commercial lease may be more involved; we will discuss that briefly below. But in both instances, the landlord tries to exert control over who has the right to exclusive possession. Interestingly, the reason that the landlord finds it necessary to insert this sort of language is that, at common law, the tenant had an *absolute right* to assign his lease or sublease the premises.

> ➢ **The Default Rule:** The tenant has a right to transfer.

Historically, leases were treated more as conveyances than contracts. As we have seen though, this basic approach to the nature of the lease has been changing and, generally speaking, the lease is increasingly seen as a contract. Yet, there is a striking area of agreement between property law and contract law. Under both approaches, a tenant has the right to transfer his rights under the lease (whether by sublease or assignment), if the lease does not otherwise preclude the transfer. To put it another way, if the lease is silent on the subject, the tenant can transfer.

The property law rationale is this: property law "abhors" a restraint on alienation. In more modern language we might simply say that property law resists restrictions on sale or transfer of real property or interests in real property. The contract law rationale is this: contract law assumes parties *expected* a right to assign the lease. Under this baseline rule permitting the tenant to transfer the lease, the tenant does not owe any duty to the landlord to use care when locating an assignee. *See* Shadeland Dev. Corp. v. Meek, 489 N.E.2d 1192 (Ind. Ct. App. 1986) (the tenant assigned a lease of a hotel property to an *insolvent* party; the court held that the tenant had no duty to select a tenant financially capable of paying rent when due).

If the landlord wishes to restrict the tenant's ability to transfer, he must *expressly* limit the tenant in the lease. This rule applies to both residential and commercial leases. Consider why the landlord might wish to do so in a residential lease. Assume you lease one unit in a duplex (a house with two separate units). Your landlord lives in the other unit. Prior to leasing to you, the landlord looks you over and decides that you are not too terribly objectionable. That's important to him because he lives in the very same building, although in a separate unit. This is a rather intimate distance. Your landlord will see you every day; he will hear you through the walls; and he will encounter your friends. The fact that he approves of you does not mean that he will approve of someone to whom you transferred the lease. He would like the chance to look every tenant in the eye and make a decision about whether to lease to that particular individual. If you are unrestricted, you might assign your lease rights to a drummer in a heavy metal band. While some landlords might love heavy metal, this is the last person that your landlord desires to see living next door.

A different but equally important dynamic causes a *commercial* landlord to restrict the tenant's ability to transfer. Imagine a large, high-end shopping center. We will call this the "Old Mall." Old Mall contains two "anchor" tenants. These are large department stores that attract significant numbers of shoppers. Smaller retail tenants located between the anchor tenants depend on the department stores to generate foot traffic.

Assume that both of the anchor tenants are truly high-end: one is Nordstrom and the other is Neiman Marcus. These department stores attract very affluent shoppers. Not surprisingly, the smaller tenants who lease space in the shopping center are high-end as well: expensive jewelry and watch stores (think Tiffany and Tourneau), boutique clothing stores, and internationally known fashion stores such as Versace and Coach. The location experts for the stores know that individuals who shop at Neiman Marcus also shop at smaller expensive stores. If Neiman Marcus has a "good year," so will the smaller stores in Old Mall. Owners of shopping centers try to develop a solid "tenant mix." In other words, stores that cater to high-end shoppers want the other stores, and the mall as a whole, to exude luxury. Similarly, owners of stores that cater to cost-conscious shoppers desire to be in a mall that will attract these buyers. Quite a bit of analysis goes into the development of these retail malls and shopping centers, and landlords and tenants sign leases with defined expectations.

Nordstrom
Daniel Bogart

Add one more fact: retail stores pay rent based on a percentage of their revenues. Thus, a store that sells more goods will pay more rent to the landlord. The owner of the Old Mall wants a tenant mix that will maximize his total rents from all tenants.

Now imagine that a new and even fancier shopping mall opens down the street from Old Mall. We will call this shopping center "New Mall." The owner of New Mall would like to attract high-end tenants to its property. The owner of New Mall makes a very attractive offer to both Nordstrom and Neiman Marcus to relocate to the New Mall location; the two anchor tenants each accept. Nordstrom and Neiman Marcus, not wanting to make redundant lease payments, each finds a store interested in taking an assignment of its lease in Old Mall. Nordstrom announces that it is going to assign to Target. Neiman Marcus announces it is going to assign to JC Penny.

If you were the landlord of Old Mall, how would you react? If you were Versace, Coach, or Tourneau, and you presently leased space in Old Mall, would you be pleased? Look into a crystal ball: can you divine the fate of Old Mall?

You can see now that in the commercial environment, perhaps even more than in the residential context, the landlord will want to include a restriction on the tenant's ability to transfer. What would such a restriction say?

In some leases (both residential and commercial), the landlord will include an express limitation on the tenant's ability to transfer the lease or the premises to a third party. Typically, the lease will state that "tenant may not transfer, assign or sublease without the prior written consent of the landlord." This is sometimes called a "silent consent clause," because it says nothing about the permissible reasons for refusing consent; in fact, the language seems to allow landlord to refuse for any reason. Tenants may negotiate, especially in the commercial sphere, for language that requires the landlord to act reasonably. Even in the absence of that limiting language, however, some courts *imply* a *reasonableness requirement* into the consent provision. In those states, some leases therefore include explicit language negating the implied duty to act reasonably ("consent may be withheld for any reason").

⌨ What language, if any, does the Sample Commercial Lease on the Simulation employ? Does it restrict the tenant's ability to assign and/or sublease?

As you might imagine, lawyers representing the landlord face a difficult task in advising their clients whether it is possible to reject the tenant's request to assign or sublease; the advice will directly affect the client's income. This inquiry takes on a very urgent note in the commercial sphere, because commercial leases can involve a tremendous amount of money, and a tenant's assignment of a commercial lease might affect the financial health of the larger office park or shopping center. *See* Brent C. Shaffer, *Counseling the Client on the Reasonableness Consent Standard to Assignments*, Prac. Real Est. Law., July 2003, at 7. Mr. Shaffer provides a very thoughtful practitioner's template for negotiating these provisions. Mr. Shaffer explains:

> When drafting, negotiating, and interpreting leases, commercial leasing lawyers encounter few words more often than "reasonable." These frequent encounters are seldom pleasant. Reasonableness is a relative term. It means different things to different people, and the reputation of the word for engendering litigation is only enhanced in landlord consents to commercial lease assignments of tenants' interests. Indeed, if you have occasion to research common commercial lease clauses, you will find an amazing paucity of reported decisions, with one notable exception. That exception is express and implied reasonableness standards in lease assignment and sublease clauses. Here, you will find almost 100 reported cases from various jurisdictions. Therefore, a landlord is in dire need of counsel when a tenant requests consent to an assignment of the tenant's interest in its lease.

Query: What happens if a lease states: "Tenant may not assign his interest in the lease without the prior written consent of landlord." The tenant then enters into a sublease with a third party. Has the tenant violated the lease? *See* 24 Broad Street Corp. v. Quinn, 87 A.2d 759 (Pa. Super. Ct. 1952).

For a scholarly discussion of the topic, you might read Joshua Stein, *Assignment and Subletting Restrictions in Leases and What They Mean in the Real World*, 44 Real Prop. Tr. & Est. L.J. 1 (2009); Murray S. Levin, *Withholding Consent to Assignment: The Changing Rights of the Commercial Landlord*, 30 DePaul L. Rev. 109 (1980).

The modern trend toward requiring the landlord to be reasonable when granting or withholding consent to assignment or sublease is based in part on the property law's bias against restraints on alienation. It is also based on §205 of the Restatement (Second) of Contracts, which requires parties to a contract to act in good faith and deal fairly with one another in the performance of the contract. To the extent that a lease is viewed under the lens of contract law, then, we should ask about the reasonable expectations of parties entering into a particular contract. The modern landlord is looking for a financially stable and capable tenant. Therefore, the ability of the transferee to pay the rent is the primary consideration in the reasonableness decision. The Restatement (Second) of Property: Landlord and Tenant §15.2 (1977) echoes this view. *See also* Kendall v. Ernest Pestana, Inc., 709 P.2d 837 (Cal. 1985).

What other reasons for landlord's refusal should a court deem "reasonable"? Consider the following consent situations:

▇ PROBLEM: "BLOOD MONEY"

> ➤ Clarke owns Rama Travels, a travel agency, and leases space in an office center owned by Smith.
> ➤ Clarke is nearing retirement age. Clarke therefore locates Ursula, who agrees to buy his business.
> ➤ The lease between Rama Travels and Smith includes Provision 5, which reads as follows: "Tenant may not transfer, assign or sublease the lease or premises without the prior written consent of Landlord."
> ➤ Clarke requests that Smith consent to an assignment of the lease to Ursula. Without the assignment, Ursula will not purchase the business.
> ➤ Smith refuses, stating: "Provision 5 is my license to steal. If you want my consent, Clarke, you must give me 10 percent of the purchase price. Consider the 10 percent fee my blood money. I have the right to say no just because I feel like it. If you want to retire, pay up."

Clarke visits you and asks for advice. Is Smith entitled to demand the money? *See* Schweiso v. Williams, 198 Cal. Rptr. 238 (Cal. Ct. App. 1984).

The older common law rule allowed a landlord to deny consent for any reason if the lease required consent. This remains the majority rule, but the law is in transition. "[A] substantial number of courts have concluded that the landlord has an implied duty to be reasonable whenever the parties provide that the landlord has the right to consent prior to any assignment or sublet." 1 Andrew R. Berman, Friedman on Leases §7:3.4[D][1] (6th ed. 2017). *See also* Campbell

v. Westdahl, 715 P.2d 288 (Ariz. Ct. App. 1985). The California Supreme Court determined that the landlord was subject to an implied duty to be reasonable in Kendall v. Ernest Pestana, Inc. 709 P.2d 837 (Cal. 1985). However, the California legislature later specifically overruled *Kendall* by statute, stating that *Kendall* frustrated "the expectations of the parties, with the result of impairing commerce and economic development." *See* Cal. Civ. Code §1995.270 (West 2010). Consider the more modern contract-oriented understanding of a leasehold. What does the landlord expect? How does this affect your answer?

Video Problem: Request for Landlord's Approval

📹 In this video, which is available on the Simulation, a tenant approaches the landlord for approval of an assignment of the lease. The proposed assignee would not be a "run-of-the-mill tenant." Do you think that the landlord should consent to the request? Where is the line between dislike of a proposed assignee and a reasonable commercial concern about the impact of the assignment? Did the tenant make any mistakes in her approach?

Courts imposing a standard of commercial reasonableness generally state "[a]rbitrary considerations of personal taste, convenience, or sensibility are not proper criteria for withholding consent under such a lease provision." List v. Dahnke, 638 P.2d 824, 825 (Colo. App. 1981). How would you apply the commercial reasonableness test to the following problem?

■ PROBLEM: TRANSFER TO THE IDEOLOGICALLY UNDESIRABLE TENANT

- ➤ Yoga Studio leases space in a shopping center owned by University. The shopping center is located across from a set of University-owned dorms and near the University campus, to serve the needs of the students (food, stores, and other typical student haunts). Yoga Studio's lease contains a provision stating: "Tenant may not transfer, assign or sublease the lease or premises without the prior written consent of Landlord."
- ➤ Yoga Studio's business is floundering and it seeks an assignee to take over the space. With the help of a broker, Yoga Studio locates Planned Parenthood as a potential assignee. Planned Parenthood is a national organization and is in a much stronger financial position than Yoga Studio.
- ➤ Yoga Studio requests consent to assign the lease to Planned Parenthood. Planned Parenthood will provide health counseling to students and will

provide to students, upon request, contraceptives. It will counsel students about a range of pregnancy-related issues, including abortion, although it will not perform abortion services at that location. University is religiously affiliated. Yoga Studio's request is reported in the student-run University newspaper, and becomes a source of controversy. Many students, alumni, and trustees of University staunchly oppose some of the activities and advice provided by Planned Parenthood.

Assume that University asks for your advice. The President and Board of Trustees would like to deny consent. Is University permitted to deny the tenant's request for consent to an assignment to Planned Parenthood? What is reasonable under the circumstances? *See* American Book Co. v. Yeshiva Univ. Dev. Found. Inc., 297 N.Y.S.2d 156 (N.Y. App. Div. 1969). *See also* Krieger v. Helmsley-Spear, Inc., 302 A.2d 129, 129 (N.J. 1973) (a clause requiring landlord to be reasonable in consenting to tenant's request for assignment or sublease "is for the protection of the landlord in its ownership and operation of the particular property—not for its general economic protection"); Econ. Rentals, Inc. v. Garcia, 819 P.2d 1306, 1317 (N.M. 1991) (the landlord's decision to deny consent "must relate to the ownership and operation of the leased property, not the lessor's general economic interest").

Now consider again the example of the high-end shopping center. When would it be acceptable for the landlord to deny the request of a tenant in that center to assign or sublease the space? What factors do you think that the landlord may consider if the lease requires the landlord's consent to transfer?

> **Practice Tip: Drafting**
>
> How can University counsel in the problem above protect her client's interest when drafting future leases? Landlords generally take one of two approaches when drafting provisions governing the tenant's right to transfer the lease. First, the landlord may include a provision simply stating that "Tenant must obtain Landlord's consent to transfer, for any reason, or for no reason." Should such a "sole discretion" clause be enforceable? *See* Susan E. Myster, *Protecting Landlord Control of Transfers: The Status of "Sole Discretion" Clauses in California Commercial Leases*, 35 Santa Clara L. Rev. 845 (1995). Second, the landlord may include a provision in the lease requiring landlord to be reasonable, but then define reasonableness in such a way as to make most of landlord's decisions acceptable. 💻 An example of one such provision can be found on the Simulation.

Reasonableness depends on the context, including the other provisions of the lease. Consider the following problem.

■ PROBLEM: COMPETITION FROM TENANT

> ➢ Tenant is an outpatient surgical medical practice.
> ➢ Tenant leases space in a mixed-use commercial development known as the "Center." The tenants in the Center include retail stores, restaurants,

and some professional offices, including doctors' and lawyers' offices. Developer is landlord for all leases in the Center.

➤ Hospital is the major hospital in the region and is located adjacent to the Center. Many of the doctors who have offices in the Center also have "privileges" to see patients in the Hospital.

➤ Hospital purchases the Center and becomes landlord for all leases in the Center. The Tenant's lease contains two pertinent provisions:

  ▪ "*Use*. Tenant shall use and occupy the Leased Premises for outpatient surgical procedures and general medical and physician's offices, including related uses and for other purposes reasonably acceptable to Landlord."

  ▪ "*Assignment*. Tenant may not assign the lease without the prior written consent of Landlord, which consent shall not be unreasonably withheld."

➤ Tenant ceases doing business as a surgical center and requests that Hospital consent to assignment of the lease to OccMed, Inc. OccMed is an occupational medical clinic that provides services on contract to industry and businesses. These services largely focus on workers' compensation patients, but OccMed does accept walk-in patients for its services. The services include urgent care, primary care, physical examinations, x-rays, diagnostic and drug testing, and minor surgical procedures.

➤ Hospital denies the request for consent to assignment and in a letter to Tenant explains that it intends to open an occupational medicine wing to the Hospital, and therefore does not wish to have a tenant in the Center directly competing with Hospital's intended use.

Assume that you represent Tenant. Advise your client. Can Hospital rightly decline consent? What is the impact of the Use provision in the lease? *See* Tenet HealthSystem Surgical, L.L.C. v. Jefferson Parish Hosp. Serv. Dist. No. 1, 426 F.3d 738 (5th Cir. 2005).

🖥 Take a look again at the Sample Residential and Commercial Lease Agreements that we presented earlier in this chapter and that are available on the Simulation. Each addresses the ability of the tenant to transfer the premises. In both the Sample Commercial and Residential Lease Agreements, the tenant is required to obtain consent of the landlord to transfer. There are some real differences between the goals and language of the two documents. Why?

We have presented you with several problems that focus on commercial leases. There are more cases in the commercial context, because of the significant financial interests at stake. But we do not want to ignore the plight of the residential tenant. In fact, we started this section by pointing out what might motivate a residential landlord to say "no" to his tenant's request to transfer the tenant's interest in the lease. Must the landlord be reasonable when considering the request, and what does "reasonable" mean in the residential context?

■ PROBLEM: THE RESIDENTIAL TENANT

➤ Daniel owns a 20-unit older apartment building. Units have small floor plans and are not the "open" style developed today. Most of the tenants are couples whose children have grown; many of the tenants are elderly.

➤ Daniel leases an apartment to Jerry for a term of two years at a rental rate of $500 per month. Jerry is a married law professor, but he is considerably younger than the typical tenant in the apartment building.

➤ Jerry's lease contains the following provision: "Tenant may not assign, sublease, or otherwise transfer the premises or the lease without the prior written consent of Landlord."

➤ Jerry receives an offer to teach at a school in another state, and approaches Daniel to obtain consent to assign the lease to Greg, a drummer for a local rock band. Greg has financial statements showing his ability to pay the rent.

➤ Daniel takes one look at Greg, who very much looks the part of a rock band drummer, and simply says "absolutely not, no way!"

Jerry asks for your advice. May Daniel withhold consent? Does the modern rule requiring landlord to be reasonable when withholding consent make sense in the residential scenario?

The Restatement provides generally, as to both residential and commercial leases, that the landlord cannot withhold consent "unreasonably" to tenant's request to transfer, unless the lease includes "a freely negotiated provision [that] gives the landlord an absolute right to withhold consent." Restatement (Second) of Property: Landlord and Tenant §15.2 (1977). *But see* Slavin v. Rent Control Bd. of Brookline, 548 N.E.2d 1226 (Mass. 1990) (refusing to apply a rule that landlords must be reasonable in responding to requests for transfer in residential leases). What is reasonable in the commercial context may be unreasonable in the residential context. Imagine that Andy, the owner of a home, spends a lifetime travelling and acquiring rare artwork when doing so. Andy takes a year-long trip, and leases his house to his stable and mature friend Emily during that time. Now assume that Emily wishes to assign the lease to a college student, who also happens to be president of his fraternity. Would it be reasonable for Andy to deny Emily's request for consent to the assignment?

What happens to the subtenant if the lease between the landlord and tenant terminates? Does the sublease also fail? After all, the general rule is that you can sell only what you own. You would think that a tenant could grant only

An Invitation for Discrimination

Basically, when approached by the tenant for consent to an assignment or sublease, the landlord wants the ability to discriminate—to select among tenants. This is entirely allowed, so long as the landlord is not doing so for *illegal* reasons. We will look at the Fair Housing Act and other laws designed to prevent landlord from engaging in illegal discrimination in the last section of this chapter.

as much right in a leased premises as the tenant was given by landlord and no more. Imagine that Jerry leases a building to Daniel to be used as a hotel. Jerry includes a provision in the lease that gives Jerry the right to cancel the lease if Daniel becomes insolvent (a very sensible provision). Daniel then subleases to Bill. Daniel promptly goes insolvent and Jerry cancels the lease. What happens to Bill?

In short, Bill is out of luck; the sublease comes to an end. The lease between Jerry and Daniel is often called the "prime lease." The lease is "prime" in the sense that it is the first or senior lease. The lease between Daniel and Bill is the sublease. If the prime lease fails because of Daniel's default or because some right in the prime lease gives the landlord the right to terminate the lease, then Bill's sublease also dies. This is a risk of being a subtenant, and you probably already knew this. If you sublease a friend's apartment, you must have suspected that the end of your friend's lease would terminate your sublease as well. *See* Isidore Paiewonsky Assocs. v. Sharp Props., Inc., 998 F.2d 145 (3d Cir. 1993).

This general rule is subject to an exception. If the tenant under the prime lease *surrenders* the premises to the landlord prior to the end of the term, and the landlord accepts, then the landlord accepts surrender *with the sublease in tow*. In other words, the sublease continues. *See* 1 Andrew R. Berman, Friedman on Leases §7:7.3 (6th ed. 2017) ("The prime tenant has no power to destroy the estate that he created.").

E DISCRIMINATION IN LEASING OF REAL PROPERTY (AND MORE GENERALLY, HOUSING)

Imagine that a prospective tenant wants to lease a residential apartment in North Carolina. On the day that the tenant applies to lease the apartment, she is wearing a Duke University sweatshirt. The landlord attended the University of North Carolina at Chapel Hill, and, for lack of any better words, simply *hates* Duke. The landlord immediately rejects the tenant, and for good measure, slams the door in her face. Assume that the prospective tenant has the financial ability to pay rent as it comes due. By saying "no," the landlord is discriminating against the tenant. *What you must understand is that most forms of discrimination are legal, although they may be unfair or unwarranted*. It is important to recognize the line between legal and illegal discrimination. Is it legal for a landlord to refuse to lease or disapprove transfer to a person who went to a university that the landlord despises? Can a landlord discriminate against you because she "doesn't like lawyers"?

In this section, we will look at illegal discrimination in the context of leasing real property. Without an explicit legal basis providing otherwise, *discrimination is permissible*. Therefore, the key is finding one of several statutes or constitutional amendments that renders a particular act of discrimination illegal.

1. Reconstruction and Afterward

The historical focus of most laws limiting discrimination in housing has been race, although in time the focus has expanded to cover discrimination based on other factors, including gender, ethnicity, disability and national origin. This pernicious behavior has an old place in American society. Prior to the mid-twentieth century, it was common for deeds to contain restrictions limiting ownership of real property to white individuals. It was just as common for owners of homes and apartments to tell applicants for rental units—directly to their faces, unabashedly in advertisements, or on crude signs on buildings or houses—that the owners would not sell or lease to persons of color.

The Civil War brought Reconstruction to the South, and ratification of what are commonly known as the "Reconstruction Amendments" to the U.S. Constitution. These include the Thirteenth, Fourteenth, and Fifteenth Amendments. Taken as a package, they were intended to terminate slavery and provide for equal treatment of freed slaves. The Thirteenth Amendment, ratified at the conclusion of the Civil War in 1865, officially ended slavery. The Fourteenth Amendment, ratified in 1868, provided many new individual protections, including the Equal Protection Clause. The Fifteenth Amendment enfranchised prior slaves and all male citizens regardless of race, color, or most specifically "previous condition of servitude."

Section 1 of the Fourteenth Amendment states:

> All persons born or naturalized in the United States, and subject to the jurisdiction thereof, are citizens of the United States and of the State wherein they reside. No State shall make or enforce any law which shall abridge the privileges or immunities of citizens of the United States; nor shall any State deprive any person of life, liberty, or property, without due process of law; *nor deny to any person within its jurisdiction the equal protection of the laws.*

(Emphasis added.) We will leave it to your Constitutional Law professors to take you through equal protection analysis. Our only goal at this point is to note that the Fourteenth Amendment applies to behavior involving *state action* (including sub-entities of the state, such as cities and counties). Thus, a city that enacted laws limiting the ability of persons of color to buy real property in a particular locale would violate the Equal Protection Clause. A public university that discriminated in dormitory housing would also run into Fourteenth Amendment problems.

In Shelley v. Kraemer, 334 U.S. 1 (1948), the Supreme Court held that, although the Fourteenth Amendment did not prohibit private persons from entering into and voluntarily complying with racially restrictive covenants, enforcement of such covenants by a court would constitute state action and therefore violate the Equal Protection Clause. Thus, the Fourteenth Amendment indirectly reaches private restrictions as well.

In addition to the Fourteenth Amendment, Congress passed the Civil Rights Act of 1866, 42 U.S.C. §1982, which was directed squarely at the right of freed slaves to use and own property. The Civil Rights Act of 1866 provides:

All citizens of the United States shall have the same right, in every State and Territory, as is enjoyed by white citizens thereof to inherit, purchase, lease, sell, hold, and convey real and personal property.

The terminology of the Civil Rights Act of 1866 speaks to time and place: it states that all citizens (which would include, following the ratification of the Thirteenth Amendment, freed slaves) have the same right to own, inherit, lease, purchase, and sell real and personal property as do "white citizens." The Act is therefore a response to Emancipation. The language is broad, covering racial discrimination in any real estate context. Furthermore, the Civil Rights Act of 1866 does not require that the discrimination result from state action; it applies to private behavior such as sales and leases.

An unfortunately all-too-common sign prior
to the Fair Housing Act
©Leonard Freed/Magnum Photos

Reconstruction lasted until 1877. It then was followed by the shameful erection of both private restrictions and public laws that blatantly defied the Civil

Rights Act of 1866, the Fourteenth and Fifteenth Amendments, and their general objectives. Individuals in the North and the South routinely refused to sell or lease to persons of color, immigrants, persons of particular religious backgrounds, and so on. The Civil Rights Act of 1866 was rendered a beast without teeth. Not until a century later, in Jones v. Alfred H. Mayer Co., 392 U.S. 409 (1968), did the Supreme Court hold that the Civil Rights Act of 1866 prohibited racially discriminatory sales and leasing practices in private transactions. In *Jones*, the Court explained that the Civil Rights Act of 1866 was an exercise of congressional power pursuant to the Thirteenth Amendment, reinforcing the idea that the Civil Rights Act is limited to instances of discrimination based on race.

Given what you now know, would you expect the Civil Rights Act of 1866 or the Fourteenth Amendment to protect the alumna of one university from the rather cruel decision of the graduate of the rival university not to sell or lease real property to her?

2. The Fair Housing Act

In 1968, Congress supplemented the Civil Rights Act of 1866 by enacting a legislative regime aimed at eliminating a broad range of discrimination in housing. The Fair Housing Act, 42 U.S.C. §§3601-3631 (2013), is one of the most important pieces of legislation of the twentieth century and has had wide application. As we look at the Fair Housing Act, keep two things in mind:

1) First, as a statutory construct, the Fair Housing Act is limited to the forms of discrimination designated in the language of the statute. A court may not add to the list of prohibited behaviors as it might do when interpreting a more general law or a constitutional amendment.

2) Second, and unlike the Fourteenth Amendment or the Civil Rights Act of 1866, the Fair Housing Act provides a specific set of remedies, including damages. This particular feature adds real and intimidating teeth, as well as an incentive for individuals who are subjected to illegal discrimination to sue.

a. Application of the Fair Housing Act

You may think of property law as primarily based in common law. The reality is that statutes (state and federal) are very much part of real property law, and the real property lawyer's practice. The Fair Housing Act is one such example. A good property lawyer must be capable of doing solid statutory analysis. We have reprinted sections of the Fair Housing Act below. Read over the statutory language carefully, and then attempt to answer the problems that follow. In each case, *locate the specific, pertinent provisions* in the Fair Housing Act that allow you to answer the question.

Selected Sections of the Fair Housing Act

Section 3601 provides "It is the policy of the United States to provide, within constitutional limitations, for fair housing throughout the United States."

Section 3602 provides pertinent definitions, including:

(b) "Dwelling" means any building, structure, or portion thereof which is occupied as, or designed or intended for occupancy as, a residence by one or more families, and any vacant land which is offered for sale or lease for the construction or location thereon of any such building, structure, or portion thereof.

(c) "Family" includes a single individual.

(d) "Person" includes one or more individuals, corporations, partnerships, associations, labor organizations, legal representatives, mutual companies, joint-stock companies, trusts, unincorporated organizations, trustees, trustees in cases under Title 11, receivers, and fiduciaries.

(e) "To rent" includes to lease, to sublease, to let and otherwise to grant for a consideration the right to occupy premises not owned by the occupant.

(f) "Discriminatory housing practice" means an act that is unlawful under section 3604, 3605, 3606, or 3617 of this title.

(h) "Handicap" means, with respect to a person—

(1) a physical or mental impairment which substantially limits one or more of such person's major life activities,

(2) a record of having such an impairment, or

(3) being regarded as having such an impairment,

but such term does not include current, illegal use of or addiction to a controlled substance (as defined in section 802 of Title 21).

. . .

(k) "Familial status" means one or more individuals (who have not attained the age of 18 years) being domiciled with—

(1) a parent or another person having legal custody of such individual or individuals; or

(2) the designee of such parent or other person having such custody, with the written permission of such parent or other person.

Section 3603 exempts certain behavior:

(b) Exemptions

Nothing in section 3604 of this title (other than subsection (c)) shall apply to—

(1) any single-family house sold or rented by an owner: *Provided*, That such private individual owner does not own more than three such single-family houses at any one

time: *Provided further*, That in the case of the sale of any such single-family house by a private individual owner not residing in such house at the time of such sale or who was not the most recent resident of such house prior to such sale, the exemption granted by this subsection shall apply only with respect to one such sale within any twenty-four month period: *Provided further*, That such bona fide private individual owner does not own any interest in, nor is there owned or reserved on his behalf, under any express or voluntary agreement, title to or any right to all or a portion of the proceeds from the sale or rental of, more than three such single-family houses at any one time: *Provided further*, That after December 31, 1969, the sale or rental of any such single-family house shall be excepted from the application of this subchapter only if such house is sold or rented (A) without the use in any manner of the sales or rental facilities or the sales or rental services of any real estate broker, agent, or salesman, or of such facilities or services of any person in the business of selling or renting dwellings, or of any employee or agent of any such broker, agent, salesman, or person and (B) without the publication, posting or mailing, after notice, of any advertisement or written notice in violation of section 3604(c) of this title; but nothing in this proviso shall prohibit the use of attorneys, escrow agents, abstractors, title companies, and other such professional assistance as necessary to perfect or transfer the title, or

(2) rooms or units in dwellings containing living quarters occupied or intended to be occupied by no more than four families living independently of each other, if the owner actually maintains and occupies one of such living quarters as his residence.

Section 3604 provides the operative language:

As made applicable by section 3603 of this title and except as exempted by sections 3603(b) and 3607 of this title, it shall be unlawful—

(a) To refuse to sell or rent after the making of a bona fide offer, or to refuse to negotiate for the sale or rental of, or otherwise make unavailable or deny, a dwelling to any person because of race, color, religion, sex, familial status, or national origin.

(b) To discriminate against any person in the terms, conditions, or privileges of sale or rental of a dwelling, or in the provision of services or facilities in connection therewith, because of race, color, religion, sex, familial status, or national origin.

(c) To make, print, or publish, or cause to be made, printed, or published any notice, statement, or advertisement, with respect to the sale or rental of a dwelling that indicates any preference, limitation, or discrimination based on race, color, religion, sex, handicap, familial status, or national origin, or an intention to make any such preference, limitation, or discrimination.

(d) To represent to any person because of race, color, religion, sex, handicap, familial status, or national origin that any dwelling is not available for inspection, sale, or rental when such dwelling is in fact so available.

(e) For profit, to induce or attempt to induce any person to sell or rent any dwelling by representations regarding the entry or prospective entry into the neighborhood of a person or persons of a particular race, color, religion, sex, handicap, familial status, or national origin.

(f)(1) To discriminate in the sale or rental, or to otherwise make unavailable or deny, a dwelling to any buyer or renter because of a handicap of—

(A) that buyer or renter,

(B) a person residing in or intending to reside in that dwelling after it is so sold, rented, or made available; or

(C) any person associated with that buyer or renter.

(2) To discriminate against any person in the terms, conditions, or privileges of sale or rental of a dwelling, or in the provision of services or facilities in connection with such dwelling, because of a handicap of—

(A) that person; or

(B) a person residing in or intending to reside in that dwelling after it is so sold, rented, or made available; or

(C) any person associated with that person.

(3) For purposes of this subsection, discrimination includes—

(A) a refusal to permit, at the expense of the handicapped person, reasonable modifications of existing premises occupied or to be occupied by such person if such modifications may be necessary to afford such person full enjoyment of the premises except that, in the case of a rental, the landlord may where it is reasonable to do so condition permission for a modification on the renter agreeing to restore the interior of the premises to the condition that existed before the modification, reasonable wear and tear excepted.

(B) a refusal to make reasonable accommodations in rules, policies, practices, or services, when such accommodations may be necessary to afford such person equal opportunity to use and enjoy a dwelling;

. . .

Section 3607 exempts religious organizations and private clubs:

(a) Nothing in this subchapter shall prohibit a religious organization, association, or society, or any nonprofit institution or organization operated, supervised or controlled by or in conjunction with a religious organization, association, or society, from limiting the sale, rental or occupancy of dwellings which it owns or operates for other than a commercial purpose to persons of the same religion, or from giving preference to such persons, unless membership in such religion is restricted on account of race, color, or national origin. Nor shall anything in this subchapter prohibit a private club not in fact open to the public, which as an incident to its primary purpose or purposes provides lodgings which it owns or operates for other than a commercial purpose, from limiting the rental or occupancy of such lodgings to its members or from giving preference to its members.

◼ PROBLEM: THE CIVIL RIGHTS ACT OF 1866 AND THE FAIR HOUSING ACT

Arnold is the owner and landlord of a 20-unit apartment building. Pedro was born in the same town as Arnold, but Pedro's parents were immigrants from Colombia. Which of the following constitute illegal discrimination under the Civil Rights Act of 1866 or the Fair Housing Act?

1. Pedro works with a leasing broker and the broker shows Apartment 5 to Pedro. Pedro likes the apartment and offers to lease the unit. As a standard practice, the broker provides Arnold with a copy of Pedro's most recent pay stub, demonstrating Pedro's ability to pay the rent. Arnold sees Pedro's name on the proposed lease and inquires about Pedro's background. Arnold then tells his office assistant: "I just do not like renting to folks who come from south of the border," and rejects Pedro as a tenant. *See* Jones v. Alfred H. Mayer Co., 392 U.S. 409 (1968); Patel v. Holley House Motels, 483 F. Supp. 374 (S.D. Ala. 1979). What if Arnold says nothing, but simply sees Pedro's name, and then rejects Pedro as a tenant? *See* Bouley v. Young-Sabourin, 394 F. Supp. 2d 675 (D. Vt. 2005).

2. The apartment is part of a three-unit building. Arnold lives in one of the units. Arnold refuses to lease to Pedro for the reason specified in the initial fact pattern (the landlord is aware that Pedro's family immigrated from Columbia).

3. Arnold places an advertisement on an internet bulletin board reading as follows: "Apartment available. Full kitchen and one full bathroom. English speaking applicants only. Email arnold@landlord.com." *See* Veles v. Lindow, No. CV-96-20245, 2000 WL 1807851 (9th Cir. Nov. 1, 2000) (unpublished opinion). What if Arnold expands the advertisement to include the statement that "Landlord is a patriotic, red-blooded American"?

4. Pedro and his life partner Hugo make an offer for the apartment. For purposes of this problem, you may assume that the apartment building has ten units. Arnold responds in a letter stating: "Pedro, I couldn't care less about your race or ethnicity, but I disapprove of same-sex couples." Arnold refuses to lease to Pedro. *See* Smith v. Avanti, 249 F. Supp. 3d 1194 (D. Colo. 2017).

5. Pedro leases the apartment from Arnold. One year into the lease, other residents begin to notice a foul smell emanating from the apartment. One tenant reports to the landlord that Pedro has begun to accumulate newspapers, magazines, clothes, and general junk at an alarming rate. Pedro is hoarding. Arnold informs Pedro that he is in violation of a lease provision requiring Pedro to "keep and maintain the Premises in a sanitary and healthy condition." Pedro responds to Arnold that he is presently seeking psychiatric help for his behavior and has been informed that he has a recognized mental illness. In his letter to Arnold, Pedro asks for additional time to remedy the problem, given his proactive attempts to manage his illness. Arnold ignores the letter and seeks an order for eviction. *See* Douglas v. Kriegsfeld Corp., 884 A.2d 1109 (D.C. Ct. App. 2005). *See also* Christopher C. Ligatti, *Cluttered Apartments and Complicated Tenancies: A Collaborative Intervention Approach to Tenant "Hoarding" Under the Fair Housing Act*, 46 Suffolk U. L. Rev. 79 (2013).

> ### Reasonable Accommodations
>
> The Fair Housing Act requires the landlord to make "reasonable accommodations in rules, policies, practices, or services, when such accommodations may be necessary [for the individual] to use and enjoy a dwelling" and that failure to do so is discriminatory. 42 U.S.C. §3604(f)(3)(B) (2013). The tenant's request for the accommodation may be oral. The landlord must then determine if the accommodation is both feasible and not unduly burdensome and costly.

■ ■ ■

Private clubs receive limited protection under the Fair Housing Act, but state law may extend beyond federal law and restrict discriminatory behavior by such institutions. These laws may be far-reaching. For example, New Jersey law bars the ability of private clubs to engage in discriminatory behavior, and this has been extended to prohibit the customary practice of one of the nation's oldest and most prestigious universities. *See* Frank v. Ivy Club, 576 A.2d 241 (N.J. 1990) (applying New Jersey statute to prevent longstanding discriminatory policy of restricting membership by gender at "eating clubs"). Also, note that the Fair Housing Act gives the owner of a single-family house the right to discriminate once every 24 months in the sale or rental of the house. If the discrimination is offensive, why does the statute give property owners one shot every 24 months?

Congress significantly amended the Fair Housing Act in 1988. Among other notable changes, that amendment added disabled individuals and families with children to the list of protected classes of plaintiffs. The Amendment also substituted a new Section 3605, addressing discrimination in the financing of residential real estate. *See generally,* James A. Kushner, *The Fair Housing Amendments of 1988: The Second Generation of Fair Housing,* 42 Vand. L. Rev. 1048, 1092-96 (1989).

You might believe that invidious housing discrimination was limited historically to the American Southeast. Nothing could be further from the truth. Egregious racial and ethnic discrimination was pervasive throughout the U.S. For example, carefully review the poster shown on page 403, used to market "Hartley's North Park" in San Diego, California. This residential subdivision was developed between 1910 and 1915. The poster touts an "up to date restricted residence district" complete with access to two streetcar lines, and invites potential purchasers to "watch the growth of buildings and values." The entire point of this poster is to entice purchasers. With this objective in mind, the developer included in the poster verbatim the restrictions that would appear in deeds to subdivision lots. Read these restrictions, and focus specifically on Restriction 14. Restrictions such as this one were used throughout the U.S. This poster forces us to confront the ugly and profound history of housing discrimination as practiced for many years in the U.S.

In Shelley v. Kraemer, 334 U.S. 1 (1948), the Supreme Court invalidated a covenant that was very similar to Restriction 14 as shown on the Hartley's North Park poster. (Actually, the covenant in *Shelley* was worded in an even uglier manner.) Therefore, following *Shelley,* the racially restrictive covenant in deeds to lots in the Hartley's North Park subdivision would be void and unenforceable. Assume, nevertheless, that the subdivision developer continued to use the Hartley's North Park marketing poster after the decision in *Shelley.* The poster alone would violate the Fair Housing Act. Can you see why this is so?

b. *Disparate Treatment v. Disparate Impact*

The Fair Housing Act addresses critical societal issues. The goal of a well-crafted statutory regime is to provide parties and their attorneys with clear guidance as to the proper elements of an action, standards of proof, and defenses. But even here, questions arise.

A tenant (or any other Fair Housing Act plaintiff) may choose one of two approaches to prove a claim. Under the first, the tenant must show that the landlord *intended* to discriminate against a person protected by the statute. This type of claim is termed *disparate treatment.* "To make out a *prima facie* case of disparate treatment under § 3604(a), plaintiffs must show that (1) they are members of a class protected by the FHA; (2) they sought, and were qualified, to rent (or continue renting) the dwellings in question; (3) defendants refused to rent to plaintiffs; and (4) the housing was put on the market or was rented to other tenants." Khalil v. Farish Corp., 452 F. Supp. 2d 203 (W.D.N.Y. 2006). Not surprisingly,

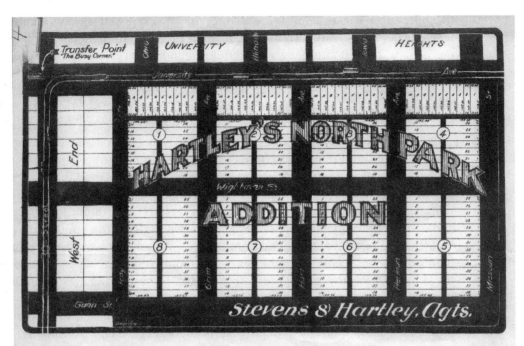

TWO CAR LINES (No. 1 and No. 2, same distance each way) will take you to "Hartley's North Park," the most up-to-date restricted residence district in San Diego. Streets graded and surfaced with decomposed granite; sidewalks and curbs, ornamental corner posts, etc.

Building restrictions $2000, except property facing on University avenue, which will be sold in 25-foot lots for business purposes. Watch the growth of buildings and values.

RESERVATIONS AND RESTRICTIONS AS FOLLOWS:

Reservations and Restrictions as follows:

FIRST: The property hereby conveyed shall be used for residence purposes only and exclusively.

SECOND: Said property shall be used for but one private residence, and no more than one residence or dwelling shall be permitted thereon at any one time. No private residence shall be erected on said premises unless such residence shall have at least a street frontage of fifty feet.

THIRD: No building or structure pertaining to, or for the conduct of any business of any kind whatever shall be erected or placed on said property, or be allowed to be erected or placed on said property.

FOURTH: No double-house, tenement house, lodging-house, boarding-house, club-house, apartment house, flats, hotels, theatre, church, school, store, nor any kind of building or residence, except a residence for use as a single private residence, shall be erected, placed or maintained on said property.

FIFTH: No residence, nor any part thereof, erected or placed on said property, shall at any time be used for any business purpose or purposes, or for any purpose other than a single private residence.

SIXTH: No residence shall be placed or erected on said property which shall cost less than Two Thousand Dollars.

SEVENTH: The residence to be built or placed upon said property, shall front on..................................., as designated on said map.

EIGHTH: The front line of said residence, including porch and piazza, but not including front steps, shall be placed on a line not less than Twenty-five feet from the nearest point of the front line of said property, except if said property fronts on Ray Street, the said front line of said residence as aforesaid, shall be placed on a line not less than twenty feet from such nearest point of such front line of said property.

NINTH: The side lines of said residence, including porch and piazza, but not including steps, shall be placed on a line not less than five feet from the nearest side line of said property.

TENTH: No building or addition to any building, shall be placed or erected on said premises nearer the front line thereof than..feet nor within five feet of the side lines of said property.

ELEVENTH: No garage, barn, or other outbuilding, shall be placed on said property within seventy-five feet of the front line of said property, nor within.......................... feet of the..........................side line of said property.

TWELFTH: No intoxicating liquors of any kind or character shall be sold, or permitted to be sold, on said property, and no sale thereof on said property shall be made, permitted or allowed.

THIRTEENTH: No male poultry or farm animals of any kind (except horses) shall be kept or allowed to be kept on said premises hereby conveyed.

FOURTEENTH: No conveyance, transfer, or lease of said property, nor any lease of any building that may be placed thereon, shall be made to any person not belonging to the Caucasian race or being one of that race, and neither the said property nor any building thereon shall be used or occupied by any person not belonging to the Caucasian race, as owner, lessee or tenant, nor in any other capacity except as servant.

FIFTEENTH: No fence or hedge over five feet high shall be permitted or allowed on said property, except on rear twenty-five feet which shall not exceed eight feet in height. No fence or hedge shall be allowed within twenty-five feet of the front property line of said lot; except a fence or hedge may be allowed to extend within twenty feet of the front line of the lot or lots that front on Ray Street.

STEVENS & HARTLEY

SOLE AGENTS

Branch Office, 30th St. and University Ave.   911 THIRD ST., SAN DIEGO, CAL.

A high resolution version of the Hartley's North Park marketing poster may also be viewed on the Simulation.

defendants, such as residential landlords, typically avoid actively announcing an illegal bias (e.g., leaving a smoking gun such as an email demonstrating racial prejudice). To put it another way, potential defendants try hard to avoid walking into Fair Housing Act litigation.

Although courts permit plaintiffs to point to circumstantial evidence to help bolster their claims (*see* Winfield v. City of New York, No. 15CV5236-LTS-DCF, 2016 WL 6208564 (S.D.N.Y. Oct. 24, 2016)) proving a disparate treatment claim can be difficult. For example, in Greater New Orleans Fair Hous. Action Ctr. v. Hotard, 275 F. Supp. 3d 776 (E.D. La. 2017), a nonprofit organization with a mission of helping low-income renters obtain housing claimed that a residential landlord treated potential renters who were black less favorably than white renters. The nonprofit used equally qualified "testers" to attempt to lease units and demonstrate the landlord's discriminatory practices. The nonprofit argued that the landlord did not respond promptly or favorably to black testers over the phone. However, according to the court, the plaintiff could not demonstrate that the landlord knew the race of the testers when communicating over the phone, a defect the court termed "fatal."

Given the difficulty of proving disparate treatment, courts permit the plaintiff to pursue a second approach to proving a violation of the Fair Housing Act: The tenant may demonstrate through statistical evidence that the behavior of the landlord disproportionately affected a protected group, such as individuals of a particular ethnicity or race. Courts describe this type of Fair Housing Act violation as resting on *disparate impact*. "In contrast to a disparate-treatment case, where a 'plaintiff must establish that the defendant had a discriminatory intent or motive,' a plaintiff bringing a disparate-impact claim challenges practices that have a 'disproportionately adverse effect on minorities' and are otherwise unjustified by a legitimate rationale." Tex. Dep't of Hous. & Cmty. Affairs v. Inclusive Cmtys. Project, Inc., 135 S. Ct. 2507, 2513 (2015), *quoting* Ricci v. DeStefano, 557 U.S. 557, 577 (2009). To succeed based on disparate impact, the plaintiff must demonstrate that the practice or rule in question was outwardly neutral—in other words, that on its face, the practice or rule does not appear to discriminate against a protected class of individuals.

Disparate impact claims have been controversial. Not long after publication of the first edition of this text, a case challenging the manner in which the State of Texas allocated low-income housing development tax credits wound its way up to the United States Supreme Court. Inclusive Communities Project, a nonprofit corporation with a mission of aiding low income individuals and families to secure housing, alleged that Texas had allocated too many low income housing development tax credits to largely minority inner city areas, and too few to mostly white Texas suburbia, limiting the ability of non-white individuals to find housing in the suburbs. Inclusive Communities Project used statistical evidence to demonstrate the negative impact on classes of individuals protected by the Fair Housing Act. Texas argued that the Fair Housing Act required a showing of actual discriminatory intent and that a claim under the Fair Housing Act could not be based on disparate impact alone. Ultimately, the Court validated disparate impact analysis, in Tex. Dep't of Hous. and Cmty. Affairs v. Inclusive Cmtys. Project, Inc., 135 S. Ct. 2507 (2015).

In his majority opinion, Justice Kennedy explained that

> [A]ntidiscrimination laws must be construed to encompass disparate-impact claims when their text refers to the consequences of actions and not just to the mindset of actors, and where that interpretation is consistent with statutory purpose. These cases also teach that disparate-impact liability must be limited so employers and other regulated entities are able to make the practical business choices and profit-related decisions that sustain a vibrant and dynamic free-enterprise system. And before rejecting a business justification—or, in the case of a governmental entity, an analogous public interest—a court must determine that a plaintiff has shown that there is "an available alternative . . . practice that has less disparate impact and serves the [entity's] legitimate needs."

*Inclusive Cmtys. Project Inc.,*135 S. Ct. at 2518., *quoting* Ricci v. DeStefano, 557 U.S. 557, 578 (2009). Plaintiffs cannot bring disparate impact claims under a federal discrimination statue, unless the statutory language "refers to the consequences of actions and not just to the mindset of actors." Is this true of the Fair Housing Act? Reread §3604(a). Can you pinpoint the precise language in this provision that would permit proof of a claim by disparate impact evidence?

Consider the following Problem:

■ PROBLEM: REDEVELOPMENT AT THE EXPENSE OF PROTECTED TENANTS

Manuel and Olivia are a young Mexican-American couple who live in the Sun View Apartment Building in the city of Apple. The Sun View Apartment Building is located in Pine Bluff, an older neighborhood in Apple. Apple is not an ethnically diverse city, and Latin American residents make up approximately 8 percent of the town's population. Pine Bluff is a less affluent neighborhood and is 56 percent Latin American. Apple is undergoing a period of revitalization and growth. Over the last several years, some local politicians and neighborhood groups have complained in the media and at Apple City Council hearings that day-laborers have moved in increasing numbers to the City of Apple. Some of the day-laborers are Latin American and reside largely in Pine Bluff. These politicians and neighborhood groups argue that the presence of day-laborers inhibits development of Apple and diminishes property values. Local fair housing advocacy groups suspect a darker explanation for the anti-day laborer sentiment. The Apple City Council institutes regulations limiting activities of day-laborers by, among other things, fencing in the sites used by day-laborers to wait for offers of day employment and enacting traffic laws that prohibit contractors from picking up day-laborers. Bill Smith, a prominent anti-day laborer radio personality wins the office of Mayor of Apple. Smith then persuades the Apple City Council to adopt the "Pine Bluff Redevelopment Plan." Under the Pine Bluff Redevelopment Plan, Apple approves "high value" multi-use and residential development and, as a result, private developers purchase property in Pine Bluff for the purpose of constructing high-rent shopping and residential buildings. One such developer, Apple Partners, purchases the Sun View Apartment Building, the building in which Manuel and Olivia live. Apple Partners then informs tenants that their leases in Sun View Apartment Building will not be renewed. When Manuel and Olivia's lease expires, they are forced to move to an apartment in a nearby neighborhood, at a higher rental, and with less space. Manuel and Olivia ask for your advice. Do they have recourse pursuant to the Fair Housing Act? *See* Rivera v. Incorporated Village of Farmingdale, 571 F. Supp. 2d 359 (E.D.N.Y. 2008).

c. Missteps Happen

Business people face a host of state and federal regulations. It is possible to unknowingly step close to, and possibly cross, the statutory line separating legal from illegal discrimination.

One of the authors of this book represented a client who was in the business of developing golf course communities in a bedroom county of Atlanta, Georgia. The client owned significant undeveloped land in this county and planned, over time, to develop a number of upscale, gated communities. These communities would include all the usual and desirable amenities. The developer faced a problem, though. How do you reach potential buyers and persuade them to move to an unfinished project that is a difficult drive from work centers in the city? Here is the approach taken by the developer: it put up billboards along highways inviting passersby to visit the development. The billboards showed the façade of a beautiful home, the name of the development, the location, including county, of the project, and a phone number (this occurred in prehistoric times, before the internet and web sites). The billboards included the Fair Housing Act symbol: the little house that indicates that the property owner abides by the Fair Housing Act. Finally, the billboards depicted a very happy nuclear family: a father, mother, son, and daughter. The family was all white. Can you make a claim that the developer violated the Fair Housing Act? Would it matter whether the same picture accompanied the ads for the development in the newspaper? *See* Miami Valley Fair Hous. Ctr., Inc. v. Connor Grp., 805 F. Supp. 2d 396 (S.D. Ohio 2011); Tyus v. Urban Search Mgmt., 102 F.3d 256 (7th Cir. 1996). *See also* 24 C.F.R. §100.75 (2017).

SUMMARY

The Nature of the Lease

- A lease is a *conveyance* of a property interest: the landlord transfers to tenant his exclusive right of possession of real property for a period of time.
- The lease creates a future interest—a *reversion*—in the landlord.
- The tenant's *exclusive right to possession* limits even the landlord's right to enter the premises.
- A lease should be distinguished from the purely contractual *license*; a license is a personal and revocable right to use property.

- A lease may be viewed as a construct of either (or both) *property law* or *contract law*, with significant implications for the rights of the landlord and the tenant. The modern view that a lease is properly evaluated under contract law is increasingly dominant in lease law.

Categories of Leases

- There are three types of "true" leases: tenancies for a *term of years*, *periodic* tenancies, and tenancies *at will*.
- A term of years ends at a date certain; a periodic tenancy terminates upon notice equal to the period of the term; and a tenancy at will terminates at the discretion of either party.
- The *length of notice* for periodic tenancies has been limited today by judicial rule or local statute, and often is a maximum of six months, even if the period is a year.
- A tenant who remains in the premises when the lease terminates is known as a *tenant at sufferance*, and the landlord may elect to treat the tenant at sufferance as a trespasser and evict the tenant, or to treat the tenant as a holdover tenant under a new lease.

Lease Obligations and Rights

- The lease imposes obligations on both tenant and landlord, and grants rights to them as well.
- In American Rule jurisdictions, the landlord need grant the tenant only the legal *right to possession* on the day the term is to commence; in English Rule jurisdictions, the landlord must place tenant in *actual, physical possession*.
- It is the tenant's job to remove any trespasser who commences possession *after* the term begins.
- Under the older common law, so long as the landlord did not breach the peace, the landlord was permitted to resort to *self-help* to remove the holdover tenant or tenant who had breached the lease. Today, most jurisdictions require the landlord to obtain a court order via *summary proceedings* and have the sheriff remove the tenant.
- The tenant's right of exclusive possession comes with two obligations, at a minimum: the obligation to pay rent and the obligation not to waste the property.
- Lease covenants are said to be *independent*: the failure of the landlord to abide by promises he makes to the tenant in the lease does not release the tenant from his obligation to pay rent.
- The one universally accepted dependent covenant is the landlord's *covenant of quiet enjoyment*—the landlord's obligation to permit tenant to remain "quietly in possession" of the premises, without interference by landlord or any person acting through or on behalf of landlord.
- When the tenant *abandons* the premises, the landlord may elect to accept surrender, terminating the tenancy, or continue to hold the tenant to the lease.
- If the landlord elects to continue the lease after tenant's abandonment, the older property-oriented rule does not require landlord to *mitigate damages* by attempting to find a replacement tenant.

- The newer contract rule requires landlord to take *reasonable steps to mitigate* the damages from tenant's abandonment of the space.
- Tenant also has a duty not to *waste* the leased premises. Waste is a tort and landlord may collect compensatory and, in some cases, punitive damages as a result of waste caused or permitted by tenant.

Lease Transfer

- The tenant may wish to transfer his right to exclusive possession to a third person; this will occur by either *assignment* or *sublease*.
- The tenant has an *absolute right to assign or sublease*, unless the lease specifies otherwise.
- An *assignment* is usually deemed to be a transfer of the tenant's entire interest for the remainder of the term; in a *sublease*, the tenant retains a right, however slim, to retake possession.
- The tenant continues to be personally liable to landlord for the rent after an assignment or sublease, unless the landlord *releases* the tenant from liability.
- An *assignee* is liable to the landlord under property law for rent so long as he is in possession and has not assigned to a new party.
- The sub-landlord and sub-tenant owe one another the same duties as a landlord and tenant owe one another.
- Under a modern rule, if the tenant must obtain landlord's consent to transfer, then some jurisdictions require the landlord to be *reasonable* when rejecting the tenant's request.
- The lease may define what is "reasonable," or it may grant the landlord the express right to withhold consent for "any reason."

Illegal Discrimination in Leasing

- The landlord may not *illegally discriminate* against tenants or prospective tenants. Depending on the nature of the discrimination, the act might be barred by the Equal Protection Clause of the Fourteenth Amendment to the U.S. Constitution, the Civil Rights Act of 1866, or the federal Fair Housing Act.
- The *Civil Rights Act of 1866* bars racial discrimination in private leasing arrangements; the Equal Protection Clause bars discrimination involving *state action*.
- The *Fair Housing Act* prohibits discrimination against statutorily identified groups; this list cannot be expanded judicially.
- The Fair Housing Act contains a number of *exceptions and exemptions*, including a protection for a landlord who leases units in a building of four units or less, where the landlord actually occupies one of the units.
- It is never acceptable for a landlord to *advertise* or demonstrate an illegal preference, even if the actual discrimination might be otherwise protected by an exception or exemption.
- A Fair Housing Act claim may be predicated on evidence of *disparate treatment* or *disparate impact*.

PART III

Transfer of Ownership

I n Chapter 2 of this book, we looked at an assortment of mechanisms by which you might come to own property. However, in that chapter, we did not examine the most common means of obtaining ownership of an interest in real property: by purchase.

In Chapter 7, we examine the *real property purchase and sale transaction*. We present concepts and legal doctrine in Chapter 7 along the timeline of the transaction: starting with the moment that an owner of real property decides to sell his land and hires a broker to help him do so, until the closing of the sale and afterward. Each phase of the real estate transaction is associated with a set of particular legal issues, including the Statute of Frauds, the nature of title to property, *caveat emptor* ("buyer beware"), and the fundamentals of the deed. We will also examine the real property purchase and sale contract; this document is the heart of "the deal."

One of the most important concerns of a purchaser of real property is *title*. The purchaser wants to be certain (or as certain as possible) that she is really obtaining the legal interest for which she bargained. Chapter 8 is devoted to the system upon which we rely to ascertain the nature of seller's title. Every jurisdiction maintains a system allowing purchasers to record publicly documents that transfer an interest in real property, as well as "recording statutes" that create the necessary incentive for buyers to do so. We lay the foundation for you to understand a title search, and we will even present you with an opportunity to conduct a title search on your own.

Finally, in Chapter 9, we will examine the *loan transaction*. Notice that we refer above to the purchaser of "an interest in real property." If you borrow money from a bank in order to purchase a home, the bank will ask you to provide collateral for the loan. This collateral is ordinarily a mortgage on the real property you have purchased. A mortgage is an interest in real property, and allows the bank to sell the property in satisfaction of the loan if you default. The bank purchases this interest in real property as part of the loan. The lender therefore has the same need to ascertain the state of the borrower's title as does the purchaser of the seller's title. Few individuals or businesses are able to purchase real property without taking out a loan and mortgaging the real property as collateral. In practice, the loan transaction can be very complex and involve a number of documents. However, we look at the two primary documents in this chapter: the promissory note and the mortgage. If the borrower repays his loan, the lender releases the mortgage and the borrower and lender go their separate ways. Unfortunately, the harsh reality is that some borrowers are unable to repay their loans. As a result, the lender may be forced to foreclose and sell the property. The bulk of Chapter 9 examines the end point of the failed loan transaction—foreclosure.

The Real Estate Purchase and Sale Transaction

> Buy land, they aren't making any more of it.
> —*Will Rogers (or maybe Mark Twain)*

INTRODUCTION: LAWYERS AND TRANSACTIONS

1. Viewing the Purchase and Sale as a Transaction, Not a Lawsuit

There are few events in the lives of businesses or of individuals that are as important, scary, exciting, and risky as the purchase of real property. Residential purchasers invest their dreams of a future in their home purchases. In both commercial and residential contexts, buyers and sellers take a gamble on property values: purchasers hope that the property will appreciate in value, and sellers hope to sell at "the peak of the market." Of course, purchasers and sellers cannot both be right; someone will get the better half of the deal.

And if a purchaser of property buys "more real property than she can afford"—that is, if the purchaser takes on a larger loan than she can pay on a monthly basis to finance the purchase—that purchaser may ultimately discover that she is standing on the wrong end of a foreclosure action. This hard and often life-shattering lesson was learned by hundreds of thousands of homeowners following the great recession in 2008.

The successful purchase and sale of real property therefore calls for clear vision; it is not for the faint of heart.

In the vast majority of cases, the real property transaction is really two transactions in one: the purchase transaction and the loan transaction. Few individuals or businesses have the wealth to purchase real property in cash. In the vast majority of real property purchases, buyers obtain loans in order to finance real property purchases. As a result, purchase transactions are almost always accompanied by loan transactions. We look at the loan transaction, and most specifically the law of mortgages, in Chapter 9.

2. What Lawyers Do: An Initial Comment

The parties to the real estate purchase/loan transaction all hope to increase their wealth (or to limit their losses). The stakes for the parties are very high. An attorney representing a party in this transaction handles the wealth, money, and hopes of her client.

Therefore, it is not surprising that these transactions generate significant litigation after the fact. Disappointed buyers in particular are very quick to "pull the trigger" and sue the seller, as well as the title company, surveyor, home inspector, broker, every lawyer involved in the transaction, and just about anyone else with a pocket and some money.

There is a basic divide between commercial and residential real estate transactions. In a commercial context, lawyers often are involved in all stages of the real estate transaction. Lawyers represent purchasers, sellers, and lenders, and sometimes real estate brokers. A lawyer representing a party in a real estate purchase/loan transaction must understand basic property law concepts of first-in-time and possession. But the real property transaction is not a neatly segregated part of property law. This transaction calls for mastery of contract law, including the Statute of Frauds, *caveat emptor* ("buyer beware"), and title issues, including the concept of marketable title. The real property transaction is document-driven, and a real estate lawyer will need a familiarity with the primary documents involved in the transaction, including the contract, deed, mortgage, and note.

By contrast, lawyers play less of a role in residential transactions. Parties typically sign form contracts provided by brokers. The broker often uses these contracts as a method of conveying offers to the seller. The purchaser signs the contract, which is delivered by the broker to the seller. The seller accepts the offer by signing the contract.

The purchaser and seller are typically (but not always) represented by attorneys in commercial transactions, but much less frequently in residential transactions. In some jurisdictions, lawyers close residential transactions, while in others, such as California, closings are left to escrow or title companies. Nevertheless, there is nothing to prevent a residential purchaser or seller from hiring a lawyer to give advice, even in jurisdictions in which a title or escrow company handles the closing.

As we move through this chapter, we will examine the law as it affects both the residential and commercial transaction. The baseline law is usually the same in residential and commercial transactions, but the expectations of the parties and the language in transactional documents are often significantly different.

Finally, the real property transaction is just that—a *transaction*. It is not litigation, comprised of parties in an adversarial judicial process. Real estate transactions do sometimes fail (or in the parlance of real estate lawyers, "crater") and result in litigation. However, although this is always a possibility, it is not the norm. Unlike litigation, a transaction succeeds because all parties to the transaction find it in their best interests to "close," that is, to exchange money for ownership of property. Each side agrees to close because it believes that it has received what it wants, even if one side may in fact out-negotiate the other.

The mindset of attorneys to a real estate transaction is therefore different from that of a litigation attorney. Transactional lawyers such as real estate attorneys are paid to protect their client's interests, *while helping to get the deal done*. This only happens if the attorney can work with, and not against, attorneys on the other side of the table.

3. The Transaction Timeline

This chapter is structured in the same order as a purchase and sale transaction. There are four phases of the purchase and sale transaction: *pre-contract period*, *contract/executory period*, *closing*, and *post-closing*. Each phase requires lawyers to anticipate risks, to understand substantive legal issues, and to take specific

Timeline Along the Border

You will notice that the border of this chapter shows a continual timeline. This timeline will allow you to keep track of our place in the real estate transaction.

action. Disputes may arise among parties (and often do) at specific points along the timeline. Lawyers associate substantive legal issues and types of disputes with points along the trajectory of the transaction. We believe that presenting this material in this fashion will help you understand and retain the law underlying real property transactions.

A few preliminary definitions will be helpful to you.

- **Pre-contract period.** The time period preceding the moment at which the owner of real property executes a contract for sale with her purchaser is commonly called the *pre-contract* phase of the transaction. During this time period, brokers play a central role in helping the seller locate a ready, willing, and able purchaser.

- **Contract/executory period.** The time period immediately following the *execution* (signing) of the contract until the moment of closing is known as the *executory period*. In this context, executory means *not fully performed*. In other words, the seller has yet to give the purchaser the deed, and the purchaser has yet to give the seller the complete purchase price. During the executory period, the purchaser will investigate title, and to the extent permitted by the contract, perform physical inspections of the property. Indeed, at each step along the timeline, the parties will complete tasks assigned to them by the contract.

Gifts Happen

We focus on sales of real property in this chapter, but in some instances a donor simply skips the contract and makes a gift of real property to a donee by deed. The deed might state that the deed was delivered in consideration of "love and affection." There are other types of non-sales transfers of real property as well (e.g., to settle a divorce case).

- **Closing.** The contract *closes* when the parties each complete performance as required and the seller delivers title, in exchange for the purchaser tendering full consideration.

- **Post-closing.** The period of time following closing, when the purchaser has taken ownership of the property, is called the *post-closing* phase of the transaction. All sorts of nasty problems can crop up post-closing, primarily with respect to title to the real property, or with respect to the physical condition of the property. When this happens, the buyer will look to (and possibly sue) the seller, the title insurance company, and professionals involved in the transaction.

A typical real property lawyer will be engaged in many transactions at any given time, and will have to track details for each transaction on a daily and weekly basis. This is why lawyers representing parties to a real estate transaction think in terms of timelines. The purchase and sale, and the loan follow along mostly parallel timelines, but implicate different legal issues and documents.

B THE PRE-CONTRACT PERIOD—THE BROKER

Legal issues arise prior to execution of the contract between the buyer and the seller. We will focus on the intermediary who helps make the deal happen, the broker. In many, but certainly not all instances, a real estate broker will guide a seller of property to an interested purchaser.

The job of the broker is to locate a "ready, willing, and able" purchaser for the seller's property, and to help persuade the purchaser to make an offer at a price acceptable to seller. *Brokers make deals happen.*

The ultimate goal of the broker is to be paid his commission, and the broker will want the commission to be as high as possible. For this reason, the broker will work hard to increase the total pool of potential buyers, given the nature of the property. In other words, the more possible buyers for the property the broker can locate, the better for the seller. The price of the property will increase as the number of interested parties climbs.

We spend time on brokers, and the law surrounding the earning of a commission and the duties of a broker, because these individuals are crucial to real property sales in the United States. And, to some real extent, we focus on brokers because broker claims to commissions, and sellers' refusals to pay commissions, have led to disputes and litigation.

1. Listing Agreements

The broker and seller will enter into a *listing agreement.* This agreement will set out the duration of the broker's service, the commission rate, and listing price of the property. The listing price is the price at which the seller agrees to accept a purchaser's offer. The broker who signs a listing agreement with the seller is known as the listing broker. Brokers are usually compensated with a commission; this is a payment equal to a fixed percentage of the sale price. For example, if the commission is 6 percent and the house sells for $100,000, then the broker will receive $6,000 in commission payment. Although the listing agreement sets a listing price, the seller is typically free to accept a lower sales price, which of course results in a lower commission for the broker.

The duration of the listing agreement is important to both the seller and the broker. The broker will want to have enough time to reasonably attempt to sell the property. Seller will view the broker much as the owner of a football team views the coach: in the same way that a team owner may want to replace a coach after a losing season, a real property seller wants the ability to drop the broker in favor of someone new if the property is not sold in the seller's time frame.

PRE-CONTRACT

CONTRACT/EXECUTORY

CLOSING

POST-CLOSING

There are three primary forms of listing agreements: *exclusive* listing agreements, *exclusive agency* listing agreements, and *open* listing agreements. Brokers favor exclusive listing agreements because these guarantee a commission if the seller enters into an agreement with a purchaser during the term of the listing, no matter who locates the purchaser. In an exclusive agency listing, the seller agrees to work exclusively with the listing broker; as a result, the listing broker will earn a commission if the seller conveys to a purchaser located by another broker. However, the seller may locate the purchaser without owing a commission to the listing broker. In an open listing, the seller makes no promises of exclusivity at all to the broker; the broker who locates a purchaser acceptable to the seller earns a commission.

Listing Agreement

⌨ You may view an exclusive listing agreement on the Simulation. This form was created by the North Carolina Association of REALTORS. This type of listing agreement is often used in the residential sales context.

Broker versus Agent

You will often see references to real estate *brokers* and real estate *agents*. States require individuals who represent sellers in real property transactions to be licensed, and licensing typically requires an individual to meet educational standards and pass a test. This is true for both "brokers" and "agents." A broker is the party who technically lists property. A broker may have one or more sales agents as employees. The broker's license requires a greater degree of knowledge and may require a minimum number of years in the industry. An agent must work for a broker.

2. The Commission

Brokers show property only because they anticipate being paid. The seller and the broker will sometimes dispute whether and when the broker earned a commission. The initial standard operating procedure for resolving these disputes is to examine the listing agreement.

According to a longstanding common law rule, the broker earns her commission as soon as she locates a "ready, willing, and able" purchaser, even if later the purchaser contracts a nasty case of "cold feet" and refuses to consummate the transaction. In other words, the broker expects to be paid once her work is done. From the broker's perspective, she completes her work when she finds a purchaser acceptable to the seller. If the purchaser does not "show up at the altar," well, that is the seller's worry. This older rule is under attack. Consider the following problem.

■ PROBLEM: THE "NO SHOW"

> ➤ Broker specializes in selling residential property on Nantucket Island. The island is a small place, at least in terms of the number of property sellers and purchasers. Samantha wishes to sell her home on the island and lists the property with Broker. The listing agreement sets a listing price of $110,000 and a 5 percent commission.
> ➤ Broker locates Paul, who counteroffers with a proposed purchase price of $105,000. Broker presents this counteroffer to Samantha, and Samantha accepts the offer. Paul and Samantha sign a contract with a purchase price of $105,000. The contract calls for a February 1 closing. Paul tenders a check in the amount of $1,000 as a down payment at the time he signs the contract.
> ➤ After signing the contract, Samantha realizes that she needs to stay in her home a bit longer and requests that Paul agree to extend the date for closing until March 1. Paul refuses the request.
> ➤ Samantha appears at the regularly scheduled February 1 closing date, deed in hand, ready to sell and convey her island home. However, Paul is a "no show" and does not attend the closing or purchase the property. Broker also attends the scheduled closing. When it is clear that Paul will not show, Broker states to Samantha: "Well, that is a shame. I am sure that you were hoping the deal would close. Nevertheless, you owe me a commission. Please give me my check."

Does Samantha owe Broker a commission, and if so, in what amount? *See* Tristram's Landing, Inc. v. Wait, 327 N.E.2d 727 (Mass. 1975).

■   ■   ■

The more modern and increasingly popular rule, established by the seminal case of Ellsworth Dobbs, Inc. v. Johnson, 236 A.2d 843 (N.J. 1967), demands that the broker locate a ready, willing, and able purchaser, that the parties execute a binding contract for sale and purchase, *and that the purchaser show up at closing, tender payment, and consummate the transaction.* The *Ellsworth Dobbs* court famously stated, "The house-owner wants to find a man who will actually buy his house and pay for it. He does not want a man who will only make an offer or sign a contract. He wants a purchaser 'able to purchase and able to complete as well.'" *Id.* at 854. Can you see the economic rationale for the new rule?

There is an exception to the newer rule that a broker earns a commission only if the purchaser completes the transaction. If the seller causes the purchaser to back out, or takes steps that the seller should realize would cause a reasonable purchaser to refuse to close, then the seller must pay the broker a commission. If this were not the rule, then any seller getting cold feet would be able to walk away from a transaction without paying the commission.

PRE-CONTRACT

CONTRACT/EXECUTORY

CLOSING

POST-CLOSING

■ PROBLEM: A FOCUS ON SELLER BEHAVIOR

> Sidney and Broker enter into a listing agreement for the sale of Sidney's apartment building. The listing price is $1 million. The term of the listing agreement is six months, and the commission rate is 6 percent.

> Broker locates Patricia, a local property investor. Patricia must obtain a loan in order to buy the property.

> There are four apartments in the building, and each is occupied by a tenant pursuant to a periodic tenancy lease agreement. Patricia tours the property and asks about the rental rates paid by tenants. Patricia intends to obtain a loan to provide the necessary amount of money to purchase the apartment building. Patricia calculates that the rent she will receive from the four tenants will cover her mortgage payment and leave a small profit.

> Patricia signs a purchase and sale contract with Sidney on August 1 at the listing price, with a closing set for September 1.

> One week before closing, Patricia visits the property for the purpose of making a list of "things to do" once the property transaction is complete. During her visit she chances to meet Ms. Smith, one of the four tenants. Ms. Smith informs Patricia that she plans to give notice and terminate her lease, as allowed by her lease agreement. Ms. Smith explains: "Sidney sent us a letter on August 2 informing us that he was increasing rents by 10 percent at the end of the term. That is just too much. I am willing to bet that the other tenants feel just the same as I do." Patricia confronts Sidney about the letter. Sidney admits that "I was not sure that our deal would close, and if I am left as owner, I want more rent from my tenants."

> Patricia goes back to her office and does the math. If even one tenant terminates, and if she has difficulty replacing that tenant at the present rent rate, Patricia will be unable to make payments on her loan.

Patricia does not show up at closing and fails to complete the purchase of the apartment building. Broker demands a commission. What results would you expect under the older common law and the *Ellsworth Dobbs* rule? *See* Drake v. Hosley, 713 P.2d 1203 (Alaska 1986); Dworak v. Michals, 320 N.W.2d 485 (Neb. 1982).

3. Fiduciary Duties

If you are a seller of real property and hire a broker, how can you be sure that your broker is acting in your interest? For example, how can you be sure that the broker will not tell a prospective purchaser your "minimum acceptable price"? If

What Is a Moral Hazard?

Whenever one person controls the wealth or property of another, it is possible that the person controlling the wealth will treat that wealth or property with less care or concern than he might treat his own. For example, if a real estate broker suggests a purchaser for seller's property at a price lower than the market rate, or gives away the seller's confidential information, it is the seller who bears the cost. Fiduciary duties force the broker to treat the property as if it were his own.

a purchaser has access to this information, the purchaser would be able to buy the property at its lowest price, to your distinct disadvantage.

Lawyers, trustees, and brokers are all *fiduciaries*. Each professional, in the manner of her profession, manages and preserves the wealth or assets belonging to another person. The seller hires a broker and entrusts the broker with the important job of locating a buyer for seller's property, and more specifically, a *reliable* buyer who will pay a price that satisfies seller. The seller is therefore the *beneficiary* of the broker's fiduciary duties. The primary fiduciary duties that a broker owes to the seller are the duty of care, the duty of loyalty, and the duty of disclosure.

Broker's Duties to Seller

Because the broker's contract is with the seller, the broker's fiduciary duty is to the seller. The primary duties to the seller include:

- **Duty of care.** The broker owes the seller a duty to act with the level of care of a hypothetical competent broker specializing in the sale of real property under like circumstances.
- **Duty of loyalty.** The broker must (1) not engage in self-dealing (placing the broker's interests above the seller's), (2) maintain client confidences, and (3) avoid conflicts of interest.
- **Duty to disclose all offers.** The broker must disclose all non-frivolous offers to the seller, including offers below the listing price, so that seller may determine whether or not to accept any such offers.

A broker who breaches a fiduciary duty to the seller is not entitled to a commission. And if the seller discovers that the broker breached the fiduciary duty after paying the broker the commission, the broker can be forced to pay back or "disgorge" this amount to the seller.

HAYMES v. ROGERS

219 P.2d 339 (1950)
Supreme Court of Arizona

DeConcini, Justice.

Kelley Rogers, hereinafter called appellee, brought an action against L.F. Haymes, hereinafter referred to as appellant, seeking to recover a real estate

PRE-CONTRACT

CONTRACT/EXECUTORY

CLOSING

POST-CLOSING

commission in the sum of $425. The case was tried before a jury which returned a verdict in favor of appellee. The said appellant owned a piece of realty which he had listed for sale with the appellee, real estate broker, for the sum of $9,500. The listing card which appellant signed provided that the commission to be paid appellee for selling the property was to be five (5%) per cent of the total selling price. Tom Kolouch was employed by the said appellee as a real estate salesman, and is hereafter referred to as "salesman."

On February 4, 1948, the said salesman contacted Mr. and Mrs. Louis Pour, prospective clients. He showed them various parcels of real estate, made an appointment with them for the following day in order to show them appellant's property. The salesman then drew a diagram of the said property in order to enable the Pours to locate and identify it the next day for their appointment. The Pours, however, proceeded to go to appellant's property that very day and encountering the appellant, negotiated directly with him and purchased the property for the price of $8,500. The transcript of evidence (testimony) reveals that the appellant knew the Pours had been sent to him through the efforts of appellee's salesman but he did not know it until they verbally agreed on a sale and appellant had accepted a $50 deposit. Upon learning that fact he told the Pours that he would take care of the salesman.

Appellant makes several assignments of error and propositions of law. However we need only to consider whether the trial court was in error by refusing to grant a motion for an instructed verdict in favor of the defendant.

One of the propositions of law relied upon by the appellant is as follows: "The law requires that a real estate broker employed to sell land must act in entire good faith and in the interest of his employer, and if he induces the prospective buyer to believe that the property can be bought for less, he thereby fails to discharge that duty and forfeits all his rights to claim commission and compensation for his work."

There is no doubt that the above proposition of law is correct. A real estate agent owes the duty of utmost good faith and loyalty to his principal. The immediate problem here is whether the above proposition is applicable to the facts in this instance. The question is, is it a breach of a fiduciary duty and a betrayal of loyalty for a real estate broker to inform a prospective purchaser that a piece of realty may be purchased for less than the list price? We believe that such conduct is a breach of faith and contrary to the interests of his principal, and, therefore, is a violation of the fiduciary relationship existing between agent and principal which will preclude the agent from recovering a commission therefrom.

The facts here are clear and undisputed. The salesman informed the purchasers that he had an offer of $8,250 for the property from another purchaser which he was about to submit to appellant. He further told them he thought appellant would not take $8,250 but would probably sell for a price between $8,250 and $9,500 and that they in all probability could get it for $8,500. The agent was entirely without justification in informing the purchasers that the property might be bought for $8,500, since that placed the purchasers at a distinct advantage in bargaining with the principal as to the purchase price of the realty. As a general rule an agent knows through his contacts with his principal, how anxious he is to sell and whether or not the principal will accept less than the listed price. To inform a third person of that fact is a clear breach of duty and loyalty owed by the fiduciary to his principal. Such misconduct and breach of duty results in the agent's losing his right to compensation for services to which he would otherwise be entitled.

. . .

> In Alford v. Creagh, 7 Ala. App. 358, 62 So. 254, the court lays down these rules: "The law requires that a real estate agent, employed to sell land, must act in entire good faith and in the interest of his employer. *Henderson v. Vincent*, 84 Ala. 99, 101, 4 So. 180. To this end he must exact from the purchaser the price, the terms, and conditions of sale which his employer has fixed. 23 Am. & Eng. Ency. Law (2d Ed.) p. 902. If he fails to do this, but induces the prospective purchaser to believe that the property can be bought for less, he fails to discharge that duty to his principal that good faith demands. Such conduct on the broker's part is well calculated to lead the purchaser to stand out and thereby either force from the seller a lower price than that fixed or delay the sale, even if he finally buys at the price fixed, both detrimental to the interest of the seller. . . . The real estate agent loses his right to commissions where, in his dealings in reference to the subject-matter of his employment, he is guilty of either fraud or bad faith towards his employer. 23 Am. & Eng. Ency. Law (2d Ed.) p. 921."

This determination makes a consideration of the other grounds for appeal unnecessary. Under the circumstances the court should have directed a verdict for the defendant, appellant.

Judgment reversed.

LA PRADE, C.J., and STANFORD and PHELPS, JJ., concur.

UDALL, Justice (dissenting).

I dissent for the reason that as I construe the record in the instant case the facts do not disclose such bad faith or gross misconduct on the part of the broker as to disentitle him to compensation.

There is no disagreement between us as to the high standard which the law prescribes must be maintained in dealings between an agent and his principal. . . . The difficulty comes in applying the law to the facts of this case.

The great majority of the reported cases denying a brokerage fee involve instances where (1) the agent acts adversely for the purpose of securing a secret profit for himself or otherwise advancing his own welfare at the expense of that of his employer; (2) an agent disclosing the necessitous circumstances of his principal; (3) the agent is guilty of fraud or dishonesty in the transaction of his agency; (4) his conduct is disobedient or constitutes a wilful and deliberate breach of his contract of service; or (5) where he withholds information from his principal which it is his duty to disclose.

. . .

Two of the other cases referred to [in the majority opinion] are also readily distinguishable. In Alford v. Creagh, 7 Ala. App. 358, 62 So. 254, there was underhanded dealing on the part of the broker by his endeavoring to buy the property for his own benefit. In the case of Harvey v. Lindsay, 117 Mich. 267, 75 N.W. 627, 629, the decision turned upon the refusal of the trial court to direct a verdict for the defendants, the appellate court concluded "We are not satisfied that bad faith was conclusively proven." The judgment allowing the broker's fee was therefore affirmed.

An analysis of the testimony before us, when taken as it must be in the light most favorable to a sustaining of the judgment, shows but four questionable matters. First, the agent advised his principal, before the Pours came onto the scene, that in his opinion the listed sales price of $9500 was excessive. This statement was made after repeated efforts to sell to others at the list price had failed. I can see nothing improper in this. Second, the agent advised Pour (the ultimate purchaser whom he had procured) that his principal, the owner, then had on his desk for acceptance or rejection an offer of $8,250 which offer, in his opinion, the seller would not accept. There may have been some impropriety in this disclosure of his principal's business but I cannot read into this slip such gross misconduct as to warrant denying him compensation. Third, complaint is made that the broker failed to exert his best efforts to effect a sale to the Pours at the list price of $9500. In my opinion there is no merit to this contention because it is clear that the broker did advise the prospective purchasers that the owner's asking price was $9500 and it further appears that appellant perfected the sale with the Pours the evening of the first day they were contacted and before the broker's salesman had an opportunity to keep an appointment for the following day at 1:00 P.M., when he was to show them the property in question. It is unthinkable to believe that any purchaser would buy property without first seeing it. The majority evidently do not base the reversal upon any of these derelictions so finally we consider what is urged as the broker's most serious breach of duty to act in good faith and for the interest of the appellant, to wit, his unauthorized statement that the owner might accept less than the list price. To keep the record straight I quote from the cross-examination of salesman Tom Kolouch:

"Q. And you also told them at that time that you were pretty sure if they would offer $8500 for the property that they would get it? A. I told them they might try $8500. I didn't tell them for sure they would get it because I wasn't setting a price on the other man's property. Q. And you told them if they would offer $8500 that they might get the property? A. They might have, yes. Q. And there wasn't anything said at that time about their offering $9500 for the property? A. I told them the price was $9500 on our list." and the following is Mr. Pour's version of the matter: "Q. He told you to go out there and offer $8500 for the property? A. No, he told me it was listed for more, but he didn't think this offer would go through, and if I met somewhere in between I might get it."

. . .

In effect, as I view it, all the appellee intended by his statements to the Pours was to hold their interest in the property until he could show it to them and the parties could be brought together. I understand it to be the law that the ultimate duty of the broker toward his principal is to procure a purchaser ready, willing and able to purchase upon terms agreed upon by the owner and the purchaser. How then can it be said that the effort of the broker in the instant case in attempting to interest a purchaser and bring the purchaser and owner together by stating that the property might possibly be purchased for less than the quoted price (something which every prospective purchaser would be justified in assuming and which is a hope in the mind of every buyer) amounted to a breach of his duty to act for his principal's best interest? Will not the court's opinion be construed as holding that if a broker states to a purchaser or even indicates in any manner that property might be acquired for less than the listed price his right to a commission is thereby forfeited? If such be the declared law of this state it will certainly give a wide avenue of escape to unscrupulous realty owners from paying what is justly owed to agents who have been the immediate and efficient cause of the sale of their property.

It would be a most naive purchaser who would not know or assume without being told that the owner of realty might sell for less than the original asking price. In my opinion this broker's conduct does not disclose such bad faith or gross misconduct on his part as to warrant a forfeiture of all right to a commission. Particularly is this true where, as here, it is shown that the owner primarily refused to pay the usual 5% commission and thus brought on the lawsuit, because the broker would not agree to split the fee with him. Certainly the appellee was the procuring cause of the sale to the Pours as he put them in touch with the owners. The case was fairly tried to a jury and by their verdict it is apparent they found no evidence of bad faith or gross misconduct on the part of appellee. To me it seems erroneous for this court to now declare that the conduct heretofore enumerated, as a matter of law is such as to warrant denying all compensation to the broker.

I would affirm the judgment as entered by the learned trial court.

■ POINTS TO CONSIDER

1. **Tell your client's story.** In many respects, the broker in *Haymes* is a more sympathetic party than the apparently aggrieved seller. If you represented the broker in *Haymes*, how would you present a narrative on your client's behalf?

2. **Getting to yes.** The court flatly says that the broker and salesman violated the duty of loyalty by disclosing what the seller thought might be an acceptable price for the seller. This is the result that most courts would reach. But think for a moment about what this really means. What is the job of the broker? If a broker works with a seller who has "stars in his eyes" (believes that his property is worth more than it really is), what can and should the broker do? In the normal course of real estate deals, do you imagine that brokers often suggest that potential purchasers offer a particular price, or that

they only rarely do so? What if Kolouch had merely told the Pours that the seller "might take less" than the listing price, rather than suggesting a specific price? Is that so different from what actually occurred? *See* Gerald Korngold, *Real Estate Brokers Are Not "Fiduciaries": A Call for Developing a New Legal Framework*, 40 Real Est. L.J. 376 (2011).

■ PROBLEMS: SCENARIOS TESTING THE SCOPE OF FIDUCIARY DUTIES

The broker's other primary fiduciary duties are the duty of care and the duty to disclose all offers to seller. Consider the following scenarios. Do you think that the broker violated a fiduciary duty to the seller, and if so, which duty?

1. Jones owns property and meets with Broker to discuss property that Jones wishes to list for sale. Broker explains that he has "evaluated the market" and suggests a listing price of $100,000. Jones agrees and lists property for sale with Broker at a 5 percent commission rate. Two weeks after the property is publicly listed and advertised for sale, Smith signs a contract to purchase the property at the listing price. The sale takes place within 30 days, without a hitch, and Broker receives his $5,000 (5 percent) commission. One month after purchasing the property, Smith contracts to sell the property to Brown for $300,000. That sale takes place as scheduled. Jones discovers the later conveyance to Brown and is irate. May he force the Broker to disgorge (that is, return to Jones) his commission?

2. Tricia is an associate in a law firm in Des Moines. She informs Broker that she has received a fantastic job offer in Los Angeles, but the terms of the offer require her to begin work in L.A. virtually immediately. Tricia owns a modest ranch-style home in Des Moines. Apartment rental rates, and home values, are considerably higher in L.A. than in Des Moines. Broker tells Tricia that her house should be listed for $120,000. Other similar homes in the same neighborhood as Tricia's have been selling in the range of $105,000 to $110,000. Tricia moves to L.A. One day after Tricia moves to L.A., a story appears in the Des Moines newspaper under the headline "UPS Considering Move to Des Moines." According to the story, UPS is earnestly examining a move from Atlanta to the less congested and much more affordable Midwest. The newspaper article suggests that the decision will come within six to eight weeks, and if UPS chooses Des Moines, home values in that city will increase significantly. As a result, Broker does not schedule any Sunday house showings. Broker does receive an offer of $99,000, but Broker deems this amount to be so low as to not warrant Tricia's attention and does not inform Tricia of the offer. Tricia is successful in her new job, but because she cannot afford to pay rent while also paying her existing mortgage/note payment in Des Moines, she is forced to sleep on the couch of a friend until her Des Moines house is sold. UPS ultimately chooses

Des Moines, and Broker secures a sale price above the listing price, at $140,000. Tricia becomes aware that UPS has moved to Des Moines only after closing. Can she force disgorgement of the commission?

4. A Few Final Broker Issues

Purchaser's confusion. As you know, a broker and a seller will enter into a written listing agreement. In the residential context, there are often two brokers involved in the transaction. The *listing broker* enters into the listing agreement with seller. The listing broker places her sign in front of the seller's house, promotes and advertises the house for sale, and shows the home. Often a different broker will take a prospective purchaser to see many homes, including the seller's home. The prospective purchaser comes to rely on the advice of this broker, and may come to believe that this person owes purchaser legal duties. If the purchaser buys the home, the second broker is known as the *selling broker.*

The listing broker and selling broker will share the commission. In fact, in every jurisdiction, licensed brokers participate in a community-wide Multiple Listing Service (MLS) agreement, in whidch they agree in advance to share commissions for residential transactions in this manner. Basic agency law considers both the listing broker and the selling broker as agents of seller; therefore, both brokers' fiduciary obligations flow to the seller. This results from the listing agreement and the fact that the seller pays the commission, which the listing and selling broker split. The selling broker is therefore a "sub-agent" of the listing broker.

> ### Commercial Brokers
>
> There is often a single broker in commercial transactions, although there can certainly be more than one broker. However, there is no Multiple Listing Service for commercial transactions. If a purchaser uses a broker, the listing broker and selling broker will negotiate the division of the commission.

A purchaser is sometimes *shocked* to discover that the agent who has been taking the purchaser on home tours technically works for the seller. After all, if the selling broker owes fiduciary duties to the seller, the selling broker might "emphasize" the nice features of a home or neighborhood when showing a property to the purchaser, or minimize the drawbacks of a property.

The possibility that purchaser might believe that the selling broker represents the purchaser and not the seller is real, but this problem may be alleviated or reduced by one of several approaches. Recall that the purchaser will often tell her selling broker the confidential high price the purchaser is willing to offer. In some states, the selling broker is required to maintain confidential information of the purchaser.

Alternatively, the purchaser might hire a true *buyer's broker*. In this case, the buyer's broker only owes fiduciary duties to the purchaser. This solution is

PRE-CONTRACT
CONTRACT/EXECUTORY
CLOSING
POST-CLOSING

especially clean if the purchaser pays her broker directly, but this is not the usual practice. Instead, the buyer's broker typically receives a portion of the listing broker's commission. The listing brokers and buyer's broker negotiate over a division of the commission. 💻 An example of a form listing agreement providing for a buyer's broker can be found on the Simulation.

Many jurisdictions require brokers to present disclosure forms to the purchaser. These forms explain the nature of the relationship between the parties. A number of jurisdictions permit what is known as *dual agency*, in which a single broker is permitted to act as broker for both parties, so long as the broker discloses this status to the parties and the parties agree. *See, e.g.,* Horiike v. Coldwell Banker Residential Brokerage Co., 383 P.3d 1094 (Cal. 2016) (explaining and applying disclosure requirements under Cal. Civ. Code §2079). *See generally,* Bruce Zucker and Kiren Dosanjh Zucker, *Both Sides of the Fence: Legal and Ethical Implications of Dual Agency in Real Estate Transactions,* 45 Real Est. L. J. 153 (2016).

Theoretically, a broker is required to meet the duties of care and loyalty to each party. You can see how difficult this might be; if the transaction fails, one or perhaps both parties will claim that the broker was disloyal. Some states have developed what are termed *transaction brokers* to represent both purchaser and seller. The transaction broker provides "limited representation to a buyer, a seller, or both, in a real estate transaction, but does not represent either in a fiduciary capacity or as a single agent." Fla. Stat. §475.01(1)(l) (2017).

These approaches are discussed more fully in advanced Real Estate Law courses.

■ PROBLEM: DOES THE BROKER OWE FIDUCIARY DUTIES TO THE PURCHASER?

Pam recently moved to a new city and state. She has no real knowledge of the city and therefore hires Greg as a real estate broker to show her homes in a variety of neighborhoods. She is also selective about homes and wants a house with historical and architectural flair. Greg takes Pam to see over 20 homes and patiently explains the features of each. Finally, Greg takes Pam to see Seller's home. Bob is the listing agent. Bob and Greg help Pam tour the home. The listing price is $105,000. Pam is entranced, but she is not sure that the listing price is fair. She tells Greg that she can only really afford $100,000 but would strongly prefer to go no higher than $95,000. Greg responds, "I will go talk to Bob and see what I can do." Greg returns and says that Seller has lowered the price to "$100,000, but no lower." Greg further says, "I think that this is the seller's floor price. You may lose the house if you do not act quickly." Pam accepts the price of $100,000. After the closing, Pam learns that Greg told Bob that Pam's maximum price was $100,000 and this is why Seller chose that amount. Pam is angry. What is Pam's position vis-à-vis Greg? How might Pam have avoided any confusion and received the service from Greg that she truly desired?

PRE-CONTRACT

CONTRACT/EXECUTORY

CLOSING

POST-CLOSING

THE CONTRACT/EXECUTORY PERIOD

Execution (signature) of the contract by the parties signifies the start of the executory period. The executory period concludes when the seller and purchaser close the transaction. *Closing* is the event at which the seller and the purchaser exchange a deed to the property for money.

The contract will obligate the seller to convey title to the property to the purchaser, by one of several forms of deed. In return, the purchaser will agree to tender specified consideration as payment. The contract will set out a description for the property, the identities of the purchaser and seller, the consideration purchaser will pay to buyer, the description of the real property that is the subject of the sale, the timing of the transaction, and any number of promises and conditions.

The word *executory* has a particular meaning; it is not a word that is used often by non-lawyers. Promises that are unfulfilled are executory. The purchaser's promise to pay consideration is executory until the moment of closing when the purchaser tenders the purchase price. The seller's promise is executory until the moment of closing when the seller has transferred title.

The executory period is created and limited by the contract. The purchaser will use this time period to examine the state of seller's title, because, after all, the seller can only sell what she owns. To the degree permitted by the contract, the purchaser will inspect the physical condition of the property. The purchaser will also line up financing.

The contract not only sets deadlines for closing, it also creates a set of tasks for both the seller and the purchaser. For example, the contract may require the seller to deliver to purchaser an updated *survey* of the property. This is especially common in commercial property transactions. The survey helps the purchaser identify different types of problems that relate to the real property. The survey may reveal that the property does not contain the promised amount of acreage, or that the boundary lines are not actually in the locations anticipated by the purchaser. It does not do the purchaser any good if the purchaser (or more likely the purchaser's attorney) does not have time to really look the survey over in advance of closing.

Real estate contracts often contain *contingency* provisions. These provisions make a party's contract obligations contingent on the happening of an event or determination of facts. One of the most important "contingency" provisions conditions the purchaser's obligation to buy the property on her ability to obtain a loan. This contingency condition will specify the total loan amount, the maximum interest rate, and the term of the loan (e.g., 15 years). If the purchaser cannot obtain a loan that meets these criteria, she can withdraw from the contract.

At the time the parties sign the contract, the purchaser typically tenders a small percentage of the sale price as *earnest money*. This is not actually necessary to create an enforceable contract because the contract is one of bilateral promises. However, the seller usually requires some payment, to be held in escrow, to show that the purchaser is serious about the agreement. The seller may also treat the earnest money as liquidated damages, in the event of purchaser's breach, as we discuss below. If the deal goes through, the earnest money is credited against the amount the purchaser owes at closing.

1. The Enforceable Contract and the Statute of Frauds

If the executory period begins with the execution of a contract, then it is important to recognize what is required to create an *enforceable* contract. Real property transactions include elements of both contract and property law. The property portion of the transaction is known as the *conveyance*. The seller signs and delivers a deed that conveys her interest in the real property to the purchaser. However, the agreement that sets up the conveyance is contractual in nature, and it is governed by contract law. As a result, for a contract to be a contract at all, *there must be an agreement*: offer and acceptance, and a meeting of the minds on the nature of the transaction.

The key language in any contract for sale of property is the exchange of promises—that seller agrees to convey the property and purchaser agrees to tender consideration. Here is how that language reads in the well-crafted but basic form of real property sales contract: "Seller agrees to sell the Real Property to Buyer, and Buyer agrees to buy the Real Property from Seller, on the terms and subject to the conditions set forth in this Agreement." 🖥 We have provided a Sample Purchase and Sale Agreement that you can view on the Simulation.

The *Statute of Frauds* dates back to an enactment of the English Parliament in 1677. The Statute of Frauds requires that parties to certain agreements place their agreements or memoranda of agreements in writing. Under the Statute of Frauds, parties to an agreement for a contract in land or an interest in land cannot bring an action on the agreement "unless the agreement upon which such action shall be brought or some memorandum or note thereof shall be in writing, and signed by the party to be charged therewith."

This statutory language can be seen as having two component parts. The first requires an agreement, or a note or memorandum thereof, to be in writing and signed by the party to be charged (e.g., to be sued). The second part applies the Statute to contracts for the sale of land or an interest in land. Simply put, under the Statute of Frauds, one party to the contract cannot enforce against the other an oral agreement to sell or to buy real property. The Statute of Frauds has been translated into modern-day law in the statutes of many, but not all, states. In jurisdictions in which the Statute of Frauds is not actually rendered into legislation, courts adopt it as part of the common law and cite to the Restatement (Second) of Contracts §129 (1981).

The name of the rule—the Statute of Frauds—gives away its primary purpose: to prevent one party from claiming, fraudulently, that she did (or did not) agree to buy or sell real property, or to prevent a party from misrepresenting the terms of the agreement. The Statue of Frauds requires parties to place their understanding in writing and then sign the agreement; in other words, the Statute of Frauds forces the purchaser and the seller to place their cards on the table. In practice, this means that both parties understand the terms of the deal—how much the property costs, precisely what property is to be conveyed, and so on.

Real property is included in the Statute of Frauds because it is often the most significant and valuable asset in the portfolio of many individuals. This is also true of many businesses. Imagine a company that owns many car dealerships in a particular city or region. The company may own the real property on which each of the individual dealerships sits. This kind of real property is often visible and valuable.

The Statute of Frauds applies to agreements to transfer any interest in real property, not only a conveyance of the entire fee, but also mortgages, long-term leases, conveyances of fee simple, easements, and real covenants. Leases covered by the Statute of Frauds originally had a minimum term of one year. However, in some jurisdictions today the Statute of Frauds is limited to leases of a term of greater length, often three years.

We want to know that a person selling real property really means to do so. If she reduces to writing her intent with "all the particulars," and signs the document, we know that the seller understands the significance of her decision and intends to follow through. Perhaps just as importantly, the possibility for misunderstanding and fraud is diminished.

a. The Basics

Price, Parties, and Property Must Be Described to Satisfy the Statute of Frauds

- **Price.** The contract must fix a price in a set dollar amount or provide a means (or formula) of determining the dollar amount.
- **Parties.** The contract must identify the purchaser and the seller.
- **Property.** The contract must describe the property sufficiently to allow a third person to locate the boundaries.

The Statute of Frauds, as it is applied today, typically requires that parties set out in writing the following minimal information: the identities of the parties to the contract (parties); the consideration to be paid in exchange for the conveyance (price); and the real property that is to be conveyed (property.) In each case (parties, price, and property), the description in the contract must be sufficient to allow a third person (i.e., a judge) to unambiguously determine the intent of the parties. Information that helps identify the intent of the parties *but is not contained in the contract* is called "parol" evidence. As noted above, the Statute of Frauds also requires at a minimum that the party to be charged sign the contract.

Many courts today also require a real estate contract to include in writing other provisions key to the parties' understanding. For example, many real estate contracts include a loan contingency provision that allows the purchaser to condition his obligation to buy the property on obtaining a sufficient loan. This provision is central to many real estate transactions. Some courts would hold that ambiguity in the drafting of this provision renders the entire contract unenforceable.

Price is usually easy for parties to reflect in a contract. It is typically a specified sum. On occasion, a contract will state the price of property as "fair market value." This phrase implies that the parties will use a mechanism to find fair market price at the time of closing—usually this involves the hiring of appraisers. This mechanism can create litigation if the appraisers for purchaser and seller disagree.

Still, price can be a problem in some contracts. Consider contracts for the sale of "income producing" property such as office buildings and shopping centers. Income producing property contains tenants who pay rent; the purchaser takes over as landlord when he purchases the real property. Contracts for the sale of income producing real property sometimes represent price in a formula or equation rather than a straightforward dollar amount. The formula will reflect the rate of income produced by the property and will be based on assumptions about whether tenants will pay rent on time and whether the space will be occupied. If these assumptions are not clearly described, the contract might fail.

① yes - no fixed $ amount
② maybe - was the property described in the writing?

S AND PRICE

into a contract in which purchaser agrees to
e office tower contains rent-paying tenants.
e tower is shown as a formula: "The purchase
qual to the average rentals for the equivalent
building in the same market."
te the transaction.

to avoid performance? *See* Behrends v. White
.2d 227 (N.Y. App. Div. 2008).

■   ■   ■

milarly easy. In most cases, the purchaser and seller are easily identified. But individuals who draft contracts sometimes err here as well. Assume that two people are married and wish to buy real property. They may buy the property in one of several ways. One of the spouses may take title solely in her name, or the spouses may take title in a form of co-tenancy. Perhaps the spouses do not really know how they wish to take title. Consider

PRE-CONTRACT

CONTRACT/EXECUTORY

CLOSING

POST-CLOSING

the following: at the time the spouses execute the contract, the spouses sign as "husband, or husband and wife in co-tenancy, as grantees." Do you think that the contract is enforceable against the purchasers?

■ PROBLEM: TRUST BUT VERIFY

> ➢ Marcia is a new resident of Des Moines, Iowa, and is in the market for a home. Marcia sees a "for sale by owner" sign in front of a modest but well-kept ranch-style home dating to the 1950s. She knocks on the door and is admitted to the house by a young man. The young man identifies himself as Daniel Greene and then gives her a tour of the home. Marcia is intrigued by the home and asks about its history. Daniel explains: "This was my parents' house. My dad died ten years ago, and my mother passed away four months ago. It's mine now."
> ➢ Marcia makes an offer of $150,000 for the house; Daniel accepts Marcia's offer. Marcia signs the contract for sale of the home as "purchaser" and Daniel signs as "seller."
> ➢ During the executory period, Marcia discovers that Daniel is a trustee of the "Greene Family Trust," and that the Greene Family Trust has title to the property. As trustee, Daniel has discretion to sell the house. Land values in the area rise following the execution of the contract between Daniel and Marcia. Daniel delivers a letter to Marcia informing her that, "as trustee, I have decided that the deal is not in the interest of the trust and I will not close the sale."

Marcia approaches you for advice. May Daniel avoid performance?

■   ■   ■

The primary source of conflict is the third and final P—**property**—or the land description. The description of the property in the contract must be such that a third person (again, a court) could locate the boundaries of the property without resort to parol evidence.

If, for example, the purchaser wishes to purchase the seller's entire multi-million-dollar estate, the last thing the purchaser wishes to discover after the fact is that the deed conveyed the land on which the swimming pools sits, but not the house. The lawyer's job is to make sure that the contract, and later the deed, correctly describe the property. A lawyer who does not take care with land description is a stone's throw away from a malpractice suit for breach of the duty of care. It is vitally important for a contract for sale of real property to accurately describe the property.

To work through land transactions, you must understand the ways in which real property can be described in writing. This is of paramount importance to the Statute of Frauds.

b. The Description of Real Property

We will pay special attention to the mechanisms used to describe real property, and particularly metes and bounds legal descriptions. What a court demands in terms of property description for purposes of a deed may be stricter than what courts require in connection with the contract. When evaluating a real property contract, the goal of the courts is to determine the intent of the parties. By contrast, the deed actually conveys the real property, and courts allow little in the way of wiggle room; courts demand precision.

i. Metes and Bounds. You have already encountered some of the important players in a real estate transaction (seller, purchaser, and broker). An additional player is the registered *surveying engineer*. The surveyor is a professional who uses specialized equipment to physically examine the property and information gleaned from documents in the chain of title to the property (prior deeds and such). The surveyor will also look for natural and man-made "monuments" when evaluating the property. The surveyor then draws a map of the property showing boundary lines. The survey may be very bare bones (showing only the boundary lines) or "as built" (depicting all structures and important physical elements on the property). The survey may show other crucial information, such as the location of the property in a flood zone. However, for purposes of the Statute of Frauds, the key information is that of boundary lines.

Once a surveyor creates the survey, either the surveyor or a lawyer will translate the survey into a written description—this is often called a *metes and bounds legal description.*

Imagine that you take the survey and actually walk the boundary lines, all while dictating your travels. You would start by identifying an easily recognizable "place of beginning"—perhaps the intersection of two roads—then you would walk in a clockwise manner around the boundaries until you returned to your starting point. If you identified each segment (known as "calls") of your walk around the property, noting the course (direction) and distance, and the stopping point of each segment, you would create a running description of the property that any third person could later use to locate the boundaries. Your references to courses and distances would all be taken from the engineering notations on the survey.

A metes and bounds description of property will satisfy the Statute of Frauds only if it *ends* where it *starts*. If the description omits an obvious call that is reflected on the survey, the court

How to Read a Survey: See a Real Survey and Legal Description

⌨ You can view an interactive high definition version of a survey and legal description by visiting the Simulation. You will also see some instructions on how you can read the survey with legal description. The survey shows a parcel of undeveloped land that borders two roads. The legal description begins at the intersection of the roads. As you click on each "call" in the legal description, the associated link in the boundary will highlight on the survey.

will probably simply say the parties made a clerical error in the description and enforce the contract.

The parties may go to the trouble of ordering a survey, but this does not mean that the contract is enforceable. Under the right circumstances, the court may be forced to resort to parol evidence in order to locate a satisfactory description. Consider the following case:

CRAWLEY v. HATHAWAY

721 N.E.2d 1208 (1999)
Appellate Court of Illinois

Justice McCULLOUGH delivered the opinion of the court:

In April 1996, plaintiff, Douglas W. Crawley, sued defendant, Mark Hathaway, for specific performance of a written contract involving the sale of real property from Hathaway to Crawley. In January 1999, after the parties had engaged in discovery, Hathaway filed a motion for summary judgment, alleging section 2 of the Frauds Act (740 ILCS 80/2 (West 1998)), often referred to as the "Statute of Frauds," as a defense. In February 1999, Crawley moved to strike Hathaway's motion as untimely. The trial court denied that motion and ultimately granted Hathaway's motion for summary judgment. Crawley appeals, arguing that the trial court erred by (1) determining that the Statute of Frauds bars enforcement of the purported contract and (2) permitting Hathaway to untimely raise the Statute of Frauds in his motion for summary judgment. We reverse and remand.

During the spring of 1995, the parties negotiated Crawley's possible purchase of property owned by Hathaway. Around the beginning of June 1995, Hathaway prepared and the parties signed a handwritten document (hereinafter the document) that is the subject of this litigation. The document, in its entirety and in the following format, reads as follows:

> "Agreement to Buy
> 100 Acres More or less,
> 83 acres of pasture & timber and 19
> acres of tillable ground
> For $90,000
> Seller Mark Hathaway
> Buyer Doug Crawley"

When the document was executed, Crawley gave Hathaway as down payment a check for $7,500, which Hathaway cashed. Hathaway then contacted a banker in an effort to help Crawley obtain financing.

Hathaway did not know the exact acreage he was selling but believed it to be "100 acres[,] more or less." The land consisted of woods and tillable ground that was in pasture and hay.

In August 1995, Hathaway commissioned a survey to acquire a legal description of the property and picked a beginning point for the survey to be done. Both parties were present during the performance of the survey and directed the surveyor as to the boundary lines for the land that was contemplated as the subject of the sale. This survey was completed in October 1995. Between October 1995 and January 1996, Hathaway changed his mind about the sale because he believed the area surveyed exceeded the size of what he intended to sell. In January 1996, Hathaway refused to transfer the property to Crawley and instead listed it with a real estate broker at a price of $150,000. The acreage on that listing was "127 acres more or less."

In January 1997, Crawley filed a request for admission of facts and genuineness of document pursuant to Supreme Court Rule 216 (134 Ill. 2d R. 216). Because Hathaway did not respond, Crawley's request for admission of facts stands admitted, establishing the following facts in this case: (1) Hathaway drafted the document; (2) Hathaway owned the property that was the subject of the document; (3) Hathaway provided a legal description by ordering a survey; (4) Hathaway received a $7,500 down payment from Crawley; and (5) Hathaway later contracted to sell the land to a third party. Subsequently, the court considered (over Crawley's objection) Hathaway's January 1999 motion for summary judgment and granted that motion.

Summary judgment is appropriate only when the pleadings, depositions, admissions, and affidavits, if any, demonstrate that no genuine issue exists as to any material fact and the moving party is entitled to judgment as a matter of law. Hubble v. O'Connor, 291 Ill. App. 3d 974, 979, 225 Ill. Dec. 825, 684 N.E.2d 816, 820 (1997). The Statute of Frauds provides, in pertinent part, as follows: "No action shall be brought to charge any person upon any contract for the sale of lands ... unless such contract or some memorandum or note thereof shall be in writing, and signed by the party to be charged therewith. ... " 740 ILCS 80/2 (West 1998).

In Callaghan v. Miller, 17 Ill. 2d 595, 599, 162 N.E.2d 422, 424 (1959), the supreme court addressed what a purported written contract for real property needed to contain to comply with the Statute of Frauds:

> "The memorandum is sufficient to satisfy the Statute of Frauds if it contains upon its face the names of the vendor and the vendee, a description of the property sufficiently definite to identify the same as the subject matter of the contract, the price, terms and conditions of the sale, and the signature of the party to be charged."

The subject matter of the contract in *Callaghan*, 17 Ill. 2d at 599, 162 N.E.2d at 424, was described as follows:

> "'[T]he Altha Martin property located on Route 25, north of the city of Batavia, Illinois (not in corporation). This area comprises five acres more or less. The space now occupied by 20 trailers[,] is properly licensed and zoned by the State of Illinois and Kane County Zoning Dept. (non-conforming use).'"

The supreme court in *Callaghan* affirmed the trial court's rejection of the Statute of Frauds argument and wrote the following:

> "There is nothing in the record to indicate that some other tract was the subject matter of this memorandum. Moreover, parol evidence is admissible to identify the subject matter of the contract or memorandum. It is not necessary in contracts for the sale of real estate that it should be so described as to admit of no doubt as to what it is." *Callaghan*, 17 Ill. 2d at 599, 162 N.E.2d at 424.

More recently, the appellate court in Guel v. Bullock, 127 Ill. App. 3d 36, 39-40, 82 Ill. Dec. 264, 468 N.E.2d 811, 814 (1984), was presented with the argument that a purported real estate contract did not comply with the Statute of Frauds because the contract's description of the property in question was uncertain and ambiguous. The purported contract in *Guel* involved the sale "'of the property commonly known as 8427 S. Euclid'" for a certain sum of money. *Guel*, 127 Ill. App. 3d at 39, 82 Ill. Dec. 264, 468 N.E.2d at 813. The defendant in *Guel* argued that the document at issue was an insufficient contract because it failed to specify the county or state of the subject property. The appellate court rejected this argument and, citing *Callaghan*, wrote, "Under the Statute of Frauds in this State, parol evidence may be used to clarify the terms of a written contract." *Guel*, 127 Ill. App. 3d at 40, 82 Ill. Dec. 264, 468 N.E.2d at 814. Significantly, the appellate court added the following:

> "This is not to say that parol evidence may be used to supply missing terms. Only when the contract itself evinces the fact that the parties intended to be bound and that they agreed on the essential terms may parol evidence be introduced. See Corbin, Contracts sec. 499, at 689 (1950)." *Guel*, 127 Ill. App. 3d at 40, 82 Ill. Dec. 264, 468 N.E.2d at 814.

In granting summary judgment, the trial court in the present case found that the document did not describe the land with sufficient particularity and incorrectly reasoned that extrinsic evidence could not be used to overcome this deficiency.

The land survey completed in October 1995 may be considered when determining whether the document constitutes a valid contract. The writing required by the Statute of Frauds may include one or more documents that collectively contain a description of the property. *Hubble*, 291 Ill. App. 3d at 983, 225 Ill. Dec. 825, 684 N.E.2d at 823, quoting Prodromos v. Poulos, 202 Ill. App. 3d 1024, 1028, 148 Ill. Dec. 345, 560 N.E.2d 942, 946 (1990). "A writing sufficient to satisfy the Statute of Frauds need not itself be a valid contract, but only evidence of one." Melrose Park National Bank v. Carr, 249 Ill. App. 3d 9, 15-16, 188 Ill. Dec. 269, 618 N.E.2d 839, 843 (1993). The land is sufficiently described in the writings when that description will enable a surveyor, with the aid of extrinsic evidence, to locate the property. Thomas v. Moore, 55 Ill. App. 3d 907, 911, 12 Ill. Dec. 898, 370 N.E.2d 809, 811-12 (1977).

In Werling v. Grosse, 76 Ill. App. 3d 834, 841, 32 Ill. Dec. 399, 395 N.E.2d 629, 634 (1979), the writings described the property only as "'my farm,'" but that was

PRE-CONTRACT

CONTRACT/EXECUTORY

CLOSING

POST-CLOSING

deemed sufficient because the description could be made certain by the aid of extrinsic evidence and the property located. In Moore v. Pickett, 62 Ill. 158, 161, 1871 WL 8346 (1871), a letter that was the subject of the litigation did not specify the subject property, but the surrounding facts and circumstances served to identify the subject matter of the letter as the premises in question.

In McConnell v. Brillhart, 17 Ill. 354, 362 (1856), the court discussed the use of parol evidence in relation to the Statute of Frauds as follows:

> "The intention [of the parties] is to govern, and latent ambiguities may be explained, if any exist. The court may, therefore, inquire into the circumstances surrounding the parties, to gather every material fact relating to the person, who claims to be interested, and to the property which is claimed as the subject of disposition, for the purpose of identifying the person or thing intended, or the quantity of interest, where a knowledge of extrinsic facts, can in any way be made ancillary to the right interpretation of the words used. 1 Greenl. Ev., Secs. 287, 288, note 3, p. 364. As a description, 'one half of the farm on which he, said Moses, then dwelt,' parol admitted to show the land he lived on. Doolittle v. Blakesley, 4 Day R. 265; Venable v. McDonald, 4 Dana R. 336."

As a result, the court in *McConnell* found enforceable an agreement to sell a half section contiguous to Dr. Michener's because that description was susceptible of identification by parol evidence. *McConnell*, 17 Ill. at 363.

In this case, the document signed in June 1995 does not refer to any land survey, and the October 1995 land survey does not refer to the document. Although a contract may consist of several writings, they must be connected in some definite manner, physically or otherwise, so that it is clear they relate to the same matter. Davito v. Blakely, 96 Ill. App. 2d 196, 201-02, 238 N.E.2d 410, 413 (1968). Nevertheless, the survey and the testimony regarding the survey are admissible as evidence of the intention of the parties.

Hathaway testified in his deposition that he and Crawley met with the surveyor at the time the survey was initiated. At that time, Hathaway identified for the surveyor the point at which the survey was to begin. Hathaway told the surveyor to follow the road to the north, then follow the road to the east to the tracks, follow the tracks on to the north boundary, and then complete the survey by following the tree line. Hathaway admitted it was his intention to sell to Crawley the wooded area and 19 acres of pasture encompassed by the survey. From this evidence and the resultant survey, the trier of fact could reasonably conclude that the parties knew exactly what property was intended to be conveyed even though Hathaway was unaware of how many acres it covered.

The purpose of the Statute of Frauds is to prevent fraud, not facilitate it. Courts will refuse to apply the Statute of Frauds if the result would be to perpetrate a fraud. Union Mutual Life Insurance Co. v. White, 106 Ill. 67, 73, 1883 WL 10185 (1883); *Davito*, 96 Ill. App. 2d at 201, 238 N.E.2d at 413; 413; Conness v. Conness, 94 Ill. App. 2d 281, 284, 236 N.E.2d 753, 754-55 (1968).

In this case, because the survey and parol evidence may be admitted to identify the property subject to the contract, a genuine issue of material fact remained and summary judgment should not have been granted. Since we reverse the summary judgment on the merits, we need not consider whether the trial court committed an abuse of discretion by denying a motion to strike Hathaway's motion for summary judgment.

The judgment of the circuit court of Vermilion County is reversed, and the cause is remanded for further proceedings.

Reversed and remanded.

. . .

Justice STEIGMANN, dissenting:

I respectfully dissent.

The particular document before us is so bereft of any meaningful description that the majority's resort to parol evidence amounts to "supply[ing] missing terms" of the purported contract, contrary to the sound analysis of the *Guel* court. *Guel*, 127 Ill. App. 3d at 40, 82 Ill. Dec. 264, 468 N.E.2d at 814. The document contained no description whatsoever of the property to be sold, except for a statement that the property contains 100 acres "more or less," consisting of 83 acres of pasture and timber and 19 acres of tillable ground. This description contains nary a clue as to where this property might be located. Further obscuring the issue, this "description" does not identify Hathaway as the "owner" of the property but as the "seller." The two are not equivalent. Hathaway could fully comply with the written terms of the document by purchasing any 83 acres of woods and 19 acres of tillable land and selling it to Crawley. Hathaway could meet the description of "seller" even if he were acting as an agent for some other, unnamed owner.

In a big, largely rural state like Illinois, the description contained in the document could undoubtedly be applied to hundreds, perhaps thousands, of parcels of land. Because the law governing the Statute of Frauds permits Crawley to use parol evidence only to clarify the terms of the purported contract, not to supply missing terms, this court should agree with the trial court's decision to grant Hathaway summary judgment.

We should also reject Crawley's argument that the land survey completed in October 1995 may be considered when determining whether the document constitutes a valid contract. The document, signed in June 1995, does not refer to any land survey, and the October 1995 land survey does not refer to the document. Although a contract may consist of several writings, they must be connected in some definite manner, physically or otherwise, so that it is clear they relate to the same matter. *Davito*, 96 Ill. App. 2d at 201-02, 238 N.E.2d at 413. Hathaway is correct that unless the land survey somehow indicates that it is to be attached as a supplement to the document, it may not be considered as part of the document. The land survey does not so indicate. Thus, the document and the land survey cannot be read together to create an enforceable contract that would satisfy the Statute of Frauds.

■ POINTS TO CONSIDER

1. **An enforceable description.** In the absence of the survey, would the description contained in the contract in *Hathaway* have been sufficient? Can you determine from the opinion what the court considered to be the bare

PRE-CONTRACT

CONTRACT/EXECUTORY

CLOSING

POST-CLOSING

minimum information that a property description must contain in order to be enforceable? Do you think that the court would have been stricter in its demand for clarity in description, or in its willingness to accept the survey as parol evidence, if the drafter had been an attorney?

2. **The Statute of Frauds protects both parties.** Who took advantage of the Statute in *Hathaway*? You might think that this doctrine is protective solely of purchaser. In fact, the Statute of Frauds is intended to protect both parties, and may be employed by both the seller and purchaser. *See, e.g.,* Ray v. Frasure, 200 P.3d 1174 (Idaho 2009) (mere street address not sufficient description of real property to permit enforcement of contract against seller). This can lead to a counterintuitive result. As a policy matter, we would like to see less litigation over real estate contracts, furthering our fundamental principle of certainty. If this is so, then we would expect to see rules that reduce the likelihood of disputes over the size and boundaries of property that is the subject of a real estate contract. Reading *Hathaway*, does it appear that the Statute of Frauds furthers this policy, at least as applied to the facts of that case?

3. **The parol evidence rule.** You encountered or will encounter the parol evidence rule in your contracts course. Essentially, the parol evidence rule makes inadmissible any written or oral evidence that somehow varies or contradicts a written contract that is otherwise complete on its face. To put it another way, parties and courts must work with the language of the contract. The parol evidence rule furthers a policy of judicial efficiency. It is much easier and faster for a court to apply the law to the contract as written. Unlike the Statue of Frauds, the parol evidence rule is not intended to preclude fraud; rather, it is intended to allow for a more efficient adversarial process. If a contract is incomplete on its face, and there is a clear intention to incorporate other written material, courts will look beyond the contract at this external— parol—evidence. *Hathaway* is as much about the parol evidence rule as it is about the Statute of Frauds. How do the two rules interact in *Hathaway*?

   Not all scholars agree that the parol evidence rule promotes judicial efficiency. *See* Susan J. Martin-Davidson, *Yes, Judge Kozinski, There Is A Parol Evidence Rule in California - the Lessons of A Pyrrhic Victory*, 25 Sw. U. L. Rev. 1, 72 (1995). In her article, Professor Martin-Davidson argues that "the parol evidence rule cannot be justified because it operates fairly and efficiently to reduce the cost of contract litigation. Any research into the cases or the many treatises and articles which have examined its practical effects proves the opposite. A parol evidence objection is more likely to spur protracted disputes about its proper application. The rule should be abolished."

4. **The real impact of parol evidence.** Look back at the rather primitive contract in dispute in *Hathaway*. This is not something a competent lawyer would have drafted. If you were limited simply to the language of the contract, would you be able to locate the boundaries of the real property? If your answer is

"no," then you will see the necessity and value of parol evidence. There is only an enforceable contract if the court can read the survey into the written agreement. That raises the million-dollar question: why was the court willing to admit the survey at all? The agreement that Hathaway drafted does not refer to the survey. According to the court, when is it proper to allow this type of parol evidence? The dissent draws a very different rule where the survey is concerned. What does the dissent demand in practical terms? The parol evidence rule is subject to defenses and exceptions. The court will admit parol evidence that contradicts or varies the terms of the contract if the evidence suggests fraud or mutual mistake. A court interpreting the final written agreement may examine a written agreement that is otherwise not attached if it is referenced in the final contract. For example, home purchase contracts sometimes refer to loan commitments. The court may complete the purchase agreement by examining the loan commitment. This is nothing more than the basic contract law rule that an agreement may be comprised of more than one memorandum.

5. **More or less.** The contract between the parties explicitly stated that Hathway would convey "100 acres more or less." What is the effect of that last phrase?

> ### Practice Tip: Integration Clauses
>
> Many contracts include an "integration clause." This provision expressly states that the written agreement is the entirety of the agreement of the parties. In essence, this reduces the parol evidence rule to a provision in the contract, and limits the ability of one party to argue for an exception to the rule. ⌨ Section 10.17 of the Sample Purchase and Sale Agreement, available on the Simulation, presents an example of an integration clause.

ii. Recorded Plat. A *plat* is a survey, created by a surveying engineer, of a subdivision created under local law. For example, assume that a developer creates El Camino Estates, a large 100-lot residential gated subdivision. The developer will ask the surveyor to create a single survey showing all the roads and lots, with engineering notation for each lot. The plat must be approved by the local authority (city or county) as meeting all its requirements, such as lot size, streets, and sidewalks. The plat will then be recorded in the county courthouse of the county in which the subdivision sits. Plats are recorded in large numbered books called plat books. Once the subdivision is legally created and the plat is recorded, it is easy for the developer to describe, in contracts and deeds, the individual lots the developer wishes to sell.

Assume that the developer contracts to sell Lot 2 to Jerry Anderson. The developer will refer to the "Lot 2, as shown on that certain plat of El Camino Estates, created by Daniel Bogart, registered Land Surveyor, recorded in Plat Book 3, Page 10, in the Orange County Courthouse." It will be similarly easy for later owners of lots in El Camino Estates to describe their properties when selling to future purchasers. Jerry Anderson will include the same property description in the deed if he later sells his lot to Ben Jones.

iii U.S. Government Survey. Thomas Jefferson had the idea of facilitating the transfer of property by instituting a uniform system of reference based on a *comprehensive government survey.* Enacted in 1785, the government survey covers 30 western and southern states, which were largely unsettled at the time. Of course, you should recall from *Johnson v. M'Intosh* that, although devoid of settlements of westerners, Native American tribes populated this region. The survey divides all the land in this area into six-mile square *townships,* which are designated by their distance from a principal meridian (running vertically) and a base line (running horizontally). There are 37 principal meridians encompassed by the survey. Each township is then further divided into 36, one-square-mile *sections* (640 acres each).

A reference to the government survey therefore enables a purchase contract or deed to describe land anywhere within the survey area by a relatively short reference. For example, the sale of 160 acres in Warren County, Iowa, is described as the NW1/4 of Section 34, Township 76 N, Range 24W of the 5th principal meridian. This township is located 76 townships north of the range line that goes through Arkansas, and 24 townships west of the meridian that runs through the eastern part of Iowa. As you can see, reference to the survey is most useful for describing large tracts of undeveloped land in rural areas and is typically used for that sort of transaction.

For more information, see https://nationalmap.gov/small_scale/a_plss.html.

■ PROBLEMS: THE STATUTE OF FRAUDS AND DESCRIPTION OF REAL PROPERTY

1. **The absent exhibit.** In an August 1 contract between seller and purchaser, seller agrees to convey to purchaser, for $500,000, a parcel of undeveloped land. The land is described in the contract as "all that tract of land lying and being along Highway 10, Orange County, recorded in Plat Book 10, Page 12; see Exhibit A attached." The seller commissioned a survey on which the recorded plat is based and the plat is recorded in the plat book and at the page referenced. However, there is no Exhibit A actually attached to the contract. Seller receives a competing offer of $750,000 on August 10 and informs purchaser that seller will not show at closing. Purchaser asks you for advice. Is the contract valid or void under the Statute of Frauds? *See* Oconee Land & Timber, LLC v. Buchanan, 686 S.E.2d 452 (Ga. Ct. App. 2009). Can you see a motive behind a seller's failure to attach the exhibit?

2. **The lonely street address.** Seller agrees to sell to purchaser property described only as "101 West Maple Street, Atlanta, Georgia, 30329." Seller then receives a higher offer on the property and reneges on the sale to purchaser. Is

the contract enforceable? Should the court permit parol evidence? As we will see, one party to a land sales agreement may ask the court to force the other party to complete the transaction. This is known as an action for *specific performance*. *See* Key Design, Inc. v. Moser, 983 P.2d 653 (Wash. 1999). Should the result be different if the seller admits in testimony at trial or in its filings that it intended particular property and that there was in fact a meeting of the minds?

c. *Exceptions to the Statute of Frauds*

The Statute of Frauds promotes sound policy. It requires parties to reduce to writing the essential elements of their agreements concerning transfers of interest in real property. The Statute of Frauds forces individuals (and their lawyers) to think through the goals and terms of a deal. And it helps prevent fraud because an alleged purchaser or seller cannot claim to have a right to buy or sell property based on hard-to-prove oral agreements. But the Statue has its shortcomings, as the prior section makes clear. The greatest flaw is simply that a party may refuse to close, even though *she damn well knew she agreed to buy or sell the land*. She can do this if one or more key terms were not sufficiently reduced to writing.

When one party breaches the contract, the other can sue for damages, or may seek to enforce the contract, otherwise known as an action for *specific performance*. In other words, if the seller breaches the contract, the purchaser may ask the court to force the seller to convey the property and accept the purchase price. Specific performance is an *equitable remedy* that the court grants in its discretion. Specific performance is one of the primary remedies that purchasers and sellers seek from one another after a breach; we will discuss specific performance below following *Hickey v. Green*, and in the section of this chapter on remedies.

Here is the basic question: is it possible for the party who wishes to close a real property transaction to force the recalcitrant party back to the table and consummate the deal? To put it another way, are there exceptions to the Statute of Frauds? Imagine that purchaser and seller agree on a sale of real property. Seller then informs purchaser that seller will not close the transaction. Seller argues that the description of property in the contract was not sufficient to allow a third person to find the property's boundaries. A court may order specific performance of the contract if purchaser can demonstrate that the purchaser has partly performed the contract.

Part performance rests on two possible rationales. First, the purchaser's part performance may demonstrate to a court that the purchaser detrimentally relied on the agreement, and as a result it would be decidedly unfair to deny enforcement. Second, the part performance may simply act as evidence of the agreement that substitutes for a writing that would be otherwise required under the Statute. A court applying the evidence-based rationale of part performance will focus on the behavior of the party who seeks to enforce the contract and ask whether that party's behavior is strong evidence that a contract existed.

Read *Hickey v. Green* below. On which of these theories of part performance is this opinion based?

HICKEY v. GREEN

442 N.E.2d 37 (1982)
Massachusetts Court of Appeals

Before Perretta, Cutter and Kass, JJ.

Cutter, Justice.

This case is before us on a stipulation of facts (with various attached documents). A Superior Court judge has adopted the agreed facts as "findings." We are in the same position as was the trial judge (who received no evidence and saw and heard no witnesses).

Mrs. Gladys Green owns a lot (Lot S) in the Manomet section of Plymouth. In July, 1980, she advertised it for sale. On July 11 and 12, Hickey and his wife discussed with Mrs. Green purchasing Lot S and "orally agreed to a sale" for $15,000. Mrs. Green on July 12 accepted a deposit check of $500, marked by Hickey on the back, "Deposit on Lot . . . Massasoit Ave. Manomet . . . Subject to Variance from Town of Plymouth." Mrs. Green's brother and agent "was under the impression that a zoning variance was needed and [had] advised . . . Hickey to write" the quoted language on the deposit check. It turned out, however, by July 16 that no variance would be required. Hickey had left the payee line of the deposit check blank, because of uncertainty whether Mrs. Green or her brother was to receive the check and asked "Mrs. Green to fill in the appropriate name." Mrs. Green held the check, did not fill in the payee's name, and neither cashed nor endorsed it. Hickey "stated to Mrs. Green that his intention was to sell his home and build on Mrs. Green's lot."

"Relying upon the arrangements . . . with Mrs. Green," the Hickeys advertised their house on Sachem Road in newspapers on three days in July, 1980, and agreed with a purchaser for its sale and took from him a deposit check for $500 which they deposited in their own account.[1] On July 24, Mrs. Green told Hickey that she "no longer intended to sell her property to him" but had decided to sell to another for $16,000. Hickey told Mrs. Green that he had already sold his house and offered her $16,000 for Lot S. Mrs. Green refused this offer.

The Hickeys filed this complaint seeking specific performance. Mrs. Green asserts that relief is barred by the Statute of Frauds contained in G.L. c. 259, §1. The trial judge granted specific performance.[2] Mrs. Green has appealed.

---

[1] On the back of the check was noted above the Hickeys' signatures endorsing the check "Deposit on Purchase of property at Sachem Rd. and First St., Manomet, Ma. Sale price, $44,000."

[2] The judgment ordered Mrs. Green to convey Lot S to the Hickeys but, probably by inadvertence, it failed to include an order that it be conveyed only upon payment by the grantees of the admittedly agreed price of $15,000.

The present rule applicable in most jurisdictions in the United States is succinctly set forth in Restatement (Second) of Contracts, §129 (1981). The section reads, "A contract for the transfer of an interest in land may be specifically enforced notwithstanding failure to comply with the Statute of Frauds if it is established that the party seeking enforcement, *in reasonable reliance on the contract* and on the continuing assent of the party against whom enforcement is sought, *has so changed his position that injustice can be avoided only by specific enforcement*" (emphasis supplied).[3]

The earlier Massachusetts decisions laid down somewhat strict requirements for an estoppel precluding the assertion of the Statute of Frauds. See, e.g., Glass v. Hulbert, 102 Mass. 24, 31-32, 43-44 (1869); Davis v. Downer, 210 Mass. 573, 576-577, 97 N.E. 90 (1912); Hazelton v. Lewis, 267 Mass. 533, 538-540, 166 N.E. 876 (1929); Andrews v. Charon, 289 Mass. 1, 5-7, 193 N.E. 737 (1935), where specific performance was granted upon a consideration of "the effect of all the facts in combination"; Winstanley v. Chapman, 325 Mass. 130, 133, 89 N.E.2d 506 (1949); Park, Real Estate Law, §883 (1981). See also Curran v. Magee, 244 Mass. 1, 4-6, 138 N.E. 1 (1923); Chase v. Aetna Rubber Co., 321 Mass. 721, 724, 75 N.E.2d 637 (1947). Compare Gadsby v. Gadsby, 275 Mass. 159, 167-168, 175 N.E. 495 (1931); Nichols v. Sanborn, 320 Mass. 436, 438-439, 70 N.E.2d 1 (1946). Frequently there has been an actual change of possession and improvement of the transferred property, as well as full payment of the full purchase price, or one or more of these elements.

It is stated in Park, Real Estate Law, §883, at 334, that the "more recent decisions . . . indicate a trend on the part of the [Supreme Judicial C]ourt to find that the circumstances warrant specific performance." This appears to be a correct perception. See Fisher v. MacDonald, 332 Mass. 727, 729, 127 N.E.2d 484 (1955), where specific performance was granted upon a showing that the purchaser "was put into possession and . . . [had] furnished part of the consideration in money and services"; Orlando v. Ottaviani, 337 Mass. 157, 161-162, 148 N.E.2d 373 (1958), where specific performance was granted to the former holder of an option to buy a strip of land fifteen feet wide, important to the option holder, and the option had been surrendered in reliance upon an oral promise to convey the strip made by the purchaser of a larger parcel of which the fifteen-foot

---

[3] Comments *a* and *b* to §129, read (in part): "*a*. . . . This section restates what is widely known as the 'part performance doctrine.' Part performance is not an accurate designation of such acts as taking possession and making improvements when the contract does not provide for such acts, but such acts regularly bring the doctrine into play. The doctrine is contrary to the words of the Statute of Frauds, but it was established by English courts of equity soon after the enactment of the Statute. Payment of purchase-money, without more, was once thought sufficient to justify specific enforcement, but a contrary view now prevails, since in such cases restitution is an adequate remedy. . . . Enforcement has . . . been justified on the ground that repudiation after 'part performance' amounts to a 'virtual fraud.' A more accurate statement is that courts with equitable powers are vested by tradition with what in substance is a dispensing power based on the promisee's reliance, *a discretion to be exercised with caution* in the light of all the circumstances . . . [emphasis supplied].

"*b*. . . . Two distinct elements enter into the application of the rule of this Section: first, the extent to which the evidentiary function of the statutory formalities is fulfilled by the conduct of the parties; second, the reliance of the promisee, providing a compelling substantive basis for relief in addition to the expectations created by the promise."

PRE-CONTRACT
CONTRACT/EXECUTORY
CLOSING
POST-CLOSING

strip was a part; Cellucci v. Sun Oil Co., 2 Mass. App. 722, 727-728, 320 N.E.2d 919 (1974), S.C., 368 Mass. 811, 331 N.E.2d 813 (1975). Compare Young v. Reed, 6 Mass. App. 18, 20-21, 371 N.E.2d 1378 (1978), where the questions arose on the defendants' motion for summary judgment and the summary judgment granted was reversed, so that the full facts could be developed at trial; Fitzsimmons v. Kerrigan, 9 Mass. App. 928, 404 N.E.2d 127 (1980). Compare also D'Ambrosio v. Rizzo, 12 Mass. App. _____, Mass. App. Ct. Adv. 1539, 425 N.E.2d 369 (1981).

The present facts reveal a simple case of a proposed purchase of a residential vacant lot, where the vendor, Mrs. Green, knew that the Hickeys were planning to sell their former home (possibly to obtain funds to pay her) and build on Lot S. The Hickeys, relying on Mrs. Green's oral promise, moved rapidly to make their sale without obtaining any adequate memorandum of the terms of what appears to have been intended to be a quick cash sale of Lot S. So rapid was action by the Hickeys that, by July 21, less than ten days after giving their deposit to Mrs. Green, they had accepted a deposit check for the sale of their house, endorsed the check, and placed it in their bank account. Above their signatures endorsing the check was a memorandum probably sufficient to satisfy the Statute of Frauds under A.B.C. Auto Parts, Inc. v. Moran, 359 Mass. 327, 329-331, 268 N.E.2d 844 (1971). *Cf.* Guarino v. Zyfers, 9 Mass. App. 874, 401 N.E.2d 857 (1980). At the very least, the Hickeys had bound themselves in a manner in which, to avoid a transfer of their own house, they might have had to engage in expensive litigation. No attorney has been shown to have been used either in the transaction between Mrs. Green and the Hickeys or in that between the Hickeys and their purchaser.

There is no denial by Mrs. Green of the oral contract between her and the Hickeys. This, under §129 of the Restatement, is of some significance.[4] There can be no doubt (a) that Mrs. Green made the promise on which the Hickeys so promptly relied, and also (b) she, nearly as promptly, but not promptly enough, repudiated it because she had a better opportunity. The stipulated facts require the conclusion that in equity Mrs. Green's conduct cannot be condoned. This is not a case where either party is shown to have contemplated the negotiation of a purchase and sale agreement. If a written agreement had been expected, even by only one party, or would have been natural (because of the participation by lawyers or otherwise), a different situation might have existed. It is a permissible inference from the agreed facts that the rapid sale of the Hickeys' house was both appropriate and expected. These are not circumstances where negotiations fairly can be seen as inchoate. Compare Tull v. Mister Donut Development Corp., 7 Mass. App. 626, 630-632, 389 N.E.2d 447 (1979).

---

[4] Comment *d* of Restatement (Second) of Contracts, §129, reads "*d. . . .* Where specific enforcement is rested on a transfer of possession plus either part payment of the price or the making of improvements, it is commonly said that the action taken by the purchaser must be unequivocally referable to the oral agreement. But this requirement is not insisted on *if the making of the promise is admitted or is clearly proved. The promisee must act in reasonable reliance on the promise, before the promisor has repudiated* it, and the action must be such that the remedy of restitution is inadequate. If these requirements are met, *neither taking of possession nor payment of money nor the making of improvements is essential . . .*" (emphasis supplied).

We recognize that specific enforcement of Mrs. Green's promise to convey Lot S may well go somewhat beyond the circumstances considered in the *Fisher* case, 332 Mass. 727, and in the *Orlando* case, 337 Mass. 157, 148 N.E.2d 373, where specific performance was granted. It may seem (perhaps because the present facts are less complicated) to extend the principles stated in the *Cellucci* case (see esp. 2 Mass. App. at 728, 320 N.E.2d 919). We recognize also the cautionary language about granting specific performance in comment *a* to §129 of the Restatement (see note [3], *supra*). No public interest behind G.L. c. 259, §1, however, in the simple circumstances before us, will be violated if Mrs. Green fairly is held to her precise bargain by principles of equitable estoppel, subject to the considerations mentioned below.

Over two years have passed since July, 1980, and over a year since the trial judge's findings were filed on July 6, 1981. At that time, the principal agreed facts of record bearing upon the extent of the injury to the Hickeys (because of their reliance on Mrs. Green's promise to convey Lot S) were those based on the Hickeys' new obligation to convey their house to a purchaser. Performance of that agreement had been extended to May 1, 1981. If that agreement has been abrogated or modified since the trial, the case may take on a different posture. If enforcement of that agreement still will be sought, or if that agreement has been carried out, the conveyance of Lot S by Mrs. Green should be required now.

The case, in any event, must be remanded to the trial judge for the purpose of amending the judgment to require conveyance of Lot S by Mrs. Green only upon payment to her in cash within a stated period of the balance of the agreed price of $15,000. The trial judge, however, in her discretion and upon proper offers of proof by counsel, may reopen the record to receive, in addition to the presently stipulated facts, a stipulation or evidence concerning the present status of the Hickeys' apparent obligation to sell their house. If the circumstances have changed, it will be open to the trial judge to require of Mrs. Green, instead of specific performance, only full restitution to the Hickeys of all costs reasonably caused to them in respect of these transactions (including advertising costs, deposits, and their reasonable costs for this litigation) with interest. The case is remanded to the Superior Court Department for further action consistent with this opinion. The Hickeys are to have costs of this appeal.

So ordered.

■ POINTS TO CONSIDER

1. **Change in position as part performance.** The older common rule is that purchasers would have to take possession and/or make substantial improvements to the subject property to take advantage of the part performance exception to the Statute of Frauds. Carefully review the facts of this case. What precisely was the Hickeys' part performance? How can we say that the Hickeys partly performed the contract if they did not take possession of Mrs. Green's lot?

2. **Specific performance is not automatic.** It is not clear that the Hickeys will be able to specifically enforce the contract with Mrs. Green. Specific performance is a remedy the court grants in equity. In order to be eligible for this remedy, the Hickeys must be able to show that (1) they acted in good faith and "with clean hands," and (2) they will be able to tender the sale price. As a rule, purchasers are entitled to an order for specific performance when the seller of real property breaches because the law (and courts) assume that real property is unique. Therefore, the Hickeys would not be satisfied merely by a payment of money damages. The Hickeys are not given the immediate grant of specific performance. The trial court is instructed on remand to check the "status" of the Hickeys' present house before forcing Mrs. Green to deliver the deed. What must the Hickeys show, and why, before they can obtain the final order?

3. **A closer look at the Restatement.** As the court in *Hickey* notes, §129 of the Restatement (Second) of Contracts (1981) sets out the part performance exception to the Statute of Frauds. Comment d to that section normally requires that the part performance of the party seeking to enforce the oral contract must be "exclusively referable" to the contract. *See also*, Bradshaw v. McBride, 649 P.2d 74, 79 (Utah 1982). This means that "[t]he performance must be one that is in some degree evidential of the existence of a contract and not readily explainable on any other ground." Martin v. Scholl, 678 P.2d 274, 275 (Utah 1983) (internal quotation marks omitted). Are there actions in this case that meet this test?

4. **Consider the following hypothetical.** Assume that Harry knocks on your door and says, "Hey, I love your house, I'll give you $100,000 for it." You politely decline, saying the house is not for sale. A few days later, you get a letter with a check from Harry for $1,000, with a note indicating it is "a deposit on your house, per our agreement for $100,000 price." You laugh at his lunacy and put the check in your desk drawer. A few days later, you hear that Harry has sold his house and is telling his friends he has bought yours. Does Harry have a case against you for specific performance? The Hickeys wrote Mrs. Green a check and sold their house. Isn't that what Harry did in the hypothetical? What's the difference?

5. **Estoppel.** Part performance is not the only defense a party may have against application of the Statute of Frauds. A court may employ the terminology of estoppel. The parties to a transaction value certainty: they wish to know that when they sign on the dotted line, so to speak, that the transaction will conclude as anticipated. Furthermore, the parties anticipate a closing on terms to which they agreed. The written agreement gives the parties the assurance that they require. However, certainty is only one possible policy that the law promotes. Estoppel provides a safety valve of sorts, and ensures *fairness* in situations in which one party is harmed as a result of the behavior of the other. The injured party must show that he substantially altered his position to his

detriment. If the injured party can make this showing, then the party deny-ing existence of the contract may be equitably "estopped" from asserting the Statute of Frauds.

6. **Make your best case for an unsympathetic party.** Assume that you are Mrs. Green's attorney. There is one decent, but perhaps not winning, argu-ment left in your quiver. Consider "detrimental reliance" and "estoppel." Now think about the decision that the Hickeys made to sell their own house, and argue on Mrs. Green's behalf.

7. **One final question.** What happens if the Hickeys do not sell their house as they agreed to do?

2. Title Examination and Marketable Title

Two activities directly related to title take place during the executory period: the investigation and examination of title, and the obtaining of a title insurance company's commitment to issue a title policy. Some transactions involve a third activity: obtaining a new or revised survey. Purchasers do not want nor expect surprises, especially in connection with title to the property they intend to pur-chase. The law requires that the seller deliver "marketable title" at closing, or the purchaser can walk away from the transaction and demand return of his ear-nest money.

We define "marketable title" in the section immediately below. For now, it is enough to consider marketable title as fee simple absolute that is not subject to title claims superior to the seller.

In most contracts, seller is subject to an *express* obligation to deliver market-able title at closing, less certain specific encumbrances that purchaser agrees to accept (for instance, existing access easements that affect the property).

However, even when the contract does not place an express title obligation on seller, seller is subject to an *implied* obligation to deliver marketable title at closing. The implied obligation to deliver marketable title at closing is therefore a default rule, and it can be altered in the contract by the parties.

Title issues are largely matters of public record. This means that the purchaser can check the records without the permission of the seller. If you are interested in buying a home, you do not need the seller's permission to check the records. You can do this effectively if you know the name of the owner and the location of the property. We will look at how you actually do a title search in Chapter 8.

In some transactions, particularly commercial sales, the purchase contract may limit the time during which purchaser can object to title defects, so that seller has an adequate time to attempt to cure those defects before the closing date. In essence, by agreeing to this title inspection language in the contract, the purchaser will have waived his ability to object to any title defect the purchaser could have found in an inspection but failed to conduct, and the purchaser will

PRE-CONTRACT

CONTRACT/EXECUTORY

CLOSING

POST-CLOSING

Abstract versus Examination

In the title review process, there are two primary steps: abstract and examination. A title abstracting service will accumulate all public records relevant to title to an interest in property. The service will issue a report that will include entries for all deeds, easements, mortgages, servitudes, and other matters that affect the title to property. This is the "abstract." A professional—often, but not always, a lawyer—will examine the title abstract and determine the "state of title" on which the purchaser will rely.

have waived his ability to object to a title problem he finds after the title search period expires. The inspection provision has the effect of lighting a fire under the purchaser to complete a search and shortening the time period during which purchaser can locate problems in title.

The purchaser's lawyer will be on the lookout for myriad complications when conducting an *examination of title* to property. For example, title to property under contract may be owned by more than one person over time (where one person has a present estate and another has a future interest) or by more than one person at the same time (where parties share a form of co-tenancy, such as joint tenants). Title may be subject to imperfections (e.g., encumbrances or future interests held by third persons). Other complications may arise as well. A careful review of a deed may reveal problems with the legal description. In some instances, simple errors, such as a title owner's misspelled name, may creep into the records. These errors may manifest as title problems.

It is the job of the purchaser's attorney to give her client a solid understanding of the state of the seller's title, and then arrange protection for purchaser's title if the sale closes.

The abstract may be performed by a title insurance company or a title abstractor. However, if a lawyer is hired to *examine* title, the lawyer cannot "outsource" her fiduciary duty. The ultimate obligation to inform the purchaser of the state of title belongs to the purchaser's lawyer.

The lawyer can help control the purchaser's risk "on the back end" by obtaining a title insurance policy for her client, and by providing the client an opinion of counsel (a letter from the lawyer to the purchaser describing the nature of title). We will look at title insurance and lawyer's title opinions later in this chapter.

a. Marketable Title

Marketable title can also be viewed as a closing issue. Seller has a duty to deliver marketable title at closing, making the obligation a closing issue. Why then do we examine marketable title during the executory period? The answer is simple and relates to the title search. Purchaser will examine title *prior to closing* to determine whether seller has marketable title. The purchaser will object to problems (usually called "defects") in title during the executory period.

What then is marketable title? Generally speaking, marketable title does not require truly perfect title, free from any attack, no matter how unlikely to succeed. Instead, courts ask whether a reasonable third person in the purchaser's position would refuse to close if the purchaser were aware of the defect. If so, the title is not marketable. In practical terms, marketable title means fee simple absolute ownership, which is free from defects such as easements and mortgages. Although case opinions will state the meaning of marketable title in many different ways, it is the combination of three elements or ideas:

Elements of Marketable Title

1. **The seller must be the "record owner" of the property the seller intends to sell.** In other words, if the seller is John Black, then the last deed recorded in the deed room in the chain of title must be to John Black.
2. **The seller must have fee simple absolute ownership of the property, without encumbrances or limitations of any kind.**
3. **By purchasing the property, the purchaser will not be placed into a non-frivolous prospect of litigation over ownership.** To put it another way, the purchaser is not required to "buy a lawsuit" when buying the property.

■ PROBLEM: NAME CHANGES

> ➤ Delia Simmons purchases a house one day after graduating from law school. The public record shows "Delia Simmons" as grantee.
> ➤ Delia Simmons marries George Smith and changes her name to Delia Smith.
> ➤ Delia Smith enters into a contract to sell her house to Paul Jones.

Does Delia have marketable title? Review the elements of marketable title above.

Fortunately, state bar associations adopt guidelines known as "title standards" that resolve the impediment to marketable title described in the problem.

Consider Colorado's Real Estate Title Standard 9.1.2 ("Evidence of Name Change.") That Standard provides that Delia's title would be marketable if reflected as follows:

> In an instrument executed by such person after such name change and recorded in the county in which such real property is located, stating that the two names refer to the same person (such as "Mary Smith, formerly Mary Jones") in the identification of the grantor in the body of the instrument and in either (1) the signature or (2) the acknowledgment.

PRE-CONTRACT

CONTRACT/EXECUTORY

CLOSING

POST-CLOSING

Practice Tip

Title standards allow lawyers to provide assurances about the state of title in the face of often minor uncertainties of title, *without subjecting the lawyer to significant risk of legal malpractice.* Title standards serve as proof that the bench and bar may have changed, but at heart, the practice of law remains a guild!

In other words, in Colorado, Delia Smith would record a written, signed, and notarized statement that she is the same person as Delia Simmons. The title standard would view this as sufficient to meet the first element of marketable title.

Title standards help "clear title" by providing rules that parties and their attorneys can use or actions they can take to essentially overcome what would otherwise be a flaw in title. This is important for two reasons: (1) title standards allow deals to close and (2) title standards insulate lawyers from malpractice for breach of the duty of care.

➤ Assume a purchaser sues her attorney after buying real property and alleges that her attorney recommended that purchaser close the transaction notwithstanding an alleged title problem. The attorney's behavior will be judged against that of the hypothetical, competent real estate attorney. If that hypothetical attorney would have taken the same action as the lawyer being sued, then the lawyer did not breach the duty of care. The title standards are created by a committee of *lawyers* expert in their field. Therefore, title standards reflect the views of marketability held by competent attorneys. If a lawyer for purchaser in a specific transaction gives advice reasonably based on the title standards, *then by definition the lawyer did not breach the duty of care.*

The second element of marketable title states that the purchaser is entitled to title clear of any *encumbrances.* Encumbrances include any interest in the real property owned by another party. If the property is subject to an easement, for instance, then the seller cannot convey marketable title.

b. Contract Title

The requirement that the seller deliver marketable title to the purchaser is a default rule. It is implied in every real property contract, *but the parties can choose to change the standard as they see fit.* In other words, the purchaser and seller can agree that the purchaser will deliver something other than marketable title, or they may simply redefine what marketable title means in a particular transaction.

The most common manner in which parties modify the meaning of marketable title in the contract is to specify precisely which defects in title the purchaser is willing to accept. In commercial sales, for instance, the seller often knows that property is subject to easements for utilities. The contract signed by the parties will state that seller must deliver marketable title, with the exception of the known utility easements.

Most commercial real estate contracts limit the definition of marketable title by excluding certain "permitted exceptions" to title. These exceptions are usually added as an exhibit to the contract and include known easements for access or utilities. The permitted exception list may be modified by the time the deal closes, as a result of the purchaser's title search. If the purchaser discovers additional encumbrances not shown on the exhibit attached to the contract, the purchaser and seller will negotiate a reduction in the purchase price to reflect the value of the defects in title. The parties will then add the newly discovered easements, liens, and defects to the list of permitted exceptions. This exhibit will be attached to the deed seller delivers to the purchaser at closing. ⌨ Review Section 2.6 of the Sample Purchase and Sale Agreement, which is available on the Simulation, and you will see how one well-crafted contract anticipates a set of permitted exceptions to title.

If the purchaser believes that the seller does not have marketable title, the purchaser can refuse to close. As you can imagine, purchaser's refusal to close virtually invites seller to file a lawsuit against purchaser for breach of the contract. The purchaser's decision not to close is therefore a high-stakes gamble: if the court sides with the seller, the court may force the purchaser to the closing table (via an action for specific performance) or the court may award damages.

> ### Insurable Title
>
> One species of contract title is "insurable title." The parties will sometimes agree that purchaser will accept insurable title rather than marketable title. Insurable title is title that a title insurance company is willing to insure. Do you see any way this might present a problem for a purchaser?

In California and some other states, marketability of title must be demonstrated *solely from the public records*. Therefore, in those states, adverse possession cannot serve as the basis of marketability unless the adverse possessor files a suit to quiet title and obtains a judgment of good title. In other states, the question will turn on whether an attack on the rights of the seller by an adverse possessor is remote and unlikely to occur. If possession is well established in the hands of the seller for a very long period of time without dispute, some courts might hold the title marketable.

■ PROBLEM: CAN ADVERSE POSSESSION PROVIDE THE BASIS FOR SELLER'S MARKETABLE TITLE?

➤ Seller and Purchaser enter into a contract for the sale of fifteen acres of land. Seller presently occupies a small building on the property, and operates a country store.

➤ Purchaser intends to build a shopping center on the property.

➤ Purchaser performs a title search, and the search reveals that a portion of the property was subject to a 70-year-old possibility of reverter in the

> descendants of a prior owner of the property that the property shall be used only for residential purposes.
> ➤ Purchaser informs Seller that Purchaser's title search revealed a title defect and demands to be let "off the hook."
> ➤ Seller responds by sending Purchaser a letter stating the following: "Please be advised that Seller has been in open and notorious possession of the property, for twenty-one years, adverse to the legal interest of the descendants of the prior owner, and that Seller entered into possession with full knowledge of the right of entry. Seller is therefore an adverse possessor of the property, and has marketable title."

May Seller insist that Purchaser close the transaction? *See* Conklin v. Davi, 388 A.2d 598 (N.J. 1978).

The lawyer for purchaser has a heavy responsibility: she must accurately inform the purchaser of the title risks with respect to seller's property. Assume that a lawyer determines that the property under contract carries minimal or no title risks. The purchaser must be confident in her lawyer's judgment that seller has marketable title. And here is the problem: marketable title issues are rarely easy or garden-variety. Marketable title issues can crop up in a variety of ways. For example, the purchaser may discover prior to closing that the property is subject to a restrictive covenant or servitude, or to a regulatory prohibition, both of which reduce the attractiveness of the property. Consider *Lohmeyer v. Bower*, below. Which of the three elements of marketable title were at issue?

Practice Tip

Lawyers for the seller should disclose in the contract all possible exceptions to title, and therefore limit the ability of the purchaser to rescind. Some title defects (for example, reciprocal easements in a retail property with neighboring properties) actually increase the value of property.

LOHMEYER v. BOWER

227 P.2d 102 (1951)
Supreme Court of Kansas

[Dr. Lohmeyer was a purchaser under a contract with Bower for a small house in the City of Emporia, Kansas. The house sat on Lot 37 of the "Berkeley Hills Addition" subdivision. In the contract, Bower promised to deliver a warranty deed to Dr. Lohmeyer at closing, along with an abstract of title, demonstrating "good, merchantable title or an Owners Policy of Title Insurance in the amount of the sale price, guaranteeing said title to [Lohmeyer], free and clear of all encumbrances except special taxes, subject, however, to all restrictions and easements of record applying to this property, it being understood that [Bower] shall have sufficient time to bring said abstract to date or obtain Report for Title Insurance and to correct any imperfections in the title if there be such imperfections."

After signing the contract, Dr. Lohmeyer hired a lawyer to examine the abstract of title delivered by Bower. The abstract revealed that in 1926 the developer of Berkeley Hills Addition subjected Lot 37 to a restrictive covenant requiring any house built on the lot to be two stories. The house sitting on Lot 37 at the time Dr. Lohmeyer contracted to purchase the property was one story only. The abstract also revealed that the City of Emporia's zoning ordinance included "set back" requirements that applied to Lot 37. These "set backs" required that a house situated on Lot 37 must be at least three feet from the rear or side lot lines. Bower's house sat a mere 18 inches from one of the lot lines, in violation of the zoning ordinance.

Dr. Lohmeyer informed Bower of the problems. Bower offered to correct the zoning violation by purchasing a two-foot-wide swath of land along the lot line from Bower's neighbor. This would have the effect of moving the lot line two feet away from the house. Dr. Lohmeyer rejected this offer, and instead brought suit to rescind the contract. As part of the suit, Dr. Lohmeyer demanded a return of his down payment. Bower took a diametrically opposed position and brought a counterclaim for specific performance. The trial court found for Bower and specifically enforced the contract. Dr. Lohmeyer appealed.]

PARKER, Justice.

. . .

With contentions advanced by appellees with respect to the force and effect to be given certain portions of the stipulation disposed of it can now be stated we are convinced a fair construction of its terms compels the conclusion that on the date of the execution of the contract the house on the real estate in controversy was a one story frame dwelling which had been moved there in violation of section 2 of the dedication restrictions providing that any residence erected on Lot 37 should be of the height of a two story residence and that it had been placed within 18 inches of the side or rear lot line of such lot in violation of section 5-224, supra, prohibiting the erection of such building within three feet of such line.

There can be no doubt regarding what constitutes a marketable or merchantable title in this jurisdiction. This court has been called on to pass upon that question on numerous occasions. See our recent decision in Peatling v. Baird, 168 Kan. 528, 213 P.2d 1015, 1016, and cases there cited, wherein we held:

> "A marketable title to real estate is one which is free from reasonable doubt, and a title is doubtful and unmarketable if it exposes the party holding it to the hazard of litigation.
>
> "To render the title to real estate unmarketable, the defect of which the purchaser complains must be of a substantial character and one from which he may

PRE-CONTRACT

CONTRACT/EXECUTORY

CLOSING

POST-CLOSING

suffer injury. Mere immaterial defects which do not diminish in quantity, quality or value the property contracted for, constitute no ground upon which the purchaser may reject the title. Facts must be known at the time which fairly raise a reasonable doubt as to the title; a mere possibility or conjecture that such a state of facts may be developed at some future time is not sufficient." (Syl ¶¶1, 2)

Under the rule just stated, and in the face of facts such as are here involved, we have little difficulty in concluding that the violation of section 5-224 of the ordinances of the city of Emporia as well as the violation of the restrictions imposed by the dedication declaration so encumber the title to Lot 37 as to expose the party holding it to the hazard of litigation and make such title doubtful and unmarketable. It follows, since, as we have indicated, the appellees had contracted to convey such real estate to appellant by warranty deed with an abstract of title showing good merchantable title, free and clear of all encumbrances, that they cannot convey the title contracted for and that the trial court should have rendered judgment rescinding the contract. This, we may add is so, notwithstanding the contract provides the conveyance was to be made subject to all restrictions and easements of record, for, as we have seen, it is the violation of the restrictions imposed by both the ordinance and the dedication declaration, not the existence of those restrictions, that renders the title unmarketable. The decision just announced is not without precedent or unsupported by sound authority.

In Moyer v. De Vincentis Const. Co., 107 Pa. Super. 588, 164 A. 111, involving facts, circumstances, and issues almost identical to those here involved, so far as violation of the ordinance is concerned, the plaintiff (vendee) sued to recover money advanced on the purchase price pursuant to the agreement on the ground that violation of a zoning ordinance had made title to the property involved under its terms unmarketable. The court upheld the plaintiff's position and in the opinion said:

> "We are of the opinion that a proper construction of the agreement of sale supports the position of appellant, the vendee in the agreement. The vendor agreed to furnish a good and marketable title free from liens and incumbrances, excepting existing restrictions and easements, if any. As applied to the facts of the case in hand, vendee agreed to purchase the premises subject to the zoning ordinance, but not to purchase the premises, when the house was built in violation of the terms of that ordinance.
>
> "The facts lend weight to the force of this construction. It appears from the pleadings that the premises to be conveyed embraced not only the bare land, but an entire parcel of real estate which included a semidetached dwelling. The description is not by metes and bounds but by house number. The vendee could not take possession without immediately becoming a violator of the law and subject to suit, with a penalty of $25 for every day the building remained in position overlapping the protected area.
>
> "The title was not marketable, not because of an existing zoning ordinance, but because a building had been constructed upon the lot in violation of that ordinance...." 107 Pa. Super. at page 592, 164 A. at page 112.

To the same effect is 66 C.J. 912 §592, where the following statement appears: "Existing violations of building restrictions imposed by law warrant rejection of title by a purchaser contracting for a conveyance free of encumbrances. The fact that the premises to be conveyed violate tenement house regulations is ground for rejection of title where the contract of sale expressly provided against the existence of such violations...." See, also, Moran v. Borrello, 132 A. 510, 4 N.J. Misc. 344.

With respect to covenants and restrictions similar to those involved in the dedication declaration, notwithstanding the agreement—as here—excepted restrictions of record, see Chesebro v. Moers, 233 N.Y. 75, 134 N.E. 842, 21 A.L.R. 1270, holding that the violation by a property owner of covenants restricting the distance from front and rear lines within which buildings may be placed renders the title to such property unmarketable.

See, also, Hebb v. Severson, 32 Wash. 2d 159, 201 P.2d 156, which holds, that where a contract provided that building and use restrictions general to the district should not be deemed restrictions, the purchaser's knowledge of such restrictions did not estop him from rescinding the contract of purchase on subsequent discovery that the position of the house on the lot involved violated such restrictions. At page 172 of 32 Wash. 2d, at page 162 of 201 P.2d it is said:

> "Finally, the fact that the contract contains a provision that protective restrictions shall not be deemed encumbrances cannot aid the respondents. It is not the existence of protective restrictions, as shown by the record, that constitutes the encumbrances alleged by the appellants; but, rather, it is the presently existing violation of one of these restrictions that constitutes such encumbrance, in and of itself. The authorities so hold, on the rationale, to which we subscribe, that to force a vendee to accept property which in its present state violates a building restriction without a showing that the restriction is unenforcible, would in effect compel the vendee to buy a lawsuit. 66 C.J. 911, Vendor and Purchaser, §590; Dichter v. Issacson, 4. N.J. Misc. 297; 132 A. 481, [Affirmed, 104 N.J.L. 167,] 138 A. 920; Chesebro v. Moers, 233 N.Y. 75, 134 N.E. 842, 21 A.L.R. 1270."

Finally appellees point to the contract which, it must be conceded, provides they shall have time to correct imperfections in the title and contend that even if it be held the restrictions and the ordinance have been violated they are entitled to time in which to correct those imperfections. Assuming, without deciding, they might remedy the violation of the ordinance by buying additional ground the short and simple answer to their contention with respect to the violation of the restrictions imposed by the dedication declaration is that any changes in the house would compel the purchaser to take something that he did not contract to buy.

Conclusions heretofore announced require reversal of the judgment with directions to the trial court to cancel and set aside the contract and render such judgment as may be equitable and proper under the issues raised by the pleadings.

It is so ordered.

PRE-CONTRACT

CONTRACT/EXECUTORY

CLOSING

POST-CLOSING

■ POINTS TO CONSIDER

1. **How mistakes happen.** It may seem odd that the one-story house in *Lohmeyer* stood on a lot that was subject to a recorded and very explicit covenant that only a two-story house could be built on the property. How could this even happen? Keep in mind that lawyers are not involved in all aspects of our everyday lives. This is a good thing, the authors suppose. But the absence of lawyers from important decision making has consequences. It turns out that Bower *moved* an existing one-story house to Lot 37 that had originally been built on another piece of land. Apparently, Bower never thought to consult a lawyer about the legal consequences of this move.

2. **Carefully distinguish between zoning and restrictive covenants.** Generally, *zoning regulations* that apply to property and exist at the time the purchaser and seller enter into a contract are not considered encumbrances on property. This is true even if the regulation restricts use or development of the property, because governmental restrictions are not deemed defects in title.

   In modern society, property owners expect, or should expect, that the government can reasonably interfere with use and development of property to advance the general well-being of the community. In constitutional terms (as we will see in Chapter 13), zoning derives from the police power reserved to the States, and is therefore permitted to protect the public's health, safety, and welfare. For example, a set-back is important because it prohibits houses from being too close together. This may allow fire and safety personnel to move quickly through a subdivision if necessary, and perhaps keep a fire from spreading from house to house. *See* Michael J. Garrison & J. David Reitzel, *Zoning Restrictions and Marketability of Title*, 35 Real Est. L.J. 257 (2006).

   Unlike zoning, *restrictive covenants* that exist at the time of execution of the contract are *per se* encumbrances and therefore defects in title, unless the purchaser expressly agrees to accept such covenants in the purchase agreement. This is true even if the purchaser *actually knew* about the covenants when he entered into the contract. The interesting thing is that zoning and covenants often prohibit exactly the same behavior by a property owner. Why is the former not a defect in title, while the latter is? Some modern courts are beginning to consider covenants violations of marketable title only if they unreasonably interfere with the purchaser's "intended and announced purposes" for buying the property. *See, e.g.,* Caselli v. Messina, 567 N.Y.S.2d 972 (N.Y. App. Term. 1990). Do you think this rule makes more sense and comports with most parties' expectations?

   The court in *Lohmeyer* concludes that, although a zoning regulation on property is not a defect in title, the *existing violation* of a zoning regulation constitutes a defect. Not all jurisdictions abide by a rule that a violation of zoning is a defect in title. *See* Voorheesville Rod & Gun Club, Inc. v. E.W. Tompkins Co., Inc., 626 N.E.2d 917 (N.Y. 1993) (the existence of a zoning violation will be deemed a defect in title only if the "contract expressly provides that the seller warrants and represents that, upon purchase, the property will not be in violation of any zoning ordinance. . . . ").

3. **The difference between contract title and pure marketable title can be huge.** Ordinarily, the *mere existence* of the restrictive covenant on a parcel of real property would limit marketable title. This was not true in *Lohmeyer*. A restrictive covenant applied to Lot 37. Why wasn't the covenant a violation of marketable title? Look back at the contract in *Lohmeyer*. What exactly was the violation of marketable title? *See also* Henley v. MacDonald, 971 So. 2d 998 (Fla. Dist. Ct. App. 2008).The *Lohmeyer* contract is an example of an agreement in which parties changed the definition of marketable title as it applied to their transaction. Bower was required to deliver to Dr. Lohmeyer a deed conveying "good merchantable title . . . free and clear of all encumbrances . . . *subject, however, to all restrictions and easements of record applying to this property.* . . ." The modification is contained in the italicized language. There is no indication that Dr. Lohmeyer had an attorney prior to signing the contract, only afterward. What do you think of the modification? Assume that you are Dr. Lohmeyer's lawyer, and Dr. Lohmeyer shows you this provision of the contract *before* execution. How would you advise your client?

4. **The requirement of marketable title creates the possibility for opportunistic behavior.** What happens if the purchaser discovers a problem with seller's title prior to closing? Can the purchaser rescind the contract? In some instances, the seller might be able to fix a title problem by payment of money. For instance, if the property is subject to a minor easement, the seller may want the opportunity to terminate the easement by paying the easement owner money. Think for a moment about what this means in practice. Assume that the seller of real property approaches the owner of the easement and asks: "Would you be willing to release the easement? I need to terminate the easement in order to sell my house." How do you expect that the easement owner will react?

> ### Merchantable Title
>
> Note that the contract in *Lohmeyer* required the seller to deliver "merchantable title." This phrase carries the same meaning as marketable title.

5. **Limited damages for failure to deliver marketable title.** The main remedy sought by Dr. Lohmeyer was rescission of the contract and return of earnest money. The issue arose in *Lohmeyer* pre-closing. It is generally easier to persuade a court to rescind a contract before the seller and purchaser have exchanged deed for money. Might a purchaser also be entitled to damages for the seller's failure to deliver marketable title? The normal rule of contracts for a breach not related to title is that the seller pays the purchaser "benefit-of-the-bargain"

PRE-CONTRACT

CONTRACT/EXECUTORY

CLOSING

POST-CLOSING

damages. However, in many jurisdictions, if the seller is unable to deliver marketable title, damages are limited to returning the purchaser's earnest money and paying the purchaser's costs (such as the appraisal and title examination fee). This rule is based on an older English case, Flureau v. Thornhill, 96 Eng. Rep. 635 (C.P. 1776). However, if the purchaser can show that the seller deliberately harmed title in order to back out of the transaction, the purchaser will be entitled to benefit-of-the-bargain damages. Some courts reject the *Flureau* rule and allow the purchaser to pursue normal contract law damages.

6. **The role of the lawyer.** Consider the role of the lawyer in the *Lohmeyer* transaction. The lawyer, a "Mr. Roscoe Graves," demonstrated care and diligence and allowed Dr. Lohmeyer to make an informed decision to not close on the purchase of Bower's house. In fact, Mr. Graves wrote a letter to Dr. Lohmeyer carefully pointing out the defects in title. It was not Mr. Graves's job to tell Dr. Lohmeyer to refuse to close; it was Mr. Graves's job to inform Dr. Lohmeyer that there were problems inherent in Bower's title to property, and assess the likelihood that actual litigation would result. Sellers often close even though there is an issue. They understand the risks and make the determination that the property is worth the possibility of title trouble after the fact. What do you think Dr. Lohmeyer's response would have been if he had not been explicitly told about the set-back violations and covenant problems, and closed on the transaction?

   The lawyer's evaluation of title implicates the lawyer's duty of care. The lawyer's advice to her client will be judged against the standard of a hypothetical real estate lawyer expert in her field. This is a high standard. If in a particular transaction a lawyer fails to meet this burden, she will be liable for malpractice and negligence to her client. This is why good real estate lawyers sweat all the details associated with title, and also why lawyers' title opinions are often filled with caveats and provisos. For example, lawyers always inform clients in title opinion letters that they cannot verify whether deeds in the seller's chain of title are forged or real.

   Lawyers grapple with marketable title issues in practice on a constant basis. These problems are often resolved by the parties, either because one party lowers a price, or because the purchaser obtains title insurance specifically covering the particular risk. In some cases, the defects can be cured by obtaining waivers of questionable interests or affidavits clearing ambiguities in the title records. Could the defects in *Lohmeyer* be cured? Normally, unless the purchaser agrees to an extension, the seller has until the closing date to make title marketable.

3.   Quality of Property—*Caveat Emptor*

Here is a pattern that we sometimes see real property transactions follow: purchaser finds property, purchaser falls in love with property, purchaser signs contract to buy property, purchaser falls out of love with property, purchaser seeks

PRE-CONTRACT

CONTRACT/EXECUTORY

CLOSING

POST-CLOSING

lawyer's help in "getting out of the contract." The problem with this drama is that once the purchaser signs the contract, the purchaser is subject to a legal doctrine known as *caveat emptor*—"buyer beware." Essentially, under this ages-old doctrine, the buyer must accept the property in its existing condition regardless of any defects in physical quality. As a result, the seller had no duty to disclose defects in the condition of the premises.

The doctrine of *caveat emptor* does not act alone. The purchaser sometimes faces other formidable obstacles when trying to persuade a court to provide purchaser a remedy in connection with a defect in the property's physical quality. The right fact pattern might implicate not only the doctrine of *caveat emptor*, but also the parol evidence rule and the Statute of Frauds. Taken together, these rules and doctrines contributed at common law to a lack of remedy for a purchaser unhappy with the quality of property that she contracted to purchase.

The common law quite seriously said to the prospective purchaser of real property: "buy the property if you wish, but do not complain afterwards." One cornerstone to this regime was the idea that the seller was not obligated to disclose defects in the quality of property. If the seller knew that a nest of vampires lived in the dirt basement below the house, at common law the seller had no property law-based obligation to inform the purchaser.

This fit with the original English common law understanding of the transaction. At common law, the typical agrarian purchaser had the ability to fix and maintain his real property, and it was assumed that this purchaser would take the property "as is." The seller of land with a barn assumed that the purchaser could discern problems with the property and would fix whatever problems the purchaser discovered after the sale. The purchaser had the same set of expectations.

The expectations of parties to a real property contract are different today. Most purchasers of residential and commercial property do not have the knowledge or the ability to discern defects in property without the help of an expert, and they do not want to buy property needing immediate and unexpected repairs. It is therefore important that modern purchasers have the ability to discover any problems in advance of closing.

As a result, the law on disclosure has changed in virtually every jurisdiction. States now

> ### Patent versus Latent Defects
>
> A *patent* defect is one that is obvious or discoverable upon a reasonable inspection. A *latent* defect is one that is hidden, concealed, or not discoverable upon a reasonable inspection.

require sellers to disclose, at minimum, *defects that would not be discoverable by a reasonable inspection and that materially affect the value of the property*. Indeed, the seller may commit fraud if the seller intentionally conceals a defect from prospective purchasers. If the seller is unaware of a particular latent problem, but nevertheless affirmatively asserts that the property does not have that problem, the seller will have negligently misrepresented the quality of the property. Not surprisingly, this behavior is known as *negligent misrepresentation*.

Some real property purchase contracts contain *"as is" clauses*. These provisions essentially say that the purchaser will accept the property no matter what defects in quality the purchaser finds prior to or after closing. This is a powerfully protective provision for seller. A purchaser should sign a contract containing this provision only if he believes he really knows the property and decides that it is worth the risk of a defect. In some jurisdictions, as-is clauses protect the seller from claims that seller negligently misrepresented the quality of the property. However, as-is clauses are no defense against allegations of outright fraud by the seller. ⌨ You can see how an "as-is" provision is incorporated into a well-drafted commercial real property contract by examining Section 3.7 of the Sample Purchase and Sale Agreement that is available on the Simulation.

In addition, many states today impose *specific statutory disclosure* requirements for sales of property. The seller can usually satisfy the requirements by honestly completing an approved disclosure form. *See* New York's Property Condition Disclosure Act, N.Y. Real Prop. Law §§460-67 (McKinney 2015). That Act, like many others, has been criticized for providing sellers with loopholes and therefore not demanding adequate disclosure to purchasers. *See* Philip Lucrezia, *New York's Property Condition Disclosure Act: Extensive Loopholes Leave Buyers and Sellers of Residential Real Property Governed by the Common Law*, 77 St. John's L. Rev. 401 (2003). These statutes may require disclosure of a laundry list of problems, including termite and pest infestations, structural problems, and water damage and mold. ⌨ You may see the disclosure form required in California by Cal. Civ. Code §1102.6 (West 2007 & Supp. 2018) by visiting the Simulation. You will also see a disclosure form in use in residential transactions in North Carolina.

Many, but not all, of these statutes focus on residential transactions. Commercial purchasers are often thought to have a greater opportunity, and therefore greater responsibility, to discover quality problems in property. Moreover, commercial properties vary widely, while residential transactions are fairly uniform. Thus, commercial parties can and should deal with disclosure obligations in the purchase contract. *See* Kathleen M. Tomcho, *Commercial Real Estate Buyer Beware: Sellers May Have the Right to Remain Silent*, 70 S. Cal. L. Rev. 1571 (1997).

Before we move on, we want to hone in on a critical aspect of *caveat emptor* and the duty to disclose: the matter of timing.

A defect in the quality of property will typically emerge either during the executory period or during the period following closing. For example, a prospective purchaser may discover a defect during the executory period when visiting the property or during the purchaser's professional home inspection. To the extent that a problem crops up during this phase of the transaction, it is likely to be blatant (observable mold, for example). However, in the vast majority of cases, a purchaser will discover a defect in property following the closing and *after* taking possession. It is then that the purchaser will confront odors that were too slight to notice during a brief tour with the broker, or will see how rain collects in a basement during a rare but heavy storm.

What you must understand is that the doctrine of *caveat emptor* and the seller's duty to disclose remain the same regardless of when the defect in property emerges. However, the relative *leverage* of the purchaser radically diminishes if she learns of the problem after closing. Prior to closing, the seller holds the purchaser's earnest money, and purchaser runs the risk of losing this amount in a dispute. This is bad news for the purchaser, but at least, from the purchaser's perspective, the earnest money is only a fraction of the sale price.

This risk of losing earnest money pales in comparison to the loss faced by the purchaser following closing. At this point, the purchaser will have paid the *entire sale price* to the seller. Persuading a court to rescind a fully-performed contract, when the purchaser is in possession, is a much more difficult task. And it is hard to imagine many scenarios in which the seller voluntarily repays the purchaser the sale price and agrees to take back the deed.

CASE SUMMARY: Stambovsky v. Ackley, 572 N.Y.S.2d 672 (N.Y. App. Div. 1991)

In *Stambovsky v. Ackley*, New York adopted the duty to disclose latent defects, in a case involving unusual circumstances. The purchaser complained that the house the seller contracted to sell to him was haunted! The prospective purchaser in *Stambovsky* learned of the home's ghostly reputation prior to closing, and asked a court to rescind the contract. Proof of this defect ordinarily would be difficult to demonstrate. However, the court in *Stambovsky* accepted the allegation that the home was haunted as true "as a matter of law," because the seller had promoted the house as haunted during her ownership. Regardless of whether the home really was haunted, the house had a seller-generated reputation that affected its market value, making the ghosts a material defect.

The court held for the prospective purchaser and rejected the seller's defense of *caveat emptor*. The court explained:

> The doctrine of caveat emptor requires that a buyer act prudently to assess the fitness and value of his purchase and operates to bar the purchaser who fails to exercise due care from seeking the equitable remedy of rescission. . . . *Where a condition which has been created by the seller materially impairs the value of the contract and is peculiarly within the knowledge of the seller or unlikely to be discovered by a prudent purchaser exercising due care with respect to the subject transaction, nondisclosure constitutes a basis for rescission as a matter of equity.* Any other outcome places upon the buyer not merely the obligation to exercise care in his purchase but rather to be omniscient with respect to any fact which may affect the bargain. No practical purpose is served by imposing such a burden upon a purchaser. To the contrary, it encourages predatory business practice and offends the principle that equity will suffer no wrong to be without a remedy.

Stambovsky v. Ackley, 572 N.Y.S.2d 672, 676 (N.Y. App. Div. 1991) (emphasis added). The court determined that the seller created the public image of the house as haunted, and that this was not a condition that a buyer could have discovered upon a reasonable inspection. Therefore, the seller should have disclosed the condition. The court permitted the purchaser to rescind.

Does *Stambovsky* stand for a rule that a seller must always disclose paranormal activity she may have experienced in her house? If not, why not?

a. Discovering the Problem

The obligation to disclose latent defects raises some of the most difficult *caveat emptor* problems. It is not always easy to discern whether a problem is discoverable by purchaser (*patent*) or non-discoverable (*latent*). The modern legal rule places the risk of loss on the purchaser if the defect could have been discovered. This rule presumes that the purchaser either had an opportunity, before or after signing the contract, to investigate the property, or that the purchaser simply agreed in the contract to take the property with whatever defects it may contain.

In the section on title examination, we told you that the purchaser has the right to investigate the public records to locate title issues regardless of whether the contract provides this right. By contrast, the purchaser has no right to enter and investigate the seller's property to locate defects in the quality of the property (water damage, leaking roofs, open pits to hell in the basement, that sort of thing) unless the purchaser negotiates this right in the contract or unless a statute provides this right as a matter of law (for example, to permit inspection for termite damage). Usually, this means that the purchaser will hire a professional expert to evaluate real property and structures in order to discover problems.

Sometimes the seller permits the purchaser to enter the property and investigate its quality (whether it has any defects, such as leaky roofs) before signing the contract. The typical practice, however, is that the seller grants purchaser the right to investigate such matters only after execution of the contract. 🖥 For example, Section 4.1 of the Sample Purchase and Sale Agreement, which you can view on the Simulation, provides:

> **Access to Real Property.** From the Mutual Execution Date until the end of the Contingency Period (or, if earlier, until this Agreement is terminated), Buyer and Buyer's designees shall have access to the Real Property for the purpose of conducting such environmental and other tests and investigations as Buyer deems appropriate. If after conducting such tests and investigations Buyer exercises any right to terminate this Agreement, Buyer shall forthwith correct any dangerous or abnormal condition on the Real Property caused by Buyer's tests, including but not necessarily limited to plugging any holes drilled in the course of soil sampling.

Due Diligence

In the commercial world, all of the investigation into the property by purchaser (investigation of the state of title, quality of the property, whether tenants are paying their rents, etc.) are collectively referred to as "due diligence."

The purchaser's contractual right to enter the property and investigate prior to closing is time-limited. If the purchaser does not object to some aspect of the quality of the property within the stated time limit, the purchaser is deemed to have waived this right. In other words, the purchaser is deemed to accept the property with the defect. For example, in a residential sale, if the inspector finds a problem (and he very often does), the purchaser will present the inspection report to the seller. The seller may agree to fix the problem or negotiate a reduced price for the property. In the alternative, the seller may indicate that he will not fix the problem or reduce the price, and the buyer will have to decide whether the problem is significant enough to back away or attempt to force the seller to fix it.

A well-written inspection clause should specify the seller's obligations in the event the inspection reveals defects. Some contracts give the purchaser a right to walk away from the deal altogether (and take back the earnest money) if the problems found by the inspector would cost in excess of a pre-set amount of money.

■ PROBLEM: WATER IN THE BASEMENT

> On January 1, Daniel contracts to purchase Jerry's house and related property. The contract provides Daniel with a right to conduct a physical inspection of real property within 30 days of execution of the contract.
> On January 15, Daniel visits Jerry's home and is admitted to all parts of the house, including the basement. Daniel notices that the basement has been repainted and the floor is newly carpeted. The basement has been renovated to be a recreation room; it even includes a pool table. Everything looks great to Daniel's eye.
> On February 13, an inch of water collects in a corner of the basement during a heavy rain storm.

Assume that Daniel visits you for legal advice. What questions would you ask him? What is Daniel's position vis-a`-vis Jerry? *See* Wilhite v. Mays, 232 S.E.2d 141 (Ga. Ct. App. 1976) (defective septic and sewer system).

Now let's add one new element to the Problem. Assume that in the contract for sale, Daniel agreed to take the property "as-is." Would this change your answer? *See* Goddard v. Stabile, 924 N.E.2d 868 (Ohio Ct. App. 2009).

b. *The Seller's Representations*

The purchaser may ask questions when inspecting property. Sometimes, the seller simply volunteers information. This happens more often in the residential context. What happens if the representations later prove false?

PRE-CONTRACT

CONTRACT/EXECUTORY

CLOSING

POST-CLOSING

■ PROBLEM: PHYSICAL QUALITY AND THE EFFECT OF REPRESENTATIONS

> ➤ Brenda is 30 years old and is ready to move out of her one-bedroom apartment. Brenda decides that she has the income necessary to purchase a house and enlists the aid of a broker. The broker takes her to see numerous properties, but ultimately she focuses her attention on a pretty, ranch-style house in an older neighborhood.

> ➤ The seller, Norma, is an older woman. Norma lived in the house with her husband from the time the house was built. Norma's husband died recently, and Norma wishes to move into a retirement community.

> ➤ Brenda takes a tour of the house in the company of Norma. The interior of the home has been newly repainted; the kitchen and bathroom floors are new. Brenda notices air fresheners in many of the rooms, especially in the small master bedroom. Brenda asks why Norma uses so many air fresheners. Norma responds, "Well, this is an older house. These little machines really keep the place inviting and happy."

> ➤ Brenda makes an offer for the property, which Norma accepts. Brenda and Norma sign a contract. The contract permits Brenda to hire a home inspector, and to make objections based on the inspection report within fifteen days following the inspection. Brenda hires an inspector; the inspection report reveals no major flaws.

> ➤ Twenty days after the home inspection, and just a day before closing, Norma permits Brenda to transfer some of her personal belongings into the house, to get a jump on the move. Brenda begins to put linens into an empty linen closet. The closet is newly repainted. Brenda notices a loose board in the back of the closet, and jiggles it to see if it is in need of repair. The board comes loose, revealing a dark black patch, which Brenda immediately recognizes as mold.

> ➤ Brenda asks Norma if she can have her inspector re-enter the house for a second inspection. Norma declines, stating, "The contract allowed you to enter one time and make a report, and you have already done that."

If you were advising Brenda on her position vis-à-vis Norma, what would you say?

■ PROBLEM: OTHER TYPICAL QUALITY ISSUES

Assume that the following simple fact patterns arise prior to, or after, closing. Does the seller have an obligation to disclose?

1) The kitchen is infested with cockroaches.
2) The attic is full of mice.

3) The bottom two steps of the front porch are cracking and ready to collapse.
4) Some of the pipes in the basement are wrapped with asbestos insulation.
5) Five of the double-hung windows do not open and it will cost $1,000 to repair them.

Practice Tip

Representations are subject to the duty of *continuing accuracy*. Facts represented by the seller at the time the contract is signed might change prior to closing. For example, the property may be subjected to a condemnation action after the contract is signed.

c. Stigma Cases

Most cases involving *caveat emptor* concern physical defects. However, as we saw in *Stambovsky*, the haunted house case, some problems with real property are reputational in nature rather than physical. These defects may reduce property value. Courts sometimes use more colorful language and suggest that these defects "stigmatize" property.

Stigmatized property cases present issues of the seller's obligation to disclose and the purchaser's obligation to uncover reasonably discoverable defects. However, they do so in a more difficult and in many instances a more emotionally charged context than run-of-the-mill instances of physical defects. *Van Camp v. Bradford* is very much that sort of case. This case does not lend itself to easy answers; rather, it presents hard questions. You should approach *Van Camp* as though you were an attorney representing one of the parties, and you should do so with sensitivity and compassion.

VAN CAMP v. BRADFORD

623 N.E.2d 731 (1993)
Court of Common Pleas of Ohio, Butler County

MICHAEL J. SAGE, Judge.

This matter comes before this court on three motions filed by the defendants. The defendants in this case are Connie Bradford, the original owner/seller; Campbell Realty World (hereinafter "Realty World"), the selling/listing agency; William Campbell, the owner of Realty World; Martin Patton, the agent of Realty World; West Shell Realtors, Inc., the cooperating agency (hereinafter "West Shell"); and Robert Hoff, the cooperating agent of West Shell. Counsel have agreed that these motions are to be treated as Civ. R. 56(C) motions for summary judgment.

I

This case arises from the sale of a residence located at 6027 Arcade Drive, Fairfield, Ohio. On or about October 30, 1991, a renter's daughter was raped at knifepoint in the residence owned by defendant Bradford. On or about December 20, 1991, another rape occurred in a neighboring home at 2499 E. Highland Drive; that same day, defendant Bradford listed the house for sale with defendant Realty World.

Plaintiff Kitty Van Camp submitted a written offer to purchase the home on February 4, 1992. Before closing and during a walk-through inspection of the premises with defendant Bradford, and defendant Patton and defendant Hoff present, plaintiff noticed bars on the basement windows. In response to plaintiff's inquiry regarding the purpose and necessity of the bars on the windows, defendant Bradford stated that a break-in had occurred sixteen years earlier, but that there was currently no problem with the residence. Plaintiff stated that she would like to remove the bars for cosmetic purposes, but Bradford advised her not to do so, as it was in plaintiff's best interests to leave the bars in place.

The closing on the property took place on February 21, 1992. At this time, the perpetrator of the crimes was still at large. While moving into the home, a neighbor informed plaintiff that the daughter of the last occupant had been raped in October, and that another brutal rape had occurred shortly before Christmas, in 1991. Two more rapes occurred in June and August 1992 at a nearby home, 5886 Coachmont Drive, Fairfield. Plaintiff's house was burglarized on April 8, 1992, and threatening phone calls were received by plaintiff in July 1992. Police reports submitted by plaintiff confirm that all of these crimes did in fact take place.

Plaintiff, after being informed of the rapes in her home and the surrounding neighborhood, confronted defendant Campbell, who acknowledged that he, defendant Patton, and defendant Hoff were all aware of the rapes, including the rape at the subject property.

Plaintiff filed her complaint on May 25, 1992, alleging that the defendants knew of the unsafe character of the residence and neighborhood, failed to disclose, and concealed these material facts, which would have influenced her decision to buy the property. Plaintiff seeks damages from all defendants for mental stress and anguish, for the decreased value of the property, for fraud and negligence, and for equitable relief.

The defendants have filed for summary judgment, arguing primarily that the doctrine of *caveat emptor* is a complete defense in a suit seeking recovery for the "stigma" attached to or the "psychological impairment" of a piece of property. Defendants also claim that a cause of action for property defects that are neither a physical or legal impairment does not exist in Ohio.

II

The rule that a seller is generally under no duty to disclose material facts about the subject matter of a sale unless a specific exception exists originates from the doctrine of *caveat emptor.* Powell, The Seller's Duty to Disclose in Sales of Commercial Property (Summer 1990), 28 Am. Bus. L.J. 245, at 248. At least since 1956, the principle of *caveat emptor* has been consistently applied in Ohio to sales of real estate relative to conditions discoverable by the buyer, or open to observation upon an investigation of the property. Traverse v. Long (1956), 165 Ohio St. 249, 59 O.O. 325, 135 N.E.2d 256. One of the earliest Ohio cases upholding this principle held that since repairs to an area of filled-in land were clearly visible upon inspection, the plaintiffs knew of the defect and *caveat emptor* was an applicable defense to their claim. *Id.* Similarly, in 1974, the Franklin County Court of Appeals held that since the seller generally has no affirmative duty to disclose patent material defects, the defendants were not liable for failing to disclose that the residence in question was serviced by well water and not city water, since the well itself and the defects in the well were both readily observable. Klott v. Assoc. Real Estate (1974), 41 Ohio App. 2d 118, 121, 70 O.O.2d 129, 131, 322 N.E.2d 690, 692.

Five years later, however, the Supreme Court of Ohio held that latent defects do give rise to a duty on the part of the seller, and constitute an exception to the application of *caveat emptor.* Miles v. McSwegin (1979), 58 Ohio St. 2d 97, 100, 12 O.O.3d 108, 110, 388 N.E.2d 1367, 1369. When latent defects are coupled with misrepresentations or concealment, the doctrine of *caveat emptor* does not preclude recovery for fraud. Finomore v. Epstein (1984), 18 Ohio App. 3d 88, 18 OBR 403, 481 N.E.2d 1193. Fraudulent concealment exists where a vendor fails to disclose sources of peril of which he is aware, if such a source is not discoverable by the vendee. Klott, 41 Ohio App. 2d at 121, 70 O.O.2d at 131, 322 N.E.2d at 692. Thus, the Supreme Court of Ohio held that the plaintiffs could sue for termites discovered after the real estate agent made the representation that the house was a "good solid home," especially since the seller was personally aware of the problem prior to the sale. See *Miles.* The nature of the defect and the ability of the parties to determine through a reasonable inspection that a defect exists are key to determining whether or not the defect is latent. *Id.,* 58 Ohio St. 2d at 101, 12 O.O.3d at 110, 388 N.E.2d at 1369.

In the 1983 case of Kaye v. Buehrle, the Summit County Court of Appeals affirmed a directed verdict in favor of the defendants and upheld the validity of a real estate "as is" disclaimer clause. Kaye v. Buehrle (1983), 8 Ohio App. 3d 381, 8 OBR 495, 457 N.E.2d 373. Such disclaimer clauses bar suit for passive nondisclosure, but will not protect a defendant from positive misrepresentation or concealment. *Id.* The court found, however, that the defendants did not make any statement or false representation regarding the condition of the basement, which suffered extensive flooding after the plaintiffs purchased the property.

PRE-CONTRACT

CONTRACT/EXECUTORY

CLOSING

POST-CLOSING

The following year, the Cuyahoga County Court of Appeals held that *caveat emptor* did not preclude the purchaser of two tracts of land from recovering for fraud due to a latent defect in the form of a blemished title, since a misrepresentation had accompanied the latent defect. See *Finomore*. The plaintiff in that case testified that the owner had told him that the lots were "free and clear," yet the evidence indicated that a small mortgage on the property was outstanding at the time of the sale.

In contrast to the national trend, Ohio has recently upheld the doctrine of *caveat emptor* with regard to real estate sales. Layman v. Binns (1988), 35 Ohio St. 3d 176, 519 N.E.2d 642 ("we are not disposed to abolish the doctrine of *caveat emptor*" and "[t]he doctrine of *caveat emptor*, although virtually abolished in the area of personal property, remains a viable rule of law in real estate sales"); see, also, Jones, Risk Allocation and the Sale of Defective Used Housing in Ohio—Should Silence Be Golden? (1991), 20 Cap. U. L. Rev. 215. Conditions traditionally limiting the application of the doctrine, however, were also vigorously upheld in the court's opinion: the property defect must be open to observation or discoverable upon a reasonable inspection, the purchaser must have an unimpeded opportunity to examine the property and the vendor may not engage in fraud. *Layman* at 179, 519 N.E.2d at 645. The court held that, unlike a latent defect, the structural defect of the basement wall at issue was "highly visible," and the corrective I-beams supporting the wall were open to observation by the plaintiffs. The court further acknowledged that an affirmative misrepresentation or misstatement of a material fact by the sellers regarding the condition of the wall would have precluded the application of *caveat emptor*, but found that no such statement was made by the defendants during the transaction.

With the recent enactment of R.C. 5302.30, the Ohio legislature has taken a bold step toward ameliorating the harsh application of *caveat emptor* in even patent defect real estate transactions. For sales conducted on or after July 1, 1993, the statute requires a seller of residential property to provide each prospective buyer, or his/her agent, with a prescribed disclosure form regarding various aspects of the property. Even though the official disclosure form has not yet been formally established, preliminary drafts indicate that its purpose is to disclose material matters regarding not only the physical condition of the property, but also title, survey and other matters. Sidor, Ohio's New Seller Disclosure Law (May/June 1993), Ohio Lawyer, at 8. If the seller fails to provide the disclosure form, the statute grants the buyer the powerful remedy of rescission. With this initiative, the Ohio legislature has seriously undermined the doctrine of *caveat emptor* as previously applied.

Virtually all of the case law regarding the buyer's duties under *caveat emptor* focuses on physical property defects. Thus, the case at bar is unique in that it presents issues regarding duty and liability for a so-called psychological defect in the property, namely, that the property was rendered unsafe for habitation by the plaintiff due to the serious crimes that had occurred in and near the residence.

The stigma associated with the residence at 6027 Arcade Drive is analogous to the latent property defects that have become an exception to the strict application of *caveat emptor*. Due to the intangible nature of the defect at issue here, a prospective buyer would have been unable to determine from a walk-through of the house in 1992 that it was the site of a serious, unsolved violent crime. Clearly, any psychological stigma that may be attached to a residence is even more undiscoverable than the existence of termites in a home, see *Miles,* or a defect in the title to the property, see *Finomore,* both of which have been deemed latent defects despite the fact that they could have been discovered through a professional inspection or title search.

Defendants' argument that the defect at issue here was readily discoverable lacks merit. Checking police records in order to ascertain the relative safety of a neighborhood or a particular residence would not be an action undertaken by even the most prudent of purchasers. When viewed in conjunction with a potential misrepresentation or concealment on the part of defendant Bradford regarding the relative safety of the home, the latent nature of the defect at issue here renders the defense of *caveat emptor* inapplicable.

III

The case *sub judice* raises the question whether Ohio should recognize a cause of action for residential property tainted by stigmatizing events that have occurred on and near the premises. The only reported case involving a psychological property defect was heard in California by the Third District Court of Appeals, and involved a house that had been the site of multiple murders ten years prior to its sale to the plaintiff. Reed v. King (1983), 145 Cal. App. 3d 261, 193 Cal. Rptr. 130. The Third District held that the plaintiff buyer did have a cause of action capable of surviving the seller's motion to dismiss. The determinative issue in that case was whether the failure to disclose the murders was material. *Id.*

The California court "saw no principled basis for making the duty to disclose turn upon the character of the information," and held that the failure to disclose the murders was a material fact that could conceivably depress the value of the property. *Id.* at 267, 193 Cal. Rptr. at 133. The Third District then stated that the plaintiff could recover in her suit for rescission and damages if she was successful in proving the allegation that the murders did in fact cause a measurable decrease in the market value of the property.[5]

The unreported opinion in Brannon v. Mueller Realty & Notaries (Oct. 24, 1984), Hamilton App. No. C-830876, unreported, 1984 WL 7018, is the only Ohio decision that deals with a defect that is neither a legal nor physical impairment of property. The husband of defendant Constance Barrett had committed suicide in their home

---

[5] For an interesting discussion and analysis of this case, see Note, Reed v. King: *Fraudulent Nondisclosure of a Multiple Murder in a Real Estate Transaction* (1984), 45 U. Pitt. L. Rev. 877.

prior to its sale to the plaintiffs. In response to Linda Brannon's inquiry regarding the whereabouts of the owners, the real estate agent reportedly answered that Constance Barrett and her family moved out of the house after her husband died of an unexpected heart attack.

The Hamilton County Court of Appeals analyzed the case by discussing the elements required in order to prove fraudulent inducement warranting rescission, namely misrepresentation or concealment of a material fact that justifiably induced the party to enter into the bargain to his/her detriment. *Brannon* at 7. Although the court acknowledged that the agent had misrepresented the facts, the plaintiffs' claim nevertheless failed, since the court determined that the nature by which a former owner died was not a material misrepresentation that would affect the conduct of a reasonable person attempting to purchase. *Brannon* at 8. Further, the court noted that even though Gerald Brannon was ignorant regarding the suicide until a month after the transfer, Linda Brannon had full knowledge of the suicide prior to signing the contract, and therefore the agent's misrepresentation could not have induced her decision to effect the sale. *Brannon* at 6.

By engaging in this analysis, an Ohio Court of Appeals has tacitly asserted that a remedy for stigmatized residential property is available in certain circumstances. This *de facto* recognition of a cause of action for psychologically tainted property is the natural culmination of the trend regarding property disclosure in Ohio, and will be upheld by this court.[6]

IV

Clearly defining the cause of action for stigmatized property is necessary in order to protect the stability of contracts and prevent limitless recovery for insubstantial harms and irrational fears: misrepresentation, concealment or nondisclosure of a material fact by a seller of residential property in response to an affirmative inquiry is evidence of a breach of duty on the part of the seller. After inquiry, if the buyer justifiably relied on the misrepresentation or nondisclosure, or was induced or misled into effecting the sale to his/her detriment and damage, the buyer has met the burden of proof required to withstand a summary judgment motion.

Fraud may be committed by suppression or concealment, as well as by expression of a falsehood. *Klott,* 41 Ohio App. 2d at 121, 70 O.O.2d at 131, 322 N.E.2d at 692 (citing 24 Ohio Jurisprudence 2d [1957] 676, Fraud and Deceit, Section 74). Even an innocent misrepresentation may, under the appropriate circumstances, justify rescission in the interests of fairness. *Brannon* at 7.

The misrepresentation, however, must be regarding a material fact. As adopted by the *Brannon* court, a misrepresentation of fact is material when it would be likely, under the circumstances, to affect the conduct of a reasonable person with

---

[6] For an excellent summary of the trend regarding nondisclosure and *caveat emptor* in Ohio, see Kafker (1986), Sell and Tell: The Fall and Revival of the Rule on Nondisclosure in Sales of Used Real Property, 12 U. Dayton L. Rev. 57, 63-65.

reference to the transaction in question. *Brannon* at 8 (citing Restatement of the Law, Contracts [1932] 891, Section 470[2]). When determining whether or not a particular fact is material to the transaction at issue, the *Brannon* court highlighted the importance of augmenting this objective test with subjective considerations. When the individual making the misrepresentation is aware that the recipient is peculiarly disposed to attach importance to a particular subject, subjective considerations have a bearing on the subject matter; in such an instance, the misrepresentation should be deemed material, regardless of its significance to a reasonable person under similar circumstances. *Brannon* at 9.

When a seller receives an affirmative inquiry regarding the condition of a piece of property, the buyer is entitled to a truthful answer. In contrast to the holding in *Klott v. Assoc. Real Estate*, the defective-water-well case, in *Foust v. Valleybrook Realty Co.*, the fact that the plaintiffs specifically inquired regarding the sanitary sewer system was the underpinning for the court's affirmance of the trial court's finding of fraud. See Foust v. Valleybrook Realty Co. (1981), 4 Ohio App. 3d 164, 4 OBR 264, 446 N.E.2d 1122. One who responds to an inquiry is guilty of fraud if he gives equivocal, evasive or misleading answers calculated to convey a false impression, even though the answer may be literally true. 37 American Jurisprudence 2d (1968) 207, Fraud and Deceit, Section 150. Responding honestly to an affirmative inquiry regarding the condition of a residence is a lighter burden than the voluntary disclosure of a defect mandated by *caveat emptor*, particularly when knowledge of a stigmatizing defect is within the ready personal or actual knowledge of the seller at the time of the inquiry.

The misrepresentation or nondisclosure of the seller must cause justifiable reliance on the part of the buyer, and damage must result as a consequence of the fraudulent transaction. Both of these requirements will serve as effective limitations on seller liability and will function to prevent the bringing of meritless claims. In determining whether reliance is justifiable, courts consider the various circumstances involved, such as the nature of the transaction, the form and materiality of the representation, the relationship of the parties, the respective intelligence, experience, age, and mental and physical condition of the parties, and their respective knowledge and means of knowledge. *Finomore*, 18 Ohio App. 3d at 90, 18 OBR at 405-406, 481 N.E.2d at 1195. When a fiduciary relationship exists, as between a realty agent and a client, the client is entitled to rely upon the representations of the realty agent. *Id.*; see, also, *Foust*. In the absence of a fiduciary relationship, the law requires a person to exercise proper vigilance in his dealings, so that where one is put on notice as to any doubt as to the truth of a representation, the person is under a duty to reasonably investigate before relying thereon. *Id.*, 4 Ohio App. 3d at 165, 4 OBR at 265, 446 N.E.2d at 1124. The prevailing trend in misrepresentation cases, however, is to place a minimal duty on the buyer to investigate and discover the true facts about the property. See Powell, *supra*, at 258.

A seller who is under a duty to disclose facts and fails to do so will be held liable for damages directly and proximately resulting from his silence. See, *e.g.*, *Kaye*, 8 Ohio App. 3d at 382, 8 OBR at 495, 457 N.E.2d at 375; *Miles*, 58 Ohio St. 2d at 100,

12 O.O.3d at 110, 388 N.E.2d at 1369. A person injured by fraud is entitled to such damages as will fairly compensate him for the wrong suffered. See *Foust*, 4 Ohio App. 3d at 166, 4 OBR at 266, 446 N.E.2d at 1125 (citing 25 Ohio Jurisprudence 2d [1957] 32, Fraud and Deceit, Section 201). As an additional safeguard, objective tangible harm must be demonstrated to still the concern that permitting cases of this nature to go forward will open the floodgates to rescission on subjective and idiosyncratic grounds. Accord *Reed*, 145 Cal. App. 3d at 268, 193 Cal. Rptr. at 134.

V

The defendants in this case have argued that the prevailing trend across the nation regarding property disclosure is evidenced by the nondisclosure statutes that have been enacted in twenty states and the District of Columbia.[7] Defendants also contend that these statutes imply that a cause of action for tainted property in Ohio is necessarily barred.

These statutes generally state that sellers of real estate are not liable for failing to disclose stigmatizing events, such as the fact that a homicide, suicide, felony or death by AIDS occurred in the residence.[8] Ohio has not adopted a nondisclosure statute of this nature.

It is the opinion of this court that the nondisclosure statutes as enacted in other states still require a good faith response to an inquiry regarding a potential psychological impairment: these statutes were enacted solely to insulate sellers from liability for any failure to *voluntarily* and automatically disclose information regarding potential stigmas associated with property. As aptly stated by Representative Prague during the public hearings discussing Connecticut's newly adopted nondisclosure statute, "It seems to me that anybody selling a house would have to answer truthfully when a buyer asks a question. I mean, why should we tell you what the realtor should say or shouldn't say, or should reveal and shouldn't reveal. He should reveal anything that is asked of him." See An Act Concerning Psychologically Impacted Property, hearings on S.B. 390 before the Insurance and Real Estate Committee Hearings, Conn. General Assembly, March 6, 1990, at 254.

Nondisclosure statutes are not designed to allow sellers to make false representations regarding property defects in response to affirmative questioning by the buyer. In fact, the statutes enacted in Rhode Island, South Carolina and Georgia specifically state that the nondisclosure provision is not to be interpreted as authorization for an agent to make any misrepresentation of fact or a false

---

[7] California (Cal. Civ. Code 1710.2); Colorado (C.R.S. 38-35.5-101); Connecticut (Conn. Gen. Stats. 20-329cc *et seq.*); Delaware (24 Del. C. 2929); District of Columbia (D.C. Code 45-1936); Illinois (Ill. Rev. Stat. ch. 111, ¶5831.1); Georgia (O.C.G.A. 44-1-16); Louisiana (La. R. S. 37:1468); Maryland (Md. Code Ann., Business Occupations and Professions, 16-322.1 and Real Property, 2-120); Missouri (R.S. Mo. 442.600); Nevada (Nev. Rev. Stat. 40.565); New Mexico (N.M. Stat. Ann. 47-13-2); North Carolina (N.C. Gen. Stat. 39-50); Oklahoma (59 Okla. St. 858-513); Oregon (O.R.S. 93.275); Rhode Island (R.I. Gen. Laws 5-20.8-6); South Carolina (S.C. Ann. 40-57-270); Tennessee (Tenn. Code Ann. 66-5-110); Utah (Utah Code Ann. 57-1-37); Virginia (Va. Code Ann. 55-524), and Wisconsin (Wis. Stat. 452.23).

[8] For more information regarding nondisclosure statutes, see McEvoy (Jan./Feb. 1992), Stigmatized Property: What a Buyer Should Know, 48 J. Mo. Bar 57.

statement.[9] In addition, two other statutes contain a specific provision that codifies *Brannon*'s "peculiarly disposed" concept whereby subjective considerations may make a fact material with regard to a particular transaction: in Connecticut or Oklahoma, if in the process of making an offer, a purchaser or lessee advises an owner in writing that knowledge of a psychological impact is important to his decision to purchase, the owner through his agent shall report in writing any findings to the purchaser or lessee. See Conn. Gen. Stats. 20-329cc et seq.; 59 Okla. Stat. 858-513. In fact, the burden on the real estate agent under this type of statute is potentially greater than the minimal duty imposed by this court in that, once asked, an agent in Connecticut or Oklahoma potentially has the affirmative duty to seek out from the seller the information sought by the buyer, rather than merely disclosing his or her actual knowledge without the duty of further inquiry.

Thus, since the nondisclosure statutes of other states merely protect sellers from the burden of voluntary disclosure regarding psychological defects, and since several states have specific provisions designed to uphold honesty in residential sales transactions, the duty described in this opinion is well within the range delineated and envisioned by other state legislatures.

VI

A cause of action for stigmatized property, as previously defined and limited, is warranted in the case at bar. At this point, it is necessary to analyze the elements of the cause of action for stigmatized property in the context of the defendants' summary judgment motions, and in light of the facts of the case *sub judice*.

A motion for summary judgment shall be granted when there is no genuine issue of any material fact and the moving party is entitled to judgment as a matter of law. Summary judgment shall not be granted unless it appears from the evidence that reasonable minds could come to but one conclusion and that conclusion is adverse to the party against whom the motion is made. In reviewing a motion for summary judgment, the inferences to be drawn from the underlying facts must be viewed in the light most favorable to the opposing party. Civ. R. 56(C); Temple v. Wean United, Inc. (1977), 50 Ohio St. 2d 317, 4 O.O.3d 466, 364 N.E.2d 267.

Summary judgment is a procedural device to terminate litigation and to avoid a formal trial where there is nothing left to try. It must be awarded with caution, resolving doubts and construing evidence against the moving party, and granted only when it appears from the evidentiary material that reasonable minds can reach only an adverse conclusion as to the party opposing the motion. Norris v. Ohio Std. Oil Co. (1982), 70 Ohio St. 2d 1, 24 O.O.3d 1, 433 N.E.2d 615. Because summary judgment is a procedural device to terminate litigation, it must be awarded with caution. Doubts must be resolved in favor of the nonmoving party. Osborne v. Lyles (1992), 63 Ohio St. 3d 326, 587 N.E.2d 825.

---

[9] For example, Rhode Island's statute reads: "...under no circumstances, shall this provision be interpreted as or used as authorization for an agent or seller to make any misrepresentation of fact or false statement." See R.I. Gen. Laws 5-20.8-6(B).

PRE-CONTRACT

CONTRACT/EXECUTORY

CLOSING

POST-CLOSING

Construing the evidence in the light most favorable to the plaintiff, the court finds that the plaintiff has met her initial burden of proof. The court must accept plaintiff's evidence that a rape occurred in the residence at 6027 Arcade Drive, and that several other crimes occurred in close proximity to the property. Further, the court must accept plaintiff's allegation that all of the defendants involved knew that these crimes had occurred, yet failed to disclose this knowledge to the plaintiff.

Reasonable minds could construe the plaintiff's question regarding the bars on the basement windows as an affirmative inquiry directed at ascertaining the safety of the premises, and defendant Bradford's statements regarding the reason for the bars to be a misrepresentation or a nondisclosure of their current purpose. Upon the plaintiff's inquiry, defendant Bradford was simply required to tell the truth. A more difficult case would arise had there been no evidence to indicate that the plaintiff had solicited information regarding the safety of the residence.

Further, both the plaintiff and defendant Bradford are single mothers with teenage daughters. This fact alone may be sufficient to make disclosure of the rape a material fact with regard to the sale of the property at Arcade Drive, or at least may be sufficient to demonstrate that defendant Bradford should have known that the plaintiff was "peculiarly disposed" to attach importance to the subject of female-targeted crimes. Thus, a potential misrepresentation in response to plaintiff's affirmative inquiry regarding a material fact placed a duty of honesty upon the seller, and plaintiff has shouldered her initial burden in coming forward.

Numerous questions of material fact remain regarding the conversation that took place between plaintiff and defendant Bradford, and these questions preclude a granting of summary judgment. Trial is necessary to at least determine (1) whether the plaintiff did in fact inquire regarding the safety of the premises; (2) whether defendant Bradford did in fact misrepresent or fail to disclose a material fact; (3) whether plaintiff relied upon defendant Bradford's representations regarding the safety of the residence when deciding to purchase the property at 6027 Arcade Drive; (4) whether plaintiff was put on notice that there was a potential problem regarding the safety of the residence; (5) whether plaintiff reasonably conducted her duty of inspection and further inquiry when examining the property for defects; and (6) the extent and nature of plaintiff's damages. Since reasonable minds could easily come to differing conclusions regarding the evidence, defendant Bradford's motion for summary judgment is hereby DENIED.

By contrast, however, the court finds as a matter of law that the inquiry of plaintiff was directed solely to the homeowner, defendant Bradford: she alone responded to plaintiff's question regarding the safety of the residence. The real estate defendants had no duty to affirmatively speak up and disclose their knowledge of the crimes simply because they were in the room at the time the inquiry was made. Had the real estate agents similarly misrepresented or failed to disclose a material fact upon an inquiry directed to them, summary judgment in their favor would not be warranted. Even construing the facts in the light most favorable to the plaintiff, however, the court must nevertheless find that this factually distinguishable situation simply did not transpire in this case. Thus, since reasonable minds could come to but one conclusion regarding the evidence, and that conclusion is adverse to the plaintiff, the summary judgment motions of defendants Realty World, Campbell, Patton, and defendants West Shell and Hoff are hereby GRANTED.

So ordered.

■ POINTS TO CONSIDER

1. **Duty to disclose.** Does the duty to disclose described in *Van Camp* follow the modern position? For example, what if plaintiff had not asked about the bars on the window? Would an "as is" clause in the contract have changed the result in this case?

2. **Post-closing discovery.** The reputational latent defect in *Van Camp* was discovered by the purchaser post-closing although the breach—the failure to disclose—occured prior to closing. These types of defects appear more often post-closing simply because the purchaser will more likely encounter a reputational defect as her familiarity with the property and the locale in which the property is located grows over time. This usually happens after the purchaser takes possession. In *Stambovsky*, the ghost case, the reputational defect appeared before closing. The court in that case granted a purchaser rescission of contract *before closing*. Do you think the timing of the discovery of the defect makes any difference?

3. **Should we require a *physical* defect?** Think about the fact pattern in *Van Camp*. Why did the court consider the defect latent? The court suggests that Van Camp could not reasonably have discovered the string of crimes in and around the house. Is this really true? Imagine that you are in Van Camp's position. Do you think that the rationale for disclosure of "reputational" defects is really equivalent to the rationale for disclosure of physical defects, such as a leaky basement? Other courts have rescinded contracts post-closing where the purchaser discovered that the property had been the scene of a multiple murder (Reed v. King, 193 Cal. Rptr. 130 (Cal. Ct. App. 1983)), and where the purchaser learned that the property may have been the location of a cemetery (Rhee v. Highland Dev. Corp., 958 A.2d 385 (Md. Ct. Spec. App. 2008)). *See also* Marc Ben-Ezra & Asher Perlin, *Stigma Busters: A Primer on Selling Haunted Houses and Other Stigmatized Property*, Prob. & Prop., May/June 2005, at 59.

   State statutes may affect the outcomes of these types of cases. *See, e.g.,* Milliken v. Jacono, 60 A. 3d 133 (Pa. Super. Ct. 2012) (seller not required to disclose that property was site of murder/suicide). In *Milliken*, the court construed Pennsylvania's disclosure statute. That statute requires seller to disclose all "material defects" to purchaser. 68 Pa.Cons.Stat. § 7102 defines a material defect as "a problem with a residential real property or any portion of it that would have a significant adverse impact on the value of the property or that involves an unreasonable risk to people on the property. The fact that a structural element, system or subsystem is near, at or beyond the end of the normal useful life of such a structural element, system or subsystem is not by itself a material defect." On its face, a murder/suicide might seem to fit within the definition of material defect: the tragic event might have a significant adverse impact on the value of the property. 68 Pa.Cons.Stat. § 7304 presents a sixteen item laundry list of "material defects," all of which are either physical in nature, or present legal impediments to use and enjoyment of the property. None of the sixteen listed defects is reputational.

The *Milliken* court held that a very serious reputational problem was *not* a material defect. The court reasoned that the Pennsylvania legislature would have included a reference to reputational or stigmatized property if that had been its intention. The court's reluctance to identify stigmatized property as defective is evident in the court's largely rhetorical questions. The court asked, for example, "how recent must the murder be that the seller must inform the buyer? What if the murder happened 100 years ago?" Do you think that the court's concern is well-placed?

In some cases, state legislatures have crafted provisions that address reputational defects. For example, *see* Cal. Civ. Code § 1710.2 (West 2010 & Supp. 2016) ("Subject to subdivision (d), an owner of real property or his or her agent, or any agent of a transferee of real property, is not required to disclose either of the following to the transferee, as these are not material facts that require disclosure: (A) The occurrence of an occupant's death upon the real property or the manner of death where the death has occurred more than three years prior to the date the transferee offers to purchase, lease, or rent the real property."). What does the California statute imply about the seller's duty to disclose deaths in the property *within* three years of sale?

4. **The narrative matters.** To some extent, whether you think a problem with real property is a defect that must be disclosed depends on which party you happen to represent. How would you frame your narrative explaining your client's position if you represented the purchaser in *Van Camp*? How would you frame your client's position if you represented the seller? On which facts did the court focus to find in the purchaser's favor?

5. **Must the defect exist in or on the property, or can it be "off-site"?** What if the crimes and assaults described in *Van Camp* had all occurred in the house next door to Bradford? Would and should the court find that Bradford was under the obligation to disclose this fact? In other words, would these crimes be deemed latent defects in the property?

6. **Should the brokers disclose?** Think back to the broker materials earlier in this chapter. Are you comfortable with the court's decision that the brokers were not liable to Van Camp? In what scenario would the brokers face a responsibility to disclose? *See generally,* Thomas J. Miceli, Katherine A. Pancak, and C. F. Sirmans, *Evolving Property Condition Disclosure Duties: Caveat Procurator?,* 39 Real Est. L. J. 464 (2011); Paula C. Murray, *Aids, Ghost, Murder: Must Real Estate Brokers and Sellers Disclose?,* 27 Wake Forest L. Rev. 689 (1992).

4. Getting the Loan

In Chapter 9, we will examine the loan transaction and mortgage law. In this section, we look only at provisions contained in the real estate contract that relate to the purchaser's ability to obtain a loan.

It is the rare real estate purchaser who has enough cash on hand to purchase real property without a loan. Even people who can afford to pay cash are loath to forgo the healthy tax deductions that a borrower may utilize when buying real property. In the loan transaction, the purchaser of property also becomes a borrower. The purchaser will want the contract to include a provision conditioning her obligation to buy the property on her ability to obtain a loan at terms she can afford.

a. The Loan—Some Basic Elements

A purchaser of real property will have a choice of lenders and loans, depending on her credit-worthiness. Financial institutions earn money on these deals because they charge fees for originating the loan, charge interest on repayment of the principal, and obtain additional fees if they "sell the loan" to another party.

On occasion, a purchaser will not procure a loan from a financial institution and will instead purchase the property from the seller on credit. This is known as *seller financing*. The purchaser will receive a deed from the seller, and contemporaneously give the seller a promissory note and mortgage just as she would give to a lending institution. A common form of seller financing is the *contract for deed* or *installment land contract* in which the seller does not convey title until the entire debt is paid.

In the residential sphere, many loans are for either 15-year or 30-year terms. For example, a purchaser with a good credit rating may discover that she is eligible for a 30-year "fixed" (meaning equal monthly installments) loan at a rate of 4 percent per year. If she has a poor credit rating, she may discover that her loan terms are considerably worse (perhaps 30 years fixed at 7 percent per year). The unfavorable loan terms will translate into a much higher monthly payment for the same total amount borrowed. Loans are amortized. This means that, although the monthly payment remains the same, the percentage of the payment allocated to principal is lower at the start of the loan term, but increases as the loan ages. Commercial loans tend to be shorter in length and carry higher interest rates.

Residential purchasers currently receive a federal income tax deduction for the interest payments on their loans. This means, to some extent, that the federal government subsidizes the purchase of homes by forgoing the collection of considerable tax revenues.

Today, there are many types of loan arrangements marketed to borrowers of residential property. One of the most common is the adjustable rate loan. Adjustable rate loans usually have the same overall loan term as fixed rate loans

PRE-CONTRACT

CONTRACT/EXECUTORY

CLOSING

POST-CLOSING

(e.g., 15 or 30 years). However, these loans provide the borrower a much lower "introductory rate" for an initial period (e.g., 5 or 7 years), which is "reset"—adjusted upward—at the end of the initial period. The new rate is usually based on a formula; the purchaser's interest rate will jump to a set number of percentage points above the prime lending rate. This is a useful mechanism for individuals who cannot afford a large initial loan payment and expect to have a greater financial ability in the future.

As we will see in Chapter 9, adjustable rate mortgages carry real risks for purchasers, particularly if the value of real estate falls and interest rates rise after the loan is made.

Purchasers (the borrowers in the real estate sale transaction) receive money from lenders in exchange for a promise to repay the principal amount with interest over time. Lenders are, or at least, should be careful in their loan decisions. They will lend money only if they know (1) the loan is backed by collateral, and (2) they can take the collateral from the purchaser quickly if the purchaser defaults.

The purchaser pays a fee and the lender promises, in a letter or agreement, to provide a loan at certain terms, secured by real property the borrower intends to purchase. The purchaser will sign an assortment of documents, but the primary documents are the promissory note and the mortgage. The *promissory note* is a creature of contract law and reduces the borrower's promise to repay into a written contract. The *mortgage* is a creature of property law and imposes a lien on real property. If the purchaser defaults on the promissory note, the mortgage allows the lender to "foreclose the lien"—that is, to sell the property at an auction in satisfaction of the outstanding balance of the note. In the parlance of real estate lawyers, "the note evidences the loan, and the mortgage secures it."

Of course, the loan transaction is more complicated than this brief description suggests. For example, the loan transaction for commercial property will usually include a document assigning rental money from tenants to the lender, in the event of a default. At this stage in our review of the real property transaction, however, it is enough to know that the lender wants documents that protect its interests.

b. The Loan Contingency Provision

The purchaser does not want to be in a position where she is obligated to buy property but does not have the money to do so. Therefore, unless the purchaser plans to pay in cash, the real property purchase and sale contract should contain an express contingency provision that makes the purchaser's obligation to close contingent on purchaser's ability to obtain a loan at an interest rate and in an amount that satisfies the purchaser's needs. The purchaser will not know exactly what loan she will obtain until she approaches the lending institution. The purchaser will typically do this once she and the seller sign the contract. The real estate contract will require the purchaser to seek to obtain the loan commitment within a fixed number of days following execution. The lender will also require an independent appraisal of the property's value to confirm the property's market value.

Here is the point of the loan contingency provision: if the purchaser cannot get a loan on terms she desires, the seller must return the purchaser's earnest money, and purchaser will "walk" away from the transaction without repercussion. For this reason, the purchaser desires a tightly defined set of favorable terms in the loan contingency provision, allowing the purchaser more freedom to walk away from the transaction. The seller has a diametrically opposed objective. The seller desires the terms to be stated in as generous a manner as possible—in other words, to cast a wide net. This will increase the likelihood that the purchaser will successfully obtain the loan. As is so often the case, there is room for misunderstanding, poor drafting, and litigation in connection with this provision.

■ PROBLEM: IS THE LOAN CONTINGENCY PROVISION NARROWLY OR BROADLY DRAFTED?

> ➤ On January 1, Daniel Bogart signs a contract to purchase Jerry Anderson's house in Des Moines, Iowa. Bogart pays Anderson earnest money in the amount of $5,000. The contract sets the closing date as February 1.
> ➤ The contract contains the following provision: "This agreement is contingent upon purchaser obtaining a loan in connection with the purchase of the subject property at 80 percent of the purchase price, said loan to be for a period of 30 years (in 360 consecutive fixed monthly payments), at a rate not to exceed 3.5 percent interest per annum."
> ➤ Daniel Bogart approaches every major lending institution and is turned down by all. As a result, Bogart writes a letter to Anderson stating: "I have been unable to obtain a loan on the terms listed in our contract, and pursuant to the loan contingency provision, I hereby inform you that the contract is now terminated and you must return my earnest money to me."
> ➤ Anderson responds with a letter to Bogart stating: "The contract is not terminated. I hereby agree to lend you 80 percent of the purchase price, for a fixed 30-year term, at 3.5 percent interest."

Must Bogart close and accept the loan from Anderson? Courts are not in agreement. *Compare* Gardner v. Padro, 517 N.E.2d 1131 (Ill. Ct. App. 1987) (purchaser is not obligated to accept seller financing) with Duncan v. Rossuck, 621 So. 2d 1313 (Ala. 1993) (purchaser required

Draft the Language

In the problem, Daniel Bogart may find that he is forced to accept his seller, Jerry Anderson, as his lender. You should know that having Anderson as a lender is no picnic! How would you draft the purchase contract to better protect Bogart?

PRE-CONTRACT

CONTRACT/EXECUTORY

CLOSING

POST-CLOSING

to accept seller financing). Why would Bogart object to having Anderson as a lender?

Recall from our earlier discussion of the Statute of Frauds that some courts have held that the failure to complete or fill in the necessary parameters of the loan contingency provision in a form real estate contract will render it unenforceable. Courts now view loan terms as critical to real property contracts—at least with respect to residential transactions.

5. Equitable Conversion

The executory period poses a set of very real risks for purchaser and seller. One perpetual worry of both purchaser and seller is that the property will suffer a "casualty" prior to closing. In this context, casualty means an event that causes significant destruction to the real property. In a residential transaction, purchaser and seller might worry that the house will burn down, or will be hit by a tornado, or perhaps will be severely vandalized. Whatever the event, the purchaser will ask her attorney this question: "Now that the property has been damaged, I no longer want to complete the purchase. Must I do so?" Under the well-established rule of *equitable conversion*, the answer for purchaser is unfortunately *yes*. In fact, under the common law rule, the purchaser must pay the entire price set out in the contract. This doctrine appears to be the majority rule.

The doctrine of equitable conversion creates a powerful and destructive disincentive: the seller continues to possess the property during the executory period, but knows that he can force the purchaser to buy the property at full price even if it suffers damage during the executory period. The seller now has no incentive, other than a moral obligation, to take care of the real property in his possession.

How is it that a purchaser can be saddled with property that has been destroyed? Under equitable conversion doctrine, the moment the purchaser signs the contract to buy the real property, she is deemed the "beneficial" or "equitable" owner. From and after the moment the seller signs the contract, the law treats the seller as "mere record owner." The word "mere" is a giveaway; it indicates that the seller's ties to the property are diminished. *See* Brush Grocery Kart, Inc. v. Sure Fine Market, Inc., 47 P.3d 680 (Colo. 2002) (purchaser forced to specifically perform contract after property damaged during severe hail storm; purchaser required to pay full purchase price without abatement).

The theory behind equitable conversion is straightforward, if misguided. Assume that seller and purchaser sign a contract for the sale of residential property and that the date for closing arrives. Assume also that the property is intact; it has not been destroyed. Instead, the purchaser chooses not to close solely because she has changed her mind. The seller may seek specific performance of the contract. Specific performance is an equity-based remedy, forcing the purchaser to pay the purchase price, accept the deed, and take the property. Courts reasoned that, because the seller would have the right to force a breaching purchaser to buy property, the purchaser became all but the owner at the time she signed the contract.

> ➤ The maxim "equity regards as done, that which ought to be done," captures the essence of equitable conversion.

The problem with this rationale is that it assumes that seller will in fact have a remedy of specific performance. But it is not clear that seller always has this right. Some courts are reluctant to grant specific performance to sellers, asserting that sellers only need money (i.e., damages) to make them whole. Finally, seller can obtain specific performance, which is an equitable remedy, only if the seller has "clean hands." It is possible that the seller misled the purchaser about many things, including the quality of the property. In any of these instances, seller would be denied specific performance. The doctrine of equitable conversion rests on a very insubstantial assumption. Indeed, it has been called "another emperor with no clothes, or at least the product of some fairly circular reasoning." *See* Tanya D. Marsh, *Sometimes Blackacre is a Widget: Rethinking Commercial Real Estate Contract Remedies*, 88 Neb. L. Rev. 635, 684 (2010).

Contrast the doctrine of equitable conversion with the risk-of-loss rule for other forms of tangible property. Equitable conversion—which applies only to real property—runs contrary to the ordinary contract rule. If Bogart agrees to sell his fabulous yacht to Anderson and one day before the day of closing, the yacht sinks, then Anderson does not have to show up and buy the ship, which now sits at the bottom of the ocean. The yacht—the subject matter of the transaction—was destroyed. The ordinary contract rule for personal property is that a purchaser is not required to close the transaction if the subject property is destroyed.

Draft the Language

Assume that you represent a prospective purchaser of real property in an equitable conversion jurisdiction. Your client explains that "the seller is 80 years old. He runs a dental lab in his basement, and continuously operates Bunsen burners. I'm worried that the old man is going to burn the place down before I close the purchase." Draft a provision to include in the contract that will protect your client.

Equitable conversion is the majority rule. However, a number of jurisdictions have adopted the Uniform Vendor and Purchaser Risk Act (1935). This model statute places the risk of loss on the party in *possession* (who is almost always the seller) until the conveyance of title. If purchaser accepts possession prior to closing, the risk of loss for damage to the real property transfers to purchaser. Other courts have adopted variations of these rules. Some provide that if the damage to the property is not "substantial," then purchaser or seller can specifically enforce the contract, so long as the purchaser receives abatement in the price—that is, a reduction in the price that equals the amount of the loss.

■ PROBLEM: MINNESOTA WINTER

> ➤ Bogart executes a contract to purchase a warehouse and parking lot from Anderson in Minneapolis, Minnesota, for a price of $4 million; closing is scheduled for January 15. The warehouse is presently vacant. Anderson does not maintain service contracts for clearing snow off the property (including both the building and parking lot).
> ➤ Bogart intends to convert the building to be used as a location for a "big box" retailer such as a Costco or Wal-Mart.
> ➤ Two weeks prior to closing, Bogart informs Anderson that some of the construction materials that Bogart ordered for renovation of the warehouse have arrived early. Bogart asks Anderson whether he may enter the property early to place the materials in a corner of the empty space. Anderson agrees and gives Bogart a key. With Anderson's permission, Bogart's contractor enters the space on two occasions and places two small loads of building supplies in a corner of the warehouse.
> ➤ One day before the date set for closing, a major winter storm pounds the Midwest, dumping more than three feet of snow on Minneapolis in a mere four hours. The roof of the warehouse buckles under the weight of the snow. Bogart asks his contractor for an estimate for repairing the damage and is told: "Well, to be honest, the roof makes that building. It is going to cost you $500,000 to repair it."

Bogart asks you for legal advice; he does not wish to purchase the building now that the roof has caved in. Must Bogart appear on January 15 and purchase the real property? If so, how much must he pay? Assume that Bogart does not carry insurance on the property, but Anderson does. Can you see the possibility of a double recovery for Anderson? We will look at this question below. As a general matter, though, courts do not like enabling parties like Anderson to profit twice.

■ PROBLEM: EQUITABLE CONVERSION AND THE LIFE ESTATE

In 2001, Ferne wrote a will granting her daughter Suzanne a life estate in her property, Blackacre. In 2014, Ferne's health deteriorated and her children agreed that she needed to move into a nursing home. To raise money, on January 1, 2014, her son, George, pursuant to a power of attorney, entered into a contract to sell Blackacre to Eliot, subject to the contingency that Eliot sell his own house to finance the transaction. On February 1, Eliot notified George that his house had sold, so they set a closing date for Blackacre of March 1. On February 15, Ferne deeded a life estate to Blackacre to Suzanne, who recorded it promptly. On March 1, George deeded Blackacre to Eliot. Suzanne claims that Eliot's ownership of Blackacre is subject to her life estate. Should she prevail? *See* Estate of Clark, 447

N.W.2d 549 (Iowa Ct. App. 1989). Would the case be different if the conveyance to Suzanne had occurred on January 15th instead?

Keep in mind that jurisdictional rules governing risk of loss are default rules. The parties are always free to negotiate a different rule in their contract. The parties should make clear exactly who bears the risk of loss, and when the risk may shift from one party to another. Furthermore, they should make clear who has a duty to insure and what happens to insurance proceeds paid on account of a loss. ⌨ Take a minute to review the Sample Purchase and Sale Agreement that is available on the Simulation. Can you find the language addressing risk of loss during the executory period? What exactly does the Agreement say and mean?

People do not always buy insurance, even when they should. A seller should maintain policies on property during the executory period. If the seller does maintain insurance, then courts will give the insurance proceeds to the purchaser, unless the seller has used the proceeds to actually repair the property. The court will use the equitable device of a "constructive trust." The court will treat the seller as if the seller is a trustee of the insurance money, and the purchaser as if she is the beneficiary. But what if the seller simply chooses to cut expenses and forgo insurance? The purchaser is deemed, as equitable owner, to have an insurable interest in the real property. If the jurisdiction follows the doctrine of equitable conversion and the contract does not require the seller to insure during the executory period, the purchaser should do so to protect against the possibility that seller has let seller's policy lapse.

■ PROBLEM: CAN A PURCHASER OF REAL PROPERTY COLLECT CASUALTY INSURANCE TWICE FOR THE SAME EVENT?

➤ Jerry Anderson agrees to purchase a house from Daniel Bogart. The real property is located in an equitable conversion jurisdiction.

➤ Bogart maintains an insurance policy on the property during the executory period. Anderson purchases an insurance policy on the property as well.

➤ The house burns down one day before closing.

➤ Anderson demands and receives payment of insurance proceeds from Anderson's insurer. Anderson then demands that the court create a constructive trust and deliver Bogart's insurance proceeds to Anderson.

Is Anderson entitled to double payment? Reach for the sensible answer, and you will be right. But there is always the chance a court will do something that seems devoid of sense. *See* Vogel v. N. Assurance Co., 219 F.2d 409 (3d Cir. 1955).

6. Remedies

There is something special about transactions involving real property that elicits intense litigation when a transaction fails. Real property defines individuals and is identified with businesses. We invest real property with passion and with hope, and we feel its loss sharply. Our time with the real estate contract would be incomplete without a discussion of what remedies a party might seek when alleging a breach by the other party to the agreement. In disputes involving real property, individuals want money or the property itself, and often both.

We discuss remedies for breach of the contract during the executory phase of the contract because in most cases the matter arises here. One party backs out of the transaction: the seller, by failing to convey title, or the buyer, by failing to tender payment. We could view this as a closing matter, because the parties are required to perform at closing. However, remedies for breach prior to closing are best discussed here, because, to be blunt, *the whole problem is that a closing does not take place.*

We will look at two types of remedy: contractual (damages) and equitable. Discussion of remedies is often separated in this way, but in a sense this is artificial. Equitable remedies such as specific performance exist because of the contract. We have already discussed specific performance, the primary equitable remedy, and will reduce the remedy to its elements later in this section.

> **Practice Tip**
>
> Attorneys often pursue more than one remedy. In some cases, remedies may be mutually exclusive; if so, lawyers will plead "in the alternative." This means that the attorney will demand one remedy, but at the same time ask the court to award a different remedy if the first is not granted.

a. Damages

Purchasers and sellers may ask for damages. Damages are based in contract and represent a cash payment intended to make the aggrieved party whole. Damage awards fall into several categories, including benefit of the bargain, liquidated damages, costs of resale, and costs of ownership. Benefit-of-the-bargain damages and liquidated damages are available to both the seller and purchaser, depending on the contract and the facts. Costs of resale and costs of ownership are available only to the seller.

Most law students and in fact most property owners think in terms of lost profits (more commonly known as the *benefit of the bargain*) when evaluating damages. As we will see, a purchaser or seller may breach the contract, but this does not automatically mean that the other party will be entitled to benefit-of-the-bargain damages. Generally speaking, parties breach real property contracts because they come to believe that they have made a poor bargain. The whole point of a contract, however, is that both parties take a risk: the purchaser takes the risk after signing the contract that the property will drop in value; the seller takes the risk that the property will appreciate in value. The value of benefit-of-the-bargain damages is that it places the breaching party in the position it would have been if the transaction had closed.

Liquidated damages are specific damage amounts that the parties agree to in advance and set out in the contract. The idea is that the parties know that, in the event of breach, damages may be difficult to prove and litigating over the issue is undesirable. So, instead, they reach an agreement in advance about the remedy for a breach. In other words, the parties "liquidate" the damages at the outset. Courts generally enforce such agreements in the real estate context, as long as (1) the damages to be expected were difficult to ascertain at the time the parties entered into the contract, and (2) the damages provided are reasonable. *See, e.g.,* HH East Parcel, LLC v. Handy and Harman, Inc., 947 A.2d 916, 927 (Conn. 2008) (liquidated damages must be "not greatly disproportionate to the amount of the damage which, as the parties looked forward, seemed to be the presumable loss which would be sustained . . . in the event of a breach. . . . "). Consider the application of that test in the following case.

ROSCOE-GILL v. NEWMAN

937 P.2d 673 (1997)
Arizona Court of Appeals

PELANDER, PRESIDING Judge.

The key issue in this case is whether a seller in a real estate sales transaction is bound by and limited to a liquidated damage provision in the parties' contract or instead may avoid the provision and recover from the buyer a greater amount of damages allegedly caused by the latter's breach. After granting summary judgment for the buyer on that issue, the trial court entered a stipulated judgment for the seller, plaintiff/appellant Carolyn Roscoe-Gill, in the amount of the liquidated damages specified in the contract. She appeals from that judgment. For the reasons stated below, we affirm.

We view the evidence and all reasonable inferences therefrom in the light most favorable to plaintiff. Angus Medical Co. v. Digital Equip. Corp., 173 Ariz. 159, 840 P.2d 1024 (App. 1992). Plaintiff owned a ranch in Greenlee County, Arizona. In September 1994, she entered into a written agreement to sell the ranch to defendants/appellees, Charles Newman (Newman) and his wife, Bonnie. The agreement, which was drafted by plaintiff's attorney, provided for a $380,000 purchase price, $5,000 of which was to be paid as earnest money when escrow opened. The agreement contained the following liquidated damage provision:

> *DEFAULT BY BUYER.* If Buyer defaults hereunder, actual damages to Seller will be difficult to calculate, but Buyer and Seller agree that the Earnest Money is a reasonable approximation thereof. Accordingly, if Buyer defaults, Seller may terminate this Agreement and Escrow Agent shall pay to Seller the Earnest Money.

On the initial closing date of November 2, 1994, Newman informed plaintiff and her attorney that he could not complete the purchase at that time because he had not received money expected from the sale of his farms in Mexico. Plaintiff and her attorney agreed to extend the closing date to December 7 and negotiated several conditions. The purchase price was increased to $404,000; Newman's corporation, defendant T-Link Ranches, was substituted as buyer; and Newman was to provide a caretaker and properly manage the ranch until the sale closed.

Defendants still were unable to close on December 7, and thereafter plaintiff agreed to extend the closing date two more times. Plaintiff and her attorney consented to and documented each extension in a written agreement. In none of the extensions did plaintiff obtain an agreement to increase the liquidated damages amount. After Newman failed to close on the final, extended date, January 30, 1995, plaintiff declared a breach and terminated the escrow in March 1995. Faced with a pending foreclosure and trustee's sale, plaintiff ultimately sold the ranch under financially pressured circumstances to a new purchaser for $260,000.

Plaintiff filed suit against defendants for breach of contract in April 1995, seeking damages exceeding $140,000.[10] The parties filed cross-motions for summary judgment on the issue of whether the liquidated damages clause limited plaintiff's damages to the $5,000 earnest money deposit. The trial court granted defendants' motion and denied plaintiff's, ruling that "[i]f the liquidated damages clause was to be set aside during the period of extensions, that should have been expressed between the parties." The parties then stipulated to judgment for plaintiff in the amount of $5,000, and this appeal followed.

When liquidated damages are specified in a contract, the terms of the contract generally control. Davis v. Tucson Arizona Boys Choir Soc., 137 Ariz. 228, 233, 669 P.2d 1005, 1010 (App. 1983); Roy H. Long Realty Co. v. Vanderkolk, 26 Ariz. App. 226, 228, 547 P.2d 497, 499 (1976). This court has previously noted that "[a] provision for the forfeiture of earnest money on breach of a contract to purchase real estate has been held a stipulation for liquidated damages." Lyons v. Philippart, 140 Ariz. 36, 38, 680 P.2d 172, 174 (App. 1983). A contractual clause that fixes an unreasonably large sum of liquidated damages, however, is unenforceable because it is deemed to be a penalty. Restatement (Second) of Contracts §356 (1981); Pima Sav. and Loan Ass'n v. Rampello, 168 Ariz. 297, 299, 812 P.2d 1115, 1117 (App. 1991). Plaintiff contends that the liquidated damage amount provided in the subject contract is an unenforceable penalty because it is too low. She relies in part on comment a to §356 of the Restatement, which provides that "[a] term that fixes an unreasonably small amount of damages may be unenforceable as unconscionable."

There are no Arizona cases directly on point. The Washington Supreme Court, however, has held that a seller in a real estate sales transaction cannot seek to avoid a contractual liquidated damages clause on grounds that it constitutes a

---

[10] Plaintiff claimed as damages the $120,000 difference between the original sale price of $380,000 and the actual sale price of $260,000, plus $20,000 in interest and lost discounts, $10,000 in additional legal fees, and payments for taking care of the ranch.

penalty because it is too low. *See* Mahoney v. Tingley, 85 Wash. 2d 95, 529 P.2d 1068 (1975). As that court stated:

> A penalty exists where there is an attempt to enforce an obligation to pay a sum fixed by agreement of the parties as a punishment for the failure to fulfill some primary contractual obligation. In this case, it is not the party in default who seeks relief from an excessively high liquidated damages provision. Rather, the provision operates to limit the recovery of the party who incurred a loss as a result of the other parties' breach. There being no element of punishment involved, it cannot be said that plaintiff is being penalized in any sense.

85 Wash. 2d at 98, 529 P.2d at 1070 (citations omitted). The court noted that, in making an earnest money agreement, the seller "can simply demand more protection—a larger deposit of earnest money—or even dispense with a liquidated damages provision altogether." *Id.* at 100, 529 P.2d at 1071. It then concluded that, in the absence of extraordinary circumstances such as fraud by the buyer, "a seller who chooses to utilize the device of liquidated damages in an earnest money agreement, with its attendant features of certainty and reliance upon the limitation, cannot avoid the effect of that agreement." . . .

We agree with the reasoning and conclusion in *Mahoney*. The principle under which unreasonably excessive liquidated damage clauses are deemed punitive and therefore unenforceable does not apply to liquidated damage provisions that are claimed to be insufficient. The primary purpose of contractual liquidated damage provisions is to avoid the parties having to litigate, and courts or juries having to decide, what would be a fair and reasonable damage award in the event of a breach. *Rampello*, 168 Ariz. at 299, 812 P.2d at 1117. Adopting plaintiff's position would undermine that purpose, unduly infringe on the parties' right to contract, and inject uncertainty into their contractual dealings. We hold that, in the absence of a clear showing by the seller of fraud, duress or unconscionability, liquidated damage provisions are not subject to challenge based on their being inadequate to compensate for damages actually incurred.

Plaintiff presented no evidence to support a claim of unconscionability or fraud on Newman's part, nor did she assert such claims in her complaint or summary judgment motion. Plaintiff emphasizes that Newman continually promised to complete the purchase, consistently expressed a desire to own the ranch, and represented that this was a "done deal" and that he could obtain financing elsewhere if his money from Mexico did not materialize. According to plaintiff, but for those assurances, she would not have extended the closing date.

Such facts do not support an actionable claim of fraud. *See* Staheli v. Kauffman, 122 Ariz. 380, 383, 595 P.2d 172, 175 (1979) (actual fraud cannot be predicated on unfulfilled future promises); McAlister v. Citibank (Arizona), 171 Ariz. 207, 215, 829 P.2d 1253, 1261 (App. 1992). Nor do those facts render the liquidated damage provision unconscionable. See H.S. Perlin Co., Inc. v. Morse Signal Devices, 209 Cal. App. 3d 1289, 258 Cal. Rptr. 1 (1989); *cf.*Maxwell v. Fidelity Fin. Serv., Inc., 184 Ariz. 82, 87-91, 907 P.2d 51, 56-60 (1995).

Finally, based on Newman's repeated assurances to close on the deal, plaintiff asserts defendants are equitably estopped from using the liquidated damages clause to limit her recovery of actual damages. "Equitable estoppel involves, generally speaking, an affirmative misrepresentation of a present fact or state of facts and detrimental reliance by another thereon." Tiffany Inc. v. W.M.K. Transit Mix, Inc., 16 Ariz. App. 415, 419, 493 P.2d 1220, 1224 (1972). As noted above, there is no evidence in the record that Newman made affirmative misrepresentations of present fact when he requested extensions of the closing date. Plaintiff could have conditioned the closing date extensions on larger earnest money deposits or the elimination of the liquidated damages provision. *See, e.g.,* Kendrick v. Alexander, 844 S.W.2d 187 (Tenn. App. 1992) (court upheld $50,000 increase in amount of liquidated damages added in consideration for seller's agreement to several extensions of closing date). We also note that plaintiff's counsel drafted the sale agreement and that, while plaintiff was represented by counsel throughout the parties' negotiations, Newman was not.[11]

In addressing the plaintiff/seller's equitable estoppel argument in *Mahoney*, the Washington court stated:

> [The buyers'] request merely tended to confirm their intention to complete the transaction, and plaintiff could rely on nothing more than the defendants' agreement to meet their obligations under the earnest money agreement. Upon defendants' breach of the agreement, the extent of defendants' liability was fixed by the liquidated damages clause. Therefore, the doctrine of equitable estoppel is not applicable in this case.

85 Wash. 2d at 101, 529 P.2d at 1072. Similarly, we reject plaintiff's equitable estoppel claim here. We affirm the trial court's judgment and, in our discretion, decline defendants' request for attorney's fees on appeal.

DRUKE, C.J., and LIVERMORE, J., concur.

■ POINTS TO CONSIDER

1. **Calculating benefit-of-the-bargain damages.** The seller in *Roscoe-Gill* wanted full benefit-of-the-bargain damages, and you can see why she would. The purchaser typically backs out of a deal because he comes to believe that he is buying property for more than what the property is worth. When seller sues purchaser for breach of a real property contract, the amount of benefit-of-the-bargain damages is equal to the price shown in the contract less the fair market value of the property on the date of breach. If the seller breaches the contract, the formula is inversed: the amount of benefit-of-the-bargain

---

[11] Plaintiff's counsel during the subject transaction was different than counsel who represents her in this case.

damages is equal to the fair market value of the property less the price shown in the contract. How did the seller in *Roscoe-Gill* arrive at the $140,000 damage amount?

Notice the use of the phrase *fair market value*. Determination of benefit-of-the-bargain damages depends

Date of Breach

When fixing benefit-of-the-bargain damages, courts look at the value of property on the date of breach. Usually, this means the closing date. Of course, parties sometimes breach contracts prior to closing.

on establishing the market value of the property as of a particular date. There is no Greek God of Valuations standing ready to tell parties and courts how much alternative purchasers would have been willing to spend on real property as of particular dates. As a result, we are often left with a battle of experts and appraisers. In negotiations and eventual litigation, purchasers and sellers hire experts to determine how much property was worth at the date of breach. This is not an easy process. *Appraisers* look at comparable properties (commonly called "comparables" in the trade). If the property that is subject to the breach is a two-story house of approximately 2,000 square feet of space built in 1980 in a particular subdivision, appraisers will try to find three or more similar properties that sold within a recent time period in that locale to establish the fair market value. Unfortunately, properties are not identical and rarely are perfectly interchangeable. This is particularly true for commercial properties. As a result, the purchaser's experts may generate a very different set of comparables from the seller's. Appraisers, attorneys, and courts will often look at property values along a trajectory. Were property values rising or falling at the time set for performance, and if so, how sharply?

2. **Liquidated damages.** Due to the liquidated damages provision, the purchaser in *Roscoe-Gill* only lost his $5,000 in earnest money, a small percentage of the contract price. When a court enforces a liquidated damages provision, it is delegating responsibility for determining the remedy to the parties. For this reason, courts look at the language and effect of these provisions very carefully. What is the rationale for allowing purchasers and sellers to limit damages to a liquidated amount? Liquidated damages are mutually exclusive from benefit-of-the-bargain damages. If one party agrees to accept liquidated damages, it hopes that it has not undervalued the actual amount of damages that could result from the other party's breach. By agreeing to liquidated damages, that party forgoes a claim for benefit-of-the-bargain damages. This is therefore one more example of parties taking a risk. There is absolutely no reason that this remedy must be mutual. If the seller has greater bargaining power, then the seller will not agree to be limited to liquidated damages if the purchaser defaults. However, the same seller may say to the purchaser: "I will agree to sell you my property only if you agree to be limited to liquidated damages if I breach."

3. **Tracking the language.** Courts usually state that they are unwilling to enforce a liquidated damages provision unless it provides for a reasonable amount given the nature of the transaction. In addition, courts provide that the damages expected from a breach must have been difficult to ascertain. *See, e.g.,* 5907 Blvd. LLC v. West N.Y. Suites, LLC, No. L-5870-09, 2013 WL 3762695 (N.J. Super. Ct. App. Div., July 19, 2013); HH East Parcel, LLC v. Handy and Harman, Inc., 947 A.2d 916 (Conn. 2008). In the give-and-take of real estate negotiations, it more likely that the party with the greater leverage fixes the liquidated damages amount and the other party compromises. A thoughtful lawyer drafting a liquidated damages provision will try to increase the likelihood that the provision will be enforced by tracking the language of the test announced by courts in that jurisdiction. *See generally,* Larry A. Dimatteo, *A Theory of Efficient Penalty: Eliminating the Law of Liquidated Damages,* 38 Am. Bus. L. J. 633, 673 (2001) ("The drafting attorney pays homage to the dictates of liquidated damages law in order to enhance the likelihood of enforceability."). Did the liquidated damages provision at issue in *Roscoe-Gill* expressly track the elements required in that jurisdiction? How would you draft the language of a liquidated damages provision in a jurisdiction and situation similar to that in *Roscoe-Gill,* having read the opinion?

4. **Liquidated damages or penalty?** When courts refuse to enforce these provisions, they usually do so by declaring the provisions to be "unenforceable penalties" rather than enforceable liquidated damages. There is a common dividing line between a penalty and damages: 10 percent of the purchase price. In other words, for reasons that few scholars or courts can really articulate, there is the assumption that a damage amount of less than 10 percent is reasonable and presumptively enforceable; an amount over 10 percent is often deemed void as a penalty. *See* Kraft v. Michael, 70 A.2d 424 (Pa. Super. Ct. 1950). Keep in mind that the liquidated damage amount is often the earnest money. For this reason, purchasers should strive to give the seller as little earnest money as is necessary. How does this comport with the purchaser's behavior in *Roscoe-Gill?* The purchaser may never see this money again. Of course, if the deal closes, the seller will apply the earnest money against the purchase price.

5. **Seller can claim other damages.** There are two additional forms of damages to which the seller may lay claim. First, if the purchaser breaches, the seller will ask for "costs of resale." For example, the purchaser may have hired a lawyer to prepare for closing. The seller knew he would face this cost once, but he did not expect to have to do so twice. The seller will eventually sell the property to a new purchaser, but will have to pay the lawyer again in connection with preparing for closing. The seller is entitled to receive these repeat costs. Second, the seller is often, but not always, entitled to costs of holding on to property after the breach of the failed transaction. These are often known as *carrying costs.* For example, the seller will be forced to continue insuring the property against fire damage and tort liability. If the sale had gone through as scheduled, these would have been purchaser's responsibilities. There is a

caveat to seller's ability to receive this form of damages: the seller can legitimately claim this amount only if the carrying costs exceed the seller's profit from having held on to the property. It is true that the seller wanted to unload the property and the purchaser negated the agreement. But assume that, serendipitously, the value of the property appreciates after purchaser breaches, and then the seller sells to a third party at double the original sale price. *The seller cannot retrieve damages associated with carrying costs if seller profited from carrying the property!* Look back at *Roscoe-Gill.* Did the seller demand these additional damages?

b. Equitable Remedies

English courts long ago recognized that contract remedies might be limiting. Although theoretically money damages make parties whole, the courts in equity believed that real property was intrinsically different. This made sense in a place such as common law England, in which wealth and status were tied to real property. As a result, the courts remedied breach of real property contracts in a fashion that was meant to do more than make a party whole monetarily, but instead was intended to do justice for the parties at a more profound level. As you go through this section, think about what fundamental property policies in modern society might be furthered by equitable remedies.

All equitable remedies share at least one characteristic: a party requesting that a court do equity must come to the court "with clean hands."

i. Specific Performance. We have already examined the remedy of *specific performance* in the context of both the Statute of Frauds (in our discussion of *Hickey v. Green*) and the doctrine of equitable conversion. Specific performance is the primary mechanism by which courts do justice in this manner. Keep in mind the basic requirements of, and the rationale for, a purchaser's action for specific performance.

■ PROBLEM: THE CONDO

- ➤ Betty signs a contract with Developer to purchase Unit 101 in Heavenly Estates Condominium Community. Heavenly Estates includes 500 units total.
- ➤ There are four model units in Heavenly Estates, and Unit 101 is a "Model A." Model A units consist of 1,500 square feet of space.
- ➤ Model A units differ only with respect to exterior trim details and type of flooring used in the kitchen and family room.
- ➤ Developer refuses to convey Unit 101 to Betty on the date of closing.
- ➤ As of the date of closing, 30 Model A units in Heavenly Estates are unsold and remain on the market.

Betty visits you to ask for your advice. What remedies are available to Betty? *See* Giannini v. First Nat. Bank of Des Plaines, 483 N.E.2d 924 (Ill. App. Ct.1985) (permitting purchaser to specifically enforce contract to buy condominium unit).

■ ■ ■

In order to obtain specific performance, the party requesting the remedy must be in a position to complete her side of the bargain: in the case of the purchaser, she must be in a position to tender the purchase price.

The seller is also entitled to specific performance if the purchaser breaches the contract and fails to show at closing. However, the seller faces more of an uphill battle. Older opinions granting the seller specific performance were based on a rationale of *mutuality*. Seller was entitled to specific performance simply because purchaser had this remedy if seller breached. This is not a principled basis for granting specific performance to seller. Today, courts and scholars focus on the fact that, when purchaser breaches, seller is forced to retain possession of real property, and with possession comes costs and risks. For example, the seller will have continued liability for torts arising from property ownership and will have to pay taxes and maintenance costs.

Benefit-of-the-bargain damages and specific performance are mutually exclusive remedies. If the purchaser is able to force the seller to specifically perform the contract (and exchange the deed for the sales price), then the purchaser has obtained the benefit of the bargain.

ii. Reformation and Rescission. Reformation or rescission of the contract are two additional equitable remedies.

A party will seek *reformation* of a contract if it contains a *mistake* made mutually by the parties to the contract or if one party is the subject of *fraud*. In negotiating a sophisticated commercial real estate sales contract, lawyers for purchaser and seller will exchange several iterations of the contract, as the parties inch toward an agreeable finished product. Purchaser and seller do not sign until they have agreed on final language. The problem is that there may have been several prior incarnations of the contract. What happens if, by mere error, the lawyers present the purchaser and seller with one of the intermediate drafts for signature? This contract will not really embody the agreement of the parties. Presumably, both parties understood and wished the final negotiated agreement to be the signed contract. This is an example of a *mutual mistake* of the parties. A court will reform the contract to reflect the final agreement.

This does not violate the parol evidence rule because, by definition, the contract is merely being reformed so that the proper information is shown within the four corners of the document.

> ➤ Keep in mind that reformation cannot be based solely on one party's error. The mistake must be on the part of both parties.

The older common law was quite stingy and rarely allowed the *rescission* of contracts. Today, a court may rescind the agreement—in other words, terminate the contract—on the grounds of fraud, mutual mistake, or impossibility of performance.

Rescission places purchaser and seller into their original pre-contract position. In essence, this means that the seller must return the purchaser's earnest money, and neither party may enforce the contract. A court may equitably rescind a real property contract if the purchaser can demonstrate that the seller committed a fraud or misrepresented the property. The court can also grant rescission if it turns out that the parties entered into the contract under a mutual misunderstanding as to a material fact about the property, or that performance will be impossible. Finally, courts will also rescind the contract if the seller cannot deliver marketable title.

You should distinguish the remedy of equitable rescission from express termination or rescission rights that parties place into the contract. The scope of an *express rescission right* is governed by the terms negotiated by the parties.

Even if the contract does not contain an express rescission provision, the parties can both "fall out of love" with the deal after signing the contract and mutually choose to terminate the transaction. Interestingly, although the Statute of Frauds requires the contract for real estate to be in writing, the usual rule is that a mutual agreement to rescind does not have to be in writing.

Although there is no ironclad rule, many courts would prefer to reform a contract where possible rather than rescind it.

■ PROBLEM: REMEDIES

> Bogart Real Estate Development owns a retail and office park. Anderson Fitness operates fitness clubs. Bogart Development negotiates to sell Anderson Fitness a portion of its retail park, to be used as a fitness center. There is a building on the property, with a ceiling height of ten feet.

> Anderson Fitness initially offers $1,800,000 for the property. Anderson Fitness also informs Bogart Development that the developer would have to raise the existing ceiling height of the property to 12 feet, so that the property would have the same basic dimensions and aesthetics as other Anderson Fitness studios. Bogart Development agrees to make this improvement, but demands an increase in the purchase price, to $2,000,000. Anderson Fitness agrees.

> Anderson Fitness then delivers $10,000 as earnest money and signs a "deposit agreement" that, by its terms, "is not the final purchase and sale agreement but rather is preparatory to the execution of a complete purchase and sale agreement." The deposit agreement sets the purchase price at $2,000,000.

PRE-CONTRACT

CONTRACT/EXECUTORY

CLOSING

POST-CLOSING

> Daniel Bogart, the chief executive officer of Bogart Development, informs Jerry Anderson, the CEO of Anderson Fitness, that both the increased purchase price and promise to raise the ceiling height will be reflected in the final contract. Bogart Real Estate Developers delivers a contract to Anderson Fitness, which Jerry Anderson signs. After execution, Anderson discovers that the contract included the purchase price of $2,000,000, but did not include a promise that Bogart Development would raise the ceiling height of the property prior to closing.

Assume you represent Anderson Fitness. Your client no longer trusts Bogart Development. Please advise your client on his rights under the circumstances. *See* Goodall v. Whispering Woods Ctr., L.L.C., 990 So. 2d 695 (Fla. Dist. Ct. App. 2008). Do you need to know more about your client's view of seller to answer the question?

D CLOSING

Law school textbooks are filled with case opinions. By definition, these describe transactions that failed. However, in the real world, most transactions successfully close, and only a minority result in litigation. Casebooks operate on law students' perceptions in much the same way that the local news operates on the perceptions of TV viewers. If you watch local news, you will see inordinate coverage of stories on violent crime, high-speed chases, and the like. Viewers can be forgiven for overestimating the rate of crime based on the emphasis on these stories in the daily newscasts. You can be similarly forgiven for thinking that a lawsuit sits at the end of every real estate negotiation. Most deals close, and usually without drama.

In this section, we will look at the closing phase of the transaction. A number of activities take place at closing, and these activities implicate important legal rules. Chief among these activities is the transfer of the deed to the purchaser. This is the moment at which seller conveys an interest in real property in exchange for money. The seller will sign and deliver the deed at closing, and the purchaser (or the lender, on purchaser's behalf) will tender the remaining consideration. You must understand at a minimum what constitutes a valid "delivery" of the deed. The deed must conform to the Statute of Frauds. With a bit of tweaking, everything you have learned about the Statute of Frauds in the section on the real estate contract applies to the deed.

Practice Tip

The lawyer and the lawyer's assistants will focus on careful preparation of documents in advance of closing. They will lay out documents on conference tables, with signature lines tabbed for easy access. Lawyers will pay special attention to formalities, such as notarial acknowledgments.

As we will see, closing also triggers the "merger doctrine." The seller is obligated to deliver marketable title at closing, unless the parties agreed otherwise in their contract. The promises that the seller made to the purchaser with respect to title prior to closing, either in writing or orally, are generally deemed to "merge" into the deed.

Real estate closings always include what we might call the "Law and Order" moment. If you have watched any TV at all, you have probably seen this criminal justice drama. The show is famous among other things for a distinctive sound. Whenever prosecutors or police reach a pivotal moment or grasp an important fact, the viewer hears a foreboding sound: a cross between a gavel striking and a deep drum beat. This is the sound that real property lawyers hear in their heads as the parties exchange money for a deed; the leverage and legal rights of the parties change at this moment *irrevocably*.

At closing, the title insurance company will "mark down" a title commitment in advance of issuing a title insurance policy. The commitment, sometimes called a "binder," is a document that commits the title insurance company to issue a title insurance policy, so long as certain conditions (such as the delivery of a survey) are met and so long as the purchaser pays the title insurance company a one-time premium. In most cases, the title insurance company will issue two policies—one to the purchaser and one to the lender. Together with deed warranties, title insurance protects the quality of the purchaser's title after closing. We look at title insurance and other forms of title assurance in the section discussing the post-closing phase of the transaction.

The various players in the transaction will be paid at closing. The lender who makes the purchase possible will fund the deal. Out of these funds, the purchaser will disburse proceeds and fees to the seller, the broker, the surveyor, and the attorneys. If there are any prior mortgages, those lenders will be paid directly in exchange for a release of their mortgages.

1. The Deed

When lawyers who do not practice real estate law encounter the topic of deeds, perhaps in a litigation matter, their eyes tend to glaze over. This should not be the case. Deeds are fundamental legal documents, used to convey real property interests.

Because deeds convey interests in real property, they are subject to the Statute of Frauds. Deeds must therefore identify the parties and the property in a transaction, and be signed by the party to be charged, the grantor. The grantee doesn't sign the deed because it is an instrument of conveyance.

Unlike real estate contracts, however, deeds are not required to show the actual price paid for property. In fact, a deed need not recite any *consideration* at all in order to be valid. However, typically the drafter will include some statement that consideration was paid, in order to have prima facie evidence that the grantee is a bona fide purchaser. Because the deed will be a public document (unlike most contracts), the parties usually prefer to avoid stating the exact consideration.

> ➤ A deed in a sale transaction often simply states the grantor is conveying "for ten dollars and other good and valuable consideration." If the grantor is making a gift of real property, the deed may recite that the conveyance is "for love and affection

We noted above that the property description in the contract for sale need not be a "legal" description, as long as the court can ascertain the property the parties intended to convey. By contrast, the description of real property attached or included in a deed should be the precise legal description, using one of the three methods we described earlier (metes and bounds, reference to a recorded plat, or reference to government survey).

Sample Texas Deed

🖥 The sample Texas deed is also available on the Simulation.

Deeds must include conveyancing language: these are the specific words that indicate that the grantor is transferring an interest in real property to the grantee. These words replace the ritual of livery of seisin. As an example, here is a sample deed form promulgated by the bar of the State of Texas. We have placed the granting language in bold.

General Warranty Deed

Notice of confidentiality rights: If you are a natural person, you may remove or strike any or all of the following information from any instrument that transfers an interest in real property before it is filed for record in the public records: your Social Security number or your driver's license number.

Date:

Grantor:

Grantor's Mailing Address:

Grantee:

Grantee's Mailing Address:

Consideration:

Property (including any improvements):

Reservations from Conveyance:

Exceptions to Conveyance and Warranty:

Grantor, for the Consideration and subject to the Reservations from Conveyance and the Exceptions to Conveyance and Warranty, grants, sells, and conveys to Grantee the Property, together with all and singular the rights and appurtenances thereto in any way belonging, to have and to hold it to Grantee and Grantee's heirs, successors, and assigns forever. Grantor binds Grantor and Grantor's heirs and successors to warrant and forever defend all and singular the Property to Grantee and Grantee's heirs, successors, and assigns against every person whomsoever lawfully claiming or to claim the same or any part thereof, except as to the Reservations from Conveyance and the Exceptions to Conveyance and Warranty.

When the context requires, singular nouns and pronouns include the plural.

_____
[Name of grantor]

_____
[Name of grantee]

▪ PROBLEM: DEEDS AND FUTURE TENSE

➤ Sam conveys real property to Paul by deed.

➤ Sam's deed recites that "Sam, Grantor, for ten dollars and other good and valuable consideration, will grant, sell, and convey to Paul, Grantee, the Property, and all appurtenances thereto, to have and to hold as Grantee's and Grantee's heirs, successors and assigns, forever.

Did Paul receive a valid and enforceable deed?

▪   ▪   ▪

Most lawyers avoid problems with deeds by using documents that are either statutorily approved, or customarily employed, in their jurisdictions. In some jurisdictions, statutes require that specific information must be used to identify grantors, including addresses and (if the grantor is an individual) whether the grantor is married. Why would it make sense to require a statement of the grantor's marital status?

An acknowledgment by a notary public is not required for a deed to validly transfer property, but it is typically required in order to record a deed. Recordation is crucially important for imparting constructive notice of the transaction. We will discuss acknowledgments and notaries in Chapter 8. Recordation, however, is not required for the deed to be valid.

A few states, including Florida, require two witnesses to the grantor's signature on a deed. Fla. Stat. Ann. §689.01 (2017). In other states, such as Texas,

PRE-CONTRACT

CONTRACT/EXECUTORY

CLOSING

POST-CLOSING

PRE-CONTRACT
CONTRACT/EXECUTORY
CLOSING
POST-CLOSING

witnesses may be used instead of a notarial acknowledgment in order to make the deed eligible for recording.

You should view the deed from two perspectives: the elements required for delivery of a deed, and the protections different types of deeds provide after closing if the purchaser discovers a defect in title to the property. The first issue—the delivery of the deed—is a closing issue, and is discussed in this section. The second issue—protections provided by deeds to purchasers after closing—is a post-closing issue. We will look at this aspect of deeds in the last section of this chapter.

Elements of a Deed

Valid deeds must contain the following elements:

- description of the property;
- identification of the grantor and grantee (or grantors and grantees);
- language demonstrating the grantor's intent to make a present transfer and conveyance; and
- signature of the grantor.

a. Delivery

A deed must be delivered to be effective. We already have seen that delivery of personal property (for purposes of a gift) must be made manually, if possible. In other words, the personal property must be physically handed over to the donee. Similarly, there must be a delivery of a deed for a conveyance (whether a gift or sale) to be valid; but what delivery of a deed means for real property is different than the meaning of that term in the context of personal property.

In feudal England, before the age of presumed literacy, "livery of seisin" was required in order to mark a conveyance of real property. The grantor would hand a twig and clod of dirt to the grantee to serve as evidence of the transfer of the property. Today, the law presumes that grantors and grantees can read and write, and instead permits the transfer of real property *only* if represented in a written product. The deed, just like the clod of dirt in livery of seisin, is usually handed over in order to complete the transfer.

Delivery of the deed is typically accomplished by manual delivery, accompanied by words indicating an intent to transfer the property immediately. Indeed, in most states the recordation of a deed raises a presumption of delivery. However, delivery may also be accomplished by an unambiguous statement or action by the grantor indicating his intention to presently relinquish his ownership and control of the property. *This may occur even though the deed has not been physically handed over or recorded.*

Real property owners may try to dispose of their real property as a matter of estate planning. This is thoughtful behavior, and if done correctly, can solve problems for surviving family members. There is nothing wrong with a person conveying property *prior to death* to friends and family, as the donor contemplates her own passing. That said, the Statute of Wills requires a will, subject to formal requirements such as witnesses, to effect a transfer *at the time of a person's death*. Sometimes it is hard to tell whether the grantor intended to convey prior to death or at the time of death. This creates the possibility of dispute among family members. Consider *Rosengrant v. Rosengrant*.

ROSENGRANT v. ROSENGRANT

629 P.2d 800 (1981)
Court of Appeals of Oklahoma

Boydston, Judge.

This is an appeal by J.W. (Jay) Rosengrant from the trial court's decision to cancel and set aside a warranty deed which attempted to vest title in him to certain property owned by his aunt and uncle, Mildred and Harold Rosengrant. The trial court held the deed was invalid for want of legal delivery. We affirm that decision.

Harold and Mildred were a retired couple living on a farm southeast of Tecumseh, Oklahoma. They had no children of their own but had six nieces and nephews through Harold's deceased brother. One of these nephews was Jay Rosengrant. He and his wife lived a short distance from Harold and Mildred and helped the elderly couple from time to time with their chores.

In 1971, it was discovered that Mildred had cancer. In July, 1972 Mildred and Harold went to Mexico to obtain laetrile treatments accompanied by Jay's wife. Jay remained behind to care for the farm.

Shortly before this trip, on June 23, 1972, Mildred had called Jay and asked him to meet her and Harold at Farmers and Merchants Bank in Tecumseh. Upon arriving at the bank, Harold introduced Jay to his banker J.E. Vanlandengham who presented Harold and Mildred with a deed to their farm which he had prepared according to their instructions. Both Harold and Mildred signed the deed and informed Jay that they were going to give him "the place," but that they wanted Jay to leave the deed at the bank with Mr. Vanlandengham and when "something happened" to them,[12] he was to take it to Shawnee and record it and "it" would be theirs. Harold personally handed the deed to Jay to "make this legal." Jay accepted the deed and then handed it back to the banker who told him he would put it in an envelope and keep it in the vault until he called for it.

In July, 1974, when Mildred's death was imminent, Jay and Harold conferred with an attorney concerning the legality of the transaction. The attorney advised them it should be sufficient but if Harold anticipated problems he should draw up a will.

---

[12] Common euphemism meaning their deaths.

In 1976, Harold discovered he had lung cancer. In August and December 1977, Harold put $10,000 into two certificates of deposit in joint tenancy with Jay.

Harold died January 28, 1978. On February 2, Jay and his wife went to the bank to inventory the contents of the safety deposit box. They also requested the envelope containing the deed which was retrieved from the collection file of the bank.

Jay went to Shawnee the next day and recorded the deed.

The petition to cancel and set aside the deed was filed February 22, 1978, alleging that the deed was void in that it was never legally delivered and alternatively that since it was to be operative only upon recordation after the death of the grantors it was a testamentary instrument and was void for failure to comply with the Statute of Wills.

The trial court found the deed was null and void for failure of legal delivery. The dispositive issue raised on appeal is whether the trial court erred in so ruling. We hold it did not and affirm the judgment.

The facts surrounding the transaction which took place at the bank were uncontroverted. It is the interpretation of the meaning and legal result of the transaction which is the issue to be determined by this court on appeal.

In cases involving attempted transfers such as this, it is the grantor's intent at the time the deed is delivered which is of primary and controlling importance. It is the function of this court to weigh the evidence presented at trial as to grantor's intent and unless the trial court's decision is clearly against the weight of the evidence, to uphold that finding.[13]

The grantor and banker were both dead at the time of trial. Consequently, the only testimony regarding the transaction was supplied by the grantee, Jay. The pertinent part of his testimony is as follows:

A: (A)nd was going to hand it back to Mr. Vanlandingham (sic), and he wouldn't take it.

Q: What did Mr. Vanlandingham (sic) say?

A: Well, he laughed then and said that "We got to make this legal," or something like that. And said, "You'll have to give it to Jay and let Jay give it back to me."

Q: And what did Harold do with the document?

A: He gave it to me.

Q: Did you hold it?

A: Yes.

Q: Then what did you do with it?

A: Mr. Vanlandingham (sic), I believe, told me I ought to look at it.

Q: And you looked at it?

A: Yes.

Q: And then what did you do with it?

A: I handed it to Mr. Vanlandingham (sic).

Q: And what did he do with the document?

A: He had it in his hand, I believe, when we left.

Q: Do you recall seeing the envelope at any time during this transaction?

---

[13] Blagg v. Rutledge, 207 Okl. 559, 251 P.2d 196 (1952).

A: I never saw the envelope. But Mr. Vanlandingham (sic) told me when I handed it to him, said, "Jay, I'll put this in an envelope and keep it in a vault for you until you call for it."

A: Well, Harold told me while Mildred was signing the deed that they were going to deed me the farm, but they wanted me to leave the deed at the bank with Van, and that when something happened to them that I would go to the bank and pick it up and take it to Shawnee to the court house and record it, and it would be mine. (emphasis added)

When the deed was retrieved, it was contained in an envelope on which was typed: "J.W. Rosengrant—or Harold H. Rosengrant."

The import of the writing on the envelope is clear. It creates an inescapable conclusion that the deed was, in fact, retrievable at any time by Harold before his death. The bank teller's testimony as to the custom and usage of the bank leaves no other conclusion but that at any time Harold was free to retrieve the deed. There was, if not an expressed, an implied agreement between the banker and Harold that the grant was not to take effect until two conditions occurred [—] the death of both grantors and the recordation of the deed.

In support of this conclusion conduct relative to the property is significant and was correctly considered by the court. Evidence was presented to show that after the deed was filed Harold continued to farm, use and control the property. Further, he continued to pay taxes on it until his death and claimed it as his homestead.

Grantee confuses the issues involved herein by relying upon grantors' goodwill toward him and his wife as if it were a controlling factor. From a fair review of the record it is apparent Jay and his wife were very attentive, kind and helpful to this elderly couple. The donative intent on the part of grantors is undeniable. We believe they fully intended to reward Jay and his wife for their kindness. Nevertheless, where a grantor delivers a deed under which he reserves a right of retrieval and attaches to that delivery the condition that the deed is to become operative only after the death of grantors and further continues to use the property as if no transfer had occurred grantor's actions are nothing more than an attempt to employ the deed as if it were a will. Under Oklahoma law this cannot be done. The ritualistic "delivery of the deed" to the grantee and his redelivery of it to the third party for safe keeping created under these circumstances only a symbolic delivery. It amounted to a pro forma attempt to comply with the legal aspects of delivery. Based on all the facts and circumstances the true intent of the parties is expressed by the notation on the envelope and by the later conduct of the parties in relation to the land. Legal delivery is not just a symbolic gesture. It necessarily carries all the force and consequence of absolute, outright ownership at the time of delivery or it is no delivery at all.[14]

---

[14] In Anderson v. Mauk, Okl., 67 P.2d 429 (1937), the court stated:

(I)t is the established law in this jurisdiction that when the owner of land executes a deed during his lifetime and delivers the same to a third party (who acts as a depository rather than an agent of the property owner) with instructions to deliver the deed to the grantee therein named upon his death, intending at the time of delivery to forever part with all lawful right and power to retake or repossess the deed, or to thereafter control the same, the delivery to the third party thus made is sufficient to operate as a valid conveyance of real estate.

PRE-CONTRACT

CONTRACT/EXECUTORY

CLOSING

POST-CLOSING

The trial court interpreted the envelope literally. The clear implication is that grantor intended to continue to exercise control and that the grant was not to take effect until such time as both he and his wife had died and the deed had been recorded. From a complete review of the record and weighing of the evidence we find the trial court's judgment is not clearly against the weight of the evidence. Costs of appeal are taxed to appellant.

BACON, P.J., concurs and BRIGHTMIRE, J., concurs specially.

BRIGHTMIRE, Judge, concurring specially.

In a dispute of this kind dealing with the issue of whether an unrecorded deed placed in the custody of a third party is a valid conveyance to the named grantee at that time or is deposited for some other reason, such as in trust or for a testamentary purpose, the fact finder often has a particularly tough job trying to determine what the true facts are.

The law, on the other hand, is relatively clear. A valid in praesenti conveyance requires two things: (1) actual or constructive delivery of the deed to the grantee or to a third party; and (2) an intention by the grantor to divest himself of the conveyed interest. Here the trial judge found there was no delivery despite the testimony of Jay Rosengrant to the contrary that one of the grantors handed the deed to him at the suggestion of banker J.E. Vanlandengham.

So the question is, was the trial court bound to find the fact to be as Rosengrant stated? In my opinion he was not for several reasons. Of the four persons present at the bank meeting in question only Rosengrant survives which, when coupled with the self-serving nature of the nephew's statements, served to cast a suspicious cloud over his testimony. And this, when considered along with other circumstances detailed in the majority opinion, would have justified the fact finder in disbelieving it. I personally have trouble with the delivery testimony in spite of the apparent "corroboration" of the lawyer, Jeff Diamond. The only reason I can see for Vanlandengham suggesting such a physical delivery would be to assure the accomplishment of a valid conveyance of the property at that time. But if the grantors intended that then why did they simply give it to the named grantee and tell him to record it? Why did they go through the delivery motion in the presence of Vanlandengham and then give the deed to the banker? Why did the banker write on the envelope containing the deed that it was to be given to either the grantee "or" a grantor? The fact that the grantors continued to occupy the land, paid taxes on it, offered to sell it once and otherwise treated it as their own justifies an inference that they did not make an actual delivery of the deed to the named grantee. Or, if they did, they directed that it be left in the custody of the banker with the intent of reserving a de facto life estate or of retaining a power of revocation by instructing the banker to return it to them if they requested it during their lifetimes or to give it to the named grantee upon their deaths. In either case, the deed failed as a valid conveyance.

I therefore join in affirming the trial court's judgment.

■ POINTS TO CONSIDER

1. **Delivery.** Did a valid delivery take place in *Rosengrant*? Look back at the definition of delivery at the start of this section. "[E]ffective legal delivery of a deed requires (1) intent by the grantor to make a present transfer and (2) a transfer of dominion and control." Blancett v. Blancett, 102 P.3d 640, 642 (N.M. 2004). *See also,* Hammack v. Coffelt Land Title, Inc., 348 S.W.3d 75 (Mo. Ct. App. 2011). What do you think Mr. Vanlandengham was doing and why?

2. **The deed as a testamentary device.** The Statute of Wills requires that parties who seek to pass property at death do so in a written instrument meeting certain formalities, such as the use of witnesses. This is done to ensure that property moves to the persons intended by the decedent and to prevent fraud on heirs. Was Harold attempting to pass property at the time of his death or before? At the time of the trial, both Mr. Vanlandengham and Harold were dead. Of the three parties present for Mr. Vanlandengham's deed ritual, only Jay remained alive. Does this matter? What could Jay have done if he had been truly mercenary and understood the mechanics of delivery?

3. **Compare to revocable deeds.** Harold would like to "settle" his farm on his nephew Jay, but would also like to retain a life estate, and the right to revoke the deed if he changes his mind. Harold would also like to be able to get a mortgage or sell off part of the land without getting Jay's consent. He could accomplish this in a will, of course, but he wants the deed to be effective immediately on his death and not wait for the probate process. Can you think of another approach that would meet Harold's goal? The obvious answer is to use a revocable trust. But many states also provide by statute or court decision for "enhanced life estate deeds," "revocable deeds," or "transfer on death (TOD)" deeds.[15] These deeds allow the grantor to transfer the property to a grantee, but also retain both a life interest and the right to revoke the deed. *See, e.g.,* Ariz. Rev. Stat. Ann. §33-405 (2014); Tennant v. John Tennant Mem'l Home, 140 P. 242 (Cal. 1914). Such a deed also allows the life tenant to sell or encumber the property without the consent of the remaindermen. Do you see any reason why such deeds should not be allowed?

4. **Intent required for delivery of a deed.** Delivery occurs only when the grantor exhibits an *intention* to relinquish control over the deed. It is not necessary for the grantor to intend to relinquish control over the deed at the time the deed is created; the grantor may decide to convey and relinquish control a day, a week, or a month after drafting the instrument. *See, e.g.* Montgomery v. Callison, 700 S.E.2d 507 (W. Va. 2010) (grantor's act of placing deed in a

---

[15] These revocable deeds are also known in some states as "Lady Bird" deeds. Apparently, the name originated because President Lyndon Johnson used such a deed to transfer property to his wife, Claudia "Lady Bird" Johnson.

safe deposit box and later giving key to grantee established grantor's intent to deliver deed). We can think of a number of scenarios that test the idea. Consider the following: Father announces loudly at a party for his son, who has just graduated from law school, that "I hereby grant my vacation home in Florida to you, dear Son. I have placed the deed to the house in the top locked drawer of my desk at work." Shortly thereafter, Son embarrasses himself at the party and Father changes his mind about the gift. Has Father delivered the deed? Would it make a difference if Father had given the deed to his lawyer to be recorded the next week?

5. **Escrows, delivery, and robots.** Commercial real estate transactions often use escrow agreements and escrow agents (and some residential transactions do as well). The parties deliver the important signed documents, and cash, into the hands of the escrow agent. The escrow agent is essentially a robot and must act in strict compliance with an escrow agreement. The agent will disburse funds to seller and other parties such as the broker, hand over the deed to the buyer, and deliver the note and mortgage to the lender, when and if the escrow agent receives all the promised documents and money by a specific date and time. The escrow agent has no choice in the matter. Does the seller's handing over of a signed deed to the escrow agent constitute delivery? *See* Reicherter v. McCauley, 283 P.3d 219 (Kan. Ct. App. 2012) (deed delivered when given to lawyer for recordation).

b. *Acceptance*

The grantee may not want the real property. This sometimes happens in the gift scenario. For example, a donor may wish to gift environmentally contaminated property to a nonprofit organization. The grantee of the deed may refuse to accept the deed. Acceptance is presumed because property is valuable. Recall, however, that acceptance is always a rebuttable presumption.

Video Problem: The Deal that "Craters" at Closing

Transactions should not fall apart at the closing, but occasionally they do. You might jump ahead a bit and read the material on deed warranties in the section on post-closing before viewing this video, which is available on the Simulation. In this scenario, the seller's lawyer takes advantage of an ambiguity in the contract and presents purchaser a warranty deed at closing to which the purchaser's lawyer objects. The result is *not* pretty.

2. The Merger Doctrine

The merger doctrine eviscerates seller's pre-closing promise to deliver marketable title. The purchaser is left with other mechanisms to protect his title after closing, which may or may not provide the purchaser relief.

When the purchaser accepts the deed to real property, courts say that "the contract merges into the deed." With few exceptions, any promises regarding title that seller made in the contract disappear. The purchaser is left only with any warranties contained in the conveyancing deed.

■ PROBLEM: THE SURPRISE EASEMENT

> ➤ Jerry Anderson agrees to sell his home to Daniel Bogart, and in the contract agrees that Bogart will receive marketable title at closing. The transaction closes and Bogart accepts the deed.
> ➤ After taking possession of the property, Bogart sees his next-door neighbor crossing the far end of Bogart's property to access a public road. Bogart intercepts the neighbor to tell him to leave the property. The neighbor responds: "I purchased an easement from Bill Smith, who owned your home long before Jerry Anderson, to cross this property to reach the road. Leave me be."
> ➤ Bogart hurries to the County Recorder's office and discovers that, in fact, Smith had conveyed an easement to the neighbor. The easement was negligently omitted from the title search that was performed on Bogart's behalf prior to closing.

Bogart asks you for your advice. What is his position vis-à-vis Anderson? Has Anderson breached his promise to deliver marketable title to Bogart? Would the result be different if Bogart had the conversation with the neighbor before closing? As we will see, Bogart's ability to sue Anderson may be limited, depending on whether Bogart received a general warranty deed or a limited warranty deed.

■   ■   ■

An older application of the merger doctrine permitted it to wipe out *all* promises, even promises about the quality of the property. In other words, the doctrine suggested that a deed really and fully replaced the contract. If the point of the deed is to memorialize title, then it seems odd that courts would interpret the merger doctrine in such a way as to wipe out promises about the quality of property.

This expansive view of the merger doctrine has been replaced in many jurisdictions by an approach that limits the doctrine to *title* promises. These courts typically state that promises that are only "collateral" to the conveyance (the transfer of title by deed) do not merge into the deed. Courts disagree about what the "collateral agreement" exception includes.

PRE-CONTRACT

CONTRACT/EXECUTORY

CLOSING

POST-CLOSING

■ PROBLEM: PROMISES COLLATERAL TO THE CONVEYANCE

> Samantha enters into a contract to sell her home to Paul. Samantha expressly warrants in the contract that the furnace and heating system in her house will be in operating condition at the time Paul takes possession.
> Closing takes place and Paul takes possession.
> Paul discovers after taking possession that the utility company had discontinued service to the home because the company determined the heating system was unsafe and posed a threat of carbon monoxide poisoning to anyone living there.

Paul visits you for advice. Can Paul pursue Samantha on the warranty she made in the contract? *See* Neppl v. Murphy, 736 N.E.2d 1174 (Ill. App. Ct. 2000).

■ ■ ■

Some courts continue to apply the doctrine of merger to promises regarding the quality of the premises. For example, in Arnold v. Wilkins, 876 N.Y.S.2d 780 (N.Y. App. Div. 2009), a purchaser of a residential home discovered after closing that the sewage system serving the home was defective and needed to be replaced. In the contract between the seller and purchaser, the seller promised that the sewage system was in good working order. The reader can appreciate the purchaser's distinct unhappiness at his discovery; but unhappiness, however legitimate, does not make for a successful legal action. The court held that the seller's promise that the sewage system was in good working order was merged into the deed at closing. In other words, the seller's promise to provide a working sewage system to the house simply vanished. *But see* Clackamas Cnty. Serv. Dist. No. 1v. Am. Guaranty Life Ins. Co., 711 P.2d 980 (Or. Ct. App. 1985) (sewage system warranties not merged into deed.).

The parties may agree in the contract, or after the contract is signed, that specific promises will "survive closing" and do not merge into the deed. Indeed, the court in *Arnold v. Wilkins* specifically noted that the purchaser could have inserted a provision in the sale contract stating that seller's promise to deliver a working sewage system would "survive closing" but failed to do so. Courts also refuse to apply the merger doctrine to promises that are fraudulent in nature or that result from a mutual mistake of the parties.

The best general discussion of the merger doctrine remains Lawrence Berger, *Merger by Deed—What Provisions of a Contract for the Sale of Land Survive the Closing?*, 21 Real Est. L.J. 22 (1992) (finding a host of legal precepts underlying merger doctrine cases, including

Exceptions to Merger Doctrine

Promises that do not merge include:

■ promises collateral to conveyance;
■ promises parties expressly denote as "surviving closing";
■ promises that are subject to mutual mistake of fact;
■ promises extracted by fraud.

the parol evidence rule, the doctrine of substituted performance, and accord and satisfaction). For a nice critique of the merger doctrine, you might read Michael Madison, *The Real Properties of Contract Law*, 82 B.U. L. Rev. 405 (2002). The doctrine has come under repeated fire. *See* Paul Teich, *A Second Call for Abolition of the Rule of Merger by Deed*, 71 U. Det. Mercy L. Rev. 543 (1994).

E   POST-CLOSING

After purchasing a house, the purchaser may discover significant issues affecting the real property. These problems may be classified typically as defects either in the quality of the property or in the title to property. Unfortunately for the purchaser, discovery of defects after closing may be too late.

1. Title Assurance

You can see why it is important to the purchaser to have a means to protect the state of title to real property post-closing: the merger doctrine undermines the promises that seller made to purchaser in the contract. The purchaser may take possession of property, only to discover that she has not purchased fee simple absolute. Keep in mind that the promises that the seller made to purchaser prior to closing are merged into the deed, unless one of the exceptions to merger applies. This means that the purchaser must look to deed warranties and other forms of title assurance for protection.

The purchaser should do a thorough title examination during the executory period to look for any defects. But some title defects may not have been revealed by the search. For example, it is possible that a grantor in the chain of title failed to obtain the necessary signature of a spouse, or that a long-lost relative of one of the grantors in the chain of title emerges to claim an interest by inheritance. Perhaps a neighbor asserts title to part of the property by adverse possession. The kinds of title issues that can arise are as limitless as the number of properties that are transferred each year. In each case, the purchaser (now owner) of the property hopes that one of several devices will protect her title. This is often referred to as "title assurance." We will look at several of these devices, but we will concentrate on deed warranties.

a. Deed Protections

We discussed deeds in the section on closing. We made the general point then: the seller must deliver to purchaser an enforceable deed to close the transaction. But it is after closing that the purchaser may look to the deed (and to the grantor) if title is defective. It is at this point that you really need to distinguish between types of deeds and the protections they afford.

You should think about two questions when evaluating deed protections and the protections they provide to purchasers. The first issue is substantive: what specific warranties are contained in deeds, and what do these warranties mean? The second issue is time-bound: is the grantor liable only for defects that arose *during* the term of his possession, or also for defects that arose *before* the grantor obtained possession?

i. Quitclaim Deeds. There are three types of deeds: quitclaim, general warranty, and limited (or special) warranty. Let's look at the quitclaim deed first. Quitclaim deeds are odd little beasts. They are by far the least attractive form of deed from the purchaser's perspective. A quitclaim deed contains no promises whatsoever regarding title. In a quitclaim deed, the grantor says this to the grantee: "I hereby convey to you the property described in the deed, to the extent that I own it. However, at least in the deed, I do not represent that I own the property at all or guarantee the state of my title." In every jurisdiction, quitclaim deeds are enforceable to convey title.

When Are Quitclaim Deeds Used?

This form of deed is especially useful in some common situations:

- **To "clear title."** When parties discover a flaw in title records and approach a third party who arguably owns an interest in the property, to request that the third party release the interest.
- **In divorce or other settlements.** For example, Wife and Husband may agree that Husband gets the house while Wife gets the yacht. Wife needs to quitclaim her interest in the house to Husband to complete the settlement.
- **To effectuate gifts.** If grantor does not receive consideration for the transfer, warranties of title are inappropriate.

The development of real property can be messy. Developers may assemble several tracts of land to create a single tract large enough for construction of a shopping mall. On occasion, a combination of title search and survey work will reveal that a boundary line is "fuzzy"—that there is more than one possible "correct location" for the boundary line. This will leave a sliver of land whose ownership is in doubt. As a result, the developer will need to locate any third person who might own the land—even if ownership is unlikely—and have that person release his or her interest. The developer will use a quitclaim deed, because that third person will not be willing to give any sort of warranty with respect to the conveyance. Of course, nothing comes for free. The developer will almost certainly have to pay the third person money to obtain the quitclaim deed.

■ PROBLEM: THE UNSCRUPULOUS SELLER

Assume that Andy Jones, a local handyman, is the lucky winner of a weekly state lottery. He does not win "mega millions" but he does receive $200,000. The city newspaper picks up the story and Andy's win becomes well known. Stephanie Smalls reads the local paper and sees an opportunity to make some money. She approaches Andy and explains: "I own a nice tract of land left to me by my parents. It would be a perfect place for you to build a home. I can part with it for $100,000." Andy visits the property and decides that the offer is a good one. He enters into a contract to purchase the property from Stephanie. In the contract, Stephanie warrants that Stephanie Smalls "has marketable title to the property and purchaser will receive marketable title at closing." The contract further provides that Stephanie Smalls will "convey title by quitclaim deed." One day after closing, Andy receives a letter from a different individual named Stephanie Smalls, who claims to own the property just purchased by Andy. Apparently, and improbably, there are two people named Stephanie Smalls, and the "Stephanie Smalls" who sold the property to Andy was not in fact the record owner. Did Stephanie's title promise merge into the deed? Does it matter that Andy agreed to take a quitclaim deed?

ii. General Warranty Deeds. Unlike quitclaim deeds, general warranty deeds contain specific protections for the grantee of the deed. General warranty deeds contain two sets of warranties: present warranties (promises that are breached, if at all, at the time of conveyance) and future warranties (promises that are breached, if at all, at some point following conveyance). ⌨ You can examine a Sample General Warranty Deed on the Simulation. This document is a copy of an actual deed, publicly recorded in Williamson County, Tennessee. The Sample General Warranty Deed includes a legal description of the real property and a statement of limitations, exceptions and encumbrances.

Here are the present and future warranties of title contained in a general warranty deed:

Present Warranties (Also Known as *Covenants* of Title)

1. **Seisin.** Grantor warrants that he has rightful freehold possession (i.e., that he is the owner of the property in fee simple absolute).
2. **Authority to convey.** Grantor warrants that he has the authority to convey the interest in property. For example, in a trust situation, the trustee may hold legal title, but not have the right to convey the property.
3. **No encumbrances.** Grantor warrants that there are no encumbrances at time of conveyance affecting title to the real property.

PRE-CONTRACT

CONTRACT/EXECUTORY

CLOSING

POST-CLOSING

Future Warranties

1. **Defense (also known as covenant of general warranty).** Grantor warrants that he will appear in court and defend grantee against a third person alleging a superior title.
2. **Quiet enjoyment.** Grantor asserts that grantee will not be disturbed in possession by someone with superior title.
3. **Further assurances.** Grantor promises to take action as necessary to correct a title problem that would otherwise be a violation of the present warranties.

Deed warranties are tied to the concept of marketable title, which we first encountered in the section on the executory phase of the purchase and sale transaction. The present warranties essentially state that grantor has marketable title at closing. Keep in mind, though, that the scope of these warranties may be varied by the deed itself. In other words, the grantor and grantee may agree that the warranty (or covenant) against encumbrances excludes specified easements or mortgages. These "permitted exceptions" will be attached as an exhibit to the deed.

A present warranty is breached, if at all, at the time the deed is delivered. Courts have traditionally held that because present covenants are breached at the moment the deed is delivered, the benefit of present covenants do not run to *remote grantees*. In other words, the only party who can sue on the breach is the immediate grantee under the deed.

Future warranties are triggered after delivery of the deed. This occurs when a third party actually asserts superior title. The future warranty of quiet enjoyment requires either a physical or constructive eviction to trigger protections for the deed grantee. A future warranty may be triggered many years after the delivery of the deed when a third party asserts superior title. Future warranties anticipate that the grantee under a warranty deed may have transferred title in the interim. These warranties therefore run with the land and benefit remote grantees.

The warranties in the deed are meant to provide the grantee of the deed with recourse (an ability to sue) if it later turns out that there is a defect in title. However, suing on the deed warranties has significant limitations. For example, if the defect occurs years later, it may be difficult to find the grantor and she may be judgment-proof. In addition, a grantee suing under one of the present warranties, or under the future warranty of quiet enjoyment, is limited to the price the grantor received for the property.

Remote Grantee

A remote grantee is a grantee who did not receive title directly from the grantor. Assume that Anderson conveys Blackacre to Bogart, who then conveys it to Carter. Carter is a remote grantee in respect to Anderson, because he did not receive the property directly from Anderson. You can also refer to Anderson as a *remote grantor* in respect to Carter.

PRE-CONTRACT

CONTRACT/EXECUTORY

CLOSING

POST-CLOSING

For example, assume that Anderson paid Bogart $100,000 for a deed to Blackacre in 2000. By 2020, the property has appreciated and is now worth $200,000. At that point, a third party, Carter, demonstrates that he has superior title to Anderson and wins Blackacre in a suit to quiet title. Assume further that the title problem—Carter's superior right—arose during or prior to Bogart's period of ownership. As a result, Anderson sues Bogart under the present warranties and the future warranty of quiet enjoyment. Anderson loses $200,000 worth of property, but he can only recover $100,000 from Bogart, because this is the consideration Bogart received for the warranty.

The modern trend is to find a breach of the title warranty only if the violation results in a loss of value to the purchaser. The grantee under a warranty deed will always say that there was a loss of value; the grantor will usually say that the problem, to the extent it exists, does not impact the value of the real property.

■ PROBLEM: AN EASEMENT IN THE WRONG LOCATION

> ➢ Smith purchases residential real property from Jones, knowing that the property is subject to an ingress/egress easement, which allows the neighbor to cross the property to reach a road.
> ➢ However, the deed, as executed and delivered to Smith, shows the easement in the wrong location.
> ➢ After closing, the neighbor begins to cross the property at a location different from the one shown in the deed.

Assume that Smith sues Jones on the deed warranties. What result do you anticipate? *See* McCormick v. Crane, 37 A.3d 295 (Me. 2012).

■ ■ ■

The *further assurances warranty* requires the grantor to take action after closing as necessary to protect grantee's title. Can you imagine how that situation might arise? Assume that, after closing, purchaser discovers a discrepancy in the chain of title—perhaps the seller was married and never obtained the signature of his spouse. The seller might need to either file an affidavit regarding the terms of his divorce, or obtain a release from his spouse, to clear up the defect.

■ PROBLEM: PRESENT AND FUTURE WARRANTIES

In 2010, Smith sells an 80-acre tract of land to Anderson. The land is valuable in part because of subsurface minerals. In the deed to Anderson, Smith reserves a two-thirds interest in the subsurface mineral rights, including coal. This deed was properly recorded. In 2020, Anderson sells the property to Bogart via a general warranty deed containing the present and future warranties listed above.

The deed does not contain any exceptions to the warranties. In 2030, Bogart contracts to sell his mineral rights to Big Coal Company, including the right to extract coal. Big Coal Company performs a title search during the executory period of the contract and discovers that Bogart owns only a one-third interest in the mineral rights, and that Smith owns the remaining two-thirds interest. The jurisdiction in which the land is located has a ten-year statute of limitations for actions on the deed warranties, which begins to run at the time the cause of action arose. Big Coal Company backs out of the transaction on the basis that Bogart does not own complete mineral rights. Assume that you represent Bogart in a suit against Anderson for breach of title warranties. Do you have good news or bad news to deliver to your client? *See* Brown v. Lober, 389 N.E.2d 1188 (Ill. 1979).

In recent years, some jurisdictions have approved warranty deeds with streamlined language. These convey all of the protections and obligations generally associated with warranty deeds.

iii. Limited (or Special) Warranty Deeds

> *General warranty deed.* Protects grantee against encumbrances and defects in title that arose at any time before the conveyance.
>
> *Limited warranty deed* (or *special warranty deed*). Protects grantee against encumbrances and defects in title made by, through, or under the immediate grantor only.

The *general warranty deed* is the most attractive form of deed to purchaser. The warranties will cover any title defects created during the grantor's period of ownership, *and also interests created by prior grantors in the chain of title*. For example, assume Mary bought Blackacre in 2010 and conveyed it by general warranty deed to Norbert in 2020. If Norbert discovers shortly thereafter that Olive, who owned the property just prior to Mary, granted an easement in 2008 to the next-door neighbor, Norbert can sue Mary for this encumbrance, even though she didn't create it and it arose before she even owned Blackacre. The *limited warranty deed* is the compromise deed. The actual warranties in the limited warranty deed are identical to those in the general warranty deed. *However, the time period of coverage is limited to defects created by the grantor of the deed, or during her ownership.* The grantor makes no promises about defects that arose prior to grantor's ownership.

Suing Down the Line

Remember that grantors of general warranty deeds are liable to remote grantees for the breach of future warranties of title. Similarly, grantors of limited warranty deeds are liable to remote grantees, if the defect is one that arose during their ownership.

If you are selling real property, you would want to incur as little risk as necessary when transferring title. In the residential sphere, general warranty deeds are often the norm. But in the commercial arena, a seller may insist on a limited warranty deed. One very sophisticated commercial real estate lawyer explained that "In the author's days as in-house counsel for major institutional real-estate owners and lenders (Prudential, Travelers, and Bank of America), there were strict instructions that, in connection with sales of company-owned property, the company was only to give a special or limited warranty deed (or a "deed with covenant against grantor's own acts") and never, EVER give the buyer a general warranty deed." John C. Murray, *Special and Limited Warranty Deeds (with Form)*, 20 Prac. Real Est. Law. 27 (2004). Whether the seller will be able to limit the purchaser to a limited warranty deed, rather than a general warranty deed, is dependent on the relative leverage of the parties. Mr. Murray represented the largest commercial entities, and he carried the weight of that bargaining power into his negotiations.

■ PROBLEM: LIABILITY AND THE TYPE OF DEED

- ➤ Able conveys BogartAcre by general warranty deed to Baker.
- ➤ Baker conveys by limited warranty deed to Charley.
- ➤ Charley conveys by general warranty deed to David.

1. During David's ownership of BogartAcre, Xena claims to have a mortgage created by Able. Assuming the court finds the mortgage to be a valid encumbrance on BogartAcre, which of the prior owners of BogartAcre will be liable to David under deeds in the chain of title?

2. Assume the same fact pattern, but Xena claims that Baker gave the mortgage to Xena.

3. Assume that Baker conveys BogartAcre by quitclaim deed to Charley and not by limited warranty deed. Xena claims a mortgage on the property that she alleges was made by Able. Which of the prior owners will be liable under the deeds in the chain of title? This change in facts highlights the issue of a "break in the chain of warranties." There are two possible answers and they depend on the effect of the quitclaim deed.

b. *Other Forms of Title Assurance*

Interests in Real Property

Deeds may contain fee ownership to real property. However, "interests in real property" is a broader category than just fee. Lenders receive a mortgage from the borrower entitling the lender to foreclose and take title if the borrower defaults. Lenders therefore have an interest in real property; lenders typically obtain title insurance to cover this interest.

The purchaser of property may discover the worst title problems—the kind that make him think that he may not really own the property at all—after giving the seller consideration and taking the deed. A good title search might turn up some of these unpleasant surprises, but life has a way of throwing purchasers of real property curveballs; title defects sometimes come to light after money and deed change hands. Because the deed warranties have significant limitations, purchasers also rely on other mechanisms to assure title.

In addition to deed warranties, there are four other types of title assurance that are important to the purchaser of interests in real property:

- title insurance;
- attorney title opinions;
- title abstractor liability;
- adverse possession.

i. Title Insurance. It is almost axiomatic that you can procure insurance for just about anything of value that you may own. You may insure your house against fire and your health against illness. Opera stars insure their voices and pianists insure their fingers. The most valuable part of the average person's portfolio of wealth is her real property. Yet, the real property is *her* property only to the extent it is grounded in good title. It should come as no surprise that the purchasers of interests in real property can *insure title* to those interests.

The primary reason a purchaser obtains title insurance is because she is not sure that a title search revealed existing title defects prior to closing. The purchaser tries to reduce the risk of a title defect by performing a title search (or having one performed). But in the end, the system of public records is not perfect, and a host of problems, including forgeries and fraud in the chain of title, may ultimately invalidate the purchaser's title. Title insurance covers these risks. *See* Marietta Morris Maxfield, *Why You Need Title Insurance*, Prob. & Prop., May/June 2001, at 8.

In contrast to a malpractice lawsuit against a lawyer for a faulty title opinion, a purchaser of title insurance does not need to show that the insurance company was negligent to be entitled to a payout. What matters is the insurance contract. If there is a defect in title not covered by exceptions in the insurance contract, then the title insurance company must pay the insured.

Title insurance is standardized. Insurers use a basic form that is promulgated by the American Land Title Association (ALTA). ALTA publishes a set of standard "endorsements" as well. An endorsement is a statement by the title insurance company that it will insure a specific type of title problem that would otherwise be excepted from coverage. Endorsements cost extra. There are some problems that are so unusual that there is no standard endorsement. However, title insurance companies are willing to insure just about any defect and issue an endorsement, if the price is right.

Title Insurance

⌨ Visit the Simulation to see the current American Land Title Association Insurance form policy.

The purchaser of the title insurance pays a single insurance premium based on the face value of the policy, usually stated at a rate of x dollars per thousand dollars of insurance. Think about this for a moment: life insurance and health insurance companies receive a constant stream of premium payments. What incentives are created when a title insurance company receives a single premium at the time of a transaction, but no money afterward?

The title insurance company will either hire an independent contractor to perform a title search and discover defects, or perform the title search itself. Some title insurance companies maintain proprietary "title plants." These are confidential data rooms in which the title insurance company keeps copies of recorded documents in each county. These are not "public records," although they may be more efficient and accurate records of the state of title in a county. This is also why title insurance companies are willing to issue policies; they have confidence in their own records.

As you can imagine, title insurance companies write a huge number of policies each year. They are therefore in the constant business of researching titles. What happens if they make a mistake? The insured party, either the property owner or the lender, will make a claim on the insurance contract. Assuming that the claim is valid and that there are no applicable exceptions or defenses, the title insurance company will pay out an amount equal to the damages resulting from the defect, but no more than the face amount of the policy. The problem is that property often appreciates over time. If the defect results in a total loss in value, then the insurance contract may only cover a portion of the loss.

Assume title to a shopping center was originally insured for $10 million, but that within five years of acquiring the property, the property has appreciated in value and is worth $20 million. The title insurer did a poor title search and negligently failed to discover a mortgage that was duly recorded and applied to the property. If this defect in title results in the purchaser losing the property altogether, then the title insurance policy will pay out only the face value of $10 million. Should the crestfallen title policy owner have any other recourse against the title insurance company? If there is no real remedy in contract law (the insured receives only $10 million), would it make sense to allow the purchaser to also sue the title insurance company in tort for the negligent search? *See* Bank of Cal. N.A. v. First Am. Title Ins. Co., 826 P.2d 1126 (Alaska 1992).

The title insurance policy will reflect the title search. If the title search reveals several recorded easements, the policy will specifically "except" (in other words, exclude) those easements from the coverage of the policy.

As explained in an earlier section of this chapter, the title insurance company initially provides a commitment to issue title insurance. The parties purchasing title insurance—the owner or lender, and usually both—each pay a single premium at closing. Assuming that the purchaser has provided information necessary to satisfy the title insurance company, the title insurance agent then "marks down" the commitment (sometimes called a binder) to delete exceptions to coverage.

For example, the title commitment will except from coverage any title defect that would have been revealed by an accurate survey. The purchaser can deliver an accurate survey to the title insurance agent before closing, and in time for

PRE-CONTRACT

CONTRACT/EXECUTORY

CLOSING

POST-CLOSING

PRE-CONTRACT

CONTRACT/EXECUTORY

CLOSING

POST-CLOSING

the agent to do a thorough review. If the survey does not disclose any additional title defects, the agent will literally "mark through" the exception listed on the title insurance commitment at closing. The final title insurance policy will not contain the exception. In the vast majority of cases, the insurer will remove the exceptions to coverage listed in the chart above (thus making the policy more robust from the purchaser's point of view), if the insurer is presented with information that satisfies its need to reduce risk.

Some Common Exceptions to Title Coverage in the Initial Title Insurance Commitment	What the Exceptions Really Mean
Rights or claims of parties in possession not shown by the public records	The title insurance company will not insure against the rights of adverse possessors.
Encroachments, overlaps, boundary line disputes, and any matters that would be disclosed by an accurate survey and inspection of the premises	The title insurance company is concerned that the description of the real property is inaccurate or that some defect would be noticeable by a visual inspection.
Easements, claims of easements, not shown by the public records	There might be implied easements not subject to the Statute of Frauds; seller will provide an affidavit stating no such easements exist, to the best of his knowledge.
Any lien, or right to a lien, for services, labor, or material heretofore furnished, imposed by law and not shown by public records	Contractors may have provided goods or services for the improvement of the property that under state law will not be recorded until after closing; these are "hidden liens."
Taxes or assessments that are not shown as existing liens by the public records	Fear of the ultimate hidden liens: federal, state or local tax liens

When an insured party discovers a title defect after closing, he will demand that the title insurance company pay up. If the defect is clear and unambiguous, the title insurance company will typically do so. However, if the defect is somehow unusual, the title insurance company will look to the insuring provisions to see if the defect is covered, and then to the exceptions on the policy to see whether the defect has been excepted. The title insurance company may argue that the defect is not covered.

For example, in Kayfirst Corp. v. Wash. Terminal Co., 813 F. Supp. 67 (D.D.C. 1993), large underground footings supporting an elevated train physically encroached into the property of an adjacent parcel of real property. The owner of the adjacent parcel wished to construct a building on the site. The owner of the adjacent parcel discovered the footings when doing excavation work in preparation for constructing its building; this discovery seriously limited plans to develop the site. The landowner made a claim pursuant to its title insurance policy. The title insurance company rejected the claim and refused to pay on the policy. The court determined that a physical encroachment is in fact a defect in title; it is akin to a trespass and therefore makes the property unmarketable. The title insurance policy excepted defects that would be revealed by an accurate survey. However, the court acknowledged that an encroachment of this kind—deep and underground—would never be revealed by a survey. As a result, the court held that the title insurance policy of the owner of the adjacent parcel covered the loss associated with this encroachment.

ii. Attorney Title Opinions. A purchaser of real property will often ask an attorney to write opinion letters stating that, in the attorney's opinion, the purchaser has acquired good title, subject to any identified encumbrances. Lenders also demand letters of this sort, especially in the world of commercial real estate where property values are high. This is true even though the purchaser and the lender also obtain title insurance. In most jurisdictions, title insurance has replaced the need for attorney title opinions in residential transactions.[16] *See* J. Carmichael Calder & S.H. Spencer Compton, *What You Need to Know About Title Insurance in International Real Estate Transactions*, Prac. Real Est. Law., Mar. 2005, at 5. In California and some other jurisdictions, lawyers are excluded from residential transactions altogether, as escrow and title companies close all residential real estate deals.

If the lawyer's title opinion letter later proves incorrect (if it turns out that there is an unsatisfied mortgage lien, for example), the purchaser may sue her lawyer for negligence. Keep in mind that the lawyer will be liable only if the lawyer violated his duty of care. The standard for lawyer negligence is often described as the care normally exercised by a hypothetical lawyer expert in the field. The opinion is written to the purchaser and/or lender and will specifically disclaim liability to any other persons who read and rely on the letter.

iii. Title Abstractor Liability. If the title fails, the purchaser might want to sue someone other than the attorney who issued the title opinion and the title insurance company. The attorney's liability must have been due to malpractice. The title insurance company's liability is likely limited to the face amount of the policy, and the defect may fall within one of the exceptions to coverage.

The opinion of the attorney or the title insurance company's policy might be based on an abstract of title, a document prepared by a title abstractor. The

---

[16] In Iowa, however, attorney title opinions are the primary form of title assurance, as title insurance is prohibited by statute.

PRE-CONTRACT

CONTRACT/EXECUTORY

CLOSING

POST-CLOSING

abstractor collects and summarizes all public records that might affect title to the real property. These include materials in the county recorder's office, but also tax lien notices and filings in bankruptcy court, divorce and family law court, and probate court, just to name a few. The abstractor does not have to render a legal opinion, but she must catch the "things that matter." This calls for real judgment and skill.

The abstractor will be subject to tort liability if that person negligently failed to note an issue with title. The abstractor's duty of care will be based on the expected results of a search conducted by a hypothetical competent abstractor under the same circumstances.

iv. Adverse Possession. Your initial introduction to adverse possession posited a trespasser knowingly taking over the property belonging to someone else. In other words, we tend to think of Mr. Lutz, from *Van Valkenburgh v. Lutz*, taking possession of a triangular tract of land to farm vegetables, and chasing children off the property with an iron bar. This is a colorful setting for the doctrine, but it does not really depict how the doctrine usually arises in practice.

All too often, especially in commercial real estate development, a title search reveals that the seller cannot establish clear title to some portion of property. Lawyers for the purchaser will explain the problem to their client, and the client will make an informed decision about whether to complete the closing.

If the portion of the property about which there is unclear title has been in the hands of the seller, or seller's predecessor, for the statutory period of time, and used in an uninterrupted fashion, there may be a plausible claim that the property has been adversely possessed. Of course, to provide this level of "comfort," attorneys advising the purchaser must be aware of the elements of the doctrine at play in that jurisdiction. However, even in the absence of all the elements necessary to prove adverse possession, purchasers will often take comfort in the simple fact that no party has challenged the seller's title to the disputed parcel over some significant period of time.

■ PROBLEM: THE UNOWNED SLIVER OF LAND

> Supermall Developer intends to buy three adjacent parcels of farm land from three different sellers in order to build a shopping center on the collected parcels. The present owners of the property are unrelated, and their individual properties do not have a common grantor.
> Supermall Developer enters into three contracts with the three sellers on the same day.

> ➤ Supermall Developer hires a title search company as well as a surveyor during the executory period. The search shows that there is a place at the center of the three tracts where all three parcels join up; this point of contact lies smack dab in the middle of the future shopping center. The survey and title search reveal a small triangular tract at that location—no more than five square feet in total land—that does not appear in the chain of title of *any* of the three sellers.
> ➤ The three sellers have owned their properties for more than 21 years, and at least one of the sellers has been farming the land continuously during that period.

Supermall asks for your advice about whether Supermall should proceed to purchase the three tracts of land. Is there any information that you would like to know to answer the question? What is the best course of action for Supermall Developer? Think about the other forms of title assurance as you formulate an answer.

2. Problems with Quality

The purchaser sometimes discovers problems with the quality of real property after closing. In fact, in the residential sphere, physical defects are far more likely to occur than title defects. If you or your family have purchased a house, you know that not everything may have been as it was promised to be: you may have discovered after taking possession that the water never gets warm quickly in the showers; the upstairs is as hot as Hades and is unbearable in the summer; and the basement collects rain water in even the lightest spring shower. As discussed earlier in this chapter, court decisions or statutes have eroded the doctrine of *caveat emptor* and place an obligation on sellers to disclose certain defects in quality. In this section, we discuss warranties of quality that may be express or implied in the contract.

At one time, courts might have employed the merger doctrine to terminate many of the promises the seller may have made about the quality of the property. As we have already seen, however, the more modern approach is to apply the merger doctrine only to promises related to the conveyance of title. A seller's promise that a basement never leaks during rainstorms connects to the quality of the property, not title, and therefore a court may find it is not merged away.

Let's be honest here: if a seller receives a call from the purchaser after closing, it can only be bad news. The purchaser will not call to tell the seller just how much she loves the house. The purchaser will call to complain about all the problems purchaser has found, and to demand cash to fix the defects. Therefore the seller wants protection. Depending on the facts, the seller will point to two common law lines of defense: (a) express warranties of quality must be clear and unambiguous, and (b) there are no implied warranties in contracts for the sale of real property.

a. Express Warranties

The common law of property was stingy to purchaser. If a purchaser wanted a warranty regarding the quality of the premises, then the warranty would have to be *expressly stated* in the contract and indicate that it *survives closing*. Any such promise must be an "affirmation of fact" and not just a statement of the seller's opinion. To put it another way, the purchaser must demonstrate that the seller made an unequivocal statement of fact intended to induce the purchaser to enter into the transaction. Courts will sometimes explain that the seller's statement must be peculiarly within the knowledge of the seller.

■ PROBLEM: THE MISSING SEPTIC SYSTEM

Jerry Anderson decides to move to a more rural area of Iowa to get away from the hectic city life. He sees an ad for real property owned by Daniel Bogart. Bogart, who is 70 years old, has lived in the house and on the property since he was a child, and inherited the property upon the death of his parents. Bogart listed the house with a broker. Anderson visits Bogart on a weekend; the agent is not at the property during the meeting. Bogart presents Anderson with the pre-printed contract created by the real estate agent. The form includes a category and a space entitled "sewerage." The agent typed above this space the word "septic." Bogart takes Anderson on a tour. The real property consists of 10 acres of land and a 100-year-old house. During the tour, Anderson asks Bogart about the location of the septic tank, and whether the septic tank had been "recently pumped." Bogart points at the northwest corner of the property and responds, "I haven't pumped the tank, but I do use a bunch of chemicals to keep it in working order." Anderson signs the contract and purchases the property. One year later, Anderson contacts a local septic service company and instructs the employee to pump the tank. The septic service digs up the northwest corner of the property looking for a septic tank, but to the surprise of all, none can be located. Instead, the septic service locates several pipes running from the home to a far corner of the property, at the end of which is an area filled with debris and outflow. Anderson instructs the septic service to install a septic system, and then sends a bill for the costs to Bogart. What results do you expect? *See* Garriffa v. Taylor, 675 P.2d 1284 (Wyo. 1984).

b. Implied Warranties

Common law courts did not imply any warranties into purchase and sale transactions. This remains largely the rule today, with one exception: the *implied warranty of quality* for new construction. You may see similarities to the implied warranty of habitability we discussed in the landlord-tenant context.

In many transactions, the seller is also the builder. Property sold by a builder/seller must meet minimal standards of workman-like quality. Imagine buying a house, only to discover that it is not level. You place your child in a high chair that sits on casters, and it rolls unexpectedly from one side of a room to the other. The baby might be thrilled, but you will not be so happy. Courts are not in agreement as to whether this implied warranty of quality may be waived, but many do allow waiver if it is clear and knowingly given. *See* Bankston v. McKenzie, 698 S.W.2d 799 (Ark. 1985); Tibbitts v. Openshaw, 425 P.2d 160 (Utah 1967). The implied warranty is a creature of both tort and contract law. The purchaser can sue for damages, including punitive damages.

In most jurisdictions, the defect must be latent—that is, it must be a defect that could not have been discovered upon reasonable inspection. The defect must also be significant (minor defects don't qualify). Why do you think that courts have created the implied warranty of quality for new homes, but do not imply a similar warranty for sales of existing homes?

One difficult issue commonly arises with respect to this warranty: assume that ACME Builder constructs a home and sells it to Jerry Anderson. Shortly thereafter, Anderson sells the home to you. The defect appears only after you buy the house, not before. Can you sue the builder? *See* Nichols v. R.R. Beaufort & Assocs., Inc., 727 A.2d 174 (R.I. 1999).

SUMMARY

■ The purchase and sale transaction can be reduced to four phases: pre-contract, executory period, closing, and post-closing.

Pre-Contract Period

■ Seller typically employs a broker pre-contract to locate a willing buyer at the seller's terms or terms the seller will accept. The broker and seller execute a *listing agreement*, setting commission rate and listing price. There are three types of listing agreements (exclusive, exclusive agency, and open).
■ Brokers owe the seller *fiduciary duties* of care, loyalty, and disclosure of bids. Brokers have limited duties to the purchaser.
■ The broker earns a *commission* upon finding a *ready, willing, and able* purchaser. Under a modern rule, the broker earns a commission only if the transaction closes.

Contract/Executory Period

■ The *executory period* begins at the moment the parties sign the contract and ends at closing. During the executory period, the purchaser will investigate the state of title and the quality of the property, and line up financing.

■ The executory period arises only if there is a binding contract that satisfies the Statute of Frauds. The *Statute of Frauds* requires all contracts (or a memorandum thereof) for the conveyance of real property to be in writing and signed by the party to be charged. At a minimum, the writing must identify *price, parties, and property*.

■ The Statute of Frauds is subject to *defenses* of part performance, estoppel, and fraud.

■ Contracts for the sale of real property are subject to the *parol evidence* rule. Oral promises made to the purchaser that are not placed in the contract are deemed beyond enforcement as an evidentiary matter.

■ The seller must deliver *marketable title* at closing; therefore the purchaser will investigate seller's title prior to closing to ascertain whether it meets the standard.

■ *Marketable title* requires that seller deliver fee simple absolute and insure that the purchaser will not be subject to a non-frivolous possibility of a lawsuit regarding title.

■ The parties may agree in the contract to modify the standard of title that will be delivered to purchaser, to include a set of permitted exceptions. One such standard is *insurable title*—title that could be insured by a title insurance company.

■ A purchaser is subject to the doctrine of *caveat emptor*—"buyer beware."

■ The purchaser's *physical inspection* of property must usually be completed within a limited period of time following execution of the contract.

■ The seller is subject to an *implied duty to disclose* defects that would not be discoverable upon a reasonable inspection.

■ The purchaser will seek financing during the executory period and will make purchaser's performance under the purchase contract contingent upon successfully securing the loan commitment. The purchaser will try to tightly confine the terms of the *loan contingency provision*.

■ The real property may be damaged or destroyed by fire or tornado or by myriad other events. The common law rule of *equitable conversion* placed the risk of loss on the purchaser. The purchaser would be required to pay the full price and accept the deed. The more modern rule places risk of loss on the seller until closing or until the purchaser takes possession prior to closing.

■ Courts in equitable conversion jurisdictions move *insurance proceeds* to the purchaser under the constructive trust doctrine.

■ A purchaser or seller who breaches the contract may be subject to the equitable remedy of *specific performance* or the contract remedy of *damages*.

■ The parties may choose in advance, in the contract, to *liquidate damages*, so long as the amount chosen is not an invalid penalty.

■ Depending on the valuation of the property at the time of breach, purchaser or seller may be entitled to *benefit-of-the-bargain damages*.

Closing

- Closing occurs when the parties *complete performance* by exchanging the deed for consideration.
- The deed is the instrument of conveyance. The *deed* must describe the property, identify the grantor and grantee, and be signed by the grantor.
- *Delivery* requires an act that evinces the grantor's intent to sever his interest in the property; acceptance is presumed (although the presumption is rebuttable).
- *Merger doctrine* suggests that title promises made by seller prior to closing "merge into the deed." A seller's promises about the quality of property are typically deemed "collateral" to the conveyance and not merged into the deed. However, some courts continue to apply the doctrine to promises concerning quality of property.
- The purchaser may assert that certain promises *survive closing* if that is stated in the contract, or if the nature of the promises requires that they survive. In addition, promises induced by fraud are not merged.

Post-Closing

- After closing, the purchaser will take possession and may discover a legion of problems affecting either *quality* or *title* to the property.
- The purchaser will want various forms of *title assurance*, including warranties in the deed, title insurance, attorney title opinions, and title abstractor liability.
- There are *three forms of deeds*: general warranty deeds, limited warranty deeds, and quitclaim deeds.
- *Quitclaim deeds* make no promises whatsoever to the grantee about the state of title.
- *Warranty deeds* contain two sets of promises: present covenants that are breached at the time the deed is granted, if at all; and future covenants that are breached at the time superior title is asserted.
- The grantor *warrants* that he has marketable title and authority to convey, promises to defend the grantee if a party asserting a superior right later makes a claim on the property, and promises to take action to protect grantee's title.
- *Limited warranty deeds* protect the grantee against defects in title arising during the term of the grantor's ownership. *General warranty deeds* protect the grantee against defects in title arising prior to the conveyance, whether arising during grantor's ownership or before.
- *Damages* under the marketable title promises of a warranty deed are limited to the consideration received by the grantor.
- *Title insurance* is a contract between a title insurance company and the insured, which may be the purchaser or the lender. The title insurance company will pay up to the face amount of the policy for defects covered by

the policy and not subject to one of the listed exceptions. The title insurance policy will cover defects such as forgeries in the chain of title.

- Attorneys will often write *title opinions* for the benefit of purchasers and lenders describing the state of title. Lawyers may miss a title defect and therefore be subject to suits for malpractice. Attorneys will be held to the duty of care of a lawyer specializing in real estate practice.

- *Title abstractors* may similarly be sued for failing to discover a defect in title during a title search. Abstractors will be subject to a duty of care of an abstractor specializing in the business of title search.

- The usual rule is that title insurance companies will not be subject to suit for negligence in performance of a *title examination*, and instead, the insured will have resort only to the face value of the policy.

- Purchasers may also rely on the doctrine of adverse possession as a means of title assurance.

- Absent seller fraud, misrepresentation, or failure to disclose a defect, caveat emptor applies post-closing to eliminate the purchaser's objection to a defect in the quality of property.

- A purchaser may rely on express, written warranties about the quality of property. A warranty must be "an affirmation of fact" and not merely the seller's opinion.

- The common law denied purchasers of real property any implied warranties. However, under a more modern approach, and particularly in residential transactions, some courts imply a warranty of quality into sales involving *new construction*.

Recording

> WHEREAS divers persons as dayly experience informeth doe closely and privately convey over their estates by way of mortgage not delivering possession whereby the creditors are defrauded and defeated of their just debts not having knowledge of the same, *Be it therefore enacted and confirmed,* for redresse of the like inconveniencies hereafter that what person or persons soever . . . hereafter shall make or pass over any conveyance as aforesaid of any part or parcell of his estate in any other way or manner then what shall be done and acknowledged at a quarter court or monethly court and there registred such conveyance shall be adjudged fraudulent and to all intents and purposes void and of none effect.
>
> —*Act XII, 1 Laws of Va. 248, 248-49 (Hening 1642)*

A INTRODUCTION

In this chapter, we look at the systems used by purchasers, lenders, and others to examine the state of title to property. We have already touched upon the importance and place of title examination in Chapter 7, which was devoted to real estate transactions. However, we reserved the discussion of the actual mechanics of the search and the law underlying priority of instruments; we will address those issues here.

Title is of paramount importance to any party buying or receiving an interest in real property. Consider purchase and loan transactions. In the purchase transaction, the purchaser pays seller the sale price. In the loan transaction, the lender gives the borrower loan proceeds. *In both instances, these parties act in anticipation of receiving something valuable in return.* The seller conveys purchaser the property by deed. The borrower conveys to the lender a lien in the form of a mortgage, deed of trust, or other instrument that enables the lender to foreclose title to the borrower's property. As you know, the seller must be in a position to deliver marketable title to property at closing, unless the contract provides otherwise. The lender anticipates that the mortgage will encumber property that the borrower really does own. These expectations lead purchaser and lender to examine title carefully. In other words, purchaser and lender will want to know if the "state of title" to property that seller transfers matches the purchaser's or lender's expectations.

It is a truism in the law that the seller can convey only what the seller owns. This truism raises the question, *what does the seller own?* The purchaser, for instance, will want to know whether the seller can demonstrate that there is an unbroken chain of ownership of the property that extends from the seller to predecessor owners back in time, and that the seller's property interest is not subject to unanticipated and pre-existing rights, such as easements and mortgages. Similarly, a lender may choose not to lend to a borrower if borrower's title is somehow in doubt or subject to an unanticipated interest, such as a prior mortgage.

Future Interests

There are other limitations on title. You know from the discussion of future interests that a seller may own something less than fee simple absolute, such as a fee simple subject to an executory interest.

The purchaser of real property, or a lender making a loan secured by real property, may allay these concerns via an examination of public records that affect title. The most important recorded documents are instruments conveying interests in real property such as deeds, recorded in the county recorder's office. Sometimes a search will disclose competing interests in real property. A court will determine the relative rights of parties by application of jurisdictional rules, known as *recording statutes.* In this chapter, we will examine both the system of recordation and the application of recording statutes. The searching of public records and determination of title is a complicated and, to a real extent, inefficient process. We will conclude this chapter by briefly examining two legislative approaches intended to reform title searching—Torrens registration and marketable title acts.

B RECORDATION

In the mid-1980s, Arthur Leff, a professor at Yale University Law School, began writing his own legal dictionary. He intended to create a comprehensive and erudite dictionary that would bring clarity to the law. Professor Leff died before he could complete the task. However, he did manage to make his way through the "Cs" before his passing. The Yale Law Journal published his unfinished work in *The Leff Dictionary of Law: A Fragment*, 94 Yale L.J. 1855 (1985). Professor Leff's passing, and his ambitious dictionary project, were the subject of thoughtful essays written by his colleagues. *See* Robert M. Cover, Comment, *Arthur's Words*, 94 Yale L.J. 1848 (1985) and Joseph W. Bishop, Comment, *Arthur Leff as a Lexicographer*, 94 Yale L.J. 1843 (1985). Here is part of Professor Leff's definition for the letter "B":

> b. Second letter of the English alphabet but, unlike a, blessedly not a preposition in any known Western language. . . . Also, another frequent participant in **legal hypotheticals**, with a tendency toward victimization, as in "A hits B."

Arthur Alan Leff, *The Leff Dictionary of Law: A Fragment*, 94 Yale L.J. 1855, 2113 (1985) (emphasis in the original). Professor Leff was nowhere more accurate in his description of B than in the area of recording of property interests. Consider the following hypothetical:

> ➤ O, the owner of Blackacre, conveys Blackacre by deed to A as grantee. A gives O $100,000 as consideration for the deed.
> ➤ One month later, O creates a second deed to Blackacre, this time naming B as grantee. B gives O $100,000 consideration for the deed.
> ➤ O disappears with the money, and A and B each claim ownership of Blackacre.

In property law parlance, we would present the hypothetical in simpler terms:

> ➤ O to A;
> ➤ Then O to B.

As between A and B, the English common law held that A owned Blackacre. The basic property law rule of *first-in-time* determines A to be the winner. O conveyed the interest in Blackacre first to A and therefore had nothing left to convey to B. B owns nothing but a lawsuit in fraud against O for selling something he no longer owned.

Now let's add to the hypothetical:

> ➤ After taking the deed to Blackacre, A places the deed in a desk drawer. Blackacre is raw land (that is, undeveloped real property with no structures or tenants on it). B does not know A personally and O does not inform B that O previously conveyed Blackacre. In the normal course of events, there is no way that B can learn of the prior transfer to A. B is "innocent," but according to the rule of first-in-time, B loses. This is true even though a deed in A's desk drawer is beyond B's discovery.

As Professor Leff might have said, B seems destined to play the victim.

In England, there were no public records that B could search, prior to giving O money, to determine if O still owned the land. Surprisingly, such recording systems were implemented in England only in the last century. By contrast, in every American jurisdiction, instruments affecting title are recorded in county recorder offices. Counties are required by state statute to maintain such records.[1] If A records his deed, then B can presumably find evidence of the prior transfer and avoid his unfortunate interaction with O. The goal of creating a system for recording instruments affecting title to real property is to force A to record his deed, thus putting the world on notice of the prior transfer.

With the creation of *centralized recording*, A becomes the "low cost avoider." This means that it is easy for A to take steps to avoid a dispute; all A needs to do is to pay a small recording fee and invest minimal time to record his deed. States have also adopted what are commonly known as recording statutes. These statutes create the necessary incentive to encourage grantees to record instruments affecting real property. We will discuss the operation of the recording statutes after we look at the mechanics of a records search.

---

[1] We will refer to the county recorder because, in most states, recording is the responsibility of the county, or county equivalent (such as the parish, in Louisiana). Some states have different systems, however: in Connecticut, for example, town clerks are responsible for keeping property records. Conn. Gen. Stat. §7-23(2017).

Fire destroys the Webster County (Mississippi) Courthouse on January 17, 2013. Deeds and other documents suffered smoke and water damage, but ultimately firefighters were able to save them. Other counties have not been as fortunate. Webster County has since digitized all of their records.

Photo by Joel McNeece/Calhoun County Journal

The establishment of county recorders' offices benefits society broadly, and not just individuals searching title. People lose important documents: they can be destroyed in house fires or floods, or in myriad other ways. A system of private property depends on stable and reliable proof of ownership. The recorder's office (or "record room") preserves records.

Record rooms protect the ordering of important private property rights against loss of instruments. Our system of recording documents affecting title promotes one of the most important property policies—certainty—and reduces the transactions costs associated with real estate sales and loans.

Keep in mind that copies of deeds and other instruments are physical records. Recordation helps achieve the goal of certainty of title only if these records are kept safely. For the most part, these records do not reside "in the cloud." In a few instances, fires and earthquakes have destroyed record rooms. This catastrophic loss of records leads to lasting litigation over ownership of property.

1. The Indexes

The early statutes merely required counties to maintain record rooms, but not *indexes* of records. This was probably sufficient in times when land did not change hands quickly. Today, a large county, such as Orange County, California, may see thousands of documents recorded each day. Local officials in the county recorder's office photocopy real property documents such as deeds, mortgages, easements, and other documents affecting title to real property, stamp a date and time of recordation, and place them in books for public review. Although these books include a variety of instruments, they are commonly known as deed books. Each deed book is separately numbered, and each instrument is simply placed in the book *seriatim* in the order received.

Bedford County, Tennessee, deed room
Register of Deeds, Bedford County, Tennessee

As you now know, parties will search the public records, or have professionals do this for them, in order to determine the state of title. However, the party searching title will only be able to do so if there is a means to locate individual records affecting specific real property. In other words, there must be a system of indexing the documents. If the index is accurate, then a party searching title will be able to locate relevant instruments. A massive number of instruments convey, encumber

Which Public Records?

The primary records affecting title are located in the county recorder's office. But other records affect title as well. Bankruptcy orders can affect title, and so can probate and divorce orders. These other records are also checked during a title search.

or affect title. It would be impossible to find every document that relates to specific property unless there is a system for doing so.

There are two types of indexes: grantor/grantee-based indexes and tract indexes. Each of these systems is intended to allow searchers to find instruments relevant to title for specific property. The two systems work quite differently, however.

a. Grantor/Grantee Indexes

The grantor/grantee indexes are the most commonly used indexing system. This system is actually comprised of two indexes: the grantee/grantor index and the grantor/grantee index. Each of these indexes allows a searcher to locate instruments affecting title to property. They must be used together to work properly.

The *grantee/grantor* index is a book compiled in final form annually (and supplemented daily) by the clerk of the local recording office. This index lists every person who has been a *grantee* of an interest in real property by recorded instrument in the jurisdiction, alphabetically by last name. The index then provides crucial information: the name of the grantor of the interest, the deed book and page number in the deed book in which a copy of the instrument is located, the date on which the instrument was recorded, the type of instrument recorded (a deed, mortgage, etc.), and often a short description (in the case of a deed, the description may simply be a short description of the identity of the property by street address). The *grantor/grantee* index is almost identical, except that it lists all *grantors* of interest in property by recorded instrument, alphabetically, by the last name of the grantor. This index will likewise show the name of the grantee taking the interest, the date on which the instrument was recorded, the type of instrument, the deed book and page in which the instrument can be found, and a description of the property.

Searching the Grantor/Grantee Indexes

Let's do a skeletal record search. Assume that you intend to purchase a home from Jerry Anderson in Fulton County, Georgia. You will do a title search in order to determine whether Jerry has marketable title. Your contract may require you to complete the search within a short period of time following execution. The property is "Lot 4 of Ridgeline Subdivision." Let's further assume that you forgo hiring a professional title searcher (not a very good idea, actually) and perform the search yourself. You need to determine whether Jerry Anderson has title to sell the property to you, and if so, the quality of Jerry's title. You would therefore trek to the recorder's office at the Fulton County Courthouse.

A title search is a kind of detective work. You must first look backward in time to determine whether Jerry Anderson purchased the property from a lawful owner, and whether that owner purchased from a predecessor who similarly owned the property, and continue this process over and over. Theoretically, you must search all the way back to the origin or "root of title"; this would be the moment at which the sovereign first granted the property to a private party. Since Georgia was one of the original colonies, the root moment of title would be old indeed. But as we will see, a statute or title standard typically allows a far shorter search, often 40, 50 or 60 years.

In the example above, Jerry Anderson is (allegedly) the present owner; we would therefore begin our search with him. If the year is 2020, you would start with the grantee/grantor index for the year 2020, searching the last name "Anderson." You would look among the many Andersons for "Anderson, Jerry." We know that in order to have title, Jerry Anderson must have been the grantee under a deed of the property at some point, and we work our way backward until we find the deed in which that conveyance took place. In our search we do not find "Anderson, Jerry" in the 2020 index; nor do we find him in any of the indexes for 2020-2003. But we do find a reference to "Anderson, Jerry" in the 2002 grantee/grantor index. "Bogart, Daniel" is shown as the grantor, and the index further states that "Anderson, Jerry" was the grantee, under a deed of property having the correct legal description, recorded on February 1, 2002. The index reports that instrument as appearing at deed book 300, page 2.

> **Backward/Forward**
>
> The grantee/grantor index allows you to search *backward* in time. The grantor/grantee index then allows you to search *forward* in time.

It is not enough to find the correct reference in the index. We must then check the actual deed book 300, page 2, and examine the recorded document shown on that page. Sure enough, we discover a copy of a general warranty deed by which Daniel Bogart conveyed to Jerry Anderson property having the correct legal description. As we will see later, it will be important for you to read the deed to see if it contains any restrictions or easements, because these affect the state of title.

In addition, you will also want to check the date of the deed, because the conveyance may have actually occurred on a date prior to the recording date. If, for example, the deed were dated April 1, 2001, Anderson actually became owner of the property on that date, assuming the deed was delivered on that date, rather than on the date of recording. To simplify our example, though, from now on you should assume that the recording date is also the date of the conveyance.

Grantee	Grantor	Date Recorded	Instrument	Description	Book	Page
Anderson, Jerry	Bogart, Daniel	February 1, 2002	Deed	Lot 4, RL Sub	300	2
Bogart, Daniel	Smith, Linda	March 1, 1954	Deed	Lot 4, RL Sub	150	35

So far, all we have determined is that your seller purchased the property on February 1, 2002 from Daniel Bogart. From whom, and when did

Daniel Bogart receive title? We must now begin searching to discover this information. You would do this by searching under the last name Bogart in the grantee/grantor index, looking for the instrument by which he acquired ownership. Searching again in the 2002 grantee/grantor index (to catch any transaction involving Daniel Bogart prior to February 1, 2002) and then in each grantee/grantor index for the years 2001 through 1955, we find no mention of "Bogart, Daniel" as grantee of a deed to the property. But in the search of the grantee/grantor index for 1954 we find a reference to "Bogart, Daniel" as grantee, and "Smith, Linda" as grantor, of a deed to the property. The index shows that deed recorded on March 1, 1954, and entered in deed book 150 at page 35 (see table above). You take down that actual deed book and, sure enough, you see the deed from Linda Smith to Daniel Bogart. The description of the property matches the property Jerry Anderson plans to sell to you.

You could go back further in time, although that would be time-consuming. If you had employed a title searcher, such a search would have been much more expensive. The search backward via the grantee/grantor index establishes the chain of ownership of the property, as well as defects that are obvious in the text of the actual instruments that the searcher finds, such as easements and servitudes that might be reserved or created in the instruments.

Title Standards: Allowing for a Sane Title Search

The title standard for the State of Georgia says that a competent real estate attorney or title searcher would need to search back only to a "root of title" consisting of a conveyance that occurred more than 50 years ago. Title Standards (State Bar of Georgia, 2016). The root of title would be a starting point conveyance of the property interest in the seller's chain of title. It is possible that searching back further will reveal a defect in title, but it would be nearly impossible to do this with every transaction. A lawyer or title searcher may confidently limit her search in most cases to the period provided by the title standard.

Having gone back the requisite time period for a standard title search, you would switch to the grantor/grantee index to "bring the search forward." It is at this point that you may discover unanticipated conveyances and defects. In our example, you searched backward and found that Linda Smith granted the property to Daniel Bogart by deed on March 1, 1954, shown in deed book 150, page 35. In other words, you know that as of March 1, 1954, Daniel Bogart owned the property. You would therefore begin searching, by last name, the 1954 grantor/grantee index, and all the years following, up to February 1, 2002, to see if Daniel Bogart conveyed the property or an interest in the property following March 1, 1954.

Grantor	Grantee	Date Recorded	Instrument	Description	Book	Page
Smith, Linda	Bogart, Daniel	March 1, 1954	Deed	Lot 4, RL Sub	150	35
Bogart, Daniel	Big Bank	June 1, 1995	Mortgage	Lot 4, RL Sub	200	31
Bogart, Daniel	Anderson, Jerry	February 1, 2002	Deed	Lot 4, RL Sub	300	2

You already know that Daniel Bogart sold the property by deed to Jerry Anderson in 2002; you learned this from the grantee/grantor index. The question is whether Daniel Bogart conveyed an interest in the property *before* selling the property to Jerry Anderson.

As it happens, when reviewing the 1995 grantor/grantee index, you discover an entry under "Bogart, Daniel." The index entry identifies "Big Bank" as the grantee of a mortgage recorded June 1, 1995, and identifies the property that you wish to buy from Jerry Anderson as the subject of the mortgage. It gives a deed book and page of 200/31 (see table above). You take down deed book 200 and turn to page 31. When you do, you discover a copy of a mortgage securing a 30-year loan and promissory note in the amount of $50,000. Your search of the records finds no "accord and satisfaction" or release of the mortgage. Therefore, it would appear that the mortgage is still valid and enforceable.

A party purchasing real property takes subject to existing recorded mortgages, unless the mortgages are released. Jerry Anderson does not have marketable title, unless he obtains a release of the mortgage, because the property is subject to an encumbrance—Big Bank's mortgage.

Note again that the mortgage would be discovered only by moving forward in the grantor/grantee index, and not when moving backward in the grantee/grantor index. Can you now see why?

Now, if you think about it, your search is incomplete if you limit your search as shown immediately above. Look at the mortgage to Big Bank, recorded June 1, 1995. Jerry Anderson proposes to sell the property to you in 2020. Quite a few years have passed after the creation of the mortgage. Lenders often transfer their mortgages. *It is not clear that Big Bank is the present owner of the mortgage.* You would want to know who presently owns the mortgage interest. To do so, you will have to examine Big Bank as grantor in the grantor/grantee index from June 1, 1995 and forward. You will have to do this until you reach the present moment. If you had found other mortgages, easements, and conveyances, you would similarly need to search forward to see who presently owns those interests, and whether the interests have been discharged or released.

In an actual record and title search, then, the searcher will take notes on all instruments affecting title to the property found in the index, in order to create as complete a picture as possible of the state of title. As noted in prior chapters, this is often called an "abstract of title." For example, rather than including the entire 30-page mortgage on the property, the abstractor will typically prepare only a one-page summary of the mortgage, containing the relevant details such as the names of mortgagor and mortgagee, date, amount, and so on.

Look back at the information from the charts for the grantee/grantor and grantor/grantee indexes above. By going backward and forward in time, and searching title, you will discern the *chain of title.* This phrase suggests that title can be seen as a series of connected links. The links must reach back, unbroken, for the requisite period of time (depending on the jurisdiction), and each link can be seen to convey a form of fee or some lesser interest.

b. Tract Index

A few jurisdictions maintain or permit *tract indexes.* This form of index simplifies the search process considerably. A tract index identifies a specific parcel of property ("the tract") by an identification number. These numbers correspond to a single file in which the county recording office places all instruments affecting that tract. Theoretically, a searcher would then need only to pull out the folder for a specific parcel in order to find all deeds, mortgages, easements, and other documents relating to the title of the tract.

Tract indexes are not the prevalent form of public indexing system. Most deeds created prior to the advent of modern subdivisions include metes-and-bounds legal descriptions, making the identification of property by tract number very difficult. And property sometimes changes in boundary and size, as a grantor sells slivers over time. A tract index assumes some certainty about property description, when there is often ambiguity. Moreover, even in a tract system, the searcher will have to search the grantor's name to discover whether any judgment liens might apply to the property.

The key point, though, is that in jurisdictions that permit and maintain tract indexes, these indexes are part of the public recording system, and should be searched in addition to the grantor/grantee indexes.

In recent years, some jurisdictions have moved to a form of computerized tract index. In this system, each parcel is assigned an identification number. How numbers are assigned is itself problematic: they are not based on existing legal descriptions but instead on other sources of information. For example, the county recorder may use numbers assigned to parcels by the tax assessor. The authors cannot predict how quickly and how thoroughly this transition will occur, although it is clear that some jurisdictions are moving more quickly than others. It is doubtful, given the fact that other identification methods are so historically rooted in recording of title (particularly metes-and-bounds descriptions), that tract indexes will become the legal norm anytime soon.

2. Computerized Records and Searching

The authors came of "law practice age" before the widespread use of computers. Back then, any person seeking to search title did so physically, by visiting the county recorder's office and other locations in which official records were kept. Today, many county recorders have spurred a transformational shift in the recordation and searching of records: they have—on a county-by-county basis—begun the process of placing indexes and scanned copies of instruments affecting title online, permitting remote searching of title records.

Digitizing and placing records online is a costly process. The problem is that a title searcher must be able to look backward in time at documents that were recorded many years ago. To make computerized searching worthwhile, the county recorder must take the time, and more importantly, invest the money, to scan and index instruments that are *decades* old. There was a time that scholars believed that this simply would not occur, but in fact, some counties have progressed rapidly in recent years. If you want to learn more about the changing nature of recordation and the use of technology, you might read Charles Szypszak, *Real Estate Records, the Captive Public, and Opportunities for the Public Good*, 43 Gonz. L. Rev. 5 (2007).

For instance, the Jackson County, Missouri, Recorder's Office has an accessible online site that allows the searching of title records. You should take the time to look at this site; it makes the search process much easier. But do not be fooled—a good title search requires skill and judgment, no matter how easy a county recorder may make it to locate records. The home page for the recorder is http://www.jacksongov.org/323/Searching-Documents-Online. After entering the site, you will have the choice of Official Public Records (the real property title records), Marriage Records, and Uniform Commercial Code filings. If you enter the Official Public Records (which you can access with the direct address http://records.jacksongov.org/RealEstate/SearchEntry.aspx), you will see a search page, a copy of which we have included on the following page.

Practice Tip

Assume that you are hired to discover whether Mr. and Mrs. Homer R. and Juanita Peek presently own Lot 1 in the "Old Town of Sibley," which is a subdivision in Jackson County, Missouri. Use the publicly available records and indexes from the Jackson County Recorder's Office. You can enter names in the field for grantee or grantor and search backward or forward. If you do a solid search, you should discover that the Peeks purchased the property from a husband and wife, the Gresses. Juanita Peek died in 1994, followed by Homer in 2004. The property was ultimately conveyed by Mr. Peek's "successor in interest," a Ms. Tammy Ham, to Jackson County in 2006. See if you can construct a rudimentary abstract demonstrating the chain of title from the Gresses to the County.

Jackson County, Missouri, Recorder of Deeds Official Public Records online search page
Senior Deputy County Counselor, Jackson County, Missouri

Note that the search page provides fields for grantor and grantee, by last name. This means that the Jackson County online database essentially combines the grantor/grantee and grantee/grantor indexes. You can search either the grantor or grantee by last name from the same page. The database allows the searcher to narrow a search by entering a field for type of instrument (deed of trust, warranty deed, easement, etc.), dates filed, and so on. As to the date field, a searcher may narrow a search by looking at instruments filed within a single-year period or over a multiple-year period. The page provides different means for locating parcels of property, including by lot in subdivision or by U.S. Government Survey.

C RECORDING STATUTES

Every jurisdiction has enacted a recording statute. The goal of the recording statute is to force parties who receive a conveyance of an interest in real property to record the interest publicly. Think about a basic hypothetical: O sells a farm to A first-in-time by deed, which A does not record. O then contracts to sell the farm to B by deed. This scenario presents the real possibility that B will complete the transaction, pay good money, and only then discover that O no longer owned the farm. To help B avoid this result, the recording statute encourages A to take the minimal step of recording A's interest, so that B will be on notice of it. If A does not do this, B may be awarded title to the property as a good faith purchaser.

There are three types of recording statutes: race, notice, and race-notice. We will discuss each below.

First-in-Time as Default Rule

Each of the three types of recording statutes provides a "safe harbor" for the subsequent purchaser, but only if she meets the requirements of the statute. If the subsequent purchaser is unable to take advantage of the statute, she is subject to the common law default rule of first-in-time.

Recording statutes guide the decisions of parties anticipating the purchase of property interests. Think for a moment about some of the material from Chapter 2. In *Pierson v. Post*, a hunter who had invested the most effort when hunting a fox lost his action against an interloping hunter who mortally wounded the fox. Do you recall the policies that motivated the *Pierson* court? Do you detect a "sympathetic echo" in the manner in which the recording statutes resolve disputes between subsequent purchasers and owners of prior unrecorded interests? Policy questions abound with respect to the methods of acquiring property examined in Chapter 2; these questions are just as relevant to recording acts.

1. Types of Recording Statutes

a. Race

The first type of recording statute is known as a pure "race" statute. A race statute gives title to the party who wins the race to record the instrument conveying the interest.

Assume the basic fact pattern of O to A, by deed, which deed A does not record. O then conveys to B by deed, which deed B does not record. O has obviously engaged in inappropriate and possibly fraudulent behavior, but the parties left holding the bag are A and B. If, after the conveyance from O to B, A records A's deed before B records hers, *A wins* in a dispute between A and B. Conversely, if B records her deed first, *B wins*.

Only Delaware, Louisiana, and North Carolina employ a pure race statute. The other states are split fairly evenly between the notice and race-notice types of recording acts.

Here are examples of race statutes from Delaware and North Carolina:

Del. Code Ann. tit. 25, §2106 (2009):

A mortgage, or a conveyance in the nature of a mortgage, of lands or tenements shall have priority according to the time of recording it in the proper office, without respect to the time of its being sealed and delivered, and shall be a lien from the time of recording it and not before.

N.C. Gen. Stat. §47-18(a) (2017):

No (i) conveyance of land, or (ii) contract to convey, or (iii) option to convey, or (iv) lease of land for more than three years shall be valid to pass any property interest as against lien creditors or purchasers for a valuable consideration from the donor, bargainer or lesser[sic] but from the time of registration thereof in the county where the land lies. . . . Unless otherwise stated either on the registered instrument or on a separate registered instrument duly executed by the party whose priority interest is adversely affected, (i) instruments registered in the office of the register of deeds shall have priority based on the order of registration as determined by the time of registration. . . .

Read over the statutes. Do they just come out and say "where two parties claim an interest from the same grantor, the first to record wins"? What specific language indicates that these are race recording statutes?

The race statute is not necessarily fair; it is, however, efficient. As we will see, race statutes value *certainty* over fairness. If O conveys Blackacre to both A and B, uncertainty about which of these conveyance occurred first may arise in a variety of ways. However, there is no uncertainty about the date and time stamp on a recorded document. It will tell us whether A or B recorded first—in some cases down to the second. Of course, if two competing instruments are apparently recorded at the same moment, then the race statute does not resolve the question of priority; courts grant equal priority to the conveyances. *See, e.g.*, Baer v. Douglas, No. D057811, 2012 WL 917190 (Cal. Ct. App. Mar. 19, 2012) (two deeds of trust with 3:09 P.M. time stamp); First Bank v. E. W. Bank, 132 Cal. Rptr. 3d 267 (Cal. Ct. App. 2011) (trust deeds deposited before business hours both given 8:00 A.M. time stamps; instruments therefore have equal priority).

To see the race statute in action, let's look at one admittedly extreme scenario. Assume that Jerry Anderson is an older man (perhaps in his 90s) and dependent on public transportation. Assume also that Daniel Bogart is much younger (say, in his 20s). Bogart is Anderson's next-door neighbor in an apartment complex. On January 1, Ben Smith sells a condominium unit to Anderson and delivers a deed to Anderson that same day. Anderson pays $500,000 consideration. The purchase is completed at 5 P.M., and the county recorder's office is closed. Anderson is therefore unable to record the deed that day. Later that evening, in a conversation in the elevator to the apartment building, Anderson tells Bogart: "I've grown tired of living in this run-down apartment building. I just bought a condominium unit from Ben Smith and I plan to move in next week. Ben did not ask a high price. He seemed a little shifty to me, but who cares, now that I have the deed?"

Bogart approaches Smith early the following morning, January 2, about the condominium unit. Smith, sensing an opportunity to make a windfall from his property, sells the condominium unit to Bogart; Bogart also pays consideration and receives a deed from Smith.

On January 3, Bogart knocks on Anderson's door. When Anderson opens the door, Bogart waves his deed from Smith in Anderson's face and says: "Look old man. Smith just conveyed to me the same condominium unit that he sold to you. I think I'll go down and record my deed. I plan to walk real slowly down to the county recorder's office." Upset, Anderson, who uses a walker, rushes to the bus station to take a bus to the county recorder's office, which is located in the courthouse. The fastest route from the bus is up the steps of the courthouse, rather than the ramp, and Anderson moves as quickly he can up the stairs toward the door. As Anderson approaches the midway point on the stairs, Bogart appears, and marching backward tells Anderson: "Man, you move slowly. I have been waiting for an hour for you to arrive." Laughing, Bogart darts up the stairs and records his deed. The condominium unit is located in a race statute jurisdiction.

In an action between Anderson and Bogart, a court will deem Bogart's deed superior, even though the conveyance to Anderson was first in time. Put simply, Bogart won the race to record his deed in the county recorder's office. It does not matter that Bogart knew of the prior deed to Anderson; Bogart's knowledge is irrelevant. Indeed, Bogart had *actual knowledge* of Anderson's prior interest and took advantage of this knowledge. The race statute permits, and may even reward, this behavior.[2] *See* New Bar P'ship v. Martin, 729 S.E.2d 675, 685-86 (N.C. Ct. App. 2012) (actual knowledge of previous transaction does not defeat title of subsequent purchaser who was first to record; until interest recorded, third parties may act as if no interest exists).

■ PROBLEMS: RACE RECORDING STATUTE

1. What happens if no one records in a race statute jurisdiction?

    ➤ O to A, A does not record;
    ➤ O to B, B does not record.

In an action between A and B, who has superior title in a race statute jurisdiction?

2. A "wakes up."

    ➤ O to A, A does not record;
    ➤ O to B, B does not record;
    ➤ A records.

In an action between A and B, who has superior title in a race statute jurisdiction?

---

[2] Of course, Anderson should be able to recover his money from Smith, if he can find him, and if Smith is solvent.

b. Notice

In a notice statute jurisdiction, a subsequent purchaser's interest is superior to an earlier conveyance from the same grantor, if the subsequent purchaser took the property without notice at the time of the purchase. The question is not *who recorded first*, but instead, *what did the subsequent purchaser know, and when did he know it?*

Assume that O conveys Blackacre to A for consideration, then O conveys Blackacre to B for consideration. In a notice jurisdiction, B wins in an action between A and B if at the time of B's purchase of Blackacre, B did not have notice of the earlier conveyance to A. As we will see, notice may be actual, constructive, or inquiry. In the scenario above involving Old Man Anderson, in which Bogart beat Anderson to the county recorder's office to record his deed, Bogart had actual notice of grantor's earlier conveyance to Anderson. Anderson lost in a race statute jurisdiction, *but Anderson would win in a notice statute jurisdiction.*

Here are examples of notice recording statutes from Arizona and Texas:

Ariz. Rev. Stat. Ann. §33-412 (2014):

A. All bargains, sales and other conveyances whatever of lands, tenements and hereditaments, whether made for passing an estate of freehold or inheritance or an estate for a term of years, and deeds of settlement upon marriage, whether of land, money or other personal property, and deeds of trust and mortgages of whatever kind, shall be void as to creditors and subsequent purchasers for valuable consideration without notice, unless they are acknowledged and recorded in the office of the county recorder as required by law.

B. Unrecorded instruments, as between the parties and their heirs, and as to all subsequent purchasers with notice thereof, or without valuable consideration, shall be valid and binding.

Tex. Prop. Code Ann. §13.001 (West 2014):

(a) A conveyance of real property or an interest in real property or a mortgage or deed of trust is void as to a creditor or to a subsequent purchaser for a valuable consideration without notice unless the instrument has been acknowledged, sworn to, or proved and filed for record as required by law.

(b) The unrecorded instrument is binding on a party to the instrument, on the party's heirs, and on a subsequent purchaser who does not pay a valuable consideration or who has notice of the instrument.

Both statutes limit protections to creditors or "subsequent purchasers for valuable consideration without notice." Often, statutes and case opinions refer simply to *bona fide purchasers* (also known as "good faith purchasers"). In either

Focus on the Subsequent Purchaser

The recording statutes are intended to protect subsequent purchasers of an interest; these statutes act as safe harbors for later grantees from the first-in-time default rule. Therefore, you should begin your inquiry by (1) determining the type of statute in place in the jurisdiction and (2) locating the subsequent purchaser of the interest.

case, the language indicates that the benefit of the statute is limited to persons who paid real consideration and who, at the time of the purchase, had no notice of the previous transaction.

Look carefully at the statutes. Does either require the subsequent purchaser without notice to record her deed to obtain priority? The answer is no. The statutes provide that the subsequent purchaser has priority unless the *prior* grantee records. We ask whether the subsequent grantee purchased the property, and whether at the time of purchase, she had notice. Notice statutes do not require the subsequent purchaser to actually record her conveyance in order to defeat the prior unrecorded interest.

For example, assume the following conveyances in a notice statute jurisdiction:

➢ O to A; A does not record;
➢ O to B; B does not have notice and B does not record.

In an action between A and B over ownership of the interest in property, B wins, because B purchased without notice. Whether B records his deed is irrelevant to B's title in a dispute with A. However, if B fails to record his deed from O, then B runs the very real risk that O will do to B what O did to A:

➢ O to A; A does not record;
➢ O to B; B does not have notice and does not record;
➢ O to C; C does not have notice and does not record.

C wins in a dispute over ownership among the parties. The notice statute encourages each grantee to record the deed or face the possibility of losing title to a subsequent bona fide purchaser.

As is often the case in life, status carries perks. A bona fide purchaser—that is, a subsequent purchaser without notice—has the ability to extend his privileged position to a third person who has notice or would be deemed to have notice. This is known as the *shelter rule*. For example, assume the following:

➢ O to A; A does not record;
➢ O to B; B does not have notice;
➢ B to C; C has actual notice of the O to A conveyance.

C steps into the shoes of B and is said to be "sheltered" by the fact that B took without notice. We want individuals who rely on the recording statute to be in a position to sell the property that they have paid good money to purchase. This happens only if B can shelter his purchaser.

Finally, there is an important timing issue for us to address: at what moment does a subsequent purchaser acquire notice? Assume that Oliver owns property in a notice jurisdiction. Oliver then engages in the following conveyances:

> ➢ Time 1: O to A, by deed; A does not record;
> ➢ Time 2: B pays O for property, but has yet to receive the deed;
> ➢ Time 3: A personally informs B of the Time 1 conveyance;
> ➢ Time 4: O to B, by deed.

We care about the moment that B pays consideration. We ask—as of that point in time—did B have notice? If the answer is no, then B has satisfied the requirement of the notice statutes. The fact that B later is notified of the prior conveyance becomes irrelevant. This is the majority rule, although some courts in notice jurisdictions adopt a stricter standard and require that O complete the conveyance of the property to B. In other words, these courts ask whether B knew about the prior conveyance at the time O conveyed title by deed to B. We will expand on this discussion of payment of consideration below in Section C.

c. Race-Notice

Race-notice statutes are the third and final category of recording statute. In essence, these statutes combine the critical elements of both race and notice recording statutes. To take priority over prior conveyances, a subsequent purchaser must show that (1) she recorded her interest first *and* (2) she took without notice of the prior conveyance at the time of her purchase.

Here are examples of race-notice statutes from Hawaii and Utah:

Haw. Rev. Stat. §502-83 (2006):

All deeds, leases for a term of more than one year, mortgages of any interest in real estate, or other conveyances of real estate within the State, shall be recorded in the bureau of conveyances. Every such conveyance not so recorded is void as against any subsequent purchaser, lessee, or mortgagee, in good faith and for a valuable consideration, not having actual notice of the conveyance of the same real estate, or any portion thereof, or interest therein, whose conveyance is first duly recorded.

Utah Code Ann. §57-3-103 (West 2017):

Each document not recorded as provided in this title is void as against any subsequent purchaser of the same real property, or any portion of it, if:

> (1) the subsequent purchaser purchased the property in good faith and for a valuable consideration; and
>
> (2) the subsequent purchaser's document is first duly recorded.

Review the language of these two statutes and you will see the phrases "good faith" (the notice element) and "first duly recorded" (the timing element). Good faith may be used interchangeably with "bona fide." In each case, purchaser must take an interest without notice of a prior-in-time transfer. The requirement that a subsequent interest be "first duly recorded" means exactly what it says: the subsequent purchaser may obtain a senior position only if he records his interest first.

For example, consider the following conveyance:

➢ O to A; A fails to record;
➢ O to B; B takes without notice;
➢ A records.

In a pure notice jurisdiction, B would defeat A because of the lack of notice. However, in a race-notice jurisdiction, although B purchased the property without notice, A nevertheless recorded before B. A would win.

Now consider a second possibility:

➢ O to A; A fails to record;
➢ O to B; B records, *but B has notice of the prior transfer to A.*

The Least Generous Statute

The race-notice statute creates the highest hurdle for a subsequent purchaser to overcome to defeat the prior conveyance. It carries the limiting factors of both race and notice statutes.

In a pure race jurisdiction, B would defeat A, because B recorded first. However, in a race-notice jurisdiction, A will win because B had notice, notwithstanding the fact that B recorded first.

■ PROBLEM: RECORDING STATUTES

O's friend A loans him $25,000 and O grants A a mortgage on Blackacre in return. A neglects to record it immediately, however. Shortly thereafter, O decides to sell Blackacre to B, who has no knowledge of A's mortgage. B doesn't record either. A hears of the sale to B and immediately records her mortgage. Several days later, B finally records his deed. O defaults on the loan and A seeks to foreclose on Blackacre. Under each of the types of recording statutes, determine if Blackacre is subject to A's mortgage.

■ ■ ■

The purpose of recording statutes is to incentivize owners of interests in real property to record their instruments. Consider again the basic hypothetical of O to A, then O to B. The idea is to force the grantee of an interest in real property (A) to give notice of her interest to the rest of the world—or more specifically to give notice to a party who receives an interest later in time (B). The three types of recording statutes have one thing in common: if A does not record, they permit B to win! In other words, even though the conveyance to B is second-in-time, the statutes supersede the rule of first-in-time and award the superior right to B.

Let's take a look at a case that demonstrates the operation of the recording rooms and indexes, and the interaction between the process of recording and recording statutes. The grantor/grantee indexes are the mechanisms for providing notice, in most jurisdictions. What must the index do to provide notice and protect our friend "B," the subsequent purchaser? Consider *Luthi v. Evans*, below.

LUTHI v. EVANS

576 P.2d 1064 (1978)
Supreme Court of Kansas

PRAGER, Justice:

On February 1, 1971, Grace V. Owens was the owner of interests in a number of oil and gas leases located in Coffey county. On that date Owens, by a written instrument designated "Assignment of Interest in Oil and Gas Leases," assigned to defendant International Tours, Inc. (hereinafter Tours) all of such oil and gas interests. This assignment provided as follows:

"ASSIGNMENT OF INTEREST IN OIL AND GAS LEASES
"KNOW ALL MEN BY THESE PRESENTS:
"That the undersigned Grace Vannocker Owens, formerly Grace Vannocker, Connie Sue Vannocker, formerly Connie Sue Wilson, Larry R. Vannocker, sometimes known as Larry Vannocker, individually and also doing business as Glacier Petroleum Company and Vannocker Oil Company, hereinafter called Assignors, for and in consideration of $100.00 and other valuable consideration, the receipt whereof is hereby acknowledged, do hereby sell, assign, transfer and set over unto International Tours, Inc., a Delaware Corporation, hereinafter called Assignee, all their right, title, and interest (which includes all overriding royalty interest and working interest) in and to the following Oil and Gas Leases located in Coffey County, Kansas, more particularly specified as follows, to-wit:

"(Lease descriptions and recording data on 7 oil and gas leases not involved in this appeal are stated here.)

"Together with the rights incident thereto and the personal property thereon, appurtenant thereto or used or obtained in connection therewith.

"And for the same consideration the Assignors covenant with the Assignee, his heirs, successors or assigns: That the Assignors are the lawful owners of and has good title to the interest above assigned in and to said Lease, estate, rights and property, free and clear from all liens, encumbrances or adverse claims; That said Lease is valid and subsisting Lease on the land above described, and all rentals and royalties due thereunder have been paid and all conditions necessary to keep the same in full force have been duly performed, and that the Assignor will warrant and forever defend the same against all persons whomsoever, lawfully claiming or to claim the same.

Assignors intend to convey, and by this instrument convey, to the Assignee all interest of whatsoever nature in all working interests and overriding royalty interest in all Oil and Gas Leases in Coffey County, Kansas, owned by them whether or not the same are specifically enumerated above with all oil field and oil and gas lease equipment owned by them in said County whether or not located on the leases above described, or elsewhere in storage in said County, but title is warranted only to the specific interests above specified, and assignors retain their title to all minerals in place and the corresponding royalty (commonly referred to as land owners royalty) attributable thereto.

"The effective date of this Assignment is February 1, 1971, at 7:00 o'clock A.M.

"/s/ Grace Vannocker Owens

"Grace Vannocker Owens

"Connie Sue Vannocker

"Larry R. Vannocker

"(Acknowledgment by Grace Vannocker Owens before notary public with seal impressed thereon dated Feb. 5, 1971, appears here.)" (Emphasis supplied.)

This assignment was filed for record in the office of the register of deeds of Coffey county on February 16, 1971.

It is important to note that in the first paragraph of the assignment, seven oil and gas leases were specifically described. Those leases are not involved on this appeal. In addition to the seven leases specifically described in the first paragraph, Owens was also the owner of a working interest in an oil and gas lease known as the Kufahl lease which was located on land in Coffey county. The Kufahl lease was not one of the leases specifically described in the assignment.

The second paragraph of the assignment states that the assignors intended to convey, and by this instrument conveyed to the assignee, "all interest of whatsoever nature in all working interests and overriding royalty interest in all Oil and Gas Leases in Coffey County, Kansas, owned by them whether or not the same are specifically enumerated above. . . ." The interest of Grace V. Owens in the Kufahl lease, being located in Coffey county, would be included under this general description.

On January 30, 1975, the same Grace V. Owens executed and delivered a second assignment of her working interest in the Kufahl lease to the defendant, J. R. Burris. Prior to the date of that assignment, Burris personally checked the records in the office of the register of deeds and, following the date of the assignment to him, Burris secured an abstract and title to the real estate in question. Neither his personal inspection nor the abstract of title reflected the prior assignment to Tours.

The controversy on this appeal is between Tours and Burris over ownership of what had previously been Owens's interest in the Kufahl lease. It is the position of Tours that the assignment dated February 1, 1971, effectively conveyed from Owens to Tours, Owens's working interest in the Kufahl lease by virtue of the general description contained in paragraph two of that assignment. Tours then contends that the recording of that assignment in the office of the register of deeds of Coffey county gave constructive notice of such conveyance to subsequent purchasers, including Burris. Hence, Tours reasons, it is the owner of Owens's working interest in the Kufahl lease.

Burris admits that the general description and language used in the second paragraph of Owens's assignment to Tours was sufficient to effect a valid transfer of the Owens interest in the Kufahl lease to Tours as between the parties to that instrument. Burris contends, however, that the general language contained in the second paragraph of the assignment to Tours, as recorded, which failed to state with specificity the names of the lessor and lessee, the date of the lease, any legal description, and the recording data, was not sufficient to give constructive notice to a subsequent innocent purchaser for value without actual notice of the prior assignment. Burris argues that as a result of those omissions in the assignment to Tours, it was impossible for the register of deeds of Coffey county to identify the real estate involved and to make the proper entries in the numerical index. Accordingly, even though he checked the records at the courthouse, Burris was unaware of the assignment of the Kufahl lease to Tours and he did not learn of the prior conveyance until after he had purchased the rights from Grace V. Owens. The abstract of title also failed to reflect the prior assignment to Tours. Burris maintains that as a result of the omissions and the inadequate description of the interest in real estate to be assigned under the second paragraph of the assignment to Tours, the Tours assignment, as recorded, was not sufficient to give constructive notice to a subsequent innocent purchaser for value. It is upon this point that Burris prevailed before the district court. On appeal, the Court of Appeals held the general description contained in the assignment to Tours to be sufficient, when recorded, to give constructive notice to a subsequent purchaser for value, including Burris.

At the outset, it should be noted that a deed or other instrument in writing which is intended to convey an interest in real estate and which describes the property to be conveyed as "all of the grantor's property in a certain county," is commonly referred to as a "Mother Hubbard" instrument. The language used in the second paragraph of the assignment from Owens to Tours in which the assignor conveyed to the assignee "all interest of whatsoever nature in all working interests . . . in all Oil and Gas Leases in Coffey County, Kansas," is an example of a "Mother Hubbard" clause. The so-called "Mother Hubbard" clauses or descriptions are seldom used in this state, but in the past have been found to be convenient for death bed transfers and in situations where time is of the essence and specific information concerning the legal description of property to be conveyed is not available. Instruments of conveyance containing a description of the real estate conveyed in the form of a "Mother Hubbard" clause have been upheld in Kansas for many years as between the parties to the instrument. (In re Estate of Crawford, 176 Kan. 537, 271 P.2d 240; Bryant v. Fordyce, 147 Kan. 586, 78 P.2d 32.)

The parties in this case agree, and the Court of Appeals held, that the second paragraph of the assignment from Owens to Tours, providing that the assignors convey to the assignee all interests in all oil and gas leases in Coffey County, Kansas, owned by them, constituted a valid transfer of the Owens interest in the Kufahl lease to Tours as between the parties to that instrument. We agree. We also agree with the parties and the Court of Appeals that a single instrument, properly executed, acknowledged, and delivered, may convey separate tracts by specific description and by general description capable of being made specific, where the clear intent of the language used is to do so. We agree that a subsequent purchaser, who has actual notice or knowledge of such an instrument, is bound thereby and takes subject to the rights of the assignee or grantor.

This case involves a legal question which is one of first impression in this court. As noted above, the issue presented is whether or not the recording of an instrument of conveyance which uses a "Mother Hubbard" clause to describe the property conveyed, constitutes constructive notice to a subsequent purchaser. The determination of this issue requires us to examine the pertinent Kansas statutes covering the conveyance of interests in land and the statutory provisions for recording the same. . . .

The recordation of instruments of conveyance and the effect of recordation is covered in part by K.S.A. 58-2221, 58-2222, and 58-2223. These statutes are directly involved in this case and are as follows:

> "58-2221. Recordation of instruments conveying or affecting real estate; duties of register of deeds. Every instrument in writing that conveys real estate, any estate or interest created by an oil and gas lease, or whereby any real estate may be affected, proved or acknowledged, and certified in the manner hereinbefore prescribed, may be recorded in the office of register of deeds of the county in which such real estate is situated: Provided, It shall be the duty of the register of deeds to file the same for record immediately, and in those counties where a numerical index is maintained in his or her office the register of deeds shall compare such instrument, before copying the same in the record, with the last record of transfer in his or her office of the property described and if the register of deeds finds such instrument contains apparent errors, he or she shall not record the same until he or she shall have notified the grantee where such notice is reasonably possible.

> "The grantor, lessor, grantee or lessee or any other person conveying or receiving real property or other interest in real property upon recording the instrument in the office of register of deeds shall furnish the register of deeds the full name and last known post-office address of the person to whom the property is conveyed or his or her designee. The register of deeds shall forward such information to the county clerk of the county who shall make any necessary changes in address records for mailing tax statements."

> "58-2222. Same; filing imparts notice. Every such instrument in writing, certified and recorded in the manner hereinbefore prescribed, shall, from the time of filing the same with the register of deeds for record, impart notice to all persons of the contents thereof; and all subsequent purchasers and mortgagees shall be deemed to purchase with notice."

> "58-2223. Same; unrecorded instrument valid only between parties having actual notice. No such instrument in writing shall be valid, except between the parties thereto, and such as have actual notice thereof, until the same shall be deposited with the register of deeds for record."

It is the position of Tours that the statutes contained in Chapter 58, Article 22, of K.S.A. are the only statutes which are material for a determination of this case and that statutory provisions in other chapters need not be examined. Simply stated, it is the position of Tours that the assignment from Owens to Tours was properly executed and acknowledged as required by the statutes and constituted a valid transfer of the Owens interest in the Kufahl lease to Tours. This instrument, when filed for record in full compliance with the provisions of K.S.A. 58-2221, imparted constructive notice to all subsequent purchasers, including Burris, who are deemed to purchase with notice under K.S.A. 58-2222. This was the position taken by the Court of Appeals.

Burris maintains that our examination must extend beyond the statutes set forth above. It is his position that we must also consider the Kansas statutes which govern the custody and the recordation of instruments of conveyance, and the duties of the register of deeds in regard thereto, as contained at K.S.A. 19-1201 through K.S.A. 19-1219. We will discuss only those statutes which we deem pertinent in the present controversy. K.S.A. 19-1204 makes it the duty of the register of deeds in each county to take custody of and preserve all of the records in his office and to record all instruments authorized by law to be recorded. K.S.A. 19-1205 requires the register of deeds to keep a general index, direct and inverted, in his office. The register is required to record in the general index under the appropriate heading the names of grantors and grantees, the nature of the instrument, the volume and page where recorded, and, where appropriate, a description of the tract.

K.S.A. 19-1207 requires the register to keep a book of plats with an index thereof. K.S.A. 19-1209 provides that the county commissioners of any county may order the register of deeds to furnish a numerical index containing "the name of the instrument, the name of the grantor, the name of the grantee, a brief description of the property and the volume and page in which each instrument indexed is recorded." K.S.A. 19-1210 makes it the duty of the register to make correct entries in the numerical index, of all instruments recorded concerning real estate, under the appropriate headings, and "in the subdivision devoted to the particular quarter section described in the instrument making the conveyance."

At this point we should refer back to K.S.A. 58-2221 which is set forth above. That statute makes it the duty of the register of deeds in those counties where a numerical index is maintained to compare any instrument offered for recordation, before copying the same in the record, with the last record of transfer in his office of the property described; if the register of deeds finds that such instrument contains apparent errors, he shall not record the same until he shall have notified the grantee where such notice is reasonably possible. The second paragraph of K.S.A. 58-2221 requires either the grantor or grantee, upon recording the instrument in the office of the register of deeds, to furnish the register of deeds the full name and last known post-office address of the person to whom the property is conveyed. The register of deeds is required to forward the necessary information to the county clerk who shall make any necessary changes in address records for mailing tax statements. These two provisions in K.S.A. 58-2221 show a legislative intent that instruments of conveyance should describe the land conveyed with sufficient specificity to enable the register of deeds to determine the correctness of the description from the numerical index and also to make it possible to make any necessary changes in address records for mailing tax statements.

We have concluded that the statutes contained in K.S.A. Chapter 58 pertaining to conveyances of land and the statutes contained in Chapter 19 pertaining to recordation of instruments of conveyance constitute an overall legislative scheme or plan and should be construed together as statutes *in pari materia*. (City of Overland Park v. Nikias, 209 Kan. 643, 498 P.2d 56.) It also seems obvious to us that the purpose of the statutes authorizing the recording of instruments of conveyance is to impart to a subsequent purchaser notice of instruments which affect the title to a specific tract of land in which the subsequent purchaser is interested at the time. From a reading of all of the statutory provisions together, we have concluded that the legislature intended that recorded instruments of conveyance, to impart constructive notice to a subsequent purchaser or mortgagee, should describe the land conveyed with sufficient specificity so that the specific land conveyed can be identified. As noted above, K.S.A. 58-2203 and 58-2204 require a deed to describe the premises. A description of the property conveyed should be considered sufficient if it identifies the property or affords the means of identification within the instrument itself or by specific reference to other instruments recorded in the office of the register of deeds. Such a specific description of the property conveyed is required in order to impart constructive notice to a subsequent purchaser.

[The *Luthi* court uses the Latin phrase *in pari materia*. This is a rule of statutory construction, and it is an important one at that. Sometimes several statutes seem to relate to the same set of issues, even if they are not always presented in a legal code as an orderly package. This rule asks the court to make sense of the statutes by reading them together. The patchwork of state statutes that govern the process for recordation of real property interests, and rights of subsequent purchasers, are to be read *in pari materia*.—EDS.]

Again, we wish to emphasize that an instrument which contains a "Mother Hubbard" clause, describing the property conveyed in the general language involved here, is valid, enforceable, and effectively transfers the entire property interest as between the parties to the instrument. Such a transfer is not effective as to subsequent purchasers and mortgagees unless they have actual knowledge of the transfer. If, because of emergency, it becomes necessary to use a "Mother Hubbard" clause in an instrument of conveyance, the grantee may take steps to protect his title against subsequent purchasers. He may take possession of the property. Also, as soon as a specific description can be obtained, the grantee may identify the specific property covered by the conveyance by filing an affidavit or other appropriate instrument or document with the register of deeds.

We also wish to make it clear that in situations where an instrument of conveyance containing a sufficient description of the property conveyed is duly recorded but not properly indexed, the fact that it was not properly indexed by the register of deeds will not prevent constructive notice under the provisions of K.S.A. 58-2222. (*See* Gas Co. v. Harris, 79 Kan. 167, 100 P. 72.)

From what we have said above, it follows that the recording of the assignment from Owens to Tours, which did not describe with sufficient specificity the property covered by the conveyance, was not sufficient to impart constructive notice to a subsequent purchaser such as J. R. Burris in the present case. Since Burris had no actual knowledge of the prior assignment from Owens to Tours, the later assignment to Burris prevails over the assignment from Owens to Tours.

The judgment of the Court of Appeals is reversed and the judgment of the district court is affirmed.

■ POINTS TO CONSIDER

1. **Identify the specific type of recording statute.** Look back at the opinion in *Luthi v. Evans*. What type of recording act does Kansas employ? How can you tell? Would the case have come out differently if Kansas had a different type of recording act? The first step in working with these kinds of problems is to identify the parties in an almost mechanical way: in *Luthi v. Evans*, who occupies the positions of O (the grantor), A (the first-in-time grantee), and B (the subsequent purchaser)?

2. **Why was recording not enough?** In *Luthi v. Evans*, Tours did what a purchaser is supposed to do—it recorded its interest. Why was that not enough to put Burris on notice?

3. **The description in the index matters.** Look back at the Kansas statutes. They do more than establish the type of recording statute at play. All jurisdictions today maintain indexes. However, some state statutes require only that the county governments maintain record rooms, *but do not require indexes*. Does Kansas require the maintenance of indexes? An index is valuable only if it allows the hypothetical title searcher to find relevant records. How do you think the court would have ruled if Kansas had been a jurisdiction that did not statutorily require the maintenance of an index?

4. **Unrecorded conveyances are valid; the question is their effect vis-à-vis subsequent purchasers.** Note that the court says that as between Owens and Tours, the Mother Hubbard clause effectively transferred the Kufahl lease to Tours. Assume that if instead of conveying the interest to Burris, Owens simply sent Tours a letter. The letter states: "I know that I included a Mother Hubbard clause in the assignment of leases to you, but I do not think it permits you any rights in the Kufahl lease. We believe the description in the record room index insufficiently describes the Kufahl lease." What response do you expect from Tours?

5. **Surprise: bureaucrats can make mistakes. What happens when they screw up the index?** Toward the end of the opinion, the court states: "We also wish to make it clear that in situations where an instrument of conveyance containing a sufficient description of the property conveyed is duly recorded but not properly indexed, the fact that it was not properly indexed by the register of deeds will not prevent constructive notice under the provisions of K.S.A. 58-2222." What!? Let's make this statement concrete: rather

than use a Mother Hubbard clause, assume that Owens described the Kufahl lease properly by reference to specific property in the assignment to Tours. Tours presents the assignment to the county clerk for recordation, but the clerk indexes the assignment under "Mowens" rather than "Owens." Owens then contracts to assign the Kufahl lease to Burris. Burris searches the record room using the indexes. Will he find the earlier conveyance to Tours? How is that different from what occurred in the *Luthi* case? Should that type of error be treated any differently? *See* Miller v. Simonson, 92 P.3d 537 (Idaho, 2004) (properly recorded instrument is constructive notice to later purchaser, even though indexed under the wrong name).

It is equally possible for the recorder to correctly index a deed or assignment, but fail to place the instrument in a deed book. Most courts hold that the entry alone in the index is not constructive notice. That said, if a party does a title search, and discovers the entry even though there is no corresponding deed in the deed book, the searcher will have inquiry notice. This is a variant of actual notice; the entry in the index is a red flag. The title searcher is on notice of whatever he would learn from asking the grantee of the interest what the grantee owns. We discuss inquiry notice in the section that follows.

6. **Remember what we told you at the start of this book: possession is crucial.** Assume that Tours was physically working the Kufahl lease at the time Owens sold that interest to Burris. Would this have affected the outcome?

2. Recording Statutes Protect Purchasers (and Sometimes Lien Creditors)

Recording statutes explicitly protect purchasers. This makes sense. The recording statutes act as a safe harbor from the default common law rule of first-in-time. If the statute is going to dispossess the prior grantee, then at least we should demand that the subsequent grantee *purchase* the property interest. Statutes typically require that the purchaser give "valuable consideration." Courts do not insist that a subsequent purchaser pay fair market value for the property interest. But neither are courts willing to protect a subsequent purchaser who paid only a meager amount in connection with a prior conveyance. The courts vary on the exact language, but often they will demand that the subsequent purchaser pay a meaningful or substantial price in exchange for the conveyance.

Whether the subsequent purchaser really "paid" consideration can be a hard question. For example, consider the scenario of the installment land contract. At times, a purchaser may be unable (or simply not want) to take out a traditional loan from a lender. The purchaser may instead choose, with the cooperation of the seller, to buy the property on credit. This type of loan is known as "seller financing." In other words, the seller becomes the lender. The clean way to accomplish this sort of transaction is for the seller to convey title in a deed to the purchaser, and for purchaser to deliver a promissory note and mortgage to the seller, just as the purchaser would have done with respect to a typical lender. However, in some instances—often involving farm land—the purchaser and seller execute a contract for sale of the property. The closing date is set for a number of years following execution of the contract. In the interim, the purchaser occupies the property and makes periodic installment payments to the seller. At the end of the executory period, the seller delivers the deed to the purchaser.

Tomlinson v. Clarke, below, involves just such an installment contract. In Washington State, these installment contracts are sometimes referred to as executory contracts.

TOMLINSON v. CLARKE

803 P.2d 828 (1991)
Court of Appeals of Washington

[Tomlinson owned land in Snohomish County, Washington. On March 23, 1979, Tomlinson conveyed one parcel to the Whitsells via an installment contract. The Whitsells did not record their contract immediately in the county recorder's office, instead waiting until October 19, 1982 to do so. The description of the property attached to the Whitsells' installment contract included a 125-foot length of shore land along Lake Stevens. Apparently, the Whitsells only intended to purchase a 50-foot length of land along the lake, but at the time the contract was executed no one noticed the error.

On December 26, 1979 (after the Whitsells signed their contract, but before they recorded it), Tomlinson sold a second parcel of land, to the Clarkes. This transaction was also an installment land sale contract. Although the Clarkes' transaction involved a separate parcel, the legal description overlapped that of the Whitsells' parcel: the legal description attached to the Clarke contract covered the same 125 feet of shore land along Lake Stevens. There were no facts indicating that the Clarkes were actually aware of the prior transfer to the Whitsells, and because the Whitsells had not recorded their contract, the Clarkes were not constructively on notice of the prior transfer. The Clarkes recorded their contract on February 8, 1980. The Clarkes discovered the prior conveyance to the Whitsells in 1985. At dispute was the 50 feet of land along the shore of Lake Stevens that the Whitsells believed that they purchased in 1979. The trial court held that the Clarkes were not bona fide purchasers entitled to the protection of the recording statute.

At that time, the recording statute for the State of Washington, Wash. Rev. Code §65.08.080, read as follows:

> An executory contract for the sale or purchase of real property or an instrument granting a power to convey real property as the agent or attorney for the owner of the property, when acknowledged (with the acknowledgment certified) in the manner to

entitle a conveyance to be recorded, may be recorded in the office of the recording officer of any county in which any of the real property to which it relates is situated, and when so recorded shall be notice to all persons of the rights of the vendee under the contract.]

COLEMAN, Presiding Chief Judge.

. . .

We first decide whether a vendee may acquire the status of a bona fide purchaser after purchasing real property through an executory contract and recording the contract, but before acquiring legal title by making all of the installment payments.

One of the earliest Washington cases purporting to settle the law on the matter was Ashford v. Reese, 132 Wash. 649, 233 P. 29 (1925), *overruled by* Cascade Sec. Bank v. Butler, 88 Wash. 2d 777, 567 P.2d 631 (1977). In *Ashford*, the court held that a vendee to an executory contract for the sale of real property did not bear the risk of loss for that property. *Ashford*, 132 Wash. at 650-51, 233 P. 29. That court relied on precedent which had held that an executory contract of sale in Washington conveyed no title or interest, either legal or equitable, to the vendee. *Ashford*, at 650-51, 233 P. 29 (*citing* Schaefer v. E.F. Gregory Co., 112 Wash. 408, 192 P. 968 (1920)).

. . .

A long line of cases ensued, whittling away the broad *Ashford* holding and granting the vendees of executory contracts of sale a wide variety of rights and interests, including the recognition that such vendees have "'substantial rights,'" a "'valid and subsisting interest in property,'" and a "'claim or lien' on the land[.]" (Citations omitted.) *Cascade*, 88 Wash. 2d at 781, 567 P.2d 631. In addition, the Washington Supreme Court has acknowledged in various decisions that such vendees have the right to possess, control, and cultivate the land; that their interest in the land is mortgageable; and that their interest is personal property for purposes of inheritance taxes, succession, and administration. *See Cascade*, at 782, 567 P.2d 631.

Cascade prospectively overruled *Ashford* and held that "a real estate contract vendee's interest is 'real estate' within the meaning of the judgment lien statute." *Cascade*, at 782, 567 P.2d 631. In so holding, the court emphasized that the cases decided after *Ashford* determined the rights and interests of vendors and vendees "based upon a realistic examination of the nature of the interest in a particular context." *Cascade*, at 784, 567 P.2d 631. In the present case, the Clarkes argue that in the context of a properly recorded executory contract, a vendee's rights should include the status of bona fide purchaser for value regardless of the executory nature of the contract or the fact that legal title would not vest in the vendee until the contract was fulfilled.

To support their argument, the Clarkes cite In re McDaniel, 89 B.R. 861 (Bkrtcy. E.D. Wash. 1988), a bankruptcy case that thoroughly analyzed the Washington law regarding the interests created by an executory real estate contract. That court concluded that under such a contract, a vendee acquires a property interest in the real estate, while the vendor possesses a lien-type security device. *McDaniel*, at 869.

Moreover, the Clarkes note that executory real estate contracts were deemed to be conveyances in Terry v. Born, 24 Wash. App. 652, 653-54, 604 P.2d 504 (1979). *Terry*, like *McDaniel*, also stated that "[a] contract seller's retention of title is a security device functionally similar to a real estate mortgage or deed of trust." *Terry*, at 655, 604 P.2d 504.

The Whitsells, in response, assert that under Peterson v. Paulson, 24 Wash. 2d 166, 163 P.2d 830 (1945), a bona fide purchaser for value "must have paid the purchase price and have acquired the legal title without notice of [any] prior equity." *Peterson*, at 180, 163 P.2d 830.[3] The Whitsells argue that because neither they nor the Clarkes made all of the necessary payments under their respective executory contracts or received legal title for the disputed parcel of land, neither of the two parties could claim status as a bona fide purchaser.

In addition, the Whitsells rely on Reed v. Eller, 33 Wash. App. 820, 664 P.2d 515 (1983), which held that a vendee of an executory contract must first obtain legal title by paying the full contract price before acquiring the status of a bona fide purchaser. *Reed*, at 827, 664 P.2d 515. *Reed* further concluded in a footnote that *Cascade* had not *sub silentio* overruled *Peterson* and, thus, did not eliminate the requirement of having legal title before qualifying as a bona fide purchaser. *Reed*, at 827 n.2, 664 P.2d 515.

We expressly decline to follow *Reed*. That court failed to give proper weight to the Supreme Court's holding in *Cascade* and its unavoidable weakening of *Peterson* and other cases that relied upon *Ashford* as the prevailing law.[4] In *Cascade*, the court recognized that in many previous cases it had "defined and classified the interest of vendors and vendees for a variety of purposes . . . based upon a realistic examination of the nature of the interest in a particular context." *Cascade*, 88 Wash. 2d at 784, 567 P.2d 631. Such a realistic examination of the issue presented here leads us to conclude that a vendee to an executory contract should have the same opportunity to enjoy the protection of bona fide purchaser status as someone financing the transaction in some other way, such as through a deed.

Further, *Reed* gave no consideration to what was then RCW 65.08.080, a provision that granted executory contracts the protection of the Recording Act even though such a contract was not yet termed a "conveyance." It is significant that the Legislature promptly expressed its disapproval of the *Reed* holding by repealing what was formerly RCW 65.08.080 and amending the Recording Act to make indisputably clear that executory contracts were property conveyances afforded the full protection of the Recording Act. Thus, an executory contract for the sale

---

[3] *Peterson* noted, however, that although purchasers of real property under an executory contract do not acquire any title or interest in the property until the contract is fully performed, such contracts "do create and vest in the vendee an enforcible [sic] right against the land which is subject to the contract." *Peterson*, at 178-79, 163 P.2d 830.

[4] *See, e.g.*, McVean v. Coe, 12 Wash. App. 738, 742-43, 532 P.2d 629 (1975) (in reliance upon Kendrick v. Davis, 75 Wash. 2d 456, 464, 452 P.2d 222 (1969), *Peterson*, and former RCW 65.08.080, the *McVean* court concluded that recording an executory contract does not affect another party's prior, unrecorded equitable interest).

of real estate is a conveyance and may be recorded as all other conveyances are recorded, and

> [e]very such conveyance not so recorded is void as against any subsequent purchaser or mortgagee in good faith and for valuable consideration from the same vendor . . . of the same real property or any portion thereof whose conveyance is first duly recorded.

RCW 65.08.070. Consequently, a vendee of an executory real estate contract who has no notice of competing interests in the property at issue and who properly records the executory contract may acquire the status of bona fide purchaser.[5]

. . .

The trial court's judgment regarding the Clarkes' interest in the disputed parcel is reversed and the cause remanded for entry of an order identifying the Clarkes as bona fide purchasers of the property with an interest superior to that of the Whitsells.

■ POINTS TO CONSIDER

1. **What type of recording statute does Washington employ?** Reread the language of the statute. It should be easy to determine.

2. **Can you be a purchaser without taking title?** In this case, neither the Clarkes nor the Whitsells took title via a deed from Tomlinson. This complicates the issue of determining whether the Clarkes were "subsequent purchasers" entitled to the protection of the recording act. How is it that the court finds a "contract" to suffice for purposes of that state's recording statute? If a contract does suffice, who is the subsequent purchaser? In order to take advantage of the recording statute, you must show that you are subsequent in time to any other party claiming a right in the property through the grantor.

3. **Missing facts.** The facts as related by the court in *Tomlinson* do not reveal what percentage of the sale price the Clarkes or the Whitsells had paid to Tomlinson by the time of the litigation. It would seem that both parties made payments to Tomlinson. Should we care if the Whitsells paid 90 percent of the installment payments and the Clarkes had paid only 5 percent?

4. **Three possible approaches to resolving title disputes involving installment land contracts.** Professors William Stoebuck and Dale Whitman explain that there are three possible approaches to protect competing parties in cases such as *Tomlinson*. William B. Stoebuck & Dale A. Whitman, The Law of Property §11.10, at 890-91 (3d ed. 2000). A court might award title to

---

[5] After reviewing a comparable series of cases under California law, the Ninth Circuit likewise held that a purchaser under an uncompleted land sale contract was not automatically precluded from enjoying the status of bona fide purchaser merely because of the nature of the conveyance. *See* Perry v. O'Donnell, 749 F.2d 1346, 1350-51 (9th Cir. 1984).

the first-in-time installment contract purchaser, the Whitsells, and require the Whitsells to reimburse in cash the Clarkes an amount equal to the installment payments the Clarkes had made to date to Tomlinson. Second, a court might award the Clarkes title, but require the Clarkes to make their final installment payments to the Whitsells. Finally, the court might act in Solomon-like fashion and award fractional shares to the Whitsells and the Clarkes, in amounts representative of their payments to Tomlinson. The courts are split between the first two approaches; there is apparently little enthusiasm for creating a co-tenancy among the warring parties, which would result from employing the third method. Which approach did the court in *Tomlinson* seem to take?

■ PROBLEMS: RECORDING

Assume that the jurisdiction has a notice recording statute:

1. O is getting older, so she decides to ensure that her daughter A gets Blackacre without going through probate. She executes a quitclaim deed "to A and her heirs, subject to life estate in O." A records the deed immediately. O continues in sole possession of Blackacre, as before. Shortly thereafter, O's friend B agrees to lend O $50,000 and takes a promissory note and a mortgage on Blackacre to secure the debt, having no knowledge of the conveyance to A. O then dies. Is B's interest superior to A's?

2. Assume, in the previous problem, that B obtained the mortgage *before* the conveyance to A, but failed to record it. A then took without knowledge of B's mortgage and recorded her deed right away. What result?

■   ■   ■

One question commonly arises in recording statute disputes: are persons who obtained interests in property, because civil statutes award them a lien, treated as "purchasers" in the same sense as persons who bought property in the traditional manner? The most prominent of these non-traditional purchasers are holders of judicial liens. The common law rule is that only purchasers and mortgagees in the traditional sense (people who pay consideration) are "purchasers" for the purposes of the recording statute. However, some recording statutes specifically raise lien creditors to the status of "purchasers."

Judgment Creditors and Other Statutory Lien Creditors

A successful plaintiff in a civil law suit obtains a lien against real property of the defendant in the county in which the lawsuit is filed, allowing the plaintiff to pursue and sell the property in satisfaction of the judgment. The judgment will award a specific amount of money (a "sum certain") against a particular defendant. The judgment creditor can sell the real property owned by the defendant to the extent of the outstanding judgment award. Some creditors, such as a county owed taxes by the property owner, have liens against real property of the debtor by operation of statute. These are known as statutory lien creditors.

For example, assume that Owen owns real property in a notice statute jurisdiction. The statute does not specifically address the rights of lien and judgment creditors. On January 1, while driving to the store, Owen hits a pedestrian, Bogart. Bogart files suit in tort against Owen on January 2. One month later, on February 1, Owen sells his real property to Smith, conveying his property by warranty deed. Smith does not record his deed. On August 1, Bogart wins a lawsuit in negligence against Owen in the county in which the real property is located. On the date that Bogart wins his suit, he has no notice of the earlier conveyance to Smith. Bogart does not know Smith personally and has no reason to suspect that Owen is no longer owner. Bogart's judgment acts as a lien against all real property of Owen, now known as the "judgment debtor," located in in the county in which the judgment is obtained. However, even though the judicial process grants Bogart a lien right, Bogart is not a "purchaser." Smith has the superior interest. It is true that Smith failed to record his deed, but the recording statute only comes to the aid of subsequent purchasers. Bogart is left to the common law default rule of first-in-time, and Smith was first.[6]

Some recording statutes specifically raise lien and judgment creditors to the level of traditional purchasers. Recall Texas's notice recording statute. It states: "A conveyance of real property or an interest in real property or a mortgage or deed of trust is void as to *a creditor* or to a subsequent purchaser for a valuable consideration without notice. . . ." If the facts of the problem above occurred in Harris County, Texas, Bogart would have the superior interest. *See* TPEA No. 5 Credit Union v. Solis, 605 S.W.2d 381 (Tex. App. 1980).

Many creditors, such as credit unions, extend credit based on the property owned by the debtor, as shown by public records. If the debtor already has conveyed that property to others, by unrecorded deed, significant fairness issues would result. Does it make sense, however, to extend the same reasoning to tort creditors such as Bogart? Did Bogart take into account the recorded property interests of Owen before "entering into" the auto accident? Would an economist view Bogart as an unwilling "purchaser" of a right to sue and obtain a lien on Owen's property? Can you see the connection between this issue and the discussion of creditor's rights with regard to tenancy by the entirety property in Chapter 4?

---

[6] Bogart might be able to set aside the conveyance under the Uniform Fraudulent Transfers Act, which most states have adopted, if Owen did not receive fair market value for the property. But we are discussing only the recording act application here.

3. What Does Notice Really Mean?

Both notice and race-notice statutes require a subsequent purchaser to take his or her interest without notice of the prior conveyance in order to assert superior title. What does "notice" mean? As always, think in terms of the basic hypothetical:

> ➢ O to A, then
> ➢ O to B.

The question becomes: did B have notice of the O-to-A transfer?

Courts typically suggest that a purchaser may be held to have one of three types of "notice": actual notice, constructive notice, and inquiry notice.

Categories of Notice

- **Actual notice.** Notice arises when B is personally aware of the prior transfer.
- **Constructive notice.** B is deemed to have notice if the title flaw would have been revealed by a competent title search, whether or not B actually performs the search.
- **Inquiry notice.** B has notice of any fact that would have been revealed had B made a reasonable inquiry, if facts suggest the possibility that there is a flaw in title.

---

a. Actual Notice

If B is personally aware of the prior O-to-A transfer, then B has *actual notice*. In our earlier example of old man Anderson who loses the race to the county recorder's office, Anderson told Bogart that he had purchased the real property. Bogart therefore had actual notice of the earlier transfer. Actual notice may also occur if a person sees a deed, even though it is not properly recorded. You cannot be a bona fide purchaser if you know about the previous transaction.

b. Constructive Notice

As we discussed with regard to constructive possession, the word "constructive" means something implied and *deemed* to be true by law rather than actually true. *Constructive notice arises purely as a result of the recording system.* The law assumes that individuals can search title records properly and discover title flaws. If an individual purchasing property fails to search title, that person is presumably following a course of his own choosing. Therefore, the law deems a person to know whatever he would have learned from an appropriate search of title records. B will be held to constructively know whatever B would have turned up had he searched title. If a competent title search would reveal that a predecessor in interest to the seller mortgaged the property, or conveyed an easement, B is deemed to have notice of the mortgage or easement.

c. Inquiry Notice

Sometimes there is a *red flag* that suggests that the prospective purchaser of an interest should be worried about the state of the seller's title. However, there is no recorded document in the chain of title revealing the title flaw. In other words, facts exist that would cause a reasonable person to be concerned. In such cases, we say that the purchaser has *inquiry notice* of the title flaw. The purchaser will be on notice of anything that a reasonable inquiry would reveal. Professors Donald Kochan and James Smith explain inquiry notice in a more colorful manner:

> Consider this analogy. If you buy a box of fruit and at the time of purchase something smells rotten, but you never open the box to investigate whether the produce is bad, you cannot be heard to later complain that you didn't know the fruit was inedible. Or, if you buy a 16-ounce box of chocolates, but when you pick it up it feels a little light, you cannot be heard to complain that it was a few truffles short.

Donald J. Kochan and James Charles Smith, *When Inquiring Minds Ought to Know*, Prob. & Prop., July/Aug. 2017, at 57; *When Inquiring Minds Ought to Know, Part II*, Prob. & Prop., Jan./Feb. 2018, at 48 (together providing an excellent discussion of inquiry notice).

Inquiry notice arises in one of two ways:

1) a *surrounding circumstance* or fact on the ground leads a reasonable person to wonder about the seller's title; or
2) a *reference in the public records* may not definitively reveal the existence of a prior transfer, but hints at one.

In general, courts say that inquiry notice exists if the purchaser is in possession of facts or information that would lead a reasonable person to ask whether there might be some interest outside the record chain of title that affects title to the property. These facts may indicate any number of title issues. Here are a few examples: an unrecorded mortgage, the possibility that property might be adversely possessed by someone other than the record owner, and the existence of an easement by necessity.

i. Inquiry Notice from Surrounding Circumstances

Inquiry notice can arise when circumstances should make the purchaser aware that there might be a title flaw. For example, if the purchaser, upon a physical inspection of the property, sees train tracks running through the property, he should realize that the railroad might have an easement.

Courts generally hold that *possession provides inquiry notice of rights held by occupiers* whose occupation is inconsistent with record ownership. Consider the

---

Searches of Records and Actual/Inquiry Notice

If a person searches the records and actually sees a document that undermines title, that person will have notice. This will be either actual notice or inquiry notice. If the document definitively reveals a title flaw (for example, a mortgage), the searcher has actual notice. If the document refers to a possible flaw, then the searcher has inquiry notice. For example, a deed may refer to an easement, even though the easement itself is not found in the records.

---

sale of a house. Anderson contracts to sell his private residence to Bogart. Bogart does a title search, and the search reveals "clean title." Bogart has a question about the maintenance of the landscaping and decides to pay an unannounced visit to Anderson at the house during the executory period. Someone other than Anderson answers the door in a bathrobe and Anderson is nowhere to be seen. A reasonable person would inquire of the man answering the door in the bathrobe why he, and not Anderson, appears to be living in the home. Many courts state that the mere presence of a "party in possession" other than the record title owner is a red flag that requires inquiry. The inquiry may put the issue to rest, or it may suggest a true title flaw. If Bogart fails to inquire and it turns out that Anderson conveyed the property to the man in the bathrobe in an unrecorded installment contract, Bogart would be deemed to have inquiry notice of the bathrobe man's interest.

> ➤ It is not necessary that Bogart actually visit the home to be on inquiry notice of the interests of parties in possession. We assume that Bogart, as a reasonable purchaser, would determine whether there were parties in possession with interests contrary to the record owner.

Let's look at some problems to define the boundaries of inquiry notice. The first problem is easy, or at least it should be. In each case you should ask, "Would the facts cause a reasonable person to suspect that there has been an earlier, unrecorded conveyance of a property interest?"

■ PROBLEM: ADJACENT LAND IS OCCUPIED

Sam owns farmland and a farmhouse on a 20-acre parcel in the Midwest (the "Land.") The following occurs:

> **Time 1:** Sam conveys the Land to Paul by quitclaim deed. Paul records the deed that same day. Paul pays one-half of the consideration for the Land at the time of the sale and is required to pay the remainder a year later. In addition, Paul permits Sam to reside in the farmhouse until Sam makes the final one-half payment of consideration. The farmhouse includes 5 of the 20 acres.
> **Time 2:** Paul fails to pay the remaining consideration for the Land as agreed, and as a result conveys the Land by quitclaim deed back to Sam. Sam does not record this deed. Sam continues to reside in the farmhouse.
> **Time 3:** Paul enters into a contract to sell the Land to Tom. The contract specifically excepts the 5-acre portion of the Land on which the farmhouse is located. The parties enter into the contract during the peak of winter. Snow covers the ground, and there is no external indication on the farm-land that that anyone is actively farming the Land. Paul explains to Tom that he is excepting the 5-acre farmhouse from the property conveyed by the contract because "my brother-in-law lives in that house, and he is old and just needs a place to live."
> **Time 4:** Paul conveys the Land, minus the 5-acre farmhouse property, to Tom by warranty deed.
> **Time 5:** Sam records the Time 2 quitclaim deed from Paul.
> The jurisdiction in which the property is located is race-notice.

Sam discovers to his great dismay that Paul has conveyed the Land (minus the 5-acre farmhouse) to Tom. Evaluate Sam's position and advise him on actions that he may take, if any. *See* Wiseth v. Thorson, No. A12-0798, 2013 WL 490782 (Minn. Ct. App., Feb. 11, 2013) (*rev. denied*).

▮ PROBLEM: DISPUTED PARKING LOT

Church and Bank own property on contiguous parcels; in other words, they are direct next-door neighbors and their property lines touch. A bank building sits on the Bank property and a church sits on the Church property. Consider the following additional facts:

> **1964:** Church begins to use, without permission, a portion of Bank property for overflow parking (the "Parking Lot").
> **1970:** Sam Smith purchases and occupies property on the other side of the Bank property and not adjoining the Church property.
> **1985:** Church buys the Parking Lot from the Bank to construct more permanent parking; conveyance of Parking Lot occurs by warranty deed but the Church does not record the deed.
> **1986:** Church makes substantial improvements, including paving and painting lines on the Parking Lot.

> ➤ Other businesses and individuals use the Parking Lot in addition to the Church.
> ➤ **1999**: Smith enters into a contract to purchase the Bank property. During the executory period, Bank delivers to Smith a survey. The survey shows the Parking Lot as part of the Bank property and not Church property.
> ➤ **2000**: Smith purchases Bank property; the description of the land included in the warranty deed from Bank to Smith includes the Parking Lot. Smith records his deed.
> ➤ **2001**: Smith sends a letter to Church demanding that Church cease using the Parking Lot.
> ➤ The jurisdiction in which property is located is race-notice.

One can find other issues buried in this fact set (including adverse possession), but let's focus on recording. Examine the chain of events. Who occupies the superior position with respect to the Parking Lot: Mr. Smith or the Church? *See* Milledgeville United Methodist Church v. Melton, 388 S.W. 3d 280 (Tenn. Ct. App. 2012).

■ PROBLEM: DEVELOPER PERMITS NON-OWNERS TO OCCUPY CONDO UNITS AS PART OF MARKETING CAMPAIGN

Developer builds Golden Gate Condominium ("Golden Gate"), a 150-unit condominium property. Golden Gate is located in a beach town overbuilt with such projects. As a part of its efforts to sell units in the condominium and to make it look less like a losing proposition, Developer permits individuals to occupy a number of the units on a hotel-like basis; in other words, the Developer charges the occupants daily rates.

> ➤ **January 1, 2020**: Amy executes a contract to purchase Unit 100 in Golden Gate from Developer for $500,000. Amy does not record this contract. Amy pays $1,000 on the date of purchase and agrees to pay the remainder over a five-year period. The contract provides that Golden Gate will deliver to Amy a deed to Unit 100 when Amy makes her final payment of the purchase price.
> ➤ **February 1, 2020**: With permission of Developer, Amy takes possession and moves in to Unit 100.
> ➤ **January 1, 2021**: Developer obtains a $5 million loan from Bank, secured by a mortgage on the real property, in order to make improvements to Golden Gate Condominium. Bank records the mortgage.
> ➤ **January 1, 2024**: Amy pays the remainder of the consideration for the purchase. Developer delivers a deed to Unit 100. Amy records the deed.

> ➤ **April 1, 2024**: Developer defaults on debt to Bank, and Bank forecloses its mortgage lien on Golden Gate Condominium, including Unit 100.
> ➤ This is a notice jurisdiction.

Amy intervenes in the foreclosure action and claims that her interest in Unit 100 is superior to that of the Bank. Is she right? Make the best case possible for the Bank and then for Amy. What is Amy really asking Bank to do in order to employ the benefit of the notice statute? *See* Waldorff Ins. & Bonding, Inc. v. Eglin Nat'l Bank, 453 So. 2d 1383 (Fla. Dist. Ct. App. 1984).

Make sure you correctly identify the subsequent purchaser and the prior purchaser. Does it matter whether Amy paid consideration?

■   ■   ■

Consider the rationale underlying the recording statutes for just a moment: we want those people who have been conveyed interests in real property to record their interests. This furthers important property policies of certainty and fairness: it puts all prospective purchasers in a position to determine the status of title, and make informed decisions when dealing with any party claiming to own an interest in the real property. If the owner of the prior interest fails to record, we only shed "crocodile tears" if the application of the recording act terminates that person's interest in favor of a subsequent purchaser without notice. Conversely, if the prior grantee records, the subsequent purchaser loses because he has constructive notice: the subsequent purchaser has notice based on what he would have found in the public records had he bothered to search. *However, this rationale makes no sense if the owner of a prior interest was not in a position to record her interest.* The recording statutes rely on the idea that the owner of a prior interest had a *recordable* document.

In the problem, Amy had a contract, and not a deed. Should this matter? Contracts such as Amy's usually may be recorded if they are properly acknowledged. For example, in Florida, the jurisdiction in which *Waldorf* arose, parties may record contracts if they meet recording formalities. However, in many instances sellers do not acknowledge (i.e., "notarize") contracts, for the simple reason that they do not want purchasers to record their contracts. Contracts contain the terms of the deal, and one or both of the parties may want the terms to be confidential. Would it matter if Amy had not yet gone into possession?

ii. Inquiry Notice from a Reference in the Record. Normally, we think of public records as providing constructive notice, as described above. We have also noted that public records might provide actual notice in a limited number of instances: a purchaser actually searching title will have actual notice of whatever she sees if she physically searches the records, even if the document the purchaser finds should never have been recorded in the first place. But is it possible for a subsequent purchaser to be subject to *inquiry notice* based on something in the public records? The answer is yes, and this can lead to troubling results. Consider the following:

◼ PROBLEM: REFERENCE TO A DOCUMENT AFFECTING TITLE IN THE PUBLIC RECORDS

➢ **2020:** Olive conveys Blackacre to her niece Alice for life, giving remainder to her nephew George. Alice does not record this deed and later misplaces it.

➢ **2026:** Olive is diagnosed in the early stages of Alzheimer's and gives Ellie power of attorney over her affairs. Alice consults Ellie about the lost deed, and Ellie agrees to replace it. Ellie mistakenly believes that the original deed gave Alice fee simple in Blackacre. As a result, Ellie drafts a new deed granting Alice fee simple. That document is titled "Replacement Deed" and states that "this Replacement Deed is a replacement for the deed originally granting Alice Blackacre in 2020, which deed was subsequently lost." Alice records the Replacement Deed.

➢ **2027:** Alice sells Blackacre to Carter for fair market value. Carter records his deed.

➢ **2029:** Alice dies and her executor locates the original deed in the bottom of a chest in Alice's attic. The executor records this deed.

➢ Here is the recording statute in effect: "Civil Code Section 100 (Recording). Every conveyance of real property within this State hereafter made, which shall not be recorded as provided in this chapter, shall be void as against any subsequent purchaser, in good faith and for a valuable consideration of the same real property, or any portion thereof, where his or her own conveyance shall be first duly recorded.

George claims that he owns Blackacre and brings a suit to quiet title. Should George prevail? If you represent George, do you have good news or bad news to deliver to him? Start by answering the following questions: What type of recording statute is reflected in the problem? Who is the subsequent purchaser? *See* Harper v. Paradise, 210 S.E.2d 710 (Ga. 1974).

◼   ◼   ◼

Recording statute issues may arise in any number of scenarios. The order of recording is especially important in the area of mortgage law (a subject we will address in the next chapter). When a borrower defaults on a loan secured by a mortgage, the lender may choose to foreclose its lien on the property. It is common for owners of real property to take out several loans, all secured by mortgages on the same property. The priority of the mortgages is determined by the order in which the mortgages are recorded and by the recording statute.

◼ PROBLEM: THE CREDIT REPORT

Marvin borrows $200,000 from Major Bank on January 1, 2020, and secures this loan with a mortgage on his home. Major Bank fails to record the mortgage. Four years later, on January 1, 2024, Marvin applies for a loan in the amount of $400,000 from

Renovation Bank. Marvin proposes to secure the loan with a mortgage on his home. The Renovation Bank loan application asks Marvin to disclose any prior loans or mortgages affecting his property, but he does not list the prior mortgage to Major Bank. Renovation Bank follows a set procedure when evaluating loan applications. As part of this procedure, Renovation Bank orders a credit report on Marvin. That credit report includes the following notation: "1/1/20, Major B, $200,000, conventional real." Renovation Bank also performed a title search of Marvin's home, which did not reveal Major Bank's mortgage, because it was unrecorded. Renovation Bank decides to make the loan, and Marvin gives Renovation Bank a note and a mortgage on his home to secure the loan. Renovation Bank records the mortgage.

Marvin ultimately defaults on his loan to Renovation Bank, and as a result, Renovation Bank brings an action to foreclose its mortgage. As we will see in Chapter 9, if Renovation Bank is the senior mortgage, foreclosure wipes out all junior interests. Marvin's home is located in a race-notice jurisdiction. Assume that you represent Major Bank. You may join the foreclosure action to protect your interest. What is your client's position? What arguments might you make on Major Bank's behalf, and what response would you expect of Renovation Bank? *See* Metropolitan Nat'l Bank v. Jemal, No. F-52618-10, 2013 WL 5299489 (N.J. Sup. Ct. App. Div., Sept. 23, 2013).

4. Getting Documents into the Records

The fact that you are fortunate enough to be the purchaser or donee of an interest in property does not mean that you are entitled to record your interest. As we have already learned, with the exceptions of leases of less than a year, all transfers of real property interests must be in writing. States add to this by requiring that deeds and other instruments meet certain formalities in order to be recorded.

For example, state statutes require that the grantor's signature on a deed must be notarized. This requirement is intended to eliminate or diminish the possibility that the deed is a forgery. Most state statutes require only that deeds or other instruments of conveyance be "acknowledged" before a notary to be entitled to be recorded. This means that the deed might be signed many years earlier, but as long as the signer *appears* and *acknowledges* his signature to the notary, it can be notarized. Cal. Civ. Code §1189 (West 2007 & Supp. 2018). Consult your local statute carefully to determine the proper form of notarization required.

Notary

Notaries are individuals appointed by the state pursuant to statute to perform ministerial acts of determining identity, informing individuals who sign important documents such as deeds of the seriousness of execution, and to make sure that anyone signing is not subject to intimidation or duress. Notaries are impartial witnesses. You will often find that assistants, paralegals, and others who are "close to the action" in transactions and litigation are certified as notaries. The most important act of notaries is often simply to request that parties executing documents produce identification, such as drivers' licenses, to ensure that they are really the persons named in the document.

As you can imagine, people occasionally screw up formalities. This can mean that a court may not treat a deed that appears in the public records as properly recorded. Recall the purpose of recordation: to place subsequent parties on notice of the earlier conveyance.

Assume that a prospective purchaser of real property checks the public records. The prospective purchaser will act on what he discovers. It is possible, however, that a prior conveyance in the seller's chain may appear to meet formality requirements, but in fact contain a latent (that is, non-obvious) defect. What happens then? Ordinarily, a deed or mortgage recorded in the chain of title gives constructive notice to later purchasers of interests in the property. Should this rule govern in cases in which the defect in formalities was not the kind of thing a title searcher would be able to discover?

One of the most common formality failures occurs when an acknowledgment to a deed recorded in the chain of title harbors a latent defect. Keep in mind that a latent defect does not affect the parties to the deed: *as between the parties, the deed transfers seisin to the grantee.* What is the effect of a deed with a latent defect in the acknowledgment *on later purchasers without notice?* Should courts treat later purchasers as having constructive notice of the deed?

ALL CAPACITY ACKNOWLEDGMENT

> A notary public or other officer completing this certificate verifies only the identity of the individual who signed the document to which this certificate is attached, and not the truthfulness, accuracy, or validity of that document.

STATE OF _____

COUNTY OF _____

On _____ before me, _____,
             (Date)   (Name and title of the officer)

personally appeared _____,
                                            (Name of person signing)
who proved to me on the basis of satisfactory evidence to be the person(s) whose name(s) is/are subscribed to the within instrument and acknowledged to me that he/she/they executed the same in his/her/their authorized capacity(ies), and that by his/her/their signature(s) on the instrument the person(s), or the entity upon behalf of which the person(s) acted, executed the instrument.

I certify under PENALTY OF PERJURY under the laws of the State of California that the foregoing paragraph is true and correct.

WITNESS my hand and official seal.

_____
      Signature of officer

                                                         (Seal)

Sample acknowledgment form authorized by
Cal Civ. Code §1189 (West 2007 & Supp. 2018)

A majority of courts answer in the affirmative; that is, *these courts treat a deed with a latent defect in the acknowledgment as constructive notice to later purchasers. See* In re Bearhouse, Inc., 99 B.R. 926 (Bankr. D. Ark. 1989) ("If the clerk is under a duty to record an acknowledged instrument that is regular on its face, the recording must constitute constructive notice to third parties if the concept of constructive notice is to have any practical application"); Mills v. Damson Oil Corp., 437 So. 2d 1005 (Miss. 1983) (defectively acknowledged but recorded deed provides constructive notice). *See also* H.D. Warren, Annotation, *Record of Instrument Without Sufficient Acknowledgment as Notice*, 59 A.L.R.2d 1299 (1958) ("The general rule, as established by the numerical weight of authority, is that a defect in the acknowledgment of an instrument required for recordation, which is not apparent on the face of the instrument, as acknowledged, does not prevent the recordation from being constructive notice to persons who may be affected by the transaction recorded.").

This answer makes sense, because it forces purchasers to rely on public records when there is no obvious reason to distrust what they might find there. A rule treating a latent defect in the acknowledgment as constructive notice furthers public policies of bringing certainty to land records and of allowing efficient transfer of interests in property. However, as with all legal rules, it is best to see how this majority rule actually operates in practice.

■ PROBLEM: A DEFECTIVE ACKNOWLEDGMENT AND A FAMILY FIGHT

- ➤ George, Sr. has seven children and owns a large tract of land consisting of undeveloped land, farmland, and a farmhouse.
- ➤ George, Sr. conveys the bulk of the property, consisting of the farmland and farmhouse, to his son, George, Jr. but reserves to himself a smaller 5.64 acre tract of undeveloped land.
- ➤ George, Sr. appoints his daughter, Georgia, as power of attorney, with authority to sell, convey, or mortgage the 5.64 acre tract.
- ➤ George, Sr. verbally informs Georgia not long after executing the power of attorney that he wishes Georgia to convey the remaining 5.64 acres to all of his children, *excluding George, Jr.* George, Sr. explains that it is his intention to provide for the remaining six siblings.
- ➤ Georgia acts immediately and conveys the 5.64 acres by warranty deed to herself and her siblings, excluding George, Jr. Georgia does not sign the deed in her own name, but rather signs as "George, Sr."
- ➤ The warranty deed executed by Georgia is notarized and acknowledged with a standard form acknowledgment block, such as the one on page 567 above. The acknowledgment states that *George, Sr.* appeared before the notary. That deed is recorded and indexed in the county recorder's office.
- ➤ George, Sr. then leases the 5.64 acre tract to George, Jr. for a period of 25 years.

> ▷ The recording statute for the jurisdiction in which the real property is located reads as follows: "Every such instrument in writing, certified, and recorded in the manner hereinbefore prescribed, shall, from the time of filing the same with the register of deeds for record, impart notice to all persons of the contents thereof; and all subsequent purchasers and mortgagees shall be deemed to purchase with notice."

Assume that you represent George, Jr. He asks whether his right as tenant in the 5.64 acres is superior to the rights of his six siblings pursuant to the warranty deed? *See* Hildebrandt v. Hildebrandt, 683 P.2d 1288 (Kan. Ct. App. 1984) (and yes, in *Hildebrandt*, the father was named George, Sr., son George, Jr. and daughter, Georgia, although none of the other children were named "George" or a variation thereof). When responding to your client, you might consider a series of questions: What is a power of attorney, and what rights does the power grant Georgia vis-à-vis execution of the deed? What would the public records reveal upon a search by George, Jr.? What is the effect of Georgia's decision to execute the deed in her father's name? What is a "proper" acknowledgment? Finally, what is the impact of the recording statute provided at the end of the Problem?

Some courts are less willing to view an instrument recorded with a defective acknowledgment as constructive notice of a prior interest. Consider *Allen v. Allen*, below.

ALLEN v. ALLEN

16 N.E.3d 1078 (2014)
Appeals Court of Massachusetts

KATZMANN, J.

This case concerns competing claims between adult siblings for the ownership of the house formerly owned by their now-deceased parents. Harold Allen, Jr., (Harold) traces his ownership to a July, 2001, deed (July deed) from the siblings' mother, Ethel Allen (Ethel). Harold's sister Deborah Allen (Deborah) claims ownership by virtue of a November, 2001, deed (November deed) from Ethel to the Allen Realty Trust (Trust), of which Deborah was a cotrustee along with Ethel.

Deborah brought an action alleging that the July deed was forged and claiming that the property was rightfully hers.[7] Following a jury-waived trial, a judge of the Land Court determined that, because the acknowledgment of the July deed was defective, its recording did not give constructive notice to Deborah of the

---

[7] The rights of other siblings, who, along with Deborah, are beneficiaries of the Trust, are also affected by the determination as to which deed is valid. Deborah's complaint does not purport to divest the other siblings of their interest in the property.

conveyance and the deed was not enforceable against her. This is an issue of first impression, not yet addressed by our appellate courts.

...

We affirm.

BACKGROUND

We summarize the relevant facts as found by the judge in his memorandum of decision and postjudgment order, supplemented as necessary with undisputed facts from the record. We reserve certain details for discussion with the specific issues raised.

Deborah and Harold are two of the six children of Ethel and Harold Allen, Sr. (Harold, Sr.). Harold, Sr., and Ethel owned a house at 257 Marrett Road, in Lexington, and lived in that home for many years. Over the course of their marriage, Harold, Sr., and Ethel created numerous estate plans, which consistently excluded their two sons, Harold and Lawrence, because Harold, Sr., and Ethel had provided for them through lifetime gifts.[8] After Harold, Sr., died, Ethel continued this pattern.[9]

The events at the center of this dispute occurred during 2001. In late April, 2001, Ethel began the process of moving from her Lexington home to live with one of her daughters, Nancy Oldro, in Nashua, New Hampshire. After evaluating conflicting testimony, the judge concluded that Ethel had fully moved in by mid-July, 2001.

Harold traces his claim to a deed Ethel executed on July 23, 2001, conveying the house to Harold and to Ethel as joint tenants with a right of survivorship. This deed is the subject of the present dispute. Attorney Paul Maloy prepared the deed and signed a certificate of acknowledgment, dated July 23, 2001, which reads: "Then personally appeared the above named Ethel M. Allen and acknowledged the foregoing instrument to be her free act and deed, before me, [/s] Paul F. Maloy—Notary Public." Maloy recorded the deed on August 10, 2001. We reserve further details regarding the execution and acknowledgment of the deed for the discussion below.

On November 30, 2001, Ethel established the Allen Realty Trust and executed a deed conveying the Lexington property to herself and to Deborah as cotrustees of the Trust, reserving a life estate for herself. She specified that the property would be sold upon her death and the proceeds divided among several of her descendants, including Deborah.[10] This deed was recorded on February 8, 2002.

Only after Ethel died on December 20, 2009, did Harold reveal the July 23, 2001, deed. Neither Deborah nor her sister Nancy nor the attorney who prepared the November deed had discovered the July conveyance.[11] In January, 2010, Deborah commenced the present action, disputing Harold's claim to the property. After a trial

---

[8] In 1987, Harold, Sr., transferred a one-third ownership stake in the family home heating oil business, Sherwood Oil Co., Inc., to Harold and a one-third ownership stake in the business to Lawrence.

[9] Ethel's final will, executed on February 28, 2008, stated: "I have intentionally and not as the result of any accident or mistake, made no specific provision for my sons, LARRY ALLEN and HAROLD J. ALLEN, Jr., and their issue, not for lack of love or affection, but rather because my sons have been provided for by my late Husband and myself."

[10] Once again, she did not include Harold or Lawrence as a beneficiary.

[11] The judge noted that the conveyances to Harold and the trustees were both for nominal consideration, and observed, "[T]here is nothing to suggest that the Trustees looked in the Registry before taking their deed, or had

that included forensic testimony regarding the July deed, the judge found that Ethel's signature on the July deed was authentic. But he determined that, contrary to the certificate of acknowledgment on the deed, Ethel never appeared before Attorney Maloy to acknowledge the deed. The judge found that, instead, she had signed the deed in front of Harold, who then brought it to Maloy for his signature. Harold appeals from the judgment and from the denial of his postjudgment motions.[12]

STANDARD OF REVIEW

"In reviewing a matter wherein the trial judge was the finder of fact, '[t]he findings of fact ... are accepted unless they are clearly erroneous[] [and] [w]e review the judge's legal conclusions de novo.'" *Crown v. Kobrick Offshore Fund, Ltd.*, 85 Mass.App.Ct. 214, 224, 8 N.E.3d 281 (2014), quoting from *T.W. Nickerson, Inc. v. Fleet Natl. Bank*, 456 Mass. 562, 569, 924 N.E.2d 696 (2010) (citations omitted).

. . .

DISCUSSION

1. The recording statute

a. Latent defect in certificate of acknowledgment[13]

"[O]rdinarily an acknowledgment is not an essential part of a deed; but if it is desired to record the deed in order to charge the world with notice of the conveyance, then it is necessary that the deed be acknowledged and that a certificate reciting this fact be attached to the deed. Doubtless, that is the principal function of a certificate of acknowledgment." *McOuatt v. McOuatt*, 320 Mass. 410, 413–414, 69 N.E.2d 806 (1946) (*McOuatt*). See G.L. c. 183, § 4, as appearing in St.1973, c. 205 ("A conveyance ... shall not be valid as against any person, except the grantor or lessor, his heirs and devisees and persons having actual notice of it, unless it ... is recorded in the registry of deeds for the county or district in which the land to which it relates lies"); *Gordon v. Gordon*, 8 Mass.App.Ct. 860, 862–863, 398 N.E.2d 497 (1979) ("[T]itle to real estate may be transferred by a deed which has not been acknowledged, and such deed is good against the grantor and his heirs and those having actual notice").

The certificate of acknowledgment "furnishes formal proof of the authenticity of the execution of the instrument when presented for recording." *Id.* at 862, 398 N.E.2d 497, citing *McOuatt*, 320 Mass. at 413–414, 69 N.E.2d 806. "The certificate of acknowledgment is of evidentiary character, and the taking of the acknowledgment has always been regarded in this Commonwealth as a ministerial and not as a judicial act and the recitals contained in the certificate may be contradicted." *McOuatt, supra* at 413, 69 N.E.2d 806.

---

any compelling reason to do so, given the estate planning context of their acquisition of title. A genuine third party purchaser for value, on the other hand, would have been remiss in not consulting the record before paying consideration."

[12] Harold makes no separate argument with respect to the denial of his postjudgment motions.

[13] On appeal, Harold argues that the judge's consideration of this issue exceeded the scope of the pleadings. See part 2, infra. Because we determine that the issue was fairly litigated, we first consider the issue on the merits.

In *McOuatt,* the Supreme Judicial Court held that where an acknowledgment had not actually occurred, a facially correct certificate of acknowledgment failed to satisfy the statutory requirement that in order for a deed conveying property between spouses to be valid, it must be acknowledged and recorded.[14] *McOuatt, supra* at 415–416, 69 N.E.2d 806 (applying the then-existing version of G.L. c. 209, § 3). Here, as in *McOuatt,* the deed included a facially correct certificate of acknowledgment, with the required signature and recitals, and was recorded. Also, as in *McOuatt,* the judge here concluded that the acknowledgment never actually occurred.

Notwithstanding the facially correct certificate of acknowledgment, because the July deed was never actually acknowledged, it was not entitled to be recorded. See G.L. c. 183, § 29 ("No deed shall be recorded unless a certificate of its acknowledgment or of the proof of its due execution, made as hereinafter provided, is endorsed upon or annexed to it");[15] *Dole v. Thurlow,* 53 Mass. 157, 12 Metcalf. 157, 163 (1846) ("[A]s a prerequisite to recording, acknowledgment, or proof by one or more subscribing witnesses, was necessary. Actual recording, without one of these prerequisites, would not give effect to the deed").

An improvidently recorded deed cannot give constructive notice of the conveyance. See *Graves v. Graves,* 72 Mass. 391, 6 Gray 391, 392–393 (1856) (where assignment was recorded notwithstanding fact that it had not been acknowledged, court held that the assignment was improvidently recorded, the recorded document did "not operate as constructive notice of the execution of the assignment . . . as against [a] . . . creditor . . . ; and therefore the title of the . . . creditor, though subsequent in time, takes precedence").

As in *McOuatt,* the facially correct certificate of acknowledgment does not remedy the absence of a proper acknowledgment. See *McOuatt, supra* at 413, 415, 69 N.E.2d 806. Indeed, as the judge here observed, to determine otherwise would reward a grantee who records a deed that falsely purports to be acknowledged. And, pursuant to *Graves,* an improvidently recorded deed cannot provide constructive notice to subsequent grantees. We therefore conclude that the latent defect in the certificate of acknowledgment of the July deed prevented it from giving constructive notice to Deborah of the prior conveyance.

Harold argues that, even if the July deed was not properly acknowledged, that defect does not affect his claim to the property. He argues, first, that he was not required to record the July deed in order for it to provide superior title, and, second, that the recording statute's safe harbor provision protects his right to the property given the time that elapsed between the recording of the July deed and the action on appeal here. We disagree with both contentions.

---

[14] Because the conveyance was void on these grounds, that court did not reach the question we face today regarding constructive notice to subsequent grantees.

[15] Harold makes no argument that the July deed was recorded with a certificate proving its due execution.

b. Requirement to record deed

As we have noted, the recording statute provides:

"A conveyance . . . shall not be valid as against any person, except the grantor or lessor, his heirs and devisees and persons having actual notice of it, unless it . . . is recorded in the registry of deeds for the county or district in which the land to which it relates lies." G.L. c. 183, § 4.

Harold argues that proper recording is not required for the July deed to be valid against Deborah because she qualifies both as the grantor's heir and as the grantor's devisee. But Deborah's status as Ethel's heir (as her daughter) and devisee (as a named beneficiary of other property under Ethel's will) does not determine whether the requirement to record applies to this transaction. Deborah did not receive the disputed property by virtue of either of these statuses; she received it through an inter vivos transfer. Harold does not point to any authority establishing that a grantee's status as an heir or devisee, with respect to *unrelated* property, eliminates the protections of the recording statute for that grantee. We conclude that it does not.

"We interpret a statute according to 'all its words construed by the ordinary and approved usage of the language, considered in connection with the cause of its enactment, the mischief or imperfection to be remedied and the main object to be accomplished, to the end that the purpose of its framers may be effectuated.'" *Johnson v. Kindred Healthcare, Inc.,* 466 Mass. 779, 783, 2 N.E.3d 849 (2014), quoting from *Board of Educ. v. Assessor of Worcester,* 368 Mass. 511, 513, 333 N.E.2d 450 (1975). The purpose of the recording statute is "to allow persons without actual knowledge to the contrary to rely upon registry records." *Moore v. Gerrity Co.,* 62 Mass.App. Ct. 522, 526, 818 N.E.2d 213 (2004). The enforceability of unrecorded deeds against the grantors, as well their heirs and devisees, is closely linked with the rationale for enforcing unrecorded deeds against those with actual knowledge—preventing fraud. . . . Interpreting the statute as Harold suggests would undermine the purpose of the statute, removing protection for grantees like Deborah who were uninvolved with the original conveyance and had no knowledge of it. That result cannot be what the Legislature intended in establishing the recording system.

Harold also argues that proper recording is not required for the July deed to be valid against Deborah because she had actual notice of the prior conveyance. This argument also fails. The burden of showing actual notice is on Harold. *Tramontozzi v. D'Amicis,* 344 Mass. 514, 517, 183 N.E.2d 295 (1962). Actual notice is to be "construed with considerable strictness [and mere] [k]nowledge of facts which would ordinarily put a party upon inquiry is not enough." *Ibid.,* quoting from *McCarthy v. Lane,* 301 Mass. 125, 128, 16 N.E.2d 683 (1938). Deborah did not know of the prior conveyance at the time the November deed was executed. Nor did she or any of her siblings who were beneficiaries of the Trust know of the prior conveyance to Harold at any point before Harold revealed its existence after Ethel's death, eight years later. Harold's argument that Deborah had knowledge by virtue of Ethel's knowledge is unavailing. The question we face is not whether the conveyance to Harold is valid against *Ethel,* but, rather, its validity against *Deborah*. Harold has not carried his burden of showing that Deborah had actual notice.[16]

. . .

Judgment affirmed.

Order denying postjudgment motions affirmed.

■ POINTS TO CONSIDER

1. **Patently defective acknowledgments.** The *Allen* and *Hildebrandt* courts disagree on the legal impact of a *latently* defective acknowledgment. Yet both courts agree that a *patently* defective acknowledgment does *not* act as constructive notice to later purchasers of interests in property. For example, imagine that a grantee records a deed but the acknowledgment block (date, name of notary, notary signature, and notary stamp) are left totally blank. These are obvious *patent* defects. If the grantee takes the deed to the county recorder's office, and the clerk records the deed, the clerk has committed an error. (We should not be surprised, though; these sorts of errors happen all the time.) A court will not deem a later purchaser to have constructive notice of a deed containing this patently defective acknowledgment.

   This result may seem odd to you. After all, a title searcher will see a recorded deed, whether or not the acknowledgment is obviously defective. A grantee's or title searcher's discovery of the deed when actively conducting a search will be deemed either actual notice of the deed, or at the least, inquiry notice that an effective prior transfer may have occurred. The question we address in this section is whether a grantee would have *constructive* notice of the prior deed, in the absence of a search. The rule—that a patently defective deed acknowledgment is not constructive notice to later grantees—serves public policy. This rule increases the likelihood that only genuine documents untouched by fraud make their way into the public records.

2. **Carefully follow the chain of events and find the "subsequent purchaser."** When working through recording act cases and problems, you should identify carefully each conveyance, one step at a time. Note the parties, the nature of the instrument, and whether and when the instrument was recorded. Who is the subsequent grantee in *Allen*? Does it matter that the subsequent grantee was not a subsequent *purchaser*?

---

[16] In his reply brief, Harold further argues that Deborah had actual notice because Ethel's knowledge of her prior conveyance to Harold should be attributed to Deborah given that Ethel also conveyed the property to herself and to Deborah as cotrustees. "Any issue raised for the first time in an appellant's reply brief comes too late, and we do not consider it." Pasquale v. Casale, 72 Mass.App.Ct. 729, 738, 893 N.E.2d 1263 (2008), quoting from Assessors of Boston v. Ogden Suffolk Downs, Inc., 398 Mass. 604, 608 n. 3, 499 N.E.2d 1200 (1986). Even if we considered this argument, it would fail. Even if the knowledge of one cotrustee can be attributed to other cotrustees in certain circumstances, we would not do so here, where the disputed knowledge pertains to an event that occurred before the cotrustee relationship began.

3. **The crucial question: What would Deborah have seen when checking the records?** Put yourself in Deborah's shoes. The trust received a deed to Ethel's house. Deborah could have completed a title search prior to accepting the conveyance. Is the flaw in the acknowledgment in the July 23, 2001 deed from Ethel to Harold, Jr. something that would pop out in a title search? Ethel signed the deed, but not in the presence of the notary. The notary then signed the acknowledgment affirming Ethel's presence. Is the inaccuracy in the acknowledgment something that Deborah could have reasonably discovered from just looking at the records? Does the rule adopted in *Allen* support or undermine the goals of recording system? Who was the lowest cost-avoider in this case? As we pointed out at the start of this section, *Allen* represents a minority rule.

4. **Reading between the lines.** Look carefully again at the parties in both the Problem (based on *Hildebrandt*) and in *Allen*. In each, we see a frustrated family member disputing the rights of siblings—George, Jr. in the Problem and Harold, Jr. in *Allen*. The two courts adopt opposing rules. Do the contrary positions taken by these two courts help or stymie George, Jr. and Harold, Jr.? What lesson do you take from this comparison? In cases such as *Hildebrandt* and *Allen*, we often see one member of the family alleging that a sibling has taken advantage of a parent. How does this dynamic surface in *Allen*?

5. Chain of Title

Imagine that you represent a prospective purchaser of real property. You will have a number of tasks to perform in connection with the purchase, but, as we have said previously, perhaps none is as important as determining whether seller is really the "owner." The seller shows you a valid and recorded deed by which the seller purchased the property. Will this be sufficient for you to give your client the "go ahead"? The answer is no. You must go further, and demonstrate to your client the following: that seller can trace his ownership, in an unbroken set of conveyancing documents, back a requisite period of time. Each "link"—that is, each period from one conveyance to the next—must be discoverable via a search of public records. This is the chain of title.

The concept of chain of title furthers twin goals: *efficiency* (reducing the time and money spent on title searches to that which is most likely to turn up defects in title), and *certainty* (allowing purchasers of title to proceed with their transactions, or refrain from closing, confident that they have made correct assumptions about the state of title).

In order to promote these goals, you will examine the period of ownership (the "link in the chain") for a predecessor in title starting at the date that person was conveyed title and ending at the point that predecessor in title conveyed his interest away and a deed reflecting this conveyance is recorded.

Think about chain of title in the context of a hypothetical. Assume that Olivia purchased Blackacre from Xander more than 50 years ago. Olivia recorded this deed. Pursuant to title standards (see our earlier discussion in this chapter), the local jurisdiction does not require title searches to extend past a deed establishing title more than 50 years before. The Xander to Olivia deed is therefore deemed the "root of title." Olivia conveyed her property by deed to Anderson, which deed was immediately recorded. Anderson then sold Blackacre to Bogart, who immediately recorded his deed. You represent Carlos, who is a prospective purchaser.

> ➤ Time 1: X to O (recorded, root of title)
> ➤ Time 2: O to A (recorded)
> ➤ Time 3: A to B (recorded)

If you search on Carlos's behalf, you would move backward in the grantee/grantor index and find an unbroken "chain" of conveyances ending in Xander. You would then begin to search forward; but between which dates would you search under each owner's name in the grantor/grantee index? Recall that in searching forward you may find unexpected conveyances (either of fee or something else, such as mortgages or easements). If you believe that the indexes are accurate, and you also believe in efficiency, you would search under each owner's name beginning at the point at which a person was conveyed her interest, and ending when she conveyed the property away and that conveyance was recorded.

To put it another way: why would you ever search the name of a person to see if he conveyed an easement in it, or disposed of the property, before that person even owned it?

a. Missing Links

Sometimes a search reveals that the chain ends in a "dead end." In other words, the search of the public records reflects that a predecessor in title was never actually conveyed a recorded interest. In other cases, the records appear complete to the title searcher, even though there are recorded documents "outside the chain."

i. Wild Deed. This is the easiest of scenarios. We will put it simply: if there is no record evidencing your seller's title, *don't buy.* Let's change the facts of our original example. Assume that in Time 2, Anderson purchased Blackacre from Olivia, but Anderson *failed to record.* Then in Time 3, Bogart purchased the property from Anderson, and Bogart did record. Your client Carlos wishes to purchase Blackacre, but instead of purchasing Blackacre from Bogart, Carlos signs a contract to purchase the property from *Olivia.*

> ➤ Time 1: X to O (recorded, root of title)
> ➤ Time 2: O to A (unrecorded)
> ➤ Time 3: A to B (recorded)

When conducting a title search for Carlos, will you discover the recorded Anderson to Bogart deed? The answer is no. You will not discover the Anderson to Bogart deed in the public records, even though it is recorded, because it is apparently unconnected to Olivia. You will search Olivia's name in the grantee/grantor index and find the Time 1 conveyance. Then you will search Olivia's name forward in the grantor/grantee index and find . . . nothing. The Anderson to Bogart deed is a "wild deed." It cannot impart constructive notice for a title search of Blackacre.

ii. Late-Recorded Deed. Let's modify the fact pattern and the parties. Assume that Olivia conveyed the property to Anderson in Time 1 by deed, but Anderson simply forgot to record his deed. In Time 2, Olivia conveyed the property again, even though she had already sold it to Anderson, this time to Bogart. Bogart was actually aware of the prior conveyance to Anderson, because Olivia told Bogart about the sale. Bogart recorded immediately. In Time 3, Anderson woke up and recorded his Time 1 deed from Olivia. In Time 4, Bogart conveys the property to Carlos, and Carlos immediately records. Who should win in a dispute between Carlos and Anderson?

> ➤ Time 1: O to A (deed not recorded)
> ➤ Time 2: O to B (deed recorded), with actual notice of O to A conveyance
> ➤ Time 3: A records Time 1 deed
> ➤ Time 4: B to C (deed recorded)

"Chain of title" is a concept. Chain of title suggests that documents are recorded if they are discoverable in the ordinary course of a search. In this case, the deed to Anderson was recorded before the conveyance to Carlos, so arguably Carlos should have constructive notice of that deed. However, would a title searcher for Carlos examine the grantor/grantee index under Olivia's name in Time 3 and find the deed to Anderson? Why would the title searcher do so? After all, it appears from the public records that Olivia conveyed the property to Bogart in Time 2. From that time on, the searcher would look under Bogart's name in the grantor index. Thus, even though Bogart was not a bona fide purchaser, Carlos would be.

iii. Early-Recorded Deed. The early-recorded deed is simply a variation of the transaction above, but in this scenario, one party records a deed *before* her predecessor-in-interest actually acquired the property:

> ➤ Time 1: Olivia conveys to Anderson (deed recorded)
> ➤ Time 2: Xander conveys to Olivia (deed recorded)

If we were to stop here, and resolve a dispute over ownership of the property between Olivia and Anderson, the courts will resolve the problem fairly easily. Courts apply an equitable doctrine known as *estoppel by deed* to protect Anderson. Equity treats that as done which ought to be done. In this case, assuming Olivia used a warranty deed when conveying to Anderson, Anderson would have the benefit of future warranties, including the warranty requiring Olivia to take steps to perfect Anderson's title. Presumably, Anderson would demand that Olivia take the step of recording a new deed conveying title to Anderson. For this reason, the law applies an equitable doctrine to estop Olivia from denying that she made the conveyance in Time 1. As between Olivia and Anderson, Anderson wins.

The real problem arises if in Time 3 *Olivia conveys to Bogart*, and Bogart and Anderson dispute title.

> Time 3: Olivia conveys to Bogart (deed recorded)

If you were in Bogart's shoes, and prior to purchasing property from Olivia you conducted a title search, would you have found the Time 1 deed from Olivia to Anderson? If you apply the reasoning of chain of title, the answer is a resounding no. Why is this so? Recall that the purpose of the county recorder offices is to allow an earlier purchaser of an interest in property to alert the world of his purchase. Has Olivia "put the world on notice"? Most courts would award ownership to Bogart, even if arguably there is constructive notice: Bogart purchased the property from Olivia after Anderson recorded his title. Anderson's deed is in the public records, but it is not really discoverable.

Early-Recorded Deed Scenario

The early-recorded deed scenario is not just a theoretical problem; it occurs in practice. *See, e.g.*, In re Heaver, 473 B.R. 734 (Bankr. N.D. Ill. 2012).

> Time 1: Borrower grants mortgage on Blackacre to Bank, mortgage recorded
> Time 2: O conveys Blackacre to Borrower, deed recorded
> Time 3: Borrower conveys Blackacre to A

Is Blackacre subject to the mortgage? What is A's argument?

We should make two points with respect to both early-recorded and late-recorded deeds. First, in each case the subsequent purchaser really is the more innocent of the parties. Look back at the initial early-recorded deed hypothetical. Anderson could have performed a title search and discovered that he was purchasing from an owner who did not have record title. There is no record, at the time that Anderson purchased his interest from Olivia, that Olivia owned anything. Similarly, with respect to the late-recorded deed, Anderson failed to record immediately when receiving his interest. We prefer, for policy reasons, to burden the party who can help avoid the dispute at the lowest cost. Treating the early-recorded and late-recorded deeds as not recorded—or at least as not imparting constructive notice—accomplishes this objective.

Second, these particular problems tend to disappear if the jurisdiction utilizes a tract index rather than grantee/grantor and grantor/grantee indexes. If a deed is recorded late, but is nevertheless identified in the tract file, then the subsequent purchaser will take with notice.

b. *Competing Chains of Title*

The "last man standing" often (but not always) wins disputes involving competing interests in property. This means that in a dispute between two individuals, each claiming a superior right in real property via a separate chain of title, the person who successfully occupies the position of "subsequent purchaser" is more likely to win.

■ PROBLEM: FINDING THE CHAIN OF TITLE

Bogart owns Lot 1 in Purgatory Heights. Consider the following set of events:

> ➤ Time 1: Bogart delivers a deed for Lot 1 to Anderson for $100,000. The deed shows Bogart as "Grantor" but leaves the name of "Grantee" blank. Anderson does not record this deed.
> ➤ Time 2: Bogart delivers a deed for Lot 1 to Sisk for $100,000. This deed correctly shows Bogart as "Grantor" and Sisk as "Grantee." Sisk does not record this deed.
> ➤ Time 3: Sisk delivers a deed for Lot 1 to Howe for $200,000. Howe records his deed.
> ➤ Time 4: Anderson fills his name into the Time 1 deed as "Grantee" and records.
> ➤ Time 5: Sisk records his Time 2 deed from Bogart.

Howe brings an action to quiet title against Anderson to determine the true owner of Lot 1. Assume that this is a race-notice jurisdiction. Who should win?

The first step to finding an answer to the problem is to identify the subsequent purchaser. Recall that the race-notice statute only protects purchasers who took without notice of an earlier transfer and recorded first. Is Anderson the subsequent purchaser, or is it Howe? Howe acquired a deed to Lot 1 in Time 3, and Anderson apparently did so in Time 1, so we would assume that Howe is the subsequent purchaser. This is the best answer.

However, in a well-known case, Board of Educ. of Minneapolis v. Hughes, 136 N.W. 1095 (Minn. 1912), the court held, under essentially the same facts, that Anderson was the subsequent purchaser! The court explained that Anderson became a purchaser when he filled his name in the deed. This is not a good rule, and other courts might reach a different result. Why should they do so? Most courts would say that conveyance occurs when money changes hands. In the problem, Anderson paid his $100,000 in Time 1. If the court considers Howe to be the subsequent purchaser, who wins under a race-notice statute?

c. Deeds from a Common Grantor

As we will discuss in Chapter 11, developers often create restrictions on property called "covenants" to create a uniform and harmonious neighborhood. The covenants might cover everything from the permissible uses of the property (e.g., single-family residential use only), to aesthetic issues (e.g., the appearance and size of any buildings). In modern developments, developers commonly create a set of restrictions when they subdivide the property into lots. Developers record this "declaration of covenants, conditions, and restrictions" contemporaneously with a plat map, showing the location of lots. This declaration thus becomes part of the chain of title of every lot in the subdivision.

However, some developers, especially in older subdivisions, did not record a declaration, but rather just included the covenants in individual deeds granted to lot purchasers. This method works, as long as the developer places the same restrictions in each deed. Consider the following problem, though:

◼ PROBLEM: RESTRICTIONS IN DEEDS FROM A DEVELOPER

> **2020**: Bogart develops "Bogartville Estates," a 300-lot residential subdivision.
> **2021**: Bogart conveys Lots 1-8 to eight purchasers. In each warranty deed, Bogart restricts the use of the lots to "residential purposes only" and specifically prohibits "professional office use."
> **2022**: Bogart conveys Lot 9 to Anderson by warranty deed. This deed contains the following restriction: "Lot 9 is hereby restricted to residential and not professional use; *Grantor hereby imposes on all remaining lots owned by Grantor the identical restriction that such lots will be used for residential and not professional purposes.*"
> **2023**: Bogart conveys Lots 10-20 to 11 purchasers with the same deed restrictions as Lots 1-8.
> **2024**: Bogart conveys Lot 21 to Sisk. The deed does not contain any restrictions on use.

> ➤ **2025**: Sisk begins using the property for his accounting practice. The neighbors complain to Bogart about the additional traffic and parked cars. Bogart notifies Sisk that he is in violation of the covenants restricting his property, and Sisk replies, "What covenants? There was no restriction in my deed."

Assume that you represent Sisk. Must he cease operating his professional accounting practice out of his home? In a normal title search, would Sisk discover and examine the mutual restriction in the 2022 deed to Anderson? Would it make sense to require him to find such restrictions? If your answer is yes, what are the implications for the scope of title searching? *See* Guillette v. Daly Dry Wall, Inc., 325 N.E.2d 572 (Mass. 1975).

Your first answer may be that Sisk would not see the restriction applying to all remaining lots of Bogart (including Lot 21). After all, in a title search, Sisk would have no reason to search the title to lots other than his own. Nevertheless, some courts follow the Massachusetts view (forcefully defended in *Guillette*) that restrictions in prior deeds out from a common grantor are part of the purchaser's chain of title. The doctrine appears to be limited to properties owned by the common grantor that are related, such as those in a subdivision. Other courts reject this expanded version of the chain of title, fearing the burden that this requirement would place on title searchers. *See, e.g.,* Spring Lakes, Ltd. v. O.F.M. Co., 467 N.E.2d 537 (Ohio 1984). Which do you think is the better view?

ATTEMPTS TO IMPROVE CERTAINTY OF TITLE: TORRENS REGISTRATION AND MARKETABLE TITLE ACTS

The quality of title assurance in the United States varies—state by state and county by county. Most states employ a combination of recording statutes and searching mechanisms that have existed, often unchanged, for decades, if not longer. A few jurisdictions provide tract indexes as an alternative to traditional grantee/grantor and grantor/grantee indexes. Some county recorder's offices have invested in computerized searching mechanisms; these have improved the efficiency and certainty of title investigation. However, this development has come about haltingly. To further complicate matters, some jurisdictions provide that mis-indexed documents are constructive notice to subsequent purchasers, even if no competent title searcher would discover them. As a result, we are left with a hodge-podge of title assurance practice and law.

As we have seen, title to land is made marketable by the use of title insurance, title opinions, and abstracting. However, one could clearly imagine more efficient systems. Indeed, scholars have dreamed of the day in which title to real property might be transferred as cheaply and speedily as the transfer of title to an automobile.

Whether that day will ever arrive is open to question, but efforts at dramatically reducing the cost of ascertaining title have been implemented in the United States, with varying success. We will spend just a little time with a couple of these measures: Torrens registration and the marketable title acts.

1. Torrens Registration

What if title to land were like title to cars? If you have ever sold your automobile, then you have "signed over" your title certificate to your buyer. The buyer will submit that certificate (in accordance with particular state rules and laws) to the Department of Motor Vehicles and receive a new certificate with the buyer's name on it. Generally speaking, your purchaser can be assured that she has good title to the car because the certificate is a state-registered document; there can be only one owner of the car at a time.

Similarly, if you owned a home and the land on which it sits, and possessed a "certificate" of title that could be transferred, then presumably title searching as we know it would be a thing of the past. The transaction costs associated with selling property would fall, and purchasers would obtain greater certainty in title they purchased.

An Australian politician, Richard Torrens, conceived of this type of title system to real property in the mid-1800s. His idea was a success, first in Australia, and then throughout the British Empire.

However, U.S. jurisdictions have been much less welcoming of Torrens registration. Here is the reason: A system of title registration must have a starting point. Each title must be recognized by the state so that a certificate can be issued. *To do so, Torrens registration requires the property owner to bring a lawsuit to determine the ownership of property.* The lawsuit is essentially a suit to quiet title provided by Torrens statute. This registration of title fixes initial ownership. If there are competing claims, as is often the case, then one or more parties will see their interests diminished or destroyed. Due process requires that anyone with an interest in the real property have an opportunity to assert and defend her claim. This means that every "registered" parcel of land has, as its root of title, a lawsuit. As you can imagine, this is an expensive process. The end-product of the Torrens suit is a court judgment declaring the true owner of real property. The property owner then submits this judgment to the state for registration, and a certificate follows.

Fewer than ten states have Torrens statutes today, and it appears that these statutes are used only in a very few places, including Hennepin County, Minnesota (essentially Minneapolis), Cook County, Illinois (Chicago), and Hawaii. *See* Stoebuck & Whitman, The Law of Property §11.15, at 923-25 (3d ed. 2000). The idea of Torrens registration is attractive; costs are the problem. The states that adopted Torrens registration statutes do not pay for the title lawsuits that underpin registration. *Property owners bear this burden.* Nor did states and counties appropriate money to help with the bureaucratic costs associated with transferring title from the normal index system to the Torrens registration model.

Torrens registration continues to have both detractors and proponents. *See, e.g.,* John V. Orth, *Torrens Title in North Carolina—Maybe a Hundred Years Is Long Enough*, 39 Campbell L. Rev. 271, 286 (2017); Kimball Foster, *Certificate of Possessory Title: A Sensible Addition to Minnesota's Successful Torrens System*, 40 Wm. Mitchell L. Rev. 112 (2013).

> **Query:** Why do you think that policy makers and legislators believed that property owners would invest time and money with Torrens suits and registration? What economic principle does the failure of property owners to employ Torrens, where available, seem to implicate?

Today, computerization of records is beginning to allow for at least some of the efficiencies that scholars had hoped would be afforded by Torrens registration. Although technology has come slowly to American title assurance, the world of the internet is encroaching inexorably into county recorders' offices. This has lessened the need and the demand for Torrens registration. *See* John L. McCormack, *Torrens and Recording: Land Title Assurance in the Computer Age*, 18 Wm. Mitchell L. Rev. 61 (1992).

2. Marketable Title Acts

Torrens registration represents an attempt to replace the existing system of title searching and assurance of title based on public records with a new system of title registration. If this process has failed to gain significant traction in the United States, it may be due not only to cost, but also to a general entrenched notion among lawyers and real estate professionals about how title should be ascertained and transferred. To be blunt, lawyers are used to doing things a certain way, and scholars who have pushed for Torrens have been tilting at a windmill. If so, then one might expect a less radical attempt to garner more success. This is in fact the case. Twenty jurisdictions have adopted legislation known as marketable title acts, intended to provide both certainty of title and a more limited title search.

The Minnesota Marketable Title Act provides:

> As against a claim of title based upon a source of title, which source has then been of record at least 40 years, no action affecting the possession or title of any real estate shall be commenced by a person, partnership, corporation, other legal entity, state, or any political division thereof, to enforce any right, claim, interest, incumbrance, or lien founded upon any instrument, event or transaction which was executed or occurred more than 40 years prior to the commencement of such action, unless within 40 years after such execution or occurrence there has been recorded in the office of the county recorder in the county in which the real estate affected is situated, a notice sworn to by the claimant or the claimant's agent or attorney setting forth the

name of the claimant, a description of the real estate affected and of the instrument, event or transaction on which such claim is founded, and stating whether the right, claim, interest, incumbrance, or lien is mature or immature.

Minn. Stat. §541.023 (2018).

Marketable title acts extinguish older property interests, limiting the search period. Most of these acts choose a time period of somewhere between 30 and 50 years. Conn. Gen. Stat. §47-33b(e) (2017) (40 years); Iowa Code §614.31 (2019) (40 years); Fla. Stat. §712.02 (2018) (30 years).

Marketable title acts exist side-by-side with traditional recording statutes. These acts eliminate certain older claims that would otherwise detract from marketable title. In other words, marketable title acts treat these older defects in title as though they magically evaporated. Interests not terminated by the marketable title act (either because the owner of the interest preserves the interests with a filing, or because the interests are within the root of title) remain subject to the ordinary operation of the recording statutes.

The key to marketable title acts is the concept of the "root of title." An individual contemplating a purchase of property will be required to examine seller's chain of title records back to the root of title. *The root of title for any particular chain of title will be the most recent deed that transfers fee simple at or prior to the time period established by the statute.*

Consider the following example: Daniel Bogart intends to purchase real property from Jerry Anderson in a jurisdiction with a 40-year marketable title act. If, on January 1, 2020, you were to search public records for a 60-year period (whether grantee/grantor or tract indexes), you would see the following:

> ➢ **January 1, 1960**: Mavis to Helga (deed of fee)
> ➢ **January 1, 1965**: Helga to Franklin (easement)
> ➢ **December 25, 1978**: Helga to Jerry (deed of fee)

The root of title will be the first conveyance that is at least 40 years from the date of search; this would be the December 25, 1978 deed from Helga to Jerry. The searcher need not consider the January 1, 1960 conveyance from Mavis to Helga or the January 1, 1965 easement from Helga to Franklin. Those instruments are irrelevant, because they pre-date the root of title. The marketable title act is considerably more powerful than a title standard. In many jurisdictions, title searchers are deemed to have performed a competent search if they limit the search to a period designated by the title standard (often around 40 years). However, a title standard only helps insulate the searcher from liability by trying to define what constitutes "marketable" title a buyer should accept. It does not extinguish older interests. The marketable title act *extinguishes* the older interests.

The actual mechanism for protecting subsequent purchasers under the marketable title acts varies depending on the jurisdiction. In some, the act affirmatively states that a record owner who meets the requirements of the act has marketable title. In others, it is a bit more indirect; these jurisdictions provide a statute of limitations that bars claims that reach back before the period designated by the statute. The result is the same, however, as the subsequent purchaser who can show a chain of title within the confines of the act is "safe" from old but otherwise valid interests. Thus, the January 1, 1965 easement in the example above would have had continuing vitality in jurisdictions without a marketable title act (although a searcher might not be required to search and find the easement if that instrument was older than the title standard). *However, in a marketable title act jurisdiction, the easement is simply gone—"poof"!* Keep in mind the usual common law rule that easements are not terminated by mere non-use. The marketable title act undermines this common law rule, at least as to easements that precede the root of title.

If the rationale for the marketable title act is to shorten the period of a title search and to increase certainty of title for those individuals contemplating purchasing property or an interest in property, how would you answer the following problems?

■ PROBLEM: ROOT OF TITLE INSTRUMENT IS A FORGERY

> ➤ Jane intends to purchase real property from Daniel in a jurisdiction with a 40-year marketable title act. Jane performs a public records search on January 1, 2020.
> ➤ The search reveals a deed from Bill to Daniel recorded on January 1, 1978. The records also show Bill received title to the property in a deed from Jerry, recorded January 1, 1969.
> ➤ Jane purchases the property from Daniel on February 1, 2020.
> ➤ Jerry brings an action to quiet title claiming that the January 1,1969 deed was a total forgery (and has indisputable proof to back up this claim).

Who has title to the property, Jerry or Jane? *See* City of Miami v. St. Joe Paper Co., 364 So. 2d 439 (Fla. 1978). *See generally*, William B. Stoebuck & Dale A. Whitman, The Law of Property §11.12, at 903 (3d ed. 2000).

■ PROBLEM: TWO CHAINS OF TITLE

> ➤ James intends to purchase from Daniel property in a jurisdiction with a 40-year marketable title act.
> ➤ James performs a title search on January 1, 2020.
> ➤ The search reveals that Ed conveyed title to Daniel, by deed dated and recorded on October 1, 1978.
> ➤ James purchases the property on February 1, 2020.

> ➤ Ann brings an action to quiet title. Ann asserts that she purchased the property by deed dated and recorded January 1, 1969, from Wendy, and that Wendy purchased the property from Vivian by deed dated and recorded January 1, 1955 (these deeds do in fact exist in the public records).

As between Ann and James, who has title? On what basis do we choose the winner? *Compare* Roberts v. Feitz, 933 N.E.2d 456 (Ind. Ct. App. 2010) and Exchange Nat'l Bank v. Lawndale Nat'l Bank, 243 N.E. 2d 193 (Ill.1968).

To see the significance of the marketable title act, consider its impact on one of the most basic title problems (one that we have already seen): the wild deed. In a marketable title act jurisdiction, a wild deed of sufficient age (one that serves as the root of title) *may actually establish title. See* Esterholdt v. Pacificorp, 301 P.3d 1086, 1091 (Wyo. 2013) ("We cannot find anything in the Act that suggests that a wild deed cannot be the root of title for a contestant in a controversy under the Act. In fact, such an interpretation would render the methodology of the Act pointless.") This stands in stark contrast to the normal treatment of a wild deed by the recording statutes.

Curative Acts and Other Title-Clearing Statutes

Marketable title acts do not stand alone as statutes intended to shorten search periods and improve the certainty of title. Many states maintain curative acts that fix formality issues, such as inadequate acknowledgments, in deeds and other instruments. Other statutes terminate specific types of very old instruments, such as mortgages.

The marketable title act works effectively, but it does not wipe out all interests that precede the root of title. Marketable title acts typically protect governmental interests. Furthermore, some versions of the act permit the holders of old interests to keep those interests alive, either by rerecording the interests, or by filing a notice of intent to keep the interests alive. In addition, interests that pre-date the root of title are not terminated if the interests are referenced in another instrument that would be found in the chain of title within the statutory period.

Recall the initial fact pattern that we presented in the material on marketable title acts:

> ➤ **January 1, 1960**: Mavis to Helga (deed of fee)
> ➤ **January 1, 1965**: Helga to Franklin (easement)
> ➤ **December 25, 1978**: Helga to Jerry (deed of fee)

We said that a purchaser of the property in January of 2020 would take the property free and clear of the January 1, 1965 easement. Assume one additional fact—that the December 25, 1978 deed contained the following language: "Grantor hereby conveys the fee to grantee, subject to the easement created by Helga and recorded January 1, 1965." The reference to the easement is made in the root of title instrument and would be found in a search. The easement survives.

SUMMARY

- Documents transferring interests in land may be recorded in county recorders' offices and other public offices, such as probate courts; the status of title may be revealed by a search of these records.
- The primary indexing systems for recorded title instruments are the *grantee/grantor* and *grantor/grantee* indexes. Some jurisdictions use *tract* indexes.
- A search of the grantee/grantor and grantor/grantee indexes takes the searcher backward to the root of title, and then forward to discover any other conveyances, including easements, mortgages, or other encumbrances.
- Parties record documents in order to perfect a superior interest in property; they are encouraged to do so by *recording statutes*.
- Recording statutes protect subsequent purchasers of interests from prior unrecorded interests.
- There are three types of recording statutes: *race*, *notice*, and *race-notice*: (1) *race statutes* protect the first grantee to properly record an interest; (2) *notice statutes* protect subsequent purchasers who take without notice of a prior conveyance; and (3) *race-notice statutes* only protect subsequent purchasers against prior conveyances, if the subsequent purchaser records first and takes without notice at the time of payment.
- There are three categories of notice: *actual*, *constructive*, and *inquiry*.
- *Constructive notice* arises because a document affecting title is publicly recorded.
- *Inquiry notice* arises when a subsequent purchaser would reasonably suspect the existence of a prior conveyance.
- Inquiry notice may arise from a *reference in the record* to a prior conveyance, or from *surrounding circumstances*, such as occupancy of the property by a person other than the record owner.
- Many courts consider documents affecting title to be recorded when accepted by the county recorder, even if they are not properly indexed.
- Documents affecting interests in real property must be notarized and must meet other formality requirements in order to be recorded.
- A recorded document affecting title to real property with a *patent* defect in the acknowledgment does not constitute constructive notice to later purchasers.
- Many, but not all courts permit a recorded instrument with a *latent* defect in the acknowledgment to constitute constructive notice to later purchasers of an interest in the property.
- Some of the most difficult recording problems involve the chain of title, and include the wild deed, the early-recorded deed, and the late-recorded deed.
- The chain of title may include restrictions in deeds from a *common grantor*, even if the deed to the property in question does not actually contain the restriction. This typically arises because the common grantor has developed a subdivision.

- Jurisdictions have attempted to improve on the title search system by adopting either Torrens registration or marketable title acts, although the latter have been more successful.

- *Torrens registration* requires a lawsuit to produce a certificate of title; *marketable title acts* limit the title search to a relatively recent root of title.

- In marketable title jurisdictions, owners of old easements, mortgages, and other encumbrances may keep these alive by *recording a notice of intent* to do so in the chain of title, or rerecording their interests.

- In marketable title jurisdictions, encumbrances and deeds that pre-date the root-of-title deed are ineffective, with the exception of instruments referenced in instruments recorded after the root of title and certain interests, such as those owned by the government, specifically excepted by the acts.

The Loan Transaction

> "I know exactly who I am talking to, Mr. Croker." Croker's voice was low and strong, but Harry's high grinding whine cut through it. "I'm talking to an individual who owes this bank half a billion dollars and six other banks and two insurance companies two hundred and eighty-five million more, that's who I am talking to. And you know, there's an old saying here in Atlanta, too, and that saying is 'Money talks, and b******t walks,' and the time has come to talk with money, Mr. Croker."
>
> —*Tom Wolfe, A Man in Full 48 (1998)*

A INTRODUCTION

Some people have money, others need money (often to buy things they otherwise cannot afford). Of course, the problem is that the people with money do not usually like to part with it. It is from this continuous dynamic that the loan transaction is born. A lender will part with money only because it expects to be repaid by the borrower, with interest. Unfortunately, the lender cannot know with certainty that the borrower will pay back the loan. To ensure repayment, the lender will insist that the borrower provide collateral for the loan. *Collateral* is property of one form or another that is pledged to the lender as security in the event the borrower does not repay the loan.

The loan transaction can exist in a huge array of scenarios. Consider a person charged with a crime and sent to jail to await trial. The defendant may arrange for a bail bondsman to provide the necessary money to make bail and secure a release pending trial. Of course, this is just a loan. The defendant must repay the loan, with interest. If the defendant skips town, then the bail bondsman will take the collateral (it may be a house, a car, or just about anything else) as repayment, and then send a bounty hunter to locate the defendant.

As a text for a first-year Property course, this book focuses upon loans secured by real property. This chapter connects directly to material in the preceding chapter on the real estate transaction. The loan may be necessary for the purchase of real property.

In this chapter, we will examine the two basic documents that, taken together, comprise the loan transaction: the promissory note, which is the promise to pay back the loan by a certain date, with interest; and the mortgage, which encumbers the real property with a security interest. It is important to distinguish carefully between the promissory note, which is a creature of contract law, and the mortgage, which is a creature of property law. A different set of legal issues attaches to the operation and enforcement of each of these two documents. However, our primary focus will be the mortgage.

The loan may extend well beyond the closing date for the purchase and sale transaction, often as long as 30 years in the residential context. If things go well, the loan ends when the borrower makes final payment. If things go poorly, the loan ends when the borrower defaults on payments and the lender forecloses its lien on the real property (and perhaps takes personal property of the borrower).

The Loan Transaction Timeline

- Lender Commits to Issue Loan via Loan Commitment Letter
- Lender Performs Due Diligence—Examines Borrower's Financials and Appraises Collateral
- Lender Performs Title Search—Often Combined with Borrower/Purchaser's Title Search
- Closing—Lender Disburses Money, Existing Mortgage Loans Paid Off and Documents (Mortgage and Note) Executed and Delivered
- If Things Go Well—Borrower Pays Loan and Lender Executes Accord and Satisfaction of Mortgage
- If Things Go Badly—Borrower Defaults and Lender Forecloses, or Takes Steps Just Short of Foreclosure, Including Acceptance of "Deed in Lieu"

The loan transaction therefore creates an ongoing relationship between borrower and lender, and depending on the duration of the promissory note, this relationship may go on for many years. Relationships, in life and in business, place obligations on the parties. We will examine what the loan relationship means to both the borrower and the lender.

B   HISTORY AND TERMINOLOGY

Loan transactions have existed in "civilized" society for a very long time. Romans permitted loans and interest. The English common law, however, on which our mortgage law is based, originally forbade lenders from charging interest. The law was heavily influenced by religion, and the Church declared interest to be sinful usury. In the feudal system, in which only a few people owned land via the Crown, there was a limited demand for individuals to borrow money and even more limited ability of individuals to pledge any collateral. Wealth was tied to real property, and given that England is an island, real property stayed in the hands of a few. There was no market to speak of for real property. However, as a mercantile class in England grew, the need for money to finance transactions grew with it. The modern world is an entirely different place; loans are made routinely. But some of the older religiously based rules quietly persist, such as the stricture against usury, described below.

The Mantra

Lawyers often say: "The note evidences the loan, and the mortgage secures it."

The *promissory note* is the written contract that memorializes the loan and the obligation of the borrower to repay. It contains payment terms and dates for payment. If a borrower defaults by failing to make a payment, then the lender may enforce the contract in the form of a lawsuit and pursue the assets of the borrower in satisfaction of the debt, as in any other breach of contract case. The borrower makes a promise to repay the loan and is therefore a *promisor*. The borrower makes this promise to the lender, and the lender is therefore called the *promisee*.

A *mortgage* secures the loan. Assume that Bill borrows $100,000 from Lisa and signs a promissory note requiring him to repay the loan in 360 equal monthly installments (in other words, Bill has a 30-year period to repay). Assume further that Bill fails to make payments for the first three months of the fifth year of the loan. If the only document that Lisa has in her possession from Bill is the promissory note, then Lisa will be forced to bring a traditional lawsuit against Bill for repayment. This suit requires Lisa to serve a complaint, to present evidence of Bill's default, and to otherwise engage Bill, as defendant, as she would in any other lawsuit. All Lisa wants is her money back, but she will be forced to wait, and litigate, if she wishes to succeed. Moreover, the promissory note would not prevent Bill from selling the property to someone else and spending the sale proceeds, so that by the time Lisa wins the suit he could be "judgment proof," i.e., have no assets Lisa could attach to satisfy the promissory note obligation.

A *mortgage* allows Lisa to circumvent this process and ensure that the real property will not be sold without satisfying the debt. A mortgage provides Lisa with the right to take real property in satisfaction of the defaulted note quickly and prior to a suit on the note. In addition, it ensures that, regardless of what other assets Bill may have, the lender will always be able to claim the real property to satisfy the debt.

The mortgage conveys an interest in real property—the right to take title—and therefore must satisfy the Statute of Frauds. This right is known as a *lien*. If Lisa enforces her mortgage, we say that she is *foreclosing* her lien. Lisa is referred to as the *mortgagee*, because she has taken a mortgage on the property, and Bill is referred to as the *mortgagor*, because he has mortgaged his property to Lisa.

C   THE PROMISSORY NOTE—THE WRITTEN OBLIGATION TO REPAY

The promissory note is a contract. Like any other contract, it must identify the parties and consideration, and describe the obligations to be performed. It must be signed by the party against whom it is to be enforced. The borrower signs the promissory note; the lender does not. The key terms for the note are the amount borrowed, the duration of payment, and the interest rate. A court is likely to hold a note unenforceable if it is missing one of these key terms. In addition, the promissory note will describe what events constitute an event of default and the lender's remedy for default. In some real estate loans, the promissory note will reference the mortgage and the collateral.

Here is a simple promissory note:

PROMISSORY NOTE

$_____   City, State
                                              _____, 20_____

FOR VALUE RECEIVED, _____, an _____ ("Borrower"), promises to pay to the order of _____, an _____ ("Lender"), its successors or assigns, at its office at _____, the principal sum of _____ Dollars ($_____) together with interest on the principal balance as provided herein.

This Note shall be amortized over a period of _____ (_____) months, with interest on the principal balance remaining unpaid from time to time accruing from the date hereof at the rate of _____ percent (_____%) per annum, without relief from valuation or appraisement laws. Monthly payment of principal and interest in the amount of _____ Dollars ($_____) shall commence on the 1st day of _____, 20_____, and shall be due and payable on the 1st day of each month thereafter for ___ ____ (_____) additional consecutive months. The entire unpaid principal balance, along with all accrued interest and other amounts due under this Note, shall be due and payable on the 1st day of _____, 20_____ (the "Maturity Date").

All payments shall be applied first to the payment of all accrued and unpaid interest and the balance, if any, shall be applied to the reduction of the outstanding principal balance of this Note. All or any portion of the unpaid principal and unpaid and accruing interest on this Note may be pre-paid by Borrower at any time, without penalty for prepayment, by a payment to Lender in immediately available dollars.

At the option of Lender, all obligations hereunder shall become immediately due and payable without notice or demand upon the occurrence of any of the following events (each an "Event of Default"): (i) any default in the payment of this Note and the failure to cure such default within ten (10) days of the date payment is due; (ii) death, dissolution, termination of existence, insolvency, business failure, the filing of a petition in bankruptcy or for the appointment of a receiver of any part of the property of Borrower or any member of Borrower, or any assignment for the benefit or creditors by or against Borrower or any member of Borrower; (iii) upon the Borrower filing, or having filed against it, a petition in bankruptcy or for reorganization or arrangement or for the appointment of a receiver or trustee of all or a portion of the Borrower's property, or if the Borrower makes an assignment for the benefit of creditors.

Presentment for payment, notice of dishonor, protest and notice of protest are hereby waived by Borrower and any and all others who may at any time become liable for the payment of all or any part of this obligation. This Note shall be the joint and several obligation of all Borrowers and endorsers, and shall be binding upon them and their heirs, personal representatives, successors and assigns.

No delay or omission on the part of Lender in the exercise of any right or remedy shall operate as a waiver thereof, and no single or partial exercise by Lender of any right or remedy shall preclude other or further exercise thereof or of any other right or remedy.

Borrower agrees to pay all costs of collection, including all attorneys' fees, in case the principal of this Note or any payment on the principal or any interest thereon is not paid by any applicable due date, and to pay all costs, including attorneys' fees, in the event it becomes necessary to protect the security hereof, regardless of whether suit be brought, all without relief from valuation or appraisement laws or Lender may at Lender's option elect to add said attorneys' fees and expenses to the principal balance of said obligations.

Notwithstanding any provision herein or in any instrument now or hereafter securing this Note, the total liability for payments in the nature of interest shall not exceed the limits now imposed by the usury laws of the State of _____.

The rights and remedies of Lender, whether provided for in this Note, the Letter of Credit, or the Guaranty or otherwise available to Lender at law or in equity, shall be cumulative and concurrent, and may be pursued singly, successively, or together.

The indebtedness evidenced by this Note was originated, negotiated, and consummated within the State of _____; all payment, repayment, and performance of the terms and obligations of this Note shall take place within the State of _____, and the laws of the State of _____ shall control and apply.

Time shall be of the essence with respect to all of Borrower's obligations hereunder.

Executed and delivered this _____ day of _____, 20_____.

"Borrower"

_____,

an _____

Signature:_____

Name:_____

Title:_____

Consider a few aspects of this promissory note:

Default. What happens if the borrower fails to make a payment when due? Is the borrower immediately in default? Notice the "acceleration" clause—in the event of default, may the lender go after the entire debt or just the portion then due?

Authority to sign. Assume that Nine Princes Corporation borrows $1 million from Big Bank to purchase real estate. Who should sign the promissory note? If you represented Big Bank, what would you want to know prior to accepting the promissory note?

Place yourself in the shoes of the lender for a moment. No doubt, you want the borrower to repay the loan. But the point of the promissory note is that it makes your borrower personally liable on the debt. If the borrower fails to repay, you may sue your borrower for the debt. Once you win your judgment, you become a judgment creditor and you will be able to pursue any of the borrower's nonexempt personal assets in satisfaction of the debt. This is in addition to any rights accorded by the mortgage, discussed below.

Practice Tip: Non-Recourse Loans

Some loans are "non-recourse." This means that the lender agrees that, if the borrower fails to repay the loan, the lender will be limited to taking the mortgaged property and will not pursue the personal assets of the debtor. The borrower will pay additional consideration at the outset of the loan to obtain "non-recourse status." *See* Gregory M. Stein, *The Scope of the Borrower's Liability in a Nonrecourse Real Estate Loan*, 55 Wash. & Lee L. Rev. 1207 (1998). The promissory note may therefore contain language that makes the loan non-recourse. Here is an example of one such provision:

> *Nonrecourse.* Borrower has no personal liability under this Note. Lender's rights and remedies shall be limited to the Collateral. If Lender obtains a judgment under this Note, Lender may enforce it only against the Collateral.

Usury; Borrower Protection

A loan that requires payment at an interest rate higher than the maximum specified by state law is called *usurious*. Usury laws are provided either in a state's statutes or in the state constitution. *See* Cal. Const. art. XV, §1; Tenn. Const. art. XI, §7, both setting the maximum interest at 10 percent. These laws serve a public policy that assumes, as one court put it, that "desperately poor people" will sign notes on unconscionable terms, because they have no choice. *See* Schneider v. Phelps, 359 N.E.2d 1361, 1365 (N.Y. 1977). In other words, individuals of little means who need access to cash will sometimes agree to outrageous repayment terms. State usury laws are not uniform. States that maintain laws against usury define it differently and penalize the activities in a variety of ways. Usury leads not only to civil actions, but in some states, to criminal actions as well.

Imagine that you borrowed money from Anderson. He charged a rate you think may be usurious. You may have also provided Anderson with a mortgage on real property as collateral. Your allegation that the loan is usurious may arise at one of two times. You may take pre-emptive action by bringing a lawsuit alleging a violation of usury law prior to going into default on the promissory note, and therefore before his attempt to foreclose on his mortgage lien. It is also possible that you will fail to pay, and as a result Anderson will declare you in default and initiate foreclosure proceedings. You may bring your usury suit at this moment as well, or raise it as a defense to a foreclosure action.

The borrower's *remedy* will vary significantly by state.

- In some states, the lender is permitted to collect interest up to the maximum amount provided by law. In those states, it is as though the court rewrites the promissory note to reflect a lower interest rate.
- Other states require the payment of principal only.
- Less than a handful of states maintain the oldest of rules and cancel the borrower's obligation to pay back the loan obligation altogether. *See* Conn. Gen. Stat. §37-8 (2017); N.Y. Gen. Oblig. §5-511 (McKinney 2012 & Supp. 2018). *See also* Haworth v. Dieffenbach, 38 A.3d 1203 (Conn. App. Ct. 2012), and Behette v. Grant, 820 N.Y.S.2d 841 (N.Y. Sup. Ct. 2005).

Which remedy do you think is most appropriate? Should it depend on the circumstances?

Federal law regulating loans pre-empts state usury laws with respect to most first mortgages on residential real estate. Depository Institutions Deregulation and Monetary Control Act of 1980, 12 U.S.C. §1735f-7. However, state usury laws are still applicable to second or third loans on residential property, and to commercial loans. In addition, states were allowed to "opt out" of the federal standards, and 15 states did so. *See* Donald C. Lampe, *Federal Preemption and the Future of Mortgage Loan Regulation*, 59 Bus. Law. 1207, 1210 n.22 (2004).

Sometimes usury issues arise in the context of variable rate loans. Recall from Chapter 7 that real property loans come in many flavors. Some are *fixed rate*—meaning that the interest rate stays the same over the life of the loan. Other loans are *adjustable rate*—meaning that at some point during the term the loan "resets" at a different, usually higher, interest rate.

■ PROBLEM: ADJUSTABLE RATE LOANS AND USURY

Bob is a newly minted lawyer and has opened his own law practice. He has a modest income but expects to see his income rise as his law practice (hopefully) flourishes. Bob purchases a small commercial building to use as his office. He finances his purchase with a $100,000 loan from Lender Bank, signing a variable rate promissory note and a mortgage covering the property. The promissory note requires Bob to repay Lender Bank the $100,000 in 120 monthly installments. This is therefore a ten-year loan. Interest for the first 84 months is set at 6 percent. The interest rate will reset in the 85th month (the first month of the eighth year of the loan) at 2 points above the then-published Prime Rate.

As a result of rapid changes in the economy, interest rates zoom upward in the seventh year of the loan; inflation is a severe problem in the market. Interest rates for commercial loans now commonly run at 9 percent. The Prime Rate at the time the interest rate resets is 8.5 percent. The loan therefore resets for the last three years at 10.5 percent. The state constitution sets a usury level at a flat interest rate of 10 percent. Bob does a quick calculation and determines that, over the life of the loan, the interest rate will average below 10 percent.

Bob asks for your advice. *See, e.g.,* Norstar Bank v. Pickard & Anderson, 529 N.Y.S. 2d 667 (N.Y. App. Div. 1988).

Take a look at the simple promissory note reprinted earlier in this chapter. Is it likely that a loan transaction that uses that form of promissory note will be usurious?

D   THE MORTGAGE—THE PLEDGE OF COLLATERAL

Back to Future Interests

The original mortgage was really just a deed granting title to the lender, while giving the borrower a right in the future to retake possession. It was an early form of a fee simple subject to condition subsequent (in which the full payment on Law Day gave the borrower a right of entry) or a fee simple determinable (in which the full payment on Law Day automatically gave the borrower the right of possession).

In fourteenth- and fifteenth-century England, when loans were rare, a borrower would not simply pledge his real property as collateral. Instead, the borrower would convey the property by deed to the lender. The deed would contain a future interest (either a right of entry or a possibility of reverter), or at least the lender would covenant to reconvey the property upon payment of the debt. In the event that the borrower repaid the loan, the borrower would be able to retake title. The date set for repayment was called *Law Day*.

However, the borrower often failed to have the necessary cash on the date set for repayment of his loan. Under the terms of the conveyance, this meant his right to the property was terminated. Left with no remedy "at law," the borrower would approach the Chancellor and request that the Chancellor act in equity to allow the borrower additional time to pay. If the borrower could come up with the cash, the borrower would be allowed to reclaim his property. Borrowers found a friend in the court of equity; the practice of granting an extension became common by the end of the seventeenth century. This right is still known as the *equity of redemption*.

In time, lenders demanded that the Chancellor in Equity set an outside time limit by which borrowers would have to find the cash to redeem their property, and if the funds could not be located, the right to redeem would be cut off entirely. This final due date and the process by which the equity of redemption is terminated (i.e., foreclosed) is known as *foreclosure*.

The idea of the equity of redemption remains crucial today. Prior to foreclosure, borrowers can always redeem their property and terminate the lender's lien right by making full payment. Foreclosure rules are now statutory and carefully regulated by law. In addition, many states provide the debtor a statutory right to redeem for a certain period of time (typically six months to a year) even *after* foreclosure. *See, e.g.*, Fla. Stat. §45.0315 (2018). We discuss the statutory right of redemption below.

1. What Is a Mortgage?

Mortgage Document

⌨ Mortgage documents are typically longer than promissory notes, and rather than reprinting one in the text, we have made one very solid but simple Commercial Mortgage Agreement available electronically. Residential forms are often standardized. You can see the forms, by state, used by the Federal National Mortgage Association ("Fannie Mae") by going to https://www. fanniemae.com/singlefamily/security-instruments. You might pick a state, say North Carolina, and find and look over the form.

A *mortgage* is an instrument that conveys an interest in real property to serve as security for a loan. This interest allows the lender to take or sell the property in satisfaction of the debt if the borrower does not fulfill his obligation to repay the loan. In the vast majority of loan transactions, a mortgage is easy to spot. The document creating the security interest in real property will be titled mortgage, deed of trust, or deed to secure debt.

2. Mortgage Theories

The purpose of a mortgage is to provide a lender with collateral that he can sell in the event the borrower defaults on the loan. Courts and commentators identify two theories to explain the property interest that the borrower conveys to the lender. We will describe these two theories, but for your purposes, you should know that the outcomes are largely the same, notwithstanding the theory adopted in a jurisdiction. Like a rose, a mortgage is a mortgage, regardless of the theory that underlies it.

Some states adopt a *title theory* of mortgages. This theory emanates from the original common law transaction that saw a borrower convey title by deed to a lender, with a future interest in the borrower.

The majority of states now rely on what is known as *lien theory*. Pursuant to lien theory, a mortgage conveyance is understood to create a lien allowing the lender to take or sell the property in satisfaction of the debt if the borrower does not make good on its obligation to repay. Title theory is a minority rule, and today lien theory is the most common approach.

> ➤ Even in the few jurisdictions that apply title theory, courts recognize that the purpose of the mortgage is to secure a debt. It is *not considered a true conveyance of title. See, e.g.*, City of Fort Smith v. Carter, 270 S.W.3d

822, 825 (Ark. 2008) ("Our court has long held that despite the fact that a mortgagee has legal title to the mortgaged land, the mortgagee does not have absolute title thereto and does not have the right to possess the land until the mortgagor defaults on the mortgage."); Mortgage Elec. Registration Sys., Inc. v. Saunders, 2 A.3d 289 (Me. 2010) (stating that Maine is a "title theory" state in which lender holds title, but Borrower has "the right to possession"); Case v. St. Mary's Bank, 63 A.3d 1209 (N.H. 2013) (holding title for security did not make lender the landlord of property).

One distinction between lien theory and title theory concerns the ability of the lender to take possession of the property, and perhaps rental derived from the property, after the borrower defaults *but before the lender forecloses.* Imagine that the borrower owns a large office tower and collects rent from a large number of tenants. Purchasers of office buildings ordinarily borrow money to finance the purchase, and must make a monthly mortgage payment to the lender. These types of borrowers depend on rental payments from tenants to make their monthly mortgage payments. If the total rental income that a borrower takes in from tenants is insufficient to pay its monthly mortgage payment, the borrower will default on the promissory note to the lender. Yet, even after default to the lender, the borrower will continue collecting rent. After all, why would a landlord (the borrower) stop taking monthly rent from its tenants?

Furthermore, after defaulting on the promissory note, the borrower may cease to physically maintain the office building as it should. This lowers the value of the mortgaged property upon which the lender will ultimately foreclose. Indeed, the borrower may divert this income stream to other purposes, such as maintaining other properties not subject to the mortgage. Lenders hate this behavior, and refer to it as a borrower "milking" the property. Here is where mortgage theory matters: in a title theory state, it is typically easier for a lender to obtain possession of the real property and rental stream pre-foreclosure than it is in a lien theory state.

An extensive discussion of lien and title theory is beyond the scope of first-year Property; you may consider the distinction more thoroughly in an upper-level real estate transactions course.

E   FORECLOSURE

The borrower who obtains a loan from a lender and gives a mortgage to secure the promissory note is in a relationship: one based in the expectation of repayment, but a relationship all the same. The borrower—now a mortgagor—does not obtain a loan believing that the end point of the relationship will be a foreclosure. Think of a marriage for a moment. We know that many marriages unfortunately end in divorce, but this is not what the parties expect when they make their marital commitments. And for what it is worth, except for periods of significant economic recession, the rate of default on loans is much lower than the rate of divorce. (The authors are not suggesting that readers borrow and lend rather than marry, but one supposes that the implication is there.)

Foreclosure sign
Mark Avery/Reuters/Landov

As we said at the outset of this chapter, foreclosure lies at the end of the failed lending relationship. In fact, it is quite a bit more than that. The foreclosure process to a large degree defines the lending relationship. If a loan goes well and is paid off, the mortgagee records a satisfaction and release of the mortgage lien and the parties go their separate ways. There is really not much to do or say about a good loan. *Almost everything we see in the mortgage law arena is about the loan that goes bad.*

Lenders do not always foreclose on loans in default. Sometimes the lender and borrower will reach an accord that averts the foreclosure action. In commercial loan transactions, the lender may be willing to "work out" a loan with a borrower. In other words, the lender may wish instead to modify the loan to make it possible for the borrower to hang on. For example, the lender may grant the borrower a lower interest rate or a longer time for payment. The lender may do this to avoid a time-consuming and expensive foreclosure process, or to avoid foreclosing on property it will have a hard time selling. There is almost always a catch to a loan workout, from the borrower's perspective. An individual associated with the borrower may have to give a personal guarantee, or the borrower may have to provide additional collateral. *See generally* Daniel B. Bogart, *Games Lawyers Play: Waivers of the Automatic Stay in Bankruptcy and the Single Asset Loan Workout*, 43 UCLA L. Rev. 1117 (1996). If a foreclosure seems inevitable, the lender may agree to take a "deed in lieu" of foreclosure from the borrower and in so doing, take title. Typically, this means that the lender has agreed to forgive any deficiency. In this scenario, both parties agree it is best to end the relationship, and do so without the expense of conducting a foreclosure sale.

The quotation from Tom Wolfe's *A Man in Full*, at the start of this chapter, was a description of a very unpleasant loan workout meeting between a fictional Georgia property developer and his bank. The developer was personally liable for a humongous loan, and in addition to losing his real property, the developer was required to turn over virtually all of his personal assets.

Following the great recession of 2008, hundreds of thousands of Americans learned the hard reality of foreclosure. They lost homes and personal property, and saw their credit ratings and equity evaporate. They lost enormous personal wealth. Today, many homeowners remain "under water": the values of their homes have depreciated to the point that the properties are worth less than the respective outstanding loan debts. To put it another way, if these homeowners sell their homes, the sales will not generate enough cash to repay the outstanding debts.

In many parts of the country, home values have risen, and have reached pre-2008 levels. Nevertheless, this increase in home values occurred after the largest number of home foreclosures in American history. To the extent that home values have risen, it has benefited those people lucky enough to have retained their homes, or speculators who purchased property at the bottom of the market.

We will look at several topics in this section. First, we will examine the controlling rules of foreclosure sales, which describe how money flows to the various parties affected by a foreclosure, what happens to liens on the property, and the rights of mortgagees to pursue other assets of the mortgagor in satisfaction of a deficiency if the foreclosure auction brings in less than the outstanding loan. Most of the time, a borrower defaulting on a note and mortgage has more than one creditor and has pledged the property as collateral for more than one loan. How is the money divvyed up when one of these mortgagees forecloses its lien at an auction? We will then distinguish between the judicial foreclosure process, which is carried out in the form of a lawsuit, and the private foreclosure process, which results from a "power of sale" granted to the lender.

Foreclosed development
© David Becker/ZUMA Press/Corbis

Finally, we will look at challenges to the foreclosure process from the particular viewpoint of the mortgagor losing his property. Was the process fair and legal? Did it bring in enough money to be valid? Did the mortgagee "chill the bidding"?

1. Conducting a Sale—and Doing the Math

A mortgage gives the mortgagee the right to foreclose on the secured property in the event of a default. Foreclosure includes the sale of the secured property at auction, in order to pay off the debt.

In the end, a foreclosure sale is not only about possession of the property but also about *money*. The liens of the lender who forecloses and all junior interest holders are destroyed, and they will each want part of the sale proceeds (assuming that there are any). And of course, the borrower's right in the property is terminated as well. The borrower hopes to receive some cash from the sale. As we see below, the borrower is living in a fantasy land if the borrower really believes that there is cash waiting for him at the conclusion of a foreclosure sale. If there is money left over for the borrower after paying off all creditors entitled to be paid from the sale, then this suggests that the borrower could have sold the property outright and avoided foreclosure.

The lender/mortgagee often purchases the property at the auction. You may wonder why the mortgagee would do so: why buy unattractive property in a bad market? The mortgagee may be planning to hold on to the property and hope that property values rise. However, land speculation is not a primary reason that the mortgagee bids. The mortgagee, alone among all bidders at the auction, has *play money* with which to bid. Imagine that Debby defaults on her note and mortgage to First Bank. The outstanding amount of the promissory note is $100,000 at the time of Debby's default. First Bank may bid up to $100,000 without having to come up with actual cash, because each dollar it bids offsets the amount of the loan. This works only for the mortgagee foreclosing his loan; all other bidders must come up with cash.

In some cases, the cash generated by a foreclosure sale is less than the amount of the outstanding debt owed to the foreclosing lender. Recall that the borrower signed a promissory note to the lender making the borrower personally liable for the debt. If the foreclosure sale of the property does not pay off the debt, then in some states the lender may be entitled to a *deficiency judgment* against the borrower for the difference. A lender who obtains a deficiency judgment is a judgment creditor and can seek a writ of execution against the borrower's other assets. We will examine the nature of deficiency judgments in greater detail in later sections of this chapter. For now, it is enough to know that the foreclosing lender may obtain a personal judgment against the borrower as a result of the foreclosure.

Recordation of Mortgages

Mortgages convey interests in real property. These documents may be recorded in the county recorder's office, thus alerting any party who wishes to take an interest in the property of the earlier conveyance of a preexisting lien right. The note, which evidences the obligation to pay, is not a property interest and is therefore not recordable. Priority—whether one mortgage is senior or junior to another—is usually determined by the order in which the mortgages are recorded.

You will see below six rules that control foreclosure sales. These rules generally apply to both judicial and non-judicial foreclosure. If you understand and can apply these rules, then you grasp the key truths of the foreclosure process.

Six Controlling Rules of Foreclosure Sales

1. A lender can foreclose a loan only if the borrower is in default.
2. Foreclosure terminates the lien of the lender who brings the foreclosure action and all interests in the property *junior* to the lender's mortgage lien.
3. Foreclosure does not terminate any lien or property interests held by parties who are *senior* to the lender who brings the foreclosure action.
4. Money from the foreclosure sale pays off the debt of the lender who brings the foreclosure first, then travels downward to junior creditors and lastly the borrower by the rule of "absolute priority." The rule of

absolute priority provides that each creditor is paid in full before any junior lender receives a penny.

5. Interest holders who are senior to the foreclosing lender never receive money from the foreclosure sale (because their liens remain intact).

6. The only lender eligible for a *deficiency judgment* is the lender bringing the foreclosure action. The borrower may owe other lenders money, but those lenders cannot obtain judgments based on the foreclosure.

Practice Tip: Adding to the Balance

Most loan documents (notes and mortgages) contain language that adds the lender's cost of foreclosing to the outstanding debt balance. For example, the lender's attorneys' fees and court costs may be recovered from the foreclosure sale proceeds. From the perspective of a borrower losing property to foreclosure, this just adds salt to the wound.

Let's try out one hypothetical, and then a problem, to test your ability to apply these rules.

Jerry purchases Blackacre for $300,000 by borrowing $250,000 from State Bank and using $50,000 of his own money. State Bank records its mortgage. One year later, Jerry decides to renovate his home and borrows $50,000 from CrazyEddy Lending secured by a mortgage on Blackacre. CrazyEddy immediately records its mortgage. Finally, Jerry decides to take a cruise to Costa Rica. Jerry borrows $20,000 for the trip from University Credit Union, a loan secured by a third mortgage on Blackacre, which University immediately records. Jerry defaults on his loan from CrazyEddy Lending, but is current on his other two loans. Only CrazyEddy may bring a foreclosure action. At the time of CrazyEddy foreclosure, Jerry owes the following to his lenders:

StateBank	$200,000
CrazyEddy Lending	$40,000
University Credit Union	$20,000

Assume further that, if it were totally free and clear of liens and encumbrances, Blackacre would have a current fair market value of $230,000. A third person will bid $30,000 at the CrazyEddy foreclosure sale. Why is this the correct bid? What would happen to the sale proceeds? Will any of the lenders receive a deficiency judgment?

■ PROBLEMS: THE FORECLOSURE SALE

Modify the facts in the hypothetical above as follows:

➤ Same facts, except that Jerry defaults on his loan to State Bank instead of CrazyEddy, and State Bank forecloses. How much should a third person bid at the auction, and is any lender eligible for a deficiency judgment?

> ➤ Same facts, except Jerry defaults on his loan to University Credit Union, but not on his loans to the other lenders. University Credit Union forecloses. At the time of foreclosure, the property has a fair market value, if totally free of liens and mortgages, of $250,000. Jerry owes State Bank $220,000, CrazyEddy $40,000 and University Credit Union $20,000. How much will a third person bid at the auction, and is any lender eligible for a deficiency judgment? Does it make sense for University Credit Union to foreclose in this scenario?

All Junior Interests Are Destroyed

Mortgages are not the only junior interests destroyed by a foreclosure. Generally, any real property interest recorded after the recordation of the mortgage being foreclosed will also be terminated. For example, an *easement*, recorded after the recording date of the mortgage being foreclosed, would be extinguished by the foreclosure. *See* Restatement (Third) of Property: Mortgages §7.1, cmt. a (1997).

Practice Tip: Drafting to Make It Easier to Declare a Default

A mortgagee may bring an action to foreclose its lien only if the mortgagor is in default. This seems like a basic rule and it is. But it is also an easy rule to forget. Therefore, the mortgagee will draft the promissory note and mortgage to give itself wide leeway to declare a default, so that the mortgagee may, if it wishes, start the foreclosure process.

2. Judicial and Non-Judicial Foreclosure

A mortgagee may foreclose its lien in one of two ways: in a process known as *judicial foreclosure*, or in a process carried out by the lender or its nominee known as *non-judicial foreclosure*. A non-judicial foreclosure authorizes the lender to foreclose on the property without going to court and can be done only pursuant to a "power of sale" provision in the mortgage document. In both judicial and non-judicial foreclosure, the property of the mortgagor will be auctioned to pay off the outstanding debt owed on the promissory note.

This is a change from the harsh common law foreclosure process known as *strict foreclosure*. This process was not borrower-friendly. In strict foreclosure, there was no auction; instead, the borrower was required to pay by a particular date. If the borrower could not do so, the lender took the property in satisfaction of the debt, even if the property was worth more than the debt at the time of foreclosure. In contrast, an auction allows the debtor the chance to recover the property's value in excess of the debt.

There are important common aspects to judicial and non-judicial foreclosure. For example, regardless of whether a lender elects to judicially or non-judicially foreclose on property, the borrower has an equity of redemption that the borrower may exercise until the actual foreclosure auction. In other words, the borrower may bring the foreclosure process to a halt by paying the past due amounts of the loan (and accumulated foreclosure costs). Today, lenders routinely include an *acceleration provision* in promissory notes. This provision requires the borrower to pay the *entire* amount of the outstanding debt to redeem her property and stop the foreclosure.

Acceleration

Take another look at the promissory note reprinted at the start of this chapter. See if you can find the provision in that promissory note giving the lender the right to accelerate the loan in the event the borrower defaults.

Assume that Olivia borrows $100,000 from the Bank to purchase a house and provides the Bank with a promissory note to evidence the loan and a mortgage on the property as security. Assume further that Olivia defaults on the promissory note and that at the time she defaults, Olivia is in default by $8,000, but owes a total of $70,000 on the note. The Bank initiates the foreclosure process. A modern promissory note will contain a clause permitting the Bank to accelerate Olivia's entire indebtedness. The Bank will most definitely do so, and in order to exercise her equity of redemption, *Olivia would have to pay the Bank the entire $70,000 plus accumulated fees and costs to redeem her property.*

The manner in which non-judicial foreclosure terminates the borrower's rights in property is crucially different from judicial foreclosure: a lender, or in the case of a deed of trust, the trustee, foreclosing a power of sale has the burden of notifying parties of the foreclosure and of the conducting of the auction. The court does not supervise the process as it would in a judicial foreclosure. The lender conducting a non-judicial foreclosure has a duty to the borrower to conduct the foreclosure strictly according to statutory requirements. State statutes typically require the lender to advertise the property for sale repeatedly for a period of time preceding the foreclosure. Usually, this is accomplished with a bland advertisement in the legal notices section in a newspaper of general circulation. The advertisement will give the address and basic description of the property; the time, date, and place of the foreclosure auction; information regarding the loan being foreclosed; and contact information for the attorney or party conducting the foreclosure. The statutes specify when and where the auction must take place. For example, Georgia requires foreclosure sales to take place between the hours of 10 A.M. and 4 P.M. on the first Tuesday of the month. Ga. Code Ann. §9-13-161 (2015 & Supp. 2018).

a. Judicial Foreclosure

In every state, the mortgagee may bring an action for *judicial foreclosure* upon default. This means that the foreclosure is a lawsuit. The mortgagee becomes the plaintiff and the mortgagor, and perhaps guarantors of the promissory note, if there are any, become defendants. Once the mortgagee establishes adequate proof of the mortgage and default, the process concludes with an auction of the property carried out under the auspices of the court. Judicial foreclosure terminates the mortgagor's equity of redemption. Indeed, the end result of the process is that the court issues a foreclosure deed. This deed resembles a quitclaim deed (because it does not contain warranties) and grants title to the auction purchaser. *Why do you think that the courts use what essentially amounts to a quitclaim deed to transfer title at a foreclosure?*

In many states, the sale of the property and issuance of the foreclosure deed terminates the mortgagor's right to the property.

> ➤ In those states that provide a *statutory right of redemption*, the foreclosure sale marks the *start of the time period* in which the mortgagor may redeem pursuant to the statute. In those states, if the mortgagor does not redeem, the mortgagor's rights in the property terminate at the end of the statutory redemption period.

Because judicial foreclosure is a lawsuit, and stands to deprive the mortgagor of his right to possession and title, the mortgagor is entitled to due process. As you know, foreclosure also terminates all interests junior to the lien of the party foreclosing. Any party whose interest might be terminated is similarly entitled to due process, including junior creditors.

For example, assume that Ursula borrows $100,000 from First Bank to purchase a house. Ursula signs a promissory note to evidence the loan and provides First Bank a mortgage covering the house as security. First Bank records the mortgage in the county recorder's office. Two years after granting the note and mortgage to First Bank, Ursula decides to renovate the kitchen of the house and obtains a second loan on the home in the amount of $30,000 from Renovation Bank. Ursula provides Renovation Bank with a promissory note for this amount and a mortgage covering the property. Renovation Bank immediately records the mortgage in the county recorder's office. Finally, one year later, Ursula grants an express easement to Daniel allowing Daniel to access a public road by crossing Ursula's property. Daniel immediately records the easement in the county recorder's office.

The Renovation Bank mortgage and the easement to Daniel are both *subsequently recorded* and therefore "junior" to the First Bank mortgage. Both Renovation Bank and Daniel would have discovered the earlier First Bank mortgage if they had performed a competent title search of the property. One of the most important rules is that a foreclosure by the senior lienholder, in this case First Bank, will "wipe out" junior mortgage liens and other junior interests. If that happens, Renovation Bank will lose its mortgage lien, and it will be left only with its promissory note. This is the reason that all junior interest holders, such as Renovation Bank and Daniel, must be given notice of a judicial foreclosure proceeding; otherwise, they will not have been given due process prior to the termination of their interests.

Practice Tip

If a senior mortgagee forecloses but for some reason fails to join a junior mortgagee, then the senior mortgagee can foreclose again, after meeting all necessary requirements for foreclosure in that jurisdiction, to wipe out the party mistakenly omitted.

Junior mortgagees are considered *necessary parties*. A party is necessary if the foreclosure will wipe out that party's interest. In the example, Daniel and Renovation Bank are both necessary parties. The foreclosure of the senior mortgagee's lien will be valid, but it will not apply against any junior interest that was not joined to the foreclosure action. It is necessary to join Renovation Bank, in order to terminate its mortgage lien, and Daniel, to terminate his easement. Ursula, the mortgagor, is a special kind of necessary party. If the mortgagee fails to join the mortgagor in the foreclosure action, then the entire foreclosure is wholly void as to all parties.

Some parties are not "necessary," but they are "proper." It may be beneficial to the party foreclosing to join a party even though that person's interest is not wiped out by the foreclosure. Consider the following problem:

■ PROBLEM: SENIOR MORTGAGES AND "PROPER PARTIES"

➢ On January 1, 2020, Garth purchases a restaurant located in an ornate Victorian mansion and finances the purchase with a $100,000 variable rate 15-year loan from Big Bank. Garth provides Big Bank a promissory note and a mortgage. Big Bank immediately records the mortgage in the county recorder's office. The interest rate required under the note is 6 percent for the first 10 years, to be reset at a rate "5 percent above prime" beginning the first month of the eleventh year.

➢ On January 1, 2026, Garth borrows $50,000 from Mr. Monday Finance Co. to cover the cost of renovating an imposing iron gate surrounding the mansion. Garth provides Mr. Monday Finance Co. with a promissory note and mortgage, which Mr. Monday Finance Co. immediately records in the county recorder's office.

➢ On January 1, 2030, the interest rate for the Big Bank loan resets at 15 percent. The jurisdiction in which the property is located maintains a statute declaring as usurious any loan in excess of 14 percent.

➢ Garth continues to pay his mortgage payments to Big Bank, but defaults on his payments to Mr. Monday Finance Co.

The lending officer for Mr. Monday Finance Co. asks for your advice. He would like to foreclose and take the property. What is your advice?

b. Non-Judicial Foreclosure

Lawsuits take time. This is certainly true of judicial foreclosure, which is just a type of lawsuit. In addition, a judicial foreclosure takes place under the watchful eye of the court. The mortgagee does not like to wait or to be subjected to the scrutiny of a court. The mortgagee would rather just take the property.

For this reason, most lenders will, in jurisdictions that permit the practice, demand from the borrower a mortgage document containing a *power of sale*. This means that the borrower grants the lender, upon borrower's default, a right to sell the property at a private sale in satisfaction of the debt. The mortgage document containing a power of sale is titled a "deed of trust," a "security deed," or a "deed to secure debt." The deed of trust permits a third-party trustee chosen by the lender to conduct a private sale and foreclose against the borrower; a security deed permits the lender itself to conduct the private sale and foreclose. Whatever the name, though, these are still just security devices, and are mortgages in substance if not in form. Indeed, in some states, the document containing the power of sale is simply titled mortgage. The power of sale allows the mortgagee (or a trustee) to hold a foreclosure sale without invoking the judicial mechanism.

> **Judicial Foreclosure Is Always an Option**
>
> A lender may choose to foreclose a deed with power of sale through the judicial process, if it wishes to do so. The courts will recognize the security or trust deed as a mortgage.

The mechanisms of non-judicial foreclosure vary significantly from jurisdiction to jurisdiction. Some require the use of a trustee, and others do not. Some prevent the lender from obtaining a deficiency judgment (more about that below) after a non-judicial foreclosure, while others allow it. The standards for notice, times, dates of sale, and other mechanics of sale also vary widely. The Uniform Law Commission adopted the Uniform Nonjudicial Foreclosure Act in 2002, and this was in turn approved by the American Bar Association. The Act distinguishes between residential debtors and all other debtors, and provides particular protections to the former. The Act has been controversial. *See* Dale A. Whitman, *Reforming Foreclosure: The Uniform Nonjudicial Foreclosure Act*, 53 Duke L.J. 1399 (2004) (Professor Whitman was one of the drafters of the Act).

One of the authors of this textbook acted on behalf of lenders at non-judicial foreclosures and sold at auction numerous commercial properties. At each such event, the author's client—the lender—was the only bidder. And at each such event, the author bid only the outstanding debt due under the foreclosed mortgage, plus expenses. The auction took place, pursuant to local law, *on the courthouse steps* of the county in which the property was located. The entire scene was surreal: attorneys were required by statute to recite their "scripts" between certain hours in public—although in most cases, no one was listening except other attorneys. The author was under strict instructions that, in the *very* unlikely

Video Problem: Foreclosure Sale

🎥 In this video, which is available on the Simulation, a lawyer for the lender forecloses against a borrower's property "on the courthouse steps." The video describes the requirements for a foreclosure sale as set forth by local statute. The lawyer recites the foreclosure notice and then conducts an auction. A lawyer is supposed to dot every "i" and cross every "t" when conducting a sale. Assume that you represent the borrower whose property is being sold. What advice do you have for your client? Do you detect any defects in the lawyer's performance, and if so, what impact would this have on the sale and the sale price?

event that an additional bidder showed up at the foreclosure and announced an intention to enter a bid, the author was required to briefly delay the start of the bidding and contact the lender for instructions. The author had *absolutely no authority* to spend actual, new cash of the client without approval; the author was allowed only to bid in an amount equal to the outstanding debt, which would be credited against the debt. Why do you think no one else showed up to bid on these properties?

i. Price. Now that you have a sense of how money flows to the various parties to a foreclosure, you understand how important it is for the foreclosure sale to generate a significant sale price. The higher the sale price generated by the foreclosure auction, the more likely creditors will be paid, and the less likely the borrower will owe a deficiency judgment.

The hypothetical and the problems in the prior section titled "Conducting a Sale—and Doing the Math" assumed that the foreclosure auction would bring in fair market value. However, foreclosure is not an environment conducive to bringing in a high sale value; the foreclosure world is dominated by distressed borrowers and anxious creditors. The borrower almost always thinks that the price generated by a foreclosure sale is too low. The borrower gauges the foreclosure price against the price she imagines she would have received if the borrower had hired a broker to show the property, if the property looked well maintained, and if the borrower could wait for an offer she found acceptable. Yet, these are not generally attributes of the foreclosure sale process. In reality, the property often looks worn and is sold quickly, and a broker is only rarely involved. Only those buyers who can pay cash can bid. As a result, courts do not lightly invalidate foreclosure sales on the basis of low price alone.

Courts utilize different rules to test the sale price of foreclosed property. Some will invalidate the sale if the price is so low that it "shocks the conscience." The *borrower's* conscience is not the measure; the question is whether the price is so low that the court—an objective third party—would be scandalized by the amount paid by the purchaser at the foreclosure auction. A scandalously low price suggests fraud of some kind or collusion between the lender and the purchaser.

➢ In Crown Life Ins. Co. v. Candlewood, Ltd., 818 P.2d 411, 415 (N.M. 1991), property with a value between $880,000 and $1,200,000 sold pursuant to a power of sale for *$200,010*, which amounted to somewhere between 14 and 23 percent of the property's estimated value. Only two bidders actually participated. The outstanding amount of the foreclosed loan at the time of the sale was $1 million, and the lender instructed its agent conducting the foreclosure to bid in the amount of the debt. The agent misunderstood his instructions, however, and began bidding at *zero* dollars. The bidding edged up to a final but minimal bid of $200,010. The winning bid was placed by a party other than the lender. The court ruled for the borrower, explaining "however insensitive the court's conscience, this disparity, under the circumstances of this case, should shock it." Was the mistake of the lender's agent, in starting the bidding at zero dollars, a procedural error? Should the fact that the lender's agent made such an obvious error matter to the court?

In many cases, however, it would appear difficult to shock the conscience of courts. *See, e.g.*, CS Assets, LLC v. W. Beach, LLC, 370 Fed. App'x 45, 46 (11th Cir. 2010) (declining, under Alabama law, to set aside lender's acquisition of property in a foreclosure where sales price paid was 20 percent, 30 percent, or 66 percent of fair market value, depending on the appraisal used, and where there was no indication that fraud, bad faith, or lack of notice tainted the auction); Charter Bank v. Francoeur, 287 P.3d 333, 341-43 (N.M. Ct. App. 2012) *cert. granted*, 296 P.3d 491(N.M. 2012), *cert. quashed*, 301 P.3d 859 (N.M. 2013) (district court did not abuse its discretion in deciding that a sales price of $100,000—48.7 percent of the $206,000 appraised value of the home—did not shock the conscience where no deficiency judgment resulted, because the sale price was greater than the amount borrower owed on the loan).

The American Law Institute adopted a more modern terminology to explain when it is appropriate to invalidate foreclosure sales based purely on price. Section 8.3 of the Restatement (Third) of Property: Mortgages provides:

(a) A foreclosure sale price obtained pursuant to a foreclosure proceeding that is otherwise regularly conducted in compliance with applicable law does not render the foreclosure defective unless the price is *grossly inadequate.*

(b) Subsection (a) applies to both power of sale and judicial foreclosure proceedings.

Restatement (Third) of Property: Mortgages § 8.3 (1997) (emphasis added). The Restatement does not provide a tidy definition of a "grossly inadequate" price, admitting that gross inadequacy "cannot be precisely defined in terms of a specific percentage of fair market value." Instead, the Restatement provides that, generally,

a court is warranted in invalidating a sale where the price is less than 20 percent of fair market value and, absent other foreclosure defects, is usually not warranted in invalidating a sale that yields in excess of that amount. While the trial court's judgment in matters of price adequacy is entitled to considerable deference, in extreme cases a price may be so low (typically well under 20% of fair market value) that it

Fire Sales

It is true that a foreclosure today routinely involves an auction of the property. But foreclosure sales look more like fire sales in most instances than true auctions. Often the only bidding party is the lender. Property subject to foreclosure may be in lousy shape, and few lenders hire brokers or market the property in any serious way. Foreclosure sales do not typically generate what we might otherwise call "fair market values."

would be an abuse of discretion for the court to refuse to invalidate it.

Restatement (Third) of Property: Mortgages § 8.3, cmt. b (1997).

Sometimes a foreclosure sale price is very low, but not so low as to be grossly inadequate or shock the conscience. When this happens, a court may still invalidate the sale, but only if the foreclosure sale was somehow tainted by procedural irregularity. "Such defects may include, for example, chilled bidding, an improper time or place of sale, fraudulent conduct by the mortgagee, a defective notice of sale, or selling too much or too little of the mortgaged real estate." Restatement (Third) of Property: Mortgages § 8.3, cmt. c (1997).

Where should courts draw the line when considering a claim that the foreclosure price is too low? What policies should drive the court in formulating an appropriate rule? Does the choice of rule have an impact on the outcome?

■ PROBLEM: A BID FOR THE OUTSTANDING BALANCE

➤ Shopping Center Developer borrows $5 million from Regional Bank in order to purchase a local strip shopping center. Shopping Center Developer executes a promissory note in favor of Regional Bank in the amount of $5 million, as well as a deed of trust covering the strip shopping center.

➤ One year following the purchase, a key tenant of the strip shopping center unexpectedly quits its space and ceases to make rental payments. Shopping Center Developer is not able to find an adequate substitute tenant, and as a result, defaults on the promissory note.

➤ Regional Bank initiates a non-judicial foreclosure. Regional Bank and the foreclosure trustee follow all statutory procedures for foreclosure, including advertising as required by the statute, and do not otherwise preclude or discourage additional bidders at the foreclosure sale.

➤ Shopping Center Developer hires a land appraiser prior to the foreclosure sale, and the appraiser's report indicates that the property has a fair market value of $10 million.

➤ Regional Bank purchases the strip shopping center at the foreclosure sale, bidding in the outstanding balance of the loan, $3.7 million.

Assume that you represent Shopping Center Developer and that your client asks for your advice. Can Shopping Center Developer successfully challenge the foreclosure sale, and if so, on what basis? Does your answer change depending on whether you employ the language of the Restatement or older terminology that focuses on a sale price that "shocks the conscience"?

Now let's modify the Problem as follows:

> The foreclosure statute requires foreclosure auctions to take place between the hours of 10 a.m. and 4 p.m. on the first Tuesday of each month. The statute permits the trustee to advertise in advance the specific anticipated time that the auction will take place.
> The trustee advertises that the auction will take place on the first Tuesday of June at 10:30 a.m.
> The foreclosure trustee arrives at the auction location on the first Tuesday in June, at 10:15 a.m. Prior to the auction, at 10:20 a.m., two individuals identify themselves to the trustee as anticipated third-party bidders.
> Without providing a reason, the trustee then delays the auction by 1½ hours. When the auction commences at noon, the two third-party bidders are no longer present.
> All other facts from the Problem remain the same, and Regional Bank purchases the property as described in the Problem above.

Again, Shopping Center Developer asks for your advice. Is your client in a better position under the modified fact pattern, and if so, why? *See* J. Ashley Corp. v. Burson, 750 A.2d 618 (Md. Ct. App. 2000).

Valuation Matters: The Battle of Appraisers

The value that matters to a despondent borrower watching as the lender forecloses on the property is the value of the property on the date of the foreclosure sale. Can you see why the lender and the borrower will present entirely different valuations, if a dispute arises as to the validity of the sale?

A borrower litigates the validity of the foreclosure sale because the borrower is genuinely dissatisfied with the sale price. A low sale price places the behavior of the lender in the sale process front and center and forces us to ask: What duties does the lender owe the borrower, if any, to obtain an advantageous sale price? Consider the following case.

MURPHY v. FINANCIAL DEVELOPMENT CORP.

495 A.2d 1245 (1985)
Supreme Court of New Hampshire

DOUGLAS, JUSTICE.

The plaintiffs brought this action seeking to set aside the foreclosure sale of their home, or, in the alternative, money damages. The Superior Court (Bean, J.), adopting the recommendation of a Master (R. Peter Shapiro, Esq.), entered a judgment for the plaintiffs in the amount of $27,000 against two of the defendants, Financial Development Corporation and Colonial Deposit Company (the lenders).

The plaintiffs purchased a house in Nashua in 1966, financing it by means of a mortgage loan. They refinanced the loan in March of 1980, executing a new promissory note and a power of sale mortgage, with Financial Development Corporation as mortgagee. The note and mortgage were later assigned to Colonial Deposit Company.

In February of 1981, the plaintiff Richard Murphy became unemployed. By September of 1981, the plaintiffs were seven months in arrears on their mortgage payments, and had also failed to pay substantial amounts in utility assessments and real estate taxes. After discussing unsuccessfully with the plaintiffs proposals for revising the payment schedule, rewriting the note, and arranging alternative financing, the lenders gave notice on October 6, 1981, of their intent to foreclose.

During the following weeks, the plaintiffs made a concerted effort to avoid foreclosure. They paid the seven months' mortgage arrearage, but failed to pay some $643.18 in costs and legal fees associated with the foreclosure proceedings. The lenders scheduled the foreclosure sale for November 10, 1981, at the site of the subject property. They complied with all of the statutory requirements for notice. *See* RSA 479:25.

At the plaintiffs' request, the lenders agreed to postpone the sale until December 15, 1981. They advised the plaintiffs that this would entail an additional cost of $100, and that the sale would proceed unless the lenders received payment of $743.18, as well as all mortgage payments then due, by December 15. Notice of the postponement was posted on the subject property on November 10 at the originally scheduled time of the sale, and was also posted at the Nashua City Hall and Post Office. No prospective bidders were present for the scheduled sale.

In late November, the plaintiffs paid the mortgage payment which had been due in October, but made no further payments to the lenders. An attempt by the lenders to arrange new financing for the plaintiffs through a third party failed when the plaintiffs refused to agree to pay for a new appraisal of the property. Early on the morning of December 15, 1981, the plaintiffs tried to obtain a further postponement, but were advised by the lenders' attorney that it was impossible unless the costs and legal fees were paid.

At the plaintiffs' request, the attorney called the president of Financial Development Corporation, who also refused to postpone the sale. Further calls by the plaintiffs to the lenders' offices were equally unavailing.

The sale proceeded as scheduled at 10:00 A.M. on December 15, at the site of the property. Although it had snowed the previous night, the weather was clear and warm at the time of the sale, and the roads were clear. The only parties present were the plaintiffs, a representative of the lenders, and an attorney, Morgan Hollis, who had been engaged to conduct the sale because the lenders' attorney, who lived in Dover, had been apprehensive about the weather the night before. The lenders' representative made the only bid at the sale. That bid of $27,000, roughly the amount owed on the mortgage, plus costs and fees, was accepted and the sale concluded.

Later that same day, Attorney Hollis encountered one of his clients, William Dube, a representative of the defendant Southern New Hampshire Home Traders, Inc. (Southern). On being informed of the sale, Mr. Dube contacted the lenders and offered to buy the property for $27,000. The lenders rejected the offer and made a counter offer of $40,000. Within two days a purchase price of $38,000 was agreed upon by Mr. Dube and the lenders and the sale was subsequently completed.

The plaintiffs commenced this action on February 5, 1982. The lenders moved to dismiss, arguing that any action was barred because the plaintiffs had failed to petition for an injunction prior to the sale. The master denied the motion. After hearing the evidence, he ruled for the plaintiffs, finding that the lenders had "failed to exercise good faith and due diligence in obtaining a fair price for the subject property at the foreclosure sale...."

The master also ruled that Southern was a bona fide purchaser for value, and thus had acquired legal title to the house. That ruling is not at issue here. He assessed monetary damages against the lenders equal to "the difference between the fair market value of the subject property on the date of the foreclosure and the price obtained at said sale."

Having found the fair market value to be $54,000, he assessed damages accordingly at $27,000. He further ruled that "[t]he bad faith of the 'Lenders' warrants an award of legal fees." The lenders appealed.

[The court first disposed of a procedural issue.]

The second issue before us is whether the master erred in concluding that the lenders had failed to comply with the often-repeated rule that a mortgagee executing a power of sale is bound both by the statutory procedural requirements *and* by a duty to protect the interests of the mortgagor through the exercise of good faith and due diligence. *See, e.g.*, Carrols Equities Corp. v. Della Jacova, 126 N.H. 116, 489 A.2d 116 (1985); Proctor v. Bank of N.H., 123 N.H. 395, 464 A.2d 263 (1983); Meredith v. Fisher, 121 N.H. 856, 435 A.2d 536 (1981); Lakes Region Fin. Corp. v. Goodhue Boat Yard, Inc., 118 N.H. 103, 382 A.2d 1108 (1978); Wheeler v. Slocinski, 82 N.H. 211, 131 A. 598 (1926). We will not overturn a master's findings and rulings "unless they are unsupported by the evidence or are erroneous as a matter of law." Summit Electric, Inc. v. Pepin Brothers Const., Inc., 121 N.H. 203, 206, 427 A.2d 505, 507 (1981).

The master found that the lenders, throughout the time prior to the sale, "did not mislead or deal unfairly with the plaintiffs." They engaged in serious efforts to avoid foreclosure through new financing, and agreed to one postponement of the sale. The basis for the master's decision was his conclusion that the lenders had failed to exercise good faith and due diligence in obtaining a fair price for the property.

This court's past decisions have not dealt consistently with the question whether the mortgagee's duty amounts to that of a fiduciary or trustee. *Compare* Pearson v. Gooch, 69 N.H. 208, 209, 40 A. 390, 390-91 (1897) and Merrimack

Industrial Trust v. First Nat. Bank of Boston, 121 N.H. 197, 201, 427 A.2d 500, 504 (1981) (duty amounts to that of a fiduciary or trustee) *with* Silver v. First National Bank, 108 N.H. 390, 391, 236 A.2d 493, 494-95 (1967) *and* Proctor v. Bank of N.H., *supra* 123 N.H. at 400, 464 A.2d at 266 (duty does not amount to that of a fiduciary or trustee). This may be an inevitable result of the mortgagee's dual role as seller and potential buyer at the foreclosure sale, and of the conflicting interests involved. *See* Wheeler v. Slocinski, 82 N.H. at 214, 131 A. at 600.

We need not label a duty, however, in order to define it. In his role as a seller, the mortgagee's duty of good faith and due diligence is essentially that of a fiduciary. Such a view is in keeping with "[t]he 'trend ... towards liberalizing the term [fiduciary] in order to prevent unjust enrichment.'" Lash v. Cheshire County Savings Bank, Inc., 124 N.H. 435, 438, 474 A.2d 980, 981 (1984) (quoting Cornwell v. Cornwell, 116 N.H. 205, 209, 356 A.2d 683, 686 (1976)).

A mortgagee, therefore, must exert every reasonable effort to obtain "a fair and reasonable price under the circumstances," Reconstruction Finance Corp. v. Faulkner, 101 N.H. 352, 361, 143 A.2d 403, 410 (1958), even to the extent, if necessary, of adjourning the sale or of establishing "an upset price below which he will not accept any offer." Lakes Region Fin. Corp. v. Goodhue Boat Yard, Inc., 118 N.H. at 107, 382 A.2d at 1111.

What constitutes a fair price, or whether the mortgagee must establish an upset price, adjourn the sale, or make other reasonable efforts to assure a fair price, depends on the circumstances of each case. Inadequacy of price alone is not sufficient to demonstrate bad faith unless the price is so low as to shock the judicial conscience. Mueller v. Simmons, 634 S.W.2d 533, 536 (Mo. App. 1982); Rife v. Woolfolk, 289 S.E.2d 220, 223 (W. Va. 1982); Travelers Indem. Co. v. Heim, 218 Neb. 326, 352 N.W.2d 921, 923-24 (1984).

We must decide, in the present case, whether the evidence supports the finding of the master that the lenders failed to exercise good faith and due diligence in obtaining a fair price for the plaintiffs' property.

We first note that "[t]he duties of good faith and due diligence are distinct.... One may be observed and not the other, and any inquiry as to their breach calls for a separate consideration of each." Wheeler v. Slocinski, 82 N.H. at 213, 131 A. at 600. In order "to constitute bad faith there must be an intentional disregard of duty or a purpose to injure." *Id.* at 214, 131 A. at 600-01.

There is insufficient evidence in the record to support the master's finding that the lenders acted in bad faith in failing to obtain a fair price for the plaintiffs' property. The lenders complied with the statutory requirements of notice and otherwise conducted the sale in compliance with statutory provisions. The lenders postponed the sale one time and did not bid with knowledge of any immediately available subsequent purchaser. Further, there is no evidence indicating an intent on the part of the lenders to injure the mortgagor by, for example, discouraging other buyers.

There is ample evidence in the record, however, to support the master's finding that the lenders failed to exercise due diligence in obtaining a fair price. "The issue of the lack of due diligence is whether a reasonable man in the [lenders'] place would have adjourned the sale," *id.* at 215, 131 A. at 601, or taken other measures to receive a fair price.

In early 1980, the plaintiffs' home was appraised at $46,000. At the time of the foreclosure sale on December 15, 1981, the lenders had not had the house reappraised to take into account improvements and appreciation. The master found that a reasonable person in the place of the lenders would have realized that the plaintiffs' equity in the property was at least $19,000, the difference between the 1980 appraised value of $46,000 and the amount owed on the mortgage totaling approximately $27,000.

At the foreclosure sale, the lenders were the only bidders. The master found that their bid of $27,000 "was sufficient to cover all monies due and did not create a deficiency balance" but "did not provide for a return of any of the plaintiffs' equity."

Further, the master found that the lenders "had reason to know" that "they stood to make a substantial profit on a quick turnaround sale." On the day of the sale, the lenders offered to sell the foreclosed property to William Dube for $40,000. Within two days after the foreclosure sale, they did in fact agree to sell it to Dube for $38,000. It was not necessary for the master to find that the lenders knew of a specific potential buyer before the sale in order to show lack of good faith or due diligence as the lenders contend. The fact that the lenders offered the property for sale at a price sizably above that for which they had purchased it, only a few hours before, supports the master's finding that the lenders had reason to know, at the time of the foreclosure sale, that they could make a substantial profit on a quick turnaround sale. For this reason, they should have taken more measures to ensure receiving a higher price at the sale.

While a mortgagee may not always be required to secure a portion of the mortgagor's equity, such an obligation did exist in this case. The substantial amount of equity which the plaintiffs had in their property, the knowledge of the lenders as to the appraised value of the property, and the plaintiffs' efforts to forestall foreclosure by paying the mortgage arrearage within weeks of the sale, all support the master's conclusion that the lenders had a fiduciary duty to take more reasonable steps than they did to protect the plaintiffs' equity by attempting to obtain a fair price for the property. They could have established an appropriate upset price to assure a minimum bid. They also could have postponed the auction and advertised commercially by display advertising in order to assure that bidders other than themselves would be present.

Instead, as Theodore DiStefano, an officer of both lending institutions testified, the lenders made no attempt to obtain fair market value for the property but were concerned *only* with making themselves "whole." On the facts of this case, such disregard for the interests of the mortgagors was a breach of duty by the mortgagees.

Although the lenders *did* comply with the statutory requirements of notice of the foreclosure sale, these efforts were not sufficient in this case to demonstrate due diligence. At the time of the initially scheduled sale, the extent of the lenders' efforts to publicize the sale of the property was publication of a legal notice of the mortgagees' sale at public auction on November 10, published once a week for three weeks in the Nashua Telegraph, plus postings in public places. The lenders did not advertise, publish, or otherwise give notice to the general public of postponement of the sale to December 15, 1981, other than by posting notices at the plaintiffs' house, at the post office, and at city hall. That these efforts to advertise were ineffective is evidenced by the fact that no one, other than the lenders, appeared at the sale to bid on the property. This fact allowed the lenders to purchase the property at a minimal price and then to profit substantially in a quick turnaround sale.

We recognize a need to give guidance to a trial court which must determine whether a mortgagee who has complied with the strict letter of the statutory law has nevertheless violated his additional duties of good faith and due diligence. A finding that the mortgagee had, or should have had, knowledge of his ability to get a higher price at an adjourned sale is the most conclusive evidence of such a violation. *See* Lakes Region Fin. Corp. v. Goodhue Boat Yard, Inc., 118 N.H. at 107-08, 382 A.2d at 1111.

More generally, we are in agreement with the official Commissioners' Comment to section 3-508 of the Uniform Land Transactions Act:

> "The requirement that the sale be conducted in a reasonable manner, including the advertising aspects, requires that the person conducting the sale use the ordinary methods of making buyers aware that are used when an owner is voluntarily selling his land. Thus an advertisement in the portion of a daily newspaper where these ads are placed or, in appropriate cases such as the sale of an industrial plant, a display advertisement in the financial sections of the daily newspaper may be the most reasonable method. In other cases employment of a professional real estate agent may be the more reasonable method. It is unlikely that an advertisement in a legal publication among other legal notices would qualify as a commercially reasonable method of sale advertising."

13 Uniform Laws Annotated 704 (West 1980). As discussed above, the lenders met neither of these guidelines.

While agreeing with the master that the lenders failed to exercise due diligence in this case, we find that he erred as a matter of law in awarding damages equal to "the difference between the fair market value of the subject property ... and the price obtained at [the] sale."

Such a formula may well be the appropriate measure where *bad faith* is found. *See* Danvers Savings Bank v. Hammer, 122 N.H. 1, 5, 440 A.2d 435, 438 (1982). In such a case, a mortgagee's conduct amounts to more than mere negligence. Damages based upon the *fair market value*, a figure in excess of a *fair* price, will more readily induce mortgagees to perform their duties properly. A "fair" price may or may not yield a figure close to fair market value; however, it will be that price arrived at as a result of due diligence by the mortgagee.

Where, as here, however, a mortgagee fails to exercise due diligence, the proper assessment of damages is the difference between a fair price for the property and the price obtained at the foreclosure sale. We have held, where lack of due diligence has been found, that "the test is not 'fair market value' as in eminent domain cases nor is the mortgagee bound to give credit for the highest possible amount which might be obtained under different circumstances, as at an owner's sale." Silver v. First National Bank, 108 N.H. 390, 392, 236 A.2d 493, 495 (1967) (quoting Reconstruction Finance Corp. v. Faulkner, 101 N.H. 352, 361, 143 A.2d 403, 410 (1958)) (citation omitted). Accordingly, we remand to the trial court for a reassessment of damages consistent with this opinion.

Because we concluded above that there was no "bad faith or obstinate, unjust, vexatious, wanton, or oppressive conduct," on the part of the lenders, we see no reason to stray from our general rule that the prevailing litigant is not entitled to collect attorney's fees from the loser. Harkeem v. Adams, 117 N.H. 687, 688, 377 A.2d 617, 617 (1977). Therefore, we reverse this part of the master's decision.

Reversed in part; affirmed in part; remanded.

BROCK, J., dissented; the others concurred.

BROCK, JUSTICE, dissenting:

I agree with the majority that a mortgagee, in its role as seller at a foreclosure sale, has a fiduciary duty to the mortgagor. I also agree with the majority's more specific analysis of that duty, including its references to the commissioners' comment to the U.L.T.A., as well as those to *Wheeler* and other decisions of this court.

On the record presently before us, however, I cannot see any support for the master's finding that the lenders here failed to exercise due diligence as we have defined that term. I would remand the case to the superior court for further findings of fact.

Specifically, the master made no findings regarding what an "owner ... voluntarily selling his land" would have done that the lenders here did not do, in order to obtain a fair price. The master's report stated that the lenders "did not establish an upset price or minimum bid," and that they "did not cause the property to be reappraised," but there is nothing in the record to show that an owner conducting a voluntary sale would have done these things.

Nor is there anything to indicate what an appropriate upset price would have been under the conditions present here. The master correctly noted that "[a] foreclosure sale ... usually produces a price less than the property's fair market value," so it is virtually certain that any upset price would have been less than that amount.

I also cannot accept the majority's statement that the lenders' offer to sell the house for $40,000 constitutes support for a finding that they "should have taken more measures to ensure receiving a fair price at the sale." The offer was certainly relevant to the question of what the lenders knew about the house's value. Standing alone, however, it says nothing about what a reasonable person in the lenders' position would have done to ensure a fair price under the circumstances of this particular sale.

The master, in fact, found that the lenders "did not mislead or deal unfairly with the plaintiffs" until the sale itself. He did not find, as the majority appears to assume, that the lenders should have adjourned the sale a second time. Although the report nowhere states specifically *what* the lenders should have done, its clear implication is that they should have made a higher bid at the foreclosure sale.

There is no authority for such a conclusion. The mortgagee's fiduciary duty extends only to its role as a *seller.* Once the mortgagee has exerted every reasonable effort to obtain a fair price (which may sometimes include setting an upset price and adjourning the sale if no bidder meets that price), it has no further obligation in its role as a potential buyer. *See generally* 1 Glenn on Mortgages §108.1, at 652-53 (1943).

As the majority notes, a low price is not of itself sufficient to invalidate a foreclosure sale, unless the price is "so low as to shock the judicial conscience." The price here was clearly not that low. *Cf.* Shipp Corp., Inc. v. Charpilloz, 414 So. 2d 1122, 1124 (Fla. Dist. Ct. App. 1982) (bid of $1.1 million was not grossly inadequate compared to a market value of between $2.8 and $3.2 million).

Because it is unclear whether the master applied the correct standard regarding the mortgagee's duty, and because the record as presently constituted cannot support a determination that the lenders violated that standard, I respectfully dissent.

■ POINTS TO CONSIDER

1. **The test in *Murphy*.** According to the court in *Murphy*, what price must a lender or its agent obtain at the foreclosure sale? What are the implications of this rule under the particular facts in *Murphy*? Would the holding in *Murphy* change in a non-judicial foreclosure involving more run-of-the-mill facts? *See also* Wansley v. First Nat'l Bank of Vicksburg, 566 So. 2d 1218 (Miss. 1990). In *Wansley*, the borrower went into default on a promissory note and a trust deed. The trustee foreclosed, and the mortgagee purchased the property at the auction for approximately 71 percent of the outstanding debt. The mortgagee then pursued the borrower for a deficiency judgment to recover, from the borrower's personal assets, the difference between the foreclosure sale price and the outstanding balance of the loan. Here was the problem, though: it turned out that the trustee who conducted the foreclosure sale was a part owner of the mortgagee, and therefore stood to gain by the sale of the property at a low price followed by a deficiency judgment. Should this matter?

2. **Fiduciary duties.** A lender foreclosing directly pursuant to a power of sale has the same fiduciary responsibility to the borrower as a trustee does under a deed of trust. "Courts frequently state that a trustee in a deed of trust is a fiduciary for both the borrower-trustor and lender-beneficiary and must act impartially between them." Grant S. Nelson et al., Real Estate Finance Law §7.22, at 656 (6th ed. 2015).What does this mean in the context of a foreclosure process and sale? What is the duty of a deed trustee in a non-judicial foreclosure to the borrower? Does the lender (or in the case of

a deed of trust, the trustee) have a fiduciary duty to the borrower to obtain a high foreclosure sale price? Many courts answer in the negative. One court stated: "In Texas, a special relationship does not normally exist between a borrower and a lender, and when one has been found, it has rested on extraneous facts and conduct, such as excessive lender control over, or influence in, the borrower's business activities." Greater Sw. Office Park, Ltd. v. Tex. Commerce Nat'l Ass'n, 786 S.W.2d 386, 391 (Tex. Ct. App. 1990). *See also* Stephens, Partain & Cunningham v. Hollis, 242 Cal. Rptr. 251, 255 (Cal. Ct. App. 1987) ("Although commonly called a "trustee," a trustee under a deed of trust is not the kind of trustee identified in former Civil Code section 2229. Just as a panda is not an ordinary bear, a trustee of a deed of trust is not an ordinary trustee."). Does the court in *Murphy* hold this view of the lender's fiduciary obligation to the borrower? Assume that the court in *Murphy* applied the approach that the lender is *not* in a fiduciary relationship with the borrower, and thus has no duty to obtain a high price at the sale, absent special circumstances. Would this have changed the result in that case?

3. **Bank policy.** Some lenders adopt an *institutional policy* of bidding less than the fair market value of property at a foreclosure auction. For example, a lender may follow a policy of bidding no more than 70 percent of the fair market value of properties on which it foreclosed. Keep in mind that often the lender is the only bidder, and to the extent that the lender's bid is below the outstanding debt owed by the borrower, the lender does not have to come up with actual cash. The lender can simply offset the amount it bids against the outstanding debt. Should we require the lender to bid in a higher amount, closer to fair market value? Does the lender have a duty to the borrower to bid at all, or to bid a high value, at the foreclosure sale? If a lender bids only 70 percent of the value of a property—as a matter of policy—is it engaging in a fraud on the borrower?

4. **Different narratives.** It is a natural inclination to try to distinguish the "good guy" from the "bad guy" in litigated disputes, and this might seem like an especially easy thing to do when the dispute involves a lender's foreclosure of a borrower's home. But the story is not always so simple. Can you cast a forgiving light on the lender's behavior in *Murphy*? What was the lender's failure? Now assume that you represent the borrower in *Murphy* post-foreclosure: can you create a narrative, based on the facts of the case, that suggests that the lender in fact acted in bad faith?

5. **Remedies for invalidated non-judicial foreclosure.** A borrower who believes the sale to be defective in some way may bring an action in equity to set aside the sale. However, even if the sale is invalidated, the lender's lien is not destroyed. There is no "double jeopardy" rule for defaulting borrowers. A murderer, once acquitted, cannot be retried for murder. By contrast, a borrower is not "acquitted" if the foreclosure sale is invalidated. The lender's lien continues on the property. The lender then will begin the foreclosure process

again, and hopefully, having learned from its past error, will do so properly. To put it another way, the invalidation of the sale is at best a stay of execution. In some egregious instances, where the borrower can demonstrate the lender's bad faith, the borrower may be able to obtain money damages. For example, in addition to invalidating the sale, the borrower may be entitled to money damages if the lender foreclosed on property knowing that the debt had been paid.

6. **Statutory right of redemption.** If you are the borrower, and the lender has just foreclosed on your property, you probably think that all is lost and the ship has fully and finally gone down. And you may be right. The foreclosure has the effect of terminating your equity of redemption. After the sale, even if you put together the money necessary to redeem the property, you no longer have the right in equity to do so. However, in many jurisdictions, statutes provide you the right to redeem the property *even after the foreclosure sale.* These statutes are not uniform in content or approach. Typically, redemption statutes permit the borrower to redeem her property from the party who purchased it at foreclosure, by tendering to the purchaser the entire foreclosure sale price, interest at a rate set by statute, plus costs.

    The borrower cannot wait indefinitely to exercise her statutory redemption rights; the statutes set a time period in which she must act. Some of these statutes allow the borrower to wait a year or more, while some may require the borrower to act in a period of a few months. Many of these statutes *allow the borrower to remain in possession until the time period expires.* Think about what this means to the purchaser at the foreclosure sale. What does the purchaser own, prior to the running of the statute, if the borrower is still in possession and has a statutory right to redeem? In a few states, junior lienholders who were wiped out by the foreclosure may exercise the statutory right to redeem, but in most cases the right is limited to the borrower.

    Do you think these statutes are fair? What is the point of providing a statutory right to redeem post foreclosure? Consider the *Murphy* case above. We have seen that borrowers may be very, very close to having enough money to bring a loan current or pay a debt, and still fall short. Recall also that foreclosure sales are fire sales, and that borrowers subject to foreclosure are not in a solid financial position. What effect do you think these statutes have on foreclosure prices, and on the willingness of lenders to make loans secured by real property?

    Some scholars worry that the redemption statutes increase the uncertainty of the titles purchasers obtain at foreclosure sales, which lowers foreclosure prices. *See* Terrence M. Clauretie, *State Foreclosure Laws, Risk Shifting, and the Private Mortgage Insurance Industry,* 56 J. Risk & Ins. 544 (1989). *See also* James B. Hughes, Jr., *Taking Personal Responsibility: A Different View of Mortgage Anti-Deficiency and Redemption Statutes,* 39 Ariz. L. Rev. 117, 122-23 (1997). Other scholars are less certain that the statutes have had such an effect. *See* Patrick B. Bauer, *Judicial Foreclosure and Statutory Redemption: The*

Soundness of Iowa's Traditional Preference for Protection over Credit, 71 Iowa L. Rev. 1 (1985). Here is a final question: If the borrower remains in possession pursuant to the statutory right of redemption for a period of time, can the borrower physically alter the property? What rights and obligations does the borrower have with respect to the physical quality of the property?

ii. Deficiency Judgments.   In most foreclosures, the sale of the property does not generate a high enough sale price to pay the outstanding balance of the loan owed to the foreclosing lender. That lender may be entitled to a judgment in the amount of the deficiency. This is a judgment against the mortgagor/borrower and entitles the lender to pursue the borrower's personal assets in satisfaction of the debt. The lender may execute and levy against the borrower's personal assets in the county in which the foreclosure action takes place. The lender also may take a certified copy of the judgment to other counties and pursue the borrower's personal assets elsewhere. In fact, pursuant to the Full Faith and Credit Provision of the U.S. Constitution, the lender may pursue the borrower in other states. The deficiency judgment is therefore a very powerful tool for the lender. Let's talk a bit more about the nature of the deficiency judgment.

If the foreclosure is judicial, the court may grant the deficiency judgment in the same proceeding after the sale is conducted. In a non-judicial foreclosure, the lender will have to bring a separate action for a deficiency judgment after the foreclosure sale. Before it will grant a deficiency judgment, the court will carefully review the foreclosure process and the result. Some jurisdictions consider the foreclosure sale price as relevant in the court's decision to confirm the deficiency and grant a judgment. To put it another way, *the foreclosure sale may be valid, but the lender may not be successful in obtaining a judgment for the debt, if the price is not fair.*

Unscrupulous lenders see deficiency judgments as an opportunity to "double dip" at the expense of distressed borrowers. Recall that, at the foreclosure, the lender may purchase the property at an amount equal to the outstanding balance of the loan. As a result, the lender may realize a profit upon the eventual sale of the property. After all, the lender purchased the property below what would have been a market price. This is a bitter pill for the borrower. But as is often the case, *things can be so much worse.*

Consider what happens instead if the lender *bids less than the outstanding balance of the loan* and wins the auction. The lender will sell the property, again at a profit. If confirmed by a court, the lender will also obtain a deficiency judgment against the borrower for the difference between the balance of the loan and the foreclosure sale price. In essence, lender receives double payment for this differential, *because the lender will recoup the same amount on the resale. See generally,* Dale A. Whitman, *Preventing Creditor Abuse of Deficiency Judgments: Some Good (and Not-so-Good) Approaches,* 72 Wash. & Lee L. Rev. Online 92 (2015); Alan M. Weinberger, *Tools of Ignorance: An Appraisal of Deficiency Judgments,* 72 Wash. & Lee L. Rev. 829 (2015); Judy Gedge, *Should Deficiency Judgments Be Banned? Teaching Materials Designed to Promote an Informed Student Debate,* 19 J.L. Bus. & Ethics 65 (2013).

Some jurisdictions maintain *anti-deficiency statutes* that prohibit lenders from seeking deficiency judgments. In some states, these statutes prohibit deficiency judgments only with respect to residential mortgages or non-judicial foreclosures. For example, in California, a lender may not pursue a deficiency judgment against certain owner-occupied residential housing. Additionally, in California, a lender may not obtain a deficiency judgment in a non-judicial foreclosure. Cal. Civ. Proc. Code §580b (West 2011 & Supp. 2018). The California Supreme Court explained the rationale of its anti-deficiency statute in this way: "The purposes are to discourage land sales that are unsound because the land is overvalued and, in the event of a depression in land values, to prevent the aggravation of the downturn that would result if defaulting purchasers lost the land and were burdened with personal liability." Bargioni v. Hill, 378 P.2d 593, 594 (Cal. 1963). What are the downsides of anti-deficiency legislation?

California requires the lender to join in one legal action all causes of action to enforce a real estate mortgage and note. Cal. Civ. Proc. §726 (West 2015 & Supp. 2018). This limitation is known as the "one-action rule." Assume that a lender received a note and deed of trust from the borrower in connection with a loan. Pursuant to the one action rule, the lender cannot choose to enforce only the note and "waive the security"; the lender must foreclose the loan first, and only then pursue any deficiency. *See* Western Fuel Co. v. Sanford G. Lewald Co., 210 P. 419 (Cal. 1922). Only a minority of states maintain a one-action rule.

■ PROBLEM: A BID FOR LESS THAN THE DEBT

> Tom Ward borrows $15 million from Delaney Bank to purchase a shopping center, providing Delaney Bank a promissory note and deed of trust. Ward defaults on the loan and Delaney Bank forecloses its deed of trust. At the foreclosure sale, conducted by a deed trustee, Delaney Bank bids $1 million and wins the auction; Delaney Bank is the sole bidder. At the time of the sale, Ward owes Delaney Bank $10 million on his promissory note.
>   > After the foreclosure, Ward discovers that, one day before the foreclosure sale, Delaney Bank contracted to sell the property to a developer for $8 million.
>   > Delaney Bank sues Ward for a deficiency judgment.

Cash Only! No "IOUs"

Purchasers at a foreclosure sale cannot pay with an IOU. They must bring cash—or a statutorily accepted cash substitute. The idea is that bidding parties must be on an equal playing field and be in a position to *immediately* tender payment to terminate the mortgage lien. How do you think that this requirement affects the possible set of bidders?

Ward asks for your advice. *See* Regional Inv. Co. v. Willis, 572 S.W.2d 191 (Mo. Ct. App. 1978).

iii. Chilling the Bids.   Lenders and trustees must be careful to abide by statutory rules governing power-of-sale foreclosure. The purpose of the foreclosure auction is to produce a high sale value for the property, in order to pay off as much of the borrower's outstanding debt as possible. The last thing that the lender should do is discourage bids. This behavior is commonly known as "chilling the bids." However, lenders are not always so careful.

Practice Tip: The Lawyer's Response to a Common Question

Very often an attorney places the statutorily required foreclosure advertisement on behalf of her client, the lender, and conducts the sale. The attorney's contact information appears in the body of the advertisement. Parties interested in purchasing the property at the foreclosure sale may call the attorney and ask about the quality of the property. Can you see a problem? If the attorney answers that the property is "pretty run down," the borrower may claim the lender chilled the bidding. The better answer—and the standard practice—is for the attorney to tell the interested party that "this property is being foreclosed; you must view the property and reach your own conclusion."

■ PROBLEM: INACCURATE POWER-OF-SALE ADVERTISEMENT

Alice borrowed $150,000 from Big Bank to purchase Blackacre. Big Bank properly recorded its mortgage. Thereafter, Alice borrowed another $50,000 from Little Bank, whose mortgage specifically indicated it was subject to Big Bank's mortgage. In time, Alice paid off the loan to Big Bank and recorded a release of Big Bank's mortgage. Alice then defaulted on the Little Bank loan and Little Bank foreclosed under a power-of-sale provision. Little Bank's notices and advertisements indicated that Blackacre would be sold "subject to a senior lien in favor of Big Bank, recorded in book 327, page 399, of the Apple County records." This statement was an error: a recorded Big Bank mortgage does appear at book 327, page 399, but that mortgage referred to another property and a borrower other than Alice. After Little Bank sold Blackacre at the foreclosure sale, Alice sought to set aside the sale based on this error. Should she be able to do so?

Assume that you represent Alice. What is your advice? *See* Racette v. Bank of Am., N.A., 733 S.E.2d 457 (Ga. Ct. App. 2012).

626 Part III Transfer of Ownership

3. Moving to the Front of the Line

As we saw in the section titled "Conducting a Sale—and Doing the Math," it is always better for a lender to be earlier in time. Is there a way for one lender to move to the front of the line? The answer is yes; one lender may agree to be *subordinate* to the position of others. The subordination provision may be contained in the mortgage itself or in a separate document.

Lenders who are earlier in time may agree to subordinate their rights to a later-in-time lender. We see this quite often in the commercial context. Consider the following problem.

■ PROBLEM: SHOPPING CENTER IN THE MIDDLE OF NOWHERE

Daniel wants to buy Farmer's land, which is now a wheat field, to build a shopping center, but Daniel does not have sufficient cash. He convinces Farmer that the land will be worth much more—and Daniel will pay more—if it can be developed. Farmer and Daniel agree to a $2 million purchase price financed entirely by Farmer. In other words, Daniel provides no cash up front; instead, he will give only a promissory note and a mortgage to Farmer. In addition, Daniel explains that he will need to obtain a construction loan to build the shopping center and plans to borrow $10 million for this purpose from MegaBank. MegaBank will not loan this money to Daniel unless its lien is senior to all others. However, Daniel can't get the MegaBank loan at all until he has title to Blackacre (thus, the mortgage to Farmer will also have to come first). Therefore, Daniel proposes to add the following language to Farmer's mortgage: "Farmer understands and acknowledges that Daniel may obtain loans in connection with the real property for the purpose of improving said property. Farmer hereby subordinates this mortgage to any such future security instruments."

Farmer asks for your advice. Do you foresee any problems if Farmer signs the mortgage containing this subordination provision?

F WASTE

We earlier introduced the topic of waste in the context of co-tenants, future interests, and leaseholds. The co-tenant relationship, the life tenant/remainderman relationship, the landlord/tenant relationship, and the lender/borrower relationship all have something in common: one party is in possession of real property, while another party may or will come into possession sometime in the future. The party in possession is said to hold a duty to parties who are not yet in possession to avoid damaging or destroying the real property. If the party in possession

Waste and Externalities

If you currently possess property, but know that one day someone else will take possession, what incentive do you have to treat the property well? You may feel some of the pain and discomfort caused by a fire to the property; however, the lion's share of the pain will accrue to the party who comes into ultimate and permanent ownership. In other words, most of the costs of the fire are external to you. By making you pay damages for harm you cause to the property, waste doctrine forces you to internalize these externalities and encourages you to treat the property as if you hold it in fee simple.

acts in a deliberate manner to destroy or reduce the value of property, we say that he is engaging in "affirmative" or "voluntary" waste. If the party in possession simply "stands by" as things fall apart without taking steps to protect property, we say that he is engaging in "passive" or "permissive" waste.

The doctrine of waste applies to the mortgage relationship as well. The mortgagor borrows money and secures the loan with a mortgage on real property. If the mortgagor does not repay the loan as required, then the mortgagee will declare the note in default and foreclose the mortgage. In the end, this means that the mortgagee will sell the property at auction. The mortgagee may buy the property or a third party may purchase the property, *but either way, the borrower—the mortgagor—loses possession.* Therefore, the mortgagor of property is subject to waste doctrine as well.

Nevertheless, the concept of waste in a mortgage situation is different from the concept of waste in other situations. The expectations of a homeowner to use, renovate, and alter real property that she owns subject to a mortgage are quite different from that of a tenant subject to a lease. The homeowner reasonably expects that she will never face foreclosure, while a tenant knows that his tenancy will end. Furthermore, a homeowner assumes that she has the ability to use the property as she sees fit. These are largely correct assumptions. And in fact, the rule typically remains that the homeowner may do with property whatever one would consider normal in the context of ownership without committing waste. *See* William B. Stoebuck & Dale E. Whitman, The Law of Property §4.4, at 159–60 (3d ed. 2000).

Exactly what constitutes waste in a mortgage relationship? If the mortgagor owns a Frank Lloyd Wright home and "renovates" the home by knocking indiscriminate holes in the exterior walls for the purpose of providing "natural air conditioning," then it is probably easy for the mortgagee to prove waste. The general rule is that physical alterations to property that reduce its value constitute waste. This idea is repeated in the Restatement of Property. *See* Restatement (Third) of Property: Mortgages §4.6(a)(1) (1997). But what constitutes waste is not always so obvious. A mortgagor can do many things that do not physically alter the mortgaged property, but might reduce its value.

One scholar explains that "[a]lthough tenants and life tenants are the types of possessors most likely to come to mind in waste cases, the universe of potential waste defendants also includes mortgagors. Unlike the more obvious voluntary waste cases, in which the borrower actively harms the property, permissive waste cases present borrowers that allow the property to deteriorate without taking adequate action to mitigate the resulting damage. Rather than removing sinks and copper piping, the borrower might merely fail to repair the inevitable dripping faucets and leaky pipes, shortcomings which seem less blameworthy." *See* Gregory M. Stein, *The Scope of the Borrower's Liability in a Nonrecourse Real Estate Loan*, 55 Wash. & Lee L. Rev. 1207, 1262 (1998).

The Restatement takes an aggressive position and removes many of the older common law shackles that confined waste doctrine. We suggest that you read through §4.6 of the Restatement (Third) of Property: Mortgages (1997), and then attempt the Problems that follow.

---

§ 4.6 Waste

(a) Waste occurs when, without the mortgagee's consent, the mortgagor:
  (1) physically changes the real estate, whether negligently or intentionally, in a manner that reduces its value;
  (2) fails to maintain and repair the real estate in a reasonable manner, except for repair of casualty damage or acts of third parties not the fault of the mortgagor;
  (3) fails to pay before delinquency property taxes or governmental assessments secured by a lien having priority over the mortgage;
  (4) materially fails to comply with covenants in the mortgage respecting the physical care, maintenance, construction, demolition, or insurance against casualty of the real estate or improvements on it; or
  (5) retains possession of rents to which the mortgagee has the right of possession under § 4.2.

(b) The following remedies for waste by the mortgagor are available to the mortgagee as necessary to give complete redress:
  (1) foreclosure or the exercise of other remedies available under the mortgage for default on the secured obligation, if the waste has impaired the mortgagee's security;
  (2) an injunction prohibiting future waste or requiring correction of waste already committed, but only to the extent that the waste has impaired or threatens to impair the mortgagee's security; and
  (3) recovery of damages, limited by the amount of the waste, to the extent that the waste has impaired the mortgagee's security.

(c) If the mortgage relationship has ended at the time the mortgagee claims waste, an impairment of security exists if the value of the real estate is less than the sum of the mortgage obligation and the obligations secured by any liens senior to the mortgage. If the mortgage relationship continues to exist at the time the mortgagee claims waste, an impairment of security exists if the ratio of the mortgage obligation to the real estate's value is above its scheduled level. In such cases, the mortgagee may restore the ratio of the mortgage obligation to the real estate's value to its scheduled level by obtaining an order compelling correction of the waste or by recovery of damages, limited by the amount of the waste.

(d) Waste occurs when a person other than the mortgagor physically changes the real estate, whether negligently or intentionally, in a manner that reduces its value. Such a person may be held liable for damages and may be subjected to an injunction prohibiting future waste or requiring correction of waste already committed. If the waste was committed with the mortgagor's consent, liability exists only if the person committing it had actual knowledge of the existence of the mortgage.

(e) Persons who acquire possessory estates other than leaseholds in the real estate subject to the mortgage are liable for waste on the same basis as the mortgagor.

▰ PROBLEMS: WASTE OR NOT WASTE?

Keep in mind one of the goals of the lender: the lender wants assurance that the security it takes when making the loan will have value if it becomes necessary to foreclose on the property. Do you think that the borrower in the following scenarios has wasted the property interest of the lender who holds a mortgage on the property?

1. Nations Bank, a major national lending institution, holds a mortgage on a hotel owned by TripleTree. A trade journal reports that the TripleTree is in financial trouble. Nations Bank makes inquiries and discovers that TripleTree has not paid real estate taxes on the mortgaged property. *See* Travelers Ins. Co. v. 633 Third Assocs., 14 F.3d 114 (2d Cir. 1994); Krone v. Goff, 127 Cal. Rptr. 390 (Cal. Ct. App. 1975).

2. Big Pines owns 1,000 acres of timber land in Minnesota and is in the business of cutting that timber for profit. Big Pines obtains a 10-year loan of $1 million from the First Minnesota Bank, secured by a mortgage on the property. First Minnesota Bank was aware that Big Pines would use the land for timber-cutting purposes, and in fact took this timber use into consideration when making the loan. At the time First Minnesota Bank made its loan, Big Pines had been harvesting 1,000 trees a year from the land. Beginning in the third year of the loan, Big Pines starts harvesting 10,000 trees a year. *See* Judkins v. Woodman, 17 A. 298 (Me. 1889); Manke v. Prautsch, 401 P.2d 680 (Nev. 1965).

3. Jim DiGriz obtained a loan from Harry Harrison Lending and secured the loan with a mortgage on a San Francisco apartment building. A truly nasty earthquake (registering 7.0 on the Richter scale) hits San Francisco, damaging the apartment building. After the earthquake, DiGriz does not take steps to repair the building. *See* Krone v. Goff, *supra.*

Remedies for Waste: Damages and Injunctions

A mortgagee may bring an action in waste before or after foreclosure. If the mortgagee becomes aware of the mortgagor's actions, or inactions, that are wasteful prior to foreclosure, the mortgagee may ask the court for both damages and an injunction to prevent the mortgagor from continuing to engage in the destructive activity. Courts previously denied the mortgagee damages for waste prior to foreclosure, but this position has been receding and is not the rule adopted by the

Restatement. Sometimes the mortgagee discovers the waste only after foreclosure, and then there is little that the mortgagee can do other than demand damages.

There is one truly significant difference between the application of waste doctrine to landlords and lenders/mortgagees. In the case of a lease, the landlord recovers damages in connection with *destruction of the property*, and may recover an amount that equals the *total amount* of the damage. By contrast, the only thing that the lender bargains for is *security for the loan*. The mortgagee therefore recovers damages only to the degree that the waste "impairs his security." *See* Restatement (Third) of Property: Mortgages §4.6(b) (1997). What this means, basically, is that the mortgagee's damage award is capped at the amount still owing on the promissory note, plus expenses. Think of it this way: the mortgagee is never entitled to recover from the mortgagor an amount greater than the loan the mortgagor borrowed. Even if the dollar value of the waste exceeds the loan, the loan is the total sum for which the lender bargained. If the mortgagor repays the loan, the mortgagee/lender is made whole.

> **Practice Tip: The Mortgage Document Controls**
>
> The mortgage document will often explicitly address waste. 🖥 Look back at the Commercial Mortgage Agreement that is available on the Simulation. What constitutes waste under that mortgage, and what remedies does the mortgage grant to the lender? Can the mortgagee inspect the property to determine if the mortgagor is committing waste? How is waste treated under the Fannie Mae residential form?

G DISGUISED MORTGAGES

As we saw in our discussion of the foreclosure process, lenders gain significant rights in a mortgage document, particularly the ability to accelerate the debt and to foreclose on the property quickly if borrower defaults. However, the foreclosure process, although relatively swift, retains protections for the benefit of the borrower. At the very least, foreclosure requires that the lender auction off the property in an attempt to obtain a price that will pay off the debt. In addition, even after the foreclosure sale, many states allow the borrower a statutory redemption period.

Some lenders would rather just take the borrower's property immediately upon default and avoid the foreclosure and redemption process. Is there a way that lenders can do this?

LEE v. BEAGELL

19 N.Y.S.2d 613 (1940)
New York Supreme Court

DEYO, JUSTICE.

A somewhat novel situation is presented in this action to redeem mortgaged premises. It seems that in 1936 the plaintiff, for a valuable consideration, purchased the property involved from the defendants Theodore and Florence Beagell. The plaintiff received a warranty deed and entered into possession. The deed, however, was not recorded. Some three years later, on March 18, 1939, the plaintiff borrowed $50 from Mr. Beagell, which she agreed to repay in weekly installments of $2.50, together with interest at 6 per cent and as security for the loan, she deposited the title deed, still unrecorded, with Mr. Beagell. It was apparently understood that if the plaintiff failed to repay the loan the property would belong to Mr. Beagell. The plaintiff did not pay, and on September 8, 1939, after the twenty-week period had expired, Mr. and Mrs. Beagell executed and delivered a deed of the same premises to the defendants George and Hazel Card, with the understanding that if the plaintiff paid off the indebtedness on or before February 1, 1940, the deed to the Cards would be destroyed and the deed to the plaintiff would be redelivered to her. The defendants say that the plaintiff had knowledge of this agreement and the court assumes that to be a fact. The plaintiff failed to pay the indebtedness and on February 2, 1940, the deed to the Cards was recorded. No tender of the amount due on the loan was made until after February 2, 1940. The plaintiff remained in possession of the premises throughout and is still in possession of them. Under these facts both parties move for judgment. The plaintiff maintains that the transaction constituted an equitable mortgage in favor of the defendants. The defendants maintain that on failure to pay the indebtedness they became vested with the title to the premises.

The execution and delivery of the deed by the Beagells on June 29, 1936, vested title to the premises in the plaintiff. No further act was necessary. The failure to record the deed in no way affected its validity as between the parties nor as against any other party excepting a purchaser in good faith, for a valuable consideration and without notice of the unrecorded conveyance. Real Property Law §291....

The redelivery of the deed to Beagell did not divest the plaintiff of the title she had thus acquired, since it is well established by statute and by the decisions that title cannot be conveyed except by a written instrument or by operation of law. Real Property Law, §242. "A deed once delivered and accepted, its redelivery by the grantee will not revest the legal title in the grantor." Herrmann v. Jorgenson, 263 N.Y. 348, at page 354, 189 N.E. 449, at page 451.

What then did Beagell acquire when the title deed was deposited with him as security for the loan? It is axiomatic that a conveyance absolute in form, if intended merely as security for an obligation, will be construed in equity as a mortgage. Peugh v. Davis, 96 U.S. 332, 24 L. Ed. 775; Nestell v. Hart, 202 N.Y. 280, 95 N.E. 703; Mooney v. Byrne, 163 N.Y. 86, 57 N.E. 163; Thompson v. Lewis, 2d Dept. 1918, 182 App. Div. 556, 169 N.Y.S. 501. The defendant admits this principle of law, but insists that it applies only in those cases where the equitable mortgagor executed a conveyance. True, that is the situation in the ordinary case, but the court does not deem it to be an essential prerequisite to the granting of the relief herein sought. "The whole doctrine of equitable mortgages is founded upon that cardinal maxim of equity which regards that as done which has been agreed to be done and ought to have been done. In order to apply this maxim according to its true meaning, the court will treat the subject-matter, as to collateral consequences and incidents, in the same manner as if the final acts contemplated by the parties had been executed exactly as they ought to have been, and not as the parties might have executed them, always regarding the substance, and not the form, of the transaction." Sprague v. Cochran, 144 N.Y. 104, at page 114, 38 N.E. 1000, at page 1002.

No authority is presented and the court has found none which limits the doctrine of equitable mortgages to those instances where the equitable mortgagor has executed a written instrument. In fact, courts of equity have found an equitable mortgage to exist in a variety of cases, even though no writing exists. Sprague v. Cochran, supra; Smith v. Smith, 125 N.Y. 224, 26 N.E. 259. Although the creation of equitable mortgages by the deposit of title deeds has not been recognized in this State to the extent that it is in England, nevertheless, the courts have not hesitated to utilize this method of attaining justice when the equities so require....

In Chase v. Peck, 21 N.Y. 581, Denio, J., said at page 584: "The courts of equity in this State have adopted the general doctrines of the English Chancery upon this subject, as upon many others. The cases of a mortgage created by a writing not sufficient to convey the premises, or by a deposit of title deeds, have not been frequent with us; but the doctrine has been applied in a few instances, and I do not find any judgment or dictum by which it has ever been questioned."

The question is one of intention to be decided from a consideration of the whole transaction and not from any particular feature of it. Dickens v. Heston, 53 Idaho 91, 21 P.2d 905, 90 A.L.R. 953. Clearly, it was the intention of the parties that Beagell should have a lien on the property as security for the debt, at the very least. The plaintiff remained the owner of the legal estate and Beagell had a lien in the nature of an equitable mortgage. This lien could not be changed into a legal estate by an agreement of the parties to cut off the right of redemption. Thompson v. Lewis, 2d Dept. 1918, 182 App. Div. 556, 169 N.Y.S. 501. The equity of redemption is inseparably associated with the mortgage be it legal or equitable, and cannot be cut off or impaired by any subsequent acts of the equitable mortgagee. Mooney v. Byrne, supra; Massari v. Girardi, 119 Misc. 607, 197 N.Y.S. 751. Since the defendants George and Hazel Card had knowledge that the title deed was deposited with Beagell as security only, and since the plaintiff was at all times in possession of the premises, they could not and did not become bona fide purchasers in good faith and they succeeded only to the rights which Beagell had in the premises, which was a lien in the nature of an equitable mortgage. An action to redeem may be maintained against a mortgagee, whether in or out of possession. Reich v. Cochran, 213 N.Y. 416, 107 N.E. 1029; Sumner v. Sumner, 2d Dept. 1926, 217 App. Div. 163, 216 N.Y.S. 389.

Judgment will be granted directing the defendants to execute, acknowledge and deliver to the plaintiff a good and sufficient deed or conveyance of their interest in said property upon payment by the plaintiff to the defendants of the amount still due and unpaid upon the loan with interest on same, together with the costs of this action. If the parties cannot agree upon the amount due upon the loan, an accounting may be had which will be referred to an official referee.

Judgment on the pleadings in accordance with the foregoing. No motion costs are allowed either party.

■ POINTS TO CONSIDER

1. **What is an equitable mortgage?** You have probably heard the old adage that "if it walks like a duck, and quacks like a duck, it's probably a duck." Courts view mortgages in much the same way. From time to time, lenders have tried to coerce borrowers into waiving their equity of redemption at the inception of the loan. One way lenders do this is by disguising a mortgage transaction as something else. This practice is generically called "clogging the equity of redemption," and as we saw in *Beagell*, courts will not enforce these arrangements as anything other than mortgages. *See* John C. Murray, *Clogging Revisited*, 33 Real Prop. Prob. & Tr. J. 279 (1998). It is the substance of the relationship, and not what it is called or how it is styled, that matters. What is the essence of a mortgage of real property? Why is the transaction between Ms. Lee and the Beagells deemed a mortgage by the court? On the face of it, it appears that all Ms. Lee did was allow the Beagells to hold on to a deed. This is not "purchase money lending" because the loan money was not used to purchase the property. Note that the court refers to the arrangement as an "equitable" mortgage. Why does it employ this terminology? Why do we care about the intent of the parties?

   Equitable mortgages may arise in any number of scenarios. *See, e.g.,* Flack v. McClure, 565 N.E.2d 131 (Ill. App. Ct. 1990) (delivery of quitclaim deed determined to be an equitable mortgage securing a $9,000 loan, rather than an actual sale); Essex Prop. Services, Inc. v. Wood, 587 A.2d 1337 (N.J. Super. Ct. 1991) (sale/leaseback of home construed to create an equitable mortgage and not a landlord/tenant relationship; mortgagee prohibited from evicting borrower pursuant to summary proceedings statute).

2. **What is old is new again.** The *Beagell* court begins by saying that the fact pattern in the case is novel. Recall that originally a mortgage involved the conveyance of real property by deed to the lender (along with possession) and a reversionary interest in the borrower. Does this remind you of the fact pattern in *Beagell*?

3. **A layperson's assumptions about the operation of deeds can be very wrong.** Both Ms. Lee and the Beagells made an assumption about the effect of Ms. Lee handing back her unrecorded deed to the Beagells. This assumption was totally wrong. What was their basic misunderstanding about the operation of deeds?

4. **A review of recording statutes.** The *Beagall* opinion cites a section of New York Code for this proposition: "The failure to record the deed in no way affected its validity as between the parties nor as against any other party excepting a purchaser in good faith, for a valuable consideration and without notice of the unrecorded conveyance." N.Y. Real Prop. Law §291 (McKinney 2006 & Supp. 2018). What type of recording statute is this? The Beagells executed a deed to a second purchaser—the Cards—who were therefore subsequent purchasers. Why weren't the Cards protected under the recording statute against Ms. Lee's prior but unrecorded deed?

5. **If the court finds that a mortgage exists, then the remedy follows.** What happens to Ms. Lee if the court fails to conclude that a mortgage exists? Ms. Lee simply loses her property altogether! Is this the appropriate result? We do not know how much the property originally cost, only the amount of the loan. Assume, for the sake of argument, that Lee purchased the property from the Beagells for $500. If the court accepted the Beagells' argument, failure to pay a *$50 loan* results in a total loss of the property, and no foreclosure auction. If the court finds a mortgage, however, then at least the lender must follow foreclosure procedure and auction off the property; we hope that the auction would have brought in more than $50.

■ PROBLEM: A DISGUISED MORTGAGE?

Zelazny, Inc., a maker of premium playing cards, decides to move to a larger facility due to the growth of its business. Zelazny negotiates a 10-year lease of a 10,000-square-foot building, owned by Amber Developers. Although commercial rental rates in the area range between $25 and $30 per square foot per year, the lease specifies that Zelazny will pay Amber Developers $50 per square foot. In addition, the lease provides Zelazny with an option to purchase the building at the end of the 10-year term, for a purchase price of $100. In Year 6 of the lease, the economy is rocked by a severe recession, and consumers reduce purchases of high quality playing cards. As a result, Zelazny's revenues fall, and it fails to make rent payments in January and February of that year. Amber Developers declares the lease in default and the purchase option void, and commences eviction proceedings against Zelazny.

The president of Zelazny, Inc. asks for your advice. How do you respond? For a discussion of options to purchase as "disguised mortgages," *see* Ronald Benton Brown, *An Examination of Real Estate Purchase Options*, 12 Nova L. Rev. 147, 197 (1987).

Compare the fact pattern in the problem to *Beagell*. In the problem, there is an actual document—a lease with an option to purchase. Was there an equivalent document in *Beagell*? Does this matter?

SUMMARY

- A *promissory note* is a creature of contract law and memorializes the borrower's promise to repay a loan to the lender; the promissory note identifies the parties, the amount of the loan, and the obligations of the borrower.
- In some states, a loan that charges interest rates above a rate set by law are deemed *usurious* and illegal. States that penalize usurious loans differ on the borrower's remedy. Some states limit the lender to collecting interest at the maximum rate allowed by law, while a few states actually eliminate the borrower's obligation to repay the principal of the loan.
- A *mortgage* is a creature of property law and secures the promissory note by providing an interest in real property as collateral for the loan; the lender may sell the property in satisfaction of the loan by a process known as foreclosure.
- The party pledging an interest in real estate in a mortgage is known as a mortgagor, and the party to whom the interest is conveyed is known as a mortgagee.
- The borrower always has the right to "redeem" the property by paying the loan prior to foreclosure; this is known as the *equity of redemption*.
- Modern loan documents and promissory notes typically contain *acceleration clauses* that permit the lender to declare the entire loan amount due upon default. The borrower must therefore pay the entire loan to redeem the property prior to foreclosure.
- There are two basic explanations of the nature of a mortgage: *title theory* and *lien theory*. Title theory styles a mortgage as a conveyance of title, while lien theory treats the mortgage as the grant of a security interest only.
- *Foreclosure* terminates the lien of the mortgage that is foreclosed, as well as all interests in the property that are junior to the foreclosed mortgage.
- The *foreclosure sale* generates cash that is distributed according to a set of rules: the proceeds go first to the foreclosing lender, and then downward to junior interest holders and the borrower by the rule of absolute priority. Money never travels upward to senior lien holders.
- Lenders with mortgages covering the same property prefer to be earlier in time to record and have a higher priority; a lender may agree to *subordinate* its position.
- *Foreclosure process* may be either *judicial* or *non-judicial*.
- A *judicial foreclosure* results from a lawsuit on the note and mortgage.
- Due process requires that the mortgagee join all *necessary parties*; the party is "necessary" if the foreclosure will wipe out that party's interest.
- If a necessary party is not joined to the action, the foreclosure will not affect that party's lien rights in the property. A foreclosure action that fails to join the mortgagor mortgagee may also join *proper parties*, such as senior lienholders. A is simply void.
- Most states permit *non-judicial foreclosure*: the mortgage will contain a *power of sale* permitting the mortgagee or a designated trustee to sell the property in satisfaction of the debt upon the borrower's default. In some states, the

mortgagor conveys the security interest in the property by *deed to secure debt*, permitting the mortgagee/lender to foreclose. In others, the security interest in the property is conveyed by a *deed of trust*, permitting a trustee to foreclose.

- The mortgagee must be careful to follow all of the statutory requirements for notice and timing in a non-judicial foreclosure.

- In both non-judicial and judicial foreclosure actions, the lender must avoid *chilling bids*, or run the risk of seeing the foreclosure sale invalidated.

- Foreclosures do not typically generate high sale prices because the property is "distressed," and a foreclosure sale will be invalidated only if the price is so low as to *shock the conscience of the court.*

- Some courts invalidate foreclosure if the winning bid is grossly inadequate and is accompanied by an *irregularity* in foreclosure process.

- Courts vary on the level of duty that the foreclosing lender has to the borrower in a non-judicial foreclosure. Some hold that the lender has no duty at all, while others hold that the foreclosing lender has a *fiduciary duty* to the borrower to obtain a fair and reasonable price under the circumstances.

- If a foreclosure sale generates less cash than the outstanding indebtedness, the lender may be entitled to a *deficiency judgment*, allowing the lender to proceed as a judgment creditor directly against the personal assets of the debtor. Only the lender that forecloses is entitled to a deficiency judgment. Some states limit or prohibit deficiency judgments.

- In a non-judicial foreclosure proceeding, to obtain a deficiency judgment the lender must *confirm* the winning bid in court, which in some jurisdictions requires that the lender demonstrate to the court that the sale price was fair.

- Many jurisdictions grant the mortgagor (and in some cases, holders of interests in property junior to the mortgagee) a right of *statutory redemption.*

- The mortgagor may not *waste* the real property. Waste is generally considered to result from physical alterations that lower the value of property, but waste may result from other actions, such as the failure to pay property taxes.

- *Damages* for the borrower's waste are typically limited to the amount of the loan.

- Some arrangements are *disguised (or equitable) mortgages* and will be treated as mortgages by courts. If the purpose of an arrangement is to provide security for a loan, it will be deemed a mortgage.

PART IV

Servitudes

*S*ervitudes encompass legal rights and obligations that are attached to and burden the land. The recognized categories of servitudes include *easements, profits, licenses,* and *real covenants.*

These are *nonpossessory* interests, unlike a lease, which gives the lessee the right of possession. Nevertheless, servitudes are like the thread that binds together the patchwork quilt of land ownership into a workable, flexible fabric. Often these interests are extremely important. Blackacre may be landlocked and therefore useless without a right-of-way over Whiteacre to reach the road. A promise attached to Whiteacre, limiting its use to residential purposes only, may protect Blackacre from having Wal-Mart locate next door. Next time you turn on the gas in your stove, think about the property rights required to get that product from its source to your kitchen.

We begin with a basic introduction to the recognized types of servitudes:

1. EASEMENTS

An *easement* is defined as the right to use the property of another for a specific purpose. The most common easement is a "right-of-way," which gives the holder the right to cross another's land. Utility companies own easements for power lines or pipelines. The city may have an easement across your front yard for a sidewalk or stormwater drainage. A business may need an easement to give its customers or delivery trucks better access to its property.

An easement is an interest in land. As such, it is subject to the Statute of Frauds and the recording acts. We will study the creation, scope, and termination of easements in Chapter 10.

2. PROFITS

A *profit à prendre* is a "super-easement," in the sense that it couples the right to enter the property of another with the right to remove something, such as minerals, timber, or game. A mere easement would not allow the holder to carry off the products of the land. The term was derived from the "law French" used in the English legal system after the Norman Conquest (the translation of "profit à prendre" is "right of taking"). Modern courts often shorten the term to "profit." For the most part, the rules regarding the creation and interpretation of profits are identical to those for easements. Therefore, we will not study them separately but will note any differences in the chapter on easements.

Often a landowner will use a lease rather than a profit to give someone the right to extract minerals or timber from her property. In addition, the right to hunt or fish often is given in the form of a license (discussed below) rather than a profit.

3. LICENSES

In contrast with an easement or profit à prendre, a license is not an interest in land, but rather is a transient, personal privilege. A license constitutes permission to enter the property of another for a particular purpose. A license is usually held to be *revocable* and *unassignable* (without consent) unless the parties agree otherwise. When you buy a ticket to a Lakers game, you are given a license to occupy a particular seat. That privilege is revocable, however; if you begin to make obscene gestures or throw popcorn on the referees, you may be asked to leave.

Assume you are out working on your farm and a neighbor asks if he can hunt pheasant in the pasture. If you say yes, you have just given your neighbor a license. Because it is not an interest in land, it need not adhere to the Statute of Frauds; thus, a license can be granted orally. You can also decide at any time to revoke the neighbor's privilege. It is also unassignable—you gave permission to your neighbor, because you know him and trust him. He cannot now call up his cousin, whom you don't like and don't trust, and assign the license to her.

Of course, if you purchased a license, the terms of the license will be established by the purchase agreement. That may include the conditions under which the license may be revoked and assigned. The back of your ticket to a sporting or entertainment event, for example, may contain these conditions.

What differences do you see between licenses, leases, and profits? For example, why would a landowner prefer using a license or lease to convey a right to hunt rather than a profit?

4. REAL COVENANTS (AND EQUITABLE SERVITUDES)

A covenant is simply another term for a contractual promise, such as a covenant not to compete found in an employment contract. In property law, a *real covenant* refers to a promise relating to the land, which adheres to the title and "runs with the land" rather than remaining with the original promisor or promisee.

> ➤ In other words, *real* covenants deal with *real* property.

When Alice sells Blackacre to Clarisse, she may make any number of promises. She may promise to provide Clarisse with an updated abstract of title, she may promise to fix the broken board on the back deck, or she may promise to leave the pool table in the basement. Those are merely personal covenants, for which Alice alone is responsible. In contrast, a real covenant is one that relates to the use of the land itself. For example, the most common real covenant restricts the property to residential use, often single-family.

Historically, developers created housing subdivisions with few restrictions. In older neighborhoods, you may find that zoning ordinances, rather than covenants, are the primary constraint on the use of property. Modern subdivisions, however, typically include a much more comprehensive set of "covenants, conditions, and restrictions" (CC&Rs), which may govern everything from the type of shingles you use on your roof to the placement of satellite dishes. Many modern housing developments create homeowners associations to enforce and amend the covenants, giving rise to numerous legal questions over the association's authority.

For now, you should try to distinguish a covenant from an easement. Recall that an *easement is a grant of a property interest,* giving the holder the right to do something on another's land, or to prevent the other landowner from doing something. By contrast, *a real covenant is a promise respecting land.* Typically, Alice would grant a right-of-way to Bart in the form of an easement, but Bart may then promise, in the form of a covenant, to maintain the right-of-way. Bart's promise could not really be stated in terms of an easement—he is undertaking a duty with respect to the land.

Because of some crusty legal impediments, which we will learn shortly, courts sometimes hold that a real covenant cannot be enforced at law by or against a subsequent owner of the property. Nevertheless, the court may be willing to use its authority in equity to hold the landowner to the covenant. In that case, the covenant is enforced as an *equitable servitude.*

We will explore real covenants and equitable servitudes in detail in Chapter 11.

Problem: Distinguishing Types of Servitudes. Developer Offut sold a house to Wynn in a subdivision that included an apartment complex with a swimming pool. In order to induce Wynn to pay a slightly higher price for the house, Offut said he would throw in the right to use the swimming pool. The purchase contract included the following language: "Use of apartment swimming pool to be available to purchaser and his family." Several years later, Wynn sold the house to Bunn. Bunn was denied access to the pool, and Offut indicated the privilege was only intended to be for the Wynns, not subsequent purchasers of the house. Which type of interest did Wynn have? Why does it matter? *See* Bunn v. Offut, 222 S.E.2d 522 (Va. 1976).

Easements

> Roads, lanes, paths. We use them without reflecting how they are some of man's oldest inscriptions upon the landscape, how they are evidence of the wedding between men and their environment.
> —*Geoffrey Grigson, Freedom of the Parish 158 (1954)*

An *easement* gives the holder the right to do something on the property of another or the right to keep the other owner from doing something on his property. Easements therefore allow multiple parties to have rights with respect to land without actually owning the land itself. In this way, easements are vitally important to enable property to function efficiently in a complex modern world. In this chapter, we will discuss the various ways in which easements may be created, issues regarding their scope, and how they may be terminated.

But first, let's go over some terminology and basic principles:

Suppose Alice, who owns Blackacre, holds a right-of-way easement over adjacent Whiteacre, owned by Bart, so that she can reach a nearby road. We say that Blackacre is the *dominant* parcel or tenement, which has the benefit of the easement, while Whiteacre is the *servient* tenement, which bears the burden of the easement. We also would classify this type of easement as *appurtenant*, because it benefits a particular property (Blackacre) and is therefore attached to the title to Blackacre, rather than belonging to Alice personally.[1]

---

[1] Although an appurtenant easement usually benefits adjacent property, the dominant parcel need not be adjacent. For example, the right-of-way over Whiteacre used by Alice might be a shortcut between County Road A and County Road B, enabling her to more easily reach Blackacre, which is several miles down County Road B. It would still be appurtenant to Blackacre, because it benefits that parcel.

Therefore, if Alice conveys Blackacre to Clarisse, in a deed that does not mention the easement, does Clarisse now have the right to use the right-of-way? Absolutely, because the easement is appurtenant to Blackacre, which Clarisse now owns. How about if Bart now conveys Whiteacre to David? As long as David had notice of the easement (actual, constructive, or inquiry), he will be bound by it as well.

An easement *in gross*, on the other hand, does not benefit any particular property. Instead, an easement in gross *benefits a particular party.* MegaGas Company, for example, may have an easement through Blackacre for a pipeline transporting petroleum products from Canada to Texas. The easement is in gross and MegaGas may *assign* its rights to another company.

Affirmative easements allow the holder of the benefit *to do something* on the servient tenement. A *right-of-way* is the most common type of affirmative easement. In contrast, a *negative easement* allows the holder to *prevent* the servient landowner from making otherwise permissible use of her own land. For example, a negative "set-back" type of easement would prevent an owner from building too close to the property line. In our example, Alice could have a negative easement on Whiteacre that prevents Bart from building within 30 feet of the property line. This would not give Alice the right to use or enter upon that 30 feet, but only to object if Bart tried to build on it. Because the easement benefits Blackacre, it would be appurtenant.

Another common type of negative easement is a *conservation easement*, which leaves the fee ownership of the property in the landowner but prevents the development of the property. Similarly, a historic preservation easement prevents a building owner from destroying or modifying the structure. *See* United States v. Blackman, 613 S.E.2d 442 (Va. 2005) (explaining and recognizing as valid conservation and historic preservation easements).

These types of negative easements are typically in gross, with the benefit held by an organization, such as the Nature Conservancy.

We will discuss the creation, interpretation, and termination of easements in detail below.

■ PROBLEM: COMPARING PROFITS À PRENDRE

A *profit* may be either appurtenant or in gross, and it is sometimes difficult to tell which was intended. For example, assume Alice owns both Blackacre and Whiteacre. She conveys Whiteacre to Bart and, in the deed, also grants to Bart a right to hunt on Blackacre. A few years later, Bart sells Whiteacre to David—can David now hunt on Blackacre? The answer depends on whether the parties intended the profit to be appurtenant or in gross.

Certainly, the fact that the interest was created in the deed to Whiteacre suggests it is appurtenant, but that presumption could be rebutted by language indicating that the right was intended to be personal to Bart. *See* Merriam

v. First Nat'l Bank of Akron, 587 So. 2d 584 (Fla. Dist. Ct. App. 1991). One question would be if the right benefited the land rather than the person—for example, the right to take water on Blackacre for the use of cattle on Whiteacre would be appurtenant. *See* Goss v. C.A.N. Wildlife Trust, Inc., 852 A.2d 996 (Md. Ct. Spec. App. 2004) (profit to hunt and fish clearly intended to benefit adjacent land used for hunting camp). If the profit is appurtenant, it cannot be transferred without also conveying the land to which it is attached.

If the profit is in gross—that is, personal to Bart—can he simply assign it to David? Many courts say, without much analysis, that a profit in gross is assignable and inheritable. *See, e.g.*, Hanson v. Fergus Falls Nat'l Bank, 65 N.W.2d 857 (Minn. 1954) (hunting rights). On the other hand, some courts would focus on the grantor's intent. *See Merriam, supra.* In that case, Bart could not assign the profit to David unless the right to assign was clearly intended—for example, in the original document creating the profit (e.g., the grantee was "Bart, his successors and assigns").

A CREATION OF EASEMENTS

Easements are most often created in a deed, by express grant or reservation. Expressly created easements are preferable, because details such as scope and location can be carefully delineated. Nevertheless, as we will see, even a carefully worded grant may raise questions regarding interpretation, especially as circumstances change.

In many cases, however, the parties never formalize their easement agreement in writing. In that case, the party seeking recognition of an easement will need to rely on one of the other methods of creation. Here is a summary of ways to create easements:

Easement Creation

1. **Express:** A writing meeting the requirements of the Statute of Frauds.
2. **Estoppel:** The dominant tenant reasonably relied to his detriment on the servient tenant's promise.
3. **Implied:** These situations arise when a grantor splits a piece of property into pieces and conveys one of the parcels. The court might determine that an easement was implied in the conveyance in two situations:
   - **By prior use:** if a particular use of the servient parcel already existed and was reasonably necessary to the use and enjoyment of the dominant parcel.
   - **By necessity:** if an easement became necessary due to the conveyance.

> **4. Prescription:** Similar to adverse possession, the dominant tenant uses the servient parcel without permission for the prescriptive period. Also related to this category are easements established by custom and implied dedication.

1. Express Easements

The clearest way to create an easement is by written grant or reservation, either by deed or by will. Assume that Alice, the owner of Blackacre, sells her adjacent property, Whiteacre, to Bart. If Alice wants Bart to have a right-of-way over Blackacre, she could include a *grant* of that easement in the deed to Whiteacre. In contrast, if she wants to retain a right-of-way over Whiteacre, she may do so by a *reservation* or *exception* in the deed to Bart. Technically, an exception is used by a grantor to preserve a *pre-existing* right, while a reservation creates a *new* right.

> ➤ For example, if Alice had previously granted an easement over Whiteacre to her neighbor Carl, she would then convey Whiteacre to Bart, with an exception for Carl's easement.
> ➤ If Alice wanted to create a new easement over Whiteacre for her own benefit, she would convey Whiteacre to Bart, but reserve a right-of-way.

However, courts and lawyers sometimes use the terms *reservation* and *exception* interchangeably.

Because an express easement is an interest in land, it cannot be created orally, but only by a writing that complies with the Statute of Frauds. Thus, at a minimum, the writing must:

- properly identify the parties (grantor and grantee);
- describe the property burdened and benefited by the easement;
- indicate an intent to create an easement; and
- be signed by the grantor.

The writing *should* also specify the location, extent, and proper use (scope) of the easement. However, if the express grant merely gives the grantee a "right-of-way" over Blackacre, a court will usually fix the boundaries of the easement if the parties cannot agree. In such a case, the court will attempt to discern the parties' intent and give the grantee the "right to such way as is reasonably necessary and convenient for the purposes for which it is granted." Mugar v. Mass. Bay Transp. Auth., 552 N.E.2d 121, 123 (Mass. App. Ct. 1990) (quoting Pratt v. Sanger, 4 Gray 84, 88 (1855)).

Assume that Alice, the owner of Blackacre, is selling her adjacent property, Whiteacre, to Bart. Bart wants the deal to include a right-of-way over Blackacre, so he can easily reach the main road. Assume you are drafting this express easement. Consider the following issues:

1) *Location.* The grantor will want to ensure that the easement is located in a way that minimizes the disruption of current use of the property, as well as potential future uses. The grantee, on the other hand, will want to ensure the easement is convenient for its intended purpose. Alice may want to include a provision allowing her to relocate the easement if it interferes with her future plans.

2) *Width.* A right-of-way that was sufficient for ingress and egress in the days of horses and buggies may not suffice for cars, and certainly not for recreational vehicles.

3) *Scope.* What exactly are permitted and prohibited uses? For example, is the purpose of the easement solely for *ingress* and *egress*, or does it include parking? *See* Cochran v. Hoffman, 971 N.E.2d 670 (Ind. Ct. App. 2012) (right-of-way for "all purposes of travel" held to include right to park because it was not limited to ingress and egress). Do the parties contemplate that the right-of-way will benefit one single-family house only? What if Bart decides to build an apartment house on his land? Or Wal-Mart buys Whiteacre from Bart and builds a store? Can Wal-Mart now use the right-of-way for its daily traffic of delivery trucks?

> **Ingress and Egress**
>
> Ingress and egress are fancy legal ways of saying "entrance" and "exit." Collectively, ingress and egress grant a right of *access* to property. A right-of-way limited to ingress and egress typically does not allow parking or storage, but only coming and going.

4) *Duration.* Do the parties contemplate a perpetual easement or only a temporary one? For example, Bart may need the easement only until the construction of his house and new driveway is complete. Or Alice may be willing to allow Bart to cross her property for a while, but wants him to eventually find a different route. If no duration is stated, the easement is presumed to be perpetual. Technically, to create a perpetual easement, the grant should include words of inheritance ("to Bart, his heirs and assigns"), but modern courts will look at the intent of the parties if those words are not used. If the easement is limited to a *particular purpose*, the easement will terminate when the purpose is fulfilled or ceases to exist. *See, e.g.,* Pyramid Dev., L.L.C. v. D & J Assocs., 553 S.E.2d 725 (Va. 2001) (easement to reach railroad spur terminated when rail service discontinued).

5) *Maintenance and improvement.* Who will be responsible for maintenance of the right-of-way? What if Bart wants to dump gravel on what was previously a dirt track? What if he wants to pave it? What if Bart calls to complain that an old oak tree is interfering with his access and he wants to cut it down (or wants Alice to cut it down, which will cost her $1,000)? *See* Mayer v. Smith, 350 P.3d 1191 (N.M. Ct. App. 2015)(ingress/egress easement implied right to clear trees from right-of-way).

6) *Termination.* As noted, the easement will be deemed perpetual unless otherwise stated or implied. We will learn that it is possible, but difficult, to terminate an easement due to misuse or abandonment. It may be best to specify the exact circumstances that would allow Alice to terminate the easement.

Preparing to Practice

Your client, Rancher, has been contacted by the Great Plains Pipeline Company, which is building a long-distance pipeline to carry petroleum products from Canada to Texas. The planned route goes through Rancher's 1,000-acre ranch. The pipeline company offers to purchase a right-of-way easement through the ranch. The language of the easement states:

> Grantor, his heirs, successors and assigns, for consideration of Ten Dollars and other valuable consideration, the receipt and sufficiency of which is hereby acknowledged, does hereby grant and convey to Great Plains Pipeline Company, its successors and assigns a permanent easement to survey, construct, operate, maintain, repair and replace one or more pipelines for the transportation of petroleum products and all related above and below ground appurtenances. The permanent easement shall consist of a 50-foot width along a route to be selected by Grantee over and across the Property, described as follows: [property legal description]. The easement includes the right of access for construction, repair, and replacement of the pipeline. Grantor agrees not to excavate, build, or plant trees or shrubs on the right-of-way.

Your client has been offered what he considers fair consideration for this pipeline, "considering I won't even see the darn thing after it's been buried." He has asked you to look over the easement and suggest any changes necessary to protect his interests. *What is your advice?*

Creating Easements in "Strangers to the Deed"

A common problem arises when a landowner wants to use the deed to one party to reserve an easement for a third party. Assume that Alice's next-door neighbor, Tristan, has been using a dirt road over Whiteacre to reach his property, Greenacre, for many years. Alice and Tristan have never formalized the arrangement. (How would you classify it?) Alice wants to make sure the arrangement continues after she sells Whiteacre to Bart, so she includes in the deed to Whiteacre the following language: "Alice hereby conveys Whiteacre to Bart, in fee simple, with the exception of an easement in favor of Tristan for the dirt road." Has she accomplished her intention?

To make matters worse, parties sometimes try to include this sort of interest as a warranty exception—for example, "Alice warrants to Bart that she has good title free and clear of all encumbrances, with the exception of an easement in favor of Tristan."

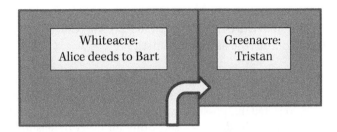

There are some problems with what Alice has tried to do. First, including the easement as an exception to her conveyance to Bart would be perfectly proper, *if* she had already created the easement by an express grant to Tristan. The problem is, she has never done that. This is a deed to Bart, delivered to Bart—how can it create an interest in Tristan? A warranty exception doesn't include any granting language; it simply makes Bart aware of previously created encumbrances that the grantor is excepting from the covenant against encumbrances.

The common law rule is that a grantor cannot create an interest in a third party, a so-called stranger to the deed. In a deed, the grantor is conveying an interest to the grantee; she may hold part of that conveyance back for herself, but cannot at the same time convey that reserved interest to someone else. As the court explained in Jolynne Corp. v. Michels, 446 S.E.2d 494, 502 (W. Va. 1994):

Make the Connection

This situation also creates problems for title searchers—how would this instrument be indexed? If you were looking for an easement in favor of Tristan, would you find it?

> Many deeds contain exceptions and reservations that restrict the interest passed by the grantor. However, neither exceptions nor reservations can create a right to the transferred property in persons who are strangers to the deed, because "property cannot be conveyed by reservation" and "property which is excepted is not granted." Erwin v. Bethlehem Steel Corporation, 134 W. Va. 900, 916, 62 S.E.2d 337, 346 (1950) (quoting 26 C.J.S., Deeds, §§140c and 140a). Syl. pt. 3, *Erwin* states:
>
>> A reservation or an exception in favor of a stranger to a conveyance does not serve to recognize or confirm a right which does not exist in his favor when the conveyance which contains such reservation or exception is made.

Id. at 502. Some recent cases confirming this common law rule include Conway v. Miller, 232 P.3d 390 (Mont. 2010) (words of exception or reservation are not words of grant and may not convey right-of-way to third party); Dichter v. Devers,

891 N.Y.S.2d 426 (N.Y. App. Div. 2009) (same). *Cf.* Peters v. Smolian, 12 N.Y.S.3d 824 (N.Y. App. Div. 2015) (rule does not apply to right of first refusal created in third party).

Although this result has a logical appeal, some courts now allow deeds to create an interest in a third party. For these courts, the technical error on the part of the grantor should not overcome clear indications of intent. In Willard v. First Church of Christ, Scientist, 498 P.2d 987 (Cal. 1972), the court denigrated the origins of the rule as anachronistic:

> The rule . . . was based on feudal considerations. . . . While a reservation could theoretically vest an interest in a third party, the early common law courts vigorously rejected this possibility, apparently because they mistrusted and wished to limit conveyance by deed as a substitute for livery by seisin. Insofar as this mistrust was the foundation of the rule, it is clearly an inapposite feudal shackle today.
>
> California early adhered to this common law rule. . . . In considering our continued adherence to it, we must realize that our courts no longer feel constricted by feudal forms of conveyancing. Rather, our primary objective in construing a conveyance is to try to give effect to the intent of the grantor. . . . In general, therefore, grants are to be interpreted in the same way as other contracts and not according to rigid feudal standards. . . . The common law rule conflicts with the modern approach to construing deeds because it can frustrate the grantor's intent. Moreover, it produces an inequitable result because the original grantee has presumably paid a reduced price for title to the encumbered property.

Id. at 989-90. *See also* Minton v. Long, 19 S.W.3d 231 (Ct. App. Tenn. 1999). The Restatement (Third) of Property: Servitudes agrees with the result in *Willard*, because the common law rule "frustrates intent and has little utility." Restatement (Third) of Property: Servitudes §2.6 (2000). The Restatement suggests that courts retaining the rule do so because they believe that "stability is more important than merit."

Do you agree that the common law rule has no merit? Even if you were in a jurisdiction following the Restatement approach, would you advise your client to create an easement to C by using a reservation in a deed to B?

■ PROBLEM: STRANGER TO THE DEED

Genevieve McGuigan owned a vacant lot that she had allowed a church to use for parking during services. She sold the lot to Petersen, but included a provision in the deed that it was "subject to an easement for automobile parking during church hours for the benefit of the church [identified by location]." She reduced the price of the lot by about a third because of this agreement. A short time later, Petersen sold the lot to Willard, who wants to build on the lot. He sues to quiet title and wants the court to declare that McGuigan's attempt to create an interest in a third party in her deed to Petersen was ineffective. How should the court rule? *See Willard, supra.*

Creation by Plat Reference

In many cases, a deed from a developer will simply refer to a subdivision plat, which contains a survey map showing the location of the easements across each lot. Is the reference to the plat sufficient to create the easements? Probably, especially if the deed contains language such as "subject to easements as shown on plat." Other things shown on the plat map, such as streets or parks, may benefit the landowner. In most cases the court will hold that an easement exists as to roads, streets, or parks appearing on the plat, either by express grant/reservation, by implication, or by estoppel. *See, e.g.,* Lindsay v. Annapolis Roads Property Owners Ass'n, 64 A.3d 916 (Md. 2013) (right-of-way shown on plat referenced by deed created implied easement); Zywickiel v. Historic Westside Vill. Partners, LLC, 721 S.E.2d 617 (Ga. Ct. App. 2011) (street easement shown on recorded plat, referenced by deed, were established by express grant); Yorlum Properties Ltd. v. Lincoln County, 311 P.3d 748, 755 (Mont. 2013) (under easement-by-reference doctrine explicit reference in the deed to a plat on which easement is clearly depicted sufficient); Carrier v. Kirchheimer, No. 2009-CA-002163-MR, 2012 WL 1232940 (Ky. Ct. App. 2012) (street appearing on plat deemed dedicated to public use by estoppel). The Restatement agrees that plats showing common areas and streets imply servitudes for those elements. Restatement (Third) of Property: Servitudes §2.13 (2000).

Although a court might allow an easement to be created by denotation on a plat map, this method may raise questions as to the intentions of the parties. Consider these problems:

■ PROBLEMS: CREATION BY PLAT REFERENCE

1. Only two end lots in a horseshoe-shaped subdivision in St. Petersburg, Florida, actually border Boca Ciega Bay. The plat of the subdivision showed a right-of-way over one of those lots, called Lot A. The right-of-way was marked only "easement for ingress and egress and utilities" and led from the main street in the subdivision to the water's edge. The deeds from the developers to each owner of a lot in the subdivision referred to the plat map, but did not specifically mention the easement. The original owners of Lot A paved this right-of-way and used it as their driveway, but also allowed other residents of the subdivision to use it to reach the bay. The new owners of Lot A have grown tired of their neighbors traipsing across their property and hanging out to watch sunsets or fireworks displays. Because of a recently installed seawall, the beach has eroded to the extent that there is nowhere, other than on Lot A, for the neighbors to go once they reach the end of the easement. The Lot A owners have installed a gate across the right-of-way and locked it. The neighbors sue for the right to cross, watch sunsets, and to build a dock at the end of the easement so they can launch kayaks and fish. Who should win? *See* Brannon v. Boldt, 958 So. 2d 367 (Fla. Dist. Ct. App. 2007).

2. Marina bought Lot 11 in the Cherokee Camp subdivision. The recorded plat of the subdivision shows a lake and a soccer field. While Lot 11 is not adjacent to either the lake or the field, Marina assumed the use of these amenities was available to all owners in the subdivision. However, when Marina tried to fish in the lake and use the soccer field for her daughter's soccer team practice, she was prohibited from doing so by the subdivision developer, who retained fee simple ownership to the lake and field. Marina claims an implied easement to use the lake and field, based on the plat map. Should she win? Is there any other evidence you would consider relevant to this issue? *See* Camp Cherokee, Inc. v. Marina Lane, LLC, 729 S.E.2d 510 (Ga. Ct. App. 2012); De Castro v. Durrell, 671 S.E.2d 244 (Ga. Ct. App. 2008).

3. In 1970, a plat for the Greenwood subdivision showed an easement marked "utility." For many years, this easement was used by the City for municipal-owned gas and electric conveyances. In recent years, the City has stopped using the easement and is willing to release it, so that the landowners can build on that section of the property. Would you advise the landowners to rely on this release? Who, in fact, is the grantee of the easement rights created by the plat reference?

2. Easement by Estoppel

Suppose Alice owns a 40-acre tract of rural land called Blackacre, with frontage on County Road. There is a dirt track, leading back to the portions of Blackacre farthest from County Road, which Alice uses occasionally to get to the pond in that area. Alice receives a letter from Bart, who owns Whiteacre, adjacent to Blackacre, asking if he could use the dirt track to reach the back part of Whiteacre. Bart's letter says, "As you know, there is a lot of hilly, marshy land on my property and it is often really difficult to drive over." Being a neighborly sort, Alice writes back saying, "Bart, you certainly have my permission to use the dirt track on Blackacre to reach your land."

Several years later, Alice sells Blackacre to Carly. Carly values her privacy and tells Bart he may no longer drive over Blackacre. Bart claims that Alice gave him an easement and that the signed letter fulfills the Statute of Frauds. Carly claims it was just a license. Which was it? Do you see the difference it makes? *See* Rowan v. Riley, 72 P.3d 889 (Idaho 2003) (easement or license determined by grantor's intent, discerned from language and surrounding circumstances). *See also* Dalliance Real Estate, Inc. v. Covert, 1 N.E.3d 850 (Ohio 2013) ("perpetual license" basically same as easement).

If Alice's permission had been oral, it would certainly be deemed a license because it was not in writing. But suppose during the time Alice owned the property, Bart built an expensive, two-story house on the hill in the back portion of his property. He also installed a driveway leading down to Alice's dirt track. Now when Carly tells Bart to stop using the road, Bart replies, "Well, Alice said I could use the dirt track and you know, now that I've built this house and driveway, I really need to continue to use it." Can Bart now claim an easement over Blackacre?

The Restatement indicates that an *easement by estoppel* may arise if injustice would otherwise result when:

> the owner or occupier permitted another to use that land under circumstances in which it was reasonable to foresee that the user would substantially change position believing that the permission would not be revoked, and the user did substantially change position in reasonable reliance on that belief[.]

Restatement (Third) of Property: Servitudes §2.10 (2000).

➤ Just as in any estoppel case, the court will not invoke its equitable power absent *substantial injustice*—for example, in the problem above, how difficult will it be for Bart to simply find another way off of his property?

➤ In addition, there must be *substantial, reasonable reliance.* Reasonableness is a difficult question in these cases—would you build an expensive house based only on an oral license of indeterminate length? On the other hand, courts recognize that many neighbors rely on handshake deals and might be offended by a request to reduce the understanding to a formal written agreement.

Would it make a difference to your application of this doctrine to the problem above if Bart mentioned, in asking for Alice's permission, that he was planning to build a house on Whiteacre? Would it matter if Bart indicated that instead of being merely difficult, it was "well-nigh impossible" to get back to that area any other way? The Restatement includes an example very much like this and suggests that an easement by estoppel would be justified because "it should have been apparent that permission for a permanent use was sought." Do you agree?

On the other hand, the Restatement also counsels that "courts should be very cautious in establishing servitudes on the basis of estoppel because they tend to penalize neighborly cooperation, and they undercut the policies encouraging the use of written documents for land transactions." Using our policy menu, we would say that the application of the estoppel doctrine tends to favor *fairness* over *certainty*.

Estoppel cases do not always involve a surface right-of-way. In this case, the parties argued over a sewer easement. Do you agree that an easement by estoppel was appropriate?

KIENZLE v. MYERS

853 N.E.2d 1203 (2006)
Court of Appeals of Ohio

This is an appeal from a summary judgment issued by the Wood County Court of Common Pleas in a property dispute. Because we conclude that a property owner's reasonable reliance on an adjacent owner's permission for use ripened into an easement by estoppel, we reverse in part and affirm in part.

Jo An Van Duyne . . . and Ruth Bauer were friends and neighbors on adjoining property on West River Road in Perrysburg. In 1981, following construction of a public sewer line along West River Road, both Van Duyne and Bauer were required by law to connect to the public system.

For Bauer, a direct connection to the River Road sewer line meant that her driveway would have to be excavated, at substantial cost and inconvenience. The two women talked and reached an accommodation. They agreed that Bauer would install her sewer through a 96-foot-long trench from her home to Van Duyne's property, where it would share a 207-foot trench with Van Duyne's connector line to the street. Because of the hilly topography of the area, the pipes were buried at a depth of five and one-half feet. Each party bore her own tap and assessment fees. It is not clear from the record as to whether there was any sharing of excavation or installation costs for the sewer line.

In 1982, Jo An Van Duyne's daughter and son-in-law, Susan S. and David W. Kienzle, moved into her River Road property. In 1987, appellee, Susan S. Kienzle Trust, acquired the property. In 1989, appellants, Michael P. and Joan Myers, acquired the Bauer property.

On November 5, 2003, counsel for the Kienzles sent a letter to appellants advising them that the Kienzles had "decided to terminate the revocable license" by which appellants' sewer pipe crossed the Kienzle property. The letter directed appellants to "make other arrangements" within 30 days. Subsequent letters from David Kienzle threatened to "cap" the sewer line absent certain concessions.

On March 26, 2004, appellee sued appellants, seeking to quiet title with respect to appellants' "encroachment" across appellee's property and to enjoin further trespass, as well as damages. . . .

Following discovery, appellee was granted partial summary judgment. The trial court rejected appellants' assertion that their use of appellee's property was by easement. . . .

Concerning an easement by estoppel, we have stated: "An easement by estoppel may be found when an owner of property misleads or causes another in any way to change the other's position to his or her prejudice. Monroe Bowling Lanes v. Woodsfield Livestock Sales, 17 Ohio App. 2d 146, 244 N.E.2d 762 (1969). 'Where an owner of land, without objection, permits another to expend money in reliance upon a supposed easement, when in justice and equity the former ought to have disclaimed his conflicting rights, he is estopped to deny the easement.' Id. at 151, 244 N.E.2d 762. . . .

"'A servitude is established if the permission is given under such circumstances that the person who gives it should reasonably foresee that the recipient will substantially change position on the basis of that permission, believing that the permission is not revocable.' Id. at 145, 244 N.E.2d 762." Schmiehausen, 2004 WL 1367278 at ¶21-26.

In Schmiehausen, a couple purchased a 28-acre parcel with the intention to subdivide. After the purchase, the couple discovered that the land was diagonally bisected by a 900-foot long, 12-inch diameter drainage pipe belonging to a neighboring farmer. Discovery of the pipe resulted in the need to redesign the site plan at some expense. The couple sued the seller, asserting a violation of general warranty covenants.

There was evidence in the trial court that the neighboring farmer and the seller's predecessor in interest reached a gentleman's agreement for installation of the pipe. The farmer then hired a contractor to install it. The trial court found an easement and awarded damages on the breach of warranty. We affirmed, noting that installation of a 12-inch diameter pipe, 900-feet long, involved a substantial cost by the farmer in reliance on the predecessor in interest's agreement to permit its installation. We concluded that "[a]pplying either Restatement Section 2.10(1) or Ohio case law, an easement by estoppel was created by the transaction between [the farmer] and [the sellers'] predecessor in interest." *Schmiehausen*, 2004 WL 1367278 at ¶54.

In this matter, the trial court distinguished *Schmiehausen* as follows:

> ". . . The easement claimant in *Schmiehausen* expended a substantial cost. In this case, Bauer's expenditure was meager and would have been much larger if she had to destroy and reconstruct her driveway to bury the sewer pipe on her own property.
>
> "The Court also finds that Defendants cannot establish all the elements necessary to prove estoppel either under common law or the broader Restatement standard. Under common law, an easement claimant must establish reasonable reliance upon a representation, resulting in actual prejudice. In this case, it is undisputed that the construction of the sewer pipe was with Van Duyne's permission. There is no evidence of misrepresentation. There is also no evidence of prejudice. Bauer actually received a benefit by not having to destroy her driveway. Defendants produced evidence showing that Bauer secured permits and spent money for the construction of the sewer pipe. The Court does not find actual prejudice from such facts. Bauer would have made those expenditures, regardless of the location of the sewer line.
>
> "The Court also finds that Defendants cannot establish easement by estoppel under the Restatement standard. The rule under the Restatement is prefaced by the phrase '[i]f injustice can be avoided only by establishment of a servitude.' It is apparent to the Court that the broader Restatement approach was crafted to cover fact situations where otherwise justice cannot be accomplished. The Court believes that this phrase was particularly applied in *Schmiehausen*. The easement claimant in *Schmiehausen* was the original party that expended the substantial cost of buying a 900 foot long drainage on the neighbor's property. . . . The facts in this case are inapposite. The parties are not the original actors in the transaction that created the alleged easement. There is no allegation of concealment or personal substantial expenditure related to the creation of the easement. Therefore, the facts in the present case are not sufficient to fulfill the particular requirement that injustice can be avoided only by establishment of easement by estoppel."

We disagree with the trial court's analysis. There is no requirement for an easement by estoppel in the common law that a property owner must mislead or misrepresent. The rule simply states that if an owner misleads or causes another in any way to change his or her position to that party's prejudice, the owner is estopped from denying the existence of an easement. . . . While permissive use may prevent an easement by prescription from arising, in another context an owner's grant of permission for land use may act as an inducement for another to act, especially when the permission granted is for an act not easily undone.

In *Schmiehausen*, for example, it was permission from the original property owner that induced the neighboring farmer to install 900 feet of large-diameter drainage tile. Moreover, from the scope of the act for which permission was granted it may be reasonably inferred that neither party expected the project to be transient or temporary. Thus, when the farmer expended money to complete the project, the owner was estopped from denying existence of an easement.

In the present matter, Jo An Van Duyne gave Ruth Bauer permission to install her sewer line in the same trench as Van Duyne's. There was testimony in the damage phase that plastic sewer lines have a 50-year expected lifespan. It can be reasonably inferred that neither party anticipated that burying a sewer pipe in a five and one-half foot deep trench would be a transient or temporary event. Thus, Van Duyne's permission reasonably induced appellants' predecessor in interest to change her position.

The trial court also refused to find prejudice in that Bauer would have had to pay for the construction of the sewer pipe even had she located it on her own property. Again, we disagree with this analysis. "Prejudice," in this context, is used as a synonym for "detriment." That is, Bauer relied upon Van Duyne's permission to her prejudice or detriment. This may be shown not only by the expenditures of funds but by the forbearance of some right to which one might otherwise be entitled.

While it is true that, in any event, Bauer would have had to spend money to connect to the public sewer, it is also true that but for Van Duyne's acquiescence to Bauer's use of her property, Bauer would have linked to the sewer wholly on her own property. Thus, Bauer's decision to cross Van Duyne's land constituted a change in position which placed her access to the public sewer out of her control. As the present lawsuit suggests, this decision disadvantaged Bauer.

With respect to the Restatement formulation, . . . we find the trial court's attempt to distinguish unpersuasive. It would seem that the equities would favor not disturbing a 25-year-old arrangement which seems to have only recently concerned anyone. . . .

Accordingly, appellants' first assignment of error [regarding establishment of easement by estoppel] is well taken. . . .

Judgment affirmed in part and reversed in part, and cause remanded.

■ POINTS TO CONSIDER

1. **Foreseeable reliance.** The Restatement approach to estoppel considers the probable expectations of the parties at the time permission was granted. In *Kienzle*, the court found that evidence concerning the longevity of the plastic pipe used for the sewer line was relevant to that question. How? That evidence came in only in the damages phase of the trial, so

neither party thought that evidence was relevant to the issue of whether an easement by estoppel existed. What other evidence helped establish the easement here?

The court's reliance on the 50-year lifespan of plastic sewer pipe raises an important point—how long does the interest granted by the court last? Most easements are considered to be perpetual, but if we call this an irrevocable license, based on detrimental reliance, it should last no longer than necessary for the reliance interest to be recovered. In other words, when the sewer line wears out and it is time to replace it, should the owner of the dominant parcel be able to continue to use the servient parcel? *See* Tatum v. Dance, 605 So. 2d 110, 113 (Fla. Dist. Ct. App. 1992) (irrevocable license, unlike easement, limited to duration necessary to prevent inequity). Similarly, easements implied by necessity terminate when the necessity ends.

2. **The opposite view.** Assume Ruth proposed the use of Jo An's sewer line, as the case suggests, and Jo An said, "Sure, why not?" But then Ruth, having had first-year Property, drafts up an easement that would allow the use of the sewer line in perpetuity. She takes it over to Jo An and asks her to sign it before a notary, so it can be recorded. Jo An asks: "Why? Don't you trust me?" Ruth replies, "Well, you might not live here forever and I don't want to spend the money to build this sewer line unless the deal is formalized." Slightly offended, Jo An says she will take the easement to her lawyer to see what she says. If you were that lawyer, what would you say? Is it possible that when push comes to shove, the owner of the servient tenement may have second thoughts about granting a perpetual, irrevocable, property interest to someone for free? Does forcing the parties to "put it in writing" encourage them to consider more carefully their intentions? Does that change your opinion on whether *Kienzle* was correctly decided?

   Not all jurisdictions accept the idea of an irrevocable license. In Kitchen v. Kitchen, 641 N.W.2d 245, 249-50 (Mich. 2002), the Michigan Supreme Court reaffirmed its position against easements by estoppel. According to the court, allowing oral licenses to become irrevocable, and thereby equivalent to easements, would undermine the Statute of Frauds.

3. **Neighborly behavior.** Think back to our first example involving Alice's neighbor Bart. Does the result in *Kienzle* suggest that, by agreeing to let him use her dirt track, she is in danger of being held to a perpetual easement by estoppel if he starts building a house? Do cases like *Kienzle* make it less likely that she will say yes? Can Alice consent but still protect her interests?

▪ PROBLEMS: EASEMENTS BY ESTOPPEL

1. Access to Greenacre, owned by Gertie, consists of a 150-foot long driveway over Brownacre, for which there is an express easement for access. 20 years

ago, when the two properties were first developed, Gertie began landscaping the area around the 30-foot wide access easement. Eventually, she installed an irrigation system and lights. Betty, who owned Brownacre, never said anything about it and seemed to appreciate the beautiful plantings. However, Bertram recently bought Brownacre and he now wants Gertie to stop planting outside the easement boundary, noting that the easement is for access only. Has Gertie established an easement? Richardson v. Franc, 233 Cal.App.4th 744 (Cal. Ct. App. 2015).

2. The Tiersteins were interested in buying a house in Thousand Oaks, which had a gorgeous view of the surrounding mountains and valley. When they inspected the property, they noticed that the next-door neighbors, the Reisers, had a row of bushes along the back fence that could potentially interfere with the view. They spoke with neighbor Ron Reiser, who said that he always kept the bushes trimmed below the fence line and would continue to do so. The Tiersteins then bought the property for $670,000. For four years, there was no problem, but now after a falling out between the neighbors, Ron refuses to trim the bushes or allow anyone else to do so. The bushes have reached a point, eight inches above the fence line, where they are beginning to block the Tiersteins' view. Can the Tiersteins claim a negative easement of view? *See* Tierstein v. Reiser, No. B223570, 2012 WL 579495 (Cal. Ct. App. 2012). How does this relate to our discussion of spite fences (and spite bushes) in Chapter 1?

3. Easements Implied by Prior Use or Necessity

Assume Alice owns two adjacent properties, Blackacre and Whiteacre. If Alice conveys Whiteacre to Bart, in certain circumstances Bart may be able to claim that an easement over Blackacre was implied as part of the deal. The doctrine focuses on what we believe the parties intended at the time of the conveyance, even though they failed to create an easement in a writing meeting the Statute of Frauds.

A court might imply an easement if Alice was already using Blackacre to service Whiteacre, such that a normal buyer would assume that the use would continue. This is the *easement implied by prior use*. Another circumstance would be if the conveyance of Whiteacre to Bart made an easement over Blackacre necessary. This would be an *easement implied by necessity*.

In both cases, the easement must arise when a *common owner* (Alice, in our example) splits her property and conveys part of it to someone else.

In an *easement implied by prior use*, the common owner must have been using part of her property for the benefit of another part of her property. Because you can't have an easement over your own property, this is sometimes called a *quasi-easement*. This prior use must have been *apparent and continuous*—so that the parties to the conveyance had constructive notice of it. In addition, the use must be *reasonably necessary* to the continued enjoyment of the dominant parcel, such that the parties must have expected its use to continue after the conveyance.

Easement Implied by Prior Use

- *common owner* (originally one owner owned both burdened and benefited parcels)
- prior to splitting property, use of part of property to benefit another part (*quasi-easement*)
- use was *apparent and continuous*
- use was *reasonably necessary*

The *implied easement by necessity* is similar, except that the use did not pre-exist the conveyance; in fact, the need for the easement did not arise until the property was divided. In addition, most courts require that the conveyance made the easement *strictly necessary*, so that the parties must have contemplated such an arrangement. Other courts require only a *reasonable* necessity, although the difference between these two standards in many cases may not be significant. *See, e.g.*, Brook v. Bonnett, 185 P.3d 346 (Nev. 2008) (mere inconvenience will not meet standard of reasonable necessity). Note that the necessity must arise *at the time of* the conveyance; a necessity that arises later will not suffice.

Easement Implied by Necessity

- *common owner*
- use is *strictly necessary* (although some courts use lower standard)
- necessity for easement *arose when property divided*

The next case illustrates that, while both types of implied easements require a showing of some necessity, the degree of necessity required differs.

BOYD v. BELLSOUTH TELEPHONE TELEGRAPH CO.

633 S.E.2d 136 (2006)
Supreme Court of South Carolina

[Caroline Boyd filed a declaratory judgment action seeking an easement across BellSouth's property.]

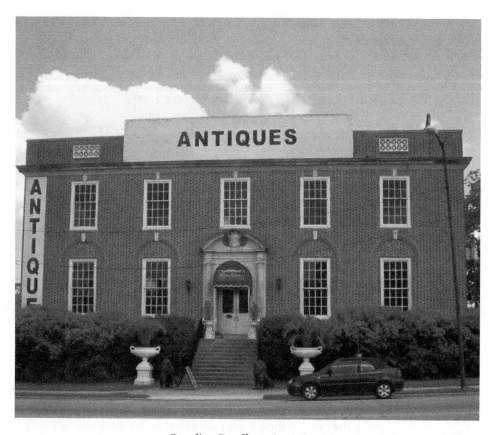

Caroline Boyd's antique store

Back entrance to the Boyd antique store made accessible by easement
Photos provided by Rodney Hair

FACTUAL AND PROCEDURAL BACKGROUND

In 1923, BellSouth's predecessor, AT & T, completed construction of a three-story building on its property in Denmark, South Carolina. BellSouth's original lot was bordered on the north by Otis Street, on the west by Carolina Highway, and on the east by Beech Avenue. At some point during BellSouth's ownership, a driveway was constructed which ran from the rear of the building to Beech Avenue. A gate was erected at the end of the driveway on Beech Avenue.

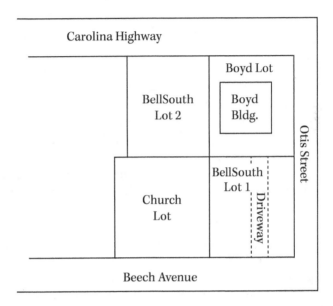

In 1988, BellSouth severed the lot into two parcels and sold the western parcel with the building to the City of Denmark (Denmark). Denmark's parcel was bordered by Otis Street and Carolina Highway. In 1991, Denmark sold its parcel to John Boyd, who later conveyed the parcel to his wife, Caroline Boyd. Boyd used the building as an antique store.

Denmark and Boyd used BellSouth's gate and driveway to access the rear entrance of the building. After September 11, 2001, BellSouth decided to construct a fence between the two parcels for security reasons. This fence would prohibit Boyd from using BellSouth's existing gate and driveway to access the rear entrance of the building.

Boyd then brought this declaratory judgment action contending she had an easement implied by prior use, implied by necessity, or by equitable estoppel over BellSouth's parcel. The special referee granted BellSouth's motion for summary judgment on all claims.

Boyd appealed. The Court of Appeals affirmed the special referee's grant of summary judgment for BellSouth on the easement by necessity claim and reversed the grant of summary judgment for BellSouth on the claims for an easement implied by prior use and by equitable estoppel....

We granted BellSouth's petition for writ of certiorari to review the Court of Appeals' decision concerning the easement implied by prior use and equitable estoppel.

. . .

LAW AND ANALYSIS

I. Easement Implied by Prior Use

. . .

A. Recognition of Claim

While other authorities plainly identify easements by prior use, necessity, and prescription as three types of easements, South Carolina case law has not clearly distinguished between these types of easements. See 25 Am. Jur. 2d Easements and Licenses 22, 30, 39 (generally describing easements by prior use, necessity, and prescription). Moreover, although easements by implication have been recognized in South Carolina, an easement implied by prior use has never been explicitly recognized.

The intent of the parties, as shown by all the facts and circumstances under which a conveyance was made, may give rise to an easement by implication. Hamilton v. CCM, Inc., 274 S.C. 152, 158, 263 S.E.2d 378, 381 (1980). Whatever easements are created by implication must be determined as of the time of the severance of the ownership of the tracts involved. Clemson Univ. v. First Provident Corp., 260 S.C. 640, 652, 197 S.E.2d 914, 920 (1973). Easements may be implied by necessity, by prior use, from map or boundary references, or from a general plan. . . .

The party asserting the right to an easement implied by prior use must establish the following: (1) unity of title; (2) severance of title; (2) [sic] the prior use was in existence at the time of unity of title; (3) the prior use was not merely temporary or casual; (4) the prior use was apparent or known to the parties; (5) the prior use was necessary in that there could be no other reasonable mode of enjoying the dominant tenement without the prior use; and (6) the common grantor indicated an intent to continue the prior use after severance of title. See Elliott v. Rhett, 39 S.C.L. (5 Rich.) 405 (1852) ("Apart from all considerations of time, there is implied, upon the severance of a heritage, a grant of all those continuous and apparent easements, which have in fact been used by the owner during the unity, though they have had no legal existence as easements. . . ."). . . .

The party asserting the right of an easement by necessity must demonstrate: (1) unity of title, (2) severance of title, and (3) necessity. Kennedy v. Bedenbaugh, 352 S.C. 56, 60, 572 S.E.2d 452, 454 (2002). . . .

A prescriptive easement is not implied by law but is established by the conduct of the dominant tenement owner; however, easements by prior use and by necessity are implied by law. *Clemson Univ.*, 260 S.C. at 652, 197 S.E.2d at 919; 12 S.C. Jur. Easements 10; 25 Am. Jur. 2d Easements and Licenses 22, 30. An easement by necessity does not require a preexisting use during unity of title; whereas an easement by prior use does impose this requirement. 25 Am. Jur. 2d Easements and Licenses §32; 28A C.J.S. Easements §92. An easement implied by prior use will not be extinguished if the easement is no longer necessary, but an easement by necessity will be extinguished once the necessity ends. 25 Am. Jur. 2d Easements and Licenses §§29, 35.

Easements by prescription, implied by prior use, and implied by necessity have different elements and are applicable to different factual scenarios; thus, an easement implied by prior use has not been subsumed by other types of easements. . . .

B. Summary Judgment

If an easement implied by prior use is recognized, BellSouth contends the Court of Appeals erred in finding a genuine issue of material fact existed as to the necessity element of easement implied by prior use because the court simultaneously found Boyd did not meet the necessity element of easement by necessity.

The necessity required for easement by necessity must be actual, real, and reasonable as distinguished from convenient, but need not be absolute and irresistible. . . . The necessity element of easement by necessity must exist at the time of the severance and the party claiming the right to an easement must not create the necessity when it would not otherwise exist. . . .

For an easement implied by prior use, necessity means "there could be no other reasonable mode of enjoying the dominant tenement without this easement. . . ." The necessity element of easement implied by prior use must be determined at the time of the severance. 25 Am. Jur. 2d Easements and Licenses 29; 28A C.J.S. Easements 69; *see, e.g.*, Norken Corp. v. McGahan, 823 P.2d 622 (Alaska 1991) (remanding case for determination of whether necessity element for easement implied by prior use met at the time of severance).

While the necessity elements for the two types of easements obviously are similar, the need required for an easement by prior use may be less than required for an easement by necessity. *See* Russakoff v. Scruggs, 241 Va. 135, 400 S.E.2d 529, 533 (1991) (easement implied by prior use "requires a showing of need which, by definition, may be less than that required for establishing an easement by necessity, but must be something more than simple convenience"); Granite Props. Ltd. v. Manns, 140 Ill. App. 3d 561, 94 Ill. Dec. 353, 487 N.E.2d 1230 (1986) (a greater degree of necessity may be required for easement by necessity than for easement by prior use); 28A C.J.S. Easements 92 (same). This lesser showing of necessity may stem in part from an often unspoken realization on the part of the fact finder that a prior use indicates a need for a particular easement. See Michael V. Hernandez,

Restating Implied, Prescriptive, and Statutory Easements, 40 Real Prop. Prob. & Tr. J. 75 (2005) ("The easement implied by prior use is based on the maxim...whatever is necessary and related is appended....").

Viewed in the light most favorable to Boyd, the evidence indicates BellSouth at one time commonly owned the two parcels at issue and used the driveway to access the rear entrance of the building. Upon severance of the two parcels, Boyd's parcel, then owned by Denmark, was bounded on two sides by public streets. The evidence indicates there are two entrances to Boyd's building. During the past 50 years, the rear entrance and loading docks have been generally accessible from Beech Avenue by using BellSouth's driveway and have been used to deliver large items to the basement of the building. There is evidence the front entrance does not provide access to the basement for the delivery of large items because the stairways and hallways are too narrow. The evidence also indicates an alternate driveway to the building would be infeasible, impractical, and very costly. Thus, there is a genuine issue of material fact that without this particular easement, there could be no other reasonable mode of enjoying the dominant tenement at the time of severance. *Crosland*, 32 S.C. at 133, 10 S.E. at 875.

II. Easement by Equitable Estoppel

BellSouth argues the Court of Appeals erred by reversing the grant of summary judgment on the claim for easement by estoppel because Boyd failed to establish the elements of equitable estoppel. We agree.

The essential elements of equitable estoppel as related to the party estopped are: (1) conduct which amounts to a false representation or concealment of material facts, or, at least, which is calculated to convey the impression that the facts are otherwise than, and inconsistent with, those which the party subsequently attempts to assert; (2) intention, or at least expectation, that such conduct shall be acted upon by the other party; and (3) knowledge, actual or constructive, of the real facts. As related to the party claiming the estoppel, they are: (1) lack of knowledge and of the means of knowledge of the truth as to the facts in question; (2) reliance upon the conduct of the party estopped; and (3) action based thereon of such a character as to change his position prejudicially. S. Dev. Land and Golf Co. v. S.C. Pub. Serv. Auth., 311 S.C. 29, 33, 426 S.E.2d 748, 750 (1993); *see, e.g.*, O'Cain v. O'Cain, 322 S.C. 551, 473 S.E.2d 460 (Ct. App. 1996) (landowner was equitably estopped from denying adjoining landowner use of driveway).

"A properly recorded title normally precludes an equitable estoppel against assertion of that title due to the requirement that the party raising the estoppel be ignorant of the true state of title or reasonable means of discovering it." Binkley v. Rabon Creek Watershed Conservation Dist. of Fountain Inn, 348 S.C. 58, 71, 558 S.E.2d 902, 909 (Ct. App. 2001) (internal citation omitted). "One with knowledge of the truth or the means by which with reasonable diligence he could acquire knowledge cannot claim to have been misled." *S. Dev. Land and Golf Co.*, 311 S.C. at 34, 426 S.E.2d at 751.

The special referee determined Boyd did not establish that she and her predecessors lacked knowledge because the chain of title revealed there was no such easement. Therefore, the special referee concluded Boyd and her predecessors could not have been misled by any representations BellSouth made regarding the use of the driveway and granted summary judgment for BellSouth.

Viewing the evidence in a light most favorable to Boyd, the Court of Appeals found the evidence indicated when Boyd's husband made the decision to purchase the property, he relied on a representation by BellSouth that he would have access to the driveway. The Court of Appeals also found Boyd's husband was acting as a joint venturer with her in the antique store during the negotiations and purchase, and concluded summary judgment was improperly granted. . . .

Viewing the evidence in the light most favorable to Boyd, Boyd assumed she would always have access to the rear of the building via BellSouth's driveway. The fact that there was not an easement allowing Boyd to cross BellSouth's property was a matter of public record, which Boyd and her predecessors in title had knowledge of or at least the means to obtain the knowledge. *Carolina Land Co.*, 265 S.C. at 107, 217 S.E.2d at 20 ("Law imputes to purchaser who proposes to acquire title to real estate notice of recitals contained in any properly recorded instrument in writing which forms link in chain of title to property proposed to be acquired."). Boyd failed to show the elements of estoppel and summary judgment was properly granted to BellSouth on this claim.

CONCLUSION

We affirm the Court of Appeals' reversal of the grant of summary judgment on the easement implied by prior use and remand for further proceedings consistent with this opinion. We reverse the Court of Appeals' reversal of the grant of summary judgment on the easement by equitable estoppel.

Affirmed in part; Reversed in part.

■ POINTS TO CONSIDER

1   **Easement by estoppel revisited.** Does the South Carolina court use a different test for an easement by estoppel than the Ohio court did in *Kienzle*? Would Boyd have a good case for an easement by estoppel under the Ohio test?

2   **Necessity.** How would you summarize the difference between the degree of necessity required for an easement implied by prior use, compared to an easement by necessity? Why is there a difference? Does Boyd have a case for an easement by necessity here?

3. **Grant or reservation?** Do you think that courts would apply the tests for implied easements more strictly in the case of an implied *grant* of an easement or an implied *reservation*? In other words, when Alice conveys Whiteacre

to Bart, would a court be more likely to imply an easement for Bart over Blackacre, or to imply an easement in favor of Alice over Whiteacre? Why? Which was at issue in *BellSouth*?

4. **Condemnation statutes.** In many states, if a parcel becomes landlocked, the owner can force an adjacent property owner to grant a right-of-way for ingress and egress. Unlike an implied easement by necessity, however, the landlocked property owner must *compensate* the servient owner for the fair market value of the easement. *See, e.g.,* Tenn. Code. Ann. §54-14-101 (West 2017). What property policies are furthered by these statutes? On the other hand, thinking back to *Jacque v. Steenberg Homes* in Chapter 1, what property policies do such statutes ignore? Think carefully about economic efficiency and how the Coase theorem might apply in these circumstances.

◼ PROBLEMS: EASEMENTS BY NECESSITY

1. Dupont sold a portion (Parcel A) of his property (Blackacre) to Whiteside. The north side of Parcel A bordered a scenic river, while the south side fronted a public road. Whiteside planned to build his house to have a view of the river. In order to access that northern portion, he would like to use a road that already exists on Dupont's Blackacre property. To build his own road, he would have to traverse about 700 feet of wetlands, which would require getting a permit from the government (an uncertain and expensive proposition). In addition, filling the wetland would make building the road difficult, although not impossible. The cost of constructing the road is estimated to be about $90,000. Does Whiteside have a good claim for an implied easement by necessity over Blackacre? *Compare* Dupont v. Whiteside, 721 So. 2d 1259 (Fla. Dist. Ct. App. 1998) (no easement by necessity), *with* Keene v. Jackson, 732 So. 2d 1138 (Fla. Dist. Ct. App. 1999) (easement by necessity to reach portion of property separated by creek).

2. In 2010, Matthews owned a piece of rural property called Greenacre. He sold a piece of Greenacre, called Parcel B, to Duff. At the time of this sale, Matthews could reach the county road from Greenacre by using a four-wheel-drive vehicle over a rough trail through a mountain pass. In 2018, however, a landslide rendered the trail impassable. Duff's tract, Parcel B, provides easy access to the county road, and Matthews now seeks a declaration that he has an implied easement by necessity over Duff's property. What result? Duff v. Matthews, 311 S.W.2d 637 (Tex. 1958).

3. In 1828, Richard Richardson died, leaving his property bordering State route 736 to Yancey and Palmer by will. The probate court subdivided the property and gave Yancey a parcel that was landlocked. Yancey was thereafter awarded an implied easement by necessity. In 2018, the present owners of the Yancey property would

like to expand the easement to allow tractor-trailers to harvest timber, claiming that the necessary scope of the easement has now evolved due to the size of modern timber-harvesting trucks. Should the easement be expanded? *See* Palmer v. R.A. Yancey Lumber Corporation, 803 S.E.2d 742 (Va. 2017).

4. In 1893, Ebeneezer Coe divided his land (Blueacre) on a peninsula on Rangeley Lake in Maine into parcels and conveyed the piece on the tip (Parcel C) of the peninsula to Abner Toothaker. Coe retained the remainder of Blueacre. Parcel C was without road access and could be reached only by boat or by crossing Greenacre on horseback or on foot (or in winter, with cross-country skis or snowshoes). In 2005, the current owners of the Toothaker property (Parcel C) sought an easement by necessity over Blueacre. What result? Welch v. State, 908 A.2d 1207 (Me. 2006). *Compare* Stansbury v. MDR Dev., L.L.C., 889 A.2d 403 (Md. 2006) (water access does not preclude easement by necessity). Does your answer depend on how the property was being used at the time of severance? *See* Davidson v. Collins, 195 So.3d 825 (Miss. Ct. App. 2015) (access solely by water sufficient for recreational use land).

4. Easement by Prescription

Easements by prescription (or *prescriptive easements*) may arise by the adverse use of another's property under a doctrine very similar to adverse possession, except that the right is established by continual *use* rather than *occupation* of the property. In order to establish an easement by prescription, the user must establish the use that is *adverse* (i.e., without the owner's permission), *open and notorious*, and *continuous* for the *period of prescription*. Just as with adverse possession, the required period of adverse use is established by a limitations statute, which in most states is the same limitations provision for recovery of land or ejectment used to establish adverse possession. In some states, statutes establish a different period for prescription. *Compare* Ga. Code Ann. §44-9-54 (West 2017) (prescriptive period seven years), *with* Ga. Code Ann. §44-5-163 (West 2017) (20 years required for adverse possession without color of title).

Some jurisdictions add a requirement that the use be "exclusive." In this context, however, exclusive use does not mean that the claimant must be the only one using the easement, or that the user must exclude the dominant owner. It is sometimes said that exclusivity means only that the use must not be dependent on another's rights or that the claimant must use the easement "as his own" rather than as a member of the general public. *See, e.g.,* Tubbs v. E & E Flood Farms, L.P., 13 A.3d 759 (Del. Ch. 2011); *see also* K & H Hideaway, LLC v. Cheloha, 885 N.W.2d 760 (Neb. Ct. App. 2016). A substantial number of jurisdictions simply dispense with the exclusivity requirement altogether. *See, e.g.,* Gardner v. Baird, 871 A.2d 949 (R.I. 2005); Brannock v. Lotus Fund, 367 P.3d 888 (N.M. Ct. App. 2015).

A couple of the elements of prescriptive easements bear further discussion. First, how does a user prove "adversity"? Assume that Bart, the owner of Whiteacre, starts driving down a path over adjacent Blackacre to reach County Road 1 after a flood makes the driveway on his property impassable. Alice sees him use the path on many occasions, but says nothing. When she is out in the yard, she sometimes waves when he drives by. The use continues for the prescriptive period. *Has Bart established an easement?*

A key component would be whether Bart can establish that the use was *adverse.* Most jurisdictions *presume* adversity in the absence of any other explanation.

> ➢ For example, in Brown v. Ware, 630 P.2d 545 (Ariz. Ct. App. 1981), the trial court denied a prescriptive easement over a road used for about 30 years by various neighbors (including, believe it or not, a family of Van Valkenburghs) because it found that the use was by the owner's "neighborly indulgence" and therefore was permissive. The appellate court overruled and held an easement by prescription did exist. If the other requirements are met, "the use will be *presumed to be adverse* and in order to overcome such presumption the owner of the servient estate. . .ha[s] the burden of showing that the use was permissive." *Id.* at 547.
>
> ➢ How would the servient owner establish permission? Could Alice do it in our example?

Some states do not follow this presumption and instead place the burden on the user to establish adversity. In the following case, the court explains the reasons it is adopting this minority rule. In such a jurisdiction, how would Bart establish adversity?

O'DELL v. STEGALL

703 S.E.2d 561 (2010)
Supreme Court of Appeals of West Virginia

KETCHUM, Justice.

Two-and-a-half centuries ago, in the days of Thomas Fairfax and John Savage, the doctrine of prescriptive easements took root in our common law. When estates were so large that the boundaries were unknown, and vast tracts were owned by individuals who never set foot on the land, it was reasonable and economical for the law to reward a diligent user of the land with an easement by prescription at the expense of the absentee owner. . . .

But in today's world, our law on the doctrine of prescriptive easements is a tangled mass of weeds. The doctrine essentially rewards a trespasser, and grants the trespasser the right to use another's land without compensation. Such a significant imposition on the rights of modern landowners discourages neighborly conduct, and does not square with the modern ideal that we live in a congested but sophisticated, peaceful society. . . .

I. FACTS AND BACKGROUND

. . . This case concerns a private, 25-foot-wide gravel lane that borders on the northern edges of both the defendants' property and the plaintiff's property. The defendants do not own the gravel lane, but it is their only access to a public highway (the Leetown Pike/Route 15).

The central question is whether the plaintiff has a legal right to use the gravel lane for ingress to and egress from the *north* side of his home. The plaintiff already has access to the Leetown Pike/Route 15 by way of his own driveway across his property on the *south* side of his home. The plaintiff does not know who owns the land beneath the gravel lane, but he insists that he has a prescriptive easement to use the lane as an additional access to his property from the Leetown Pike. The defendants retort that the plaintiff does not have a prescriptive easement, and assert that the plaintiff's use will cause wear and tear to the gravel lane which the defendants are contractually obligated to repair. . . .

A. History of the Gravel Lane

In 1890, Isaac Strider acquired a 23-acre tract of land along the Leetown Pike. Beginning in 1893, Mr. Strider divided parts of the tract into numerous smaller residential lots for sale. Four of these lots, which now border the gravel lane at issue, were created between 1893 and 1911. . . .As best we can discern from the record, Mr. Strider retained all of the land to the east of the four lots, and he used the gravel lane as one way to access the remainder of his 23-acre tract from the Leetown Pike. (See Figure 1.)

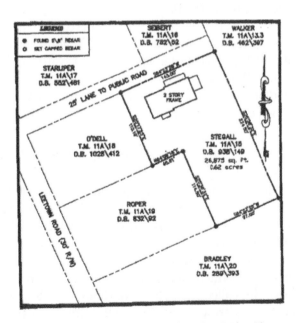

Figure 1 showing the orientation of plaintiff Michael O'Dell's property and the property of defendants Robert and Virginia Stegall to the gravel lane, marked here on the "25' Lane to Public Road."

The first of the four lots, conveyed in 1893, is about 1 acres in size, borders the Leetown Pike and now borders the north side of the gravel lane. The 1893 deed from Mr. Strider makes no mention of the gravel lane. The current owners of the lot, Clifford E. and Mary Belle Starliper, have lived on the lot for over 50 years and claim no ownership interest or other right in the gravel lane.

The second of the four lots (about ½ acre in size) was conveyed by Mr. Strider in 1898, borders the Leetown Pike/Route 15, and borders the south side of the gravel lane. The 1898 deed makes no mention of the gravel lane. Although the lot is now owned by plaintiff O'Dell, . . . the lot was originally used by the German Baptist Brethren Church. The trial testimony suggested that in the decades before 1999, churchgoers used the gravel lane at least twice a week to access a parking lot at the rear of the church. This testimony did not reveal if the use was with the permission of the owner of the gravel lane, or whether the churchgoers were trespassing. . . .

Mr. Strider conveyed the fourth lot—the southern landlocked lot which is now owned by the defendants—in 1911. The plat with the 1911 deed shows that the fourth lot (about ½ acre in size) borders on the gravel lane, which is labeled in the plat as a "lane to public road." While the deed apparently contains no wording creating an explicit right for the owner of the lot to use the gravel lane, it appears that since 1911 all of the owners of the defendants' lot have used the gravel lane to access the Leetown Pike.

As we discuss later in the opinion, while the defendants do not have an explicit, written easement to use the gravel lane to access their property, the record supports the conclusion that the defendants have an easement implied by both necessity and by prior use. *See* Cobb v. Daugherty, 225 W. Va. 435, 693 S.E.2d 800 (2010) (defining easements implied by necessity, and easements implied by a prior use of the land).

In 1988, three parties with property bordering the gravel lane. . .agreed, "for themselves, their heirs and assigns," that they would "maintain the road surface of the 25 foot wide road and right of way in its present state of repair by sharing equally the cost of maintenance and repairs." As the current owners of one of the landlocked lots, the defendants agree that they are bound by the 1988 road maintenance agreement. . . .

B. The Lawsuit to Establish a Prescriptive Easement

In 2008, numerous disagreements arose between plaintiff O'Dell and the defendant Stegalls. Essentially, the plaintiff claimed that he had the right to use the gravel lane to access a horseshoe-shaped driveway on the northern edge of his land. This horseshoe-shaped driveway appears to have been partially constructed and connected to the gravel lane sometime after 1999. The defendants objected to the plaintiff's use of the gravel lane to access the horseshoe-shaped driveway, called the police two times, and threatened to have the plaintiff prosecuted for trespassing. The defendants also took several photographs of the plaintiff driving on the gravel lane, and tape-recorded a conversation that they had with the plaintiff about his use of the lane, while the plaintiff and one of the defendants were standing on the lane.

In response to the defendants' objections, plaintiff Michael O'Dell filed the instant lawsuit in September 2008 against all of his neighbors who border the gravel lane....

The primary count in the plaintiff's complaint sought to "quiet title by way of a prescriptive easement" allowing the plaintiff to use the gravel lane. The plaintiff claimed that the gravel lane had, "by its nature and duration of its open, continuous, notorious and adverse use, as to any owner of the parcel" become a "community driveway servicing as an ingress and egress easement" to the plaintiff's property....

After a three-day trial, on June 11, 2009, the jury concluded that the plaintiff had established a prescriptive easement to use the gravel lane as an "ordinary access to his residence."...

III. DISCUSSION

The defendants, Robert and Virginia Stegall, assert on appeal that the jury's verdict is wrong for a host of different reasons, but their central argument boils down to this: the plaintiff failed to prove he had a prescriptive easement to use the gravel lane to access his property.... After carefully reviewing the trial record, we agree.

To understand why, we begin with a primer to clear up the morass that is our case law on the doctrine of prescriptive easements.

A. The Law of Prescriptive Easements

... "Prescriptive easements are based on the notion that if one uses the property of another for a certain period without permission and the owner fails to prevent such use, the prolonged usage should be treated as conclusive evidence that the use is by right." Jon W. Bruce & James W. Ely, Jr., The Law of Easements and Licenses in Land, §5:1 (2010).

> Prescription doctrine rewards the long-time user of property and penalizes the property owner who sleeps on his or her rights. In its positive aspect, the rationale for prescription is that it rewards the person who has made productive use of the land, it fulfills expectations fostered by long use, and it conforms titles to actual use of the property. The doctrine protects the expectations of purchasers and creditors who act on the basis of the apparent ownerships suggested by the actual uses of the land.

Restatement (Third) of Property (Servitudes), §2.17, cmt. c....

(1) Elements of the Prescriptive Easement Doctrine

[A] person claiming a prescriptive easement must prove each of the following elements: (1) the adverse use of another's land; (2) that the adverse use was continuous and uninterrupted for at least ten years; (3) that the adverse use was actually known to the owner of the land, or so open, notorious and visible that a reasonable owner of the land would have noticed the use; and (4) the reasonably identified starting point, ending point, line, and width of the land that was adversely used, and the manner or purpose for which the land was adversely used.

(2) *Burden of Proof*

... "It is axiomatic that easements by prescription are not favored in law because they necessarily work losses or forfeitures of the rights of others." Zimmerman v. Newport, 416 P.2d 622, 629 (Okl. 1966). "In this important matter, of subjecting, without pay, one man's land for the use of another, we must remember that the claimant carries the burden of proof, and he must show a use as of right, a hostile, adversary use, clearly show it." Crosier v. Brown, 66 W.Va. at 277, 66 S.E. at 328. ...

Accordingly, we hold that a person claiming a prescriptive easement must establish each element of prescriptive use as a necessary and independent fact by clear and convincing evidence, and the failure to establish any one element is fatal to the claim.

We now turn to the definitions of the four elements that a person claiming a prescriptive easement is required to establish.

(3) *"Adverse Use" of Another's Land Defined*

A person claiming a prescriptive easement must first show that his or her use of the servient estate was "adverse" to the rights of the true owner. Without the requirement of adversity, "licenses would grow into grants of the fee, and permissive occupations of land become conveyances of it. 'It would shock that sense of right,' Chief Justice Marshall said ... 'if a possession which was permissive and entirely consistent with the title of another should silently bar that title.'" District of Columbia v. Robinson, 180 U.S. 92, 100 (1901), quoting Kirk v. Smith ex dem Penn, 22 U.S. 241 (1824).

But what does "adverse" truly mean? ... Our cases discussing prescriptive easements have lobbed around the words "adverse" and "hostile," but have never attempted to posit a forthright definition to guide a finder of fact. ...

Moreover, instead of defining "adverse use," in many of our early cases this Court simply presumed that a claimant's use of another's property was adverse, if the claimant had otherwise proven the remaining elements of the prescriptive easement doctrine. In doing so, the Court shifted the burden of proof from the claimant to the landowner, who had to prove that the servient estate had not been used adversely (e.g., the land had been used with permission). ... This Court has never—until this case—addressed or attempted to explain this incongruity in our law.

The term "adverse use" does not imply that the person claiming a prescriptive easement has animosity, personal hostility, or ill will toward the landowner; the uncommunicated mental state of the person is irrelevant. Instead, adverse use is measured by the observable actions and statements of the person claiming a prescriptive easement and the owner of the land. ...

"Adverse use" generally means the "use of property as the owner himself would exercise, entirely disregarding the claims of others, asking permission from no one[.]" Malnati v. Ramstead, 50 Wash. 2d 105, 108, 309 P.2d 754 (1957). Use of a servient estate is adverse "when a party . . . has received no permission from the owner of the soil, and uses the way as the owner would use it, disregarding his claims entirely, using it as though he owned the property himself." Blanchard v. Moulton, 63 Me. 434, 437 (1873).

Our examination of authoritative texts, treatises, Dean Fisher's authoritative article on easements in West Virginia,[2] and cases from other jurisdictions indicates that an "adverse use" of land is, at its root, one that is against the rights of the landowner as distinguished from one that is under the rights of the landowner. . . .

The Restatement offers the following definition of the term "adverse":

> An "adverse" use . . . is a use made without the consent of the landowner, or holder of the property interest used, and without other authorization. Adverse uses create causes of action in tort for interference with property rights. The causes of action are usually actions for trespass, nuisance, or waste.

Restatement (Third) of Property (Servitudes), §2.16, cmt. b. . . .

When a property owner gives another person permission to use his or her property, the law implies that a license was intended. Restatement (Third) of Property (Servitudes), cmt. f. Unless additional facts suggest otherwise, it is assumed that the parties intended that the property owner retain the right to revoke the license at any time. Boyd v. Woolwine, 40 W. Va. 282, 286, 21 S.E. 1020, 1021 (1895) ("[T]he mere permission by the owner of the land to the public to pass over the road is, without more, to be regarded as a license revocable at his pleasure."). . . . Permission may be inferred "from the neighborly relation of the parties, or from other circumstances." 4 Powell on Real Estate, §34.10[2][a].[3]

For examples of "other circumstances," see Restatement (Third) of Property (Servitudes), §2.16 cmt. g ("Evidence that the claimed servient estate was wild, unenclosed, vacant land overcomes the presumption of prescriptive use in many states, creating a presumption that the use was permissive. Evidence that the use was made in common with the owner of the land, or that the road over which a right of way is claimed was constructed by the owner for his own use, may also overcome the presumption of prescriptive use."). . . .

Easements by prescription are not favored in the law, because they essentially reward a trespasser and allow the taking of another's property without

---

[2] John W. Fisher, II, "A Survey of the Law of Easements in West Virginia," 112 W. Va. L. Rev. 637 (2010).

[3] For examples of "neighborly relations," see, e.g., Keebler v. Harding, 247 Mont. 518, 523, 807 P.2d 1354, 1358 (1991) ("evidence of a local custom of neighborly accommodation or courtesy, without more, is sufficient to establish permissive use."); Reed v. Soltys, 106 Mich. App. 341, 347-48, 308 N.W.2d 201, 204 (1981) ("Acquiescence for a long term of years between adjoining owners in mutual use of a driveway does not create title in either party for the reason that the use is not hostile or adverse."); Burrows v. Dintlemann, 41 Ill. App. 3d 83, 85, 353 N.E.2d 708, 710 (1976) ("[E]vidence of the neighborly relationship between the parties . . . may give rise to a rebuttable presumption that the land was used by the permission of the owner.").

compensation. In this modern age, it does little to encourage civility between neighbors to have a rule whereby a landowner, who allows his neighbor to use some part of his land, runs the risk that the use may transmogrify into a legally-binding prescriptive use merely by the passage of time. Such a rule, as this case demonstrates, encourages expensive litigation between neighbors to either obtain some legal injunction to stop the use of the land, or obtain a legal ruling definitively establishing an easement. Worse, such a rule might impel neighbors to resort to aggressive, extra-legal acts in defense of their property.[4]

We therefore hold that the burden of proving adverse use is upon the party who is claiming a prescriptive easement against the interests of the true owner of the land. To the extent our prior cases suggest that proof of adverse use is not required, or that the continuous and uninterrupted use of another's land for ten years is presumed to be adverse, they are hereby overruled. The landowner has no burden of proof. It is the person claiming the prescriptive easement who must prove, by clear and convincing evidence, that the use of the land was adverse to the true owner of the land....

(4) "Continuous and Uninterrupted" Defined

The second element of the prescriptive easement doctrine requires that the person claiming a prescriptive easement show that the adverse use of the servient estate was continuous and uninterrupted for at least ten years....

In the context of prescriptive easements, "[f]or a use to be continuous, it is critical that there be no break in the attitude of mind of the claimant or the claimant's predecessor which would amount to a recognition of subordination to the servient owner's consent or an abandonment of the use in response to the servient owner's demand." Wehde v. Regional Transp. Authority, 237 Ill. App. 3d 664, 680-81, 604 N.E.2d 446, 458 (1992). A claimant's use of another's land need not be regular, constant, or daily in order to be "continuous." "[T]he evidence need not show a constant use in order to establish continuity; rather, continuity is established if the evidence shows a settled course of conduct indicating an attitude of mind on the part of the user or users that the use is the exercise of a property right." Keefer v. Jones, 467 Pa. 544, 548, 359 A.2d 735, 737 (1976). "All that is necessary is that the use be as often as required by the nature of the use and the needs of the claimant." Richards v. Pines Ranch, Inc., 559 P.2d 948, 949 (Utah 1977)....

The establishment of a prescriptive easement also requires that the claimant's adverse use of another's property must be "uninterrupted" for ten years.

---

[4] For example, in State v. Cook, 204 W. Va. 591, 515 S.E.2d 127 (1999), the defendant and her husband built a fence along the edge of their property. The defendant's neighbors tore down the fence, placed roofing nails in the defendant's driveway, and bulldozed dirt and rocks onto the property. Upon learning that defendant had called the police, one neighbor began to violently beat the defendant's husband. In defense of her husband, the defendant shot and killed the neighbor. *See also* Farmers and Mechanics Mut. Ins. Co. of West Virginia v. Cook, 210 W. Va. 394, 557 S.E.2d 801 (2001).

A use can only be interrupted by the landowner "asserting ownership before the prescriptive period has expired." Bruce & Ely, supra, §5:15. "Actions by a third person do not interrupt an adverse usage because they do not represent an assertion of dominion by the owner. Moreover, brief interruptions caused by natural forces or construction projects do not negate continuity of usage." *Id.* (Footnote added). A claimant's adverse use may be interrupted by the owner of the servient estate physically blocking the way during the prescriptive period, or by the owner instituting successful legal proceedings. . . .

However, mere unheeded requests, protests, objections, or threats of prosecution or litigation by a landowner that the claimant stop are insufficient to interrupt an adverse usage. These actions must result in the interruption of the use, no matter how brief. "Indeed, complaints may strengthen the conclusion that the claimant's use was hostile." Bruce & Ely, supra, 5:16. . . .

(5)   "Known" or "Notorious and Visible" Adverse Use Defined

To create a prescriptive easement, the claimant's adverse use must either be actually known to the rightful owner of the servient estate, or be open and notorious so that a reasonable owner would have been on notice of the adverse use. "If a right of way is claimed by prescription, the claimant should allege and prove that over the prescriptive period, without interruption, he (or a predecessor in title) used the way with such open frequency as to notify its owner of the purpose to subject his land to the use." Syllabus Point 1, in part, Nutter v. Kerby, 120 W. Va. 532, 199 S.E. 455 (1938). . . .

"Of course, where the landowner has actual knowledge of the adverse claim, the use need not be open and notorious." Bruce & Ely, supra, §5:13. *See, e.g.,* Conley v. Conley, 168 W. Va. 500, 502, 285 S.E.2d 140, 142 (1981) (per curiam) (claimant had established a prescriptive easement to use a gas line across the servient estate because the use of the line was "obvious to all parties involved"). . . .

(6)   Identifying the Line, Width, Starting and Ending Points, and Use of the Easement

Our law is clear that "[a] right of way acquired by prescription for one purpose cannot be broadened or diverted, and its character and extent are determined by the use made of it during the period of prescription." Syllabus Point 3, Monk v. Gillenwater, 141 W. Va. 27, 87 S.E.2d 537 (1955). "When an easement has been acquired by prescription, the extent of the right so acquired is measured and determined by the extent of the user out of which it originated." Syllabus Point 4, Foreman v. Greenburg, 88 W. Va. 376, 106 S.E. 876 (1921). "The precise location of an easement sought to be established should be described either by metes and bounds or in some other definite way." Syllabus Point 1, in part, Nutter v. Kerby, 120 W. Va. 532, 199 S.E. 455 (1938). . . .

B. The Lack of Evidence at Trial of a Prescriptive Easement

We now turn to the assertion by the defendants, Robert and Virginia Stegall, that plaintiff Michael O'Dell failed to establish a prescriptive easement.

As we have previously related, the plaintiff introduced the testimony of several individuals who stated that the front part of the gravel lane had, for many decades prior to 1999, been regularly used by churchgoers approximately twice a week to access a parking lot at the rear of the church. . . .

First and foremost, the plaintiff failed to show that his use of the gravel lane was adverse, that is, that it was wrongful and made without the express or implied permission of the rightful owner of the land. In part, this is because the plaintiff wholly failed to show that the defendants owned the land upon which the gravel lane rests. "The essence of an adverse use is that such use be made of the land of another." Keller v. Hartman, 175 W. Va. 418, 424, 333 S.E.2d 89, 95 (1985). Without question, the owner of the alleged servient estate is an indispensable party to a lawsuit to establish an easement across that estate.

The 1899 deed of the third lot (now owned by Ms. Seibert) clearly identifies the gravel lane as being owned by "I.H. Strider," and the deed conveyed a right to use the gravel lane "for ingress and egress 25 ft. wide running from the said lot through the land of I.H. Strider[.]" At no point did the plaintiff ever identify for the jury the current successor to Mr. Strider, or otherwise suggest who the current owner of the gravel lane might be.[5] When plaintiff's counsel was asked at oral argument before this Court, he conceded that none of the parties knows who owns the gravel roadway. We therefore believe that the plaintiff failed to prove any use of the gravel lane was adverse to the owner of the servient estate over which the alleged prescriptive easement crosses.

Furthermore, the plaintiff failed to show that the prior use of the gravel lane, by himself and his predecessors, was in any way wrongful toward, or without the express or implied permission of, the owner of the servient estate. The plaintiff was required to prove that his actions (and the actions of his predecessors) amounted to trespassing, and that the owner—whoever it might be—would have wanted to prevent the plaintiff's use, or the churchgoers' use, by resorting to the law. We can conceive that when Mr. Strider deeded the plaintiff's lot to the German Baptist Brethren Church in 1898, he gave implicit or explicit permission for churchgoers to use the lane. Nothing in the record suggests that the churchgoers' use of the gravel lane was anything more than a neighborly accommodation by the owner of the gravel lane. . . .

---

[5] While the record does not suggest who currently owns the land upon which the gravel lane sits, it does appear that the dismissed defendants Donald and Patricia Walker are the current successors to Mr. Strider, in that they now own what appears to be the remainder of Mr. Strider's 23-acre tract. Therefore, they may also own the servient estate. However, the Walkers have settled with the plaintiff. The settlement agreement stated that they have no interest in the gravel lane. The plaintiff's action against the Walkers has been dismissed with prejudice—and, accordingly, any suit by the plaintiff (or his successors) against the Walkers (or their successors) to establish ownership of the gravel lane would likely be barred by principles of res judicata or issue preclusion (i.e., collateral estoppel).

... The plaintiff also did not introduce clear evidence that the use for which he sought the easement was similar to the alleged adverse use during the prescriptive period. The plaintiff introduced evidence that churchgoers used the gravel lane approximately twice a week to access a parking lot at the rear of the building—a parking lot that apparently no longer exists. The plaintiff sought a prescriptive easement to use the gravel lane daily to access the side of the building. The plaintiff bore the burden of proving how his proposed daily use of the gravel lane was reasonably similar to the churchgoers' twice-a-week use of the lane. Likewise, the plaintiff bore the burden of showing how his proposed access to the side of the building was reasonably similar to the churchgoers' use of the lane to access the parking lot that used to be at the rear of the building. The plaintiff would only have been entitled to use the gravel lane for the purposes encompassed within the original ten-year prescriptive period; he was not entitled to increase the burden on the servient estate.

In sum, we conclude that the plaintiff failed to establish, by clear and convincing evidence, that a prescriptive easement was created to use the gravel lane to access a horseshoe driveway at the north side of his home for routine ingress and egress. . . .

While the defendants do not own the gravel lane, the evidence presented demonstrates that the defendants have an easement to use the lane to access the Leetown Pike/Route 15 that is implied, either by necessity or by prior use of the lane. . . .

The record establishes a prior common ownership of the defendants' lot and Mr. Strider's 23-acre tract, as well as a severance in 1911. On the one hand, at the time the defendants' lot was created, it was strictly necessary, and continues to be necessary, for the defendants to be able to use the gravel lane to access a public highway. Hence, the defendants have an easement implied by necessity. On the other hand, in 1911, the gravel lane had clearly and obviously been in existence (as was evidenced by the 1899 deed of the third lot that gave the owner an express easement), the 1911 deed referred to the lane as a "lane to public road," and the lane was necessary in 1911 for the reasonable enjoyment of the defendants' lot. Hence, the defendants can also establish an easement implied by a prior use of the gravel lane to access their lot.

Accordingly, the jury's verdict must be reversed and the case remanded for entry of judgment in favor of the defendants.

■ POINTS TO CONSIDER

1. **Why did the plaintiff lose?** Plaintiff could show in this case that the road had been used for at least ten years on a regular basis by his predecessors in title. What element(s) of prescription were missing? With respect to adversity, the majority of courts presume adversity from the use of property in the way the true owner would use it. Would the case have come out the same in a jurisdiction following the majority rule regarding a presumption of adversity?

See, e.g., Cramer v. Jenkins, 399 S.W.2d 15, 17 (Mo. 1966); Wertz-Black v. Guesa USA, LLC, 524 S.W.3d 68 (Mo. Ct. App. 2017) (adversity is inferred from use until rebutted by evidence of permission). Which rule do you think is better supported by property policy? Do you agree that it was essential to establish the ownership of the servient estate and that the servient owner is an indispensable party in prescription cases? What if the title to the underlying estate is unclear, as it seems to be here—does that mean prescription can never be established? Isn't one purpose of adverse possession and prescription to conform the title to current use and clear up questions about title? Why do you think the court was willing to declare that defendants had an easement by necessity or prior use over the same property, despite the failure to prove ownership of the servient estate and to join the servient owner? If the defendants don't own the servient estate, how do they have any authority to stop plaintiff from using the drive? Do you agree with the court's antagonism toward prescriptive rights? Can you imagine how the doctrine of prescription might be used in a positive way to confirm long-held access rights not shown on the records?

2. **Evidence.** Assume you use a private road for the prescriptive period without any thought or care about who the owner is and whether she minds. How would you prove adversity? Do you have to make some declaration? Do you have to show you ignored pleas to stop? If one purpose of prescription is to punish a landowner who sleeps on her rights, shouldn't the burden be on her to find out your intentions?

3. **Monitoring costs.** Because the law allows the acquisition of easements by prescription, landowners must be vigilant in monitoring their property, to ensure that no one is using it improperly. These monitoring costs might not be high for a residential lot in town, but what about an owner of thousands of acres of ranchland or timber? Having to constantly monitor the property might be problematic, especially for absentee owners. Should the rule vary depending on what type of land it is?

4. **Posting.** What is the effect of posting "No Trespassing" signs on your property? These signs commonly found on rural property might seem a bit odd at first—after all, we don't require you to post a "No Stealing" sign on your car to avoid theft. Nevertheless, in some states, you have implied permission to enter private land to fish or hunt, unless the landowner specifically denies permission or has posted signs. *See, e.g.*, Ariz. Rev. Stat. Ann. §17-304 (2017) (no criminal trespass for hunting or fishing unless land posted or you are requested to leave); N.D. Cent. Code Ann. §20.1-01-18 (West 2018) (permission of landowner required to enter for hunting only if posted). *See also* Mark R. Sigmon, *Hunting and Posting on Private Land in America*, 54 Duke L. J. 549 (2004).

© ejmphotos - Fotolia.com.

In California, posting helps avoid easements by prescription:

> No use by any person or persons, no matter how long continued, of any land, shall ever ripen into an easement by prescription, if the owner of such property posts at each entrance to the property or at intervals of not more than 200 feet along the boundary a sign reading substantially as follows: "Right to pass by permission, and subject to control, of owner: Section 1008, Civil Code."

Cal. Civ. Code §1008 (West 2018). What is the difference between this sign and a "No Trespassing" sign?

5. **Implied dedication.** When a developer creates a subdivision, the streets and sidewalks are often expressly *dedicated* to the public, through the local government. Other land in the subdivision may be dedicated for parks or other public purposes. If a landowner allows the public to use a particular road or path for a long period of time, a court may hold that public dedication has been *implied*. Some courts require evidence of *donative intent*, along with the extensive period of use. For example, donative intent might be inferred if the landowner allows the local government to maintain or improve the right-of-way, or makes some representation about the public's use. *See* Gold

Coast Neighborhood Association v. State, 403 P.3d 214 (Haw. 2017) (implied dedication based on not only public use, but also government's actions and statements asserting control over path); Scown v. Neie, 225 S.W.3d 303 (Tex. App. 2006) (implied dedication where county maintained road); Jergens v. Stanley, 277 S.E.2d 651 (Ga. 1981) (same).

■ PROBLEMS: PRESCRIPTIVE EASEMENTS

For the following prescriptive easement problems, assume the jurisdiction has a ten-year statute of limitations.

1. In 1995, Bart installed a sewer pipe on his ten-acre rural estate, Whiteacre, while his neighbor Alice, the owner of the adjacent property Blackacre, was out of the country. Bart was mistaken about the location of the property line, however, so the pipe actually crosses about 30 feet of Blackacre on its way to the road. Bart plants grass and by the time Alice returns, the intrusion was hardly noticeable. In any case, Alice wasn't sure of the exact location of the property line either. In 2017, Alice split off a section of her land and sold it to Carter. A short time later, Carter discovers the pipe when he starts to dig his foundation. He asks Bart to move the pipe, which will cost $20,000. Bart claims an easement by prescription. Does he have one?

2. In 2005, Bart began using a path over Alice's property, Blackacre, to move his cattle from his barn to a pasture on his property, Whiteacre. He does this about a dozen times each year and Alice has never objected. In 2013, however, Alice installs a gate across the path so that her new flock of sheep won't escape. She asks Bart not to use the path when the gate is closed. Bart complies for a few weeks, but then decides that as long as he closes the gate after him, it won't be a problem. Alice sees him using the path again but does nothing. This continues for another two years. Has Bart established an easement?

3. In 2017, Cathy bought a house adjacent to the Alpine Country Club from Bart, who had owned the house since 2008, when it was built. During Bart's ownership, golfers would often hit errant shots that landed in his back yard and he allowed them to come onto his property to retrieve the balls. In fact, there is some suggestion that the golf course developer who sold Bart his lot allowed him to build so close to the course with the understanding that some golfer intrusion was inevitable and would be tolerated. Cathy did not appreciate the invasion of her privacy, however, so she immediately put up a sign in her yard: "Private Property. Do Not Enter." Old habits die hard, apparently, because many golfers ignored the sign. In 2019, Cathy decided to put up a fence to keep the golfers out. The Alpine believes the fence makes the hole harder to play

because it blocks the view of the green and leaves very little room for error on that side of the fairway. Can Alpine claim an easement by prescription? *See* MacDonald Props., Inc. v. Bel-Air Country Club, 140 Cal. Rptr. 367 (Cal. Ct. App. 1977); Chewelah Golf and Country Club Ass'n v. Willia, 184 Wash. App. 1015 (2014).

Putting It Together: Easements, Notice, and a Beatle

If Alice, the owner of Blackacre, grants an easement to Bart, the owner of Whiteacre, and Bart records the easement, subsequent owners of Blackacre have constructive notice. Alice will be listed as the grantor, and if Blackacre is properly described, any title searcher using the grantor/grantee index should find this encumbrance. Thus, when Alice sells Blackacre to Clarisse, Clarisse will be bound by the easement, even if the deed from Alice does not mention it.

In some cases, however, the easement may be harder to find and issues of notice arise. A good example is the case involving former Beatle George Harrison's property on Maui. Clog Holdings v. Bailey, 992 P.2d 69 (Haw. 2000) (opinion withdrawn pending reconsideration). In 1976, the Baileys decided to divide their oceanfront property into three lots. Lot 49 (a 63-acre estate) contained all of the oceanfront, while the other two lots (12 and 48) had no water frontage. In selling lots 12 and 48, the Baileys included an easement over Lot 49 so that the owners of those lots could reach the shoreline. The easement, however, was included only in the purchase contract, which was not recorded; no easement was included in the recorded deeds to those lots. The court ruled, however, that the contract contained sufficient granting language to constitute an express easement.

Later, George Harrison (using a company he owned) purchased Lot 49. A real estate agent claimed that she told Harrison about the easement, but he did not recall that. In addition, the purchase agreement Harrison signed contained the following language:

> Seller agrees to convey the property with warranties vesting marketable title in the buyer, free and clear of all liens and encumbrances *except 10 foot pedestrian easement at the northerly end of property in favor of Parcels 12, 13, & 48* and any covenants, easements, reservations, restrictions now of record which do not materially affect the value of the property.

Id. at 76. The title searchers did not find the easement, however, because it was not recorded or even mentioned in the recorded deeds to Lots 12 and 48.

Harrison built a house near the easement, so he would have the best view of the water. After he moved in, he began to get annoyed with people using the path (at its closest point, about 100 feet from his house) who would stop and gawk. In 1999, while Harrison was away, someone using the path broke into his house, made herself a pizza, and did some laundry.

Harrison filed suit to quiet his title to the path. He claimed that he was a bona fide purchaser, because the easement was not recorded. The owners of Lots 12 and 48, including Ralph Waite (who played Grandpa Walton on a very popular 1970s TV series, *The Waltons*), said Harrison was bound by the easement. Who is right? Even if the easement exists, could you see any issues regarding scope and location?

Postscript: During the appeal of this case, Harrison was diagnosed with lung cancer and underwent extensive treatment. The Hawaii Supreme Court reached an initial decision, holding that the easement existed in favor of Lots 12 and 48, and that Harrison had notice. The court thereafter withdrew its opinion, pending reconsideration. In the meantime, on June 7, 2001, the parties reached a confidential settlement. George Harrison died November 29, 2001.

Beachfront Access

Many difficult and important easement issues arise in the context of public access to the beachfront. Coastal states must balance the rights of the public to access the water and sand against the private property rights of beachfront landowners. Similar problems occur in noncoastal states regarding access to the shores of other types of navigable waters, such as lakes and rivers.

Coastal states typically draw the border between public and private property at the *mean high tide line*. The portion of the beach below the high tide line is public trust property, while the land above it is capable of private ownership. Thus, the wet sand area, which at high tide is under water, is open to the public, while the area of dry sand beach may be owned by the adjacent landowner and shut off from public use.

The property line of beachfront property changes as the beachfront changes. If sand is added to the beach through *accretion* and the mean high tide moves seaward, the beachfront landowner gains land. Conversely, the landowner's property decreases as the beachfront recedes through erosion. If there is an *avulsion*, however, which is a rapid, dramatic change due to a flood or hurricane, the property line generally does not change. After an avulsive event, the private owner's land may be partially underwater, leaving the public without any beachfront. Conversely, a large area of dry

Accretion and Avulsion

The distinction between accretion and avulsion has deep historic roots:

"if th[e] gain be by little and little, by small and imperceptible degrees, it shall go to the owner of the land adjoining" but if the change be "sudden and considerable, in this case it belongs to the king."

—*2 William Blackstone, Commentaries *262.*

sand, now owned by the public, may be exposed. *See* Severance v. Patterson, 370 S.W.3d 705, 722-723 (Tex. 2012).

The dry sand/wet sand boundary line sets up potential conflicts over beach access. The public often would like to walk along or sit upon the dry sand area. At high tide, in fact, there might be no other way to enjoy the beachfront. If the area is a public beach, this presents no problem. If the adjacent land is privately owned, however, the private owner may prevent public access. States use various legal doctrines, such as prescription, implied dedication, and custom, to determine the extent of public access rights.

You will find significant differences among the states' approaches to this issue:

> **Texas.** In Texas, for example, the legislature codified common law in the Open Beaches Act, which declared public beaches to include private dry sand areas "to which the public has acquired the right of use or easement to or over the area by prescription, dedication, presumption, or has retained a right by virtue of continuous right in the public since time immemorial, as recognized in law and custom." Tex. Nat. Res. Code Ann. §61.011 (West 2017).

> **Oregon.** The Oregon Supreme Court held that the public had acquired open access to the state's dry sand beaches under the doctrine of *custom*, which requires use to be so ancient "that the memory of man runneth not to the contrary." State ex rel. Thornton v. Hay, 462 P.2d 671, 677 (Or. 1969) (paraphrasing Blackstone). The court described the use of the beach:

The dry-sand area in Oregon has been enjoyed by the general public as a recreational adjunct of the wet-sand or foreshore area since the beginning of the state's political history. The first European settlers on these shores found the aboriginal inhabitants using the foreshore for clam-digging and the dry-sand area for their cooking fires. The newcomers continued these customs after statehood. Thus, from the time of the earliest settlement to the present day, the general public has assumed that the dry-sand area was a part of the public beach, and the public has used the dry-sand area for picnics, gathering wood, building warming fires, and generally as a headquarters from which to supervise children or to range out over the foreshore as the tides advance and recede.

Public beach sign
Vetstein Law Group, P.C.

Id. at 673. Hawaii follows a similar approach.

➤ **New Jersey.** In Matthews v. Bay Head Improvement Ass'n, 471 A.2d 355 (N.J. 1984), the New Jersey Supreme Court relied on the *public trust* doctrine to uphold public rights to dry sand beaches. The public trust doctrine has its origins in Roman law, which provided: "By the law of nature these things are common to mankind—the air, running water, the sea and consequently the shores of the sea." J. Inst. 2.1.1. Certainly, this is the basis for public rights to the wet sand portion of the beach, but the New Jersey Supreme Court noted that exercising this right requires some use of the dry sand portion as well:

> Exercise of the public's right to swim and bathe below the mean high water mark may depend upon a right to pass across the upland beach. Without some means of access the public right to use the foreshore would be meaningless. To say that the public trust doctrine entitles the public to swim in the ocean and to use the foreshore in connection therewith without assuring the public of a feasible access route would seriously impinge on, if not effectively eliminate, the rights of the public trust doctrine. This does not mean the public has an unrestricted right to cross at will over any and all property bordering on the common property. The public interest is satisfied so long as there is reasonable access to the sea.

Id. at 364. Note the uncertainty inherent in New Jersey's test—what constitutes "reasonable access to the sea"? For further discussion, see Timothy M. Mulvaney & Brian Weeks, *"Waterlocked": Public Access to New Jersey's Coastline*, 34 Ecology L.Q. 579 (2007).

➤ **Florida.** Florida takes a more restrictive approach to public access to the dry sand beach. The state recognizes that public rights may be acquired by prescription, implied dedication, or custom, but the fulfillment of those requirements must be established on a beach-by-beach basis. In City of Daytona Beach v. Tona-Rama, Inc., 294 So. 2d 73 (Fla. 1974), the Florida Supreme Court held that public use of a portion of Daytona beach for many years would not ripen into an easement by prescription, because there was no proof of adversity and the presumption of permissive use favored the landowner. It did, however, recognize a limited right established by custom where "the recreational use of the sandy area . . . has been ancient, reasonable, without interruption and free from dispute. . . ." *Id.* at 78.

Spring Break Research Project

Next time you head to Florida, notice that some Florida beachfront hotels will not allow non-guests to use their dry sand beachfront; while you may consider this rude, consider the legal consequences if the hotel did not vigilantly police its private beach.

What differences do you see in these approaches to public access? For more discussion of these doctrines and the potential impact of climate change, see Celeste Pagano, *Where's the Beach? Coastal Access in the Age of Rising Tides*, 42 Sw. L. Rev. 1 (2012).

B SCOPE AND TERMINATION

Unless otherwise stated, easements are typically deemed to be of perpetual duration. Perpetuity, you realize, is a very long time. At some point, circumstances may change. The dominant tenant may wish to use the easement in a different way, for different purposes. This will involve questions of the scope of the easement. On the other hand, the servient tenant may want to terminate the easement.

Termination of Easements

Here are the most common ways to terminate an easement:

1. **Release.** The dominant tenant agrees to relinquish the easement. This should be in writing, to meet the Statute of Frauds, and recorded, so that the title is clear (which means it must have a notarial acknowledgment).
2. **Expiration.** If the original easement was only for a certain period of time, it ends upon the expiration of that time period. In addition, if the easement was for a particular purpose, such as to reach a mine, it ends when the purpose has been fulfilled (e.g., the mine is played out). Similarly, an easement by necessity ends when it is no longer necessary.
3. **Abandonment.** This requires more than just a period of non-use; the court must have some indication (express or implied) that the dominant tenant *intended* to abandon the easement.
4. **Merger.** If the dominant and servient parcels come to be owned by the same person, the easement is automatically extinguished, because a landowner cannot have an easement over her own land.
5. **Estoppel.** Just as in easement creation, the easement may be terminated if the dominant tenant makes a promise to release the easement, which the servient owner relies on to her detriment.
6. **Condemnation.** If the government acquires the servient tenement by eminent domain (for example, for a road or a government building), it may also forcibly terminate an easement on the property, although it must pay the dominant owner just compensation.
7. **Prescription.** Just as in easement creation, the owner of the servient estate may terminate an easement by blocking the dominant tenant's use of it for the prescriptive period.

> **8. Notice.** A subsequent purchaser of the servient tenement who takes title without notice of the easement may be a bona fide purchaser under the jurisdiction's recording act, and thus not be bound.

■ PROBLEM: THE MAGIC DISAPPEARING EASEMENT

Alice owns adjacent properties Blackacre and Whiteacre. In 2005, she conveys Whiteacre to her son, Bart, and includes an easement over Blackacre. In 2010, Bart decides to move to Australia, and he conveys Whiteacre back to his mother, but his deed doesn't mention the easement. In 2019, Alice sells Whiteacre to Charlie. Charlie wants to use the easement, which he notes was properly recorded and has never been released. Alice says the easement "is no good, Charlie, so don't try it." Is she right?

1. Misuse

Another way an easement might be terminated is through misuse. Typically, the remedy in such cases is an injunction against further misuse along with damages for any harm caused to the servient owner by the previous conduct. However, the court may also terminate the easement if the misuse is *intentional and frequent*, or if the misuse is likely to continue.

The misuse issue brings us back to questions of *scope*. The dominant owner misuses the easement only when the use exceeds the easement's scope—i.e., the permissible use for which the easement was established. As we noted at the outset, the drafter of an express easement should carefully delineate the proper uses and location of the easement and try, to the extent possible, to anticipate future developments.

Inevitably, however, questions of scope will occur. For example, assume Alice granted Bart a right-of-way over Blackacre to reach Whiteacre, when it was rural property with a small hunting cabin that Bart used only occasionally. Forty years later, should the right-of-way be construed to allow access to a subdivision of 20 residences? Or to a large commercial building supply store now built on Whiteacre?

These questions will depend on the exact language of the easement and the express or implied intent of the parties regarding its scope. In general, courts allow for the *natural evolution* of easement use, given changes in technology, as long as the burden on the servient owner is not appreciably increased. For example, a century-old grant of access for horse-drawn carriages would now be construed to allow vehicular traffic. *See, e.g.,* Stevens v. Anderson, 393 A.2d 158 (Me. 1978) (1915 grant for "cattle teams and foot passengers" construed to permit motor vehicles); In re Garza, 893 N.W.2d 1 (Wis. 2017) (even though 1969 easement specified use of wood transmission poles, the owner of the easement could update to steel poles as long as it did not create an undue burden on the servient owner).

Another common issue is whether a right-of-way may be used to *benefit land other than the original dominant tenement.* We know that an appurtenant easement is attached to a particular parcel of dominant land, and the *general rule* is that the easement may not be used for the benefit of other land. Are there circumstances, however, that call for a little flexibility in enforcing that rule?

The following influential case suggests that the general rule, or at least the *remedy* for its violation, is not always clear-cut. The dispute takes place in a beautiful area of Washington State near the Hood Canal, frequently used for vacation cabins.

BROWN v. VOSS

715 P.2d 514 (1986)
Supreme Court of Washington

The question posed is to what extent, if any, the holder of a private road easement can traverse the servient estate to reach not only the original dominant estate, but a subsequently acquired parcel when those two combined parcels are used in such a way that there is no increase in the burden on the servient estate. The trial court denied the injunction sought by the owners of the servient estate. The Court of Appeals reversed. . . . We reverse the Court of Appeals and reinstate the judgment of the trial court.

A portion of an exhibit depicts the involved parcels.

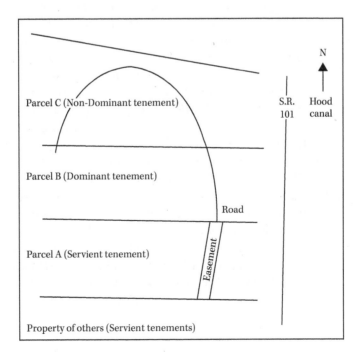

In 1952 the predecessors in title of parcel A granted to the predecessor owners of parcel B a private road easement across parcel A for "ingress to and egress from" parcel B. Defendants acquired parcel A in 1973. Plaintiffs [Will and Jean Brown] bought parcel B on April 1, 1977 and parcel C on July 31, 1977, but from two different owners. Apparently the previous owners of parcel C were not parties to the easement grant.

When plaintiffs acquired parcel B a single family dwelling was situated thereon. They intended to remove that residence and replace it with a single family dwelling which would straddle the boundary line common to parcels B and C.

Plaintiffs began clearing both parcels B and C and moving fill materials in November 1977. Defendants first sought to bar plaintiff's use of the easement in April 1979 by which time plaintiffs had spent more than $11,000 in developing their property for building.

Defendants [Fred and Hattie Voss] placed logs, a concrete sump and a chain link fence within the easement. Plaintiffs sued for removal of the obstructions, an injunction against defendant's interference with their use of the easement and damages. Defendants counterclaimed for damages and an injunction against plaintiffs using the easement other than for parcel B.

The trial court awarded each party $1 in damages. The award against the plaintiffs was for a slight inadvertent trespass outside the easement.

. . .The easement in this case was created by express grant. Accordingly, the extent of the right acquired is to be determined from the terms of the grant properly construed to give effect to the intention of the parties. *See* Zobrist v. Culp, 95 Wash. 2d 556, 561, 627 P.2d 1308 (1981); Seattle v. Nazarenus, 60 Wash. 2d 657, 665, 374 P.2d 1014 (1962). By the express terms of the 1952 grant, the predecessor owners of parcel B acquired a private road easement across parcel A and the right to use the easement for ingress to and egress from parcel B. Both plaintiffs and defendants agree that the 1952 grant created an easement appurtenant to parcel B as the dominant estate. Thus, plaintiffs, as owners of the dominant estate, acquired rights in the use of the easement for ingress to and egress from parcel B.

However, plaintiffs have no such easement rights in connection with their ownership of parcel C, which was not a part of the original dominant estate under the terms of the 1952 grant. As a general rule, an easement appurtenant to one parcel of land may not be extended by the owner of the dominant estate to other parcels owned by him, whether adjoining or distinct tracts, to which the easement is not appurtenant. [citations omitted]

Plaintiffs, nonetheless, contend that extension of the use of the easement for the benefit of nondominant property does not constitute a misuse of the easement, where as here, there is no evidence of an increase in the burden on the servient estate. We do not agree. If an easement is appurtenant to a particular parcel of land, any extension thereof to other parcels is a misuse of the easement. . . . As noted by one court in a factually similar case, "[I]n this context this classic rule of property law is directed to the rights of the respective parties rather than the actual burden on the servitude." National Lead Co. v. Kanawha Block Co., 288

F. Supp. 357, 364 (S.D. W. Va. 1968), *aff'd*, 409 F.2d 1309 (4th Cir. 1969). Under the express language of the 1952 grant, plaintiffs only have rights in the use of the easement for the benefit of parcel B. Although, as plaintiffs contend, their planned use of the easement to gain access to a single family residence located partially on parcel B and partially on parcel C is perhaps no more than technical misuse of the easement, we conclude that it is misuse nonetheless.

However, it does not follow from this conclusion alone that defendants are entitled to injunctive relief. Since the awards of $1 in damages were not appealed, only the denial of an injunction to defendants is in issue. Some fundamental principles applicable to a request for an injunction must be considered. (1) The proceeding is equitable and addressed to the sound discretion of the trial court. (2) The trial court is vested with a broad discretionary power to shape and fashion injunctive relief to fit the particular facts, circumstances, and equities of the case before it. Appellate courts give great weight to the trial court's exercise of that discretion. (3) One of the essential criteria for injunctive relief is actual and substantial injury sustained by the person seeking the injunction. Washington Fed'n of State Employees v. State, 99 Wash. 2d 878, 665 P.2d 1337 (1983); Port of Seattle v. Int'l Longshoremen's Union, 52 Wash. 2d 317, 324 P.2d 1099 (1958).

The trial court found as facts, upon substantial evidence, that plaintiffs have acted reasonably in the development of their property, that there is and was no damage to the defendants from plaintiffs' use of the easement, that there was no increase in the volume of travel on the easement, that there was no increase in the burden on the servient estate, that defendants sat by for more than a year while plaintiffs expended more than $11,000 on their project, and that defendants' counterclaim was an effort to gain "leverage" against plaintiffs' claim. In addition, the court found from the evidence that plaintiffs would suffer considerable hardship if the injunction were granted whereas no appreciable hardship or damages would flow to defendants from its denial. Finally, the court limited plaintiffs' use of the combined parcels solely to the same purpose for which the original parcel was used—i.e., for a single family residence.

Neither this court nor the Court of Appeals may substitute its effort to make findings of fact for those supported findings of the trial court. State v. Marchand, 62 Wash. 2d 767, 770, 384 P.2d 865 (1963); Thorndike v. Hesperian Orchards, Inc., 54 Wash. 2d 570, 575, 343 P.2d 183 (1959). Therefore, the only valid issue is whether, under these established facts, as a matter of law, the trial court abused its discretion in denying defendants' request for injunctive relief. Based upon the equities of the case, as found by the trial court, we are persuaded that the trial court acted within its discretion. The Court of Appeals is reversed and the trial court is affirmed.

DOLLIVER, C.J., and ANDERSEN, UTTER, CALLOW, PEARSON and DURHAM, JJ., concur.

DORE, JUSTICE (dissenting).

The majority correctly finds that an extension of this easement to nondominant property is a misuse of the easement. The majority, nonetheless, holds that the owners of the servient estate are not entitled to injunctive relief. I dissent. . . .

The majority grants the privilege to extend the agreement to nondominant property on the basis that the trial court found no appreciable hardship or damage to the servient owners. However, as conceded by the majority, any extension of the use of an easement to benefit a nondominant estate constitutes a misuse of the easement. Misuse of an easement is a trespass. . . . The Brown's use of the easement to benefit parcel C, especially if they build their home as planned, would involve a continuing trespass for which damages would be difficult to measure. Injunctive relief is the appropriate remedy under these circumstances. . . . Thus, the fact that an extension of the easement to nondominant property would not increase the burden on the servient estate does not warrant a denial of injunctive relief.

The Browns are responsible for the hardship of creating a landlocked parcel. They knew or should have known from the public records that the easement was not appurtenant to parcel C. *See* Seattle v. Nazarenus, 60 Wash. 2d 657, 670, 374 P.2d 1014 (1962). In encroachment cases this factor is significant. As stated by the court in Bach v. Sarich, 74 Wash. 2d 575, 582, 445 P.2d 648 (1968): "The benefit of the doctrine of balancing the equities, or relative hardship, is reserved for the innocent defendant who proceeds without knowledge or warning that his structure encroaches upon another's property or property rights."

In addition, an injunction would not interfere with the Brown's right to use the easement as expressly granted, i.e., for access to parcel B. An injunction would merely require the Browns to acquire access to parcel C if they want to build a home that straddles parcels B and C. One possibility would be to condemn a private way of necessity over their existing easement in an action under RCW 8.24.010. *See* Brown v. McAnally, 97 Wash. 2d 360, 644 P.2d 1153 (1982).

I would affirm the Court of Appeals decision as a correct application of the law of easements. If the Browns desire access to their landlocked parcel they have the benefit of the statutory procedure for condemnation of a private way of necessity.

GOODLOE, J. concur with DORE, J.

■ POINTS TO CONSIDER

1. **The traditional rule.** The dissent in *Brown* favors the traditional, majority rule, which adopts a bright-line approach enjoining *any use* of an easement to benefit a *non-dominant parcel*. Among the classic cases so holding is Penn Bowling Recreation Ctr. v. Hot Shoppes, 179 F.2d 64 (D.D.C. 1950), in which the dominant tenant constructed a building housing a bowling alley and restaurant, which extended onto non-dominant property. The portion of the building on the adjacent property included a luncheonette. The right-of-way was used to bring in supplies that were used in the luncheonette and

to take out trash. Even though the area served was smaller than the original dominant parcel and there was no evidence of increased burden, the court adhered to the bright-line rule. In fact, because it was difficult to tell whether the easement was being used for the luncheonette, the court authorized an injunction on all use "until the building is so altered or changed that that part of it which is on the dominant tenement may enjoy the easement without permitting its enjoyment by the other part of the building having no right thereto." *Id.* at 67.

2. **A more flexible rule.** Although the traditional rule remains that an easement may not be used to benefit a non-dominant parcel, the Washington Supreme Court is not alone in finding exceptions to the rule. For example, the Connecticut Supreme Court has adopted a more flexible intent test. In Abington Limited Partnership v. Heublein, 778 A.2d 885 (Conn. 2001), the federal government acquired the dominant parcel (just over six acres) in 1955 for use as a radar-tracking installation, and acquired an access easement at the same time. In the 1970s, the parcel was conveyed to the Science Center, which used it for holding classes and educational programs. In 1991, the Science Center constructed a 20,000-square-foot building on an adjacent parcel of about 14 acres. The building held administrative offices, classrooms, television studios, and a planetarium. The Science Center used the original easement to access both of these parcels. The Connecticut Supreme Court refused to enjoin the use of the easement for the non-dominant parcel. Instead of adopting a bright-line test that limited the use of the easement to the original dominant parcel, the court examined whether the parties, at the time the easement was created, *reasonably contemplated* it might be used for the benefit of adjacent property "not formally within the terms of the easement." *Id.* at 894. The court found that, given the nature of the government's original use, the servient owner should have anticipated its use might extend beyond the borders of the original parcel. The use would not be allowed if it overburdened the servitude. The court noted that the original easement contemplated use for Cold War military operations, which would presumably be much more burdensome than Science Center traffic. In addition, there was no evidence that traffic had increased since the opening of the new building. The court noted: "The manner, frequency, and intensity of the beneficiary's use of the servient estate may change over time to take advantage of developments in technology and to accommodate normal development of the dominant estate or enterprise benefited by the servitude." 778 A.2d at 895. Assume you represent Alice and are charged with drafting the language for a right-of-way easement over Blackacre to benefit Whiteacre, owned by Bart. What provisions might you include in light of decisions such as *Abingdon*? *See also* Ettinger v. Pomeroy Limited Partnership, 97 A.3d 1133 (N.H. 2014) (remanding for extrinsic evidence on whether parties contemplated that easement might eventually serve non-dominant parcel).

3. **Policy.** The majority in *Brown* uses a liability rule, while the dissent favors a property rule. What property policies support the rules favored by the

majority and dissent in *Brown*, or the rule in *Abingdon*? Can you see any parallels between *Brown* and *Jacque v. Steenberg Homes* from Chapter 1?

4. **Estoppel.** In *Brown*, the Browns expended a considerable amount clearing and preparing the land for development before the Vosses objected. Why couldn't the Browns claim an easement by estoppel to benefit parcel C?

5. **Division of the dominant parcel.** Carefully distinguish between what happened in *Brown* and the division of the dominant parcel into multiple parcels. Would it be permissible for the Browns to divide Parcel B into two pieces and sell one to another party so that two households would be using the easement? The right of way can serve the divided land "only if the easement can be enjoyed as to the separate parcels without any additional burden upon the servient tenement." 10 A.L.R.3d 960, § 4 (1966). The Restatement indicates that an "increase in the number of persons holding the benefit of the servitude alone does not constitute an unreasonable increase in the burden [.]" Restatement (Third) of Property: Servitudes § 5.7 cmt. c. *See* Mayer v. Smith, 350 P.3d 1191, 1199 (N.M. Ct. App. 2015) (finding that providing ingress/egress to two residences instead of one did not increase burden on servient estate).

■ PROBLEMS: MISUSE

1. Blackacre is bordered by State Street on the South and Whiteacre on the north. O, who owned both Blackacre and Whiteacre, deeded Blackacre in 1854 to A, but reserved a "right-of-way 16 feet in width with the right of free ingress and egress for all purposes" in favor of Whiteacre. In 1999, a church built a new sanctuary on land adjacent to Whiteacre. It also purchased Whiteacre, which it turned into a parking lot. The church intends to use the right-of-way over Blackacre so that worshipers can easily reach the parking lot from State Street. Is that permissible? *See* Heartz v. City of Concord, 808 A.2d 76 (N.H. 2002).

2. In 1949, Albert granted Hill Electric Company (HEC) an easement over Blackacre "for the purpose of constructing and maintaining an electric transmission or distribution line." In 2013, HEC entered into a joint use agreement with Marcus Cable Systems, which would allow the cable provider to attach its cable lines to the electric company's poles. The current owner of Blackacre, Bertha, claims that the cable lines are an unauthorized trespass. Marcus Cable claims that the use is a partial assignment of HEC's easement rights, are within the scope of that easement, and in any event, do not present any further burden to Bertha's use of her land. What do you think? *Compare* Marcus Cable Assocs. v. Krohn, 90 S.W.3d 697, 707-08 (Tex. 2002) (easement for electricity does not confer right for cable wires), *with id.* at 711-12 (Hecht, J., dissenting) (easement should be interpreted to allow technological advances that do not cause greater burden). *See* Barfield v. Sho-Me Power Electric Cooperative, 852 F.3d 795, 801-02 (8th Cir. 2017) (addition of fiber optic cables was outside the scope of electricity easement).

2. Abandonment: The Rails to Trails Context

As rail transportation expanded across the country in the 1800s, railways acquired thousands of miles of property rights in the rail corridors. Although some of these rights were deeded in fee, the vast majority were right-of-way easements, often limited to "railroad purposes only."

In the last half of the twentieth century, as rail transportation needs diminished, rail corridors began to fall into disuse. Rather than simply abandon these corridors, in many cases they were converted to public recreational use as hiking and biking trails. Congress facilitated this "rails to trails" movement by amending the National Trails System Act in 1983 to allow the federal Surface Transportation Board to certify "railbanking" projects, which authorize the "interim" use of the rail line for recreational trails, pending possible future railway operations. 16 U.S.C. §1247 (2014). In 2018, there were over 2000 rail-trails open, covering over 23,000 miles, with about 800 additional projects in the works.

These projects sometimes present difficult issues regarding the scope of easements and termination by abandonment. Consider the following hypothetical (based loosely on an actual case) to get a sense of how these issues are resolved:

Rails to Trails, a Hypothetical

Bike trail
Photo by Jerry Anderson

In 1880, Hiram Forbes granted an easement to the Union Pacific Railroad (UP) for the operation of a rail line through his 640-acre ranch in Utah.

The easement was one mile in length and was limited to "railroad purposes only."

UP stopped using this line in 1980. In 1988, the railroad pulled up all of the rails and cross-ties along the route. The railroad maintained, however, that at that point it had not decided whether it might want to resume its use of the route. In 1998, pursuant to the Trails Act, the federal Surface Transportation Board issued UP a Certificate of Interim Trail Use, authorizing the right-of-way to be used as a bicycle trail. Under the Trails Act, the Board must "preserve established railroad rights-of-way for future reactivation of rail service" by prohibiting abandonment if the railroad enters into an agreement for trail use, reserving the right to reclaim the right-of-way should there ever be a proposal to reactivate the line for rail service. *See* 16 U.S.C. §1247(d) (2018). UP negotiated an agreement with the Davis County Conservation Board, whereby that group would undertake all maintenance and responsibility for the trail.

The Forbes property is now owned by Forbes's great-great-granddaughter Inez Toscano. Toscano claims that the use of the easement as a bike trail constitutes a misuse of the easement because it is beyond its scope. In addition, she claims that the railroad has abandoned the easement, such that it should be deemed terminated and its full use should revert to her, as the owner of the servient estate. Finally, Toscano argues that if federal law authorizes the transfer of the right-of-way to a new owner (i.e., Davis County) for new purposes (i.e., recreation), the government owes her compensation for this new easement. *Do you agree?*

> ➢ In the Trails Act, Congress indicated that interim trail use "shall not be treated, for any purposes of any law or rule of law, as an abandonment of the use of such rights-of-way for railroad purposes." *Does that affect your answer?*

In Preseault v. Interstate Commerce Commission, 494 U.S. 1, 14-16 (1990), the Supreme Court held that if the Trails Act prevents the termination of easements that would otherwise be terminated by abandonment or misuse, the servient owner can obtain compensation for a taking of property rights. For examples of the many cases seeking compensation for rails to trails conversions, see Toscano v. United States, 107 Fed. Cl. 179 (2013); Arnold v. United States, 137 Fed. Cl. 524 (2018).

■ **Scope of easement.** Do you see the importance of considering the exact language used in the easement deed? For example, if the deed conveyed only a right-of-way without specifying railroad use, how would the case be impacted? What if the scope was limited to "transportation" use? *See* Washington Wildlife Pres., Inc. v. State, 329 N.W.2d 543 (Minn. 1983) (recreational trail use constituted transportation within scope of railroad easement). *Compare* James v. United States, 130 Fed.Cl. 707 (2017) (railbanking not consistent with "railroad use"). Is the new use more, or less, of a burden on the servient estate than the railroad use? Should that matter?

■ **Abandonment.** At what point, if any, did UP's actions constitute abandonment of its easement? While non-use alone does not normally indicate an intent to abandon, what about the removal of the rails and ties? Again, do you see the importance of covering this point in the easement grant? In State ex rel. Dep't of Natural Res. v. Hess, 665 N.W.2d 560 (Minn. Ct. App. 2003), the Minnesota Court of Appeals determined that a railroad easement was terminated where the deed specified that removal of rails would constitute abandonment. The Minnesota Supreme Court reversed, on the basis that the deed conveyed a fee simple determinable, rather than an easement, and the possibility of reverter was extinguished by operation of the state's Marketable Title Act. State v. Hess, 684 N.W.2d 414 (Minn. 2004).

The authors of one law review article argue that courts should, where possible, construe the railroad's interest as fee title rather than as a limited easement for a particular purpose:

> Property law doctrines, first and foremost, try to prevent upsetting settled expectations. Finding fee title in the railroad would further the public policy of quieting title that underlies our doctrines of adverse possession, the rule against forfeitures, marketable title acts, the rule against perpetuities, and rules against transfers of future interests. This is especially true when there is little, if any, expectation on the part of adjoining landowners to receive the windfall of a rail corridor.
>
> Moreover, a strong public interest exists in preserving these corridors for trails and utilities. . . . Many of these corridors were assembled with public funding, public land, and eminent domain powers. They are, in a fundamental way, public assets. To the extent that deed construction can further protect the public's interest, especially when the cost to landowners is minimal, the courts have an obligation to realize that the public is a party to these cases as well. When landowners do not have title to the corridor land, heirs of the grantor are long gone, and the corridor can continue to provide vital public utility, recreational, environmental, and transportation services, there is no reason to continue the century-old anti-railroad animus that prevailed in the days of frontier expansion. Precedents lose their legitimacy when times change.

Danaya C. Wright & Jeffrey M. Hester, *Pipes, Wires, and Bicycles: Rails-to-Trails, Utility Licenses, and the Shifting Scope of Railroad Easements from the Nineteenth to the Twenty-First Centuries*, 27 Ecology L.Q. 351, 385 (2000). Do you see the connection to the other subjects we have studied, such as the Rule Against Perpetuities and adverse possession? Do you agree with the authors' conclusions?

3. Easement Valuation

Assume that the court in our Forbes bike trail example concluded that the railroad's easement terminated due to abandonment and that the county's recreational use constituted a new easement, for which the government must give Toscano just compensation. How do you value an easement?

Traditionally, courts hold that an value may be ascertained by comparing the value of the servient estate before and after it is burdened by the easement. If a reasonable buyer would pay $500,000 for Blackacre without a bike trail, but only $450,000 for the property with the trail, the easement would be worth $50,000.

If that is the case, reconsider Misuse Problem 2 above, concerning the cable company's "piggybacking" on the electric company's easement. Assuming we find that adding the cable line is a misuse of the easement for which the servient owner deserves compensation, what should the amount of compensation be? Would you pay any less for property that has four wires running across the poles on the land, rather than just three wires? What if the cable ran through an underground conduit?

In Gulf Power Co. v. United States, 187 F.3d 1324 (11th Cir. 1999), the court upheld a federal law requiring utility companies to share their poles with cable companies. 47 U.S.C. §224(f) (2018). The statute allows the Federal Communications Commission to determine the rate of compensation to provide to utility companies for this burden on their easement rights. The maximum compensation is measured by the percentage of space occupied by the cable, times the cost of the construction and operation of the pole to which the cable is attached.

SUMMARY

- *Servitudes* include easements, real covenants, equitable servitudes, licenses, and profits à prendre.
- An *easement* is an interest in land that allows the holder to use the property of another. The easement may be *affirmative*, allowing the dominant tenant to do something on the servient land, or it may be *negative*, allowing the dominant tenant to prevent a particular use of the servient land.
- Easements may be created expressly, either by deed or will. In creating an *express* easement, the drafter should consider issues of scope, location, duration, maintenance, and termination.
- Some jurisdictions do not allow A, in deeding Blackacre to B, to reserve an easement in C, a *stranger to the deed*. Although the modern trend is to reject this rule, better practice would be to create the easement to C in a separate deed before conveying Blackacre to B.

- Easements may be created by marking them on a *plat*, especially if the deed refers to the plat, although this method may raise questions about the intention of the grantor regarding scope.
- Easements may created by *estoppel*, if the dominant owner substantially changes position in reliance on a promise to use the land that the user reasonably believed would not be revoked.
- An easement may be *implied* when a common grantor conveys part of her land, in two circumstances.
  - □ An *easement by prior use* may arise if the grantor, at the time of conveyance, was using the servient part of her land to benefit the dominant part, in a way that was reasonably necessary for its use and enjoyment, such that it was implied the use would continue.
  - □ An *easement by necessity* arises if the conveyance of part of the property makes an easement necessary. The necessity must arise at the time of the conveyance. Many courts require strict necessity, such that the parties must have intended an easement to be part of the transaction.
- An easement may be acquired *by prescription*, through adverse, continuous, open, and notorious use for the statutory period. Some jurisdictions presume adversity based on continued use, which puts the burden on the servient owner to prove that the use was by permission.
- The public owns the wet sand part of the *beach* adjacent to navigable water, while the dry sand part of the beach may be privately owned. The public may acquire access to the dry sand beach through the doctrines of prescription, custom, implied dedication, or the public trust doctrine.
- Easements may be *terminated* by release, expiration, abandonment, merger, estoppel, condemnation, prescription, or acquisition of the servient estate by a bona fide purchaser without notice. An easement may also be terminated by repeated and intentional misuse.
- In determining the *scope* of an easement, courts allow for natural evolution, given changes in technology, as long as the burden on the servient owner is not appreciably increased. Most courts prohibit the easement to be used for the benefit of a non-dominant parcel. A few courts, however, have shown some flexibility, based either on the lack of harm to the dominant tenant or the implied intentions of the original parties.
- The use of old *railway easements* as bike trails raises significant questions regarding whether trail use is within the scope of the original grant, and whether it demonstrates an *intent to abandon* the easement.

Real Covenants and Equitable Servitudes

> Chaos was the law of nature; order was the dream of men.
> —*Henry B. Adams, The Education of Henry Adams 451 (1918)*

A *real covenant* is a promise respecting the use of land. The covenant is an important legal tool for solidifying private agreements and expectations regarding acceptable landowner behavior. For example, Albert might be willing to sell off a piece of his farm to Bella, so she can build a house, but he won't do it unless he can be assured she won't use it to build a convenience store or a hog lot. A commercial developer might use covenants to ensure that each parcel of its planned shopping district fits into its harmonious design. Regrettably, covenants have also been used negatively; for example, covenants prohibiting conveyances to persons of various ethnic, racial, or religious groups can be found in many old deeds.

Today, real covenants have become more comprehensive and much more common. Most housing developments built today take the form of what is known as a common-interest community (CIC). In a CIC, the residents share the ownership of certain common areas and share obligations regarding maintenance. A CIC might be a gated community, which limits entry to neighborhood residents and their guests. It might be a condominium development, in which residents own individual units in fee simple and common areas as tenants in common. In almost every new residential development, a developer files a set of covenants that govern a wide range of landowner behavior—everything from what kind of shingles can be used to where you have to park your car. In addition, the covenants usually provide for a system of governance, including how the covenants will be enforced and amended.

Modern Covenants

In modern housing developments, the developer will record a Declaration of Covenants, Conditions, and Restrictions (CC&Rs) with the plat. These set out not only the restrictions on use, but also provide for a homeowners association (HOA), along with a Board of Directors empowered to enact more specific bylaws. 🖥 Some examples of modern covenants can be found on the Simulation.

Celebration, a planned community near Disney World, has a 166-page Declaration of CC&Rs. The bylaws include a restriction limiting window coverings visible from the exterior to white or off-white in color. Owners must also promptly remove from porches any plants that die. Trash cans can't be placed on the curb for pick-up before 7 P.M. the night before. Owners can't place a "For Sale" sign in the yard unless they first submit an application and have the sign approved by the HOA.

Because restrictive covenants have become so pervasive in modern housing, legal issues surrounding them have become increasingly important. In this chapter, we will study how covenants are created and enforced. In addition, we will study the common-interest community structure and how courts are developing rules to control arbitrary behavior by CIC governing bodies.

Typically, a contract is enforceable only by the original promisee against the original promisor. When a promise is made respecting the use of land, however, the parties usually intend for it to bind, and benefit, not only the current landowners but their successors as well. The parties intend, in other words, for the covenant to "run with the land" rather than being considered solely a personal contract.

Historically, however, courts were reluctant to allow covenants to bind subsequent owners. As we learned in the future interests chapter, courts want to promote the free alienability of land, and to ensure it may be used in the most economically beneficial way to meet the current needs of society. Property burdened by numerous restrictions on how it can be used may be less able to meet those goals. Therefore, courts initially developed tests that made it harder for covenants to run with the land as a matter of law. Nevertheless, covenants proved to be popular and courts eventually recognized that these restrictions often enhance, rather than detract from, a property's value. Because the restrictions would be of little value unless they bind, and benefit, subsequent owners, courts found ways around the common law rules limiting real covenants. The result, as you will see, is a bit of a mess.

In the modern world, we need to strike a balance between enforcing covenants that are valuable and useful, while still being able to trim away those restrictions that have proven unduly burdensome or unfair. Many scholars suggest that the courts should junk the old rules and use the unified approach to all servitudes adopted by the Restatement (Third) of Property, which focuses on granting relief from covenants that offend our policy goals. The Restatement radically departs from the established common law in many respects. While some state courts have begun to move in the direction suggested by the Restatement, for now we are stuck with learning an anachronistic framework that courts try to stretch (and often contort) to serve modern needs.

A REAL COVENANTS—RUNNING WITH THE LAND AT LAW

Suppose Alice owns Blackacre, a country estate. She decides to carve out a few acres of Blackacre to sell to Bart, and she calls this parcel Whiteacre. Blackacre is her home, however, and she wants to make sure Bart will not use Whiteacre for anything other than residential use. So, in the deed to Whiteacre, she includes the following language: "Grantee, along with his heirs and assigns, hereby covenants to use Whiteacre for single-family residential purposes only."

As between the original parties, Alice and Bart, the enforceability of this promise centers on whether it meets the Statute of Frauds. Here, the promise was in writing, but you might have a question about whether it was signed by the party to be bound—Bart. Typically, the grantee of property does not sign a deed, only the grantor does. However, courts have ruled that Bart's acceptance of the deed is sufficient to bind him to its terms.

Shortly after purchasing Whiteacre, however, Bart is transferred to Cleveland and finds that he is no longer interested in building a house on Whiteacre. Moreover, he has received a handsome offer from DayMart, which thinks Whiteacre would make a marvelous location for a new convenience store/gas station. The deal is soon done, and DayMart starts to build. Alice, who can see the store from her living room window, is irate and sues to enjoin the construction of the convenience store. Should she win? Moreover, if Alice dies and her daughter Carly inherits Blackacre, can Carly enforce the covenant against DayMart?

The question is whether the burden of the covenant runs to DayMart and the benefit of the covenant runs to Carly. In graphical terms, the parties may be depicted like this:

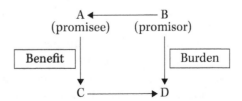

At common law, courts held that a covenant would not run with the land at law, unless it met the following five-part test:

Running with the Land—At Law

1. **Intent.** The parties must intend for the covenant to run with the land. Language such as "successors and assigns" signifies that intent explicitly, but courts will also imply intent from the surrounding circumstances, including the type or purpose of the covenant at issue.
2. **Touch and concern the land.** This factor attempts to distinguish between promises that are personal in nature and those that have to do with the use and enjoyment of the land itself. For example, assume Alice agreed to sell Whiteacre for a lower purchase price if Bart would agree to use her excavating company to dig his basement when he builds his house. After Bart sells to DayMart, does it need to use Alice's company or is that a personal promise?
3. **Horizontal privity.** Historically, courts required some connection between the original promisor and promisee *beyond the covenant itself*. Courts accepted three types of horizontal privity:
   - *Grantor/grantee or "successive" privity.* This means that the covenanting parties were the grantor and grantee of the land to which the covenant pertained. "In other words, the covenant must be part of a transaction that also includes the transfer of an interest in land that is either benefited or burdened by the covenant." Sonoma Dev., Inc. v. Miller, 515 S.E.2d 577, 580 (Va. 1999). "Horizontal privity exists where the covenant was created as part of a conveyance of real property between creating parties." BM-Clarence Cardwell, Inc. v. Cocca Dev., Ltd., 65 N.E.3d 829 (Ohio Ct. App. 2016). In our example, Alice conveyed Whiteacre to Bart, so they have this type of horizontal privity.

   OR
   - *Mutual privity.* The parties both have a legal interest in the land affected by the covenant. For example, if Bart had an easement over Blackacre and covenanted with Alice to maintain it, there would be horizontal privity because both Alice and Bart have a legal interest in Blackacre.

   OR
   - Landlord-*tenant privity.* These parties could make covenants in a lease that will bind subsequent owners of the rental property and sub-tenants or assignees of the lessee.
4. **Vertical privity.** Looking at our diagram, this type of privity is "vertical" in the sense that it requires a connection between the successive owners of the benefited property (A and C) and burdened property (B and D). This requires that the party succeed to the same interest in land burdened or benefited by the covenant. *See* Harrison v. Westview Partners, LLC, 913 N.Y.S.2d 364 (N.Y. App. Div. 2010) (this prong

met when "there has been a continuous succession of conveyances between the original covenanter and the party now sought to be burdened").

The Restatement summarizes the current judicial thought on vertical privity:

> To establish vertical privity, a chain of title must be established between the original covenantor or covenantee and the person claimed to be bound by the covenant or entitled to its benefit. For "strict" vertical privity, the successor must hold the same estate (in durational, not geographical, terms) as the original party to the servitude; for "relaxed" vertical privity, the successor may hold a lesser estate carved out of the estate held by the original party. Lessees of the person holding the same estate as an original party to the covenant and life tenants of property in which the remainder or reversion is the same estate as that of an original party to the covenant are not in strict vertical privity, but meet the requirement for relaxed vertical privity.

Restatement (Third) of Prop.: Servitudes § 5.2 cmt. b. (2000).

Although rarely an issue, some cases have found that a lack of vertical privity prevented covenant enforcement. *See* Biggs Ditch Co. v. Jongste, 149 P.2d 1 (Cal. 1944) (owner of easement acquired by prescription not bound by covenant); Runyon v. Paley, 416 S.E.2d 177, 185 (N.C. 1992) (no vertical privity where plaintiff was not successor in interest of any land owned by covenantee at time covenant entered into); Winn-Dixie Stores, Inc. v. Dolgencorp, LLC, 746 F.3d 1008 (11th Cir. 2014)(applying strict vertical privity, lessee not bound by covenant entered into by landlord).

5. **Notice.** Just like other encumbrances on real estate, a bona fide purchaser who takes without notice of the covenants is not bound by them. This is relevant only to the running of the *burden* of the covenants; a subsequent owner is entitled to the benefit of covenants even if she had no notice of them.

We will discuss the application of this traditional test below.

B   EQUITABLE SERVITUDES

Of the requirements for covenants to run with the land, horizontal privity is undoubtedly the hardest to understand and least likely to be enforced by modern courts. The original British version of horizontal privity required some continuing relationship, such as landlord-tenant, between the grantor and grantee. American courts loosened up the concept a little, but still required more of a connection between the original grantor and grantee than the covenant itself. Under the American version of horizontal privity, the covenant had to be part of a transfer of the real estate involved or it had to be supported by some other interest in the land, such as an easement.

The upshot of the horizontal privity rule was that *neighbors could not enter into a covenant* between themselves that would run with the land, unless there was some other mutual property interest to support the covenant. Assume that Alice and Bart were adjacent landowners, who were afraid of encroaching commercial development from a nearby city. If they decided to enter into a mutually binding covenant agreement to limit their property to residential use, it would not be binding on subsequent purchasers under this rule. If Bart sold his property to Daymart, it could build a convenience store on the land and Alice could not enforce the covenant against it.

Many courts either never adopted or subsequently abandoned the horizontal privity requirement, and the Restatement finds no value in it. Restatement (Third) of Property: Servitudes §2.4 (2000). *See, e.g.,* Gallagher v. Bell, 516 A.2d 1028 (Md. Ct. Spec. App. 1986) (adopting "modern and . . . more rational view" that horizontal privity not required for covenant to run at law).

Horizontal privity is not completely a dead letter, however:

> ➤ In Cunningham v. City of Greensboro, 711 S.E.2d 477 (N.C. Ct. App. 2011), the court held that a subdivision's utility agreements were not real covenants running with the land in part because of a lack of horizontal privity.
> ➤ In Bremmeyer Excavating, Inc. v. McKenna, 721 P.2d 567 (Wash. Ct. App. 1988), the court held that an agreement regarding excavation services did not run with the land in part because the promise was entered into *after* the conveyance of the land involved, thereby negating horizontal privity.

See also In re Sabine Oil & Gas Corporation, 2018 WL 2386902 (2d Cir. 2018) (applying Texas law, restrictive covenant did not run with land because no horizontal privity); Deep Water Brewing LLC v. Fairway Res., 215 P.3d 990, 1007 (Wash. Ct. App. 2009) (horizontal privity required for running of covenant).

One way courts found to avoid the horizontal privity requirement was to enforce the promise in equity as an *equitable servitude.* Although courts initially erected barriers to real covenants in order to protect the alienability of land, in the nineteenth century they began to realize some of the benefits of private land use restrictions. The equitable servitude concept developed to give courts the flexibility to enforce desirable covenants in the interests of justice.

English courts first recognized equitable servitudes in the following landmark case, involving Leicester Square in the heart of London. The promise could not be enforced at law because of a lack of horizontal privity, yet the court decided to hold the subsequent owner to the promise. What policies do you think drove the court to change its strict rules against covenant enforcement?

TULK v. MOXHAY

41 Eng. Rep. 1143 (Ch. 1848)
Court of Chancery, England

In the year 1808 the Plaintiff, being then the owner in fee of the vacant piece of ground in Leicester Square, as well as of several of the houses forming the Square, sold the piece of ground by the description of "Leicester Square garden or pleasure ground, with the equestrian statue then standing in the centre thereof, and the iron railing and stone work round the same," to one Elms in fee: and the deed of conveyance contained a covenant by Elms, for himself, his heirs, and assigns, with the Plaintiff, his heirs, executors, and administrators, "that Elms, his heirs, and assigns should, and would from time to time, and at all times thereafter at his and their own costs and charges, keep and maintain the said piece of ground and square garden, and the iron railing round the same in its then form, and in sufficient and proper repair as a square garden and pleasure ground, in an open state, uncovered with any buildings, in neat and ornamental order; and that it should be lawful for the inhabitants of Leicester Square, tenants of the Plaintiff, on payment of a reasonable rent for the same, to have keys at their own expense and the privilege of admission therewith at any time or times into the said square garden and pleasure ground."

The piece of land so conveyed passed by divers mesne conveyances into the hands of the Defendant, whose purchase deed contained no similar covenant with his vendor: but he admitted that he had purchased with notice of the covenant in the deed of 1808.

The Defendant having manifested an intention to alter the character of the square garden, and asserted a right, if he thought fit, to build upon it, the Plaintiff, who still remained owner of several houses in the square, filed this bill for an injunction; and an injunction was granted by the Master of the Rolls to restrain the Defendant from converting or using the piece of ground and square garden, and the iron railing round the same, to or for any other purpose than as a square garden and pleasure ground in an open state, and uncovered with buildings.

On a motion, now made, to discharge that order, Mr. R. Palmer, for the Defendant, contended that the covenant did not run with the land, so as to be binding at law upon a purchaser from the covenantor. . . .

Leicester Square, c. 1808
Private Collection/©Look and Learn/The Bridgeman Art Library

Leicester Square, today
©migstock/Alamy

The Lord Chancellor [COTTENHAM], (without calling upon the other side).

That this Court has jurisdiction to enforce a contract between the owner of land and his neighbour purchasing a part of it, that the latter shall either use or abstain from using the land purchased in a particular way, is what I never knew disputed. Here there is no question about the contract: the owner of certain houses in the square sells the land adjoining, with a covenant from the purchaser not to use it for any other purpose than as a square garden. And it is now contended, not that the vendee could violate that contract, but that he might sell the piece of land, and that the purchaser from him may violate it without this Court having any power to interfere. If that were so, it would be impossible for an owner of land to sell part of it without incurring the risk of rendering what he retains worthless. It is said that, the covenant being one which does not run with the land, this Court cannot enforce it; but the question is, not whether the covenant runs with the land, but whether a party shall be permitted to use the land in a manner inconsistent with the contract entered into by his vendor, and with notice of which he purchased. Of course, the price would be affected by the covenant, and nothing could be more inequitable than that the original purchaser should be able to sell the property the next day for a greater price, in consideration of the assignee being allowed to escape from the liability which he had himself undertaken.

That the question does not depend upon whether the covenant runs with the land is evident from this, that if there was a mere agreement and no covenant, this Court would enforce it against a party purchasing with notice of it; for if an equity is attached to the property by the owner, no one purchasing with notice of that equity can stand in a different situation from the party from whom he purchased. . . .

I think the cases cited before the Vice-Chancellor and this decision of the Master of the Rolls perfectly right, and, therefore, that this motion must be refused, with costs.

■ POINTS TO CONSIDER

1. **Identify the interests.** What exactly were the interests created by the language in the deed from Tulk to Elms? Were the interests *affirmative* or *negative* in nature?

2. **Horizontal privity.** Go through the requirements for covenants to run with the land at law and determine whether they were met by these covenants. Why did the court in *Tulk* have to resort to equity? Because the covenant was part of a conveyance of property from Tulk to Elms, there was horizontal privity under modern American standards. In England at that time, however, the only kind of horizontal privity recognized was landlord-tenant, so this covenant would not have run with the land at law.

3. Equitable servitudes in America. American courts followed the lead of their English cousins later in the nineteenth century, when courts of equity began to give effect to restrictions that did not meet the precise legal requirements for running with the land at law.For example, in Eckhart v. Irons, 20 N.E. 687 (Ill. 1889), the court enforced against a subsequent purchaser a clause in a deed requiring the grantee to refrain from building on or obstructing a space within 20 feet of the street. The court held that its equitable power could be used to fulfill the clear intention of the parties:

> Restrictions on the use of property held in fee are not favored; yet, where the intent of the parties is clearly manifested in the creation of restrictions or limitations upon the use of the grantee for the benefit of the grantor, his heirs or assigns, a court of equity will enforce the same. . . . Equity, looking beyond the mere form, and into the substance, will give effect to the intent of the parties when it can be found, and in such cases will disregard mere technical distinction.

Id. at 692.

Requirements for an Equitable Servitude

An equitable servitude does not require privity. Instead, courts typically enforce a covenant in equity where it meets the following conditions:

1) *Intent.* The parties must intend that the promise bind subsequent owners;
2) *Touch and concern.* The promise must have to do with the ownership and use of the property rather than a personal obligation; and
3) *Notice.* The burdened party must have notice of the restriction.

Because of the rise of equitable servitudes, the privity requirement has lost its importance, even in those jurisdictions that retain it.[1] Note, however, that the enforcement of an equitable servitude is not a given, even where these three conditions are met. *See, e.g.,* Lakewood Racquet Club, Inc. v. Jensen, 232 P.3d 1147 (Wash. Ct. App. 2010) (declining to exercise equitable powers to enforce covenant). Remember that the parties are asking a court to invoke its *equitable powers* to enforce a restriction that does meet legal requirements.

Remedies. The difference between law and equity historically determined the type of remedy available: equity would grant an *injunction* against the violation of a servitude, for example, while *damages* were available only at law. Modern courts, however, have largely abandoned that distinction, such that either remedy—injunction or damages—should be available regardless of whether the covenant runs at law or in equity. Restatement (Third) of Property: Servitudes §8.2 (2000).

---

[1] The concept of privity remains important in states like Virginia, which appears to limit the concept of equitable servitude to cases involving a common scheme of development.

C   THE TOUCH AND CONCERN REQUIREMENT

The requirement that the promise "touch and concern" the land in order to run can be rather amorphous and confusing. As noted above, this element attempts to identify those promises which *relate to the land itself* and should therefore attach to it, rather than those that are merely *personal* and should remain with the original promisor or promisee.

In cases involving *negative* covenants, applying the test is usually simple: a promise to *restrict the use* of the land clearly has to do with the property itself rather than the person who happens to own it:

> ➤ Grantee covenants to limit the use of Blackacre to *residential use only*. The covenant touches and concerns the land because it relates to the use of the property.

With regard to *affirmative* covenants, however, problems with the test arise more often. Because these promises require the landowner to *do* something, they seem more like personal obligations. English courts historically held categorically that affirmative covenants did not run with the land; until the mid-twentieth century, many American jurisdictions followed this rule.

> ➤ For example, in Miller v. Clary, 103 N.E. 1114 (N.Y. 1913), Phoenix Mills owned a flour mill powered by a water wheel. In 1873, Phoenix Mills sold other land it owned adjacent to the mill. In the deed, Phoenix *promised to provide power* from its water wheel to the grantee and to construct a shaft to carry the power. Forty years later, both properties were owned by subsequent owners, and no power was being supplied to the adjacent land. The court held that "the rule that affirmative covenants accompanying conveyances of land are not enforceable against subsequent owners is a wise one." *Id.* at 1117. Therefore, it refused to require the current owners of the servient land to construct a new shaft to carry the power.

Does the *Miller* rule make sense? Imagine that the properties in question had not passed to subsequent owners, but were still, 40 years later, owned by the original grantor and grantee. Is the problem, in other words, that the covenant has become anachronistic and unduly burdensome, rather than the fact that the property has changed hands?

A very similar case arose in Niagara Mohawk Power Corp. v. Allied Healthcare Products, Inc., 29 N.Y.S.3d 568 (N.Y. App. Div. 2016), where the court considered an affirmative covenant to supply free power entered into in 1899. Although the court found that all of the criteria for running with the land were met, it found the covenant subject to an implied duration, because otherwise the covenant would be "an 'onerous burden in perpetuity' disfavored by the law." *Id.,* at 574.

In the following case, the New York Court of Appeals had to decide whether to retain its rule against the running of affirmative covenants and whether covenants to pay fees touch and concern the land. In modern housing developments, a typical affirmative covenant requires the landowner to pay a periodic fee to the homeowners association (HOA) for the maintenance of common areas. In 1938, however, such affirmative covenants to pay money were relatively new. The court's attempt to elucidate the touch and concern requirement was influential and helped open the door for such HOA covenants; it also helps illustrate why the Restatement recommends abandoning the touch and concern requirement completely.

NEPONSIT PROPERTY OWNERS' ASSOCIATION, INC. v. EMIGRANT INDUSTRIAL SAVINGS BANK

15 N.E.2d 793 (1938)
Court of Appeals of New York

LEHMAN, Judge.

The plaintiff, as assignee of Neponsit Realty Company, has brought this action to foreclose a lien upon land which the defendant owns. The lien, it is alleged, arises from a covenant, condition or charge contained in a deed of conveyance of the land from Neponsit Realty Company to a predecessor in title of the defendant. The defendant purchased the land at a judicial sale. The referee's deed to the defendant and every deed in the defendant's chain of title since the conveyance of the land by Neponsit Realty Company purports to convey the property subject to the covenant, condition or charge contained in the original deed. . . .

It appears that in January, 1911, Neponsit Realty Company, as owner of a tract of land in Queens county, caused to be filed in the office of the clerk of the county a map of the land. The tract was developed for a strictly residential community, and Neponsit Realty Company conveyed lots in the tract to purchasers, describing such lots by reference to the filed map and to roads and streets shown thereon. In 1917, Neponsit Realty Company conveyed the land now owned by the defendant to Robert Oldner Deyer and his wife by deed which contained the covenant upon which the plaintiff's cause of action is based.

Postcard showing front entrance to Neponsit development
Courtesy of rockawaymemories.com

That covenant provides:

"And the party of the second part for the party of the second part and the heirs, successors and assigns of the party of the second part further covenants that the property conveyed by this deed shall be subject to an annual charge in such an amount as will be fixed by the party of the first part, its successors and assigns, not, however exceeding in any year the sum of four ($4.00) Dollars per lot 20x100 feet. The assigns of the party of the first part may include a Property Owners' Association which may hereafter be organized for the purposes referred to in this paragraph, and in case such association is organized the sums in this paragraph provided for shall be payable to such association. The party of the second part for the party of the second part and the heirs, successors and assigns of the party of the second part covenants that they will pay this charge to the party of the first part, its successors and assigns on the first day of May in each and every year, and further covenants that said charge shall on said date in each year become a lien on the land and shall continue to be such lien until fully paid. Such charge shall be payable to the party of the first part or its successors or assigns, and shall be devoted to the maintenance of the roads, paths, parks, beach, sewers and such other public purposes as shall from time to time be determined by the party of the first part, its successors or assigns. And the party of the second part by the acceptance of this deed hereby expressly vests in the party of the first part, its successors and assigns, the right and power to bring all actions against the owner of the premises hereby conveyed or any part thereof for the collection of such charge and to enforce the aforesaid lien therefor.

"These covenants shall run with the land and shall be construed as real covenants running with the land until January 31st, 1940, when they shall cease and determine."

Every subsequent deed of conveyance of the property in the defendant's chain of title, including the deed from the referee to the defendant, contained, as we have said, a provision that they were made subject to covenants and restrictions of former deeds of record.

There can be no doubt that Neponsit Realty Company intended that the covenant should run with the land and should be enforceable by a property owners association against every owner of property in the residential tract which the realty company was then developing. The language of the covenant admits of no other construction. Regardless of the intention of the parties, a covenant will run with the land and will be enforceable against a subsequent purchaser of the land at the suit of one who claims the benefit of the covenant, only if the covenant complies with certain legal requirements. These requirements rest upon ancient rules and precedents. The age-old essentials of a real covenant, aside from the form of the covenant, may be summarily formulated as follows: (1) It must appear that grantor and grantee intended that the covenant should run with the land; (2) it must appear that the covenant is one "touching" or "concerning" the land with which it runs; (3) it must appear that there is "privity of estate" between the promisee or party claiming the benefit of the covenant and the right to enforce it, and the promisor or party who rests under the burden of the covenant. Clark on Covenants and Interests Running with Land, p. 74. Although the deeds of Neponsit Realty Company conveying lots in the tract it developed "contained a provision to the effect that the covenants ran with the land, such provision in the absence of the other legal requirements is insufficient to accomplish such a purpose." Morgan Lake Co. v. New York, N. H. & H. R. R. Co., 262 N.Y. 234, 238, 186 N.E. 685, 686. In his opinion in that case, Judge Crane posed but found it unnecessary to decide many of the questions which the court must consider in this case.

The covenant in this case is intended to create a charge or obligation to pay a fixed sum of money to be "devoted to the maintenance of the roads, paths, parks, beach, sewers and such other public purposes as shall from time to time be determined by the party of the first part [the grantor], its successors or assigns." It is an affirmative covenant to pay money for use in connection with, but not upon, the land which it is said is subject to the burden of the covenant. Does such a covenant "touch" or "concern" the land? These terms are not part of a statutory definition, a limitation placed by the State upon the power of the courts to enforce covenants intended to run with the land by the parties who entered into the covenants. Rather they are words used by courts in England in old cases to describe a limitation which the courts themselves created or to formulate a test which the courts have devised and which the courts voluntarily apply. *Cf.* Spencer's Case, Coke, vol. 3, part 5, 16a; Mayor of Congleton v. Pattison, 10 East 130. In truth such a description or test so formulated is too vague to be of much assistance and judges and academic scholars alike have struggled, not with entire success, to formulate a test at once more satisfactory and more accurate. "It has been found impossible to state any absolute tests to determine what covenants touch and concern land and what do not. The question is one for the court to determine in the exercise of its best judgment upon the facts of each case." Clark, op. cit. p. 76.

. . . It has been often said that a covenant to pay a sum of money is a personal affirmative covenant which usually does not concern or touch the land. Such statements are based upon English decisions which hold in effect that only covenants, which compel the covenanter to submit to some restriction on the use of his property, touch or concern the land, and that the burden of a covenant which requires the covenanter to do an affirmative act, even on his own land, for the benefit of the owner of a "dominant" estate, does not run with his land. Miller v. Clary, 210 N.Y. 127, 103 N.E. 1114. In that case the court pointed out that in many jurisdictions of this country the narrow English rule has been criticized and a more liberal and flexible rule has been substituted. In this State the courts have not gone so far. We have not abandoned the historic distinction drawn by the English courts. So this court has recently said: "Subject to a few exceptions not important at this time, there is now in this state a settled rule of law that a covenant to do an affirmative act, as distinguished from a covenant merely negative in effect, does not run with the land so as to charge the burden of performance on a subsequent grantee [citing cases]. This is so though the burden of such a covenant is laid upon the very parcel which is the subject-matter of the conveyance." Guaranty Trust Co. of New York v. New York & Queens County Ry. Co., 253 N.Y. 190, 204, 170 N.E. 887, 892, opinion by Cardozo, Ch. J.

. . . It has been suggested that a covenant which runs with the land must affect the legal relations—the advantages and the burdens—of the parties to the covenant, as owners of particular parcels of land and not merely as members of the community in general, such as taxpayers or owners of other land. Clark, ip. cit. p. 76. Cf. Professor Bigelow's article on The Contents of Covenants in Leases, 12 Mich. L. Rev. 639; 30 Law Quarterly Review, 319. That method of approach has the merit of realism. The test is based on the effect of the covenant rather than on technical distinctions. Does the covenant impose, on the one hand, a burden upon an interest in land, which on the other hand increases the value of a different interest in the same or related land?

Even though we accept that approach and test, it still remains true that whether a particular covenant is sufficiently connected with the use of land to run with the land, must be in many cases a question of degree. A promise to pay for something to be done in connection with the promisor's land does not differ essentially from a promise by the promisor to do the thing himself, and both promises constitute, in a substantial sense, a restriction upon the owner's right to use the land, and a burden upon the legal interest of the owner. On the other hand, a covenant to perform or pay for the performance of an affirmative act disconnected with the use of the land cannot ordinarily touch or concern the land in any substantial degree. Thus, unless we exalt technical form over substance, the distinction between covenants which run with land and covenants which are personal, must depend upon the effect of the covenant on the legal rights which otherwise would flow from ownership of land and which are connected with the land. The problem then is: Does the covenant in purpose and effect substantially alter these rights? . . .

Looking at the problem presented in this case from the same point of view and stressing the intent and substantial effect of the covenant rather than its form, it seems clear that the covenant may properly be said to touch and concern the land of the defendant and its burden should run with the land. True, it calls for payment of a sum of money to be expended for "public purposes" upon land other than the land conveyed by Neponsit Realty Company to plaintiff's predecessor in title. By that conveyance the grantee, however, obtained not only title to particular lots, but an easement or right of common enjoyment with other property owners in roads, beaches, public parks or spaces and improvements in the same tract. For full enjoyment in common by the defendant and other property owners of these easements or rights, the roads and public places must be maintained. In order that the burden of maintaining public improvements should rest upon the land benefited by the improvements, the grantor exacted from the grantee of the land with its appurtenant easement or right of enjoyment a covenant that the burden of paying the cost should be inseparably attached to the land which enjoys the benefit. It is plain that any distinction or definition which would exclude such a covenant from the classification of covenants which "touch" or "concern" the land would be based on form and not on substance.

Another difficulty remains. Though between the grantor and the grantee there was privity of estate, the covenant provides that its benefit shall run to the assigns of the grantor who "may include a Property Owners' Association which may hereafter be organized for the purposes referred to in this paragraph." The plaintiff has been organized to receive the sums payable by the property owners and to expend them for the benefit of such owners. Various definitions have been formulated of "privity of estate" in connection with covenants that run with the land, but none of such definitions seems to cover the relationship between the plaintiff and the defendant in this case. The plaintiff has not succeeded to the ownership of any property of the grantor. It does not appear that it ever had title to the streets or public places upon which charges which are payable to it must be expended. It does not appear that it owns any other property in the residential tract to which any easement or right of enjoyment in such property is appurtenant. It is created solely to act as the assignee of the benefit of the covenant, and it has no interest of its own in the enforcement of the covenant.

The arguments that under such circumstances the plaintiff has no right of action to enforce a covenant running with the land are all based upon a distinction between the corporate property owners association and the property owners for whose benefit the association has been formed. If that distinction may be ignored, then the basis of the arguments is destroyed. How far privity of estate in technical form is necessary to enforce in equity a restrictive covenant upon the use of land, presents an interesting question. Enforcement of such covenants rests upon equitable principles (Tulk v. Moxhay, 2 Phillips, 774; Trustees of Columbia College v. Lynch, 70 N.Y. 440; Korn v. Campbell, 192 N.Y. 490, 85 N.E. 687), and at times, at least, the violation "of the restrictive covenant may be restrained at the suit of one who owns property or for whose benefit the restriction was established, irrespective of whether there were privity either of estate or of contract between the parties, or whether an action at law were maintainable." Chesebro v. Moers, 233 N.Y. 75, 80, 134 N.E. 842, 843. . . .

The corporate plaintiff has been formed as a convenient instrument by which the property owners may advance their common interests. We do not ignore the corporate form when we recognize that the Neponsit Property Owners' Association, Inc., is acting as the agent or representative of the Neponsit property owners. As we have said in another case: when Neponsit Property Owners' Association, Inc., "was formed, the property owners were expected to, and have looked to that organization as the medium through which enjoyment of their common right might be preserved equally for all." Matter of City of New York, Public Beach, Borough of Queens, 269 N.Y. 64, 75, 199 N.E. 5, 9. . . . In substance if not in form the covenant is a restrictive covenant which touches and concerns the defendant's land, and in substance, if not in form, there is privity of estate between the plaintiff and the defendant. . . .

The order should be affirmed, with costs, and the certified questions answered in the affirmative.

■ POINTS TO CONSIDER

1. **Touch and concern** What test does the *Neponsit* court use to distinguish between personal agreements and those promises that touch and concern the land? Does the court's attempt to clarify the touch and concern requirement

work? Under the court's test, does the covenant to construct a shaft to convey power in *Miller v. Clary* touch and concern the land?

2. **Time limit.** One way to prevent covenants from becoming outdated is to include a "sunset" provision, under which the covenants will expire after a certain time period. The Neponsit covenant contained such an expiration clause. Would you recommend that approach as a covenant drafter?

3. **Restatement approach.** Recognizing that the touch and concern requirement is difficult to apply and does not address the central concerns regarding the enforceability of covenants, the Restatement abandons the requirement and substitutes the following test:

> A servitude created as provided in Chapter 2 is valid unless it is illegal or unconstitutional or violates public policy.
>
> Servitudes that are invalid because they violate public policy include, but are not limited to:
>
>   1) a servitude that is arbitrary, spiteful, or capricious;
>   2) a servitude that unreasonably burdens a fundamental constitutional right;
>   3) a servitude that imposes an unreasonable restraint on alienation . . . ;
>   4) a servitude that imposes an unreasonable restraint on trade or competition . . . ; and
>   5) a servitude that is unconscionable. . . .

Restatement (Third) of Property: Servitudes §3.1 (2000). Note that this test applies not to the "running" of covenants to subsequent purchasers, but to the enforceability of any covenant, even as to the original parties to the promise.

Is the Restatement "public policy" test too broad? How should it be interpreted? In Terrien v. Zwit, 648 N.W.2d 602 (Mich. 2002), defendants operated day care centers in their homes, which were restricted by covenant to residential use. The trial court held that the covenant violated the state's public policy favoring such uses. The court of appeals affirmed by interpreting day care use in a home to be "residential" in nature. The Michigan Supreme Court reversed. Although the court agreed that covenants that violate public policy are void, it held that the category must be narrowly construed:

> In defining "public policy," it is clear to us that this term must be more than a different nomenclature for describing the personal preferences of individual judges, for the proper exercise of the judicial power is to determine from objective legal sources what public policy is, and not to simply assert what such policy ought to be on the basis of the subjective views of individual judges. . . .
>
> In identifying the boundaries of public policy, we believe that the focus of the judiciary must ultimately be upon the policies that, in fact, have been adopted by the

public through our various legal processes, and are reflected in our state and federal constitutions, our statutes, and the common law.

Id. at 608. The dissent would have affirmed, using this test: "Public policy is what is just, right, reasonable, and equitable for society as a whole." *Id.* at 620; *see also* Southwind Homeowners Ass'n v. Burden, 810 N.W.2d 714 (Neb. 2012) (public policy favoring in-home daycare did not negate covenants prohibiting them). Do you think the covenant should be upheld? Do you see how the common restriction limiting the property to "residential use" could be deemed ambiguous?

■ PROBLEMS: TOUCH AND CONCERN VERSUS RESTATEMENT APPROACH

Consider the differences between the touch and concern test and the Restatement test by applying them to attempts to enforce the following covenants:

1. Developer owns Blackacre and wants to subdivide it to create a coherent commercial area. Developer sells Parcel A to ABC Corp., with a covenant requiring it to be used for a discount store or similar commercial use. In return, Developer promises not to use the remaining part of Blackacre for a discount store that would compete. ABC Corp. transfers Parcel A to K-Mart, Inc., which builds the discount store. A few years later, Developer sells another piece of Blackacre to Dollar General, which plans to build a discount store.

2. Artis bought a lot in the Green Acres subdivision in 1973 and agreed to be bound by a set of covenants that included a prohibition on solar collectors. At that time, solar power was limited to large box-type thermal units. Artis sold the lot in 2010 to Brianna, who wants to install a flat thin-film photovoltaic solar panel on her roof.

3. The Elysian Fields subdivision has covenants designed to promote a uniform, pleasant appearance. One of these covenants prohibits the flying of flags and the posting of any signs. The HOA has fined Carl, in accordance with the Association's bylaws, for flying a Swedish flag and posting a sign in his yard stating his support for a candidate in the next election.

4. Raintree Village created a subdivision surrounding a golf course, called the Raintree Country Club. The recorded covenants required each lot owner to be a member of the club and pay club dues. A subsequent owner of Lot 12 refused to pay the dues, which have increased dramatically, on the ground that he did not play golf and would not use the club.

5. Bremmeyer sells a lot to Parks, in which Parks agrees to use Bremmeyer's business for any excavation and fill work to prepare the land for development.

Parks then sells the lot to McKenna, who does not want to use Bremmeyer's company.

Who may enforce the covenant? In our original diagram, A, the owner of Blackacre, conveyed Whiteacre to B and included a covenant. The covenant could be enforced by the promisee (A) and anyone who succeeded to the ownership of Blackacre, the benefited land, in accordance with vertical privity. In the more typical context, however, the original grantor A would be the developer of a subdivision. In that case, who can enforce the covenants? Certainly, the developer could enforce the covenants, if it retained any ownership of property in the subdivision. The covenants might also specify that an HOA would be empowered to enforce the covenants, and the *Neponsit* case endorsed that approach. In general, courts also allow any landowner in the subdivision who is benefited by a "common scheme" of restrictions to enforce them against other lot owners. *See, e.g.,* Rice v. Coholan, 695 S.E.2d 484 (N.C. Ct. App. 2010); Bessemer v. Gersten, 381 So. 2d 1344 (Fla. 1980) (right to enforce covenant belongs to holder of benefited land).

Because the ability to enforce requires the ownership of benefited land, a developer who sells all of its property within the subdivision may no longer enforce the covenants. Anyone outside the development, who did not succeed to land owned by the grantee of the original promise, cannot enforce the covenant, even if she is indirectly benefited by it. King v. Ebrens, 804 N.E.2d 821 (Ind. Ct. App. 2004). *See also* In re Midsouth Golf, LLC, 549 B.R. 156 (Bankr. E.D.N.C. 2016) ("where the covenant is sought to be enforced by someone not a party to the covenant or against someone not a party to the covenant, the party seeking to enforce the covenant must show that he has a sufficient legal relationship with the party against whom enforcement is sought to be entitled to enforce the covenant").

Questions regarding *standing to sue* may also arise if a development proceeds in phases and a landowner from Phase 1 wants to enforce a covenant against a landowner in Phase 2. Rooney v. Peoples Bank of Arapahoe Cnty., 513 P.2d 1077 (Colo. App. 1973).

Note that for the benefit to run to a subsequent owner, the benefit side of the covenant must touch and concern the land. Usually, if the burden fulfills the touch and concern requirement, the benefit will as well. However, think about the covenant in problem 5 above, which requires the covenantor to use the developer's company for excavation. Even if a court found that the burden touched and concerned the burdened land, the benefit would surely not pass to whomever the developer sold its remaining land.

D IMPLIED COVENANTS

Most covenants are created when a developer is subdividing a tract of land into lots. Short covenants, such as "residential use only," can be simply written into a deed in any conveyance. For more extensive restrictions, the developer drafts a "declaration of covenants" and records it along with the subdivision plat. At that point, no covenants have actually been created, because you can't create a covenant on your own land; there is no "party of the second part" on the other side. When the developer begins to sell the lots, each deed should contain a reference to the declaration, thereby incorporating those covenants into the transaction.

In some cases, the developer will neglect to incorporate the covenants into each deed. If so, the court may still hold the unrestricted lot to the recorded covenants by implication, if there is a *"general scheme" of development*. Sometimes these implied covenants are called "reciprocal servitudes" because the court in equity decides it would be unfair to allow a lot to receive the benefit of the restrictions on the neighboring lots without also being bound thereby. A number of states[2] refer to these implied covenants as *reciprocal negative easements*, although that term seems to unnecessarily confuse easements with covenants. We will refer to them as *implied covenants*.

> ➢ For example, in Varney v. Fletcher, 213 A.2d 905 (N.H. 1965), a landowner divided his land into 100 lots. All but 15-18 of the lots were conveyed subject to a covenant limiting their use to residential purposes only. The defendants bought a lot whose deed did not contain the covenant and intended to use it for a beauty salon. The court granted an injunction against the defendants, based on an implied covenant:

> > The law is well settled in this jurisdiction that building [or use] restrictions inserted in deed can create enforceable equitable servitudes. . . . If an original owner has adopted a *general scheme for development* or subdivision of a certain tract or parcel of land and has inserted in his deeds of lots therefrom uniform restrictions intended by him and by the purchasers to be imposed on each lot for the benefit of all other lots included in the general plan, *reciprocal servitudes are thereby created on all the lots in the development.* . . . The existence of such an intent can be ascertained from the language of the instruments, the conduct of the parties, and the surrounding circumstances.

> *Id.* at 907 (quoting Bouley v. City of Nashua, 205 A.2d 34, 36 (N.H. 1964)) (emphasis added).

The "general plan of development" concept may be used not only to imply a covenant on a lot in the subdivision, but also may put the lot owner on *inquiry notice* as to the existence of the covenants.

---

[2] These states include Alabama, Maryland, Minnesota, Michigan, Texas, and Vermont. *See, e.g.,* Hun Es Tu Malade? No. 16, LLC v. Tucker, 963 So. 2d 55 (Ala. 2006).

➤ Assume Alice is buying Lot 1 in the Green Acres subdivision. She examines the chain of title to Lot 1 and does not see any reference to any covenants in the deeds. She does notice, however, that there is a uniform pattern of development—all of the other lots have single-family residences. A court may find that she should have examined the deeds from the developer to those other lots to determine if there was a *pattern of restrictions* such that her lot was subject to an implied covenant.

➤ Of course, if the developer filed a declaration of covenants along with the subdivision plat, this inquiry would be easier and a court would be more likely to hold Alice to this duty.

Implied covenants rest on enforcing the *reasonable expectations* of those who bought lots subject to restrictions on use—did they have a legitimate expectation that the remainder of the development would be similarly restricted? In this way, the implied covenant doctrine resembles the estoppel decisions.

Preparing to Practice: Implied Covenants

Nora Notte comes to your office with a land use problem. She has lived for many years in a modest house on Melrose Avenue, on Lot 43 of the Spring Hill subdivision, a development of 48 half-acre lots. Her mother, Mona Notte, bought the property from the developer, Sam Springer, in 1980. The deed from Sam to Mona indicated that the conveyance was subject to a covenant to use the lot "for residential purposes only." Nora inherited the property in 2000, when her mother died.

For this entire period, the property next door, Lot 44, has been vacant. Because it was a larger corner lot and had some rough terrain, the developer initially had trouble selling it. In 1995, Sam finally sold the lot to Josie Alba. Josie had just become a certified public accountant and was thinking about using the property for a combination residence/accounting office. Ultimately, however, she was unable to secure a loan and her plans never materialized. In 2005, she sold the lot to Miguel Balas, who plans to build an Argentinian restaurant on Lot 44.

The parcel is currently zoned R-3, which allows all kinds of residential use, from apartments to single-family homes. Miguel filed an application to rezone the parcel to C-1, which would allow his restaurant. He believes he has an attractive, low-impact design that will fit well into the neighborhood, and his preliminary discussions with zoning officials have been favorable. The city has been looking for more commercial development in this area to attract people to a nearby shopping district.

Nora assumed that Lot 44 was restricted by a covenant like the one limiting her lot to residential use only. However, Miguel informed her that neither the deed he received from Josie nor the deed Josie received from Sam contained any restrictions on use.

> Does Nora have any grounds for asserting that there is an implied covenant on Lot 44? What additional evidence would you want to have in order to make your case on Nora's behalf? If you represented Miguel instead, what arguments could you make in response?
>
> Does it matter that the city seems to want the restaurant there? Would the change in zoning affect Nora's case?

E   TERMINATION OR MODIFICATION OF COVENANTS

A covenant is like super-glue—once it is created and attached to property, it is awfully hard to detach. In the previous problem, for example, assume that a court finds that Lot 44 is bound by a covenant limiting the use of the property to residential. In order to use the property for his restaurant, Miguel would need to obtain a *release* of the covenant from all of the owners who could enforce it. In his case, that would mean he would need 47 other lot owners to agree. If he was able to get 46 signatures on the release, but one owner held out, the covenant would still be valid.

In economic terms, we recognize that the *transaction costs* of reaching an agreement to modify or release a covenant can be prohibitive. In any multilateral bargaining situation, *hold-outs* may prevent the transaction. A hold-out recognizes that the transaction will fail without her participation and therefore tries to extort a price above the market value of her individual interest. In a subdivision, where every owner must agree to release the covenant, chances are increased that one or more parties may take hold-out positions. Thus, even if Miguel's use of the property may not adversely affect the other lots and would greatly increase the value of his lot (thus meeting our requirements for economic efficiency), the parties may be unable to reach an agreement.

Covenants may also terminate under the doctrine of *waiver* or *acquiescence*, due to a failure to enforce the restrictions. The toleration of minor violations does not result in the loss of the right to prevent more substantial violations, however. Pietrowski v. Dufrane, 634 N.W.2d 109 (Wis. Ct. App. 2001) (permitting small sheds to be constructed did not waive right to prevent two-car garage); Myers v. Armstrong, 324 P.3d 388 (N.M. Ct. App. 2014)(impacts of previous violations were trivial in comparison and did not constitute waiver). To constitute waiver, the previous pattern of nonenforcement must indicate an *intent to abandon* the restriction. Farmington Woods HOA v. Wolf, 817 N.W.2d 768 (Neb. 2012).

Are there any other circumstances in which a court should step in to modify or terminate a covenant? Times change and what once seemed to be a logical restriction may no longer make sense. A quiet suburb may now be in the middle of a bustling city. A new highway may come through a neighborhood, making residential use no longer as appropriate as commercial or industrial. Nevertheless, courts are reluctant to disturb agreed-upon restrictions.

> ➤ **Most use this test:** A *change in conditions* justifies a refusal to enforce the covenant only where the change is so substantial that *the original purpose of the restriction can no longer be accomplished.* This requires a finding that the covenant has ceased to be valuable to the benefited lots. If those lot owners cared enough to bring suit for an injunction, it's difficult for a court to find that the covenant has no value.

CASE SUMMARY: Vernon Township Volunteer Fire Department, Inc. v. Connor, 855 A.2d 873 (Pa. 2004)

In 1946, the owners of the Culbertson Subdivision agreed to a restrictive covenant prohibiting the sale of alcoholic beverages on any lot. In 1997, the Fire Department purchased a 3.25-acre parcel in the subdivision for the purpose of building a new truck room and social hall, which would sell alcohol to club members (volunteer firefighters and their guests). Although the restriction was recorded, the Fire Department didn't know about the covenant until after it had commenced construction. The Department then obtained a release of the restriction from 68 of the 77 parcels in the subdivision. Some of the remaining owners, however, wanted the restriction to be enforced. The Department argued that changed conditions had rendered the covenant obsolete.

The Department stressed the following evidence:

- three alcohol-serving establishments were now located in the immediate vicinity;
- 90 percent of the lot owners agreed to waive the restriction, so it has little value;
- none of the lot owners relied upon the restriction when purchasing his or her property.

The Pennsylvania Supreme Court found this evidence insufficient to render the covenant a nullity:

[T]he existence of three other liquor-serving establishments located outside of the Culbertson Subdivision does not warrant a finding of changed circumstances to invalidate the restrictive covenant. . . . [C]hanged conditions outside of the restricted tract do not necessarily impair the value of an alcohol restriction to the residents of the restricted tract. The stated purpose of the restrictive covenant was to protect the "health, peace, safety and welfare" of the occupants of the land by preventing the sale of alcoholic beverages within the tract. The original signatories clearly intended to protect themselves and their heirs from the vices of alcohol consumption by restricting the sale of alcohol within the

Culbertson Subdivision. As the trial court noted, "[i]f people are not drinking at establishments in the neighborhood, they are not exhibiting objectionable behavior which accompanies overdrinking, like public drunkenness and driving under the influence." Trial Court Opinion, 8/29/01, at 7. Thus, Appellants will continue to benefit from the restriction as long as alcohol is not sold within the restricted tract.

Id. at 882. In dissent, Justice Castille disagreed with the majority's narrow focus on changes inside the subdivision and found that the fact that almost all of the property owners were willing to release the covenant strong evidence that it had "outlived its usefulness." "Anachronisms," the dissent concluded, "need not persist for their own sake." *Id.* at 884.

Do you agree? Would you feel differently about the case if the court terminated the covenants only on the condition that the Fire Department agreed to pay compensation to the dissenters (in other words, used a liability rule instead of a property rule)? *See* Restatement (Third) of Property: Servitudes §7.10 (2000) (court may award compensation to lot owners harmed by termination of covenant due to changed conditions).

Recognizing the need to occasionally modify covenants and the transaction costs of doing so, modern covenants often build in devices to make this process easier. For example, the covenants may provide for amendment by a majority or super-majority of lot owners, rather than requiring unanimous agreement. How would such a provision have changed the result in *Vernon Township*?

Over twenty states have a statutory "Marketable Record Title Act," which erases interests that do not appear in the chain of title traced back to a root transaction 30-50 years prior. *See, e.g.*, Fla. Fla. Stat. Ann. §§ 712.01 *et.seq.* (2018). To preserve covenants, the HOA should therefore record a notice in the chain of title sometime before the expiration of the marketable title period (i.e., every 30-50 years). The effect of these laws is to "weed out" old covenants and other restrictions that no longer serve the interests of the benefitted parties. Is this the best way to deal with anachronistic restrictions?

COMMON-INTEREST COMMUNITIES AND HOMEOWNERS ASSOCIATIONS

As noted earlier, modern developments often take the form of a common-interest community (CIC), for example, single-family residences and townhouses in a gated or non-gated subdivision, or condominiums in a high-rise building. In any form, the individual owners in the development become members of a homeowners association (HOA). As set forth in the Declaration of Covenants, Conditions, and Restrictions (CC&Rs), the HOA typically provides for the election of a governing board, which has the authority to enforce the covenants and determine the fees to be charged for the maintenance of common property. The

Board may adopt bylaws, which clarify or fill in the details of more general covenants. For example, the covenants may empower the Board to enact "reasonable pet restrictions" or "regulations regarding the use of common areas." The HOA may also have the power to modify the covenants.

The flexibility provided by these governance provisions helps avoid the problem of archaic covenants that are difficult to terminate or modify. However, they also raise the potential of unfair treatment of individual owners by the majority. In addition, greater flexibility can upset the settled expectations of property owners. The next case deals with a *major modification* of a development's covenants, which was agreed to by a vote of the HOA. Does the court strike the right balance between certainty and fairness?

HUGHES v. NEW LIFE DEVELOPMENT CORP.

387 S.W.3d 453 (Tenn. 2012)
Supreme Court of Tennessee

... This is a case involving two families who purchased lots in a new subdivision that advertised permanent access to a set of dedicated wilderness preserves on the property surrounding their homesites. After the land was sold to a new developer, that developer began making plans to convert that land to a golf course and dozens of additional home sites. The homeowners sued to protect the wilderness preserves, hoping that the courts would enforce what the homeowners believed was a restrictive covenant on the land.

Cooley's Rift is a private residential development near Monteagle, Tennessee. The original developer of Cooley's Rift was Raoul Land and Development Company ("Raoul Land Development"). On November 6, 2002, Raoul Land Development recorded a plat ("the 2002 plat") for Cooley's Rift Subdivision Phase I that showed twenty-four delineated lots, roads accessing the lots, a lake bordering some of the lots, and a surrounding area of land.

Days later, Raoul Land Development recorded a Declaration of Covenants and Restrictions ("the Declaration") for Cooley's Rift. The Declaration stated in its introduction that Raoul Land Development would cause to be incorporated the Cooley's Rift Homeowners' Association ("the Association") to exercise certain functions set out in the Declaration. The Declaration also specifically referenced bylaws ("the Bylaws") for the Association, indicating that the initial text of the Bylaws was attached to and made a part of the Declaration. ...

Douglas and Lynne Hughes purchased a lot in Cooley's Rift from Raoul Land Development, as did Guy and Louise Hubbs (collectively "the Homeowners"). According to the Homeowners, promotional materials for the development indicated that Cooley's Rift, which comprised approximately 1,450 acres of land, would have only eighty homesites, up to eight acres in size each, and would have nearly 1,000 acres preserved in perpetuity. The promotional materials, however, also indicated that the design concept was preliminary in nature and was subject to change by the developer without notice.

Raoul Land Development did not complete the Cooley's Rift development. Although the record does not specifically address the reason, the parties have indicated that the one-time president of Raoul Land Development, Gaston C. Raoul, III, passed away. Regardless, on September 6, 2005, Raoul Land Development conveyed to New Life Development Corporation ("New Life") eleven unimproved lots in the subdivision and approximately 1,400 acres of undeveloped land surrounding the platted lots. . . .

New Life eventually undertook to continue development of the real property it had purchased from Raoul Land Development. On June 24, 2006, New Life convened a special meeting of the Association. Present at the meeting were representatives of New Life, which owned eleven platted lots and surrounding acreage, and the owners of nine of the remaining thirteen platted lots. At this meeting, New Life presented a conceptual development plan, subject to change, that depicted an eighteen-hole golf course and approximately 650 homesites.

On April 16, 2007, the Homeowners filed suit against New Life in the Chancery Court for Franklin County. They alleged that New Life had announced an intention to develop its property in ways that violated the Declaration and the general plan created by Raoul Land Development. . . . The Homeowners alleged that, in purchasing their lots, they had reasonably relied upon the representations of Raoul Land Development that Cooley's Rift would be developed in accordance with its general plan. Specifically, according to the Homeowners, this general plan contained two forest preserves that were to remain undeveloped: an East Preserve and a West Preserve. The Homeowners further alleged that New Life took title subject to the plan. . . .

[The trial court initially ruled against the Homeowners, on the ground that the express covenants applied only to the platted lots in the initial plat. In addition, the court found there were no implied covenants, because the Declaration contained a disclaimer of any such implied covenants. The court of appeals reversed on the issue of an implied covenant, finding the disclaimer ambiguous. In response, New Life initiated an amendment of the Declaration to eliminate the ambiguity and solidify its plans.]

On May 26, 2009, the Association's board of directors ("the Board") issued a notice of a special meeting of the Association to consider proposed amendments to the Charter and the Declaration. Accompanying the notice was a letter from the President of the Association (also a member of the Board) which specifically referenced the ongoing litigation and stated that one of the purposes of the amendments was to address the ambiguity that had been pointed out by the Court of Appeals. [The Declaration specifically provided that it may be amended with the approval of 75 percent of owners in attendance or represented at a meeting.]

. . . Thereafter, the amendments to the Charter and Declaration were adopted with nineteen of twenty-two votes in favor [86 percent approval. Because the developer is entitled to five votes per homesite it still owned, the vote was actually 63 in favor to 3 opposed (95 percent approval)]. . . .

The trial court, in granting a summary judgment to New Life after the remand by the Court of Appeals and the adoption of the amendments to the Declaration, found that "the amendments defining common properties and excluding wilderness preserves with hiking and riding trails have resolved any ambiguities with regard to implied restrictive covenants that might exist under a general plan of development." . . .

On appeal, the Court of Appeals again reversed the trial court's judgment and remanded the case for further proceedings. The Court of Appeals . . . concluded that because the amendments were adopted by less than 100% of the property owners in the subdivision, the amendments were subject to judicial review under a "reasonableness" standard. The Court of Appeals therefore remanded for the trial court to determine whether the amendments "are reasonable in light of the original intent of the contracting parties and the totality of the surrounding circumstances, including whether the purchasers were apprised that such amendments could be made and whether the amendments materially change the character of the development."

. . . We respectfully decline to adopt this [reasonableness] approach.

C.

A property owner's right to own, use, and enjoy private property is a fundamental right. . . . Not surprisingly, then, Tennessee law does not favor restrictive covenants, because they are in derogation of the rights of free use and enjoyment of property. . . .

Nevertheless, residential developments subject to restrictive covenants and governed by homeowners' associations, such as Cooley's Rift, have rapidly proliferated in recent decades. Lee Anne Fennell, Contracting Communities, 2004 U. Ill. L. Rev. 829, 829 (2004) ("Fennell"). The concept dates back to at least the eighteenth-century English practice of building a cluster of homes around a common square. Fennell, 2004 U. Ill. L. Rev. at 834-35. Yet only in the last fifty years has the practice accelerated in the United States. According to the Community Associations Institute, more than 63,000,000 Americans live in an estimated 323,600 association-governed communities. See Industry Data, http://www.caionline.org/info/research/Pages/default.aspx (last visited Oct. 24, 2012). These residential developments are diverse, comprising everything from a single condominium building to a large neighborhood of single-family homes. What they all have in common, however, is the practice of using restrictive covenants to privately control land use. Fennell, 2004 U. Ill. L. Rev. at 830.

Many such communities are created by a single developer who, before selling any individual units in the community, drafts and records a master deed or declaration of covenants and restrictions intended to bind each purchaser in the community. Stewart E. Sterk, Minority Protection in Residential Private Governments, 77 B.U. L. Rev. 273, 277 (1997) ("Sterk"). The developer also creates an association to govern the community and drafts bylaws for the association, which typically provide for a board of directors, define the scope of the board's power, and specify the procedures the board must follow in its everyday governance of the community. Sterk, 77 B.U. L. Rev. at 277-78. Notably, the declaration often provides for its own amendment. Sterk, 77 B.U. L. Rev. at 277.

The development of Cooley's Rift is not unlike the typical scenario just described. It was begun by Raoul Land Development, which recorded the Declaration and created the Association. The Declaration provided for its own amendment, without substantive limitation, by a 75% super-majority of the Association. We have already determined that the Association amended the Declaration in accordance with the applicable procedures. What we are now called upon to examine is the extent to which the courts will sit in judgment of the private decision-making in this community structure.

D.

The restrictive covenants in the Declaration in this case are property interests that run with the land, but they arise from a series of overlapping contractual transactions. *See* Maples Homeowners Ass'n v. T & R Nashville Ltd. P'ship, 993 S.W.2d 36, 38-39 (Tenn. Ct. App. 1998). Accordingly, they should be viewed as contracts and examined as such....

Contract law in Tennessee plainly reflects the public policy allowing competent parties to strike their own bargains.... Courts do not concern themselves with the wisdom or folly of a contract,... and they cannot countenance disregarding contractual provisions simply because a party later finds the contract to be unwise or unsatisfactory....

These contract principles, applied in the context of a private residential development with covenants that are expressly subject to amendment without substantive limitation, yield the conclusion that a homeowner should not be heard to complain when, as anticipated by the recorded declaration of covenants, the homeowners' association amends the declaration. See Sterk, 77 B.U. L. Rev. at 282. When a purchaser buys into such a community, the purchaser buys not only subject to the express covenants in the declaration, but also subject to the amendment provisions of the declaration. Sterk, 77 B.U. L. Rev. at 282. And, of course, a potential homeowner concerned about community association governance has the option to purchase a home not subject to association governance. Sterk, 77 B.U. L. Rev. at 301. As one commentator has noted, people who live in private developments "are not just opting for private ordering in the form of covenants, but also are opting for a privatized form of collective decision making that can undo, replace, modify, or augment the private ordering already achieved." Fennell, 2004 U. Ill. L. Rev. at 848.

For this reason, we decline to subject the amendments to the Declaration in this case, adopted by the requisite 75% super-majority, to the "reasonableness" test as announced by the Court of Appeals. We acknowledge that a homeowner's

Lockean exchange of personal rights for the advantages afforded by private residential communities does not operate to wholly preclude judicial review of the majority's decision.[3] However, because of the respect Tennessee law affords private contracting parties, we are reticent [*sic*—court means "reluctant"] to inject the courts too deeply into the affairs of a majoritarian association that parties freely choose to enter.[4]

As cited by the Court of Appeals, other jurisdictions have implemented various permutations of "reasonableness" review of non-unanimous amendments to restrictive covenants. *See, e.g.*, Miller v. Miller's Landing, L.L.C., 29 So. 3d 228, 235 (Ala. Civ. App. 2009) (finding amendment of restrictive covenant by supermajority of homeowners' association subject to reasonableness test); Armstrong v. Ledges Homeowners Ass'n, 360 N.C. 547, 633 S.E.2d 78, 87 (2006) (finding that every amendment of restrictive covenants by homeowners' association must be reasonable in light of the contracting parties' original intent); Bay Island Towers, Inc. v. Bay Island-Siesta Ass'n, 316 So. 2d 574, 575-76 (Fla. Dist. Ct. App. 1975) (finding modification of restrictive covenants by majority of owners valid if not unreasonable with respect to the general scheme of the development).

We note that some of these cases involve amendments authorized by a simple majority vote. . . . We further note that some of the cases imposing a "reasonableness" test involve amendments made solely by a developer pursuant to a retained power rather than by a vote of a homeowners' association. *See, e.g.*, Holiday Pines Prop. Owners Ass'n v. Wetherington, 596 So. 2d 84, 87 (Fla. Dist. Ct. App. 1992) (stating that a developer's reserved power to modify restrictive covenants must be exercised in a reasonable manner so as not to destroy the general plan of development). . . .

It also bears mentioning that there is no clear "reasonableness" standard among the other jurisdictions. For example, in *Miller v. Miller's Landing, L.L.C.*, the court stated that in assessing what constitutes a reasonable manner consistent with the general plan of development, courts must look to the language of the covenants, their apparent import, and the surrounding facts, such as (1) whether the amendment was enacted in compliance with procedural requirements, (2) whether the amendment was enacted in a reasonable manner, e.g., whether the majority of owners acted with due regard for the rights of minority owners, and (3) whether the amendment represents a good faith attempt to adapt to changing circumstances. Miller v. Miller's Landing, L.L.C., 29 So. 3d at 236. In contrast, in *Armstrong v. Ledges Homeowners Ass'n*, the court stated simply that reasonableness may be ascertained from the language of the original declaration of covenants, deeds, and plats, together with other objective circumstances

---

[3] See Note, Judicial Review of Condominium Rulemaking, 94 Harv. L. Rev. 647, 659 n. 60 (1981) (citing J. Locke, Two Treatises of Government §§95, 99 (T. Cooke ed. 1947) ("Whosoever . . . out of a state of nature unite into a community must be understood to give up all the power necessary to the ends for which they unite in society to the majority.")).

[4] As one commentator has queried, "The scope of association power may not be unlimited, but how do we decide what that scope is? Why are courts better situated to make that decision than the majority of homeowners as represented by their association?" Sterk, 77 B.U. L. Rev. at 287.

surrounding the parties' bargain, including the nature and character of the community, and that courts reviewing a disputed amendment must consider both the legitimate needs of the homeowners' association and the legitimate expectations of lot owners. Armstrong v. Ledges Homeowners Ass'n, 633 S.E.2d at 88. Yet another standard evaluates (1) whether the decision is arbitrary or capricious, (2) whether the decision is discriminatory or evenhanded, and (3) whether the decision is made in good faith for the common welfare of the owners. Worthinglen Condo. Unit Owners' Ass'n v. Brown, 57 Ohio App. 3d 73, 566 N.E.2d 1275, 1277-78 (1989); *see also* Buckingham v. Weston Vill. Homeowners Ass'n, 1997 N.D. 237, ¶11, 571 N.W.2d 842, 845 (applying same three-part test to amendments to bylaws).

By way of contrast, we note that some jurisdictions do not appear to employ a "reasonableness" test as described above. For example, the Texas Court of Appeals evaluated an amendment to restrictive covenants that removed certain undeveloped lots from the legal description of lands subject to the declaration. Bryant v. Lake Highlands Dev. Co. of Texas, 618 S.W.2d 921, 922 (Tex. Civ. App. 1981). . . . [C]entral to the court's decision was the recognition that the plaintiffs had purchased their lots subject to declarations which included a right of amendment, and thus the plaintiffs had no guarantee that the declaration would not be amended. *Id.*, at 923.

Likewise, the Missouri Court of Appeals reviewed an amendment to restrictive covenants that changed a restriction against subdividing lots. LaBrayere v. LaBrayere, 676 S.W.2d 522, 524 (Mo. Ct. App. 1984). . . . The court upheld the amendment, stating that "plaintiff disregards the fact that her property rights as owner . . . are subject to the terms imposed by that subdivision's restrictions" and that "the restrictions [permit] the owners . . . to change, modify or amend the restrictions." *Id.*, at 525. . . .

Lastly, the Illinois Court of Appeals expressly rejected a "reasonableness" test in a case involving a homeowners' association that adopted uniformly applicable amendments to a declaration to restrict leasing. Apple II Condo. Ass'n v. Worth Bank & Trust Co., 277 Ill. App. 3d 345, 659 N.E.2d 93, 98 (1995). The court distinguished between amendments adopted by a board of an association, which are valid only if affirmatively shown to be reasonable in purpose and application, and amendments adopted by association members. For amendments adopted by the association's membership, the court stated that "we will presume that the restriction is valid and uphold it unless it can be shown that the restriction is arbitrary, against public policy or violates some fundamental constitutional right of the unit owners." *Id.*, 659 N.E.2d at 99.

We find these latter three cases instructive. Accordingly, we hold that the amendments to the Declaration in this case, uniform in application and adopted in conformance with the 75% super-majority procedures of the Declaration and the Bylaws, are subject to judicial review principally under an arbitrary and capricious standard. . . .[5]

---

[5] In so holding, we do not suggest that amendments which are against public policy, such as amendments which restrict ownership on the basis of race, are valid.

F.

We now examine the amendments in this case for any indication that they are arbitrary or capricious. In its broadest sense, the arbitrary and capricious standard requires the reviewing court to determine whether there has been a clear error in judgment. An arbitrary or capricious decision is one that is not based on any course of reasoning or exercise of judgment, or one that disregards the facts or circumstances of the case without some basis that would lead a reasonable person to reach the same conclusion.

. . . The Homeowners assert that . . . the amendments afford New Life "the unilateral authority to dictate the use of every piece of property within Cooley's Rift Preserve and to change the Express Restrictive Covenants at its whim" goes too far. The amendments afford the Board and the Developer the authority to consent in writing to certain varying uses of parcels of property, including non-residential use, multi-family use, and re-subdivision of homesites. We, however, do not view the amendments as granting New Life the unilateral authority to dictate the use of every piece of property and to change the express restrictive covenants at its whim.

In evaluating the amendments, we note that they were properly adopted by in excess of a 75% super-majority of the Association. The notice to the members of the Association regarding the proposed amendments specifically identified the Homeowners' lawsuit, Case No. 18,444, and the dispute over the meaning and the impact of the Declaration in light of the first opinion of the Court of Appeals. The notice indicated that it was in the best interest of the Association that the terms of the Declaration be clear. In short, the record before this Court does not demonstrate anything arbitrary or capricious about the amendments.

G.

Having determined that the amendments were properly adopted and survive judicial review, we turn to the question of whether the amended Declaration supports the implication of restrictions as to New Life's undeveloped land outside the platted subdivision. The trial court found no basis for implied restrictive covenants arising from a general plan or scheme based on the amended Declaration and granted New Life a summary judgment as to the Homeowners' claims in that regard. We agree with the trial court.

The construction of restrictive covenants, like other written contracts, is a question of law. The amended Declaration no longer (1) references an intention to develop the Property as a residential community featuring wilderness preserves, (2) refers to a requirement for the Developer to adhere to a master plan with respect to the general location and approximate acreage of Common Properties, or (3) defines Common Properties as including wilderness preserve areas. What remains in the Declaration is (1) an express disclaimer of implied reciprocal covenants "with respect to lands which have been retained by the Developer for future development," (2) an express statement that the Developer may revise its development plan at any time, and (3) the Developer's reserved right to use or convey its property outside the platted subdivision with different restrictions than set forth in the Declaration or with no restrictions.

We are also mindful that courts construe restrictive covenants strictly because they are in derogation of the right to free use and enjoyment of property. Any doubt concerning the applicability of a restrictive covenant will be resolved against the restriction. When the terms of a covenant may be construed in more than one way, courts must resolve any ambiguity against the party seeking to enforce the restriction and in a manner which advances the unrestricted use of the property.

Based on all of these circumstances, we can only conclude that the amended Declaration does not serve as the basis for implied restrictive covenants, based on a general plan or scheme, applicable to New Life's property outside the platted lots. Having discerned no genuine issue of material fact in dispute, we affirm the trial court's grant of a summary judgment in favor of New Life on this claim.

V.

The final issue we are called upon to address involves the Homeowners' claim that there are implied restrictive covenants arising from the 2002 plat that are applicable to New Life's property outside the platted subdivision. . . . In short, the Homeowners assert that the 2002 plat identified the forest preserves, and thus there arose an implied restrictive covenant prohibiting development on these areas. New Life asserts that the 2002 plat did not legibly identify the forest preserves, and thus no implied restrictive covenant arose. . . .

The 2002 plat consists of five sheets. Sheet 1 is a view of what appears to be the entire tract of land, including land surrounding the delineated lots of the subdivision. Because of the smaller scale on Sheet 1, virtually no writing on it with respect to the tract of land is legible. . . .

Sheets 2 through 5 are closer views of the platted lots and the area immediately surrounding them. The writing on Sheets 2 through 5 is plainly legible. The sheets delineate twenty-four lots designated as numbered "tracts." They show named streets servicing the lots, including Cooley's Rift Boulevard, Lake Louisa Loop, Brow Road, and Connector Road, all of which are noted on the plat as private streets. . . . Sheets 2 through 5 contain printed words outside the boundaries of the platted lots, usually alongside the aforementioned streets, which state "Cooley's Rift Mountain Preserve—Future Development," "Raoul Land Company—Future Development," "Raoul Land Company," or simply "Future Development." However, Sheets 2 through 5 contain no designation of an East Preserve or a West Preserve.

C.

Restrictive covenants may be implied by reference to a plat. The Homeowners liken this case to that of Stracener v. Bailey, 737 S.W.2d 536 (Tenn. Ct. App. 1986). In *Stracener*, two plats, each one for a separate phase of a residential development, contained language on the plat but outside the boundaries of the platted subdivision. The language designated an area as "Future Park" in one instance and "Reserved for Future Park" in the other. *Id.* at 537. The court held that the original developer, by designating the area in question as a "Future Park" or "Reserved for Future Park," and then selling lots according to the plats, had created a restriction on the use of the property for any purpose inconsistent with that designation. *Id.* at 539.

This case is quite different from *Stracener*. Unlike in *Stracener*, the 2002 plat in this case bears no legible reference to forest preserves. Sheets 2 through 5, which contain no illegible writing, contain no reference whatsoever to forest preserves. Sheet 1 contains virtually no legible writing with respect to the tract, and not surprisingly contains no legible reference to an East Preserve or a West Preserve. Thus, having examined all five sheets comprising the 2002 plat, we can only conclude that the 2002 plat does not clearly designate an East Preserve or a West Preserve in the manner the plats in *Stracener* designated a future park.

Recognizing this problem, the Homeowners advance a novel argument to buttress their claim that the 2002 plat supports the imposition of implied restrictive covenants. The Homeowners contend that what was on the 2002 plat was sufficient enough to put New Life on inquiry notice to determine what any illegible markings on the plat actually were. The Homeowners assert that had New Life contacted the surveyor, it would have led to the discovery of an unrecorded version of the plat containing legible writing designating an East Preserve and a West Preserve.

Tennessee recognizes the concept of inquiry notice. We have stated that "another kind of notice occupying what amounts to a middle ground between constructive notice and actual notice is recognized as inquiry notice." Blevins v. Johnson Cnty., 746 S.W.2d 678, 683 (Tenn. 1988). . . . [I]nquiry notice means that "whatever is sufficient to put a person on inquiry" is "notice of all the facts to which that inquiry will lead," when pursued "with reasonable diligence and good faith." *Id.* (quoting City Fin. Co. v. Perry, 195 Tenn. 81, 84, 257 S.W.2d 1, 2 (1953)); Stracener v. Bailey, 737 S.W.2d at 539. . . .

There is no legible reference on the 2002 plat in the record to an East Preserve or a West Preserve. Our examination of the 2002 plat convinces us that the visible "legends" on Sheet 1 are indeed more like "blobs." Inquiry notice can be derived under circumstances where there exists a clear reference on a recorded instrument directing observers to an identifiable unrecorded instrument. *See* Texas Co. v. Aycock, 227 S.W.2d at 45-46 (finding inquiry notice of the terms of an unrecorded lease where the deed contained a clear reference to the lease). These are not the circumstances of this case. Absent a clear reference to the forest preserves on the 2002 plat, we conclude that New Life was not put on inquiry notice of the dedication and acreage of an East Preserve and a West Preserve. Regardless of whether the 2002 plat is characterized as containing "blobs" or "blurry words," the facts and circumstances are not "sufficiently pertinent in character to enable reasonably cautious and prudent persons to investigate and ascertain" the ultimate facts. *Id.*, 227 S.W.2d at 46. The "blobs" or "blurry words" on Sheet 1 of the 2002 plat signify nothing of importance to an observer and direct the observer nowhere.

Accordingly, we agree with the trial court that there are no material facts in dispute. We affirm the trial court's grant of a summary judgment in favor of New Life on the Homeowners' claim that the 2002 plat serves as the basis for implied restrictive covenants as to New Life's property outside the platted subdivision.

■ POINTS TO CONSIDER

1. **Bait and switch?** The original Cooley's Rift plan called for only 80 homesites and a 1,000-acre forest preserve. The new plan called for 650 homesites and a golf course. Consider whether the following Restatement provision applies in this circumstance:

   > A developer may not exercise a power to amend or modify the declaration in a way that would materially change the character of the development or the burdens on the existing community members unless the declaration fairly apprises purchasers that the power could be used for the kind of change proposed.

   Restatement (Third) of Property: Servitudes §6.20 (2000). Do you agree that the new plan for Cooley's Rift would "materially change the character of the development"? Does the Restatement prohibit all such changes? If you represented the first purchasers of lots in this development, how could you better protect their expectations concerning the forest preserve?

2. **What should be the test?** You can see that courts are split on the level of scrutiny to be accorded to modifications of restrictive covenants. Should they be treated the same as the covenants in the original declaration? What fundamental property policies support a requirement of "reasonableness"? What policies favor a more lenient "arbitrary and capricious" standard?

CASE SUMMARY: Nahrstedt v. Lakeside Village Condominium Association, Inc., 878 P.2d 1275 (Cal. 1994)

Many cases on restrictive covenants involve condominiums, a very common form of CIC, which deserves a brief introduction. We are quite used to the idea of dividing land ownership with vertical lines to create Blackacre and give the owner dominion from the heavens to the center of the earth (recall our discussion of the *ad coelum* doctrine in Chapter 1). In addition, anything attached to the land belongs to the owner of the land. The idea of dividing property *horizontally* and allowing separate ownership of the different strata created has ancient roots, but was generally accepted in the United States only in the latter half of the twentieth century.

In a condominium, individual owners have fee simple title to their particular units and own the common areas as tenants in common with the other unit owners. Because the owners are therefore financially dependent on each other and may be significantly impacted by each other's behavior, condo developments often contain some very restrictive covenants. Many states now have legislation (some modeled on the Uniform Condominium Act (1980)) that recognizes and regulates this form of ownership. *See generally* Robert G. Natelson, Law of Property Owners Associations (1989).

Nahrstedt v. Lakeside Vill. Condo. Ass'n involved the enforcement of a covenant in the condominium context, although its holding applies to any common-interest community. Plaintiff Natore Nahrstedt purchased a condominium unit in Lakeside Village and moved in with her three cats.[6] A covenant in the Village's original declaration prohibited all pets except fish and birds. After the HOA enforced the restriction against her, Nahrstedt challenged it as unreasonable as applied to her cats, which were kept indoors and could not bother anyone. The HOA argued that the pet restriction was justified because it "furthers the collective 'health, happiness and peace of mind' of persons living in close proximity."

The California Supreme Court distinguished between restrictions contained in the original declaration and those adopted by later amendment. Restrictions in the recorded declaration have a presumption of validity and are enforceable unless "they are wholly arbitrary, violate a fundamental public policy, or impose a burden on the use of affected land that far outweighs any benefit." *Id.* at 1287. In addition, the court held that, in making this determination, "the focus is on the restriction's effect on the project as a whole, not on the individual homeowner." *Id.* at 1290. The court outlined the policy reasons for its approach:

> Refusing to enforce the CC & R's contained in a recorded declaration, or enforcing them only after protracted litigation that would require justification of their application on a case-by-case basis, would impose great strain on the social fabric of the common interest development. It would frustrate owners who had purchased their units in reliance on the CC & R's. It would put the owners and the homeowners association in the difficult and divisive position of deciding whether particular CC & R's should be applied to a particular owner. Here, for example, deciding whether a particular animal is "confined to an owner's unit and create[s] no noise, odor, or nuisance" is a fact-intensive determination that can only be made by examining in detail the behavior of the particular animal and the behavior of the particular owner. Homeowners associations are ill-equipped to make such investigations, and any decision they might make in a particular case could be divisive or subject to claims of partiality.

Id. at 1289-90.

---

[6] You can see pictures of the complex at www.lakesidevillagecondominiums.com.

The dissent, in contrast, found the restriction arbitrary and would have refused to enforce it against Nahrstedt:

> Given the substantial benefits derived from pet ownership, the undue burden on the use of property imposed on condominium owners who can maintain pets within the confines of their units without creating a nuisance or disturbing the quiet enjoyment of others substantially outweighs whatever meager utility the restriction may serve in the abstract.

Id. at 1292-93 (Arabian, J., dissenting). *Do you agree?*

In a later case, the California Supreme Court ruled that it was bound by statute to apply its deferential standard of review to *amendments to the Declaration* as well. Villa De Las Palmas HOA v. Terifaj, 90 P.3d 1223 (Cal. 2004) (pet restriction in amended declaration not unreasonable). *Do you think that amendments to the Declaration should be subject to a stricter standard?*

■ PROBLEMS: RESTRICTIVE COVENANTS

In *Nahrstedt*, the plaintiff was on notice of the pet restriction when she bought her condominium, because it was contained in the original declaration. Does the test vary when the facts change? Assume the Green Acres subdivision has a covenant prohibiting homeowners from having more than one dog. Oscar had only one dog when he bought his house in Green Acres, but recently took in a stray he would like to adopt. The Green Acres Homeowners Association, however, says he must get rid of it.

Consider whether the following circumstances impact the *degree of scrutiny* the court should give a covenant:

a) The covenant was contained in the original declaration.

b) The covenant was not in the original declaration, but the covenant was added before Oscar bought his property.

c) The covenant was added to the declaration after Oscar bought his lot, by a vote of the HOA Board.

d) The covenant was added to the declaration after Oscar bought his lot, by a vote of a majority of the Green Acres homeowners.

e) Same as d), but the vote was by a supermajority of over 75 percent of the homeowners.

f) The covenant was added by the developer after Oscar bought his lot, pursuant to a clause giving the developer the right to make amendments.

g) The covenant is directed only at dogs "of the pit bull or Rottweiler breeds" and Oscar's dog happens to be a pit bull terrier.

■ PROBLEMS: REASONABLENESS

Assume that the court adopts a "reasonableness" test for amendments to restrictive covenants. Would the following covenants meet that test? Does the restriction need to be reasonable only on its face or as applied to a particular homeowner?

1. The HOA enacted a restriction prohibiting residents from parking recreational vehicles anywhere on their lots or on the street. Charlene owns a camper and does not want to get rid of it. She parks it beside her garage and believes it is not unsightly. Holleman v. Mission Trace HOA, 556 S.W.2d 632 (Tex. App. 1977).

2. The HOA enacted a restriction prohibiting residents from using satellite dishes. Paul argues that his dish will be of the modern, small variety and will be located on the back of his house where it can't be seen by other residents. Mountain Park HOA v. Tydings, 864 P.2d 392 (Wash Ct. App. 1993).

3. The original Declaration provided that undeveloped lots owned by builders would have to pay only 25 percent of the normal homeowner annual assessment, and payment could be deferred until the lot was sold to a homeowner. The provision was intended to encourage builders to buy lots in the subdivision, even if they weren't ready to build immediately. Five years later, only three of the subdivision's 44 lots remained vacant and owned by builders. The HOA adopted an amendment eliminating the reduced assessment and the deferred payment. Wallach v. Linville Owners Ass'n, 234 N.C.App. 632, 760 S.E.2d 23 (2014).

Are HOAs Like Cities?

For many homeowners, the restrictions imposed by restrictive covenants may be more intrusive than the ordinances of the municipality they live in. In fact, HOAs have much in common with local governmental institutions. Should we use the same standards, then, to judge the regulations and enforcement activities of HOAs as we do for local government?

Professor Robert Ellickson was one of the first to explore this analogy and its implications:

> Both cities and homeowners associations regulate the conduct of residents. Both may have rules requiring that dogs be kept on leashes, that residential structures be built in a Colonial style, or that external noise from social gatherings cease at 8:00 P.M. Nevertheless, courts rightly use different standards in reviewing the substantive validity of public and private rules.

In the case of public rules, the basic federal constitutional constraints arise from the due process and equal protection clauses of the fourteenth amendment. More often than not, the constitutional issue is whether the contested regulation is rationally related to a legitimate state interest. In the hands of most state and federal courts, this test now usually proves undemanding.

Because the fourteenth amendment only applies when state action is present, one might expect even greater judicial deference to the substantive validity of private regulations. In fact, however, courts are more vigorous in their examination of the validity of certain types of private regulations. Prevailing common-law and statutory rules ask courts to scrutinize the "reasonableness" of private regulations—an apparent invitation to Lochnerian activism. This active judicial review is inappropriate when the provisions contained in an association's original governing documents are at issue, but it is fully appropriate when litigants challenge amendments to those documents.

The initial members of a homeowners association, by their voluntary acts of joining, unanimously consent to the provisions in the association's original governing documents. [T]his unanimous ratification elevates those documents to the legal status of a private "constitution." The original documents—which today typically include a declaration of covenants, articles of association (or incorporation), and bylaws—are a true social contract. The feature of unanimous ratification distinguishes these documents from and gives them greater legal robustness than non-unanimously adopted public constitutions, not to mention the hypothetical social contracts of Rousseau or Rawls.

In most instances, familiar principles of contract law justify strict judicial enforcement of the provisions of a private constitution. Strict enforcement protects members' reliance interests. By allowing the establishment of, and subsequently protecting the integrity of, diverse types of private residential communities, courts can provide genuine choice among a range of stable living arrangements. Proper legal nourishment could enable private associations to supply quasi-public goods, such as local parks and security services, that in the past have been more frequently supplied by cities. This could lead in turn to a reduced role for the city—the more coercive (less consensual) form of residential organization. . . .

When courts are asked to rule on the validity of an association's actions to flesh out and apply its original constitution, they currently apply the previously mentioned test of "reasonableness." The association's governing documents or a state statute may call for application of the reasonableness standard; if not, courts imply the standard as a matter of law into the original constitution. The reasonableness standard applies to several types of association actions. It constrains all administrative actions—for example, an association's decision to expel a member, to veto the transfer of a membership, or to deny approval of architectural plans. In addition, it constrains the substance of all "legislation" that an association adopts by procedures less cumbersome than the association's procedures for a constitutional amendment. "Legislation" would include, for example, house rules that a board of directors might adopt under an express grant of authority in the original declaration.

"Reasonable," the most ubiquitous legal adjective, is not self-defining. In reviewing an association's legislative or administrative decisions, many judges have viewed the "reasonableness" standard as entitling them to undertake an independent cost-benefit analysis of the decision under review and to invalidate association decisions that are not cost-justified by general societal standards. This variant of reasonableness review ignores the contractarian underpinnings of the private association. As some courts have recognized, respect for private ordering requires a court applying the reasonableness standard to comb the association's original documents to find the association's collective purposes, and then to determine whether the association's actions have been consonant with those purposes.

Robert C. Ellickson, *Cities and Homeowners Associations*, 130 U. Penn. L. Rev. 1519, 1526-30 (1982). *See also* Stewart E. Sterk, *Minority Protection in Residential Private Governments*, 77 B.U. L. Rev. 273, 277 (1997).

Can you explain how a court's approach to covenant enforcement implicates our fundamental policies of fairness, efficiency, certainty, and personhood?

SUMMARY

- *Real covenants* are promises respecting the use of land. To be valid between the original parties, the covenant must meet the requisites of the Statute of Frauds, although the grantee's acceptance of a deed containing covenants substitutes for the required signature.
- Traditionally, for a covenant to *run with the land* to subsequent owners, the original parties must have *intended* the covenant to run; it must *touch and concern* the land; there must have been *horizontal privity* between the original parties and *vertical privity* with the subsequent owners; and the party bearing the burden must have had *notice*.
- *Horizontal privity* requires that the covenant arose in connection with a conveyance of the underlying property or that the holder of the benefit had some other interest, such as an easement, in the burdened property. Most, but not all, modern jurisdictions have either dispensed with the horizontal privity requirement or avoided it by using an equitable servitude, which is merely a covenant enforced in equity.
- An *equitable servitude* requires that there be an intent to bind and benefit subsequent owners; that the promise touches and concerns the land; and that the burdened owner had notice.
- The *touch and concern* requirement attempts to distinguish between covenants that relate to the land itself and those that are merely personal obligations. Unfortunately, the requirement is sometimes difficult to apply, and courts have used it to curtail covenants that have become unduly burdensome or violate public policy. The Restatement suggests eliminating the requirement and substitutes a test that holds covenants unenforceable that violate *public policy*.
- Covenants may be *implied* on lots with a uniform pattern of restrictions within a *common scheme* of development.

- A covenant may be *terminated* by a *release* from all those who may enforce it. A covenant may be terminated by *waiver*, if substantial violations have been allowed.
- A covenant may be terminated by a *change in conditions*, such that the restriction no longer has value to the benefited land.
- *Common-interest communities* often provide for an extensive set of covenants, along with an amendment and enforcement process.
- Many jurisdictions refuse to enforce covenants in the original declaration only if they are *unconstitutional or totally arbitrary*.
- With respect to later *amendments*, however, some courts use a *reasonableness* requirement. The test for reasonableness varies, and factors may include whether the amendment required a super-majority vote and whether the benefits of the covenant outweighed its burdens.

PART V

Land Use Control

I n the next three chapters, we will discuss various ways to restrict an owner's use of her land. By now, you have grounds to question Blackstone's definition of property as the "sole and despotic dominion" of property by the owner, "in total exclusion of the right of any other individual in the universe." In fact, one person's use of property may affect others, perhaps substantially and harmfully. In a civilized society, there must be limits on property use that cause undue harm, in order to enable harmonious and productive development. On the other hand, the Constitution prevents governmental control of land use from exceeding certain boundaries.

This part, therefore, introduces the various *methods of land use control* and the *constitutional limitations* on governmental land use regulations.

> ➤ Assume that Alice is building a house on Blackacre, which is out in the country. Alice wants to ensure that adjacent Whiteacre, owned by Bart, will not be used for anything, such as a feedlot, that would diminish her use and enjoyment of her property. There are *three basic ways* in which she could attempt to accomplish this goal.

In the previous chapter, we studied the first way. One of the most prevalent and useful tools to limit land use is through servitudes. These *private land use controls*, in the form of restrictive covenants or easements, are usually preferred because they are voluntary and can be narrowly tailored to particular circumstances. Thus, Alice and Bart could enter into a covenant mutually agreeing to restrictions on their land. The previous chapter discussed the advantages and limitations of servitudes, so Part V will focus on other means of land use control. We will discuss, however, the interplay between private land use controls and the other methods.

Second, Alice could sue Bart for a *nuisance* if he attempts to use his land in a way that adversely affects her. In a nuisance case, the court is called upon to decide whether Bart's use is a substantial and unreasonable interference with Alice's use and enjoyment of her land. Thus, we call this *judicial land use control*, because it is based primarily on common law—a judge's determination of whether a particular use of land is proper in this location. As we will see, judicial control of land use is necessary to fill in the gaps of our other methods, but it has significant drawbacks that limit its effectiveness in modern society. For example, nuisance judgments are *ad hoc* rather than comprehensive, and typically *ex post* (after the fact), rather than *ex ante* (before the fact), leading to unpredictability and uncertainty. We will describe the common law of nuisance in Chapter 12.

Our third method, *governmental land use control,* is usually more comprehensive and lets prospective owners know ahead of time what uses of land are permissible. It is no surprise, therefore, that the importance of nuisance law has diminished as governmental land use control has increased. In Chapter 13, we will study *zoning* as the primary form of government control. We must recognize, however, that many other laws, from the federal level down to the municipal level, may limit your use of land. For example, the federal Clean Water Act may prohibit you from filling in a wetland or a state law may limit how close a feedlot may be to residential areas.

> ➤ In our example, Alice should determine whether local zoning ordinances or other laws limit Bart's use of his land. If the area is zoned residential, for example, then her worries about incompatible uses of Whiteacre will be substantially diminished. State statutes may limit Bart's ability to construct a feedlot near a residence as well.
>
> ➤ Even though the area may be zoned residential, can you think of any reasons why Alice also would like a covenant to guard against undesirable uses of Bart's land?

As we study governmental control of land use, you may begin to wonder whether this power has any limits. Land use regulations have the potential to significantly impact a landowner's investment and expectations. If the county zones Bart's property for residential use, it may completely destroy his plans. In fact, the government's authority over land use includes the ultimate power to take property away from a private owner, using the power of *eminent domain.*

Therefore, in Chapter 14, we consider the significant *limitations on government power* contained in the federal and state constitutions. For example, the constitutions limit when the government can use its eminent domain power, and they ensure that property owners are fairly compensated. We will also discover that, even if property is not physically taken, government regulations may become so onerous that the Constitution requires the owner to be compensated for the decline in the property's value. These *constitutional aspects of government land use regulation* are the subject of the final chapter of this book and conveniently cause us to revisit the foundational principles we discussed in Chapter 1.

The Forms of Land Use Control

1. **Private:** Restrictive covenants or other servitudes, in which parties agree to limit use.
2. **Judicial:** Common law, primarily through nuisance doctrine, controls unreasonable uses.
3. **Governmental:** Federal, state, or local laws, such as zoning, that limit land use. Governmental controls are in turn constrained by constitutional limitations.

CHAPTER 12

Judicial Land Use Control: Nuisance

A. Introduction

B. The Restatement Nuisance Test: Balancing the Utilities

C. "Substantial Harm" Test Compared

D. Effect of Zoning or Covenants on Nuisance Analysis

E. Questions of Remedy

F. Public Nuisance

> A nuisance may be merely a right thing in the wrong place—like a pig in the parlor instead of the barnyard.
> —*Justice Sutherland, Village of Euclid v. Ambler Realty Co.*

A INTRODUCTION

The *common law of nuisance* is the primary method of invoking judicial power to curtail injurious uses of land. Nuisance is a *tort*, but because it involves land, it lies at the intersection between property law and tort law.

A *private nuisance* exists when a landowner *substantially and unreasonably interferes with the use and enjoyment of the land of another.* "The law of private nuisance rests on the concept embodied in the ancient legal maxim *Sic utere tuo ut alienum non laedas* [often shortened to *sic utero tuo*], meaning, in essence, that every person should so use his own property as not to injure that of another." Morgan v. High Penn Oil Co., 77 S.E.2d 682 (N.C. 1953).

The Restatement of Torts specifies that a nuisance must be *nontrespassory*—to distinguish a cause of action for nuisance from the *physical* intrusions handled under trespass law. Often the line between nuisance and trespass is hard to draw, however. For example, a neighbor's feedlot may cause odors and dust, and manure may pollute the stream running through your land. The manure is a physical invasion, and technically the dust is invading your land as well. Even the odors are caused by hydrogen sulfide and ammonia molecules entering your airspace. Therefore, lawsuits often include claims based on both of these theories. Some courts do not limit nuisance to nontrespassory interference. *See* Rancho Viejo LLC v. Tres Amigos Viejos LLC, 123 Cal. Rptr. 2d 479, 486-87 (Cal. Ct. App. 2002).

A private nuisance affects one landowner or at most a small number of neighboring properties. A *public nuisance* has a more widespread impact that affects the public in general. Traditionally, public nuisance cases could be brought only by a public prosecutor or by a private plaintiff who was *specially affected* by the harm. Public nuisance claims are often based on violations of statutes or ordinances. In this chapter, we will concentrate on private nuisance, although many of the concepts are relevant to public nuisance cases as well. At the end of the chapter, we point out the major differences in public nuisance claims, along with a discussion of some recent, novel uses of the doctrine.

Analyzing Nuisance Cases

It is helpful to divide your analysis in nuisance cases into two questions:

1. Does a nuisance exist?
2. If a nuisance exists, what should be the remedy—damages or an injunction?

Many American courts have changed their approach to both of these questions over time. Early American decisions took a *substantial harm* approach to nuisance law: if A's use of her land substantially interfered with B's use and enjoyment of his land, A's use was a nuisance and must be enjoined. B should not have to put up with noise, dust, stench, or other consequences of A's activities. The courts used the term *unreasonable* interference mostly to refer to the *degree* of harm caused.

Modern courts tend to take a more nuanced view. With regard to the test for nuisance, the Restatement of Torts agrees that only an *unreasonable* interference should be actionable, but the test for unreasonableness takes into account the conduct of both the plaintiff and defendant. The fact that two land uses are in conflict doesn't necessarily tell us which one is causing the problem—in other words, "it takes two to tango."

> ➤ The Restatement test is described as a *balance of utilities*, which defines conduct as unreasonable if the "*gravity of the harm [to the plaintiff] outweighs the utility of the [defendant]'s conduct.*" Restatement (Second) of Torts §826(a) (1979) (emphasis added).

In balancing harm versus utility, the Restatement suggests that a number of factors should be considered (emphasis added):

Restatement (Second) of Torts §827 (1979)

In determining the *gravity of the harm* from an intentional invasion of another's interest in the use and enjoyment of land, the following factors are important:

    (a) the extent of the harm involved;

    (b) the character of the harm involved;

    (c) the social value that the law attaches to the type of use or enjoyment invaded;

    (d) the suitability of the particular use or enjoyment invaded to the character of the locality; and

    (e) the burden on the person harmed of avoiding the harm.

Restatement (Second) of Torts §828 (1979)

In determining the *utility of conduct* that causes an intentional invasion of another's interest in the use and enjoyment of land, the following factors are important:

    (a) the social value that the law attaches to the primary purpose of the conduct;

    (b) the suitability of the conduct to the character of the locality; and

    (c) the impracticability of preventing or avoiding the invasion.

Think about the factors that the Restatement identifies as important to the balance of the utilities calculus. In what ways do these considerations go beyond the traditional "substantial harm" test?

Note that this test applies only to an *intentional* interference—but don't let that mislead you. In this context, the term *intentional* does not mean that the defendant intended to cause harm to her neighbor. Rather, it means only that the defendant's *conduct* is purposeful—for example, our friend Bart may intentionally construct a feedlot on Whiteacre. He doesn't intend for it to cause harm to Alice—in fact, he hopes it doesn't—but certainly his conduct was intentional. As the Restatement explains:

> An invasion of another's interest in the use and enjoyment of land is intentional when the actor: a) acts for the purpose of causing it, or b) knows that it is resulting or is substantially certain to result from his conduct.

Restatement (Second) of Torts §825 (1979).

Unintentional conduct may also constitute a nuisance, if the defendant is negligent or reckless, or engages in an abnormally dangerous condition or activity. Restatement (Second) of Torts §822(b) (1979). Bart may construct a feedlot which, if it is properly maintained, will not cause any harm. However, if Bart neglects his waste containment system and manure leaks into the creek, Alice could charge him with an unintentional nuisance.

The judicial approach to the *remedy for nuisance* has also evolved. Even if a nuisance is found, many courts have moved away from automatic imposition of an injunction, reasoning that damages may be a more appropriate remedy in some cases. In other words, these courts use a *liability rule* rather than a *property rule*. In these cases, the defendant's activity causing the harm might be so valuable to society that enjoining it would be undesirable.

The Restatement states that the decision to award injunctive relief should be based on a *balance of equities,* considering primarily:

the harm to the plaintiff if an injunction is denied
weighed against
the hardship to the defendant if an injunction is granted

In considering the equities, the court will also weigh the good or bad faith of the actors, as well as *impacts on third parties and the public in general.* Restatement (Second) of Torts §941 (1979). We will consider this trend more fully below.

■ PROBLEM: CONTRASTING APPROACHES TO NUISANCE

Alice owns Blackacre, while Bart owns the adjacent property, Whiteacre. Alice decides to build a resort hotel on Blackacre. Bart decides to use Whiteacre as a large feedlot for 1,000 head of cattle. The feedlot will naturally produce significant odors that most people do not want to smell when they are relaxing by the pool of a resort hotel; it will also destroy the scenic view and increase noise. *Can Alice enjoin Bart's feedlot as a nuisance?*

1. **Nuisance test.** First, determine whether a court would hold that Bart's use constitutes a nuisance at all. Apply the substantial harm test and then the Restatement balancing test. This is undoubtedly a land use conflict between incompatible uses, but is it necessarily the case that Bart's use should be called a nuisance? Do any of the following facts change your conclusion regarding the proper result in this case?
   ■ Bart's parents began using Whiteacre as a feedlot in 1950. Bart took over the operation in 1990 and it has not increased significantly in size since that time. Blackacre had been used as cropland until 2009, when Alice bought it and began building her resort.
   ■ Bart has taken a number of steps to reduce the impacts of his use, including planting a row of large evergreen trees on the edges of his property to shield the animals from view and help disperse the odors. He also improved manure collection structures and increased manure collection frequency. Alice, on the other hand, built her pool close to Bart's property instead of at other possible locations farther away.

■ Whiteacre is located five miles away from the nearest incorporated city, and the area is currently not zoned by the county.

Can you think of any other facts that might be relevant to the decision? How do you characterize the "social value" of these competing uses?

2. **Remedy.** Assume that the court believes that Bart's feedlot constitutes a nuisance. Should the court enjoin it or allow it to continue upon the payment of damages? Would you want to know the size of each operation? How much they contribute to the local economy? How many employees they have? Does it matter whether this case is in an area of Florida where tourism is vitally important, or in an area of Texas known for its production of high-quality beef?

B THE RESTATEMENT NUISANCE TEST: BALANCING THE UTILITIES

As set out above, the Restatement approach to nuisance directs the court to consider not only the harm caused to the plaintiff, but the relative *social utility* of each party's conduct. The following case, involving an interference with solar power, illustrates how social policy may affect the nuisance decision. As you read the case, think about whether the Restatement test opens the door to "judicial activism," as the dissent suggests.

PRAH v. MARETTI

321 N.W.2d 182 (1982)
Supreme Court of Wisconsin

ABRAHAMSON, Justice.

This appeal from a judgment of the circuit court for Waukesha county . . . , as presenting an issue of first impression, namely, whether an owner of a solar-heated residence states a claim upon which relief can be granted when he asserts that his neighbor's proposed construction of a residence (which conforms to existing deed restrictions and local ordinances) interferes with his access to an unobstructed path for sunlight across the neighbor's property. This case thus involves a conflict between one landowner (Glenn Prah, the plaintiff) interested in unobstructed access to sunlight across adjoining property as a natural source of energy and an adjoining landowner (Richard D. Maretti, the defendant) interested in the development of his land.

The circuit court concluded that the plaintiff presented no claim upon which relief could be granted and granted summary judgment for the defendant. We reverse the judgment of the circuit court and remand the cause to the circuit court for further proceedings.

According to the complaint, the plaintiff is the owner of a residence which was constructed during the years 1978-1979. The complaint alleges that the residence has a solar system which includes collectors on the roof to supply energy for heat and hot water and that after the plaintiff built his solar-heated house, the defendant purchased the lot adjacent to and immediately to the south of the plaintiff's lot and commenced planning construction of a home. The complaint further states that when the plaintiff learned of defendant's plans to build the house he advised the defendant that if the house were built at the proposed location, defendant's house would substantially and adversely affect the integrity of plaintiff's solar system and could cause plaintiff other damage. Nevertheless, the defendant began construction. The complaint further alleges that the plaintiff is entitled to "unrestricted use of the sun and its solar power" and demands judgment for injunctive relief and damages. . . .

The record made on the motion reveals the following additional facts: Plaintiff's home was the first residence built in the subdivision, and although plaintiff did not build his house in the center of the lot it was built in accordance with applicable restrictions. Plaintiff advised defendant that if the defendant's home were built at the proposed site it would cause a shadowing effect on the solar collectors which would reduce the efficiency of the system and possibly damage the system. To avoid these adverse effects, plaintiff requested defendant to locate his home an additional several feet away from the plaintiff's lot line, the exact number being disputed. Plaintiff and defendant failed to reach an agreement on the location of defendant's home before defendant started construction. The Architectural Control Committee and the Planning Commission of the City of Muskego approved the defendant's plans for his home, including its location on the lot. After such approval, the defendant apparently changed the grade of the property without prior notice to the Architectural Control Committee. The problem with defendant's proposed construction, as far as the plaintiff's interests are concerned, arises from a combination of the grade and the distance of defendant's home from the defendant's lot line. . . .

. . . We consider first whether the complaint states a claim for relief based on common law private nuisance. This state has long recognized that an owner of land does not have an absolute or unlimited right to use the land in a way which injures the rights of others. The rights of neighboring landowners are relative; the uses by one must not unreasonably impair the uses or enjoyment of the other.[1]

---

[1] In Abdella v. Smith, 34 Wis. 2d 393, 399, 149 N.W.2d 537 (1967), this court quoted with approval Dean Prosser's description of the judicial balancing of the reciprocal rights and privileges of neighbors in the use of their land:

> Most of the litigation as to private nuisance has dealt with the conflicting interests of landowners and the question of the reasonableness of the defendant's conduct: The defendant's privilege of making a reasonable use of his own property for his own benefit and conducting his affairs in his own way is no less important than the plaintiff's right to use and enjoy his premises. The two are correlative and interdependent, and neither is entitled to prevail entirely, at the expense of the other. Some balance must be struck between the two. The plaintiff must be expected to endure some inconvenience rather than curtail the defendant's freedom of action, and the defendant must so use his own property that he causes no unreasonable harm to the plaintiff. The law of private nuisance is very largely a series of adjustments to limit the reciprocal rights and privileges of both. In every case the court must make a comparative evaluation of the conflicting interests according to objective legal standards, and the gravity of the harm to the plaintiff must be weighed against the utility of the defendant's conduct.

Prosser, Law of Torts, §89, p. 596 (2d ed. 1971) (citations omitted).

... When one landowner's use of his or her property unreasonably interferes with another's enjoyment of his or her property, that use is said to be a private nuisance....

The private nuisance doctrine has traditionally been employed in this state to balance the rights of landowners, and this court has recently adopted the analysis of private nuisance set forth in the Restatement (Second) of Torts.... The Restatement defines private nuisance as "a nontrespassory invasion of another's interest in the private use and enjoyment of land." Restatement (Second) of Torts sec. 821D (1977). The phrase "interest in the private use and enjoyment of land" as used in sec. 821D is broadly defined to include any disturbance of the enjoyment of property....

Although the defendant's obstruction of the plaintiff's access to sunlight appears to fall within the Restatement's broad concept of a private nuisance as a nontrespassory invasion of another's interest in the private use and enjoyment of land, the defendant asserts that he has a right to develop his property in compliance with statutes, ordinances and private covenants without regard to the effect of such development upon the plaintiff's access to sunlight. In essence, the defendant is asking this court to hold that the private nuisance doctrine is not applicable in the instant case and that his right to develop his land is a right which is *per se* superior to his neighbor's interest in access to sunlight. This position is expressed in the maxim "*cujus est solum, ejus est usque ad coelum et ad infernos*," that is, the owner of land owns up to the sky and down to the center of the earth. The rights of the surface owner are, however, not unlimited. U.S. v. Causby, 328 U.S. 256, 260-1 (1946)....

At English common law a landowner could acquire a right to receive sunlight across adjoining land by both express agreement and under the judge-made doctrine of "ancient lights." Under the doctrine of ancient lights if the landowner had received sunlight across adjoining property for a specified period of time, the landowner was entitled to continue to receive unobstructed access to sunlight across the adjoining property. Under the doctrine the landowner acquired a negative prescriptive easement and could prevent the adjoining landowner from obstructing access to light.[2]

Although American courts have not been as receptive to protecting a landowner's access to sunlight as the English courts, American courts have afforded some protection to a landowner's interest in access to sunlight. American courts honor express easements to sunlight. American courts initially enforced the English common law doctrine of ancient lights, but later every state which considered the doctrine repudiated it as inconsistent with the needs of a developing country....

---

[2] Pfeiffer, *Ancient Lights: Legal Protection of Access to Solar Energy*, 68 ABAJ 288 (1982). No American common law state recognizes a landowner's right to acquire an easement of light by prescription. Comment, *Solar Lights: Guaranteeing a Place in the Sun*, 57 Ore. L. Rev. 94, 112 (1977).

Many jurisdictions in this country have protected a landowner from malicious obstruction of access to light (the spite fence cases) under the common law private nuisance doctrine.[3] If an activity is motivated by malice it lacks utility and the harm it causes others outweighs any social values.... Thus a landowner's interest in sunlight has been protected in this country by common law private nuisance law at least in the narrow context of the modern American rule invalidating spite fences. *See, e.g.,* Sundowner, Inc. v. King, 95 Idaho 367, 509 P.2d 785 (1973); Restatement (Second) of Torts, §829 (1977).

This court's reluctance in the nineteenth and early part of the twentieth century to provide broader protection for a landowner's access to sunlight was premised on three policy considerations. First, the right of landowners to use their property as they wished, as long as they did not cause physical damage to a neighbor, was jealously guarded. Metzger v. Hochrein, 107 Wis. 267, 272, 83 N.W. 308 (1900).

Second, sunlight was valued only for aesthetic enjoyment or as illumination. Since artificial light could be used for illumination, loss of sunlight was at most a personal annoyance which was given little, if any, weight by society.

Third, society had a significant interest in not restricting or impeding land development. Dillman v. Hoffman, 38 Wis. 559, 574 (1875). This court repeatedly emphasized that in the growth period of the nineteenth and early twentieth centuries change is to be expected and is essential to property and that recognition of a right to sunlight would hinder property development....

Considering these three policies, this court concluded that in the absence of an express agreement granting access to sunlight, a landowner's obstruction of another's access to sunlight was not actionable. Miller v. Hoeschler, *supra*, 126 Wis. at 271, 105 N.W. 790; Depner v. United States National Bank, *supra*, 202 Wis. at 410, 232 N.W. 851. These three policies are no longer fully accepted or applicable. They reflect factual circumstances and social priorities that are now obsolete.

First, society has increasingly regulated the use of land by the landowner for the general welfare. Euclid v. Ambler Realty Co., 272 U.S. 365 (1926); Just v. Marinette, 56 Wis. 2d 7, 201 N.W.2d 761 (1972).

Second, access to sunlight has taken on a new significance in recent years. In this case the plaintiff seeks to protect access to sunlight, not for aesthetic reasons or as a source of illumination but as a source of energy. Access to sunlight as an energy source is of significance both to the landowner who invests in solar collectors and to a society which has an interest in developing alternative sources of energy.[4]

---

[3] In several of the spite fence cases, courts have recognized the property owner's interest in sunlight. Hornsby v. Smith, 191 Ga. 491, 500, 13 S.E.2d 20 (1941) ("the air and light no matter from which direction they come are God-given, and are essential to the life, comfort, and happiness of everyone"); Burke v. Smith, 69 Mich. 380, 389, 37 N.W. 838 (1888) ("the right to breathe the air and enjoy the sunshine, is a natural one"); Barger v. Barringer, 151 N.C. 433, 437, 66 S.E. 439 (1909) ("light and air are as much a necessity as water, and all are the common heritage of mankind").

[4] State and federal governments are encouraging the use of the sun as a significant source of energy. In this state the legislature has granted tax benefits to encourage the utilization of solar energy.... The federal government has also recognized the importance of solar energy and currently encourages its utilization by means of tax benefits, direct subsidies and government loans for solar projects....

Third, the policy of favoring unhindered private development in an expanding economy is no longer in harmony with the realities of our society. State v. Deetz, 66 Wis. 2d 1, 224 N.W.2d 407 (1974). The need for easy and rapid development is not as great today as it once was, while our perception of the value of sunlight as a source of energy has increased significantly.

Courts should not implement obsolete policies that have lost their vigor over the course of the years. The law of private nuisance is better suited to resolve landowners' disputes about property development in the 1980's than is a rigid rule which does not recognize a landowner's interest in access to sunlight. As we said in Ballstadt v. Pagel, 202 Wis. 484, 489, 232 N.W. 862 (1930), "What is regarded in law as constituting a nuisance in modern times would no doubt have been tolerated without question in former times."... We recognized in *Deetz* that common law rules adapt to changing social values and conditions....

Yet the defendant would have us ignore the flexible private nuisance law as a means of resolving the dispute between the landowners in this case and would have us adopt an approach, already abandoned in *Deetz*, of favoring the unrestricted development of land and of applying a rigid and inflexible rule protecting his right to build on his land and disregarding any interest of the plaintiff in the use and enjoyment of his land. This we refuse to do.[5]

Private nuisance law, the law traditionally used to adjudicate conflicts between private landowners, has the flexibility to protect both a landowner's right of access to sunlight and another landowner's right to develop land. Private nuisance law is better suited to regulate access to sunlight in modern society and is more in harmony with legislative policy and the prior decisions of this court than is an inflexible doctrine of non-recognition of any interest in access to sunlight across adjoining land.

We therefore hold that private nuisance law, that is, the reasonable use doctrine as set forth in the Restatement, is applicable to the instant case. Recognition of a nuisance claim for unreasonable obstruction of access to

---

[5] Defendant's position that a landowner's interest in access to sunlight across adjoining land is not "legally enforceable" and is therefore excluded per se from private nuisance law was adopted in Fontainebleau Hotel Corp. v. Forty-five Twenty-five, Inc., 114 So. 2d 357 (Fla. App. 1959), *cert. den.* 117 So. 2d 842 (Fla. 1960). The Florida district court of appeals permitted construction of a building which cast a shadow on a neighboring hotel's swimming pool. The court asserted that nuisance law protects only those interests "which [are] recognized and protected by law," and that there is no legally recognized or protected right to access to sunlight. A property owner does not, said the Florida court, in the absence of a contract or statute, acquire a presumptive or implied right to the free flow of light and air across adjoining land. The Florida court then concluded that a lawful structure which causes injury to another by cutting off light and air—whether or not erected partly for spite—does not give rise to a cause of action for damages or for an injunction. *See also* People ex rel. Hoogasian v. Sears, Roebuck & Co., 52 Ill. 2d 301, 287 N.E.2d 677 (1972).

We do not find the reasoning of *Fontainebleau* persuasive.... The court did not explain why an owner's interest in unobstructed light should not be protected or in what manner an owner's interest in unobstructed sunlight differs from an owner's interest in being free from obtrusive noises or smells or differs from an owner's interest in unobstructed use of water. The recognition of a *per se* exception to private nuisance law may invite unreasonable behavior.

sunlight will not prevent land development or unduly hinder the use of adjoining land. It will promote the reasonable use and enjoyment of land in a manner suitable to the 1980's. That obstruction of access to light might be found to constitute a nuisance in certain circumstances does not mean that it will be or must be found to constitute a nuisance under all circumstances. The result in each case depends on whether the conduct complained of is unreasonable.

Accordingly we hold that the plaintiff in this case has stated a claim under which relief can be granted. Nonetheless we do not determine whether the plaintiff in this case is entitled to relief. In order to be entitled to relief the plaintiff must prove the elements required to establish actionable nuisance, and the conduct of the defendant herein must be judged by the reasonable use doctrine. . . .

Although the memorandum decision of the circuit court in the instant case is unclear, it appears that the circuit court recognized that the common law private nuisance doctrine was applicable but concluded that defendant's conduct was not unreasonable. The circuit court apparently attempted to balance the utility of the defendant's conduct with the gravity of the harm. Sec. 826, Restatement (Second) of Torts (1977). The defendant urges us to accept the circuit court's balance as adequate. We decline to do so.

The circuit court concluded that because the defendant's proposed house was in conformity with zoning regulations, building codes and deed restrictions, the defendant's use of the land was reasonable. This court has concluded that a landowner's compliance with zoning laws does not automatically bar a nuisance claim. Compliance with the law "is not the controlling factor, though it is, of course, entitled to some weight." Bie v. Ingersoll, 27 Wis. 2d 490, 495, 135 N.W.2d 250 (1965). The circuit court also concluded that the plaintiff could have avoided any harm by locating his own house in a better place. Again, plaintiff's ability to avoid the harm is a relevant but not a conclusive factor. See §§826, 827, 828, Restatement (Second) of Torts (1977).

Furthermore, our examination of the record leads us to conclude that the record does not furnish an adequate basis for the circuit court to apply the proper legal principles on summary judgment. The application of the reasonable use standard in nuisance cases normally requires a full exposition of all underlying facts and circumstances. Too little is known in this case of such matters as the extent of the harm to the plaintiff, the suitability of solar heat in that neighborhood, the availability of remedies to the plaintiff, and the costs to the defendant of avoiding the harm. Summary judgment is not an appropriate procedural vehicle in this case when the circuit court must weigh evidence which has not been presented at trial. . . .

The judgment of the circuit court is reversed and the cause remanded for proceedings not inconsistent with this opinion.

CALLOW, Justice (dissenting).

The majority has adopted the Restatement's reasonable use doctrine to grant an owner of a solar heated home a cause of action against his neighbor who, in acting entirely within the applicable ordinances and statutes, seeks to design and build his home in such a location that it may, at various times during the day, shade the plaintiff's solar collector, thereby impeding the efficiency of his heating system during several months of the year. Because I believe the facts of this case clearly reveal that a cause of action for private nuisance will not lie, I dissent.

The majority arrives at its conclusion that the common law private nuisance doctrine is applicable by analogizing this situation with the spite fence cases which protect a landowner from malicious obstruction of access to light. . . . Clearly, the spite fence cases, as their name implies, require malice which is not claimed in this case.

The majority then concludes that this court's past reluctance to extend protection to a landowner's access to sunlight beyond the spite fence cases is based on obsolete policies which have lost their vigor over the course of the years. . . . The majority has failed to convince me that these policies are obsolete.

It is a fundamental principle of law that a "landowner owns at least as much of the space above the ground as he can occupy or use in connection with the land." United States v. Causby, 328 U.S. 256, 264 (1946). . . . I firmly believe that a landowner's right to use his property within the limits of ordinances, statutes, and restrictions of record where such use is necessary to serve his legitimate needs is a fundamental precept of a free society which this court should strive to uphold. . . .

In the instant case, we are dealing with an action which seeks to restrict the defendant's private right to use his property, notwithstanding a complete lack of notice of restriction to the defendant and the defendant's compliance with applicable ordinances and statutes. The plaintiff who knew of the potential problem before the defendant acquired the land seeks to impose such use restriction to accommodate his personal, private benefit—a benefit which could have been accommodated by the plaintiff locating his home in a different place on his property or by acquiring the land in question when it was for sale prior to its acquisition by the defendant.

I know of no cases repudiating policies favoring the right of a landowner to use his property as he lawfully desires or which declare such policies are "no longer fully accepted or applicable" in this context.[6] The right of a property owner to lawful enjoyment of his property should be vigorously protected, particularly in those cases where the adjacent property owner could have insulated himself from the alleged problem by acquiring the land as a defense to the potential problem or by provident use of his own property.

The majority concludes that sunlight has not heretofore been accorded the status of a source of energy, and consequently it has taken on a new significance in recent years. Solar energy for home heating is at this time sparingly used and of questionable economic value because solar collectors are not mass produced, and consequently, they are very costly. Their limited efficiency may explain the lack of production.

---

[6] Perhaps one reason courts have been hesitant to recognize a cause of action for solar blockage is that such a suit would normally only occur between two abutting landowners, and it is hoped that neighbors will compromise and reach agreement between themselves. . . .

Regarding the third policy the majority apparently believes is obsolete (that society has a significant interest in not restricting land development), it cites State v. Deetz, 66 Wis. 2d 1, 224 N.W.2d 407 (1974)....I note that this court in *Deetz* stated: "The reasonable use rule retains ... a policy of favoring land improvement and development." *Id.* at 20, 224 N.W.2d 407....

I would submit that any policy decisions in this area are best left for the legislature....

The legislature has recently acted in this area. Chapter 354, Laws of 1981 (effective May 7, 1982), was enacted to provide the underlying legislation enabling local governments to enact ordinances establishing procedures for guaranteeing access to sunlight. This court's intrusion into an area where legislative action is being taken is unwarranted, and it may undermine a legislative scheme for orderly development not yet fully operational.

Chapter 354, Laws of 1981, sec. 66.032, provides specific conditions for solar access permits. In part that section provides for impermissible interference with solar collectors within specific limitations: [describing procedure].

This legislative scheme would deal with the type of problem presented in the present case and precludes the need for judicial activism in this area....

In order for a nuisance to be actionable in the instant case, the defendant's conduct must be "intentional and unreasonable." [7] It is impossible for me to accept the majority's conclusion that Mr. Maretti, in lawfully seeking to construct his home, may be intentionally and unreasonably interfering with the plaintiff's access to sunlight. In addressing the "unreasonableness" component of the actor's conduct, it is important to note that "[t]here is liability for a nuisance only to those to whom it causes significant harm, of a kind that would be suffered by a normal person in the community or by property in normal condition and used for a normal purpose." Restatement (Second) of Torts §821F (1979)....

I conclude that plaintiff's solar heating system is an unusually sensitive use. In other words, the defendant's proposed construction of his home, under ordinary circumstances, would not interfere with the use and enjoyment of the usual person's property. See W. Prosser, supra, §87 at 578-79. "The plaintiff cannot, by devoting his own land to an unusually sensitive use, such as a drive-in motion picture theater easily affected by light, make a nuisance out of conduct of the adjoining defendant which would otherwise be harmless." *Id.* at 579 (footnote omitted).

... The majority ... cites *Bie v. Ingersoll,* supra, for the proposition that compliance with the law is not the controlling factor in evaluating a nuisance claim. I note that *Bie* involved the operation of an asphalt plant from which dust and odors permeated the plaintiff's adjoining residence. The defendants asserted that, because the property occupied by the asphalt plant was zoned for industrial use, the plant could not constitute a nuisance. This court concluded that

---

[7] Unintentional conduct may also be actionable if the plaintiff asserts negligence or recklessness or if an abnormally dangerous condition or activity exists. Restatement (Second) of Torts §822(b) (1979). The plaintiff's complaint does not specify whether the defendant's conduct was intentional, negligent, or reckless.

the zoning classification was not the controlling factor. "It is rather 'the peculiar nature and the location of the business, not the fact that it is a business, that constitutes the private nuisance.'" 27 Wis. 2d at 495, 135 N.W.2d 250. The *Bie* case is clearly distinguishable from the case at bar. Here, the defendant seeks to build his home in compliance with all existing laws, and it will have no "peculiar nature." ...

... I believe the facts of the instant controversy present the classic case of the owner of a solar collector who fails to take any action to protect his investment. There is nothing in the record to indicate that Mr. Prah disclosed his situation to Mr. Maretti prior to Maretti's purchase of the lot or attempted to secure protection for his solar collector prior to Maretti's submission of his building plans to the architectural committee. Such inaction should be considered a significant factor in determining whether a cause of action exists.

... I do not believe that an adjacent lot owner should be obliged to experience the substantial economic loss resulting from the lot being rendered unbuildable by the contour of the land as it relates to the location and design of the adjoining home using solar collectors.[8]

... Because I do not believe that the facts of the present case give rise to a cause of action for private nuisance, I dissent.

■ POINTS TO CONSIDER

1. **Restatement test.** As you know, the Restatement test balances the harm to the plaintiff versus the utility of the defendant's conduct. Upon remand in this case, what facts do you think the trial court should weigh in striking that balance? Can some of the concerns raised by the dissent be taken care of by considering them in the balancing process? Do you think that the Restatement approach, with its emphasis on the social value of each party's use, allows courts too much of an opportunity to inject their own policy preferences into the determination of nuisance? Does the "substantial harm" approach avoid that criticism?

2. **Unusually sensitive uses.** Do you agree with the dissent that solar collectors, at least in 1982, were unusually sensitive uses? Are they still? Why should a sensitive use deserve less protection from nuisance law?

3. **Economic efficiency.** Note that the Restatement approach relies on some of our fundamental property policies, such as fairness (who was there first, who could have avoided the harm most easily) and economic efficiency. In fact, the "balancing of utilities" terminology suggests that the whole objective is to maximize the value of competing land uses. Assume the evidence shows that

---

[8] Mr. Prah could have avoided this litigation by building his own home in the center of his lot instead of only ten feet from the Maretti lot line and/or by purchasing the adjoining lot for his own protection. Mr. Maretti has already moved the proposed location of his home over an additional ten feet to accommodate Mr. Prah's solar collector, and he testified that moving the home any further would interfere with his view of the lake on which the property faces.

Maretti's house would be worth $30,000 less if he has to build it on another part of his lot where it will have no view. If Maretti doesn't move the house, on the other hand, Prah's solar collectors will produce less energy, requiring Prah to spend about $1,000 more per year on additional energy costs.[9] Do these numbers make Maretti's conduct seem more reasonable? If the damage to Prah is $3,000 per year and Maretti's property value would decline by only $10,000 if he moved, does your opinion change? We don't know what the real numbers were in this case—the majority points out that this evidence needs to be presented on remand. In contrast, the dissent emphasized fairness—he believed Prah is acquiring the solar rights for free. Do you agree? Is ensuring that your lot has solar access any different than ensuring that your lot has transportation access? The dissent also thinks the courts should let the parties bargain in these situations. Prah should be willing to pay Maretti enough to acquire what is essentially a negative easement, presumably at a price that will make both parties better off. If parties can't reach such an agreement, we can assume it is because the restriction is not economically efficient (in other words, it will not increase the value of Prah's property enough to make up for the detriment to Maretti). In addition, allowing the parties to bargain will account for any personal value Maretti attaches to the view, which might not be accounted for in property value evidence. Do you agree? Do you see how the Coase theorem may have influenced the dissent?

4. **Certainty.** Which opinion best furthers our policy of certainty in property transactions? After *Prah*, what additional concerns do you have when you buy a vacant lot in a residential area in Wisconsin? What steps would you have to take to alleviate these concerns?

5. **Comparative institutional analysis.** The dissent notes that the legislature enacted statutory measures in the area of solar collector interference. Which institution—the legislature or the courts—is best able to balance the rights of solar collector owners and their neighbors? What advantages does the legislative solution have? What effect should it have on the common law nuisance action?

6. **Solar power and the courts.** Although *Prah* provides an excellent example of the social utility approach championed by the Restatement, it does not necessarily represent the position taken by most courts on nuisance liability for blocking solar collectors. One commentator recently concluded that "despite the publicity, *Prah* has not had a significant impact on solar access law. Wisconsin courts have cited it only for its unrelated holding on summary judgment, and only two or three courts outside of Wisconsin have cited *Prah* favorably for its findings on nuisance." Sara C. Bronin, *Solar Rights*, 89 B.U. L. Rev. 1217, 1254 (2009). Why do you suppose court recognition of solar rights has not gained more traction?

---

[9] The lump sum present value of this additional cost, at a 5 percent interest rate, over 30 years, would be just over $15,000.

"SUBSTANTIAL HARM" TEST COMPARED

Many American jurisdictions continue to use the "substantial harm" test rather than the Restatement balancing approach to nuisance. The substantial harm approach focuses on the degree of harm caused by the offending use, rather than examining the comparative social utility of the competing uses. For example, the Virginia Supreme Court defined its nuisance test as follows:

> When a business enterprise, even though lawful, becomes obnoxious to occupants of neighboring dwellings and renders enjoyment of the structures uncomfortable by virtue of, for example, smoke, cinders, dust, noise, offensive odors, or noxious gases, the operation of such business is a nuisance. . . . The term "nuisance" includes "everything that endangers life or health, or obstructs the reasonable and comfortable use of property."

Bowers v. Westvaco Corp., 419 S.E.2d 661 (Va. 1992). *See also* Washington Suburban Sanitary Comm'n v. CAE-Link Corp., 622 A.2d 745, 750 (Md. 1993) ("where a trade or business as carried on interferes with the reasonable and comfortable enjoyment by another of his property, a wrong is done to a neighboring owner for which an action lies. . . ." "[I]t makes no difference that the business [is] lawful and one useful to the public and conducted in the most approved method").

What makes a harm "substantial" is of course difficult to define. Courts that use this test note that sensory offenses can qualify, but "discomfort and annoyance must, however, be significant and of a kind that would be suffered by a normal person in the community." Collett v. Cordovana, 772 S.E.2d 584 (Va. 2015).

Some courts using the substantial harm test at least *consider* the utility of the offensive conduct in determining whether it is unreasonable. However, they do not explicitly *balance* the harm versus the utility of the conduct.

A prime example of the traditional substantial harm approach is Morgan v. High Penn Oil Co., 77 S.E.2d 682 (N.C. 1953). The court upheld a trial court's judgment that an oil refinery constituted a nuisance with respect to plaintiffs' property, which included a house, restaurant, and trailer park. The refinery argued that it was operating a lawful enterprise without negligence. The court determined, however, that the evidence supported a finding of nuisance, because the refinery "intentionally and unreasonably caused noxious gases and odors to escape onto the nine acres of the plaintiffs to such a degree as to impair in a substantial manner the plaintiffs' use and enjoyment of their land." *Id.* at 690. The court made no attempt to balance the relative social utility of the uses involved.

Courts using the substantial harm approach often refer to a category of harms labeled nuisances *per se*, which are always nuisances regardless of circumstances. In contrast, a nuisance *per accidens* is actionable only because of its location, its manner of operation, or other circumstances. For example, a use that violates a zoning or other law is often held to be a nuisance *per se*—there is really nothing more plaintiff needs to prove to show that the conduct is unreasonable.

See, e.g., Soupal v. Shady View, Inc., 672 N.W.2d 171 (Mich. 2003) (commercial use in area zoned single-family residential constituted nuisance *per se*); Tiegs v. Watts, 954 P.2d 877 (Wash. 1998) (violation of pollution permit). Be aware, however, that courts sometimes misuse the nuisance *per se* term and some courts find the whole concept inappropriate, noting that the nuisance determination should always depend on the circumstances. Coyote Flats, L.L.C. v. Sanborn Cnty. Comm'n, 596 N.W.2d 347, 354 n.13 (S.D. 1999).

> ➤ What are the relative merits of the "substantial harm" approach as compared with the Restatement approach? Why has the Restatement balance-of-utilities approach failed to win over more state courts? Note that, under the Restatement approach, a landowner might have to put up with significant harm—if the activity causing the harm has sufficient social value. Is that fair?

In response to criticism of its approach, the Second Restatement added an alternative provision that provides for damages, regardless of the utility of the activity, "if the harm resulting from the invasion is severe and greater than the other should be able to bear without compensation." Restatement (Second) of Torts §829A (1979). This provision does not allow the victim to enjoin the nuisance, however. Do you see why the drafters chose that balance?

■ PROBLEMS: IS THIS A NUISANCE?

Consider whether a nuisance should be found in the following problems, under the Restatement balancing-of-utilities approach, and compare the possible result under the traditional "substantial harm" test:

1. Sowers announced he was building a wind turbine on his residential property to reduce his energy costs. His neighbors, the Halls, sued for an injunction, alleging that the turbine would be a nuisance based on blocking the view, shadow flicker (alternating light and dark shadows occurring as the turbine rotates), and noise approximating the "hum of a highway." *See* Sowers v. Forest Hills Subdivision, 294 P.3d 427 (Nev. 2013). *See also* Renner Kincaid Walker, *The Answer, My Friend, Is Blowin' in the Wind: Nuisance Suits and the Perplexing Future of American Wind Farms*, 16 Drake. J. Agric. L. 509 (2011) (suggesting that legislatures enact nuisance immunity law for wind energy).

2. Episcopal Community Services opened a center to provide free meals to indigent persons, on property adjacent to a residential neighborhood. Neighbors complain that the center attracts many undesirable transients to the area, who trespass in neighbors' yards and sometimes urinate, drink alcohol, or

litter. Some residents have been annoyed or frightened by the transients and have had to increase their vigilance with respect to their property and children. The center's property is properly zoned for this use. *See* Armory Park Neighborhood Ass'n v. Episcopal Cmty. Servs., 712 P.2d 914 (Ariz. 1985).

3. Osborne owned three residential lots in a subdivision of Little Rock, Arkansas. Every Christmas, he created spectacular light displays. Starting with 1,000 lights in 1986, the display got bigger every year, until it reached over 3 million lights in 1993. Neighbors complained that sightseer traffic backed up so far that it took them two hours to make a trip to the corner grocery store. *See* Osborne v. Power, 908 S.W.2d 340 (Ark. 1995).

4. Belhumeur sues Zilm, his next-door neighbor, alleging that a tree on Zilm's property contains a large colony of very aggressive wild bees, which constitutes a nuisance. Belhumeur has become afraid to go near that portion of his property, for fear of being stung, but Zilm refuses to take down the tree or otherwise act to remove the bees. *See* Belhumeur v. Zilm, 949 A.2d 162 (N.H. 2008); Patricia E. Salkin, *Honey, It's All the Buzz: Regulating Neighborhood Beehives*, 39 B.C. Envtl. Aff. L. Rev. 55 (2012). *See also* Christmas v. Exxon Mobil Corp., 138 So.3d 123 (Miss. 2014)(infestation of alligators attracted to neighbor's land did not constitute nuisance).

5. Bode Tower constructs a new cell tower on its land for use by local companies to help fill a gap in reception. The company obtained all of the proper permits. Laubenstein, who owned land nearby, complained that the tower, including its flashing warning lights, was visually unappealing and ruined his view. Laubenstein v. Bode Tower, L.L.C., 392 P.3d 706 (Okla. 2016).

The Moral Nuisance?

Does nuisance law cover offenses to morals? Assume that Odette Naturale bought a small beachfront guesthouse and began advertising a "clothing optional" experience, catering specifically to "swingers." Her next-door neighbors, Glen and Teri Powers, are horrified by the spectacle now presented every time they sit on their back porch or walk on the beach. Can they sue O. Naturale for a nuisance? *See* Mark v. State Dep't of Fish & Wildlife, 158 Or.App. 355, 974 P.2d 716 (1999)(public nudity and sexual activity can support a nuisance claim); John Copeland Nagle, *Moral Nuisances*, 50 Emory L.J. 265 (2001).

If you think the Powers have a good case, what other harms to morality might be sufficient to sustain a nuisance claim? A sex offender moving into the neighborhood? A meeting house for a neo-Nazi group? Harry L. Stephens, Jr., *The Convicted Child Sex Offender Nearby: Does Private Nuisance Provide a Remedy for Neighbors?*, 44 N. Ky. L. Rev. 105 (2017).

D   EFFECT OF ZONING OR COVENANTS ON NUISANCE ANALYSIS

As the court explained in *Prah v. Maretti*, the general rule is that a nuisance suit is *not precluded* merely because a particular activity is allowed by law (such as zoning) or by private restrictions on land use, such as covenants, or homeowners association (HOA) bylaws. Nevertheless, because nuisance rests on a determination of *unreasonableness*, compliance with zoning or other restrictions can be good evidence of the social utility of the defendant's conduct. In addition, a statute that directly addresses the conflicting uses may *displace* the common law, due to the concept of *legislative supremacy*.

Two *funeral parlor cases* decided by the Arkansas Supreme Court illustrate how the increasing prevalence of zoning led courts to retreat from the nuisance arena.

➤ In Powell v. Taylor, 263 S.W.2d 906 (Ark. 1954), the court found that a funeral home in an "essentially residential" neighborhood could be enjoined as a nuisance, because "its continuous suggestion of death and dead bodies tends to destroy the comfort and repose sought in home ownership." *Id.* at 907. The opinion is remarkable for its early recognition that nuisance law protects mental health and aesthetic interests as well as the more physical harms (e.g., soot or vibrations) traditionally recognized.

➤ Yet 23 years later, in Elston v. Paal, 550 S.W.2d 771 (Ark. 1977), the same court, in an opinion written by the same judge, held that a funeral home operating in a residential district was not a nuisance. Although the court did not explicitly overrule *Powell*, it was clearly reluctant to enjoin a business that was allowed by city zoning.

➤ In the years between 1954 and 1977, zoning laws had become much more prevalent, shifting the primary burden of deciding "proper" land use from the courts to city councils. Does the transition from judicial to legislative zoning make sense? And, by the way, do you think a funeral parlor is a nuisance in a residential area?

Note, however, that compliance with zoning ordinances does not *preclude* a nuisance claim. For example, even though Bart's land may be in an agricultural zone, which allows feedlots, under the circumstances this particular feedlot, on this particular property, may be an unreasonable use.

There is a similar relationship between nuisance suits and *covenants or HOA bylaws*. Should nuisance law be used to resolve disputes between owners in a common-interest community? Courts typically hold that compliance with covenants and bylaws does not preclude a nuisance claim. *See, e.g.*, Keane v. Pachter, 598 N.E.2d 1067 (Ind. Ct. App. 1992) (board's consent for installation of tile floor not determinative in nuisance suit by neighbor to abate noise). Nevertheless, courts are reluctant to become involved where an HOA has specifically addressed a particular conflict:

➢ For example, in Ewan v. Maccherone, 927 N.Y.S.2d 274 (N.Y. App. Term 2011), plaintiffs claimed that, due to their neighbors' excessive smoking and an inadequate ventilation system, "secondhand smoke fills [plaintiffs'] kitchen, bedroom and living room, causing them to vacate their unit often at night." *Id.* at 275. Even accepting these allegations as true, however, the court noted: "Critically, defendants were not prohibited from smoking inside their apartment by any existing statute, condominium rule or bylaw. Nor was there any statute, rule or bylaw imposing upon defendants an obligation to ensure that their cigarette smoke did not drift into other residences." *Id.* at 275. The court indicated that people living in multiple-unit buildings had to expect more annoyances. *See also* Feinstein v. Rickman, 26 N.Y.S.3d 135 (N.Y. App. Div 2016).

➢ In Winchell v. Burch, 688 N.E.2d 1053 (Ohio Ct. App. 1996), plaintiff claimed that defendant built a nonconforming deck on her condo that encroached into common areas. The court found the deck to constitute a private nuisance, but delegated the question of remedy to the condominium association. The association board thereafter approved the deck and the court vacated the finding of nuisance. Does it make sense for the court to defer to the board in cases like this?

Preparing to Practice

Assume your client, Paradise Condominiums, asks you to review a draft of a proposed Declaration, which will constitute the governing document for the development. The draft includes the following paragraph:

11. *Nuisances.* No owner shall use his unit, or permit it to be used, in any manner which constitutes or causes an unreasonable amount of annoyance to the occupant of another unit, or which would not be consistent with the maintenance of the highest standards for a first-class residential condominium, nor permit the premises to be used in a disorderly or unlawful way. The use of each unit shall be consistent with existing laws and the condominium documents, and occupants shall at all times conduct themselves in a peaceful and orderly manner.

Should you consider additional clauses to help resolve disputes such as those noted above between unit owners? Can you draft the language?

■ PROBLEM: INTERPLAY BETWEEN STATUTE AND NUISANCE

Plasko owns a 28-acre farm, part of which he uses to raise corn. During the ripening season, he uses a mechanical noisemaking device called a "corn cannon" to scare away birds from the crop. It emits a noise like a gunshot, from 7 A.M. to 8 P.M., at five-minute intervals. Maykut's house lies about 600 feet from Plasko's cannon, which greatly disturbs him. Maykut has sued Plasko, seeking an injunction based on nuisance. Plasko argues that he has a permit to fire the cannon, which is authorized by state law as long as it fired more than 500 feet from any residence. What result? Maykut v. Plasko, 365 A.2d 1114 (Conn. 1976).

E   QUESTIONS OF REMEDY

Once a nuisance is found to exist, the court must then decide what to do about it. Historically, the remedy was simple: a nuisance is a tort that must be enjoined. The Restatement, on the other hand, conditions injunctive relief on a *balance of the equities*—which examines primarily the relative hardship to the defendant if an injunction is granted versus the hardship to the plaintiff if an injunction is denied. Restatement (Second) of Torts §941 (1979). The Restatement also suggests that the motives of the actors as well as the interests of third parties and the public in general should be taken into account in determining whether an injunction is appropriate. Restatement (Second) of Torts §942 (1979).

> **Get the Right Balance!**
>
> Students sometimes confuse the Restatement test for nuisance—*the balance of utilities*—with the Restatement test for injunctive relief—*the balance of equities*. Note carefully how they are different and make sure you use the right test at the right time!

The following case represents the most prominent and influential example of the judicial shift away from the common law's automatic injunction remedy. The cement plant at issue was clearly causing significant harm to the plaintiffs, who lived nearby, and the plant did not appeal the finding that its operation constituted a nuisance. Nevertheless, the court refused to grant an injunction. Pay close attention to the court's reasoning—what sort of nuisance case would merit an injunction after *Boomer*?

B O O M E R v. A T L A N T I C C E M E N T C O .

257 N.E.2d 870 (1970)
Court of Appeals of New York

BERGAN, Judge.

Defendant operates a large cement plant near Albany. These are actions for injunction and damages by neighboring land owners alleging injury to property from dirt, smoke and vibration emanating from the plant. A nuisance has been found after trial, temporary damages have been allowed; but an injunction has been denied.

The public concern with air pollution arising from many sources in industry and in transportation is currently accorded ever wider recognition accompanied by a growing sense of responsibility in State and Federal Governments to control it. Cement plants are obvious sources of air pollution in the neighborhoods where they operate.

But there is now before the court private litigation in which individual property owners have sought specific relief from a single plant operation. The threshold question raised by the division of view on this appeal is whether the court should resolve the litigation between the parties now before it as equitably as seems possible; or whether, seeking promotion of the general public welfare, it should channel private litigation into broad public objectives.

A court performs its essential function when it decides the rights of parties before it. Its decision of private controversies may sometimes greatly affect public issues. Large questions of law are often resolved by the manner in which private litigation is decided. But this is normally an incident to the court's main function to settle controversy. It is a rare exercise of judicial power to use a decision in private litigation as a purposeful mechanism to achieve direct public objectives greatly beyond the rights and interests before the court.

Effective control of air pollution is a problem presently far from solution even with the full public and financial powers of government. In large measure adequate technical procedures are yet to be developed and some that appear possible may be economically impracticable.

It seems apparent that the amelioration of air pollution will depend on technical research in great depth; on a carefully balanced consideration of the economic impact of close regulation; and of the actual effect on public health. It is likely to require massive public expenditure and to demand more than any local community can accomplish and to depend on regional and interstate controls.

A court should not try to do this on its own as a by-product of private litigation and it seems manifest that the judicial establishment is neither equipped in the limited nature of any judgment it can pronounce nor prepared to lay down and implement an effective policy for the elimination of air pollution. This is an area beyond the circumference of one private lawsuit. It is a direct responsibility for government and should not thus be undertaken as an incident to solving a dispute between property owners and a single cement plant—one of many—in the Hudson River valley.

The cement making operations of defendant have been found by the court of Special Term to have damaged the nearby properties of plaintiffs in these two actions. That court, as it has been noted, accordingly found defendant maintained a nuisance and this has been affirmed at the Appellate Division. The total damage to plaintiffs' properties is, however, relatively small in comparison with the value of defendant's operation and with the consequences of the injunction which plaintiffs seek.

The ground for the denial of injunction, notwithstanding the finding both that there is a nuisance and that plaintiffs have been damaged substantially, is the large disparity in economic consequences of the nuisance and of the injunction. This theory cannot, however, be sustained without overruling a doctrine which has been consistently reaffirmed in several leading cases in this court and which has never been disavowed here, namely that where a nuisance +has been found and where there has been any substantial damage shown by the party complaining an injunction will be granted.

The rule in New York has been that such a nuisance will be enjoined although marked disparity be shown in economic consequence between the effect of the injunction and the effect of the nuisance.

The problem of disparity in economic consequence was sharply in focus in Whalen v. Union Bag & Paper Co., 208 N.Y. 1, 101 N.E. 805. A pulp mill entailing an investment of more than a million dollars polluted a stream in which plaintiff, who owned a farm, was "a lower riparian owner." The economic loss to plaintiff from this pollution was small. This court, reversing the Appellate Division, reinstated the injunction granted by the Special Term against the argument of the mill owner that in view of "the slight advantage to plaintiff and the great loss that will be inflicted on defendant" an injunction should not be granted. "Such a balancing of injuries cannot be justified by the circumstances of this case," Judge Werner noted (p. 4, 101 N.E. p. 805). He continued: "Although the damage to the plaintiff may be slight as compared with the defendant's expense of abating the condition, that is not a good reason for refusing an injunction" (p. 5, 101 N.E. p. 806). . . .

Although the court at Special Term and the Appellate Division held that injunction should be denied, it was found that plaintiffs had been damaged in various specific amounts up to the time of the trial and damages to the respective plaintiffs were awarded for those amounts. The effect of this was, injunction having been denied, plaintiffs could maintain successive actions at law for damages thereafter as further damage was incurred.

The court at Special Term also found the amount of permanent damage attributable to each plaintiff, for the guidance of the parties in the event both sides stipulated to the payment and acceptance of such permanent damage as a settlement of all the controversies among the parties. The total of permanent damages to all plaintiffs thus found was $185,000. This basis of adjustment has not resulted in any stipulation by the parties.

This result at Special Term and at the Appellate Division is a departure from a rule that has become settled; but to follow the rule literally in these cases would be to close down the plant at once. This court is fully agreed to avoid that immediately drastic remedy; the difference in view is how best to avoid it.[10]

One alternative is to grant the injunction but postpone its effect to a specified future date to give opportunity for technical advances to permit defendant to eliminate the nuisance; another is to grant the injunction conditioned on the payment

---

[10] Respondent's investment in the plant is in excess of $45,000,000. There are over 300 people employed there.

of permanent damages to plaintiffs which would compensate them for the total economic loss to their property present and future caused by defendant's operations. For reasons which will be developed the court chooses the latter alternative.

If the injunction were to be granted unless within a short period—e.g., 18 months—the nuisance be abated by improved methods, there would be no assurance that any significant technical improvement would occur.

The parties could settle this private litigation at any time if defendant paid enough money and the imminent threat of closing the plant would build up the pressure on defendant. If there were no improved techniques found, there would inevitably be applications to the court at Special Term for extensions of time to perform on showing of good faith efforts to find such techniques.

Moreover, techniques to eliminate dust and other annoying by-products of cement making are unlikely to be developed by any research the defendant can undertake within any short period, but will depend on the total resources of the cement industry nation-wide and throughout the world. The problem is universal wherever cement is made.

For obvious reasons the rate of the research is beyond control of defendant. If at the end of 18 months the whole industry has not found a technical solution a court would be hard put to close down this one cement plant if due regard be given to equitable principles.

On the other hand, to grant the injunction unless defendant pays plaintiffs such permanent damages as may be fixed by the court seems to do justice between the contending parties. All of the attributions of economic loss to the properties on which plaintiffs' complaints are based will have been redressed.

The nuisance complained of by these plaintiffs may have other public or private consequences, but these particular parties are the only ones who have sought remedies and the judgment proposed will fully redress them. The limitation of relief granted is a limitation only within the four corners of these actions and does not foreclose public health or other public agencies from seeking proper relief in a proper court.

It seems reasonable to think that the risk of being required to pay permanent damages to injured property owners by cement plant owners would itself be a reasonable effective spur to research for improved techniques to minimize nuisance....

Thus it seems fair to both sides to grant permanent damages to plaintiffs which will terminate this private litigation. The theory of damage is the "servitude on land" of plaintiffs imposed by defendant's nuisance. (*See* United States v. Causby, 328 U.S. 256, 261, 262, 267, where the term "servitude" addressed to the land was used by Justice Douglas relating to the effect of airplane noise on property near an airport.) The judgment, by allowance of permanent damages imposing a servitude on land, which is the basis of the actions, would preclude future recovery by plaintiffs or their grantees. ... This should be placed beyond debate by a provision of the judgment that the payment by defendant and the acceptance by plaintiffs of permanent damages found by the court shall be in compensation for a servitude on the land....

The orders should be reversed, without costs, and the cases remitted to Supreme Court, Albany County to grant an injunction which shall be vacated upon payment by defendant of such amounts of permanent damage to the respective plaintiffs as shall for this purpose be determined by the court.

JASEN, Judge (dissenting).

I agree with the majority that a reversal is required here, but I do not subscribe to the newly enunciated doctrine of assessment of permanent damages, in lieu of an injunction, where substantial property rights have been impaired by the creation of a nuisance.

It has long been the rule in this State, as the majority acknowledges, that a nuisance which results in substantial continuing damage to neighbors must be enjoined.... To now change the rule to permit the cement company to continue polluting the air indefinitely upon the payment of permanent damages is, in my opinion, compounding the magnitude of a very serious problem in our State and Nation today.

In recognition of this problem, the Legislature of this State has enacted the Air Pollution Control Act declaring that it is the State policy to require the use of all available and reasonable methods to prevent and control air pollution (Public Health Law §1265[11]). The harmful nature and widespread occurrence of air pollution have been extensively documented. Congressional hearings have revealed that air pollution causes substantial property damage, as well as being a contributing factor to a rising incidence of lung cancer, emphysema, bronchitis and asthma.

The specific problem faced here is known as particulate contamination because of the fine dust particles emanating from defendant's cement plant. The particular type of nuisance is not new, having appeared in many cases for at least the past 60 years. It is interesting to note that cement production has recently been identified as a significant source of particulate contamination in the Hudson Valley. This type of pollution, wherein very small particles escape and stay in the atmosphere, has been denominated as the type of air pollution which produces the greatest hazard to human health. We have thus a nuisance which not only is damaging to the plaintiffs, but also is decidedly harmful to the general public.

I see grave dangers in overruling our long-established rule of granting an injunction where a nuisance results in substantial continuing damage. In permitting the injunction to become inoperative upon the payment of permanent damages, the majority is, in effect, licensing a continuing wrong. It is the same as saying to the cement company, you may continue to do harm to your neighbors so long as you pay a fee for it. Furthermore, once such permanent damages are assessed and paid, the incentive to alleviate the wrong would be eliminated, thereby continuing air pollution of an area without abatement....

---

[11] See also, Air Quality Act of 1967, 81 U.S. Stat. 485 (1967).

This kind of inverse condemnation . . . may not be invoked by a private person or corporation for private gain or advantage. Inverse condemnation should only be permitted when the public is primarily served in the taking or impairment of property. . . . The promotion of the interests of the polluting cement company has, in my opinion, no public use or benefit.

Nor is it constitutionally permissible to impose servitude on land, without consent of the owner, by payment of permanent damages where the continuing impairment of the land is for a private use. . . . This is made clear by the State Constitution (art. I, §7, subd. (a)) which provides that "(p)rivate property shall not be taken for *public* use without just compensation" (emphasis added). It is, of course, significant that the section makes no mention of taking for a *private* use.

In sum, then, by constitutional mandate as well as by judicial pronouncement, the permanent impairment of private property for private purposes is not authorized in the absence of clearly demonstrated public benefit and use.

I would enjoin the defendant cement company from continuing the discharge of dust particles upon its neighbors' properties unless, within 18 months, the cement company abated this nuisance.

It is not my intention to cause the removal of the cement plant from the Albany area, but to recognize the urgency of the problem stemming from this stationary source of air pollution, and to allow the company a specified period of time to develop a means to alleviate this nuisance.

I am aware that the trial court found that the most modern dust control devices available have been installed in defendant's plant, but, I submit, this does not mean that better and more effective dust control devices could not be developed within the time allowed to abate the pollution.

Moreover, I believe it is incumbent upon the defendant to develop such devices, since the cement company, at the time the plant commenced production (1962), was well aware of the plaintiffs' presence in the area, as well as the probable consequences of its contemplated operation. Yet, it still chose to build and operate the plant at this site.

In a day when there is a growing concern for clean air, highly developed industry should not expect acquiescence by the courts, but should, instead, plan its operations to eliminate contamination of our air and damage to its neighbors. . . .

■ POINTS TO CONSIDER

1. **Nuisance?** Was the cement plant in *Boomer* a nuisance at all? The court does not address that issue, because the defendant did not appeal the trial court's finding of nuisance, which was "based solely on the cement plant's substantial interference with the plaintiffs' use and enjoyment of their properties, without consideration of its utility." Jeff L. Lewin, Boomer *and the American Law of Nuisance: Past, Present, and Future*, 54 Alb. L. Rev. 189, 220 (1990). If a court applied the Restatement "balance of utilities" test to these facts, how do you think it would rule?

2. **Comparative institutional analysis.** The majority believes that this type of issue requires a legislative, rather than judicial, solution. What characteristics of this case factor into the decision regarding the proper forum? Are there any current issues of widespread harm you consider similar?

3. **Coase Theorem.** The Coase Theorem suggests that, in the absence of transaction costs, the parties will bargain to reach an efficient outcome regardless of the legal rule adopted.[12] In this case, the court could simply order an injunction, forcing the cement plant to pay the plaintiffs a sufficient amount to account for their damages. Certainly, if their damages are $185,000 and the value of the plant is $45 million, an amount between those two figures should adequately compensate the plaintiffs and avoid a plant shutdown. This approach avoids having the court attempt to assess the real harm to the plaintiff, including personhood harms, which are difficult to quantify. Why did the court reject that solution here? Why did the court use a liability rule here and a property rule in *Jacque v. Steenberg Homes*?

4. **Servitude.** Both the majority and the dissent consider the "right to pollute" granted to the cement plant to be the equivalent of a servitude (i.e., an easement) on the plaintiff's land. Does the analogy make sense to you? In what circumstances do we usually force landowners to grant easements involuntarily? Are those circumstances similar to the situation in this case?

5. **Other possible remedies.** The dissent urged the court to enjoin the nuisance unless the defendant took steps to abate the harm within 18 months. What problems do you see with this remedy?

Practice Tip: Thinking Like a Lawyer

Consider how important the potential remedy will be in advising your client. In our example of Alice's resort hotel and Bart's feedlot, what remedy do you think Alice will want? If she can obtain only damages, how should they be measured? If the damages are limited to the difference in property value, plaintiff may not recover enough to make the costs of litigation worthwhile. *See, e.g.*, Baldwin v. McClendon, 288 So. 2d 761 (Ala. 1974) (hog lot causing noxious odors that sickened neighbors could continue upon payment of $3,000, representing loss of property value); Behar v. Quaker Ridge Golf Club, Inc., 42 N.Y.S.3d 538 (N.Y. App. Div. 2016) (golf balls hit into backyard; loss in property value damages, $5,580). If you were plaintiff's lawyer, what would you argue is the proper measure of damages? If an injunction is granted, is there still an argument for damages as well?

---

[12] *See* Ronald Coase, The Firm, the Market, and the Law (Univ. of Chi. Press 1988).

F   PUBLIC NUISANCE

As we mentioned in the introduction, this chapter focuses on private nuisance as the primary common law restriction on land use. One significant limitation on private nuisance, however, is that it is *only* available to another *landowner*—the plaintiff must show an unreasonable interference with the use and enjoyment of her own land. The doctrine of *public nuisance*, however, is available for conduct that affects the public in general.

Assume that Cassie is an avid kayaker and she is appalled at the feedlot Bart is running on Whiteacre, which is polluting her favorite recreational river. Cassie could not maintain a private nuisance action against Bart, even though it is significantly affecting her use and enjoyment of the river, because it is not interfering with the use of her land.

Nevertheless, she might be able to maintain a *public nuisance* action against Bart, or convince the local authorities to do so. The Restatement defines a public nuisance as follows:

> (1) A public nuisance is an unreasonable interference with a right common to the general public.
>
> (2) Circumstances that may sustain a holding that an interference with a public right is unreasonable include the following:
>
> > (a) Whether the conduct involves a significant interference with the public health, the public safety, the public peace, the public comfort or the public convenience, or
> >
> > (b) whether the conduct is proscribed by a statute, ordinance or administrative regulation, or
> >
> > (c) whether the conduct is of a continuing nature or has produced a permanent or long-lasting effect, and, as the actor knows or has reason to know, has a significant effect upon the public right.

Restatement (Second) of Torts §821B (1979).

Public nuisance actions are often brought by government authorities. Municipalities are typically given broad authority, pursuant to their police power, to define what constitutes a public nuisance and to take abatement action. Abatement action could include not only going to court to seek injunctive relief, but also simply ordering landowners to clean up property or cease activity causing the nuisance. *See, e.g.,* City of S. Milwaukee v. Kester, 830 N.W.2d 710 (Wis. Ct. App. 2013) (sex offender violation of residential restrictions was public nuisance *per se*).

In fact, many courts hold that public nuisance actions may be brought *only* by governmental authorities, unless an individual plaintiff can show she suffered *special harm*, of a kind different from that suffered as a member of the general public. Burton v. Dominion Nuclear Conn., Inc., 23 A.3d 1176 (Conn. 2011) (plaintiff could not bring public nuisance claim against nuclear power plant because alleged harms were suffered by all members of public who used public lands); Hale v. Ward County, 848 N.W.2d 245 (N.D. 2014)(plaintiff could not bring public nuisance claim against shooting range; merely driving occasionally on road near shooting range did not constitute "special harm"); Restatement (Second) of Torts §821C (1979). Some modern courts are moving away from the special harm requirement, especially in cases seeking injunctive relief only. Otherwise, in many cases a public nuisance claim could be brought only by a public official. Does our friend Cassie the kayaker have a special harm that would allow her to sue for a public nuisance?

Litigants have recently used public nuisance law as a tool to achieve social reform goals. For example, in the area of *climate change*, plaintiffs have brought several cases alleging that the greenhouse gas emissions of the defendants (mostly large power plants) cause widespread harm to public health and welfare (for example, by contributing to the destruction of infrastructure, public lands, and the habitat of endangered species). The suits have attempted to obtain both damages for the harm caused and injunctive relief to abate the nuisance. Thus far, however, the suits have not been able to overcome significant roadblocks. *See, e.g.*, American Elec. Power Co. v. Connecticut, 564 U.S. 410 (2011) (federal common law of nuisance displaced by the Clean Air Act); Native Vill. of Kivalina v. ExxonMobil Corp., 696 F.3d 849 (9th Cir. 2012) (same; irrelevant whether suit seeks damages or injunctive relief).

Other novel uses of public nuisance theory involve litigation against firearms and lead paint manufacturers. *See, e.g.*, City of Chi. v. Beretta U.S.A. Corp., 821 N.E.2d 1099 (Ill. 2004) (dismissing public nuisance claim against gun manufacturer because no evidence that it carried out lawful act in unreasonable manner); KS&E Sports v. Runnels, 72 N.E.3d 892 (Ind. 2017) (public nuisance claim for the sale of firearms survived motion to dismiss); State v. Lead Indus. Ass'n, Inc., 951 A.2d 428 (R.I. 2008) (overturning public nuisance verdict against lead pigment manufacturers).[13]

Do you think courts should allow public nuisance law to be used in this manner? Why or why not? How would you distinguish these cases from other uses of public nuisance law?

SUMMARY

■ A *private nuisance* exists when a landowner creates a substantial, unreasonable, nontrespassory interference with the use and enjoyment of another's land.

■ The Restatement of Torts defines an unreasonable interference as one in which the gravity of the harm to the plaintiff outweighs the utility of the defendant's conduct. This *balance of utilities* analysis requires a court to weigh the suitability and social value of each party's land use.

---

[13] On December 16, 2013, a trial court in California ordered several lead paint manufacturers to pay $1.1 billion in damages on public nuisance grounds. California v. Atlantic Richfield Co., 1-00-CV-788657 (Cal. Super. Ct. Santa Clara).

- In contrast, many courts use the more traditional *substantial harm* approach, which focuses more on the degree of interference caused by the defendant, although social utility may be considered as a factor by some courts.

- The fact that a particular use is allowed by *zoning or restrictive covenants* does not automatically preclude a court from declaring the use a nuisance, although it may be good evidence of reasonableness. If a homeowners association has specifically dealt with a particular conflict, however, courts are reluctant to intervene.

- In deciding the remedy for a nuisance, courts have moved away from automatically granting an injunction. The Restatement suggests a *balancing of equities*, weighing the harm caused to the plaintiff if no injunction were granted against the harm to the defendant and the public if the use were to be enjoined.

- A *public nuisance* is an unreasonable interference with a right common to the general public. Such actions are often based on violations of statutes or local ordinances and are brought by public officials.

- Many courts do not allow private plaintiffs to bring public nuisance actions unless they can show *special harm*, different from that suffered by the general public.

- Recently, plaintiffs have brought public nuisance actions to achieve *social reform goals* in the areas of climate change, firearms, and lead paint, albeit with limited success.

CHAPTER 13

Legislative Land Use Control: An Introduction to Zoning

> We shape our buildings, and afterwards our buildings shape us.
> —*Winston Churchill*
>
> Cities have the capability of providing something for everybody, only because, and only when, they are created by everybody.
> —*Jane Jacobs, The Death and Life of Great American Cities 238 (1961)*

A INTRODUCTION

In the last chapter, the court in *Boomer* recognized that some problems involving incompatible land uses are more amenable to resolution through legislative control, which has some advantages over case-by-case adjudication. In general, the legislature is able to consider issues of proper land use more comprehensively, and sometimes may be able to prevent problems before they arise. Moreover, land use decisions made by legislative bodies are more democratic and usually are reached only after considering public input.

Therefore, the importance and breadth of legislative land use controls have greatly increased over the last century. Legislative controls range from federal protections of wetlands or endangered species, to state regulations on siting of landfills or power plants, to local ordinances prohibiting farm animals or open burning within city limits. These land use controls can be specific—directed at particular undesirable uses or activities—or general, such as subdivision and zoning regulations.

In this chapter, we introduce you to the most prevalent form of land use control—zoning. By understanding the basics of zoning, you will have a good grasp of a factor that plays a role in virtually every real estate deal. Moreover, you will also understand the balance between the public interest and the individual landowner inherent in all disputes involving land use control.

First, we will take you through a brief history of zoning, to give you some perspective. Next, you will learn about some of the constitutional limits on the government's ability to regulate how you use your land. Then we will work through the basics of zoning procedure, so you will understand the actors and issues involved. Finally, we focus on two of the most commonly litigated zoning issues: the variance and the nonconforming use.

B   A BRIEF HISTORY OF ZONING

Today, it is difficult to imagine a world before zoning controls. We tend to take these laws for granted now. Prospective purchasers of real estate, at least in urban areas, know to check the zoning classification of property they want to buy, to ensure that it corresponds to their plans.

But the widespread adoption (and acceptance) of comprehensive zoning ordinances is a relatively recent phenomenon. In fact, the idea that the government can tell you exactly what your land can be used for runs contrary to the American spirit of individualism. Moreover, as our study of *Village of Euclid v. Ambler Realty Co.*(below) will reveal, the constitutionality of intrusive government limitations on property use was initially in some doubt. In order to fully understand the significance of *Euclid* and gain some perspective on the issue, it is useful to briefly consider the history and origins of zoning in the United States.

At the turn of the twentieth century, *comprehensive* zoning ordinances, which designated the permissible uses of each parcel in the city limits, did not exist. Instead, cities had long employed narrowly focused, nuisance-type controls to separate the most noxious uses from residential or commercial areas. The Supreme Court noted in 1872 that the police power could certainly be used to protect the public from these harms:

> Unwholesome trades, slaughter-houses, operations offensive to the senses, the deposit of powder, the application of steam power to propel cars, the building with combustible materials, and the burial of the dead, may all," says Chancellor Kent, "be interdicted by law, in the midst of dense masses of population, on the general and rational principle, that every person ought so to use his property as not to injure his neighbors; and that private interests must be made subservient to the general interests of the community.

Slaughter-House Cases, 83 U.S. 36, 62 (1872) (quoting Chancellor James Kent, 2 Commentaries on American Law 340 (1826)).

Before the 1900s, cities were able to deal with incompatible land uses without a comprehensive approach, merely by targeting specific types of noxious uses. If a tannery or rendering plant caused unpleasant odors, the city could banish it to a rural area. If smoke began to irritate the residents, the city could enact smoke controls or ban certain types of fuel. In other words, rather than thinking holistically about what uses of land should go where, cities simply reacted to the most significant problems as they arose.

By the early 1900s, however, the desire for more comprehensive *urban planning* began to grow. City planning allows officials not only to separate conflicting uses to the extent possible, but also to design efficient and aesthetically pleasing communities. For example, planners can ensure that industries are located near railways and highways, and away from urban areas, so that big trucks don't rumble through residential streets. If officials know where concentrations of people will live, they can plan for the schools, libraries, water, sewer, fire, and police protection those residents will need. They can ensure that adequate shopping is located nearby and that transportation routes are sufficient to avoid gridlock.

A city plan, however, is of little value unless it is implemented by ordinances restricting the uses that can be made of land in particular areas. Thus, good urban planning includes comprehensive zoning—the designation of districts restricted to particular kinds of property use, such as residential, commercial, or industrial. In addition to zoning ordinances, *subdivision ordinances* mandate the details of new housing developments, such as streets, sidewalks, sewers, and streetlights.

The twentieth-century push for comprehensive planning resulted from the confluence of a number of historical developments. Think about how these factors contributed:

- The *advent of skyscrapers* allowed a much greater concentration of people to work and live in a smaller space, increasing urban conflicts. In 1885, the Home Insurance Building in Chicago stretched to nine stories; in 1890, the New York World (Pulitzer) building more than doubled that size and took the title of tallest building. Many other skyscrapers, such as New York's Manhattan Life Insurance, Flatiron, and American Surety buildings, were all completed in this era.

- *City populations were exploding.* Between 1860 and 1910, the number of Americans living in cities increased almost seven-fold, while the number of cities with over 50,000 inhabitants grew from 16 to 109. In just one decade (1860-1870), the population of Chicago more than doubled.[1] The increased population, which resulted from increased immigration and movement from rural areas, often crowded into substandard tenement housing.

---

[1] Richard Hofstadter, The Age of Reform: From Bryan to F.D.R. 173 (1st ed. 1955).

- In the *Progressive era* (1890-1920), society placed more faith in the ability of government and professionals to solve a wide range of social problems, such as slums and traffic congestion.
- Urban planners began to push the *City Beautiful*, the idea that planning could not only deal with social ills, but could also make cities aesthetically pleasant places in which to live and work.

Skyscraper History

Skyscrapers began to be built in the late 1800s due to several developments.

- Elevators had become much safer and were now powered by electricity. (Can you imagine skyscrapers with stairs?)
- Advances in structural steel manufacture improved building materials.
- Engineering developments solved issues of load-bearing capacity of taller buildings.
- Land prices made building up, instead of out, more desirable.

Imagine your house next to a three-story office building. Now imagine your house next to the Woolworth Building. As you can see, skyscrapers helped bring the issue of incompatible land uses to a head.

Woolworth Building, c.1913
Library of Congress

In 1916, New York City adopted the first city-wide regulation of tall buildings, and its provisions began to be copied elsewhere. In 1926, the concept of comprehensive planning and zoning was immensely furthered by the publication of a Standard State Zoning Enabling Act (SSZEA),[2] developed by an advisory committee appointed by Secretary of Commerce (later President) Herbert Hoover. The

---

[2] American Law Inst., Standard State Zoning Enabling Act, *reprinted in* Model Land Dev. Code 210 (Tent. Draft No. 1, 1968) (hereinafter SSZEA).

SSZEA made it relatively easy for states to delegate authority over planning and zoning to their municipal governments.

In the courts, however, zoning was receiving mixed reviews. For example, in Goldman v. Crowther, 128 A. 50 (Md. 1925), the Maryland Court of Appeals struck down Baltimore's comprehensive zoning ordinance. In that case, Daniel Goldman used the basement of his four-story house as a tailor shop, repairing used clothing by hand and with a sewing machine. The City of Baltimore, however, prohibited such commercial use in a residential zone, much like a typical zoning ordinance today. The court held that such a blanket restriction on all commercial uses could not be justified under the police power:

> [The zoning law's] only apparent purpose was to prevent the encroachment of business establishments of any kind upon residential territory, regardless of whether they affected in any degree the public health, morals, safety, or welfare. In effecting that purpose they take from the property owner the right to use his property for any purpose not sanctioned by the letter of the ordinance or allowed by the practically unfettered discretion of the board of zoning appeals, and deprive him of privileges guaranteed by article 23 of the Maryland Bill of Rights.

Id. at 60.

Similarly, the Supreme Court of Texas struck down Dallas's zoning ordinance in Spann v. City of Dallas, 235 S.W. 513 (Tex. 1921). Spann bought a lot, intending to use it for commercial purposes. However, the lot was later zoned residential, reducing its value from $8,500 to $4,500. The court held that, while private property rights can be limited by the police power, there was no justification for restricting lawful, inoffensive uses of property:

> The ordinance takes no heed of the character of business to be conducted in the store house which it condemns. It disregards utterly the fact that the business may be legitimate, altogether lawful, in no way harmful and even serve the convenience of the neighborhood. Its prohibition is absolute.
>
> ... The ordinance visits upon ordinary retail stores, engaged in a useful business, conducted in an orderly manner, frequented and availed of by respectable people, and doubtless serving as a convenience to many, all the proscription visited upon common nuisances.
>
> ... But it is not the law of this land that a man may be deprived of the lawful use of his property because his tastes are not in accord with those of his neighbors. The law is that he may use it as he chooses, regardless of their tastes, if in its use he does not harm them.

Id. at 514-16. *See also* Ignaciunas v. Risley, 121 A. 783 (N.J. 1923) (police power cannot support zoning imposing blanket ban of stores from residential areas).

These state court decisions set the stage for a constitutional challenge in the United States Supreme Court.

CONSTITUTIONAL ISSUES: *VILLAGE OF EUCLID v. AMBLER REALTY CO.*

The zoning case that found its way to the Court in 1926 involved the Village of Euclid, a suburb of Cleveland, Ohio. Feeling development pressure from the nearby big city, Euclid adopted a comprehensive zoning ordinance, involving a set of use, height, and area restrictions not much different from modern zoning provisions. The constitutional challenge to this ordinance became the most famous zoning case in American history—Village of Euclid v. Ambler Realty Co., 272 U.S. 365 (1926).

The background of the *Euclid* case includes some behind-the-scenes drama.[3] While initially arguing that all comprehensive zoning was unconstitutional, at oral argument the attorney for Ambler Realty adopted a more moderate position emphasizing the unfairness and impact on the landowner in this particular case. The attorney for the Village of Euclid, James Metzenbaum, worried as he took the train home to Cleveland from Washington, D.C., that his opponent's argument had persuaded the Court. As the train wound its way through a snowstorm, the time for motions was running out. Metzenbaum was able to throw a note out the window to a railroad workman, asking for a telegram to be sent to the Supreme Court requesting permission to file a reply brief.[4] The telegram got through in time and the request was granted, perhaps changing the course of zoning history!

After both sides filed reply briefs, the Supreme Court took the unusual step of asking the parties to re-argue the case. One account suggests that Alfred Bettman, a friend of Chief Justice Taft's, wanted to file an amicus brief on behalf of the National Conference of City Planning, and a re-argument would give him that opportunity. Bettman's brief turned out to be very influential. *See* Timothy Alan Fluck, Euclid v. Ambler: *A Retrospective*, 52 J. Am. Plan. Ass'n 326, 332 (1986).

Another account, by Justice Stone's law clerk at the time, suggested that Justice Sutherland was in the process of writing an opinion that would have declared Euclid's zoning unconstitutional, but began to be shaken in his conviction by the arguments of other justices. Since Sutherland had been absent at the first oral argument, he wanted an opportunity to hear both sides. Alfred McCormack, *A Law Clerk's Recollection*, 46 Colum. L. Rev. 710, 712 (1946).

In any event, after the second oral argument, the Supreme Court issued the following opinion *upholding the concept of comprehensive zoning*. As you read this landmark decision, consider how close the Court came, it seems, to the opposite result. If it had, what impact would that have had on what the United States looks like today, and on our daily lives? Consider, too, whether this decision means that *all* zoning is constitutional, or whether potential challenges remain.

---

[3] For a fascinating account of the history of zoning and *Euclid, see* Michael Allan Wolf, The Zoning of America: *Euclid v. Ambler* (2008).
[4] *Id.* at 1-2.

VILLAGE OF EUCLID v. AMBLER REALTY CO.

272 U.S. 365 (1926)
Supreme Court of the United States

Mr. Justice SUTHERLAND delivered the opinion of the Court.

The village of Euclid is an Ohio municipal corporation. It adjoins and practically is a suburb of the city of Cleveland. Its estimated population is between 5,000 and 10,000, and its area from 12 to 14 square miles, the greater part of which is farm lands or unimproved acreage. It lies, roughly, in the form of a parallelogram measuring approximately 3 ½ miles each way....

Appellee is the owner of a tract of land containing 68 acres, situated in the westerly end of the village, abutting on Euclid Avenue to the south and the Nickel Plate Railroad to the north. Adjoining this tract, both on the east and on the west, there have been laid out restricted residential plats upon which residences have been erected.

On November 13, 1922, an ordinance was adopted by the village council, establishing a comprehensive zoning plan for regulating and restricting the location of trades, industries, apartment houses, two-family houses, single family houses, etc., the lot area to be built upon, the size and height of buildings, etc.

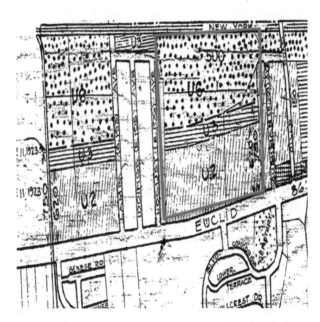

The original 1922 Euclid Village zoning map shows Ambler Realty's property just right of center, above Euclid Avenue, marked by the red box.

The entire area of the village is divided by the ordinance into six classes of use districts, denominated U-1 to U-6, inclusive; three classes of height districts, denominated H-1 to H-3, inclusive; and four classes of area districts, denominated A-1 to A-4, inclusive. The use districts are classified in respect of the buildings which may be erected within their respective limits, as follows: U-1 is restricted to single family dwellings, public parks [and similar uses]; U-2 is extended to include two-family dwellings; U-3 is further extended to include apartment houses, hotels, [and similar multi-family or group uses]; U-4 is further extended to include banks, offices, [and other commercial uses]; U-5 is further extended to include . . . warehouses, [and other light industrial uses]; U-6 is further extended to include plants for sewage disposal and for producing gas, [and other heavy industrial] and manufacturing and industrial operations of any kind other than, and any public utility not included in, a class U-1, U-2, U-3, U-4, or U-5 use. There is a seventh class of uses which is prohibited altogether.

Class U-1 is the only district in which buildings are restricted to those enumerated. In the other classes the uses are cumulative—that is to say, uses in class U-2 include those enumerated in the preceding class U-1; class U-3 includes uses enumerated in the preceding classes, U-2, and U-1; and so on. In addition to the enumerated uses, the ordinance provides for accessory uses; that is, for uses customarily incident to the principal use, such as private garages. Many regulations are provided in respect of such accessory uses.

The height districts are classified as follows: In class H-1, buildings are limited to a height of 2 ½ stories, or 35 feet; in class H-2, to 4 stories, or 50 feet; in class H-3, to 80 feet. To all of these, certain exceptions are made, as in the case of church spires, water tanks, etc.

The classification of area districts is: In A-1 districts, dwellings or apartment houses to accommodate more than one family must have at least 5,000 square feet for interior lots and at least 4,000 square feet for corner lots; in A-2 districts, the area must be at least 2,500 square feet for interior lots, and 2,000 square feet for corner lots; in A-3 districts, the limits are 1,250 and 1,000 square feet, respectively; in A-4 districts, the limits are 900 and 700 square feet, respectively. The ordinance contains, in great variety and detail, provisions in respect of width of lots, front, side, and rear yards, and other matters, including restrictions and regulations as to the use of billboards, signboards, and advertising signs. . . .

Appellee's tract of land comes under U-2, U-3 and U-6. The first strip of 620 feet immediately north of Euclid Avenue falls in class U-2, the next 130 feet to the north, in U-3, and the remainder in U-6. The uses of the first 620 feet, therefore, do not include apartment houses, hotels, churches, schools, or other public and semipublic buildings, or other uses enumerated in respect of U-3 to U-6, inclusive. The uses of the next 130 feet include all of these, but exclude industries, theaters, banks, shops, and the various other uses set forth in respect of U-4 to U-6, inclusive. . . .

The enforcement of the ordinance is intrusted to the inspector of buildings, under rules and regulations of the board of zoning appeals. Meetings of the board are public, and minutes of its proceedings are kept. It is authorized to adopt rules and regulations to carry into effect provisions of the ordinance. Decisions of the inspector of buildings may be appealed to the board by any person claiming to be adversely affected by any such decision. The board is given power in specific cases of practical difficulty or unnecessary hardship to interpret the ordinance in harmony with its general purpose and intent, so that the public health, safety and general welfare may be secure and substantial justice done. . . .

The ordinance is assailed on the grounds that it is in derogation of section 1 of the Fourteenth Amendment to the federal Constitution in that it deprives appellee of liberty and property without due process of law and denies it the equal protection of the law, and that it offends against certain provisions of the Constitution of the state of Ohio. The prayer of the bill is for an injunction restraining the enforcement of the ordinance and all attempts to impose or maintain as to appellee's property any of the restrictions, limitations or conditions. The court below held the ordinance to be unconstitutional and void, and enjoined its enforcement, 297 F. 307.

Before proceeding to a consideration of the case, it is necessary to determine the scope of the inquiry. The bill alleges that the tract of land in question is vacant and has been held for years for the purpose of selling and developing it for industrial uses, for which it is especially adapted, being immediately in the path or progressive industrial development; that for such uses it has a market value of about $10,000 per acre, but if the use be limited to residential purposes the market value is not in excess of $2,500 per acre; that the first 200 feet of the parcel back from Euclid Avenue, if unrestricted in respect of use, has a value of $150 per front foot, but if limited to residential uses, and ordinary mercantile business be excluded therefrom, its value is not in excess of $50 per front foot.

It is specifically averred that the ordinance attempts to restrict and control the lawful uses of appellee's land, so as to confiscate and destroy a great part of its value; that it is being enforced in accordance with its terms; that prospective buyers of land for industrial, commercial, and residential uses in the metropolitan district of Cleveland are deterred from buying any part of this land because of the existence of the ordinance and the necessity thereby entailed of conducting burdensome and expensive litigation in order to vindicate the right to use the land for lawful and legitimate purposes; that the ordinance constitutes a cloud upon the land, reduces and destroys its value, and has the effect of diverting the normal industrial, commercial, and residential development thereof to other and less favorable locations.

The record goes no farther than to show, as the lower court found, that the normal and reasonably to be expected use and development of that part of appellee's land adjoining Euclid Avenue is for general trade and commercial purposes, particularly retail stores and like establishments, and that the normal and reasonably to be expected use and development of the residue of the land is for industrial and trade purposes. Whatever injury is inflicted by the mere existence and threatened enforcement of the ordinance is due to restrictions in respect of these and similar uses, to which perhaps should be added—if not included in the foregoing—restrictions in respect of apartment houses. . . .

We proceed, then, to a consideration of those provisions of the ordinance to which the case as it is made relates, first disposing of a preliminary matter.

A motion was made in the court below to dismiss the bill on the ground that, because complainant (appellee) had made no effort to obtain a building permit or apply to the zoning board of appeals for relief, as it might have done under the terms of the ordinance, the suit was premature. The motion was properly overruled, the effect of the allegations of the bill is that the ordinance of its own force operates greatly to reduce the value of appellee's lands and destroy their marketability for industrial, commercial and residential uses, and the attack is directed, not against any specific provision or provisions, but against the ordinance as an entirety. . . .

It is not necessary to set forth the provisions of the Ohio Constitution which are thought to be infringed. The question is the same under both Constitutions, namely, as stated by appellee: Is the ordinance invalid, in that it violates the constitutional protection "to the right of property in the appellee by attempted regulations under the guise of the police power, which are unreasonable and confiscatory"?

Building zone laws are of modern origin. They began in this country about 25 years ago. Until recent years, urban life was comparatively simple; but, with the great increase and concentration of population, problems have developed, and constantly are developing, which require, and will continue to require, additional restrictions in respect of the use and occupation of private lands in urban communities. Regulations, the wisdom, necessity, and validity of which, as applied to existing conditions, are so apparent that they are now uniformly sustained, a century ago, or even half a century ago, probably would have been rejected as arbitrary and oppressive. Such regulations are sustained, under the complex conditions of our day, for reasons analogous to those which justify traffic regulations, which, before the advent of automobiles and rapid transit street railways, would have been condemned as fatally arbitrary and unreasonable. And in this there is no inconsistency, for, while the meaning of constitutional guaranties never varies, the scope of their application must expand or contract to meet the new and different conditions which are constantly coming within the field of their operation. In a changing world it is impossible that it should be otherwise. But although a degree of elasticity is thus imparted, not to the meaning, but to the application of constitutional principles, statutes and ordinances, which, after giving due weight to the new conditions, are found clearly not to conform to the Constitution, of course, must fall.

The ordinance now under review, and all similar laws and regulations, must find their justification in some aspect of the police power, asserted for the public welfare. The line which in this field separates the legitimate from the illegitimate assumption of power is not capable of precise delimitation. It varies with circumstances and conditions. A regulatory zoning ordinance, which would be clearly valid as applied to the great cities, might be clearly invalid as applied to rural communities. In solving doubts, the maxim "sic utere tuo ut alienum non laedas," which lies at the foundation of so much of the common law of nuisances, ordinarily will furnish a fairly helpful clew. And the law of nuisances, likewise, may be consulted, not for the purpose of controlling, but for the helpful aid of its analogies in the process of ascertaining the scope of, the power. Thus the question whether the power exists to forbid the erection of a building of a particular kind or for a particular use, like the question whether a particular thing is a nuisance, is to be determined, not by an abstract consideration of the building or of the thing considered apart, but by considering it in connection with the circumstances and the locality. Sturgis v. Bridgeman, L. R. 11 Ch. 852, 865. A nuisance may be merely a right thing in the wrong place, like a pig in the parlor instead of the barnyard. If the validity of the legislative classification for zoning purposes be fairly debatable, the legislative judgment must be allowed to control. Radice v. New York, 264 U.S. 292, 294.

There is no serious difference of opinion in respect of the validity of laws and regulations fixing the height of buildings within reasonable limits, the character of materials and methods of construction, and the adjoining area which must be left open, in order to minimize the danger of fire or collapse, the evils of overcrowding and the like, and excluding from residential sections offensive trades, industries and structures likely to create nuisances. . . .

Here, however, the exclusion is in general terms of all industrial establishments, and it may thereby happen that not only offensive or dangerous industries will be excluded, but those which are neither offensive nor dangerous will share the same fate. But this is no more than happens in respect of many practice-forbidding laws which this court has upheld, although drawn in general terms so as to include individual cases that may turn out to be innocuous in themselves. Hebe Co. v. Shaw, 248 U.S. 297, 303; Pierce Oil Corp. v. City of Hope, 248 U.S. 498, 500. The inclusion of a reasonable margin, to insure effective enforcement, will not put upon a law, otherwise valid, the stamp of invalidity. Such laws may also find their justification in the fact that, in some fields, the bad fades into the good by such insensible degrees that the two are not capable of being readily distinguished and separated in terms of legislation. In the light of these considerations, we are not prepared to say that the end in view was not sufficient to justify the general rule of the ordinance, although some industries of an innocent character might fall within the proscribed class. . . .

It is said that the village of Euclid is a mere suburb of the city of Cleveland; that the industrial development of that city has now reached and in some degree extended into the village, and in the obvious course of things will soon absorb the entire area for industrial enterprises; that the effect of the ordinance is to divert this natural development elsewhere, with the consequent loss of increased values to the owners of the lands within the village borders. But the village, though physically a suburb of Cleveland, is politically a separate municipality, with powers of its own and authority to govern itself as it sees fit, within the limits of the organic law of its creation and the state and federal Constitutions. Its governing authorities, presumably representing a majority of its inhabitants and voicing their will, have determined, not that industrial development shall cease at its boundaries, but that the course of such development shall proceed within definitely fixed lines. If it be a proper exercise of the police power to relegate industrial establishments to localities separated from residential sections, it is not easy to find a sufficient reason for denying the power because the effect of its exercise is to divert an industrial flow from the course which it would follow, to the injury of the residential public, if left alone, to another course where such injury will be obviated. It is not meant by this, however, to exclude the possibility of cases where the general public interest would so far outweigh the interest of the municipality that the municipality would not be allowed to stand in the way.

We find no difficulty in sustaining restrictions of the kind thus far reviewed. The serious question in the case arises over the provisions of the ordinance excluding from residential districts apartment houses, business houses, retail stores and shops, and other like establishments. This question involves the validity of what is really the crux of the more recent zoning legislation, namely, the creation and maintenance of residential districts, from which business and trade of every sort, including hotels and apartment houses, are excluded. Upon that question this court has not thus far spoken. The decisions of the state courts are numerous and conflicting; but those which broadly sustain the power greatly outnumber those which deny it altogether or narrowly limit it, and it is very apparent that there is a constantly increasing tendency in the direction of the broader view. . . .

The matter of zoning has received much attention at the hands of commissions and experts, and the results of their investigations have been set forth in comprehensive reports. These reports which bear every evidence of painstaking consideration, concur in the view that the segregation of residential, business and industrial buildings will make it easier to provide fire apparatus suitable for the character and intensity of the development in each section; that it will increase the safety and security of home life, greatly tend to prevent street accidents, especially to children, by reducing the traffic and resulting confusion in residential sections, decrease noise and other conditions which produce or intensify nervous disorders, preserve a more favorable environment in which to rear children, etc. With particular reference to apartment houses, it is pointed out that the development of detached house sections is greatly retarded by the coming of apartment houses, which has sometimes resulted in destroying the entire section for private house purposes; that in such sections very often the apartment house is a mere parasite, constructed in order to take advantage of the open spaces and attractive surroundings created by the residential character of the district. Moreover, the coming of one apartment house is followed by others, interfering by their height and bulk with the free circulation of air and monopolizing the rays of the sun which otherwise would fall upon the smaller homes, and bringing, as their necessary accompaniments, the disturbing noises incident to increased traffic and business, and the occupation, by means of moving and parked automobiles, of larger portions of the streets, thus detracting from their safety and depriving children of the privilege of quiet and open spaces for play, enjoyed by those in more favored localities—until, finally, the residential character of the neighborhood and its desirability as a place of detached residences are utterly destroyed. Under these circumstances, apartment houses, which in a different environment would be not only entirely unobjectionable but highly desirable, come very near to being nuisances.

If these reasons, thus summarized, do not demonstrate the wisdom or sound policy in all respects of those restrictions which we have indicated as pertinent to the inquiry, at least, the reasons are sufficiently cogent to preclude us from saying, as it must be said before the ordinance can be declared unconstitutional, that such provisions are clearly arbitrary and unreasonable, having no substantial relation to the public health, safety, morals, or general welfare. . . .

It is true that when, if ever, the provisions set forth in the ordinance in tedious and minute detail, come to be concretely applied to particular premises, including those of the appellee, or to particular conditions, or to be considered in connection with specific complaints, some of them, or even many of them, may be found to be clearly arbitrary and unreasonable. But where the equitable remedy of injunction is sought, as it is here, not upon the ground of a present infringement or denial of a specific right, or of a particular injury in process of actual execution, but upon the broad ground that the mere existence and threatened enforcement of the ordinance, by materially and adversely affecting values and curtailing the opportunities of the market, constitute a present and irreparable injury, the court will not scrutinize its provisions, sentence by sentence, to ascertain by a process of piecemeal dissection whether there may be, here and there, provisions of a minor character, or relating to matters of administration, or not shown to contribute to the injury complained of, which, if attacked separately, might not withstand the test of constitutionality. . . . Under these circumstances, therefore, it is enough for us to determine, as we do, that the ordinance in its general scope and dominant features, so far as its provisions are here involved, is a valid exercise of authority, leaving other provisions to be dealt with as cases arise directly involving them. . . .

Decree reversed.

Mr. Justice VAN DEVANTER, Mr. Justice MCREYNOLDS, and Mr. Justice BUTLER dissent.

■ POINTS TO CONSIDER

1. **Policy.** The background of *Euclid* indicates that the constitutionality of comprehensive zoning was in significant doubt. The lower court, after all, had ruled the ordinance unconstitutional, and some accounts indicate that the majority of Supreme Court justices leaned in the same direction. Justice Sutherland, in fact, was part of a conservative group of justices known as the Four Horsemen (including the three dissenters in *Euclid*) who opposed much of Franklin Roosevelt's New Deal legislation. What policy reasons would cause a noted conservative jurist to decide that this degree of government intrusion into private property rights was permissible?

2. **Substantive due process.** You may not have had Constitutional Law yet. The *Euclid* decision rests on the Due Process Clause of the Constitution found in the Fourteenth Amendment: "nor shall any State deprive any person of life, liberty, or property, without due process of law" (the Fifth Amendment applies the same restriction to the federal government). The Supreme Court has interpreted "due process" to require that every law bear a rational relationship to a legitimate governmental purpose. This is called the *substantive due process* test because it is focused on the content of the law. By contrast, *procedural due process* is focused on the fairness of the process, such as providing adequate notice and an opportunity to be heard. What is the legitimate governmental interest put forward by the Village of Euclid here? What is the argument of Ambler Realty that the zoning scheme does not meet the substantive due process test?

3. **Facial versus as-applied challenges.** The Court emphasized that its decision upholding the validity of comprehensive zoning was limited to a *facial* challenge to the ordinance at issue. The Court left open the possibility that the ordinance might be found unconstitutionally arbitrary and unreasonable *as applied* to a particular property. Yet, the Supreme Court had evidence that the ordinance as applied to Amber Realty's property would significantly reduce its property value, and that residential use was already established on similarly situated surrounding properties. Given that, what sort of case might fail an "as applied" challenge? Just two years after *Euclid*, in Nectow v. City of Cambridge, 277 U.S. 183 (1928), the Court struck down a zoning ordinance as applied to particular property. The ordinance placed a small strip of plaintiff's property in a residential zone, which the master (a person appointed to review the situation) determined left the land with "no practical use." *Id.* at 187. Justice Sutherland again wrote the (very brief) opinion, which rested upon a finding of the master "that the health, safety, convenience, and general welfare of the inhabitants of the part of the city affected will not be promoted by the disposition made by the ordinance of the locus in question." *Id.* at 188. Does *Nectow* suggest that Amber Realty could win an as-applied challenge with respect to its property? Does *Nectow* mean that a city will have to show, for each restricted lot, that the prohibited uses would impact the public's health, safety or welfare in some way?

4. **The rest of the story.** The Village of Euclid has now grown from a hamlet of between 5,000 to 10,000 population at the time of this case to a town of 49,000 people, according to the 2010 census. The "farm lands and unimproved acreage" the Court describes have long since disappeared. The Village thus has experienced just the sort of growth the ordinance was adopted to manage. Things do not always go according to plan, however. The attorney for the Village of Euclid, James Metzenbaum, lived on Euclid Avenue himself, and envisioned that it would become a quiet, residential boulevard. Nevertheless, market forces had other ideas—several years after the Supreme Court's decision, Ambler Realty's land was rezoned for industrial use. The site is now

the home of a variety of commercial and industrial uses. Garrett Power, *The Advent of Zoning*, 4 Plan. Persp. 10 (1989). Does the inability of Euclid's city planners to create a residential boulevard affect your view of the efficacy of zoning?

5. **Zoning today.** After *Euclid*, assisted by the SSZEA, comprehensive zoning spread throughout the country. Today, every major city in the United States (with the exception of Houston), and the vast majority of smaller cities, have a comprehensive zoning ordinance. Outside of city limits, many counties have zoning, although you can find many rural counties that do not. Houston provides an interesting illustration of how communities might have dealt with the situation had *Euclid* come out the other way. While the city does not have a comprehensive zoning ordinance delineating single-use districts, it does have ordinances regulating development (e.g., lot size, minimum parking requirements, street size). In addition, developers rely on private covenants to protect neighborhoods from commercial or industrial intrusion.

▓ PROBLEMS: SUBSTANTIVE DUE PROCESS AND ZONING

1. **Zoning out manufactured homes.** Coweta County adopted an ordinance prohibiting the placement of manufactured homes on property in any residential zone. Manufactured housing could be used only in mobile home parks. Cannon purchased a one-acre residential lot, on which he applied for permission to build a manufactured house, which he claimed would be as aesthetically pleasing and safe as a site-built house. After the county denied his application, he sued, claiming that the restriction violated substantive due process. Can the County justify this restriction under the police power? What result under *Euclid* and *Nectow*? *Compare* Cannon v. Coweta Cnty., 389 S.E.2d 329 (Ga. 1990) (striking down ordinance as unconstitutional), *with* King v. City of Bainbridge, 577 S.E.2d 772 (Ga. 2003) (overruling *Cannon*).

2. **No permitted uses zone.** The Town of Rhine established an area zoned B-2, which allowed no uses as of right—all uses were deemed "conditional," and the owner had to apply for a conditional use permit for any proposed use, which had to be approved by the town's Plan Commission. The Off-Highway Vehicle Club purchased 80 acres of land it intended to use for all-terrain vehicle (ATV) recreation and hunting. The Club was issued a conditional use permit that allowed ATV activity only on Wednesdays and Fridays until 6 P.M. (i.e., no evenings, weekends, or holidays, when club members most wanted to ride). The Club challenged the B-2 zone as arbitrary and unrelated to any permissible governmental interest. Conditional use permits have been repeatedly upheld as a zoning device, but can the Town make all uses in a zone conditional? *See* Town of Rhine v. Bizzell, 751 N.W.2d 780 (Wis. 2008).

3. **Large lot zoning.** Jaylin bought an 18-acre parcel of undeveloped land in the town of Moreland, on which he intended to build 29 houses on half-acre lots. Moreland's zoning ordinance required two-acre minimum lots in this district due to deep ravines and steep slopes. Jaylin challenged the requirement as arbitrary and unrelated to a legitimate governmental purpose. He pointed out that his half-acre development would be designed to have no more adverse impact on the environment than two-acre lots. In addition, he presented evidence that there was no market for two-acre lots in this area of town because many surrounding houses were older, less expensive, and built on smaller lots. Should Jaylin win an as-applied challenge? *Jaylin Invs., Inc. v. Moreland Hills,* 839 N.E.2d 903 (Ohio 2006).

The Downsides of Zoning

We understand that, after *Euclid,* comprehensive zoning is an established and accepted concept. Justice Sutherland did a good job of detailing the advantages of zoning. Can you list them?

Nevertheless, before we move on, it is useful to consider whether there are disadvantages to *Euclid* and the triumph of comprehensive zoning. Understanding the disadvantages to this approach may help us—as lawyers, judges, legislators, or simply citizens—to avoid some of its pitfalls. Which, if any, of the following concern you?

- **Interference with market.** Our system uses the free market to allocate resources such as land, to ensure they get to the "highest and best use." If the market values land along Euclid Avenue more highly for commercial use than residential use, is it better to trust the market, rather than city officials, to determine the best use of that land?
- **Environmental impacts.** What are the consequences of completely separating industrial, commercial, and residential uses? Would you walk to a neighborhood café or tailor?
- **Barriers to entry for small business.** Think about Goldman, the tailor. Now that he can't use his house for his business, what increased costs does he face? What other small businesses might be affected by prohibiting commercial uses in residential areas?
- **Discrimination.** Giving local boards power to decide how property can be used opens up the potential for unequal treatment and favoritism. A local developer might get a variance while one from out of town may not. In addition, zoning may allow economic segregation (minimum lot-size restrictions, for example, may keep out lower-income buyers).
- **Spillover effects.** The Court in *Euclid* was sympathetic to the Village's effort to protect itself from the "natural flow" of industrial activity coming from Cleveland. However, by limiting the space available

to industry, what effect does Euclid's action have on other nearby suburbs?

Is it possible for zoning law or judicial review to ameliorate any of these zoning downsides?

Other Constitutional Issues

Although courts today are very deferential to zoning ordinances, and the general validity of comprehensive zoning is no longer in question, many other constitutional issues are implicated by zoning decisions. We will save most of those issues for Constitutional Law classes or upper-level courses in land use law. Nevertheless, we will give you some examples of how zoning ordinances might present other kinds of *constitutional problems*:

- **First Amendment: Religion.** Suppose a church wants to locate in a residential zone that prohibits public meeting places; does that zoning restriction impermissibly burden the free exercise of religion? *See* Maum Meditation House of Truth v. Lake County, Ill., 55 F.Supp.3d 1081 (N.D. Ill. 2014)(content-neutral restrictions on meeting places upheld).What if the city prohibits animal sacrifices, central to the Santeria faith, in most areas of the city? Church of the Lukumi Babalu Aye, Inc. v. City of Hialeah, 508 U.S. 520 (1993).
- **First Amendment: Speech.** Can a city prohibit the display of political signs in residential zones to eliminate "clutter"? City of Ladue v. Gilleo, 512 U.S. 43 (1994). Could it at least limit the duration of such displays to the period before an election? Painesville Bldg. Dep't v. Dworken & Bernstein Co., 733 N.E.2d 1152 (Ohio 2000). Do prohibitions on "adult entertainment" venues violate freedom of expression? MJJG Restaurant, LLC v. Horry County, S.C., 11 F.Supp.3d 541 (D. S.C. 2014) (upholding adult entertainment zoning against first amendment challenge).
- **Fourteenth Amendment: Equal protection.** Zoning officials must be evenhanded in enacting and applying land use controls. To prevail on equal protection grounds, a claimant must show that similarly situated persons received disparate treatment, and that the disparate treatment did not bear a rational relationship to a legitimate government purpose. Stricter scrutiny will be used for claims of disparate treatment involving a "suspect class" such as race, national origin, or religion, or those involving fundamental rights. For example:
  - ☐ Village of Willowbrook v. Olech, 528 U.S. 562 (2000). Olech stated a claim for violation of equal protection when the Village demanded a 33-foot easement for her water hookup instead of the 15-foot easement normally demanded.

☐ Chabad of Nova, Inc. v. City of Cooper City, 575 F. Supp. 2d 1280 (S.D. Fla. 2008). Chabad entered into a lease of a store in a shopping center, intending to use it for a Jewish Orthodox Chabad Outreach Center, serving nearby college students. City claimed this violated its prohibition on religious assembly uses in a business district. Using strict scrutiny, court held that this prohibition violated equal protection. Similar uses were allowed in the business zone and City could not justify the difference.

▪ **Fifth Amendment: Takings.** The most significant limitation on land use regulation is the Takings Clause of the Fifth Amendment, which prohibits regulations that deprive owners of their property—either directly or indirectly—without just compensation. In other words, if the Village of Euclid ordinance had made it impossible for Ambler Realty to make any valuable use of its property, the Constitution probably would require the government to compensate the company for its loss. We will consider that complex issue in depth in Chapter 14.

D   THE ZONING PROCESS

Every lawyer who deals in land use issues must have a fundamental understanding of the zoning process. Although there are many state variations, the basic structure of the process is typically based on the State City Planning Enabling Act, published in 1928, and the Standard State Zoning Enabling Act (SSZEA) of 1924. We will describe that structure, but you should understand that your state may use a slightly different process, with different terms or governmental bodies. We will use the term *city* or *municipality*, but the process is usually similar at the county or township level.

Comprehensive Planning

The zoning process begins with the development of a comprehensive plan for the area. The plan is a policy document that sets out the community's long-term goals and strategies for achieving them. Thus, it attempts to forecast future growth and how to accommodate it. The process addresses issues such as transportation and public services (including schools, fire protection, police, sewers, and utilities). For example, planners may consider questions such as:

▪ As the population grows, will we need more parks and recreation areas? Where should they go?
▪ How can we revitalize the deteriorating inner city?
▪ Should we expand our public transportation system and if so, how?

As you can see, these issues go far beyond zoning, but certainly mapping out areas where residential, commercial, and industrial growth would be best accommodated is a central part of the comprehensive plan.

Comprehensive Plans

⌨ To get a good idea of what comprehensive plans look like, check the book's Simulation for some examples. As you can see, there may be several plans in different areas, such as transportation or economic development, which taken together constitute the city's comprehensive plan.

Developing the plan is a lengthy process, requiring input from citizens as well as experts in many fields. Ultimately, a group of citizens called the Planning and Zoning Commission (P&Z) is charged with putting together the final product, which then goes to the city council for final approval. As you might imagine, the comprehensive plan must be periodically updated to account for changing conditions; thus, planning becomes a more or less continuous, rather than static, process.

In most jurisdictions, the comprehensive plan is not "law," but merely a *policy document* setting forth recommendations for the future. The city council must implement the plan by enacting ordinances or taking other actions (such as acquiring land for parks or open space). Although the plan may show that a particular area—now zoned Agricultural—would be a good place for future housing development, implementing that recommendation requires the council to amend the zoning classification of the area. In many cases, that won't be done until a developer asks the council to rezone a particular tract.

The Relationship Between Planning and Zoning

What happens if the city rezones property to a different classification than called for by the comprehensive plan? What if the city adopts a zoning ordinance without adopting a separate comprehensive plan? In other words, is comprehensive planning required, and what effect does it have on individual zoning decisions?

States have adopted a variety of positions on the status of comprehensive planning. The SSZEA included a phrase requiring zoning to be "in accordance with a comprehensive plan." Many states, therefore, included that provision in their enabling statutes. Courts interpret this requirement in different ways, however:

- **No separate plan required; plan is advisory only.** In many jurisdictions, courts are willing to find that the requirement of a comprehensive plan is satisfied if the municipality approaches the zoning question in a nonarbitrary way, by considering the community's interests rather than those of a particular landowner. A good example is Konigsberg v. Board of Aldermen, 930 A.2d 1, 19 (Conn. 2007):

  The requirement of a comprehensive plan is generally satisfied when the zoning authority acts with the intention of promoting the best interests of the entire community. . . . It is established that the comprehensive plan is to be found in the zoning regulations themselves and the zoning map. . . .

See also PTL, L.L.C. v. Chicago Cnty. Bd. of Comm'rs, 656 N.W.2d 567, 575 (Minn. Ct. App. 2003) (comprehensive plan is merely advisory, not binding). Even in these jurisdictions, however, a zoning action that is inconsistent with the comprehensive plan might be held to be arbitrary (and therefore invalid) if the city doesn't have a good reason for its decision.

■ **Separate plan required; substantial compliance with plan required.** Some jurisdictions accord a comprehensive plan a much more central place in the process. Once a plan is adopted, it must be followed. As the Montana Supreme Court has explained, some deviation from the plan is acceptable under this standard, but the plan cannot be ignored:

The vital role given the planning boards by these statutes cannot be undercut by giving the governing body the freedom to ignore the product of these boards—the master plan. We hold that the governmental unit, when zoning, must substantially adhere to the master plan. . . .

To require strict compliance with the master plan would result in a master plan so unworkable that it would have to be constantly changed to comply with the realities. The master plan is, after all, a plan. On the other hand, to require no compliance at all would defeat the whole idea of planning. Why have a plan if the local governmental units are free to ignore it at any time? The statutes are clear enough to send the message that in reaching zoning decisions, the local governmental unit should at least substantially comply with the comprehensive plan (or master plan).

Little v. Bd. of Cnty. Comm'rs of Flathead Cnty., 631 P.2d 1282, 1293 (Mont. 1981). In these jurisdictions, if a zoning ordinance significantly conflicts with the comprehensive plan, the municipality must first go through the process of amending the plan to make it consistent.

For a good summary of cases on this issue, see Edward J. Sullivan, *Recent Developments in Comprehensive Planning Law*, 43 Urb. Law. 823 (2011). *See also* RNDT, LLC v. City of Bloomington, 861 N.W.2d 71, 79-88 (Minn. 2015)(Justice Anderson's concurrence laments the modern trend requiring greater compliance with a comprehensive plan, which is "a broad, forward-looking document that is not designed to support specific land-use decisions.")

■ PROBLEM: IN ACCORDANCE WITH A COMPREHENSIVE PLAN

Ervin plans to convert three acres of his agricultural land into an indoor shooting range, where he will also sell some guns, ammunition, and accessories. The range will generate some noise, along with vehicular traffic equivalent to ten single-family homes. The property is zoned Rural Agricultural, which allows "recreational uses." Aldridge lives next door and objects to the facility. The County decides to permit it, as a valid recreational use. Aldridge argues that the comprehensive plan specifies that only *non-commercial* recreational uses should be allowed in the county's rural areas. Does the County have to interpret the zoning ordinance to be consistent with this statement in the comprehensive plan? Would the various approaches discussed above lead to different results in this case? *See* Aldridge v. Jackson Twp., 983 A.2d 247, 258-59 (Pa. Commw. Ct. 2009).

Zoning

The SSZEA provided authority for the legislative body of cities (typically the city council) to divide the municipality into districts and to regulate the height and size of buildings, the size of lots and the percentage that may be occupied, the density of population, and the use to be made of the structures and land within each district. SSZEA §§1, 2. The regulations must be uniform within each district.

The P&Z Commission is usually given the task of recommending the initial boundaries of each district and the regulations to be enforced in each. SSZEA §6. Any amendments to the zoning classifications also go through the P&Z Commission. The city council, however, must take final action on the initial zoning scheme and any amendments thereto.[5]

Modern zoning districts may include a variety of different categories of residential, commercial, and industrial use zones. For example, typical zoning districts may include:

- **A-1**: agricultural
- **R-1**: single-family residential
- **R-2**: single-family or duplex
- **R-3**: apartments and other forms of multi-family
- **C-1**: low impact or neighborhood commercial
- **C-2**: higher impact commercial (shopping center, downtown, highway)
- **M-1**: light industrial
- **M-2**: heavy industrial

Larger cities usually have even more categories of districts. In addition, the city might have special zoning classifications for mobile home parks or historic districts. In addition to specifying the uses permitted in each district, the ordinance will include other restrictions, such as limits on signs or requirements for parking. It may specify how many toilets and how much floor space must be provided for residents of group homes. It may specify the minimum lot size and setback requirements (depth of front and side yards) and limit the height of buildings.

Sample Zoning Ordinance

⌨ Check out a typical zoning ordinance and maps on the Simulation.

---

[5] In a few states, P&Z decisions have more weight. For example, in Connecticut, the decisions of the zoning commission on adoption and amendment of zoning regulations are final. Conn. Gen. Stat. §8-1-8-3 (2018). In Kentucky, the commission's recommendation on zoning amendments becomes final unless the city council votes to overrule it within 90 days. Ky. Rev. Stat. Ann. §100.211 (West 2018).

Flexibility. Zoning districts usually are fairly large and encompass many different properties within their boundaries. Not all of these properties will be uniform in size or circumstances. Moreover, the appropriate classification may change over time as the city develops. Zoning ordinances provide for several mechanisms to provide the necessary flexibility to fine-tune and modify these categories:

- **Zoning amendments.** The property owner may apply to actually rezone a parcel of land, changing its classification. For example, as the city expands, the owner of property originally zoned agricultural may seek to have it rezoned R-3 so that apartment houses may be built on the land. A corner grocery store may seek to rezone an adjacent parcel from R-3 to C-1, so it can expand its parking area.
- **Variances.** The property owner may want to seek relief from a particular requirement of the zone. This may be an *areavariance*: for example, allowing the landowner to have a smaller side yard due to the size or shape of the lot. Or he may seek a *use variance*, allowing a particular use that ordinarily would not be allowed in that zone (for example, a child care business in a residential zone).
  - ☐ Variances differ from zoning amendments in that the property remains in its original zoning classification. A variance to permit child care, for example, would not allow any other type of commercial use on the property.
  - ☐ Variances are not favored, because they are *ad hoc* exceptions to the generally applicable law. Thus, in most jurisdictions they are granted only upon a showing of *unnecessary hardship*.
  - ☐ Variances usually are granted by another citizen board, called the Board of Zoning Adjustment (BZA).
- **Special permit or conditional uses**. Many ordinances single out particular uses as conditionally allowed, subject to approval by the BZA. For example, the ordinance may provide that bed-and-breakfast uses are allowed in agricultural zones, but require the landowner to obtain individual approval. The process allows the BZA to ensure that the landowner's plans for parking, number of guests, and signage do not have an adverse effect on neighbors.

Although a full-scale excursion into the intricacies of zoning practice is beyond the scope of the first-year course, we want to delve into a couple of common issues that arise in this area. In examining the law of variances and nonconforming uses, you will also learn more about the overall function and purpose of zoning ordinances.

1. Variances

Standard zoning provisions allow an administrative body (typically the Board of Zoning Adjustment) to provide relief from provisions of the zoning ordinance in cases of *unnecessary hardship*. How this term is defined varies by jurisdiction.

The test normally entails consideration of *both* the burden on the landowner if the variance is not granted balanced against the impact on the neighborhood/public if the variance is granted.

One question is how much of a burden constitutes "hardship": some jurisdictions require the landowner to prove that no economic use of the property could be made without a variance, while others are not as strict. Second, note that *even if* there is significant hardship, it does not merit a variance unless the hardship is *unnecessary*—which means that the purposes of the ordinance can be accomplished despite the variance. If the impact on the neighbors will be too great, no variance should be granted regardless of the degree of hardship.

The following case concerns a vacant lot in Old Town Alexandria—a very desirable historic district just across the Potomac from Washington, D.C. *Martin* illustrates that there is more to the variance test than merely showing that compliance would be difficult. As you read the case, consider why the court refused to uphold a plan that two city boards had approved.

MARTIN v. CITY OF ALEXANDRIA

743 S.E.2d 139 (2013)
Supreme Court of Virginia

Opinion by Justice MCCLANAHAN.

H. Curtiss Martin and Virginia Drewry (Martin) appeal from the circuit court's judgment upholding the decision of the Board of Zoning Appeals of the City of Alexandria (BZA) granting side and rear yard variances to James and Christine Garner (Garners). Because the BZA's decision was contrary to law, we conclude the circuit court erred.

I. BACKGROUND

> **Visualizing Dimensions**
>
> It is easy to let your eyes run over dimensions like those mentioned in this case. To get a rough idea of how narrow the lot in question is, you might think about 10 yards on a football field. With the set-backs, the building width would be only 26 feet—less than 9 yards.

The Garners seek side and rear yard variances in connection with a proposed design of a single family home on their property located at 122 Prince Street in the City of Alexandria. The property has 36 feet of frontage along Prince Street and is 44.33 feet deep. It is zoned RM[6] and is required to have two five-foot side yards and a 16-foot rear yard under the Zoning Ordinance of the City of Alexandria (Zoning Ordinance). See Zoning Ordinance §§3-1108(C)(1), 3-1106(A)(3)(a). Located on the 100 block of Prince Street known as "Captain's Row," the property is also subject to the Zoning

---

[6] RM is a medium-density residential zone, which allows single-family, two-family, and townhouse dwellings.—EDS.

Ordinance requirements for the Old and Historic Alexandria District (Historic District Ordinance). The Historic District Ordinance requires the issuance of a certificate of appropriateness from the Old and Historic Alexandria District Board of Architectural Review (BAR) for new construction.[7]

Adjoining the Garners' property on the east is the property owned by Martin, located at 118 Prince Street.[8] The home built on the property located at 126 Prince Street, which adjoins the Garners' property to the west, is one of the City's only remaining examples of late 18th century rough sawn wood used as siding. Preserving a view of this wall is a factor in the BAR's decision to issue a certificate of appropriateness for any home design the Garners might submit.

Vacant lot and adjacent houses involved in the Martin case. Notice the historic wood siding discussed in the opinion.
Photo provided by Prof. Cathy Lesser Mansfield

---

[7] In passing upon the appropriateness of any "proposed construction, reconstruction, alteration or restoration of buildings or structures," the BAR shall consider numerous features and factors including the "height, mass and scale of buildings or structures," "the impact upon the historic setting, streetscape or environs," and "the extent to which the building or structure will preserve or protect historic places and areas of historic interests in the city." Historic District Ordinance §10-105(A)(2)(a), (c), (e).

[8] An eight-foot wide alley separates the properties owned by the Garners and Martin, who are parties to proceedings initiated by the Garners to determine title to the alley. See Martin v. Garner, 286 Va. 76, 745 S.E.2d 419 (2013) (this day decided). For the purposes of the current BZA application, the Garners have agreed that their side yard is calculated without regard to any portion of the alley.

In 2003, the Garners applied for a side yard variance of five feet and a rear yard variance of 16 feet. City staff recommended denial of the application based on its opinion that the strict application of the Zoning Ordinance would not result in undue hardship to the property. According to the staff analysis, "[t]he lot is level and there is no condition of the lot which restricts the reasonable use or development of a new single-family dwelling." Further, City staff noted "[t]he lot is a large buildable lot that can be developed without the need of a variance. The lot's characteristics are similar to other lots within this section of Prince Street." In addition, City staff explained that "[g]ranting the variance will be detrimental to the adjacent property to the east [Martin's property]" because the neighbor "will now view 44.3 feet of building wall." The City deferred action on the Garners' application pursuant to the Garners' request due to ongoing legal issues pertaining to the title to the alley running between the Garners' and Martin's properties.

...In 2011, the Garners submitted the current application seeking a three-foot side yard variance and a 13-foot rear yard variance. The design for the proposed home was submitted to the BAR which approved the Garners' application for a certificate of appropriateness. In connection with the Garners' variance application, the Historic Preservation Manager, Al Cox, submitted a memo to the BZA relaying the BAR's decision on the design of the home proposed by the Garners. Cox stated that the BAR "found the height, mass, scale and architectural style to be appropriate for the historic character of the block" and "the general design and arrangement of the building on the east side of the site adjacent to the alley was consistent with the historic setting, streetscape, and environs" following "the historic development patterns in the [Historic District]."

At the BZA hearing on the Garners' variance application, the BZA received the report of the City staff describing the proposed house as a "two-and-one-half story, three-bay, brick townhouse in a late Federal architectural style" to be "located on the front property line facing Prince Street, 2.00 feet from the west edge of the private alley, 11.00 feet from the west side property line and 3.00 feet from the rear property line." Thus, a "variance of 3.00 feet from the west edge of the private alley and 13.00 feet from the rear property line is required." Noting that "Captain's Row is an especially important street in Alexandria," City staff supported the two variances "not only because the result is a good development compatible with its historic context, but also because the applicants' case meets the legal standards for the grant of a variance."

In particular, staff stated that because this application concerns "a new house in Old Town and on the 100 block of Prince Street," it is unique since "[t]he zoning regulations and requirements in the Old and Historic District are designed to apply to old buildings."... According to staff, "the RM zone regulations ... are especially intended to apply to additions to historic buildings, and are rarely used for new houses on vacant lots." In addition, the Garners' lot is shallower than two-thirds of the other lots on Captain's Row.

In its report, City staff stated that having two five-foot side yards "would actually call more attention to the proposed house because it would appear to be the only single family detached house on a block of row houses" and the proposed location "will maintain the historic sense of open space immediately adjacent to 126 and 130 Prince Street and allow the historic rough sawn siding on that east wall to be clearly visible." Staff supported the rear yard variance because "it is far preferable to have the public view of a house with a narrower, more historically appropriate width and depth, than a shallow house with an architecturally grand, four-bay wide frontage." According to staff, "[i]f the house were modified to meet both zoning and BAR requirements, it would be very small relative to the other houses on the block. While the RM zone provides for such dimensions, it was not designed primarily for the construction of new houses."

In the Garners' application and at the hearing before the BZA, they advanced four primary factors justifying the variances. First, the Garners asserted that their property is the only vacant buildable lot on the 100 block of Prince Street. Second, they pointed out that their property is wider and more shallow than most of the other lots in the RM zone. Third, they noted that their property is adjacent to the historic siding on the home located at 126 Prince Street. Finally, they argued that these factors, in combination with the enforcement of the RM zoning regulations and the Historic District Ordinance would amount to a clearly demonstrable hardship. The Garners contended they "cannot build a house with two side yard setbacks and a sizeable rear yard without resulting in an atypical footprint from other houses located in the historic block of Prince Street." According to the Garners, "[t]he BAR confirmed this in their deliberations and approval of a certificate of appropriateness for the proposed home on the lot."

At the hearing, opponents of the variances pointed out to the BZA that the City staff had submitted a home design that conformed to the Zoning Ordinance and that could be built on the Garners' property. Neither this design, nor any other design conforming to the requirements of the Zoning Ordinance, however, was submitted by the Garners to the BAR for a certificate of appropriateness. At the conclusion of the hearing, the BZA voted to approve the application. Martin appealed the decision of the BZA to the circuit court, which upheld it.

II. ANALYSIS

A. City Charter Provisions

The Alexandria City Charter (City Charter) governs appeals from the BZA. It provides that the circuit court "may reverse or modify the decision reviewed . . . when it is satisfied that the decision of the board is contrary to law or that its decision is arbitrary and constitutes an abuse of discretion." City Charter §9.21. . . .

The City Charter defines the powers of the BZA and provides that the BZA may authorize a variance "when, owing to special conditions a literal enforcement of the provisions will result in unnecessary hardship; provided that the spirit of the ordinance shall be observed and substantial justice done," upon the property owner's showing of at least one of the following conditions and one of the following justifications:

When a property owner can show that his property was acquired in good faith and where by reason of the exceptional narrowness, shallowness, size or shape of a specific piece of property at the time of the effective date of the ordinance, or where by reason of the exceptional topographical condition or other extraordinary situation, or condition of such piece of property, or of the use or development of property immediately adjacent thereto, the strict application of the terms of the ordinance would effectively prohibit or unreasonably restrict the use of property or where the board is satisfied, upon the evidence heard by it, that the granting of such variance will alleviate a clearly demonstrable hardship,[9] as distinguished from a special privilege or convenience sought by the applicant, provided that all variances shall be in harmony with the intended spirit and purpose of the ordinance.

City Charter §9.18(b).

"[N]ot only must an applicant show the existence of at least one of [these] several 'special conditions' which would cause compliance with a zoning ordinance to result in an 'unnecessary hardship,' but the board of zoning appeals must find that the [following] three enumerated tests are satisfied." Packer v. Hornsby, 221 Va. 117, 121, 267 S.E.2d 140, 142 (1980).... Specifically, the BZA must find:

> (1) That the strict application of the ordinance would produce undue hardship.
> (2) That such hardship is not shared generally by other properties in the same zone and the same vicinity and is not created by the owner of such property.
> (3) That the authorization of such variance will not be of substantial detriment to adjacent property and that the character of the zone will not be changed by the granting of the variance.

City Charter §9.18(b). Finally, the City Charter provides that

> [n]o variance shall be authorized unless the board finds that the condition or situation of the property concerned or the intended use of the property is not of so general or recurring a nature as to make reasonably practicable the formulation of a general regulation to be adopted as an amendment to the ordinance.

City Charter §9.18(b).

B. Evidence to Support Variances

Noting that where the City Charter formerly required proof of a "hardship approaching confiscation" it was amended to require only a showing of a "clearly

---

[9] Code §15.2-2309(2), which contains virtually identical language, and the City Charter previously permitted a BZA to grant a variance only where it would "alleviate a clearly demonstrable hardship approaching confiscation." See Former Code §15.2-2309(2) (2008) (emphasis added). In 2009, the General Assembly removed "approaching confiscation," from the statewide statutory provision, 2009 Acts ch. 206, and the same change was implemented by the Legislature in an amendment to the City Charter the following year. 2010 Acts ch. 221. City staff relied, in part, upon the elimination of this language to justify its change in position regarding the Garners' request for the variances.

demonstrable hardship," the Garners contend that the BZA may now authorize variances in instances that previously were not authorized. Their argument ignores, however, the fact that the amendment did not alter the remainder of Section 9.18(b) of the Charter, which "requires a board of zoning appeals, prior to approving a variance, to make certain findings of fact, which we deemed 'crucial'" in discussing the analogous statewide statutory provisions in Code §15.2-2309. Hendrix v. Board of Zoning Appeals, 222 Va. 57, 60, 278 S.E.2d 814, 816 (1981) (citing *Packer*, 221 Va. at 121, 267 S.E.2d at 142).

Thus, notwithstanding that the BZA need not find a hardship "approaching confiscation" to grant a variance, the BZA still must find that (i) "the strict application of the terms of the ordinance would effectively prohibit or unreasonably restrict the use of property," or "the granting of such variance will alleviate a clearly demonstrable hardship, as distinguished from a special privilege or convenience"; (ii) "all variances [are] in harmony with the intended spirit and purpose of the ordinance"; (iii) "the strict application of the ordinance would produce an undue hardship"; (iv) the "hardship is not shared generally by other properties in the same zone and the same vicinity"; and (v) "the condition or situation of the property . . . is not of so general or recurring a nature as to make reasonably practicable the formulation of a general regulation to be adopted as an amendment to the ordinance." City Charter §9.18(b).

We review the Garners' four primary justifications for the variances and whether the BZA could properly have found them to satisfy all of the requirements of section 9.18(b) of the City Charter.

1. Condition of Lot Being Vacant in a District Where Most Surrounding Properties Are Already Developed

The Garners first argue that they face a unique hardship because they seek to build a new home on a vacant lot subject to both the RM *Zoning* Ordinance and the Historic District Ordinance, where most of the surrounding properties are already developed.

Contrary to the repeated assertions made by City staff that "[t]he zoning regulations and requirements in the Old and Historic District are designed to apply to old buildings," the City's Zoning Ordinance was expressly intended to apply to new structures. Zoning Ordinance §1-200(B) ("All buildings and structures erected hereafter . . . shall be subject to all regulations of this ordinance.") In fact, granting a variance because a property owner is erecting a new structure would render the Zoning Ordinance meaningless. We have rejected interpretations of a statute that "would render the entire statute meaningless." Stone v. Liberty Mut. Ins. Co., 253 Va. 12, 20, 478 S.E.2d 883, 887 (1996). Therefore, the decision of the BZA cannot be upheld on this ground.

2. Condition of Lot Being Shallow and Wide

The Garners next argue that a variance is justified because their lot is exceptionally wide and shallow as compared to other lots on the 100 block of Prince

Street. City staff reported that "[o]n the 100 block of Prince Street, two-thirds of the lots are deeper than the [Garners'] property." The Garners' argument, therefore, is that they face a hardship because, when compared with other properties on the block, their relatively more shallow lot makes it difficult to build a home that satisfies the rear yard requirement.

We rejected a similar argument in *Packer* where "[t]he premise for the Board's decision was that the [applicants] should be entitled to build as close to the ocean as 'the average of the houses along this block.'" 221 Va. at 122, 267 S.E.2d at 143. We held that

> [i]f, as the Board concluded, one owner of the property complying with a restriction should be allowed to conform his structure to neighboring nonconforming structures, then every such owner would be entitled to do so. A board of zoning appeals could, by granting variances piecemeal, ultimately nullify a zoning restriction throughout the zoning district. But the statute provides that "all variances shall be in harmony with the intended spirit and purpose of the ordinance."

Id. at 122-23, 267 S.E.2d at 143.

Likewise, the Garners' argument, if accepted, would justify variances for the one-third of the properties that are even more shallow than the Garners' property, yet still conform to the zoning ordinance, resulting in the "granting [of] variances piecemeal" that would "ultimately nullify" the zoning ordinance requiring a rear yard, thereby conflicting with the "intended spirit and purpose of the ordinance." *Id.* Since the City Charter prohibited the BZA from issuing a variance not "in harmony with the intended spirit and purpose of the ordinance," the BZA's decision cannot be upheld on this ground. City Charter §9.18(b).

3. *Condition of the Property as Being Subject to Historic District Ordinance*

Finally, the Garners contend that their property is "undevelopable" because alternative designs would not comply with both the Historic District Ordinance and the Zoning Ordinance.[10]

The BZA was presented with evidence that because the siding of the home at 126 Prince Street is of historical value, the Garners' property is immediately adjacent to a property of extraordinary condition. The Garners argue that because the BAR considers the visibility of the neighboring wall in deciding whether to approve any home design the Garners might propose, they face a unique challenge in creating a design that both satisfies the BAR and conforms to the RM Zoning Ordinance.

As the Garners admitted during the BZA hearing, they have the option of submitting to the BAR a conforming design that would not require variances,

---

[10] Because the Garners' third justification—the historic siding on the home adjacent to their property—relates to their claim of hardship resulting from being subject to both the Historic District Ordinance and Zoning Ordinance, we combine their third and fourth justifications for discussion.

and they have not done so. Consequently, it is mere speculation that the BAR would not approve this design or any other design that conforms to the Zoning Ordinance. Thus, there was no factual support for the Garners' claim that their property, by being located next to the historic wall, makes it uniquely more difficult to build a structure that both satisfies the BAR and conforms to the RM zoning regulations. Accordingly, the BZA's decision cannot be upheld on this ground. *See Hopkins*, 197 Va. at 205, 89 S.E.2d at 3 (action that is "unsupported by facts, [i]s an illegal action" by a board of zoning appeals).

Without support for that fundamental premise, the Garners' argument is instead simply that because it is difficult to both satisfy the BAR and comply with the RM zoning regulations, any design that the BAR approves should be granted the necessary variances. But all properties in the Old and Historic District are subject to both the RM zoning regulations and Historic District Ordinance. Under the Charter, the BZA may grant a variance only if it finds "that the condition or situation of the property concerned or the intended use of the property is not of so general or recurring a nature as to make reasonably practicable the formulation of a general regulation to be adopted as an amendment to the ordinance." City Charter §9.18(b)....

> In passing upon requests for variances, a board of zoning appeals exercises the limited function of insuring that a landowner does not suffer a severe hardship not generally shared by other property holders in the same district or vicinity. The power to resolve recurring zoning problems shared generally by those in the same district is vested in the legislative arm of the local governing body.

Hendrix, 222 Va. at 61, 278 S.E.2d at 817.

Because being subject to both sets of ordinances is a condition shared by every other property holder in the same zone, this condition was "of so general or recurring a nature as to make reasonably practicable the formulation of a general regulation to be adopted as an amendment to the ordinance." City Charter §9.18(b); see Code §15.2-2309. Moreover, authorization of the variance upon this ground would amount to a policy judgment that structures built in the Old and Historic District should only be subject to approval of the BAR and need not comply with the RM Zoning Ordinance and would, therefore, constitute an " 'administrative infringement upon the legislative prerogatives of the local governing body.' " *Hendrix*, 222 Va. At 61, 278 S.E.2d at 817 (quoting *Packer*, 221 Va. At 123, 267 S.E.2d at 143).

III. CONCLUSION

In sum, none of the conditions asserted by the Garners to justify their application for a variance satisfied the requirements of City Charter §9.18(b). Accordingly, the decision of the BZA was contrary to law. Therefore, we will reverse the judgment of the circuit court and enter final judgment for Martin.

Reversed and final judgment.

■ POINTS TO CONSIDER

1. **Purpose of variance.** What is the function of the variance provision? Why does the variance test require the hardship to be "special," in that it is not shared by the other property owners in the area? What do you think the court means by its statement that the BZA's actions constituted "administrative infringement upon the legislative prerogatives of the local governing body"? Remember that the BZA is a group of unelected citizens, typically appointed by the city council. Does that help explain the court's determination to limit this body's authority?

2. **Defining "unnecessary hardship."** Is it enough for the landowner to show that compliance would be difficult? What else does the landowner need to prove? Why does the test require more than just hardship?

Are Zoning Boards Skewed?

A recent study found that zoning boards, such as the BZA in this case, generally are not comprised of a cross-section of the community. Rather, they are often dominated by white-collar professionals and those with some interest in real estate (e.g., agents, mortgage brokers, architects, and developers).[11] Does this affect your opinion regarding the degree of deference courts should accord BZA decisions?

3. **Variances and "takings."** In the final chapter, we will cover the Takings Clause of the Constitution, which prohibits governmental actions that deprive owners of private property without just compensation. Court decisions interpret this clause to mean that if a zoning ordinance effectively prohibits any economic use of property, it constitutes a "taking" and the property owner must be compensated. In this case, the state and local variance provisions originally applied only when the hardship imposed by a zoning provision approached "confiscation." Do you see why? Does the amended provision apply to cases beyond those constitutionally requiring a variance?

4. **Use versus area variances.** Be aware that many states use a more lenient *practical difficulties* test for an *area* variance, as opposed to a use variance. The enabling acts of many states allow for variances in cases of both "unnecessary hardship" and "practical difficulties." For some courts, the two terms are interchangeable, but others have interpreted this language to require a lower burden for area variances. As the Delaware Supreme Court explained:

> We hold that the Superior Court correctly distinguished the two types of variances and prescribed a less burdensome test where an area variance is in issue. . . . Many states, with comparable statutory provisions, have adopted such an interpretation. [citing cases from Michigan, Rhode Island, D.C., and Maryland]. The rationale, which we approve, is that a use variance changes the character of the zoned district by permitting an otherwise proscribed use, whereas an area variance concerns only the

---

[11] *See* Jerry L. Anderson, Aaron E. Brees & Emily C. Reninger, *A Study of American Zoning Board Composition and Public Attitudes Toward Zoning Issues*, 40 Urb. Law. 689 (2008).

practical difficulty in using the particular property for a permitted use. Accordingly, given the differing purposes and effects of the two types of variance, a lesser standard of the owner's "exceptional practical difficulties" is appropriate for obtaining an area variance.

Board of Adjustment of New Castle Cnty. v. Kwik-Check Realty, Inc., 389 A.2d 1289, 1291 (Del. 1978) (citations omitted). Would the Garners have prevailed on their Old Town Alexandria variance if the Virginia court had used a "practical difficulties" test instead?

CASE SUMMARY: State ex rel. Ziervogel v. Washington County Board of Adjustment, 676 N.W.2d 401 (Wis. 2004)

Wisconsin went through an interesting evolution of its standard for area variances, which illustrates the importance of the test used and why area variances might be treated more leniently.

In Snyder v. Waukesha Cnty. Zoning Bd. of Adjustment, 247 N.W.2d 98, 102 (Wis. 1976), the state supreme court had defined the term *unnecessary hardship* differently for use and area variances. However, 22 years later, in 1998, the court reversed course and established a single standard, interpreting the statutory language of "unreasonable hardship" to require that "no reasonable use of property" would remain unless a variance were to be granted. The standard applied to both use and area variances. State v. Kenosha Cnty. Bd. of Adjustment, 577 N.W.2d 813 (Wis. 1998).

In 2004, in *Ziervogel*, the court reconsidered this position yet again and reinstated its 1976 opinion that area variances should in fact be treated differently:

> We now conclude that the distinctions in purpose and effect of use and area zoning make the perpetuation of a single, highly-restrictive "no reasonable use of the property" standard for all variances unworkable and unfair. . . .
>
> Restricting the availability of variances to those property owners who would have "no reasonable use" of their property without a variance may be justifiable in use variance cases, given the purpose of use zoning and the substantial effect of use variances on neighborhood character. But applying the same strict "no reasonable use" standard to area variance applications is unjustifiable. The "no reasonable use" standard is largely disconnected from the purpose of area zoning, fails to consider the lesser effect of area variances on neighborhood character, and operates to virtually eliminate the statutory discretion of local boards of adjustment to do justice in individual cases. . . .
>
> We now reaffirm the *Snyder* standard for unnecessary hardship in area variance cases: "[w]hen considering an area variance, the question of whether unnecessary hardship . . . exists is best explained as '[w]hether compliance with the strict letter of the restrictions governing area, set backs, frontage, height, bulk or density would unreasonably prevent the owner from using the property for a permitted purpose or would render conformity with such restrictions unnecessarily burdensome.'" *Snyder*, 74 Wis. 2d at 475, 247 N.W.2d 98 (quoting 2 Rathkopf, The Law of Zoning & Planning §45-28 (3d ed. 1972)). Whether this standard is met in individual cases depends upon

a consideration of the purpose of the zoning restriction in question, its effect on the property, and the effect of a variance on the neighborhood and the larger public interest.

676 N.W.2d at 404. Thus, in Wisconsin the "unnecessary hardship" standard is applied to both types of variances, but the degree of hardship required for an area variance is much lower than for a use variance.

Practice Tip: Getting a Variance

Even though the legal standard for variances appears to be tough to meet, studies consistently show that the majority of variance applications are granted. *See* David W. Owens, *The Zoning Variance: Reappraisal and Recommendations for Reform of a Much-Maligned Tool*, 29 Colum. J. Envtl. L. 279 (2004) (studies indicate 70-80 percent approval rate).

Talking to the neighbors before making the application and responding to any concerns they might have is key. Most boards report that neighborhood opposition has a significant influence on whether a variance is granted or denied. One study found, for example, that variance denial rates were three times higher when neighbors appeared in opposition.[12]

A variance granted without meeting the requisite standard would not withstand judicial review, but if the neighbors don't oppose it, it's likely no one will appeal it. That might explain the high approval rates.

■ PROBLEMS: VARIANCES

1. In 2010, Valerie purchased Blackacre, a one-acre tract of land on the outskirts of Freeport. In 2015, she granted an easement to a gas company for a pipeline running diagonally through the northwest corner of Blackacre. The pipeline was buried, but the easement agreement prevents her from building any improvements within 25 feet on either side of the pipe location. She now wants to build a house on Blackacre, but the position of the pipeline means that a house similar to others in the area (three- or four-bedroom ranch with two-car attached garage) will require her to build about ten feet from the eastern property line adjoining Whiteacre, owned by her neighbor, Ernest. The Freeport zoning ordinance for this district requires that any structure be set back 25 feet from all boundary lines. Can Valerie get a variance, despite Ernest's objections? What additional facts would you want to know if you represented Valerie or Ernest?

---

[12] H. Bornong & Bradley R. Peyton, *Contemporary Studies Project, Rural Land Use Regulation in Iowa: An Empirical Analysis of County Board of Adjustment Practices*, 68 Iowa L. Rev. 1083, 1197 (1983).

2. Jiang operates a restaurant on Greenacre, which is zoned commercial (C-1). He recently bought the lot next door, Whiteacre, which is zoned R-3. Jiang would like to tear down an old dilapidated apartment house on Whiteacre and use the lot for parking, so he can expand his restaurant on Greenacre. He claims that unless he can expand, the restaurant will go under. In addition, repairing the house to make it tenantable is not feasible, with the low market rates for rent in this neighborhood. The neighbors on the other side of Whiteacre object to his application for a variance. They say the parking lot will harm them with noise and lights. Should the variance be granted? If Jiang does not get the variance, does he have other options?

Video Problem: Variance Hearing

In this video, which is available on the Simulation, Beacon House requests a variance so that it may convert an old sorority house into a home for disabled veterans. Like many zoning issues, this application raises many emotional issues on both sides. Imagine you are the city attorney advising the Board of Zoning Adjustment—how would you advise the board regarding the "unnecessary hardship" variance standard in this situation?

2. Nonconforming Uses

Assume Dexter has a farm a mile outside the city limits of Hopeville. For many years, he has operated a farm implement repair shop in a converted barn, which brings in good money to supplement his farm income. The county has no zoning, so the use was perfectly legal. Hopeville is rapidly expanding in Dexter's direction, however, and his land was recently annexed into the city. The city then zoned the property R-4, Estate Residential, which calls for houses on large lots. The zone does not allow any commercial uses, such as repair shops. Should Dexter be allowed to continue his shop, despite the new restrictions? For how long?

Dexter's repair shop is an example of a *nonconforming use*. Most zoning ordinances allow such uses to continue, despite the fact that they violate the zoning ordinance for that district. The nonconforming use was in place before the ordinance made it illegal, so the theory is that the owner has a "vested right" to continue the use. Nonconforming uses arise in a variety of circumstances:

- when the city or county adopts a zoning ordinance for the first time, many uses are already in place and may not fit neatly into the desired pattern;
- when a city annexes additional land into the city limits and thus zones it for the first time;
- when the city rezones a particular area—uses previously allowed in an agricultural zone on the edge of town, for example, no longer conform when urban growth results in a zoning change to commercial or residential;
- when the city decides to target particular uses, such as mobile homes, junkyards, or adult businesses, in areas where they were previously allowed.

Usually, nonconforming uses have no specified termination date—as long as the use continues, it is exempt. However, the goal is to eventually get rid of the "blemish" on the zoning map, so most ordinances also specify that the right will be lost in the event the use is *abandoned* or a nonconforming building is *destroyed*. In addition, they usually prohibit any *change or expansion* of the use. For example, Dexter could not transform his small repair shop into a Jiffy Lube or a parts store. The exact language of the ordinance will be important in deciding cases of that nature.

Note that the privilege to continue applies to the "use," not to the landowner personally. So, as Dexter approached retirement, after running his shop for many years, he could sell it to someone much younger, or have his grandson take over. Thus, the use could continue indefinitely.

a. Amortization

In many cases, the long-term continuance of a nonconforming use may be tolerated, because it may not conflict greatly with the surrounding area and those who buy neighboring property know that the use is there. In some cases, however, the city may decide that the conflict is too great, such that the nonconformity can no longer be allowed to continue.

Municipalities developed a technique called *amortization* to deal with this problem. The idea is to give the nonconforming use a reasonable period of time to discontinue the use. The owner can therefore recover (at least theoretically) the amount he invested in reliance on the previous state of the law. The approach aims to balance fairness to the individual against the needs of the community (the public interest).

In a majority of jurisdictions, amortization is allowed, as long as the deadline for discontinuance is *reasonable*. The *test for reasonableness* depends on the circumstances. The court will consider the period of time allowed and the amount of investment to be recovered, along with the degree of conflict the use presents. The closer a nonconforming use is to being a nuisance, the shorter the period can be.

The following case illustrates the use of amortization, but in this case the ordinance has a twist: instead of allowing a definite period, the use is allowed to continue until ownership changes hands. As noted above, typically nonconforming use ordinances protect the *use*, not the *owner*. Can amortization be based on who owns the property?

VILLAGE OF VALATIE v. SMITH

632 N.E.2d 1264 (1994)
Court of Appeals of New York

SIMONS, Judge.

This appeal challenges the facial validity of chapter 85 of the Village Code of the Village of Valatie, a local law that terminates the nonconforming use of a mobile home upon the transfer of ownership of either the mobile home or the land upon which it sits. Defendant argues that it is unconstitutional for the Village to use a change in ownership as the termination date for a nonconforming use. We conclude, however, that defendant has failed to carry her burden of showing that the local law is unreasonable on its face. Accordingly, we modify the order of the Appellate Division by denying defendant's cross motion for summary judgment.

In 1968, the Village enacted chapter 85 to prohibit the placement of mobile homes outside mobile home parks. Under the law, any existing mobile home located outside a park which met certain health standards was allowed to remain as a nonconforming use until either ownership of the land or ownership of the mobile home changed. According to the Village, six mobile homes, including one owned by defendant's father, fell within this exception at the time the law was passed.

In 1989, defendant inherited the mobile home from her father and the Village instituted this action to enforce the law and have the unit removed. Both the Village and defendant moved . . . for summary judgment. The court granted defendant's motion and denied the Village's. The court characterized defendant's mobile home as a lawful nonconforming use—i.e., a use that was legally in place at the time the municipality enacted legislation prohibiting the use. Reasoning that the right to continue a nonconforming use runs with the land, the court held that the portion of the ordinance setting termination at the transfer of ownership was unconstitutional. The Appellate Division affirmed. The Court acknowledged that a municipality had the authority to phase out a nonconforming use with an "amortization period," but it concluded that this particular law was unreasonable, and therefore unconstitutional, because the period of time allowed "bears no relationship to the use of the land or the investment in that use."

Preliminarily . . . there is no question that municipalities may enact laws reasonably limiting the duration of nonconforming uses. . . . Thus, the narrow issue is whether the Village acted unreasonably by establishing an amortization period that uses the transfer of ownership as an end point.

The policy of allowing nonconforming uses to continue originated in concerns that the application of land use regulations to uses existing prior to the regulations' enactment might be construed as confiscatory and unconstitutional. While it was initially assumed that nonconforming uses would disappear with time, just the opposite proved to be true in many instances, with the nonconforming use thriving in the absence of any new lawful competition. In light of the problems presented by continuing nonconforming uses, this Court has characterized the law's allowance of such uses as a "grudging tolerance," and we have recognized the right of municipalities to take reasonable measures to eliminate them.

Most often, elimination has been effected by establishing amortization periods, at the conclusion of which the nonconforming use must end. As commentators have noted, the term "amortization period" is somewhat misleading. "Amortization" properly refers to a liquidation, but in this context the owner is not required to take any particular financial step. "Amortization period" simply designates a period of time granted to owners of nonconforming uses during which they may phase out their operations as they see fit and make other arrangements. It is, in effect, a grace period, putting owners on fair notice of the law and giving them a fair opportunity to recoup their investment. Though the amortization period is typically discussed in terms of protecting the owners' financial interests, it serves more generally to protect "an individual's interest in maintaining the present use" of the property.

The validity of an amortization period depends on its reasonableness. We have avoided any fixed formula for determining what constitutes a reasonable period. Instead, we have held that an amortization period is presumed valid, and the owner must carry the heavy burden of overcoming that presumption by demonstrating that the loss suffered is so substantial that it outweighs the public benefit to be gained by the exercise of the police power. Using this approach, courts have declared valid a variety of amortization periods. Indeed, in some circumstances, no amortization period at all is required. In other circumstances, the amortization period may vary in duration among the affected properties. We have also held that an amortization period may validly come to an end at the occurrence of an event as unpredictable as the destruction of the nonconforming use by fire.

Defendant here does not challenge the local law's constitutionality under our established balancing test for amortization periods—i.e., whether the individual loss outweighs the public benefit. Instead, the challenge is a more basic due process claim: that the means of eliminating nonconforming uses is not reasonably related to the Village's legitimate interest in land use planning. More particularly, defendant makes two arguments: first, that the length of an amortization period must be related either to land use objectives or to the financial recoupment needs of the owner and, second, that the local law violates the principle that zoning is to regulate land use rather than ownership. Neither argument withstands analysis.

We have never required that the length of the amortization period be based on a municipality's land use objectives. To the contrary, the periods are routinely calculated to protect the rights of individual owners at the temporary expense of public land use objectives. Typically, the period of time allowed has been measured for reasonableness by considering whether the owners had adequate time to recoup their investment in the use. Patently, such protection of an individual's interest is unrelated to land use objectives. Indeed, were land use objectives the only permissible criteria for scheduling amortization, the law would require immediate elimination of nonconforming uses in all instances. Instead, the setting of the amortization period involves balancing the interests of the individual and those of the public. Thus, the real issue here is whether it was irrational for the Village, in striking that balance, to consider a nonfinancial interest of the individual owners—specifically, the individual's interest in not being displaced involuntarily.

It is significant that the six properties involved here are residential. In our previous cases dealing with amortization, we have focused almost exclusively on commercial properties, where the owner's interest is easily reduced to financial considerations. The same may not be true for the owners of residential properties, especially in instances where the property is the primary residence of the owner. Simply being able to recoup one's financial investment may be a secondary concern to staying in a neighborhood or remaining on a particular piece of land. Indeed, when mobile homes are involved, there may actually be little or no financial loss, given that the owner often will be able to relocate the structure and sell the land for legal development. Here, rather than focusing solely on financial recoupment, the Village apparently took a broader view of "an individual's interest in maintaining the present use" of the property. It enacted a law that allowed owners to keep their mobile homes in place until they decided to sell, even though they may have recouped their investment long ago. By doing so, it saved the owners from a forced relocation at the end of a predetermined amortization period set by the Village. Defendant has not demonstrated why such an approach is irrational or explained why a municipality should be barred constitutionally from considering the nonfinancial interests of the owners in setting an amortization schedule. Thus, on this motion for summary judgment and the present record, defendant has failed to overcome the presumption of the law's validity and prove, as she must, unconstitutionality beyond a reasonable doubt.

Equally unavailing on this facial challenge is defendant's contention that the law might prevent some owners from recouping their investment. Defendant raises the hypothetical concern that in some circumstances owners might not have adequate time to recoup—for instance, if a sale took place shortly after the law's enactment. Whatever the validity of that concern, it is not relevant to this facial challenge to the law. Defendant has not claimed that she was so injured, and her argument must fall to the general principle that a litigant cannot sustain a facial challenge to a law when that law is constitutional in its application to that litigant.

Defendant's second argument is premised on the "fundamental rule that zoning deals basically with land use and not with the person who owns or occupies it." In essence, the rule is a prohibition against *ad hominem* zoning decisions (see Matter of Dexter v. Town Bd., 36 N.Y.2d 102, 324 N.E.2d 870). In *Dexter*, for instance, a zoning change needed to allow a supermarket was to be effective only if a certain corporation developed the site. We voided the action on the ground that the identity of the site's owner was irrelevant to its suitability for a certain type of development. Likewise, variances to accommodate the personal physical needs of the occupants have been denied on the basis that such needs are unrelated to land use (see Matter of Fuhst v. Foley, 45 N.Y.2d 441, 382 N.E.2d 756). In the present case, defendant claims that the Village's amortization scheme is similarly personal in that the right to the nonconforming use is enjoyed only by those who owned the property in 1968 and cannot be transferred.

Defendant misconstrues the nature of the prohibition against *ad hominem*-zoning. The hallmark of cases like *Dexter* and *Fuhst* (supra) is that an identifiable individual is singled out for special treatment in land use regulation. No such individualized treatment is involved in the present case. All similarly situated owners are treated identically. The same is true for all prospective buyers. The only preferential treatment identified by defendant is that the owner in 1968 has rights that no future owner will enjoy. But the law has long recognized the special status of those who have a preexisting use at the time land controls are adopted. Indeed, the allowance of a nonconforming use in the first instance is based on that recognition. To the extent that defendant's argument is an attack on special treatment for the owners of nonconforming uses it flies in the face of established law.

In fact, what defendant is actually arguing is that the Village should not be allowed to infringe on an owner's ability to transfer the right to continue a non-conforming use. It is true that, in the absence of amortization legislation, the right to continue a nonconforming use runs with the land. However, once a valid amortization scheme is enacted, the right ends at the termination of the amortization period. As a practical matter, that means the owner of record during the amortization period will enjoy a right that cannot be transferred to a subsequent owner once the period passes. In such circumstances, the law is not rendered invalid because the original owner no longer has a right to transfer or because the original owner and subsequent owners have received disparate treatment under the land use regulations.

Here, of course, the absence of the right at the time of transfer is not left to the happenstance of when the owner decides to sell but is an explicit part of the legislative plan. But that difference does not change the test for the validity of an amortization period. The test remains whether the period unreasonably inflicts a substantial loss on the owner or fails to comport to the reasonableness required by due process. Put simply, there is no independent requirement that the right to continue the nonconforming use be available for transfer at a given time. That is true whether the right to continue the nonconforming use is terminated by the passage of time, destruction of the use, abandonment or, as here, transfer of ownership. Thus, the mere fact that the right cannot be transferred or that later owners are treated disparately from the original owner is insufficient to sustain defendant's facial challenge to the ordinance.

Nor can we subscribe to the Appellate Division's theory that the amortization period here is unreasonable because it may be too long. In the Appellate Division's view, an open-ended amortization schedule does not reasonably advance land use objectives. The Appellate Division noted that if a corporation owned one of the mobile homes here, the amortization period would be limitless in theory. The Village answers by stating that all six mobile homes were owned by individuals, and thus amortization would end, at the latest, upon their deaths. . . .

Thus, we conclude that defendant has failed to prevail on her facial challenge to the Village law. As to the remaining issues raised, further factual development is necessary.

Accordingly, the order of the Appellate Division should be modified, without costs, by denying defendant's cross motion for summary judgment and, as so modified, affirmed.

■ POINTS TO CONSIDER

1. **The minority rule.** Note that *Village of Valatie* applies the majority rule, which holds that amortization of nonconforming uses is permissible if a reasonable period is allowed. A *minority* of jurisdictions, however, hold that the whole concept of amortization is *unconstitutional*. These courts reason that requiring the cessation of a nonconforming use deprives the owner of a vested property right, which must be compensated under the Constitution. As we will learn in Chapter 14, the Constitution requires compensation when government action deprives an owner of valuable property rights. For that reason, municipalities can't immediately shut down nonconforming uses, without compensation, because taking away the vested right to a use would be a "taking" of a property right. These courts hold that delaying the governmental deprivation of vested rights for a period of time does not magically make it constitutional. *See, e.g.,* PA Nw. Distribs., Inc. v. Zoning Hearing Bd., 584 A.2d 1372, 1375 (Pa. 1991) ("[a] lawful nonconforming use establishes in the property owner a vested property right which cannot be abrogated or destroyed, unless it is a nuisance, it is abandoned, or it is extinguished by eminent domain.").

   As the Missouri Supreme Court said:

   > [I]t would be a strange and novel doctrine indeed which would approve a municipality taking private property for public use without compensation if the property was not too valuable and the taking was not too soon. . . .

   Hoffman v. Kinealy, 389 S.W.2d 745, 753 (Mo. 1965); *see also* Heck v. City of Pacific, 447 S.W.3d 202 (Mo. Ct. App. 2014). Which view do you support? Assume that you are a city official (or a city attorney) in a state, such as Missouri or Pennsylvania, that does not allow amortization. How do you deal with nonconforming uses, such as junkyards or mobile homes, that you believe need to be phased out?

2. **Reasonableness.** In judging whether the amortization ordinance is reasonable, what factors do the courts consider? In what way do those factors implicate our fundamental property goals? How can the court determine the ordinance is reasonable when the exact amortization period allowed is indeterminate? Does the "personhood" theory play a part in the decision?

3. **Sticks in the bundle.** Remember in Chapter 1 we said that in some situations, property rights might include some, but not all, of the sticks in the bundle? In *Village of Valatie*, which sticks are missing from the bundle held by the owners of manufactured homes?

■ PROBLEMS: AMORTIZATION

For the following problems, assume that the jurisdiction follows the majority rule, which allows amortization of nonconforming uses if a reasonable period is allowed. What arguments could you make, on either side, regarding the reasonableness of the following amortization provisions?

1. The City of Dogwood decided that the presence of adult businesses in the downtown area was contributing to the decay of the urban core and detracting from the City's ability to attract conventions and new business to the area. The Dogwood City Council passed a new ordinance banning adult businesses in the "Downtown Commercial" zone and giving existing adult businesses in that district six months to cease operations. Two such businesses, Earl's Dance Parlor and A-1 Adult Books, challenge the ordinance as unreasonable.

2. Arnold has operated an automobile salvage yard on Blackacre since 1985. The nearby town of Arborville annexed the property in 1995 and zoned it for light commercial, which made Arnold's junkyard a nonconforming use. A strip mall is now located next door and a fast-food restaurant is planned for across the road. The city tried to negotiate a buy-out of Arnold's business, but he refused. The city then enacted an ordinance requiring all salvage yards in commercial districts to cease operations within 18 months.

b. *Abandonment*

The privilege of continuing a nonconforming use is lost if the owner *abandons* the use. As we know from other contexts, such as easements, the term *abandonment* generally connotes not only the cessation of a use, but also the *intent* to permanently discontinue it. In the context of a nonconforming use, courts often read abandonment ordinances to require an intent to abandon. Where there is a long period of non-use, however, a court might shift the burden to the landowner to show an intent to continue, and *infer an intent to abandon* from a lack of activity. *See, e.g.*, Burlington Sand & Gravel, Inc. v. Town of Harvard, 528 N.E.2d 889 (Mass. App. Ct. 1988).

Modern ordinances tend to be stated in terms of *discontinuance* rather than abandonment. Discontinuance refers to a particular period of non-use (e.g., six months or a year) after which the nonconforming status is lost. In some states, this type of ordinance still requires some evidence of intent to abandon. In others, the period of non-use eliminates the need to prove an intent to abandon. *See, e.g.*, Prudco Realty Corp. v. Palermo, 455 N.E.2d 483 (N.Y. 1983); Rodehorst Brothers v. City of Norfolk Bd. of Adjustment, 844 N.W.2d 755 (Neb. 2014) (discontinuance statute does not require intent to abandon). In others, it establishes a rebuttable presumption: the burden shifts to the landowner to prove an intent to continue. Some courts also say that the nonconforming use should not be lost if the discontinuance was involuntary. *See* Boles v. City of Chattanooga, 892 S.W.2d 416 (Tenn. Ct. App. 1994).

■ PROBLEM: ABANDONMENT

Charlie had, for many years, operated a streetside hotdog stand in a busy commercial area. He leased part of a parking lot owned by Big Bank and built a small wooden structure opening out on the sidewalk. In 2010, the City amended the zoning code to prohibit street vendors, but allowed Charlie to continue as a nonconforming use. In May 2018, the City found that Charlie had violated several provisions of the health code and ordered him to shut down until he had made several alterations in the floor drain and ventilation system. Charlie had a little trouble finding a contractor to make the repairs and then winter came, during which he usually closed for several months anyway. In the meantime, his lease expired and he had some trouble renegotiating a new one. By June 2019, however, he was ready to go. At that point, the City ordered Charlie to cease, based on the one-year discontinuance provision of the city code. What result?

Preparing to Practice Class Exercise: Nonconforming Use

For many years, King Coal Company operated a small coal mine on 200 acres called (appropriately) Blackacre, in an unzoned portion of Monroe County. In 1995, as the coal became harder to mine and the market collapsed, King discontinued mining. During the next two decades, residential development began to sprout up near Blackacre. In 2019, King sold Blackacre to MegaDump, which planned to use the large holes in the ground as a landfill. MegaDump also acquired Whiteacre, a 100-acre tract adjacent to Blackacre, where it planned to eventually expand its operation. MegaDump paid $800,000 for the two properties, plus additional sums for engineering studies and environmental permits. MegaDump planned to develop four parts of Blackacre and one part of Whiteacre as a landfill. It completed work to prepare Phase 1, by building a road, and excavating and lining the pit.

Just as it was about to begin operation, however, the local residents convinced the county Board of Supervisors to zone the area Estate Residential, a classification that explicitly prohibited all mining and landfill uses.

Monroe County ordinances include the following:

Section 501: A nonconforming use certificate shall be issued to permit the continuance of nonconforming uses. A nonconforming use is defined as: Any continuous, lawful land use having commenced prior to the time of adoption, revision or amendment of the zoning ordinance, but which fails, by reason of such adoption, revision, or amendment, to conform to the present requirements of the zoning district.

Section 502: A legal nonconforming land use may be continued from the time that legal nonconforming land use is established, except that:

A. No such use shall be expanded, enlarged, increased, or extended to occupy a greater area than that occupied when the legal nonconforming use was established.

B. No such use may be intensified over the level of use that existed at the time the legal nonconforming use was established.

C. The legal nonconforming use may be changed to a use of a similar or more restricted nature, subject to a use certificate in each case.

In addition, the price of coal has gone back up and MegaDump wants to lease part of the site to a coal company for continued mining. The neighbors oppose that plan as well.

Is MegaDump entitled to nonconforming use status? If so, to what extent? *See* Vulcan Materials Co. v. Greenville Cnty. Bd. of Zoning Appeals, 536 S.E.2d 892 (S.C. Ct. App. 2000).

You will be assigned to represent MegaDump, Monroe County, or the neighbors. Meet with the other parties to discuss your party's position and determine whether any agreement can be negotiated. In attempting to negotiate a resolution, think not only about the legal position and *rights* of each party, but also about the *interests* of each party and whether there are possibilities for cooperative problem-solving. As you prepare, think about the following advice:

> Rather than simply stating their positions, which are often in opposition to one another, parties should focus on their interests. Positions are the outcomes people believe will satisfy their underlying interests. Interests explain why people care about an issue, what motivates them, and what they deem important. . . .
>
> Processes that help parties tease out interests, invent options based on those interests, and find ways to select options that meet the shared interests are most likely to result in stable, wise, and fair outcomes. If well identified, interests can serve as the building blocks for options and approaches to satisfy the parties.

Sean Nolon, Ona Ferguson & Pat Field, Land in Conflict: Managing and Resolving Land Use Disputes 14 (2013).

SUMMARY

■ American cities began to adopt *comprehensive zoning ordinances* in the early twentieth century, as land use conflicts became more frequent and city planning began to be more desirable.

■ The Supreme Court in *Euclid v. Ambler Realty Co.* held that, in general, comprehensive zoning ordinances did not violate the Due Process Clause of the Constitution.

- Nevertheless, particular applications of zoning ordinances could be held unconstitutional if found not to be *rationally related* to legitimate police power objectives such as promoting health, safety, and welfare.

- Zoning has many *advantages*, including separating conflicting land uses and allowing for efficient planning of transportation and government services.

- However, zoning can have *disadvantages* as well, including interference with market forces leading to inefficient land use and impacts on the environment and small businesses.

- Zoning ordinances may run into other constitutional problems, such as interfering with the *freedom of religion or speech* under the First Amendment, or violating the *Equal Protection Clause* of the Fourteenth Amendment through unequal treatment.

- State enabling acts typically require zoning to be done "in accordance with a comprehensive plan." A *comprehensive plan* is a policy document that sets out the community's long-term goals and strategies for achieving them.

- However, some states do not require a separate plan to be produced apart from the comprehensive zoning ordinance. Even when a separate comprehensive plan is produced, most states consider them *advisory* only.

- Comprehensive zoning ordinances typically divide the city into various *use districts*, such as gradations of residential, commercial, and industrial, and may also include height and area districts.

- To provide sufficient flexibility, a landowner may seek to rezone a particular tract through a *zoning amendment*. Typically, a zoning amendment must go through the Planning and Zoning Commission and be approved by the city council.

- In addition, a landowner may seek a *use or area variance* from the Board of Zoning Adjustment, to seek relief from particular zoning requirements. A variance should be granted only upon a finding of *unnecessary hardship*, which requires an examination of the impact on the landowner, as well as the harm to the neighbors if the variance were to be granted.

- Jurisdictions vary as to how strictly they interpret the variance test. In some jurisdictions, a lower standard of *practical difficulties* is used for area variances.

- Zoning ordinances usually allow pre-existing *nonconforming uses* to continue, based on a concept of vested rights. However, most jurisdictions do not allow the owner to expand or modify a nonconforming use, or rebuild if a nonconforming building is destroyed. The right to continue may also be lost by *abandoning* the use, although jurisdictions differ as to whether this requires proof of an intent to abandon.

- Most jurisdictions allow *amortization* of nonconforming uses, in which the owner is given a certain period of time to cease, as long as the period given is reasonable under the circumstances. Some jurisdictions, however, consider this to be an unconstitutional taking of property rights without just compensation.

CHAPTER 14

Constitutional Limitations on Land Use Control: The Takings Clause

> [N]or shall private property be taken for public use, without just compensation.
>
> —*U.S. Const. amend. V*

The final chapter of this book takes us back, in a way, to the concepts we discussed in Chapter 1. The introductory material stressed that, for many important policy reasons, the protection of property constitutes one of the foundational goals of our government. Not surprisingly, then, the Constitution contains some important protections for property owners. As we have already discussed, the Due Process Clauses of the Fifth and Fourteenth Amendments provide a significant procedural and substantive check on governmental control of property. First Amendment rights may also be implicated by land use controls that infringe on speech or religion.

In this chapter, we discuss the constitutional limitation on government *deprivations* of property, contained in what is known as the *Takings Clause* of the Fifth Amendment (quoted above). While the Fifth Amendment applies directly only to the federal government, the Takings Clause is applied to the states (and their subdivisions, such as cities and counties) by incorporation through the Fourteenth Amendment.

The strength of these constitutional property protections depends on those fundamental questions we asked in the first chapter: what constitutes a property interest, and when has it been "taken" so that compensation is required? In *Pierson v. Post*, the court had to call on notions of fairness, certainty, and efficiency to determine when a hunter had been deprived of a property interest in a fox.[1] Similarly, in this chapter, we use the same policies to determine how far the government can go in limiting and "redefining" the bundle of property rights before it must compensate the owner.

Remember, we are dealing with one of the most coercive of governmental powers—the ability to deprive you of your property. Under what circumstances should that be allowed?

To understand what's at stake, let's start with this example:

➤ Novak owns 80 acres of land called Blackacre in Coffey County. He grows organic vegetables and sells them to local restaurants. The County's biggest employer, an appliance manufacturer called Juneco, sits just across the road from Blackacre. Over the last several years, it has made several attempts to buy Blackacre, so it can expand its operations, but Novak is unwilling to sell. He grew up on this land, and it has been in his family for three generations. Moreover, he has finally gotten the soil and irrigation just the way he wants it for organic farming, and he likes the proximity of his land to the restaurants he supplies.

➤ Now, however, the County has notified him that it is considering taking his land by eminent domain for a new "industrial park," and then selling or leasing it to Juneco. Recently, Juneco has threatened to close its plant and move to Mexico unless it is able to expand. Given the number of jobs Juneco provides, the County considers the deal vital to its economic interests. The county will give Novak fair market value for his land, of course.

➤ Coincidentally, Novak is also thinking about expansion. His customer list is growing and he will soon be unable to keep up with demand. Ten of his acres lie near the Mucky River; so far, they have been too soggy to be farmed. Novak plans to truck in some fill dirt to raise the elevation of the land, so he can cultivate it. He is told that he needs a "dredge and fill" permit, because those acres are classified as wetlands. He applies, but permission is denied. The government believes that filling the wetlands will cause too much environmental harm to the Mucky River's ecosystem, which includes some endangered species. Novak complains that he now is stuck with ten acres that are virtually worthless, and the permit denial is costing him thousands of dollars a year in potential profits.

---

[1] Pierson v. Post, 3 Cai. R. 175, 178-79 (1805).

Are these governmental actions constitutional? Novak's situation illustrates the two main types of problems implicating the Takings Clause: eminent domain and regulatory takings. Coffey County's proposal to forcibly acquire Blackacre is an example of *eminent domain.* Read the Fifth Amendment, printed above, one more time. You should see that it contains two important limitations on this type of government action: Novak must be given *just compensation,* and the taking must be for a *public use.* In this case, Novak questions whether any compensation would be "just." This land is special to him—he knows that the market price will never compensate him for the personal value he attaches to this land. He also questions whether the county's plan for Blackacre—giving it to another private party—really constitutes a valid "public use."

Novak's wetlands problem raises the issue of *regulatory takings.* The government isn't physically confiscating Novak's property, and title is still in his name. Yet, the government's *restrictions on use*—one of the most important sticks in the bundle—have virtually destroyed the value of those ten acres. Instead of an *explicit* taking of Novak's property, in this case the government's actions might be deemed to have indirectly or *impliedly "taken"* those ten acres. Does Novak deserve just compensation for this deprivation of his property rights? We will consider the difficult issue of regulatory takings in the last part of this chapter.

A   EMINENT DOMAIN

We will begin by exploring the limitations on the government's use of its eminent domain power. First, where does this power come from? Although seemingly implied by the Fifth Amendment, the federal Constitution does not contain an explicit authorization allowing the government to take property by eminent domain; most state constitutions are similar. Nevertheless, the Supreme Court has consistently held that the power is *inherent* in the concept of *sovereignty*:

> The power to take private property for public uses, generally termed the right of eminent domain, belongs to every independent government. It is an incident of sovereignty, and . . . requires no constitutional recognition. The provision found in the Fifth Amendment to the federal constitution, and in the constitutions of the several states, for just compensation for the property taken, is merely a limitation upon the use of the power. It is no part of the power itself, but a condition upon which the power may be exercised.

United States v. Jones, 109 U.S. 513, 518 (1883). Other courts have noted that the power of eminent domain is a "necessity of government." People v. Adirondack Ry. Co., 54 N.E. 689, 692 (N.Y. 1899) (power "essential to [state's] existence").

Do you agree that the power of eminent domain is "essential"? If you wanted to build a new supermarket, for example, you would have to negotiate with the property owner or owners in an attempt to assemble an adequate parcel of land in the best location. Transaction costs would typically increase with the size of the project and limited options for locations. Now think about governmental projects, such as building a new post office, a new highway, or a new school. Should we expect the government to negotiate with willing sellers to accomplish these plans?

State governments delegate their eminent domain power by statute to local governments, to public utilities, to public universities, or even private individuals for quasi-public purposes. These examples of *eminent domain authority* may remind you of some of the issues we've covered in previous chapters:

> ➢ Remember the problem of natural gas storage we explored in Chapter 2? Some states authorize gas companies to use eminent domain to acquire underground storage capacity for natural gas. *See* In re Central N.Y. Oil & Gas Co., LLC, 969 N.Y.S.2d 174 (N.Y. App. Div. 2013).
> ➢ Remember the problem, discussed in Chapter 10, of the landlocked landowner and the limitations on establishing a common law easement by necessity? Many states allow private individuals whose property is landlocked to use eminent domain to force a neighbor to grant an easement for access. *See, e.g.,* Wash. Rev. Code §8.24.010 (2018) (condemnation allowed for "private way of necessity").
> ➢ Remember our discussion in Chapter 2 of "prior appropriation" of water rights, which allows non-riparian landowners to acquire property rights in water? How do they get the water to their land? In some western states, private parties may use eminent domain to acquire easements for the pipes or ditches needed to convey water to their land for irrigation purposes. *See* Telford Lands LLC v. Cain, 303 P.3d 1237 (Idaho 2013).

The language of these *statutory authorizations* must be carefully considered, because these eminent domain powers often contain important limitations and special procedures that must be used.

Condemnation

The use of eminent domain is referred to as a *condemnation* of private property. In our example, the County would be the *condemnor* and Novak would be the *condemnee.* You may associate the word "condemned" with property that is in uninhabitable condition. In the legal sense, however, any time government takes property by eminent domain, it has *condemned* it. Thus, the legal procedure used is called a *condemnation action.*

1. Just Compensation

If the County is allowed to take Novak's farm, the Constitution says he is entitled to "just compensation." How will that be calculated?

It is often said that "just compensation" means the owner is entitled to the property's *fair market value.* The Supreme Court has said:

Just compensation includes all elements of value that inhere in the property, but it does not exceed market value fairly determined. The sum required to be paid the owner does not depend upon the uses to which he has devoted his land but is to be arrived at upon just consideration of all the uses for which it is suitable. The highest and most profitable use for which the property is adaptable and needed or likely to be needed in the reasonably near future is to be considered, not necessarily as the measure of value, but to the full extent that the prospect of demand for such use affects the market value while the property is privately held.

Olson v. United States, 292 U.S. 246, 255 (1934). The idea is to estimate the amount a willing buyer would pay a willing seller in a voluntary, open market sale. The estimate is based on the *highest and best use* of the land, not necessarily its current use.

Comparable sales are the preferred method of determining fair market value. However, in some cases, comparable sales are not available, so other methods must be used. For example, if the property is producing income, an income capitalization method might be used to estimate the net cash flow and reduce it to present value. Assume a condemnation will destroy a billboard on Novak's property that he has rented out. It might be difficult to get "comparable" sales of billboards; a better value might be obtained by capitalizing the expected income stream (reducing it to a lump sum present value).

Many states use a procedure requiring the appointment of commissioners to make an initial assessment of just compensation. *See, e.g.*, Ala. Code §18-1A-279 (2017); Ky. Rev. Stat. Ann. §416.580 (West 2018). The commissioners then report to the court, which enters judgment based on their assessment. The condemnee may appeal this determination: the question of *the right to condemn* is usually a question of law for the judge, while the *amount of just compensation* may be determined by a jury. *See, e.g.*, Gamble v. State, 266 So. 2d 286 (Ala. 1972); Ala. Code §18-1A-283 (2017). So, in deciding whether to accept a condemnation offer, a condemnee like Novak should assess the possibility of convincing a jury to award higher compensation.

Practice Tip

Just because parties have the power of eminent domain doesn't mean they won't negotiate on the price or other terms. Condemnors would much rather reach a voluntary sales agreement to avoid the lengthy, expensive condemnation process.

■ PROBLEM: JUST COMPENSATION

In the example of Novak above, assume that Blackacre consists of 80 acres of land (60 tillable acres) and a three-bedroom wood-frame house. The County introduces evidence showing that, based on comparable sales in the area, Blackacre would sell for about $800,000. Novak would like the jury to consider that the recent construction of a nearby highway has made the area more attractive to developers who want to build subdivisions. He also would like the jury to consider the $50,000 he just spent on a new irrigation system for his organic vegetables. Above all, he would like the jury to consider that this property has been in his family for many generations and has significant sentimental value to him. Should this evidence be admissible?

Putting It Together: Eminent Domain and Servitudes

In 2000, Kaija and Albert Jensen bought Lot 15 in the Rolling Hills Subdivision and built their residence on it. They felt good about the fact that all of the lots in the subdivision were bound by a set of restrictive covenants requiring that the property be used "for single-family residential purposes only." Lots 19 and 20, located just behind the Jensens' lot, had not yet been developed or sold, but the Jensens knew the lots were bound by the covenants.

In 2014, Lots 19 and 20 were condemned by the local school district, which intended to use them (along with some other adjacent land) for a new elementary school. This use would obviously violate the covenant on the land and upset the Jensens' settled expectations. Can the school district violate the covenants? If so, must it compensate the Jensens and any other subdivision owners damaged by the covenant violation?

The school district also plans to condemn a five-acre piece of Whiteacre, adjacent to the Rolling Hills Subdivision, to use as the school's playground and parking lot. Whiteacre is owned by Greta Green. In 2005, Greta placed a "conservation easement" on her land, which she donated to the Nature Conservancy. The easement obligated her to refrain from any development or disturbance of the land. The easement lowered the value of Whiteacre from $5,000 per acre as developable land, to $1,000 per acre as preserve land. Greta took a tax deduction based on that amount.

Can the school district simply "override" that conservation easement? How much should the district pay for Whiteacre, and who should get the money?

2. The "Public Use" Limitation

Many people whose property is subject to condemnation are very upset—this is a forced sale and may be a dislocation from their home or business. They often seek the advice of attorneys about what they can do to stop the action. In most cases, the answer is simple: not much. Unless there happens to be an endangered species on the property that would prevent the government from building its proposed highway or school, there is usually nothing you can do to prevent the taking.

The only limitation specified in the Constitution, other than the just compensation requirement, is that the taking must be for a *public use.*

What does *public use* mean? In most cases, this limitation is easily met, because the public will actually be *using* the condemned property for a highway, or a public library, or a post office, or a park, for example. Condemnation also is commonly used for railroads, telecommunications, and utilities: in those cases,

Practice Tip: Defending Condemnation

If you are representing the condemnee, you may not be able to stop the condemnation, but you should always:

- ▓ ensure that the condemnor has proper statutory authority and stays within the limits of that authority;
- ▓ ensure that the condemnor follows the proper statutory procedure;
- ▓ ensure that the condemnee is paid just compensation;
- ▓ negotiate terms (location or timing, for example) to reduce the impact on the condemnee as much as possible.

even though the ownership of the property may be in private hands, a *public service* is being provided.

Questions arise, however, when property is taken from one private party and given to another, such that the public does not use the property at all. Think about the example of Novak described above. Is there a public use involved in taking the property from Novak and selling it to Juneco?

In a series of cases, the Supreme Court has held that, with regard to the limitation in the *federal* Constitution, *public use* should be read broadly to mean *public purpose*:

➢ In Berman v. Parker, 348 U.S. 26 (1954), the Court considered Congress's plan for urban redevelopment in Washington, D.C. In order to clear out a large area of the city it considered "blighted," Congress gave a redevelopment agency the authority to condemn that entire area. Part of it would then be used for traditional public uses such as schools or parks, but some of it would be leased or sold to private parties whose proposed uses (such as apartments or department stores) fit the redevelopment plan. The owner of a department store in the designated area challenged the condemnation, arguing that *his* property was not blighted.[2] The Court unanimously held that urban redevelopment constituted a valid public purpose, which met the "public use" limitation:

> It is within the power of the legislature to determine that the community should be beautiful as well as healthy, spacious as well as clean, well-balanced as well as carefully patrolled. In the present case, the Congress and its authorized agencies have made determinations that take into account a wide variety of values. It is not for us to reappraise them. If those who govern the District of Columbia decide that the Nation's Capital should be beautiful as well as sanitary, there is nothing in the Fifth Amendment that stands in the way.
>
> Once the object is within the authority of Congress, the right to realize it through the exercise of eminent domain is clear. For the power of eminent domain is merely the means to the end.

Id. at 33. The Court thus gave its blessing to a forced transfer from one private party to another, in furtherance of urban redevelopment efforts. It held that the public use requirement was met even though the public

---

[2] The department store was at 712 Fourth Street, S.W., which now appears to be a private apartment building. The entire redevelopment displaced approximately 1,500 businesses and 23,000 residents from 560 acres of land.

would not be actually owning, or even using, all of the property, and even though not every individual property taken was blighted.

> In Hawaii Hous. Auth. v. Midkiff, 467 U.S. 229 (1984), the Court considered a Hawaii statute intended to help alleviate a land oligopoly—a concentration of property ownership in the hands of very few landowners. Under the statute, in certain circumstances, a lessee of property could ask the government to condemn fee title from the lessor and transfer it to the lessee upon payment of just compensation to the lessor. Understand what this means: renter B could force landlord A to sell a rented house to her, even though A didn't want to sell! Justice O'Connor's opinion for a unanimous Supreme Court upheld the Hawaii statute:

> The mere fact that property taken outright by eminent domain is transferred in the first instance to private beneficiaries does not condemn that taking as having only a private purpose. The Court long ago rejected any literal requirement that condemned property be put into use for the general public. "It is not essential that the entire community, nor even any considerable portion, . . . directly enjoy or participate in any improvement in order [for it] to constitute a public use." Rindge Co. v. Los Angeles, 262 U.S., at 707. . . . The Act advances its purposes without the State's taking actual possession of the land. In such cases, government does not itself have to use property to legitimate the taking; it is only the taking's purpose, and not its mechanics, that must pass scrutiny under the Public Use Clause.

> *Id.* at 243-44.

Thus, after *Berman* and *Midkiff,* it seemed that *public use* really meant *public purpose.* As long as the legislative body could articulate a legitimate governmental goal furthered by taking the property, it would pass muster.

Those precedents set the stage for the next case, a controversial decision that tested the limits of the Court's public use jurisprudence. *Kelo v. City of New London* involved the condemnation of an area that definitely was *not* "blighted," solely for the purpose of *economic development.* Is this case different, in any material way, from *Berman* or *Midkiff?* If not, why then did Justice O'Connor, who wrote the Court's unanimous opinion in *Midkiff,* dissent so emphatically in *Kelo?* Pay close attention to Justice Kennedy's concurrence, which—not unusually—provides the fifth vote in this case. Does the public use clause provide any meaningful limitation on government condemnations after *Kelo?*

KELO v. CITY OF NEW LONDON

545 U.S. 469 (2005)
Supreme Court of the United States

Justice STEVENS delivered the opinion of the Court.

In 2000, the city of New London approved a development plan that, in the words of the Supreme Court of Connecticut, was "projected to create in excess of

1,000 jobs, to increase tax and other revenues, and to revitalize an economically distressed city, including its downtown and waterfront areas." 268 Conn. 1, 5, 843 A.2d 500, 507 (2004). In assembling the land needed for this project, the city's development agent has purchased property from willing sellers and proposes to use the power of eminent domain to acquire the remainder of the property from unwilling owners in exchange for just compensation. The question presented is whether the city's proposed disposition of this property qualifies as a "public use" within the meaning of the Takings Clause of the Fifth Amendment to the Constitution.

I

The city of New London (hereinafter City) sits at the junction of the Thames River and the Long Island Sound in southeastern Connecticut. Decades of economic decline led a state agency in 1990 to designate the City a "distressed municipality." In 1996, the Federal Government closed the Naval Undersea Warfare Center, which had been located in the Fort Trumbull area of the City and had employed over 1,500 people. In 1998, the City's unemployment rate was nearly double that of the State, and its population of just under 24,000 residents was at its lowest since 1920.

These conditions prompted state and local officials to target New London, and particularly its Fort Trumbull area, for economic revitalization. To this end, respondent New London Development Corporation (NLDC), a private nonprofit entity established some years earlier to assist the City in planning economic development, was reactivated. In January 1998, the State authorized a $5.35 million bond issue to support the NLDC's planning activities and a $10 million bond issue toward the creation of a Fort Trumbull State Park. In February, the pharmaceutical company Pfizer Inc. announced that it would build a $300 million research facility on a site immediately adjacent to Fort Trumbull; local planners hoped that Pfizer would draw new business to the area, thereby serving as a catalyst to the area's rejuvenation. After receiving initial approval from the city council, the. . .NLDC finalized an integrated development plan focused on 90 acres of the Fort Trumbull area.

The Fort Trumbull area is situated on a peninsula that juts into the Thames River. The area comprises approximately 115 privately owned properties, as well as the 32 acres of land formerly occupied by the naval facility (Trumbull State Park now occupies 18 of those 32 acres). The development plan included a waterfront conference hotel, marinas, 80 new residences, a Coast Guard museum, office and retail space.

The NLDC intended the development plan to capitalize on the arrival of the Pfizer facility and the new commerce it was expected to attract. In addition to creating jobs, generating tax revenue, and helping to "build momentum for the revitalization of downtown New London," *id.*, at 92, the plan was also designed to make the City more attractive and to create leisure and recreational opportunities on the waterfront and in the park.

The city council approved the plan in January 2000, and designated the NLDC as its development agent in charge of implementation. *See* Conn. Gen. Stat. §8-188 (2005). The city council also authorized the NLDC to purchase property or to acquire property by exercising eminent domain in the City's name. §8-193. The NLDC successfully negotiated the purchase of most of the real estate in the 90-acre area, but its negotiations with petitioners failed. As a consequence, in November 2000, the NLDC initiated the condemnation proceedings that gave rise to this case.

II

Petitioner Susette Kelo has lived in the Fort Trumbull area since 1997. She has made extensive improvements to her house, which she prizes for its water view. Petitioner Wilhelmina Dery was born in her Fort Trumbull house in 1918 and has lived there her entire life. Her husband Charles (also a petitioner) has lived in the house since they married some 60 years ago. In all, the nine petitioners own 15 properties in Fort Trumbull. . . . Ten of the parcels are occupied by the owner or a family member; the other five are held as investment properties. There is no allegation that any of these properties is blighted or otherwise in poor condition; rather, they were condemned only because they happen to be located in the development area.

In December 2000, petitioners brought this action in the New London Superior Court. They claimed, among other things, that the taking of their properties would violate the "public use" restriction in the Fifth Amendment.

[T]he Supreme Court of Connecticut . . . held, over a dissent, that all of the City's proposed takings were valid. It began by upholding the lower court's determination that the takings were authorized by chapter 132, the State's municipal development statute. See Conn. Gen. Stat. §8-186 et seq. (2005). That statute expresses a legislative determination that the taking of land, even developed land, as part of an economic development project is a "public use" and in the "public interest." Next, relying on cases such as Hawaii Housing Authority v. Midkiff, 467 U.S. 229 (1984), and Berman v. Parker, 348 U.S. 26 (1954), the court held that such economic development qualified as a valid public use under both the Federal and State Constitutions. . . .

We granted certiorari to determine whether a city's decision to take property for the purpose of economic development satisfies the "public use" requirement of the Fifth Amendment.

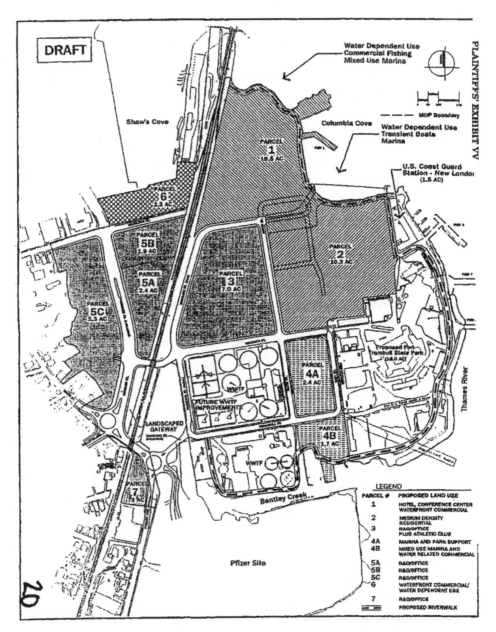

New London Redevelopment Plan Plaintiffs' properties are located on residential streets in Parcels 3 and 4A

Kelo v. City of New London, Exhibit VV, Joint Appendix, 2004 WL 2967525, at 4

III

Two polar propositions are perfectly clear. On the one hand, it has long been accepted that the sovereign may not take the property of A for the sole purpose of transferring it to another private party B, even though A is paid just compensation. On the other hand, it is equally clear that a State may transfer property from one private party to another if future "use by the public" is the purpose of the taking; the condemnation of land for a railroad with common-carrier duties is a familiar example. Neither of these propositions, however, determines the disposition of this case.

As for the first proposition, the City would no doubt be forbidden from taking petitioners' land for the purpose of conferring a private benefit on a particular private party. See *Midkiff*, 467 U.S., at 245 ("A purely private taking could not withstand the scrutiny of the public use requirement; it would serve no legitimate purpose of government and would thus be void"); Missouri Pacific R. Co. v. Nebraska, 164 U.S. 403 (1896). Nor would the City be allowed to take property under the mere pretext of a public purpose, when its actual purpose was to bestow a private benefit. The takings before us, however, would be executed pursuant to a "carefully considered" development plan. 268 Conn., at 54, 843 A.2d, at 536. The trial judge and all the members of the Supreme Court of Connecticut agreed that there was no evidence of an illegitimate purpose in this case. Therefore, as was true of the statute challenged in *Midkiff*, 467 U.S., at 245, the City's development plan was not adopted "to benefit a particular class of identifiable individuals."

On the other hand, this is not a case in which the City is planning to open the condemned land—at least not in its entirety—to use by the general public. Nor will the private lessees of the land in any sense be required to operate like common carriers, making their services available to all comers. But although such a projected use would be sufficient to satisfy the public use requirement, this "Court long ago rejected any literal requirement that condemned property be put into use for the general public." *Id.*, at 244. Indeed, while many state courts in the mid-19th century endorsed "use by the public" as the proper definition of public use, that narrow view steadily eroded over time. Not only was the "use by the public" test difficult to administer (e.g., what proportion of the public need have access to the property? at what price?),[3] but it proved to be impractical given the diverse and always evolving needs of society. Accordingly, when this Court began applying the Fifth Amendment to the States at the close of the 19th century, it embraced the broader and more natural interpretation of public use as "public purpose." See, e.g., Fallbrook Irrigation Dist. v. Bradley, 164 U.S. 112, 158-164 (1896).

---

[3] See, e.g., Dayton Gold & Silver Mining Co. v. Seawell, 11 Nev. 394, 410 (1876) ("If public occupation and enjoyment of the object for which land is to be condemned furnishes the only and true test for the right of eminent domain, then the legislature would certainly have the constitutional authority to condemn the lands of any private citizen for the purpose of building hotels and theaters. Why not? A hotel is used by the public as much as a railroad. The public have the same right, upon payment of a fixed compensation, to seek rest and refreshment at a public inn as they have to travel upon a railroad").

The disposition of this case therefore turns on the question whether the City's development plan serves a "public purpose." Without exception, our cases have defined that concept broadly, reflecting our longstanding policy of deference to legislative judgments in this field.

In Berman v. Parker, 348 U.S. 26 (1954), this Court upheld a redevelopment plan targeting a blighted area of Washington, D.C. . . . The public use underlying the taking was unequivocally affirmed. . . .

In Hawaii Housing Authority v. Midkiff, 467 U.S. 229 (1984), the Court . . . rejected the contention that the mere fact that the State immediately transferred the properties to private individuals upon condemnation somehow diminished the public character of the taking. "[I]t is only the taking's purpose, and not its mechanics," we explained, "that matters in determining public use. *Id.*, at 244. . . .

Viewed as a whole, our jurisprudence has recognized that the needs of society have varied between different parts of the Nation, just as they have evolved over time in response to changed circumstances. Our earliest cases in particular embodied a strong theme of federalism, emphasizing the "great respect" that we owe to state legislatures and state courts in discerning local public needs. See Hairston v. Danville & Western R. Co., 208 U.S. 598, 606-07 (1908), noting that these needs were likely to vary depending on a State's "resources, the capacity of the soil, the relative importance of industries to the general public welfare, and the long-established methods and habits of the people"). For more than a century, our public use jurisprudence has wisely eschewed rigid formulas and intrusive scrutiny in favor of affording legislatures broad latitude in determining what public needs justify the use of the takings power.

IV

Those who govern the City were not confronted with the need to remove blight in the Fort Trumbull area, but their determination that the area was sufficiently distressed to justify a program of economic rejuvenation is entitled to our deference. The City has carefully formulated an economic development plan that it believes will provide appreciable benefits to the community, including—but by no means limited to—new jobs and increased tax revenue. As with other exercises in urban planning and development,[4] the City is endeavoring to coordinate a variety of commercial, residential, and recreational uses of land, with the hope that they will form a whole greater than the sum of its parts. To effectuate this plan, the City has invoked a state statute that specifically authorizes the use of eminent domain to promote economic development. Given the comprehensive character of the plan, the thorough deliberation that preceded its adoption, and the limited scope of our review, it is appropriate for us, as it was in *Berman*, to resolve the challenges of the individual owners, not on a piecemeal basis, but rather in light of the entire plan. Because that plan unquestionably serves a

---

[4] Cf. Village of Euclid v. Ambler Realty Co., 272 U.S. 365 (1926).

public purpose, the takings challenged here satisfy the public use requirement of the Fifth Amendment.

To avoid this result, petitioners urge us to adopt a new bright-line rule that economic development does not qualify as a public use. Putting aside the unpersuasive suggestion that the City's plan will provide only purely economic benefits, neither precedent nor logic supports petitioners' proposal. Promoting economic development is a traditional and long-accepted function of government. There is, moreover, no principled way of distinguishing economic development from the other public purposes that we have recognized. In our cases upholding takings that facilitated agriculture and mining, for example, we emphasized the importance of those industries to the welfare of the States in question, *see, e.g., Strickley*, 200 U.S. 527; in *Berman*, we endorsed the purpose of transforming a blighted area into a "well-balanced" community through redevelopment, 348 U.S., at 33; in *Midkiff*, we upheld the interest in breaking up a land oligopoly that "created artificial deterrents to the normal functioning of the State's residential land market," 467 U.S., at 242; and in *Monsanto*, we accepted Congress' purpose of eliminating a "significant barrier to entry in the pesticide market," 467 U.S., at 1014-1015. It would be incongruous to hold that the City's interest in the economic benefits to be derived from the development of the Fort Trumbull area has less of a public character than any of those other interests. Clearly, there is no basis for exempting economic development from our traditionally broad understanding of public purpose.

Petitioners contend that using eminent domain for economic development impermissibly blurs the boundary between public and private takings. Again, our cases foreclose this objection. Quite simply, the government's pursuit of a public purpose will often benefit individual private parties. For example, in *Midkiff*, the forced transfer of property conferred a direct and significant benefit on those lessees who were previously unable to purchase their homes. . . . The owner of the department store in *Berman* objected to "taking from one businessman for the benefit of another businessman," 348 U.S., at 33, referring to the fact that under the redevelopment plan land would be leased or sold to private developers for redevelopment. Our rejection of that contention has particular relevance to the instant case: "The public end may be as well or better served through an agency of private enterprise than through a department of government—or so the Congress might conclude. We cannot say that public ownership is the sole method of promoting the public purposes of community redevelopment projects." *Id.*, at 33-34.[5]

---

[5] Nor do our cases support Justice O'Connor's novel theory that the government may only take property and transfer it to private parties when the initial taking eliminates some "harmful property use." There was nothing "harmful" about the nonblighted department store at issue in *Berman*, 348 U.S. 26; nothing "harmful" about the lands at issue in the mining and agriculture cases, *see, e.g., Strickley*, 200 U.S. 527, 26 S. Ct. 301; see also nn. 9, 11, supra; and certainly nothing "harmful" about the trade secrets owned by the pesticide manufacturers in *Monsanto*, 467 U.S. 986. In each case, the public purpose we upheld depended on a private party's future use of the concededly nonharmful property that was taken. By focusing on a property's future use, as opposed to its past use, our cases are faithful to the text of the Takings Clause.

It is further argued that without a bright-line rule nothing would stop a city from transferring citizen A's property to citizen B for the sole reason that citizen B will put the property to a more productive use and thus pay more taxes. Such a one-to-one transfer of property, executed outside the confines of an integrated development plan, is not presented in this case. While such an unusual exercise of government power would certainly raise a suspicion that a private purpose was afoot, the hypothetical cases posited by petitioners can be confronted if and when they arise. They do not warrant the crafting of an artificial restriction on the concept of public use.

Alternatively, petitioners maintain that for takings of this kind we should require a "reasonable certainty" that the expected public benefits will actually accrue. Such a rule, however, would represent an even greater departure from our precedent. "When the legislature's purpose is legitimate and its means are not irrational, our cases make clear that empirical debates over the wisdom of takings—no less than debates over the wisdom of other kinds of socioeconomic legislation—are not to be carried out in the federal courts." *Midkiff*, 467 U.S., at 242-243. . . . Orderly implementation of a comprehensive redevelopment plan obviously requires that the legal rights of all interested parties be established before new construction can be commenced. A constitutional rule that required postponement of the judicial approval of every condemnation until the likelihood of success of the plan had been assured would unquestionably impose a significant impediment to the successful consummation of many such plans.

Just as we decline to second-guess the City's considered judgments about the efficacy of its development plan, we also decline to second-guess the City's determinations as to what lands it needs to acquire in order to effectuate the project. "It is not for the courts to oversee the choice of the boundary line nor to sit in review on the size of a particular project area. Once the question of the public purpose has been decided, the amount and character of land to be taken for the project and the need for a particular tract to complete the integrated plan rests in the discretion of the legislative branch." *Berman*, 348 U.S., at 35-36.

In affirming the City's authority to take petitioners' properties, we do not minimize the hardship that condemnations may entail, notwithstanding the payment of just compensation. We emphasize that nothing in our opinion precludes any State from placing further restrictions on its exercise of the takings power. Indeed, many States already impose "public use" requirements that are stricter than the federal baseline. Some of these requirements have been established as a matter of state constitutional law, while others are expressed in state eminent domain statutes that carefully limit the grounds upon which takings may be exercised.[6] As the submissions of the parties and their amici make clear, the necessity and wisdom of using eminent domain to promote economic development are certainly matters of legitimate public debate. This Court's authority,

---

[6] Under California law, for instance, a city may only take land for economic development purposes in blighted areas. Cal. Health & Safety Code Ann. §§33030-33037 (West 1999). See, e.g., Redevelopment Agency of Chula Vista v. Rados Bros., 95 Cal. App. 4th 309, 115 Cal. Rptr. 2d 234 (2002).

however, extends only to determining whether the City's proposed condemnations are for a "public use" within the meaning of the Fifth Amendment to the Federal Constitution. Because over a century of our case law interpreting that provision dictates an affirmative answer to that question, we may not grant petitioners the relief that they seek.

The judgment of the Supreme Court of Connecticut is affirmed.

It is so ordered.

Justice KENNEDY, concurring.

I join the opinion for the Court and add these further observations.

This Court has declared that a taking should be upheld as consistent with the Public Use Clause, U.S. Const., Amdt. 5, as long as it is "rationally related to a conceivable public purpose." Hawaii Housing Authority v. Midkiff, 467 U.S. 229, 241 (1984). . . . The determination that a rational-basis standard of review is appropriate does not, however, alter the fact that transfers intended to confer benefits on particular, favored private entities, and with only incidental or pretextual public benefits, are forbidden by the Public Use Clause.

A court applying rational-basis review under the Public Use Clause should strike down a taking that, by a clear showing, is intended to favor a particular private party, with only incidental or pretextual public benefits, just as a court applying rational-basis review under the Equal Protection Clause must strike down a government classification that is clearly intended to injure a particular class of private parties, with only incidental or pretextual public justifications. . . .

A court confronted with a plausible accusation of impermissible favoritism to private parties should treat the objection as a serious one and review the record to see if it has merit, though with the presumption that the government's actions were reasonable and intended to serve a public purpose. Here, the trial court conducted a careful and extensive inquiry into "whether, in fact, the development plan is of primary benefit to . . . the developer [i.e., Corcoran Jennison], and private businesses which may eventually locate in the plan area [e.g., Pfizer], and in that regard, only of incidental benefit to the city." App. to Pet. for Cert. 261. . . .

The trial court concluded, based on these findings, that benefiting Pfizer was not "the primary motivation or effect of this development plan"; instead, "the primary motivation for [respondents] was to take advantage of Pfizer's presence." Id., at 276. Likewise, the trial court concluded that "[t]here is nothing in the record to indicate that . . . [respondents] were motivated by a desire to aid [other] particular private entities." Id., at 278. . . . This case, then, survives the meaningful rational-basis review that in my view is required under the Public Use Clause. . . .

My agreement with the Court that a presumption of invalidity is not warranted for economic development takings in general, or for the particular takings at issue in this case, does not foreclose the possibility that a more stringent standard of review than that announced in Berman and Midkiff might be appropriate for a more narrowly drawn category of takings. There may be private transfers in which the risk of undetected impermissible favoritism of private parties is so acute that a presumption (rebuttable or otherwise) of invalidity is warranted under the Public Use Clause. . . .

This is not the occasion for conjecture as to what sort of cases might justify a more demanding standard, but it is appropriate to underscore aspects of the instant case that convince me no departure from *Berman* and *Midkiff* is appropriate here. This taking occurred in the context of a comprehensive development plan meant to address a serious citywide depression, and the projected economic benefits of the project cannot be characterized as *de minimis*. The identities of most of the private beneficiaries were unknown at the time the city formulated its plans. The city complied with elaborate procedural requirements that facilitate review of the record and inquiry into the city's purposes. In sum, while there may be categories of cases in which the transfers are so suspicious, or the procedures employed so prone to abuse, or the purported benefits are so trivial or implausible, that courts should presume an impermissible private purpose, no such circumstances are present in this case.

. . . For the foregoing reasons, I join in the Court's opinion.

Justice O'CONNOR, with whom THE CHIEF JUSTICE, Justice SCALIA, and Justice THOMAS join, dissenting.

Over two centuries ago, just after the Bill of Rights was ratified, Justice Chase wrote:

> "An ACT of the Legislature (for I cannot call it a law) contrary to the great first principles of the social compact, cannot be considered a rightful exercise of legislative authority. . . . A few instances will suffice to explain what I mean. . . . [A] law that takes property from A. and gives it to B: It is against all reason and justice, for a people to entrust a Legislature with SUCH powers; and, therefore, it cannot be presumed that they have done it." Calder v. Bull, 3 Dall. 386, 388 (1798) (emphasis deleted).

Today the Court abandons this long-held, basic limitation on government power. Under the banner of economic development, all private property is now vulnerable to being taken and transferred to another private owner, so long as it might be upgraded—i.e., given to an owner who will use it in a way that the legislature deems more beneficial to the public—in the process. To reason, as the Court does, that the incidental public benefits resulting from the subsequent ordinary use of private property render economic development takings "for public use" is to wash out any distinction between private and public use of property—and thereby effectively to delete the words "for public use" from the Takings Clause of the Fifth Amendment. Accordingly I respectfully dissent.

Where is the line between "public" and "private" property use? We give considerable deference to legislatures' determinations about what governmental activities will advantage the public. But were the political branches the sole arbiters of the public-private distinction, the Public Use Clause would amount to little more than hortatory fluff. An external, judicial check on how the public use requirement is interpreted, however limited, is necessary if this constraint on government power is to retain any meaning. See Cincinnati v. Vester, 281 U.S. 439, 446 (1930) ("It is well established that . . . the question [of] what is a public use is a judicial one"). . . .

The Court's holdings in *Berman* and *Midkiff* were true to the principle underlying the Public Use Clause. In both those cases, the extraordinary, precondemnation use of the targeted property inflicted affirmative harm on society—in *Berman* through blight resulting from extreme poverty and in *Midkiff* through oligopoly resulting from extreme wealth. And in both cases, the relevant legislative body had found that eliminating the existing property use was necessary to remedy the harm. Thus a public purpose was realized when the harmful use was eliminated. Because each taking directly achieved a public benefit, it did not matter that the property was turned over to private use. Here, in contrast, New London does not claim that Susette Kelo's and Wilhelmina Dery's well-maintained homes are the source of any social harm. Indeed, it could not so claim without adopting the absurd argument that any single-family home that might be razed to make way for an apartment building, or any church that might be replaced with a retail store, or any small business that might be more lucrative if it were instead part of a national franchise, is inherently harmful to society and thus within the government's power to condemn.

In moving away from our decisions sanctioning the condemnation of harmful property use, the Court today significantly expands the meaning of public use. It holds that the sovereign may take private property currently put to ordinary private use, and give it over for new, ordinary private use, so long as the new use is predicted to generate some secondary benefit for the public—such as increased tax revenue, more jobs, maybe even esthetic pleasure. But nearly any lawful use of real private property can be said to generate some incidental benefit to the public. Thus, if predicted (or even guaranteed) positive side effects are enough to render transfer from one private party to another constitutional, then the words "for public use" do not realistically exclude any takings, and thus do not exert any constraint on the eminent domain power. . . .

The specter of condemnation hangs over all property. Nothing is to prevent the State from replacing any Motel 6 with a Ritz-Carlton, any home with a shopping mall, or any farm with a factory. Cf. Bugryn v. Bristol, 63 Conn. App. 98, 774 A.2d 1042 (2001) (taking the homes and farm of four owners in their 70's and 80's and giving it to an "industrial park"); 99 Cents Only Stores v. Lancaster Redevelopment Agency, 237 F. Supp. 2d 1123 (C.D. Cal. 2001) (attempted taking of 99 Cents store to replace with a Costco); Poletown Neighborhood Council v. Detroit, 410 Mich. 616, 304 N.W.2d 455 (1981) (taking a working-class, immigrant community in Detroit and giving it to a General Motors assembly plant), overruled by County of Wayne v. Hathcock, 471 Mich. 445, 684 N.W.2d 765 (2004); Brief for Becket Fund for Religious Liberty as Amicus Curiae 4-11 (describing takings of religious institutions' properties); Institute for Justice, D. Berliner, Public Power, Private Gain: A Five-Year, State-by-State Report Examining the Abuse of Eminent Domain (2003) (collecting accounts of economic development takings). . . .

* * *

Any property may now be taken for the benefit of another private party, but the fallout from this decision will not be random. The beneficiaries are likely to be those citizens with disproportionate influence and power in the political process, including large corporations and development firms. As for the victims, the government now has license to transfer property from those with fewer resources to those with more. The Founders cannot have intended this perverse result. "[T]hat alone is a just government," wrote James Madison, "which impartially secures to every man, whatever is his own." For the National Gazette, Property (Mar. 27, 1792), reprinted in 14 Papers of James Madison 266 (R. Rutland et al. eds. 1983).

I would hold that the takings in both Parcel 3 and Parcel 4A are unconstitutional, reverse the judgment of the Supreme Court of Connecticut, and remand for further proceedings.

Justice THOMAS, dissenting.

... Today's decision is simply the latest in a string of our cases construing the Public Use Clause to be a virtual nullity, without the slightest nod to its original meaning. In my view, the Public Use Clause, originally understood, is a meaningful limit on the government's eminent domain power. Our cases have strayed from the Clause's original meaning, and I would reconsider them. ...

The most natural reading of the Clause is that it allows the government to take property only if the government owns, or the public has a legal right to use, the property, as opposed to taking it for any public purpose or necessity whatsoever. ...

... The "public purpose" test applied by *Berman* and *Midkiff* also cannot be applied in principled manner. "When we depart from the natural import of the term 'public use,' and substitute for the simple idea of a public possession and occupation, that of public utility, public interest, common benefit, general advantage or convenience ... we are afloat without any certain principle to guide us." Bloodgood v. Mohawk & Hudson R. Co., 18 Wend. 9, 60-61 (N.Y. 1837) (opinion of Tracy, Sen.).

... The consequences of today's decision are not difficult to predict, and promise to be harmful. So-called "urban renewal" programs provide some compensation for the properties they take, but no compensation is possible for the subjective value of these lands to the individuals displaced and the indignity inflicted by uprooting them from their homes. Allowing the government to take property solely for public purposes is bad enough, but extending the concept of public purpose to encompass any economically beneficial goal guarantees that these losses will fall disproportionately on poor communities. Those communities are not only systematically less likely to put their lands to the highest and best social use, but are also the least politically powerful. If ever there were justification for intrusive judicial review of constitutional provisions that protect "discrete and insular minorities," United States v. Carolene Products Co.,

304 U.S. 144, 152, n.4 (1938), surely that principle would apply with great force to the powerless groups and individuals the Public Use Clause protects. The deferential standard this Court has adopted for the Public Use Clause is therefore deeply perverse. . . .

When faced with a clash of constitutional principle and a line of unreasoned cases wholly divorced from the text, history, and structure of our founding document, we should not hesitate to resolve the tension in favor of the Constitution's original meaning. For the reasons I have given, and for the reasons given in Justice O'Connor's dissent, the conflict of principle raised by this boundless use of the eminent domain power should be resolved in petitioners' favor. I would reverse the judgment of the Connecticut Supreme Court.

■ POINTS TO CONSIDER

1. **Federalism.** The term *federalism* describes the relationship between the two top tiers (federal and state) in our system of government. The U.S. Constitution grants only limited authority to the national government, while reserving all remaining power to the states. Advocates for stronger states' rights suggest that the Supreme Court should more narrowly interpret constitutional clauses that give the federal government power and should accord state sovereignty more respect. How does federalism play a role in the *Kelo* decision? Do you think it influenced Justice Kennedy's decision to join his more liberal colleagues in this case?

2. **Does the public use limitation have any teeth?** Can you imagine any circumstances in which the majority would find a violation of the public use clause? Consider carefully the opinion of Justice Kennedy, the deciding vote: What test does he use to judge the legitimacy of transfers to private parties? What facts in this case led him to conclude that the New London confiscation passed muster?

3. **Dissenting voices.** Justice O'Connor wrote the Court's opinion in *Midkiff*, upholding a transfer from one private owner to another, as long as there was a valid public purpose. Why does she find, in her vigorous dissent, that this precedent does not validate the transfer here? What test for public use does she favor? What problems does the majority see with her proposed rule? Despite the fact that Justice O'Connor's opinion did not win the day in this case, you should still pay attention to it for a couple of reasons. State courts may use her approach in interpreting similar provisions of their state constitutions.[7]

---

[7] In fact, some state courts have already cited Justice O'Connor's dissent in adopting narrower "public use" interpretations. *See, e.g.,* Board of Cnty. Comm'rs of Muskogee Cnty. v. Lowery, 136 P.3d 639, 647 (Okla. 2006); In re Condemnation by Redev. Auth. of Lawrence Cnty., 962 A.2d 1257, 1264 (Pa. Commw. Ct. 2008); Norwood v. Horney, 853 N.E.2d 1115, 1140 (Ohio 2006).

Legislatures might use it as a basis for adopting statutory limits on eminent domain. Furthermore, as you know, dissenting opinions might at some point in the future become majority positions and, in any event, might influence how later courts interpret the majority rule (e.g., to avoid some of the problems the dissent raises). Justice Thomas's dissent diverges even further from the majority, suggesting that *Berman* and *Midkiff* should be reconsidered, because they strayed too far from the original meaning of the public use limitation. What test would Justice Thomas use for "public use"? Is such a limitation workable? Should that matter?

■ PROBLEMS: PUBLIC USE LIMITATION

1. **Trade secrets.** Can the government force a company to divulge its trade secrets to help another company? Before a pesticide can be sold, Congress requires it to be registered with the Environmental Protection Agency (EPA) to ensure that it does not present an unreasonable risk to health and the environment. Therefore, the manufacturer must submit voluminous data on the laboratory testing it has performed. Assume that Company A submits an application for registration of a pesticide, containing test data that cost $23 million and took years to produce. Thus, Company A considers the data a valuable trade secret. Later, Company B submits an application for a very similar pesticide. Company B wants EPA to disclose Company A's data, so it can use it to support its own application. A federal statute provides that EPA must disclose the data, as long as Company B adequately compensates Company A. Company A objects to being forced to reveal its trade secrets to a competitor and argues that this "taking" of its intellectual property rights violates the public use limitation. EPA argues that the sharing of data promotes competition by avoiding the delay necessary to reproduce the data. Is there a valid public use? *See* Ruckelshaus v. Monsanto, 467 U.S. 986 (1984).

2. **University expansion.** For many years, Bogart University has hosted a popular track meet, called the Bogart Relays. The annual event draws competitors and spectators from around the country. Bogart University wants to continue its prominent position, as well as possibly attract even larger events, like national championships. To do so, Bogart's facilities need to be expanded and more parking needs to be provided. Bogart University has a plan involving the property just to the north of the stadium, which now has six single-family houses on it. Five of the six landowners are willing to sell, but the sixth, Wilma, refuses a very generous offer, because "she likes it here and is too old to move." Bogart University asks the City to condemn Wilma's house and transfer it to the university so it can proceed with the plan. Is that a public use? Does your opinion change if the university wanted the

land for law school dorms instead? Does it matter whether the university is private or public? *See* Kaur v. N.Y. State Urban Dev. Corp., 933 N.E.2d 721 (N.Y. 2010).

3. **Easements by necessity.** Some states allow a private landowner to condemn a right-of-way over the land of another, if his property would otherwise be landlocked. Compensation must be provided, of course. In this case, an easement is taken from A and transferred to B. Is there a public use involved? What if you apply Justice O'Connor's test instead? Justice Thomas's? Would it matter if the statute required any such right-of-way to be "open to the public," even though as a practical matter no one but B would actually use it? *See* Lockridge v. Adrian, 638 So. 2d 766 (Ala. 1994).

State Responses to Kelo

Justice Stevens emphasized in *Kelo* that the majority's decision did not preclude states from taking action to restrict the use of eminent domain. Indeed, he noted that some state constitutions and statutes already contained more restrictive provisions. States quickly accepted Stevens's invitation to take action. Indeed, the *Kelo* decision "generated a massive backlash from across the political spectrum," which "probably resulted in more new state legislation than any other Supreme Court decision in history." Ilya Somin, *The Limits of Backlash: Assessing the Political Response to* Kelo, 93 Minn. L. Rev. 2100, 2101-02 (2009). As of 2009, 43 states had enacted some type of post-*Kelo* reform. *Id.* Given the relative breadth of the federal "public use" limitation, state restrictions have become the deciding source of law in many post-*Kelo* cases:

State constitutions

- Some state constitutions contain different, more restrictive, language than the federal constitution. For example, Arizona's constitution states explicitly that, with certain limited exceptions, "[p]rivate property shall not be taken for private use." Ariz. Const., art. II, §17 (1970).
- Many states interpret their constitutions more narrowly, even if the language is no more restrictive than the federal version. For example, in Board of Cnty. Comm'rs of Muskogee Cnty. v. Lowery, 136 P.3d 639 (Okla. 2006), the Oklahoma Supreme Court determined that the state constitution's public use restriction, which was similar to the federal clause, should be interpreted to prohibit takings solely for economic development. The court struck down the county's condemnation of a water pipeline easement to provide cooling water for the benefit of a privately owned power plant.
- States that interpret their constitutions to require more than economic development to meet public use restrictions include

Arizona,[8] Arkansas,[9] Florida,[10] Illinois,[11] Oklahoma,[12] Ohio,[13] South Carolina,[14] Michigan,[15] and Maine.[16]

State statutory reforms

■ **Limiting public use definition.** Some state legislatures amended their eminent domain statutes to simply prohibit takings solely for economic development. For example, in 2006 Missouri enacted a statute that provides explicitly: "No condemning authority shall acquire private property through the process of eminent domain for solely economic development purposes." Mo. Rev. Stat. §523.271 (2016). The impact of this limitation became clear when the Missouri Supreme Court held that this statute basically prevented the state's port authorities from advancing their purposes through eminent domain. The port authorities had been established by state statute precisely for the purpose of promoting economic development in port areas along the Missouri and Mississippi rivers. State ex rel. Jackson v. Dolan, 398 S.W.3d 472 (Mo. 2013).

□ Many of these states continue to allow redevelopment of "blighted" areas. Thus, how "blight" is defined may determine whether eminent domain may be used in *Kelo*-type cases. *See, e.g.*, Nev. Rev. Stat. §37.010 (2017) (banning private-to-private takings, except in cases of blight, which is broadly defined).

■ **Enhanced compensation.** Another type of post-*Kelo* reform centered on improving compensation requirements, which indirectly would discourage the use of eminent domain absent compelling need. Imagine your home has been taken and the government offers you fair market value. What costs are not reflected in this amount? You will need to buy a new house, so you will have costs, such as title search and closing fees. You may not be able to obtain the same financing package. You will have relocation costs. And, as we discussed previously, you may have a sentimental attachment to your property that is not reflected in fair market value. So, some states require condemnors to pay relocation costs and a percentage above fair market value to reflect the intangible costs of an involuntary transfer. *See, e.g.*, Iowa Code §6B.54 (2018) (condemnor should pay relocation costs or offer 130 percent of fair market value); Md. Code Ann. Real Prop. §12-202 (2018). Do these provisions respond, at least in part, to the

---

[8] *See* Bailey v. Myers, 76 P.3d 898 (Ariz. Ct. App. 2003).

[9] *See* Little Rock v. Raines, 411 S.W.2d 486 (Ark. 1967).

[10] *See* State v. Miami Beach Redev. Agency, 392 So. 2d 875 (Fla. Dist. Ct. App. 1980).

[11] *See* Southwestern Ill. Dev. Auth. v. Nat'l City Envtl., L.L.C., 768 N.E.2d 1 (Ill. 2002).

[12] *See Lowery*, 136 P.3d at 650-51.

[13] *See* Norwood v. Horney, 853 N.E.2d 1115 (Ohio 2006).

[14] *See* Georgia Dep't of Transp. v. Jasper Cnty., 586 S.E.2d 853 (S.C. 2003).

[15] *See* Country of Wayne v. Hathcock, 684 N.W.2d 765 (Mich. 2004).

[16] *See* Opinion of the Justices, 131 A.2d 904 (Me. 1957).

concerns raised by Justice Thomas in his *Kelo* dissent? Would they help our client Novak?

■ As a policy matter, do you think these legislative reforms are desirable? *See* Abraham Bell & Gideon Parchomovsky, *The Uselessness of Public Use*, 106 Colum. L. Rev. 1412 (2006).

Preparing to Practice: Applying Legislative Reforms

After *Kelo*, the Texas legislature enacted this provision limiting the use of eminent domain:

(b) A governmental or private entity may not take private property through the use of eminent domain if the taking:

(1) confers a private benefit on a particular private party through the use of the property; [or]

(2) is for a public use that is merely a pretext to confer a private benefit on a particular private party; [or]

(3) is for economic development purposes, unless the economic development is a secondary purpose resulting from municipal community development or municipal urban renewal activities to eliminate an existing affirmative harm on society from slum or blighted areas....

Tex. Gov't Code §2206.001 (2017).

The City of Eastville, Texas, would like to improve the attractiveness of its waterfront by developing a new "fish market" with adjoining shops and restaurants. The waterfront has long been in decline and is now full of largely vacant buildings and lots. A local developer, Clive Walker, will construct, own, and operate the new development. Most of the required land has been acquired, except for land occupied by Total Seafood, where shrimp trawlers offload their catches for processing. Total Seafood's building is rather unsightly, but is not dilapidated. It is, however, out of keeping with the City's new master plan for this area. After negotiations with Total Seafood failed, the City started eminent domain proceedings to condemn the property.

Assume you are the attorney for Total Seafood. Analyze whether the *Kelo* decision, or the new Texas legislation, affects the City's ability to condemn your client's property in this case.

B   REGULATORY TAKINGS

To begin our consideration of the "regulatory taking" concept, think for a moment about the problems confronting those who care about Lake Tahoe, a jewel of a lake lying on the border between California and Nevada. One of the lake's signal characteristics is its pristine, crystal-clear water, which Mark Twain described as "not *merely* transparent, but dazzlingly, brilliantly so." [17] The Lake Tahoe Basin area has become a favorite destination of many vacationers, who engage in water sports in the summer and snow skiing in the winter. In addition to its beauty, its proximity to large metropolitan markets like Sacramento and San Francisco make it very desirable for vacation homes.

Lake Tahoe
© Mariusz Blach - Fotolia.com

Unfortunately, the lake's popularity also threatens the very qualities that make it unique. Burgeoning development around the lake has greatly increased runoff loadings of sediment and nutrients that produce algae. Development in the Basin therefore could turn the blue lake green and opaque, ruining its outstanding beauty.

---

[17] Mark Twain, *Roughing It*, 174-75 (1872).

California and Nevada entered into an interstate compact, called the Tahoe Regional Planning Compact, for the purpose of protecting and conserving the lake, in part by regulating development in the Basin. A bi-state entity, the Tahoe Regional Planning Agency (TRPA), was given authority to adopt land use ordinances.

TRPA established certain areas, called Stream Environment Zones (SEZ), in which development would be particularly harmful, given their proximity to the streams running into the lake. TRPA's regulations allow no additional land coverage or permanent land disturbance on parcels located in those SEZ zones.

Bernadine Suitum, along with her husband, purchased an undeveloped lot near the Nevada shore of Lake Tahoe long before these development restrictions were put in place. The couple planned to build a retirement home there. After some setbacks, including the illness and death of her husband, Mrs. Suitum was finally able to realize her dreams, as the neighbors on three sides of her Tahoe property did long ago. When she submitted her plans, however, she was told her property was in a newly designated SEZ, on which no construction would be allowed.

On one hand, we surely sympathize with the TRPA's objectives—after all, if development is not controlled, everyone—including Suitum—will be worse off. There is no doubt that the regulation has a valid, even vital, public purpose.

But on the other hand, what about Suitum? Is it fair to suddenly cut off her right to use her parcel, destroying her property's value, when many others have already built? Shouldn't she at least be compensated for the loss of her investment in this lot? Has her private property basically been converted to a water pollution filter for the other landowners?

Yet, even though we feel for Suitum, can we afford to compensate everyone who is caught by the changing rules, especially if many others are in the same situation? As we learned in *Euclid*, government regulations often impact property values, for better or for worse. Is this just part of the risk of land investment, especially in a sensitive area?

The Tahoe example, roughly taken from the facts of a real case, presents the central problem of regulatory takings cases. On one side, there is usually a very strong public interest at stake—the preservation of endangered species or wetlands, for example—but on the other, a strong private property interest as well. When, if ever, should the government have to compensate the landowner for the loss of property value caused by regulation?

As you can see, the answer to this question may depend on your view of the importance of private property rights vis-à-vis the public interest. As we know from Chapter 1, both of those interests are balanced in determining the nature of property. It should not surprise you, therefore, that this area has produced a lot of closely divided Supreme Court decisions, along with a doctrine that seems to fluctuate considerably with the changing composition of the Court.

1. *Pennsylvania Coal* and the Rise of the "Regulatory Taking" Concept

To understand the importance of our first regulatory takings case, Pennsylvania Coal v. Mahon, 260 U.S. 393 (1922), a brief history is required. *Pennsylvania Coal* began the Court's recognition of "regulatory" takings, the idea that government laws restricting land use could require compensation, even though the property itself had not been physically taken. Until the Court's 1922 decision, the Takings Clause had been applied only to actual confiscations or physical occupation of property by the government.

Even before *Pennsylvania Coal*, the Supreme Court had recognized that the Takings Clause protected property that was physically destroyed without being actually confiscated. In Pumpelly v. Green Bay & Mississippi Canal Co., 80 U.S. 166 (1871), the Court considered whether the Takings Clause was implicated when the construction of a dam caused Pumpelly's property to be flooded. The defense argued that the legal title of the property remained in Pumpelly and that the public made no actual use of his property. The Court declared:

> It would be a very curious and unsatisfactory result, if in construing a provision of constitutional law, always understood to have been adopted for protection and security to the rights of the individual as against the government, . . . it shall be held that if the government refrains from the absolute conversion of real property to the uses of the public it can destroy its value entirely, can inflict irreparable and permanent injury to any extent, can, in effect, subject it to total destruction without making any compensation, because, in the narrowest sense of that word, it is not *taken* for the public use.

Id. at 177-78.

Thus, the Court in *Pumpelly* recognized that the word "take" in the Constitution must be construed to include more than the actual transfer of property ownership to the government. Still, that case involved *physical* destruction or invasion of property by the government. In contrast, government laws that restricted the use of property, and thereby *diminished its value*, were treated differently.

Prior to *Pennsylvania Coal*, the Supreme Court limited its scrutiny of land use restrictions to a *substantive due process* analysis: as long as the regulatory restriction had a rational relationship to a legitimate governmental interest, the Court upheld it. Thus, the *police power*—which enabled the government to protect the health, safety, and welfare of the citizens—defined the permissible extent of land use regulation.

For example, consider the following cases:

> ➢ Mugler v. Kansas, 123 U.S. 623 (1887). The State of Kansas prohibited the manufacture of intoxicating beverages. Mugler claimed that this restriction rendered his brewery valueless. The Court, however, rejected his claim that the state must compensate him for his loss:
>
> > This interpretation of the fourteenth amendment is inadmissible. It cannot be supposed that the states intended, by adopting that amendment, to impose restraints upon the exercise of their powers for the protection of the safety, health, or morals of the community.

Id. at 664. The Court reached a similar conclusion in upholding Pennsylvania's prohibition on the manufacture or sale of margarine, an obvious dairy protectionist measure, which a margarine manufacturer claimed had destroyed his investment. Powell v. Pennsylvania, 127 U.S. 678 (1888).

➤ Hadacheck v. Sebastian, 239 U.S. 394 (1915). Hadacheck's land, which he used for brickmaking, was annexed into the City of Los Angeles. As the residential area grew, the city enacted an ordinance prohibiting the manufacture of bricks in that district. Hadacheck alleged that the restriction reduced the value of his property from $800,000 to $60,000. The Court declined to restrict the government's ability to exercise its police power:

> It is to be remembered that we are dealing with one of the most essential powers of government, one that is the least limitable. It may, indeed, seem harsh in its exercise, usually is on some individual, but the imperative necessity for its existence precludes any limitation upon it when not exerted arbitrarily. A vested interest cannot be asserted against it because of conditions once obtaining.... To so hold would preclude development and fix a city forever in its primitive conditions. There must be progress, and if in its march private interests are in the way, they must yield to the good of the community.

Id. at 410.

➤ Reinman v. City of Little Rock, 237 U.S. 171 (1915). Little Rock enacted an ordinance prohibiting livery stables in what it called "the greatest shopping district in the entire state of Arkansas." Reinman complained that the value of his stable was thereby destroyed. The Court upheld the ordinance:

> Granting that [the livery stable] is not a nuisance *per se*, it is clearly within the police power of the state to regulate the business, and to that end to declare that in particular circumstances and in particular localities a livery stable shall be deemed a nuisance in fact and in law, provided this power is not exerted arbitrarily, or with unjust discrimination, so as to infringe upon rights guaranteed by the 14th Amendment.

Id. at 177.

Thus, in a long line of cases, the Supreme Court had upheld regulations by state and local governments that had profound effects on private property. As long as the regulation could be justified by its reasonable relationship to the police power, the impact on the landowner was irrelevant.

So, *Pennsylvania Coal* is a landmark because, for the first time, the Supreme Court recognized that the just compensation requirement of the Takings Clause presents an *additional* limitation on government regulation. Even if a law has a valid public purpose, even if it rationally furthers a legitimate state interest, the Takings Clause may require compensation be provided to affected property owners.

Two icons in legal history, Justice Oliver Wendell Holmes and Justice Louis Brandeis, eloquently present the two sides of this important question. Virtually every sentence of these two opinions has been quoted thousands of times since. The tension between the public interest and private property rights, which the two jurists stake out in this case, never has been, and never will be, fully resolved.

PENNSYLVANIA COAL CO. v. MAHON

260 U.S. 393 (1922)
Supreme Court of the United States

[In 1878, the Pennsylvania Coal Company conveyed the surface rights to a tract of land to H.J. Mahon, but retained the mineral rights underneath. In the deed, Mahon accepted the risk of coal mining on the property and waived any claim he might have for damages resulting therefrom. In 1921, the Commonwealth of Pennsylvania enacted the Kohler Act, which prohibited the mining of coal in a manner that would cause the surface under a structure used for human habitation to subside. When Pennsylvania Coal notified Mahon that it intended to begin mining under his land, upon which he had built a house, he brought suit for an injunction based on the Kohler Act restriction. The trial court rejected his claim, holding that the Kohler Act was unconstitutional as applied to these facts, because the law did not provide compensation to Pennsylvania Coal for the loss of its coal that had to be left in place. The Pennsylvania Supreme Court reversed, holding that the Act was constitutional under the police power and compensation was not required.

Pennsylvania Coal (now designated "plaintiff in error"—or petitioner, in today's terminology) appealed the ruling to the U.S. Supreme Court. The Mahons (respondents) are now called "defendants in error."]

Mr. Justice HOLMES delivered the opinion of the Court.

This is a bill in equity brought by the defendants in error to prevent the Pennsylvania Coal Company from mining under their property in such way as to remove the supports and cause a subsidence of the surface and of their house. The bill sets out a deed executed by the Coal Company in 1878, under which the plaintiffs claim. The deed conveys the surface but in express terms reserves the right to remove all the coal under the same and the grantee takes the premises with the risk and waives all claim for damages that may arise from mining out the coal. But the plaintiffs say that whatever may have been the Coal Company's rights, they were taken away by an Act of Pennsylvania, approved May 27, 1921, commonly known there as the Kohler Act. . . .

The statute forbids the mining of anthracite coal in such way as to cause the subsidence of, among other things, any structure used as a human habitation, with certain exceptions, including among them land where the surface is owned by the owner of the underlying coal and is distant more than one hundred and fifty feet from any improved property belonging to any other person. As applied to this case the statute is admitted to destroy previously existing rights of property and contract. The question is whether the police power can be stretched so far.

Government hardly could go on if to some extent values incident to property could not be diminished without paying for every such change in the general law. As long recognized some values are enjoyed under an implied limitation and must yield to the police power. But obviously the implied limitation must have its limits or the contract and due process clauses are gone. One fact for consideration in determining such limits is the extent of the diminution. When it reaches a certain magnitude, in most if not in all cases there must be an exercise of eminent domain and compensation to sustain the act. So the question depends upon the particular facts. The greatest weight is given to the judgment of the legislature but it always is open to interested parties to contend that the legislature has gone beyond its constitutional power.

This is the case of a single private house. No doubt there is a public interest even in this, as there is in every purchase and sale and in all that happens within the commonwealth. Some existing rights may be modified even in such a case. Rideout v. Knox, 148 Mass. 368, 19 N.E. 390. But usually in ordinary private affairs the public interest does not warrant much of this kind of interference. A source of damage to such a house is not a public nuisance even if similar damage is inflicted on others in different places. The damage is not common or public. Wesson v. Washburn Iron Co., 13 Allen (Mass.) 95, 103, 90 Am. Dec. 181. The extent of the public interest is shown by the statute to be limited, since the statute ordinarily does not apply to land when the surface is owned by the owner of the coal. Furthermore, it is not justified as a protection of personal safety. That could be provided for by notice. Indeed the very foundation of this bill is that the defendant gave timely notice of its intent to mine under the house. On the other hand the extent of the taking is great. It purports to abolish what is recognized in Pennsylvania as an estate in land—a very valuable estate—and what is declared by the Court below to be a contract hitherto binding the plaintiffs. If we were called upon to deal with the plaintiffs' position alone we should think it clear that the statute does not disclose a public interest sufficient to warrant so extensive a destruction of the defendant's constitutionally protected rights.

But the case has been treated as one in which the general validity of the act should be discussed. . . .

It is our opinion that the act cannot be sustained as an exercise of the police power, so far as it affects the mining of coal under streets or cities in places where the right to mine such coal has been reserved. As said in a Pennsylvania case, "For practical purposes, the right to coal consists in the right to mine it." Commonwealth v. Clearview Coal Co., 256 Pa. 328, 331, 100 Atl. 820. What makes the right to mine coal valuable is that it can be exercised with profit. To make it commercially impracticable to mine certain coal has very nearly the same effect for constitutional purposes as appropriating or destroying it. This we think that we are warranted in assuming that the statute does.

It is true that in Plymouth Coal Co. v. Pennsylvania, 232 U.S. 531, it was held competent for the legislature to require a pillar of coal to be left along the line of adjoining property, that with the pillar on the other side of the line would be a barrier sufficient for the safety of the employees of either mine in case the other should be abandoned and allowed to fill with water. But that was a requirement for the safety of employees invited into the mine, and secured an average reciprocity of advantage that has been recognized as a justification of various laws.

The rights of the public in a street purchased or laid out by eminent domain are those that it has paid for. If in any case its representatives have been so short sighted as to acquire only surface rights without the right of support we see no more authority for supplying the latter without compensation than there was for taking the right of way in the first place and refusing to pay for it because the public wanted it very much. The protection of private property in the Fifth Amendment presupposes that it is wanted for public use, but provides that it shall not be taken for such use without compensation. . . . When this seemingly absolute protection is found to be qualified by the police power, the natural tendency of human nature is to extend the qualification more and more until at last private property disappears. But that cannot be accomplished in this way under the Constitution of the United States.

The general rule at least is that while property may be regulated to a certain extent, if regulation goes too far it will be recognized as a taking. It may be doubted how far exceptional cases, like the blowing up of a house to stop a conflagration, go—and if they go beyond the general rule, whether they do not stand as much upon tradition as upon principle. Bowditch v. Boston, 101 U.S. 16. In general it is not plain that a man's misfortunes or necessities will justify his shifting the damages to his neighbor's shoulders. . . . We are in danger of forgetting that a strong public desire to improve the public condition is not enough to warrant achieving the desire by a shorter cut than the constitutional way of paying for the change. As we already have said this is a question of degree—and therefore cannot be disposed of by general propositions. But we regard this as going beyond any of the cases decided by this Court. . . .

We assume, of course, that the statute was passed upon the conviction that an exigency existed that would warrant it, and we assume that an exigency exists that would warrant the exercise of eminent domain. But the question at bottom is upon whom the loss of the changes desired should fall. So far as private persons or communities have seen fit to take the risk of acquiring only surface rights, we cannot see that the fact that their risk has become a danger warrants the giving to them greater rights than they bought.

Decree reversed.

Mr. Justice BRANDEIS dissenting.

The Kohler Act prohibits, under certain conditions, the mining of anthracite coal within the limits of a city in such a manner or to such an extent "as to cause the . . . subsidence of . . . any dwelling or other structure used as a human habitation, or any factory, store, or other industrial or mercantile establishment in which human labor is employed." Act Pa. May 27, 1921, §1 (P. L. 1198). Coal in place is land, and the right of the owner to use his land is not absolute. He may not so use it as to create a public nuisance, and uses, once harmless, may, owing to changed conditions, seriously threaten the public welfare. Whenever they do, the Legislature has power to prohibit such uses without paying compensation; and the power to prohibit extends alike to the manner, the character and the purpose of the use. Are we justified in declaring that the Legislature of Pennsylvania has, in restricting the right to mine anthracite, exercised this power so arbitrarily as to violate the Fourteenth Amendment?

Every restriction upon the use of property imposed in the exercise of the police power deprives the owner of some right theretofore enjoyed, and is, in that sense, an abridgment by the state of rights in property without making compensation. But restriction imposed to protect the public health, safety or morals from dangers threatened is not a taking. The restriction here in question is merely the prohibition of a noxious use. The property so restricted remains in the possession of its owner. The state does not appropriate it or make any use of it. The state merely prevents the owner from making a use which interferes with paramount rights of the public. Whenever the use prohibited ceases to be noxious—as it may because of further change in local or social conditions—the restriction will have to be removed and the owner will again be free to enjoy his property as heretofore.

The restriction upon the use of this property cannot, of course, be lawfully imposed, unless its purpose is to protect the public. But the purpose of a restriction does not cease to be public, because incidentally some private persons may thereby receive gratuitously valuable special benefits. Thus, owners of low buildings may obtain, through statutory restrictions upon the height of neighboring structures, benefits equivalent to an easement of light and air. Furthermore, a restriction, though imposed for a public purpose, will not be lawful, unless the restriction is an appropriate means to the public end. But to keep coal in place is surely an appropriate means of preventing subsidence of the surface; and ordinarily it is the only available means. Restriction upon use does not become inappropriate as a means, merely because it deprives the owner of the only use to which the property can then be profitably put. The liquor and the oleomargarine cases settled that. Mugler v. Kansas, 123 U.S. 623; Powell v. Pennsylvania, 127 U.S. 678, 682. See also Hadacheck v. Los Angeles, 239 U.S. 394; Pierce Oil Corporation v. City of Hope, 248 U.S. 498. Nor is a restriction imposed through exercise of the police power inappropriate as a means, merely because the same end might be effected through exercise of the power of eminent domain, or otherwise at public expense. Every restriction upon the height of buildings might be secured through acquiring by eminent domain the right of each owner to build above the limiting height; but it is settled that the state need not resort to that power. If by mining anthracite coal the owner would necessarily unloose poisonous gases, I suppose no one would doubt the power of the state to prevent the mining, without buying his coal fields. And why may not the state, likewise, without paying compensation, prohibit one from digging so deep or excavating so near the surface, as to expose the community to like dangers? In the latter case, as in the former, carrying on the business would be a public nuisance.

It is said that one fact for consideration in determining whether the limits of the police power have been exceeded is the extent of the resulting diminution in value, and that here the restriction destroys existing rights of property and contract. But values are relative. If we are to consider the value of the coal kept in place by the restriction, we should compare it with the value of all other parts of the land. That is, with the value not of the coal alone, but with the value of the whole property. The rights of an owner as against the public are not increased by dividing the interests in his property into surface and subsoil. The sum of the rights in the parts can not be greater than the rights in the whole. The estate of an owner in land is grandiloquently described as extending *ab orco usque ad coelum*. But I suppose no one would contend that by selling his interest above 100 feet from the surface he could prevent the state from limiting, by the police power, the height of structures in a city. And why should a sale of underground rights bar the state's power? For aught that appears the value of the coal kept in place by the restriction may be negligible as compared with the value of the whole property, or even as compared with that part of it which is represented by the coal remaining in place and which may be extracted despite the statute. . . . Where the surface and the coal belong to the same person, self-interest would ordinarily prevent mining to such an extent as to cause a subsidence. It was, doubtless, for this reason that the Legislature, estimating the degrees of danger, deemed statutory restriction unnecessary for the public safety under such conditions.

It is said that this is a case of a single dwelling house, that the restriction upon mining abolishes a valuable estate hitherto secured by a contract with the plaintiffs, and that the restriction upon mining cannot be justified as a protection of personal safety, since that could be provided for by notice. The propriety of deferring a good deal to tribunals on the spot has been repeatedly recognized. May we say that notice would afford adequate protection of the public safety where the Legislature and the highest court of the state, with greater knowledge of local conditions, have declared, in effect, that it would not? If the public safety is imperiled, surely neither grant, nor contract, can prevail against the exercise of the police power. . . . Nor can existing contracts between private individuals preclude exercise of the police power. "One whose rights, such as they are, are subject to state restriction cannot remove them from the power of the state by making a contract about them." Hudson Water Co. v. McCarter, 209 U.S. 349. . . .

This case involves only mining which causes subsidence of a dwelling house. But the Kohler Act contains provisions in addition to that quoted above; and as to these, also, an opinion is expressed. These provisions deal with mining under cities to such an extent as to cause subsidence of [public buildings, places of assemblage, public streets, or public easements.]

A prohibition of mining which causes subsidence of such structures and facilities is obviously enacted for a public purpose; and it seems, likewise, clear that mere notice of intention to mine would not in this connection secure the public safety. Yet it is said that these provisions of the act cannot be sustained as an exercise of the police power where the right to mine such coal has been reserved. The conclusion seems to rest upon the assumption that in order to justify such exercise of the police power there must be "an average reciprocity of advantage" as between the owner of the property restricted and the rest of the community; and that here such reciprocity is absent. Reciprocity of advantage is an important consideration, and may even be an essential, where the state's power is exercised for the purpose of conferring benefits upon the property of a neighborhood, as in drainage projects or upon adjoining owners as by party wall provisions. But where the police power is exercised, not to confer benefits upon property owners but to protect the public from detriment and danger, there is in my opinion, no room for considering reciprocity of advantage. There was no reciprocal advantage to the owner prohibited from using his oil tanks in [*Pierce Oil*]; his brickyard, in [*Hadacheck*]; his livery stable, in

Sinkhole
AP Photo/Charlie Riedel

[*Reinman*]; his billiard hall, in [*Murphy*]; his oleomargarine factory, in [*Powell*]; his brewery, in [*Mugler*]; unless it be the advantage of living and doing business in a civilized community. That reciprocal advantage is given by the act to the coal operators.

■ POINTS TO CONSIDER

1. **The takings test.** Justice Holmes recognizes that not every government regulation that reduces the value of property requires compensation. "Government could hardly go on," he admits, if that were the case. So how do we recognize those cases that do require compensation? What factors in this case led Justice Holmes to conclude that the regulation went "too far"?

2. **A "single private house."** In this case, as Justice Holmes emphasized, the parties had already allocated the risk of subsidence in a private transaction. Is this case as much about impairment of contracts as it is about property law? Would the case have come out differently if the coal company had not included the express waiver of subsidence damages in its deed of the surface estate? Can you think of other instances in which we override private contractual arrangements, due to the public interest at stake?

3. **Nuisance rationale.** Consider carefully the dissenting opinion of Justice Brandeis. He sets out the "nuisance rationale," which provides that government should not have to pay to prevent an owner from making harmful uses

of property. After all, if a court could enjoin a particular use as a nuisance, why can't the legislature do the same? This remains an important consideration in takings jurisprudence. Why does Justice Holmes believe this case is not covered by the nuisance exception?

4. **Severability.** Justice Brandeis points out a problem that continues to plague takings analysis: when weighing the impact of a government regulation on the private property owner, what is the relevant parcel to be considered? For example, in this case, do you consider:

   - only the value of the coal required to be left in place?
   - the value of the coal that can be mined in addition to the coal left in place?
   - the value of the entire parcel (the surface in addition to the subsurface)?
   - the value of all the coal rights owned by the coal company throughout Pennsylvania?

The latest Supreme Court attempt to resolve this issue is Murr v. Wisconsin, discussed below.

The impact on the coal company's property rights is 100 percent if only the value of the coal left in place is considered, but diminishes considerably if one takes a broader view of the property at issue.If one party owned both the surface and subsurface in this case, would there have been a taking? If not, does it make sense to have the issue turn on the fact that the subsurface rights have been severed?

5. **Reciprocity of advantage.** What do you make of the debate between Holmes and Brandeis concerning "reciprocity of advantage"? In some cases, the burden of a restriction is offset by the benefit conferred by similar restrictions on others. A set-back requirement prohibiting you from building within ten feet of the property line certainly prevents you from making full use of your land, but any decrease in value is offset by the knowledge that your neighbor can't crowd your property line either. All landowners are similarly burdened and benefited.In the coal mining context, if one person owned the entire bundle of sticks in Blackacre, the impact on the coal rights might be offset by the value of restrictions on the neighbors. No one wants to live in a neighborhood with a bunch of sinkholes. But when the coal rights have been severed from the surface rights, how does the reciprocity calculus change? Again, should a takings claim depend on how the property interests have been divided?

2. The *Penn Central* Balancing Test

The two opinions in *Pennsylvania Coal* nicely frame the central balance in takings analysis. On one side, Justice Holmes emphasizes the need to protect private property from destruction by government regulation. For all the reasons we set out in Chapter 1—certainty, fairness, economic efficiency, personhood—property rights must be protected. Owners have to feel secure, in making property investments, that they will be able to actually make valuable use of the property they purchase. In countries where uncompensated government *expropriation* (i.e., taking of private property) often occurs, attracting capital investment becomes extremely difficult.

On the other side, Justice Brandeis captures the public interest at stake. Government must be able to regulate to protect the public health and safety, and to promote the public welfare. Pennsylvania wants to be known as the Keystone State, not the Sinkhole State. Of course, the Takings Clause doesn't *prevent* the state from regulating subsidence—it just requires that private property owners be *compensated* for the resulting losses. But can the state afford to regulate if has to purchase all the coal required to be left in place? And, as a matter of fairness, should the public have to pay to stop a noxious use of property?

The Takings Clause is the fulcrum on which these two very important interests are balanced. Nevertheless, while *Pennsylvania Coal* does a wonderful job of describing both sides of the balance, in the end we are left with a vague test for determining when compensation is required. Justice Holmes said only that when regulation "goes too far" and the extent of diminution in property value "reaches a certain magnitude," a taking has occurred.

In the half-century following *Pennsylvania Coal*, the Court did little to clarify the test. Then, in our next case, *Penn Central Transportation Co. v. New York City*, the Court attempted to articulate the factors to be weighed in determining when a taking has occurred and compensation is required. The case, involving the historic Grand Central terminal building in New York City, gave us the framework still used today for analyzing takings claims.

PENN CENTRAL TRANSPORTATION CO. v. NEW YORK CITY

438 U.S. 104 (1978)
Supreme Court of the United States

Mr. Justice BRENNAN delivered the opinion of the Court.

The question presented is whether a city may, as part of a comprehensive program to preserve historic landmarks and historic districts, place restrictions on the development of individual historic landmarks—in addition to those imposed by applicable zoning ordinances—without effecting a "taking" requiring the payment of "just compensation." Specifically, we must decide whether the application of New York City's Landmarks Preservation Law to the parcel of land occupied by Grand Central Terminal has "taken" its owners' property in violation of the Fifth and Fourteenth Amendments.

Over the past 50 years, all 50 States and over 500 municipalities have enacted laws to encourage or require the preservation of buildings and areas with historic or aesthetic importance. These nationwide legislative efforts have been precipitated by two concerns. The first is recognition that, in recent years, large numbers of historic structures, landmarks, and areas have been destroyed without adequate consideration of either the values represented therein or the possibility of preserving the destroyed properties for use in economically productive ways. The second is a widely shared belief that structures with special historic, cultural, or architectural significance enhance the quality of life for all. . . .

The New York City law is typical of many urban landmark laws in that its primary method of achieving its goals is not by acquisitions of historic properties, but rather by involving public entities in land-use decisions affecting these properties and providing services, standards, controls, and incentives that will encourage preservation by private owners and users. . . .

In the event an owner wishes to alter a landmark site, three separate procedures are available through which administrative approval may be obtained. First, the owner may apply to the Commission for a "certificate of no effect on protected architectural features": that is, for an order approving the improvement or alteration on the ground that it will not change or affect any architectural feature of the landmark and will be in harmony therewith. . . . Denial of the certificate is subject to judicial review.

Second, the owner may apply to the Commission for a certificate of "appropriateness." . . . Such certificates will be granted if the Commission concludes—focusing upon aesthetic, historical, and architectural values—that the proposed construction on the landmark site would not unduly hinder the protection, enhancement, perpetuation, and use of the landmark. Again, denial of the certificate is subject to judicial review. Moreover, the owner who is denied either a certificate of no exterior effect or a certificate of appropriateness may submit an alternative or modified plan for approval. The final procedure—seeking a certificate of appropriateness on the ground of "insufficient return," . . .—provides special mechanisms . . . to ensure that designation does not cause economic hardship. . . .

This case involves the application of New York City's Landmarks Preservation Law to Grand Central Terminal (Terminal). The Terminal, which is owned by the Penn Central Transportation Co. and its affiliates (Penn Central), is one of New York City's most famous buildings. Opened in 1913, it is regarded not only as providing an ingenious engineering solution to the problems presented by urban railroad stations, but also as a magnificent example of the French beaux-arts style.

. . . The Terminal itself is an eight-story structure which Penn Central uses as a railroad station and in which it rents space not needed for railroad purposes to a variety of commercial interests. . . .

Grand Central Terminal

On January 22, 1968, appellant Penn Central, to increase its income, entered into a renewable 50-year lease and sublease agreement with appellant UGP Properties, Inc. (UGP). . . . Under the terms of the agreement, UGP was to construct a multistory office building above the Terminal. UGP promised to pay Penn Central $1 million annually during construction and at least $3 million annually thereafter. The rentals would be offset in part by a loss of some $700,000 to $1 million in net rentals presently received from concessionaires displaced by the new building.

Appellants UGP and Penn Central then applied to the Commission for permission to construct an office building atop the Terminal. Two separate plans, both designed by architect Marcel Breuer and both apparently satisfying the terms of the applicable zoning ordinance, were submitted to the Commission for approval. The first, Breuer I, provided for the construction of a 55-story office building, to be cantilevered above the existing facade and to rest on the roof of the Terminal. The second, Breuer II Revised, called for tearing down a portion of the Terminal that included the 42d Street facade, stripping off some of the remaining features of the Terminal's facade, and constructing a 53-story office building. The Commission denied a certificate of no exterior effect on September 20, 1968. Appellants then applied for a certificate of "appropriateness" as to both proposals. After four days of hearings at which over 80 witnesses testified, the Commission denied this application as to both proposals. . . .

The issues presented by appellants are (1) whether the restrictions imposed by New York City's law upon appellants' exploitation of the Terminal site effect a "taking" of appellants' property for a public use within the meaning of the Fifth Amendment, which of course is made applicable to the States through the Fourteenth Amendment, . . . and, (2), if so, whether the transferable development rights afforded appellants constitute "just compensation" within the meaning of the Fifth Amendment. We need only address the question whether a "taking" has occurred.

Before considering appellants' specific contentions, it will be useful to review the factors that have shaped the jurisprudence of the Fifth Amendment injunction "nor shall private property be taken for public use, without just compensation." The question of what constitutes a "taking" for purposes of the Fifth Amendment has proved to be a problem of considerable difficulty. While this Court has recognized that the "Fifth Amendment's guarantee . . . [is] designed to bar Government from forcing some people alone to bear public burdens which, in all fairness and justice, should be borne by the public as a whole," Armstrong v. United States, 364 U.S. 40, 49 (1960), this Court, quite simply, has been unable to develop any "set formula" for determining when "justice and fairness" require that economic injuries caused by public action be compensated by the government, rather than remain disproportionately concentrated on a few persons. *See* Goldblatt v. Hempstead, 369 U.S. 590, 594 (1962). Indeed, we have frequently observed that whether a particular restriction will be rendered invalid by the government's failure to pay for any losses proximately caused by it depends largely "upon the particular circumstances [in that] case." United States v. Central Eureka Mining Co., 357 U.S. 155, 168 (1958); *see* United States v. Caltex, Inc., 344 U.S. 149, 156 (1952).

In engaging in these essentially ad hoc, factual inquiries, the Court's decisions have identified several factors that have particular significance. The economic impact of the regulation on the claimant and, particularly, the extent to which the regulation has interfered with distinct investment-backed expectations are, of course, relevant considerations. *See* Goldblatt v. Hempstead, *supra*, 369 U.S., at 594. So, too, is the character of the governmental action. A "taking" may more readily be found when the interference with property can be characterized as a physical invasion by government, *see, e.g.*, United States v. Causby, 328 U.S. 256 (1946), than when interference arises from some public program adjusting the benefits and burdens of economic life to promote the common good. . . .

In contending that the New York City law has "taken" their property in violation of the Fifth and Fourteenth Amendments, appellants make a series of arguments, which, while tailored to the facts of this case, essentially urge that any substantial restriction imposed pursuant to a landmark law must be accompanied by just compensation if it is to be constitutional. . . .

They first observe that the airspace above the Terminal is a valuable property interest, citing *United States v. Causby, supra*. They urge that the Landmarks Law has deprived them of any gainful use of their "air rights" above the Terminal and that, irrespective of the value of the remainder of their parcel, the city has "taken" their right to this superadjacent airspace, thus entitling them to "just compensation" measured by the fair market value of these air rights. . . .

"Taking" jurisprudence does not divide a single parcel into discrete segments and attempt to determine whether rights in a particular segment have been entirely abrogated. In deciding whether a particular governmental action has effected a taking, this Court focuses rather both on the character of the action and on the nature and extent of the interference with rights in the parcel as a whole—here, the city tax block designated as the "landmark site."

Secondly, appellants, focusing on the character and impact of the New York City law, argue that it effects a "taking" because its operation has significantly diminished the value of the Terminal site. . . .

It is, of course, true that the Landmarks Law has a more severe impact on some landowners than on others, but that in itself does not mean that the law effects a "taking." Legislation designed to promote the general welfare commonly burdens some more than others. The owners of the brickyard in *Hadacheck*, of the cedar trees in *Miller v. Schoene*, and of the gravel and sand mine in *Goldblatt v. Hempstead*, were uniquely burdened by the legislation sustained in those cases. Similarly, zoning laws often affect some property owners more severely than others but have not been held to be invalid on that account. For example, the property owner in *Euclid* who wished to use its property for industrial purposes was affected far more severely by the ordinance than its neighbors who wished to use their land for residences.

In any event, appellants' repeated suggestions that they are solely burdened and unbenefited is factually inaccurate. This contention overlooks the fact that the New York City law applies to vast numbers of structures in the city in addition to the Terminal—all the structures contained in the 31 historic districts and over 400 individual landmarks, many of which are close to the Terminal. Unless we are to reject the judgment of the New York City Council that the preservation of landmarks benefits all New York citizens and all structures, both economically and by improving the quality of life in the city as a whole—which we are unwilling to do—we cannot conclude that the owners of the Terminal have in no sense been benefited by the Landmarks Law. . . .

. . . We now must consider whether the interference with appellants' property is of such a magnitude that "there must be an exercise of eminent domain and compensation to sustain [it]." Pennsylvania Coal Co. v. Mahon, 260 U.S., at 413. That inquiry may be narrowed to the question of the severity of the impact of the law on appellants' parcel, and its resolution in turn requires a careful assessment of the impact of the regulation on the Terminal site. . . . Its designation as a landmark not only permits but contemplates that appellants may continue to use the property precisely as it has been used for the past 65 years: as a railroad terminal containing office space and concessions. So the law does not interfere with what must be regarded as Penn Central's primary expectation concerning the use of the parcel. More importantly, on this record, we must regard the New York City law as permitting Penn Central not only to profit from the Terminal but also to obtain a "reasonable return" on its investment. . . .

On this record, we conclude that the application of New York City's Landmarks Law has not effected a "taking" of appellants' property. The restrictions imposed are substantially related to the promotion of the general welfare and not only permit reasonable beneficial use of the landmark site but also afford appellants opportunities further to enhance not only the Terminal site proper but also other properties.

Affirmed.

Mr. Justice REHNQUIST, with whom THE CHIEF JUSTICE and Mr. Justice STEVENS join, dissenting.

Of the over one million buildings and structures in the city of New York, appellees have singled out 400 for designation as official landmarks. The owner of a building might initially be pleased that his property has been chosen by a distinguished committee of architects, historians, and city planners for such a singular distinction. But he may well discover, as appellant Penn Central Transportation Co. did here, that the landmark designation imposes upon him a substantial cost, with little or no offsetting benefit except for the honor of the designation. The question in this case is whether the cost associated with the city of New York's desire to preserve a limited number of "landmarks" within its borders must be borne by all of its taxpayers or whether it can instead be imposed entirely on the owners of the individual properties.

Only in the most superficial sense of the word can this case be said to involve "zoning." Typical zoning restrictions may, it is true, so limit the prospective uses of a piece of property as to diminish the value of that property in the abstract because it may not be used for the forbidden purposes. But any such abstract decrease in value will more than likely be at least partially offset by an increase in value which flows from similar restrictions as to use on neighboring properties. All property owners in a designated area are placed under the same restrictions, not only for the benefit of the municipality as a whole but also for the common benefit of one another. In the words of Mr. Justice Holmes, speaking for the Court in Pennsylvania Coal Co. v. Mahon, 260 U.S. 393, 415 (1922), there is "an average reciprocity of advantage."

Where a relatively few individual buildings, all separated from one another, are singled out and treated differently from surrounding buildings, no such reciprocity exists. The cost to the property owner which results from the imposition of restrictions applicable only to his property and not that of his neighbors may be substantial—in this case, several million dollars—with no comparable reciprocal benefits. And the cost associated with landmark legislation is likely to be of a completely different order of magnitude than that which results from the imposition of normal zoning restrictions. Unlike the regime affected by the latter, the landowner is not simply prohibited from using his property for certain purposes, while allowed to use it for all other purposes. Under the historic-landmark preservation scheme adopted by New York, the property owner is under an affirmative duty to *preserve* his property *as a landmark* at his own expense. . . .

While neighboring landowners are free to use their land and "air rights" in any way consistent with the broad boundaries of New York zoning, Penn Central, absent the permission of appellees, must forever maintain its property in its present state. The property has been thus subjected to a nonconsensual servitude not borne by any neighboring or similar properties. . . .

As early as 1887, the Court recognized that the government can prevent a property owner from using his property to injure others without having to compensate the owner for the value of the forbidden use. . . .

The nuisance exception to the taking guarantee is not coterminous with the police power itself. The question is whether the forbidden use is dangerous to the safety, health, or welfare of others. . . .

Appellees are not prohibiting a nuisance. The record is clear that the proposed addition to the Grand Central Terminal would be in full compliance with zoning, height limitations, and other health and safety requirements. Instead, appellees are seeking to preserve what they believe to be an outstanding example of beaux-arts architecture. Penn Central is prevented from further developing its property basically because *too good* a job was done in designing and building it. The city of New York, because of its unadorned admiration for the design, has decided that the owners of the building must preserve it unchanged for the benefit of sightseeing New Yorkers and tourists. . . .

As Mr. Justice Holmes pointed out in *Pennsylvania Coal Co. v. Mahon*, "the question at bottom" in an eminent domain case "is upon whom the loss of the changes desired should fall." 260 U.S., at 416. The benefits that appellees believe will flow from preservation of the Grand Central Terminal will accrue to all the citizens of New York City. There is no reason to believe that appellants will enjoy a substantially greater share of these benefits. If the cost of preserving Grand Central Terminal were spread evenly across the entire population of the city of New York, the burden per person would be in cents per year—a minor cost appellees would surely concede for the benefit accrued. Instead, however, appellees would impose the entire cost of several million dollars per year on Penn Central. But it is precisely this sort of discrimination that the Fifth Amendment prohibits. . . .

■ POINTS TO CONSIDER

1. **The *Penn Central* balancing test.** How would you state the test for determining when a regulatory taking has occurred after *Penn Central*? Can you state with more clarity now what factors a court should consider in weighing the public interest and the harm to the landowner? The Supreme Court has often summarized the takings test as "bar[ring] Government from forcing some people alone to bear public burdens which, in all fairness and justice, should be borne by the public as a whole." Armstrong v. United States, 364 U.S. 40, 49 (1960). Explain how the following factors, which Justice O'Connor has

labeled "vexing subsidiary questions,"[18] come into play, to determine when "fairness and justice" demand that the property owner be compensated:

Impact on Property Owner: Diminution in Value	Public Interest: Character of Governmental Action
reciprocity of advantage	physical invasion
singling out	economic regulation
investment-backed expectations, reasonable return	nuisance or noxious use prevention
severance: relevant parcel	

2. **Sinkholes revisited.** The Court provided a striking example of how the *Penn Central* balancing test may be applied in Keystone Bituminous Coal Ass'n v. DeBenedictis, 480 U.S. 470 (1987). The Court considered a Pennsylvania statute (called the Subsidence Act) that required 50 percent of coal to be left in place under certain structures to provide surface support. Sound familiar? The challengers thought the case was a straightforward application of *Pennsylvania Coal*. Four members of the Court agreed that the case was "strikingly similar" to, and controlled by, *Pennsylvania Coal*. The majority in *Keystone*, however, applied the *Penn Central* balancing test and upheld the new subsidence law. How did the *Keystone* majority distinguish *Pennsylvania Coal*?

   ▪ **Character of the government action.** The Court found the purpose here was "harm-preventing" rather than "benefit-conferring." The law applied to all property, even where one person owned both surface and mineral rights and was directed at safety concerns.
   ▪ **Impact on property owner.** Instead of focusing only on the value of the coal left in place, the Court noted that the amount of coal regulated by the statute was less than 2 percent of the 1.4 billion tons petitioners owned in 13 mines.

   In *Pennsylvania Coal*, Justice Holmes focused on the fact that the Kohler Act negated a pre-existing transaction that had specifically allocated the risk. In contrast, the *Keystone* majority focused on the fact that the law protected the public from harm while still allowing coal mining companies a substantial profit. As in *Penn Central*, the coal companies still could earn a reasonable return on their investment. Thus, the Court focused on the substantial economic value *remaining*, rather than on the value of what was taken.

   Nevertheless, the *Keystone* majority did not overrule *Pennsylvania Coal*, at least explicitly—*Pennsylvania Coal* remains the seminal case in the regulatory takings area.

---

[18] Lingle v. Chevron U.S.A., 533 U.S. 528, 539 (2005).

TDRs

The *Penn Central* case mentions transferable development rights (TDRs), which the majority believed softened the law's economic impact. TDRs allow the owner of restricted property to sell development rights to the owners of other parcels, who are then able to use their property more intensively (in terms of height or density, for example) than they otherwise would.

➤ For example, assume Angie owns property with a wetland. The law prohibits her from building on the wetland but gives her TDRs as compensation. Bart owns property located in a zone that allows only 10-story structures. Bart may be able to buy TDRs from Angie and build a 15-story building instead. This *market-based* mechanism attempts to shift the costs of preservation onto those who want more intense growth.

■ PROBLEMS: APPLYING *PENN CENTRAL*

Practice Tip: Inverse Condemnation

When a *state* government entity has taken or damaged your client's property by regulation, your remedy might be to file an *inverse condemnation* suit. "Inverse condemnation is simply a device to force a governmental body to exercise its power of condemnation, even though it may have no desire to do so." Smith v. City of Charlotte, 339 S.E.2d 844, 847 (N.C. Ct. App. 1986). In some states, this cause of action is specifically provided by statute; in others, it is matter of common law.

   If the governmental actor is *federal*, the *Tucker Act* gives the property owner a claim for damages in the U.S. Court of Federal Claims. 28 U.S.C. §1491(a)(1) (2018). Although this court is located in Washington, D.C., it can hold trials across the country, where the cause of action arose.

1. Bart owned a game farm in Montana, on which he raised elk and then charged customers to shoot them. The farm was required to obtain a license from the state and was highly regulated due to the risk of chronic wasting disease at such operations. Bart obtained a license in 1997, and over the next few years invested about half a million dollars in the acquisition of stock and improvements to his land, such as fencing. In 2000, however, Montana voters enacted an initiative measure that prohibited the transfer of game farm licenses and prohibited charging fees for the shooting of game animals at such facilities. Although Bart can still harvest the elk and sell the meat, he estimates he has lost about $4,000 per head as a result of the restrictions. In addition, the value of his ranch has decreased by about 70 percent, due to the restrictions on shooting and the inability to transfer his license. Has a taking occurred? *See* Kafka v. Mont. Dep't of Fish, Wildlife & Parks, 201 P.3d 8 (Mont. 2008). *See also* Brakke v. Iowa Dep't of Nat. Res., 897 N.W.2d 522 (Iowa 2017) (no taking because of 5-year quarantine of whitetail deer preserve due to chronic wasting disease).

2. **Suitum revisited.** How would you apply the *Penn Central* balancing test to the Lake Tahoe situation set out in the introduction to this section? Suitum claimed that when the Tahoe Regional Planning Agency placed her property in an SEZ zone, it destroyed the value of the lot. TRPA tried to soften the blow to Suitum by granting her TDRs, although their value was uncertain. Do "fairness and justice" demand that Suitum be compensated?

3. **Uber and Lyft.** For many years, the City regulated taxicabs by imposed licensing requirements, fixing the overall number of licenses, capping fares, requiring insurance, and prescribing vehicle standards. Because the city's regulation made them a scarce, valuable resource, a taxicab license (known as a "medallion") traded for approximately $340,000 on the open market. Recently, entities such as Uber and Lyft began offering rides outside of this regulated system. The City responded, eventually, by requiring drivers to register, provide proof of insurance, and disclose rates. It did not, however, limit the number of operators and the flooded market has now completely undermined the taxicab medallion market, rendering them practically worthless. Taxicab drivers filed a class action against the City, alleging that the failure to protect their licenses from competition constituted a taking of their property. Do they have a case? Checker Cab Operators, Inc. v. Miami-Dade County, 899 F.3d 908 (11th Cir. 2018).

3. Categorical Takings: *Loretto* and *Lucas*

Although the *Penn Central* decision established a framework for analyzing takings claims, you can tell that the test remained extremely indeterminate and malleable (as the majority and dissent in *Keystone* illustrated). In an effort to create some clarity, the Court developed two categories of cases, which avoided the need for ad hoc balancing: (a) *permanent physical occupations*, and (b) 100 percent diminutions in value (called *total takings*).

a. Permanent Physical Occupation

The physical occupation category was recognized in Loretto v. Teleprompter Manhattan CATV Corp., 458 U.S. 419 (1982). The owner of an apartment building in New York City challenged a state statute that required her to allow a cable company to install facilities on her property. The intrusion was admittedly small—cable wire and boxes taking up about 1½ cubic feet of space. Moreover, the public interest was fairly strong—ensuring that tenants could have access to cable and that the expansion of cable service would not be held up by landlords who engaged in price-gouging.

Nevertheless, the Court refused to engage in *Penn Central* balancing:

> [W]hen the "character of the governmental action," is a permanent physical occupation of property, our cases uniformly have found a taking to the extent of the occupation, without regard to whether the action achieves an important public benefit or has only minimal economic impact on the owner.
>
> . . . Such an appropriation is perhaps the most serious form of invasion of an owner's property interests. To borrow a metaphor, the government does not simply take a single "strand" from the "bundle" of property rights: it chops through the bundle, taking a slice of every strand.

Id. at 434-35. Thus, any government action that authorizes a permanent physical occupation of private property is a taking, period. The only question is the amount of just compensation. In that regard, Loretto's victory for New York landlords may have been ephemeral—absent special circumstances, the New York State Commission on Cable Television determined that $1 constituted just compensation for cable installations.

CASE SUMMARY: Horne v. Department of Agriculture, 135 S. Ct. 2419 (2015)

Marvin Horne, Laura Horne, and their family are raisin growers. The Agricultural Marketing Agreement Act of 1937 authorizes the Secretary of Agriculture to promulgate "marketing orders" to help maintain stable markets for particular agricultural products. The marketing order for raisins required growers like the Hornes to set aside a certain percentage of their crop for the account of the Government, which then either sold them in noncompetitive markets, donated them, or disposed of them.

The Hornes refused to comply with the marketing order on the ground that it constituted an uncompensated taking of private property. The Government fined the Hornes the fair market value of the raisins as well as additional civil penalties for their failure to obey the raisin marketing order. The Ninth Circuit held that the requirement was not a taking, because it was simply a condition imposed in exchange for the government's ordering of the raisin market for the benefit of all growers. 750 F.3d 1128, 1143 (9th Cir. 2014).

The Supreme Court reversed, holding that the marketing order effected a physical confiscation of personal property without just compensation. Chief Justice Roberts noted that the Fifth Amendment requires that the Government pay just compensation for takings of personal property as well as real property. Instead of analyzing the case as a regulatory requirement, Roberts viewed it as a physical appropriation of the raisins, which triggered the *per se* takings analysis of *Loretto*. He noted: "Actual raisins are transferred from the growers to the Government. Title to the raisins passes to the Raisin Committee." 135 S. Ct., at 2428.

In dissent, Justice Sotomayor noted that government agents were not "storming raisin farms in the dark of night to load raisins onto trucks." Instead, the order

> simply requires the Hornes to set aside a portion of their raisins. . . . And it does so to facilitate two classic regulatory goals. One is the regulatory purpose of limiting the quantity of raisins that can be sold on the market. The other is the regulatory purpose of arranging the orderly disposition of those raisins whose sale would otherwise exceed the cap. The Hornes and the Court both concede that a cap on the quantity of raisins that the Hornes can sell would not be a *per se* taking.

Id. at 2442 (Sotomayor, J., dissenting). Because the agency could achieve the same result by placing a limit on how many raisins the Hornes could grow, Justice Sotomayor found the Court's focus on the government's arrangement to dispose of the excess raisins troubling.

Chief Justice Roberts replied:

> A physical taking of raisins and a regulatory limit on production may have the same economic impact on a grower. The Constitution, however, is concerned with means as well as ends. The Government has broad powers, but the means it uses to achieve its ends must be "consist[ent] with the letter and spirit of the constitution." *McCulloch v. Maryland*, 4 Wheat. 316, 421, 4 L.Ed. 579 (1819).

Id. at 2428.

■ PROBLEM: APPLYING *LORETTO*

The federal Environmental Protection Agency (EPA) discovered an old hazardous waste dump on the property adjacent to Hendler's. It requested permission from Hendler to install a series of groundwater monitoring wells on his property, so that it could determine the extent of the contamination and the efficacy of cleanup efforts. Hendler refused, so EPA issued an administrative order granting itself access, as authorized by statute. After EPA installed five monitoring wells, Hendler brought suit demanding compensation for a taking. EPA argued that the intrusion was temporary, minimal and, in any event, intended to help protect Hendler's own property. How would you apply *Loretto* to this case? *See* Hendler v. United States, 952 F.2d 1364 (Fed. Cir. 1991); Waverley View Investors, LLC v. U.S., 135 Fed. Cl. 750 (2018).

b. "Total Takings"

The second category of "per se" takings was recognized (or perhaps "created") by the Supreme Court in the following beachfront development case. Justice Scalia clearly wanted to establish a bright-line test in an area fraught with uncertainty—did he succeed?

LUCAS v. SOUTH CAROLINA COASTAL COUNCIL

505 U.S. 1003 (1992)
Supreme Court of the United States

Justice SCALIA delivered the opinion of the Court.

In 1986, petitioner David H. Lucas paid $975,000 for two residential lots on the Isle of Palms in Charleston County, South Carolina, on which he intended to build single-family homes. In 1988, however, the South Carolina Legislature enacted the

Beachfront Management Act, which had the direct effect of barring petitioner from erecting any permanent habitable structures on his two parcels. A state trial court found that this prohibition rendered Lucas's parcels "valueless." This case requires us to decide whether the Act's dramatic effect on the economic value of Lucas's lots accomplished a taking of private property under the Fifth and Fourteenth Amendments requiring the payment of "just compensation." U.S. Const., Amdt. 5.

South Carolina's expressed interest in intensively managing development activities in the so-called "coastal zone" dates from 1977 when, in the aftermath of Congress's passage of the federal Coastal Zone Management Act of 1972, the legislature enacted a Coastal Zone Management Act of its own. In its original form, the South Carolina Act required owners of coastal zone land that qualified as a "critical area" (defined in the legislation to include beaches and immediately adjacent sand dunes) to obtain a permit from the newly created South Carolina Coastal Council (Council) (respondent here) prior to committing the land to a "use other than the use the critical area was devoted to on [September 28, 1977]."

In the late 1970s, Lucas and others began extensive residential development of the Isle of Palms, a barrier island situated eastward of the city of Charleston. Toward the close of the development cycle for one residential subdivision known as "Beachwood East," Lucas in 1986 purchased the two lots at issue in this litigation for his own account. No portion of the lots, which were located approximately 300 feet from the beach, qualified as a "critical area" under the 1977 Act; accordingly, at the time Lucas acquired these parcels, he was not legally obliged to obtain a permit from the Council in advance of any development activity. His intention with respect to the lots was to do what the owners of the immediately adjacent parcels had already done: erect single-family residences. He commissioned architectural drawings for this purpose.

The Beachfront Management Act brought Lucas's plans to an abrupt end. Under that 1988 legislation, the Council was directed to establish a "baseline" connecting the landward-most "point[s] of erosion ... during the past forty years" in the region of the Isle of Palms that includes Lucas's lots. In action not challenged here, the Council fixed this baseline landward of Lucas's parcels. That was significant, for under the Act construction of occupiable improvements[19] was flatly prohibited seaward of a line drawn 20 feet landward of, and parallel to, the baseline. The Act provided no exceptions.

Lucas promptly filed suit in the South Carolina Court of Common Pleas, contending that the Beachfront Management Act's construction bar effected a taking of his property without just compensation. Lucas did not take issue with the validity of the Act as a lawful exercise of South Carolina's police power, but contended that the Act's complete extinguishment of his property's value entitled him to compensation regardless of whether the legislature had acted in furtherance of legitimate police power objectives. Following a bench trial, the court agreed. Among its factual determinations was the finding that ... the

---

[19] The Act did allow the construction of certain nonhabitable improvements, *e.g.*, "wooden walkways no larger in width than six feet," and "small wooden decks no larger than one hundred forty-four square feet."

Part of "Wild Dunes" resort on Isles of Palms, SC, 11/94

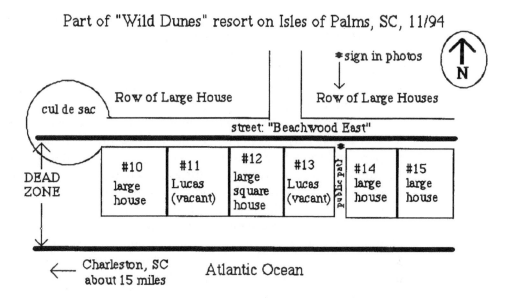

David Lucas's two lots
Map and photo courtesy of Prof. William A. Fischel

Beachfront Management Act decreed a permanent ban on construction insofar as Lucas's lots were concerned, and that this prohibition "deprive[d] Lucas of any reasonable economic use of the lots, . . . eliminated the unrestricted right of use, and render[ed] them valueless." *Id.* at 37. The court thus concluded that Lucas's properties had been "taken" by operation of the Act, and it ordered respondent to pay "just compensation" in the amount of $1,232,387.50. *Id.* at 40.

The Supreme Court of South Carolina reversed. It found dispositive what it described as Lucas's concession "that the Beachfront Management Act [was] properly and validly designed to preserve . . . South Carolina's beaches." Failing an attack on the validity of the statute as such, the court believed itself bound to accept the "uncontested . . . findings" of the South Carolina Legislature that new construction in the coastal zone—such as petitioner intended—threatened this public resource. The court ruled that when a regulation respecting the use of property is designed "to prevent serious public harm," 304 S.C. 376, 383, 404 S.E.2d, at 899 (citing, inter alia, Mugler v. Kansas, 123 U.S. 623 (1887)), no compensation is owing under the Takings Clause regardless of the regulation's effect on the property's value.

Prior to Justice Holmes's exposition in Pennsylvania Coal Co. v. Mahon, 260 U.S. 393 (1922), it was generally thought that the Takings Clause reached only a "direct appropriation" of property, Legal Tender Cases, 12 Wall. 457, 551 (1871), or the functional equivalent of a "practical ouster of [the owner's] possession," Transportation Co. v. Chicago, 99 U.S. 635, 642 (1879). *See also* Gibson v. United States, 166 U.S. 269, 275-276 (1897). Justice Holmes recognized in *Mahon*, however, that if the protection against physical appropriations of private property was to be meaningfully enforced, the government's power to redefine the range of interests included in the ownership of property was necessarily constrained by constitutional limits. 260 U.S., at 414-415. . . .

Nevertheless, our decision in *Mahon* offered little insight into when, and under what circumstances, a given regulation would be seen as going "too far" for purposes of the Fifth Amendment. In 70-odd years of succeeding "regulatory takings" jurisprudence, we have generally eschewed any "'set formula'" for determining how far is too far, preferring to "engag[e] in . . . essentially ad hoc, factual inquiries." Penn Central Transportation Co. v. New York City, 438 U.S. 104, 124 (1978) (quoting Goldblatt v. Hempstead, 369 U.S. 590, 594 (1962)). . . .

We have, however, described at least two discrete categories of regulatory action as compensable without case-specific inquiry into the public interest advanced in support of the restraint. The first encompasses regulations that compel the property owner to suffer a physical "invasion" of his property. In general (at least with regard to permanent invasions), no matter how minute the intrusion, and no matter how weighty the public purpose behind it, we have required compensation. . . .

The second situation in which we have found categorical treatment appropriate is where regulation denies all economically beneficial or productive use of land. *See Agins*, 447 U.S., at 260. . . . As we have said on numerous occasions, the Fifth Amendment is violated when land-use regulation "does not substantially advance legitimate state interests *or denies an owner economically viable use of his land." Agins, supra,* 447 U.S., at 260 (citations omitted) (emphasis added).[20]

We have never set forth the justification for this rule. Perhaps it is simply, as Justice Brennan suggested, that total deprivation of beneficial use is, from the landowner's point of view, the equivalent of a physical appropriation. *See* San Diego Gas & Electric Co. v. San Diego, 450 U.S., at 652. "[F]or what is the land but the profits thereof[?]" 1 E. Coke, Institutes, ch. 1, §1 (1st Am. ed. 1812). Surely, at least, in the extraordinary circumstance when no productive or economically beneficial use of land is permitted, it is less realistic to indulge our usual assumption that the legislature is simply "adjusting the benefits and burdens of economic life," *Penn Central Transportation Co.,* 438 U.S., at 124, in a manner that secures an "average reciprocity of advantage" to everyone concerned, Pennsylvania Coal Co. v. Mahon, 260 U.S., at 415. And the functional basis for permitting the government, by regulation, to affect property values without compensation—that "Government hardly could go on if to some extent values incident to property could not be diminished without paying for every such change in the general law," *id.* at 413—does not apply to the relatively rare situations where the government has deprived a landowner of all economically beneficial uses.

On the other side of the balance, affirmatively supporting a compensation requirement, is the fact that regulations that leave the owner of land without economically beneficial or productive options for its use—typically, as here, by requiring land to be left substantially in its natural state—carry with them a heightened risk that private property is being pressed into some form of public service under the guise of mitigating serious public harm. *See, e.g.,* Annicelli v. South Kingstown, 463 A.2d 133, 140-141 (R.I. 1983) (prohibition on construction adjacent to beach justified on twin grounds of safety and "conservation of open space"); Morris County Land Improvement Co. v. Parsippany-Troy Hills Township, 40 N.J. 539, 552-553, 193 A.2d 232, 240 (1963) (prohibition on filling marshlands imposed in order to preserve region as water detention basin and create wildlife refuge). . . . The many statutes on the books, both state and federal, that provide for the use of eminent domain to impose servitudes on private scenic lands preventing developmental uses, or to acquire such lands altogether, suggest the practical equivalence in this setting of negative regulation and appropriation. . . .

---

[20] Regrettably, the rhetorical force of our "deprivation of all economically feasible use" rule is greater than its precision, since the rule does not make clear the "property interest" against which the loss of value is to be measured. When, for example, a regulation requires a developer to leave 90% of a rural tract in its natural state, it is unclear whether we would analyze the situation as one in which the owner has been deprived of all economically beneficial use of the burdened portion of the tract, or as one in which the owner has suffered a mere diminution in value of the tract as a whole. (For an extreme—and, we think, unsupportable—view of the relevant calculus, *see* Penn Central Transportation Co. v. New York City, 366 N.E.2d 1271, 1276-1277 (1977), aff'd, 438 U.S. 104 (1978), where the state court examined the diminution in a particular parcel's value produced by a municipal ordinance in light of total value of the takings claimant's other holdings in the vicinity.) . . . The answer to this difficult question may lie in how the owner's reasonable expectations have been shaped by the State's law of property—i.e., whether and to what degree the State's law has accorded legal recognition and protection to the particular interest in land with respect to which the takings claimant alleges a diminution in (or elimination of) value. . . .

We think, in short, that there are good reasons for our frequently expressed belief that when the owner of real property has been called upon to sacrifice all economically beneficial uses in the name of the common good, that is, to leave his property economically idle, he has suffered a taking.[21]

. . . It is correct that many of our prior opinions have suggested that "harmful or noxious uses" of property may be proscribed by government regulation without the requirement of compensation. For a number of reasons, however, we think the South Carolina Supreme Court was too quick to conclude that that principle decides the present case. The "harmful or noxious uses" principle was the Court's early attempt to describe in theoretical terms why government may, consistent with the Takings Clause, affect property values by regulation without incurring an obligation to compensate—a reality we nowadays acknowledge explicitly with respect to the full scope of the State's police power.

. . . The transition from our early focus on control of "noxious" uses to our contemporary understanding of the broad realm within which government may regulate without compensation was an easy one, since the distinction between "harm-preventing" and "benefit-conferring" regulation is often in the eye of the beholder. It is quite possible, for example, to describe in either fashion the ecological, economic, and esthetic concerns that inspired the South Carolina Legislature in the present case. One could say that imposing a servitude on Lucas's land is necessary in order to prevent his use of it from "harming" South Carolina's ecological resources; or, instead, in order to achieve the "benefits" of an ecological preserve. . . . Whether Lucas's construction of single-family residences on his parcels should be described as bringing "harm" to South Carolina's adjacent ecological resources thus depends principally upon whether the describer believes that the State's use interest in nurturing those resources is so important that any competing adjacent use must yield.[22]

When it is understood that "prevention of harmful use" was merely our early formulation of the police power justification necessary to sustain (without compensation) any regulatory diminution in value; and that the distinction between regulation that "prevents harmful use" and that which "confers benefits" is difficult, if not impossible, to discern on an objective, value-free basis; it becomes self-evident that noxious-use logic cannot serve as a touchstone to distinguish regulatory "takings"—which require compensation—from regulatory deprivations that do not require compensation. *A fortiori* the legislature's recitation of

---

[21] Justice Stevens criticizes the "deprivation of all economically beneficial use" rule as "wholly arbitrary," in that "[the] landowner whose property is diminished in value 95% recovers nothing," while the landowner who suffers a complete elimination of value "recovers the land's full value." This analysis errs in its assumption that the landowner whose deprivation is one step short of complete is not entitled to compensation. Such an owner might not be able to claim the benefit of our categorical formulation, but, as we have acknowledged time and again, "[t]he economic impact of the regulation on the claimant and . . . the extent to which the regulation has interfered with distinct investment-backed expectations" are keenly relevant to takings analysis generally. Penn Central Transportation Co. v. New York City, 438 U.S. 104, 124 (1978). . . .

[22] In Justice Blackmun's view, even with respect to regulations that deprive an owner of all developmental or economically beneficial land uses, the test for required compensation is whether the legislature has recited a harm-preventing justification for its action. Since such a justification can be formulated in practically every case, this amounts to a test of whether the legislature has a stupid staff. We think the Takings Clause requires courts to do more than insist upon artful harm-preventing characterizations.

a noxious-use justification cannot be the basis for departing from our categorical rule that total regulatory takings must be compensated. If it were, departure would virtually always be allowed. . . .

Where the State seeks to sustain regulation that deprives land of all economically beneficial use, we think it may resist compensation only if the logically antecedent inquiry into the nature of the owner's estate shows that the proscribed use interests were not part of his title to begin with. This accords, we think, with our "takings" jurisprudence, which has traditionally been guided by the understandings of our citizens regarding the content of, and the State's power over, the "bundle of rights" that they acquire when they obtain title to property. . . . [W]e think the notion pressed by the Council that title is somehow held subject to the "implied limitation" that the State may subsequently eliminate all economically valuable use is inconsistent with the historical compact recorded in the Takings Clause that has become part of our constitutional culture.[23]

. . . Any limitation so severe cannot be newly legislated or decreed (without compensation), but must inhere in the title itself, in the restrictions that background principles of the State's law of property and nuisance already place upon land ownership. A law or decree with such an effect must, in other words, do no more than duplicate the result that could have been achieved in the courts—by adjacent landowners (or other uniquely affected persons) under the State's law of private nuisance, or by the State under its complementary power to abate nuisances that affect the public generally, or otherwise.

On this analysis, the owner of a lake-bed, for example, would not be entitled to compensation when he is denied the requisite permit to engage in a land-filling operation that would have the effect of flooding others' land. Nor the corporate owner of a nuclear generating plant, when it is directed to remove all improvements from its land upon discovery that the plant sits astride an earthquake fault. Such regulatory action may well have the effect of eliminating the land's only economically productive use, but it does not proscribe a productive use that was previously permissible under relevant property and nuisance principles. The use of these properties for what are now expressly prohibited purposes was always unlawful, and (subject to other constitutional limitations) it was open to the State at any point to make the implication of those background principles of nuisance and property law explicit. . . . When, however, a regulation that declares "off-limits" all economically productive or beneficial uses of land goes beyond what the relevant background principles would dictate, compensation must be paid to sustain it.

The "total taking" inquiry we require today will ordinarily entail (as the application of state nuisance law ordinarily entails) analysis of, among other things,

---

[23] . . . Justice Blackmun is correct that early constitutional theorists did not believe the Takings Clause embraced regulations of property at all, but even he does not suggest (explicitly, at least) that we renounce the Court's contrary conclusion in *Mahon*. Since the text of the Clause can be read to encompass regulatory as well as physical deprivations (in contrast to the text originally proposed by Madison, see Speech Proposing Bill of Rights (June 8, 1789), in 12 J. Madison, The Papers of James Madison 201 (C. Hobson, R. Rutland, W. Rachal, & J. Sisson ed. 1979) ("No person shall be . . . obliged to relinquish his property, where it may be necessary for public use, without a just compensation"), we decline to do so as well.

the degree of harm to public lands and resources, or adjacent private property, posed by the claimant's proposed activities, *see, e.g.,* Restatement (Second) of Torts §§826, 827, the social value of the claimant's activities and their suitability to the locality in question, *see, e.g., id.,* §§828(a) and (b), 831, and the relative ease with which the alleged harm can be avoided through measures taken by the claimant and the government (or adjacent private landowners) alike, *see, e.g., id.,* §§827(e), 828(c), 830. The fact that a particular use has long been engaged in by similarly situated owners ordinarily imports a lack of any common-law prohibition (though changed circumstances or new knowledge may make what was previously permissible no longer so, *see id.,* §827, Comment g. So also does the fact that other land-owners, similarly situated, are permitted to continue the use denied to the claimant.

It seems unlikely that common-law principles would have prevented the erection of any habitable or productive improvements on petitioner's land; they rarely support prohibition of the "essential use" of land, Curtin v. Benson, 222 U.S. 78, 86 (1911). The question, however, is one of state law to be dealt with on remand. We emphasize that to win its case South Carolina must do more than proffer the legislature's declaration that the uses Lucas desires are inconsistent with the public interest, or the conclusory assertion that they violate a common-law maxim such as *sic utere tuo ut alienum non laedas.* As we have said, a "State, by *ipse dixit,* may not transform private property into public property without compensation. . . ." Webb's Fabulous Pharmacies, Inc. v. Beckwith, 449 U.S. 155, 164 (1980). Instead, as it would be required to do if it sought to restrain Lucas in a common-law action for public nuisance, South Carolina must identify background principles of nuisance and property law that prohibit the uses he now intends in the circumstances in which the property is presently found. Only on this showing can the State fairly claim that, in proscribing all such beneficial uses, the Beachfront Management Act is taking nothing.[24]

* * *

The judgment is reversed, and the case is remanded for proceedings not inconsistent with this opinion.

So ordered.

---

[24] Justice Blackmun decries our reliance on background nuisance principles at least in part because he believes those principles to be as manipulable as we find the "harm prevention"/"benefit conferral" dichotomy. There is no doubt some leeway in a court's interpretation of what existing state law permits—but not remotely as much, we think, as in a legislative crafting of the reasons for its confiscatory regulation. We stress that an affirmative decree eliminating all economically beneficial uses may be defended only if an objectively reasonable application of relevant precedents would exclude those beneficial uses in the circumstances in which the land is presently found.

Justice KENNEDY, concurring in the judgment.

The South Carolina Court of Common Pleas found that petitioner's real property has been rendered valueless by the State's regulation. The finding appears to presume that the property has no significant market value or resale potential. This is a curious finding, and I share the reservations of some of my colleagues about a finding that a beach-front lot loses all value because of a development restriction.

The finding of no value must be considered under the Takings Clause by reference to the owner's reasonable, investment-backed expectations. The Takings Clause, while conferring substantial protection on property owners, does not eliminate the police power of the State to enact limitations on the use of their property. The rights conferred by the Takings Clause and the police power of the State may coexist without conflict. Property is bought and sold, investments are made, subject to the State's power to regulate. Where a taking is alleged from regulations which deprive the property of all value, the test must be whether the deprivation is contrary to reasonable, investment-backed expectations.

There is an inherent tendency towards circularity in this synthesis, of course; for if the owner's reasonable expectations are shaped by what courts allow as a proper exercise of governmental authority, property tends to become what courts say it is. Some circularity must be tolerated in these matters, however, as it is in other spheres. *E.g.*, Katz v. United States, 389 U.S. 347 (1967) (Fourth Amendment protections defined by reasonable expectations of privacy). The definition, moreover, is not circular in its entirety. The expectations protected by the Constitution are based on objective rules and customs that can be understood as reasonable by all parties involved.

In my view, reasonable expectations must be understood in light of the whole of our legal tradition. The common law of nuisance is too narrow a confine for the exercise of regulatory power in a complex and interdependent society. The State should not be prevented from enacting new regulatory initiatives in response to changing conditions, and courts must consider all reasonable expectations whatever their source. The Takings Clause does not require a static body of state property law; it protects private expectations to ensure private investment. I agree with the Court that nuisance prevention accords with the most common expectations of property owners who face regulation, but I do not believe this can be the sole source of state authority to impose severe restrictions. Coastal property may present such unique concerns for a fragile land system that the State can go further in regulating its development and use than the common law of nuisance might otherwise permit.

The Supreme Court of South Carolina erred, in my view, by reciting the general purposes for which the state regulations were enacted without a determination that they were in accord with the owner's reasonable expectations and therefore sufficient to support a severe restriction on specific parcels of property. The promotion of tourism, for instance, ought not to suffice to deprive specific property of all value without a corresponding duty to compensate. Furthermore, the means, as well as the ends, of regulation must accord with the owner's reasonable expectations. Here, the State did not act until after the property had been zoned for individual lot development and most other parcels had been improved, throwing the whole burden of the regulation on the remaining lots. This too must be measured in the balance. *See* Pennsylvania Coal Co. v. Mahon, 260 U.S. 393, 416 (1922).

With these observations, I concur in the judgment of the Court.

Justice BLACKMUN, dissenting.

Today the Court launches a missile to kill a mouse.

The State of South Carolina prohibited petitioner Lucas from building a permanent structure on his property from 1988 to 1990. Relying on an unreviewed (and implausible) state trial court finding that this restriction left Lucas' property valueless, this Court granted review to determine whether compensation must be paid in cases where the State prohibits all economic use of real estate. According to the Court, such an occasion never has arisen in any of our prior cases, and the Court imagines that it will arise "relatively rarely" or only in "extraordinary circumstances." Almost certainly it did not happen in this case.

Nonetheless, the Court presses on to decide the issue, and as it does, it ignores its jurisdictional limits, remakes its traditional rules of review, and creates simultaneously a new categorical rule and an exception (neither of which is rooted in our prior case law, common law, or common sense). I protest not only the Court's decision, but each step taken to reach it. More fundamentally, I question the Court's wisdom in issuing sweeping new rules to decide such a narrow case. Surely, as Justice Kennedy demonstrates, the Court could have reached the result it wanted without inflicting this damage upon our Takings Clause jurisprudence.

My fear is that the Court's new policies will spread beyond the narrow confines of the present case. For that reason, I, like the Court, will give far greater attention to this case than its narrow scope suggests—not because I can intercept the Court's missile, or save the targeted mouse, but because I hope perhaps to limit the collateral damage.

In 1972 Congress passed the Coastal Zone Management Act. 16 U.S.C. §1451 et seq. The Act was designed to provide States with money and incentives to carry out Congress' goal of protecting the public from shoreline erosion and coastal hazards. In the 1980 amendments to the Act, Congress directed States to enhance their coastal programs by "[p]reventing or significantly reducing threats to life and the destruction of property by eliminating development and redevelopment in high-hazard areas." [25] 16 U.S.C. §1456b(a)(2).

---

[25] The country has come to recognize that uncontrolled beachfront development can cause serious damage to life and property. Hurricane Hugo's September 1989 attack upon South Carolina's coastline, for example, caused 29 deaths and approximately $6 billion in property damage, much of it the result of uncontrolled beachfront development. See Zalkin, *Shifting Sands and Shifting Doctrines: The Supreme Court's Changing Takings Doctrine and South Carolina's Coastal Zone Statute*, 79 Calif. L. Rev. 205, 212-213 (1991). The beachfront buildings are not only themselves destroyed in such a storm, "but they are often driven, like battering rams, into adjacent inland homes." *Ibid.* Moreover, the development often destroys the natural sand dune barriers that provide storm breaks. *Ibid.*

South Carolina began implementing the congressional directive by enacting the South Carolina Coastal Zone Management Act of 1977. Under the 1977 Act, any construction activity in what was designated the "critical area" required a permit from the South Carolina Coastal Council (Council), and the construction of any habitable structure was prohibited. The 1977 critical area was relatively narrow.

This effort did not stop the loss of shoreline. In October 1986, the Council appointed a "Blue Ribbon Committee on Beachfront Management" to investigate beach erosion and propose possible solutions. In March 1987, the Committee found that South Carolina's beaches were "critically eroding," and proposed land-use restrictions. In response, South Carolina enacted the Beachfront Management Act on July 1, 1988. The 1988 Act did not change the uses permitted within the designated critical areas. Rather, it enlarged those areas to encompass the distance from the mean high watermark to a setback line established on the basis of "the best scientific and historical data" available.

Petitioner Lucas is a contractor, manager, and part owner of the Wild Dune development on the Isle of Palms. He has lived there since 1978. In December 1986, he purchased two of the last four pieces of vacant property in the development. The area is notoriously unstable. In roughly half of the last 40 years, all or part of petitioner's property was part of the beach or flooded twice daily by the ebb and flow of the tide.

... If the state legislature is correct that the prohibition on building in front of the setback line prevents serious harm, then, under this Court's prior cases, the Act is constitutional. "Long ago it was recognized that all property in this country is held under the implied obligation that the owner's use of it shall not be injurious to the community, and the Takings Clause did not transform that principle to one that requires compensation whenever the State asserts its power to enforce it." Keystone Bituminous Coal Assn. v. DeBenedictis, 480 U.S. 470, 491-492 (1987) (internal quotation marks omitted). The Court consistently has upheld regulations imposed to arrest a significant threat to the common welfare, whatever their economic effect on the owner.

Petitioner never challenged the legislature's findings that a building ban was necessary to protect property and life. Nor did he contend that the threatened harm was not sufficiently serious to make building a house in a particular location a "harmful" use, that the legislature had not made sufficient findings, or that the legislature was motivated by anything other than a desire to minimize damage to coastal areas.

Nothing in the record undermines the General Assembly's assessment that prohibitions on building in front of the setback line are necessary to protect people and property from storms, high tides, and beach erosion. Because that legislative determination cannot be disregarded in the absence of such evidence, and because its determination of harm to life and property from building is sufficient to prohibit that use under this Court's cases, the South Carolina Supreme Court correctly found no taking. ...

The Court creates its new takings jurisprudence based on the trial court's finding that the property had lost all economic value. This finding is almost certainly erroneous. Petitioner still can enjoy other attributes of ownership, such as the right to exclude others, "one of the most essential sticks in the bundle of rights that are commonly characterized as property." Kaiser Aetna v. United States, 444 U.S. 164, 176 (1979). Petitioner can picnic, swim, camp in a tent, or live on the property in a movable trailer. State courts frequently have recognized that land has economic value where the only residual economic uses are recreation or camping. Petitioner also retains the right to alienate the land, which would have value for neighbors and for those prepared to enjoy proximity to the ocean without a house.

Yet the trial court, apparently believing that "less value" and "valueless" could be used interchangeably, found the property "valueless." . . .

The Court also alters the long-settled rules of review.

The South Carolina Supreme Court's decision to defer to legislative judgments in the absence of a challenge from petitioner comports with one of this Court's oldest maxims: "[T]he existence of facts supporting the legislative judgment is to be presumed." United States v. Carolene Products Co., 304 U.S. 144, 152 (1938). . . .

Rather than invoking these traditional rules, the Court decides the State has the burden to convince the courts that its legislative judgments are correct. Despite Lucas' complete failure to contest the legislature's findings of serious harm to life and property if a permanent structure is built, the Court decides that the legislative findings are not sufficient to justify the use prohibition. Instead, the Court "emphasize[s]" the State must do more than merely proffer its legislative judgments to avoid invalidating its law. In this case, apparently, the State now has the burden of showing the regulation is not a taking. The Court offers no justification for its sudden hostility toward state legislators, and I doubt that it could.

The Court does not reject the South Carolina Supreme Court's decision simply on the basis of its disbelief and distrust of the legislature's findings. It also takes the opportunity to create a new scheme for regulations that eliminate all economic value. From now on, there is a categorical rule finding these regulations to be a taking unless the use they prohibit is a background common-law nuisance or property principle.

I first question the Court's rationale in creating a category that obviates a "case-specific inquiry into the public interest advanced," if all economic value has been lost. If one fact about the Court's takings jurisprudence can be stated without contradiction, it is that "the particular circumstances of each case" determine whether a specific restriction will be rendered invalid by the government's failure to pay compensation. United States v. Central Eureka Mining Co., 357 U.S. 155, 168 (1958). This is so because although we have articulated certain factors to be considered, including the economic impact on the property owner, the ultimate conclusion "necessarily requires a weighing of private and public interests." *Agins*, 447 U.S., at 261. When the government regulation prevents the owner from any economically valuable use of his property, the private interest is unquestionably substantial, but we have never before held that no public interest can outweigh it. Instead the Court's prior decisions "uniformly reject the proposition that diminution in property value, standing alone, can establish a 'taking.'" Penn Central Transp. Co. v. New York City, 438 U.S. 104, 131 (1978).

This Court repeatedly has recognized the ability of government, in certain circumstances, to regulate property without compensation no matter how adverse the financial effect on the owner may be [discussing *Mugler, Powell, Hadacheck, Miller*, and *Goldblatt*]. . . .

These cases rest on the principle that the State has full power to prohibit an owner's use of property if it is harmful to the public. "[S]ince no individual has a right to use his property so as to create a nuisance or otherwise harm others, the State has not 'taken' anything when it asserts its power to enjoin the nuisance-like activity." *Keystone Bituminous Coal*, 480 U.S., at 491, n. 20. It would make no sense under this theory to suggest that an owner has a constitutionally protected right to harm others, if only he makes the proper showing of economic loss. *See* Pennsylvania Coal Co. v. Mahon, 260 U.S. 393, 418 (1922) (Brandeis, J., dissenting) ("Restriction upon [harmful] use does not become inappropriate as a means, merely because it deprives the owner of the only use to which the property can then be profitably put").

Ultimately even the Court cannot embrace the full implications of its *per se* rule: It eventually agrees that there cannot be a categorical rule for a taking based on economic value that wholly disregards the public need asserted. Instead, the Court decides that it will permit a State to regulate all economic value only if the State prohibits uses that would not be permitted under "background principles of nuisance and property law."

Until today, the Court explicitly had rejected the contention that the government's power to act without paying compensation turns on whether the prohibited activity is a common-law nuisance. The brewery closed in *Mugler* itself was not a common-law nuisance, and the Court specifically stated that it was the role of the legislature to determine what measures would be appropriate for the protection of public health and safety. *See* 123 U.S., at 661. . . . Instead the Court has relied in the past, as the South Carolina court has done here, on legislative judgments of what constitutes a harm. . . .

The threshold inquiry for imposition of the Court's new rule, "deprivation of all economically valuable use," itself cannot be determined objectively. As the Court admits, whether the owner has been deprived of all economic value of his property will depend on how "property" is defined. . . .

Even more perplexing, however, is the Court's reliance on common-law principles of nuisance in its quest for a value-free takings jurisprudence. In determining what is a nuisance at common law, state courts make exactly the decision that the Court finds so troubling when made by the South Carolina General Assembly today: They determine whether the use is harmful. Common-law public and private nuisance law is simply a determination whether a particular use causes harm. See Prosser, Private Action for Public Nuisance, 52 Va. L. Rev. 997

(1966) ("Nuisance is a French word which means nothing more than harm"). There is nothing magical in the reasoning of judges long dead. They determined a harm in the same way as state judges and legislatures do today. If judges in the 18th and 19th centuries can distinguish a harm from a benefit, why not judges in the 20th century, and if judges can, why not legislators? There simply is no reason to believe that new interpretations of the hoary common-law nuisance doctrine will be particularly "objective" or "value free." Once one abandons the level of generality of *sic utere tuo ut alienum non laedas*, one searches in vain, I think, for anything resembling a principle in the common law of nuisance.

Finally, the Court justifies its new rule that the legislature may not deprive a property owner of the only economically valuable use of his land, even if the legislature finds it to be a harmful use, because such action is not part of the "long recognized" "understandings of our citizens." These "understandings" permit such regulation only if the use is a nuisance under the common law. Any other course is "inconsistent with the historical compact recorded in the Takings Clause." It is not clear from the Court's opinion where our "historical compact" or "citizens' understanding" comes from, but it does not appear to be history.

The principle that the State should compensate individuals for property taken for public use was not widely established in America at the time of the Revolution.

> "The colonists . . . inherited . . . a concept of property which permitted extensive regulation of the use of that property for the public benefit—regulation that could even go so far as to deny all productive use of the property to the owner if, as Coke himself stated, the regulation 'extends to the public benefit . . . for this is for the public, and every one hath benefit by it.'" F. Bosselman, D. Callies, & J. Banta, The Taking Issue 80-81 (1973), quoting The Case of the King's Prerogative in Saltpetre, 12 Co. Rep. 12-13 (1606). . . .

Although, prior to the adoption of the Bill of Rights, America was replete with land-use regulations describing which activities were considered noxious and forbidden . . . the Fifth Amendment's Takings Clause originally did not extend to regulations of property, whatever the effect. . . .[26]

In short, I find no clear and accepted "historical compact" or "understanding of our citizens" justifying the Court's new takings doctrine. . . .

I dissent.

Justice STEVENS, dissenting.

. . .

---

[26] James Madison, author of the Takings Clause, apparently intended it to apply only to direct, physical takings of property by the Federal Government. See Treanor, *The Origins and Original Significance of the Just Compensation Clause of the Fifth Amendment*, 94 Yale L.J. 694, 711 (1985). Professor Sax argues that although "contemporaneous commentary upon the meaning of the compensation clause is in very short supply," 74 Yale L.J., at 58, the "few authorities that are available" indicate that the Clause was "designed to prevent arbitrary government action," not to protect economic value. *Id.*, at 58-60.

Like many bright-line rules, the categorical rule established in this case is only "categorical" for a page or two in the U.S. Reports. No sooner does the Court state that "total regulatory takings must be compensated," than it quickly establishes an exception to that rule.

The exception provides that a regulation that renders property valueless is not a taking if it prohibits uses of property that were not "previously permissible under relevant property and nuisance principles." The Court thus rejects the basic holding in Mugler v. Kansas, 123 U.S. 623, (1887). There we held that a state-wide statute that prohibited the owner of a brewery from making alcoholic beverages did not effect a taking, even though the use of the property had been perfectly lawful and caused no public harm before the statute was enacted. We squarely rejected the rule the Court adopts today:

> It is true, that, when the defendants . . . erected their breweries, the laws of the State did not forbid the manufacture of intoxicating liquors. But the State did not thereby give any assurance, or come under an obligation, that its legislation upon that subject would remain unchanged. [T]he supervision of the public health and the public morals is a governmental power, "continuing in its nature," and "to be dealt with as the special exigencies of the moment may require"; . . . "for this purpose, the largest legislative discretion is allowed, and the discretion cannot be parted with any more than the power itself."

Id., at 669. . . .

The Court's holding today effectively freezes the State's common law, denying the legislature much of its traditional power to revise the law governing the rights and uses of property. Until today, I had thought that we had long abandoned this approach to constitutional law. More than a century ago we recognized that "the great office of statutes is to remedy defects in the common law as they are developed, and to adapt it to the changes of time and circumstances." Munn v. Illinois, 94 U.S. 113, 134 (1877). . . .

Arresting the development of the common law is not only a departure from our prior decisions; it is also profoundly unwise. The human condition is one of constant learning and evolution—both moral and practical. Legislatures implement that new learning; in doing so they must often revise the definition of property and the rights of property owners. Thus, when the Nation came to understand that slavery was morally wrong and mandated the emancipation of all slaves, it, in effect, redefined "property." On a lesser scale, our ongoing self-education produces similar changes in the rights of property owners: New appreciation of the significance of endangered species, *see, e.g.*, Andrus v. Allard, 444 U.S. 51 (1979); the importance of wetlands, *see, e.g.*, 16 U.S.C. §3801 *et seq.*; and the vulnerability of coastal lands, *see, e.g.*, 16 U.S.C. §1451 *et seq.*, shapes our evolving understandings of property rights.

Of course, some legislative redefinitions of property will effect a taking and must be compensated—but it certainly cannot be the case that every movement away from common law does so. There is no reason, and less sense, in such an absolute rule. We live in a world in which changes in the economy and the environment occur with increasing frequency and importance. If it was wise a century ago to allow government "'the largest legislative discretion'" to deal with "'the special exigencies of the moment,'" *Mugler*, 123 U.S., at 669, it is imperative to do so today. The rule that should govern a decision in a case of this kind should focus on the future, not the past.[27]

The Court's categorical approach rule will, I fear, greatly hamper the efforts of local officials and planners who must deal with increasingly complex problems in land-use and environmental regulation. As this case—in which the claims of an individual property owner exceed $1 million—well demonstrates, these officials face both substantial uncertainty because of the ad hoc nature of takings law and unacceptable penalties if they guess incorrectly about that law. . . .

In view of all of these factors, even assuming that petitioner's property was rendered valueless, the risk inherent in investments of the sort made by petitioner, the generality of the Act, and the compelling purpose motivating the South Carolina Legislature persuade me that the Act did not effect a taking of petitioner's property.

Accordingly, I respectfully dissent.

Statement of Justice SOUTER.

I would dismiss the writ of certiorari in this case as having been granted improvidently. After briefing and argument it is abundantly clear that an unreviewable assumption on which this case comes to us is both questionable as a conclusion of Fifth Amendment law and sufficient to frustrate the Court's ability to render certain the legal premises on which its holding rests.

■ POINTS TO CONSIDER

1. **Back to Chapter 1.** Does the debate between Scalia and the dissenters remind you of the material in Chapter 1 concerning the "evolutionary" or contingent nature of property rights? Recall in *State v. Shack*, the case involving migrant workers and the right to exclude, how the court noted that property rights depend on, and are limited by, the needs of society at the time. How does that relate to the Takings Clause and the different approaches taken by the justices in *Lucas*?

2. **Original meaning.** You might know that Justice Scalia is one of the primary proponents of using "original meaning" to interpret constitutional

---

[27] Even measured in terms of efficiency, the Court's rule is unsound. The Court today effectively establishes a form of insurance against certain changes in land-use regulations. Like other forms of insurance, the Court's rule creates a "moral hazard" and inefficiencies: In the face of uncertainty about changes in the law, developers will overinvest, safe in the knowledge that if the law changes adversely, they will be entitled to compensation. See generally Farber, *Economic Analysis and Just Compensation*, 12 Int'l Rev. of Law & Econ. 125 (1992).

provisions. Antonin Scalia, A Matter of Interpretation: Federal Courts and the Law (Amy Gutmann ed. 1997). Justice Scalia argues that constitutional provisions should be interpreted in accordance with the original meaning of the text as understood by "intelligent and informed people of the time." In this case, does Justice Scalia adopt the original meaning of the Fifth Amendment Takings Clause?

3. **100 percent diminution in value.** After *Lucas*, the determination of whether a regulation has destroyed *all economic value* of property becomes crucially important. If a total diminution has occurred, it's a taking *per se*; anything less than total diminution requires the indeterminate ad hoc balancing test of *Penn Central.*But how do you know whether *all* economic value has been destroyed? For example, in this case, do you agree that the development restriction rendered the property valueless? Would you pay anything to acquire a lot on the beach, even though you couldn't build any permanent habitable structures on it? Would the local Campfire Girls or Boy Scouts pay something? Would the homeowner across the street pay something, so they could have a private beach? Is that sort of minimal *residual value* enough to take it out of the total takings category? See the case summary of *Palazzolo*, below.

4. **Severance.** In our example at the beginning of this chapter, the government denied Novak's application to fill in 10 acres of wetlands on his 80-acre parcel. Unless those acres can be filled, Novak considers them "worthless." In applying the "total takings" test of *Lucas*, is it clear whether you should consider Novak's 10 acres in isolation or whether you should look at the 80 acres as a whole? Does the Court address that issue? Again, see the discussion of *Palazzolo*, below.

5. **Background principles.** *Lucas* holds that the total destruction of a property's economic value is a taking, *unless* the uses prohibited would not be permitted under "background principles of nuisance and property law." How is that exception different from the "noxious use" analysis favored by the dissenters? Why does Justice Kennedy think the exception is too narrow? Do you agree with Justice Blackman's critique that this exception favors *judicial* rather than *legislative* judgments as to what uses of land are harmful? Do you feel confident, after studying nuisance law in Chapter 11, that you can tell what uses could be enjoined under the common law test?

CASE SUMMARY: Palazzolo v. Rhode Island, 533 U.S. 606 (2001)

After *Lucas*, many courts interpreted the "background principles" exception to mean that a claimant could not win a takings case if the restriction on land use was in place at the time he or she purchased the property. If you bought the property with the restriction, your investment-backed expectations should have been adjusted to include that condition. In addition, some courts held the "total takings" test inapplicable if there was *any* residual value left in the property.

In *Palazzolo*, the Supreme Court rejected both of those premises. Palazzolo wanted to develop his coastal property, which included both wetland and non-wetland (upland) acreage. Palazzolo became sole owner of the property in 1978, after a corporation he and several associates formed to hold the property dissolved. He applied for a permit to fill 11 acres of marsh land. The state's coastal management council rejected his application, based on a 1971 law protecting coastal wetlands. Palazzolo alleged that the value of his property, developed as he envisioned, would be over $3 million. As restricted, however, the parcel had a residual value of just $200,000.

Rhode Island argued that Palazzolo became the owner of the property after the wetland law was enacted, which made it a "background principle" of state law under *Lucas*. Five members of the Court held that a state's restrictive regulation is not exempt from takings analysis merely because title changed hands *after* the regulation was enacted:

> Were we to accept the State's rule, the postenactment transfer of title would absolve the State of its obligation to defend any action restricting land use, no matter how extreme or unreasonable. A State would be allowed, in effect, to put an expiration date on the Takings Clause. This ought not to be the rule. Future generations, too, have a right to challenge unreasonable limitations on the use and value of land.

Id. at 627. But what did *Lucas* mean, then, by "background principles of the State's law of property and nuisance," if not state laws already in place?

Justice O'Connor, concurring in *Palazzolo*, wrote to emphasize that the *timing of the law* is a *factor* to be considered, at least:

> Today's holding does not mean that the timing of the regulation's enactment relative to the acquisition of title is immaterial to the *Penn Central* analysis. Indeed, it would be just as much error to expunge this consideration from the takings inquiry as it would be to accord it exclusive significance. Our polestar instead remains the principles set forth in *Penn Central* itself and our other cases that govern partial regulatory takings. Under these cases, interference with investment-backed expectations is one of a number of factors that a court must examine. Further, the regulatory regime in place at the time the claimant acquires the property at issue helps to shape the reasonableness of those expectations.

Id. at 633 (O'Connor, J., concurring).

Justice Scalia, however, concurred specifically to point out that he disagreed with Justice O'Connor that the timing should even be considered. Thus, the issue is still in some doubt.

As to the issue of *residual value*, the Court agreed with Palazzolo that a mere "token interest" would not take the case out of the "total taking" rubric. However, because Palazzolo could still make use of the upland acres, the Court refused to find that his land was economically valueless as required by the *Lucas* test.

Palazzolo asked the Court to focus only on the wetlands acreage, rather than the parcel as a whole, in applying the test. However, the Court refused to consider that issue, because he had not properly raised it in the courts below and in his petition for certiorari.

A year after *Palazzolo*, however, in Tahoe-Sierra Preservation Council, Inc. v. Tahoe Regional Planning Agency, 535 U.S. 302 (2002), the Court repeated with approval the admonition of *Penn Central* that "the parcel as a whole" must be considered: "'Taking' jurisprudence does not divide a single parcel into discrete segments and attempt to determine whether rights in a particular segment have been entirely abrogated." *Id.* at 327 (quoting *Penn Central*, 438 U.S. at 130-31). But what if Palazzolo had purchased only the marshland part of the property?

CASE SUMMARY: Murr v. Wisconsin, 137 S.Ct. 1933 (2017).

This case represents the Court's most definitive attempt to answer the "denominator" question: what constitutes "the parcel" when analyzing the impact of a regulation on particular property? The Murrs owned two adjacent lots along the Lower St. Croix River in Wisconsin. Their parents purchased Lot F in 1960 and built a small cabin on it. They transferred title to a plumbing company they owned. In 1963, they purchased neighboring Lot E, taking title in their own names. Eventually, the parents transferred both lots to their children. The children decided they wanted to sell off Lot E to finance a building project on Lot F, which involved moving the cabin to a different location on the lot.

State and local law, however, basically merged the lots once they came under common ownership. The government denied the Murrs' request to sell the Lot E for development purposes, which the owners claimed deprived that lot of its economic value, constituting a taking. The trial court held, however, that the lots should be considered together, and that the value of the combined property declined only 10% due to the government regulation.

The Supreme Court agreed that the two lots should be considered together for purposes of applying the takings test.

Justice Kennedy, writing for the majority, described the determination of the relevant parcel as a multi-factor inquiry:

> [N]o single consideration can supply the exclusive test for determining the denominator. Instead, courts must consider a number of factors. These include the treatment of the land under state and local law; the physical characteristics of the land; and the prospective value of the regulated land. The endeavor should determine whether reasonable expectations about property ownership would lead a landowner to anticipate that his holdings would be treated as one parcel, or, instead, as separate tracts. The inquiry is objective, and the reasonable expectations at issue derive from background customs and the whole of our legal tradition.

137 S.Ct., at 1945. Applying those factors in this case, Justice Kennedy found that the two lots should have been considered as one unit; therefore, the regulation did not amount to a taking of property.

■ PROBLEMS: APPLYING *LUCAS*

1. **Native American remains.** In 1990, Hunziker purchased 59 acres of farmland, which he intended to develop. He platted out 60 lots and began selling them. For $80,000, Fleming purchased Lot 15, on which he planned to build a house. Shortly thereafter, a Native American burial mound was discovered on the lot. Pursuant to a 1978 state law, the state archeologist examined the site and declared that the mound had been made during the Woodland period, over 1,000 years ago, and therefore had historical significance. This declaration prevented the mound and a buffer zone around it from being disturbed, effectively precluding construction. Hunziker agreed to buy back the lot from Fleming and then sued the state for a "taking" of Lot 15. Hunziker alleged that Lot 15, in its undevelopable state, is now worth about $100. Has a taking occurred? *See* Hunziker v. State, 519 N.W.2d 367 (Iowa 1994).

2. **Endangered species.** Lloyd Good purchased a 40-acre tract of undeveloped land in the Florida Keys in 1973 for $100,000. The tract contained 32 acres of wetlands and 8 acres of upland. In 1991, Good submitted a proposal to fill about 10 acres of wetlands in order to build 16 houses, along with a canal and tennis court. The federal government denied the application, based on its detrimental impact on an endangered species—the silver rice rat. The federal Endangered Species Act was enacted in December 1973, and the rice rat was listed as endangered in 1991, just as Good submitted his application. Good alleges that the property developed as proposed would be worth $2.5 million, but with the restrictions is virtually worthless (it could possibly be sold to a conservation group for about $30,000). Has a taking occurred? *See* Good v. United States, 189 F.3d 1355 (Fed. Cir. 1999).

> ## Putting It All Together—Nonconforming Uses
>
> Now that you have a thorough introduction to the Takings Clause, do you understand why local zoning ordinances usually exempt pre-existing structures and uses that do not meet the district's restrictions? Do you understand why courts allow communities greater leeway in eliminating nonconforming uses, the closer the conflicting use is to a nuisance?

4   Development Exactions: *Nollan* and *Dolan*

Most communities place conditions on the right to develop land. For example, the developer may have to agree to put in streets, sewers, water lines, and sidewalks, which are either dedicated in fee or by easement to the community. These requirements are commonly called *exactions* because they are "exacted" or demanded of the landowner in exchange for the right to build.

In most cases, developers can live with these requirements, if they are not too onerous. After all, a new development will need streets and sewers. Dedicating these improvements to the community means that the responsibility for maintenance and operation will also be transferred. But at some point, can the exactions go "too far" and become unconstitutionally burdensome? The next two cases—*Nollan* and *Dolan*—explore the limits of exactions.

NOLLAN v. CALIFORNIA COASTAL COMMISSION

483 U.S. 825 (1987)
Supreme Court of the United States

Justice SCALIA delivered the opinion of the Court.

James and Marilyn Nollan appeal from a decision of the California Court of Appeal ruling that the California Coastal Commission could condition its grant of permission to rebuild their house on their transfer to the public of an easement across their beachfront property. 177 Cal. App. 3d 719, 223 Cal. Rptr. 28 (1986). The California court rejected their claim that imposition of that condition violates the Takings Clause of the Fifth Amendment, as incorporated against the States by the Fourteenth Amendment. *Ibid.* . . .

I

The Nollans own a beachfront lot in Ventura County, California. A quarter-mile north of their property is Faria County Park, an oceanside public park with a public beach and recreation area. Another public beach area, known locally as "the Cove," lies 1,800 feet south of their lot. A concrete seawall approximately eight feet high separates the beach portion of the Nollans' property from the rest of the lot. The historic mean high tide line determines the lot's oceanside boundary.

The Nollans originally leased their property with an option to buy. The building on the lot was a small bungalow, totaling 504 square feet, which for a time they rented to summer vacationers. After years of rental use, however, the building had fallen into disrepair, and could no longer be rented out.

The Nollans' option to purchase was conditioned on their promise to demolish the bungalow and replace it. In order to do so, under [state law], they were required to obtain a coastal development permit from the California Coastal Commission. On February 25, 1982, they submitted a permit application to the Commission in which they proposed to demolish the existing structure and replace it with a three-bedroom house in keeping with the rest of the neighborhood.

The Nollans were informed that . . . the Commission staff had recommended that the permit be granted subject to the condition that they allow the public an easement to pass across a portion of their property bounded by the mean high tide line on one side, and their seawall on the other side. This would make it easier for the public to get to Faria County Park and the Cove. The Nollans protested imposition of the condition, but the Commission overruled their objections and granted the permit subject to their recordation of a deed restriction granting the easement. . . .

[The Commission] found that the new house would increase blockage of the view of the ocean, thus contributing to the development of "a 'wall' of residential structures" that would prevent the public "psychologically . . . from realizing a stretch of coastline exists nearby that they have every right to visit." The new house would also increase private use of the shorefront. These effects of construction of the house, along with other area development, would cumulatively "burden the public's ability to traverse to and along the shorefront." Therefore the Commission could properly require the Nollans to offset that burden by providing additional lateral access to the public beaches in the form of an easement across their property. The Commission also noted that it had similarly conditioned 43 out of 60 coastal development permits along the same tract of land, and that of the 17 not so conditioned, 14 had been approved when the Commission did not have administrative regulations in place allowing imposition of the condition, and the remaining 3 had not involved shorefront property.

II

Had California simply required the Nollans to make an easement across their beachfront available to the public on a permanent basis in order to increase public access to the beach, rather than conditioning their permit to rebuild their house on their agreeing to do so, we have no doubt there would have been a taking. . . . In *Loretto* we observed that where governmental action results in "[a] permanent physical occupation" of the property, by the government itself or by others, see 458 U.S., at 432-433, n. 9, "our cases uniformly have found a taking to the extent of the occupation, without regard to whether the action achieves an important public benefit or has only minimal economic impact on the owner," *id.*, at 434-435. We think a "permanent physical occupation" has occurred, for purposes of that rule, where individuals are given a permanent and continuous right to pass to and fro, so that the real property may continuously be traversed, even though no particular individual is permitted to station himself permanently upon the premises. . . .

Given, then, that requiring uncompensated conveyance of the easement outright would violate the Fourteenth Amendment, the question becomes whether requiring it to be conveyed as a condition for issuing a land-use permit alters the outcome. We have long recognized that land-use regulation does not effect a taking if it "substantially advance[s] legitimate state interests" and does not "den[y] an owner economically viable use of his land," Agins v. Tiburon, 447 U.S. 255, 260 (1980)....

The Commission argues that a permit condition that serves the same legitimate police-power purpose as a refusal to issue the permit should not be found to be a taking if the refusal to issue the permit would not constitute a taking. We agree. Thus, if the Commission attached to the permit some condition that would have protected the public's ability to see the beach notwithstanding construction of the new house—for example, a height limitation, a width restriction, or a ban on fences—so long as the Commission could have exercised its police power (as we have assumed it could) to forbid construction of the house altogether, imposition of the condition would also be constitutional. Moreover (and here we come closer to the facts of the present case), the condition would be constitutional even if it consisted of the requirement that the Nollans provide a viewing spot on their property for passersby with whose sighting of the ocean their new house would interfere. Although such a requirement, constituting a permanent grant of continuous access to the property, would have to be considered a taking if it were not attached to a development permit, the Commission's assumed power to forbid construction of the house in order to protect the public's view of the beach must surely include the power to condition construction upon some concession by the owner, even a concession of property rights, that serves the same end. If a prohibition designed to accomplish that purpose would be a legitimate exercise of the police power rather than a taking, it would be strange to conclude that providing the owner an alternative to that prohibition which accomplishes the same purpose is not.

The evident constitutional propriety disappears, however, if the condition substituted for the prohibition utterly fails to further the end advanced as the justification for the prohibition. When that essential nexus is eliminated, the situation becomes the same as if California law forbade shouting fire in a crowded theater, but granted dispensations to those willing to contribute $100 to the state treasury.... Similarly here, the lack of nexus between the condition and the original purpose of the building restriction converts that purpose to something other than what it was. The purpose then becomes, quite simply, the obtaining of an easement to serve some valid governmental purpose, but without payment of compensation. Whatever may be the outer limits of "legitimate state interests" in the takings and land-use context, this is not one of them. In short, unless the permit condition serves the same governmental purpose as the development ban, the building restriction is not a valid regulation of land use but "an out-and-out plan of extortion." J.E.D. Associates, Inc. v. Atkinson, 121 N.H. 581, 584, 432 A.2d 12, 14-15 (1981)....

III

The Commission claims that it concedes as much, and that we may sustain the condition at issue here by finding that it is reasonably related to the public need or burden that the Nollans' new house creates or to which it contributes. We can accept, for purposes of discussion, the Commission's proposed test as to how close a "fit" between the condition and the burden is required, because we find that this case does not meet even the most untailored standards. The Commission's principal contention to the contrary essentially turns on a play on the word "access." The Nollans' new house, the Commission found, will interfere with "visual access" to the beach. That in turn (along with other shorefront development) will interfere with the desire of people who drive past the Nollans' house to use the beach, thus creating a "psychological barrier" to "access." The Nollans' new house will also, by a process not altogether clear from the Commission's opinion but presumably potent enough to more than offset the effects of the psychological barrier, increase the use of the public beaches, thus creating the need for more "access." These burdens on "access" would be alleviated by a requirement that the Nollans provide "lateral access" to the beach.

Rewriting the argument to eliminate the play on words makes clear that there is nothing to it. It is quite impossible to understand how a requirement that people already on the public beaches be able to walk across the Nollans' property reduces any obstacles to viewing the beach created by the new house. It is also impossible to understand how it lowers any "psychological barrier" to using the public beaches, or how it helps to remedy any additional congestion on them caused by construction of the Nollans' new house. We therefore find that the Commission's imposition of the permit condition cannot be treated as an exercise of its land-use power for any of these purposes. . . .

[The Commission believes] that the public interest will be served by a continuous strip of publicly accessible beach along the coast. The Commission may well be right that it is a good idea, but that does not establish that the Nollans (and other coastal residents) alone can be compelled to contribute to its realization. Rather, California is free to advance its "comprehensive program," if it wishes, by using its power of eminent domain for this "public purpose," see U.S. Const., Amdt. 5; but if it wants an easement across the Nollans' property, it must pay for it.

Reversed.

Justice BRENNAN, with whom Justice MARSHALL joins, dissenting.

Appellants in this case sought to construct a new dwelling on their beach lot that would both diminish visual access to the beach and move private development closer to the public tidelands. The Commission reasonably concluded that such "buildout," both individually and cumulatively, threatens public access to the shore. It sought to offset this encroachment by obtaining assurance that the public may walk along the shoreline in order to gain access to the ocean. The Court finds this an illegitimate exercise of the police power, because it maintains that there is no reasonable relationship between the effect of the development and the condition imposed.

The first problem with this conclusion is that the Court imposes a standard of precision for the exercise of a State's police power that has been discredited for the better part of this century. Furthermore, even under the Court's cramped standard, the permit condition imposed in this case directly responds to the specific type of burden on access created by appellants' development. Finally, a review of those factors deemed most significant in takings analysis makes clear that the Commission's action implicates none of the concerns underlying the Takings Clause. The Court has thus struck down the Commission's reasonable effort to respond to intensified development along the California coast, on behalf of landowners who can make no claim that their reasonable expectations have been disrupted. The Court has, in short, given appellants a windfall at the expense of the public.

I

There can be no dispute that the police power of the States encompasses the authority to impose conditions on private development. . . . In this case, California has employed its police power in order to condition development upon preservation of public access to the ocean and tidelands. The Coastal Commission, if it had so chosen, could have denied the Nollans' request for a development permit, since the property would have remained economically viable without the requested new development. Instead, the State sought to accommodate the Nollans' desire for new development, on the condition that the development not diminish the overall amount of public access to the coastline. . . .

The Commission is charged by both the State Constitution and legislature to preserve overall public access to the California coastline. . . . The Commission has sought to discharge its responsibilities in a flexible manner. It has sought to balance private and public interests and to accept tradeoffs: to permit development that reduces access in some ways as long as other means of access are enhanced. In this case, it has determined that the Nollans' burden on access would be offset by a deed restriction that formalizes the public's right to pass along the shore. In its informed judgment, such a tradeoff would preserve the net amount of public access to the coastline. The Court's insistence on a precise fit between the forms of burden and condition on each individual parcel along the California coast would penalize the Commission for its flexibility, hampering the ability to fulfill its public trust mandate. . . .

B

. . . Even if we accept the Court's unusual demand for a precise match between the condition imposed and the specific type of burden on access created by the appellants, the State's action easily satisfies this requirement. First, the lateral access condition serves to dissipate the impression that the beach that lies behind the wall of homes along the shore is for private use only. It requires no exceptional imaginative powers to find plausible the Commission's point that the average person passing along the road in front of a phalanx of imposing permanent residences, including the appellants' new home, is likely to conclude that this particular portion of the shore is not open to the public. If, however, that person can see that numerous people are passing and repassing along the dry sand, this conveys the message that the beach is in fact open for use by the public. Furthermore, those persons who go down to the public beach a quarter-mile away will be able to look down the coastline and see that persons have continuous access to the tidelands, and will observe signs that proclaim the public's right of access over the dry sand. The burden produced by the diminution in visual access—the impression that the beach is not open to the public—is thus directly alleviated by the provision for public access over the dry sand. The Court therefore has an unrealistically limited conception of what measures could reasonably be chosen to mitigate the burden produced by a diminution of visual access....

II

The fact that the Commission's action is a legitimate exercise of the police power does not, of course, insulate it from a takings challenge, for when "regulation goes too far it will be recognized as a taking." Pennsylvania Coal Co. v. Mahon, 260 U.S. 393, 415 (1922). Conventional takings analysis underscores the implausibility of the Court's holding, for it demonstrates that this exercise of California's police power implicates none of the concerns that underlie our takings jurisprudence.

In reviewing a Takings Clause claim, we have regarded as particularly significant the nature of the governmental action and the economic impact of regulation, especially the extent to which regulation interferes with investment-backed expectations. *Penn Central*, 438 U.S., at 124.... The physical intrusion permitted by the deed restriction is minimal. The public is permitted the right to pass and repass along the coast in an area from the seawall to the mean high-tide mark.... The intrusiveness of such passage is even less than the intrusion resulting from the required dedication of a sidewalk in front of private residences, exactions which are commonplace conditions on approval of development.... Appellants can make no tenable claim that either their enjoyment of their property or its value is diminished by the public's ability merely to pass and repass a few feet closer to the seawall beyond which appellants' house is located....

Finally, the character of the regulation in this case is not unilateral government action, but a condition on approval of a development request submitted by appellants. The State has not sought to interfere with any pre-existing property interest, but has responded to appellants' proposal to intensify development on the coast. Appellants themselves chose to submit a new development application, and could claim no property interest in its approval. They were aware that approval of such development would be conditioned on preservation of adequate public access to the ocean. The State has initiated no action against appellants' property; had the Nollans' not proposed more intensive development in the coastal zone, they would never have been subject to the provision that they challenge.

Examination of the economic impact of the Commission's action reinforces the conclusion that no taking has occurred. Allowing appellants to intensify development along the coast in exchange for ensuring public access to the ocean is a classic instance of government action that produces a "reciprocity of advantage." *Pennsylvania Coal*, 260 U.S., at 415. Appellants have been allowed to replace a one-story, 521-square-foot beach home with a two-story, 1,674-square-foot residence and an attached two-car garage, resulting in development covering 2,464 square feet of the lot. Such development obviously significantly increases the value of appellants' property; appellants make no contention that this increase is offset by any diminution in value resulting from the deed restriction, much less that the restriction made the property less valuable than it would have been without the new construction. Furthermore, appellants gain an additional benefit from the Commission's permit condition program. They are able to walk along the beach beyond the confines of their own property only because the Commission has required deed restrictions as a condition of approving other new beach developments. Thus, appellants benefit both as private landowners and as members of the public from the fact that new development permit requests are conditioned on preservation of public access. . . .

With respect to the permit condition program in general, the Commission should have little difficulty in the future in utilizing its expertise to demonstrate a specific connection between provisions for access and burdens on access produced by new development. Neither the Commission in its report nor the State in its briefs and at argument highlighted the particular threat to lateral access created by appellants' development project. . . . In the future, alerted to the Court's apparently more demanding requirement, it need only make clear that a provision for public access directly responds to a particular type of burden on access created by a new development. . . .

Nonetheless it is important to point out that the Court's insistence on a precise accounting system in this case is insensitive to the fact that increasing intensity of development in many areas calls for far-sighted, comprehensive planning that takes into account both the interdependence of land uses and the cumulative impact of development. As one scholar has noted:

> "Property does not exist in isolation. Particular parcels are tied to one another in complex ways, and property is more accurately described as being inextricably part of a network of relationships that is neither limited to, nor usefully defined by, the property boundaries with which the legal system is accustomed to dealing. Frequently, use of any given parcel of property is at the same time effectively a use of, or a demand upon, property beyond the border of the user." Sax, *Takings, Private Property, and Public Rights*, 81 Yale L.J. 149, 152 (1971) (footnote omitted).

. . . State agencies therefore require considerable flexibility in responding to private desires for development in a way that guarantees the preservation of public access to the coast. They should be encouraged to regulate development in the context of the overall balance of competing uses of the shoreline. The Court today does precisely the opposite, overruling an eminently reasonable exercise of an expert state agency's judgment, substituting its own narrow view of how this balance should be struck. Its reasoning is hardly suited to the complex reality of natural resource protection in the 20th century. I can only hope that today's decision is an aberration, and that a broader vision ultimately prevails.

I dissent.

CASE SUMMARY: Dolan v. City of Tigard, 512 U.S. 374 (1994)

Although *Nollan* established that "an essential nexus" must exist between the exaction and the burden or need created by the new development, the Court did not decide how close the fit must be. The opportunity to clarify the test came seven years later in the *Dolan* case.

Florence Dolan owned a plumbing and electrical supply store adjacent to Fanno Creek in the City of Tigard. She applied for permission to double the size of the store and pave the parking lot. The City Planning Commission approved the request, on two conditions: (1) that she dedicate the portion of her property within the 100-year floodplain for improvement of the storm drainage system along Fanno Creek, and (2) that she dedicate a strip of land for a pedestrian/bicycle pathway.

Under *Nollan*, the City could show a nexus between these conditions and the redevelopment. The pavement of the parking lot would increase runoff to the nearby creek, which would be alleviated by the City's increased management of the floodplain area. The larger store would add to traffic, which could be offset by increased use of pedestrian/bike trails.

Nevertheless, the Court held that the exactions must be related to the burdens of the development not only in *kind*, but also in *degree*. The conditions must bear a *rough proportionality* to the development's impacts: "No precise mathematical calculation is required, but the city must make some sort of individualized determination that the required dedication is related both in nature and extent to the impact of the proposed development." *Id.* at 391.

The majority found that the City had not met this burden. With regard to the floodplain dedication, it had not shown why *dedicating* the greenway to the City, rather than simply leaving it undeveloped, was necessary to alleviate the additional runoff. With regard to the pathway, the City had not "met its burden of demonstrating that the additional number of vehicle and bicycle trips generated by petitioner's development reasonably relate to the city's requirement for a dedication of the pedestrian/bicycle pathway easement." *Id.* at 395. Again emphasizing that a "precise mathematical calculation" was not required, the Court nonetheless demanded that the city make "some effort to quantify its findings...beyond the conclusory statement that [the pathway] could offset some of the traffic demand generated." *Id.* at 396.

■ POINTS TO CONSIDER

1. **Subdivision ordinances.** Most cities impose significant requirements on new developments. In addition to meeting lot size and set-back requirements,

typically the developer must agree to pave streets and sidewalks, and install sewers and water mains. Many of these improvements must be dedicated to the city. Are these exactions legal after *Nollan/Dolan*? Is the lateral access easement sought in *Nollan* different from a sidewalk?

2. **Rough proportionality.** Although the Court said that mathematical precision was not required, what exactly does the City of Tigard have to do to justify its bike trail requirement?

3. **In-lieu fees.** What if the government, rather than demanding an easement, as in *Nollan* and *Dolan*, instead conditions approval of a land use permit on a monetary payment? Many jurisdictions use payments "in lieu" of in-kind exactions. Arguably, the payment of money for the privilege of development could be considered a "tax," which has never been deemed to be subject to the Takings Clause. In Koontz v. St. Johns River Water Mgmt. Dist., 133 S. Ct. 2586, (2013), the Court held that such payments were "monetary exactions," which were required to meet the *Nollan/Dolan* tests of essential nexus and rough proportionality.

■ PROBLEM: APPLYING *NOLLAN / DOLAN*

Dodge City is growing quickly, and it has few parks and recreation areas to serve its increasing population. The City Council is considering an ordinance that would require new subdivisions to set aside 5 percent of their total acreage for public recreational use. A developer of a new 80-acre subdivision, for example, would have to dedicate at least 4 acres for bike trails, or parks, or soccer fields, etc. As the City Attorney for Dodge City, how would you advise the council concerning the legality of this ordinance?

Would it make any difference if Dodge City required the developer to make a monetary contribution to a public recreation fund, in an amount equivalent to 5% of the value of the undeveloped land? What if, instead of requiring land to be set aside for public use, the City required every housing developer to dedicate at least 15% of the its units to low-income housing? *See* California Building Industry Assn. v. City of San Jose, 351 P.3d 974, 61 Cal.4th 435 (2015)(holding that affordable housing requirement is not an exaction).

5. The Next Frontier: "Judicial Takings"?

The "regulatory takings" concept prevents the *legislative branch* from changing the law in such a way that it unfairly destroys a landowner's investment based on reasonable expectations regarding use. The *executive branch* is also constrained by the Takings Clause in its interpretation and enforcement of the law. But the *judicial branch* can also make significant changes to the *common law* that interfere with settled expectations. Can such a common law shift by courts ever result in a destruction of property interests that requires compensation for a "judicial taking"?

While academics have long discussed the possibility,[28] the Supreme Court did not address the concept until Stop the Beach Renourishment, Inc. v. Florida Dep't of Envtl. Protection, 560 U.S. 702 (2010). Even though the case ultimately did not resolve the viability of judicial takings claims, the various opinions provide much fodder for discussion.

CASE SUMMARY: Stop the Beach Renourishment, Inc. v. Florida Department of Environmental Protection, 560 U.S. 702 (2010)

Stop the Beach involved a "renourishment" project, in which the government deposits massive quantities of new sand on an eroding beach. As we discussed in earlier chapters, usually a littoral landowner's property line is the mean high tide line, and when additional sand is added (by *accretion*), the landowner gains land. Under Florida's Beach and Shore Preservation Act (BSPA), however, the new sand added in a restoration project belongs to the public. In this case, the littoral owners sued, claiming that the law resulted in a "taking" of their littoral rights.

In the decision below, the Florida Supreme Court held that the restoration of critically eroded beaches under the BSPA does not unconstitutionally deprive upland owners of littoral rights without just compensation. Although the Act provides that the State may retain title to the newly created dry land directly adjacent to the water, upland owners may continue to access, use, and view the beach and water as they did prior to beach restoration. The Florida Supreme Court upheld this statutory scheme, finding that it "achieves a reasonable balance of interests and rights to uniquely valuable and volatile property interests." Walton Cnty. v. Stop the Beach Renourishment, Inc., 998 So. 2d 1102, 1115 (Fla. 2008).

In the U.S. Supreme Court, the beachfront landowners claimed that the Florida Supreme Court's decision abrogated their traditional common law littoral rights. The decision therefore amounted to a "judicial taking," without just compensation, in violation of the Fifth and Fourteenth Amendments.

The Supreme Court held 8-0 (Justice Stevens did not participate) that the Florida Supreme Court's decision was not a judicial taking of property. Nevertheless, four justices did support the idea of judicial takings.

Justice Scalia (joined by Chief Justice Roberts and Justices Thomas and Alito) declared:

> [T]he Takings Clause bars *the State* from taking private property without paying for it, no matter which branch is the instrument of the taking. . . . But the particular state *actor* is irrelevant. If a legislature *or a court* declares that what was once an established right of private property no longer exists, it has taken that property, no less than if the State had physically appropriated it or destroyed its value by regulation.

130 S. Ct. at 2602. Scalia noted that "[i]t would be absurd to allow a State to do by judicial decree what the Takings Clause forbids it to do by legislative fiat." *Id.* at 2601.

---

[28] *See* Barton H. Thompson, Jr., *Judicial Takings*, 76 Va. L. Rev. 1449 (1990).

The other four justices did not reach the issue, agreeing only that if such a judicial taking were possible, it did not occur in this case. Justice Kennedy, joined by Justice Sotomayor, indicated that there should be some restraint on the ability of courts to reallocate property rights, but that the constraint should be found in the Due Process Clause, rather than the Takings Clause. Kennedy stated that a court "would be on strong footing in ruling that a judicial decision that eliminates or substantially changes established property rights, which are a legitimate expectation of the owner, is 'arbitrary or irrational' under the Due Process Clause." *Id.* at 2615. Justices Breyer and Ginsburg declined to address the judicial takings issue.

Thus, although the Court did not establish a judicial takings doctrine in *Stop the Beach*, six justices agreed that there should be some constraint on the judicial erosion of property rights. The case has also inspired judicial takings claims in the lower courts, based on the plurality opinion. *See, e.g.*, Northern Natural Gas Co. v. ONEOK Field Servs. Co., 296 P.3d 1106 (Kan. 2013) (finding no judicial taking); Willits v. Peabody Coal Co., 400 S.W.3d 442 (Mo. Ct. App. 2013) (judicial takings claim waived). *See also* Surfrider Foundation v. Martins Beach 1, LLC, 14 Cal.App.5th 238 (2017) ("The lesson we take from *Stop the Beach* is that where it has been determined that a court action eliminates an established property right and would be considered a taking if done by the legislative or executive branches of government, it must be invalidated as unconstitutional, whether under the takings or due process clauses.").

Should a judicial takings claim be recognized? What are the drawbacks of such an approach? For a critique of the judicial takings concept, see Timothy M. Mulvaney, *The New Judicial Takings Construct*, 120 Yale L.J. Online 247, 265-66 (2011) (judicial takings concept is counter to traditional "evolutionary view of the law").

■ PROBLEM: JUDICIAL TAKING

The State of Grace has long used a "good faith" rule for determining when to recognize adverse possession of property. As you recall, this means that the possessor must have honestly believed she had good title to the property. In 2014, Alice brought suit to eject Bart from Blackacre. For 20 years Bart had cultivated and improved about 4 acres of Alice's property, because it was on his side of the fence, which Alice had negligently and erroneously erected. Bart claimed the property by adverse possession; Alice defended on the ground that Bart's possession was not in good faith. Bart admitted he knew the land wasn't his.

After reviewing the criticism of the "good faith" rule, the Grace Supreme Court decided that it was not based on sound policy. Instead, it believed that certainty and fairness require that the land should belong to the person who took care of and improved the land over a long period of time while it was neglected by the true owner. Thus, the court abandoned the "good faith" rule.

Alice now sues the State of Grace, alleging that the court's decision was a "judicial taking" of her property. Does her claim meet the test proposed by Justice Scalia in *Stop the Beach*? If she has a valid claim, who pays the damages?

SUMMARY

- The *Takings Clause* of the Fifth Amendment, applied to the states through the Fourteenth Amendment, requires the government to take private property only for *public use* and to provide *just compensation*.
- *Just compensation* means the property's fair market value, based on its highest and best use. Compensation is often based on sales of comparable property or the capitalization of the property's expected income stream.
- The power of *eminent domain* may be exercised only for *public use*, which the U.S. Supreme Court has interpreted to require a valid public purpose.
- In *Kelo*, the Court held that the government's *economic development* goals could support the use of eminent domain, even though the property taken was not blighted or otherwise harmful.
- Justice Kennedy's pivotal concurrence in *Kelo* focused on whether the taking is intended to favor a private party, with only pretextual or *incidental public benefits*.
- Many states have limited the use of eminent domain, either by statutory restrictions or by narrower interpretations of state constitutional provisions.
- *Regulatory takings* may occur when government action impairs property value without actually confiscating it.
- The U.S. Supreme Court recognized the concept of regulatory takings in *Pennsylvania Coal v. Mahon*, in which Justice Holmes said that governmental restrictions that "go too far" in diminishing property value require compensation.
- The Court's *Penn Central* decision provided factors to be considered in the *ad hoc balancing test* for regulatory takings. A court should consider the impact of the regulation on the investment-backed expectations of the landowner, along with the character of the governmental action and the nature of the public interest at stake. The Court focused on the fact that the landowner still could make an economically valuable use of the property.
- The Court has adopted two categories of cases that are deemed takings *per se*: *permanent physical occupations*, as in *Loretto*, and *total takings* (100 percent diminution in value) under *Lucas*.
- In judging the impact on the landowner, the *entire parcel* should be considered, rather than just the part affected by the regulation. In addition, the fact that a landowner acquired the property *post*-regulation does not preclude a takings claim.
- Landowners who want to develop property are often required to satisfy governmental demands for *exactions*.

- Under *Nollan*, such exactions must have an adequate *nexus* to the additional impact or burden created by the development; otherwise, they constitute a taking of property without compensation.
- Under *Dolan*, the exactions must also be *roughly proportional* to the impact created, in quantitative terms.
- A plurality of the U.S. Supreme Court recognized the concept of *judicial takings* in *Stop the Beach*. Justice Scalia suggested that a taking occurs when a court declares that a previously existing property right no longer exists. Two other justices suggested that this might be a violation of a property owner's due process rights.

Principal cases are indicated by italics.